Elementary
Information
Security

Richard E. Smith

World Headquarters
Jones & Bartlett Learning
5 Wall Street
Burlington, MA 01803
978-443-5000
info@jblearning.com
www.jblearning.com

Jones & Bartlett Learning books and products are available through most bookstores and online book-sellers. To contact Jones & Bartlett Learning directly, call 800-832-0034, fax 978-443-8000, or visit our website, www.jblearning.com.

Substantial discounts on bulk quantities of Jones & Bartlett Learning publications are available to corporations, professional associations, and other qualified organizations. For details and specific discount information, contact the special sales department at Jones & Bartlett Learning via the above contact information or send an email to specialsales@jblearning.com.

Production Credits
Publisher: Cathleen Sether
Senior Acquisitions Editor: Timothy Anderson
Managing Editor: Amy Bloom
Director of Production: Amy Rose
Production Assistant: Alyssa Lawrence
Marketing Manager: Lindsay White
V.P., Manufacturing and Inventory Control: Therese Connell
Composition: Northeast Compositors, Inc.
Cover Design: Kristin E. Parker
Rights and Permissions Manager: Katherine Crighton
Associate Photo Researcher: Lauren Miller
Cover Image: © bumihills/ShutterStock, Inc.
Printing and Binding: Malloy, Inc.
Cover Printing: Malloy, Inc.

To order this product, use ISBN: 978-1-4496-4820-6

Library of Congress Cataloging-in-Publication Data
Smith, Richard E., 1952-
  Elementary information security / Richard E. Smith.
      p. cm.
  Includes bibliographical references and index.
  ISBN 978-0-7637-6141-7 (pbk.)
  1. Computer security. I. Title.
  QA76.9.A25S652 2012
  005.8--dc22
                              2011008940

6048

Printed in the United States of America
16 15 14 13 12   10 9 8 7 6 5 4 3 2

CONTENTS

Preface   xvii

Chapter 1   Security from the Ground Up   1
  1.1   The Security Landscape   1
      1.1.1   Making Security Decisions   3
      1.1.2   The Security Process   5
      1.1.3   Continuous Improvement: A Basic Principle   6

  1.2   Process Example: Bob's Computer   7

  1.3   Assets and Risk Assessment   11
      1.3.1   What Are We Protecting?   14
      1.3.2   Security Boundaries   15
      1.3.3   Security Architecture   17
      1.3.4   Risk Assessment Overview   19

  1.4   Identifying Risks   20
      1.4.1   Threat Agents   20
      1.4.2   Security Properties, Services, and Attacks   22

  1.5   Prioritizing Risks   23
      1.5.1   Example: Risks to Alice's Laptop   24
      1.5.2   Other Risk-Assessment Processes   29

  1.6   Ethical Issues in Security Analysis   31
      1.6.1   Searching for Vulnerabilities   32
      1.6.2   Sharing or Publishing Vulnerabilities   33

  1.7   Security Example: Aircraft Hijacking   35
      1.7.1   Hijacking: A High-Level Analysis   36
      1.7.2   September 11, 2001   37

1.8   Resources   39

    1.8.1   Review Questions   41

    1.8.2   Exercises   41

Chapter 2   Controlling a Computer   43

2.1   Computers and Programs   43

    2.1.1   Input/Output   45

    2.1.2   Program Execution   47

    2.1.3   Procedures   48

2.2   Programs and Processes   49

    2.2.1   Switching Between Processes   51

    2.2.2   The Operating System   53

2.3   Buffer Overflow and the Morris Worm   54

    2.3.1   The "Finger" Overflow   55

    2.3.2   Security Alerts   59

2.4   Access Control Strategies   60

    2.4.1   Puzzles and Patterns   61

    2.4.2   Chain of Control: Another Basic Principle   63

2.5   Keeping Processes Separate   65

    2.5.1   Sharing a Program   68

    2.5.2   Sharing Data   70

2.6   Security Policy and Implementation   71

    2.6.1   Analyzing Alice's Risks   73

    2.6.2   Constructing Alice's Policy   75

    2.6.3   Alice's Security Controls   77

2.7   Security Plan: Process Protection   80

2.8   Resources   85

    2.8.1   Review Questions   86

    2.8.2   Exercises   87

Chapter 3   Controlling Files   91

3.1   The File System   91

    3.1.1   File Ownership and Access Rights   94

3.1.2   Directory Access Rights   95

3.2   Executable Files   97
3.2.1   Execution Access Rights   98
3.2.2   Computer Viruses   100
3.2.3   Macro Viruses   103
3.2.4   Modern Malware: A Rogue's Gallery   104

3.3   Sharing and Protecting Files   106
3.3.1   Policies for Sharing and Protection   108

3.4   Security Controls for Files   111
3.4.1   Deny by Default: A Basic Principle   112
3.4.2   Managing Access Rights   114
3.4.3   Capabilities   115

3.5   File Security Controls   117
3.5.1   File Permission Flags   117
3.5.2   Security Controls to Enforce Bob's Policy   120
3.5.3   States and State Diagrams   121

3.6   Patching Security Flaws   123

3.7   Process Example: The Horse   127
3.7.1   Troy: A High-Level Analysis   128
3.7.2   Analyzing the Security Failure   129

3.8   Resources   130
3.8.1   Review Questions   130
3.8.2   Exercises   131

Chapter 4   Sharing Files   135
4.1   Controlled Sharing   135
4.1.1   Basic File Sharing on Windows   137
4.1.2   User Groups   139
4.1.3   Least Privilege and Administrative Users   140

4.2   File Permission Flags   143
4.2.1   Permission Flags and Ambiguities   146
4.2.2   Permission Flag Examples   147

4.3   Access Control Lists   149

4.3.1   POSIX ACLs   151

4.3.2   Macintosh OS-X ACLs   152

4.4   Microsoft Windows ACLs   156

4.4.1   Denying Access   157

4.4.2   Default File Protection   159

4.5   A Different Trojan Horse   163

4.6   Phase Five: Monitoring the System   165

4.6.1   Logging Events   167

4.6.2   External Security Requirements   170

4.7   Resources   173

4.7.1   Review Questions   173

4.7.2   Exercises   174

Chapter 5   Storing Files   177

5.1   Phase Six: Recovery   177

5.1.1   The Aftermath of an Incident   178

5.1.2   Legal Disputes   180

5.2   Digital Evidence   181

5.2.1   Collecting Legal Evidence   182

5.2.2   Digital Evidence Procedures   184

5.3   Storing Data on a Hard Drive   185

5.3.1   Hard Drive Controller   189

5.3.2   Hard Drive Formatting   190

5.3.3   Error Detection and Correction   192

5.3.4   Hard Drive Partitions   195

5.3.5   Memory Sizes and Address Variables   197

5.4   FAT: An Example File System   200

5.4.1   Boot Blocks   201

5.4.2   Building Files from Clusters   203

5.4.3   FAT Directories   206

5.5   **Modern File Systems   207**
        5.5.1   Unix File System   209
        5.5.2   Apple's HFS Plus   211
        5.5.3   Microsoft's NTFS   212

5.6   **Input/Output and File System Software   214**
        5.6.1   Software Layering   217
        5.6.2   A Typical I/O Operation   220
        5.6.3   Security and I/O   221

5.7   **Resources   223**
        5.7.1   Review Questions   224
        5.7.2   Exercises   225

Chapter 6   Authenticating People   229
6.1   **Unlocking a Door   229**
        6.1.1   Authentication Factors   231
        6.1.2   Threats and Risks   233

6.2   **Evolution of Password Systems   237**
        6.2.1   One-Way Hash Functions   240
        6.2.2   Sniffing Credentials   243

6.3   **Password Guessing   244**
        6.3.1   Password Search Space   247
        6.3.2   Truly Random Password Selection   249
        6.3.3   Cracking Speeds   251

6.4   **Attacks on Password Bias   252**
        6.4.1   Biased Choices and Average Attack Space   254
        6.4.2   Estimating Language-Based Password Bias   257

6.5   **Authentication Tokens   258**
        6.5.1   Challenge-Response Authentication   260
        6.5.2   One-Time Password Tokens   264
        6.5.3   Token Vulnerabilities   266

6.6   **Biometric Authentication   268**
        6.6.1   Biometric Accuracy   269
        6.6.2   Biometric Vulnerabilities   271

6.7   **Authentication Policy   272**
    6.7.1   Weak and Strong Threats   272
    6.7.2   Policies for Weak Threat Environments   274
    6.7.3   Policies for Strong and Extreme Threats   276
    6.7.4   Password Selection and Handling   279

6.8   **Resources   281**
    6.8.1   Review Questions   281
    6.8.2   Exercises   282

Chapter 7   Encrypting Files   285
7.1   **Protecting the Accessible   285**
    7.1.1   Process Example: The Encrypted Diary   286
    7.1.2   Encryption Basics   287
    7.1.3   Encryption and Information States   291

7.2   **Encryption and Cryptanalysis   293**
    7.2.1   The Vigenère Cipher   294
    7.2.2   Electromechanical Encryption   296

7.3   **Computer-Based Encryption   298**
    7.3.1   Exclusive Or: A Crypto Building Block   300
    7.3.2   Stream Ciphers: Another Building Block   302
    7.3.3   Key Stream Security   305
    7.3.4   The One-Time Pad   306

7.4   **File Encryption Software   309**
    7.4.1   Built-In File Encryption   309
    7.4.2   Encryption Application Programs   311
    7.4.3   Erasing a Plaintext File   313
    7.4.4   Choosing a File Encryption Program   315

7.5   **Digital Rights Management   317**

7.6   **Resources   320**
    7.6.1   Review Questions   321
    7.6.2   Exercises   322

Chapter 8   Secret and Public Keys   325

8.1   The Key Management Challenge   325

8.1.1   Rekeying   327

8.1.2   Using Text for Encryption Keys   329

8.1.3   Key Strength   332

8.2   The Reused Key Stream Problem   333

8.2.1   Avoiding Reused Keys   335

8.2.2   Key Wrapping: Another Building Block   338

8.2.3   Separation of Duty: A Basic Principle   341

8.2.4   DVD Key Handling   343

8.3   Public-Key Cryptography   345

8.3.1   Sharing a Secret: Diffie-Hellman   348

8.3.2   Diffie-Hellman: The Basics of the Math   350

8.3.3   Elliptic Curve Cryptography   352

8.4   RSA: Rivest-Shamir-Adleman   353

8.4.1   Encapsulating Keys with RSA   354

8.4.2   An Overview of RSA Mathematics   356

8.5   Data Integrity and Digital Signatures   360

8.5.1   Detecting Malicious Changes   361

8.5.2   Detecting a Changed Hash Value   364

8.5.3   Digital Signatures   365

8.6   Publishing Public Keys   368

8.6.1   Public-Key Certificates   370

8.6.2   Chains of Certificates   371

8.6.3   Authenticated Software Updates   376

8.7   Resources

8.7.1   Review Questions   379

8.7.2   Exercises   379

Chapter 9   Encrypting Volumes   383

9.1   Securing a Volume   383

9.1.1   Risks to Volumes   384

9.1.2   Risks and Policy Trade-Offs   386

9.2   **Block Ciphers   389**
    9.2.1   Evolution of DES and AES   392
    9.2.2   The RC4 Story   395
    9.2.3   Qualities of Good Encryption Algorithms   397

9.3   **Block Cipher Modes   400**
    9.3.1   Stream Cipher Modes   402
    9.3.2   Cipher Feedback Mode   406
    9.3.3   Cipher Block Chaining   408

9.4   **Encrypting a Volume   409**
    9.4.1   Volume Encryption in Software   411
    9.4.2   Adapting an Existing Mode   413
    9.4.3   A "Tweakable" Encryption Mode   416
    9.4.4   Residual Risks   418

9.5   **Encryption in Hardware   420**
    9.5.1   The Drive Controller   421
    9.5.2   Drive Locking and Unlocking   422

9.6   **Managing Encryption Keys   423**
    9.6.1   Key Storage   425
    9.6.2   Booting an Encrypted Drive   427
    9.6.3   Residual Risks to Keys   429

9.7   **Resources   432**
    9.7.1   Review Questions   432
    9.7.2   Exercises   433

Chapter 10   Connecting Computers   435
10.1   **The Network Security Problem   435**
    10.1.1   Basic Network Attacks and Defenses   436
    10.1.2   Physical Network Protection   438
    10.1.3   Host and Network Integrity   439

10.2   **Transmitting Information   442**
    10.2.1   Message Switching   444
    10.2.2   Circuit Switching   446
    10.2.3   Packet Switching   447

10.3   Putting Bits on a Wire   450
10.3.1   Wireless Transmission   451
10.3.2   Transmitting Packets   454
10.3.3   Recovering a Lost Packet   456

10.4   Ethernet: A Modern LAN   458
10.4.1   Wiring a Small Network   460
10.4.2   Ethernet Frame Format   461
10.4.3   Finding Host Addresses   463
10.4.4   Handling Collisions   465

10.5   The Protocol Stack   467
10.5.1   Relationships Between Layers   468
10.5.2   The OSI Protocol Model   470

10.6   Network Applications   472
10.6.1   Resource Sharing   474
10.6.2   Data and File Sharing   475

10.7   Resources   478
10.7.1   Review Questions   479
10.7.2   Exercises   479

Chapter 11   Networks of Networks   481
11.1   Building Information Networks   481
11.1.1   Point-to-Point Network   483
11.1.2   Star Network   484
11.1.3   Bus Network   486
11.1.4   Tree Network   487
11.1.5   Mesh   490

11.2   Combining Computer Networks   491
11.2.1   Hopping Between Networks   493
11.2.2   Evolution of Internet Security   495
11.2.3   Internet Structure   498

11.3   Talking Between Hosts   501
11.3.1   IP Addresses   503
11.3.2   IP Packet Format   504
11.3.3   Address Resolution Protocol   506

11.4   Internet Addresses in Practice   507
        11.4.1   Addresses, Scope, and Reachability   509
        11.4.2   Private IP Addresses   510

11.5   Network Inspection Tools   512
        11.5.1   Wireshark Examples   514
        11.5.2   Mapping a LAN with Nmap   516

11.6   Resources   520
        11.6.1   Review Questions   520
        11.6.2   Exercises   521

Chapter 12   End-to-End Networking   525
12.1   "Smart" Versus "Dumb" Networks   525

12.2   Internet Transport Protocols   526
        12.2.1   Transmission Control Protocol   528
        12.2.2   Attacks on Protocols   532

12.3   Names on the Internet   535
        12.3.1   Domain Names in Practice   537
        12.3.2   Looking Up Names   539
        12.3.3   DNS Protocol   540
        12.3.4   Investigating Domain Names   543
        12.3.5   Attacking DNS   545

12.4   Internet Gateways and Firewalls   547
        12.4.1   Network Address Translation   549
        12.4.2   Filtering and Connectivity   553
        12.4.3   Software-Based Firewalls   554

12.5   Long-Distance Networking   555
        12.5.1   Older Technologies   557
        12.5.2   Mature Technologies   559
        12.5.3   Evolving Technologies   561

12.6   Resources   561
        12.6.1   Review Questions   562
        12.6.2   Exercises   563

Chapter 13   Enterprise Computing   567

    13.1   The Challenge of Community   567

        13.1.1   Companies and Information Control   568

        13.1.2   Enterprise Risks   571

        13.1.3   Social Engineering   573

    13.2   Management Process   575

        13.2.1   Security Management Standards   576

        13.2.2   Deployment Policy Directives   578

        13.2.3   Management Hierarchies and Delegation   579

        13.2.4   Managing Information Resources   581

        13.2.5   Security Audits   583

        13.2.6   Information Security Professionals   584

    13.3   Enterprise Issues   587

        13.3.1   Personnel Security   588

        13.3.2   Physical Security   592

        13.3.3   Software Security   594

    13.4   Enterprise Network Authentication   598

        13.4.1   Direct Authentication   600

        13.4.2   Indirect Authentication   602

        13.4.3   Off-Line Authentication   606

    13.5   Contingency Planning   608

        13.5.1   Data Backup and Restoration   608

        13.5.2   Handling Serious Incidents   612

        13.5.3   Disaster Preparation and Recovery   613

    13.6   Resources   616

        13.6.1   Review Questions   617

        13.6.2   Exercises   618

Chapter 14   Network Encryption   619

    14.1   Communications Security   619

        14.1.1   Crypto by Layers   621

        14.1.2   Administrative and Policy Issues   627

14.2   Crypto Keys on a Network   629
    14.2.1   Manual Keying: A Building Block   632
    14.2.2   Simple Rekeying   633
    14.2.3   Secret-Key Building Blocks   635
    14.2.4   Public-Key Building Blocks   638
    14.2.5   Public-Key Versus Secret-Key Exchanges   641

14.3   Crypto Atop the Protocol Stack   642
    14.3.1   Transport Layer Security—SSL and TLS   645
    14.3.2   SSL Handshake Protocol   647
    14.3.3   SSL Record Transmission   648

14.4   Network Layer Cryptography   651
    14.4.1   The Encapsulating Security Payload   654
    14.4.2   Implementing a VPN   656
    14.4.3   Internet Key Exchange Protocol   657

14.5   Link Encryption on 802.11 Wireless   659
    14.5.1   Wireless Packet Protection   661
    14.5.2   Security Associations   663

14.6   Encryption Policy Summary   665

14.7   Resources   668
    14.7.1   Review Questions   669
    14.7.2   Exercises   669

Chapter 15   Internet Services and Email   673
15.1   Internet Services   673

15.2   Internet Email   674
    15.2.1   Email Protocol Standards   679
    15.2.2   Tracking an Email   681
    15.2.3   Forging an Email Message   684

15.3   Email Security Problems   687
    15.3.1   Spam   688
    15.3.2   Phishing   691
    15.3.3   Email Viruses and Hoaxes   693

15.4 Enterprise Firewalls   695
      15.4.1 Controlling Internet Traffic   697
      15.4.2 Traffic-Filtering Mechanisms   698
      15.4.3 Implementing Firewall Rules   701

15.5 Enterprise Point of Presence   705
      15.5.1 POP Topology   706
      15.5.2 Attacking an Enterprise Site   709
      15.5.3 The Challenge of Real-Time Media   711

15.6 Resources   712
      15.6.1 Review Questions   713
      15.6.2 Exercises   713

Chapter 16 The World Wide Web   715
16.1 Hypertext Fundamentals   715
      16.1.1 Addressing Web Pages   719
      16.1.2 Retrieving a Static Web Page   722

16.2 Basic Web Security   724
      16.2.1 Static Website Security   728
      16.2.2 Server Authentication   730
      16.2.3 Server Masquerades   735

16.3 Dynamic Websites   738
      16.3.1 Scripts on the Web   739
      16.3.2 States and HTTP   743

16.4 Content Management Systems   746
      16.4.1 Database Management Systems   747
      16.4.2 Password Checking: A CMS Example   750
      16.4.3 Command Injection Attacks   752

16.5 Ensuring Web Security Properties   756
      16.5.1 Web Availability   757
      16.5.2 Web Privacy   758

16.6 Resources   760
      16.6.1 Review Questions   761
      16.6.2 Exercises   762

Chapter 17 Governments and Secrecy 765

   17.1 Secrecy in Government 765

      17.1.1 The Challenge of Secrecy 767

      17.1.2 Information Security and Operations 770

   17.2 Classifications and Clearances 773

      17.2.1 Security Labeling 775

      17.2.2 Security Clearances 777

      17.2.3 Classification Levels in Practice 779

      17.2.4 Compartments and Other Special Controls 780

   17.3 National Policy Issues 786

      17.3.1 Facets of National System Security 788

      17.3.2 Security Planning 790

      17.3.3 Certification and Accreditation 792

   17.4 Communications Security 793

      17.4.1 Cryptographic Technology 795

      17.4.2 Crypto Security Procedures 797

      17.4.3 Transmission Security 800

   17.5 Data Protection 803

      17.5.1 Protected Wiring 804

      17.5.2 TEMPEST 805

   17.6 Trustworthy Systems 808

      17.6.1 Integrity of Operations 810

      17.6.2 Multilevel Security 814

      17.6.3 Computer Modes of Operation 816

   17.7 Resources 818

      17.7.1 Review Questions 820

      17.7.2 Exercises 820

Appendix A Acronyms 823

Appendix B Alternative Security Terms and Concepts 833

Index 841

Credits 889

PREFACE

About the Book

The goal of this textbook is to introduce college students to information security. Security often involves social and organizational skills as well as technical understanding. To solve practical security problems, we must balance real-world risks and rewards against the cost and bother of available security techniques. This text uses continuous process improvement to integrate these elements.

Security is a broad field. Some students may excel in the technical aspects, while others may shine in the more social or process-oriented aspects. Many successful students fall between these poles. This text offers opportunities for all types of students to excel.

Introducing Technology

If we want a solid understanding of security technology, we must look closely at the underlying strengths and weaknesses of information technology itself. This requires a background in computer architecture, operating systems, and computer networking. It's hard for a typical college student to achieve breadth and depth in these subjects and still have time to really study security.

Instead of leaving a gap in students' understanding, this text provides introductions to essential technical topics. Chapter 2 explains the basics of computer operation and instruction execution. This prepares students for a description of process separation and protection, which illustrates the essential role of operating systems in enforcing security.

Chapter 5 introduces file systems and input/output in modern operating systems. This lays a foundation for forensic file system analysis. It also shows students how a modern operating system organizes a complex service. This sets the stage for Chapter 10's introduction to computer networking and protocol software.

Introducing Continuous Process Improvement

The text organizes security problem-solving around a six-phase security process. Chapter 1 introduces the process as a way of structuring information about a security event, and presents a simple approach to risk analysis. Chapter 2 introduces security policies as a way to state security objectives and security controls as a way to implement a policy. Subsequent chapters introduce system monitoring and incident response as ways to assess and improve system security.

Each step in the process builds on earlier steps. Each step also provides a chance to assess how well our work addresses our security needs. This is the essence of continuous process improvement.

In order to give students an accurate view of process improvement, the text introduces document structures that provide cross references between different steps of the process. We use elements of each earlier phase to construct information in the following phase, and we often provide a link back to earlier data to ensure complete coverage. While this may seem like nit-picking in some cases, it allows mastery of essential forms of communication in the technical and professional world.

Intended Audience

When used as a textbook, the material within is intended for lower division undergraduates, or for students in a two-year community college program. Students should have completed high school mathematics. Typical students should have also completed an introductory computing or programming course.

Instructors may want to use this book for either a one or two semester course. A one semester course would usually cover one chapter a week; the instructor may want to combine a couple of earlier chapters or skip the final chapter. Some institutions may find it more effective to teach the material over a full year. This gives the students more time to work with the concepts and to cover all topics in depth.

Following the style of my earlier books, this text focuses on diagrams and practical explanations to present fundamental concepts. This makes the material clearer to all readers and makes it more accessible to the math-phobic reader. Many concepts, particularly in cryptography, can be clearly presented in either a diagram or in mathematical notation. This text uses both, with a bias toward diagrams.

Many fundamental computing concepts are wildly abstract. This is also true in security, where we sometimes react to illusions perceived as risks. To combat this, the text incorporates a series of concrete examples played out by characters with names familiar to those who read cryptographic papers: Bob, Alice, and Eve. They are joined by additional classmates named Tina and Kevin, since different people have different security concerns.

Curriculum Standards

The material in this text is designed to fulfill curriculum requirements published by the U.S. government and the Association for Computing Machinery (ACM). In particular, this text contains all required topics for training information systems security professionals under the Information Assurance Courseware Evaluation Program (NSTISSI #4011) established by the U.S. National Security Agency (NSA). This text also provides substantial coverage of the required topics for training senior system managers (CNSSI #4012) and system administrators (CNSSI #4013).

This text also covers the core learning outcomes for information security education published in the ACM's "IT 2008" curricular recommendations for Information Technology education. As a reviewer and contributor to the published recommendations, the author is familiar with its guidelines.

Students who are interested in becoming a Certified Information System Security Professional (CISSP) may use this book as a study aid for the examination. All key areas of the CISSP Common Body of Knowledge are covered in this text. Certification requires four or five years of professional experience in addition to passing the exam.

Teaching Security

Information security is a fascinating but abstract subject. This text introduces students to real-world security problem solving, and incorporates security technology into the problem-solving process. There are many "how to" books that explain how to harden a computer system.

Many readers and most students need more than a "how to" book. They need to decide *which* security measures are most important, or how to trade off between alternatives. Such decisions often depend on what assets are at stake and what risks the computer's owner is willing to take.

The practitioner's most important task is the planning and analysis that helps choose and justify a set of security measures. In my own experience, and in that of my most capable colleagues, security systems succeed when we anticipate the principal risks and design the system to address them. In fact, once we have identified *what we want* for security (our policy requirements), we don't need security gurus to figure out *what we get* (our implementation). We just need capable programmers, testers, and administrators.

Pedagogy

As each chapter unfolds, we encounter important *key terms* indicated in bold italics. These highlight essential terms that students may encounter in the information security community. Successful students will recognize these terms. These terms are also defined on the Companion website (see next page).

The **Resources** section at the end of each chapter lists the key terms and provides review questions and exercises. The review questions help students confirm that they have absorbed the essential concepts. Some instructors may want to use these as recitation or quiz questions. The exercises give students the opportunity to solve problems based on techniques presented in the text.

Student and Instructor Resources

Each new text includes an access code that gives students access to a Companion website. The website includes multiple study tools for students, including an Interactive Glossary, Flashcards, Crossword Puzzles, and links to relevant websites for each chapter.

Instructor resources, including PowerPoint lecture outlines, Solutions to End-of-Chapter Exercises, and Test Items, are available for download at go.jblearning.com/infosec.

Acknowledgments

For graphics and other materials:

    Computer History Museum

    KeyGhost, Inc.

    Titan Missile Museum

    U.S. Library of Congress

At Jones & Bartlett Learning:

    Tim Anderson, Senior Acquisitions Editor

    Amy Rose, Director of Production

Reviewers:

    Clint Andera, Northern Star Council, Boy Scouts of America

    Lesley Atwood, MD, Allina Medical Clinic

    Beth-Ann Bloom, Minnesota Department of Health

    Jeremy Epstein, SRI International

    Daniel P. Faigin, CISSP, The Aerospace Corporation

    Daniel Feldman, University of Minnesota

    Dr. Sunil Hazari, University of West Georgia

    Dr. Cedric Jeannot, I Think Security

    Ray Kaplan, CISSP, Ray Kaplan & Associates

    John Linn, RSA Security

    Daniel W. Oehmke, State of Minnesota

    Charles Payne, Adventium

    Dr. Charles P. Pfleeger, Pfleeger Consulting Group

    Dan Thomsen, SIFT

I am also grateful for the support of my family and friends.

SECURITY FROM THE GROUND UP

ABOUT THIS CHAPTER

This chapter introduces the first steps in solving security problems. We examine the overall problems of information security and security decision making. The chapter focuses on the following topics:

- A six-phase process for managing and improving information security
- A strategy for identifying security risks
- A process for comparing and prioritizing security risks

1.1 The Security Landscape

Information security problems can be small and local and they can be international in scope, involving computers and organizations on every continent. In this book, we start with information security on a personal computer, especially the risks of misuse. As we move to later chapters, we increase our scope to sets of people and assets and to networks of computers. The progression goes like this:

- **An isolated computer**
  - The security cycle and risk assessment process (Chapter 1)
  - Computer-based access control (Chapters 2–4)
  - File systems and forensics (Chapter 5)
- **Cryptographic techniques**
  - Authentication (Chapter 6)
  - Encryption and key management (Chapters 7–9)
- **Computer networking basics**
  - Local network fundamentals (Chapter 10)
  - Internet protocols (Chapters 11–12)
- **Large-scale security**
  - Enterprise security (Chapter 13)

- Site and network encryption (Chapter 14)
- Internet services and applications (Chapters 15–16)
- Governments and secrecy (Chapter 17)

We start with an overview of security problem solving in Chapter 1. We practice examining security problems, identifying their features, and estimating risks.

In computer-based access control, we rely on computer logic to control access to protected programs and data. In Chapters 2 through 5, we build these controls up from special features of modern computers, and we rely on features of modern operating systems. Most people see this access control at work protecting files.

Authentication and encryption rely on mathematical puzzles to protect information. Conventional password systems often rely on computing techniques related to encryption. Chapters 7 through 9 use these mechanisms as building blocks to protect data stored in files and entire hard drives.

While the earlier chapters focus on individual computers, the remaining chapters consider the challenges of multiple computers used by growing user communities. Internet-based networking is a major force in information security today. It is also a complicated subject. We study it in layers, starting with local networks in Chapter 10, progressing to network interconnections in Chapter 11, and then to end-to-end Internet communications in Chapter 12.

Enterprises face a broad range of challenges that don't impact individuals. Chapter 13 examines this environment and the strategies often used to address information security in large businesses and other organizations. Enterprise security is heavily influenced by national and international standards for information security planning, auditing, and control. We will examine those standards and how they affect information security practice.

Chapters 14 through 16 complete our coverage of the Internet and its security technologies. First, we will look at network cryptography and specific techniques applied to modern, Internet-compatible systems; then we examine Internet services with a focus on email and web service.

The final chapter examines the challenges facing government information security. A classic example is the control of nuclear weapons. Other challenges arise when handling classified information (data marked "Secret" or "Top Secret," for example).

Not Just Computers Any More

Many people associate computer viruses and other security problems with desktop and laptop computers, or with company servers; problems that intrude on web surfing or other traditional computer activities. Today, however, every electronic appliance contains a computer. Many of them connect through the Internet or other networks and even let us upload "apps" or other customized programs.

This flexibility opens our products up to security risks. If we can upload an application to our personal digital assistant (PDA) or smart phone, we also can upload a virus.

We reduce the risk if we rely on reputable sources for our applications. We can choose to be more adventurous, but then we increase our risks.

As computers move into factories and utilities, security problems follow. Many industrial systems and power grids rely on supervisory control and data acquisition (SCADA) devices or programmable logic controllers (PLCs). These are special computers designed to control motors, valves, and other devices in industrial applications. Modern systems connect these systems together into a network.

In the past, SCADA and PLC system designers have tried to protect the computers by isolating their networks from the Internet and other threats. Internally, their networks relied on very weak defenses. In 2010, the Stuxnet worm appeared: a malicious program that sneaks onto isolated networks, and then seeks out and reprograms specific PLC devices (see Section 3.2.4). Stuxnet illustrates how easily a worm could attack manufacturing and utility systems.

Modern computer-controlled automobiles don't face a virus risk yet, but researchers have found vulnerabilities in their control systems. One research team found a way to track individual vehicles through the wireless tire pressure sensors. Another could trick the control system into braking or killing the engine.

1.1.1 Making Security Decisions

We all make security decisions on a daily basis. Regardless of how much—or how little—is at stake, some security decisions are hard to make. While we don't want to risk breaking or losing a piece of gold jewelry or an expensive camera, we don't leave all of our possessions in a bank vault. What is the point of spending money on a special item if we don't benefit from owning it?

Computing poses the same problem. On the one hand, a good laptop computer can be very expensive and demands protection from risk. Whenever we bring it along, we risk theft or damage. Whenever we connect it to the Internet, we risk virus and worm infestation, not to mention phishing attacks and other forms of fraud. However, we only reap the benefits of ownership when we actually take advantage of what the computer can do.

Security choices fall into three categories described here:

1. **Rule-based decisions:** These are made for us by external circumstances or established, widely accepted guidelines (example: car ignition locks).
2. **Relativistic decisions:** These try to "outdo" others who are faced with similar security problems (example: the hunter's dilemma described later).
3. **Rational decisions:** These are based on a systematic analysis of the security situation (example: the security process, described in the next section).

Some security decisions are made for us. For example, all modern automobiles include keys and locks for the ignition and doors. We rarely leave the keys in a car's ignition (Figure 1.1). Although this may seem like common sense, the behavior stems from public service advertising in the 1970s. At the time there was a barrage of ads

Rule-based security.

commanding: "Lock the door. Take the keys." While most of us find it almost painful to leave keys in the ignition, others leave keys in the ignition as a habit, particularly in rural areas. Such people are more worried about a lost key than a stolen car.

When we look at a friend's bike lock and then buy a more impressive model for ourselves, we are making a relativistic security decision. These decisions reflect the *hunter's dilemma*: You are with a group of hunters who encounter an angry bear. The bear can run faster than you can, so how do you escape? Cynics and survivors point out that you don't have to outrun the bear; you only have to outrun another hunter.

This bit of cruel wisdom suggests that you don't have to defeat all potential threats, you simply have to be harder to catch (or rob) than your neighbor. In some cases, the security may be purely cosmetic: Many businesses install fake video cameras and hope that potential shoplifters will go elsewhere to steal merchandise. Relativistic security also leads a phenomenon that security expert Bruce Schneier calls "security theater" in his 2003 book *Beyond Fear*. Security theater refers to security measures intended to make potential victims feel safe and secure without regard to their effectiveness.

Security decisions made for us—or those based on one-upmanship—are not always the best ones. In a successful outing, all hunters return unscathed, and safe neighborhoods have as little theft as possible. Moreover, if you simply try to outdo your neighbor with a more elaborate version of the same security measures, you may both overlook a completely different threat. For example, a higher fence and a stronger lock will not protect your home from a clever bit of property fraud.

Rational security decisions often reflect a mind-set called *reasoned paranoia*. This involves a continuous intellectual quest to identify potential threats and worst- case scenarios. While reason may obligate us to lock our cars, we are not obliged to set up shields to protect ourselves from meteors.

When selecting our security measures, we need to apply knowledge and reason to systematically prune back our list of risks to those we can reasonably address. It is no sin to identify a risk and fail to defend against it, but we must justify that choice by comparing the security costs against the potential damage.

1.1.2 The Security Process

Security decisions can be incredibly complex, even when we look at a relatively small and simple problem. To make a rational decision, we need to marshall the details of the problem and work through them systematically. This yields the six-phase *security process* shown in Figure 1.2.

The phases take place in order, with the later steps building on the results of earlier phases. In some cases, the results from a later phase may lead us to revisit an earlier step and revise its output.

This type of process crops up many times in other fields of computing and engineering. The *systems engineering process* is a way to plan, design, and build a large-scale system. Companies that build complicated technical products like operating systems, automobiles, or aircraft often follow a similar process.

These different processes share some crucial features:

- **Planning**: early phases lay out the project's expectations
- **Trade-off analysis**: early phases compare alternative solutions against the project's expectations to ensure the best outcome

---

1. Identify your assets.
2. Analyze the risk of attack.
3. Establish your security policy.
4. Implement your defenses.
5. Monitor your defenses.
6. Recover from attacks.

Figure 1.2

The six phases of the security process.

- **Verification:** later phases verify that the implemented system meets expectations established in earlier phases
- **Iteration:** if a later phase detects a problem with the results of earlier phases, then revisit the earlier phases to correct the problem

These processes try to ensure that resources spent on a project yield the expected result. Large projects use a lot of resources and pose a serious risk: Enterprises can't afford to invest in a project only to have it fail. These steps help organize the work among a large team and track the project's progress.

The security process serves an additional purpose; it ensures that we have systematically reviewed the risks facing the system. When we rely purely on rules or on relativist security decisions, we are assuming that we all face the same risks. For example, several organizations have the following security rule:

Never use a removable storage device in any company computer.

Companies invoke this rule for many reasons. Several recent computer viruses, including Stuxnet and Conficker, spread through infected storage drives. Companies also may lose vast amounts of sensitive company data or experience a large-scale privacy breach if someone copies the wrong information onto a removable drive.

In contrast, students use removable storage devices all the time, usually a USB drive that attaches to a universal serial bus connection. Some instructors recommend or require USB drives for particular courses. Does this expose students to an unnecessary security risk—or is that rule unnecessarily cautious? If students use antivirus software and avoid connecting their USB drive in risky situations, then the risk should be small. The security process allows us to identify risks that concern us and to avoid rules that don't really make us safer.

1.1.3 Continuous Improvement: A Basic Principle

The security process and the systems engineering process find their origin in the concept of *Continuous Improvement*. A process based on the Continuous Improvement principle never ends at the final step. Instead, any step in the process may suggest a change that will improve the result. To implement the change, we return to earlier steps in the cycle. Once we make the change, we continue the process.

Continuous Improvement is a *basic principle* of *information security*. We will encounter several such basic principles in this textbook. Security experts generally acknowledge these basic principles as fundamental building blocks for constructing and maintaining secure systems. To emphasize these principles, the textbook capitalizes them when used.

The Roots of Continuous Improvement

The modern roots of this principle are found in Japan. Following World War II, Japan rebuilt its industrial structure and Japanese companies sought a strategy to compete in international markets against more successful countries. In the 1950s, Japanese merchandise was derided for poor quality. This changed, however, over the next 30 years as a few visionary manufacturers systematically improved their quality.

These manufacturers were heavily influenced by the work of the U.S. expert W. Edwards Deming (1900–1993). While most U.S. manufacturers took haphazard approaches to quality assurance, the Japanese manufacturers embraced what they called the *Deming cycle*:

- **Plan**—Establish and document the objectives and processes needed to achieve the goals.
- **Do**—Implement the processes.
- **Check**—Measure the actual results against the expected results to find the differences.
- **Act**—Analyze the differences to determine their causes and revise the processes. If no improvements are needed, revise the scope of the cycle to require improvements.

The four letters also form the acronym "PDCA." The concept has since been adopted as part of an international standard for information security: ISO 27002, issued by the International Standards Organization. The 27002 standard lists best practices in information security. The standard is used in conjunction with ISO 27001 to certify that the information management within an organization is robust, effective, and self-correcting through continuous improvement. We will examine these standards further in Section 13.2.

The PDCA concept is based on statistical quality improvement techniques developed by Walter A. Shewhart (1891–1967) in the early 20th century. Shewhart is called "the father of statistical quality control." Some experts call the PDCA cycle the "Shewhart cycle." We can further trace the roots of this concept back to the origins of the scientific method as outlined by Francis Bacon in 1620.

The PDCA cycle is itself subject to interpretation and improvement as it is applied to different fields. In the 1980s, the Motorola Corporation crafted the "Six Sigma" process for manufacturing management through continuous improvement cycles. Six Sigma and variations of it were adopted by numerous corporations. There is also the "OODA loop," which is used in the defense and business communities. Developed by military strategist John Boyd (1927–1997), the acronym stands for "Observe, Orient, Decide, and Act."

1.2 Process Example: Bob's Computer

Bob is a new student living in a dormitory suite he shares with others. His computer sits on a desk in the suite's common area. His suitemates have physical access to it.

Initially, Bob did not implement any security on the computer. Anyone could sit down in front of it and use it. Then Bob started losing files. He concluded that someone was using the computer and, possibly through carelessness, damaging his files.

We will use Bob's computer problem to demonstrate *high-level analysis*, using the security process. In general, a high-level analysis provides a few paragraphs summarizing the important aspects of each phase. The following examination of Bob's situation may apply reasonably well to other students with a similar lifestyle.

We will perform a high-level analysis of other security incidents and situations later in the text. There are also exercises at the end of the chapter that require a high-level analysis.

ASSETS

When assessing security, the *assets* represent the physical devices, the items of information, and the services we rely on. A description of a situation should include the assets; the things or services that need protection.

Bob uses his computer to do schoolwork and for entertainment. If Bob's computer becomes unusable, it impacts his ability to work in his suite instead of relying on computer labs elsewhere on campus. Moreover, Bob has stored his most recent assignments on the computer.

RISKS

When assessing security, the *risks* are the potential situations that threaten the assets. If we have a description of a situation, the risks identify bad things that could happen to assets.

While some risks, like a tornado or hurricane, aren't blamed on people, most security risks arise because some people act maliciously. We call such people *threat agents*. We categorize them according to their likely acts and motivation: What might they do and why? For example, a thief will physically steal things, and is probably motivated by a need for cash or possessions.

Bob faces risks from specific threat agents: Someone might steal his computer, or someone might damage files on his computer. Dorm residents rarely steal each other's computers. Bob's tower unit is not a particularly expensive model, and most students already have a computer. Moreover, a locked door restricts access to the dorm by non-residents, and another locked door secures the suite from all except those who live there. It is possible that someone might be inclined to grab his computer if the doors were unlocked.

Within the suite, Bob did not expect his suitemates to bother using his computer. He knew it wasn't a particularly powerful or appealing machine, so he assumed it would be immune from abuse. As a naive new student, Bob did not expect other students to be careless with borrowed equipment, or that suitemates might play practical jokes on each others' computers.

POLICY

In general, a *security policy* describes the protection we need. Security policy also may be referred to as *security goals* or *security requirements*. When we read a description of a situation, the policy or goals identify *what* protections we want, without necessarily saying *how* the protections work. The policy reflects a balance between the value of the assets and the likelihood of damage based on the risks we identified.

The first part of Bob's policy is to avoid the theft of his computer by storing it in a place potential thieves don't enter. More precisely, Bob has identified a **boundary**, the suite he lives in, and limits access to the suite by thieves.

The second part of Bob's policy deals with *misuse* of his computer: actions that don't deprive him of the computer itself, but deprive him of the information and services it provides. His policy seeks to exclude others from using his computer. Bob initially assumes that his suitemates won't mess with his computer, so he doesn't specify a boundary to exclude them.

IMPLEMENTATION

We have described *what* protections Bob wants, and now we describe *how* he tries to achieve them. When reading a description, we see **implementation** when it identifies specific details of the protection. In this example, separate parts of the policy are addressed by separate parts of the implementation.

The first part of the policy identifies a boundary to prevent theft. The implementation describes how the boundary corresponds to genuine protective measures, and how to handle any holes in the boundary, like the doorways. Clearly, the suite's walls represent most of the boundary. Bob completes this part of the implementation by locking the suite door. His implementation further assumes that his suitemates also will keep the suite door locked.

The second part of the policy declares that other people should not use Bob's computer. Initially, Bob assumes that his suitemates won't use other peoples' possessions, even when they are sitting unattended in the suite's common area. This assumption proved wrong.

MONITORING

Security measures aren't implemented in a vacuum. Often they are just a delaying tactic, something to slow the attacker down while raising the alarm. Sometimes they only provide indications that trouble occurred and a record of the harm. This does not always tell us the entire story.

An Incident: A team of consultants visited a smaller *Fortune* 500 company to help them establish a computer security program. The company had some protections installed by rule, but very little else. The IT manager described an incident that occurred the night before: A person had connected to the main server over the Internet and located "the big spreadsheet" used to track and control the company's financial status. The spreadsheet included every possible operational detail, including salaries of all employees. The IT manager was unhappy because the visitor had changed the access permissions so that anyone in the company could read or write "the big spreadsheet" and, in particular, look at the salaries.

The consultant sighed and asked, "Can you tell me if the visitor, or anyone else, has also *modified* the spreadsheet?"

The IT manager gasped. If someone *had* modified the spreadsheet, there would be no way to tell which cells had been changed. The spreadsheet had thousands of cells.

The IT manager detected the break-in by *monitoring* the site's Internet connection. Additional monitoring might have provided a better indication of the damage the attacker did.

There are several ways to keep track of what happens to a computer. Most operating systems provide "logging" or "security auditing" services that keep track of significant events. Traditionally, such mechanisms are turned off to save resources: a detailed log requires extra computing time to create and a lot of hard disk space for storage. Separately, most file systems keep track of which files have been modified, and users can often use this feature to identify recent changes. In Bob's case, he did not try to assess what happened to his computer, nor did he take steps to collect better information if the problem were to happen again.

RECOVERY

After an attack occurs, we go through a *recovery* process. We need to assess the impact, recover whatever assets we can, and reestablish our defenses. We may need to revisit our risk analysis based on new knowledge about the risks we face. This may yield changes in our policy, implementation, or monitoring strategy.

Bob recovered from his "attack." He restored his missing files as best as he could. However, his security measures (or lack thereof) failed to protect his computer from violations of the second part of his policy. He assumed that his suitemates, and their guests, would not bother his computer, whether out of disinterest or good manners.

Initially, Bob's policy defined the security boundary to include his suite. This worked as long as he could trust his suitemates to leave his computer alone. In fact, he found that they did not meet his expectations. Thus they are actually threat agents *inside* his security boundary.

Bob's Response

To address these risks, Bob needs to identify and enforce another boundary. The valuable components must be inside the boundary, and the threat agents (Bob's suitemates) must be outside the boundary.

As we will see in later chapters, the software on a computer relies on the *integrity* of the computer's hardware. In other words, we can make Windows or any other operating system behave in surprising ways if we can interfere with the computer's processor, memory, or other internal components. Thus, Bob needs to define a boundary that includes his computer hardware. For Bob's tower unit, this corresponds to the computer's physical case.

Bob then needs to exclude, or at least control, what people do with his computer. Modern computers almost all implement a *login* feature; the computer refuses to provide services until the person supplies identifying information. The computer provides services only if it recognizes the person. This allows Bob to exclude everyone from using the computer as long as they don't open its case.

1.3 Assets and Risk Assessment

When we face simple security problems, the most common response is to apply a rule-based approach: We identify the specific risk and apply a specific security measure to defend against it. To defend against thieves walking through an open door, we put a lock on the door and keep it locked. When Bob first moved into the suite, he assumed his computer faced a low risk of damage from his suitemates. His assessment proved wrong, so he enabled password protection.

Bob didn't perform a detailed risk assessment to arrive at this conclusion, but he did recognize the asset at risk: his computer and its contents. The first step in applying reasonable security measures is to identify the assets we need to protect.

In this section, we look at identifying assets, the things you need to protect. We also take a high-level look at the *risk-assessment* process. We will look more closely at the individual steps of the risk-assessment process in later sections.

Risk assessment is not an exclusive feature of information security; it figures prominently in many disciplines. For example, ASIS International (formerly known as the American Society for Industrial Security) has developed a risk-assessment guideline for general commercial and industrial environments. This process is very similar to the one outlined here: First, we enumerate risks and then we prioritize them. An important difference, however, is how the ASIS guideline enumerates risks.

The ASIS guideline focuses on industrial and commercial enterprises. These enterprises have dealt with security risks for decades, even centuries. Many of their risks, whether universal or specific to distinctive communities and disciplines, are well known to practitioners. To produce an appropriate list of risks, the ASIS guideline focuses on commonly recognized events, like crimes reported in the area as well as natural and nonnatural disasters. This works well when risks are well established and well known.

IDENTIFYING RISKS

Information risks are not as well established; even worse, they evolve and change very rapidly. This demands a different strategy to identify risks. Instead of trying to list every specific risk, we identify them by analyzing other elements: threat agents, attacks, vulnerabilities, and defenses. We produce our list of risks by studying these elements in the context of our assets and the boundaries we've built around them. Figure 1.3 illustrates the relationship of these elements.

We encountered threat agents when analyzing Bob's situation. We don't need to identify threat agents by name; we identify them in terms of their behavior. Superficially, Bob

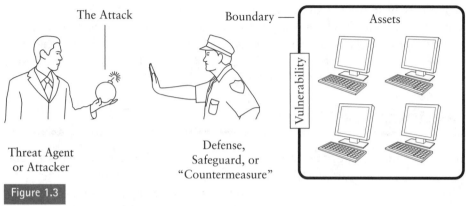

Figure 1.3

Elements of identifying risks.

faces two threat agents: thieves and meddlers. Thieves are most likely to be outside his suite and perhaps even outside the dorm. Meddlers, people who use his computer without permission and who lose his files, may be suitemates.

An *attack* is an attempt by a threat agent to exploit the assets without permission. We call a threat agent an *attacker* when action replaces inclination and the attack actually takes place. If we have defined a security boundary, then an attack may be an attempt to breach the boundary. While thefts or acts of meddling may be attacks, we need to be more specific to perform a risk assessment. Typically, we identify attacks in terms of exploited vulnerabilities and broken defenses.

A *vulnerability* is a weakness in the boundary that protects the assets from the threat agents. We often see this as an opening or other weakness in the boundary. For example, a door represents a vulnerability, because it can admit thieves into Bob's suite.

A *defense,* safeguard, or countermeasure is a security measure intended to protect the asset. The boundary is the basic defense. Additional defenses often are associated with specific vulnerabilities. For example, a door lock is a defense intended to address the vulnerability posed by a door.

FINE POINTS OF TERMINOLOGY

Threat agents and attackers both refer to people or other active entities; we distinguish them by what they *have* done, not what they might do. For example, Bob might think of all of his suitemates as threat agents of his computer. However, there has only been one attack, so far. The person who performed that attack is the attacker. A threat agent is a person who *might* attack our assets; an attacker *did* attack an asset.

A *compromised system* is one that is no longer safe to use as a result of an attack. An attack often compromises a system by disabling security measures, which increases the risk of leaking confidential information. An attack may also install software that bypasses security measures and allows the attacker to easily penetrate the system again or use it as a platform to attack other systems.

A *botnet* is a collection of compromised systems controlled remotely by the attacker. Botnets may contain thousands of computers. Each compromised system contains special software to allow the network's controller to give commands to the systems. Such systems often send "spam." By spreading the emails out among thousands of systems, the flood of email isn't detected as a flood.

Hackers

The *hacker* has become an almost mythical figure in the computing community. The term originally arose in university research labs to refer to local experts with an almost uncanny understanding of computer systems. In the 1980s, the popular press used the term to identify people who attacked computers and other systems. A lexicon has developed to identify different people involved in attacking computer systems:

- *Script kiddy*—a person who uses an attack developed by another party to attack computers. The attack may be implemented using a "scripting language," so the attacker literally executes the script to attack the computer.
- *Cracker*—a person who has learned specific attacks on computer systems and can use those specific attacks. A cracker doesn't necessarily have the technical knowledge to modify the attacks and apply them to different types of targets.
- *Phone phreak*—a person who attacks telephone systems, usually to make long distance and international calls for free. John Draper (nicknamed "Captain Crunch") was a notorious phone phreak in the early 1970s.
- *Hacker*—a person with a high degree of knowledge and skill with computing systems, including the ability to attack them if so motivated. The term arose at the Massachusetts Institute of Technology (MIT) in the 1950s and was applied to computer enthusiasts in the 1960s.
- *Black-hat hacker*—a person skilled in attacking computer systems, who uses those skills to attack a system. During the 1980s and 1990s, Kevin Mitnick became notorious for both phone phreaking and for computer break-ins. Following a prison term, Mitnick became a writer and consultant.
- *White-hat hacker*—a person skilled in attacking computer systems, who uses those skills as a security expert to help protect systems. Experts like Jeff Moss and Ray Kaplan have used their knowledge of hacking and the hacker community to bring such information to the security community.

Today, the term hacker almost always is used in the context of computer security, and the hacker is able to penetrate a system of interest. The term black hat or white hat indicates the hacker's motivation: whether he or she is inclined to attack or defend systems.

"Reformed" black-hat hackers pose a dilemma for the information security community. While their knowledge is often valuable, many companies will not hire a convicted felon to do security work, regardless of skill. There are a few well-known exceptions, including Mitnick and Frank Abnagale, the central character of the film *Catch Me if You Can* (2002).

1.3.1 What Are We Protecting?

Although it is easy to assume that Bob's main asset is his computer, the information and services the computer provides may be the most valuable assets, and not the specific physical device. If Bob has insurance on his computer or can easily replace it some other way, he still has lost his assignments and other personal items stored on it.

IDENTIFYING GOALS

To better discuss assets, let's look at overall goals and objectives in a real-world context. A company that sells clothes doesn't talk about its goals in terms of server uptime, it talks in terms of items successfully sold and not returned.

To continue analyzing Bob's problem, our first step is to identify Bob's goals, particularly those achieved by his computer, directly or indirectly. The computer might not help him play hockey or lacrosse, but it helps him stay in school so he can play more hockey and lacrosse. Thus, we've identified goals of staying in school and playing sports.

IDENTIFYING ASSETS

Now that we have identified Bob's goals, we identify computing activities and resources that support those goals. We should strive for a complete list. If we omit any goals supported by his computer, then we won't identify risks associated with those goals. Here are examples of computing activities and resources to consider as Bob's assets:

- Computer hardware—naturally, each hardware item is itself an asset.
  - Windows tower computer.
- Purchased software—each purchased software package can incur an expense if it is lost. At the least, it will cost time to reinstall software if the computer hardware fails and installation disks are available. There also may be extra purchase costs if the installation disks are lost.
  - Windows installation disk.
  - Office software installation disk.
- Computer customization—it takes time to install and organize information on a computer in a way that works efficiently. Bob takes his desktop layout very seriously. This time must be spent if a computer is lost and replaced by a new one.
- Work data—this is data developed to do work to achieve particular goals. This may be on behalf of an employer or for school.
  - Homework files.
  - Other coursework files.
- Financial data—this is data involving money and financial transactions. Its disclosure could open the risk of identity theft or embezzlement.
  - College business office information (bills, etc.).
  - Financial aid information.
  - Banking information.

- Personal data—this is data that people want to keep private and only disclose to specific people. The data could be health related or social related, including that stored on social websites.
- Student or work activities—these are computing activities associated with one's work as a student or as a person making a living. This may involve using software residing on the computer or via a network connection. Note that *activities* are different from *data*. You may be able to participate in an activity even if you lose important data related to that activity.
- Financial activities—these are computing activities that handle money, like banking and bill paying.
- Social activities—these are computing activities that involve socializing with other people.
- Research activities—these are computing activities that involve collecting data from various sources.

This list is sufficient to consider Bob's situation even though the list is not necessarily complete. Every user needs to analyze objectives individually or in terms of their organization. This asset list serves as an example.

1.3.2 Security Boundaries

Physical security is the foundation of all computer security. We need to keep our computing equipment physically protected from threat agents. If we can rely on the safety of the physical hardware, then we can focus our efforts on keeping the software secure. However, no amount of software security can redeem a system whose hardware has been compromised.

Boundaries are the essence of physical protection. A physical boundary establishes a container for our assets. We protect the assets from threat agents by denying them access to the container's contents. We measure the degree of protection by the strength of the boundary; we achieve strong protection if the boundary is very difficult to breach without permission.

LEAST PRIVILEGE: A SECOND BASIC PRINCIPLE

Asset security also depends on the people who can cross the boundary. In general, an asset is safer if we limit the number of people allowed inside its security boundary. If possible, we also restrict what each person may do to the asset. We call this *Least Privilege*. We enforce Least Privilege when we give people as few privileges as possible regarding the assets we try to protect.

EXAMPLE: BOUNDARIES IN A DORM

Figure 1.4 illustrates the boundaries of Bob's dorm. The locked front door represents a coarse version of Least Privilege; residents and staff may enter the dorm, but not the general public.

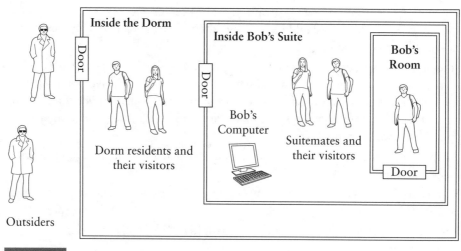

Figure 1.4

Physical boundaries of Bob's dorm.

We'd like to exclude only those people who might harm residents or steal things, but there's no practical way to do that. Within the dorm, we apply Least Privilege again on individual suites; suitemates have keys to their own suites but not to others.

Boundary security has an obvious problem: Protecting the boundary is not the same as protecting the asset itself. Sometimes we can't help but grant access to a threat agent, regardless of how careful we might be. The dorm's entrance allows some outsiders to enter as guests of residents, and we know that threat agents will enter the dorm occasionally, too. We consider suitemates to be less-significant threat agents, but Bob's experience shows that he can't trust them entirely.

Analyzing the Boundary

Boundaries consist of two parts: the "walls" and the "doorways." The walls are fixed parts of the boundary that nobody can cross, not even those allowed inside. The doorways are the parts of the boundary that allow passage. The security challenge is to allow passage through the doors without letting any threat agents through. In computing, we often refer to the doorways as interfaces between the inside and the outside.

When analyzing security, a boundary poses four questions:

1. What must a threat agent do to breach a wall?
2. How do we control the doorways to exclude threat agents?
3. How can a threat agent pass through the doorway despite our protections?
4. We are trusting those we allow inside. Exactly what are we trusting them to do—or not to do?

The point of the boundary is to keep the threat agents outside, away from our assets, and allow the trustworthy inside. The first question asks about the risk of breaching a wall. If it's practical for a threat agent to breach a wall, the risk assessment must include that risk in our Phase 2 assessment. In many cases, walls are strong enough not to be breached, and the risk is not important.

The second question asks how we control access to doorways. In a dorm or suite, the answer involves keys of some kind, either mechanical or electronic. In computing, we use special security controls built into our software. Our risk assessment identifies threat agents and in Phase 3, our policy identifies who we allow through the door. In Phase 4, our implementation decides *how* we control the door.

The third question considers the likelihood of an attacker breaking the access control or tricking it somehow. This leads to a trade-off between alternative security measures. A stronger or more sophisticated locking mechanism, or an armed guard, might further reduce the risk. Now we ask whether the cost of an attack justifies the more expensive security measures.

The Insider Threat

The fourth question asks about the ***insider threat***: What threat agents exist *inside* our security boundary? Although it is tempting to treat all threat agents as purely bad and anyone we trust as perfectly good, the world is not so simple. Some people are clearly threat agents in some cases but are trustworthy in others.

The fourth boundary question raises this point. We can trust Bob's suitemates not to steal his computer and sell it, but we can't trust them as a group to leave it entirely alone. In some cases, then, we have to specify how we trust various people and identify the situations in which those same people might pose a threat.

In some cases, we can't build a strong enough wall or door, but we can detect a breach in one or the other. We strengthen the security by installing an alarm to call for help if a breach occurs. Alarms don't provide physical protection, but they pose a risk to the attacker: Can the attack succeed and the attacker withdraw to safety before someone answers the alarm? Many attackers rely heavily on stealth, and the alarm makes a stealthy attack less likely. The alarm might not deter all attackers, but it helps us recognize when attacks occur and helps motivate a rapid response.

1.3.3 Security Architecture

We often organize a security problem by defining boundaries and doorways in one sense or another. Bob started with physical walls and doorways, and then identified his computer's case as another boundary. His "security architecture" consists of the security measures he applied and how they interact.

When we write a computer program, we establish boundaries when we put different functions into different procedures and files. We create doorways when we provide functions that different procedures may use. These decisions establish the structure of the program.

When we establish boundaries and doorways to address an information security problem, we produce an ***information security architecture***. Such an architecture often relies on boundaries *inside* the computer to protect important information and programs from error-prone or malicious programs.

Within a security architecture, we often find separate *security domains*. Each domain is a place marked out by security boundaries; each domain has its own set of security expectations. For example, Bob's suite is a security domain, and the public halls of his dorm are a different security domain. Each has its own security expectations.

We may even perform a separate security analysis on each domain. Each domain has its objectives and assets. Each domain has its policy for protecting and restricting actions. Each domain has its own trade-off to choose security over potential risk.

When we analyze a system using the six-phase security process, we are performing a *security architecture study*. As students, some of these studies assess an existing system's boundaries and security measures. Other studies may look at systems after a dramatic failure and try to pinpoint problems that led to the failure. We try to associate the failure with a flaw in one or more phases of the security process.

A high-level analysis, like the one in Section 1.2, is a simple example of a security architecture study. Instead of going into details, we explain each phase with a few paragraphs of narrative. We often do this when a particular system or incident highlights a particular security principle.

A *security plan* is an architecture study for a system that doesn't exist. The plan identifies appropriate security measures to implement the system's security policy. This information guides the builders to produce a secure system. Structurally, the plan looks like an architecture study that stops at the fourth phase. However, an effective plan also includes procedures and mechanisms that address the fifth and sixth phases: how to monitor the system and recover from security incidents.

DEFENSE IN DEPTH: A THIRD BASIC PRINCIPLE

Bob's suite doesn't connect directly to the outside. Figure 1.4 shows that a thief must traverse two separate doorways to reach his suite. Dorms used to issue special keys to residents that opened the front door to the building, the suite's door, and their individual room door. There were also "master keys" that would open any door in the building. This was a problem, because a stolen master key would bypass all security in the dorm.

Today, dorms often use one type of lock on the front door and a different type on the suite door. For example, the dorm's front door may require a "swipe card" with a magnetic stripe. There may even be a student present during the day who visually checks the ID cards that vouch for a student's identity. To reach his room, Bob would have to swipe his card through the card reader on the dorm door and use his key for the suite door.

This approach provides *Defense in Depth* because access to the suite depends on passing through multiple security mechanisms. We also use the term *layered defense* because the security domains provide layers of protection. The innermost domain has the most restricted access, surrounded by another domain with less restriction, but that still enforces *some* access restriction.

To achieve genuine depth or layering, the access points or doorways must use truly independent security mechanisms. If a master key exists that traverses all layers, then we no longer have Defense in Depth. If we use one type of credential (a key) for the suite door and a different type of credential (photo ID and/or swipe card) for the building, then we achieve Defense in Depth.

1.3.4 Risk Assessment Overview

Once we have identified the assets we want to protect, the risk assessment influences the rest of the process: policy development, implementation, monitoring, and recovery plans.

In mature industries, like construction, there are building codes and standards that tell builders how to avoid risks when building a home or other structure. Computing and software development are too new, and we don't really have a set of standards to tell us the right things to do. We can't calculate the strength, resilience, or safety factor of a network layout like we can for a roof or bridge. Sometimes we can't even tell which parts of a system need the most attention.

Risk assessment helps us identify the importance of different system components in terms of the risk of failure. In the security world, our risk assessments focus on the risk of attack or subversion by recognized threat agents.

A risk-assessment process gives people a way of working together to analyze the risks to a shared enterprise. They can argue and come to a consensus about critical parts, potential costs of disruptions, and the likelihood of attacks. Here, we use the five-step process shown in Figure 1.5.

A thorough and realistic risk assessment involves two separate activities: *identifying risks* and *prioritizing risks*. To identify risks, we look at how the risks arise and we get specific about how they turn into attacks on assets. To prioritize risks, we estimate the significance of different risks by looking at their likelihood and the impact or damage they may cause. We use a spreadsheet to collect this information and calculate the relative significance of different attacks.

- Identifying Risks
  - Step 1: Identify assets.
  - Step 2: Identify threat agents and attacks.
- Prioritizing Risks
  - Step 3: Estimate the likelihood of attacks.
  - Step 4: Estimate the impact of attacks.
  - Step 5: Calculate the relative significance of attacks.

Figure 1.5

The risk-assessment process.

Step 1 incorporates the results of the first phase of our information security process. Step 2 looks at threat agents in order to identify plausible attacks on our information. The remaining steps estimate the importance of the different attacks. We use these results to prioritize our defenses.

The purpose of this process is to put a framework around the discussion of risk, and give people a way of comparing different risks. We must prune a longer list of risks by estimating their relative values. While the process we discuss here yields very specific numerical results, we must treat the results as estimates.

1.4 Identifying Risks

When identifying risks, our focus is on threat agents and attacks: who attacks our assets and how the attacks might take place. At this point we only use vulnerabilities and defenses as extra information to help identify plausible attacks. For this example, let us look at a room where we store valuable articles, like an office or storage locker. We need to identify threat agents and attacks that affect the assets stored in the room.

Based on news reports, stories, and personal experience, most of us should be able to identify threat agents and attacks in this situation. Here is a summary:

> **Threat Agents:** Thieves and vandals
>
> **Attacks:** Theft, destruction, or damage associated with a break-in

Attack damage may involve breaking a window, a window screen, or entering through an open door.

If the assets are really valuable or an attack can cause really serious damage, then it's worthwhile to list every possible threat agent and attack. For example, banks analyze the risk of attacks through vault walls because the assets are quite valuable and portable. We decide whether to consider a particular type of attack, like those through walls, by looking at the rewards the attacker reaps with a difficult or unusual attack. The more difficult attacks may be less likely, so we balance the likelihood against the potential loss. We look at this more closely in later steps.

1.4.1 Threat Agents

To identify threat agents, we think about people in terms of their interest in attacking our assets (stealing, abusing, damaging, and so on). We don't try to profile a particular person like Jesse James or John Dillinger. Instead we try to capture a particular motivation. Some threat agents, like criminals, won't care about doing us harm for their own benefit. Our friends and family, however, may be threat agents even if they aren't intending to harm us. For example, they might accidentally do us a lot of harm when using our computers.

A threat agent list starts with classic threat agents, like thieves or vandals, and grows to incorporate stories we've heard in the news, from other people, or other sources. Here is a list of typical threat agents at the time of this book's publication:

- Property thieves—they steal physical property, like computers, hard drives, peripherals, etc.
- Vandals—they are more inclined to damage property than to steal things, but their efforts can make equipment unusable. This category can include intentional damage for political reasons or perhaps terrorism.
- Identity thieves—they steal identification information and masquerade as someone else in financial transactions.
- Botnet operators—they embed backdoor software in peoples' computers (see Section 2.3). Botnets use the back door to command the computer to send spam or perform other malicious acts.
- Embezzlers—people inside a company who are motivated to steal from the company.
- Con artists—people outside a company who steal or gain advantage through trickery instead of simple theft.
- Competitors—people who are competing against us for some limited resource: a job, sales prospects, or other things.
- Suite/room/family/housemates—people who share our living space.
- Malicious acquaintances—people we know who would be willing to do us harm for their own benefit. This could include people who share our living space.
- Maintenance crew—people who have physical access to our private living or working space. They might not usually intend to do us harm, but might do so if the benefit is large enough and the risk is small enough.
- *Administrators*—people who have administrative access to our computing resources. This may be limited to access to network resources or may include administrative access to our computer. As with maintenance people, administrators are rarely motivated to do harm to anyone in particular, but might be tempted by easy prey.
- Natural threats—actions of the natural environment that cause damage or loss, like severe weather or earthquakes, and actions possibly caused by humans but causing similar, large-scale damage, like building failures, warfare, or arson.

The final entry, natural threats, incorporates environmental risks. We don't necessarily need to include these risks; it depends on the type of analysis we must perform. If we are trying to decide between using passwords or some other form of authentication, these "natural" risks might not be necessary. The risk analysis is less work when we have a shorter list of risks. On the other hand, we need the longer list if we are looking at alternatives that affect data backups.

Every entity on the list has proven to be a threat to a computer at some point. In practice, however, a particular list should only contain realistic threats to a particular individual or enterprise. If a particular threat seems so unlikely over the span of a few years that its likelihood can't be estimated, it can be ignored.

1.4.2 Security Properties, Services, and Attacks

When looking at information, we see three general security properties, often called the *CIA properties*:

1. *Confidentiality*: Assuming there are people who should not receive this information, we should be confident that the information is not disclosed to them.
2. *Integrity*: The information has not been modified in a way to render it invalid.
3. *Availability*: We can reliably retrieve and use our information and information-related services when we need them.

We deploy security measures to preserve these properties. Some experts describe five *security services* that help maintain these properties. Note the parallel naming:

1. **Confidentiality:** Services that restrict information distribution to people explicitly authorized to receive it.
2. **Integrity:** Services to protect information against unauthorized modification or destruction. These services may be associated with notions of the relative trustworthiness of different system components.
3. **Availability:** Services to ensure that information is reliably available. In many cases these services are considered nonsecurity functions and may encompass power supply reliability or disaster recovery.
4. *Authentication*: Services that reliably establish the identity of an entity that provides information or commands to the system.
5. *Nonrepudiation*: Services that reliably indicate the origin of data or indicate that an intended recipient has definitely received a particular message.

If we look closely at these properties, we can turn each one around and ask, "What attack takes place if we don't have this particular security property or service in place?" This yields the general list of attacks shown in Figure 1.6.

The attacks listed in Figure 1.6 aren't specific enough to use in a risk analysis; you need to be able to estimate the likelihood and the effects of an attack. Instead of using these attacks "as is," we use them as a guide to identify more specific attacks whose effects we can estimate. We look at the resources we depend on, and review information we might have about the types of threats and the attacks they perform. From there, we identify more specific types of attacks. In some cases, a risk assessment can get very specific about attacks; this approach is interesting because it may be possible to test a system for vulnerability against very specific attacks.

- **Physical theft** — the computing resource itself is physically removed.
- **Denial of service (DOS)** — the use of computing data or services is lost temporarily or permanently, without damage to the physical hardware.
- *Subversion* — a program is modified to operate on the behalf of a threat agent.
- *Masquerade* — a person takes on the identity of another when using a computer.
- *Disclosure* — data that should be kept confidential is disclosed. This is the classic *passive* attack.
- *Forgery* — someone composes a bogus message and sends it to a computer. For example, a bogus order sends merchandise to the wrong recipient.

Figure 1.6

General types of attacks on information.

Once we have made a list of attacks, we line them up against our computing resources and activities. We then identify which attacks are relevant for which threats and for which resources. For example, physical theft will apply to physical computing devices and to software that is installed on specific devices. Fraudulent transactions will apply to resources associated with those transactions, like the server providing the defrauded service, or the bank supporting the fraudulent financial transaction.

1.5 Prioritizing Risks

Once we have produced our list of plausible attacks, we prioritize the attacks by comparing their individual costs over time. For example, let us calculate the possible cost of a sneak thief stealing Bob's $500 tower computer. Let's assume that on average a sneak thief manages to enter one suite in Bob's dorm once a month, and there are 100 suites in the dorm. Thus in a given month the chance is 1/100 that Bob's suite is the one targeted. To estimate the attack's significance, we multiply the likelihood of the attack over a given time period by the cost of the attack to Bob. In this case, the significance is $500 times 1/100 per month, or $5 a month.

We estimated the impact on Bob in terms of money. This is not the only way to do it. We may instead want to estimate loss in terms of time required to recover from an attack. For example, if an attack causes a student to fail a course, then arguably it will take another semester's worth of work to recover from the loss. There may be other ways to represent losses as well. The best choice is the one that captures the costs most accurately and completely. In any case, be sure to choose *only one* way of giving estimates for the cost of attacks. If some attacks are estimated in terms of money and others in terms of time, we can't accurately compare them.

We follow these steps to prioritize risks:

1. Estimate the cost of a loss caused by this attack. As just noted, choose either time or money or some alternative, and use it consistently for all attack cost estimates. The cost should include all costs that arise when recovering from the attack. For a stolen item, this includes replacement costs. For a computer, it may include the cost to reinstall third-party applications and to recover or reconstruct lost files.

2. Estimate the frequency of the event; how often the attack is likely to occur over a fixed time period. In the sneak thief example, we used a month as our time period; you can use a day, a year, or any other period, as long as you are consistent throughout your risk assessment. The frequency may yield a fraction; in the sneak thief example, the attack occurred on Bob's suite 0.01 times every month.

3. Multiply the cost times the frequency. The result is the cost over that time period. If one risk presents a $5 per month risk and another poses a $50 per month risk, then clearly the $5 per month risk isn't as critical.

Once the numbers and calculations are filled in, we can identify the biggest risks by looking for the highest risk index values.

We get simple and impressive numbers when we calculate risk in terms of money. However, the results often are misleading. Numbers by themselves carry a lot of authority, especially when they represent money. *Do not be fooled*. There are two reasons these numbers are misleading.

First, the numbers are nothing more than estimates. They are useful when comparing one to another, but don't rely on them in an absolute sense. An actual loss over time could be significantly less—or more—than this estimate.

Second, this calculation assumes that the risks and the attack events are independent of one another. This is nonsense. Some types of attacks, if successful, may increase the likelihood of further attacks. For example, shoplifters may be encouraged to steal more from a store that never catches shoplifters. Moreover, attacks of one type could influence the likelihood of attacks of another type.

Remember, the point of the process is to compare risks. The numerical values may be useful for gross comparisons, so it's best to pay the most attention to the largest differences. Relatively small differences may not be significant.

1.5.1 Example: Risks to Alice's Laptop

We now will perform a risk assessment for a situation similar to Bob's: that of the laptop computer that belongs to his classmate Alice. She uses the laptop in a school and dormitory environment. We will walk through the five steps. Unlike earlier examples, we will estimate costs in terms of time required to recoup the loss.

STEP 1: IDENTIFY COMPUTING ASSETS

We identify Alice's personal goals and then we identify computing assets that support her goals. Here are the goals:

- Finish courses successfully
- Live comfortably

Here are computing activities and resources that support Alice's goals:

- Course work on laptop computer
- Course work on shared server space, including password
- USB drive with copies of latest course work
- Proprietary software on computer
- Personalization of computer
- Bank website for managing money, including password
- Social websites for communicating with friends, including passwords

STEP 2: IDENTIFY THREAT AGENTS AND POTENTIAL ATTACKS

Here is a list of Alice's security threats (We will keep the list short in this example.):

- Malicious social acquaintances—people looking for payback or just out to have fun at Alice's expense
- Property thieves—the usual motivations: money, envy, etc.
- Identity thieves—for some thieves it is enough to steal a legitimate name and associated identity data like birth date or Social Security number, even if Alice herself doesn't have any money
- Botnet operators—every computer has some value to a botnet
- Roommates/housemates—nobody wants a war in their living space, but roommates can be careless or thoughtless

Next, we compare the generic list of attacks in Figure 1.6 to this list of threats to produce a more specific list of possible attacks. We use a table to ensure that we cover all possibilities. On one axis we list the generic attacks and on the other we list the threats, then we fill in all the plausible attacks (Table 1.1).

To fill in the table, we look at what motivates the threats, compare that against the possible attacks, and identify specific kinds of attacks those threats might perform. This yields nine specific attacks on Alice by these potential threats. The following is a brief description of each:

- Privacy breach—personal information is released that causes Alice personal damage or embarrassment.
- Stolen work—some of Alice's work is stolen and handed in by the thief.

TABLE 1.1 Identifying specific attacks by threat agents					
Possible Attacks	Malicious Acquaintances	Property Thieves	Identity Thieves	Botnet Operators	Roommates Suitemates
Physical loss		Hardware theft			Files lost
Denial of service		Files lost			Files lost
Disclosure	Privacy breach, Stolen work		Password theft		
Subversion				Back door	
Masquerade			Identity theft		
Forgery	Social forgery		Bogus purchase		

- Social forgery—someone sends false messages and makes false electronic statements masquerading as Alice, and those statements cause her personal damage or embarrassment.
- Hardware theft—someone steals Alice's laptop or other computing items, like program disks or her USB drive.
- Password theft—someone steals Alice's password. Alice realizes the theft took place before the password is misused.
- Bogus purchase—someone poses as Alice to make a purchase using a credit card or other electronic financial instrument.
- Identity theft—someone poses as Alice in one or more major financial transactions, like applying for a loan or credit card.
- Back door—someone installs backdoor software in Alice's computer so the computer may take part in a botnet.
- Files lost—someone removes, erases or otherwise damages some of Alice's files, making those files unusable. This includes physical loss of the device storing the files.

For each asset or activity, we identify the attacks that apply to it. For example, physical theft applies to Alice's laptop and to information that resides exclusively on her laptop. We assume that Alice does not really need to keep copies of course work after it is handed in, and that some course work resides on the laptop and other work resides on a shared campus server. Privacy breaches only apply to the social website, on the assumption that Alice's personal information and social activities are focused there. Note that this process requires a lot of specific information about how Alice uses computers.

STEP 3: ESTIMATE THE LIKELIHOOD OF INDIVIDUAL ATTACKS

Pick a time period (a day, a month, a year) and then estimate how often each type of attack might occur. Be sure to use the same time period for each type of attack. Use fractions or decimals as needed; if we are counting events per year and something bad occurs every 5 years, we still need to consider the risk. To keep the analysis simple for now, we assume that Alice provides little or no protection, and has no insurance on her property.

To estimate likelihood, we estimate how many times Alice might suffer the attack in an average year. Fractions indicate that the frequency is less than a year. The laptop theft assumes that an unsecured laptop might survive 3 hours on average before being stolen, considering a possible 24x7 risk. The same rate applies to botnets, since automated on-line attacks scan the Internet continuously looking for vulnerable machines. In fact, 3 hours is optimistic for botnet attacks. USB drives, on the other hand, are so cheap and common that people may either ignore them if unprotected or perhaps turn them in to the campus lost-and-found.

STEP 4: ESTIMATE THE IMPACT OF ATTACKS

If a particular attack occurs, how much will it cost Alice to recover from it? As noted earlier, our estimate must include replacement cost, labor costs, the cost of lost opportunities, money spent on alternatives, and so on. We can estimate loss either in monetary terms or in terms of the time required to recover. In this case, we will estimate in terms of recovery time: the number of days Alice requires to recover from a particular attack.

For example, if Alice's laptop is stolen, she will need to work 90 days to save enough "extra" money to replace the laptop. Replacing the proprietary software requires 30 days, assuming that for some reason installation disks aren't available. If something causes the loss of course work stored on her computer, we estimate it will take 5 days for her to replace the lost work. If another student steals some of her work and hands it in as his own, the worst case would be for the instructor to fail both students for being involved in cheating. This yields 120 days to recover: 4 months to retake the course. If Alice is subjected to bogus purchases on the Visa card she uses for ATM withdrawals from her bank, it will take her 1 day to deal with the red tape involved in reversing the charges. The bank also could keep up to $50 of the bogus charges (but few banks do this).

STEP 5: CALCULATE THE RELATIVE SIGNIFICANCE OF ATTACKS

Once we have filled in the attack likelihoods and costs, we compute the risk impact by multiplying these values together. The biggest risks have the biggest impact values. A high impact means that the potential disruption is likely and that it will affect the student for a long time. Other disruptions may be likely, but the effects won't be as long-lasting. The computed results appear in Table 1.2.

A spreadsheet provides the easiest way to systematically collect this data and perform the calculations. Any modern spreadsheet will work. We may want to use two separate

TABLE 1.2 Calculating the impact

Computing Asset/Activity	Attack	Disruption Cost	Likeli-hood	Impact
Laptop computer	Hardware theft	90.0	2,920.00	262,800
Laptop computer	Back door	3.0	2,920.00	8,760
Course work/computer	Stolen work	120.0	0.50	60
Course work/computer	Files lost	5.0	3.00	60
Course work/shared server	Stolen work	120.0	1.00	120
Course work/shared server	Password theft	0.1	6.00	1
Course work/shared server	Files lost	5.0	5.00	100
USB drive	Hardware theft	6.0	50.00	300
USB drive	Stolen work	120.0	0.50	60
USB drive	Files lost	5.0	5.00	100
Proprietary software	Hardware theft	30.0	2,920.00	87,600
Proprietary software	Files lost	3.0	1.00	3
Personalization of computer	Hardware theft	1.0	60.00	60
Personalization of computer	Files lost	1.0	3.00	3
Bank website	Password theft	0.1	720.00	72
Bank website	Identity theft	30.0	0.05	2
Bank website	Bogus purchase	1.0	0.50	1
Social websites	Privacy breach	10.0	10.00	100
Social websites	Social forgery	10.0	0.20	2

worksheets or two separate parts of the same worksheet: one to produce the list of attacks (Table 1.1) and one to calculate the impact (Table 1.2).

Spreadsheets especially are worthwhile for larger, more complex risk assessments. It is easy to sort a large spreadsheet by risk index values, which clusters the highest risks at one end of the spreadsheet for study and comparison.

In practice, we focus on the risks that we can't afford to encounter, or at least on the highest priority risks. In this case, we limit our focus to the 10 highest priority risks from Table 1.2:

1. Laptop computer: Hardware theft
2. Proprietary software: Hardware theft

3. Laptop computer: Back door

4. USB drive: Hardware theft

5. Course work/shared server: Stolen work

6. Course work/shared server: Files lost

7. USB drive: Files lost

8. Social websites: Privacy breach

9. Bank website: Password theft

10. Course work/computer: Stolen work

We will use this list later in Chapter 2 to develop a policy for protecting Alice's information resources.

1.5.2 Other Risk-Assessment Processes

The assessment process just described is streamlined for teaching purposes. In practice, though, information security professionals use similar techniques. We can study these techniques in detail by looking in other books and in online documents. Here we will introduce two in particular:

- "Risk Management Guide for Information Technology Systems," published by the U.S. National Institute of Standards and Technology (NIST) as Special Publication 800-30.
- The operationally critical threat, asset, and vulnerability evaluation (OCTAVE) process was developed at the Software Engineering Institute (SEI) of Carnegie-Mellon University (CMU).

Both of these techniques, like the ASIS technique described in Section 1.3, exist as *recommendations* and not as *standards*. This is an important distinction. Recommendations give advice and make suggestions while standards present rules and demand compliance.

NIST RECOMMENDATION

The NIST recommendation arranges risk assessment into the following nine steps. The steps incorporate phases of information security process as well as the steps of the risk-assessment process.

1. System characterization (Step 1 and Phase 1)

2. Threat identification (part of Step 2)

3. Vulnerability identification (part of Step 2)

4. Control analysis: analyzes existing or proposed security (Phase 4)

5. Likelihood determination (Step 3)

6. Impact analysis (Step 4)

7. Risk determination (Step 5)

8. Control recommendations: revisions to NIST Step 4 (Phase 4)
9. Documentation (part of all earlier steps)

The major difference from our risk assessment is that the NIST process is not part of a broader information security process. The NIST process incorporates earlier and later phases of our information security process instead of referring to a separate, more comprehensive process. The NIST process needs to stand by itself: It must be effective even if it's not being used as part of a broader information security process. This is why the NIST process considers proposed security measures and makes recommendations for additional measures.

Organizations within the U.S. government often are bound by NIST standards and recommendations. Because there is no NIST standard for an information security process, it must incorporate the essential parts of the process into other recommendations, like this one.

OCTAVE PROCESS

The OCTAVE process was developed by SEI under contract to the U.S. military and, like the NIST document, serves as a recommendation and not a standard. OCTAVE is intended more for private industry and organizations, while NIST is targeted at U.S. government organizations. SEI has published a series of papers and guidelines on OCTAVE to provide detailed examples and recommendations. To some extent, OCTAVE is intended to provide both a general framework for information security risk assessment and to provide specific recommendations for specific situations and environments.

The OCTAVE framework consists of three phases:

1. Phase 1: "Build asset-based threat profiles"—identifies assets, threats to those assets, and "organizational risks" (Steps 1 and 2)
2. Phase 2: "Identify infrastructure vulnerabilities" (part of Step 2)
3. Phase 3: "Develop security strategy and plans" (Step 3 and Phase 4)

A more recent recommendation, called OCTAVE Allegro, breaks the process into eight steps that more closely match the process used here:

1. Establish risk measurement criteria (part of Step 1).
2. Develop an information asset profile (part of Step 1).
3. Identify information asset containers (part of Step 1).
4. Identify areas of concern (part of Step 2).
5. Identify threat scenarios (part of Step 2).
6. Identify risks (part of Step 2).
7. Analyze risks (Steps 2, 3, and 4).
8. Select mitigation approach (Phase 3).

Like the NIST process, OCTAVE parallels phases of our information security process. The OCTAVE framework goes further and recommends that organizations implement OCTAVE as part of a broader information security process. Their recommendation incorporates all of the phases of our process.

OCTAVE, like NIST, also produces security recommendations. However, OCTAVE produces recommendations that are closer in intent to security policy. Instead of recommending particular controls, the step prioritizes the different risks and recommends which require security measures ("mitigation").

1.6 Ethical Issues in Security Analysis

Security analysis exists to improve system security. Students of security analysis must ensure that they themselves do not pose a risk to the systems they review.

Security analysis poses two problems. First, if seeking vulnerabilities, is the seeker authorized to do so and, in particular, does the seeker do anything illegal or potentially damaging while searching? The second problem is the question of publishing vulnerabilities: If one finds a vulnerability, what should be done with the information?

When an organization requests a security assessment, the security analyst's situation is clear:

- The analyst needs written authorization from the organization to verify that the assessment should take place.
- The analyst should use the appropriate tools to perform the assessment.
- When finished, the analyst should collect the results and report them to the appropriate people in the organization.

The assessment results could pose a risk to the organization, so they are treated as confidential. The results are only shared with the appropriate people in the organization. The analyst is obligated to protect all working notes and ensure that information about the analysis doesn't leak to others. When finished, the analyst should securely erase all information not needed for business purposes, and take strong measures to prevent any details from leaking to others.

LAWS, REGULATIONS, AND CODES OF CONDUCT

The guidance provided here may be affected by local laws and regulations, or by obligations to employers or other secrecy agreements. Here is a brief review of other obligations that might affect the handling and disclosure of security vulnerabilities.

- Legal restrictions. There are "antihacking" laws in some jurisdictions. In the United States, the Digital Millennium Copyright Act (DMCA) outlaws "circumvention" of technical measures intended to protect copyrighted data, often called *digital rights management* (DRM) mechanisms. In the United States, it may be a crime to find a vulnerability in a DRM technique and publish it.

- National security information. If the vulnerability involves a "classified" system, then the information may fall under defense secrecy restrictions discussed in Chapter 17. People who handle such information sign secrecy agreements; violating such an agreement could even be treated as criminal espionage.
- Nondisclosure agreements. Employees and people working with sensitive information on the behalf of various enterprises or other organizations often sign an agreement not to disclose information the enterprise considers sensitive. Violations may lead to lost jobs and even lawsuits.
- Codes of conduct. Many professional organizations or holders of professional certifications agree to a professional code of conduct. Violators may lose their certification or membership. In practice, however, such codes of conduct aren't used punitively but instead try to reinforce accepted standards of just and moral behavior.

Legal and ethical obligations may push a security practitioner both toward secrecy and toward disclosure. Professional standards and even laws recognize an obligation to protect the public from danger. An extreme case often arises in medical science: When people get sicker during a drug trial, is it caused by the tested drug or by something else? The researchers may be obliged to keep their research secret because of agreements with the drug company. On the other hand, the drug company may be legally and morally liable if people die because they weren't informed of this newly discovered risk.

1.6.1 Searching for Vulnerabilities

With practice, it becomes easy to identify security weaknesses in everyday life. One sees broken fences, broken locks, and other security measures that are easy to circumvent. Such observations are educational when studying security. However, these observations can pose risks both to the security analyst and to people affected by the vulnerabilities.

In general, an analyst does not pose a danger by passively observing things and making mental notes of vulnerabilities. The risks arise if the analyst makes a more overt search for vulnerabilities, like searching for unlocked homes by rattling doorknobs. Police officers and other licensed security officers might do this, but students and other civilians should not engage in suspicious behavior.

For example, there are security scanning tools that try to locate computers on a network. Some of these tools also check computers for well-known vulnerabilities. Most companies that provide computer or network services require their users and customers to comply with an *acceptable use policy* (or AUP). Most network AUPs forbid using such tools, just as some towns might have laws against "doorknob rattling." Moreover, some tools may have unfortunate side-effects, like the one in this example.

An Incident: A security analysis team was scanning a network. Part of the scan was interpreted as attempts to log in as an administrative user on the main server computer. The numerous failed logins caused the system to "lock out" the administrative user. The system had to be restarted to reestablish administrative control.

Overt and systematic security scanning should only take place when it has been explicitly authorized by those responsible for the system. It is not enough to be a professional with a feeling of responsibility for security and the expertise to perform the scan.

In 1993, Randall Schwartz, a respected programming consultant and author of several books on programming, was working for an Intel Corporation facility in Oregon. Schwartz claimed to be concerned about the quality of passwords being used at the site, particularly by managers. Without formal authorization, Schwartz made a copy of a password file and used a "password cracking" program to extract the passwords.

Intel management was not amused. They contacted local police and reported the incident as a computer crime. Schwartz was indicted under the Oregon computer abuse law and found guilty of three counts of computer abuse.

Information security can't flourish as a grassroots effort. If upper management doesn't want to address security issues, we won't gain their trust and support by locating and announcing existing security weaknesses. Not only does this increase risks by highlighting weaknesses, it also carries an implicit criticism of management priorities. Security improves when the appropriate managers and system administrators apply resources to improve it. We must keep this in mind when we take on roles as managers and administrators.

1.6.2 Sharing or Publishing Vulnerabilities

Not all vulnerabilities are found by security analysts on request by a site or vendor. In fact, many are found through a form of "freelance" security testing. Many people have earned a few minutes of fame and publicity by finding a security vulnerability, reporting it publicly, and seeing the report repeated in the national news. This was especially true in the 1990s as the general public struggled to understand the rapidly emerging technologies of the personal computer and the Internet.

Often, the initial announcements appeared in email discussion groups. Several such groups arose in the early 1990s to discuss newly uncovered vulnerabilities in computer products and Internet software. Many participants in these discussions believed that "full disclosure" of security flaws would tend to improve software security over time. Computer product vendors did not necessarily patch security flaws quickly; in fact, some did not seem to fix such flaws at all. Some computing experts hoped that the bad publicity arising from vulnerability reports would force vendors to patch security flaws promptly.

By the late 1990s, the general public had come to rely heavily on personal computers and the Internet, and security vulnerabilities had become a serious problem. Reports of security vulnerabilities often were followed by Internet-borne attacks that exploited those new vulnerabilities. This called into question the practice of full disclosure. Today, the general practice is as follows:

- Upon finding a vulnerability in a product or system, the finder reports the vulnerability to the vendor or system owner. The finder should provide enough information to reproduce the problem.
- The vendor should acknowledge the report within 7 days, and provide the finder with weekly updates until the vendor has resolved the problem.
- The vendor and the finder should jointly decide how to announce the vulnerability.
- If the vendor and finder cannot agree on the announcement, the finder will provide a general announcement 30 days after the vendor was informed. The announcement should notify customers that a vulnerability exists and, if possible, make recommendations on how to reduce the risk of attack. The announcement should *not* include details that allow an attacker to exploit the vulnerability. Some organizations that handle vulnerabilities wait 45 days before making a public announcement.
- Publication of the details of the vulnerability should be handled on a case-by-case basis.

Although many organizations recognize these guidelines, they are not the final word on vulnerability disclosure. At the Black Hat USA 2005 Briefings, a security conference, security researcher Michael Lynn described a vulnerability in Cisco's Internet *router* products. Routers provide the backbone for moving messages on the Internet; they provide the glue to connect local networks and long-distance networks into a single, global Internet.

Lynn did not provide the details of how the vulnerability worked, but he did demonstrate the vulnerability to the audience at the conference. Cisco had released a patch for the vulnerability 4 months earlier. However, Lynn's presentation still unleashed a furor, including court actions and restraining orders. As Lynn noted in his talk, many routers on the Internet still would contain the vulnerability if their owners hadn't bothered to update the router software.

Although few student analysts are likely to uncover a vulnerability with widespread implications, many will undoubtedly identify weaknesses in systems they encounter every day. Students should be careful when discussing and documenting these perceived weaknesses.

Students who are analyzing systems for training and practice also should be careful. A student exercise that examines a real system could pose a risk if it falls into the wrong hands. Therefore, it is best to avoid discussing or sharing information security class work with others, except for fellow students in information security and the instructors.

Moreover, some countries and communities may have laws or other restrictions on handling security information. Be sure to comply with local laws and regulations. Even countries that otherwise guarantee free speech may have restrictions on sharing information about security weaknesses. In the United States, for example, the DMCA makes it illegal to distribute certain types of information on how to circumvent copyright protection mechanisms.

There is an ongoing discussion in the security community about whether, when, and how to announce security vulnerabilities. In the past, there was a tradition of openness and sharing in the Internet community that biased many experts toward full disclosure. Today, however, security experts tend to keep vulnerability details secret and, at most, share it with the owners of the vulnerable system. The challenge is to decide how much to tell, and when.

1.7 Security Example: Aircraft Hijacking

Flight Captain Francis Riley might have found it amusing if it hadn't been terrifying. A strange man entered the cockpit of his airliner brandishing a handgun and a steak knife. The hijacker, a former Miami electrician, demanded that the aircraft be flown to Havana, Cuba. Riley complied.

This incident in 1961 was the first of dozens that took place over the following decades. Typically, an armed man approached the cockpit and demanded the pilot fly to Cuba. The flight crew usually complied. Once the hijacker had left the plane, the pilot refueled the plane and flew home. Most incidents ended without any loss of life or aircraft, though each one caused stress, and wasted time and aircraft fuel.

In 1961, there was no historical precedent to guide Captain Riley's response. A man threatening a pilot is a threat to an aircraft, regardless of his intentions. Riley chose to comply with the hijacker's demands. His behavior established the pattern that most pilots followed for the next 40 years.

Before 1967, no more than five aircraft hijackings took place each year worldwide, and few of them made the worldwide news. In 1968, however, over a dozen planes were hijacked from the United States to Cuba alone. The number continued to climb, with over 200 hijackings taking place in 1983.

Most hijackings followed the same script: Threaten the pilot, land at a different destination, make a press statement, and let everyone go home. However, not all hijackers acted the same. Some made different kinds of political statements by threatening passengers of particular cultural groups. In 1970, a coordinated hijacking took three airliners to Zarqua, Jordan, landing them at what was once known as Dawson's Field. Rather than relinquish the planes to an anticipated military strike against them, the hijackers unloaded the planes and blew them up. This violence dramatically raised the stakes in aviation security.

In 1971, a passenger listed as Dan Cooper hijacked a plane traveling from Portland, Oregon, to Seattle, Washington. He allowed the flight to land and off-load other passengers, but demanded that the plane take off again carrying himself, the flight crew, four parachutes, and $200,000 in cash. Cooper let himself out the aircraft's tail-mounted staircase, skydiving into oblivion. Neither he nor the money (except a few thousand dollars) were ever seen again.

1.7.1 Hijacking: A High-Level Analysis

In response to the situation as it evolved in the 1980s, the airlines, airports, and government agencies implemented antihijacking procedures for flights and airports. In the United States, the Federal Aviation Administration, or FAA, coordinated this effort. To understand the procedures established in the 1980s, we will examine the hijacking situation through our six-phase process.

ASSETS

In this case, human lives are the most important assets, and the highest priority is to protect lives. The second priority is to protect aircraft assets.

RISKS

Airplane crashes were considered the biggest risk to human life. Safety and security focused on preventing plane crashes. This focus also addressed the biggest risk to the planes themselves. It was not until they proliferated in the late 1960s that hijackings were considered significant risks.

POLICY

We address the primary risk (plane crashes) by requiring that only pilots with the appropriate licenses fly aircraft that carry passengers. We further arrange cockpit operations to reduce the risk of distractions from the flight crew's main concern: flying the aircraft safely.

We address the hijacking risk by forbidding passengers from carrying weapons on aircraft. We define a boundary that includes every aircraft's boarding door, and we forbid passengers from carrying weapons into that area.

If a hijacking occurs despite these precautions, we address the risk to life and equipment by cooperating with the hijackers.

IMPLEMENTATION

Pilot licensing is implemented through governmental agencies like the FAA and through airline policies and procedures.

To implement the security boundary around the aircraft, we define a perimeter around the airport and control access to different parts of that perimeter. Most airports have long been surrounded by fences, and the aircraft kept behind locked doors, if only to keep people from wandering onto operating runways or taking free rides. To reduce the risk of hijacking, the perimeter incorporated metal detectors to detect serious weapons such as handguns and large knives.

If a hijacking occurred despite these security measures, the flight crew was trained to cooperate with the hijacker and, in general, to comply with their demands. This became part of the FAA's training standards for flight crews, first developed in the early 1980s.

MONITORING

In this case, we have two levels of monitoring. On the individual aircraft, the flight crew monitors the situation to identify threats arising from the aircraft operation or from the people it carries. In addition, the aviation community monitors accidents and attacks against aircraft. If the threats change, then new policy recommendations emerge.

In the United States, the FAA is responsible for keeping track of all reported aircraft "incidents" and for developing recommendations on how to address them.

RECOVERY

When an incident threatens an aircraft, the pilot interprets the established policies and procedures, and decides how to respond. For hijacks, most flight crews followed the traditional guidance, and cooperated with the hijackers. In the vast majority of cases, this kept the crew, passengers, and aircraft intact.

1.7.2 September 11, 2001

From the start, these hijackings were uncharacteristically violent. In earlier cases, the hijackers limited their demands to aircraft destinations, and perhaps some others for publicity, for the release of associates, or perhaps for ransom. Hijackers avoided killing people, since people could serve as hostages. Killings occurred only after the hijackers' plans were seriously frustrated, and such killings often were staged in front of news cameras.

On September 11, those trying to deal with the hijackings had a dilemma. The professionals had been trained to follow established procedures that, in the past, had made the best of bad situations—but these hijackings posed a novel danger that their training did not address. In this case, the crucial asset at risk was, of course, human lives.

The first casualties that day were crew members on three of the flights: They were attacked with knives, and many were reported killed. On all four aircraft, the passengers and cabin crew were chased to the far end of the plane with threats of a bomb, with knives, and with Mace.

In all four aircraft, passengers and crew in the back of the plane tried to contact people on the ground using cell phones and in-cabin phones. The cabin crew who made phone calls were violating their hijack training; in a hijack situation, all communication is supposed to be coordinated by the flight crew in the cockpit. Passengers also tried contacting people via cell phone, despite rules against it, and despite technical problems that make such calls unreliable.

After 8:46 AM on September 11, it was no longer an effective policy to cooperate with hijackers, even at the risk of a plane crash and loss of all aboard. The first two targets were the twin towers of the World Trade Center (Figure 1.7). These targets yielded over 10 times as many casualties as would have resulted from simply crashing the planes themselves.

Figure 1.7

World Trade Center, September 11, 2001.

The terrorists' strategy completely changed the risk assessment regarding aircraft hijacking. As the day unfolded, many people caught up in the hijacking came to understand the changed situation (Table 1.3).

TABLE 1.3 Time line for hijackings on September 11, 2001				
Flight #	Time Hijacked (AM)	Aware of WTC Crashes?	Site of Crash	Time of Crash (AM)
American 11	8:14	No	WTC	8:46
United 175	8:42–46	Probably, around 9:00	WTC	9:03
American 77	8:51–54	Probably, around 9:20	Pentagon	9:37
United 93	9:28	Definitely, around 9:30	Shanksville, Pennsylvania	10:03

Phone calls by passengers and cabin crew have shed light on the changed perception. One passenger on United 175, the second plane to crash, reported discussions among passengers about trying to overpower the hijackers, but there wasn't enough time for passengers to implement the plan. On American 77, the passengers had perhaps 17 minutes to take action, which was apparently not enough time, either. On United 93, passengers had as much as a half hour to realize their situation, plan on retaking the cockpit, and execute the plan. The hijackers crashed the plane into a field in Pennsylvania rather than give up the cockpit.

Traditional hijacking policies did not consider the possibility of suicidal hijackers who would use the planes themselves as destructive weapons. There had been hints at such a threat before September 11; suicide bombers in surface vehicles had become a fact of life in Israel, a private plane had crashed into the White House in 1994, and intelligence agencies had heard of earlier plans (not executed) by terrorists to hit targets in Europe with planes. However, these indications arose among thousands of others that reinforced fears of more traditional attacks.

Other factors made the risk of suicide aircraft seem unlikely. Modern commercial airliners are complex devices requiring years of training and experience to fly and aim at a particular target. Commercial pilots are highly trained professionals, and not inclined to threaten the safety of their aircraft, passengers, or themselves. Modern airliners require years of training to fly, and it seemed unlikely that anyone could expend that much training for a suicide mission.

The risk only became real after it had occurred.

We cannot predict the future, but we can learn lessons from the past. We can look at what has happened, and what is happening, and see how it may relate to what we do. That is how we make effective security decisions.

1.8 Resources

 IMPORTANT TERMS INTRODUCED

administrator	CIA properties	hunter's dilemma
asset	compromised system	implementation
attack	confidentiality	information security
attacker	Continuous Improvement	architecture
authentication	cracker	insider threat
availability	defense	integrity
basic principle of information	Defense in Depth	Least Privilege
security	disclosure	login
black-hat hacker	forgery	masquerade
botnet	hacker	monitoring
boundary	high-level analysis	natural threats

nonrepudiation	script kiddy	standard
phone phreak	security architecture study	subversion
recommendation	security domain	systems engineering process
recovery	security plan	threat agent
risk	security policy	vulnerability
risk assessment	security process	white-hat hacker
router	security services	

ACRONYMS INTRODUCED (INCLUDING THE PREFACE)

ACM—Association for Computing Machinery

ASIS—American Society for Industrial Security

ATM—Automated teller machine

AUP—Acceptable use policy

CIA—Confidentiality, integrity, availability

CISSP—Certified information systems security professional

CMU—Carnegie-Mellon University

DMCA—Digital Millennium Copyright Act

DOS—Denial of service

DRM—Digital rights management

FAA—Federal Aviation Administration

ID—Identity

ISO—International Standards Organization

IT—Information technology

MIT—Massachusetts Institute of Technology

NIST—National Institute of Standards and Technology

NSA—National Security Agency

OCTAVE—Operationally critical threat, asset, and vulnerability evaluation

OODA—Observe, orient, detect, act

PDA—Personal digital assistant

PDCA—Plan, do, check, act

PLC—Programmable logic controller

SCADA—Supervisory control and data acquisition

SEI—Software Engineering Institute

USB—Universal serial bus

WTC—World Trade Center

1.8.1 Review Questions

R1. Describe the four general topics of the "security landscape" covered in this book.

R2. Describe the three strategies people often use to make security decisions.

R3. What is the hunter's dilemma?

R4. Explain the role of "reasoned paranoia" in the security process.

R5. Describe the six phases in the security process.

R6. How does the security process compare to continuous quality improvement?

R7. What is the difference between *policy* and *implementation* in the security process?

R8. Describe the relationship between assets, boundaries, threat agents, vulnerabilities, attacks, and defenses.

R9. Identify some typical information assets.

R10. Explain the concept of Least Privilege.

R11. What are the four things to assess when looking at boundaries?

R12. Describe the three *security properties* of information (hint: "CIA") and the five *security services* for protecting information.

R13. Describe the steps to take when identifying risks in a risk assessment.

R14. Describe the steps to take when assessing risks in a risk assessment.

R15. Summarize the differences between the risk-assessment process used in this chapter and the NIST and OCTAVE processes.

R16. Summarize the recommended ethical steps a security analyst takes when performing a security assessment.

R17. Summarize the recommended process for disclosing a security vulnerability.

1.8.2 Exercises

E1. Describe the physical security boundary that Bob relied on in Section 1.1. Is there a better place for the computer where he can enforce a more effective boundary?

E2. Give examples of how individuals can act as vulnerabilities, defenses, or threats to an information system.

E3. Write a summary of how desktop computers are used in your organization. The organization may be a particular portion of a larger site, like a school or college, or a department within the organization.

E4. Who do you call if something goes wrong with your computer? Provide contact

information and a summary of which problems are covered by which contacts.

E5. Draw a diagram of the physical security boundary around your current living space. Identify possible points of entry. Describe how the physical boundary is kept secure if you are not present.

E6. Select a commercial space like a store or restaurant with which you are familiar. Draw a diagram of its physical security boundary. Identify possible points of entry or exit, including emergency exits. Describe the rules (the "policy") for opening, closing, and locking those entrances. Pay special attention to public, employee-only, and emergency exits, if any.

E7.   Select a familiar organization, business, website, or computer system that is not your own. Produce a high-level security analysis using the six-phase security process. Section 1.2 provides an example of this type of high-level description.

E8.   Make a list of the really important tasks performed by your personal computer, following examples in Sections 1.3 and 1.5. If you do not own your own computer, describe one that you regularly use for class work. List the physical and information assets you rely upon to perform these tasks.

E9.   Following the example in Section 1.5, do a risk assessment of your own personal computer. Be sure to answer Exercise E8

first, and be sure that your risk assessment reflects your most important tasks and assets. Show the results in a table that uses the same format as Table 1.2.

E10.   Select a disaster or security incident that has been described in the news. Write a high-level analysis of the incident using the six-phase security process. Identify shortcomings in one or more steps of the process that could explain the incident. Be sure to focus on what *did* happen.

E11.   Using a disaster or security incident described in a film, video, or fictional story, write a high-level analysis of the incident using the six-phase security process. Identify shortcomings in one or more steps of the process that explain how the incident occurred. Be sure to focus on what *did* happen.

CONTROLLING A COMPUTER

ABOUT THIS CHAPTER

This chapter introduces fundamental mechanisms for controlling a computer's operation, and further develops the process of solving security problems. The chapter focuses on the following topics:

- An overview of the general strategies for controlling access
- "Buffer overflow": a well-known technique for subverting computer software
- The mechanisms typically used to control access within a computer
- Security planning: describing the protections needed and how to implement them

2.1 Computers and Programs

When writing a paper, we run a word-processing program. When doing calculations, we use a spreadsheet. When searching for information on the Web, we use a browser. We choose programs to do the jobs we have at hand.

Attackers also use the tools at hand. They make the computer run a program to perform the work of the attack. Sometimes an existing program will do the job. Other times they have to provide a new program. It's a matter of directing the computer to the right sequence of instructions.

Everything a computer does, right or wrong, results from running a computer program. As the computer's owner, we try to keep it under control by telling it to run the right programs: the right operating system, the right browser, the right word processor, and so on. While attackers sometimes trick a program into misbehaving, they also may provide their own programs to do the work.

Thus, computer security depends on keeping control of the computer. We try to prevent attackers from redirecting the computer to run their attack programs.

When we look at a computer's operation at the most basic level, all programs look more or less the same. A program contains sequences of *machine instructions*. Most of the instructions are absurdly simple arithmetic operations, or are driven by the result of simple arithmetic. This is true for mundane programs like word processors, as well as for the innermost workings of operating systems. It also is true for the most dangerous programs run by attackers.

THE MOTHERBOARD

If we rip open a computer and dig through the cables and enclosures, we will find a flexible plastic board covered with multicolored layers of metallic traces, physical wires, and integrated circuit packages. This is the *motherboard* (Figure 2.1). It contains the **central processing unit** (CPU), covered by a heat sink or other cooling mechanism. The CPU runs the programs that make the computer work.

Elsewhere on the motherboard, we will often find one or more *daughterboards* containing the **random access memory** (RAM) in a row of integrated circuits. In some systems, the RAM also may have heat sinks or extra cooling. Most of the time, computer programs involve the CPU and RAM exclusively.

Computer Dissection: As with most things, only dissect discarded computers. *Do not dissect a working computer without special instructions and guidance.* It's very, very easy to damage a computer while dissecting it.

The best candidate is a discarded desktop or tower computer; they usually have a single large motherboard similar to Figure 2.1. Be sure to remove the computer's power cord and leave the computer unplugged for a few days before dissecting. This ensures that any stray charges have dissipated.

After removing the outer casing, the motherboard is visible beneath the hard drives, power supply, and other assemblies. Remove those items to see the entire motherboard. Do *not* try to disassemble the power supply.

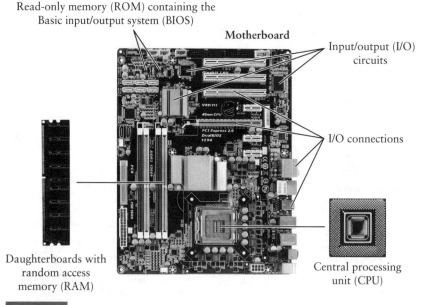

Read-only memory (ROM) containing the
Basic input/output system (BIOS)

Motherboard

Input/output (I/O) circuits

I/O connections

Daughterboards with random access memory (RAM)

Central processing unit (CPU)

Figure 2.1

The working insides of a computer.

Replacing the CPU and/or RAM: Many computers are designed to accept a variety of CPUs and RAM sizes. Such computers have published instructions for how to open the computer and locate these components. Follow such instructions exactly. *Accidents or carelessness may damage the computer.*

2.1.1 Input/Output

The remainder of the motherboard is filled with ***input/output*** (I/O) circuits. These circuits provide the electronics to connect other components to the computer. These include keyboards, mice, video displays, hard drives, printers, and so on. The I/O circuits let the CPU give commands and share data with the I/O devices. In some cases, the circuits can copy data directly between the devices and the computer's RAM.

Sprinkled on the motherboard, especially along the edges, are connections for different types of cables. A small number of large, relatively thick pins connect to the computer's power supply. The remaining pins are much smaller and connect to I/O devices. These often connect through standard cables or other connectors with well-known names:

- **USB** (Universal Serial Bus)—connects primarily to lower-speed equipment like keyboards, printers, and mice, though it also connects to high-speed external hard drives.
- **IDE** (Integrated Drive Electronics)—a wide, flat "parallel" cable that connects high-speed devices like hard drives and compact disk (CD) drives to the motherboard. This appears on older computers.
- **ATA** (Advanced Technology Attachment)—another name applied to IDE connections.
- **SATA** (Serial ATA)—a narrow, flat cable that is easier to handle than a parallel ATA cable, to connect similar devices.
- **DVI** (Digital Video Interface)—a cable that connects to a digital video display, like a flat screen display.
- **VGA** (Video Graphics Array)—a cable that connects to older video displays, including analog video monitors with "tubes."
- **PCI** (Peripheral Component Interconnect)—a wide, parallel connector that attaches a daughterboard containing I/O circuits to the motherboard.
- **10-, 100-, 1000-baseT**—a wired connection to a local area network. This is also called an "Ethernet" connection. We examine these further in Chapter 10.

When we talk about computer hardware, the word ***bus*** refers to a computer connection that allows us to attach several separate components. A USB is obviously a bus, since the word appears in its name. The IDE, ATA, and SATA connections are also busses. Video connections don't tend to use busses. The PCI connection is considered a bus, even though it manages a small number of hardware connectors in the back of the computer.

Parallel Versus Serial Wiring

Wires are cheap inside a computer. When we connect a CPU to RAM, the motherboard uses a set of parallel wires to transfer addresses and data between them. Each wire carries one bit of data or one bit of address belonging to a location in RAM. The CPU often handles data and addresses "in parallel" because the circuits work on all the bits in a word at a time. When we run wires in parallel to connect two endpoints, we call it a *parallel* connection. Older hard drives used "ribbon cables" to make a parallel link between the drive controller and RAM; the upper cable in Figure 2.2 is a parallel ATA cable.

It is cheaper and more convenient, however, to run a single wire. This provides a *serial* connection. Most modern computers use serial ATA (SATA) cables instead of the wider, parallel ones. Although parallel cables could be faster in theory, improved circuitry yields a significant performance improvement with SATA connections.

The BIOS

Another important part of the motherboard is the BIOS (*Basic Input/Output System*). The BIOS isn't actually a circuit, it is really a computer program stored in special memory, called ROM (*read-only memory*), that usually remains unchanged. Computer programs stored in ROM are often called *firmware*. When we turn on the computer's power switch and the computer starts up, the BIOS is the first program to run. Normally, the BIOS loads the operating system into RAM from the computer's hard drive and starts it running. The process of loading and starting the computer's software is called *bootstrapping*, or simply *booting*.

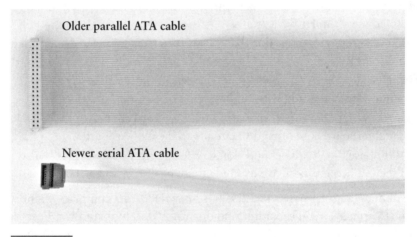

Older parallel ATA cable

Newer serial ATA cable

Figure 2.2

Older and newer ATA cables.

2.1.2 Program Execution

Every program relies on the CPU to execute its machine instructions. There is a storage location inside the CPU called the ***program counter*** (PC) that keeps track of where a program's next instruction resides. To execute the instruction, the CPU retrieves the instruction from RAM, performs the instruction, and updates the PC to point to the next instruction.

Figure 2.3 shows what happens when we execute a typical instruction. Since the PC contains 103, the CPU retrieves the instruction stored in RAM location #103. The instruction stored there says "ADD 702." The number 702 selects a RAM location whose contents are added to the CPU's running total. Location 702 contains the value 2273, while the CPU contains a running total of 3516. After executing the instruction, the CPU's running total is 5879. Once the CPU is finished with the instruction at location 103, it moves on to location 104 and executes the instruction there.

Usually, the next instruction is in the next sequential location in RAM. However, the CPU can use the results of arithmetic and other operations to change the program counter. This gives the program a way to change what happens when it encounters new data. When a computer program uses an **if, then, while, for, do,** or another loop or conditional test, the instructions in RAM tell the CPU to change the contents of the PC.

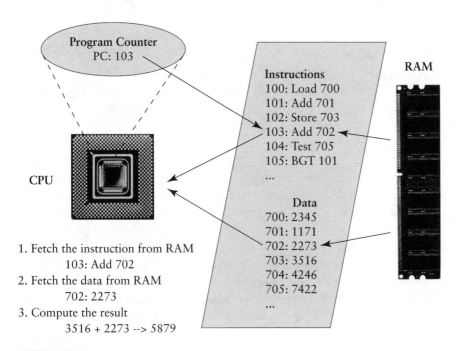

Figure 2.3

Executing a machine instruction in a computer.

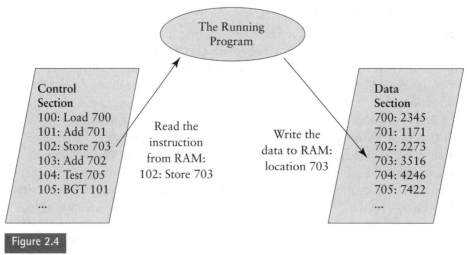

Figure 2.4

Separate control and data sections.

In Figure 2.3, we encounter some notation we will use in this book. We use parallelograms to indicate data stored in RAM. We use an oval to indicate a running program. We call a running program a *process*.

SEPARATING DATA AND CONTROL

Within RAM, we separate programs into two parts: a *control section* that contains the instructions, and a separate *data section* that contains the program's data (Figure 2.4). This distinction makes it easier to run programs reliably and efficiently.

The CPU itself doesn't always distinguish between control and data sections in RAM. If the program counter points to the data section, it retrieves instructions from there. Likewise, an instruction could treat parts of a control section as data. In practice, however, such mix-ups usually arise from a programming error or a security problem.

Although these examples show one instruction and one numeric value fitting comfortably into a single memory location, modern RAM doesn't work that way. Each location in RAM stores a single *byte*—eight bits of data. Although this is enough to store a typical character typed on a keyboard, most machine instructions require 2 or more bytes. If the instruction includes the RAM address of its data, then the instruction must set aside enough space for that address. If the program's RAM uses 4 gigabytes or less, then the RAM address alone requires 32 bits, or 4 bytes. Regardless of the instruction size, the CPU always updates the program counter to skip over an entire instruction after its execution.

2.1.3 Procedures

Modern computer programs often consist of thousands and even millions of instructions. To tame this complexity, most programs are organized into hundreds or thousands of relatively short procedures. When one part of the program needs a task performed, it often will call upon a separately written procedure to perform that task. That procedure itself may in turn call other procedures to perform smaller parts of the task. When a procedure finishes its work, it returns to the one that called it, allowing the caller to finish its own work. In other words, the *calling procedure* tells the *called procedure* to start running. Once the called procedure is finished, it returns to the point where the calling procedure left off.

When one procedure calls another, however, the computer must keep track of where the first one left off. To do this, the CPU saves the contents of the program counter in RAM. This serves as the *return address*, the location at which the CPU resumes the calling procedure. When the called procedure reaches its end, it picks up the saved return address and reloads it into the program counter. This resumes the calling procedure at the point where it left off.

THE STACK

Each procedure may itself call other procedures. The program's data section must store the return address for each procedure that calls another, in addition to each procedure's working storage. In practice, this data is stored in RAM on a *stack*, a last-in, first-out data store. The stack provides a simple, structured way to give temporary storage to a procedure, including a place to save the return address. The stack is part of the program's data section.

BUFFERS

Although most computer instructions involve arithmetic of some sort, not all data is strictly numerical. A great deal of processing involves blocks of text or other structured data, or "raw" unprocessed data that is being moved between I/O circuits like those for network connections.

A network gateway is responsible for directing network traffic that enters and leaves a site (see Chapter 11). A busy gateway for a large site transfers vast amounts of data while trying to actually "look" at as little of it as possible. The router tries to spend all of its time giving commands to the network I/O circuits. When it spends time looking at the data inside a network message, it delays the message's delivery.

When the router's I/O circuitry receives a network message, the data is read into an area in RAM. An area in RAM used for moving data is called a *buffer*. At most, the router looks at a few bytes at the beginning of the buffer and then it tells a network interface to transmit the buffer's contents across another network. Buffers always reside in a data section. If the buffer is only used inside a particular procedure, then the buffer will probably reside on the stack.

2.2 Programs and Processes

To make the most out of our computers, we run as many programs simultaneously as possible. When drafting a report or paper, people often run a word processor in one window and a web browser in the other. We rely on the *operating system* to run the processes for us and to make sure that our keystrokes and mouse clicks go to the correct program. Most systems fall into two categories: *Windows-based* systems and Unix-based systems. The Windows-based systems were developed by Microsoft. *Unix-based* systems include Apple's Macintosh OS-X, Sun's Solaris operating system, and the many variants of Linux.

Originally, people operated computers by typing individual commands to the operating system or to application programs using the computer's keyboard. When Microsoft first sold an operating system for desktop computers, it called it the Microsoft "Disk Operating System" or *MSDOS*. On Unix-based systems, users typed commands into a program to handle keyboard commands called a *shell*. Today, we may call any program that handles the operating system's keyboard commands a shell.

In modern graphics-oriented computers, many keyboard commands became drop-down menu items. However, most systems still provide a command shell to interpret keyboard commands. This is because some commands are rarely used by less-sophisticated users, and programmers never bothered to create a graphical user interface (GUI) for it. When we run the "cmd" program on Microsoft Windows, it starts up the MSDOS shell.

Figure 2.5 shows two windows running the MSDOS shell. Each window is in fact executing slightly different commands. Although both are running the same "cmd" program, each represents a separate *process* inside the computer. Each process has its own, separate RAM and program counter, even if it executes the same program as another process.

If we type a command to print out a long file in each window, we may see the output scroll past on both windows simultaneously. Although it may look as if the processes are running windows simultaneously, they may in fact be taking turns. Each turn may last for a few thousandths of a second. The switching takes place so fast that we don't see the processes take turns.

We call this type of sharing *multitasking*. Modern computers have special circuits in their CPUs to support multitasking. Modern operating systems have special multitasking software to manage these circuits and implement the sharing. Even when a computer lacks multiple CPUs or "cores," the operating system can keep several programs active at once.

If a computer contains only a single CPU, it's impossible to execute more than one program at a time. Instead, the operating system makes the programs take turns with the CPU. Each "running" program gets to use the CPU for a fraction of a second, or until it reaches a point where it must await an I/O operation. Then the operating system turns the CPU over to another program.

Process switching happens so quickly that we can't tell that programs are taking turns. This produces an "illusion of parallelism" because it appears as if the programs are running simultaneously.

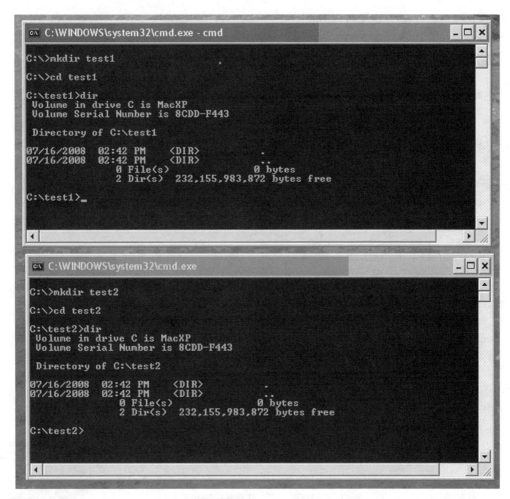

Figure 2.5

Running two processes at once.

2.2.1 Switching Between Processes

To switch between two processes, the operating system maintains a collection of data called the *process state*. This includes the program's RAM contents (control and data sections) plus the program counter and other data the program was using inside the CPU. When a particular process is actually executing, the CPU contains its program counter. The instructions contained in the executing program point at data in the program's own data section.

A process "loses" the CPU either because its time is up or because it must wait for something, like a keystroke or other I/O operation. When this happens, the operating system "dispatches" a different process. To do this, it takes the following steps:

1. Saves the program counter for the stopped process in its process state
2. Saves any other CPU data that belongs to the process in its process state
3. Locates the process state for the next process to run
4. Loads the CPU with the data needed to resume the next process
5. Once all other data is loaded and ready, the operating system loads the program counter for the next process into the CPU; this resumes the next process

Section 2.7 describes the dispatching process in detail. It also provides an example of how to describe a program's security controls.

Observing Active Processes

Most operating systems can display the system's activity by listing the currently active processes. Figure 2.6 provides part of such a list, produced using the Unix keyboard command *ps* on Apples OS-X.

The right column lists the running programs by identifying the executable file (some names are truncated). The left column lists the identity of the user or system entity who is running the program. User programs belong to user "rick," while other programs belong to system identities, including "root" and "super." The "PID" column shows the process identifier, a numerical code assigned to the process; certain keyboard commands may use the PID to select a process to control. Other columns give execution times and the percentage of CPU and RAM granted to that process.

```
$ ps aux
USER              PID   %CPU %MEM  TT   STAT STARTED      TIME COMMAND
rick              599   0.4  0.5   ??   S     9:58AM   0:12.61 /Applications/Utilities/Act
rick              235   0.4  0.5   ??   S     7:31AM   0:42.01 /System/Library/Frameworks/
_windowserver      58   0.4  1.2   ??   Ss    1:30AM   1:03.77 /System/Library/Frameworks/
rick              663   0.1  2.6   ??   S    10:10AM   0:05.72 /Applications/Firefox.app
root               26   0.0  0.0   ??   Ss    1:30AM   0:00.50 /usr/sbin/ntpd -n -g -p
root               21   0.0  0.1   ??   Ss    1:30AM   0:00.24 /usr/sbin/securityd -i
_mdnsresponder     16   0.0  0.0   ??   Ss    1:30AM   0:00.17 /usr/sbin/mDNSResponder
daemon             15   0.0  0.0   ??   Ss    1:30AM   0:01.10 /usr/sbin/distnoted
root               14   0.0  0.1   ??   Ss    1:30AM   0:01.72 /usr/sbin/configd
rick              201   0.0  0.0   ??   Ss    7:31AM   0:04.54 /sbin/launchd
super             642   0.0  0.1   ??   SNs  10:09AM   0:00.16 /System/Library/Frameworks
root              641   0.0  0.0   00   Ss   10:09AM   0:00.02 login -pf rick
_securityagent    625   0.0  0.2   ??   S    10:05AM   0:00.70 /System/Library/CoreSe
nobody            239   0.0  0.0   ??   Ss    7:31AM   0:00.01 /System/Library/PrivateFrame
rick              360   0.0  0.3   ??   S     8:56AM   0:02.22 /Applications/TextEdit.app/C
```

Figure 2.6

A partial list of processes displayed by the Unix ps command.

The ps command works on most Unix-based systems, including Macintosh OS-X. The Macintosh also has a graphics-oriented "System Monitor" application. Microsoft Windows provides a similar graphical display using its Task Manager.

2.2.2 The Operating System

When we start, stop, or monitor processes on a computer, we rely on the operating system to do all the work. The fundamental job of every operating system is to run programs, and this relies on certain basic functions:

- Process management—the work of keeping the CPU busy by giving it processes to run.
- RAM management—assign RAM to active processes and manage unused RAM to assure that it's not wasted.
- I/O management—make it easy for programs to use I/O devices through a uniform programming interface, and make it easy for computer owners to add or replace I/O devices.

These three functions appear in every operating system, from simple ones on the most basic cell phones to highly complex ones on the most sophisticated interactive desktops.

All operating systems provide a uniform programming interface through which programs can request specific services. For example, a program can request additional RAM, which might be provided as an increased size to its existing data section or as an additional, separate data section. More sophisticated operating systems, including modern Windows and Unix derivatives, allow one process to tell the operating system to start another process.

I/O System

The I/O system has a difficult job. The operating system must provide a uniform programming interface for using the keyboard, display, printer, hard drive, and any other device the user buys and wants to attach. When a program sends data to the computer's printer, the program often doesn't care who built the printer, whether it is ink jet or laser, or even whether it's black and white or color. It's up to the operating system to match these different printers to our application programs. The same problem arises when we connect cameras, cell phones, and other complex devices to our computers.

Operating systems address this problem with ***device drivers***, specialized procedures that convert an application program's requests into a form the particular device understands. When we install a new device, the operating system often installs a special device driver to work with that device. These drivers are written specifically for the device and provided to its customers. Each driver is tailored for the particular operating system and for the particular device. We examine device drivers further in Chapter 5.

Many operating systems, especially modern desktop systems, add three major components atop the I/O system:

1. File management—provide a special I/O interface to the hard drive, flash drive, or other external storage to make data easy to find and update; also manage free space on the drive to ensure there is room for new files. The OS also provides access controls (see Chapters 3 through 5).

2. User interface—manage the keyboard and display I/O to provide a way to give commands and receive responses from the operating system. On larger systems, this involves the modern GUI with a mouse, windows, menus, and other typical elements.

3. Network protocol process—manage network I/O to provide standard, Internet-oriented network services (see Chapter 10).

SECURITY

When a computer uses programs and information from many different sources, it relies on its operating system to protect programs and processes from one another. On smaller, integrated products like cell phones, the risks mostly threaten the product's application, not its computing infrastructure. In that case, the operating system itself has few, if any, security mechanisms.

Desktop systems include a standard set of security mechanisms. When processes start and run, security mechanisms keep them from hogging the CPU or damaging each others' RAM. The GUI also keeps processes from modifying each others' windows on the video display. If people log in, then they have the choice of protecting files from each other.

Those protections evolved in timesharing systems developed during the 1960s and 1970s, including the Unix system. Unfortunately, the protections don't, by themselves, always protect systems from harm.

2.3 Buffer Overflow and the Morris Worm

In a perfect world, a computer should not crash or misbehave simply because it is connected to a network and it receives the "wrong" data. The network software (the computer's protocol process) should identify a badly formed message and discard it. In practice, network software may contain flaws by which cleverly designed messages may crash the software (and perhaps the computer's operating system) or may open a *back door* for an attacker.

A back door provides a network connection by which the attacker can take control of the computer. In the film *WarGames* (1983), the story revolved around a backdoor connection found by a teen computer enthusiast. The teen thought the connection led to a computer games company, but, in fact, it led to a military computer that could launch nuclear missiles. The simplest back door gives the attacker control of a command shell, preferably one with administrative privileges. This allows the attacker to remotely control the system by typing keyboard commands.

In 1988, a graduate student at Cornell University named Robert T. Morris wrote an experimental *worm* program that could replicate itself across computers on the Internet—then a research network with 60,000 host computers. Morris did not want to remotely control these systems. He simply wanted to see if it would be possible to build a program that could distribute itself unobtrusively across the Internet. The worm would move from one computer to another by seeking a vulnerability in the next computer that would allow the worm to enter. Morris had learned about several common vulnerabilities in the Unix operating system, which was heavily used on the Internet. He programmed his worm program to take advantage of those vulnerabilities.

THE "FINGER" PROGRAM

One of the vulnerabilities Morris used was in a networking service called *finger*. The purpose of finger was to report the status of individual computer users. A person could type the keyboard command:

```
finger jsl@bu.edu
```

The command includes the user name of interest and the host computer on which the user resides, all packaged together like an email address (of course, this form often served as the user's email address).

The command starts a program that contacts the finger server at the computer *bu.edu* and asks it about the user named *jsl*. The server returns an answer that reports whether the user is currently logged in, or when last logged in, and may deliver additional information (like address and phone number) if the user jsl has provided it.

2.3.1 The "Finger" Overflow

Researchers familiar with the Unix system, and with the finger service in particular, had discovered a flaw in the software. To understand the problem, examine Figure 2.7, which shows how the finger server program arranged its data.

"finger" Data Section
1000: return address to Network
1010: some finger variables
1020: buffer for user ID
1120: more finger variables
1180: return address to finger()
1200: some network "read" variables
1260: a network "read" buffer
1400: unused space
1450: unused space

Figure 2.7

Data section for the finger service.

The finger data section shown here is actually part of its stack. When the host computer's network software recognized that it had received a finger request, it started the finger process, leaving the network software's return address in RAM at 1000, the first location on the stack. The finger process began with a procedure that set aside variables at locations 1010 and 1120. It also set aside a 100-byte buffer at location 1020 to contain the user ID (underlined in Figure 2.7).

Then the procedure called a network "read" function to retrieve the network message that just arrived. When calling the function, finger saved its return address at location 1180. The network read function created some variables starting at location 1200. (These RAM addresses are meant to illustrate what happened and are not exact.)

The finger service assumed that a user's name and host computer name would together never exceed 100 bytes, including a null character at the end. The example query shown earlier ("jsl@bu.edu") is 10 bytes long, or 11, including the trailing null. In 1988, most Internet user and host names were similarly small. The finger service did not check the size of the incoming text, assuming that users would not be inclined to type exceedingly long names.

EXPLOITING "FINGER"

Morris had heard about this flaw and was aware of how an attacker might exploit it. When the worm program started running on a particular host computer, it would try to connect across the Internet to other host computers. Then the worm would use the finger connection to try to attack the victim computer.

Figure 2.8 shows how the worm used a network connection to attack the finger service. The infected host computer (right) connected to the finger process (left). It then sent an excessively long string as the "name" of the user.

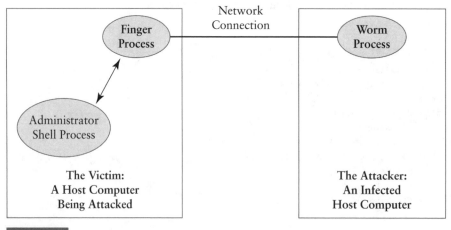

Figure 2.8

Attacking a computer via the finger process.

"finger" Data Section
1000 return address to network
1010 some finger variables
1020 jsl@bu.eduXXXXXXXXXX
1120 XXXXXXXXXXXXXXXXXX
1180 1260
1200 XXXXXXXXXXXXXXXXXX
1260 [machine instructions that]
1400 ["take over" the finger process]
1450 XXXXXXXXXXXXXXXX

Figure 2.9

Buffer overflow in the finger service.

The finger service read this string into its buffer, but the string was much longer than the buffer. Since the finger service didn't check the size of the incoming data, it simply kept copying the data into RAM past the end of the buffer's assigned space. Thus, the input string "overflowed" the buffer. In Figure 2.9, the overflow spans the variables filled with "XXX."

THE SHELLCODE

Morris carefully crafted the overflow data so that the worm process then could infect the computer it attacked. Morris had studied how the finger service used RAM and where it saved program counters for returning from procedures. He designed the overflow data to contain two essential components:

1. A sequence of computer instructions (a program called a "shellcode") would start a command shell, like "cmd" on Windows. Instead of taking commands from the keyboard, this shell took its commands from the attacking host computer. The commands traveled over the same connection it used to attack the finger service. In Figure 2.9, the shellcode program starts at location 1260 and ends before 1450.

2. A storage location contained the return address for the network read function. The overflow data overwrote the return address. Once the read function finished, it tried to return to its caller by using the address stored at location 1180. The overflow rewrote that location to point to the shellcode (location 1260).

The attack took place as follows. Morris' worm program sent a query to the computer's finger service. The query was so long that it overflowed the buffer as shown. When the finger program called the network read function, that function copied the overlong query into the too-short buffer. The message overwrote the function's return address.

When the network read function ended, it tried to return from its caller by retrieving the return address. Instead, however, that return address redirected the CPU to execute the shellcode. When executed, the shellcode started a command shell that took its commands from the opened network connection (Figure 2.8). The computer that sent the attack then gave commands to upload and install the worm program.

This attack worked because of shortcomings in the system. The first problem was that the CPU could not distinguish between instructions and data inside RAM. While some CPUs can be programmed to treat control sections as instructions and data sections as data, not all Unix systems used the technique. If the system had done so, the CPU would *not* have executed the shellcode written on the stack. Even today, not all systems and applications use this feature. On Microsoft systems, there is a specific ***data execution prevention*** (DEP) feature. The operating system provides it, but only if applications take the trouble to distinguish between their control and data sections.

Another feature of the finger process made this attack especially powerful: The finger process ran with "root" privileges. In other words, the finger process had full administrative power on the computer. Once finger was subverted, the attacker likewise had full administrative access to the computer.

This is a notable case in which Least Privilege could have reduced the damage of an attack. In essence, the finger process had "Most Privilege" instead of Least Privilege. There were ways to arrange the Unix network software so that the finger process could run with user privileges, but it was easier to give it "root" privileges. This trade-off made sense in an experimental environment, but not in the face of growing risks.

THE WORM RELEASED

The ***Morris worm*** was successful in one sense: When Morris released it in October of 1988, it soon infested about 10 percent of the machines on the Internet. Morris had included a check in the program to limit the number of copies of the worm that ran on each computer, but the check did not halt its spread. Soon dozens and even hundreds of copies of the worm were running on each infested computer. Each computer would try to infest its neighbors dozens of times, and succeed, and those neighbors returned the favor.

Buffer overflows are an ongoing problem with computer software. Some blame the C programming language, which was used to write many modern programs, protocol processes, and operating systems. The original programming libraries for C did not provide boundary checking for text-oriented input. This may have made programs more efficient when computers were smaller and slower, but the risks of buffer overflow no longer justify the efficiency gains.

Modern programming languages like Java and many scripting languages will automatically check for buffer overflow. However, many programmers still use C. Modern C libraries provide ways to check for buffer overflow, but not all programmers understand and use them.

2.3.2 Security Alerts

The Morris worm was the first Internet-wide security incident. By 9 PM of the evening of the attack, major Internet sites at Stanford University and at the Massachusetts Institute of Technology (MIT) were seeing the effects of the worm. The University of California at Berkeley was attacked around 11 PM. An expert in California reported characteristics of the attack via email early the following morning.

An informal network of experts quickly developed to analyze the worm. The network was centered around Berkeley, MIT, Purdue University, and the University of Utah. An annual meeting of Unix experts was in progress at Berkeley when the attack took place, and the participants soon went to work analyzing the attack.

Unfortunately, the analysts and victims were limited by the communications technologies available in 1988. Although the wired telephone network was unaffected by the worm, the remaining communications media were all Internet based, and the Internet was in trouble. As analysts got their own sites under control, they used Internet email and the "Usenet news" system to distribute information about the worm and defensive measures against it. However, the worm still disrupted communications with some sites. One message sent out that first morning took over 2 days to be delivered to most recipients. Without email guidance or established non-Internet contact information for other sites "in the know," site administrators were hard pressed to respond to the attack.

Some site managers voluntarily disconnected themselves from the Internet to deal with the worm. In some cases, they disconnected before they were infected. In other cases, the disconnection made it difficult to get information to combat the site's own worm infestations.

ESTABLISHING CERT

In response to the Morris worm, the United States government established its first Computer Emergency Response Team (CERT) at the Software Engineering Institute of Carnegie-Mellon University. CERT provides an official clearinghouse for reporting security vulnerabilities in computing systems. The CERT Coordination Center (CERT/CC) is a division of CERT that was established within weeks of the worm attack to coordinate the response to future Internet-wide security incidents. More recently, the U.S. Department of Homeland Security transferred the traditional CERT reporting and coordination activities to the government-operated US-CERT organization. Other countries and large entities have established their own CERT organizations. Computing vendors have their own processes for handling and reporting vulnerabilities in their products.

For several years, CERT published "CERT Advisories" to report security vulnerabilities. Organizations and security experts would use the CERT Advisory number to refer to well-known vulnerabilities. Today, we typically use "CVE numbers" taken from the Common Vulnerability Enumeration (CVE) database. This database is maintained by Mitre Corporation on behalf of the U.S. government. As with CERT Advisories, the system relies on the discovery of vulnerabilities by vendors or other interested parties, and the reporting of these vulnerabilities through the CVE process. The CVE database helps ensure that every security vulnerability has a single designation that is used consistently by all vendors, software tools, and commentators in the information security community.

Although the Morris worm attack took place in 1988, it took a decade for worm attacks to become a recurring problem on the Internet. The "Internet Storm Center" was established in 1998 to watch Internet traffic patterns and look for disruptions caused by large-scale worm attacks. It is sponsored by the SANS (SysAdmin, Audit, Network, Security) Institute, a cooperative that provides education and training in system administration and security.

2.4 Access Control Strategies

Even though the Morris worm attacked systems that implemented many access control mechanisms, these did not halt the worm's spread. To understand why, we need to examine those mechanisms. First, we look at the general problem of access control. Computer-based access control falls into four categories that correspond to these real-world situations:

- *Islands*—a potentially hostile process is marooned on an island. The process can only use resources brought to it.
- *Vaults*—a process has the right to use certain resources within a much larger repository. The process must ask for access to the resources individually, and the system checks its access permissions on a case-by-case basis.
- *Puzzles*—a process uses secret or hidden information in order to retrieve particular data items. This provides effective protection only if it is not practical to try to guess the unknown information through exhaustive trial and error.
- *Patterns*—the data items and programs made available to a process are compared against patterns associated with hostile data. If the data item matches a pattern, the system discards the data or at least blocks access to it by other processes. This technique is not very reliable and is used as a last resort.

ISLANDS

In practice, computer-based access control begins by making each process into its own *island*. If you are marooned on an island, you are restricted to the resources already there, plus whatever resources are brought to you. If we look at a process as an island, the operating system gives the process access to its own RAM and to carefully metered turns using the CPU. The island forms its own security domain, within which the process has free rein.

This type of access control is called "isolation and mediation." We isolate the process, or group of processes, to create the island. We then "mediate" its access to other resources. We try to do this with risky processes so that we may restrict the damage they might do.

VAULTS

Processes rarely operate simply as islands. Often the operating system provides access to a *vault* of computing resources. Each request is checked to ensure the process has permission to use the file or other resource. If you have a safe deposit box at a bank, the clerk may admit you to the vault, but only to the area containing your box, and only for retrieving that particular box. Section 2.5 discusses the RAM access controls applied by typical operating systems to typical processes.

2.4.1 Puzzles and Patterns

Puzzle-based access control appears in many ways in the real world and in computer systems. Its most powerful form appears in *cryptography*, or *crypto* for short. Crypto provides us with a variety of mathematical techniques to hide data through encryption or to authenticate its contents.

Another puzzle technique is called **steganography**, in which we try to hide one collection of information inside another. A simple example might be to write a message in invisible ink. Digital steganography often encodes the data in a special way and then spreads it among seemingly random data bits in another file. For example, the digital image on the left of Figure 2.10 contains the 243-word document shown at right. For every spot in the digital image, there is a binary number representing its brightness in the image. We encode the data in the low-order bits of individual spots. Changes to those bits rarely change the picture's general appearance.

Puzzles also provide a popular but less-effective form of protection called *security through obscurity* or "STO" for short. This approach often relies on hiding to keep

EMISSIONS SECURITY ASSESSMENT REQUEST (ESAR) FOR ALL CLASSIFIED SYSTEMS

The information below are EMSEC requirements that must be complied with by government contractors before the processing of classified data can begin. These are the minimum requirements established for the processing of DOD SECRET information. The processing of higher than DOD SECRET call for more stringent requirements.

(1) The contractor shall ensure that emission security (EMSEC) conditions related to this contract are minimized.

(2) The contractor shall provide countermeasure assessment data to the Contracting Officer as an ESAR. The ESAR shall provide only specific responses to the data required in paragraph 3 below. The contractor's standard security plan is unacceptable as a "standalone" ESAR response. The contractor shall NOT submit a detailed facility analysis/assessment. The ESAR information will be used to complete an EMSBC Countermeasures Assessment Review of the contractor's facility to be performed by the government EMSEC authority using current Air Force EMSEC directives.

(3) When any of the information required in paragraph 4 below changes (such as location or classification level), the contractor shall notify the contracting officer of the changes, so a new EMSEC Countermeasures Assessment Review is accomplished. The contractor shall submit to the Program Management Office a new ESAR. The new ESAR will identify the new configuration, a minimum of 30 days before beginning the change(s). The contractor shall not commence classified processing in the new configuration until receiving approval to do so from the contracting officer.

Figure 2.10

Example of steganography.

resources safe, without weighing the risk of potential attackers finding the resources through a process of searching.

> **An Incident**: Several years ago, a spreadsheet vendor provided a feature that let customers password-protect their spreadsheets. The technique used a very weak encryption technique. A programmer was looking at how the technique worked and realized that there was a very easy way to break it. He reported the problem to the vendor and expected the vendor would fix the problem and update the software.
>
> Instead, the vendor threatened the programmer with legal action if he revealed the problem to anyone else. The vendor decided it was easier to threaten legal action than to fix the problem. Of course, this did not prevent others from finding the problem on their own and making their own announcements.

Encryption becomes STO when it is easy to crack. Steganography used by itself may also qualify as STO. If it hides sensitive information, the information itself should be encrypted.

Although steganography can hide information, it isn't effective when people know where to look for it. We also must prevent potential attackers from retrieving the information.

Open Design: A Basic Principle

STO is most often famous for its failures. For example, house thieves seem to find the hidden valuables first. The opposite of STO is the principle of *Open Design*.

When we practice Open Design, we don't keep our security mechanisms secret. Instead, we build a mechanism that is strong by itself but kept secure using a component we easily change. For example, we can replace the locks on doors without replacing the doors and latches themselves.

Open Design acknowledges the fact that attackers may "reverse engineer" a device to figure out how it works. If a security device relies on STO, reverse engineering allows the attacker to bypass its protection. A well-designed security device still provides protection even after reverse engineering. For example, safecrackers know all about how safe mechanisms work. Even so, it may take them hours to open a safe unless they know its secret combination.

Open Design, however, is not the same as "open source." An open-source software package is made freely available on terms to ensure the free portions, and improvements made to them, remain available freely to everyone. While all open-source systems are also Open Design by intent, not all Open Design systems are open source.

Cryptography and Open Design

Properly designed cryptosystems use Open Design. The concept arises from *Kerckhoffs' principle*, in which we assume that potential attackers already know everything about how the cryptosystem works. All real security should rest in a changeable piece of secret information, the *key*, which we can easily change without replacing the whole system.

Kerckhoff was a 19th century French military thinker. Claude Shannon restated this principle succinctly by saying, "The enemy knows the system" in his 1949 paper

"Communication Theory of Secrecy Systems." This is sometimes called *Shannon's maxim*. This arose as part of Shannon's development of information theory and his work on the mathematical properties of cryptosystems.

If we build an access control system using puzzles and Open Design, we end up with a variation of the vault. Encryption presents a puzzle: We possess the data but it's effectively "locked up" in its encrypted form. We can retrieve the encrypted data only if we have the key.

PATTERN-BASED ACCESS CONTROL

Pattern-based access control is very common although it is notoriously unreliable. Photo ID cards provide a common real-world example: A guard or clerk compares the fuzzy photo on an ID card to the face of the person. These checks are very unreliable because the photos are rarely of high quality and are rarely updated to reflect significant changes in appearance, like changes to facial hair or hair style.

Most computers today rely on pattern-based access control to detect *malware*: programs or data whose contents may harm processes that handle it. The *computer virus* is a common example; software that replicates itself when executed. While the replication might not be designed to cause harm, it uses up resources and may damage files by accident. Moreover, modern virus writers often use the virus to compromise any system that runs it, making viruses very dangerous. We examine viruses further in Section 3.2.2.

Mathematically, there is no 100 percent reliable way to analyze a block of data or a computer program and conclusively determine what it could do. Antivirus software looks for patterns associated with known viruses and other possibly harmful data, and blocks vulnerable processes from accessing that data. Pattern matching is rarely exact, so there is always a risk of a mismatch. This can lead to either mistaking safe data as malware or failing to identify malware as such. Malware pattern detection can only block existing types of malware that the system has been shown how to detect. It is not effective against new threats.

BIOMETRICS

Another computer-based application of patterns is in *biometrics*: techniques that try to identify individual people based on personal traits like voice, fingerprints, eye features, and so on. In this case, as with malware detection, decisions are based on approximate matches. Again, we try to avoid both a mismatch of the legitimate person and a successful match against someone else. We examine biometrics further in Section 6.6.

2.4.2 Chain of Control: Another Basic Principle

When Bob starts up his computer normally, it runs the operating system on his hard drive. He then can protect the files on his hard drive by telling his operating system how to restrict access. If Bob ensures that the computer *always* runs his operating system the way he set it up, then the system will protect his files. We call this the *Chain of Control*.

If one of his suitemates boots Bob's computer from a compact disk, like a CD-ROM, his computer loses its Chain of Control. From the CD-ROM, they can start up their own operating system. That system is *not* restricted by the rules Bob established.

We retain the Chain of Control as long as the following is true:

- Whenever the computer starts, it runs software that enforces our security policy, and
- If the software we start (typically an operating system) can start other software, then that other software either:
  - Complies with the security policy, or
  - Is prevented from violating the policy by other defensive measures, like operating system restrictions on RAM and file access.

CONTROLLING THE BIOS

When a computer starts up, it starts the BIOS program stored on its motherboard (Figure 2.1). Many computers recognize a special "escape key" (sometimes this is the key marked "ESC" for "escape") that activates the BIOS user interface. This interface allows an operator to adjust certain computer features maintained by the motherboard hardware. In particular, the user interface selects the "bootstrap device" from which the BIOS loads the operating system. The term "boot" and "bootstrap" refers to the process of loading and running a program from a mass storage device like a hard drive or CD-ROM.

When most systems start up, they try to bootstrap the operating system from the first hard drive they find. If that fails, they then may search for a CD-ROM or other device. Some systems, like the Macintosh, allow the user to type a key on the keyboard (like the letter "C") to force a bootstrap from a CD-ROM.

While this type of flexibility is useful at home and in some technical environments, it can compromise the computer's Chain of Control. If this poses a real security risk, administrators may take another step: They may disable bootstrapping from any device except the approved hard drive containing the approved operating system. However, if the hard drive fails, the administrator will not be able to boot a CD-ROM with recovery software. The administrator will need to physically reconfigure the computer to install a new hard drive or to reenable the BIOS.

Administrators may further protect the Chain of Control by enabling password protection in the BIOS. This protection prevents changes to the BIOS configuration unless the operator knows the password, thereby allowing the administrator to change the boot device if there is a hardware failure.

Unfortunately, the BIOS is not the only risk to the Chain of Control. The Morris worm illustrated another risk; malicious software can exploit a software weakness that allows the software to subvert the system.

SUBVERTING THE CHAIN OF CONTROL

Here are ways to subvert the Chain of Control on Bob's computer:

- Bootstrap the computer from a different hard drive or CD-ROM. Bypass the normal operating system and use the different, bootstrapped one to modify the hard drive.

- Trick Bob into running software that attacks his files. Since he started the process, the process has full access to his files.

- Trick the operating system, or an administrator, into running a subverted program with administrative or system privileges. This often allows a program to bypass security restrictions. This is how the Morris Worm attacked through the finger process.

We can install security measures to block these vulnerabilities, but we need to decide that these are risks worth addressing.

2.5 Keeping Processes Separate

Worms and other malware aren't the only risks to computers. Operator errors and software bugs can pose as big of a threat. Operating systems use access control mechanisms to keep processes separate.

Computing pioneers didn't need computer-based access control mechanisms. In the 1940s and 1950s, users often had exclusive use of a computer while their programs were run. Access control relied exclusively on physical protection of the computer itself. Although computer users often shared the computer with others, they didn't have to share space *inside* the computer with others. As computer hardware and software became more sophisticated, designers realized they could get a computer to do more work if they ran several users' programs at once. This was the origin of multitasking.

The earliest computing systems were incredibly expensive to build and operate. A typical high-performance "mainframe" computer system in the 1960s might rent time at the rate of $100 per *second* of execution time. Today, we could *buy* an entire computer for the cost of *renting* less than a minute of 1960s mainframe time. Back then, computer owners had to keep their computers busy every moment in order to recoup the high costs. Multitasking helped keep the expensive mainframes busy.

SEPARATION MECHANISMS

Effective multitasking depended on protection to keep the processes separate. The University of Manchester, England, developed such protections for the Atlas computer in the early 1960s. In the United States, Fernando Corbató's team at MIT used similar techniques to implement the Compatible Time-Sharing System (CTSS), which allowed about 30 people to use a mainframe computer simultaneously. CTSS used a large IBM 7090 computer built by International Business Machines. These systems relied on access control mechanisms to protect processes from one another and to allow sharing of other computing resources. The protections relied on special circuits within the CPU to provide two features:

1. Two "modes" to distinguish between normal application programs and special operating system programs
2. Mechanisms to restrict a process to those specific regions of RAM assigned to it

Program Modes

The two program modes are ***user mode*** and ***kernel mode***. Most programs run in user mode; this embodies all of the CPU's standard instructions for calculating, comparing, and making decisions. A handful of special instructions are only available in kernel mode. The kernel mode instructions are used to switch the CPU between processes and to control what parts of RAM are visible to the CPU. When the operating system switches between processes, it runs a short program in kernel mode called the ***dispatcher***. The program switches the program counter and RAM permissions from the previous process to the next one (see Section 2.7).

Keep in mind that these modes are different from the "administrative" or "root" privileges referred to when discussing the Morris worm. Such access privileges are enforced by decisions of the operating system's software. The kernel and user modes are enforced by the CPU itself when instructions execute.

RAM Protection

When a process performs some work, it collects the results in RAM. In modern operating systems, each process operates in its own "island" of RAM. The island typically is implemented using a *page table* that lists all of its available RAM. When the process reaches for an instruction or data in RAM, the CPU consults the page table. If the table doesn't include that location, the CPU stops the process with a memory error. The table also indicates whether the process may write to parts of RAM as well as read them.

When a process begins, the operating system constructs a page table that lists its control and data sections. A program only touches other parts of RAM by mistake. For example, the program might reach "out of bounds" if its code contains an error. Normally, these memory restrictions don't interfere with a program's operation.

The CPU can read or write any part of RAM while in kernel mode. When the operating system switches from one program to another, it constructs a page table for the new process. The new table points to different parts of RAM than those used by other processes.

RAM protection, like page tables, and the distinction between kernel and user mode, keep the system running smoothly. They keep processes safe from one another, and to keep the operating system itself safe from misbehaving processes.

User Identities

Building on process protection, an operating system provides the "vault" from which it serves up individual files and other resources. This mechanism typically employs user identification. When a particular individual starts to use the computer, the operating system associates a simple, unique name, the ***user identity***, or user ID, with that person. When processes try to use a system's resources (files, printers, etc.) the operating system may grant or deny access according to the user's identity.

EVOLUTION OF PERSONAL COMPUTERS

Although mainframe computers were extremely popular with large corporations, universities, and defense organizations, they exceeded the budgets of many who could benefit from computing. However, the underlying cost of computing circuits dropped as the circuits changed from expensive vacuum tubes to lower-cost transistors and then to integrated circuits. By the 1960s it was possible to build a serviceable computer for less than $20,000. These were called "minicomputers." Technically, the systems were comparable to mainframes from a decade earlier, but they continued to improve as hardware technology improved.

By the late 1970s, minicomputer technology provided all of the programming features of mainframes, including process protection. Mainframes remained popular until the 1990s when all but the largest applications could be serviced by smaller scale computers.

"Microcomputers" emerged in the 1970s with the development of the microprocessor. Technically, the first microcomputers were similar to the early minicomputers, but they cost less than $2,000. As with minicomputers, these devices improved in capability as the underlying technologies improved. Modern personal computers evolved directly from early microcomputers.

SECURITY ON PERSONAL COMPUTERS

Modern process protections were rarely used on personal computers until the late 1990s. Before that, desktop operating systems were fairly simple, although some could run multiple processes. Those operating systems took as little effort as possible to make this happen, and did very little to protect one process from another. Computer viruses could easily install themselves in RAM and wreak havoc on the rest of the system. Even if the system was virus-free, the lack of protection made *all* running programs vulnerable to software bugs in *any* of the running programs.

For example, Bob's dad was running both the word processing program and the spreadsheet on his 1990-vintage computer. If a particularly nasty error arose in the word-processing program, it could damage the spreadsheet's code stored in RAM. When the spreadsheet program took its turn to run, the damaged instructions could in turn damage Dad's saved spreadsheet data. This was not a problem if programs were simple and reliable, but programs were constantly adding features. These changes made the programs larger, and often made them less reliable. Process protection made it safer to run several programs at once, and also made it easier to detect and fix software errors.

OPERATING SYSTEM SECURITY FEATURES

To summarize, a modern operating system contains the following features to run multiple processes and keep them safe and separate:

- Make different programs take turns using the CPU.
- Give separate parts of RAM to separate programs.
- Protect the RAM used by one process from damage by other processes.
- Provide a separate, window-oriented user interface for each program, so one program doesn't put its results in a different program's window.
- Grant access to files or other resources according to the user running the program.

2.5.1 Sharing a Program

We keep processes separate by putting them on individual islands. The protections between processes prevent them from interfering with one another by keeping them from sharing the same RAM. This is fine if our only concern is protection. However, there are times when it makes sense to share RAM between processes. For example, if two processes are running the same program (Figure 2.11), then we can save RAM if the processes share the same control section.

Problems arise if one process changes the control section while another process also is using it. This could cause the second process to fail. The operating system prevents such problems by setting up an access restriction on the control section; the processes may read the RAM containing the control section, but they can't write to that RAM. The CPU blocks any attempts to write to the control section. This is an example of a *read-only* (RO) access restriction.

In Figure 2.11, the arrows indicate the flow of data between each process (the ovals) and other resources. The control section is read only, so the arrow flows *from* the control section *to* the processes. The window is part of an output device, so the arrow flows *to* the window *from* the processes. The processes can both read and write their data sections, so those arrows point in both directions. We isolate each process by granting it exclusive access to its own data section, and blocking access to other data sections.

However, some processes need to share a data section with other processes. For example, networking software often will use several separate processes. These processes pass network data among one another using shared buffers in RAM. The operating system establishes shared blocks of RAM and grants full read/write access to both processes. This is the fastest and most efficient way to share data between processes.

ACCESS MATRIX

Table 2.1 takes the access permissions shown in Figure 2.11 and displays them as a two-dimensional form called an *access matrix*. Some researchers call this "Lampson's matrix" after Butler Lampson, the computer scientist who introduced the idea in 1971. Lampson developed the matrix after working on a series of time-sharing system designs,

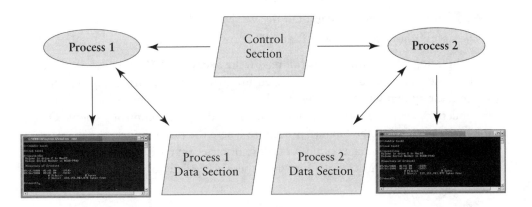

Process 1 Window

Process 2 Window

Figure 2.11

Two processes sharing a control section.

TABLE 2.1 Access matrix for processes in Figure 2.11			
Control or Data Section	Process #1	Process #2	Operating System
Program's control section	R–	R–	RW
Process #1's data section	RW	––	RW
Process #2's data section	––	RW	RW

notably with Scientific Data Systems (SDS), where he worked on the time-sharing system for their SDS 940 computer.

The access matrix shows the processes across one axis of the matrix and all sections of RAM down the other axis. When we apply it to access rights in general, the rows represent *objects* in the system, like RAM, I/O devices, or files. Columns represent *subjects*, which include any type of process in the system, or may refer to the "owners" of those processes (i.e., the users that started the processes).

ACCESS RIGHTS

Each cell in the matrix represents the ***access rights*** granted to a particular subject for interacting with a particular object. Because the matrix lists all subjects and all objects on the system, it shows all rights granted. When we talk about RAM access, the access choices include:

• Read/write access allowed (abbreviated RW)

- Read access only, no writing (omit the W; show only R-)
- No access allowed (omit both R and W; show two hyphens)

The operating system always has full read/write access to RAM used by processes it runs. This allows it to create processes, to ensure that they take turns, and to remove them from the system when they have finished execution or they misbehave.

In modern systems, programs often contain several separate control sections. One control section contains the "main" procedure where the program begins and ends. Other control sections often contain procedure libraries that are shared among many different programs. On Microsoft Windows, these are called "dynamic link libraries" and carry a ".dll" suffix.

2.5.2 Sharing Data

Modern computers often have situations where two or more processes need to work on the same data. When we need to send data to a printer or other output device, for example, our own program uses the operating system to give that data to the printer's device driver. Figure 2.12 shows how the operating system arranges this in RAM.

First, the operating system acquires a data section to share with the printer device driver. This data section holds the buffer for the data we send to the printer.

When our program produces data to be printed, the program places that data in the buffer. When the buffer is full, the operating system tells the device driver process, which then retrieves the data from the buffer and sends it to the printer.

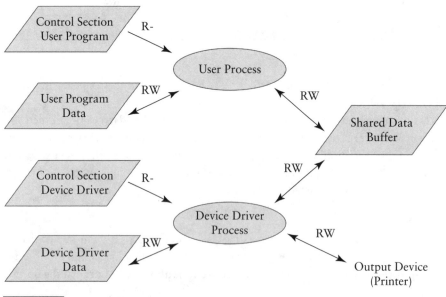

Figure 2.12

Two processes (a program and a device driver) share a data section.

TABLE 2.2 Access matrix for Figure 2.12

Control or Data Section	User Process	Device Driver Process	Operating System
User program's control section	R-	--	RW
User program's data section	RW	--	RW
Device driver's control section	--	R-	RW
Device driver's data section	--	RW	RW
Shared data buffer	RW	RW	RW

If we focus on the left and center of Figure 2.12, the two processes look simple and conventional; each has its own control section and one data section. The special part appears on the right, with the shared buffer stored in its own data section. Both processes have read and write access to it; this allows them to leave signals for each other in RAM to help keep track of the status of the output operations. Table 2.2 presents the access matrix for the system in Figure 2.12.

The device driver is part of the operating system and it's not unusual to grant the device driver full access to all of RAM, just like the rest of the operating system. It is, however, much safer for the operating system and the computer's owner if we apply Least Privilege to device drivers. In other words, we only grant the driver whatever access rights it really needs.

Microsoft's Windows NT, and then Windows 2000, were their first operating systems that provided modern process protection. Both of these systems occasionally suffered from the "Blue Screen of Death." This was a failure in which the Windows system encountered a fatal error, switched the display into a text mode (with a blue background), and printed out the CPU contents and key information from RAM. The only way to recover was to reboot the computer. Many of these "blue screen" failures were eventually traced to faulty device drivers.

One of the risks with device drivers is that they rarely are written by the operating system developers. Microsoft writes a few key drivers for Windows, but many are written by hardware manufacturers. While many driver writers are careful to follow the rules and test their software, not all are as careful.

2.6 Security Policy and Implementation

In Chapter 1, we encountered the six-phase security process, and looked at Phases 1 and 2 in detail. These phases develop a prioritized list of information security risks for a particular system, situation, or environment. Phases 3 and 4, Policy and Implementation, determine how we address those risks.

Policy describes *what we want* for security while the implementation describes *what we get*. When writing our security policy, we decide which risks we will defend against and we write requirements to address those risks. When planning our implementation, we identify the security measures we will use. We must, however, remember that the measures don't always protect as much as we might want.

For example, a household security policy might say: "We admit only family, friends, and trusted maintenance people to our house." The implementation says: "We have a lock on the door, we keep it locked, and we open the door only to admit people we know." Clearly, there are still risks to this implementation and even to this policy. By choosing a particular policy and implementation, we show less concern for the risks we aren't addressing.

In many cases, the policy and implementation evolve together as part of a *security plan* document. The plan isn't a security architecture analysis because it doesn't describe an existing system. It is the planning and design document we use to construct a secure system.

We initially develop a draft policy based on our prioritized list of risks. We then use the draft policy to plan and design the implementation. Once our design is complete, we review it to ensure that it implements the policy.

Sometimes it is hard to tell if a statement represents policy or implementation. As we make statements that describe our system, some statements are more general and others are more specific; the more specific statements represent *implementation*. Some statements "set the stage" for other statements; those preparatory statements represent *policy*.

CONSTRUCTING ALICE'S SECURITY PLAN

In the following subsections, we will develop a security plan for Alice's laptop. The plan begins with Alice's risk assessment in Section 1.5. The assessment yielded the following list of prioritized risks:

1. Laptop computer: Hardware theft
2. Proprietary software: Hardware theft
3. Laptop computer: Back door
4. USB drive: Hardware theft
5. Course work/shared server: Stolen work
6. Course work/shared server: Files lost
7. USB drive: Files lost
8. Social websites: Privacy breach
9. Bank website: Password theft
10. Course work/computer: Stolen work

Using this prioritized list of risks, we first develop policy statements for Alice's laptop. Next, we develop a list of security controls to enforce Alice's policy.

WRITING A SECURITY POLICY

To write a security policy, we enumerate our *requirements* for security. We derive these requirements from our highest security priorities based on our risk assessment. For ease of analysis and use, we write our policy as a series of individual statements. In a well-written policy, the statements have these five properties:

1. Each statement is numbered. This allows us to cross-reference the policy statements to features of our implementation. A complicated policy might use outline numbering so that statements are arranged into sections and subsections.

2. Each statement uses the word "*shall*." This is part of many standards for writing requirements. We omit "shall" only if the policy statement is somehow optional. In our examples, however, we won't have optional statements.

3. There should be a way to test the implementation to determine if the policy statement is true. When we test our implementation, the policy provides a list of features we must test.

4. Each statement identifies which prioritized risks the statement is intended to address.

5. Whenever possible, we phrase the statements in a positive and specific sense. In other words, policy statements should describe what the system *does*, instead of talking about what it *doesn't do*. Although a few policy statements may require global quantifiers like *all* or *any*, we should produce as few such statements as possible. It is harder (and less certain) to test and verify negative or global policy statements.

To develop our policy, we start with our prioritized list of risks. For each risk, we identify security requirements that, if achieved, will minimize or eliminate the risk.

2.6.1 Analyzing Alice's Risks

Alice's policy evolves directly from the risks. We identify how each risk might occur and we choose a general strategy to defend against that risk. As we analyze these risks, we focus on risks to Alice's information; we don't address other risks that apply to her personally or to other possessions of hers.

1. LAPTOP COMPUTER: HARDWARE THEFT

For this risk, we consider two possibilities: when Alice is physically using or carrying the laptop, and when Alice has left the laptop somewhere. In the first case, the laptop is safe as long as Alice isn't forced to hand it over to an attacker. This type of attack has more to do with Alice's personal safety than with information security, so we will omit it from our analysis.

In the second case, Alice needs to ensure that the laptop is secure from theft. This case is specific to Alice's information security, so we need a policy statement to address it: *(1) The laptop shall be locked up in Alice's room when not being carried.* A second statement specifies handling if she must leave it while away from home: *(2) If the laptop must be left somewhere while traveling, it shall be protected from theft.*

Depending on Alice's situation, she may want a third policy statement: *(3) There shall be an insurance policy that covers the replacement cost of the laptop in the case of loss.* Some insurance policies have deductible amounts that don't completely cover the replacement cost. Some insurance policies cover specific types of loss, like theft, but not others, like accidental damage from dropping. Depending on the insurance Alice can find and afford, she may need to modify her security policy.

2. Proprietary Software: Hardware Theft

Alice is most concerned about proprietary software installed on her laptop, so the protections from Risk 1 apply to this one, too.

There is, however a second risk. If Alice's laptop is stolen and she buys a new one, she won't want to pay to replace the proprietary installation disks as well. This yields a policy statement: *(4) Installation disks for proprietary software shall be kept in a locked drawer in Alice's room.*

3. Laptop Computer: Back Door

This is primarily a risk arising from the Internet: Alice's laptop might be infected by a worm or virus, or it may accidentally download malware when visiting a website. This risk is too complicated to fully address here, but we will address the basic problems.

First, remember how the Morris worm propagated: It exploited vulnerabilities in system software, and the worm was blocked when those vulnerabilities were patched. This yields a policy statement: *(5) The laptop shall regularly check for system security updates and install those updates.*

Second, we are all familiar with antivirus software. The software searches a computer for files or other indicators of malicious software and disables that software. This yields our next statement: *(6) The laptop shall contain and use antivirus software.* Note that antivirus software needs to be kept up-to-date, but that is covered by the previous policy statement.

4. USB Drive: Hardware Theft

Alice relies on her USB drive for moving data between her laptop and computers in campus labs. There are different ways of addressing this risk, and we will take the simplest approach: *(7) The USB drive shall be kept with the laptop at all times.* This protects the USB drive by giving it the same protection from theft as the laptop.

5. Course Work/Shared Server: Stolen Work

Some of Alice's course work resides on campus-shared servers. She is worried that another student might steal her work and hand it in. This could place her at risk of being accused of some sort of cheating. This threat bothers her enough to give it some prominence on her risk assessment.

The shared server is protected by a password, so the policy must address the shared server's password. In fact, Alice is going to have several *critical passwords* that protect information she particularly values. We will produce policy statements that apply to all these passwords. First: *(8) Critical passwords shall be protected from disclosure to others*. Second: *(9) Critical passwords shall be hard to guess*. In truth, Statement 9 is not really a positive policy statement, so it will be hard to really validate. We will discuss password policies further in Chapter 6.

There is another important aspect of password use: leaving a computer unattended while logged in. If Alice leaves a shared server connection active while on a lab computer and leaves that computer, even briefly, another student could use that connection to copy Alice's files. This yields another policy statement: *(10) Alice shall not leave a computer unattended if it is logged in using a critical password*.

6. Course Work/Shared Server: Files Lost

Another problem is that another student or some other mishap could wipe out her course work files. Although she may be able to recover from this, the time involved and the likelihood of the risk makes this worth avoiding.

We address this risk by keeping *backup* copies of Alice's course work files. This produces the following policy: *(11) Alice shall produce backup copies of all course work files in a safe place*.

2.6.2 Constructing Alice's Policy

Policy writing gets simpler as we work our way down the list of risks. Earlier policy statements often apply to the later, lower priority risks. This is true for the remaining policy statements

7. USB Drive: Files Lost

This is similar to Risk 6 and we address it with the same policy statement.

8. Social Websites: Privacy Breach

Alice's information on the social website is protected by a password. This is the same situation as in Risk 5, and we address it with the same policy statements.

9. Bank Website: Password Theft

The password to the bank website is clearly a critical password, so we address this risk with the policy statements given in Risk 5.

10. Course Work/Computer: Stolen Work

To steal Alice's work, someone would have to have physical possession of her laptop. Since she always has it in her possession, or keeps it locked up, we have addressed this risk through the policy statements applied to Risk 1.

THE POLICY

Now that we have analyzed Alice's high priority risks, we extract the policy statements from our analysis and construct the policy. The result appears in Table 2.3.

Once we have a draft of the policy, we review it against our five rules. We ensure that all risks are addressed by at least one policy statement. We also compare the policy statements against the risks to ensure that the policy fully addresses each risk.

As the policy and risk lists get longer, it becomes more challenging to process and cross-reference this information in textual form. Engineers often use spreadsheets or databases to maintain such information. While some may use a package like FileMaker or Microsoft Access, there also are specialized packages for requirements management ("Rational Doors" for example).

We follow two steps to verify that our policy is complete. First, we check the individual policy statements against the five policy rules at the beginning of this section. Second, we verify the *policy coverage*. In other words, we check each risk to ensure that at least one policy statement addresses that risk; then we look at our policy statements to

TABLE 2.3 Policy for Alice's laptop		
#	Policy Statement	Risks
1	The laptop shall be locked up in Alice's room when not being carried.	1, 2, 10
2	If the laptop must be left somewhere while traveling, it shall be protected from theft.	1, 2, 10
3	There shall be an insurance policy that covers the replacement cost of the laptop in the case of loss.	1, 2
4	Installation disks for proprietary software shall be kept in a locked drawer in Alice's room.	2
5	The laptop shall regularly check for system security updates and install those updates.	3
6	The laptop shall contain and use antivirus software.	3
7	The USB drive shall be kept with the laptop at all times.	4
8	Critical passwords shall be protected from disclosure to others.	5, 8, 9
9	Critical passwords shall be hard to guess.	5, 8, 9
10	Alice shall not leave a computer unattended if it is logged in using a critical password.	5, 8, 9
11	Alice shall produce backup copies of all course work files in a safe place.	6, 7

ensure that each one is justified by a risk. This ensures that the policy covers everything it should, and it doesn't include things it doesn't need.

2.6.3 Alice's Security Controls

When we implement a policy, our goal is to provide *security controls* to cover all requirements of the policy. The security controls are the features of the system that implement our policy. In general, security controls fall into three categories:

1. Preventative. These controls directly block actions that violate the security policy. Most designers prefer to use these controls since they directly implement parts of the policy.
2. Detective. These controls detect violations of the policy so that administrators, security officers, auditors, or investigators can see them. Some security techniques simply detect problems and can't prevent them.
3. Corrective. These controls take measures to help restore the system. Truly corrective controls are rare in information security.

To simplify the job of analyzing security, we classify controls according to the six categories listed in Figure 2.13.

- **Physical** — protection arises from physical boundaries that resist penetration. Example: a wall around a city.

- **Mechanical** — protection arises from connections that can only change through mechanical intervention that is not available to the attacker. Example: unplugging a computer from the Internet to protect it from a worm.

- **Logical** — protection is controlled by a structured set of rules or other configuration data in a computer-based security device. Example: making a read-only file writable by other users.

- **Functional** — protection arises from the design and operation of functions embedded in software. Example: a program includes instructions to cause it to exit if certain users try to run it.

- **Procedural** — protection arises from compliance with explicitly defined operating procedures. Example: a company only gives building keys to employees above a certain pay grade.

- **Cryptographic** — protection based on transformation of the data using cryptographic techniques.

Figure 2.13

Categories of security controls.

We describe each control with the following information:

- Control number—like the policy statements, we number each security control. A complicated implementation might use outline numbering so that statements are arranged into sections and subsections.
- Control category—associates each control with one of the six categories shown in Figure 2.13.
- A description of the control—what it is and how we configure it to fulfill the policy objective.
- Relationship to policy—the number of the policy statements that this control helps enforce.

We show that the policy covers the system's risks by cross-referencing the policy statements to the risk statements. When we build our list of security controls, we do the same thing: We cross reference each control to the policy statements it implements.

In Alice's case, we don't need rocket science, sophisticated technology, or software engineering to implement her security policy. We use a straightforward collection of physical, logical, and procedural controls, listed in Table 2.4. Note that the controls aren't listed in any particular order, except perhaps the order in which we formulated them. The control numbers simply allow us to keep track of them.

To verify that the design implements the policy, we review its coverage, the same way we compared the policy to the risks. Each policy statement must be addressed by at least one security control. We also need to assess the completeness with which the controls enforce the policy requirements. This is the point where vulnerabilities often arise in otherwise well-designed systems: at places where security policy requirements are only partially fulfilled.

ALICE'S BACKUP PROCEDURE

It can be very hard for people to keep backup copies of important files. Even computer experts have trouble with this. Alice uses a simple approach to ensure that she's never lost more than a few day's worth of work. As she works on her courses, she produces files on her laptop and on the school's shared file server. She occasionally moves files between the school's lab computers, the shared server, and her USB drive. Even without backups, it can be difficult to keep a collection of files up to date.

Alice uses file synchronization software to keep her files up to date. These application programs try to keep two files or folders "in sync." One folder is on the computer and one is on a USB drive or other removable hard drive. When Alice runs the program, it compares the files in the two folders. If a file in one folder is newer than the copy in the other, it replaces the older file with the newer one. Thus, if Alice updates her term paper on her USB drive and synchronizes it with her laptop, the laptop receives the newer copy of the paper.

TABLE 2.4 Alice's security controls

#	Control Category	Description	Policy Stmt.
1	Physical	Alice's room provides a secure location to store her laptop and proprietary software.	1, 4
2	Procedural	Alice never leaves her own computer unattended, except in her own room.	1, 10
3	Procedural	When carrying her laptop away from home, Alice almost always keeps it in her possession.	2
4	Procedural	If Alice must leave her laptop unattended, she stores it in a physically secure location.	2
5	Procedural	Alice has purchased an insurance policy for her laptop.	3
6	Logical	Alice's laptop is configured to automatically check for updates to her security-critical software and to automatically install such updates.	5
7	Logical	Alice has installed antivirus software and it is configured to operate automatically.	6
8	Procedural	Alice always keeps her USB drive with her laptop.	7
9	Procedural	Alice has memorized most of her critical passwords.	8
10	Physical	Alice has written a few critical passwords on a piece of paper. She keeps this paper physically protected in her wallet along with her money and other valuables.	8
11	Procedural	Alice always looks around to be sure that no one is trying to watch her type her password.	8
12	Procedural	When constructing passwords, Alice chooses two words out of a large dictionary and connects them with a digit or special character.	9
13	Logical	Alice has configured her own computer to automatically log out if she leaves it unattended for more than 15 minutes.	10
14	Procedural	Whenever Alice is finished with a computer, she ensures that she has logged out.	10
15	Procedural	Alice uses file synchronization software to keep up-to-date copies of her course work files on her laptop, desktop, and USB drive.	11
16	Procedural	Alice keeps two separate USB drives. The one she carries is always synchronized to contain the latest copies of her course work files. The second USB drive resides in her desk in her room.	11
17	Procedural	Alice swaps the two USB drives every 2 or 3 days.	11

Alice then keeps a backup copy of all her course work files by switching between two separate USB drives. One drive resides in her desk drawer at all times and she carries the other with her laptop; she switches the two every day or two.

By switching the drives, she saves the latest files in her desk. When she plugs the USB drive into her laptop, she runs the application to "sync up" her older USB drive. This replaces the older files with the latest ones. Now she can plug her USB drive into lab computers in the school and use her latest files.

There are several application programs that synchronize files. Microsoft provides its "SyncToy" application for free on its website. There are also free and low-cost synchronization programs for Macintosh and Linux systems.

Remember that there are three parts to Alice's procedure. First, she keeps copies of all of her course work on two USB drives and on her laptop. Second, she uses file synchronization software to keep the course work on her laptop in sync with a USB drive she carries. Third, she switches between USB drives every day or two, leaving one in her room. If she loses her USB drive, or worse, loses both the drive and her laptop, she still has a backup of her files in her desk drawer.

2.7 Security Plan: Process Protection

An operating system is a computer program: It is a collection of computer instructions that, when executed, provide the features we expect from the operating system. The system has separate parts to manage RAM, handle files on the hard drive, and operate I/O devices. The operating system's dispatcher chooses which processes to run. As noted earlier, a computer can have several processes running at once even if it only has a single CPU. The different processes take turns using the CPUs. The dispatcher switches between processes when one must wait while another gets to run.

We now will look at the dispatcher program as another example of a security plan. First, we develop a security policy for process protection; then we describe the basic design of the dispatcher. We also make a list of security controls provided by the dispatcher. We use the design and the list of controls to show the dispatcher fulfills the policy requirements.

To develop the policy, we naturally start by identifying assets. In this case, the assets of interest are the control and data sections used by the different processes. The functional objectives are to provide the following operating features:

1. Multiple processes may share one or more CPUs.
2. Processes may share control sections.
3. Processes do not share data sections by default, but may do so on request.

The general security objective is to prevent processes from interfering with one another. Here is the list of risks:

1. One process may accidentally or intentionally monopolize the CPU.
2. One process may write data into the RAM belonging to another process.
3. One process may read data belonging exclusively to another process.

In order to identify our security requirements, we examine the risks one by one. For each risk, we identify protections that we need to ensure. In the following discussion, policy statements appear in italics.

1. **One process may accidentally or intentionally monopolize the CPU.**

    When a process is running, the CPU is executing its instructions, one after another. The CPU will focus exclusively on that process' instructions unless the operating system interferes. Typically, the operating system has two opportunities to interfere: first, when the process asks the operating system to perform an I/O operation, and second, when the process has been running "too long" without encountering an I/O operation.

    Our first policy statement addresses the first case: *(1) When the running process requests an I/O operation, the operating system shall suspend that process from execution and give the CPU to another waiting process.*

    Our second policy statement addresses the second case: *(2) When a process has been using the CPU too long without interruption, the operating system shall interrupt that process, suspend it, and give the CPU to another waiting process.*

    We should also include another policy statement to restrict these controls to the operating system: *(3) When the operating system starts a process running, the process shall run in user mode, not kernel mode.*

2. **One process may write data into the RAM belonging to another process.**

    Before we start providing access to RAM, we need to know that we are starting with a "clean slate" with respect to RAM access. In other words, the process should have no access to RAM *except* the access we provide through the policy. We address this with the following policy statement: *(4) The operating system shall ensure that a process has no access to RAM except those it specifically enables within the policy.* In other words, the dispatcher implements Deny By Default (see Section 3.4.1). This is one of those tricky "global" policy statements, but it is essential in this situation.

    When addressing this risk specifically, there are two possibilities. First, a process may write into a control section being used by another process. We address this with the following statement: *(5) Before starting a process, the operating system shall establish read-only access to the control sections assigned to the process.*

    The second possibility is that a process may write into a data section that belongs exclusively to another process. We address this first through Policy Statement 4. Then we establish access to the process' assigned data sections: *(6) Before starting a process, the operating system shall establish read/write access to the data sections assigned to the process.*

3. **One process may read data belonging exclusively to another process.**

   This is a case where one process "eavesdrops" on another. This is not always a risk—it depends on the environment—but we have listed it as a risk in this case. However, we have already addressed it in the previous risk with Policy Statements 4 and 6.

POLICY FOR PROCESS PROTECTION

Now that we have analyzed the risks and established policy statements to address them, we organize those statements into an actual policy. The result appears in Table 2.5. All statements follow the five policy rules.

To verify coverage, we review the list of risks against the policy statements. The first risk, that of a process monopolizing the CPU, is addressed by the first three policy statements. The second risk, of processes writing to the wrong RAM, is addressed by the fourth, fifth, and sixth statements. The final risk is addressed by the fourth and sixth statements. For the coverage to correctly apply, we must be confident that each risk is fully addressed by its corresponding policy statements. This requires a clear understanding of what the risk entails and what the policy statements require.

TABLE 2.5 Policy for process protection		
#	Policy Statement	Risks
1	When the running process requests an I/O operation, the operating system shall suspend that process from execution and give the CPU to another waiting process.	1
2	When a process has been using the CPU too long without interruption, the operating system shall interrupt that process, suspend it, and give the CPU to another waiting process.	1
3	When the operating system starts a process running, the process shall run in user mode, not kernel mode.	1
4	The operating system shall ensure that a process has no access to RAM except those it specifically enables within the policy.	2, 3
5	Before starting a process, the operating system shall establish read-only access to the control sections assigned to the process.	2
6	Before starting a process, the operating system shall establish read/write access to the data sections assigned to the process.	2, 3

FUNCTIONAL SECURITY CONTROLS

It is fairly easy to construct our list of security controls as long as we can describe each control with a brief and clear description. This is true for many physical, mechanical, and procedural controls. The security controls for Alice's laptop (Table 2.4) are simple to describe, so the list of controls is sufficient to describe the security implementation.

A simple list is not adequate when the system relies on functional controls. These controls depend on elements of the system design that might not be obvious to everyone, or that may vary from one system to the next. To illustrate all of the system features that support the policy, our implementation description contains two parts: first, a *design description*, and second, a list of security controls described in terms of that design. This additional detail gives more confidence in the efficacy of the security policy.

THE DISPATCHER'S DESIGN DESCRIPTION

This software design description contains two parts: the **design features** and the **procedure**. The design features identify properties of software that are outside of its own control. In other words, this is a list of properties applied to the software externally. In this case, the operating system establishes the dispatcher's environment and enforces the design features. The software's procedure describes the steps it performs.

The Design Features

We are looking at the operating system's dispatcher because it carries the primary responsibility for restricting access by processes. The dispatcher creates, starts, and resumes processes, so it is responsible for granting access to sections of RAM. This description focuses on the task of switching the CPU from running one process to running a different one. Here are the design features of the dispatcher:

1. The dispatcher runs in kernel mode. This in turn requires that the CPU provide kernel and user modes.
2. The operating system calls the dispatcher after a process requests an I/O operation.
3. The operating system calls the dispatcher after a process gets interrupted for running too long.
4. A running process receives no access to RAM except for those access permissions established by the dispatcher. This in turn requires that the CPU be able to restrict access by user mode programs.

The Dispatching Procedure

Now, we describe the steps the dispatcher takes when switching between processes.

1. The dispatcher saves the state of the previously running process.
2. The dispatcher looks for the next process to run. If another process is waiting to run, the dispatcher runs that one. If not, it may restart the previously running process.

3. The dispatcher looks at the process state for the next process to run.

4. The dispatcher establishes read-only access to RAM containing the control sections being used by the next process.

5. The dispatcher establishes read/write access to RAM containing the data sections being used by the next process.

6. The dispatcher switches from kernel mode to user mode.

7. The dispatcher runs the next process, giving it the program counter value saved in its process state.

SECURITY CONTROLS FOR PROCESS PROTECTION

Table 2.6 lists the security controls required to protect processes. The security controls used to protect processes rely on CPU features, but they are all implemented by the dispatcher software. These controls are, therefore, *functional* controls.

We develop the list of controls by examining the statements made in the design description. There are four design features and seven steps listed in the description. We examine each one individually to see if it implements a policy statement.

TABLE 2.6 Security controls for process protection			
#	Control Category	Description	Policy Statement
1	Functional	Design Feature 2: The operating system calls the dispatcher after a process requests an I/O operation.	1
2	Functional	Design Feature 3: The operating system calls the dispatcher after a process gets interrupted for running too long.	2
3	Functional	Design Feature 4: A running process receives no access to RAM except for those access permissions established by the dispatcher.	4
4	Functional	Dispatcher Step 2: If a process is waiting to run, the dispatcher runs that one.	1, 2
5	Functional	Dispatcher Step 4: The dispatcher establishes read-only access to RAM containing the control sections being used by the next process.	5
6	Functional	Dispatcher Step 5: The dispatcher establishes read/write access to RAM containing the data sections being used by the next process.	6
7	Functional	Dispatcher Step 6: The dispatcher switches from kernel mode to user mode.	3

Now we review the list of security controls to see that they implement the policy. There is at least one control to implement each policy statement. If we compare the policy statement against the controls that implement it, we see that the controls, in general, implement the policy. However, it may be possible that the CPU doesn't provide exactly the controls we want. For example, the CPU might not be able to restrict RAM access to sufficiently small pieces, and a process might be granted unintentional access to information from other processes. Gaps between the policy's intentions and the implementation details demand attention, because they may lead to security vulnerabilities.

2.8 Resources

 IMPORTANT TERMS INTRODUCED

access matrix	finger	puzzle
access right	firmware	return address
Apple Macintosh OS-X	island	security controls
back door	Kerckhoffs' principle	serial
biometrics	kernel mode	"shall"
booting, bootstrapping	key	Shannon's maxim
buffer	machine instructions	shell
buffer overflow	malware	stack
bus	Morris worm	steganography
called procedure	motherboard	Unix-based
calling procedure	multitasking	user identity
Chain of Control	Open Design	user mode
computer virus	parallel	vault
control section	pattern	Windows-based
data section	policy coverage	worm
device driver	process	
dispatcher	process state	

ACRONYMS INTRODUCED

ATA—Advanced technology attachment

BIOS—Basic input/output system

CD—Compact disk

CERT—Computer Emergency Response Team

CERT-CC—CERT Coordination Center

CPU—Central processing unit

CTSS—Compatible Time-Sharing System

CVE—Common Vulnerability Enumeration

DEP—Data execution prevention

DVI—Digital video interface

ESC—Escape character
GUI—Graphical user interface
IBM—International Business Machines
I/O—Input/output
IDE—Integrated drive electronics
OS—Operating system
PC—Program counter
PCI—Peripheral component interconnect
PID—Process identifier
RAM—Random access memory
RO—read-only access
ROM—read-only memory
RW—Read/write access
SANS Institute—SysAdmin, Audit, Network Security Institute
SATA—Serial ATA
SDS—Scientific Data Systems
STO—Security through obscurity
VGA—Video graphics array

2.8.1 Review Questions

R1. Describe the basic components inside a computer.

R2. List the steps the CPU performs when executing an instruction.

R3. Summarize the differences between *hardware*, *firmware*, and *software*.

R4. Explain the role of control sections and data sections. Which section would a *buffer* reside in?

R5. Explain the difference between a *program* and a *process*. What information makes up the *process state*?

R6. Explain what happens when the CPU switches from one process to another.

R7. Describe the four general access control strategies.

R8. What is a *worm*? What was the intended goal of the Morris worm? What was its actual effect?

R9. When the Morris worm exploited the "finger" vulnerability, where did the shellcode reside when it executed?

R10. Explain how a buffer overflow can allow an attacker to take over a computer.

R11. Identify the basic hardware features a CPU must have in order to reliably protect processes from one another.

R12. Summarize the evolution of computers through mainframes, minicomputers, and microcomputers.

R13. Identify the basic features an operating system should have in order to reliably protect processes from one another.

R14. Describe the format and contents of an access matrix.

R15. Explain how to draw a diagram of process and data accesses, based on an access matrix.

R16. Explain how to construct an access matrix, based on a diagram of process and data accesses similar to Figure 2.11.

R17. How does a computer maintain its Chain of Control?

R18. List the five properties of a good security policy statement.

R19. Briefly explain how to construct a security policy from a list of assets and risks.

R20. Describe the six categories of security controls.

R21. List the four components of a security control that we provide when constructing a list of security controls.

R22. Describe the operation of an operating system's dispatcher process.

2.8.2 Exercises

E1. Find a discarded computer. Disassemble it and locate these parts: CPU, RAM, BIOS, I/O circuits, disk drives (hard disks, CDs, diskettes), bus connectors (USB, Firewire, SCSI, ATA, SATA, etc.).

E2. Given the following C or Java-like program, associate the lines of the program with the following four computer elements: control section, data section, I/O, program counter.

```
01 main () {
02     char x;
03
04     x = getchar();
05     if (x < '9')
06         putchar(x);
07}
```

E3. Review the access control strategies described in Section 2.4. For each strategy, find two real-world examples not described in the book. Describe those examples.

The next few exercises involve computer networking software. When a user process wants to send or receive a network message, it does *not* talk directly to the network device driver. Instead, it must talk to a process that manages *network protocols*. This process talks to the device driver on behalf of the user.

The arrangement is similar to that for device drivers (Figure 2.12 and Table 2.2), except that this third process, the protocol process, is sand-

wiched between the user process and the device driver process. We need one data buffer to share data between the user and the protocol process, and a separate data buffer to share data between the protocol process and the device driver.

E4. Draw a diagram of the process and RAM access rights required so that the user process, protocol process, and device driver can work together. Start with Figure 2.12 and modify it to include the extra process and RAM sections. Indicate access rights with arrows and labels (R and W). Be sure the access rights comply with Least Privilege.

E5. Create an access matrix showing the process and RAM access rights required so that the user process, protocol process, and device driver can work together. Start with Table 2.2 and modify it to include the extra process and RAM sections. Be sure the access rights comply with Least Privilege.

E6. Make a list of current sources for information security alerts and up-to-date reports on new security vulnerabilities. In particular, locate CERT, the CVE, and the SANS Internet Storm Center. Provide a

URL for each. Are there other significant sources of information security alerts?

E7. Check your computer's documentation or Help facility to find out how to produce a list of processes. Display a list of running processes, preferably one that lists processes run by other users and by the system itself. Print the list. Use a highlighter to mark the processes directly belonging to you.

The following program, written in the C programming language, writes data all over the data section, starting from the local variable i. Compile and run the program, then answer the questions. Note that the results vary with different compilers and different operating systems.

Note the behavior of the *while* loop. The first statement in the loop ($*j = 0;$) writes a zero to the RAM address stored in variable j. The second statement ($j = j - 1;$) moves the address downward in RAM each time the loop executes. Each step of j moves by a "short integer," which is 2 bytes (16 bits) long.

```
main () {
    short i, *j;

    j = &i;
    while(1) {
        *j = 0;
        j = j - 1;
    }
}
```

E8. Describe what happens when the program runs.

E9. Does the program behave differently if we store a nonzero value in the first statement in the *while* loop? For example, substitute 21845 (in hex, 0x5555, alternating 0s and 1s). Describe what happens. Try another numeric value and describe what happens.

E10. Does the program behave differently if we *add* 1 instead of *subtracting* 1 in the second statement? Try it while storing zeroes and find out. Describe what happens.

E11. Repeat Exercise E10, but use a nonzero value as described in Exercise E9.

E12. Give examples of how computer software can act as vulnerabilities, defenses, or threats to information systems.

E13. Write a program that reads text into an input buffer that is 10 bytes long. Run the program and type in 20 bytes. What happens? Do you get a different result if you use a different language, for example, C versus Java?

E14. Table 2.7 lists five security policy statements. Compare the statements against the five properties of properly formed policy statements. For each statement, indicate which properties the statement fails to fulfill, if any.

#	Policy Statement	Risks
	TABLE 2.7 Policy for Exercise E14	
1	Bob is granted full access to all files on his computer.	2
2	Alice shall have full access to files she creates.	2, 3
3	Access shall never be granted to thieves.	1
4	Installation disks for proprietary software shall be kept in a locked drawer in Alice's room.	
5	The laptop shall regularly check for system security updates and install those updates.	

E15. Review the situation with Bob's tower unit, as told in Chapters 1 and 2, then create a security plan for the tower unit. The plan includes the following:

a. A list of security assets and major risks based on Bob's story.

b. A security policy for Bob's tower computer.

c. A list of security controls for Bob's computer based on the policy.

E16. Write a security plan for your own information security assets. The plan includes the following:

a. A list of security assets and a risk assessment. This may reuse information produced in earlier assignments, as appropriate.

b. A security policy for your assets.

c. A list of security controls to implement your policy.

E17. Go online and look up information about the Morris worm. Identify other vulnerabilities that the worm used to propagate itself.

E18. Go online and find information about another worm that has attacked computers on the Internet. Write a brief history of that worm: when it appeared, what computers it attacked, and whether the instigator was ever identified. If available, include a description of how it attacked other computers and an estimate of how many computers were infected.

CONTROLLING FILES

ABOUT THIS CHAPTER

In this chapter, we look at access control mechanisms used to protect larger-scale resources like files and folders. The chapter focuses on these topics:

- Overview of file system technology
- Structure of executable files and viruses
- Goals and basic policies for file protection and sharing
- File security controls based on "permission flags"

3.1 The File System

Data sharing poses a problem: If people can look at *some* information on a computer, how do we prevent them from seeing *all* the information? This is the same problem as RAM protection in Chapter 2. If any user can modify any information inside the computer, we can't prevent users from reaching any of its contents.

For most people, their most important information assets reside in their files. Modern file systems keep the hard drive organized and give us a way to reliably locate and save our data.

All modern systems use a *hierarchical directory* to organize files into groups. The directory forms an inverted tree growing from the topmost directory, called the *root directory*. Many users think of files as living in *file folders* instead of directories. In practice, we use the terms interchangeably.

On Microsoft Windows, each drive has its own directory, starting at its own root. Figure 3.1 shows the root folder for a Windows system drive. We can tell it's the root because the "Address" field of the window only contains the drive letter ("C:\") and no other names.

On Unix-based systems, the system drive provides the root. The directories on all other drives appear beneath it in the hierarchy. In OS-X, there is a Volumes subdirectory that leads to the directories for individual drives.

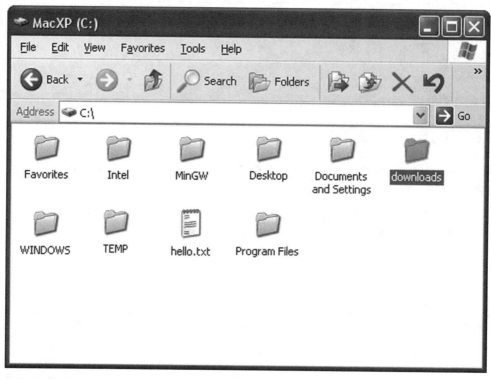

Figure 3.1
Root directory folder on Windows drive C:\.

When we click on a folder icon within a folder on our desktop, we go "down" a level in the directory hierarchy (Figure 3.2). On Windows, the "Address" field contains the directory's name following the "\" character.

DIRECTORY PATH AND FILE NAMES

Each file on a hard drive has a unique identifier made of the file's name and the list of directories leading to it. If a file is in the root directory, then we don't need a directory name to find it. All we need is the "\" character, which by itself indicates the root directory. In Figure 3.1, we see a file named "hello.txt" in the root directory. The file's entire name consists of the drive letter, a "\" character, and the file name:

```
C:\hello.txt
```

If the file is in a subdirectory, then we need both the name and the *directory path*, which leads us to the file's directory starting from the root directory. We see from Figure 3.2 that there is also a file named "hello.txt" in the "downloads" directory. To choose this file, instead of the one in the root directory, we include the path to its directory:

```
C:\downloads\hello.txt
```

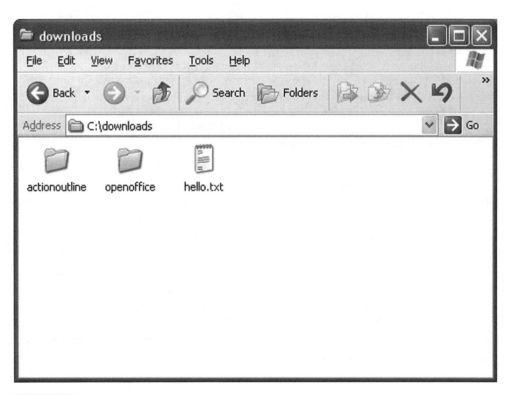

Figure 3.2

The "downloads" subdirectory.

If the file resides in a directory within the "downloads" directory, then we must include that directory in the path. Each directory name is separated by a "\" and they occur in order starting from the root directory. Not all systems use the same character to separate directory names; Table 3.1 lists the commonly used characters.

File systems, like operating systems, mostly fall into either of two categories: Windows systems and Unix-based systems. Apple's Macintosh OS-X is based on a version of Unix, but it uses a distinctive file system. Unless otherwise noted, like in Table 3.1, OS-X has the features of a Unix-based system.

TABLE 3.1 File and directory name formats

System	Separator	Character	Example File Name with Path
Macintosh	Colon	:	Mac:downloads:hello.txt
Other Unix-like systems	Slash	/	/downloads/hello.txt
Windows and MS-DOS	Back slash	\	C:\downloads\hello.txt

3.1.1 File Ownership and Access Rights

Bob has decided to share his tower computer with his suitemates. He has activated the login mechanism and constructed three logins: an administrator ("superbob"), one for his school-work ("bob"), and one for his suitemates ("suitemates"). He established a password for the first two accounts. The third account doesn't need a password. Any suite mate or guest may walk up to the computer and click on the "suitemates" name to log in.

Bob has just typed up an essay for his English class. He saved it on the hard drive. How can he protect it from injury by his suitemates?

Even though Bob shares the computer with his suitemates, he still needs to protect his files. Some desktop operating systems allow us to run without the apparent need for user identities or file protection, but most modern systems have those features built in. In older systems, we need to activate multiuser features before we can use them. Once Bob activated user identities, he needs to protect *his* files.

Modern operating systems protect files according to user identity. When Bob logs in as "bob" and presents his secret password, the system starts up a graphical interface process so Bob can run programs and use his files (Figure 3.3).

The system associates Bob's user identity with the processes he runs. When he edits an essay for English class, the word processor takes on his user identity. It then creates and modifies his files on his behalf. Since Bob created his essay file, the system naturally grants him access rights to the file.

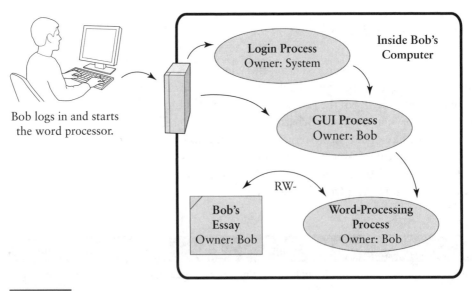

Figure 3.3

Bob's processes inherit his identity and access rights.

FILE ACCESS RIGHTS

When we looked at RAM access in Chapter 2, we focused on "read" and "write" access permissions. An operating system provides four access rights for files and most other resources:

- **Create** a new instance of the resource (for example, a new file).
- **Read** the contents of a particular resource.
- **Update** or "write" or "modify" a particular resource.
- **Delete** or destroy an existing resource.

The names of these four rights form the acronym *CRUD*. While the four rights also may apply to RAM and processes, it's more common for programs to apply them to files. When a process tries to create or use a file, it inherits whatever rights belong to the user who started the process.

Some systems also provide a right to **append** to a file; that is, add data to the end of the file without reading its contents. There also may be an **execute** right that we will examine later.

INITIAL FILE PROTECTION

A modern personal computer easily may contain hundreds of thousands of files. This multitude poses a real problem: How do we establish protections for all of them? It's not practical to set permissions individually. The system has to apply the correct permissions automatically whenever a user creates a new file or directory. Systems tend to implement either of two mechanisms to apply initial access rights:

1. Default rights. The system applies a standard set of permissions to all files a particular user creates. This is common in Unix-based systems.
2. Inherited rights. The system applies permissions inherited from one or more enclosing directories. We will see specific examples of this in Chapter 4.

3.1.2 Directory Access Rights

Directories (folders) tie together files in different parts of the hard drive. A file exists because it has a directory entry, and we must change that directory entry to delete it. Thus, we don't have full control over a file unless we have the right to change its directory entry.

Figure 3.4 shows the directory structure in which Bob's essay file resides. The file resides in Bob's personal directory (named **bob**). His personal directory resides in the system's "root" directory. To find the file, Bob's process starts at the root directory and looks for Bob's personal directory. The root directory entry leads the process to Bob's personal directory, then the process searches Bob's personal directory. The entry in that directory leads it, finally, to the file itself.

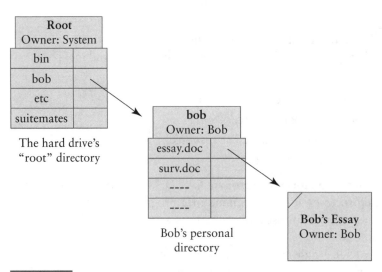

The hard drive's "root" directory

Bob's personal directory

Figure 3.4

Directory and file ownership.

Operating systems grant or deny rights in terms of *containers*. We may have the right to change the file itself; we may even own the file, but we need rights to its directory in order to change that directory entry.

The basic access rights to a directory are **read**, **write**, and **seek**. Bob has the right to read his own directory, so he can list the files in his directory and look at file details stored in that directory. Bob also can write to his own directory, so he can add, modify, or delete files listed in it.

The *seek right* is separate from the read right; it allows the user's process to search a directory for a particular name in a file's path, but not to examine the directory as a whole. This allows other users to retrieve a file from a directory even if they don't have the right to read the entire directory.

For example, the system could give Bob the right to seek file names in the root directory but withhold the right to read that directory. Bob would be able to locate his own directory by name. He would not be allowed to list the names of other files or directories in the root.

To protect the directories belonging to other users, Bob does not have the right to write to the root directory. Because of this, Bob does not have the right to delete his own directory.

Some systems provide very specific rights for managing directories, while others provide minimal rights, like read, write, and seek. Here is a detailed listing of possible rights a system could grant for access to a directory:

- **Create** a new directory—like the generic creation right.

- **Delete** a directory—like the generic deletion right. This operation can be tricky because directories contain files, and the process might not have delete rights for all of its files.
- **Seek** a directory for an entry—the right doesn't necessarily allow the process to list the names of all directory entries, or to examine properties of individual entries.
- **Read** a directory—this right allows listing of the directory as well as seeking files in it.
- **Create new files** in a directory—may be part of a generic "write" permission or a separate right.
- **Delete files** in a directory—part of a generic "write" permission or a separate right.

We can come close to implementing these distinct rights even if the system restricts us to read, write, and seek rights. The arrangement would not be able to distinguish between creating or deleting files or directories.

If the system implements these six distinct rights, it can achieve a higher degree of Least Privilege. This may or may not be important, depending on the security policy we need to enforce. If the policy doesn't need to distinguish between files and directories, then the extra rights aren't necessary. In either case, we want the system to apply protections that enforce our policy objectives.

3.2 Executable Files

When we look in our directories at the files, we must distinguish between two distinct file types:

1. Data files, like a word-processing file containing an essay, a spreadsheet, or a configuration file used by a program or the operating system.
2. Executable files that contain application programs or other programs.

An executable file contains instructions to be executed by the CPU. When we load those instructions into a control section in RAM, the CPU runs that program. This was described in Section 2.1. The program's instructions must be organized and formatted in a special "executable" file format. Although the format varies with different operating systems, they are all similar to what we see in Figure 3.5.

Every executable file begins with a "file header" that describes the structure and format of the program. The header contains these fields:

- Magic number—a standard data value that appears in the first location of the executable file. Different operating systems and different CPUs typically use different magic numbers so that the system won't accidentally run a program that can only run correctly on a different type of system.
- Program size—indications of the size of the block of machine instructions that make up the program itself.

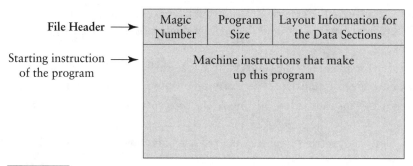

File Header ——▶

Starting instruction ——▶
of the program

Figure 3.5

Executable file format.

- Layout information—addresses and offsets to be used to lay out variables and stack locations in the program's data section.

Following the header, the rest of the file consists primarily of machine instructions. When we execute the program in a file, the operating system loads those instructions directly into a control section. When starting the program, the operating system sets the program counter to the starting address of the control section.

3.2.1 Execution Access Rights

Figure 3.6 shows what happens when Bob runs the word-processor program to edit his essay. The square boxes on the top left and right represent files. The box with the tab in the left corner is a data file, owned by Bob, that contains his essay. The plain box on the right is an executable file owned by the system that contains the word-processor program.

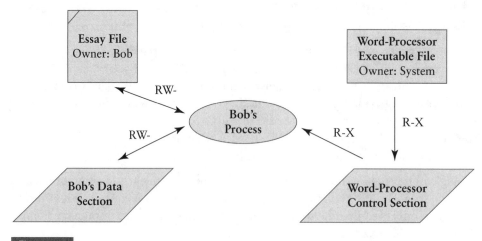

Figure 3.6

Bob executes the word processor to edit his essay.

When Bob starts the word processor, the system reads the executable file into the word-processor control section (lower right corner). As the process executes the program, it uses the data section (lower left corner) to contain working variables and to store the parts of the essay file being edited.

Bob has full ownership of his essay file and full read/write access to his data section. The file containing the word-processor program is owned by the operating system. Bob has read-only access to the file, and to its control section. When Bob starts the program, the operating system itself copies the file's instructions into the control section.

As before, we represent access rights with labeled arrows. Note that executable files and control sections may have an "X" permission. In the case of the file, this indicates the *execute right*. When present, a user may execute the file. Most modern systems provide this right. This helps implement Least Privilege; it allows a user to run a program, but does not imply the right to copy it or visually examine the executable instructions. In practice, however, most systems provide both Read and Execute permissions, because parts of the system might not respond well if they can't actually read the program file. The programmer who actually creates a program has all three rights, read, write, and execute, which yields "RWX."

TYPES OF EXECUTABLE FILES

Application programs aren't the only executable files on a typical operating system. The first and most important executable file is the "kernel" of the operating system itself. When we boot the system, the BIOS reads this file from the hard drive and loads it into RAM. From there, the rest of the operating system starts up. Any part of the operating system that may be added while the system is running must reside in its own executable file.

Here is a list of common types of executable files:

- **Application programs**—the files we execute to run useful applications. Some "system utility" programs, like those for managing and formatting hard drives, are application programs.
- **Operating system kernel**—the file the BIOS reads into RAM during the bootstrap process. This contains the machine instructions that make up the operating system's main procedures.
- **Device drivers**—custom procedures for using I/O devices.
- **Shared libraries**—useful functions that may be shared among multiple programs (dynamic link libraries in Windows).

These files, like typical executable files, contain machine instructions. To run the program, we load it into RAM and direct the CPU to execute the instructions. Some systems, however, notably those derived from Unix, also treat some text files as executable files. These are files written in a *scripting language*. These include programming languages like Perl, Python, PHP, or Lisp. The CPU can't execute these programs directly, but instead must execute the language's *interpreter* program. This is also true of programs written in versions of the Basic language, including Visual Basic. We discuss scripting languages further when we discuss computer viruses in Section 3.2.3.

A system's security depends on protecting executable files, especially operating system files. An attacker can break our Chain of Control by modifying an executable file, especially if it is a critical operating system file.

3.2.2 Computer Viruses

By 1981, the Apple II had become an incredibly popular desktop computer. Introduced at the West Coast Computer Faire in 1977, the Apple received a huge boost in sales with the introduction of "Visicalc" in 1979, the first spreadsheet program. Visicalc justified buying an Apple II for the office. Back then, hard drives were too expensive for small computers. Most computers used removable diskettes. The operating system and one or two applications could fit on a single diskette.

The computer software industry was in its infancy. People often borrowed software from one another and often copied each others' application programs. This behavior was especially rampant with computer games. Bill Gates, then the young co-founder of the tiny Microsoft Corporation, published articles urging computer users to pay for their software and shun unauthorized copies, but the sharing (called piracy today) persisted.

There was little to discourage computer users from sharing software until a few of them noticed this odd phenomenon: Their application programs grew larger and started more slowly. Closer investigation revealed that a small program attached itself to each of their application program files. When such a program was executed, it would attach a similar program to any other program files it found.

In 1983, researcher Fred Cohen performed a series of studies in which he constructed programs that replicated themselves. He used the term *computer virus* to describe them. At first, other researchers saw little relevance in this work, but soon viruses emerged as the first widespread form of computer malware.

Virus Infection

When a virus "infected" an application program, it added its own machine instructions to the end of the program's file (Figure 3.7).

By adjusting the file headers, the virus ensured that its instructions were loaded into RAM along with the application program. The virus also modified the application itself so that the virus program would run first.

When the user started up an infected application, the operating system loaded the program into RAM, including the virus. The system jumped to the start of the application, which had been modified to make the virus program run first. Here is what a typical virus did:

1. The virus searched the operating system's file directory to locate every file containing an application program. It would then inspect each application program file.

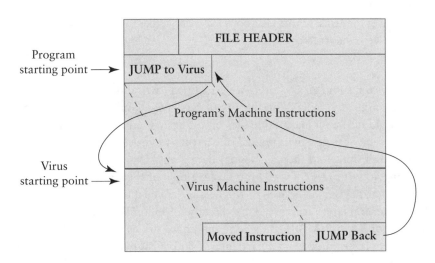

Figure 3.7

A virus infection in an executable program file.

2. If the program file had already been infected by the virus, the virus skipped to the next file.

3. If the file was not infected, the virus copied its executable instructions to the end of the file, "appending" to it. This reduced the risk of accidentally damaging the application.

4. Next, the virus modified the first instruction in the application to "Jump" to the start of the virus program. The virus also saved that first instruction, so that it would be the last instruction the virus executed itself before jumping back to resume the application. Now the file was fully "infected" and would run the virus the next time application started.

5. Once the virus had checked every application program on the system, it executed the instruction from the start of the application, and jumped back to the application program.

The computer user might see a delay before the application started, while these steps were performed—or not.

Biological viruses rely on particular techniques to infect other victims; some are airborne, some travel in food, and so on. In the case of computer viruses, infection only occurs if the victim executes the virus code. In other words, the virus subverts the Chain of Control to cause itself to be executed. There are often many ways this can happen. In the early days, viruses most often spread by running an infected application.

Originally, viruses seemed benign. Early virus authors sought persistence and replication. They found their viruses spread more effectively if they were innocuous and hard to detect. Even so, viruses made assumptions about executable files, and could damage a file if the assumptions were incorrect.

MALICIOUS VIRUSES

By the late 1980s, however, some virus writers were inclined toward destruction. The Jerusalem virus, which appeared in 1987 in the city of Jerusalem, contained a "destructive payload" that would delete all executable files on the system on Friday the 13th, starting in 1988. This type of trigger was typical of destructive viruses: They would spread for some period of time, and then a calendar date would trigger a destructive action. The Michelangelo virus (1991) was a famous example of this; it was programmed to reformat hard drives on March 6, Michelangelo's birthday.

Michelangelo, like several later viruses, did not directly infect applications. Instead, it infected the *Master Boot Record* (MBR) of diskettes and hard drives (Figure 3.8). Whenever a computer bootstrapped from a particular disk, the BIOS would first read in and execute the instructions stored on the MBR.

By that time, low-cost disk drives were common on desktop computers. The Michelangelo virus code ran whenever the system was booted from an infected disk, whether a hard drive or diskette. The virus would then modify the bootstrap data on every disk on the system so that it would execute the virus code before it bootstrapped the operating system.

Figure 3.8

A diskette infected with a virus, circa 1991.

Applications and bootstraps were not the only techniques used to spread viruses. Any time the virus writer can trick a victim into executing a program, the virus writer will use it to spread a virus. There are several ways to automatically execute a program when inserting a USB drive into a computer; several viruses use such techniques to spread between computers.

3.2.3 Macro Viruses

Whenever we write a computer program, we write it in a programming language. For us to use a particular language, we need a program that translates what we wrote into actions performed by the CPU. These "programming language programs" fall into two categories:

1. Compiler—a program that converts our program into machine language. The CPU executes the machine language. C, Java, Fortran, and Cobol are examples of compilers.
2. Interpreter—a program that "interprets" the text of our program a word at a time, and performs the actions specified in the text. Python, Visual Basic, Javascript, PHP, Lisp, and keyboard command processors are examples of interpreters.

We called interpreted languages *scripting languages* earlier. A program in a scripting language sometimes is called a *script*. For example, a file containing Unix shell commands or MSDOS commands is often called a **shell script**. Today's languages may even straddle the line between compiling and interpreting. For example, Java usually compiles the program into "bytecodes," which then are run by a highly optimized interpreter that is customized to specific CPUs and operating systems.

Adobe's Acrobat program and most web browsers understand scripts written in Javascript. Typically, the script's author ties each script to a particular event within the document. In Acrobat, a file in **Portable Document Format** (PDF) may include a script that executes when we open the document, when we reach a particular page, or when we fill in fields in a form. On a web page, the script runs when we open the page or when the mouse moves or clicks on particular items on the page.

Sometimes we call scripts **macros**, especially when we embed them in other documents. For example, many Microsoft Office applications will allow us to create a macro by recording a sequence of operations. The Office application typically translates the sequence into a Visual Basic program and saves it with the file. We can tell the application to perform the macro when particular events occur.

While these programming capabilities provide some interesting features, they also open users to attack. Most scripting languages can create files or modify other files and execute other programs. A script-oriented or macro virus uses these features to propagate the virus code.

In the early 1990s, a rumored macro virus infected Microsoft Word documents. When executed, the virus copied itself to other Word files it could find and also posted the document to the Usenet News system. This published the document worldwide for viewing by everyone who used the Usenet News system.

While macro viruses posed a serious risk for some systems, vendors largely ignored the problem until such viruses were widely distributed by email (see Chapter 16). To reduce the risk of such viruses, Microsoft introduced "Macro Virus Protection." In 2010, Adobe announced plans to reduce the risks of Javascript-based viruses embedded in Acrobat documents.

3.2.4 Modern Malware: A Rogue's Gallery

Since the 1980s, antivirus researchers and vendors have identified thousands of viruses and other forms of malware. In 2008, vendor Symantec announced that the total number passed one million. Here is a selection of malware packages:

- Waledac
- Conficker, also called Downadup
- Pushdo/Cutwail
- ZeuS
- Stuxnet

Many of these packages propagate like viruses while others propagate across networks. Here is a summary of different propagation techniques used in modern malware:

- Infect USB drives—The malware copies itself to any plugged-in USB drives. The malware then configures the drive to automatically execute the malware when the drive is inserted in a computer.
- *Drive-by downloads*—This is a network-based attack in which a user visits a web page or clicks on a pop-up window, and unintentionally downloads the malware.
- Worm propagation—The malware exploits a desktop or server vulnerability that it can reach via a network connection. The vulnerability allows the malware to install itself on the vulnerable computer (see Section 10.1.3).
- *Trojan* infection—A "Trojan" is a program that appears benign but in fact contains malware. In a Trojan infection, the malware arrives on the computer and the user is tricked into executing it. The term Trojan is derived from the story of the Trojan horse (Section 3.7).
- Email infection—Trojan malware arrives on the desktop via email, and the user executes it, causing the infection (see Section 15.3.3).

We examine the malware packages later and examine how they propagate and what they do. Many packages construct botnets (see Section 10.1.3). The botnet controller uses the network of subverted computers for malicious and often illegal purposes. We find several examples of this.

WALEDAC

Waledac constructs and manages a sophisticated and hard-to-trace botnet. The malware then provides several ways to make money from the network. Waledac is a Trojan that originally propagated primarily through email and drive-by downloads. An existing botnet operator may also download Waledac into the network of bots.

Once the network is in place, the controller may use it to do any of the following:

- Deliver spam email (see Section 15.3.1).
- Create pop-up windows that harass the computer's owner. Waledac's pop-ups usually warn of a virus infection and offers the sale of special antivirus software. The software is sold by the botnet operator, and it contains additional malware.
- Harvest authentication credentials from the PC (see Section 6.2.2).
- Perform "distributed" denial of service attacks (see Section 10.1.3).

CONFICKER, ALSO CALLED DOWNADUP

The name "Conficker" is the popular name given to a worm often called "Downadup" in the security community. Conficker propagated through millions of Windows computers in 2009; infections subsided after that. Conficker constructed a botnet, but did not itself contain software to exploit the network. Instead, botnet operators would install other malware, like Waledac, and use it to make money from the botnet.

PUSHDO/CUTWAIL

Starting in 2007, a malware organization constructed a botnet using Pushdo and Cutwail malware. Pushdo implements a botnet and supports downloading of additional malware. Cutwail implements email spam campaigns. In early 2009, Symantec's MessageLabs estimated that this botnet contained at least 1 million bots and averaged over 7 million spam messages per day.

Over the next 18 months, however, work by regulators and security researchers closed down most of the network computers used by the botnet operators to operate the botnet. This yielded a dramatic decrease in worldwide spam traffic.

ZEUS

ZeuS is a malware "product" in that its developers offer it for sale on the black market. Criminal groups purchase the software as an easy-to-use package to create a botnet focused on financial fraud.

ZeuS generally propagates via email or drive-by downloads. Email may often use social engineering techniques that direct victims to spoofed versions of popular social networking sites, like MySpace, Facebook, or LinkedIn.

When ZeuS infects a computer, it installs its "Zbot" malware, which connects the infected machine to the botnet. Zbot then steals financial credentials from the infected machine and transmits them to the botnet operator. Zbot also can use the victim's computer to perform financial transactions using the victim's credentials.

To complete the fraud, the botnet operator recruits individuals to visit banks and withdraw cash from looted accounts. These individuals, called "money mules," then forward the money to the controllers. In late 2010, the U.S. FBI announced over 100 arrests related to a ZeuS botnet, including dozens of money mules.

STUXNET

Stuxnet is a worm that targets programmable logic controllers or PLCs. Factories, refineries, oil pipelines, and the electrical power grid use PLCs to automate industrial and utility systems. These devices are often connected to Windows computers on a network, and Stuxnet propagates by attacking the Windows computers.

Stuxnet is the most sophisticated piece of malware ever found. It propagates via USB drives so that it may infect a factory network even if the network isn't connected to the Internet. The worm uses several previously unknown Windows vulnerabilities to propagate on the network. Stuxnet seeks out specific PLC models that perform specific tasks, and ignores all others. In particular, it seems to target PLCs often used to process uranium and other nuclear materials. Stuxnet modifies the PLC software and then hides itself from detection. The changes affect motor speeds in a hard-to-detect way, which would ruin whatever industrial process the motor performed.

As of late 2010, experts could identify particular steps performed by Stuxnet, but could not conclusively identify its purpose nor its creators. Stuxnet's features suggest that it is a "cyber weapon" created by a government to attack another country's nuclear development facilities. It contains no mechanisms to make money, so it is unlikely to be the product of a criminal gang. It required a lot of specific knowledge about factory control systems and knowledge of previously unreported Windows vulnerabilities. It required a team of very sophisticated software developers.

3.3 Sharing and Protecting Files

Computer sharing happens all the time. Personal computers may be cheap enough to be treated as "personal property," but computers running server software share their resources continuously with countless users. Some desktops require controlled sharing, like those in libraries or computer labs in schools. Physicians, attorneys, financial planners, and many consultants may use a home computer to process sensitive information about patients or clients; these professionals are obligated to keep this information away from family members.

Sharing always has its limits. In a shared kitchen, the household's human residents may be perfectly happy to share boxes of cereal and bins of sugar with one another, but not with their pets or with ants and mice. We prevent "undesirable" sharing by enforcing controls. In a kitchen, we control sharing by putting food in pet-proof and vermin-proof containers (Figure 3.9).

In a computer, the operating system controls the sharing. Files and folders provide the software equivalent of cabinets, boxes, and jars. The operating system controls

Figure 3.9

Controlled sharing in a kitchen.

program execution, controls RAM access, and controls access to files on the hard disk. This helps ensure the orderly and predictable behavior of the overall system.

Controls on sharing also help prevent accidental and some malicious acts from causing damage. If a person spills something in a cupboard filled with sealed containers, the mess won't contaminate other food. If a mouse can't chew into a container of raisins, then the raisins remain safe for people to eat. If a user runs a virus-infested application but lacks the rights to modify application programs, then the virus can't infect other applications.

As with all security, the challenge is to find a balance between safety and meeting the users' needs. It's not reasonable to block a user from fixing broken software simply because the same restriction might prevent a virus infection. On the other hand, there's no sense in granting access to modify applications if the user has no business modifying them.

OBJECTIVES

To create policies for sharing files, we start by identifying potential risks. To identify risks, we start with a list of objectives:

a. Provide computing facilities for authorized users

b. Preserve the Chain of Control

c. Either permit or prevent general sharing of information among the users

The third objective reflects two alternatives for file sharing: either users share their files by default or they are kept isolated by default. We develop two different policies to reflect this choice.

Threats

To develop our list of risks, we consult the list of threats in Section 1.4 and focus on those that we can address through file protection. This eliminates people who won't be logged into the computer and people who simply pose a physical threat, like theft. This leaves the following threats:

- Script kiddy—sharing a computer at a school, or possibly at work, with people who have too much time and curiosity.
- Embezzler—sharing with a coworker who is motivated to steal from the company.
- Suite/room/family/housemate—sharing with someone in our living space.
- Malicious acquaintances—sharing with someone who visits our living space, getting physical access to the computer.
- Administrators—sharing a computer at school or work where an administrator might be inclined to eavesdrop on our work or perhaps even meddle with our files.

Risks

Now we make a list of attacks based on Figure 1.6. There are six attacks in the complete list; we can omit the first attack: physical theft. We can generalize the remaining ones to capture the essence of what the threats might do on an isolated computer. This yields the following list of risks:

1. Denial of service—someone deletes some of our files or damages software, making all or part of the computer unusable.
2. Subversion—a program gets a virus infection or suffers some other malware damage.
3. Masquerade—one user logs in, trying to pretend to be another.
4. Disclosure—some of our personal data is disclosed.
5. Forgery—someone modifies one of our files without our knowledge, so their statements are presented as our own.

This list of risks is comprehensive enough to use when developing our file protection policies. It is short enough to make it unnecessary to prioritize the risks.

3.3.1 Policies for Sharing and Protection

When we look at policies for sharing on a computing system, we see two general types of policies: *global policies* and *tailored policies*. A global policy establishes file permissions to apply by default and, in particular, determines the permissions to apply when we create a new file. Typically, there are two global policies:

1. *Isolation policy*—no access granted to other users' files
2. *File-sharing policy*—read access granted to other users' files

User files aren't the only ones in the system. There are system files that might not even be visible to user programs. Most important for users, the system contains application programs and those are stored in files. To use these programs, the system must grant users the necessary rights. However, the system also must maintain the Chain of Control, so it should not grant the right to modify those programs.

Systems rarely grant both read and write access to other users' files, at least by default. Even if people are working together on the same project, it is much safer to limit the files they share completely. We need *tailored* policies to handle special cases like those. Here are examples:

- **Privacy**—block all access to certain files in a sharing environment.
- **Shared reading**—grant read-only access to certain files in an isolation environment.
- **Shared updating**—grant full access to certain files in either environment.

For now, however, we focus on global policies.

UNDERLYING SYSTEM POLICY

Regardless of the policies we establish, we will use certain policy statements in all of them. These statements form an underlying system policy that address Objectives **a** and **b** introduced in Section 3.3, and the risks associated with them. We won't make policy statements for user file protection, since that depends on the choice posed by Objective **c**.

The policy statements appear in Table 3.2. These statements apply to both user isolation and user sharing situations.

This fundamental policy addresses the first three risks. The first statement addresses denial of service. The second statement addresses masquerade. That statement also addresses disclosure and forgery indirectly, but we will address those more directly with additional policy statements. The third policy statement directly addresses denial of service and subversion.

USER ISOLATION POLICY

Let's return to Bob's predicament. He has a computer that he shares with his suitemates. He will let them use the computer but he needs to protect his own information assets.

#	Policy Statement	Risks
	TABLE 3.2 Underlying system policy for a shared computer	
1	All users shall be able to execute customary application programs and operating system service programs.	1
2	Each user shall have a separate login and, optionally, a password.	3
3	Programs shall be protected from damage or other modifications by regular users.	1, 2

TABLE 3.3 Policy for user isolation

#	Policy Statement	Risks
1	All users shall be able to execute customary application programs and operating system service programs.	1
2	Each user shall have a separate login and, optionally, a password.	4
3	Programs shall be protected from damage or other modifications by regular users.	1, 3
4	Files belonging to one user shall be protected from any access (read or write) by other users.	1, 2, 5

Bob is looking for a policy in which we adjust Objective **c** to isolate users from one another. We create the basic policy by adding one statement to the fundamental system policy. The statement directly addresses the risks of disclosure and forgery. It also addresses the risk of denial of service if one user accidentally damages a file belonging to another user. This yields the policy in Table 3.3.

However, Bob had a specific risk in mind:

6. A suite mate tampering with Bob's files.

To protect against that specific risk, we can add some more specific security policy statements to Bob's security policy. In particular, we can add policy statements to talk specifically about how Bob and his suitemates will use the computer. These additional statements appear in Table 3.4.

If Bob configures Windows in a friendly fashion, it will display a login screen that lists all users on the computer. If a suite mate clicks on "Suitemates," the computer will log in without a password. If a suite mate clicks on "Bob," the computer asks for the password.

TABLE 3.4 Policy additions for Bob's particular situation

#	Policy Statement	Risks
5	The system shall have two regular users: Bob and Suitemates.	4, 6
6	Bob shall have a password to protect his login.	2, 4, 5, 6
7	Suitemates shall not need to type in a password to log in.	1

#	Policy Statement	Risks
	TABLE 3.5 Policy for file sharing	
1	All users shall be able to execute customary application programs and operating system service programs.	1
2	Each user shall have a separate login and, optionally, a password.	4
3	Programs shall be protected from damage or other modifications by regular users.	1, 3
4	Files belonging to one user shall be readable by other users.	1
5	Files belonging to one user shall be protected from writing by other users.	1, 3, 5

This arrangement provides Bob with the safety he needs and the suitemates with access to his computer. The suitemates can't log in as Bob unless they somehow guess his password. On the other hand, they don't have to remember a password to log in as "Suitemates." When they log in as such, they won't have access to his files (per Policy 4).

USER FILE-SHARING POLICY

When people hide things, others get suspicious. There are some environments where it's more common to share information than to hide it. For example, many families want to share their information among members. Files may consist of letters, homework, family photos, and so on, and there may be bona fide reasons to share anything and everything. In engineering projects, it is fairly common to share information.

If we assume sharing is the norm, then Risk 2, disclosure, is no longer considered a risk. Instead, it becomes a "denial of service" if we can't read each others' files. This yields the policy in Table 3.5.

As with user separation, there are some systems that provide sharing by default. This is a tradition of Unix-based systems, which create file directories for individual users and, by default, grant other users access to those files. The resulting policy does not, of course, provide unrestricted sharing. A typical user-sharing policy provides *read-only* sharing, but protects files from writing except by the owner.

3.4 Security Controls for Files

In Section 2.5, we introduced the access matrix to describe access controls for processes in RAM. We can use the same matrix to describe access controls for files and other resources in an operating system. In general, the access matrix describes three things:

- What we are sharing (*objects*)

- With whom we share them (***subjects***)
- What ***rights*** each subject has to each object

If we make very precise statements about the subjects, objects, and rights we wish to implement, then the sharing is easy to implement. If we trust the system to block all accesses *except* those we specifically allow, then it's easy to verify the system's correct behavior. The more specific and mechanical we can be in our specification of subjects, objects, and rights, the more effectively we can implement and verify our policy.

In practice, however, a realistic policy statement is more abstract than that. We want our policy to associate *people* with *data*; however, that is not the same as associating *user identities* with *files*. We build mechanisms to relate the two as closely as possible, but they just aren't the same. We want to protect what is *in* the files, and not just the computer files themselves.

This is a security problem we also have with boundaries, fences, and other containers in general: The security mechanism controls what happens to the container, not the contents. For example, we could try to protect some valuables with a high fence, border alarms, and a strongly locked gate. Still, a helicopter could drop in and steal some items, bypassing the fence and raising no alarm.

We rely on a computer's operating system to protect its files. If an attacker starts the computer normally, our operating system will start up and protect our files. We still, however, face a Chain of Control risk. A system booted from a CD-ROM bypasses the hard drive's own operating system and allows unrestricted access to our files. We can rely only on operating system protections as long as two properties remain true:

1. The operating system's protections are always invoked when accessing our protected files, and
2. There is no way to bypass the operating system to access our protected files.

The terms *subject* and *object* are well-known in the information security community. They most often appear in highly formalized security specifications and aren't used routinely. We will use more specific terms like *process* or *user* instead of *subject*, and terms like *file* or *resource* instead of *object*.

3.4.1 Deny by Default: A Basic Principle

In a clean kitchen, everything has its proper place and everything is put away. Boxes and jars are closed and stored in cabinets. A few items may remain out if they are to be used soon, or if they are not going to draw insects, rodents, or other vermin.

In essence, the "default" is to deny access to vermin, at the very least. This arrangement also denies access to legitimate users (members of the household) to a small degree, because a person must take specific steps to gain access to the desired item: open a cabinet and a box or jar. A padlock provides a more explicit example: We can't open the door unless we have the key (Figure 3.10).

Figure 3.10
Deny by Default—a padlocked door.

Deny by Default provides the foundation for strong security. In computing, it means:

No access is allowed to anyone unless specifically granted.

As we saw in Section 2.4, every process starts out as an "island." A process has no access to resources unless the system gives the process a way to request them and reach them. It isn't easy to show that processes are truly isolated, but it is a fundamental design goal of every secure system. We need confidence that a system *only* grants access rights when told to do so. Otherwise we can't fully trust a system to enforce the permissions and restrictions we want.

THE OPPOSITE OF DENY BY DEFAULT

This may sound contradictory, but we can't trust a system to share things correctly unless it starts by blocking access to everything. This makes sense when we consider the opposite: a system that allows all accesses *except* the ones we specifically tell it to block. We're now faced with the challenge of listing *everyone* we might need to block. How can we possibly tell if that list is complete? Do we start a list of every person on the planet and remove the names of permitted users? This isn't practical.

For example, *content control software* (also called *censorware*) classifies Internet websites according to content, and then blocks access to types of content the customer finds unacceptable. Some private organizations use this software to discourage employees from visiting personal, shopping, and entertainment sites with their workplace computers. A few countries, notably China and Saudi Arabia, apply such filtering to *all* Internet traffic that enters and leaves the country. We examine this further in Chapter 15.

Content control software often follows a policy of *default permit*: Everything is allowed *except* sites on the prohibited list. This doesn't really block access to all "unacceptable" sites, it only blocks access to sites that have existed long enough to find their way onto the list of banned sites. Such systems can't be 100 percent effective, though they work well enough in practice to satisfy certain customers.

Islands, vaults, and other physical boundaries often implement a Deny by Default policy. People can't go through a physical fence that's too tall or risky to climb. The fence's gateway implements the permission to pass. Some fences are designed to restrict animals while others are intended to restrict people. The intended policy of a well-built fence is reflected in the structure of the fence and the lock on the gate. A fence intended to restrict animals may have a gate that people can easily operate.

3.4.2 Managing Access Rights

In order to enforce the correct access rights, the operating system needs to maintain a list of access rights. In theory, the system could maintain an access matrix. In practice, this isn't efficient.

For example, a typical Windows desktop contains over 13,000 separate files just for operating system components, and may contain five to ten times as many files for programs, media, and user-created documents. The complete access matrix might contain 100,000 rows, plus one column per user, or even one column per process. This is too large to manage.

Access rights follow well-known patterns in most systems. When one process starts another, the child process often inherits the parent's access rights, especially to files. When this happens, we can apply the same set of access rights to both the parent and its children. If we look at individual resources, particularly files, we find that the rights tend to cluster into three distinct groups: those granted to the owner, those granted to "the system" (including system administrators), and those granted to "everyone else." Files also may have a cluster of similar permissions granted to a "group" of users working on a shared project.

In other words, the access matrix contains a lot of redundant information. We can eliminate this redundancy by taking advantage of patterns in the access rights. When the system combines matching access rights, it yields a smaller set of rules that is easier to manage and enforce. Starting from the access matrix, there are two obvious strategies for combining access rights:

1. Cluster by column: associate access rights with users or processes
2. Cluster by row: associate access rights with resources like files.

When we cluster the rights by column, we implement *capability-based security*. This is common in physical, real-world security situations: Bob, for example, carries keys to let him in to his suite, start his car, and open the front door back home. Bob's access rights are embodied in the keys, and the keys stay with the owner (the subject).

If Alice attends a concert, she buys tickets, and the tickets themselves impart access to the concert.

3.4.3 Capabilities

The Atlas system at Manchester and CTSS at MIT demonstrated that a computer could run many separate users at once, keeping them safely separated. Researchers at MIT, notably Earl Van Horn and Jack Dennis, tried to identify the essential features of such systems. Van Horn coined the term *capability* to describe the access rights a particular subject had for a particular object: the information in a single cell of an access matrix. Because operating systems always kept a list of resources belonging to each process, Dennis and Van Horn suggested that access control information be kept in that list.

When an operating system implements capability-based security, it keeps the list of access rights on a per-process basis. If a process has access rights to particular files or other resources, it carries those rights with it. The process also may be able to share or transfer its access rights to other processes. To print a file, for example, Bob's word-processing program passes the right to read his file to the printer's device driver.

This approach seemed reasonable because capability-based security seems to combine both the "island" and the "vault" access control strategies. A process can only locate a resource if it is on its capability list. If the resource appears on the list, then the system controls its access even further by including or omitting the individual access rights. When Butler Lampson introduced the access matrix in 1971, he predicted that capability-based access control would be less "cumbersome" than the column-based alternative.

CAPABILITIES IN PRACTICE

Despite Lampson's prediction, capability-based security is not an obvious feature in major modern operating systems. The access controls that most of us see—those for protecting files and folders—rarely use capability lists. Several research systems were developed in the 1960s and 1970s that used capability lists, but very few commercial systems adopted them. The only really successful commercial system that used capability-based security was the IBM System/38 and its descendent, the AS-400.

We see capability-based security in more subtle places. For example, a process page table provides capabilities to use specific RAM areas. Network-based systems also use capabilities. For example, the Kerberos system (Section 13.4.2) distributes "tickets" to its users that in turn give those users access to particular resources. Microsoft Windows uses Kerberos to distribute user access rights between host computers on Windows networks. The U.S. government issues "public-key certificates" (Section 8.6) to members of the defense community. Each certificate identifies the individual and specifies certain access rights, like security clearances.

RESOURCE-ORIENTED PERMISSIONS

Most operating systems, however, use the row-oriented approach: They store access rights with files and other resources. This is a less-common approach in real-world security; we mostly see it used for handling reservations in hotels and restaurants. If Bob takes his date to a popular restaurant, the maitre d' checks his name against the list of reservations, and only grants access if Bob is on the list. To take a typical airplane flight, Alice presents a photo ID at the airport, and the airline uses it to generate her boarding pass. Her access to the plane is based on her identity, not on possessing a ticket.

Within operating systems, the obvious example of this approach is in the file system. The system stores details about access rights along with other administrative data it maintains about a file. If we wish to find out about access rights to a particular file, we look at the file's properties. On Windows, we select the file and then select "Properties" from the file's menu. The "Security" tab lists the access rights. On Macintosh OS-X, we select the file and select "Information" from the menu. A section at the bottom of the Information window lists the access rights (Figure 3.11).

OS-X provides a specific permission ("Read Only" or "Read/Write") associated with the user who owns the file and a separate permission for the rest of the world. OS-X

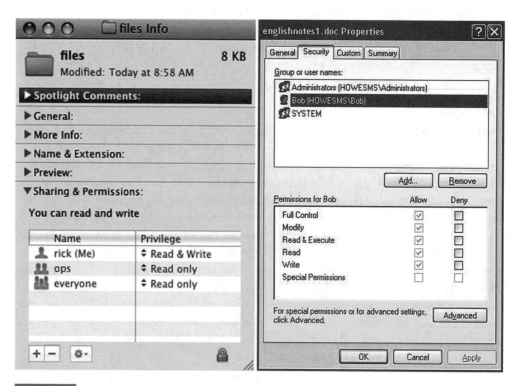

Figure 3.11

Resource-oriented permissions OS-X and Windows.

doesn't display any rights if the world has no rights. The display also shows if there are rights granted to a particular "group" of users.

3.5 File Security Controls

Let us look at the access permissions required by users on Bob's system to implement the policy for Bob's tower computer. The policy appears in Tables 3.3 and 3.4. First, let us look at access rights for executable programs. Figure 3.12 illustrates the appropriate access rights, using two executable files as examples. Regular users receive Read and Execute access. The "System" user receives full access to the file.

Figure 3.13 uses a slightly different approach to show access rights to user files. Instead of showing example files, it shows a "pile" of files to represent those belonging to the two regular users.

The two diagrams represent all of the users on Bob's system. In larger systems, we might use a single oval to represent all "regular" users and present permissions in those terms. We also could represent permissions with separate ovals to represent "the file owner," the "system," and "other users."

3.5.1 File Permission Flags

Real systems rarely use diagrams to establish access rights; instead, there is a notation or a tabular format to use. The simplest approach is to provide a set of *permission flags* to identify rights for a specific set of users.

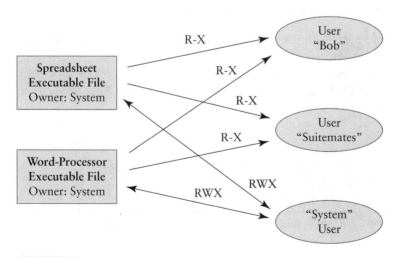

Figure 3.12

Access rights to executable files.

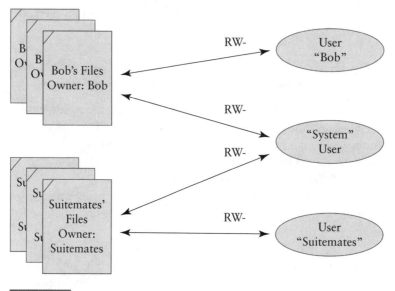

Figure 3.13
Access rights to personal files.

In Figure 3.14, we have three sets of flags. Each set specifies the basic rights of Read, Write, and Execute (or Seek for directories), and associates the rights with one of three specific classes of users:

- *Owner rights*—the user who owns the file in question
- *System rights*—privileged processes run by the system
- *World rights*—all users other than the owner and the system

This allows us to define access rights with a compact set of nine flags, along with the user identity of the file's owner.

Because the operating system already keeps track of the owner of every file and other major resources, our solution doesn't need to explicitly identify users. All it needs to do

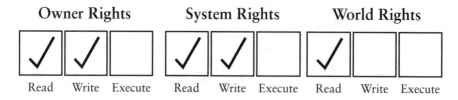

Figure 3.14
A set of file permission flags.

World Rights

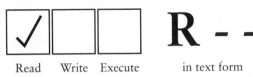

Read   Write   Execute

in text form

Flags for compact access rules.

is identify the rights granted to the owner, the system, and the rest of the user community (the "world"). A user with administrative rights receives "System" access rights to files and resources. Most systems also can grant access rights to predefined "groups" of users; we will discuss that in Chapter 4.

Although we've reduced the rights to a very compact set, they still carry a great deal of redundancy. Typically, owners get full access to their files. Administrators and privileged user identities associated with system operations, like a "System" user, typically get full access to everything. The important differences in access rights arise when we specify access rights for the rest of the user community.

In most examples and exercises in this chapter, we use a simplified set of rights called *compact access rules*. Figure 3.15 illustrates such a rule.

Compact access rules reflect two common assumptions. First, they assume that the owner of a file or folder has full access rights to it. Second, they assume that system processes, or those running under a "System" user ID, have full access rights to all files and folders on the computer. We may safely use these assumptions while working problems in this chapter.

We abbreviate a compact access rule with three letters. As shown in Figure 3.15, the letters represent read, write, and execute rights. Thus, the permission R-E allows read and execute to other users, while --- allows no access to other users.

SYSTEM AND OWNER ACCESS RIGHTS IN PRACTICE

If our examples omit owner and system access rights, we should ask some obvious questions: Why would *any* system allow us to specify owner and system access rights? Why would we ever want to restrict access by a file's owner or by the system? The answer is, of course, Least Privilege. Access restrictions sometimes make sense for individual owners or for the overall system.

For example, some owners explicitly set valuable files to be read only simply to protect the files from accidental damage. If the owner edits the file by mistake or runs a program that might change it somehow, the file system will deny access.

Operating systems are large and complex, so Least Privilege helps keep components from injuring one another. Early versions of the Unix system, for example, ran most system processes with the "root" user identity. As we saw in Section 2.3, this led to disaster when the Morris worm hit. Modern Unix systems, and their derivatives like OS-X and Linux, run as few processes as possible using the "root" user identity.

When we create a new file on Microsoft Windows, it will, by default, be accessible by the "SYSTEM" user identity and by administrators. We can remove those permissions and still, as the owner, read and write the file. The access permissions apply to any processes that belong to the "SYSTEM" user identity, while the true "kernel" of the operating system is not really restricted by such rules. Thus, we can still read and write our file even though "SYSTEM" processes cannot.

On some high-security systems, the security policy forbids administrators to look at certain types of sensitive information stored on the computer. Such systems should block access to that information, even when using a "SYSTEM" user identity, unless the specific individual is allowed to use the sensitive data. Thus, some administrators may be able to look at the highly sensitive data while others are blocked from that data.

In this chapter, we focus on simple cases and assume that both the file's owner and the system have full access rights to it. The only access rights we need to specify are for "world" access to files.

3.5.2 Security Controls to Enforce Bob's Policy

The diagrams are useful to illustrate how users can (or can't) share information on the system. To actually implement a policy, we produce a more detailed list of security controls. Bob's isolation policy, described in Tables 3.3 and 3.4, requires some general security controls and some specific access rules. These appear in the following tables.

First, we specify the general security controls in Table 3.6. These controls establish user identities and passwords on Bob's computer. These controls follow the format introduced in Section 2.6.

TABLE 3.6 Security controls to implement Bob's isolation policy			
#	Control Category	Description	Policy Statement
1	Logical	Bob has a personal user identity on the computer.	2, 5, 6
2	Logical	Bob must use a password to log in.	6
3	Logical	Suitemates have a single user identity on the computer that they all share.	2, 7
4	Logical	Suitemates do not need to use a password to log in.	7

#	File Type	File Owner	World Access	Policy Statement
TABLE 3.7 Compact access rules for Bob's isolation policy				
6	Executable programs	System	R-X	3, 4
7	Bob's data files	Bob	---	5
8	Bob's directory	Bob	---	5
9	Suitemates' data files	Suitemates	---	5
10	Suitemates' directory	Suitemates	---	5

To specify access rules, we need a different format. We will use a simple format that makes use of compact access rules; it lists the three-letter abbreviation for the "World" access rights, and also identifies the file's owner.

To simplify matters further, we list "types" of files instead of listing all files individually. We assume that the specified access rights are associated with all files of each specified type and owner. The resulting table of compact access rules appears in Table 3.7.

Note that the "File owner" column does not consistently refer to Bob even though he is the owner of the computer. The column indicates the computer user that owns the particular file. These rules assume Bob logs in as the user "Bob" and that his suitemates log in as "Suitemates." If Bob always logs in as an administrator, then he gets "System" access rights, which gives him access to every file on his computer.

3.5.3 States and State Diagrams

States and *state diagrams* give us a different way of organizing and looking at parts of a complex system. While we can always look at a system by breaking it into pieces and examining individual parts, a state diagram gives us a way to systematically break up its *behavior.*

Engineers apply state diagrams to all kinds of systems. At the circuit level, engineers can implement a diagram directly in hardware. At the system level, states and state diagrams provide a way to break complicated system behavior into separate and more comprehensible activities.

The individual "states" reduce the system's behavior into a manageable number of separate situations. The state diagram gives us a simple image of how the system behaves. For example, Figure 3.16 presents a state diagram for a door.

To create a state diagram, we look at the system and divide its behavior into a small number of completely separate conditions. Each condition becomes a "state." Then we

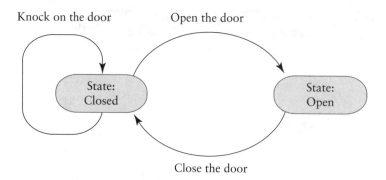

Figure 3.16

State diagram showing a door's operation.

identify events that take place, especially those that cause the system to change from one state into another.

In Figure 3.16, we have two states because a door can only be "Open" or "Closed." We have three possible events: knocking, opening, and closing. The door actually changes state when we open or close it. Knocking causes no change at all.

For the state diagram to be useful, it must capture *all* relevant and possible events, especially those that change states. Figure 3.16 presents a very limited view of a door, because it says nothing about locking or unlocking, or even about responses to knocking. In fact, knocking is clearly unnecessary, because the diagram shows the door opens and closes regardless of whether knocking took place.

INFORMATION STATES

We also talk about data or information as having states. Here are the fundamental *information states*:

- *Storage state*—the information is stored and is not currently being processed. We also call this state "data at rest."
- *Processing state*—the information is being used by an active process to make decisions or to transform the information into another form. This is "data in use."
- *Transmission state*—the information is being moved from one storage area to another. This is "data in motion."

Figure 3.17 shows a state diagram for Bob's essay file. We initially create files in an application program, so Bob creates it in the Processing state. When he saves the file, he puts it into the Storage state. If he moves it onto a removable drive, it enters the Transmission state.

In this diagram, we process either new or stored data. We save the result as stored data. We don't use processing to transport data; we simply move the data to a portable

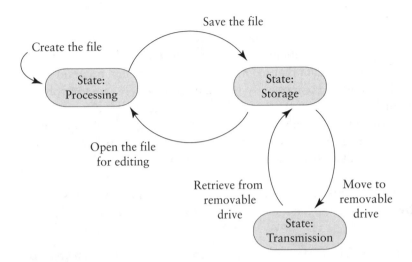

Figure 3.17

Information states of the essay file.

medium. In this environment, data never moves directly from the Processing state to the Transmission state.

A closed door has different security implications than an open one. The same is true for information states. Each reflects a different access control environment. The storage state involves files and their access rights. The processing state refers to the world of processes and RAM-based access control.

When we transmit information between programs or processes inside an operating system, the storage and processing controls protect those operations. When we move a file to removable storage, like a USB drive, we move it away from the protections enforced by our operating system. This also happens when we transmit information across a network, as we will see in Chapter 10.

3.6 Patching Security Flaws

Technical systems *always* have flaws. In the 19th century, telegraph and telephone technicians spoke of "bugs in the wire" as the source of unexplained buzzing noises and other hard-to-fix problems. We still chase bugs in technical hardware and in software.

Although system developers would like to build error-free software, this has proven impractical. Social and economic reasons encourage people to buy lower quality software at lower prices. Software vendors then provide bug fixes when existing flaws cause too much trouble, or worse, open customer computers to attack.

THE PATCHING PROCESS

Most software developers use a carefully designed process to handle bug fixes. The process collects problem reports and eventually develops a *software patch* to fix the problem. A patch is a piece of binary data that modifies the instructions in a program to correct a problem. Most modern computing systems have special software to apply patches to existing software.

The alternative to patching is to reinstall a new copy of the original software. Modern software packages often grow quite large. It is more efficient to distribute a patch, even if it contains several million bytes of data, than to replace a 100-million byte program.

There are always more problems to fix than resources to fix them. Developers use the process to prioritize flaws, develop fixes, and distribute fixes. A typical process follows these steps:

1. Collect error reports. These may come directly from individual customers, from companies that use the software, or from news reports of problems. In the worst case, error reports may come from national flaw reports, like the Common Vulnerabilities and Exposures database.

2. Prioritize errors and assign for investigation. A team of software engineers reviews the error reports and assigns the highest priority ones to engineers to investigate and to try to fix.

3. The engineer develops a fix for the software problem. This yields a change to the software containing the flaw.

4. Another team of engineers reviews proposed bug fixes for release in an upcoming patch. The team selects the fixes to include, and integrates those fixes into a new patch.

5. Test the patch. A test team applies the patch to different versions of the software and tests them for correctness and stability. The vendor doesn't want to release a bug fix that makes matters worse.

6. Release the patch. Software engineers package the bug fixes into a patch file for automatic installation. They place the patch on the vendor's website and ensure that automatic patching software can find and install it.

Many bugs may take weeks or months to work their way through this process. Higher priority bugs, like those that pose a serious security risk, may be fixed sooner. Given a sufficiently serious bug, the process may only take a matter of days.

SECURITY FLAWS AND EXPLOITS

In the ideal case, a small number of people in the security community find out about a software security flaw and the vendor develops a patch for it. The general public doesn't really learn about the flaw until the patch appears. Then a race begins between black-

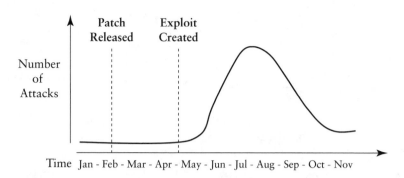

Figure 3.18

Time line for attacking unpatched flaws.

hat hackers who want to use that vulnerability to attack systems, and end users who want to patch their systems.

Many end users fail to patch their computers, even when patches are available for known vulnerabilities. Figure 3.18 summarizes the typical patching experience in the late 1990s. The vendor issues a patch in January. By March, black hats have reverse-engineered the patch to figure out the vulnerability, and they construct an *exploit*: malware that uses the vulnerability in an attack. The black hats then search out and attack the unpatched systems.

Using network scanning software, black hats could search the Internet and identify unpatched computers. The exploit software then successfully attacks those systems. Matters may have improved somewhat in recent years, since the patching process has become more efficient, reliable, and automatic. Technophobic users can set their computers to update software automatically. Even so, countless computers often go unpatched.

WINDOWS OF VULNERABILITY

Today, every potential vulnerability represents a race between the white-hat and black-hat communities. White hats, including responsible security researchers and vendors, try to find security flaws and deploy patches before exploits arise. Black hats try to identify flaws and construct exploits before the patches appear. The ideal goal for a black hat is to construct a *zero-day exploit*: one for which no patch yet exists.

Figure 3.19 illustrates this race between black hats and white hats using a state diagram. The diagram follows the history of a security vulnerability, relative to a particular piece of software installed by a particular end user. The software starts out in the Hardened state, which means that the user has patched it for all known weaknesses. The software enters the Flawed state when someone—white hat or black—finds a flaw.

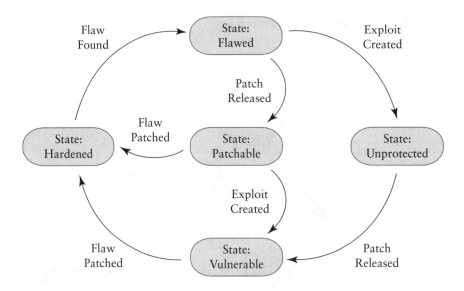

Figure 3.19

Software vulnerability state diagram.

If matters progress as shown in Figure 3.18, then the vendor releases a patch and the software enters the Patchable state. If the user immediately patches the software, it returns to the Hardened state. Otherwise, it moves to the Vulnerable state when an exploit appears.

The software remains vulnerable while an exploit exists and the software remains unpatched. We call this the *window of vulnerability*: the period of time during which a system is unprotected from an exploit. As long as the software remains unpatched in the face of a possible exploit, it is vulnerable to attack.

If, however, we face a zero-day exploit, then the software moves to the Unprotected state. The user has no choice but to be stuck in a window of vulnerability until the vendor releases the patch. The only alternative is to stop using the vulnerable software.

The Unprotected state also may arise when we install new software from a CD or other distribution media. The distribution disk may contain an older version of the software that lacks the latest patches. Thus, the newly installed software may start out in the Unprotected state.

This was a particular problem with Windows XP, the version used in the early 2000s. Various estimates in 2005 suggested that an unpatched Windows XP machine would only last a matter of minutes before being attacked on the Internet. When a user installed Windows XP from a distribution CD, the system would remain Unprotected while it connected to the Internet and downloaded the patches needed to reach a Hardened state.

3.7 Process Example: The Horse

Helen eyed the horse suspiciously. She accompanied Husband Number Three, who was known as Deiphobus, Prince of Troy.

Following Helen's kidnapping 10 years earlier (or was it an elopement—no one knew for sure), the Greeks had been making war on the city of Troy.

Now the Greek camp was empty and burned. Their ships were gone. All that remained was a huge wooden statue of a horse (Figure 3.20). The Greeks also had left a messenger; he claimed the horse was an offering to the goddess Athena for their safe trip home.

The people of Troy already had dragged the huge statue through the gates and into the city.

Helen walked around the horse with her prince, examining it closely. Were warriors hidden inside? Helen called out the names of famous Greek warriors, trying to mimic the sound of their wives' voices. No Greek voices responded. Perhaps she suspected what Odysseus told her later; he was keeping the Greeks silent while she tried to trick them into speaking.

Figure 3.20

Drawing of the Trojan horse.

Like Helen, many Trojans saw the horse as a menace. They said it should be broken up, burned, or dragged to the city's heights and pushed off, letting it fall to its ruin.

Others argued that the statue should be kept as an offering to the gods while the city celebrated its victory against the Greeks. This argument was enough to satisfy most people and the celebrations began in earnest.

Helen's suspicions were, of course, correct.

Hours later, a force of Greeks emerged from the statue. They found the city asleep after the night of festivities. The soldiers opened the city gate to admit the rest of the Greek army. Troy soon fell, as the Greeks defeated the Trojans inside the city walls.

3.7.1 Troy: A High-Level Analysis

Although the technology of the Trojan horse might not directly apply to modern computing, it is a popular symbol in computer security. When a computer program contains secret, malicious behavior that may injure its unsuspecting user, we call it a Trojan horse. For some experts, a "Trojan" virus is one that performs a damaging act in addition to spreading itself around. Other experts consider the spreading process itself to be damaging, and classify all viruses as Trojan horse programs.

However, this terminology is not relevant to this particular section: we will apply the six-part security process to the original Trojan horse.

Assets: For this discussion, we will focus on a single Trojan asset: their city. For the city to thrive, the people need food and trade, and conquerors must be kept away.

Risks: During the war, the Trojans were at risk of attack from the Greeks. The ancient city of Troy was protected by high walls that made it invulnerable to direct assaults by soldiers on foot or on horseback. Primitive weapons of the time could not breach those walls while defenders fought back.

The remaining weakness was at the city gates, which needed to be opened for trade and provisioning, and closed when the Greek army moved to attack the city.

Policy: Since we are focusing on the safety of the city of Troy itself, the security policy would simply forbid enemy warriors from entering the city. The policy would further specify the boundary to be the city's defensible walls. If the Greeks were kept outside, the Trojan defenders could rely on strong gates and high walls.

Implementation: We have specified the policy in terms of the city's boundary, and the boundary is implemented by the city's defensive walls.

The city has a main gate. Just like a door has two states, the city's defenses had two states, based on the condition of the main gate.

In the first state, the city gates were closed. We assume that the city does not contain enemy warriors. If that is true, then as long as the gate remain closed, no enemy warriors can invade the city. However, the gate cannot remain closed indefinitely. It must be opened occasionally to allow traffic for trade and provisions, or the population would starve.

In the second state, the gate was opened to allow food and traders to enter the city. Enemy warriors, however, were not allowed in the city. If any were spotted, they were captured. If an enemy army approached the city while the gate was opened, the city switched to its other state by closing its gate.

Monitoring: Trojan warriors guarded the city against the entry of Greek warriors and, in general, the Greeks stayed out. On one occasion, however, the warrior Odysseus himself dressed as a beggar and snuck into the city. Small incidents like that did not lead to disaster.

The Trojan horse allowed a team of Greek warriors into the city. Helen clearly suspected this, but her security analysis was not convincing to the rest of the city. The horse was left unguarded as the city prematurely celebrated its victory.

Recovery: Unfortunately for Troy, the final Greek attack was thoroughly successful. The archeological site attributed to Troy was destroyed in the 13th century BC and another city did not develop there for over 1200 years.

3.7.2 Analyzing the Security Failure

Let us examine the fall of Troy in terms of the process just described. The Trojans suffered failures in monitoring, in implementation, and in policy.

Monitoring: Despite the care shown by Helen and her prince in examining the horse, they did not detect the warriors hidden inside. They did not post a guard around the horse, despite their suspicions.

Implementation: There was no process in place to prevent the unusual Greek gift, the wooden horse, from being dragged into the city by the city's populace. Once the horse was in the city, it remained unguarded while the city celebrated victory over the Greeks.

Policy: The Greeks had burned their camp and their ships were gone. Many Trojans believed that the Greek threat was over and that wartime security policies no longer applied. No lookouts on the walls or guards at the city gates sounded the alarm when the Greeks marched up to the city. The populace had, in effect, nullified the policies by ignoring them.

Failures teach important lessons about security, even when the event doesn't involve computers or technology.

3.8 Resources

IMPORTANT TERMS INTRODUCED

capability	hierarchical directory	software patch
capability-based security	information states	state diagrams
censorware	interpreter	states
compact access rules	isolation policy	storage state
content control software	macro	subject
default permit	object	system rights
Deny by Default	owner rights	tailored policy
directory path	permission flags	transmission state
drive-by download	processing state	Trojan
execute right	rights	window of vulnerability
exploit	root directory	world rights
file folder	scripting language	zero-day exploit
file-sharing policy	seek right	
global policy	shell script	

ACRONYMS INTRODUCED

CRUD—Create, read, update, delete access rights

MBR—Master boot record

PDF—Adobe portable document format

RWX—Read, write, execute access rights

3.8.1 Review Questions

R1. Explain the role of a file name and path in locating a file on a hard drive.

R2. Describe the four basic access rights for files and other resources in general.

R3. Give reasons why a user would protect a file from read or write access by other users.

R4. How does the operating system decide what permissions to apply when a user creates a new file?

R5. Explain how the four basic access rights of files and directories interact.

R6. What does it mean to have "Execute" access to a file?

R7. What is "Seek" access and how is it different from "Read" access?

R8. Describe the format of an executable file.

R9. Why would we restrict access to executable files?

R10. Describe how a virus operates and spreads.

R11. Explain the difference between a virus, a worm, and a Trojan.

R12. Summarize the policy for enforcing *isolation* among users.

R13. Summarize the policy to provide *file sharing* among users.

R14. When we wish to specify file-access rights, which elements serve as *subjects* and *objects* in the access matrix?

R15. Explain the difference between a default permit policy and one that enforces Deny by Default.

R16. Name the two requirements that must remain true in order for an operating system to enforce its policy.

R17. Why do we say that "capabilities" represent the clustering of access rights "by column"?

R18. Give examples of systems that use capability-based security.

R19. Do most modern operating systems specify file permissions with a "cluster by row" or "cluster by column" strategy?

R20. Summarize the information needed to specify a file's access rights using permission flags.

R21. Describe the differences between listing customary security controls (Table 3.6) and compact access rules (Table 3.7).

R22. Describe the differences between an access matrix and a table of compact access rules.

R23. Explain how the Morris worm took advantage of a failure to use Least Privilege.

R24. Describe the components of a state diagram.

R25. List the typical steps a vendor follows to release a software patch.

R26. Explain two different situations in which a window of vulnerability might arise.

3.8.2 Exercises

E1. Search the directory on your computer. Locate the root folder. From there, locate the following files and provide the full path and file name for each:

  a. The word-processing program you typically use.

  b. A text or word-processing file in your "documents" directory (the directory in which programs typically save files for you).

  c. A file containing your "preferences" for a program like a web browser or word processor.

  d. A file you downloaded from the Internet using your browser.

E2. Can you create files in the root directory of your system? If so, create a file or folder and then delete it. If the attempt fails, describe the error message displayed.

E3. Determine whether the system you use implements an isolation policy or a user-sharing policy. Describe the steps you took to verify your conclusion.

E4. Determine whether the system you use will allow a file's owner to block access to an owned file. Create a file and try to remove the owner's Read or Write permission from the file. Did the system remove the right or not? How could you tell?

E5. Find out about antivirus software on the computer you use.

   a. Is antivirus software installed?

   b. What kind is it?

   c. Can you tell if it works? Why or why not?

   d. Has it ever reported a virus to you? If so, describe how it handled the virus.

E6. Using the story of the Trojan horse as an analogy, give two examples of "Trojan" attacks in computer systems. Explain why the examples fit the analogy of the Trojan horse.

E7. Search the Internet for information on different malware packages, like those discussed in the text. Find a description of a malware package *not* described in the text. Provide the following information about the malware:

   a. What is the malware called?

   b. How does it propagate?

   c. What does it do to the computers it infects?

E8. Bob would like to be able to look at files in the "Suitemates" folders without having to log in as Suitemates. Take these steps to create a security plan to achieve this goal.

   a. Create a revised policy to reflect this objective.

   b. Draw a diagram illustrating access rights that implement this policy.

   c. Create a table of compact access rules that implements the revised policy. Use the format shown in Table 3.7.

E9. Create a diagram portraying access rules that enforces the file-sharing policy described in Table 3.5.

E10. Create a table of compact access rules that enforces the file-sharing policy described in Table 3.5. The compact access rules should use the same format as Table 3.7.

E11. Alice's computer was infected by Virus X, which attached itself to all of her applications. Bob lent her a file-searching utility, which was stored on a USB stick. This utility, however, was infected by Virus Y, which then infected all of Alice's applications, too. Thus, each application contained *two* virus infections. Draw a diagram based on Figure 3.7 to show both infections in a single application file.

Riko is writing a program. Bob's computer contains a compiler that will take Riko's source code (the program she's written) and produce an executable program file (with a ".exe" suffix). Thus, we have three users of interest: Bob, Riko, and Suitemates, and these files: the compiler, Riko's written program, and the executable program built by the compiler. We need to implement the policy in Table 3.8.

TABLE 3.8 Policy for protecting Riko's custom program		
#	Policy Statement	Risks
1	Everyone shall have execute access to the compiler program.	1, 2
2	Riko shall have full access to the program's source code.	2, 4, 5
3	Riko shall have full access to the program's executable file.	2, 5
4	Bob shall have read and execute access to the program's executable file.	1, 2, 4, 5

Answer the following questions based on the scenario just described.

E12. Draw a diagram showing the user and file access rights that implement the file-sharing policy in Table 3.8. Create a diagram similar to Figure 3.12 that includes the correct users, files, and permissions.

Indicate access rights with arrows and labels (RWX). Be sure the access rights allow the work just described and still achieve Least Privilege.

E13. Construct an access matrix that provides the user and file access rights needed to implement the policy in Table 3.8.

SHARING FILES

ABOUT THIS CHAPTER

In this chapter, we work with the mechanisms provided by operating systems like Unix and Windows to protect files and folders. We also take a technical look at the fifth phase of the security process: monitoring the system. The chapter focuses on these topics:

- Tailoring the security policy to grant special access to individuals or groups
- Permission flags in Unix-like systems
- Access control lists in Macintosh and Windows systems
- Monitoring system events through logging

4.1 Controlled Sharing

In Section 3.3, we chose between Bob's isolation policy and a "share everything" policy. What happens if Bob needs to share files with one or two other users but not with the rest of the suite?

> Bob and his classmate Tina must collect and analyze data from surveys of other students. Because of the nature of the survey, the sociology department and the school's institutional review board require that the results remain confidential. Bob and Tina want to collect and share the results on Bob's tower computer in the suite. They must not let others in the suite read the survey data.

It is clear from Chapter 3 that we can create files and folders and establish access rights for them. We can share files with some people and hide them from others, simply by configuring the right permissions.

In security, however, it's best to be systematic. If we dive directly into a solution, we run a higher risk of making mistakes. We begin with our objectives, threats, and risks. We develop our policy before we implement the solution.

When we write the policy, we want to be more general. When we write up implementation details, we get specific. In this case, the general statements talk about the information of interest: the survey. Thus, the policy talks about the survey and who may or may not share the data. The implementation, then, talks about files, folders, users, and access rights.

1. Bob and Tina shall be able to read and modify the survey project data.

2. No one except Bob and Tina shall have access to the survey project data.

Although global restrictions, like "no one shall," sometimes are hard to verify, accurate policy statements may require them.

TAILORED FILE SECURITY POLICIES

To share the project files, Bob needs to adjust his "user isolation" security policy. Practical problems like this often arise when using "one-size-fits-all" policies like "isolate everyone" or "share everything." We address such things with tailored access policies. In Section 3.3, we identified three examples of tailored policies:

1. Privacy
2. Shared reading
3. Shared updating

There are several ways to describe a tailored policy. Here we take a systematic approach. We implement each tailored policy underneath a system-wide default policy of either isolation or sharing. The tailored policy specifies additional access rights. These new rights may add to or replace the default rights. For each new set of rights, the tailored policy needs to consider four things:

1. Which files or other resources are involved: for example, files belonging to "Project X" or perhaps "Tina's personal files."
2. Which users are granted these new rights: for example, users working on "Project X."
3. Do we Deny by Default, or do we retain the default access rights for these files?
4. What access rights do we enforce: full access, execute, read-only, or no access?

Typically the files in question will reside within a particular directory and be used by a particular group of people. When we describe the policy, however, we must be careful to describe *what we want* and not how we'll do it.

BOB'S SHARING DILEMMA

Bob needs to implement a tailored updating policy so that he can share files with Tina. But how?

For each file, we can control access by the owner, administrators, and the rest of the users. If that's all we have, there's no way to grant access to two specific users while blocking access to the rest.

Bob could solve this sharing dilemma if he always logs in to a system administration account. On some systems, these accounts use a specific user identity with a name like "system" or "root" that receives all system-related access rights. If Bob does this, the account will have full access to Tina's files. If he wants to create files to share with Tina, however, he must make Tina the owner of those files. Otherwise, he wouldn't be able to restrict access exclusively to Tina and himself.

This solution, however, poses a problem: Least Privilege. It may seem convenient to routinely log into a system as "root" or some other administrative identity, but it poses a real risk to the system. For example, if Bob unexpectedly exposes the system to a virus or malicious website while using administrative privileges, the system may quickly become compromised.

We can solve Bob's problem if we can specify additional access rights for each file and folder. There are two choices, depending on what operating system we use.

1. Keep a list of access rights for each file, called the *access control list* (ACL). Each entry in the ACL identifies a specific user, and contains a list of access rights granted to that user. This is available on modern versions of Windows and on Apple's OS-X.

2. Keep one additional set of access rights, and associate it with a *user group*. Associate a group with each file, just like we associate a user, the owner, with each file. This is available on all Unix-based systems.

Windows uses a simple version of ACLs to provide basic file sharing on "home" editions of Windows. All Unix-based systems provide group-based access controls.

4.1.1   Basic File Sharing on Windows

Windows provides a very simple mechanism for sharing files among users on a personal computer. The mechanism begins with an isolation policy; users have no access to other users' personal files. Building on the isolation policy, we assign additional permissions to selected users.

To implement tailored sharing, we first put the files in a particular folder and enable file sharing for that folder. Figure 4.1 shows how Tina shares survey files with Bob, assuming Bob's tower runs Windows Vista. The Windows 7 "Sharing Wizard" provides a similar mechanism.

First, Tina creates a folder named "Survey" to contain all of their files. Next, she selects the folder and chooses "Share..." from the menu. Windows displays the "File Sharing" window, which says "Choose people to share with." The window displays a list of users who can share files in the folder.

Because Tina created the folder, she appears in the list as the "Owner." There is a field above the table that allows Tina to add other users; there is a drop-down list of user names on the right-hand side. Tina selects Bob's name and clicks the "Add" button. Next, Tina clicks on Bob's "Permission Level" and grants Bob the "co-owner" permission, giving him the right to create, modify, and change the files in the folder.

There are four permission levels:

1. **Owner rights**: the person who owns the folder; who has full rights to read, modify, or delete anything in the folder.

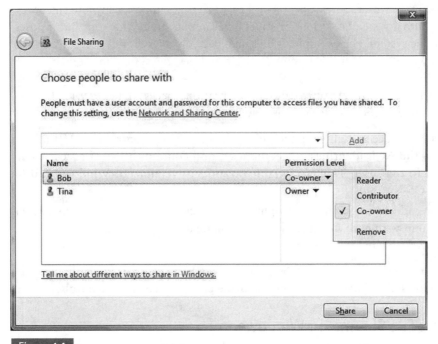

Figure 4.1

File sharing on Microsoft Windows Vista.

2. **Co-owner rights:** people who don't own the folder but receive the same rights as the owner. Windows 7 provides "Read/Write" rights instead.

3. **Contributor rights:** people with the right to create files in the folder, and to modify or delete files that they themselves have created. Windows 7 doesn't include this right

4. **Reader rights:** people with the right to read files in the folder.

When authorized users create files in the shared folder, they receive access rights for their permission level. Bob receives access rights as co-owner, which allows him to read and modify his files and Tina's files. He also can delete the files if he wants. If he was only granted permission as a contributor, he could modify the files he creates, but he couldn't make changes to Tina's files.

If someone creates a folder inside the shared folder, everything inside that new folder inherits the file-sharing permissions. Bob could create a folder for his own files, but Tina still can modify them.

4.1.2 User Groups

If Bob and Tina are using a Unix-based system or a "professional" version of Windows, they can use *group rights* to protect their files. They define a user group, which serves as another set of users for whom we specify access rights. A simple implementation adds two items to each file's access control data: the name of the file's group, and a set of flags for access rights. If a user belongs to the file's group and tries to access the file, the system applies the group access rights.

In Bob's case, he sets up a "Survey" group that contains Tina and himself (Figure 4.2). He then ensures that each file containing survey information belongs to that group. Each file in the group contains the following access information:

- File's owner: either Bob or Tina
- File's group: Survey, containing Tina and Bob
- Owner access: RW-
- System access: RW-
- Group access: RW-
- World access: ---

Editing the "Survey" user group on Windows XP Pro.

To provide access rights for groups, the system integrates group identifiers into many of the same places as user identifiers. When a process begins, it inherits a group identifier from the user who started it. When the process tries to access a file, the system checks the user identity and the group identity, and applies the specified rights if one of them matches. If neither match, the process receives any rights granted to the "world" of users.

Administrative Groups

In a sense, access permissions for the "world" represent permissions for a particular group. Likewise, some systems have one or more built-in *administrative groups* that provide special privileges for managing the system. In Windows, this is the role of the "Administrators" group. Unix-based systems often have a similar group that is sometimes called the "wheel" group.

If a system provides administrative groups, administrators can log in using personal user identities. If the identity is a member of the administrative group, the user receives administrative access to the computer's resources. This provides better control than logging in directly with a privileged user name like "root" or "SYSTEM." If administrators log in with individual, personalized identities, we can more easily track their individual actions. If an administrator performs a malicious act, we can identify the user who performed the act, even if that user was logged in as an administrator.

Even though the administrative groups give us a better way of tracking administrative actions, it's still risky to log in with such power. Many organizations provide administrators with two separate identities: one for routine activities and one for administrative tasks. The administrative identifier is a member of the administrative group. When logged in with the administrative identity, the user has full administrative powers.

When Bob set up the computer in the suite's common area, he created three separate user names: Bob, SuperBob, and Suitemates. The users Bob and Suitemates are regular users. When other suitemates use the computer, they use the Suitemates login. SuperBob is like the Bob account except that it is also in the Administrators group. When Bob and Tina started their project, Bob logged in as SuperBob and created a separate user name for Tina. He also established the Survey group containing the two of them (Figure 4.2).

4.1.3 Least Privilege and Administrative Users

Despite the risks, many people routinely log into their personal computers with full administrative powers. Some see it as their right and privilege, because they own the computer in question. More often, people simply don't realize the risks involved.

If Bob visits a malicious website or downloads a virus while logged in as an administrator, the malicious software can use full administrative privileges to infest his computer. If Bob is only logged in as a regular user, then the infestation will, at most, affect

Figure 4.3

The Task Manager's process display on Microsoft Windows.

his user environment. Many viruses are blocked when they try to infest a regular user; they depend on administrative privileges for their attacks to work.

Not all "system" accounts have unlimited rights. Some systems define several "users" that in fact represent special activities performed by the operating system. If we display the process status on Unix (the "ps" command shown in Figure 2.6), or the Task Manager on Windows (Figure 4.3), we can list all running processes along with the user names associated with those processes.

The display may show one or more special identities for running network services, including the file server or web server. Other identities, like SYSTEM and LOCAL SER-VICE, are responsible for utility processes that keep the system running. Individuals can't log in with such user names.

ADMINISTRATION BY REGULAR USERS

As an alternative to having over-powerful administrators, some operating systems provide ways of temporarily granting administrative powers to people logged in to regular user accounts. The temporary permission relies on the person authenticating as an authorized administrator. The temporary administrative privilege applies to a program started by the user and disappears when the program ends.

Figure 4.4

OS-X padlock unlocks with an administrator's password.

For years, the all-powerful Unix "root" account has been too powerful for individual users to use, but too useful to eliminate entirely. Today, Unix-based systems may have administrators who belong to administrative groups, but the administrators still must rely on "root" to make serious changes to the system. Typically, they use the *setuid* operation, which temporarily changes a user's identity.

To run a program as "root," the administrator runs the "setuid" program, specifies the new user identity to be "root," and directs it to run an administrative function under that user identity. The "setuid" function prompts for the "root" password, and starts the program if the user types the right password. Most Unix administrators today use a prepackaged "sudo" function that runs "setuid" with the identity of "root."

Apple's OS-X provides "sudo," like most Unix-based systems, but it also implements a separate mechanism for configuring sensitive parts of the system. For example, Figure 4.4 shows a screen that changes the system's behavior when restarting. To enable the "Target Disk Mode" button, the user first must click on the padlock, which demands an administrator's password. Once the user types the password, the padlock switches to "unlocked" and the system enables the button.

The same user interface allows regular users to modify many critical system preferences. OS-X uses a similar arrangement to allow regular users to adjust the rights on files and folders: Again, there is a padlock that controls the permission settings, and an administrative password unlocks that lock.

USER ACCOUNT CONTROL ON WINDOWS

Starting with Windows Vista, Microsoft's operating systems provide a similar mechanism, called user account control, or UAC for short. Whenever a user tries to run an administrative function, Windows tells the user and asks for approval. If the user is a regular, nonadministrative user, then the user must provide an administrative password before the task proceeds (Figure 4.5).

The principle behind UAC is that the really dangerous attacks on a computer begin with some extraordinary event, like using administrative privileges or making changes to critical programs in the Windows operating system. For example, the attack might try to install a back door, as described in Section 2.3. If the system always asks before

Figure 4.5
User account control pop-up window.

performing such actions, there is a better chance that a user will detect the attack and repel it.

4.2 File Permission Flags

In earlier examples, we indicated file permissions and other access rights by abbreviations: "R" for read, "W" for write, and so on. If the system granted a particular right, we showed the appropriate letter and showed a hyphen ("-") otherwise. These correspond to *file permission flags* that the system sets to "true" if the right is present and "false" otherwise.

The best-known modern implementation of file permission flags is in Unix. Ken Thompson and Dennis Ritchie at Bell Telephone Laboratories originally developed Unix in the early 1970s. Since then, Unix technology has been the foundation of many systems, including the Solaris operating system, Apple's Macintosh OS-X, and the open source Gnu and Linux software. Unix-like systems became so significant in computing that the Institute for Electrical and Electronics Engineers (IEEE) developed standards for such systems through its "Portable Operating System Interface" (POSIX) committee. Some experts refer to Unix file permissions as "POSIX file permissions."

Unix implements three file-access rights (read, write, and execute/search) for each of these three sets of identities:

1. Owner (called *user rights* in Unix)—the user who owns a file
2. Group—users belonging to the group associated with the file
3. World (called *other rights* in Unix)—all other users

Figure 4.6 illustrates Unix permission flags for a typical file. The owner typically has the right to read and write the file. Users in the file's group, and all other users, customarily receive permission to read the file but not to write it. If a file is executable, then anyone granted the right to read the file also is granted permission to execute it. In practice, most files that have execute permission also have read permission. This is not technically required in all cases, but it is customary.

Unix uses similar permission flags to protect folders, which are always called directories. To open a file listed in a particular directory or to search a directory to find another directory inside it, a user needs "execute" access to that directory. To list the contents of a directory, the user needs read access to that directory. To create or delete files, the user needs write access to the files' directory.

Figure 4.7 illustrates permission flags as they appear in text-oriented Unix "shell commands." The system prints the "$" to prompt the user for a command. The typed command appears in italics. The "ls" command lists files in the current directory. If we type "ls -l" we get the "long" directory listing shown here that includes file ownership and permissions.

The left column contains permission codes "rw-r-" and such to indicate access rights for each file. After skipping the first hyphen, the three-letter groups indicate rights for the file's owner, the file's group, and the rest of the world, respectively. File names appear in the right column. The permissions for the data files "data1.txt" and "hello.c"

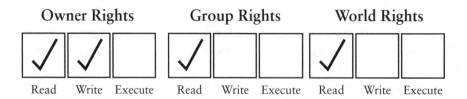

Unix file permissions for a typical file.

```
$ ls -l
total 56
-rw-r--r--@ 1 rick  ops    4321 Nov 23 08:58 data1.txt
-rwxr-xr-x  1 rick  ops   12588 Nov 23 10:19 hello
-rw-r--r--@ 1 rick  rick     59 Nov 23 10:18 hello.c
```

Figure 4.7

Unix directory listing command "ls".

match the permissions shown in Figure 4.6. The column containing "rick" denotes the files' owner, and the next column to the right identifies the owning group (either "rick" or "ops").

Unix users have several commands for adjusting a file's rights:

- chmod—short for "change mode," can change the rights granted to the owner, group, or rest of the world, for a file.
- chown—short for "change owner," changes the identity of a file's owner.
- chgrp—short for "change group," changes the identity of the group associated with a file.

Unix is not the only system that uses permission flags; the "protection codes" in the OpenVMS operating system work the same way (Figure 4.8). Like Unix, OpenVMS organizes permissions into sets of identities with access rights for each. Unlike Unix, OpenVMS provides a fourth set to specify access rights for system processes. OpenVMS also implements a fourth access right that indicates delete permission.

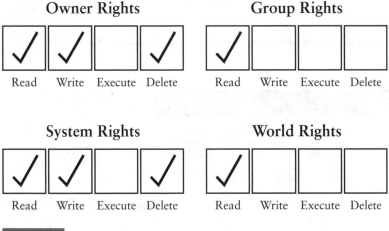

Figure 4.8

OpenVMS file permission flags.

OpenVMS was originally developed by Digital Equipment Corporation (DEC) in the mid 1970s. Today, few people use OpenVMS except to provide applications that were developed for OpenVMS many years ago. One of the principal developers of Open-VMS, Dave Cutler, was responsible for developing the modern Microsoft Windows operating systems, starting with Windows NT. In some cases, Windows inherited design features from OpenVMS. However, Windows has not included permission flags in its file security mechanisms.

Permission flags have an obvious advantage: They cover a broad range of security policies while storing a small amount of data with each file. Simple policy objectives can be solved directly with permission flags. Ambiguities arise, however, when we must tailor permissions to grant or deny access to two or more individual users or to control access by two or more groups of users.

4.2.1 Permission Flags and Ambiguities

Bob wants to create a file and allow everyone including Tina to see it, but protect it from change. The file belongs to the "Survey" group, which contains Tina and himself. Table 4.1 shows the access rules he set up. He gives the "world" read access to the file. He gives the group *no* access to the file. Will Tina be able to read the file?

Because Tina is both a member of the "Survey" group and a member of "the world," the access rights are ambiguous. On the one hand, a missing access right might mean that we should forbid access to Tina, since she's a member of the Survey group and the group is granted no access. However, Bob, the owner, is also a member of the Survey group: Should we forbid access to him, too? On the other hand, the missing rights may simply mean that Tina acquires any rights she deserves from being a member of the world.

The OpenVMS system combines the "access-allowed" permissions granted via system, owner, group, and world permissions. On OpenVMS, Bob can read the file because he is granted read access both as the owner and as a member of the owning group. In Tina's case, she can read the file because the world is allowed to read the file. The only

TABLE 4.1 Ambiguous access rules				
			Effective Access	
Identity Class	Access	Bob	Tina	World
Owner (Bob)	RW	RW		
Group (Bob and Tina)	--			
System (administrators)	RW			
World (everyone else)	R-		??	R-

way we can deny access to Tina on OpenVMS is to omit *any* access by her in any case. We must rely on Deny by Default and block access by everyone else.

Unix-based systems do this differently. If a permission flag fails to grant a particular right, then the right is denied. When checking permissions, the system selects the set of users (owner, group, or world) that best fits the user accessing the file. The choice is made as follows:

- If the "root" user accesses a file, the system grants full access to the file.
- If the file's owner accesses a file, the system applies the owner rights.
- If a group member (who is not the file's owner) accesses the file, the system applies the group rights.
- If the user is neither the owner nor a member of the file's group, the system applies the world rights.

When we apply the Unix rules to Tina, the system denies access. Unix-like systems block access to the file through *explicit denial*: Because Tina is a member of the group and the group has no access rights, Tina receives no access rights. If Bob accesses the file, however, the system applies the owner rights and grants read/write access. If a user is neither Bob nor a member of the Survey group, then the system applies world rights and allows read-only access. Tina herself would have read access if she weren't a member of the Survey group.

If Bob removes read access rights from one of his own files, he can no longer read the file, even if the rest of the world has read access. Because it is Bob's file, he can change the permissions back to allow read access, but he won't be able to read the file until he changes the permissions.

4.2.2 Permission Flag Examples

Let us return to Bob's desktop computer policy in Chapter 3 and extend it to protect his survey project files (a "tailored updating" policy). First, we review the five generic risks appearing in Section 3.3, the sixth associated with Bob, and add a seventh:

7. Disclosure of the survey files to anyone outside the project, which could compromise the privacy of the participants and get Bob, Tina, and the college in trouble.

Bob's original policy appears in Tables 3.3 and 3.4. To address the seventh risk, we add the policy statements shown in Table 4.2.

To implement this policy, we create an account for Tina and Tina establishes a password for it; then we add to the security controls listed in Table 3.7. This yields the controls listed in Table 4.3. Remember what an "X" ("execute") permission means when applied to a directory: It indicates the right to search the directory when trying to locate a file by name.

Note that we *always* specify group access permissions, even for personal files. When creating a new user, most Unix-based systems automatically create a separate group just

TABLE 4.2 Policy additions for tailored sharing of the survey files

Policy Number	Policy Statement	Risks
8	The system shall have a regular user named Tina.	4, 7
9	Tina shall have a password to protect her login.	2, 3, 4, 5, 7
10	All survey files shall belong to the "survey" group.	7
11	Only users Bob and Tina shall have access to files in the "survey" group.	4, 7
12	Bob and Tina shall have full access to all files in the "survey" group.	1, 4, 7

TABLE 4.3 Security controls for Tina and the shared project files

Control Number	File	Owner	Owning Group (members)	Access Rights			Policy Statement
				Owner	Group	World	
11	Tina's directory	Tina	Tina	RWX	RWX	---	4, 9
12	Tina's files	Tina	Tina	RWX	RW-	---	4, 9
13	Project directory	Bob or Tina	Bob, Tina	RWX	RWX	---	10, 11, 12
14	Project files	Bob or Tina	Bob, Tina	RWX	RW-	---	10, 11, 12

for that user. By default, all files created by that user belong to the user's personal group. When Bob or Tina want to create files that belong specifically to the "survey" group, they may need to explicitly assign those files to that group.

SECURITY CONTROLS FOR THE FILE-SHARING POLICY

Now let us look at the file-sharing policy described in Table 3.5. The policy grants read access to all files by default and execute access to shared application programs. Table 4.4 shows the appropriate security controls.

> **Practical Tip:** Always organize your files into separate folders according to their permissions. Bob and Tina established a shared folder, and ensured that both can add or change files in that folder. Neither Bob nor Tina should store files in that folder unless both of them should be sharing that file. If Bob starts up a separate project with someone else, he should set up a separate folder for that project.

TABLE 4.4 Security controls for the file sharing policy in Table 3.5

Control Number	File	Owner	Owning Group (members)	Owner	Group	World	Policy Statement
				Access Rights			
1	Executables	System	System	RWX	RWX	R-X	1, 3
2	User directories	User	User	RWX	RWX	R-X	4, 5
3	User files	User	User	RWX	RW-	R--	4, 5

Occasionally, either Bob or Tina should go through and set the access rights on all files (and folders) inside their shared folder. This ensures that both have access rights to everything and that nobody else has inadvertently been given access rights to anything.

4.3 Access Control Lists

In many access control problems, we have a single group of users who all need identical access rights to a particular set of files. We can easily solve such problems with group permissions. There are, however, cases where we can't use file permission flags and a single user group to achieve Least Privilege. Consider a policy that requires these three conditions:

1. Block access to the user community in general
2. Grant read-only access to one group of users
3. Grant read-write access to a second group of users

We can't do this with Unix-style permission flags and achieve Least Privilege. We might come close if we grant read-only access to everyone and read-write access to the second group. We also might come close if we create a single large group out of the first and second groups. We then grant read-write access to all, and tell members of the first group to restrain themselves. To achieve Least Privilege, however, we need access control lists or ACLs.

In Section 4.1, we introduced Windows "home edition" ACLs that grant rights to specific users. This particular implementation can solve the problem just described: We list all users individually and grant the appropriate access to each one. This is a reasonable solution if we are only controlling rights for a handful of people. It becomes impractical as the groups grow in size.

To implement the policy for larger groups, it is easier and more reliable to establish separate user groups. We then establish permissions for each group instead of setting permissions on a per-user basis. It is much easier to verify correct group membership than it is to review the access rights for dozens of individual users.

Fortunately, most modern ACL implementation can specify permissions for groups of users as well as individuals. Modern Unix-based systems that include ACLs, like Apple's OS-X, support group permissions as well as individual user permissions. Professional and "business" versions of Windows also support group permissions.

MULTICS ACLs

The Multics timesharing system was developed by a team including MIT, Bell Laboratories, General Electric, and eventually, Honeywell. The project intended to develop a timesharing system that was so reliable and easy to maintain that it served as a computing utility, much like water, telephone, or electric power systems. ACLs were one of several important security technologies pioneered by Multics. ACLs were first described in 1965 as part of the Multics file system.

Figure 4.9 displays a Multics ACL. The left column lists access rights and the right column shows the sets of users granted those access rights. Each line represents a single ACL entry that specifies access rights for a particular set of users.

The ACL uses a three-part identifier to specify each set of users. The first part is a user name, then a group name, and then an optional code to indicate a process type. The three identifiers are separated by periods. An asterisk indicates a "wild card" that matches anything in a field; an asterisk in the first field matches any user name, and one in the second field matches any group name. We use a row of three asterisks (*.*.*) to specify access rights for "everyone."

In Figure 4.9, the first two ACL entries indicate access for particular users, and the last two indicate access for particular groups. The user "SmithRE" of user group "CSCDDTB" has read, write, and execute access to the file in question. The "Backup" user, which belongs to a system process that backs up files, has read-only access to the file. Members of the group "CSCDDTB" have read-only access to the file, while members of the "SysAdmin" group have read/write access.

We can't possibly specify this set of access rights with Unix file permissions. We can easily specify the owner and group permissions, assuming that SmithRE is the file's owner and CSCDDTB is the owning group, but we can't specify permissions for the Backup user or SysAdmin group. If we were faced with this problem in practice, we might run the Backup operation as a Unix "root" process because, after all, it is a system utility process. However, this would violate Least Privilege since "root" would have

```
rew    SmithRE.CSCDDTB.*
r      Backup.SysDaemon.*
r      *.CSCDDTB.*
rw     *.SysAdmin.*
```

Figure 4.9

ACL from the Multics system.

full access to the file. We wouldn't be able to protect the file from accidental writing by the backup program.

MODERN ACL IMPLEMENTATIONS

Although there is still a strong tradition of using Unix-style permission flags in Unix-based systems, many modern systems implement ACLs. This is partly the result of U.S. government requirements. In 1983, the U.S. Department of Defense (DOD) published requirements for "trusted operating systems" titled *Trusted Computer System Evaluation Criteria*, (TCSEC), often called the **Orange Book**. One of the requirements was to provide ACLs. This requirement remained when the *Orange Book* was replaced by a new set of standards called the **Common Criteria** in 2000. Today, ACLs implement one of the following designs:

- POSIX.1e
- Apple Macintosh OS-X
- Microsoft Windows
- NFSV4

The newest of these is NFSV4, which was developed as part of a revision of the Network File System protocol. This protocol provides file service across local networks and was originally developed by Sun Microsystems. The ACL mechanism for NFSV4 is similar to POSIX, though it is designed to work well with Microsoft Windows systems. We shall take a closer look at the first three ACL implementations.

4.3.1 POSIX ACLs

As part of its standardization of Unix-like operating systems, the POSIX committee spent several years working on an ACL standard. However, the committee abandoned the standard without finishing it. The last draft was published in 1999. Even so, many Unix-based systems claim that their ACLs are based on that standard. The notable exceptions are Sun's Solaris and Apple's OS-X.

The POSIX ACL system is closely tied to Unix-style permission flags. Every POSIX ACL begins with a "minimum ACL" whose three entries exactly match the file's permission flags. There is one entry each for the file's owner, the file's group, and for everyone else. If we add access rights for another user or group beyond the first three, we produce an extended ACL. As with basic file permissions, each entry controls exactly three rights: read, write, and execute. When speaking of directories or folders, "execute" access allows the directory to be searched while trying to locate a file.

Table 4.5 lists the sets of users whose entries may appear in a POSIX ACL. The first three correspond to the minimum ACL. The next two provide entries to grant specific rights to a particular user or particular group. The final type of entry, the *mask*, helps ensure that simple Unix permissions still work safely when ACLs are added to existing systems.

TABLE 4.5 Access control entries in POSIX ACLs	
Class of Users	POSIX Entry
User who owns the file	user::rwx
Group associated with the file	group::rwx
The rest of the world	other::rwx
Specific user named user-name	user:user-name:rwx
Specific group named group-name	group:group-name:rwx
Mask applied to specific users and groups	mask::rwx

As with Unix permissions, the system searches the ACL for the most appropriate entry. The system grants or denies access according to the rights contained in that entry. This poses a simple matching problem if the access is by the file's owner or by someone specifically named in an ACL entry. It is also simple if the access doesn't match any users or groups in the ACL; the system applies the *other* access rights.

Rights may be ambiguous when a user belongs to two or more groups that appear in an ACL. Instead of searching for a single best match, the system combines the access rights granted to all of the user's groups. If *any* group receives the necessary access right, and the user belongs to that group, then the user receives that right.

For example, Tina is a member of the "CSResearch" group and the "CSHelpers" group. One group is granted "read" access to a particular folder, while the other is granted "search" (execute) access. Tina can both read and search the folder, because she receives one right from each of the two groups.

If access rights are granted to a named individual user or via group permissions, they must be further confirmed by the ACL's "mask entry." If the mask entry allows all three rights, then all rights may be granted by ACL entries. If the mask omits a right (like write access), then the ACL entries cannot grant write access to specific users or group members.

Although many Unix-based systems support POSIX ACLs, they don't necessarily work effectively. Ideally, if the system updates a file, the new version should have the same ACL as the original one. However, not all systems do this. Many Linux systems don't even support ACLs by default; the owner must install separate ACL software and activate ACLs on the hard drives.

4.3.2 Macintosh OS-X ACLs

Macintosh OS-X ACLs are built on top of standard Unix permissions and designed to work well with Windows-style ACLs (Figure 4.10). Most users interact with these ACLs

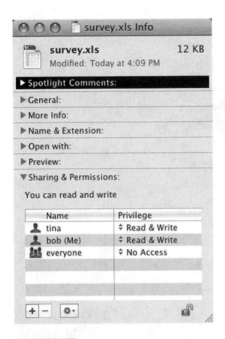

Figure 4.10

Macintosh ACL for Bob and Tina's shared file.

through the standard Macintosh GUI, known as the "Finder." Superficially, OS-X ACLs are similar to the simple Windows ACLs shown in Figure 4.1.

We start with access allowed by the owner, and we can add access rights for other users. As with the earlier example, one of the users can simply add access rights for the other. Just as Tina granted access to Bob, Bob can grant access for Tina (Figure 4.10).

To modify the ACL, we must first unlock it by clicking on the padlock in the lower right-hand corner. Unfortunately, we need administrator rights to make changes to an ACL. Thus, Bob had to type in an administrator's name and password in order to fix the ACL. Once we unlock the ACL, we add another user by clicking on the "+" box in the lower left-hand corner. The Finder then displays a list of existing users and we click on the name we wish to add.

To change the access rights in an ACL entry, we have two choices. If we want to remove all access permissions, we can delete the corresponding ACL entry. To do this, we select the corresponding row and then click on the "-" sign in the lower left.

Default rights, like those assigned to the owner, owning group, or world, can't be deleted. To remove access for one of those, we click on the corresponding entry under "Privilege" and choose the access rights we want. Figure 4.11, shows the "pop-up" menu to choose the access rights. In the example, we choose "No Access" rights for "everyone" not listed in the ACL.

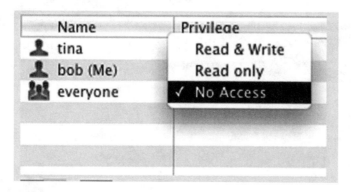

Figure 4.11

Modifying the rights on a Macintosh ACL entry.

Unlike the simple Windows ACLs described earlier, OS-X allows us to add ACL entries for groups as well as users. We first create a group by selecting "User Accounts" under the System Preferences application. We unlock the application by clicking on the padlock in the lower left and typing an administrator's password; then we click on the plus "+" sign above the padlock, and we choose to create a group. Once the group exists, we can modify its name and members by editing the screen shown in Figure 4.12.

We give the group the name "Survey" and select members by checking them in the "Membership" window. In the figure we have selected Bob and Tina as members. Note that other groups also may be members of groups.

To include a group in an ACL, we first display and unlock the ACL, then we click the plus sign to add a new entry. We select the group's name from the list, and then set the group's access rights.

When we create a new file on a Macintosh, the file grants full rights to the owner and read-only access to everyone else. This does not, however, mean that we are sharing files by default. Every user has a "home directory" that carries their user name and, within that directory, they have personal directories with names like Desktop, Documents, Downloads, Library, and Pictures. By default, other users cannot read these directories. Even if they have read access to the files themselves, they can't read the files because they can't reach them easily. Only the Public directory grants read access to users in general.

If we wish to share files with others, we either place the files in the Public directory, or in another directory that's not part of our user file directories. For example, Bob might

Choosing users for a group in Apple's OS-X.

create a "Projects" directory in the root directory that is readable by everyone. Within that directory, he creates a new directory for every project, and he sets access permissions to allow project members only.

When Tina creates a file in their shared "Survey" directory, the file will grant full access to her and read access to everyone else. This is the default behavior. The protections on its directory will protect the file from other users. The system will not, however, automatically fill in the ACL with permissions for Bob. He will be able to read the file because, by default, he receives "read" access with the rest of the world. Unlike the rest of the world, he can read the directory. This allows him to actually read the file.

Although this approach will protect their "Survey" files from being read by outsiders, it is best to explicitly change permissions to block access by people outside the group. Bob won't share his administrative password with Tina, so she can't change ACLs herself. However, she can type in a "chmod" command by hand to remove access by the world ("others") to her new files.

4.4 Microsoft Windows ACLs

ACLs first appeared in Windows operating systems with the introduction of Windows NT in 1993. The ACLs evolved over subsequent releases of "professional" versions of Windows 2000, XP, Vista, and Windows 7. Windows has produced a particularly effective ACL implementation by providing flexible and sophisticated inheritance. In most cases the file in a folder inherits access rights cleanly and simply from the enclosing directory. Files and folders automatically inherit changes made to an enclosing folder's access rights. This makes it easier to manage rights in file hierarchies.

The ACLs used in Macintosh OS-X and Sun's Solaris operating system are similar to those in Windows to ensure they work well together. Version 4 of the Network File System also adopted an ACL mechanism that is very similar to Windows. Although these ACLs are similar, each has its own interface, graphical and otherwise, for viewing and changing ACLs. In addition, these other ACLs use different techniques to inherit ACL settings and apply default rights.

On Windows, we display a file's ACL by selecting the file and choosing the "Properties" menu entry. The ACLs reside under the "Security" tab (Figure 4.13). The top pane of the ACL window lists the entries for different users or classes of users. When we click

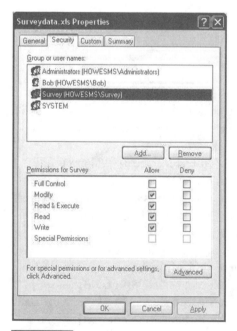

Figure 4.13

Access control list from Microsoft Windows.

on one of those entries, the lower pane displays the corresponding access rights and restrictions. A check mark under "Allow" grants that right; a check mark under "Deny" blocks that right.

As with earlier ACL examples, the access rights in Figure 4.13 can't be expressed with a set of file permission flags. The ACL describes rights for two different users, Bob and "SYSTEM," and for two different groups, "Administrators" and "Survey." Windows provides several different displays for ACLs. The display in Figure 4.13 only shows the rights for the user or group chosen in the display's upper pane. In the figure we only see the rights granted to the Survey group. We need to select the other entries individually to see the rights granted to those users or groups.

When a Windows ACL has two or more entries that apply to the current process, the access rights are combined. Let's look at a variant of the example in Table 4.1. Bob creates a file, gives the Survey group no access rights to it, but grants Read access rights to the world. Tina is in the Survey group: Can she read the file? In a Windows ACL, the *absence* of a right does not forbid access, if the ACL gives the user access some other way. Thus, Tina *can* read the file.

4.4.1 Denying Access

Windows does not deny an access right by omitting it, but it allows us to explicitly deny a right. The ACLs provide separate "Allow" and "Deny" flags (Figure 4.14). On Unix, we deny access by being silent, by failing to grant access rights. On Windows, we specifically can deny access to particular users or groups. This provides yet another opportunity to misinterpret access rights: What does it mean if one ACL entry grants access while another denies access?

Windows resolves this by always applying the Deny entries first. The system looks at the access rights being requested and the identity of the process making the request. If a Deny entry matches a user name or group associated with the process, Windows denies the specified access rights. Windows then reviews the Allow entries. If any entry matches the process owner or one of its groups, then the corresponding access rights are granted *unless* the right was previously denied through a Deny entry.

This makes Deny access convenient in some cases but tricky in others. Let us return to the example of Bob, Tina, and the Survey group. Clearly Bob wants to give read/write access to the Survey group, so he puts the appropriate rights in the ACL. After getting a stern lecture about survey privacy from his instructor, he decides to revise the ACLs. He adds an ACL entry to his Survey files to specifically deny access by the user "Suitemates." When users log in as Suitemates, they are denied access to the Survey files even if some other ACL entry grants them access by mistake. This produces the result Bob wants.

Following another stern lecture by the instructor, however, Bob gets worried. If he creates another user, then he'll have to update the ACLs to Deny that new user, too. Bob

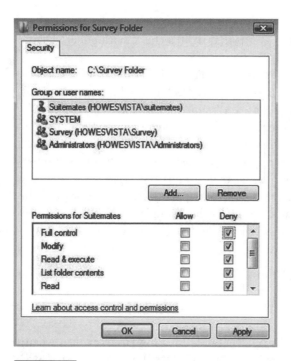

Figure 4.14

Denying access in a Windows ACL.

decides it's easier to simply Deny access by "Users" to the survey data files. He assumes that Tina will still have access since she is a member of the "Survey" group.

Instead, Windows applies all Deny ACL entries first. Because Tina (and Bob, for that matter) is a user and all Users are denied access, Tina is denied access; nobody can access the Survey files until Bob removes the Deny entry.

The Deny feature can make an ACL hard to interpret. The Multics ACL (Figure 4.9) always sorted the entries by the set of users involved, with the most specific entries first. This was the order in which the entries were applied, so it was relatively easy to interpret the ACL. The Windows ACL display in Figure 4.13 also lists the rights by the set of users involved. However, a single set of users may be subject to both Allow and Deny rights, and *all* Deny rights are applied first. Therefore, we must examine the list twice: once applying the Deny rights, and again applying the Allow rights.

DETERMINING ACCESS RIGHTS

To determine the actual rights applied to a particular file under Windows, we have two choices. First, we can manually review the rights for each user and group. We need to keep track of Allow and Deny rights, apply the Deny rights first, and apply Allow rights only if they don't contradict an earlier Deny right in the ACL. Our second choice is to click on the "Advanced" button at the bottom of the ACL window. This opens another window that gives us finer control over the access rights. If we click on the "Effective Permissions" tab in that window, we can ask Windows to determine the access rights granted to a particular user or group.

Building Effective ACLs

In general, Deny by Default yields the best approach to building ACLs. We start with no rules granting access to anyone. We add access rights required by the owner and the system, then we add access rights required by others who use the files. We won't need to use Deny entries if we haven't granted access rights we must later rescind.

Occasionally, we might encounter a case where it's more practical to use a Deny entry than to build the ACL using Deny by Default. For example, a college may have a user group for all students called, of course, "Students." As soon as people register, they are added to the group. However, there are certain items that incoming freshmen aren't allowed to use. We can implement this with Deny by Default if we create a separate group containing "Students Minus Freshmen." However, it is easier to create a separate group named "Freshmen," and create a Deny entry that applies just to Freshmen. It should be easier to move students in and out of the "Freshmen" group than to maintain a separate "Students Minus Freshmen" group.

4.4.2 Default File Protection

When we create a file, we rarely stop and think about its access rights. We assume the file will receive appropriate rights automatically. In practice, we often rely on the file's directory to protect the file for us.

In Unix-based systems, new files are assigned a default set of file protection flags. These flags usually grant the owner full access and provide read-only access to everyone else. If the file is in a private folder, like "My Documents," the folder itself is unreadable by others. Even if users are allowed to read the file, they can't actually reach it if they can't retrieve it from its folder.

Inherited Rights

Systems that support ACLs, like Apple's OS-X, often support an *inheritance* mechanism for assigning ACLs to new files. We assign the ACL we want to a particular folder. When we create new files in that folder, the files receive the inherited ACLs.

While this makes ACLs a bit more practical, there are still shortcomings. In OS-X, for example, there is no way to assign the inherited ACLs except through typed commands. The mechanism rarely is used in practice. Another problem is that the systems often use *static inheritance*. If we make any changes to the inherited ACL, we will need to manually propagate the changed ACL to all files in the folder. Mac OS-X and other Unix-based systems often provide tools to simplify the problem of changing access rights on a set of files. For example, OS-X provides a menu item "Apply to enclosed items" that applies a folder's access rights to all files and folders it contains.

Dynamic ACLs

Microsoft Windows 2000 introduced *dynamic ACLs* that inherit access rights from the enclosing folder. In other words, the files themselves don't really keep their own ACLs. Instead, they use the "parent" ACL, which is retrieved from their folder. When we create a new file, it simply inherits access rights from the folder in which we save the file.

This inheritance is *dynamic* because we can change permissions on all files in a folder just by changing permissions on the folder itself. As long as the files inside the folder inherit their ACL from the folder, we change all ACLs when we change the folder's ACL.

Thus, Bob and Tina can easily protect their survey files. First, they create a Survey Folder to hold the files. Next, they make sure that the folder does *not* inherit any permissions that let other users look in the folder, then they grant full access to the Survey group (Bob and Tina). After that, they simply have to save their survey files in the Survey Folder. The system automatically will grant them access to all the files and deny access to others.

To work with ACLs and inheritance, we need to click on the "Advanced" button in the file or folder's Security tab. Bob has created the "Survey Folder" on the root of the C: drive. Figure 4.15 shows the "Advanced" settings for the new folder.

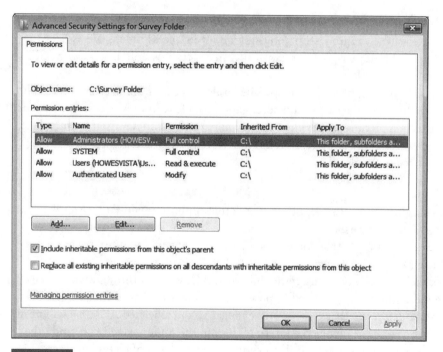

Figure 4.15

Advanced security settings for Windows ACLs.

The listing shows the default permissions established for the new folder. The right two columns describe the inheritance; the entire ACL is inherited from the C: drive root.

Note that "Users" have broad access rights to the Survey Folder. Bob's first task is to eliminate those rights. To do this, he must uncheck the first check box below the "Add" button, which says to "Include inheritable permissions from this object's parent." By unchecking that option, we eliminate the inheritance. When Bob clicks on that box, the system will ask him if the inherited rights should be copied or discarded. In practice, it may be best to copy them and then delete the unnecessary ones.

After the system copies the permissions, Bob deletes the rights for Users and Authenticated users. He leaves the rights for SYSTEM and Administrators; it isn't clear what system features will fail if we omit those. It's safest to leave system permissions in place unless we have a really compelling reason to remove them.

Finally, Bob adds an ACL entry for the Survey group, and gives it "Full control" of the files. This yields the ACL in Figure 4.16. New files or folders created in the Survey Folder will inherit this ACL. If Bob wants, he may add a Deny entry for Suitemates now or later. We saw this back in Figure 4.14. In either case, the new access rule will apply to all files and folders inside the Survey folder.

The access rights shown in a file's Security tab combine both the inherited rights and any rights we apply directly to that file. Inherited rights appear as rights with greyed-out

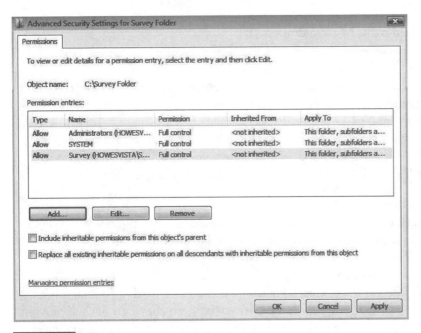

Figure 4.16

Windows ACL for Bob and Tina's survey folder.

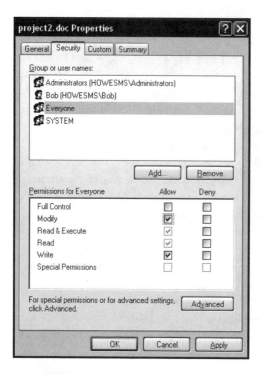

Figure 4.17

Adding to inherited rights in a Windows ACL.

boxes either checked or unchecked. If we decide to change the rights of a file, the locally assigned (not inherited) rights appear as solid boxes.

For example, in Figure 4.17 we see the access rights for "Everyone." The two greyed-out boxes show that Everyone has inherited "Read" and "Read & Execute" rights. We also have checked the "Modify" and "Write" boxes, granting those permissions to Everyone as well. Thus, Everyone can read, execute, and modify the file.

MOVING AND COPYING FILES

Dynamic inheritance obviously applies whenever we create a file; the new file inherits access rights from the enclosing folder. It also applies if we copy and/or paste a file; the destination folder establishes the access rights. To keep files protected, we must be aware of the access rights applied to the enclosing folder.

The rules are different if we *move* a file from one part of a hard drive to another. There is a subtle but important technical difference between copying a file and moving one. To move a file, we change its location in the directory hierarchy. We don't make a new copy of the file, we simply move it to a different folder. We can only move files *within* a directory or within a tree of enclosing directories. We always must copy a file if it resides on a different hard drive.

If we move a file under Microsoft Windows, the file (or folder, if we move a folder) retains its ACL, but "breaks" its inheritance relationship. The moved file or folder retains its original access rights, but those rights won't change when rights change above or around it. If we move a folder, the access rights for the files in the folder remain unchanged.

4.5 A Different Trojan Horse

> Bob has established separate user IDs on his tower computer. He has protected his homework files, including the survey file, with access controls to block unauthorized access. He has configured the BIOS so that the computer only boots from the built-in hard drive, so it always runs the operating system.
>
> One afternoon, he found a new game on his computer. One of his suitemates had added it to the "suitemates" folder. Bob liked the game. He first played it logged in as "suitemates" because that was where he found it. Then he played it a few times logged in as "bob."
>
> The next day, he found all of his secret files had been copied to the "suitemates" folder.

How did this happen? Bob established his access restrictions correctly. His computer followed the appropriate Chain of Control while it started up. Why did his information leak out anyway? It can be very hard to track down the cause of such leaks.

In this case, we will blame it on the computer game. One of Bob's suitemates had installed the game on his computer. Bob found the game and he played it regularly. At first he played it from the Suitemates login, but soon he figured out how to run it from his own login. When the program ran from Bob's login, it copied every file in his Documents folder to the Suitemates Documents folder.

In other words, the game contained malicious behavior that extracted secret information from Bob's files and revealed the information to the Suitemates. We call such a program a ***Trojan horse***, or simply a Trojan. The name is an analogy drawn from the story in Section 3.7.

Trojan horse software illustrates a common shortcoming of file-based access control. When a user runs some software, the software inherits the user's access rights. If the software wants to steal information from the user, then the user might not detect the theft.

A TROJAN HORSE PROGRAM

To understand how Bob's defenses failed, let us look at how Bob protected his files. Table 4.6 lists the access rights applied to Bob's files. Specifically, Bob granted *no access* to users other than himself. While we don't show group access permissions here, we can assume that they likewise don't grant any access rights to Suitemates. Thus, a user logged in as Suitemates can't read or write the actual secret file. At least, they can't read or write such files *directly*.

TABLE 4.6 Access rights applied to Bob's files		Effective Access	
Resources	Access Rights for "World" or "Other" Users	Bob's Processes	Suitemates' Processes
Bob's secret files	---	RW-	---
Suitemates' game file	R-X	R-X	RWX
Suitemates' copy of Bob's file	RW-	RW-	RW-

When Bob runs a program, the program starts a process. The process follows the instructions listed in the program, using the access rights belonging to Bob. If the program says, "Let's copy Bob's secret files to somewhere else," then the process follows those instructions. Bob's secret files still can't be read by Suitemates, but the process creates new copies of those files. Suitemates can read those new files.

Figure 4.18 shows how the Trojan game works. Within the figure, we divide up the resources into those on the left, belonging to Bob, and those on the right, belonging to Suitemates. The arrows and the "RWX" notations indicate the user access rights. Suitemates cannot access Bob's secret file directly because there is no arrow connecting it to the Suitemates' process.

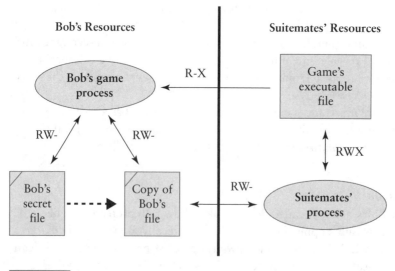

Figure 4.18

Trojan game copies one of Bob's secret files.

Whenever the game starts running, it looks to see whether it is running from Bob's login. If not, the game itself starts immediately. If Bob is running the game from his own login, however, the game activates its Trojan feature. The game looks for files in Bob's Documents folder and copies each one to the Documents folder belonging to Suitemates. Once the copying is finished, the game itself starts running. The Trojan feature may cause a slight delay in starting the game, but the delay won't be enough to arouse Bob's suspicions.

When we run a program, we implicitly trust the program's author to write a program that does us no real damage. We assume that the author isn't going to insert malicious features like the one that copies Bob's files. This implicit trust also extends to *anyone* who has the right to modify a program we run. When Bob runs the game, he is trusting his suitemates not to insert malicious features into that game. Socially, Bob's assumption might be reasonable; people avoid living with others they can't really trust.

TRANSITIVE TRUST: A BASIC PRINCIPLE

We use the term *Transitive Trust* to describe this implicit spreading of trust. If we trust a particular entity to protect our data, then we implicitly trust anyone that the entity trusts. In this case, the survey participants trust Tina and Bob to keep survey data secret. Bob trusts his computer. If we apply Transitive Trust, we see that all implicitly trust Bob's computer's defenses. Bob also implicitly trusts his suitemates with the secret data when Bob runs the game owned by Suitemates.

In Bob's story, he found the copied files in the Suitemates' Documents folder. Normally on Windows, only the owner of a Documents folder has access rights to read or change its contents. To prepare for the Trojan, however, the attacker had to make the Suitemates Documents folder writable by Bob. The copied files still were owned by Bob, they just didn't reside in one of his folders. On Windows, a new file inherits access rights from its folder. If the folder's access control list explicitly grants access to Suitemates, then new files created in the folder (by a Trojan or any other program) also will be accessible by Suitemates.

4.6 Phase Five: Monitoring the System

In our six-phase security process, we addressed phases one through four in previous chapters. Here we discuss Phase Five in which we monitor the system for correct and secure operation. There are many ways to monitor the system. The simplest approach is to set up alerts or alarms that occur when something really unusual happens.

For example, companies that use online banking often configure the software to send warning messages to cell phones when really large transactions take place. Dozens of public, nonprofit, and private enterprises have had their bank accounts looted by cyberthieves. This type of alert reports *all* large transactions, making it harder for thieves to attack without detection.

Most computing systems also provide another way to monitor the system, called *event logging*. A typical computer is a proverbial "black box": the outside gives few clues of what goes on inside. As computers have evolved, they have done more and more while displaying less and less. Early computers contained vast arrays of blinking lights, each connected to an internal signal or data item. While these lights provided a great deal of raw data about the computer's behavior, they could only display status and errors at the hardware level.

Inside a running program, the computer produces countless intermediate results we never see. The final result is our focus. We ignore everything else the computer does, except for the answers we need. The computer forgets everything else, too, unless we make it keep records.

Forgetfulness poses a security problem. If an attack occurs, we want to know everything we can about the process that performed the attack. When did it start? Who started it? What was it supposed to be doing? How did it start?

We can't answer those questions unless the computer keeps records of what it does. We store those records in a set of files called the event log or the *audit trail*. While file-based access controls provide *preventative* controls that block security violations, event logging provides *detective* controls that help us detect security violations we weren't able to block. Figure 4.19 displays an event log from Microsoft Windows.

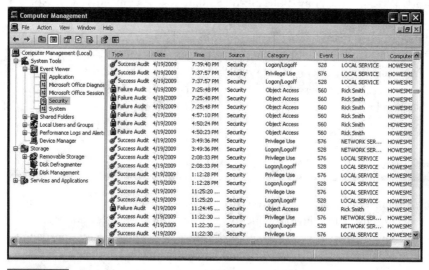

Windows security event log.

CATCHING AN INTRUDER

In an ideal world, the security system notifies us immediately when an intruder appears. We receive an alert on a cell phone or a box pops up on the computer display, announcing the problem.

Computers can't always provide such clear-cut warnings. Detection is harder when the intruder masquerades as someone else. If the intruder behaves more or less like the legitimate user, we'll only detect the intrusion by looking at larger patterns of behavior. We need to analyze the event log.

> **An Incident:** In 1986, the astronomy department of the University of California, Berkeley, owned a Unix timesharing system. Computers were expensive back then, and they paid for the machine by charging research projects $300 an hour to use it. The Unix system had a built-in mechanism that kept a log of system events. The department expanded the mechanism so that they could calculate the amount of time spent by each project and send monthly bills.
>
> The system seemed to work flawlessly until the lab manager noticed a 75-cent difference between the amount of computing time used and the amount billed. He told his new lab assistant, Clifford Stoll, to find out why. Being an astronomer by temperament, Stoll appreciated that the 75-cent difference, though small, did not make sense. It indicated a real problem with the system or its accounting. Stoll's research uncovered an intruder who was nicknamed "the Wily Hacker." Stoll ultimately tracked him across the 1980s Internet to his home in Germany.
>
> Stoll's investigation led him to other computer centers visited by the Wily Hacker, and Stoll's story took most sites by surprise. Few systems actually kept event logs of any kind, and fewer still actually bothered to look at the logs. This was true even of government and military systems the intruder visited.

Typically, we can only detect intruders if they leave evidence of their visit. For example, we might find files created while the nominal owner was out of town and out of touch. If intruders clean up after themselves, we might have no records at all. Logging gives us a separate record of what happens on our computer so that we can retrace such incidents.

4.6.1 Logging Events

An event log is no more—or less—than a data file. Whenever a significant event takes place, the system writes a brief description of that event into the log. In practice, most systems keep several separate event logs. Each operating system takes its own approach to logging, but many keep separate logs for "system" events and "security" events.

- The system log records the start-up and shutdown of the system itself and of major processes. It also may record the opening and closing of important files or other major system resources.
- The security log records all major access control requests, like logins, and all access control denials, like password failures or attempts to read protected files.

Most systems also have one or more additional logs for collecting events from application programs. These logs are very important for many organizations, because the applications perform business tasks. In a bank, for example, the software that processes account deposits and withdrawals keeps a log of all such transactions. Later, an auditing program compares account balances against the transaction log to verify correctness.

A LOG ENTRY

When something important (an *event*) takes place inside a program, the program creates a *log entry*. The program then passes the log entry to the appropriate event log. A typical log entry contains the following:

- Time and date of the event
- Source of the event—the process or system component that detected it
- User identity—a user associated with the event
- Type of event—what happened, classified into a category of events
- Event details—these vary with the type of event and the details of the occurrence

Figure 4.19 shows the Event Viewer used by Windows to display log entries. The left pane of the window gives a choice of several management displays; under Event Viewer it offers to display any of five different event logs. The figure shows the Security log, which reports access control attempts that have either succeeded or failed, yielding either a "Success Audit" or "Failure Audit" respectively.

Many organizations use these logs when they perform an ***information systems audit***. This is a formal review of the system's integrity and of the data it maintains regarding the organization's business. These audits often occur when auditing a firm's financial condition. Auditors or security experts may perform more specific security audits, which we will see in Section 13.2.5. If the system logs keep a record of all significant events, then they provide an "audit trail" by which an investigator can reconstruct what took place.

THE EVENT LOGGING MECHANISM

Figure 4.20 shows the major elements of the event logging mechanism. There are four steps in logging an event.

1. A program detects a significant event. The program constructs a log entry to describe the event, and places it in an input buffer to pass to the logging process. The program then tells the logging process that a new event has occurred.
2. The logging process retrieves the event from the buffer. If so configured, the logger may discard less-important events and only keep the more important ones.
3. The logging process writes the events to the log file. Systems may keep separate log files for different purposes. Windows, for example, keeps five separate logs.

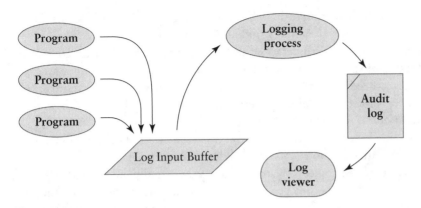

Event logging in the operating system.

4. System administrators use a log viewer to monitor the logs and discover interesting events or trends. Some systems have automated log monitors. Some administrators study the logs themselves.

The first challenge in event logging is to control the amount of information collected. Some programmers like to treat everything that happens as a significant event, and this yields vast numbers of events. As the logs grow larger, it becomes harder to see really important events. Most systems place a limit on the log files' size, because they can devour the free space on a hard drive.

In practice, we include or exclude events from the log at every point in the logging process. Programmers often include "debug" settings in their programs that increase or decrease the amount of logging performed. If the program runs well, we tell it to ignore more common events. If the program has problems, we tell it to report its behavior in greater detail.

The logger itself may also discard less-important events. Some systems include a "priority" field in each log entry, and an administrator can set the logger to discard lower priority events. On other systems, the administrator can configure the logger to keep or discard events based on the event type.

DETECTING ATTACKS BY REVIEWING THE LOGS

It isn't enough to just collect log entries, we also need to detect and respond to significant occurrences. When Berkeley was being visited by the Wily Hacker, they relied on Unix event logs to make researchers pay for their fair share of computing costs. They would not have looked at their logs and detected the Hacker's activities otherwise.

The Berkeley event logs did not contain an event record saying "The Wily Hacker was here" nor did the logger pop up a message saying "Intruder Alert!" when the Wily Hacker came to visit. Cliff Stoll simply knew there was a 75-cent anomaly in the logging and accounting records. It took a great deal of analysis to suggest the existence of the intruder, and more investigation to actually find and catch him.

Following the exposure of the Wily Hacker and the Morris worm, the U.S. government dispatched teams of experts to assess the security of government computer systems. The experts took a *red team* approach: They tested security by trying to break into the systems. They succeeded in almost every case. Even worse, they were almost never detected, no matter how obvious they were.

Two conditions contributed to the red teams' successes. First, most computer systems did not monitor or pay attention to events that might indicate an attack. While some military systems were required to keep event logs, few sites actually did so, and fewer still paid any attention to the data they collected. The second condition reflected the poor quality of computers at that time; computer behavior was very erratic. If something unusual took place, operators naturally blamed it on software failures.

Responsible system administrators no longer ignore logs. Most have tools that automatically check logs for unexpected patterns and potential problems. A few have the knowledge and insight to analyze the logs themselves. To do this, the administrator must have a good understanding of how the system works and what the different log events mean, and must be familiar with "normal" event patterns. It takes practice to effectively review event logs.

A good way to start is to look at a log and try to find evidence of known activities. For example, the Windows log identifies successful and failed login attempts. If there have been several recent login failures, the log should reflect them. If there was trouble while trying to install new software, the log should reflect the errors.

4.6.2 External Security Requirements

Early mainframe computers were staffed with operators. Although the computers often were festooned with hundreds of lights and switches, most operators relied on its console display to track the computer's behavior. The console contained a printer and its printout was called the console log. Every major event that occurred inside the computer was reported on the log. This helped the operators keep the computer running efficiently. The log also reported security relevant events, like login failures on a time-sharing system.

As computers shrank in size and cost, vendors eliminated the console and its log. This made the computers cheaper and easier to operate, but it also eliminated a lot of information about what the system was doing. When the U.S. DOD published its *Orange Book* of computer security requirements in 1983, it mandated that operating systems keep a log of security relevant events. This requirement was retained when Common Criteria evaluations replaced the *Orange Book* in the late 1990s.

This is one example of how external rules, standards, or laws specify computer security requirements. These rules often set requirements for difficult or distasteful tasks that provide important security benefits. Logging is a prime example.

LAWS, REGULATIONS, AND INDUSTRY RULES

Here is a list of recent U.S. laws, regulations, and industry rules that establish security requirements for computer systems. In general, the rules require organizations to monitor their computer systems for intrusions or other misuse, and to provide evidence that they do so.

- SOX (Sarbanes-Oxley Act), enacted by Congress in 2002, establishes requirements for financial and accounting practices.
- HIPAA (Health Insurance Portability and Accountability Act), passed in 1996, establishes security standards for certain types of health information. Rules governing HIPAA implementation call for system logging.
- GLBA (Gramm-Leach-Bliley Act), passed in 1999, requires financial institutions to protect customer information against security threats.
- FISMA (Federal Information Security Management Act), passed in 2002, requires U.S. government agencies to implement agency-wide information security programs. Government recommendations, described in NIST Special Publication SP 800-53, includes guidance on collecting and handling event logs.
- PCI DSS (Payment Card Industry Data Security Standard), an industry standard followed by everyone who issues and processes credit and debit cards. One requirement is that organizations track all accesses to network resources and cardholder data.
- ISO 27000 is a family of international standards for information security based on continuous process improvement. The standards call for continuous security monitoring both to detect security problems and to assess the effectiveness of the security processes themselves. For more information, see Section 13.2.1.

Some, but not all, of these specifically require logging and log monitoring. In practice, effective logging can show that the organization complies with more general security rules. Standards for financial accounting also may persuade an organization to keep logs, and the logs may play an important role in subsequent financial audits.

Many organizations set up their logs to meet auditing requirements. For example, the board of trustees of Bob's school require an annual audit of the school's financial status by an independent accounting firm. The firm, in turn, must audit the computers used by the school to process financial data. The audit process examines the school's security measures and uses the logs to verify that the measures have been working.

Financial audits aren't the only reason why the school keeps logs. Because the school accepts credit card transactions, the computers that handle those transactions are subject to PCI DSS requirements, and these mandate event logging. The school clinic is bound by HIPAA regulations, which also require security event logging.

EXTERNAL REQUIREMENTS AND THE SECURITY PROCESS

In our six-phase security process, we implement security measures based on earlier phases: policy, risk assessment, and ultimately on the assets we protect. When external requirements oblige us to incorporate particular security measures, we need to insert them into the process. This isn't always an easy task. What if our assessment doesn't yield any risks that these requirements address?

For example, enterprise-grade Internet firewalls (described in Section 15.4) often earn a Common Criteria certification based on a "protection profile." The profile places many requirements on the firewall product. Some of these requirements might not directly address threats the vendor has identified. This may be an error on the vendor's part or the Common Criteria evaluation may pose requirements that this particular product doesn't really need. In either case, the vendor must choose between saving money on the product implementation or earning Common Criteria certification.

To incorporate these additional requirements, we take one of three approaches:

1. Treat external requirements as a separate input to the policy.
2. Treat possible legal or contractual problems as risks.
3. Treat certifications as assets.

We do *not* want to simply add the external requirements to our policy. While this is the easiest way to do the planning and design, it may yield the most risk. For example, the external requirement may call for "strong authentication," and the implementation may simply choose a product that a vendor claims will provide "strong authentication." This solution may be more expensive than comparably strong alternatives. Moreover, the "strong authentication" may defend against the wrong types of attacks.

The first approach is also the simplest from a practical standpoint: We add to our policy by interpreting these external requirements. This allows us to integrate the external requirements with our strategy to address the threats. This works in situations where we develop a policy based on someone else's risk assessment.

The second approach acknowledges that we face risks if we ignore the external requirements. At some point, every organization makes an explicit or implicit assessment of the risks and benefits of complying with external rules. Most organizations make decisions on standards and compliance through a separate decision-making process. A few may perform a single assessment that incorporates both security risks with risks of noncompliance.

In the third approach, certifications of products and processes or regulatory compliance may be treated as assets themselves. This is the best approach when dealing with ISO certifications, since detailed requirements are often tailored to the organization. For example, the organization may be required to implement processes to track and repair flaws found in their systems, but the details of detecting and tracking flaws will be customized to the organization.

4.7 Resources

IMPORTANT TERMS INTRODUCED

administrative group	file permission flags	red team
audit trail	group rights	setuid
Common Criteria	information systems audit	Transitive Trust
event	log entry	user group
event logging	*Orange Book*	user rights
explicit denial	other rights	

ACRONYMS INTRODUCED

ACL—Access control list

DEC—Digital Equipment Corporation

DOD—Department of Defense

FISMA—Federal Information Security Management Act

GLBA—Gramm-Leach-Bliley Act

HIPAA—Health Insurance Portability and Accountability Act

IEEE—Institute of Electrical and Electronics Engineers

Multics—Multiplexed Information and Computing Service

NFSV4—Network File Service, version 4

NIST SP—NIST Special Publication

OpenVMS—Open Virtual Memory System

PCI DSS—Payment Card Industry Data Security Standard

POSIX—Portable Operating System Interface

SOX—Sarbanes-Oxley Act

TCSEC—Trusted Computer System Evaluation Criteria

UAC—User account control

4.7.1 Review Questions

R1. Summarize how each of the three tailored file security policies change the access rights of files under the two default security policies.

R2. Describe the permission levels provided in file sharing under a modern "home edition" of Windows.

R3. Explain how Windows home edition ACLs can solve Bob and Tina's security problem.

R4. Explain how the "user group" feature of Unix can solve Bob and Tina's security policy problem.

R5. Explain why it is safer for administrators to use two different accounts when working with a computer. Explain the difference between the two accounts.

R6. Describe the behavior of "sudo" on Unix. When is "sudo" used?

R7.   Describe the behavior of the padlock icon on Apple's OS-X. When is the padlock used?

R8.   Describe the behavior of user account control (UAC) on modern versions of Microsoft Windows. In what circumstances does a UAC pop-up appear?

R9.   Summarize the behavior of Unix file permission flags. Identify the sets of users that such permissions can control and what access rights are enforced for each set.

R10. Explain how Unix-like systems decide which of its three sets of access rights to apply when a particular user's process opens a file.

R11. List the columns that we need to provide when describing security controls implemented with Unix-style permission flags.

R12. Why can't we represent the file permissions shown in Figure 4.9 using Unix-style permission flags?

R13. Describe the basic features of an access control list.

R14. Compare the access rights established in Figure 4.1 with those established in Figure 4.10.

R15. Explain how access restrictions on a folder or directory can block a user's access to a file, even if the file itself may be readable by that user.

R16. List some differences between Windows ACLs and POSIX ACLs.

R17. If we create a Windows ACL in which we "Deny" all permissions to Suitemates, but we "Grant" all permissions to everyone, does Suitemates have any access to the file?

R18. When we create a file, explain how that file acquires its initial ACL under Windows.

R19. If we change the ACL for a folder under Windows, what typically happens to the ACLs for the files within that folder?

R20. Why is a program containing a Trojan considered malicious?

R21. Explain how a Trojan program can make secret data belonging to one user visible to another user.

R22. Give an example of Transitive Trust. Explain who trusts whom and why.

R23. Describe the typical contents of an entry in an event log.

R24. Describe the typical steps taken to log an event.

R25. Summarize some laws, regulations, and industry standards that lead systems to maintain event logs.

R26. Explain three ways to incorporate external security requirements into the six-phase security process.

4.7.2 Exercises

E1.   This may be most appropriate as an in-class exercise. Form teams of three or more class members with user names, for example, A, B, C, and D. Find shared hard drive space that is accessible by all team members. Then do the following:

- Team members should individually create folders that are accessible to no other team members through Deny by Default. Remove inherited access rights if needed to achieve this.

- Each team member should create a single word-processing file and store it in the new folder. The name of the file should be their user name: A creates "A.doc," B creates "B.doc," and so on. Make these files readable by the "World."

- A should add read/search access rights to its folder for B, B should add rights for C, and C for D, and so on. Be sure that *no other* access rights are granted to team members for accessing the individual folders.

- Without changing access rights or moving the word-processing files *outside* of these original folders, each student should copy other team members' files into their own folder. Repeat this until each student has a copy of all team members' files.

Describe how this took place.

Create two separate user identities on your system. Both should be regular, nonadministrative users. (You may use existing regular user identities for this if you want.) Log in as one of the users (we'll call it "user 1") and do the following:

- Create a folder on the hard drive. Put it in a place that all users can reach.

- Set access rights for this folder to allow "execute" or "search" access by the second user ("user 2") but grant "no read" access.

- Create one or two word-processing files inside that computer.

Log in as user 2 and answer the following questions about attempts to access the files.

E2.   Try to display the new folder. What happens?

E3.   Open the word-processing program. Tell it to open one of User 1's new files. Instead of browsing through folders to find the file, start from the root of the hard drive and type in the file's full path name. Describe what happens.

E4.   Log in as user 1 and remove the "search" or "execute" right from the folder. Log back in as user 2 and again open the word-processing program. Tell the word processor to open the file. Starting from the root of the hard drive and type in the file's full path name. What happens?

In Section 3.8.2, a set of problems examine a scenario in which Riko is writing a program for Bob. The program is to be protected according to the security policy given in Table 3.8. Answer the following questions based on that scenario.

E5.   Use Unix permission flags to provide security controls for Riko's file. Make the list of permissions in the format of Table 4.3.

E6.   Make a list of the advantages in solving this problem with Unix permission flags versus using Windows "professional" ACLs. Which would you prefer? Why?

E7.   Make a list of the advantages in solving this problem with Windows professional ACLs versus using Windows home edition ACLs. Which would you prefer? Why?

E8.   Apply Transitive Trust to a computer you use. Identify organizations that you implicitly trust, particularly the hardware and software vendors that provide the programs you run on your computer. Also note any users who can modify programs you would typically use, including administrative users.

E9.   (Windows Professional only.) Following the example described in Figures 4.15 and 4.16, create a Survey folder that shares files between two users. Capture and save or print out each window that pops up as you set up the correct access situation. Explain each step you take and what happens. After setting up the appropriate ACL on the folder, create a file in the folder. Use the "Advanced" display (as in Figure 4.15) to show the ACL inherited by the newly created file.

E10.   Locate the event log on your own computer. Examine the log and locate events caused by a recent action of yours (logging in, for example). Print out that part of the log, highlight the entries caused by your behavior. Explain why you believe the log entry reflects your own action.

STORING FILES

ABOUT THIS CHAPTER

In this chapter, we begin by addressing the aftermath of a security incident and follow this to the problem of file storage. Specifically, we examine the following:

- Phase six of the security process: recovering from an attack
- Fundamentals of evidence collection and preservation
- Basics of hard drives and other large-capacity devices
- Hard drive formatting
- File storage on hard drives, flash drives, and other devices
- Features of major file systems used in operating systems and for removable storage

5.1 Phase Six: Recovery

The sixth and last phase of our security process is to *Recover from an Attack*. Consider the following:

Bob and Tina occasionally use a USB drive to copy their confidential survey data file between their computers. Each time they move the file, they delete it and "Empty Trash" to ensure that it was deleted. They occasionally left the USB stick unattended in the common room. Neither Bob nor Tina thought their data was at risk because they had deleted the file.

One afternoon, an unknown person printed out a copy of the survey file and left it in the suite as a prank.

After discussing the incident, Bob and Tina concluded that someone used an *undelete* utility to retrieve the deleted survey file from the unattended USB stick.

When we write information to a file, the file system copies that information onto blocks of storage on our hard drive or flash drive. The system then saves information about the blocks' locations in the file's folder.

When we delete a file, most operating systems move it to a special folder called "trash" or "recycle." If we want to recover the file, we simply move it back to a permanent folder. After emptying the trash, the file system deletes the file from the folder, and then frees its data blocks to be reused the next time we write to the drive. Once we write new data over the old file's data blocks, it becomes almost impossible to recover the file.

However, drives often have a lot of free space. Recently freed blocks might not be reused for hours or even weeks. An ***undelete*** program tries to reconstruct a file by locating the freed data blocks before they are reused. This act also is called ***file scavenging***. Even though Bob and Tina "emptied the trash" each time they deleted the file, they didn't really remove the information from the hard drive.

Incidents and Damage

Although security problems might feel like "attacks" personally, many don't actually cause damage. Without a loss, some might argue that there really hasn't been an "attack," per se. For that reason, it's often better to refer to these events as ***incidents***, not attacks. For example, a "bicycle incident" might unhook a bicycle lock from a fence. The bicycle itself isn't damaged nor is the lock, but now it's vulnerable to theft. We can still ride, but we now have a security problem.

Bob and Tina's incident hasn't damaged them personally, and it probably won't yield any damage if the file doesn't spread further. If it does, then privacy breaches might affect the surveyed students, and the instructor might get very angry at Bob and Tina.

Bob and Tina might argue that they made a reasonable effort at protecting the data. They can describe their procedure. If they use ***digital forensics*** to analyze the USB drive, they might be able to show that their theory is plausible. The next section discusses digital forensics.

Compromised Systems

Just as a bicycle incident may render a bike vulnerable without damaging it, an incident might render Bob's computer more vulnerable to attack. For example, a suitemate might disable access permissions on system files. Bob's computer now has been *compromised*. In Victorian times, people spoke of "compromising one's reputation." This indicated that an incident had rendered the reputation suspect, even without proof of misbehavior. The "compromise" indicates that the computer is no longer trustworthy, because it *may* have been subverted.

We recover from attacks, incidents, and compromises, by taking steps to recover. The recovery process often is called ***remediation***.

Although the recovery phase may be the "last" phase of the security process, it doesn't mark its end. Each phase provides input to the next phase and suggests changes to earlier phases. The final phase almost always provides some lesson for improving earlier phases.

5.1.1 The Aftermath of an Incident

Different incidents demand different forms of recovery. The aftermath may include one or more of the following tasks:

- Identify shortcomings in our risk assessment, policy statement, or implementation in order to reduce the impact of future incidents.

- Repair any problems caused by the attack. If a Trojan program infests your computer, the repair includes removal of the Trojan.
- If the incident is caused by someone's malicious act and we can hold that person accountable, then we need to collect evidence that clearly ties the person to the incident.
- If someone is using our computer to violate laws, then we need to preserve the evidence so that a prosecutor may use it as evidence in a trial.

DIGITAL FORENSICS

We apply digital forensics when we need to collect evidence from computers and other digital storage devices. Forensic techniques recover, preserve, and analyze information from a computer system to show what its users were doing.

When we take a serious action, like firing an employee or pursuing legal measures against an attacker, we must take special care in collecting evidence. If the evidence must support legal action, then it must be admissible in court.

Questions of gathering evidence are fundamental to forensics:

- What data should we try to collect *before* a security incident that we can use as evidence after one occurs?
- What data are we allowed to collect and use as evidence from an individual's computer?
- What data can we retrieve from persistent computer memories, like hard drives and USB flash drives?

The answers depend heavily on the legal system that applies to the computers, their owners, and the perpetrators of the attack.

FAULT AND DUE DILIGENCE

If harm comes from an incident, there is often a legal or moral obligation to hold someone responsible. The attacker obviously should be held responsible and, if appropriate, should repair the damage or provide restitution. However, if the attack took advantage of carelessness, then the careless parties also may be responsible. This is an established legal concept in many communities.

If someone retrieved their files regardless of the protections they used, are Bob and Tina somehow responsible? The question revolves around whether they exercised *due diligence*; in other words, they must have taken reasonable steps to protect the files. If they could have used stronger measures and failed to, then perhaps they bear responsibility for the failure. If, on the other hand, they used the customary security measures and the community accepts those measures as adequate, then they showed due diligence. The instructor could justifiably hold them responsible if they failed to use the same security measures as others.

5.1.2 Legal Disputes

A security incident may be part of a legal dispute. If it is part of a legal dispute, then it is subject to the local legal system. If the dispute is being resolved in the United States or under a similar legal system, then we may need evidence to show what happened and, ideally, identify the people responsible.

When we present the matter to an official, whether a police officer, prosecutor, or judge, our evidence must meet local legal requirements. First, the evidence must be relevant and convincing. Second, those who review the evidence must be confident that it actually illustrates the incident under investigation. The evidence must be unchanged since the incident occurred.

Finally, we may only use information that we have legally obtained. The specific requirements vary under different legal theories and traditions. Here, we will focus on U.S. legal requirements. However, even the U.S. rules are subject to change, because this is a new area of law.

LEGAL SYSTEMS

Worldwide, legal experts classify legal systems into three categories:

1. Civil law—based on legislative enactments. Roman and Napoleonic laws are examples of this.
2. Common law—based on judicial decisions. English Common Law and the U.S. legal system follow this tradition.
3. Religious law—based on religious systems or documents. Jewish, Islamic, and Christian canon law systems are examples of this.

In practice, legal systems often reflect a blend of these systems. Traditionally, people speak of the U.S. and English legal systems as arising from common law, but today both are heavily influenced by new laws passed by legislatures.

RESOLVING A LEGAL DISPUTE

Not all incidents rise to the level of legal dispute. In the United States and in countries with similar systems, problems arising from an incident may be resolved in several ways:

- *Private action*, in which one party acts against another, based on a shared relationship. For example, an employer might discipline an employee, or a school might discipline a student, based on informal evidence that might not be admissible in court.
- *Mediation*, in which the parties rely on a third party, a mediator, to help negotiate a settlement. The mediator is not bound by particular rules of evidence and may consider evidence that is not admissible by a court.

- *Civil complaint*, in which one party files a lawsuit against another. Such matters still may be resolved privately, possibly through negotiation. If the parties go to court, then legal requirements for digital evidence must be followed precisely.
- *Criminal complaint*, in which a person is charged with breaking particular laws. The complaint sets out the facts of the matter and presents probable cause for accusing a particular person for the crime. A criminal complaint may be made by the police, a district attorney, or any interested party. If there is no plea bargain, the trial goes to court, at which point the digital evidence must fulfill all legal requirements.

Although a dispute may begin as a private action, it could escalate to mediation or to a civil case. In some cases, the incident could become a criminal complaint. The safest strategy, if legal action seems likely, is to collect evidence in a manner that preserves its admissibility in a civil or criminal court action.

A typical forensics investigator does not focus on computer or information evidence alone. The investigator will look for all kinds of evidence related to the incident under investigation: related equipment, papers, articles of clothing, latent fingerprints, and DNA, that may associate suspects with the incident. A typical investigator will follow rules outlined later to collect and secure computer data for later analysis. Investigators do not usually try to perform detailed investigations on site. Such an investigation poses the real risk of disturbing the evidence and making it impossible to distinguish between the suspect's actions and the investigator's actions.

5.2 Digital Evidence

We must collect evidence before we can use it in any dispute. If we want to use this evidence in a legal proceeding, the evidence must be *admissible*; in other words, it must meet the legal rules and standards for evidence.

We may collect evidence through surveillance or seizure. In surveillance, we watch the behavior of the threat and keep a log of activities. In seizure, we take possession of equipment involved in the dispute. The requirements for surveillance and seizure vary according to whether we act as members of law enforcement or as a private party involved in the incident.

The Fourth Amendment

Under U.S. law, surveillance and seizure are restricted by the Fourth Amendment of the Bill of Rights:

> The right of the people to be secure in their persons, houses, papers, and effects, against unreasonable searches and seizures, shall not be violated, and no Warrants shall issue, but upon probable cause, supported by Oath or affirmation, and particularly describing the place to be searched, and the persons or things to be seized.

The Fourth Amendment is, in turn, based on English common law, which treats a person's home as a "castle" intended to ensure personal safety and, if desired, seclusion. Government agents, including police officers, may intrude on one's home, but only after presenting a justifiable reason to a different official, such as a justice of the peace.

Legal Concepts

These legal principles have evolved over the centuries and even over recent decades. They promise to change further as they are applied to electronic devices. While the specific rules may change as new cases are tried, the rules will probably preserve certain concepts:

- Who performs the search. There are different rules for private citizens, for police officers, and for others performing an investigation on behalf of the government.
- Private searches. Private individuals may perform searches without warrants on equipment in their possession. Evidence they find may be admissible in court. There are some restrictions when someone else owns or routinely uses the equipment.
- Reasonable expectation of privacy. We can't arbitrarily search areas where the users expect their privacy to be protected. For example, neither police nor employers can arbitrarily wiretap telephone calls.
- Consent to search. We can eliminate the expectation of privacy in some cases, especially in the workplace. For example, we don't expect privacy when we call a service number and hear: "This call may be monitored for quality assurance purposes." Likewise, a computer's owner can display a warning that computer use may be monitored and recorded.
- Business records. If we collect data in activity logs as a routine part of doing business, then those records often are admissible in court. If we set up special logs to track an intruder, those are not business records and are not necessarily admissible as evidence.

The legal issues can be quite subtle. If we need to collect information for use in court, we must consult an expert first. Depending on the laws and recent court decisions, we may need a warrant, a court order, or a subpoena to collect information—or we might not need any court document at all, especially if we are private individuals investigating our own equipment.

5.2.1 Collecting Legal Evidence

In a purely private matter, we might be able to log in to the attacked computer, extract information from it, and present our discoveries to the attacker. This might be enough to resolve the matter. If, on the other hand, the matter goes to court, our "evidence" might not stand up. If the defendant's attorney can cast doubt on the accuracy or integrity of our evidence, a jury might not believe it even if we're allowed to present it at a trial.

To serve as evidence, we need to show that the attacked computer reflects the actions of the attacker. Whenever we use a computer, our actions make changes to it. If we use the attacked computer itself to investigate the attack, we can't always distinguish between the results of the attack and the results of the investigation. The attacker's attorney might argue that the actions of our investigation produced the evidence. It may be hard to refute that argument.

COLLECTING EVIDENCE AT THE SCENE

The digital forensic investigation takes place separately from collecting the evidence. We start by collecting the evidence and ensuring its integrity. The actual analysis is a separate step.

Let us look at the process from the point of view of the investigator who must collect evidence for a civil or criminal court case. The investigator's job is to identify the relevant evidence, collect it, and ensure its integrity. The analysis of the digital evidence must take place in a separate step under controlled conditions.

The investigator follows these steps in a single-computer environment:

- Secure the scene and all relevant digital equipment.
- Document the scene.
- Collect digital evidence.

Here is a closer look at the first two steps. The next section examines the third step.

Securing the Scene

Once we have decided we must collect evidence, we first secure the area. We must remove everyone from the scene except the people responsible for collecting the evidence. The regular occupants and residents should leave and allow the investigators to do their work.

Digital evidence is very, very sensitive to being disturbed. Therefore, we don't want anyone tampering with digital devices in the scene. Refuse all assistance with identifying or collecting digital devices.

It is particularly important to leave digital devices turned off if they already are turned off. Every time we turn on a digital device, changes may take place. We need to preserve the device so that it is exactly as it was found at the scene.

If a computer is turned on and displays a destructive process in progress, like a "Format" or "Delete" command, then you may want to unplug the computer immediately. If, however, the computer's display contains relevant evidence, you may need to photograph the display before unplugging. This is a trade-off. In some cases, it's possible to retrieve deleted files, while it's rarely possible to retrieve the display contents after the computer is turned off.

Documenting the Scene

When we document the scene of the incident, we collect information about what is there, where things are, and what condition they are in. We start by describing the geographical location of the scene; what building, floor, room, and so on. We catalog everything in the scene that's relevant: where it is, what it is, and its condition. This becomes our *evidence log*.

Photography also plays an essential role in documenting the scene. We photograph items and their relative locations. We take special care to photograph any device displays or other conditions that may disappear when we unplug things and collect them for later analysis.

When documenting digital devices, we identify what they are, what identifying marks they have, any serial numbers, and whether they are powered on or not. Photographs should clearly show the contents of any displays or screens.

As a general rule, do not move disk devices that are powered on. Some hard disk drives are sensitive to motion and may fail if we move them while running. We may need to wait and collect serial numbers later in the process, if they are not visible without closer inspection.

5.2.2 Digital Evidence Procedures

Digital items to be collected will vary with the incident, but could include:

- Computers and laptops
- USB drives and other flash memory
- Other portable or removable hard drives
- Cell phones and personal digital assistants
- GPS units

Before we collect a digital device, we need to decide if it is turned on or not. This is, of course, tricky. The main display may be blank or turned off itself while the device is still on. Each device usually poses one of these alternatives:

- *Device might be turned on but its display is blank.* We need to be sure the display power is on and then *carefully* disable any screen power savers, documenting, and photographing the display's contents at each step, then proceed as if it is turned on.
- *Device is obviously turned on.* We again carefully move the mouse to disable any screen saver, and we document and photograph any changes in the display. In most cases, we then simply unplug the computer (and remove a laptop's battery). It takes special training to collect admissible data from a running computer, then proceed as if it is turned off.
- *Device is obviously turned off.* When the device is off, we document all connections and peripherals, then we seal it in an evidence bag and ensure it is on our inventory.

As noted, the best strategy in most cases is to simply unplug a running computer. The shutdown operation in many operating systems may wipe out evidence that a forensics investigation could otherwise recover. In particular, Microsoft Windows is likely to save more information if we simply "pull the plug" than if we perform a clean "shutdown."

Authenticating a Hard Drive

There are important cases, however, where we may lose access to some evidence if we remove the power. For example, if the computer uses hard drive encryption, then we lose access to the hard drive when the drive is powered off. However, it takes special training to reliably collect evidence from a running computer.

After collecting a hard drive as evidence, the next task is to analyze its contents. However, the first question a defense attorney will ask is "How can you prove that the drive is unchanged since collected as evidence?"

We must be able to show that the drive's contents are authentic with the incident. We must be able to prove that our analysis is based on the original contents, and does not reflect side effects of our investigation. To do this, we authenticate the hard drive and any other storage devices we investigate.

We address authentication in two parts. First, we never, ever make changes to the hard drive, or to any other storage device, that we collect as evidence. Instead, we make a copy of the original drive and analyze the copy. Second, we use a utility program to calculate an *integrity check value* on the drive's data. This type of program is a standard feature in software packages for digital forensics.

The check value is a very large integer (10^{48} or larger) that we retain at full precision. The check value uses a special computation, a "one-way hash," that reliably reflects *any* change we make to the drive. We look more closely at the one-way hash in Chapter 6. We recalculate the integrity check value on our copied hard drive. As long as the recalculated value matches that of the original drive, we can present the evidence we recover from our copy.

5.3 Storing Data on a Hard Drive

While Tina and Bob probably don't need to dust their USB drive for fingerprints or identify their culprit in court, they might want to perform a detailed investigation of the USB drive. To do that, they must analyze the file system. However, before we look at the file system, we need to understand how hard drives work.

These details help us understand what information a file system provides an investigator and what information it might hide. If we can retrieve a file after deleting it, a more clever program might give someone a way to actually hide data without deleting it.

A clever computer hacker, when arranging a hard drive, might set aside space for secret file storage that isn't visible in the normal navigation windows. A really clever programmer might hide small bits of data, like encryption keys, in the "unused" space at the end of a file, or in "unusable" sections of the file system. To understand these tricks, we must understand hard drives and file systems.

Magnetic Recording and Tapes

Hard drives rely on magnetic recording. The easiest way to understand magnetic recording is to look at magnetic tapes. In both cases, the technique works the same:

When we move a magnet past a coil of wire, the coil produces a current.

The power and direction of the current indicates the strength and direction ("north" versus "south") of the magnet. This allows us to read data from a magnetized surface. The opposite also is true:

We can magnetize a metal surface if it moves past a coil of wire containing a current.

Again, the strength and direction of the magnetized surface reflects the strength and direction ("positive" versus "negative") of the current.

A magnetic tape drive moves tape back and forth between two reels. We read and write data onto the moving tape as a series of magnetized spots. The coil of wire resides in the *read/write head*, shown at the top of Figure 5.1. As the motor moves the tape, it pulls the tape across the read/write head. When reading, the tape's motion produces a current as data moves across the head.

Magnetic tapes and tape drives were the symbol of computers in the 1950s and 1960s. However, they suffered a fundamental weakness; they were limited to *sequential access*. In other words, we always encounter the data on the tape "in sequence." We can't get from the start of the tape to the middle without skipping over all of the data in between.

Hard Drive Fundamentals

Hard drives evolved in the 1950s to provide large amounts of low-cost storage for the "giant brains" of that era. Like magnetic tapes, they used magnetic techniques to store and retrieve data. Compared to magnetic tapes, hard drives provided *random access* to

Read/write
head

Tape
Reels

Figure 5.1

A simple magnetic tape drive.

Figure 5.2

A typical hard drive.

data, because it could find, retrieve, and rewrite any data on the hard drive in a relatively short time.

Figure 5.2 shows the inside of a modern hard drive. The read/write head is on the end of a long arm that hovers over the magnetized surface. The drive spins under the head to provide the motion required for reading or writing the magnetic data.

On a hard drive, we record information on the surface of a spinning disk. In fact, *disk drive* is a traditional term for a hard drive. We record the information by magnetizing spots on the surface of the drive's disk *platters*. A read/write head hovers over each platter's surface, held in place by a mechanical arm.

The hard drive's basic mechanism has not changed since the 1950s, though the speed and capacity has increased dramatically. Like other computing equipment, hard drives have benefited from *Moore's law*.

After about 5 years of watching integrated circuit development, engineer Gordon Moore published the observation that computer speed and circuit density seemed to double every year. This observation was dubbed Moore's law. After closer examination, the industry concluded that the doubling actually averages every 18 months. This rate of improvement has been sustained since the 1960s. For example, the disk on a typical hard drive today is about $3\frac{3}{4}$ in. (95 mm) in diameter, while some 1960s' hard drives were over 4 feet (1300 mm) in diameter.

Figure 5.3 illustrates the hard drive's basic geometry. We magnetize data in two dimensions on each platter. In one dimension, we move the read/write head inward or

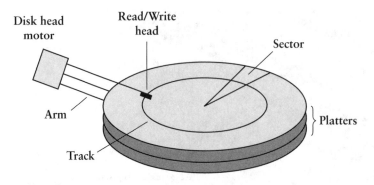

Figure 5.3

Hard drive mechanism.

outward. When it stops at a particular distance, it inscribes a magnetized ring on the platter. That ring forms a *track*. Each track contains individual blocks of data called *sectors*.

If we wanted to move from the first block to the last block on a magnetic tape, we had to wait while the drive moved the tape past every data block it contained. On a hard drive, we only need to wait for two relatively fast operations. First, the arm containing the read/write head moves from the first track to the last track. Second, we wait while the drive's spin brings the final sector under the read/write head. This was lightning fast compared to magnetic tapes, even in the 1950s.

The simplest hard drives contain a single platter and a single read/write head. We record information on only one side of such platters. Often, however, drives contain a second head to record on the other side of the platter. Some drives contain two or more platters, with an additional head for each side. Figure 5.2 shows a hard drive with two platters and four recordable surfaces.

The read/write heads are mounted on a set of arms that move together. When the drive moves the arm to a particular location on the disk surface, each head follows a matching track on its own surface. A very precise motor moves the arm assembly to specific locations on the disk surface; these locations specify the track locations.

A track represents a single ring of sectors recorded on one side of a platter. A *cylinder* represents all tracks recorded by the read/write head when it sits at a particular location. We get the highest performance out of a hard drive when all of our data resides on a single cylinder. If the data doesn't fit on a single cylinder, we optimize our performance if the data resides on adjacent cylinders.

Dissecting a Hard Drive: First, and most important, *never dissect a working hard drive.* The disk heads must hover slightly above the disk surface, and will "crash" into the surface if it tangles with an obstacle like a dust mote. It is impossible to open a hard drive without making it unusable, unless performed in a clean room by an expert.

Vendors use airtight sealing tape and several small screws to attach the drive cover to the drive body. The cover comes loose once *all* screws are removed and the tape is slit to loosen the drive cover. Note that some screws may be covered by labels.

There will always be at least one label saying "Tampering with this label will void the warranty." This is because hard drives are not designed to be opened. *Never dissect a working hard drive.*

5.3.1 Hard Drive Controller

To read and write data reliably, we must move the head assembly very precisely over the desired track. We also must be sure to read or write the correct sector on the track. Modern hard drives use a special circuit, the *drive controller,* to operate the head assembly and select the correct sector.

Figure 5.4 illustrates the parts of a controller using a *hardware block diagram.* Such diagrams show the major components in a hardware device, and the signals that pass between those components.

A modern controller resides on a circuit board packaged with the rest of the drive hardware. Typically, the hard drive accepts commands from the CPU sent to it across a high-speed bus. For example, a command may direct the drive to read data from one or more sectors. The command identifies the starting sector and the number of bytes to read. The controller moves the mechanism to the first sector and retrieves the data from the magnetized surface. As the data arrives from the mechanism, the controller transmits it back across the bus.

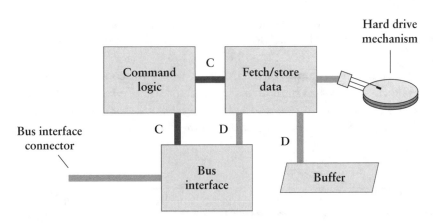

Figure 5.4

Hardware block diagram of a hard drive controller.

A controller typically contains the components shown in Figure 5.4. Connections between components carry control signals (marked "C"), data signals (marked "D"), or both. Here is a description of each component:

- **Bus interface connector**—a socket for connecting the drive to a high-speed bus, like those described in Section 2.1.1. Modern drives have a SATA connector or possibly an ATA or IDE connector.
- **Bus interface**—circuits that convert the commands and data that flow between the bus and the command logic.
- **Command logic**—circuits that convert the commands into a series of operations performed on the hard drive mechanism.
- **Buffer**—a large block of RAM that stores data temporarily on its way to or from the hard drive mechanism. The mechanical operations are time sensitive. The buffer makes it easier to synchronize the bus data transfers with the hard drive's mechanical motions.
- **Fetch/store data**—circuits that directly control the head motor to select tracks, and that retrieve or rewrite individually addressed sectors.

Hard drive speed depends on two variables: rotational speed and head motion. Modern drives in desktop computers may rotate at speeds from 5400 to 10,000 revolutions per minute (RPM), with faster drives being more expensive. Track-to-track head motion is significantly slower. While it may take microseconds to move data to or from a track without moving the head, it may take *milliseconds* to move data if the drive has to move the head between tracks. The data transfer speed is even slower if the heads must move between innermost tracks and outermost tracks.

5.3.2 Hard Drive Formatting

If we look at a hard drive before we install an operating system, the drive contains nothing except the numbered sectors. The hard drive controller uses the sector number as the sector's address.

When we perform a *low-level format* on a hard drive, we tell the controller to initialize the raw sectors themselves. Most hard drives use a sector size of 512 bytes, though some devices may have sectors as large as 2048 (2K) bytes. Each sector consists of three parts as shown in Figure 5.5: the *header*, the data, and the *check value*.

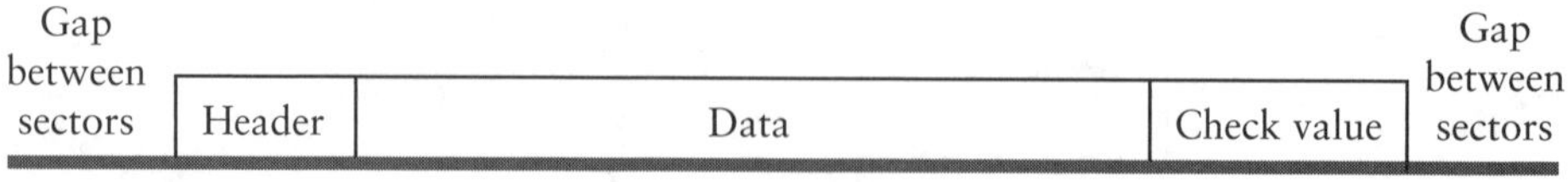

Gap between sectors	Header	Data	Check value	Gap between sectors

Figure 5.5

Low-level format of a hard drive sector.

The header contains the sector's numerical address and other information for the controller. Most drives number sectors consecutively, though older drives used to number them by track. The controller always checks the sector address when reading or writing. Although today's hard drives usually format all sectors identically, some special drives allow variations in the sector format.

The data area, naturally, contains the sector's data. The sector's check value helps the controller detect errors in the sector's data. Magnetic storage is very reliable, but the magnetic properties fail once in a while. We look closer at error detection in Section 5.3.3.

As shown in Figure 5.6, a hard drive is like a huge post office with millions of numbered boxes (the sectors). We find each box by number. We can store or retrieve a fixed amount of data via each box. When we store or retrieve data from one box, we don't affect the contents of other boxes. Unlike post office boxes, though, individual hard drive sectors rarely are large enough to store an entire file. When a file is larger than a sector, it resides in a series of boxes. To read the information, we must retrieve the data from every box in the series.

HIGH-LEVEL FORMAT

The *high-level format* of a hard drive refers to the layout of its file system. Different file systems store particular information in particular places, as described later in this chapter. Typically, the high-level format divides the hard drive into groups of sectors called *clusters* (Figure 5.6). Each file contains one or more clusters. The file system keeps track of the clusters. When we create a new file or add more data to an existing file, the system locates an unused cluster and adds it to the file.

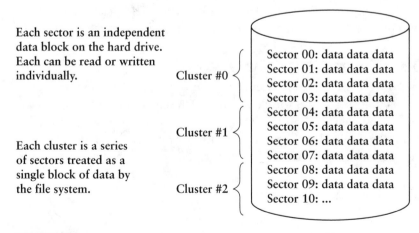

Each sector is an independent data block on the hard drive. Each can be read or written individually.

Each cluster is a series of sectors treated as a single block of data by the file system.

Cluster #0
Cluster #1
Cluster #2

Sector 00: data data data
Sector 01: data data data
Sector 02: data data data
Sector 03: data data data
Sector 04: data data data
Sector 05: data data data
Sector 06: data data data
Sector 07: data data data
Sector 08: data data data
Sector 09: data data data
Sector 10: ...

Figure 5.6

Sectors and clusters on a hard drive.

Fragmentation

A file may consist of several clusters in a row or its clusters may be scattered across the hard drive. The scattering often is called *fragmentation*. It can slow the system down when we work with those files. This is why people occasionally run a "defragment" utility on their hard drive. The utility moves the clusters in each file so that they are contiguous; this makes it faster to access the files.

Fragmentation also refers to wasted space on the hard drive. Most files contain a "fragment" of wasted space at the very end. If a file ends *exactly* at the end of a cluster, then there is no wasted space. More often, the file ends short of the end of the cluster. The remaining space can't be used in another file, so the space is wasted.

Quick Format

When we perform a "quick format" on a hard drive, we initialize the file system information. This doesn't disturb the existing sector addresses, and it ignores most of the data on the drive. Instead, it recreates all of the basic information for creating files, and gives the drive a single, empty "root" directory. If we had any files on the hard drive before reformatting, the process discards those files.

FLASH DRIVES

Mechanically, flash drives are completely different from hard drives. Flash drives are purely electronic and do not rely on magnetized surfaces or head motions. Instead, electronic circuits store data by trapping charges in a stable form for long periods of time. The name "flash" refers to an early technique of erasing previously stored data. Flash memory is often structured in blocks, similar to the way that hard drives are structured into sectors.

High-level flash-drive formatting matches those used with hard drives. Most commercial flash drives use the FAT file format described in Section 5.4. However, drive owners also may apply other formats if allowed by their operating system.

5.3.3 Error Detection and Correction

Whenever the hard drive writes data to a sector, the controller calculates a numerical check value on the data. It then writes the check value at the end of the sector. When we read a sector later, the controller repeats the calculation and checks the result against the saved check value. If the results don't match, the controller reports a data error on that sector. This prevents our software from reading incorrect data from the hard drive without realizing it.

Parity Checking

Errors have plagued computer memories since their invention. Magnetic tapes often used a simple technique called *parity checking* to detect errors. The tape drives handled data on a byte-by-byte basis, storing each byte across the width of the tape. The parity check stored an extra "parity bit" with each byte. We calculate parity by looking at the

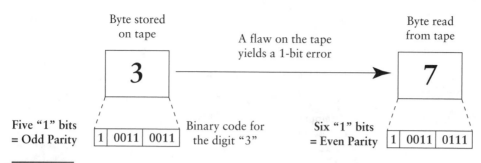

Figure 5.7

Detecting an error using odd parity on a nine-track tape.

individual bits in a byte. Each bit has a value of either 0 or 1. We count the number of bits containing the value 1.

For example, Figure 5.7 shows the data bits stored in a single byte of a "nine-track tape." The first track contained the parity bit and the remaining contained the eight data bits, one per track. On the left of the figure, the tape contains the numeric value "3" in printable text; its 9-bit code is shown as "1 0011 0011."

The nine-track tape stored data with "odd parity," which means that the parity bit is chosen to yield an odd number of 1 bits. If the remaining eight data bits had already contained an odd number of 1 bits, then the correct parity bit would be 0.

To detect an error in odd parity, we count the 1 bits, including the parity bit. The right side of Figure 5.7 shows the result of a 1-bit tape error that has changed the "3" character to a "7" character.

We detect the error by counting the bits on the tape, including the parity bit. These appear in the lower right of the figure. The character code for "7" contains an odd number of 1 bits. When we combine this with the parity bit, we have an even number of bits, yielding "even parity." The tape drive detects this as an error when reading the tape, because the byte no longer contains odd parity.

The choice of "odd is correct" and "even is wrong" is arbitrary. Some devices and systems require even parity. It is a design choice.

Unfortunately, errors aren't always limited to individual bits. Some errors may change a series of bits to all 1s or to all 0s, or otherwise affect several bits. We can rely on parity only if the most likely errors affect a single bit; it fails completely if the error changes an even number of bits.

Another problem with parity is that it uses a lot of storage: Over 11 percent of a nine-track tape's storage was used for parity checking. If we take more data into account, we can detect more errors and use less storage for error detection.

Checksums

Hard drives store blocks of data in sectors, so it makes sense to check for errors on a per-sector basis. The simplest approach is to perform a *checksum*; we use a simple rule

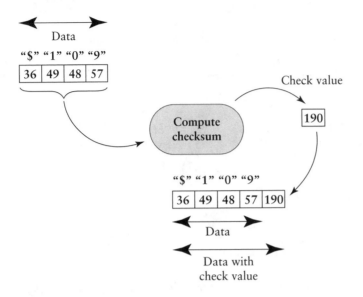

Calculating a simple checksum.

to calculate the check value from the sector's data. In Figure 5.8, for example, we have a 4-byte sector of data containing the text "$109."

To calculate the check value, we add together the character codes stored in the sector's data bytes, and discard extra bits that don't fit in an 8-bit byte. We then store the checksum in the final byte of the sector.

If we are working with hard drive sectors, then the hard drive controller calculates the checksum. When writing, it computes the value on the newly written data and writes the result at the end of the sector. When reading, it recalculates the value while reading the sector's data. The result should match the previously stored checksum. Otherwise, one or more bits in the sector have failed.

A checksum field is not limited to 8 bits; we could comfortably collect and store a 16-bit check value with a hard drive sector. Even if we store a 16-bit result, the checksum uses storage far more efficiently than parity. A hard drive sector traditionally contains 512 bytes of storage; a 16-bit checksum uses less than 1 percent of our storage for error detection.

While some older drives used simple checksums, the technique is too simple to detect many errors. For example, a checksum won't detect an error that swaps bytes. The message "$901" has the same check value as the previous correct sector and would not be detected as an error.

Cyclic Redundancy Checks

To improve error detection, more sophisticated drives computed more sophisticated check values using a *cyclic redundancy check* (CRC). A well-designed CRC detects "burst" errors, like a sequence of 0s or 1s, much more reliably than parity checking. CRCs may yield check values of 32 bits or more.

Error Correcting Codes

Parity, checksums, and CRCs are all examples of *error detecting codes* (EDCs), techniques to *detect* errors. There are also techniques that both detect *and* correct errors, called *error correcting codes* (ECCs). These can correct smaller errors in a sector and detect larger errors. An ECC yields one of the few *corrective measures* available to system designers, because it both detects a problem and corrects it in some cases.

Commercial hard drives have traditionally used CRCs to calculate sector check values. Sophisticated techniques like ECCs were used on RAMs and digital video disks (DVDs). As hard drives have increased in size and sophistication, some have adopted ECCs.

5.3.4 Hard Drive Partitions

When an operating system develops a new file system, the designers focus on a particular range of sizes. The oldest formats worked well with drives storing no more than a few megabytes (MB) of data. In 1977, Microsoft developed a system using a *file allocation table* (FAT), which became known as the "FAT File System."

Thanks to Moore's law, hard drive sizes have increased dramatically. They occasionally have exceeded the maximum size of contemporary file systems. The earliest version of FAT, now called "FAT 12," supported a maximum drive size of 15 MB. This was sufficient for the introduction of Microsoft's Disk Operating System (MS-DOS), which premiered with the first IBM PC in 1981. FAT 12 worked with the first PC hard drives, which were limited to 5 or 10 MB, but hard drives soon grew to 20 MB and larger.

The user couldn't simply tell the file system to use the larger size. The FAT 12 format really was designed for diskettes holding less than 700 KB. It had no way to deal with more than 15 MB of hard drive space. Moreover, it was risky and difficult to try to patch the file system to support larger devices.

PARTITIONING TO SUPPORT OLDER DRIVE FORMATS

Instead, vendors introduced drive *partitions*, another level of drive formatting. If the owner's OS used the FAT 12 file system, but the new hard drive held 40 MB of storage, the owner would divide the drive into three or more separate partitions (Figure 5.9). As long as no partition was larger than 15 MB, the owner could make the partitions any size and use FAT 12.

On the desktop, each partition appears as a separate device. Each partition contains its own, independent file system. We often refer to a large block of storage that contains

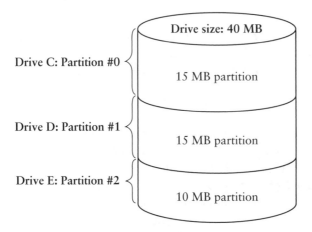

Drive C: Partition #0

Drive D: Partition #1

Drive E: Partition #2

Drive size: 40 MB

15 MB partition

15 MB partition

10 MB partition

Figure 5.9

Example of MS-DOS drive partitioning.

a single file system as a *volume*. When a hard drive contains two or more partitions, each represents a single volume. In most cases, the hard drive contains only one partition, and we may use the words "volume" and "hard drive" interchangeably.

Some users install different file systems in different partitions. Some even install different operating systems in different partitions. However, different operating systems would require special boot software to allow the user to choose which system to run.

Although not shown in Figure 5.9, a partitioned hard drive sets aside one or more sectors at the beginning to describe the partition arrangement. Microsoft uses the master boot record (MBR) to describe the partition layout. The MBR identifies the starting block of each partition.

The underlying drive hardware isn't aware of partitioning. When a device driver reads or writes sectors on the hard drive, it must adjust the sector address to match the partitioning. For example, if the driver needs to write sector 0 on drive "D" in Figure 5.9, it must find the partition's starting sector number, stored in the MBR, and add it to the desired sector address. This tells the hard drive to skip over the sectors in the "C" partition.

PARTITIONING IN MODERN SYSTEMS

As of 2011, modern file systems can easily handle typical desktop hard drives. Even so, some users and system vendors still like to partition their hard drives. Moreover, hard drive capacity continues to grow and they may exceed file system capacities again in the future. Thus, partitioning remains alive and well.

For example, some vendors use a separate partition to store a backup of the main partition. Some users set up separate partitions so that their hard drive can contain two or more different operating systems. For example, a two-partition Macintosh might contain the Windows or Linux operating system in the other partition. The user can switch operating systems by booting the other partition.

PARTITIONING AND FRAGMENTATION

In most cases, the best strategy is to format a hard drive with a single partition containing a single file system. When we divide a drive into separate partitions, we usually are stuck with the result. It is risky, and often impractical, to resize partitions after we install the file system.

If our hard drive has two or more partitions, we may run into a fragmentation problem: One partition may become too full while the other remains partly empty. We can't fix this problem with a built-in "defragment" utility. We must rearrange the files by hand to make more room, and manually move files from one partition to the other.

HIDING DATA WITH PARTITIONS

Normally an operating system tries to make as much of the hard drive available as possible. To do this, it identifies available partitions and tries to mount them as usable file systems. A casual user might not notice that the operating system only uses 100 GB of a 200 GB drive. Some people use this as a way to hide information on a computer.

There are two simple and relatively obvious ways to hide data in a system using partitions:

1. Invisible partition
2. Undersized file system

Operating systems strive to make partitions visible. If the partition contains a recognizable file system, the OS will make it visible to users. A hacker may take steps to make the partition invisible. The exact steps depend on the operating system. In some cases, it is enough to format the partition with an unrecognizable file system. For example, Unix or OS-X file systems might not be recognized by different versions of Windows. In any case, disk utilities can uncover a hidden partition.

A second approach is to create a large partition, but configure its file system to only use part of the partition. If the file system's internal data structures tell it that it mustn't exceed a particular size, then the remaining space in the partition remains free and unused. This requires special utilities to create and manage. Some disk utilities might detect a size mismatch between a file system and its partition, but not necessarily.

In either case, the hacker needs special software to store and retrieve data in this hidden area of the hard drive. The normal OS file system will not be able to access that part of the hard drive.

5.3.5 Memory Sizes and Address Variables

As we look at hard drives and other large (and growing) storage devices, we use particular words and acronyms to identify large numbers. When we talk about storage in particular, we often need to say *where* information resides; we need to express its address.

We often need to store that address in a variable; we call such things an *address variable*.

ADDRESS, INDEX, AND POINTER VARIABLES

Most programmers first encounter address variables when working with arrays. We select individual items from an array by using an *index variable*. This is the simplest type of address variable. The index value chooses which array element to use, just like an address variable chooses which memory location to use. These also are called *pointer variables*.

An important question is the *size* of an address variable. For example, if our hard drive contains 1 million sectors, then the address itself will be a number ranging between one and a million. How much space must we set aside in RAM, or in the hard drive controller, to store a number between one and a million?

This is the same problem storekeepers face when picking out a cash register for point-of-sale transactions. How large of a sale should the register handle? In general, storekeepers measure the size in terms of decimal digits; the four-digit register shown in Figure 5.10 can handle anything up to $99.99.

Many consumer electronic stores have six-digit registers to handle transactions up to $9,999.99. This handles the vast majority of purchases, but poses a problem when someone buys a really expensive home theater.

Computers don't store numbers decimally; they store numbers in binary form. Thus, we speak of variable sizes in terms of bits. To store a number between 0 and n, we need

Figure 5.10

A cash register that handles four decimal digits.

TABLE 5.1 Abbreviations for large numbers

Abbreviation	Prefix Name	Decimal Size	Size in Thousands	Binary Approximation	Address Variable Size
K	kilo-	10^3	1000	$1024 = 2^{10}$	10
M	mega-	10^6	1000^2	$1024^2 = 2^{20}$	20
G	giga-	10^9	1000^3	$1024^3 = 2^{30}$	30
T	tera-	10^{12}	1000^4	$1024^4 = 2^{40}$	40
P	peta-	10^{15}	1000^5	$1024^5 = 2^{50}$	50
E	exa-	10^{18}	1000^6	$1024^6 = 2^{60}$	60

$\log_2(n)$ bits, rounded upward. If we know that $n < 2^k$, then we can store the value n if the variable contains k bits.

MEMORY SIZE NAMES AND ACRONYMS

Table 5.1 summarizes the names and acronyms for large memory sizes. It also notes the number of bits required for an address variable that works with a memory of that size.

ESTIMATING THE NUMBER OF BITS

The fifth column of Table 5.1 illustrates an approximate relationship between decimal and binary exponents:

$$1000 \approx 1024$$
$$10^3 \approx 2^{10}$$

We use this to estimate the number of bits required by an address variable if we know the memory's size in decimal. We use the decimal exponent of the address size and convert it to the binary exponent to find the number of bits. For example, assume we have a nine-digit decimal number. To estimate the size of the address variable, we:

- Divide the number of decimal digits by 3.
- Multiply the result by 10 to estimate the number of bits.

This calculation overestimates the number of bits, because the binary result is slightly larger than the decimal one. Traditionally, RAM sizes fit a power of two, so the decimal size often implies the larger binary value. For example, a "1K" memory contains 1024 elements, and a "4K" memory contains 4096 elements. The convention broke down at 2^{16}, which some call "64K," because 64 is a power of two, and others call "65K," which is numerically more accurate.

Certain memory and address sizes crop up again and again, because the address variable fits into a convenient number of bits. Table 5.2 lists these "classic" address sizes and indicates the associated memory sizes.

On hard drives and mass storage, the technology doesn't need to match powers of two. One vendor of USB flash drives clearly states "1 GB = 1 billion bytes." A hard drive vendor's "1 terabyte" hard drive contains at least 10^{12} bytes, but falls 99 gigabytes short of 2^{40} bytes.

When we need to abbreviate a large power of two *exactly*, the standard is to affix a lowercase "i" after the uppercase abbreviation. For example:

$$2^{20} \text{ bytes} = 1 \text{ MiB}$$
$$2^{30} \text{ bytes} = 1 \text{ GiB}$$

When we talk about storage sizes, sometimes we use bits and other times we use bytes. To abbreviate the size, we use the lowercase "b" to represent bits and the uppercase "B" to represent bytes. Because 1 byte contains 8 bits:

$$64 \text{ b} = 8 \text{ B}$$

TABLE 5.2 Classic storage sizes

Address Size in Bits	Size of Memory	Description
8	256	Byte-size address
10	1024	Traditionally called "1K"
12	4096	Traditionally called "4K"
15	32,768	Traditionally called "32K"
16	65,536	Called "64K" or "65K"
24	16,777,216	Traditionally called "16 Meg"
32	4,294,967,296	4.29 gigabytes (4.29 GB)
48	281×10^{12}	281 terabytes (281 TB)
64	18.44×10^{18}	18.44 exabytes (18 EB)

5.4 FAT: An Example File System

The essentials of file system formatting are best illustrated with an example: the FAT file system. While the format dates back to the earliest personal computers, it has evolved since then. The FAT 12 format was superseded by FAT 16, which supported gigabytes of storage. Today's FAT 32 supports terabytes of disk space.

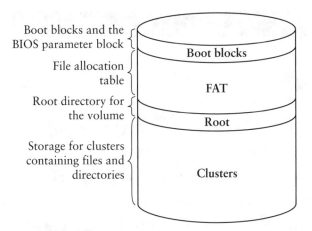

Boot blocks and the BIOS parameter block	Boot blocks
File allocation table	FAT
Root directory for the volume	Root
Storage for clusters containing files and directories	Clusters

Figure 5.11

Layout of a FAT-formatted volume.

Today, we often use FAT formatting on removable hard drives and flash memory. Most commercial digital cameras use FAT format on their storage cards. FAT provide hierarchical directories and flexible file naming. The major shortcoming is that individual FAT files must contain less than 4 gigabytes.

VOLUME LAYOUT

Figure 5.11 shows the layout of a FAT formatted volume. Sector 0, the first sector of the volume, marks the beginning of the *boot blocks*. These first sectors may contain a program to bootstrap the operating system, but they also contain variables that describe the volume's layout. Next comes the file allocation table, or FAT. This table keeps track of every cluster on the volume.

Following the FAT is the root directory, which contains entries for files and subdirectories on the volume. Each entry contains the name and the number of the first sector in the file or subdirectory. FAT directories are hierarchical, so any directory may contain entries for subdirectories.

The rest of the volume is divided into clusters to store files and subdirectories. The FAT contains one entry per cluster.

On older FAT 12 and FAT 16 volumes, the root directory had its own, dedicated set of sectors on the volume. On FAT 32, the root directory is the first file stored in the volume's clusters; it appears in roughly the same place, but there is a little more flexibility in its location.

5.4.1 Boot Blocks

The boot block resides on the first sectors of the hard drive; they are the blocks read by the BIOS when we boot from this drive. Every file system stores special information in the boot block, as well as providing room for a bootstrap program.

TABLE 5.3 Contents of the FAT 32 boot block

Offset in Bytes	Size in Bytes	Contents
0	3	A "jump" instruction to skip over the BPB data
3	8	System name, usually "MSWIN 4.1"
11	2	Number of bytes in a hard drive sector, usually 512
13	1	Number of sectors in a cluster; depends on the volume size
14	2	Number of sectors contained in the boot blocks
16	1	Number of FATs on the volume, usually 2
17	15	Variables that aren't used in FAT 32, left as spares, or used by the device driver
32	4	Total number of sectors in the volume
36	4	Total number of sectors in one FAT
40	50	Variables for other purposes, like error recovery, device driver support, and volume identification.

If we partition a hard drive, the first block contains the MBR, which itself contains a boot program. The MBR's boot program automatically redirects the boot operation to the boot block of the first "bootable" partition.

The first item stored in the FAT boot block is a "jump" instruction. If the BIOS tries to start an operating system stored on the FAT volume, it first reads a boot program from these boot blocks and then jumps to the first instruction read into RAM. This first instruction jumps over the variables FAT provides to describe the volume's format. This block of variables is called the BIOS parameter block (BPB). Table 5.3 describes the contents of this block in the FAT 32 format.

We use the information in the BPB to find the boundaries between the boot blocks, the FAT, and the cluster storage area. To find the start of the FAT, we look at offset 14, which indicates the number of sectors in the boot blocks.

THE FAT

The FAT is an array of address variables. It contains one entry for every cluster on the volume. The number associated with different FAT formats (12, 16, and 32) indicated the size of the address variables in bits. Each array entry corresponds to one cluster on the volume. The array entry's contents indicate one of the following:

- The cluster is part of a file.
- The cluster is free and may be assigned to a file that needs more space.
- The cluster contains a bad disk sector and should not be used.

Volumes often contain two FATs, one following right after the other. This is supposed to increase reliability. If the operating system keeps both FATs up to date and one is damaged by a disk error, then the system still can retrieve files by reading the undamaged FAT.

FAT FORMAT ALTERNATIVES

The file format establishes the rules for finding and storing information on the hard drive, flash drive, or other storage device. We can think of it as a map. First, it leads us to the directories, then to a file in a directory, and then through the clusters of sectors that make up the file. Table 5.4 summarizes the FAT file formats.

Note that the maximum sizes in Table 5.4 represent typical implementations that worked over multiple operating systems. Occasionally, someone would modify one operating system or another to support larger sizes, usually to satisfy a particularly important customer or vendor.

The format names or sizes (12, 16, and 32) indicate the size in bits of the address variables used to track individual clusters on the hard drive. Thus, a FAT 12 drive could only handle a few thousand clusters, because every cluster address had to fit in a 12-bit variable. By the same token, FAT 32 can only handle a quarter billion clusters, because 4 bits of the 32-bit cluster variables are used for other purposes within the file system. In theory, the maximum drive size should be the product of the maximum cluster size and the maximum number of clusters. Operating system and software restrictions may reduce the practical maximum size.

5.4.2 Building Files from Clusters

Files in most file systems, including FAT, consist of a series of clusters. The clusters themselves may be scattered across the volume. When the file system retrieves that file, however, it retrieves the clusters in the order the data appears in the file. In a file containing three clusters, the beginning of the file appears in the first cluster, the middle in the second cluster, and the end in the third cluster.

The challenge for the file system is to find a file's clusters and present them in the right order. FAT stores each file as a *cluster chain*. In other words, each FAT entry provides a "link" to connect one cluster in a file to the next cluster in that file.

TABLE 5.4 Microsoft's FAT file system formats				
Format	Introduced with OS and Year	Maximum Cluster Size	Maximum Clusters	Maximum Drive Size
FAT 12	Disk Basic, 1977	4 KB	4,077	15 MB
FAT 16	DOS 3.31, 1987	32 KB	65,517	2 GB
FAT 32	Windows 95, 1996	32 KB	268,435,437	2 TB

CLUSTER STORAGE

Cluster storage begins with the first sector following the end of the FAT area. To find the start of cluster storage, we find the size of the FAT area and add it to the area's starting point. We do that by extracting data from the BPB as follows:

- Find the number of FATs: BPB offset 16.
- Find the size of each FAT in sectors: BPB offset 36.
- Multiply the number of FATs and the size per FAT.
- Add the start of the FAT area: BPB offset 14.

For historical reasons, the first cluster in the cluster storage area is numbered 2. This first cluster almost always contains the beginning of the root directory. If the root directory contains more than one cluster, we must look in the cluster's FAT entry to find the root's next cluster.

AN EXAMPLE FAT FILE

Figure 5.12 displays a set of clusters beginning at cluster 300. The first file begins at 300 and contains the phrase "The quick brown fox jumps over the lazy dog." The text is spread across three separate clusters. A second file, containing Lincoln's Gettysburg Address, begins at cluster 302. The cluster at 305 is not being used in a file.

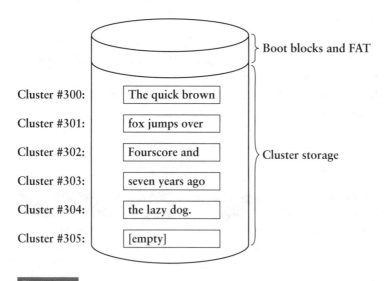

Figure 5.12

Clusters containing parts of files.

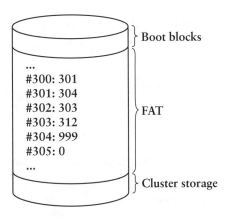

```
...
#300: 301
#301: 304
#302: 303
#303: 312
#304: 999
#305: 0
...
```

Boot blocks

FAT

Cluster storage

Figure 5.13

The FAT points to the clusters in a file.

Figure 5.13 displays the corresponding FAT entries. The first file contains three clusters (300, 301, and 304), and their FAT entries link them together. The FAT entry for 304, the file's final cluster, is too large to be a legal cluster number; this marks the end of the file. The second file contains at least two clusters (302 and 303) and links to additional clusters outside our example. Cluster 305 is unused and its FAT entry contains a 0.

If a cluster is part of a file, then its FAT entry contains the cluster number of the *next* cluster in that file. If the cluster is the last one in the file, then the FAT entry contains a special value to mark the end of the file. Either files or directories may contain two or more clusters, and both use this linking method when their contents don't fit in a single cluster.

FAT and Flash Storage

Successful low-cost flash drives first appeared in the mid-1990s, and they soon became popular components of electronic devices like digital cameras. Early flash drives ranged in size from a few megabytes to 2 gigabytes. By 2005, however, 4 gigabyte flash drives were commercially available, but they would not work in older digital products.

The problem arose from the difference between FAT 16 and FAT 32 formats. The older products used FAT 16, because it was simpler to implement and worked with the smaller memory sizes. The larger flash drives required FAT 32 to handle their full memory size. Unfortunately, the older products did not recognize the FAT 32 file format. The only solution is to use smaller devices, though it may be possible to format a newer device with FAT 16 and simply ignore storage beyond its 2 gigabyte limit.

One type of flash memory product has adopted names to reflect the different formatting standards: the secure digital (SD) card, an offshoot of the multimedia card (MMC), a flash memory in a 24 mm x 32 mm format. The card exists in these formats:

- Secure digital (SD)—up to 2 GB using FAT 16
- SD high capacity (SDHC)—4 GB to 32 GB using FAT 32
- SD extra capacity (SDXC)—32 GB to 2 TB using FAT 32

5.4.3 FAT Directories

The directories, starting with the root directory, tell us what files exist and where to find their starting clusters. Each directory in FAT 32 consists of an array of 32-byte entries. In the simplest case, each entry represents a single file or subdirectory. A typical entry contains the following:

- The name of the file or directory
- Attributes of this directory entry
- Date and time created, last examined, and last modified
- An address variable pointing to the first cluster in the file
- The total number of bytes of data in the file

The FAT directory begins with the root directory, which itself begins at cluster 2. We look in the root directory entries to find files and other directories. The "attributes" indicate whether a directory entry points to a file or to another directory. We follow links in the FAT to find additional clusters belonging to the root directory or to the other files and directories.

LONG FILE NAMES

FAT directory entries become more complicated as we look at long file names and other advanced features. The traditional FAT directory only supports file names of eight upper case characters or less, with a three-letter extension identifier. Modern FAT devices support much longer names that contain both upper- and lower-case characters.

To do this, the FAT directory sets aside a series of directory entries, one for the actual file, and additional ones to hold segments of the long name. Each "long name" entry may contain up to 13 characters. The "actual" directory entry holds a short, 11-character version of the long name plus the normal contents of the file's directory entry. The short version of the name allows older Windows and DOS systems to handle directories containing long names.

DELETING FILES

To delete a FAT file, the system takes two steps. First, it locates the file's directory entry and sets it to "empty." Some files have multiple directory entries, for example, files with long file names, and those entries also are marked as "empty." Next, the system "frees" all clusters used in the file, allowing the clusters to be used in other files.

The system marks a directory entry as empty by storing a special value (decimal 229) in the first character of its file name. The system does *not* make any other changes to the directory entry. When it is time to create a new file and give it a new entry, the system scans *all* entries in the directory to ensure that the new name is unique, and to find an existing empty entry to use. The contents of a deleted directory entry remain unchanged until the entry is reused for a new file.

To free the clusters in the file, the system follows the file's cluster chain in the FAT. For each cluster in the file, the system sets the FAT entry to 0. This marks the cluster as being free for reuse.

Undeleting a File

The most common *undelete* programs are designed to recover FAT files. To undelete a FAT file, the program starts by simply changing the first character of the deleted directory entry to a legal filename character. This retrieves the file's directory entry and its first cluster of data.

To recover the entire file, its clusters must not be fragmented. In other words, they must appear one after another on the drive, in contiguous clusters following the first cluster. In addition, the clusters must not have been allocated to another file in the mean time.

We recover the file's data by using information in its directory entry and in the FAT. The directory entry tells us the starting cluster number and the number of bytes in the file. We calculate the number of clusters by dividing the file's length by the cluster size, then we check the sequence of clusters in the FAT that start with the first cluster in the file. If all clusters are still free (i.e., their FAT entries are 0), then they most likely still contain the file's data.

5.5 Modern File Systems

Because the FAT file system is used on almost all removable storage (especially USB storage), it is probably the most common file system. However, it is not the only file system. FAT lacks many features that people need in a modern file system. For example:

- Files are limited to a size of 4 gigabytes or less.
- Smaller FAT systems (FAT 12, FAT 16) can't recover if drive errors occur in essential locations, like the root directory.
- The simple, linear directory arrangement makes it very slow to search a really large directory (e.g., one with thousands of files).
- FAT files don't identify a file's owner.
- FAT files can't support access restrictions beyond simple flags to indicate "read only," "hidden," or "system" files.

These properties explain why modern operating systems only use FAT file systems for removable storage. Access control poses a special problem. Without access restrictions, the operating system can't trust a FAT-formatted drive to protect critical files. Older versions of Microsoft Windows could be installed on FAT file systems, but those versions couldn't protect the system from tampering by a malicious user.

Three major file systems used today include:

1. Hierarchical file system plus (HFS+)—used with Apple OS-X
2. Unix file system (UFS)—used with most Unix systems
3. Windows NT file system (NTFS)—used with Windows

File systems have evolved as computers and hard drives have become larger and faster. Practical solutions for 20 megabyte hard drives in 1989 could not handle 200 gigabyte drives in 2009. As operating systems have become more complex and sophisticated, they've required more of their file systems. Most modern file systems address shortcomings encountered in FAT and in other older file systems.

FILE SYSTEM DESIGN GOALS

File systems focus on a single problem: storing information on a hard drive. This boils down to three basic challenges:

1. How to store files
2. How to find files
3. How to manage the free space on the hard drive

File storage is a deceptively simple problem. The most obvious initial solution is to simply chop the hard drive into contiguous blocks, one per file. Longer files get longer blocks, while shorter files get shorter blocks. This strategy quickly fails due to fragmentation: deleting two 1 MB files doesn't guarantee that we can now create a new 1.5 MB file. The two fragments might be in different places, preventing us from using them in a single file. Modern systems use linking strategies similar to FAT's table of cluster links.

Practically every file system used today supports hierarchical file systems. However, different systems organize their directories differently. Many, but not all, still organize subdirectories as separate files. Different choices provide different blends of simplicity and high performance.

Free-space management is important from three perspectives. First, efficient free-space management makes it fast to update files and add new data to them. Second, effective free-space management minimizes fragmentation. FAT illustrates this; the largest unused fragment in the system should be no larger than a single cluster.

Third, robust free-space management reduces the risk of losing clusters if the system crashes. A robust system may keep information about free space in multiple places, making it harder to lose track of free clusters.

Conflicting File System Objectives

As operating system designers refined their file systems, they were influenced by five objectives:

1. Make the system as simple as possible. Simple systems are the most likely to work correctly.
2. Make every action as fast as possible.
3. Make random access as efficient as possible. The earliest operating systems focused on sequential access, but this is now obsolete.
4. Make the system work effectively with hard drives of a particular size, with room to grow.
5. Make the system robust so that unexpected failures won't lose data or make the system unstable.

These objectives often are contradictory, but all are addressed to some degree. Some objectives take a priority at one point in a file system's evolution, only to be superseded later by different objectives.

The remainder of this section reviews the three file systems noted here.

5.5.1 Unix File System

The Unix file system evolved in the early 1970s. In some ways, it is simpler than FAT, and in some ways, it is more sophisticated. Like FAT, Unix sets aside space among the boot blocks to contain file system layout information. On Unix, this data is called the "superblock." Like FAT, Unix organizes the hard drive into clusters instead of constructing files out of individual sectors. Traditionally, however, Unix refers to clusters as "blocks." Like FAT, Unix also supports hierarchical directories. There are significant differences, too.

Since the introduction of Unix, several modern variations of the file system have appeared. What is today called the Unix file system, or UFS, evolved in the 1980s. Linux systems today often use an "extended" version of the file system called "ext3." Although these systems share fundamental elements of the original Unix systems, they include many changes to improve performance on larger and more demanding systems.

Inodes

The centerpiece of the Unix file system is the *inode* (pronounced "eye-node"). The inode is the data structure on the drive that describes each file. All inodes reside in a single data structure, the inode list (Figure 5.14). The inode itself tells us where to find the file's data clusters. Within the Unix operating system itself, some programs can omit the file names and handle files simply by their inode number: the index of the file's entry in the inode table.

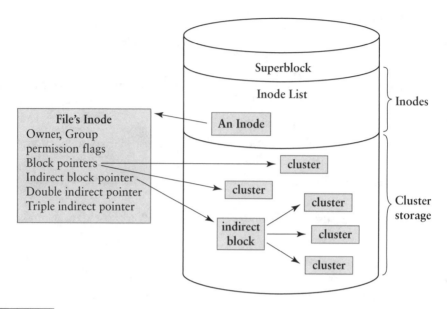

Figure 5.14

Classic Unix volume format.

To find the clusters belonging to a file, we look at the list of clusters stored in the file's inode. The inode itself points directly to the first several clusters in the file; this makes it very efficient to handle smaller files. If a file contains too many clusters to fit in that list, the inode contains a pointer to a cluster that itself contains a list of clusters. This is called an "indirect block" because each word in the cluster points to another cluster in the file. If that list overflows, too, the inode can point to *another* cluster that serves as a "double" indirect block; each word in that cluster points to an indirect block. There also can be a pointer to a "triple" indirect block whose contents point to more double indirect blocks.

The inode also contains a file's attributes. These include:

- Type of file
- Identity of the file's owner
- Associated group identifier
- File permission flags
- Access dates

DIRECTORIES

The Unix directory is much simpler than a FAT directory because the file attributes reside in the inode. Each Unix directory entry contains no more than the file's name and its inode index. In older Unix systems, the directory contained fixed-size entries. Newer versions use variable-size entries. This allows the file system to handle a mixture of longer and shorter file names efficiently. Some versions also use a technique called "hash tables" to speed up the search for file names.

Early versions of the Unix file system simply kept lists of free blocks on the hard drive. The system also managed the inode list by marking an entry as being free and reusable for another file. These techniques were not efficient enough for larger, faster systems. More recent systems use *bitmaps* to manage these resources.

A bitmap provides a compact and efficient way to keep track of a large collection of numbered items. We assign a 1-bit flag for each item. We use the item's number to locate its individual flag within the bitmap. If the item is in use, we set the flag to 0. If the item is free, we set the flag to 1. We can quickly search for a free item by looking for a word that doesn't equal 0.

Unix uses separate bitmaps to manage inodes and free clusters. For managing inodes, the bitmap contains 1 bit for each inode, indicating which ones currently belong to files. For managing free space on the hard drive, modern systems distribute the data across the hard drive to make operations more efficient. The system creates separate bitmaps for different groups of adjacent cylinders. Each group has its own bitmap to identify free clusters in that part of the drive. When a new file receives all of its clusters from a single group, we minimize the access time required to read the file's clusters.

5.5.2 Apple's HFS Plus

Apple's original hierarchical file system was introduced in 1986. It was enhanced to produce HFS+ in 1998. The HFS+ volume structure is very flexible. Each volume sets aside a few sectors at the beginning for boot blocks and for the "volume header" and a few at the end to hold a spare copy of the volume header (Figure 5.15). The rest of the volume contains clusters that belong to files.

HFS+ organizes the volume's contents around five master files. These may appear anywhere on the volume, but the volume header always contains the location of these five files. Here are the five files:

- Catalog file—contains the hierarchical directory and information about files on the volume
- Extents overflow file—contains additional information for finding clusters belonging to larger files
- Allocation file (bitmap)—indicates which clusters on the hard drive are free
- Attributes file—contains additional information about files that did not fit in the file's directory entry
- Startup file—used to boot non-Macintosh operating systems

HFS+ organizes the clusters within a file into *extents*. Each extent contains one or more contiguous clusters. The file system describes each extent with two numbers: the

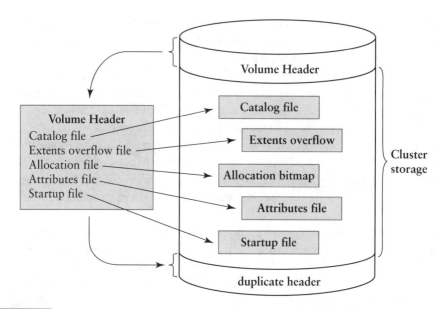

Figure 5.15

Apple's HFS+ volume format.

number of the first cluster in the extent, and the number of clusters in the extent. For example, we might have a file that contains 10 clusters arranged in three extents:

- First cluster in the extent: 100, length: three clusters
- First cluster in the extent: 107, length: four clusters
- First cluster in the extent: 115, length: three clusters

The first three clusters in the file are 100, 101, and 102, then we move to the next extent to retrieve the fourth cluster. If the system can find enough empty clusters in a row, it puts the entire file in a single extent.

Unlike earlier file systems, HFS+ directories are not simple lists of names. The directories use "balanced trees" (abbreviated "B-trees"), a data structure that stores the information efficiently and makes it much faster to search. HFS+ also uses this structure to organize the attributes file and extents overflow file.

5.5.3 Microsoft's NTFS

The *NT file system* first appeared as part of the Windows NT operating system, which was first introduced in 1993. In NTFS, the organizing principle is that "everything is a file." The first and most important file is the *master file table* or MFT. Every file, directory, or block of data on the hard drive has an entry in the MFT. While HFS+ has five essential files that are located from the boot block, an NTFS boot block points to the

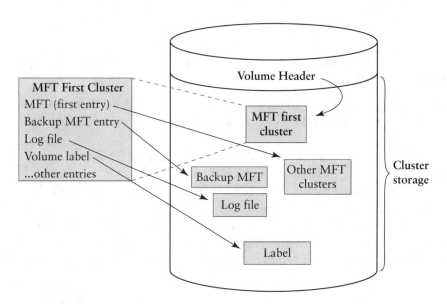

NTFS and the master file table.

single essential file: the MFT. After using that pointer to find the first cluster in the MFT, we can find everything else on the drive volume (Figure 5.16).

NTFS constructs its files out of clusters and extents, much like HFS+. The clusters in an individual file often are represented by a "run list," which is a special term for a list of extents.

The very first entry in the MFT is for the MFT itself. Because this entry contains the MFT's run list, we can use it to find additional clusters belonging to the MFT. Because the MFT is itself a file, it is easier to write utility programs to examine the MFT.

The first several entries in the MFT are assigned to specific elements of the volume:

1. The MFT itself: This entry fits in the MFT's first cluster so that we can find the subsequent clusters in the MFT.

2. A backup copy of the MFT, in case its original location suffers from a drive error.

3. A built-in log file that keeps track of changes made to the volume.

4. The volume label, including its name, identifier, and version.

5. A file describing the types of data that might appear in MFT entries on this volume. This makes it easier to handle volumes created for different versions of NTFS.

6. The root directory.

7. A bitmap identifying free clusters on the hard drive.

8. An entry for the volume's boot blocks. This lets us treat the boot blocks like any other file.

9. A list of clusters that contain bad sectors. This prevents the clusters from being allocated to new files.

In some ways, the MFT is similar to the inode table in Unix. Both tables keep one entry per file. Both systems use a file's index in the table as another way to refer to the file.

However, the MFT format is significantly different. Although all inodes have the same format, each MFT entry only shares a block of header information in common. The working contents, such as file names or lists of extents, are stored in individually formatted data items called "attribute entries." For example, a typical file contains an attribute entry that lists the file's extents. A really small file, however, may contain a different attribute entry that carries the file's actual data contents. Other attributes indicate the file's ownership, access dates, and encryption information if built-in file encryption is used.

5.6 Input/Output and File System Software

In Section 2.2.2, we looked briefly at the standard features of modern operating systems: processes, memory management, input/output, and files. Here is how the operating system provides the last two:

- The operating system provides a simple and uniform way for programs to use I/O devices or files.
- When a program performs an operation on a file, the file system software transforms it into simple, standard I/O operations performed directly on the hard drive or other storage volume.
- The I/O system converts these standard operations into the specific actions required by individual I/O devices.

As systems have evolved in complexity, I/O has likewise evolved. Originally, systems focused on reading and writing streams of text that programs processed sequentially, 1 byte at a time, or one line at a time. Hard drives, when available at all, were tiny by modern standards.

Today, the I/O system must handle massive hard drives while instantly responding to keystrokes and flicks of the mouse. A practical modern system must be able to integrate a broad range of currently available I/O products, including hundreds of different printers, keyboards, mice, hard drives, USB drives, cell phones, Bluetooth devices, and other things. Moreover, the system also must be flexible enough to be able to integrate newer devices as soon as they appear.

DEVICE INDEPENDENCE

Programming is a difficult task. I/O devices have always posed the biggest challenge. In the early days of computing, every program was custom written to work with the specific hard drives, printers, and other I/O devices on the programmer's computer. The programmer often had to rewrite parts of a program when new I/O devices appeared.

Device independence was an important feature of early operating systems. This provided programmers with a standard, uniform interface for programming I/O devices. The operating system provided specialized programs—the device drivers—that converted standard I/O requests into device-specific requests.

THE HOURGLASS

The I/O system tries to provide maximum flexibility for applications and for I/O devices. This yields the hourglass design shown in Figure 5.17. The broad range of

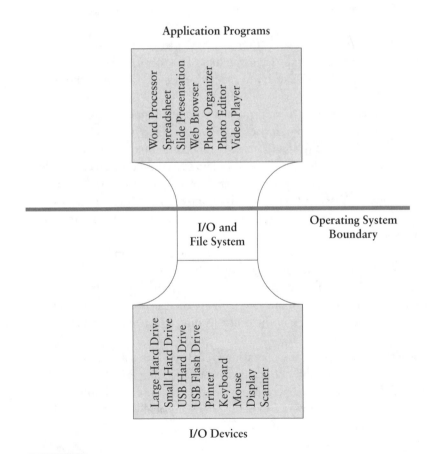

"Hourglass" structure of the I/O and file systems.

application program requirements are fulfilled by the I/O and file systems. The broad range of I/O device interfaces are mapped to the system's device driver interface.

This flexibility is demanded by the computing industry. Computer systems would be much simpler to build if everyone used the same browser software, or if all hard drive hardware worked exactly the same. The marketplace doesn't work that way in practice. Vendors flourish by providing features that competitors lack. Hardware vendors add new features and operating systems must accommodate these features. Likewise, application developers want to find new ways to use existing computing resources, and operating systems must be flexible enough to meet their needs.

FILE SYSTEM SOFTWARE

The operating system distinguishes between the file system software and the I/O system. The file system software handles the structure and organization of files on hard drives. The I/O system provides a uniform interface for performing basic I/O operations. In practice, the phrase *file system* may refer to a set of file storage formats or it may refer to the file system software that manages a particular format.

When we connect a removable drive to a computer, the operating system automatically tries to use the drive for storing and retrieving files. The software reads the boot blocks and volume labels from the drive to try to recognize the file format. If the system doesn't recognize the file format, it may ask for help. Typically, the system asks the user if the drive should be ignored, ejected, or reformatted with a recognizable file system.

If the system recognizes the file format, it tries to *mount* the file system. This connects the file system to the operating system's file software. Once mounted, we may use the user interface to navigate through directories and folders stored on the drive. The file system software saves information about the file system in RAM while it is mounted.

When the system mounts a drive, it takes exclusive control of it. Other programs, run either by users or administrators, are supposed to use the file system software for all accesses to that drive.

If a program tries to read or write to the drive directly, instead of using the file system software, there is a risk that the file system might read or write the same data block for a different purpose. This is a *concurrency problem*. If two separate programs try to use the same resource at the same time, they must coordinate their actions carefully. Otherwise, one program might undo the work of the other, leading to inconsistent data on the drive and confusion among the programs.

To remove a drive from the system, the operating system performs a *dismount* operation. This ensures that any information about the drive collected in RAM is properly written to the drive. This is why many operating systems expect users to explicitly perform an "eject" or "safely remove" operation before they physically disconnect a USB drive or other removable device.

PROGRAMMING ASSUMPTIONS

Operating systems have always made assumptions about what programmers need, and have organized the I/O requests around those assumptions. Some early systems made all

I/O devices look like punched cards and printers: 80-character blocks of input and 132-character blocks of output, always read in sequence. The Multics system tried to treat hard drives and other mass storage as extensions of RAM. The Unix I/O system had two paradigms; everything was either a sequence of bytes or a mass storage device containing addressable blocks.

Modern graphical-oriented interfaces rely on a much more sophisticated set of functions. These functions construct and manage windows on the desktop and menus of operations to perform. Modern systems organize these functions into an ***application programming interface*** (API). Internally, these operations usually are translated into basic "read" and "write" operations ("raw" I/O).

5.6.1 Software Layering

Modern operating systems are very large and staggeringly complex. Still, they are human artifacts and they follow certain design rules. In particular, most operating systems consist of ***software layers*** (Figure 5.18).

Each layer provides an API to the layer above it. Each layer relies on the API of the layer below it. At the bottom, a layer talks directly to physical resources, like I/O devices.

An Example

In Figure 5.18, the application program opens a file stored on a USB hard drive. The operation travels through four layers of I/O software to perform the operation.

First, the program calls the operating system API to open the file and to read or write the file's data.

Second, the operating system's API forwards these calls to the file system. When the user requests a file on a mounted device, the file system converts those requests into ***raw I/O*** operations. These are operations performed directly on the device, like read or write operations to specific sectors.

The file system chooses the third API layer depending on the type of device. If the device uses a more traditional mass storage interface, like ATA or SATA, then the file system passes the requests to the actual device driver. These device drivers interact directly with the device's interface circuits. In other words, the driver reads or writes data to storage registers built into the device's controller circuits. This is a privileged operation, so the device drivers run in kernel mode.

In Figure 5.18, though, the file resides on a USB drive. The file system doesn't communicate directly with the USB driver, because this driver supports a broad range of devices. The file system needs to talk to a mass storage device, so there is a separate layer of software to convert the mass storage I/O requests into USB requests. The USB hard drive software converts the file system's requests into USB operations. For the fourth layer, the hard drive software contacts the USB driver.

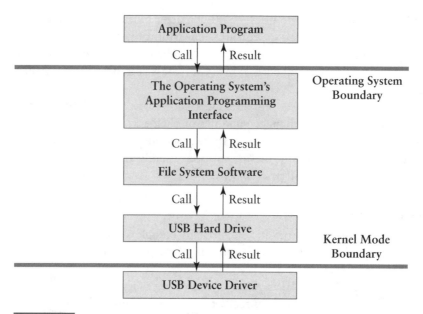

Figure 5.18

Procedure calls between operating system layers.

Layering Logic

Software designers use techniques like layering to organize large software systems. Layering is a special form of *modularity*, the notion of organizing software into separate modules, each of which contains procedures to implement specific functions.

Some systems are designed around "strict" layering, in which programs may only call procedures in the next-lower layer. All procedures in the system are assigned to layers, and no procedure may bypass one layer to talk to another. While this makes the system easier to understand, it also may make the program less efficient. For example, if a program needs to perform a specific operation that is implemented several layers lower, the request performs an extra procedure call for each layer it traverses. If the program could perform the low-level call directly, it bypasses all of those extra calls.

Layering often is enforced for security reasons. Potentially untrustworthy software resides at the top layer. It uses a tightly controlled API that checks all requests for proper form and authorization. After validating a request, the next layer passes the request to a lower, more fragile, layer of software that performs the operation efficiently without additional checking.

Within an operating system, strict layering applies in two places. First, all application programs must go through a tightly controlled API to request services from the operating system. Second, the operating system may provide strict layering between the user-mode operations it performs and kernel-mode operations, like those of device drivers.

In some cases, an I/O request may bypass a layer if appropriate. For example, a user program might have direct access to a device, like a USB flash drive. Such I/O requests bypass the file system completely. Likewise, I/O operations on a SATA hard drive won't have a separate layer between the file system and the device driver.

ABSTRACTION

Taken as a whole, computer systems are incomprehensibly complicated. The only way we can understand them is to break them into components and understand the system in terms of those components.

This approach is called *abstraction*. Instead of thinking of a computer's hardware components together in all of their complexity, we focus on the major behaviors of each one. Instead of considering how the power supply adapts to supply fluctuations while providing several different types of power to different components, we focus on the fact that it plugs in to the wall and simply feeds "the right power" to the computer's components. Instead of thinking of the CPU in terms of layers of silicon masks that exchange electrons, we think of it in terms of executing instructions and moving data around in RAM.

Figure 5.18 portrays an abstraction of the I/O system. It shows some simple features of the system's behavior and how certain components behave. It hides most of the details in order to illustrate a basic feature: that an API call is implemented by calling a series of functions that form layers.

When we use abstraction to simplify a system, we draw boundaries around its components and talk about the interactions that take place across those boundaries. To make matters simpler, we ignore interactions that aren't important for our purposes. This simplification allows us to make any system comprehensible at some level.

It is hard to hide the right amount of detail. If we do it correctly, we can examine our abstract description and use it to predict how the real system behaves. If we do it wrong, then our predictions are wrong. Successful abstraction often takes an incomprehensibly complicated system and turns it into a barely comprehensible one.

Application programming interfaces are abstractions. Instead of learning all about the programs that implement an API, the programmer simply studies the interface specifications. If the API and its specifications are written correctly, the programmer can predict what the program will do when it calls the API a particular way.

In a sense, few programmers ever see "real" I/O devices. Instead, most see a set of functions provided by the operating system. For example, all operating systems tend to treat mass storage devices as looking more or less the same. All such devices perform "read" or "write" operations with three arguments:

1. Data location in RAM
2. Data location on the device
3. Amount of data in the operation

When performing a "read" operation, the system moves the data from the given location on the device to the given location in RAM. When performing a "write," the data moves in the opposite direction. Most operating systems apply the same concept to file I/O; the data location on the device is calculated relative to the blocks of data in the file.

"Raw" I/O operations bypass the software that provides file system abstractions. Such operations won't recognize partition boundaries, files, or access restrictions.

5.6.2 A Typical I/O Operation

Here we break a typical I/O operation into 16 steps. To make matters a little more simple (more abstract as it were), we break those steps into four parts: A through D.

In this example we read a block of data from a file. We assume the file resides on a SATA hard drive, so the file system communicates directly with the driver when performing I/O. A "write" operation is subtly different in some ways, but the overall flow is similar. Likewise, different systems handle buffers, process scheduling, and other details differently. Despite subtle differences, this is how it happens in almost every modern operating system.

Part A: Call the operating system.

1. The application calls a function to read the next several bytes of data from the file. The function maintains a buffer that contains at least one cluster. If the function requires data from the next cluster, it will need to read that cluster from the file.

2. The function issues an I/O "read" operation to retrieve the next cluster from the file. The operation identifies a buffer in RAM, the buffer's size (the cluster size), and the number of the desired cluster from the file.

3. The operation performs a "trap" operation that starts an OS program running in kernel mode to handle the I/O request. Such requests often block the program from running until the I/O operation is finished. This involves scheduling and dispatching the application program's process, as described in Section 2.7.

4. The trap handler reformats the request into a format the file system can handle. It passes the request to the file system. This request identifies the file being read.

Part B: OS constructs the I/O operation.

5. The file system retrieves data about the file in order to figure out the location of the requested cluster in the file.

6. The file system constructs an I/O request to read the requested cluster from the hard drive. It converts the file's cluster number to an absolute sector address on the hard drive.

7. The file system passes the request to the device driver. The request identifies the specific drive containing the data, because most drivers may handle two or more drives, if all are of the same design.

8. The device driver identifies the physical device associated with the requested "drive." Note that a "drive" may actually be a partition on a larger device. The driver adjusts the hard drive sector address if the sector resides in a partition.

Part C: The driver starts the actual I/O device.

9. The device driver tells the device controller to start the "read" operation. It provides the controller with the sector address on the drive, the RAM address of the buffer, and the number of bytes to transfer. To do this, the driver literally writes data to registers built into the controller. These registers are connected to the controller circuits and direct the controller's actions.

10. The device controller instructs the drive mechanism to locate the appropriate cylinder and sector.

11. The mechanism starts transmitting data as soon as the sector appears under the read/write head. As the data arrives in the controller, the contoller typically stores the data in an internal buffer.

12. As data arrives in the buffer, the controller starts transferring it to the RAM location specified in the I/O request.

Part D: The I/O operation ends.

13. Once all data has been transferred to the buffer in RAM, the controller generates a special signal called an "interrupt." This signal causes a special "interrupt service routine" to run in the device driver.

14. The driver's interrupt service routine marks the I/O operation as finished. It also changes the application program's process state so that the program may resume.

15. The dispatcher sees that the application is eligible to run and, when its turn arrives, the dispatcher resumes the application program at the point following the I/O request.

16. The function in the application program retrieves the requested data and returns it to the caller within the program.

5.6.3 Security and I/O

Computer systems store all of their permanent resources on I/O devices, typically on hard drives. If application programs can perform whatever I/O they want, the programs can bypass any security measures the operating system tries to enforce. Secure operating systems often begin with restricting access to I/O devices.

RESTRICTING THE DEVICES THEMSELVES

A computer program controls an I/O device by reading or updating data registers in its device controller. In some computers, the registers appear like memory locations in RAM. Each I/O device has a set of assigned locations in RAM, and the device registers appear as storage locations. The program reads or modifies these registers by treating them just like other variables stored in RAM. This is called "memory mapped I/O."

Other computers provide a set of machine instructions to communicate with device registers. The instructions contain a numeric code that selects the device register of interest. Different machine instructions either read or write the device registers. This approach is called "programmed I/O."

Historically, not all operating systems have protected I/O devices, especially on desktop computers. The typical desktop operating system provided very few protections before the late 1990s. Many programs, especially graphics-oriented applications, relied on direct access to the hardware to achieve high performance. CPU improvements, especially in operating speeds and in built-in security mechanisms, helped reduce the impact of tightened security.

The operating system restricts access to I/O devices by blocking access to the device's registers. In memory-mapped I/O, the operating system blocks access to the RAM containing the device registers. The system restricts access to the device drivers. In programmed I/O, the CPU treats I/O operations as privileged instructions. Only kernel mode software may execute privileged instructions, and application programs never run in kernel mode. Because device drivers run in kernel mode, they may execute I/O instructions.

RESTRICTING PARAMETERS IN I/O OPERATIONS

I/O security extends beyond the problem of directly controlling devices. The I/O system plays an essential role in enforcing security at other levels, too.

For example, imagine the following: Bob and Tina both are running processes on the tower computer. What would happen if Bob's program directed the I/O system to input some data into RAM belonging to Tina's process? Or worse, the input operation might overwrite instructions inside the operating system itself. The I/O system must ensure that the process' I/O request will only affect that particular process. The I/O system has to check the RAM address used in every I/O operation and ensure that the results end up in the process' own RAM.

Likewise, the I/O system needs to check mass storage addresses to ensure they remain inside an approved range. If the process has opened a file, the file system maps the address to clusters within the file. If the address exceeds the file's permitted size, the operation fails. If the process has permission to open an entire drive partition, the system must ensure that the operation doesn't step over into a different partition.

FILE ACCESS RESTRICTIONS

The file system typically enforces the file access restrictions we studied in Chapters 3 and 4. The file system retrieves permission information when opening a file, and may refuse to open a file if the process lacks the access rights. The system marks each open file to indicate the process' access rights. This allows the file system to reject attempts to write a read-only file or to delete a file the process lacks the right to delete.

5.7 Resources

IMPORTANT TERMS INTRODUCED

abstraction	dismount	Moore's law
address variable	drive controller	mount
admissible	due diligence	partition
bitmap	evidence log	platter
boot blocks	extent	pointer variable
check value	file scavenging	private action
checksum	fragmentation	random access
civil complaint	hardware block diagram	raw I/O
cluster	header	read/write head
cluster chain	high-level format	remediation
concurrency problem	incident	sector
criminal complaint	index variable	sequential access
cylinder	inode	software layering
device independence	low-level format	track
digital forensics	mediation	undelete
disk drive	modularity	

ACRONYMS INTRODUCED

* Refer to Table 5.1 on page 199 for large number acronyms.

API—Application programming interface

B (uppercase)—Suffix indicating storage in bytes

b (lowercase)—Suffix indicating storage in bits

B-trees—Balanced trees

BPB—BIOS parameter block

CRC—Cyclic redundancy check

DVD—Digital video disk

ECC—Error correcting code

EDC—Error detecting code

FAT—File allocation table

HFS+ or HFS plus—Hierarchical file system plus

MFT—Master file table

MMC—Multimedia card

NTFS—NT file system

RPM—Revolutions per minute

SD—Secure digital

SDHC—Secure digital high capacity
SDXC—Secure digital extended capacity
UFS—Unix file system

5.7.1 Review Questions

R1. Why doesn't the last phase of the security process mark the end of the security process?

R2. Explain the four general tasks that may play a role in recovering from a security incident.

R3. Describe the basic requirements evidence must meet to be used in a legal proceeding.

R4. List and explain the three general categories of legal systems used in the world. Give an example of each.

R5. List and describe four ways of resolving a security incident that could rise to the level of a legal dispute.

R6. Explain the concept of due diligence.

R7. Does an employer in the United States have an unconditional right to search employee desks or lockers on company premises? Why or why not? Is there a way by which the employer can legally perform such searches?

R8. Describe the three steps an investigator performs when collecting forensic evidence.

R9. Is it better to perform a clean "shutdown" or simply pull the plug when collecting a computer as evidence?

R10. Explain how an investigator can examine a hard drive and still convince a court that the examination is based on the information residing on the drive when the suspect last had possession of it.

R11. Draw a diagram showing the basic components of a hard drive and its controller.

R12. Explain the difference between "high-level" and "low-level" disk formatting. When we perform a "quick format," what formatting do we perform?

R13. Describe two different ways of hiding data on a hard drive using partitions.

R14. What is the difference between 1 GB of storage and 1 GiB of storage? What is the difference between 1 KB of storage and 1 Kb of storage?

R15. Explain how to quickly convert a decimal number to a power of two by converting between decimal and binary exponents.

R16. What is Moore's law?

R17. Describe how to recover a deleted FAT file and its contents.

R18. Summarize shortcomings of the FAT file system compared to other modern file systems.

R19. List the three major hard drive storage problems addressed by file systems.

R20. Outline major similarities and differences between FAT, NTFS, Unix, and HFS+ file systems.

R21. Summarize the three strategies by which the operating system provides input/output services and a file system.

R22. Explain the relationship between device independence and device drivers.

R23. For each step in the example I/O operation described in Section 5.6.2, indicate which layer from Figure 5.18 performs the step.

R24. Indicate which layers from Figure 5.18 enforce which security measures in the I/O and file systems

5.7.2 Exercises

E1. Find the detailed technical specifications for a commercial hard drive. The specifications will identify a precise minimum or total amount of storage provided on the hard drive. Using this information, report the following:

    a. The hard drive's advertised size in bytes

    b. The exact, or minimum, number of bytes of storage actually provided by the hard drive

    c. The number of bytes of the power of two, or small multiple of a power of two, that is closest to the hard drive's advertised size

E2. Search the Internet for a description of a court action whose decision affected how computer equipment and information may be used as evidence. Describe the legal problem and the court's decision.

E3. Unix has a mechanism called a *hard link* by which it creates additional directory entries that all point to the same file. This is easy to manage because most information resides in the file's inode, including a count of the number of links. Bob is trying to create a hard link to a file in a FAT directory by duplicating the file's existing directory entry and giving it a new name. *How well will existing file read, write, and delete operations work?*

    a. Which operations work correctly if a FAT file has two directory entries?

    b. What operations won't work correctly? How do those operations fail to work correctly?

The following questions involve a forensic examination of a FAT file system. Find a "dump" utility and use it to examine the contents of a FAT file system. First, find an unused removable device, like a USB flash drive. Reformat it. Use online descriptions of the FAT format to locate the FAT and the file directories using the dump utility. Perform these exercises, print the results using the dump utility. Use a marker to highlight the results.

E4. Create a text file. Locate the file's directory entry and print it out. Locate the first cluster in the file and print it out.

E5. Create a subdirectory and place two text files in it. Locate the subdirectory you created. Print out the subdirectory.

E6. Delete a file. Locate the file's directory entry and print it out.

E7. Table 5.5 contains the partition table from the master boot record for the volume in Figure 5.9. The following is a list of sectors stored in different partitions. For each sector and partition, calculate the absolute address of the sector. (Hint: Use a spreadsheet.)

TABLE 5.5 Partition table for the drive in Figure 5.9

Partition ID	Starting Sector Number	Final Sector Number	Number of Sectors
p0	8	30,727	30,719
p1	30,728	61,447	30,719
p2	61,448	81,927	20,479

a. Partition 0, sector 1

b. Partition 0, sector 8184

c. Partition 1, sector 2040

d. Partition 1, sector 10,000

e. Partition 2, sector 1

f. Partition 2, sector 4088

The following questions involve Table 5.6, which contains part of a file allocation table. The "Cluster" column contains cluster numbers; the "Pointer" column contains the corresponding FAT entry.

The FAT entry contains one of the following: 0 to indicate a free cluster, 9999 to indicate the end of file, and any value in between indicates the next cluster in the file.

The following directory entries apply to these FAT entries:

- Name: F1, Starting Cluster: 100
- Name: F2, Starting Cluster: 106
- Name: F3, Starting Cluster: 120
- Name: F4, Starting Cluster: 126

TABLE 5.6 Part of a file allocation table

Cluster	Pointer	Cluster	Pointer	Cluster	Pointer
100	101	110	111	120	121
101	102	111	112	121	122
102	103	112	113	122	123
103	104	113	9999	123	124
104	105	114	0	124	9999
105	9999	115	0	125	0
106	107	116	117	126	127
107	108	117	118	127	128
108	109	118	119	128	129
109	116	119	9999	129	110

E8. For each file named in the directory entries, give the number of clusters in the file.

E9. We want to read individual bytes from these files. Clusters on this volume contain 4096 bytes each. For each of the following file names and byte offsets, identify the cluster that contains that byte.

a. File F1, offset 1000

b. File F2, offset 10,000

c. File F2, offset 20,000

d. File F3, offset 1000

e. File F4, offset 10,000

f. File F4, offset 20,000

E10. We are writing additional data to file F1 and need to add another cluster to the end of the file. Locate a cluster in the FAT to add to the file. List the specific changes to make to the FAT to add the sector to F1.

E11.   As in Exercise E10, we are writing data to file F2 and must add another cluster. List the specific changes to make to the FAT to add the cluster.

E12.   We are deleting File F3. List the specific changes made to the FAT to delete F3.

E13.   The engineering manager has decreed that we must discard the FAT and describe the disk contents in terms of extents. Use the FAT and file entries as they appear in Table 5.6.

  a. List the clusters in files F1 and F2 using extents.

  b. List the clusters in files F3 and F4 using extents.

  c. List all free clusters appearing in Table 5.6 using extents.

The following exercises ask about files of yours that you have not used in a while and that you *may safely modify.* You should use "About" and "Info" commands, and look at folder or directory listings to collect this information. Depending on the file system, you may be able to retrieve a creation date, reference date, and modification date.

E14.   Answer the following questions about a file stored on your computer's main hard drive: the hard drive that contains your operating system.

  a. What type of device is this: hard drive, solid state, removable, flash?

  b. What file system does the drive use? If FAT, try to determine if it is FAT 12, FAT 16, or FAT 32.

  c. Get information about the file: What dates can you retrieve and what do the dates say?

  d. Open the file with an editor or other program. Look at the file but do **not** change it. Close the file. Now, collect information about the file and report which dates, if any, have changed.

  e. Open the file again and make a minor, nondamaging change to it (for example, rotate an image left, then right). Save the file without changing the name. Now, collect the information about the file and report which dates, if any, have changed.

E15.   Answer these questions about a file of yours stored on a *removable drive* or *USB flash memory.*

  a. What type of device is this: hard drive, solid state, flash?

  b. What file system does the drive use? If FAT, try to determine if it is FAT 12, FAT 16, or FAT 32.

  c. Get information about the file: What dates can you retrieve and what do the dates say?

  d. Open the file with an editor or other program. Look at the file but do **not** change it. Close the file. Now, collect information about the file and report which dates, if any, have changed.

e. Open the file again and make a minor, nondamaging change to it (for example, rotate an image). Save the file without changing the name. Now, collect the information about the file and report which dates, if any, have changed.

E16. Find a discarded hard drive to disassemble. As you disassemble it, keep a list of every part removed or cut. Remove the cover to display the drive mechanism. Identify the major parts.

AUTHENTICATING PEOPLE

ABOUT THIS CHAPTER

In this chapter, we look at techniques to accurately associate individuals with user identities inside a computer. The discussion will focus on passwords with an introduction to other methods. The chapter examines the following topics:

- The three authentication factors: what you know, have, are
- Passwords, password bias, and average attack space
- Cryptographic building blocks: random choice, one-way hash
- Authentication devices: personal tokens and biometrics
- Basic issues in authentication policy

6.1 Unlocking a Door

We use padlocks, deadbolts, and safes to protect unattended things. We arrange it so that only authorized users may open these locks. We either restrict copies of keys to the trusted people, or we share lock combinations with only those trusted few.

In Bob's case, he lets other people use his computer, but he doesn't want their activities to affect his own work. In Figure 6.1, we break the problem down into its components. On the left we have Bob, the person who wants to use the computer. He types in a *user identity* he wishes to use, and provides a ***credential*** to prove the identity belongs to him.

On the right of the figure, we break the computer's problem into two separate mechanisms: authentication and access control.

1. Authentication—associates an individual with an identity inside the computer (this chapter).
2. Access control—checks access rights and grants access to resources (Chapters 2–4); the list of rights depends on the authenticated user identity.

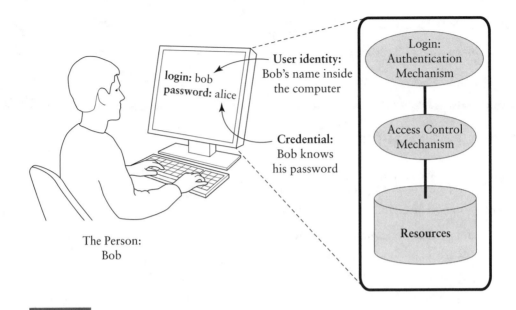

Figure 6.1

Authentication to protect computer resources.

When we look at physical locks, the bolt action provides the access control. When the bolt is locked, the door won't open and the locking mechanism keeps the bolt in place. When we supply the key or combination, we release the locking mechanism ("authentication"). When we turn the lock, we move the bolt to unlock the door ("access control").

Figure 6.2 illustrates the steps in performing an authentication. We start with Bob, the person who possesses the credential. He enters the credential into a device that converts it to computer-readable form. For passwords and PINs, the device is a keyboard. The device transmits the computer-readable credential into the computer's RAM. Inside RAM, the Login process compares the credentials against Bob's personal data stored in the computer's *authentication database*. This database contains a list of every user ID the system recognizes and the data required to authenticate each user. If they don't match, the authentication fails. If they match, Login proceeds.

Once the Login process has authenticated the user, it starts other processes on behalf of the user. Although the Login process is itself a system process, the children it starts all belong to the newly logged-in user. These processes will manage the user's desktop and handle other tasks on that user's behalf. Because these processes belong to the user, their access rights are restricted to those resources the user is allowed to use. Access control, as established by the access rights, is based on the authenticated user identity.

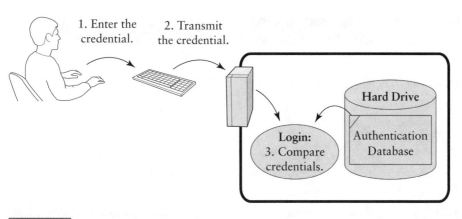

1. Enter the credential.   2. Transmit the credential.

Hard Drive

Login: 3. Compare credentials.   Authentication Database

Figure 6.2

Performing the authentication.

In authentication, our objective is to accurately tie the person to a particular user identity inside the computer. Computers make all of their decisions based on information. Thus, the computer must make its decision on information that only the authorized person can provide: the credential. It must be impractical for others to forge someone's credential.

This hard-to-forge information is often—though not always—secret information, so we call it the *base secret*. The system stores a copy of the base secret, or a specially encoded version of the base secret, in the authentication database. If an attacker acquires a copy of a user's base secret, the attacker can masquerade as that user. If the attacker has no way of retrieving or guessing the base secret, then a masquerade is much less likely.

The challenge in authentication is to establish credentials and associate them with the right people. A successful authentication system makes it as hard as possible for one user to masquerade as another by forging a credential. Over the years the computing community has developed a variety of techniques to do this, with varying degrees of success.

6.1.1 Authentication Factors

In computer systems, we recognize three fundamental strategies for authenticating people. These are called *authentication factors*:

1. Something You Know—memorized information like passwords or personal identification numbers (PINs).

2. Something You Have—an object containing a hard-to-copy base secret, like the magnetic stripe on a cash card.

TABLE 6.1 Examples of authentication techniques

Example	Factor	Base Secret	Credential
Memorized password	Know	The password itself	The password itself
Memorized PIN	Know	The PIN itself	The PIN itself
Magnetic stripe card	Have	Data on the magnetic stripe	Data on the magnetic stripe
One-time password token	Have	Internal secret	Displayed one-time password
SIM card or smart card	Have	Internal secret	Response to a mathematical handshake
USB password token	Have	Internal secret	Response to a mathematical handshake
Fingerprint	Are	Pattern derived from the owner's fingerprint	Digitized reading taken from fingerprint reader

3. Something You Are—a biometric measurement like fingerprints, voice, or eye features.

Table 6.1 gives examples of commonly used authentication techniques. Each example in the table represents a single factor. Each produces a credential. Each relies on a base secret.

Most systems use passwords, and thus they rely on only the first of the three factors. Originating with MIT's CTSS, passwords were the first effective form of computer-based authentication. Today, passwords remain the fundamental authentication technique. Even systems that use other authentication factors will have one or more password-protected logins that let administrators bypass the others.

Fernando Corbató, a key CTSS developer, saw passwords (called "private codes") as similar to combination locks that protected student lockers at MIT. Those locks were easy to crack, and Corbató did not believe that CTSS needed stronger security. Unfortunately, others in the computing community assumed that passwords could provide strong protection. In fact, secret passwords have always been vulnerable to a broad range of attacks.

TWO-FACTOR AUTHENTICATION

When we try to use an automated teller machine, we need a special object: the ATM cash card. This is an example of the second factor. An attacker can't copy the card's magnetic stripe with paper and pencil; the stripe requires special equipment to copy. Although this doesn't prevent countless thieves from buying the equipment and copying such cards, it provides slightly stronger protection than passwords. The attacker must simultaneously have both the card and the copying equipment, and this adds significantly to the effort.

In practice, ATMs won't accept the cash card by itself. The user must provide a PIN as well. The PIN is memorized information, so the ATM requires two different factors to authenticate a user. We call this *two-factor authentication*.

Two-factor authentication requires two *different* authentication factors, like a physical card plus memorized information. It isn't two-factor authentication to require two versions of the same factor, like two cards or two memorized passwords. To trick two-factor authentication, the attacker must perform two separate attacks, one for each factor. This provides a form of Defense in Depth.

Occasionally, we encounter systems that require a fingerprint, a spoken phrase, or even a peek at our face or eyes to authenticate us. These are *biometric* systems. At first glance such systems might appear to solve problems posed by the other systems. People forget passwords and lose cash cards, but they always bring their fingerprints with them. Attackers might intercept our passwords, but how can they fake our fingerprints? In fact, biometrics face their own distinct limitations. We examine them further in Section 6.6.

THREE-FACTOR AUTHENTICATION

There are a few systems that require a memorized secret, a physical token, and a biometric reading. These systems implement *three-factor authentication*. Again, to implement true three-factor authentication, we must require one factor of each type. For example, an ATM could require the cash card, the PIN, and a fingerprint reading as well. Three-factor systems are rare because the enrollment process is very difficult. Not only must we distribute cards and PINs, but we must accurately collect biometric readings.

6.1.2 Threats and Risks

Security policies rely heavily on authentication, and authentication poses its own risks. Here we focus on the specific risks and threats that affect authentication. For now, we also will focus on isolated computers like Bob's. Specifically:

- The focus is on attempts to trick the authentication system or to otherwise attack assets through the authentication system.
- We are not considering remote attacks involving either local computer networks or the Internet.
- Threats must have physical access to the system.

These features allow us to focus on a narrow range of threats. For these cases, threats fall into four categories:

1. No threat—no one sufficiently motivated to try to trick the authentication system.

2. *Weak threat*—a person with limited skills and a mild motivation to attack the authentication system.

3. *Strong threat*—a skilled person willing to invest time and money to attack the authentication system, but not inclined to cause significant damage.

4. *Extreme threat*—a person with the skill or motivation to do damage regardless of the authentication system. This includes threats who would damage or destroy the computer or people with the skill to circumvent other operating system protections.

Our risk assessment and policy will focus on the weak and strong authentication threats. We can address these threats with careful choices. The extreme threat won't be stopped by authentication alone. If we must construct a policy to resist an extreme threat, we treat it as a strong threat and work harder at covering other potential vulnerabilities.

Both weak and strong threats may appear in typical environments. There are a number of people who lack social restraint and will rifle through peoples' drawers and private spaces uninvited. Few people are motivated to penetrate further, but they exist. In a highly competitive workplace, some people will take strong measures to seek an advantage over coworkers. A strong threat can arise at home if the household is in turmoil. A family facing separation and divorce could foster a strong threat.

Risks

Though the home and workplace may face similar threats, we must address them differently. If we have our credentials in some physical form, whether as tokens, cards, or written copies of passwords, we must avoid leaving them near our computers.

At work, many people carry wallets or wear photo ID lanyards so they carry their credentials at all times. If we leave credentials or tokens unattended, they might be misused.

At home, people often leave such things unattended in a drawer or basket. We can't defend ourselves against a strong threat if we leave credentials and tokens unattended.

Figure 6.3 illustrates five basic external attacks on authentication. We will assume that Bob has a suitemate named Kevin, and that Kevin wants to masquerade as Bob:

1. Clone or borrow the credential or token.

   Kevin borrows or makes a copy of the credential itself and uses it to log in. For example, Kevin watches Bob type in his password by looking over his shoulder, and then remembering what he types (this is *shoulder surfing*). Kevin might find a copy of Bob's credential, like a password written on a slip of paper or a greasy fingerprint on a smooth surface, and use it to log in. He might also borrow an ATM card or login token.

2. Sniff the credential.

   Kevin *sniffs* the credential; he intercepts and copies it while being transmitted to the login process. Later, he replays the transmission in order to log in. For

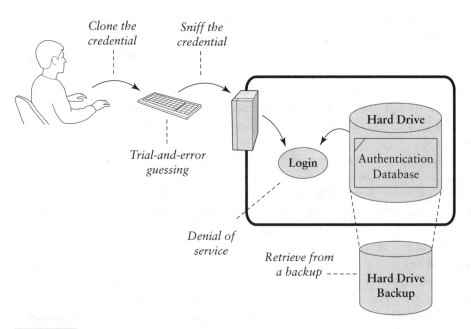

Clone the credential

Sniff the credential

Trial-and-error guessing

Login

Hard Drive

Authentication Database

Denial of service

Retrieve from a backup

Hard Drive Backup

Figure 6.3

Basic external attacks on authentication.

example, Kevin could sniff a password or the pattern generated by a biometric sensor.

3. Trial-and-error guessing.

Kevin tries to guess the data pattern that represents Bob's credential. This may be based on brute force, computer-driven guessing, or Kevin may simply guess several words or names that Bob might have chosen.

4. Denial of service.

A *denial of service* (DOS) attack either damages the system or blocks access to it by others. If the login mechanism is set up poorly, Kevin can lock Bob out by performing a series of unsuccessful logins. However, many systems will refuse access through any number of predictable events, like losing or forgetting a credential. Biometric systems may be sensitive to numerous unexpected problems, like the effects of extreme temperature or unusually dry or damp fingertips.

5. Retrieve from backup.

Kevin finds the authentication database or other information on a backup copy of Bob's hard drive and extracts the base secret from there. Most systems try to protect the authentication database from this, but there are ways to attack those protections.

In Chapter 2, we discussed process separation and protection. Clearly, if another process can read the data buffers used by the Login process, that process can sniff the credentials. This was a problem in some early password-protected systems. Modern systems routinely isolate processes to prevent access to RAM belonging to other processes. This normally prevents sniffing of credentials sent to the Login process. An attacker who can bypass RAM defenses poses an extreme threat. The attacker can use that skill to bypass other defenses. The attacker does not need to sniff passwords and masquerade as someone else.

Back in the 1960s, when CTSS was new, its developers ran into a problem. Occasionally, an unknown user would locate the password file (their authentication database), print it out, and post it on a public bulletin board. The developers took several steps to block access to this file, but the unknown user managed to bypass those defenses. In one case, the password file was swapped with the system's daily message. The password list printed itself out whenever someone logged in.

A well-designed modern system makes it much more difficult to steal a protected file like that. However, this is similar to the *retrieve from backup* attack described earlier. For now, we will not consider the problem of stealing the file itself because the file should be protected by operating system access controls. If the attacker can bypass the access controls on the password file, the attacker poses an extreme threat. The attacker does not need to masquerade as another user. The same tricks that retrieve the password file can probably retrieve other protected files.

Attack Strategy: Low Hanging Fruit

Although a few threats may target specific victims, most will settle for any profitable target they can attack. They know how to recognize common security weaknesses. When they see one, they attack. This happens in two phases:

1. The attacker scans potential targets for vulnerabilities that are easy and profitable to exploit.

2. When the attacker detects a vulnerability in a target, the attack takes place.

We call this ***low hanging fruit*** because the attacker goes after the easiest targets.

Last summer, Kevin stayed with his grandparents and was obliged to help harvest fruit with their farm workers. Most of the workers used ladders. Kevin didn't like ladders. He systematically worked his way through the orchard, grabbing all fruit on the lowest branches.

In no time, Kevin collected a few bushels, and then took the rest of the day off. Later that afternoon, he smugly presented his hand-picked bushels to his grandmother. This satisfied her demand for "working in the orchard." When she realized that Kevin wasn't popular with her other workers, she didn't have him work in the orchard itself again.

This type of attack is also called *doorknob rattling*. The attacker identifies a set of potential targets and then systematically searches them for vulnerabilities. Petty criminals do this in business districts or neighborhoods by systematically looking for unlocked homes or businesses. If the door is unlocked, the criminal robs the place. This can be a particular problem in apartment buildings.

Not all attacks are this systematic. Some attackers aren't motivated to work systematically. They don't think of themselves as criminals, but they will exploit an "opportunity" if it arises. While visiting a friend of a friend, for example, the attacker might be inclined to steal money or prescription drugs left in plain sight. These are opportunistic attacks.

> One evening, Kevin's grandmother sent him out to the cornfield to grab some fresh corn for dinner. The closest corn to the house was right along the highway. Kevin followed the highway fence looking for corn. All of the nearby stalks were stripped of their ears, probably by passing motorists. Kevin had to walk farther into the field to find ears of corn.

Attacks on computers in general, and on authentication in particular, often pursue low hanging fruit. When we assess the risk of attack, we should look at how our defenses typically work in the community of computing. We underestimate the risk if we focus on the best case.

6.2 Evolution of Password Systems

Early shared computing systems like CTSS used a combined keyboard and printer to interact with its users (the first computer terminals). These devices were often teletypes or special models of IBM's Selectric typewriters. Figure 6.4 shows Dennis Ritchie and Ken Thompson, two developers of the Unix timesharing system, using a teletype with a minicomputer. In normal operation, these terminals would echo the text the user typed by printing each character on a roll of paper. Unfortunately, this enabled the first of the five attacks just discussed.

It made perfect sense to echo the characters in most cases, but it posed a problem for passwords; once the user had typed it in, there was now a written copy of the password. A passer-by could shoulder surf and read the user name and password. Even worse, much of the printed paper was discarded after the computing session, and this would leave printed copies of passwords in trash cans.

Teletype machines allowed an easy solution: It was possible to disable the printer while typing text. Computing systems that used teletypes would disable the printer when asking for a password. Systems that used Selectric-based terminals, however, could not disable its printer. Instead, the systems would print a mask by repeatedly typing characters over the first several places on the line, making the user's typing unreadable. When the user typed in the password, the letters were typed on top of the mask. Figure 6.5 shows an example of password masking, taken from Boston University's Rax system, across the Charles River from CTSS.

The developers of CTSS did not immediately worry about the remaining attacks on passwords, despite their problems with their authentication database. The fifth attack, however, posed a worry at the University of Cambridge, England, where they were

Figure 6.4

Unix developers using a teletype.

```
*bu-rax/370  v1.0, sign on.
/id f,stdt009
*password?
▓▓▓▓▓▓▓▓
*sign-on at    20.01  17dec74 019 users
*rax will shut down at 11:00 p.m. ........
```

Figure 6.5

Masking the space for typing a password.

developing the Titan timesharing system. Their authentication database also contained all user names and passwords in the system. The Titan system was regularly copied to a backup tape, and they could not protect those tapes against weak threats within the local computing community.

PASSWORD HASHING

Roger Needham and Mike Guy, two of the Titan developers, were discussing the problem one evening at a local pub. They discussed ways of protecting the passwords with secret codes of various kinds. They finally hit upon the idea of using a "one-way cipher" function. The cipher would take a password and transform it ("hash" it) into unreadable gibberish.

Today, we call such a function a *one-way hash*. This function had two essential properties:

1. Whenever it hashed a particular password, it yielded the same gibberish every time.
2. There was no practical way to analyze the gibberish and derive the password that produced it.

The technique worked as shown in Figure 6.6. In preparation, Needham and Guy applied the hash function to the readable, plain text passwords in the password file, replacing each one with its hashed version.

Whenever a user logged in, the system collected the password and applied the hash function. Then the password checking procedure compared the hashed password against the user's hashed password stored in the password file.

Password hashing made the fifth attack, *retrieve from backup*, impractical, at least at first. In older versions of Unix, the password file itself was protected from writing, but allowed read access to all users. Unix relied on hashing to keep the passwords secret. Starting in the 1990s, however, improvements in password cracking strategies (see Section 6.4) placed even hashed passwords at risk of disclosure.

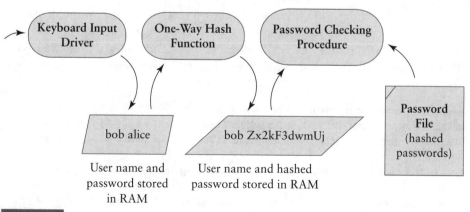

Figure 6.6

Procedure diagram of password hashing.

PROCEDURE DIAGRAMS

Note that Figure 6.6 is different from earlier diagrams in this book. It is a *procedure diagram*. So far, the other diagrams illustrated processes, and we can call those *process diagrams*. Both diagrams may work on data in RAM or in files.

In a process diagram, we show processes with ovals. The processes may all be running more or less simultaneously. Arrows show information flow between the processes.

In a procedure diagram, we show individual procedures with round-cornered rectangles. Each procedure represents a step in the larger procedure being illustrated. The procedures execute in a strict order, following the flow of data as shown by arrows.

Moreover, when we show a particular type of procedure, like a hash function, there are a specific number of inputs and outputs. Every typical implementation of a hash function has one input and one output.

PASSWORD HASHING IN PRACTICE

Password hashing on modern systems protects from the following attacks:

- *Social engineering* attacks. In these attacks, someone tries to talk a system administrator into divulging a user's password, often by posing as the user in question. Such attacks are impossible with hashed passwords. No one, including the administrator, can retrieve the password using only the hash. We explore social engineering further in Section 13.1.3.

- Stolen authentication database attacks. These are the same as classic attacks. Today, however the stakes are higher, because many users try to use the same password for many different purposes. Knowing the password for one system may help an attacker guess the right password for another system.

Modern computing systems still use passwords, but the environment is radically different from the earliest timesharing systems. Password files often reside on single-user systems as well as on personally managed websites and on larger scale systems. Some systems hash their stored passwords, while others do not. Modern Unix-based and Windows-based systems hash their passwords. Some, but not all, web-based systems hash their passwords.

> **Hint—Checking a system for plain text passwords:** Sometimes we can find out if a system stores plain text passwords. We contact the system's help desk and ask them to retrieve our lost password. If the system stores readable passwords, then there may be a way for the help desk to retrieve it.
>
> On the other hand, many help desks aren't provided the tools to retrieve passwords, regardless of whether the passwords are hashed or not. This is a sensible policy decision. It is very easy to disclose a password to the wrong person, especially if help desk operators can retrieve passwords.

6.2.1 One-Way Hash Functions

The key to successful password hashing is to use a well-written hash function. A hash function takes a larger block of data and produces a smaller result of a fixed size, called

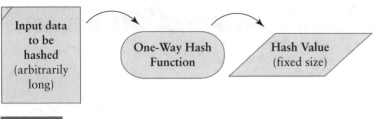

Figure 6.7

Procedure diagram of a one-way hash function.

the *hash value*. Although early hash functions worked with a few dozen bytes of data, modern hash functions can work with very large inputs, including entire documents (Figure 6.7).

In the early days of timesharing, hash functions typically were used to speed up searching for data in tables. Those hash functions were not appropriate for protecting passwords.

An early version of the Multics timesharing system used a simple hash function to protect its password file. This persisted until 1973, when the U.S. Air Force sent in a red team to probe Multics security. At a meeting reviewing their work, a member of the red team handed a slip of paper to the programmer who wrote the unfortunate hash function. The slip contained the programmer's password.

Today, we are careful to distinguish classic hash functions from modern one-way hash functions. The one-way hash is a *cryptographic function*. We use such functions to protect information against strong attacks. A well-designed cryptographic function resists trial-and-error attacks as well as analytical attacks that seek patterns in its behavior.

Years of experience have demonstrated that it's hard to construct a successful cryptographic function. The Multics programmer in the story had no real experience at designing cryptographic functions; back then very few people had such experience outside of secret government organizations like the NSA.

Modern Hash Functions

Many hash functions have appeared over the past several years. Table 6.2 summarizes major hash functions. The procedure called Message Digest 5, or MD5, was developed by Ron Rivest, a professor at MIT and prolific cryptographer. It has been widely used since the mid-1990s to protect e-commerce messages between desktop web browsers and secure web servers. MD5 distills the contents of such a message down to a 16-byte hash value.

The U.S. government also has published a series of hash procedures, called the *Secure Hash Algorithms* (SHA-x). The early versions were developed by the NSA and published as Federal Information Processing Standard 180, abbreviated FIPS-180. As of

TABLE 6.2 Modern hash functions and the size of their hash values				
Common Name	Date Introduced	Size in Bits	Size in Bytes	CURRENT USAGE
MD4	1990	128	16	No longer safe to use
MD5	1991	128	16	Used in web browsers, but unsafe
SHA-0	1993	160	20	No longer safe to use
SHA-1	1995	160	20	Used in web browsers, but unsafe
SHA-224	2002	224	28	Intended to replace SHA-1
SHA-256	2002	256	32	Intended to replace SHA-1
SHA-384	2002	384	48	Intended to replace SHA-1
SHA-512	2002	512	64	Intended to replace SHA-1

2009, the U.S. NIST published six algorithms: SHA-0, SHA-1, SHA-224, SHA-256, SHA-384, and SHA-512. The first two yield 20-byte hash values. The remaining four, all considered part of the "SHA-2" family, yield hash values whose sizes are indicated by their names.

The hash function by itself protects passwords in an authentication database. We also can use the function as an especially sensitive error detection code, like those discussed in Section 5.3.3. While checksums and CRCs work well for disk sectors or similarly sized blocks of data, a one-way hash can detect minor changes in enormous blocks of data, like programs downloaded from the Internet.

When a software publisher posts a program to be downloaded, there are risks that the user won't download the program correctly. In some cases, the program is damaged while being downloaded, and in other cases, a hacker might substitute a subverted version of the program for the legitimate one. To detect such failures, some publishers display the file's correct hash value along with the link to download the file. A careful user can use the hash procedure to calculate the file's hash and compare it with the publisher's hash value. If they match, the user downloaded the file correctly.

A CRYPTOGRAPHIC BUILDING BLOCK

However, the one-way hash isn't always easy to use by itself. It's not easy to compare hash values just by looking at them, and it's easier to have the computer do the checking. To make this work, we use the hash as a *cryptographic building block* and combine it with other functions to achieve better protection. Although there are many cryptographic functions, we will see the building blocks used in effective security systems.

To work reliably as a building block, a modern hash function must meet stronger requirements and resist more sophisticated attacks. Today, we expect a one-way hash function to perform as follows:

- If we change a document in any way, whether changing a single bit, a few bytes, or a large amount, the hash value will change in a large and unpredictable way.
- If we make a document longer or shorter, the hash value will change in a large and unpredictable way.
- If we have a hash value, we cannot construct a password or document that yields the same hash value.
- If we have a document and its hash value, we cannot build a different document that yields the same hash value.
- We cannot construct two different documents from scratch that both yield the same hash value.

A practical hash yields a unique hash value for every input. In reality this is theoretically impossible: If the hash values are only 20 bytes long and the files are 20,000 bytes long or longer, the hash values must collide once in a while. What makes hash functions work in practice is that there are far, far more hash values than there are documents. A 20-byte hash value represents a 160-bit binary number, and that number can cover a huge range of values:

$$\text{A range of 1 through } 2^{160} \cong \text{a range of 1 through } 1.46 \times 10^{48}$$

It is possible through the workings of random chance that two different documents or passwords could yield the same hash value, but it's very, very unlikely in practice.

6.2.2   Sniffing Credentials

A more recent style of attack has been to actively sniff authentication credentials as the user types them in. Sniffers exist as both hardware and software and are sometimes called *keystroke loggers*. Vendors supply a variety of justifications for customers. Parents are urged to use loggers to monitor childrens' computer use. Other vendors sell them as employee surveillance devices and, in fact, some employers use them to monitor their employees.

The lowest cost approach is, of course, to install sniffing software in the victim's computer. In some cases, sniffing software arrives unexpectedly from a worm or virus infection. Botnet software often includes a sniffer to try to retrieve authentication information for financial sites, like banks. The ZeuS botnet, for example, focuses on retrieving such information from infected computers (see Section 10.1.3). The botnet operators then use the stolen credentials in financial fraud.

Hardware keystroke loggers connect through the keyboard's cable. A typical model appears to be an innocuous extender plugged into the keyboard's USB socket (Figure 6.8). The keyboard itself plugs into a socket on the logger. Internally, the logger contains

Figure 6.8

Keystroke logger.

flash memory to collect the logged data. Physical keystroke loggers may be relatively easy to spot, assuming we know that we should look for one. However, there is no need for the devices to be large and obvious. Newer devices will be smaller and much harder to spot.

An alternative to keystroke logging is to intercept electronic signals sent by the victim's computer. Wireless keyboards, for example, transmit the keystrokes, and these transmissions may be intercepted and logged. Many such keyboards include an encryption feature, but these features often are easy to circumvent. Really sophisticated attackers could analyze stray signals generated by the computer or its peripherals; these are called TEMPEST attacks. We will discuss such matters further in Chapter 17.

Once the keystrokes have been collected, the attacker needs to sort through the data to locate passwords. In some cases, the process may be relatively obvious. For example, the password keystrokes often follow an obvious user name. In other cases, the attacker may need to use the keystroke data to identify possible passwords, and then proceed with a trial-and-error guessing attack.

6.3 Password Guessing

Password guessing takes many forms. Several unusual stories have appeared over the years on computer security discussion groups.

> **An Incident:** A woman found a coworker using her password-protected computer. She confronted the coworker, who admitted to having found her password by phoning the "Psychic Friends Hotline." A helpful psychic had told her the password.

The story is probably an urban legend, but it carries a nugget of truth. Careless or untrained computer users often choose passwords with a strong personal association. Through careful listening and observation of such people, a potential attacker can construct a list of likely passwords. Traditionally, a so-called "psychic" establishes credibility by speaking of things apparently unknown to others. Such psychics develop this information by studying and observing the target and by making shrewd guesses. This is also an effective strategy for guessing passwords.

DOD PASSWORD GUIDELINE

In 1985, the U.S. DOD's Computer Security Center published their *Password Management Guideline* (document CSC-STD-002-85). First and foremost, it required that all user identities be assigned to individual people and never shared. This meant that passwords were private secrets that likewise were never shared with others.

When the DOD guidelines were published, there were two perceived risks to passwords: disclosure (intentional or accidental) and trial-and-error guessing. Neither attack would necessarily be discovered immediately, if at all. To limit the vulnerability, the DOD guidelines recommended periodic password changes: monthly, yearly, or something in between. The recommended time frame was not based on the amount of time it would take for a masquerading attacker to do serious damage. Instead, it was calibrated to the estimated time it would take for a trial-and-error guessing attack to succeed.

INTERACTIVE GUESSING

Trial-and-error attacks take on several guises. The traditional approach was to perform successive login attempts, guessing a different password each time. A more automated form might use an automated script to feed a series of password guesses to the login command. Many systems address this by inserting time delays into the login operation. The delays may lengthen in the face of multiple failed password guesses.

Login operations also may keep a count of the number of failed password attempts. The number of failed guesses is reported to system administrators. The system may report the number of guesses directed against a particular user identity to the owner of that identity. Finally, many systems define a maximum number of guesses. When the number exceeds that threshold, the system won't allow that user identity to log in. The DOD guideline suggested a limit of five guesses in a row; some modern systems limit users to three incorrect guesses.

The restriction to three guesses may make sense on a game show or perhaps in decades past when a user only had a single password to remember. Today, a typical user may need to juggle dozens or even hundreds of password-protected accounts. Unless the user consults a written list whenever he logs in, he is not always going to enter the correct password on the first or even the second try. Matters become worse for seldom-used accounts; users can't possibly remember such passwords except by trial-and-error guessing or by consulting a saved list.

Guess restrictions may have serious side effects when applied to administrative accounts. An attacker once disabled a system by making numerous guesses to the administrator's user identity. The system locked out the administrator. The attacker then caused another problem that froze the system until an administrator cleared the problem. With the administrator locked out, there was no way to clear the problem.

NETWORK-BASED GUESSING

Attackers are not limited to interactive login guessing on some modern networking systems. For example, some older forms of Microsoft file sharing use passwords for authentication, and an attacker can try to crack a password by making successive file sharing requests, each with a different password guess. This attack takes place at network speeds.

Unfortunately, it isn't always practical to treat such attacks the same as interactive logins. On some systems, the natural behavior of the network system may make it hard to distinguish legitimate traffic from a trial-and-error guessing attack.

OFF-LINE PASSWORD CRACKING

The most powerful modern attack on passwords is the *off-line attack*, which attacks hashed passwords. We also call this *password cracking*.

For many years, Unix password files were protected from writing but not from reading. The designers relied on the hash function to protect the passwords. As systems improved, however, so did their ability to calculate password hashes very quickly. At first, Unix designers redesigned the hash function to take longer, but that was only a temporary measure. By the 1990s, Unix systems were storing password hashes in inaccessible files.

Figure 6.9 illustrates an automated attack on password hashes. For input, the attack takes one or more password hashes, like Alice's shown in the lower right-hand corner (the value "u3#"). The attack generates all possible passwords, one by one. In the figure, the attack generates three-letter passwords. It then calculates the hash for each of these passwords and compares it against the hash of the user's password. Note that Alice's hash matches the sixth hash value generated. When (if) hash values match, the attack retrieves the password it used to produce the hash (the sixth password, "aag").

This attack is much faster, and thus more dangerous, than online attacks. While an online attack may be slowed down or blocked entirely, if the attacked system detects too

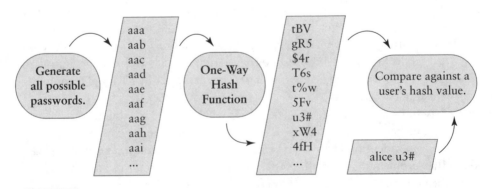

Figure 6.9

Off-line trial-and-error attack on Alice's password hash.

many bad passwords, the off-line attack proceeds at full speed. Moreover, the system under attack can't possibly detect that the off-line attack is in progress.

Modern systems try to reduce the risk of off-line attacks in two ways. First, many systems demand users create longer and more complicated passwords. Second, no modern system intentionally discloses its hashed password file to its users. Unfortunately, modern systems don't keep all encrypted and hashed passwords protected. Networking software often transmits encrypted or hashed passwords between systems. Attackers may intercept these hashed passwords and apply an off-line attack.

The good news is that off-line attacks aren't always a principal security problem. The bad news is that off-line attacks are often a major security problem. We will review the trade-offs in a later section.

6.3.1 Password Search Space

Our passwords cannot resist a guessing attack if the attacker can guess every possible password through trial and error. Whether the attack is online or off-line, it's obviously easier to try to guess a three- or four-character password than to guess a much longer one. Our first step in measuring the strength of our password system is to count the total number of possible passwords. We call this the *search space*.

The search space provides the *upper bound* for the number of guesses required to guess a particular password. If a trial-and-error attack tries every single password in the search space, the attacker is guaranteed to find the password. Statistically, the attacker is likely to guess the password long before trying all of them; on average, the attacker should only have to try half of the possible passwords before guessing the right one. It may take the attacker a very long time to search the entire search space, but the search is guaranteed to succeed eventually.

Older—and cheaper—computers could not handle both uppercase and lowercase letters. Early users chose passwords from the 26-letter alphabet. In theory, any letter in a password could be one of the 26 available letters. We calculate the search space S of different sized passwords as follows:

$$S_{OneLetter} = 26^1$$

$$S_{TwoLetters} = 26^2$$

$$S_{ThreeLetters} = 26^3$$

If we know that all passwords are of exactly the same length, then the calculation is very simple, with A representing the number of characters we can choose from (letters, digits, etc.), and L being the number of characters in the password:

$$S_{FixedLengthPassword} = A^L$$

Most systems that allow *L*-length passwords also accept shorter passwords. Traditional Unix systems, for example, accepted any password from length zero (no password) to eight characters. Although the fixed-length calculation may provide a tolerable estimate of the number of passwords, it underestimates the real number. To calculate the search space for all possible Unix passwords, we add up the search space for passwords of that length and shorter:

$$S_{8LetterPassword} = \sum_{i=1}^{8} 26^i$$

This summation produces a finite geometric progression, which we calculate by doing the sum. We also can reduce it to an equivalent and simpler algebraic form:

$$S_{8LetterPassword} = \frac{26^{8+1} - 1}{26 - 1}$$

$$S_{8LetterPassword} = 2.17 \times 10^{11}$$

This yields a great number of passwords: 217 billion worth. In the early days of passwords, this was enough to discourage the most motivated attacker, but the risks grew as computer performance improved.

We make passwords harder to crack by making the attacker work harder. We refer to this as the **work factor**. For passwords, we increase the work factor by increasing the search space:

- Increase the length of the password; allow it to contain more characters.
- Increase the size of the alphabet or **character set** from which users choose their passwords.

When we vary the password's length, character set size, or both, we use the following sum to calculate the search space; *A* being the size of the character set, and *L* being the maximum length of the password in characters.

$$S_{VaryingSize} = \sum_{i=1}^{L} A^i$$

Again, the progression has a simplified algebraic form:

$$S_{VaryingSize} = \frac{A^{L+1} - 1}{A - 1}$$

If we include both uppercase and lowercase letters in our eight-letter passwords, we double the size of the alphabet and greatly increase the search space. We make the search space even larger, of course, if our passwords include digits and punctuation. In all, today's standard ASCII character set has 94 printable characters, excluding the

		Search Space for Different Lengths		
Form of the Password or Passphrase	Number of Choices (A)	8 Characters	16 Characters	32 Characters
Single-case password	26	2.17×10^{11}	4.54×10^{22}	1.98×10^{45}
Short, single-case passphrase	27	2.82×10^{11}	7.98×10^{22}	6.36×10^{45}
Mixed-case password	52	5.45×10^{13}	2.91×10^{27}	8.33×10^{54}
Alphanumeric password	62	2.22×10^{14}	4.85×10^{28}	2.31×10^{57}
Printable ASCII password	94	6.16×10^{15}	3.76×10^{31}	1.40×10^{63}
Short, printable ASCII passphrase	95	6.63×10^{15}	4.40×10^{31}	1.94×10^{63}

TABLE 6.3 Search space for random passwords or passphrases

space character. Because words are delimited by spaces, it doesn't make sense to include spaces.

Some high-security applications use *passphrases* that use longer, multiword phrases as secrets. People might not remember a long collection of letters and punctuation, but they might remember a long text phrase. Unlike passwords, a passphrase may include spaces as well as uppercase and lowercase letters and punctuation. Table 6.3 shows the number of possible passwords or phrases given various character set sizes and password lengths.

The table illustrates password styles that yield search spaces ranging from 10^{11} to 10^{63}. Modern computational power can efficiently perform trial-and-error attacks in the range of billions and trillions (10^{12}). Problems in the quintillions (10^{18}) have been cracked, though each attack requires a number of dedicated resources.

Lacking further information, this would suggest that eight-character passwords are borderline safe, especially if we don't restrict ourselves to single-case characters. Extending passwords to 16 characters would seem to place them out of the range of current attacks. This assumes, however, that people choose random passwords. This doesn't necessarily happen in practice.

6.3.2 Truly Random Password Selection

In an ideal world, the attacker's work factor is the same as the password's search space; the only way the attacker can reliably guess a password is by trying every possible password. If we look at the probabilities, the attacker has an even chance of success after performing half as many trials as the size of the password's search space—but this is the ideal case. If passwords are *not* chosen randomly, then the attacker may exploit the bias and guess passwords faster.

When we use the word *random* in casual conversation, it often means "unplanned" or even "impulsive." People often talk about almost any hard-to-interpret information as being "random." In statistics, the word *random* refers to a collection of unbiased and uncorrelated data. That means something specific about what is in the collection, but says very little about the order in which the data appears.

In the field of security, however, we demand a really strong definition of *random*. When we require something to be random for security purposes, we can't rely on personal impulses. True randomness arises from a truly random process, like flipping a coin, rolling dice, or some other independent, unbiased action. Random events may include opening to the random page of a large book or measuring stochastic events at the electronic level inside a circuit.

This is *cryptographic randomness*. For data to be cryptographically random, it's not enough to produce a collection that's free of statistical bias in the traditional sense. The data must not be part of a computed—or computable—sequence. Random data can't be produced by a procedure. We need each choice to be produced independently from the previous one. The choices can only come from measuring truly random events.

This poses a problem inside a computer. It is easy to produce *pseudorandom numbers*. That is what we get when we call the "random" function in typical programming languages or in applications like Excel. These numbers come from a procedure best called a *pseudorandom number generator* (PRNG). These numbers are not truly random because they are determined by the procedure that generates them. Typically, these generators start from a "seed" value (often the time of day in seconds) and generate hard-to-predict numbers. In fact, the only randomness in the sequence often comes from the seed, which may or may not be random. There may be ways to unravel such sequences of numbers in a way that threatens security. When we need truly random choices, we should *not* use pseudorandom numbers.

There are many ways to generate truly random numbers, but they all require truly random inputs. For example, the four dice shown in Figure 6.10 can generate a random four-digit decimal number.

If the random numbers don't need to be secret, we can find truly random numbers on the Internet. Sites like "random.org" provide numbers generated by truly random phenomena. The website doesn't exactly roll dice to generate the numbers, but the effect is the same. Some operating systems, notably Linux, have developed "truly random sources" that carefully monitor certain types of behavior in the system and derive randomness from variations in such behavior.

There are several applications and other products that generate secret and truly random passwords from truly random input. We also can do this manually by selecting letters, digits, and punctuation randomly from large books. We randomly open the book, put our finger down, and pick the next character we find. Although this will yield hard-to-guess passwords, we still won't choose passwords that take full advantage of the

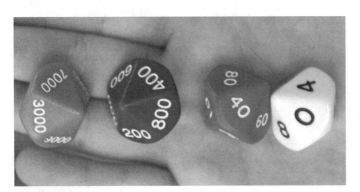

Figure 6.10

Decimal dice can produce truly random numbers.

search space. The books themselves are biased: Individual letters don't occur with the same frequency. The letter "e" will appear much more often than the letter "q" in such passwords. We will look more closely at such biases in Section 6.4.

6.3.3 Cracking Speeds

For now, we'll assume our passwords are perfectly random. If so, how big must our passwords be to resist trial-and-error attacks? If we have a hashed password file from a system restricted to single-case words of eight characters or less, then we need to hash 217 billion separate passwords. How long would that take?

Moore's law predicts that computing power doubles every 18 months, thus, our ability to crack passwords will continue to improve. Table 6.4 summarizes different degrees of cracking feasibility, based on theory and capabilities in 2011. The following paragraphs discuss the prospects of different cracking technologies.

A modern desktop computer can easily calculate 100,000 hashes (10^5) per second. It would take most of a month to hash every eight-letter word. This may be practical if the password is important enough and the delay isn't significant. If, however, we put some

TABLE 6.4 Different degrees of cracking feasibility		
Cracking Technology	Tests Completed	Estimated Time
Desktop	10^9	Hours
DES Cracker	10^{18}	Hours
Physical limit using the sun's energy	10^{75}	Ten billion years

serious computational muscle into it, we can dramatically reduce the calculation time. For example, if we throw 100 such computers at the problem, we hash all of those passwords in a little over 6 hours.

For even more serious password cracking, consider the DES Cracker. Although we will discuss its purpose and construction further in Section 7.3, for now we should appreciate its sheer speed. Designed and built in 1998, the Cracker tests encryption keys through trial and error at a rate of 88 billion keys per second (almost 10^{11}). Over ten years later, we can safely assume that it's possible to build a similar machine that cracks password hashes. At that rate, we could calculate 217 billion hashes in less than 3 seconds.

Although it seems likely that progress will continue for many years, some researchers believe computations will ultimately be limited by the fundamentals of physics. One U.S. government study examined the minimum theoretical energy requirements needed to sustain information state transitions at a physical level. The result was used to estimate the energy required to crack encryption keys. Their conclusion was that, in theory, we could test as many as 10^{75} keys or hashes, but it would take all of the energy generated by the sun over its entire lifetime. This is only a theoretical result. Some researchers suspect that "quantum computing" techniques might speed up key cracking. Today, however, we are limited to trial-and-error computation, possibly aided by testing numerous keys in parallel on separate CPUs.

6.4 Attacks on Password Bias

If our computer user community commits to using long, random passwords, attackers won't succeed very often at guessing passwords, either online or off-line. However, attackers can probably retrieve some passwords if they focus on *likely* passwords. This is the *dictionary attack*.

Researchers discussed dictionary attacks in the 1970s and 1980s, and a few systems applied simple tricks to make such attacks more difficult. In late 1988, someone actually used a dictionary attack to crack passwords and exploit them. It was, again, the Morris worm.

In Section 2.3, we saw how the Morris worm used a flaw in the "finger" process to penetrate a vulnerable computer. Not all computers ran that version of "finger," so that attack did not always succeed. If the "finger" attack failed, the worm would retrieve a computer's password file. The worm attacked Unix systems, and at that time the Unix password file was still readable to all users. The worm would try to crack any user password it could (Figure 6.11). If it succeeded, it would infest the computer via that user's login. Although no reliable numbers were collected regarding the actual achievements of the worm, observers at the time estimated that its password cracking succeeded 50 percent of the time.

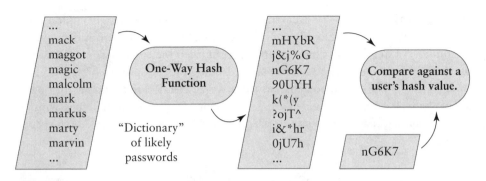

Figure 6.11

Dictionary attack by the Morris worm.

Following the worm, several researchers analyzed dictionary attacks. They constructed dictionaries, calculated hash values for each word, and compared them against genuine hashed passwords. The researchers' attacks didn't crack every password, but they often succeeded. The rates of success varied with the researcher and dictionary, but ranged from about 20 percent to about 35 percent.

Using these strategies, programmers started writing "password cracking utilities." These programs would take a hashed password file from a well-known system and try to crack the passwords. Typical programs started with a list of likely passwords, hashed them, and compared the hashed results to those in the password file. Effective programs could crack common passwords in a matter of seconds.

Many organizations recognized this as a serious risk. In response, they often passed rules to force—or at least encourage—users to select passwords that were hard to crack. With Windows 2000, Microsoft introduced tools to restrict password selection by requiring users to include a variety of uppercase and lowercase letters, digits, and punctuation characters.

The point of Microsoft's restrictions, and of similar rules enforced by other systems, is to keep people from choosing simple words from a small collection of possibilities. The rules try to force users to choose passwords containing a broad range of randomly chosen characters, instead of a work consisting entirely of letters. The rules attempt to make passwords harder to guess in order to make dictionary attacks impractical.

BIAS AND ENTROPY

Strictly speaking, a password's strength depends entirely on its uncertainty. When we measure the uncertainty in the value of a data item, we measure its *entropy*.

In physics, entropy measures the disorder in a system. In computing, it represents the amount of information you *don't* know if you don't know the value of a variable. This is also called *Shannon entropy* after the author of information theory. The entropy in a password reflects the number of different passwords that might exist in proportion to the likelihood of each one actually occurring. For example, if there are 817 billion possible passwords and all are equally likely, then the entropy is very large. But if everyone chooses from a very small collection of words instead, then the entropy is very small. We focus on the *likelihood* of particular passwords and not just on the search space.

It can be hard to calculate entropy exactly. Password selection relies on hard-to-predict personal behavior. Instead of calculating the entropy itself, we estimate password strength by estimating biases in password selection and combining it with search space calculations.

6.4.1 Biased Choices and Average Attack Space

When we calculate the search space for a particular password, we find the upper bound for the number of guesses required. This represents the attacker's "worst-case scenario" when trying to guess a password. However, attackers don't have to try all possibilities to crack some passwords. If they exploit biases in password selection, they can find passwords without having to try all the possibilities.

Average Attack Space

When attackers exploit biases in password selection, they aren't targeting individual users. Instead, they are targeting a whole community. They are relying on the fact that *some* password choices will reflect well-known biases. This is a *statistical* attack on passwords; it tries to find *any* password that it can crack without focusing on a specific user's password.

As defenders, we need to estimate the danger such attacks might pose. If the search space poses a worst-case scenario for the password attacker, we also need to estimate the work involved in the best-case scenario. The ***average attack space*** estimates the number of guesses required before success is *likely*. This estimates the ***lower bound*** for a successful attack.

For our purposes, we treat a likelihood of 50-50 or better as being likely to succeed. If we apply this to our earlier search space calculations, an attacker achieves the 50-50 likelihood after trying half of all possible passwords. In other words:

> If the search space contains all possibilities, and they are equally likely,
> then the Average Attack Space is *half* of the search space.

Biased Password Selection

When people are biased in their password selection, they choose passwords from only *part* of the total possible search space. We see a similar problem if we try to keep food stocked without actually counting cartons in the kitchen. We can estimate how quickly we use up our food by measuring the average amount we eat. In practice, however, we can't assume that we use everything at the same rate; some foods disappear much more quickly. To keep food stocked effectively, we need to replace the food most likely to be used up.

In passwords, we search most efficiently if we focus on the passwords people are most likely to choose. We can either make a list of those words or theorize about peoples' choices, and then estimate the number of passwords most likely to be chosen. This represents a "dictionary" of the likely passwords. Our biased search space *S* equals the size of this dictionary.

In practice, not everyone will choose from this biased collection. To estimate the number of guesses needed to find a biased password, we adjust the search to consider the fraction of people likely to choose from that set. We represent the fraction with *L*. This yields the *average attack space* (*V*).

$$V = \frac{S}{2 \times L}$$

Here is an example: Imagine that research at a particular site found that 1 out of 10 people chose the name of a United Nations member country as their password. There are 192 member countries. If we include the names both capitalized and uncapitalized, that yields a search space of 192 x 2 = 384 passwords.

If those are the *only* passwords allowed, then the average attack space is half of the search space, or 192.

Because only 1 out of 10 people choose from that search space, we must try 10 times as many passwords so that, on average, we regularly choose passwords from that smaller group. That yields an average attack space of 1,920.

Measuring Likelihood, Not Certainty

The result *V* estimates the average number of trial-and-error guesses the attacker must make to guess a password. The attacker may guess the password sooner or later than that, or not at all. The average attack space simply says that *statistically* the attacker is *likely* to find a password after performing that many trials.

If we need to positively guess a password, then we need to search the entire search space of possible passwords. We can't focus our attention on only the likely passwords. On average, the search may involve only guessing half of the possible passwords. On the other hand, it will never require searching more than the entire search space.

Making Independent Guesses

Our average attack space estimate only applies, however, if we respect a fundamental assumption: the estimate only applies to a large number of *independent* guesses. Each guess should randomly select a target (a victim user's password) and a candidate (a legal, randomly chosen password). If the candidate password's hash matches the target's hash, then we found a password. If not, then we randomly choose a different target and different candidate to test. We should choose both the target and the candidate randomly each time. This helps ensure that each trial is independent.

EXAMPLE: FOUR-DIGIT LUGGAGE LOCK

Figure 6.12 shows a combination lock for a lock box or a storage case. There are four digits, and the owner chooses the combination. The combination can be any number between 0000 and 9999, yielding 10,000 possible combinations.

If we assume that all combinations are equally likely, here is the average attack space calculation:

$$V_{\text{4-digit lock}} = \frac{10,000}{2 \times 1}$$

$$V_{\text{4-digit lock}} = 5000$$

If we take the attacker's point of view, we have to try at least half of the search space (5000) before it becomes likely that we guess the right combination. If we try one number every 5 seconds or so, it will take almost 7 *hours* on average to guess a combination.

A smart attacker pursues low hanging fruit. In this case, we reduce the amount of guessing if we focus on likely combinations. For example, we can easily code a date consisting of month and a day into four digits. Most people have several personal dates they remember: birthdays, anniversaries, and so on. Although we won't necessarily know which dates are significant to particular people, we dramatically reduce our guessing if we focus on the 366 possible 4-digit dates.

In the previous calculation, we could confidently say that everyone has to choose a four-digit combination from the range of 10,000 possible values. We don't really know how many people use a date as a four-digit combination, but we can make a pessimistic but plausible estimate. If we assume that only one out of four owners uses a date as a four-digit combination, we have the following average attack space:

$$V_{\text{4-digit lock}} = \frac{366}{2 \times 0.25}$$

$$V_{\text{4-digit lock}} = 732$$

A four-digit luggage lock.

At 5 seconds per trial, it will take slightly over an hour, on average, to open one of these combination locks.

Remember how the statistics work: We can't focus on a single lock or a single guessed combination. We need to randomly guess a different date each time. Likewise, we must randomly try different locks from a large collection.

For example, if we are in a room with hundreds of four-digit combination locks, it will take us an hour on average to open one, and we can't predict *which* one ahead of time. To apply our estimate correctly, we must try one lock and move to another every 5 seconds. Even then we might not succeed at the end of the hour; the statistic simply says that success is *likely*.

Moreover, the attack assumes that at least one in four owners uses a date as a combination. If all owners were vigorously indoctrinated to avoid using anything except a truly random number, and fewer than 25 percent of them ignored that advice, then the average time will be longer. If our goal is to open a specific lock and we have no reason to know how the owner chose the combination, then we can't ensure success except by planning to try every possible combination.

6.4.2 Estimating Language-Based Password Bias

We see biases in password selection because people naturally tend to choose *words* as passwords. Written words carry far less entropy than random collections of letters. For example, look at the first letter in this sentence ("F") and ask, "Which letters can possibly come next?" Spelling rules limit us to only a few choices, mostly lowercase vowels. Once we include the second letter ("Fo"), there are more possibilities, but some are much more likely than others.

If we systematically analyze typical English, we find an average entropy of perhaps three letters per character in a typical word. Thus, the practical entropy in an eight-letter English password is closer to 3^8 (3×10^3). Compare that to 10^{11}, the entropy in a password made up of eight randomly chosen lowercase letters. Even when we permit longer words, we clearly lose a great deal of entropy by choosing words.

This loss of entropy opens the way for a low hanging fruit attack. The attackers don't bother testing for all possible passwords. Instead, they use a dictionary or other list of words. If the dictionary contains lots of commonly used words, there's a good chance that the words will match some user passwords. This is the *dictionary attack*.

How dangerous can a dictionary attack be? The Morris worm used a dictionary and, according to legend, cracked about half of the passwords it examined. The legend was based on guesswork and we need better information to accurately estimate the risk.

KLEIN'S PASSWORD STUDY

In 1990, researcher Daniel Klein completed a comprehensive study of the use of words as passwords. Klein collected password files from Unix systems in the United States and the United Kingdom (UK) for an experiment in password cracking. The collection contained over 15,000 hashed passwords. First, Klein hashed each user name to see if the user had used the name as the password. He found over 300 passwords that way. Then he performed permutations of the user name and the user's proper name (also stored in the password file). Then he collected lists of proper names, place names, literary titles, mythological references, biblical terms, character names, and so on. This yielded a dictionary of over 60,000 words. Klein then produced permutations of those words by altering capitalizations, substituting letters and digits, and inserting punctuation characters. This yielded a total of over 3 million words to test. Out of the 15,000 passwords Klein examined, he cracked almost 25 percent of them.

To estimate the average attack space, we need two pieces of information. First, we need S, the range of possibilities from which users choose their passwords. Second, we need L, the likelihood that users choose from that particular range of possibilities. Klein's work provides both of those values.

With the passwords shown in Table 6.3, the likelihood is 100 percent that members of the community will be required to choose passwords from a particular set: If the system only accepts single-case letters, then that's what the passwords look like. By the same token, if it allows all 94 printable characters, some users may choose a mixture of punctuation, digits, and random letters. It is easy to calculate the average attack space for these passwords; we simply divide the search space by 2.

Klein's results estimate both the search space of likely password choices and the likelihood that people chose passwords from that search space. Klein found that 24.2 percent of users chose words in his dictionaries; similar research by others has placed the percentage in a range from 20 percent in the early 1990s to 35 percent a decade later. Here is the average attack space calculation based on Klein's experiments:

$$V_{\text{Klein}} = \frac{3,321,261}{2 \times 0.242}$$

$$V_{\text{Klein}} = 6.86 \times 10^6$$

Note that Klein's style of attack might work even if the password is required to include a mix of uppercase and lowercase letters, plus digits, plus punctuation. Klein intentionally included obvious permutations of that type. The fundamental weakness is to choose a password based on a single word.

Klein examined the possibility of testing for passwords built from pairs of words. At the time of his research, however, he could not harness the computing power needed to crack word pairs.

6.5 Authentication Tokens

Since the introduction of timesharing computers, almost every interactive computer has included a keyboard. Passwords and passphrases are popular simply because we can implement them on any of these computers. We need no extra hardware; the user types in the password and the system verifies it.

Other authentication factors require additional hardware and software. If Bob wants to use a hard-to-forge token to log in, he can't just decide to do so. He must find a hard-to-forge token, purchase it, and install the software to make it work. If he wishes to log in using a fingerprint or other biometric, he needs at least a microphone, camera, or scanner of some sort. In most cases, he must purchase a special sensor. We discuss biometric authentication in Section 6.6.

There are three types of tokens:

1. *Passive tokens*—transmit the same credential every time. These are a physical substitute for a password. The base secret they carry usually is impractical for users to memorize.
2. *Challenge-response tokens*—transmit credentials that vary according to an unpredictable "challenge" from the computer.
3. *One-time password tokens*—transmit different credentials based on an internal clock or counter.

We also call the second and third token types **active tokens** because they produce a different credential every time we use them. The authentication mechanism needs special software to match the changing credentials.

All of these can be reasonably effective for protecting a single computer. Tokens tend to be somewhat less effective in households. At home, people are inclined to leave tokens unattended. This is less likely to happen in a business setting.

PASSIVE AUTHENTICATION TOKENS

The most familiar passive tokens are credit cards and ATM cards. The same technology appears in the card keys we use to unlock hotel rooms. We also see the technology controlling access to parking garages and business doorways. In all cases, the card contains secret information associated with its owner. The card emits the secret when we present it for authentication.

Classic passive cards rely on a magnetic stripe (Figure 6.13). To read the card, the system must have a card stripe reader. When a magnetic field moves next to a coil, the motion generates a small electric current, and card stripe readers work on that principle.

We slide the card along the reader head, either by inserting it or by sliding it through a slot. The motion generates an electric current whose force and direction is based on the data stored on the stripe. The reader's electronics convert the current into a digital data stream that it transmits to the computer.

The problem with magnetic stripe cards is that attackers can forge them with easily purchased equipment. To forge a card, the attacker needs a card reader and a card programmer that costs several hundred dollars. The reader extracts data from the card and may save it for later. When convenient, the attacker can write the saved data onto another magnetic stripe card, cloning the original one.

A newer technology is the radio frequency identification (RFID) tag. While a magnetic stripe relies on motion to be read, the RFID tag relies on signals sent by a nearby

Figure 6.13

Passive authentication tokens, front and back.

RFID reader. The RFID tag is a large antenna that echoes its contents when it receives the appropriate signal. The reader asks the tag for its reading, and the tag transmits its contents. Although there are active RFID tags, the passive model is still most common. The technology occasionally appears in authentication tokens. Although it is possible for an attacker to clone an RFID credential using an RFID reader and writer, the devices cost two to three times as much as the equipment for forging magnetic stripes.

All passive authentication tokens are vulnerable to a major threat: sniffing. If attackers can sniff the credential, whether it is on a magnetic stripe or an RFID card, they can clone it and replay it later. This is why ATMs require two factor authentication: the magnetic stripe card plus the PIN.

6.5.1 Challenge-Response Authentication

Challenge-response authentication is a technique that generates a different credential each time we try to log in. If an attacker intercepts and replays such a credential, it won't work. When we log in with challenge-response authentication, the computer displays some data: the *challenge*. For authentication, we must provide a hard-to-guess answer: the *response*.

Different authentication systems produce the response in different ways. Several systems calculate the response using a token like the one in Figure 6.14. The oldest systems relied on a printed list of challenges, each with a corresponding response. Some desktop systems, including Microsoft Windows, use challenge-response for network-based authentication and calculate the response using software.

Older, hand-operated challenge-response tokens look like simple pocket calculators. To find the right login response, we type in the challenge and press the "C" (Calculate)

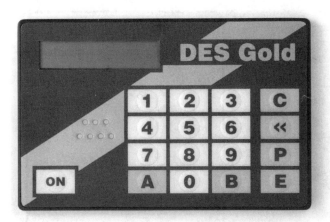

A hand-operated challenge-response token.

button. Although the token in the figure does nothing except calculate a response, some models include simple calculator operations.

Each token contains a unique base secret associated with its owner. The token combines the challenge and the base secret to calculate the response. Because each user has a different base secret, each token produces different responses to the same challenges.

Hand-operated challenge-response tokens are rarely used today. One-time password tokens are much easier to use and provide similar security (Section 6.5.2). Automated challenge-response exchanges often crop up in cryptographic systems. The USB authentication tokens we examine at the end of this section use challenge-response techniques.

The Nonce

The challenge value helps ensure that each login is different, yet each can only be performed by the owner of the correct token. We often use data for that purpose in other cryptographic techniques, and we often call the value a *nonce* instead of a challenge. In cryptography, a nonce has two important properties:

1. The value is unlikely to repeat itself.
2. An attacker can't choose the nonce's value.

The challenge value also must meet these requirements. It does not have to be secret. It may even have a predictable value. Some systems use the time of day or a counter to generate the challenge.

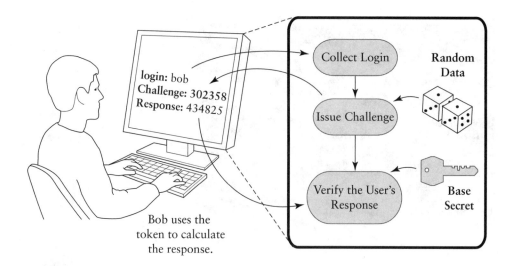

Figure 6.15

Using a challenge-response token.

IMPLEMENTING CHALLENGE-RESPONSE

Figure 6.15 shows Bob using a challenge-response token to log in to a computer. Both the token and the computer contain a matching copy of Bob's base secret. The login process takes place as follows:

1. Bob types his user name to begin the login process.
2. The computer chooses a random challenge value and displays the challenge to Bob.
3. Bob types the challenge into his token and calculates the appropriate response. This is his login credential.
4. Bob types the response into the computer instead of typing a password.
5. The computer collects Bob's credential and repeats the calculation itself. If its answer matches Bob's credential, then it logs Bob in.

ANOTHER CRYPTOGRAPHIC BUILDING BLOCK

In challenge response, the user performs an authentication calculation and the computer performs the same calculation. Both combine the base secret with a counter to generate a new credential. This technique is also called *digest authentication* and is used for website authentication in some cases.

Figure 6.16 shows a typical approach. The token places the base secret and the challenge value in adjacent RAM locations. The token applies a one-way hash function. The credential is built from part of the hash value.

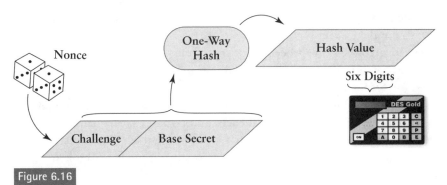

Figure 6.16

A challenge-response calculation.

Challenge response is an important cryptographic building block. It often appears in other cryptographic mechanisms. It gives us a way to prove we have the base secret without actually transmitting it. If we can avoid transmitting a secret, we reduce the risk of disclosing it by mistake.

DIRECT CONNECT TOKENS

More recent challenge-response tokens plug directly into the computer. Figure 6.17 shows recent models that use USB connections. Last summer, for example, Alice worked for a company that required her to use a USB token. The token had a clip that attached it to her lanyard with her company ID badge. When she had to log in, she unclipped the USB token and plugged it into a USB port.

Internally, the USB took part in a challenge-response exchange with the computer to prove that Alice had plugged in the correct USB token. First, the token sent the computer an identifier that indicated the token belonged to Alice. Next, the computer sent the token a challenge. Internally, the token combined the challenge with Alice's base

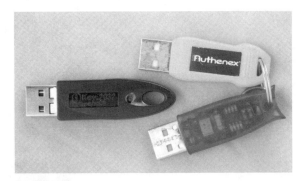

Figure 6.17

USB direct connect challenge-response tokens.

secret, using a calculation like the one shown in Figure 6.16; then the token transmitted the result to the computer.

The computer repeated the same procedure of combining the challenge with its own copy of Alice's base secret. Both calculations should produce the same result. Once the computer verifies the response, it logs Alice in.

A major advantage of USB tokens (or others that directly connect to the computer) is that they can exchange more complicated challenges and responses. The manual token was limited by what a patient user might reliably type in to the token and transcribe onto the computer's keyboard. There are no typing errors between the USB token and the computer.

Some USB tokens use *public-key cryptography* instead of using a hash calculation. In public key cryptography, the token contains a "private" secret, while the system's authentication database can store the "public" form of that secret. The public key can mathematically verify the response to a challenge, but it can't be used to actually calculate the correct response. We examine public-key cryptography in Chapter 8.

6.5.2 One-Time Password Tokens

Figure 6.18 shows a SecurID one-time password token. The token shows a six-digit credential on its display. When logging in, the user types in the credential shown by the token. The credential changes every minute, and the older credentials expire. If attackers intercept a credential, they need to use it promptly before it expires. Unlike challenge-response, there is no need to type in the challenge. We simply type in the number shown on the screen.

In fact, the one-time password uses the same general strategy as the challenge-response token. The principal difference is that it generates its own nonce. In the SecurID case, the nonce is a clock value. The token and the computer use a synchronized clock value to produce matching nonces.

Figure 6.18

One-time password token.

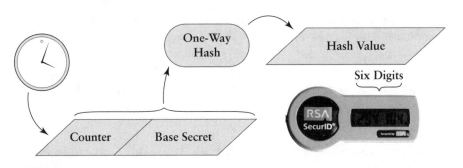

Generating a one-time password.

Other products, for example SafeWord, use a counter to generate the nonce. To log in, the user pushes a button on the token to display the next credential. During login, the computer increments its own counter to produce the corresponding nonce.

One-time password tokens combine the base secret with a clock or counter to generate new credentials. Figure 6.19 shows the calculation, which is almost identical to the challenge-response calculation. The crucial difference is that the one-time password token and the computer share a counter and use its value as the nonce. While the calculation uses a one-way hash, some products use an *encryption algorithm*, a different type of cryptographic function, which we examine in Chapter 7.

Both the clock-based and button-based techniques face a practical problem: keeping the tokens synchronized with the user's computer. Both types of products have strategies to keep tokens synchronized and to resynchronize if the counters change too much.

A TOKEN'S SEARCH SPACE

If we are looking at attacks on passive tokens, then the search space is based on the size of the token's secret. If the secret is a 10-digit decimal number, then the search space is the largest 10-digit number:

$$10^{10}$$

Often, we find the number represented in binary. To match the other examples here, we convert the binary number to decimal. For example, if the token contains a 56-bit secret, the average attack space V is half of the secret's search space:

$$V = 2^{56}/2 = 2^{56-1} = 2^{55} = 3.6 \times 10^{15}$$

When we look at active tokens, we consider two different search spaces. The tokens have an internal secret whose size often is denoted by the number of bits. We calculate its search space the same as for the secret in a passive token: 2^n for an n-bit secret.

The other space applies to the size of the credential the token produces. If the token is a SecurID or similar one-time password token, the credential is usually six decimal digits; thus, the search space is 10^6.

If the token plugs in to perform a challenge response, then the credential may be the same size as the hash function output. This may be 128 bits, 160 bits, or even longer. We calculate the search space the same way as for the internal secret.

Average Attack Space

We calculate a token's average attack space with the calculation described earlier. First, we divide the search space by two, then we scale it according to the fraction of the population who use those tokens.

Attacking One-Time Password Tokens

The relative strengths of different tokens rely more on base secret or credential sizes and less on the specific techniques being used. The only exception is for one-time password tokens. In order to simplify the synchronization problem, most one-time password systems will accept any of several credentials over a range of values. This helps adjust for variations between clocks or for excessive button pressing. In practice, however, it means that guesses have a slightly better chance of being correct, because several values may be correct in any particular instance.

Guessing a Credential

The search space for a token's credential will be a lot smaller than for its secret. This should not matter in practice, because the credential is valid only once and is validated by a server. The only way an attacker can try to crack a credential through trial and error is to request the server to check each credential it tries. Most servers are designed to detect successive attempts like that. The server may respond in one of several ways:

- Lock out the user identity that has received numerous invalid credentials during login attempts.
- Generate successively longer delays when recovering from a failed login attempt.
- Report the numerous failed logins to an administrator. The administrator then takes steps to block the attack.

Any or all of these responses may succeed in blocking an attack.

6.5.3 Token Vulnerabilities

Let us look at the five types of authentication vulnerabilities listed in Section 6.1 and how they apply to tokens.

1. **Clone or borrow the credential.**
   This is a relatively common problem with magnetic stripe tokens; an attacker acquires a magnetic stripe reader and writer, and copies mag stripe cards.

This is not a problem with active tokens because the credentials aren't supposed to work more than once. It is possible to borrow a credential, but that prevents the legitimate owner from logging in.

2. **Sniff the credential.**

The issues are the same here as for cloning, as just noted.

3. **Trial and error guessing.**

There are two cases: guessing a base secret or guessing a credential from an active token. Designers try to make both attacks impractical. Base secrets are large enough to make trial-and-error take too long. To guess a credential, the attacker must submit all of the guesses to the computer, which will recognize a pattern of trial-and-error guessing from the numerous invalid credentials.

4. **Denial of service.**

Tokens pose different availability risks than passwords, because one can physically lose a token or the token hardware can fail.

5. **Retrieve from backup.**

In most cases, the token uses a shared base secret and such tokens are vulnerable to this attack. An attacker can subvert authentication by intercepting a copy of the computer's database for authenticating tokens. The database must contain the actual base secrets in the individual tokens, or it would not be able to calculate responses or one-time passwords.

If the token uses public-key techniques (Chapter 8), it is not vulnerable to this attack. In general, this is limited to direct connect tokens.

Table 6.5 summarizes these vulnerabilities and how they affect passive, active, and public-key direct connect tokens.

None of these vulnerabilities is likely to appeal to a weak threat. A strong threat might be able to sniff and replay passive credentials or retrieve a credential database from backup, but most of these attacks are the province of an extreme threat. Tokens

TABLE 6.5 Vulnerabilities of authentication tokens			
Authentication Risk	Passive Tokens	Active Tokens	Direct Connect Public-Key Tokens
1. Clone credential	YES	no	no
2. Sniff credential	YES	no	no
3. Guessing	no	no	no
4. Denial of service	Loss/Damage	Loss/Damage	Loss/Damage
5. Retrieve from backup	YES	YES	no

clearly protect against a weak threat and will probably be effective against a strong threat. This assumes, of course, that the token's owner can keep the token protected from the threat.

6.6 Biometric Authentication

In biometric authentication, the computer collects a biometric measurement from the user, compares it to data in its authentication database, and recognizes the user if the measurement closely matches the database entry. Most biometrics require specialized readers. For example, many laptop computers incorporate fingerprint readers into their keyboards (Figure 6.20).

When a system authenticates someone using a password or token, the system performs an exact match on the credential. The system rejects the authentication on even the slightest mismatch.

In biometric authentication, the system measures some aspect of the person's body and constructs a credential from those measurements. Such measurements are never precise in the technical sense; a series of measurements may be similar, but they are almost never identical.

To perform a biometric authentication, the system first collects a measurement from the person (Figure 6.21). This is often an image of some sort: a two-dimensional repre-

biometric reader

Figure 6.20

Biometric fingerprint reader on a laptop's keyboard.

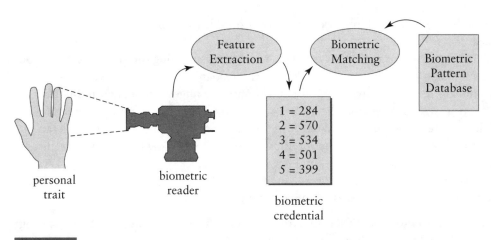

Feature
Extraction

Biometric
Matching

Biometric
Pattern
Database

1 = 284
2 = 570
3 = 534
4 = 501
5 = 399

personal
trait

biometric
reader

biometric
credential

Figure 6.21

Elements of a biometric system.

sentation of a fingerprint, an iris, the shape of the hand, or the waveform of a spoken passphrase.

The image is not, by itself, the credential. The biometric system must analyze the image to create the credential. This process is often called "feature extraction" because it distills the image down to its basic features. The process discards the "noise" inherent in such images and identifies the key features that distinguish one human from another. These features are measured and structured in a way that they can be reliably compared with other readings from the same person.

Next, the biometric system compares the credential constructed from the person to "biometric patterns" stored in the authentication database. In general, the system measures the "distance" between the credential and the pattern it has stored for that person. Typically, a measurement from the right user should yield a close match to the pattern. Thus, the distance between the pattern and the credential should be small. If the distance is too large, the system concludes that the credential does not match.

6.6.1   Biometric Accuracy

A typical human body may go through a broad range of experiences, and these cause visible changes. The body may be hot or cold due to changes of weather or clothing. Daily activities may make body parts unusually damp or dry. Fashion decisions can affect skin color, facial or body hair, or even the amount of the body that is visible to sensors.

A successful biometric sensor must be largely immune to these changes. People don't want to select clothing or decide on hand washing based on the needs of a biometric system. In any case, the biometric sensor must be able to adapt to a broad range of appearances.

A biometric sensor must always balance itself between being too strict and being too tolerant. If too strict, the sensor won't correctly recognize the people it was programmed to recognize. Authorized users will put their fingers on readers and not be authenticated. Such users may be able to succeed by trying again, but regular failures can lead a site to abandon the system. On the other hand, if the sensor is too tolerant, it may recognize one user as another or allow an unauthorized person to masquerade as someone else.

These errors play an important role in testing and assessing biometric systems. The two types of errors lead to these two measurements:

1. *False rejection rate* (FRR)—the fraction of readings that should match an existing credential template but do not match it.
2. *False acceptance rate* (FAR)—the fraction of readings that match an existing credential template but should not match it.

In the first case, false rejections, the system rejects an authorized user. Although these don't immediately compromise security, a high false rejection rate reduces the computer's availability. In the second case, false acceptances, the system authenticates the wrong person. The second measurement, the FAR, gives us a basis for estimating the average attack space for a biometric.

With a biometric, it doesn't really make sense to calculate a search space, per se. Because the FAR represents a statistical estimate, it makes more sense to calculate the average attack space from it. For simplicity, we assume that the entire population uses the biometric. We take the FAR statistic as a fraction, A_{FAR}, and use this equation:

$$V_{Biometric} = \frac{1}{2 \times A_{FAR}}$$

For example, if the FAR is 1 percent, the fraction A_{FAR} is 0.01. The average attack space is the inverse of 0.02 or 50. This suggests that, on average, we will trick the biometric sensor in one out of 50 readings from the wrong people.

Many people find biometrics fascinating, and some will buy and use them if the price is right. This has produced a marketplace in which there are many low-quality products. Vendors of such products might speak proudly of a "99 percent" or "99.9 percent" accuracy rate, suggesting a FAR on the order of 1 percent or 0.1 percent. Neither of these are especially impressive when compared to passwords.

Biometric systems often include a "sensitivity" setting that we can adjust to try to achieve particular FAR and FRR levels. The two settings, unfortunately, exist in a balance; when one goes up, the other usually goes down. Some operators seek an ideal point in which the FAR and FRR achieve the same rate.

6.6.2 Biometric Vulnerabilities

Let us look at the five types of authentication vulnerabilities listed in Section 6.1 and apply them to biometrics. Each vulnerability also indicates whether it often poses a risk in practice.

1. **Clone or borrow the credential—Often**

   This vulnerability has been very popular in motion pictures; the hero or heroine collects a fingerprint, a scan of an eye, or spoken conversation and uses it to clone the appropriate physical feature. In fact, this can often work with commercial devices. Researchers, technical magazine writers, and television experts have cloned fingerprints, faces, and even irises to fool biometric readers. Some clones required special work, while others were depressingly easy. In all cases, though, it would require a strong threat at least to carry out the attack.

2. **Sniff the credential—Often**

   Most biometric readers connect to the protected system through a cable, usually USB. If attackers have access to the hardware, they may be able to install a sniffer like those used with keyboards. Later, the attacker could transmit a sniffed credential down the same USB connection. This is more challenging if the biometric reader is physically built into the computer's case. For example, some laptops have a built-in fingerprint scanner. This attack would, at the very least, require a strong threat.

3. **Trial and error guessing—Slight**

   In this case, we present a series of biometric readings in hopes that one matches the legitimate user. For example, a group of five people can provide 50 fingerprints. This makes success likely if the fingerprint system has a FAR of 1 percent. An attack team of five people, although small, still would indicate an extreme threat.

4. **Denial of service—Possible**

   When we try to adjust a biometric system to reduce the FAR, the FRR often increases. Thus, as we try to reduce the likelihood of allowing the wrong person in, we increase the likelihood that we won't let the right people in. This is a self-inflicted difficulty, caused by trying to make the system too safe.

5. **Retrieve from backup—Possible**

   If an attacker intercepts the credential pattern database, it may be possible to forge biometric credentials, which then could be transmitted across the USB connection, pretending to be from the actual biometric reader. Some biometrics vendors argue that this is impossible or at least impractical. In practice, it appears to be a real possibility. However, there are no simple tools to do this, so it would only be the province of an extreme threat.

None of these attacks are the province of a weak threat. There are a few attacks that a strong threat might carry out, and a few that would only be mounted by an extreme threat. Therefore, biometrics are clearly usable in the face of a weak threat, and possibly in the face of a strong threat.

6.7 Authentication Policy

This chapter focuses on authentication on an isolated computer or other system. We identified four different threat levels in Section 6.1. Now we further refine our view of the threats and risks so that we may construct policy statements. We do this by answering the following questions:

- Is the computer used at home, at business locations, or both?
- For each environment, are there threats?
- For each threat, is there a weak or strong motivation?

Because we are protecting an isolated computer, people are threats only if they have direct physical access to the computer. Once they have access, the attacks may use physical, logical, or even social mechanisms. Some attackers might install simple software. The biggest risk arises from the people with the greatest motivation.

In some cases, the computer may not face any relevant threats. For example, if Alice lived alone in an apartment, a desktop computer in there would rarely need to be protected against pranks or accidents caused by roommates, friends, or family.

More often, however, a household is a small community. Even if the principal occupants are fully trustworthy, there may be guests, house sitters, or service people who pose a threat. Typically, we would think of these people as weak threats; they might be motivated to try simple attacks, but they lack the opportunity or motivation to put a lot of effort into it.

Strong threats have a stronger motivation; they will spend time, money, or both to trick the computer's authentication system. In a business, this might be an overly competitive coworker. In a troubled household, it might be a spouse facing separation or divorce. These people may put in a lot of effort, but they typically don't want to leave evidence of their actions.

An extreme threat is very highly motivated and is willing to leave evidence of the attack. Authentication by itself can't protect against such a threat. An extreme threat might simply steal the computer. If the objective is data, the threat may disassemble the computer and read the hard drive directly.

Based on these different levels of threat, we now look at how those levels affect authentication alternatives. Some attacks depend on the computer's location. Most, however, depend on the level of threat posed by people in the location.

6.7.1 Weak and Strong Threats

Of the four levels of threat, the lowest level is an environment with no threats at all. The next level poses a weak threat: Someone who is willing to try some simple tricks, but is not motivated to work hard at attacking authentication. The next level, the strong threat, is willing to spend time and money but not leave clear evidence that an attack occurred. The highest level threat, the extreme threat, doesn't care about being caught. Authentication won't protect a computer from an extreme threat who has physical access to it.

RISKS FROM WEAK THREATS

In Bob's environment, a weak threat may pose the following risks:

1. Shoulder surfing.
2. Simple trial-and-error guessing based on what is known of Bob's life and activities.
3. Search for a written copy of Bob's password that has been left near Bob's computer. These searches often succeed, especially in businesses.
4. Borrow an authentication token that's left nearby and that allows the threat to log in as Bob.

We address these threats if we follow the policy statements described here for household and business environments.

RISKS FROM STRONG THREATS

A strong threat won't steal or destroy the computer. The strong threat is not motivated or sophisticated enough to bypass the authentication mechanism. The strong threat poses the same risks as a weaker threat, in addition to the following:

5. Steal an authentication token.
6. Make a copy of a magnetic stripe card.
7. Perform large-scale trial-and-error password guessing, as opposed to limited attempts.
8. Find Bob's backup hard drive and search it for passwords.
9. Perform off-line attacks on "hashed passwords" (Section 6.2).
10. Sniff authentication credentials produced by an external device. This could include sniffing a password typed on a keyboard or sniffing the biometric reading generated by a fingerprint reader. If the attacker can collect the credential, then the credential can probably be replayed, tricking the system into thinking it came from the authorized user.
11. "Trojan login" in which the attacker displays a "login" screen on the computer and Bob logs in to it by mistake. This fake login screen appears to let him log in, but he ends up in the "Suitemates" account. This is similar to *phishing* attacks on the Internet, but is limited to trying to retrieve a password on a single computer.

12. Physically clone a biometric feature. For example, an attacker can construct a fake fingerprint that can fool many biometric fingerprint readers. Experimenters have demonstrated similar attacks on other biometric systems (Section 6.5).

EFFECT OF LOCATION

The two alternatives are household and workplace locations. These alternatives reflect typical physical security situations in these locations.

It is hard to lock things up in a home. Most locks require keys, and one's keys may be left in a pocket, on a hook, or in a drawer while at home. Thus, other members of the household may be able to use those keys and unlock those locks.

In a home, computing items tend to collect near the computer itself. Information needed to run the computer, like lists of passwords, are likely to be hidden nearby. Physical tokens required to use the computer likewise will find their way into the computer's area. Even if tokens and passwords are *not* stored nearby, they are unlikely to be physically protected. They may reside in a wallet or purse in a bedroom, farther away but occasionally unattended.

This is less of a problem for business computers. If a user relies on a physical token to log in, the token is probably taken home. Thus, the unattended computer back at work is somewhat safe. In practice, however, some people habitually write passwords on slips of paper and hide them nearby the computer.

6.7.2 Policies for Weak Threat Environments

When we apply these considerations, we yield the following policy recommendations, based on location.

A HOUSEHOLD POLICY

The policy appears in Table 6.6. This addresses the four risks from weak threats identified in the previous section.

#	Policy Statement	Risks
	TABLE 6.6 Household policy for a weak threat environment	
1	Computer working areas shall be arranged to minimize opportunities for shoulder surfing.	1
2	Passwords shall never be written down and left unsecured.	3
3	The process for choosing passwords shall yield a password that is memorable but hard to guess.	2
4	Passwords shall only be entered when threats can't watch the password being typed.	1
5	Authentication tokens shall not be used.	4

Passwords should provide ample protection in a household with a weak threat environment. Therefore, the policy says nothing about using biometrics. Because it is hard to provide around-the-clock physical custody for a token, the household policy forbids tokens.

A WORKPLACE POLICY: PASSWORDS ONLY

Table 6.7 provides a sample policy for a password-only workplace. The policy addresses the four risks from weak threats identified in the previous section.

A WORKPLACE POLICY: PASSWORDS AND TOKENS

While it's a problem to use tokens in a household, we have better options for protecting them in a workplace. This yields the sample policy in Table 6.8.

Most workers have some personal items that never leave their possession, like a wallet or building access card. We can "piggyback" authentication tokens, or even written passwords, on those to avoid leaving them unattended and unprotected. Thus, although it might not be easy to avoid leaving credentials unattended in a home, it may be possible to prevent that in the workplace.

Because we allow passwords to be written down, the passwords can be very strong, very random, and resist off-line attacks. However, we don't necessarily need to use strong passwords, because we aren't addressing strong threats.

So far, there is nothing in this policy to eliminate the use of biometrics. The policy doesn't demand biometrics, but it likewise doesn't forbid the technique. To include biometrics, we might want a policy statement that outlines whether it is a substitute for passwords or requires a password, too.

TABLE 6.7 Policy for a workplace using passwords against weak threats		
#	Policy Statement	Risks
1	Computer working areas shall be arranged to minimize opportunities for shoulder surfing.	1
2	Passwords shall only be entered when threats can't watch the password being typed.	1
3	The process for choosing passwords shall yield passwords that are hard to guess.	2
4	All written copies of passwords shall remain continuously in the possession of the owner.	3
5	Authentication tokens shall not be used.	4

#	Policy Statement	Risks
	TABLE 6.8 Policy for a workplace using tokens and passwords against weak threats	
1	Computer working areas shall be arranged to minimize opportunities for shoulder surfing.	1
2	Passwords shall only be entered when threats can't watch the password being typed.	1
3	The process for choosing passwords shall yield passwords that are hard to guess.	2
4	All written copies of passwords shall remain continuously in the possession of the owner.	3
5	Authentication tokens shall be used.	1, 3
6	Authentication tokens shall always remain in the possession of the owner, especially when the computer is unattended.	4

6.7.3 Policies for Strong and Extreme Threats

Given the greater range of attacks, we require additional policy statements to protect against stronger threats. Typically, we address this in authentication by adding authentication factors.

These policies are designed for workplaces, not households. If a household faces a strong or extreme threat, the computer owner should find a way to keep the computer physically locked up and secured against household threats. Don't depend on authentication to protect a household computer against stronger threats.

PASSWORDS ALONE FOR STRONG THREATS

To address strong threats with passwords, we address risks 7, 8, 9, 10, and 11. The other risks apply to tokens or biometrics. The resulting policy in Table 6.9 builds on the password policy in Table 6.7.

Risks 7 and 8 provide attackers with strategies for targeted trial-and-error password guessing. If we measure and report incorrect guesses, we can detect guessing attacks and perhaps identify and confront the perpetrator.

Highly complex passwords reduce the risk of a successful off-line attack. Such passwords may need to be written down; the risks inherent in that behavior are covered in the earlier password policy.

#	Policy Statement	Risks
	TABLE 6.9 Extending the password policy from Table 6.7 for strong threats	
6	The system shall keep track of failed authentication attempts and shall keep a log of such repeated attempts to report to administrators.	7, 8
7	Passwords shall be sufficiently complex to resist off-line trial-and-error attacks.	9
8	All computer keyboards shall be physically secured in a manner that protects them against hardware keystroke sniffers.	10
9	The system shall have a standard key sequence that always produces the login prompt and that can never be intercepted and faked by unauthorized programs. This is a standard feature in most modern operating systems.	11

PASSWORDS PLUS BIOMETRICS

The policy in Table 6.10 builds on the one in Table 6.7 to incorporate biometrics to address strong threats. Because we use both passwords and biometrics, we must consider Risks 7, 8, 9, 10, 11, and 12.

#	Policy Statement	Risks
	TABLE 6.10 Policy from Table 6.7 extended to apply biometrics to strong threats	
7	Routine authentication procedures shall require both a memorized password and a biometric reading.	7, 8, 9, 10, 11, 12
8	The computer shall keep track of failed authentication attempts and shall keep a log of such repeated attempts to report to administrators.	7, 8, 9, 10, 11, 12
9	The computer shall protect all of its authentication databases from reading or other access by regular users.	9
10	The computer shall have physical protections that prevent insertion of a keystroke logger between the keyboard or biometric reader and the computer.	10
11	The system shall have a standard key sequence that always produces the login prompt and that can never be intercepted and faked by unauthorized programs. This is a standard feature in most modern operating systems.	11
12	The biometric device shall be adjusted for as high of a FAR value as is practical in regular use.	12

#	Policy Statement	Risks
TABLE 6.11 Extending the token policy from Table 6.8 for strong threats		
7	Routine authentication procedures shall require both a token and a memorized password.	5, 6, 7, 10, 11
8	The system shall keep track of failed authentication attempts and shall keep a log of such repeated attempts to report to administrators.	8
9	The system shall protect all of its authentication databases from reading or other access by regular users.	9
10	The system shall have a standard key sequence that always produces the login prompt and that can never be intercepted and faked by unauthorized programs. This is a standard feature in most modern operating systems.	11

PASSWORDS PLUS TOKENS

The policy in Table 6.11 builds on the one in Table 6.8 to increase the security of token-based authentication.

CONSTRUCTING THE POLICY

To construct the policy, we evaluate the environments and the threats. If the computer spends time in a household, we apply household policy statements. If the computer spends time at work, we apply workplace policy statements. For each environment, we add in strong threat statements if there is a strong threat in that environment.

Let us start by constructing a policy for Bob's computer. The computer resides in the suite's common room. Although the attacks on it persist, none of the attacks are especially sophisticated. We can, for now, assess the threat as weak. For a weak threat in a household environment, we use the Household Policy just described. This leads Bob to choose a hard-to-guess password and memorize it.

Alice faces a different situation with her laptop. She always keeps the laptop in her possession, or it is locked in her dorm room. Her roommate is, in Alice's estimation, a weak threat. Alice has landed an impressive part-time job at a local consulting firm. The job pays really well, partly because she is required to provide her own computer. However, her workplace is clearly a strong threat environment, with consultants competing sharply for job assignments.

Alice applies the Household Policy to address her household situation, but she must combine it with the Workplace Policy and the Strong Threat Policy. Moreover, the result has to work well with her laptop. Although some laptops have built-in biometrics, her laptop does not. Alice's best alternative is to laboriously memorize a strong password.

Alice also could use a simple password together with an authentication token. Several tokens connect directly to a computer's USB port. Unlike magnetic cards, such tokens are very difficult to clone. She needs the token to protect her laptop at work, and the simple password to protect her laptop at home.

6.7.4 Password Selection and Handling

Passwords aren't perfect, but they often can do the job. When we focus on Bob's situation to protect a single, isolated computer, passwords are often highly effective. A password isn't a magic talisman that blocks extreme threats, but it will deter attackers with less skill or motivation.

Although Bob's activities have not referred to other computers, logins, or passwords, he undoubtedly has to remember other passwords. Most people today have dozens or hundreds of user name and password pairs to remember and manage. This requires a strategy, which needs to solve two problems:

1. Password selection
2. Password protection

We examine these two problems in this section. We address those problems in the light of two recommendations:

1. Choose passwords according to the risk faced by each asset.
2. Use different passwords to protect different sets of assets.

It should be clear from Section 6.4 that people typically pick passwords with strong biases. Attackers can exploit those biases to try to guess passwords. If the attacker is sufficiently motivated, a weak password won't protect the asset.

Some might argue that *all* passwords should resist strong trial-and-error attack. If we use the same password to protect all of our assets, then it makes sense to choose a hard to guess password and to take pains to memorize it. However, when faced with dozens or hundreds of different websites, desktop machines, and even combination locks, all demanding secrets to open, perhaps we can choose a few for ease of use and others for safety.

When people are faced with a vast number of secrets to keep straight, they are naturally going to use the same secret for more than one asset. The smart thing to do here is to share passwords only where it makes sense. If Alice, for example, has two or three social site logins, and she doesn't take any of them very seriously, she might choose the same password for all three. Or if she has two online bank accounts, she might use the same strong password for both. On the other hand, if she has to share one of the passwords with her father, she might want to use a different password for the other. We need to look at how the password is used as well as what it protects.

SIMPLE PASSWORDS

We often encounter assets that require little or no protection but for some reason, we are obliged to choose passwords for them. It may be sensible to pick a single, memorable password for all such cases.

Some password systems might require a mixture of uppercase and lowercase, digits, and/or punctuation. Sometimes, the simple password acquires all these bells and whistles. It may be easier to create a single complicated password for all applications than to try to remember which sites demand uppercase, or digits, or punctuation. On the other hand, some sites avoid punctuation, especially characters used in certain programming environments (notably ";").

STRONG BUT MEMORABLE PASSWORDS

These are passwords we never write down but we remember. Memorable passwords often are based on words. When we choose a word for a password, we first must avoid choosing something personal. The best approach is to open a large book and pick a longer word.

If we need a password that resists off-line attacks, we should construct it from two or three randomly selected words. Pick each word randomly, starting fresh with a different page of the book, or better, with a different book. Choose words containing five characters or more.

If the password requires a combination of letters, digits, and punctuation, use the digits or punctuation as separators between words.

Never choose a password with a strong personal association, even if you pick the word at random.

We make passwords stronger, if harder to remember, when they aren't constructed of words. One way to construct a stronger but still memorable password is to base it on a memorized phrase. We take the leading characters from the words in the phrase, and construct the password from them. For example,

'Way down upon the Swanee River, Far far away,

We copy the initial characters to form this password: 'dutSRFfa

Note that we've retained the apostrophe from the first word instead of its first letter, and we retained the capitalization. Such passwords are probably biased toward consonants, because fewer words start with vowels, but there are no dictionaries that try to attack such passwords—not yet, at least.

THE STRONGEST PASSWORDS

The strongest passwords contain randomly selected characters. These are the most difficult passwords to memorize. In practice, we generate such passwords randomly and then write them down. We keep the written copy safe at all times and destroy it after we have memorized the password.

6.8 Resources

 IMPORTANT TERMS INTRODUCED

active token	entropy	procedure diagram
authentication database	extreme threat	process diagram
authentication factors	hash value	random
average attack space	keystroke logger	search space
base secret	low hanging fruit	shoulder surfing
challenge-response token	lower bound	sniff
character set	nonce	social engineering
credential	off-line attack	strong threat
cryptographic building block	one-time password token	three-factor authentication
cryptographic function	one-way hash	two-factor authentication
cryptographic randomness	passive token	upper bound
dictionary attack	passphrase	weak threat
digest authentication	password cracking	work factor

ACRONYMS INTRODUCED

FAR—False acceptance rate

FIPS—Federal Information Processing Standard

FRR—False rejection rate

MD5—Message Digest 5

PIN—Personal identification number

PRNG—Pseudorandom number generator

RFID—Radio frequency identification

SHA-x—Secure Hash Algorithm, x is version or bit size

UK—United Kingdom

6.8.1 Review Questions

R1. Explain the difference between authentication and authorization.

R2. Describe the general steps taken during the authentication process.

R3. Identify and describe the three basic authentication factors.

R4. Explain the role of hard to forge information in authentication. Give examples of such information.

R5. Describe the type of authentication environment examined in this chapter.

R6. Explain the differences between the four levels of threats described in this chapter.

R7. Describe the five basic attacks on authentication systems.

R8. Describe how password hashing works.

R9. Why can't an attacker masquerade by using a hashed password?

R10. Describe a way to sniff passwords.

R11. Describe a way to limit trial-and-error guessing.

R12. Why might it improve security to make users change passwords periodically? What problems arise when passwords are changed periodically?

R13. Describe the operation of an off-line attack on password hashes.

R14. How do we calculate the search space in variable-length passwords given the maximum length and the number of characters in the character set?

R15. Explain the difference between "real" random number generators and "pseudo" random number generators.

R16. Explain how a dictionary attack works.

R17. Describe some biases that cause passwords to be more vulnerable to attack than they might be if they were completely random.

R18. Describe how to perform an average attack space calculation.

R19. Explain the difference between active and passive tokens.

R20. Describe how one-time password tokens determine the next password to use.

R21. Explain how challenge-response authentication works.

R22. Describe the process of performing biometric authentication.

R23. Describe FAR and FRR.

R24. How do you calculate the average attack space for a biometric?

R25. Explain how biometric systems are vulnerable to the five generic attacks on authentication systems.

R26. Summarize risks associated with weak versus strong threats.

R27. Explain how the physical location of a system affects its authentication security policy in the face of weak threats.

6.8.2 Exercises

E1. Calculate the search space for passwords in the following situations:

   a. Exactly seven characters long, chosen from uppercase and lowercase letters and digits.

   b. Seven characters or shorter, chosen from the printable ASCII character set.

   c. Exactly 14 characters long, mixed-case letters only.

   d. 14 characters or shorter, mixed-case letters only.

E2. Some password systems set a *minimum* length for passwords. We want to compare two systems in which the maximum password length is 16 characters, and passwords may contain any printable ASCII characters. One system allows passwords to be any length, while the other requires passwords to be *at least* eight characters long. Calculate the search space for these two systems. (Hint: One system reduced the search space because they *subtracted* a collection of passwords from the range of possibilities. What is the search space of the subtracted passwords?)

The following exercises describe authentication techniques and the populations that use them. Calculate the average attack space for each.

E3. Boondock Bank has an ATM with six-digit PINs. Until a year ago, all PINs were randomly assigned. Since then, an "account representative" explains the PIN process to each new customer and helps them choose a PIN. The rep says to pick a date, because they're easy to remember. Now 25 percent of all PINs are 6-digit dates.

E4. People at Barkley Corporation get to choose their own passwords. To help, there is a password choosing program that picks the password randomly from a list of 23,000 words. 60 percent of the users use this procedure.

E5. People at Foonly Corporation have a password selection program like the one in Exercise E4, but users must make passwords out of TWO words randomly chosen from the list. Assume that 60 percent of the Foonly users use this program.

E6. Marsha's company has a token-based system with 64-bit base secrets stored inside each token, yielding 1.84×10^{19} possible secrets. Everyone in the company (100 percent) has that kind of token.

E7. Joe's company has installed fingerprint sensors for logging in. The company is proud of the "proven" 99.9 percent accuracy of these machines. Everyone (100 percent) in the company uses them for logging in.

E8. Sam's company has installed fingerprint sensors that use an elaborate new matching technique. They can adjust the system's overall sensitivity to balance FAR and FRR to tolerable levels. After a lot of adjusting, the FAR is now 0.0003 though the FRR is 0.08. People find this tolerable.

E9. Some vendors required users to enter a PIN when using a challenge-response token. Redraw the diagram in Figure 6.16 to show how the calculation could incorporate a PIN.

E10. Draw a diagram showing how a computer might authenticate a user who uses a challenge-response token. Be sure to show the output of the challenge, the input of the response, and the incorporation of the base secret. Assume that the process uses a one-way hash.

E11. Following the background information provided for Alice's threat assessment and policy development in Chapters 1 and 2, do the following:

   a. Make a list of specific authentication **threats** Alice might face.

   b. Make a list of specific authentication **risks** Alice might face. For each risk, note if it applies to weak threats, strong threats, or both.

E12. Based on your answer to Exercise E11, develop an authentication policy for

Alice, assuming she faces weak authentication threats at home.

E13. Based on your answer to Exercise E11, develop an authentication policy for Alice, assuming she faces weak authentication threats at work.

E14. Based on your answer to Exercise E11, develop a complete authentication policy for Alice, assuming she faces strong authentication threats and will use passwords alone for authentication.

E15. Based on your answer to Exercise E11, develop a complete authentication policy for Alice, assuming she faces strong authentication threats and will use a password and token.

E16. Based on your answer to Exercise E11, develop a complete authentication policy for Alice, assuming she faces strong authentication threats, and will use a password and biometric.

ENCRYPTING FILES

ABOUT THIS CHAPTER

In this chapter, we introduce cryptography and encryption applications. To begin with, we use encryption as a way to protect individual files. We examine the following topics:

- Encryption fundamentals, including cryptanalysis
- Building blocks for computer-based encryption
- Features and properties of effective file encryption
- Digital rights management

7.1 Protecting the Accessible

In the previous chapters, we rely on physical and logical security measures to protect our information. These measures are not always enough. For further protection, we can use *encryption* to hide a file's contents from others. Encryption is one of several techniques classed as *cryptography* ("secret writing"). In Chapter 6, we encountered our first cryptographic function: the one-way hash. We use cryptographic functions to protect data. The only people who can share the data are those who can *decrypt* it; that is, reverse the encryption.

Encryption protects information by presenting the reader with a puzzle. Authorized readers know the puzzle's secret and can easily read the document. Unauthorized readers must take the time to solve the puzzle. We protect the document by making the puzzle hard enough to frustrate attackers.

Encryption often crops up in fiction, especially for protecting a buried treasure. The 2004 movie *National Treasure* presented the characters with a series of puzzles, including a cleverly hidden map, that were clues leading to a massive buried treasure. If we go back to 1843, we find *The Gold Bug*, written by Edgar Allen Poe, who was an accomplished amateur cryptographer. Poe's characters find an encrypted message that locates treasure buried by the pirate Captain Kidd. To find the treasure, the characters must somehow read the message.

The peculiar story of the Beale Papers may, or may not, tell of a genuine treasure hidden with encryption. In 1885, a man named James B. Ward published a pamphlet describing a set of three encrypted documents attributed to one T. J. Beale from the 1820s. An accompanying letter claimed that the encrypted documents describe the location of a treasure hidden in Bufort County, Virginia. Despite years of effort spent trying to break the puzzle, only one of the three documents has been decoded. Some experts are convinced that the papers are really a hoax.

7.1.1 Process Example: The Encrypted Diary

Treasure maps—encrypted or not—are usually the province of fiction, but every year countless children receive gifts that encourage them to create secret information: diaries. Many parents see diaries as an ideal gift for young school children; the children get to write about what they know and to improve their writing skills. The diary often becomes a privacy problem. The child writes down personal thoughts and feelings she or he does not want to share with others, and then a sibling finds the diary and reads its contents.

Children rarely protect their diaries effectively, though they certainly try. Most child diaries include a lock and key, and modern electronic versions may include keypad-controlled or even voice-controlled locks. Regardless of design, diary locks often are easy to break.

Children also try to hide their diaries: an example of Security Through Obscurity. Hiding may succeed if siblings never have enough time to search for a diary in the owner's personal space. However, it's impractical to hide a diary effectively. The child must write in a diary every day, or most days, for it to serve its purpose. Thus, the diary must be easily at hand. This limits the number of practical hiding places. Regular access increases the likelihood that a sibling might see the diary while being moved to or from its hiding place.

In 1881, a 15-year-old English girl named Beatrix Potter started keeping a diary. Unlike typical diarists, Potter developed a secret code and used it to write up her thoughts. In 1901, Potter secured literary fame by publishing *The Tale of Peter Rabbit*, a classic children's book. Let us construct a brief high-level analysis of Potter's encrypted diary.

Assets: Potter's diaries contained frank personal thoughts.

Risks: Potter was a private person who lived an isolated life. Her parents and brother rarely interacted with her. Though isolated, she was not alone; her living areas were managed by servants. This left her with almost no physically secure private space.

Policy: None of Potter's diary was to be read by others, whether servants, family members, or outsiders.

Implementation: Potter wrote all of her diary entries in code. She used the same code for all diary entries over a 15-year period. Many people might find encryption by hand too tedious to be practical. Through consistent use, however, Potter could probably write in her code as easily as in plain English.

Monitoring: Because Potter wrote in her diary regularly, she could see if the latest volume had disappeared. If one or more volumes did fall into someone else's hands, however, the encryption greatly reduced the risk of disclosure.

Recovery: If Potter lost track of her current diary volume, she could search for it. The same was true if older diary volumes went missing. There is no evidence that anyone managed to decrypt her diaries during her lifetime, so her encryption proved adequate for her personal comfort.

Fifteen years after Potter's death, a researcher found her hidden diary and decoded its contents. The actual code is relatively simple by modern standards and could be broken quickly using a computer. At the time, however, literary efforts at code breaking were performed by hand.

Potter is not the only diarist to use a code. Other diarists only used code occasionally and left most of the diary readable. Samuel Pepys, a public figure during the English Restoration in the 17th century, encrypted salacious experiences and impolitic comments about the king. Pepys didn't design a personal cipher like Potter's. Instead, he wrote in an obscure and personalized form of shorthand taught at his college.

Charles Wesley, a celebrated 18th-century clergyman, used a similar shorthand in parts of his diary. Most of his diary was published soon after his death, but the coded portions weren't decrypted until the early 21st century. The coded portions included his observations on scandal accusations made against him and on disputes with his brother, the co-founder of Methodism.

In modern computing, people can't always rely on physical possession to protect files from disclosure. Although bootleggers may not have encrypted their ledgers during Prohibition, today's FBI often encounters encrypted financial files in organized crime investigations. Increasingly, anyone who carries a laptop is encouraged, or even required by their employers, to encrypt sensitive business files. If the sensitive data is limited to a few critical files, then file encryption provides simple and practical protection.

7.1.2 Encryption Basics

Encryption transforms readable data (called the *plaintext*) into unreadable data (called the *ciphertext*) using secret information (called the key). Figure 7.1 illustrates the procedure. Our objective is to keep the readable plaintext hidden from outsiders. We only expose the plaintext when we are "inside" the safe boundary.

The encryption procedure (the *algorithm*) takes two inputs: the plaintext data and the encryption key. The procedure scrambles the data to produce the ciphertext. If we use high-quality encryption, no one will be able to interpret the ciphertext unless they have the correct key. The recipient on the right side of Figure 7.1 can retrieve the ciphertext by using the appropriate decryption algorithm and key.

The term *algorithm* should be familiar to computer science students; it is the mathematical term for a step-by-step procedure. We may use it as a synonym for "procedure" when we talk about cryptography.

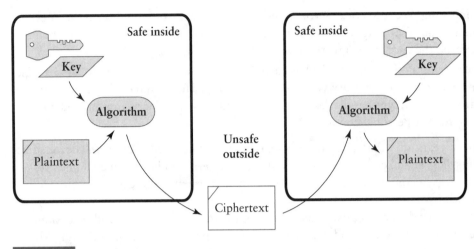

Procedure diagram of encryption.

For encryption to work, there must always be a matching decryption algorithm. These algorithms may be identical in some cases, but not always. The encryption algorithm always accepts two inputs: the plaintext and the key. The output is the ciphertext. The decryption algorithm likewise accepts two inputs: the ciphertext and the key. Likewise, the decryption algorithm yields the plaintext as output.

Following Kerckhoff's principle, we must assume that potential threats are familiar with our encryption and decryption algorithms. The secrecy of our plaintext relies *entirely* on the secrecy of the key.

CATEGORIES OF ENCRYPTION

Encryption algorithms fall into several categories (Figure 7.2). To begin with, we have *symmetric encryption* algorithms in which we use the same key for both encryption and

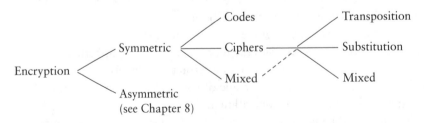

Categories of encryption algorithms.

decryption. We focus on symmetric algorithms for now. We study asymmetric (public key) algorithms in Chapter 8.

There are two categories of symmetric algorithms: codes and ciphers. In a *code*, we apply the transformation to words or phrases in the original text. For example, a military code might have a single symbol for commands like "attack" or "send reinforcements," plus individual symbols for locations, like St. Paul or Boston. For most codes, the key is a long list of phrases and code values that indicates which stands for which.

In a *cipher*, we apply the transformation to symbols in the raw text itself. For example, we could encrypt this paragraph by substituting the individual characters with different characters. The key adjusts the transformation so that it varies according to the key's value.

We classify ciphers further into transposition and substitution ciphers. In a *transposition* cipher, we rearrange the text of the message. For example, the text "hello world" might be encrypted as "drwolhel ol" through a systematic rearrangement. The original letters still appear in the ciphertext, and the cipher's key indicates the order of rearrangement. In a *substitution* cipher, the text letters remain in the same order, but individual letters are substituted with others, again according to the key. Sophisticated ciphers may combine both transposition and substitution.

Beatrix Potter's diary code was primarily a substitution cipher. She memorized a table of symbols that she systematically substituted for normal text letters. Her encryption also had "code-like" features because she occasionally substituted certain words with symbols, like the words "to" and "too" with the digit "2."

A Process View of Encryption

Alice is in Bob's statistics class. The instructor assigned another survey project, and Alice and Bob are working together. Again, they must keep the survey information confidential. They plan to share information by leaving it on a USB drive that both can reach. They plan to protect the data by encrypting it.

Figure 7.3 shows the process diagram of Bob constructing encrypted data to share with Alice. The figure shows how information is shared, or not, while passing the data between the two of them. The dark vertical bar separates Bob's resources from Alice's.

For Alice to read Bob's file, the two of them somehow must share the encryption key. The diagram doesn't show how they share the key. To keep the encrypted data secret, they must not disclose that key to others.

With encryption, we exchange the problem of protecting the file's plaintext with the problem of protecting the key.

In Potter's case, the key was a table showing which symbols were substituted for which letters or words. Potter memorized the table, and no physical copy was ever found among her possessions. While we can speculate that Potter may have had a physical copy of her key when she started encrypting her diary, she wisely destroyed it after she no longer needed it.

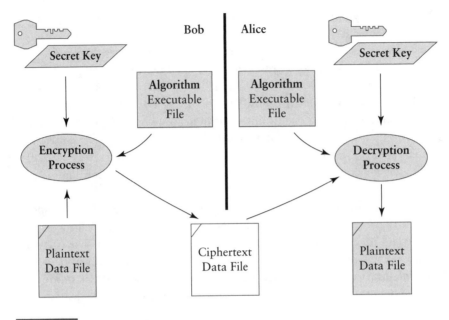

Figure 7.3

Process diagram of symmetric encryption.

Shared Secret Keys

The sender and recipient must share a *secret key* when using symmetric cryptography. This is often the most challenging part of using encryption: to protect the key from disclosure yet share it with the appropriate recipients. In some examples, we simply assume that the participants have shared the key safely. We discuss secret key handling techniques further in Chapter 8.

EFFECTIVE ENCRYPTION

Encryption succeeds when it presents a puzzle that an attacker lacks the time, resources, and motivation to solve. Encrypted diaries succeed when written by insignificant people unless the code is incredibly simple; no one will bother to try to solve the puzzle. The diaries of Beatrix Potter, Samuel Pepys, and Charles Wesley were important enough to justify the effort. This is true of all encryption: There is no point in attacking it unless the attack is trivial, or the secret information is valuable. If the attack is trivial, then the encryption gives no real protection. Weak encryption is a form of Security Through Obscurity.

The distinction between the encryption algorithm and key reflect Kerckhoff's principle. The algorithm may be known by attackers, so it must be strong enough to resist their attacks. The user keeps the key secret from attackers and can change the key if an attacker deduces a key used earlier.

Neither Potter nor Pepys nor Wesley used strong encryption, and they never changed the key that encrypted their diary entries. This was adequate for the world of hand-encoded diaries, but does not provide enough protection in the modern world of computer-based encryption.

Today, however, we can confidently protect an encrypted file from sophisticated attacks. If a diarist uses strong, computer-based encryption, the diary will be unreadable if the key is lost.

7.1.3 Encryption and Information States

In Section 3.5.3, we introduced states and state diagrams. Figure 3.17 illustrated the information states of Bob's homework file: Storage, Processing, and Transmission. When we add encryption, we place the information in new and different situations. This yields additional states.

First, we break the Storage state into two separate states: one encrypted and the other plaintext. We do the same with the Transmission state. The Processing state, however, only operates on plaintext, unless the process actually performs encryption or decryption. We're not interested in such states right now. This produces five states:

1. Plaintext Storage
2. Encrypted Storage
3. Processing
4. Plaintext Transmission
5. Encrypted Transmission

Illustrating Policy with a State Diagram

While working on their survey project together, Bob and Alice need to protect their survey file from disclosure. They also need to transmit it between their computers. They can do so with a USB drive, but they must avoid disclosing the file.

In other words, they *never* want the file to enter the Transmission state while in plaintext.

The state diagram provides us with a graphical way of illustrating this policy objective. We draw a state diagram that shows the methods by which they handle the survey data. Since our policy forbids transmission of plaintext, we omit states and arrows that might allow it. No arrows connect the Plaintext Storage state to the Transmission state.

The arrows between states need to show two types of information. First, they must show the "cause" of the state transition: the event that triggers the need to change from one state to another. Second, they should explain how the change takes place.

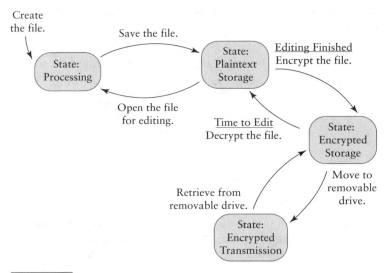

Figure 7.4

Information states using encryption.

In Figure 7.4, the arrows between states indicate both an external event to cause the transition and how the transition occurs. For example, "Open the file" reflects an action by the user that initiates processing, and it also indicates the operation that retrieves the file for processing.

Figure 7.4 illustrates a set of states and transitions intended to keep the survey file safe. Because we never want to transmit the plaintext file, we omit the Plaintext Transmission state entirely.

Note how we mark the arrows between the Plaintext Storage state and the Encrypted Storage state. Each contains an underlined phrase followed by an action. The underlined phrase describes the condition that causes the change between the two states. The second phrase indicates the action that implements the change ("encrypt" or "decrypt").

Proof of Security

When the U.S. government needs to take extreme measures to protect information, this type of analysis is a fundamental part of the process. When establishing the security policy, the designers specify every state and state change that the system should perform. Then the designers construct a similar analysis of the actual computer system. Finally, they analyze the two together using formal mathematical proof techniques. The analysts try to verify that the actual system never enters the wrong state. When older security experts spoke of systems being either "secure" or "insecure," a secure system was one that never entered a wrong ("insecure") state.

7.2 Encryption and Cryptanalysis

Encryption is deceptively simple. Anyone can create a secret code. The trick is to design a code that resists a sophisticated attack. People have been using codes for thousands of years. It seems likely that others have been breaking codes for almost as long. We call this process *cryptanalysis*. To understand encryption, we need a basic understanding of cryptanalysis.

Simple encryption is relatively easy to crack. Many newspapers publish *cryptograms*, short notes encrypted with a simple technique, as a puzzle for readers to crack. Potter's encryption was not, in fact, much more difficult than a newspaper cryptogram. To understand the basic strategy for cracking simple encryption, consider the following example:

$$
\begin{array}{r}
\text{SEND} \\
\underline{+\text{MORE}} \\
\text{MONEY}
\end{array}
$$

The visible message is in text, but we obviously have a substitution cipher: each letter corresponds to a digit. The correct decryption should yield the correct arithmetic sum. We solve the cryptogram by looking for patterns and constraints in the text. For example, the letter M must be the digit 1, because it appears on the bottom line due to a carry. If we guess that the letter O represents the value 0, then the letter S is either 8 or 9, depending on the carry from the next column. We can solve the cryptogram by applying plausible values and checking the results.

Cryptanalysts use similar tools to crack ciphers of written text. They look for patterns that naturally occur in the document's plaintext language. In English, for example, the most common letters are E, T, and A. The first step for cracking a simple cipher is to substitute those letters for the letters occurring most often in the ciphertext. Stories like Poe's *Gold Bug* describe this approach.

We also could attack the "SEND+MORE=MONEY" problem by programming a computer to generate a list of all possible assignments of digits to letters; then we tell the computer to try each possible assignment to see if the arithmetic works correctly. This requires less cleverness, but it requires a written program and a computer to run it. Once we have the program, we can easily break this kind of problem. With few important exceptions, a computer can crack any cipher people can easily apply by hand.

The simplest ciphers merely shift the letters in the alphabet. The classic example is the *Caesar cipher*, named for the Roman general and emperor. To apply the Caesar cipher, we encrypt a text message by substituting each letter with the third next letter in the alphabet: D replaces A, E replaces B, and so on. We can change the code by changing the offset. For example, another Roman shifted the alphabet by two instead of three; the shift amount alone provides the "key" for decrypting messages.

We also can vary the cipher by substituting different characters for alphabetic letters. Potter's cipher, for example, used characters she invented herself. The cipher in *The Gold Bug* substituted digits, symbols, and punctuation for letters.

While Caesar ciphers are easy to create, use, and memorize, they are also the easiest to attack. We cracked the "SEND+MORE=MONEY" code by using basic knowledge of arithmetic. We crack Caesar ciphers by using the letter frequencies noted earlier. First, we note which letters are most frequent in the ciphertext, and we use them to guess plausible shift amounts.

The same approach helps us crack other substitution ciphers, like Potter's or the one from *The Gold Bug*. We guess some characters in a message and then refine our guesses to yield readable text. Cryptanalysis becomes easier as we study larger amounts of ciphertext. A single, short message may have few or no Es, but the statistics will exert their influence as we collect more ciphertext.

This is a simple form of *frequency analysis*. As codes become more subtle and complex, cryptanalysts analyze frequencies of larger groups of letters. This helps them uncover patterns in the ciphertext. *Any* pattern may give them the insight needed to extract the message.

7.2.1 The Vigenère Cipher

We strengthen our ciphers by making frequency analysis harder. We achieve that goal by using a series of different letters to encrypt each plaintext letter. Instead of using a single alphabetic shift for encrypting every letter, we use a series of shifts. We encrypt each letter differently with each shift. This is called the **Vigenère cipher** (pronounced "Vee-zhun-air"). The Confederate Army used this type of cipher during the U.S. Civil War. To encrypt a message, the clerk used a cipher disk like the one shown in Figure 7.5.

For example, imagine that Bob wants to send the message SEND MORE FOOD to Alice, and he wants to encrypt it with a cipher disk. Bob and Alice have agreed ahead of time to use the word HUNGRY as their shared secret key. Each letter in the key represents a different shift of the alphabet. To convert the plaintext to ciphertext, we use the

Figure 7.5

A reproduction of a Confederate cipher disk.

outer disk to indicate the plaintext and the inner disk to indicate the ciphertext. Bob follows these steps:

1. Turn the inner wheel so that the first key letter, H, is under the outer disk's letter A. This sets up the inner wheel to encrypt the first plaintext letter. Figure 7.5 shows this arrangement.

2. Look for the first plaintext letter, S, on the outer disk. Its ciphertext letter appears under it: the letter Z.

3. Put "Z" in the ciphertext message.

4. Turn the inner wheel so that the second key letter, U, is under the outer disk's letter A.

5. Look for the second plaintext letter, E, on the outer disk. Its ciphertext letter appears under it: the letter Y.

6. Put "Y" in the ciphertext message.

7. Continue the series of three steps, shifting the disk for each new letter. After using the last letter in the key, start over with the first letter. Repeat until the message is fully encrypted.

We also can illustrate this process by laying down the plaintext, key stream, and ciphertext in three rows.

```
plaintext:   SENDMOREFOOD
key stream:  HUNGRYHUNGRY
ciphertext:  ZYAJDMYYSUFB
```

At the receiving end, Alice uses the same process, letter by letter, except that she looks up the ciphertext on the inner disk and replaces it with the plaintext on the outer disk. Although this is a good deal more complicated than a Caesar-like cipher, it is still vulnerable to cryptanalysis. The Confederate cipher did not prevent the Union Army from reading their messages.

Cryptanalysis takes a different approach depending on the cipher being attacked and the tricks available to attack it. Here are the general techniques:

- **Known ciphertext** or **ciphertext-only.** The analyst works exclusively from the ciphertext. The analyst doesn't have access to plaintext or to the encrypting device. This is the most common situation. Newspaper cryptograms pose this type of challenge.

- **Known plaintext.** The analyst has both the plaintext and the ciphertext for a particular message. A Vigenère cipher like that used by the Confederates cannot survive a known plaintext attack. We can derive the key easily if we have both the ciphertext and the matching plaintext.

- **Chosen plaintext.** The analyst can select plaintexts to be encrypted with the target's secret key. The analyst then tries to determine the secret key by analyzing the plaintexts and ciphertexts together. This is a powerful attack, even against modern ciphers.

The process of cracking codes, and of using knowledge gained thereby to create newer, stronger codes, has evolved into the field of *cryptology*, a more formal term for *cryptography*. In this book, we often use the word *crypto* as shorthand for these terms.

7.2.2 Electromechanical Encryption

In the 1920s, cryptographic designers developed numerous devices to encrypt and decrypt data. Some were based on cipher wheels, as seen in Figure 7.6. These are essentially mechanized versions of the simple device shown earlier in Figure 7.5.

Edward Hebern developed a different and more successful design, a *rotor machine*, that systematically scrambled the cipher alphabet each time another character was encoded. To send a message, the author typed it in to the machine, letter by letter. For

Figure 7.6

Friedman with a cipher machine.

Figure 7.7

German Enigma cipher machine.

each keystroke, the machine displayed the ciphertext letter. The machine's particular setup of rotors and interconnections served as the key.

Figure 7.7 shows the Enigma, a rotor machine used by Germany during World War II. Above the three rows of keys are three rows of lamps, one for each letter. When the operator pressed a letter key, the machine lit the corresponding letter. The switch on the upper right selected encryption or decryption. The three thumb wheels at the center top selected the starting position for the three rotors.

To decrypt a message, recipients had to set up their machines to match the sender; then they typed in the ciphertext, letter by letter. For each keystroke, the machine displayed the plaintext letter.

The incredible complexity of the machine made it virtually impossible to crack the cipher by hand, even with known plaintext. Both the Germans and the Japanese used rotor machines during World War II.

Meanwhile, however, cryptanalysts had developed strategies to attack rotor machine ciphers. William Friedman and his colleagues worked out several techniques in the 1930s. Shortly before the invasion of Poland launched World War II, Polish cryptanalysts developed a strategy for cracking the Enigma. Working with British cryptographers at Bletchley Park, the Allies improved on these techniques. During the war, Bletchley Park cracked thousands of German messages. Some historians believe this shortened the war by 2 years.

One of the reasons the Allies succeeded was that they used automatic devices, including a pioneering electronic computer, to help crack the codes through trial and error. This is how computers changed the face of encryption; they could patiently perform trial-and-error attempts to crack a code at extremely high speeds. The work at Bletchley Park is portrayed in the 2001 movie *Enigma*.

7.3 Computer-Based Encryption

Modern, computer-based encryption algorithms are far more complicated than the older mechanical or hand-operated ciphers. Their sophisticated design and operation foils traditional known-plaintext and known-ciphertext attacks. In general, the only practical attack is to try to guess the key through trial and error. This is the same as trial-and-error attacks on passwords, except that we try harder to avoid any biases in key selection. A realistic, general-purpose trial-and-error attack must examine the key's entire search space.

The Data Encryption Standard

In 1975, the U.S. government unveiled the algorithm that became the *Data Encryption Standard*, commonly called DES. The algorithm was quickly adopted by the banking industry and was the foundation of our modern electronic banking networks, from electronic funds transfers to ATMs. The DES algorithm allowed a very large number of keys:

72,057,594,037,927,900: over 72 quadrillion keys (7×10^{16})

DES, like other modern encryption algorithms, uses a binary integer as its key. We talk about the size of such keys in terms of bits: the DES keys were 56 bits long. Thus, the key could be any number between zero and 2^{56} or 72 quadrillion.

As soon as DES was announced, however, researchers argued that the key size was too small. At the time, DES seemed uncrackable, but Moore's law suggested that trial-and-error attacks might become practical within decades. Less that 20 years later, researcher David Winer proposed the design of a $1 million machine that would crack one key every 3.5 hours. The machine was never built.

In 1997, however, a collection of volunteers on the Internet worked together to crack a DES message by trial and error. The effort, nicknamed DESCHALL, used a distributed collection of tens of thousands of computers. It found the key in 5 months. The next year, a larger group cracked another DES message in 39 days. Finally, in 1998, the Electronic Frontier Foundation (EFF) unveiled their DES Cracker. At $250,000, the machine could crack a DES key in an average of less than 5 days, guessing over 92 billion keys per second.

The Advanced Encryption Standard

In 2002, the U.S. government introduced the *Advanced Encryption Standard* (AES) as the replacement for DES. AES keys come in three different sizes (Table 7.1). The smallest AES key is over twice as large as a DES key. The table also shows how long it would take to crack different sized AES keys if a modified DES Cracker could search for the keys at the same rate. A modern cracker would be significantly faster due to technology improvements. Even so, the cracking time for the smallest AES key vastly exceeds trillions of years (10^{12} years).

TABLE 7.1 AES key sizes and average cracking times		
Number of Bits in the Key	Number of Keys	Average Time Required by a DES Cracker-Style Device
128	3×10^{38}	6×10^{19} years
192	6×10^{57}	1×10^{39} years
256	1×10^{77}	2×10^{58} years

The average cracking time is the time it takes to search *half* of the total search space. This is because there are no biases in a well-chosen encryption key. Unlike passwords, we shouldn't assume that there will be biases when selecting crypto keys.

Digital cryptography succeeds when we give the attacker too many possible keys to test in a practical amount of time. We do this by using a key size that is large enough to present the attacker with too many alternatives. This is why DES is obsolete.

This also is why "exportable" software produced in the 1990s is obsolete. U.S. export laws classify encryption as a weapon of war and restrict its export. Until the end of the century, U.S. export laws effectively limited encryption keys to 40 bits in length. University researchers could crack such keys in a week using 1990s-era campus computing resources.

Predicting Cracking Speeds

According to legend, the NSA dedicates a great deal of computing power to the problem of cracking other countries' cipher keys. The precise numbers are highly classified, so we can't accurately estimate how large a key they can crack. We do, however, have hard information about how quickly various efforts could cover a search space while cracking keys:

- DESCHALL on one desktop PC: 1 million keys/second in 1997
- DES Cracker: 92 billion keys/second in 1998

If we apply Moore's law, we can estimate future cracking speeds that use similar levels of effort. Moore's law predicts that computing power doubles every 18 months; in other words, the number of keys per second should double every 18 months. If we consult Table 7.1, the time required should reduce by half every 18 months.

For example, if an optimized key cracker could try 1 million keys/second in 1997, how many can it crack per second in 2009? Here is the calculation:

$$1 \text{ million } \frac{\text{keys}}{\text{sec}} \times 2^{\left(\frac{\text{Now} - \text{Then}}{1.5} \right)}$$

$$1 \text{ million } \frac{\text{keys}}{\text{sec}} \times 2^{\left(\frac{2009 - 1998}{1.5}\right)}$$

$$= 256 \text{ million } \frac{\text{keys}}{\text{sec}}$$

Moore's law estimates that computing power increased by a factor of 256 over 12 years. Although this yields a significant improvement, it only makes a tiny dent in the strength of AES keys. Let's assume that performance improves another factor of four, giving us a 10^3 improvement in performance. Now, apply that to the time required to crack the smallest AES key in Table 7.1: over 10^{19} years. The performance improvement reduces the attack time to 10^{16} years, which remains impractical.

7.3.1 Exclusive Or: A Crypto Building Block

Computers process all data in a binary format; everything is rendered into numbers that are themselves formatted into rows of zeroes and ones. If a cipher operates in terms of fundamental symbols, then a binary cipher encrypts data by substituting zeroes and ones.

Binary encryption began with the work of Gilbert Vernam, an engineer at Western Electric in the 1920s. Vernam's goal was to provide encryption for digital teletype traffic. Although teletypes were used as early computer terminals (as in Figure 6.5), the earliest commercial models appeared around 1910.

Teletypes were electromechanical devices that converted a typist's keystrokes into a series of zeroes and ones in a standard, well-known code. At the receiving end, the teletype would type the appropriate character, typewriter style, upon receiving a particular series of zeroes and ones.

If two teletypes used the same code, one could type out any message it received from the other. The standard codes made it easy to construct a large teletype network, because compatible teletypes could transmit messages to each other. On the other hand, it also meant that anyone with the right teletype could print out any message traveling on the teletype network.

Vernam needed a way to encrypt teletype data being sent by customers who needed to keep their traffic secret. Vernam developed the simple bit-by-bit substitution cipher shown in Figure 7.8. He encrypted the message by adding each bit in the message to one bit taken from the key stream and discarding any overflow.

Vernam's bit combination operation is sometimes called a "half add." More often today we call the operation *exclusive or*, which we abbreviate **xor** or denote with the ⊕ symbol. The recipient decrypts the message by applying the same xor operation bit by bit using the same key stream.

If we look at how xor works, we see that it produces a "0" when the data and the key stream match (both 0 or both 1). It produces a "1" when the data and the key

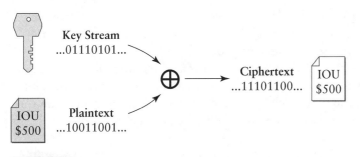

Figure 7.8

Vernam's exclusive-or cipher.

stream differ. In the following, we encrypt a series of bits with a key stream using xor. Then we decrypt it with the same key stream:

```
PLAINTEXT: 00110101
Key Stream:10101100
CIPHERTEXT:10011001
Key Stream:10101100
PLAINTEXT: 00110101
```

Figure 7.9 shows the effect of Vernam's xor encryption on a binary image. The plaintext image contains the message SEND CASH handwritten in a two-dimensional field of 0 bits (white) and 1 bits (black). We show the key stream as another binary image encoded the same way. When we combine the plaintext and key stream bit by bit using xor, we produce the ciphertext shown on the right.

The encryption seems to totally disguise the message SEND CASH. However, the key stream and the ciphertext look vaguely similar. This is because we use such a simple

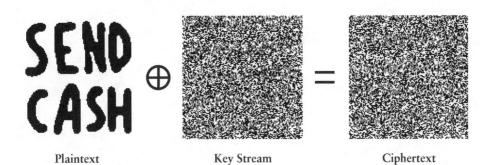

Plaintext   Key Stream   Ciphertext

Figure 7.9

Encrypting an image with xor.

transformation. The dark parts of the plaintext yield exact copies of the key stream, while the white parts yield a mirror image of the key stream. The plaintext remains secret as long as we keep the key stream secret, too.

Vernam found that the cipher worked best if they avoided repeating the key stream. As long as the senders did not use the exact same key stream to encrypt additional bits they sent, attackers had a hard time cracking the encryption, In fact, the encryption was easy to attack if they reused the key stream; we will look at this later in Section 8.2.

7.3.2 Stream Ciphers: Another Building Block

Vernam's cipher is the basis of the modern *stream cipher* (Figure 7.10). The heart of the cipher is an algorithm to generate the *key stream*, a hard-to-predict sequence of binary ones and zeroes. The algorithm generates different sequences depending on the secret key. The sequence is combined with the plaintext to produce the ciphertext. The recipient uses the same key to generate a matching key stream, and then applies xor to the message and key stream to recover the plaintext.

The key stream algorithm is the heart of every effective stream cipher. If there is a way to guess the key or the key stream, the attacker can decrypt the ciphertext. Typically, a key stream algorithm starts with the encryption key and generates a hard-to-guess sequence of bits.

If an attacker knows part of the message's plaintext, the attacker can extract that part of the key stream. Therefore, the key stream itself should not reveal the key.

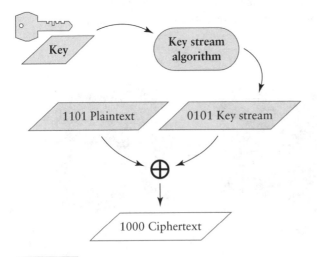

Stream cipher.

GENERATING A KEY STREAM

Recall the properties of the one-way hash we examined in Section 6.2.1. The hash output never reveals information about its input. If we were to run the encryption key through a one-way hash, the resulting hash value would not itself reveal the encryption key.

If we run that result through the hash, we get a new and different hash value. This is because the hash output should always be different from its input. Moreover, there's no easy way to invert the hash output and derive the input that produced it. Thus, we can generate a hard-to-invert data sequence with a one-way hash (Figure 7.11).

The algorithm works as follows. First, we take the secret key we want to use and we hash it. That yields the first hash value, which serves as the first group of bits in our key stream. We then feed the hash value back through the one-way hash (a "feedback" loop) to generate another hash value. This serves as the next group of bits in our key stream. If the hash generates 256 bits, then we must run the one-way hash again every time we need another 256 bits of key stream.

Unfortunately, there is a serious problem with this key stream. If attackers know part of the plaintext, they can use it to find that part of the key stream. If they know enough plaintext to recover one of the hash values, they can feed it back to the one-way hash to produce the rest of the key stream. This flaw allows them to start from a part of the message they already know and decrypt the rest of the message. This is a "known plaintext" attack.

Many documents contain predictable blocks of text near the beginning. For example, an encrypted legal document from the firm "Dewey, Cheatem, & Howe" certainly

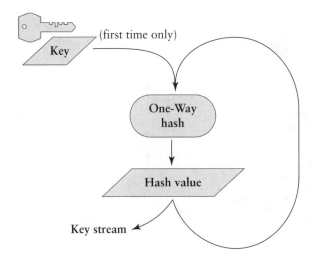

Key stream from a one-way hash.

contains the firm's name somewhere near the beginning. An attacker could guess part of the key stream by applying xor to the text "Dewey, Cheatem, & Howe" and to the ciphertext. This attack requires some trial and error, but it eventually succeeds if they guess enough plaintext.

Thus, the key stream algorithm in Figure 7.11 does not produce a secure cipher. The cipher is vulnerable to a known plaintext attack.

AN IMPROVED KEY STREAM

We can improve the cipher by hashing the secret key along with the previous hash value in each cycle, as shown in Figure 7.12.

The algorithm starts by using the key itself as the hash input. If an attacker knows some of the plaintext, he can still find that part of the key stream. Without the secret key, however, the attacker can't generate the next word in the key stream.

Although this key stream algorithm is better than the simple one-way hash, it's still not a good choice. One-way hash functions aren't really designed to generate good key streams.

A better and more efficient choice would be to use a key stream generator designed for a stream cipher. For many years, a popular choice was Rivest's Cipher 4, also known as RC4. Written in 1987 by MIT professor Ron Rivest, it has been a traditional choice in web browsers to protect messages to secure websites. RC4 requires a very simple pro-

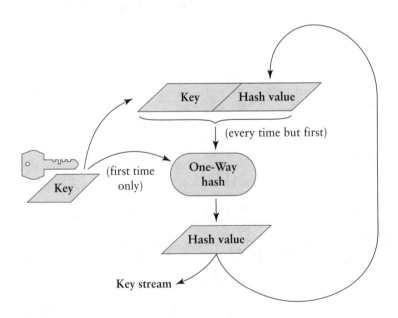

Figure 7.12

Improved key stream from a one-way hash.

gram and it generates the key stream in 8-bit bytes. Unfortunately, RC4 has not stood the test of time (see Section 9.2.2).

7.3.3 Key Stream Security

When we look at the mishmash of data that makes up an encrypted message (like the right-hand block of Figure 7.9), cryptanalysis seems like an impossible task. To crack a stream cipher, we must deduce the contents of the key stream. Some key streams are relatively easy to crack, while others are very difficult. Some are impossible to crack in practice, and some are impossible both in theory and in practice. It all depends on the amount of randomness, or entropy, in the key stream.

When we use a key stream algorithm, there is a definite limit on the entropy in the key stream. Specifically, the entropy in the key stream is limited to the entropy in the secret key we use. This is the natural result of using a fixed procedure, an algorithm, to generate numerical results. The scope of possible outputs is naturally limited by the range of initial inputs.

Thus, in a worst case, we can always reproduce a message's key stream if we know what key stream algorithm they used and we try all possible keys. This is why the DES key size was controversial. When DES was introduced, it seemed impractical to crack a 56-bit key. However, Moore's law made it clear that key cracking would get better over the next few decades. As computer speeds increased, so did the demands for an improved, U.S. government standard cipher with a larger key.

RC4 Biases

Unfortunately, a large key is not always enough to ensure security. Few crypto designers use RC4 in modern systems even though it is often used with a 128-bit key. As researchers studied RC4, they found "biases" in its behavior (see Section 9.2.2).

Pseudo-Random Number Generators

Our key stream generators, whether they are one-way hashes or RC4, serve as PRNGs, which we introduced in Section 6.3.2. Most programming libraries include a PRNG function, usually named "random()" or "rand()". Even Excel has such a function. What would happen if we used such a function to generate our key stream?

Mechanically, it seems like a practical approach. These PRNGs produce their results from an initial "seed" value. There is a function or an optional parameter that initializes the seed value. When the seed is set to a specific value, we get a predetermined sequence of pseudorandom outputs.

Remember that PRNGs are intended for games of chance, simulation, or statistical analysis. The actual sequence of values doesn't necessarily matter to these applications as long as they are "statistically random." In fact, some systems use a built-in, constant value for the seed. This yields the exact same sequence of pseudorandom numbers every time a program is run. This works badly for games of chance. Other systems initialize the seed automatically to a changing value like the system clock. If the system uses an unchanging "default" seed value, the game programmer must explicitly set the seed to some changing value, like the system time.

To create a stream cipher with the PRNG, we use the secret key as the seed value. Each time we call the PRNG, we use the resulting output as the next group of bits in the key stream. We xor the bits in the plaintext to bits from the key stream and emit the result as the ciphertext.

At the receiving end, we must run the same PRNG with the same secret key as the seed value. This generates the same key stream, which we xor with the ciphertext. This recovers the plaintext.

Technically, this produces a cipher. Unfortunately, it is unlikely to be a trustworthy cipher. A series of random numbers can be perfectly sufficient for statistical purposes but still exhibit biases that disclose other parts of the key stream, or even the key itself. Some PRNGs explicitly use their previous output value as the seed for producing the next value. This is the same as the key stream generator in Figure 7.11, and it suffers from the same weakness. A known plaintext attack could recover part of the key stream and use it to generate the rest of the key stream.

THE EFFECTS OF CIPHERTEXT ERRORS

Data storage is never perfect. As a file sits in one place on a hard drive or as it moves from one device to another, we risk data errors. The storage hardware and the operating system try hard to detect such errors, but this doesn't always work.

Potential errors pose an important question as we decrypt the data: How will a broken bit in the ciphertext affect the plaintext? Fortunately, the damage is limited in stream ciphers; if an error inverts a ciphertext bit, we see the same bit inverted after we decrypt the plaintext.

On the other hand, this poses an integrity risk to our ciphertext. An attacker can change any bit in the plaintext by changing the corresponding ciphertext bit. If the text contains some sort of promise, invoice, or IOU, the attacker can make the amounts higher or lower without detection. Thus, the stream cipher doesn't protect the data's contents; it only protects its secrecy. We need to use a separate mechanism to detect changes to the ciphertext. We will look at that problem in Chapter 8.

7.3.4 The One-Time Pad

There is, however, a way to make this encryption theoretically impossible to crack: the *one-time pad*. While a stream cipher uses a key stream algorithm to generate its key stream, a one-time pad uses a truly random stream of bits for its key stream. The sender and recipient must share that key stream in secret. They then use the key stream with the xor operation to encrypt and decrypt messages.

When properly used, it is mathematically impossible to crack a message encrypted by a one-time pad. This was first described by Claude Shannon in the 1940s as part of his development of information theory. A one-time pad is impossible to crack because knowledge of the ciphertext does not reduce uncertainty about the contents of the original, plaintext message.

The one-time pad is theoretically secure because there is no way to do a trial-and-error decryption. Because the key stream can be *anything*, there is no way to tell if a guessed decryption is correct. If we use a key stream algorithm to generate the key stream, then we can at least *theoretically* decrypt any message, just by trying all possible values of the key. Because this attack isn't practical for large secret keys, a strong, unbiased stream cipher is practical to use even if it's theoretically breakable.

People rarely use one-time pads in practice even though they are unbreakable. The best known case today is on the "hot line" that connects leaders in Washington and Moscow. Others rarely use one-time pads because they are hard to use correctly.

SOVIET ESPIONAGE AND ONE-TIME PADS

One-time pads have, however, often been used in espionage. Spies have a strong inducement to keep their messages secret, and one-time pads can be coded by hand. Soviet spies used such codes in the 1940s and 1950s. Instead of binary bits, the Soviets used a decimal number code.

The Soviets printed up the decimal one-time pads in tiny books. Each contained thousands of digits to use as key values. In both binary and decimal, the one-time pad uses "add without carry." In the decimal code, add without carry discards the overflow, as in $7 + 7 = 4$, or $8 + 8 = 6$. To decrypt the decimal code we use the opposite operation: "subtract without borrow." In the following, we encrypt a series of decimal digits using a decimal one-time pad. Then we decrypt it with the same key stream:

```
PLAINTEXT: 67519382
Key Stream:52836158
CIPHERTEXT:19345430
Key Stream:52836158
PLAINTEXT: 67519382
```

After a spy encoded a message, he or she would discard the pages of used one-time pad digits. The next message would use the remaining digits. This prevented the spy from sending two or more messages using the same key—a mistake that makes the ciphertext vulnerable to attack.

MODULAR ARITHMETIC

Mathematically, we implement the one-time pad using *modular arithmetic*. A casual explanation might suggest that we simply "round things off" in modular arithmetic. Clearly, the decimal one-time pad example shows us discarding the tens' overflow when encrypting. A different way to describe it is that we perform arithmetic on a "number circle."

Children often learn conventional arithmetic by working on a "number line." Addition or subtraction moves us to the right or left: one direction when adding and the other when subtracting.

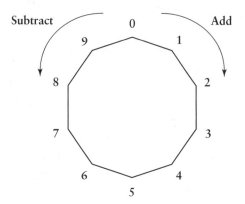

Modular arithmetic on a number circle.

In modular arithmetic, the results wrap around on themselves. We illustrate this most clearly on a number circle. Figure 7.13 shows arithmetic "modulo 10" on a number circle. This is what we used for the decimal one-time pad.

For addition, we move clockwise around the circle. This performs the same as one-time pad encryption; we add the numbers and discard the overflow. Subtraction moves counterclockwise, the same as one-time pad decryption.

If we compare the operation of the number circle to the cipher disc in Figure 7.5, we see that it, too, performs modular calculations. Most cipher disk cryptography is easy to crack, but this is because most people use weak key streams.

Modular arithmetic plays a fundamental role in many cryptographic techniques. The xor operation is a modular operation, calculating both addition and subtraction modulo 2. We also can perform modular multiplication, division, and other operations. In fact, this is the mathematical basis for public-key cryptography (Chapter 8).

PRACTICAL ONE-TIME PADS

As a practical matter, it is very difficult to create, manage, and protect a completely random key stream. If the stream leaks to an attacker, then the encryption is useless. There has to be exactly one digit of random key stream for every digit of traffic sent, so there has to be a periodic exchange of even more random digits. This inconvenience makes one-time pads rare in practice.

There is a lot of confusion about one-time pads. Some vendors use the term with their encryption products simply because one-time pads are provably secure. They believe that the term makes the product seem impenetrable. The crypto community has a name for products that make extravagant and inaccurate security claims like that: They call such products *snake oil*.

7.4 File Encryption Software

A file encryption program transforms files between plaintext and ciphertext, using keys provided to it. Some operating systems, including versions of Microsoft Windows, include a file encryption feature. In practice, however, such capabilities don't provide all the features of a separate file encryption application program.

People use file encryption in two distinct situations:

1. Protect a file while sending a copy to someone else.
2. Protect a file while it resides on the computer's hard drive. This involves three separate risks:
   a. Prevent access by a Trojan horse
   b. Prevent access by a separately booted operating system
   c. Prevent access to low-level data written to the hard drive

In the first case, we might send an electronic file via email, or we might copy it onto a USB drive and deliver it physically. When going via email, someone might intercept a copy of the file as it traverses the Internet. Effective encryption should discourage the eavesdropper from trying to read the file. If the file travels on a USB token, we may carry it by hand or send it through the mail. If we leave it unattended or plug it into an untrustworthy computer, there is no way to know for certain if someone has examined it and copied its contents.

An Incident: In the 1990s, the director of the U.S. Central Intelligence Agency (CIA) took some highly secret documents home on an early form of flash storage. He worked on them using the same computer his children used to surf the Internet. An investigation by the CIA inspector general did not find any Trojan horse programs on the computer. However, the investigation could not conclusively determine whether the information had been captured by an attacker while it was outside of the CIA headquarters.

When protecting the file on the hard drive, we also have to ensure that an eavesdropper can't retrieve the original document. This is challenging, because files leave information on the hard drive even after they are deleted.

Section 4.5 describes a Trojan horse attack on Bob's computer. When Bob is logged in and running the computer game, he wants his sensitive files to remain protected from eavesdropping. This will only protect the file if Bob is careful. For example, Bob might need to work on the file, so he decrypts it and works on it for a while. Then he gets bored and decides to play the computer game for a while. His file will be vulnerable to copying unless he remembers to encrypt it before he plays the game.

7.4.1 Built-In File Encryption

Many people use Microsoft operating systems that include a file encryption feature (it usually is limited to "Windows Professional" editions and omitted from "Home" editions). Although Windows encryption provides some useful features, it is not a cure-all. There are distinct trade-offs between using built-in file encryption and using a separate application program.

Built-in encryption is convenient, because the operating system often handles the keys for the owner. In Microsoft Windows, the user can open and save an encrypted file just like any other file. The operating system handles the keys, encryption, and decryption automatically (Figure 7.14).

For example, Bob has written an English paper ("english1a.doc") and, thanks to the odd events in his suite, he has decided to let Windows encrypt it for him. To do this, he right clicks on the file and selects "Properties" from the menu. At the bottom of the Properties window, he selects the "Advanced" button; then he checks the box marked "Encrypt contents to secure data."

Now, whenever Bob clicks on the file, Windows will open it and decrypt it for him. When he closes the file, only the encrypted form remains visible on the hard drive. This protects the encrypted files from access if an attacker boots a different operating system and tries to read files off of the hard drive.

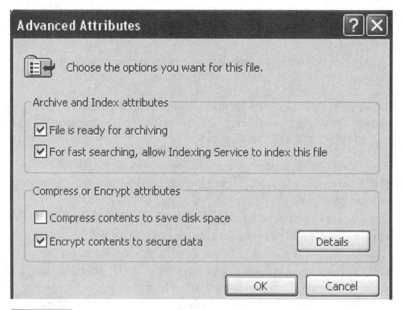

Figure 7.14
Enabling file encryption on Windows.

Windows handles the encryption key automatically. The key is stored in the file system along with the file. To prevent attackers from extracting this key from the file system, the key is itself encrypted using a separate *public key* (see Chapter 8). Windows makes this public key available to Bob whenever he logs in. If we click on the "Details" button shown in Figure 7.14, we see a list of users who can decrypt the file, each with their own copy of the encrypted key.

In security, we pay for convenience by suffering other shortcomings. In this case, the convenience reduces the security. If Bob can read the plaintext of the encrypted file simply by opening that file, then a Trojan horse can read the contents, too. Thus, the Microsoft file encryption will not protect against a Trojan horse.

However, neither can Bob share the encrypted file with people on other computers. He has no way of sharing the encryption key, so others can't decrypt the file. In particular, Windows provides no easy way of sharing the keys required to decrypt the file on a destination computer, even if running the same Windows operating system.

A final shortcoming suggests that Windows file encryption provides very limited security. Many Windows systems do not erase the plaintext data after encrypting the file. The hard drive retains scraps of the plaintext data on the disk blocks that held the decrypted file. If an attacker boots a different operating system and searches the hard drive's disk blocks, she might be able to retrieve some or all of this secret data.

7.4.2 Encryption Application Programs

From the user's point of view, an encryption application program protects a file with a memorized password. Normally, the file is unusable in its encrypted form. When the owner provides the password and the file to the encryption application, the program produces a usable copy of the plaintext file. When finished with the file, the owner must run the encryption program again to reencrypt the file.

The encryption program allows the user to select a file, provide a shared secret key, and then encrypt or decrypt the file. Figure 7.15 shows the elements of the file decryption process and the boundaries between them. The program begins as a process started by Bob. He talks to the program by way of his keyboard, which in turn talks to his file encryption process. If someone else also happens to be running the file encryption program on his computer at the same time, the program runs in a *separate* process that belongs to that other user. The separate process has its own RAM and is restricted by the other user's access rights.

To use an encryption program to protect his survey file, Bob does the following:

1. Start the encryption application program.
2. Select the file he wants to encrypt: the survey file.
3. Provide the key used to encrypt the file (usually in the form of a typed password or passphrase).
4. The program encrypts the file and saves the encrypted copy.

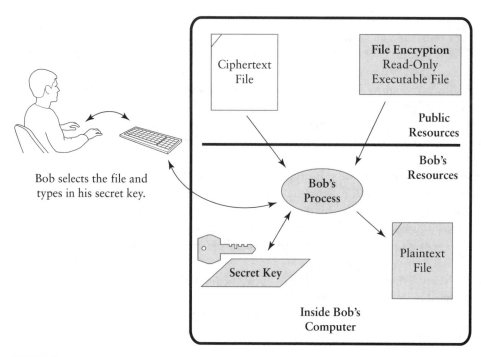

Figure 7.15
Security boundaries while decrypting a file.

5. The program erases the plaintext version of the file.
6. When finished, the program erases the key from RAM and exits.

Once the application program is finished, no one will be able to read the file without decrypting it first, not even Bob. Decryption requires the secret key. The most convenient programs use memorized passwords or passphrases as keys to encrypt and decrypt files. Such keys are not the strongest or safest, but they are the easiest to handle and share.

To decrypt a file, Bob starts the program and selects the file to decrypt via the keyboard and mouse. He also enters the file's secret key via the keyboard. The process decrypts the ciphertext file and writes the plaintext to a new file. The process sets the new file's access rights so that only Bob can use it. Once the decryption is finished, Bob exits the program, which erases the secret key before it exits.

Ensuring Secure File Encryption
The file encryption program must take several steps to ensure that it does its job effectively. Some steps involve file handling and some involve key handling.

First, the file encryption program itself must be protected from modification by arbitrary or malicious users. An easy way to bypass encryption is to either replace strong encryption with weak encryption or to disable it entirely. Few people actually examine encrypted data to ensure that it is in fact encrypted.

The program protects itself during installation. The installation program may have built-in integrity checks to test for changes made to it since it left the vendor. The installation program also sets up file permissions to prevent regular users from being able to modify the encryption program.

The program also must protect the file while in plaintext form. When it creates a plaintext version of the file, only the owner—Bob in this case—should have access to that file.

PROTECTING THE SECRET KEY

From a software and computing point of view, we only control the elements inside Bob's computer. The software can't prevent an eavesdropper (a suitemate named "Eve," for example) from shoulder surfing while Bob types his secret key. The software also can't prevent Bob from writing the key on a sticky note and leaving it on his desk.

However, the program must do whatever it can to keep the key secret. In Section 6.2, we saw how systems try to keep passwords secret by not displaying them through the GUI. The systems either fail to echo a typed password on the display, or they print a mask to obscure the text of the typed password. A file encryption program must take similar steps when collecting a secret key.

The encryption process must be very careful about handling the secret key in RAM. In particular, the key must reside only in its special location in RAM. It must not be stored anywhere else or displayed through the program's graphical interface. The key must never be copied to RAM that other processes may see. The program must ensure also that the key is never written to the hard drive.

7.4.3 Erasing a Plaintext File

After the file encryption program encrypts the plaintext file, it should actively erase the plaintext file's contents. If we delete the file, the operating system "loses" it and can't retrieve it for us. However, the actual data we wrote in the file remains on the hard drive. The disk space containing it will eventually be overwritten by new files, but the data remains undisturbed until then.

Forensic and file recovery programs often can recover deleted files. These programs look inside the file system and track down the deleted file information. Section 5.4.3 described exactly how to retrieve a deleted file on a FAT device. If the file's space on the hard drive hasn't been reused, the undelete program may be able to retrieve the deleted file.

To protect against undelete programs, the easiest solution is to literally *overwrite* the file's contents. To do this, the program writes zeros or any other data pattern over the file's contents on the hard drive. An undelete program can't possibly recover a file after we overwrite it. The hard drive's circuitry can't read anything from the hard drive except the data written most recently to it.

RISKS THAT DEMAND OVERWRITING

There are three risks related to overwriting: a Trojan horse, a reboot to a different operating system, or access to low-level signals written to the hard drive.

If we want encryption primarily to protect against Trojan horse attacks, then the encryption application doesn't need to wipe the file. A program that undeletes files requires full, unimpeded access to the hard drive. Such programs are run only by administrators. If the attacker can run such a program, then we can't protect the file with file encryption. If we apply Transitive Trust, we see that the attacker with administrative rights can modify the file encryption program so that it passes data to the attacker (the encryption keys, the plaintext files, or both).

This is a difference between the encryption application and the Windows built-in file encryption. Windows does *not* protect against a Trojan horse attack. When an application opens an encrypted file, Windows decrypts the file automatically and provides the plaintext to the program. This allows a Trojan horse to read the user's encrypted files. We must use a separate encryption application program to protect against a Trojan horse.

If we want to protect against an attacker booting a different operating system to access the hard drive, then we need to overwrite the file before we delete it. Otherwise, the attacker could boot another operating system and use it to undelete the plaintext file.

Some users store incredibly sensitive data on their computers. They do not want to take any risk of others recovering that sensitive data. If we need to protect against that, we need to work even harder at erasing the data from the hard drive.

PREVENTING LOW-LEVEL DATA RECOVERY

If we rely exclusively on the hard drive's built-in circuitry to read and write data, then it is easy to wipe the data in a file. We write new data over the old data, zeroes, ones, or a mixture, and the hard drive sees the newly written data. However, the hard drive retains subtle indicators of the drive's earlier contents.

Data recovery experts can produce high-resolution maps of the magnetic fields on a disk's surface. If the disk heads on a hard drive are not positioned exactly over a sector when writing new data, the sector's previous data may remain visible, especially in older hard drives. To counteract this, security software would try to erase the data thoroughly by rewriting each sector several times, writing a different bit pattern each time.

Modern drives, however, do not suffer from this problem. Hard drives that contain over 15 GB of storage pack their bits much more closely together. While many data recovery experts could retrieve overwritten data from older and smaller hard drives, there are no well-known techniques to retrieve overwritten data from newer drives.

Despite this, no computer program can reliably remove all sensitive data from a hard drive. When a hard drive detects an impending failure in part of the drive, it automatically copies its data to a different part of the drive. The drive marks the old section as "bad" so it isn't used for new data. From then on, there is no way to access the bad section of the drive. Low-level analysis may be able to retrieve sensitive data from the bad section. This does not pose a risk for most user communities, but it shows how persistent digital data can be.

ERASING OPTICAL MEDIA

Optical disks, either CDs or DVDs, provide an easy way to share a lot of data. They all pose a problem when we want to rid ourselves of sensitive data. The problem is more or less the same for commercially manufactured disks and for formats writable on personal computers. Here are common formats:

- CD-R—recordable CD
- CD-RW—rewritable CD
- DVD-R—recordable DVD
- DVD-RW—rewritable DVD

All of these devices work by reflecting a laser off of the disk's surface. Individual bits are distinguished by whether the laser detects a light or dark reflection. When we write on a recordable disk, the writing actually modifies a dye in the disk. When we write on a rewritable disk, we modify a special material that allows itself to be switched on and off.

The most practical way to render optical disk contents unusable is to physically destroy the disk's surface. Commercial devices may cover the surface with pits, which renders enough of the surface unusable so that a computer can't mount the disk.

It also should be possible—at least in theory—to write over either a recordable or a rewritable disk. In fact, there has been very little research on the effectiveness of such techniques. Microscopic analysis might be able to distinguish between recent and less-recent cycles. In the absence of known research results, it is best to simply destroy CDs or DVDs.

7.4.4 Choosing a File Encryption Program

If we type the term *file encryption* into an Internet search engine, we find a lot of candidates. Some entries may refer to built-in Windows encryption or to whole-disk encryption (TrueCrypt, for example), which we will examine in Chapter 9. There are countless programs that perform file encryption.

In 1989, a programmer named Phil Katz released a computer program named PKZIP, which introduced the now-popular "zip" file compression format. People typically use zip format to combine one or more files into a single, compact file for sharing with other people. In addition, PKZIP included a password-based encryption mechanism.

Unfortunately, the early versions of PKZIP did not use a modern, high-quality encryption algorithm. In 1994, researchers Biham and Kocher published a paper describing weaknesses in the encryption. Soon, others developed cracking programs that could analyze an encrypted PKZIP file and guess its password. Fortunately, the recent versions of PKZIP can support strong, modern cryptographic algorithms, as do many other programs supporting the zip format.

Cracking programs also crop up for other applications that incorporate relatively weak password protection schemes. This includes most Microsoft Office applications, which do not all use encryption when password-protecting a file.

Another program that often appears is PGP, which stands for "Pretty Good Privacy." Phil Zimmerman, the original developer, created it to exchange encrypted files using email. The program was released in 1991 in response to the fear that the U.S. Congress would pass laws forbidding the use of strong cryptography by U.S. citizens.

Originally, PGP software was free, but since then, PGP has become a commercial product. Following this freeware tradition, the PGP Corporation provides a free, limited-capability version of their software for personal, noncommercial use. PGP includes the ability to encrypt a file using a shared password or passphrase, though it also supports more sophisticated key-sharing techniques based on public keys.

Many companies that offer file and system utilities, like Norton or McAfee, also offer file encryption programs. There are also numerous freeware and shareware applications that perform file encryption.

Given all these choices, we need a way to compare the different benefits provided by the different applications. To do this, we consider a list of requirements that the file encryption program might fulfill. We use this list to produce a security checklist for the file encryption program.

Software Security Checklist

Before we look specifically at file encryption, let us look at some basic, even obvious software considerations:

- **Cost.** Can we afford the software in terms of purchase cost?
- **Compatibility.** Does the software run in our computing environment? This is challenging if we run multiple systems, like Windows, Linux, and Macintosh. We should be able to encrypt or decrypt the files on any of our systems.
- **Installation.** Did we install a genuine copy of the software? Is it protected from subversion by other users on the computer? Only the administrator should have write access to the file encryption application.
- **Usability.** Will the application fit our working style? This decision involves both the behavior of the application and the challenge of keeping the software supported and up to date.
- **Trust.** Do we trust the vendor? Some people are more inclined to trust commercial organizations. People familiar with the open-source community may be more inclined to trust open-source products if they are sure they have downloaded the correct software.

File Encryption Security Checklist

This checklist provides a list of requirements that should be met by a file encryption program.

1. The program shall use an encryption algorithm that is respected and accepted by the crypto community. Here is a list of common algorithms:
   - Advanced Encryption Standard (AES)—preferred.

- AES Candidates: Rijndael (an early version of AES), Rivest Cipher 6 (RC6), Twofish, Serpent, and MARS.
- CAST—an algorithm developed in Canada. The acronym stands for the inventors' names: Carlisle Adams and Stafford Tavares.
- International Data Encryption Algorithm (IDEA).
- Triple Data Encryption Standard (3DES)—a version of DES that applies the 56-bit algorithm three times for increased safety.

2. When the program decrypts a file and saves the result in a new plaintext file, the program shall grant access rights to the new file exclusively to the file's creator.

3. After creating an encrypted copy of a file, the program shall erase the contents of the original, plaintext file by overwriting the storage space on the hard drive. Then the program shall delete the erased file.

4. The program shall handle keys in a safe manner. We examine this problem in Chapter 8.

5. Ideally, the program shall have completed a cryptographic product evaluation by a recognized authority.

CRYPTOGRAPHIC PRODUCT EVALUATION

When we purchase other products, especially expensive or important things, we often search for expert opinions that compare alternative products. With crypto products, this comparison is especially challenging. These products can fail in many ways that weaken or eliminate the protections we require. It takes a sophisticated review process to produce an informed opinion on the quality of an encryption program.

Fortunately, there are processes and techniques for performing such evaluations. These often are established by national governments: In the United States, the recognized evaluation is a federal information processing standard, called FIPS 140-2, and administered by the NIST. Such evaluations are mandatory when the encryption is used in certain high-security environments, such as financial institutions and U.S. government organizations.

We prefer software that has completed a cryptographic evaluation because these evaluations will do some of the decision making for us. The evaluation will check the product for well-known security mistakes and weaknesses. This yields a more thorough assessment than we can make as consumers.

7.5 Digital Rights Management

When a company publishes in digital form, whether it is a computer program, music, video, or a book, they face the piracy problem: Some people may make and sell copies without paying royalties to the copyright owner. In general, the problem of sharing digital data involves Transitive Trust, because anyone can make a copy of raw bits to share with others. This problem led to digital rights management (DRM) techniques, which seek to prevent easy duplication of digital data.

In the early days of personal computing, most computer owners were hobbyists who spent money on relatively costly hardware. Back then, the cheapest diskette drive or hard drive cost more than an entire computer system costs today. Because software was relatively easy to copy, hobbyists were often inclined to "borrow" copies from friends instead of buying a copy.

Software vendors developed copy protection schemes (an early DRM technique) to reduce the piracy risk. Some built in authentication mechanisms tied to hard-to-copy information. Others distributed software on specially formatted diskettes that resisted conventional attempts to copy them. By the time computers had become a fixture in company offices, most vendors had stopped using copy protection, simply because it made matters too difficult for nontechnical users.

Video productions were first published and sold to the public in the 1970s, with the introduction of video casettes. Some video publishers worried about people making and selling their own copies of video productions. However, it proved difficult to make high-quality copies from the analog recordings. Many video publishers used a mechanism called "Macrovision" to make copying difficult. Macrovision interferes with video timing signals to prevent reliable recording without preventing playback.

The introduction of DVDs in the mid-1990s led to more sophisticated DRM techniques. Film distributors feared that digital video would make piracy rampant. The industry standard for DVD production incorporated a custom-designed DRM mechanism called the *DVD Content Scrambling System* (DVD-CSS). Every DVD player manufacturer and DVD publisher agreed to incorporate DVD-CSS. When Blu-ray disks were introduced, they incorporated a similar but much more sophisticated DRM technique.

POLICY DILEMMAS

DRM poses a dilemma because it must balance opposing interests of vendors and users. On the one hand, vendors want to preserve and enhance the income they receive from their investment in a software or media product. On the other hand, buyers want a reliable, long-lived copy of that product.

Under U.S. copyright law, there is the notion of *fair use*; the buyer has the right to use and copy a purchased, copyrighted product in certain ways. For example, the buyer can make copies to protect against losing the original. It is also legal to make limited quotations. For example, if Alice publishes an article about Dan Brown in the school paper, she can include quotations from the author's copyrighted novels as long as the quotations aren't excessive.

There is also a technical aspect to the balance between vendor and buyer: the amount of technology required to implement protections. If the vendor places too much protection on the product, nontechnical users won't be able to use the product. When Apple first started selling digitized music through their iTunes store, the music carried copy protection. The protection was removed in early 2009 to simplify downloading for music buyers.

DVD copy protection was more successful. It appeared in a broad range of DVD-related products with limited impact on end users. Overall, DVD players have worked reliably since their introduction. While the DRM technique itself has not stood the test of time, it has not prevented customers from playing DVDs on commercial DVD players. The system has worked less reliably when running on PCs.

THE DVD CONTENT SCRAMBLING SYSTEM

The DVD-CSS remains an integral part of the manufacturing and distribution of DVDs and DVD players. The design allows approved DVD players to play back the encrypted content of a commercial DVD. Every player contains a secret key to decrypt the DVD's contents. The player protects the key from disclosure, as shown in Figure 7.16.

When creating a DVD for sale, the publisher encrypts the disk's program material with randomly selected encryption keys. Those keys are themselves encrypted and written to the DVD with the program material. Every DVD player has a built-in decryption key that allows it to decrypt the keys, and then decrypt the program. We will look at DVD-CSS key handling in Section 8.2.4.

The typical consumer buys the DVD player, plugs it into the TV, and plays DVDs. The player handles all keys automatically. The player does not have to contact a third party for managing or updating its keys or algorithms.

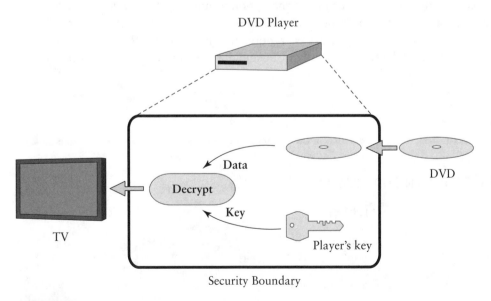

Figure 7.16

DVD content protection.

The DVD CSS arrangement has three points of vulnerability:

1. The DVD itself. It must be difficult to make a complete copy of a commercial DVD.
2. The playback signal. It must be impractical to redigitize the playback signal with acceptably high quality or to copy it onto a video casette.
3. The DVD player and its internal keys. It must be impractical to extract the keys from a player or to extract the decoded digital data stream. It also should be impractical to recover keys through brute force guessing attacks.

To prevent DVD copying, the DVD itself is formatted with an extra "invisible" track that contains a set of decryption keys used by different brands of DVD players. The track is preset to 0 in typical writable DVDs. If a computer user tries to copy a commercial DVD, typical copying techniques will not copy the invisible track.

To protect the DVD playback signal, many DVDs use the Macrovision copy protection described earlier. As video components have migrated to digital outputs, the video equipment community has so far avoided marketing consumer-grade video capture equipment that might intercept digital output from a DVD player or from newer Blu-ray players.

Internally, the DVD encases sensitive components in a hard-to-penetrate package. In many cases, DVD keys are manufactured inside integrated circuits in a way that makes them impractical to extract.

Unfortunately, the DVD technology was developed while the U.S. government enforced strong export restrictions on encryption technology. Encryption using 40 bits or less and a proprietary encryption algorithm was generally eligible for export, so DVDs adopted a 40-bit proprietary encryption algorithm. By 1999, researchers had reverse-engineered the encryption algorithm and developed practical techniques to crack DVD-CSS encryption keys.

7.6 Resources

 IMPORTANT TERMS INTRODUCED

algorithm	cryptology	plaintext
Caesar cipher	decrypt	rotor machine
cipher	encryption	secret key
ciphertext	fair use	stream cipher
code	key stream	substitution
cryptanalysis	modular arithmetic	symmetric encryption
crypto	one-time pad	transposition
cryptography	overwrite	Vigenère cipher

ACRONYMS INTRODUCED

3DES—Triple Data Encryption Standard

AES—Advanced Encryption Standard

CAST—Carlisle Adams and Stafford Tavares, creators of the CAST encryption algorithm

CD-R—Recordable CD

CD-RW—Rewritable CD

CIA—Central Intelligence Agency

DES—Data Encryption Standard

DVD-CSS—DVD Content Scrambling System

DVD-R—Recordable DVD

DVD-RW—Rewritable DVD

EFF—Electronic Frontier Foundation

IDEA—International Data Encryption Algorithm

PGP—Pretty Good Privacy

PKZIP—Phil Katz' "zip" compression program

RC4—Rivest's Cipher 4

RC6—Rivest's Cipher 6

xor—Exclusive or

7.6.1 Review Questions

R1.   Summarize the security process as applied to a personal diary.

R2.   Describe the different categories of symmetric encryption algorithms.

R3.   Outline the symmetric encryption process and explain the components involved in the process.

R4.   What is cryptanalysis? Give an example of a cryptanalytic problem.

R5.   Describe how a simple substitution cipher works, like the Caesar cipher.

R6.   Describe the components of a digital stream cipher.

R7.   Why do modern security systems avoid using RC4?

R8.   What is the difference between a stream cipher and a one-time pad?

R9.   Explain the relationship between modular arithmetic and the Caesar cipher.

R10. How do data errors in ciphertext encrypted with a stream cipher affect the decrypted plaintext?

R11. Summarize the different situations in which people use file encryption software.

R12. Compare the behavior of built-in Windows file encryption with using a separate encryption application program.

R13. Describe the steps performed when a file encryption program encrypts a file.

R14. Describe the steps performed when a file encryption program decrypts a file.

R15. Why should a file encryption program overwrite the plaintext in a file after the file has been encrypted?

R16. Summarize basic considerations for secure, trustworthy software.

R17. Summarize the basic security features of a well-written file encryption program.

7.6.2 Exercises

E1. Does your organization have a policy on using encryption? If so, describe how file encryption is used in the policy.

E2. Find an encryption policy on the Internet belonging to a large organization and describe how it addresses file encryption.

Each of the following questions presents a row of plaintext numbers followed by a row of numbers representing a keystream for a one-time pad. Apply modulo arithmetic or "xor" as needed to yield the corresponding ciphertext.

E3. 1828 7511 9151 6428 1273
1716 6143 1994 7813 4974

E4. 1 1 0 1 1 0 0 1 0 1
1 0 1 1 0 0 0 0 0 0

E5. 6305 8874 3880 4108 7125
9293 3382 6066 5317 3609

E6. 0 1 1 0 1 0 0 0 0 1
1 1 1 1 1 0 1 0 0 0

E7. Make a pro/con list of when to use file encryption and when to use file-based access control, like access control lists. In a pro/con list, you list the two alternatives ("File Encryption" and "Access Control") and then under each, make a list of features that favor choosing that alternative.

E8. Figure 7.10 shows how to *encrypt* using a stream cipher. Redraw the diagram to show how to *decrypt* using a stream cipher. Be sure to include all necessary components from the original diagram.

E9. The following give the number of bits in an encryption key. For each, calculate the number of trials, on average, it will take to crack that key in powers of ten.
a. 40 bits
b. 56 bits
c. 64 bits
d. 80 bits
e. 128 bits
f. 256 bits

E10. The following give the number of bits in an encryption key. For each, calculate the average time required to crack that key assuming we can perform 10 million attempts per second. Be sure to use time units that are reasonably close to the cracking time or specify in years if the time takes more than a year.
a. 40 bits
b. 56 bits
c. 64 bits
d. 80 bits
e. 128 bits
f. 256 bits

E11. Section 7.3 provides cracking times and speeds achieved in years past. Assume that we have updated those technologies and estimate their performance using today's capabilities. Use Moore's law to estimate today's performance based on past performance.

a. The number of years required to crack a 192-bit AES key using updated DES Cracker technology.

b. The number of keys per second tested by updated DES Cracker technology.

c. The number of keys per second tested on an updated desktop computer.

E12. Make a revised copy of Figure 7.15. Using a colored highlighter, mark all the paths along which the encryption key travels, and mark all locations in which it resides ("Spot the key"). Using a highlighter of a different color, mark all paths along which the plaintext travels, and mark all locations in which it resides ("Spot the plaintext").

E13. Hands-on: Encrypt a file using a program that performs file encryption. Use a binary editor to compare the contents of the plaintext and ciphertext versions of the same data file. See if the encryption key appears in the file.

E14. Programming: Write a simple program to perform file encryption using algorithms provided by programming language libraries. Java, for example, has extensive support for well-known encryption algorithms.

E15. Programming: Write a simple file encryption program with its own, very simple, and insecure encryption algorithm. Accept a password or phrase as input and use repetitions of that word or phrase as a key stream for a cipher that encrypts the file. Does this provide strong encryption? Why or why not?

E16. Programming: Write a simple encryption program that uses a built-in pseudorandom number generator to generate a key stream. The user provides a key that is used as the generator's "seed value." The generator will take the seed value as its initial value and should always generate the same stream of numbers from that specific value. Use the resulting stream as a key stream for a cipher to encrypt the file. Verify that the encryption program can also decrypt the file. WARNING: Do not delude yourself into believing that this provides secure encryption.

E17. Programming: Write a simple program that opens a file and overwrites all of its data to ensure that the contents can't be recovered. Provide an option to overwrite the data multiple times with different data patterns. Is it necessary to overwrite the data multiple times on your hard drive? Why or why not?

SECRET AND PUBLIC KEYS

ABOUT THIS CHAPTER

In this chapter we discuss fundamental issues and techniques for handling cryptographic keys. We also introduce the important concept of public-key cryptography. We examine the following topics:

- Managing and using secret keys
- Wrapping techniques for secret keys
- Detecting errors and protecting file integrity
- Public-key cryptography for signing data and wrapping keys
- Public-key certificates

8.1 The Key Management Challenge

When we encrypt a file, we substitute the problem of protecting the file with the problem of protecting its key. Clearly, cryptography gives us no protection if somehow threats can guess or retrieve the keys. Even worse, we might waste our security efforts if we use keys or crypto algorithms incorrectly.

Thus, we face three key management problems:

1. Sharing keys with exactly the right people, no more or less
2. Choosing keys that attackers can't guess
3. Handling keys so attackers can't guess or intercept them

The third problem itself has several facets. First, there's the key distribution problem: We need to share keys with others without risking security. Second, we need to store the keys safely so that attackers can't find copies of them. Finally, we need to use our keys and cryptographic mechanisms effectively. If we use the same key for too long, we increase the risk of successful cryptanalysis. If we set up a stream cipher incorrectly, we'll use the same key stream to encrypt two or more files, and this gives a good cryptanalyst an easy job to do.

Our key management efforts start with the following questions:

- With whom are we sharing the file?
- From whom are we protecting the file?

The answers to those questions will help us develop policies and select protections for our keys.

CRYPTONETS

When we share a key with two or more people, we refer to that group as being the *cryptonet*. Everyone within a cryptonet shares the same keys and therefore can read the same encrypted files.

A cryptonet is a classic example of Transitive Trust. We trust everyone in the cryptonet to keep the encryption key safe. We also trust all of them to protect the contents of encrypted documents. By implication, however, we also end up trusting anyone whom those people trust. Here is an example.

> Bob and Alice use a shared secret key to protect their confidential survey data. Thus, the cryptonet consists of Bob and Alice.
>
> Alice wrote down a copy of the key and she keeps it in her purse. When she returns to her room, she leaves her purse in her drawer and steps out for a moment. According to Transitive Trust, we now trust her roommate as well.

If we take an optimistic view of security, we simply might insist that the key be protected from potential attackers. However, this violates Least Privilege and overlooks potential risks of Transitive Trust. As we make the cryptonet larger, we increase the risk of someone leaking the key by accident. If we include people unnecessarily, we increase our risk unnecessarily.

Our keys are safest when we keep the cryptonet as small as possible; as Benjamin Franklin famously claimed: "Three may keep a secret if two of them are dead."

LEVELS OF RISK

In Section 6.1, we classified threats against authentication as weak, strong, and extreme. We use the same classification for threats against file encryption.

- Weak threat—a person with limited skills and a mild motivation to recover the file.
- Strong threat—a skilled person willing to invest time and money to recover the file, but not inclined to cause significant damage.
- Extreme threat—a person with the skill or motivation to do damage regardless of how the file is protected. This includes threats who would damage or destroy the computer, or people with the skill to circumvent other operating system protections.

For the most part, we will focus on strong threats. Weak threats are often discouraged by applying simple access restrictions. Extreme threats may manage to substitute Trojan horse software for our file encryption program, thus bypassing its protection.

KEY-SHARING PROCEDURES

After we establish who needs to use the keys, we need procedures to choose, handle, and distribute the keys safely.

- Do we need to plan for changing the key (*rekeying*)? How hard will it be to change the key?
- How long does a key last? What is its *cryptoperiod*?
- Key strength questions (these must be considered together):
  - Should the key be a password or a passphrase?
  - How do we maximize the entropy contained in our key?
  - How should the key be protected against a strong threat?
  - If we write the key down, will a threat have access to it?
  - Should we limit ourselves to keys we can memorize?

This discussion will focus on strong threats. Weak threats will not be inclined to attack an encrypted document. Extreme threats can find other ways of extracting the information without attacking the encryption itself.

8.1.1 Rekeying

We need to plan for changing the key on occasion. If we set things up perfectly and nothing goes wrong, it might make sense to leave an unchanged file in place, encrypted with the same key, for an extended period of time. However, trouble often crops up and we must be prepared to change the key if leaked. Moreover, we make the cryptanalyst's job easier if we use the same key to reencrypt the file after making changes.

We call the key changing process *rekeying* or *key rollover*. Here are cases in which we should rekey:

- We use the document regularly over a long period of time. Each time we use it, we introduce the risk of leaking the key. Pick a time for changing the key that balances convenience and safety.
  - a. At minimum, change the key whenever some other major event occurs. For example, the distribution of a major new version of the file might justify rekeying. Legitimate users will learn the new key. If copies of the old key leaked, then the attackers don't get access to the new version.
  - b. For safety's sake, rekey more often on larger cryptonets. A larger cryptonet poses a larger risk of disclosure. On the other hand, it is harder to distribute new keys on a larger cryptonet.
- We suspect that the key has been leaked. We don't want to wait and find out that the file itself has been leaked, so we should change the key immediately.
- A person who knows the key must leave the cryptonet. For example, Kevin worked at a company that kept administrator passwords in an encrypted file, and

Kevin knew the file's key. After he quit that job, the other administrators chose a new key.

Rekeying brings up another question: How do we *really* change the key? As long as old copies of the file reside on the hard drive somewhere, its contents are at risk, assuming that an attacker can figure out the old key. Therefore, we should be sure to delete any backup copies encrypted with the old key. This carries its own risks: We balance the risk of disclosing the file's contents against the risk of needing to refer to older versions.

CRYPTOPERIODS

U.S. government standards published by NIST recommend encrypting data with a particular secret key for no more than 2 years before changing it. If we have already encrypted data with an existing key, that data doesn't need to be reencrypted. However, we shouldn't encrypt additional data with an "old" key.

There are other limitations to using a secret key. We will see later, for example, that we shouldn't reuse the same key when encrypting with a stream cipher. We may want to use a passphrase as a memorable secret key, and it's difficult to memorize numerous passphrases. Later, we will see how "key wrapping" minimizes the need to change passphrases.

DISTRIBUTING NEW KEYS

We handle encryption keys in one of three ways: We memorize them, we write them down, or we carry them on a storage device and download them as needed. The first case applies if we *never* make a permanent copy of the key. If we never physically make a copy of the key, then we face the lowest risk of disclosure. Instead, we face a risk of losing access to the file by forgetting the exact passphrase.

It can be challenging to distribute a passphrase without writing it down. The safest way to do it is in person; the recipient should memorize it on the spot without writing it down. In some environments, telephones may be safe enough for sharing keys. This assumes potential threats can't tap our phones.

In the second and third cases, we have to keep possession of the copied key. While in our possession, we have to ensure that no one else gets a copy of the key. We share it with members of the cryptonet, but we must hide it from everyone else.

PUBLIC-KEY CRYPTOGRAPHY

Secret-key techniques provide very simple and strong mechanisms for protecting and sharing data. However, they may be impractical in some situations. Bob and Alice can use secret key techniques to share data because they've already shared a sufficiently strong secret key.

What if Bob needs to share information with Alice, but can't arrange a shared secret ahead of time? *Public-key cryptography* provides the mechanism to make this possible. Our browsers routinely use public keys to produce strongly encrypted connections for financial transactions and other private business. Although the actual connections may use AES, the keys are established using a public-key algorithm. We examine the public-key techniques later in Section 8.3.

8.1.2 Using Text for Encryption Keys

In Chapter 7, we introduced file encryption programs but deferred discussion of key handling. The simplest and most obvious technique is for the owner to handle the key as a block of text. Figure 8.1 illustrates a very simple and obvious way to do this.

File encryption programs typically expect a secret key to be a block of text typed by the user: a password or a passphrase. The encryption algorithm requires a key of a fixed size, and the passphrase might be too long or too short to fit the key size exactly.

In Figure 8.1, the program collects the passphrase in a buffer and discards extra bytes if the phrase is too long. If the phrase is too short, the program pads it with zeros. The program uses the resulting block of data as its crypto key.

A textual key is more flexible than a binary key. Cryptonet members might share a textual key orally or in text documents. A large, random, binary key would be almost impossible to memorize, even in hexadecimal notation. Cryptonet members would have to carry it around on a small USB drive or other portable storage device; if they stored it on the hard drive with the encrypted file, an attacker could find it and easily decrypt the file.

However, a binary value always has more entropy than a similar amount of text. We want as much entropy in our encryption keys as possible. A particular key may be from 56 to 256 bits long, or longer, depending on the encryption algorithm. At 8 bits per character, that yields 7 to 32 characters or more. RC4 actually accepts a variable length key up to 128 bits long. When we use a longer key, we want the attacker to face a really tough trial-and-error cracking challenge.

RC4, of course, has notorious weaknesses that make it an unlikely choice for modern security systems. If we choose a state-of-the-art cipher like the Advanced Encryption

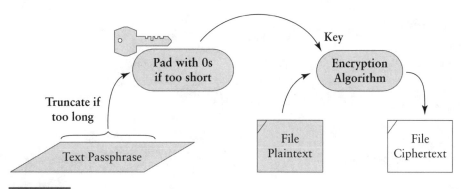

Figure 8.1

Using a passphrase for a file encryption key.

Standard (AES), then our keys may be of 128, 192, or 256 bits. A fully random 128-bit AES key should take a billion billion years to crack using today's best approaches.

If we construct our 128-bit key out of a 16-character passphrase, we limit ourselves to the entropy of our written text. As explained in Section 6.4, the average entropy of written text is about three letters per character. For a 16-character AES key, that gives us an entropy of 3^{16}, or 4×10^7 (40 million alternatives). We greatly increase the entropy if we create a random, 16-character string of ASCII: 95^{16}, or 4×10^{31}. Such random keys, however, are almost impossible to memorize. They are also very hard to type accurately. The entropy of a fully binary AES key is over 10^{38}. We lose a lot of entropy by limiting our passphrase to a short block of readable text. Realistic passphrases should contain at least 20 letters; the longer the better.

TAKING ADVANTAGE OF LONGER PASSPHRASES

Not everyone is going to want to use longer passphrases, but if people do, we must take advantage of the extra entropy. We need to compress the passphrase into a smaller block of bits from which we extract our encryption key. The obvious solution is to use a one-way hash function to hash the passphrase into a key-sized data value. This is shown in Figure 8.2.

We apply a cryptographic one-way hash function like those discussed in Section 6.2. The function serves as a building block to produce an ***internal key*** to perform the actual encryption. The internal key only exists inside the encryption process and disappears when the process is not running.

If the hash value output is too long, we discard part of the hash value and use the rest as the internal key. If the value is too short, we call the hash function a second time. We use its previous output as input. Then we concatenate the first and second hash values together to create the internal key.

This approach makes full use of the entropy in the text passphrase. Because the hash function arbitrarily can take long input texts and is indifferent to the characters used, we can use a fully punctuated sentence as a passphrase. Moreover, the one-way hash

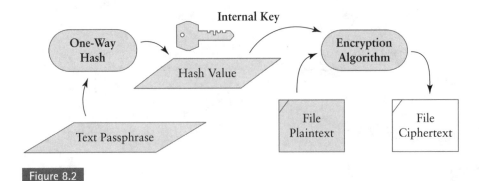

Figure 8.2

Hashing a passphrase for a file encryption key.

will yield a dramatically different key if we make even minor changes to punctuation or spelling. This makes it much easier to generate a long, hard-to-guess, but easy-to-remember passphrase. The only problem is that we must remember the capitalization, spelling, and punctuation exactly.

Because we hash the passphrase, we are not using the literal bits of the memorized passphrase. The program constructs this "internal key" from the hash value and uses it to perform the encryption. This is not a problem as long as the program follows a consistent procedure when creating the key for either encryption or decryption.

SOFTWARE CHECKLIST FOR KEY HANDLING

Here is a checklist of requirements for key handling in file encryption software. Most of these address risks to the passphrase. This checklist provides a list of properties for the software's key handling procedures.

1. The software shall support passphrases as well as passwords. (The following requirements shall assume that users typically use passphrases to protect encrypted files.)

2. The software shall allow very long passphrases, preferably allowing a length of at least 100 bytes.

3. The software shall use the full length of passphrases as long as they fit within the maximum permitted length.

4. The software shall not take other steps to reduce the entropy of a passphrase unless so directed by the user. For example, the software shall preserve the distinction between uppercase and lowercase characters, and shall preserve blanks and punctuation by default.

5. After collecting a passphrase from the user, the software shall by default store the passphrase only as long as it is needed for encryption or decryption. The software may provide an option for the user to store the passphrase in RAM for a longer period.

6. The software shall erase the passphrase from RAM as soon as it is no longer needed, unless overridden by the user's choice.

7. The software shall not write the passphrase to the hard drive unless its storage area also is protected by strong encryption.

8. When the software collects a passphrase from the user, it shall by default suppress the display of the passphrase in readable characters.

9. The software shall have an option to permit the display of a typed passphrase in readable characters.

10. The software shall avoid using the same internal encryption key to encrypt multiple files. Section 8.2 examines this problem and potential solutions.

8.1.3 Key Strength

When we encrypt a file, we choose a password or passphrase as its key. The problem of selecting a strong but memorable key is the same as that of choosing strong passwords (Section 6.7.4). It should have been clear from that discussion that a hard-to-crack secret must consist of more than a single word. If we must limit ourselves to a password, then we should construct it of two or more separate words.

It is even safer to use a passphrase. In 1990, Klein's experiments demonstrated the weakness of individual words, and he started experiments in cracking passwords constructed of pairs of words. If we use a passphrase containing more than two or three words, the result should yield a very strong key. If we simply look at the entropy in written text, we should aim for a fully punctuated passphrase of over 20 characters.

Most people should be able to come up with memorable phrases of 25 characters or more. However, if we need to share the phrase with others, we must choose a phrase that we can reliably share with others. There are two approaches to this:

1. Always write it down and share the passphrase in written form.
2. Choose text, capitalization, and punctuation that is easy to get right and hard to get wrong. This is a good idea even when we share the passphrase in writing. However, this reduces entropy, so it demands longer passphrases.

During World War II, the British operated an elaborate spying network in Germany. Each British agent memorized a long block of text, often a poem or a famous piece of prose, to use as an encryption key. These keys worked well for the most part, but occasionally the agent would remember the text differently than the decoders back at headquarters. This posed a serious challenge. In practice, however, those at headquarters often could deduce the mistaken text and decrypt the messages anyway.

The same problem can arise with secret passphrases. Even if the actual words are correctly conveyed, the file won't decrypt properly if the recipient gets the capitalization or punctuation wrong.

The real trade-off between memorization and writing down depends on the user's environment. If the written passphrases will need to reside in an unsafe location, then they must not be written down. If the strong threat will never have access to the written passphrases, then a written list might be practical.

OPERATING RECOMMENDATIONS

Because these file encryption keys are similar to passwords and passphrases, we should, in general, follow the policy recommendations outlined for passwords in Section 6.7. Here are further recommendations based on different levels of threat.

- Weak threats—file encryption should not be necessary.
- Strong threats
  a. Protect each file with a passphrase that is at least 25 characters long, including spaces.

b. Visually inspect the computer periodically to look for keystroke sniffers.

c. If possible, do not allow strong threats to have user accounts on the system containing the protected data.

- Extreme threats—such threats may bypass the encryption by attacking the system from other directions. Protection via file encryption will probably not be effective.

8.2 The Reused Key Stream Problem

Stream ciphers using the xor operation were first put into operation on teletype networks in the 1920s. Most messages were copied and transmitted from punched paper tape. The encryption key also was punched on tape. To encrypt the data, they installed a very simple circuit that computed the xor of the data and key values at each punch on the tape.

Gilbert Vernam, the developer, realized that an attacker could crack the encryption if they used the same key tape to transmit more than one message. Cryptosystem designers seem to learn this lesson all over again every generation or two.

In Section 7.3, we saw how Soviet spies used one-time pads in the 1940s. In 1998, Microsoft used the RC4 cipher to protect data transmitted across dial-up telephone connections. In both cases, the encryption method seemed reasonably strong, yet in both cases, attackers found a way to penetrate the encryption. Both made the same mistake: They encrypted their data with a *reused key stream*.

Following World War II, the far-flung Soviet spy network was hard pressed to provide one-time pads for all of its overseas agents. Each spy needed one digit of "pad" for every digit of information sent back to Moscow. This required a vast amount of typing and preparation. To save time, the pad producers made extra copies of some pads and sent them to spies in different parts of the world. This was not a problem unless an enemy cryptanalyst got hold of ciphertexts from the two different sources and matched them up.

And that is exactly what happened. Cryptanalysts at the U.S. Army Security Agency found that messages from agents in different parts of the world used the same pads for encryption. The Soviets apparently hoped that cryptanalysts in different countries would look only at messages within their own countries. The Army cryptanalysts cracked numerous messages that shed light on the atomic spy rings of the 1940s and 1950s. Notable figures, including Klaus Fuchs and the Rosenbergs appeared in those messages. At the time, however, the messages never appeared as evidence in court. The government preferred to keep the projects secret in hopes of reading more Soviet messages.

We illustrate the root of the Soviets' problem with another encryption example. Figure 8.3 encrypts the image of a smiley face. We encrypt the image using the same key stream we used earlier to encrypt the "SEND CASH" message in Figure 7.9 (Section 7.3).

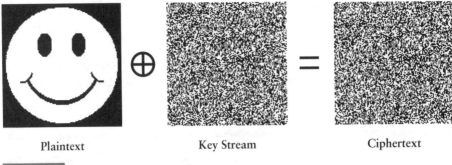

Plaintext   Key Stream   Ciphertext

Figure 8.3

Reusing the same key stream.

Now, we take the ciphertext from the "SEND CASH" message shown on the right of Figure 7.9, and the ciphertext from the smiley face message. We combine the two ciphertexts with xor, and the result appears in Figure 8.4.

The xor eliminates the key stream from both messages. What remains are the two original plaintext messages, one layered atop the other. We see this clearly when combining two images. With text, the xor combines individual characters from each message. Although the result isn't as visually dramatic as it is with images, the jumble is relatively simple for a cryptanalyst to decode.

The Army Security Agency and its successor, the NSA, used this technique to decrypt thousands of Soviet spy messages from the 1940s. Unfortunately, the agency briefed too many people on the project. Kim Philby, a senior British intelligence official, was also a Soviet spy. The Soviets corrected their encryption procedures to prevent subsequent messages from being decrypted. However, this was not the last time someone reused a key stream.

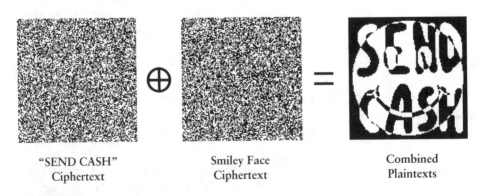

"SEND CASH"   Smiley Face   Combined
Ciphertext   Ciphertext   Plaintexts

Figure 8.4

Eliminating both key streams with xor.

In the 1990s, Microsoft introduced its version of the Point to Point Tunnelling Protocol (PPTP) to securely connect Windows computers. Microsoft's PPTP used the RC4 stream cipher in several ways. One technique derived the encryption key from a password provided at the start of the PPTP connection. PPTP would derive the same key every time the users provided that same password. Thus, an attacker could take the data sent during two separate PPTP sessions, combine them with xor, and eliminate the key stream. The attacker still would need to split out the two overlaid plaintext streams, but that is a much easier cryptanalytic task.

There are several ways to avoid this problem. In fact, Microsoft's PPTP only suffered this problem when using shorter encryption keys. When using longer keys, it used a one-way hash to combine the password with connection-specific data. Because the connection data was different in different directions and was different when new connections were made, the resulting hash yielded different keys for different connections. Well-designed encryption systems all take similar steps when using stream ciphers.

8.2.1 Avoiding Reused Keys

Figure 8.2 shows a simple way to use a passphrase as an encryption key. If the user chooses the same passphrase to encrypt two different documents, the program will use the same internal key in both cases. This will encrypt both documents with the same key stream. This makes the documents vulnerable to the attack shown in Figure 8.4.

One approach would be to simply warn the users to choose separate passphrases for separate documents. This is risky and unnecessary. People have a great deal of trouble memorizing passwords and passphrases in any case; we must not make matters more difficult. Moreover, we can design the file encryption software to use a different internal key every time it encrypts a file.

CHANGING THE INTERNAL KEY

We can, in fact, safely reuse a passphrase as long as the program uses a different internal key for each file. In Figure 8.2, we take the passphrase and hash it to produce the internal key. If we combine the passphrase with different data each time and then compute the hash, we get a different encryption key for each file.

For example, we could combine the passphrase and the file name to form a longer text string and calculate its hash. This yields a different hash, and thus a different key, for each file. However, this approach has problems. First, and most obviously, we might have two different files in different directories that have the same name, and thus the same encryption key.

Another problem may arise if we rename a file. When we try to decrypt a renamed file, the program will hash the *new* file name with the passphrase and derive a different key. We can only decrypt the file if we derive the same internal key that encrypted it. We can bypass this problem if the program adds a plaintext heading to the encrypted file, and saves the file name in the header; then it can extract the file name from that header and use the name to construct the key.

Let's assume that the program saves extra data in a file header and derives the key from the extra data. If we take this idea one step farther, we see that the program shouldn't be limited to using the file name. The extra data simply needs to be different from one file to another. The data also should not be chosen by potential attackers. We can follow those two rules and generate a new internal key every time we encrypt a file.

COMBINING THE KEY WITH A NONCE

We achieve this by saving a nonce in the file's header. Thus, we use two building blocks, the one-way hash and the nonce, to construct the internal key. This yields a highly random key that varies from one use to another, even if we use the same passphrase.

When we introduced the nonce in Section 6.5.1, we noted its two requirements, and both requirements apply here. First, we choose a different nonce so that the operation is different each time. In this case, we choose a new nonce each time we reencrypt the file. Second, we don't allow potential attackers to choose the nonce's value. We may choose either a random number that's large enough not to repeat, or we may use a counter or clock value.

Figure 8.5 shows how we create the secret key using a nonce. Each time we encrypt the file, the program constructs a new internal key. First, it accepts the passphrase; then the program chooses the nonce. The date plus the time of day is often a good choice, assuming it has always changed since the last time we saved the file.

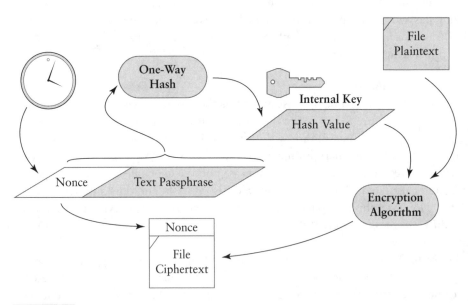

Figure 8.5

Using a nonce to construct the encryption key.

The program also can use a large random number. If so, it should use either a truly random number, or use a pseudorandom number generator that has a truly random seed. In any case, the nonce should be large enough and changeable enough so that it's unlikely to be chosen by anyone else who uses the same passphrase.

The program uses the nonce and the passphrase to construct its internal key. It combines the passphrase with the nonce and computes the hash over both of them. This hash value becomes the internal key.

When the program encrypts the file, it writes a copy of the nonce to the encrypted file, saving it in a header at the beginning. The nonce is not encrypted. It must be available as plaintext to create the internal key.

When the program decrypts the file, it reverses the process. First, it collects the passphrase as usual, then it extracts the nonce from the file being decrypted. The program constructs the internal key by hashing the passphrase and nonce together. The program must concatenate the two in *exactly* the same way to generate the same internal key.

Clearly, we are not keeping the nonce secret. It does not have to remain secret for the encryption to remain safe. All of the entropy in the file's internal encryption key resides in the text passphrase. If the passphrase is reasonably long and is kept secret, the file should be safe against cracking.

Whenever the program reencrypts a previously encrypted file, it chooses a different nonce. This yields a different internal key. Otherwise, an attacker might be able to extract information by combining the old and new encrypted files together.

SOFTWARE CHECKLIST FOR INTERNAL KEYS USING NONCES

Here is a checklist of requirements for creating and handling internal keys using nonces.

1. When encrypting a file, the software shall use an internally generated key (the *internal key*). The internal key shall be constructed from the user-supplied passphrase and an internally generated nonce.

2. When reencrypting a previously encrypted file, the software shall generate a new nonce.

3. The software shall generate the nonce in a fashion that avoids the risk of generating the same nonce when encrypting different files. For example, the nonce could be generated by a high precision time-of-day clock or by a high-quality random number generator.

4. The software shall construct the internal key by formatting the passphrase and the nonce in a uniform manner and applying a specific hash function. This ensures that a particular passphrase and nonce always will generate the same internal key.

5. After generating the internal key, the software shall store the internal key in RAM only as long as it is needed for encryption or decryption.

6. The software shall erase the internal key from RAM as soon as it is no longer needed.

7. The software shall not write the internal key to the hard drive unless its storage area also is protected by strong encryption.

These requirements only apply if we use nonces to avoid reused keys. The nonce provides a relatively simple solution to the problem, but it is not the only solution. We can increase security while avoiding reused keys if we create a completely new key every time we encrypt a file.

8.2.2 Key Wrapping: Another Building Block

When an attacker tries to crack an encryption key from known ciphertext, additional ciphertext makes the job easier. Practical attacks on RC4 rely on hundreds of thousands of bytes of ciphertext. If we encrypt a large number of files with the same passphrase, we are trusting our files to that same, small amount of entropy.

A safer way to protect these files is to generate a new, random internal key whenever we encrypt the file. We then encrypt *the key itself* using the passphrase. We call this **key wrapping**. Figure 8.6 illustrates the process.

If we choose the key randomly, then an attacker can't apply a known plaintext attack or dictionary attack to it. Moreover, we make the known ciphertext attack against the passphrase much more difficult. Such attacks require a great deal of known ciphertext.

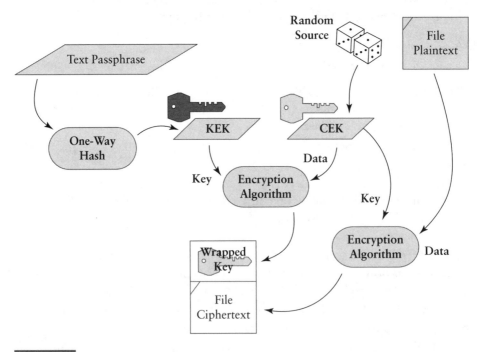

Figure 8.6

Wrapping a key: The KEK encrypts the CEK.

Here, we only encrypt individual keys with the passphrase, and that doesn't produce very much ciphertext.

Key wrapping uses two separate and unrelated keys to encrypt the file. We encrypt the actual data in the file with the ***content encryption key*** (CEK). We must generate randomly a new CEK whenever we encrypt the file. We then use the passphrase to produce a ***key encrypting key*** (KEK). We produce the wrapped key by encrypting the CEK.

Here is how we encrypt a file using wrapped keys:

1. The program collects the passphrase from the user.
2. The program hashes the password to produce the KEK.
3. The program uses a reliable source of random numbers to generate the CEK.
4. The program "wraps" the CEK by encrypting it with the KEK.
5. The program encrypts the plaintext file using the CEK as the key.
6. The program creates the encrypted file by combining the wrapped key with the ciphertext.

To decrypt the file, the program starts by opening the encrypted file and collecting the passphrase from the user. The program generates the KEK from the passphrase and "unwraps" the CEK; then the program decrypts the file's ciphertext. When the program reencrypts the file, it generates a new, random CEK and uses it to encrypt the file.

Multiple Recipients

What happens if we want to share a file with two different groups of people who have different shared passphrases? For example, Alice and Bob use the same passphrase to encrypt all of their shared project files because Bob doesn't want to memorize additional passphrases. Now they are working on another project that includes Tina. Alice wants to give Tina a different passphrase. Bob refuses to memorize another passphrase. How can we enforce Least Privilege and still share files?

They can't simply encrypt two different copies of the file: one with the passphrase shared by Alice and Bob, and another with the passphrase shared by Alice and Tina. It would be hard to keep changes updated in both copies. A better approach is to share the same ciphertext and CEK among everyone, but to wrap the CEK separately with each passphrase. The task has to be built into the file encryption program. Since Alice is the only one who knows both passphrases, she must create the initial version of the file as follows:

- Generate a CEK as usual.
- Encrypt the file as usual.
- For each passphrase, do the following:
  a. Collect the passphrase and convert it into a KEK.
  b. Wrap the CEK with this KEK.
  c. Save the wrapped key with the encrypted file and with any other wrapped keys already saved there.

When Bob retrieves the file, he uses the passphrase he always shares with Alice. Internally, the program constructs a KEK from their passphrase. This KEK decrypts one of the two wrapped keys. This yields the CEK to decrypt the actual file. When Tina retrieves the file, she uses a different passphrase. This decrypts the other wrapped key, yielding the sam KEK. Unlike files with a single passphrase, this file must reuse its CEK when encrypting new contents. Only Alice can replace the CEK, because she is the only person who knows both passphrases.

Key Wrapping and Cryptoperiods

We noted earlier that we mustn't overuse a passphrase when encrypting files. If we randomly select our encryption keys and wrap them with our passphrase, we largely eliminate the risk of overuse. We no longer use the secrecy in the passphrase itself to encrypt the files; instead, we use newly generated random keys. The passphrase only protects the keys themselves. Thus, we can use the same passphrase for the maximum cryptoperiod with a minimum of risk.

Under NIST guidelines, the maximum cryptoperiod is 2 years. After that, we should choose a new passphrase.

KEY "SPLITTING"

The simplest technique for key wrapping is called *key splitting*. It uses a randomly generated CEK and KEK and uses xor to perform the wrapping, as shown in Figure 8.7.

When we wrap keys, we perform two completely separate encryptions. The first encryption protects the data by using the CEK. The second encryption protects the CEK by using the KEK. We can use the same encryption algorithm for both, but not necessarily. Because the CEK and KEK are chosen randomly, attackers can't apply a known plaintext attack. Therefore, we can safely use the simplest possible encryption algorithm: xor.

The only difference between a split key and a wrapped key is that we use xor to encrypt the split key. In both cases, we must keep the KEK secret; if we derive the KEK from a passphrase, then we must keep the passphrase secret. We can disclose the split key to potential attackers without risking either the KEK or CEK.

SOFTWARE CHECKLIST FOR WRAPPED KEYS

Here is a checklist of requirements for using wrapped keys to avoid the risk of reusing an encryption key. Even though the requirements use the term "wrapping," they also apply to key splitting.

1. Whenever the software encrypts a file, it shall generate a new content encryption key or CEK.
2. The software shall use truly random numbers to generate the CEK.
3. The software shall use the hashed passphrase to generate the key encryption key (or KEK), which it shall use to wrap the CEK.

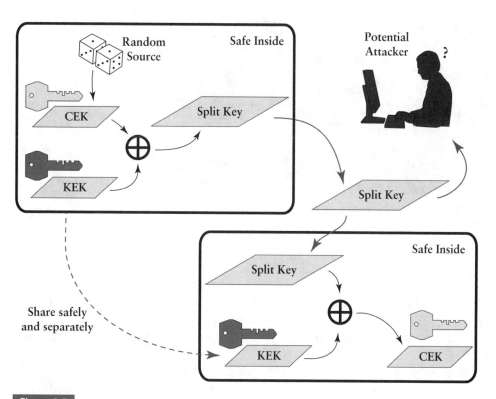

Figure 8.7

Key splitting with xor.

4. When reencrypting a previously encrypted file, the software shall generate a new CEK. Alternatively, if the software supports multiple KEKs to protect a single file, the software shall reuse the CEK to retain existing wrapped keys.

5. After creating a CEK, the software shall promptly create a wrapped copy of the CEK.

6. The software shall store the unwrapped CEK in RAM only as long as it is needed for the current encryption or decryption operation.

7. The software shall erase the unwrapped CEK from RAM as soon as the current encryption or decryption operation is finished.

8. The software shall not write the unwrapped CEK to the hard drive.

8.2.3 Separation of Duty: A Basic Principle

Sometimes we need to split a job between two or more people to ensure it's done correctly. Figure 8.8 illustrates a particularly famous and critical example. The double-padlocked file cabinet stood in the control center of a Titan II nuclear missile site from the 1960s.

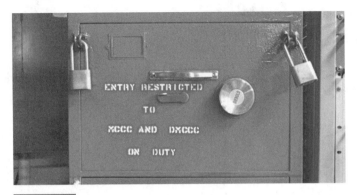

Figure 8.8

Separation of Duty for an early nuclear missile.

The file drawer contained special codes required to launch the missile. The missile commander and deputy commander each had a separate padlock securing the drawer. Both officers had to unlock the cabinet in order to retrieve the codes. If either did not believe they had received legitimate launch orders, then the codes stayed in the drawer and the missile couldn't launch.

We often have cases where we can't allow a person to act alone and take a serious action. The general solution is to break the action into steps that no single person can take independently. This is *Separation of Duty.*

However, the concept far predates nuclear weapons. It is a common tool in businesses. When paying suppliers, for example, companies break the process into multiple steps, each performed by a separate person. For example, one person enters the payments into the company ledgers, another person fills out the checks, and a third person signs the checks. Each step produces a record that auditors review periodically.

Some companies also implement Separation of Duty to authorize electronic funds transfers. One person on the team logs in and creates a transfer or a series of transfers, then a separate person logs in and separately authorizes the transfers. None of the transfers take place until both steps are finished. This reduces the risk of fraud, and also makes it more difficult for a hacker to single-handedly authorize a transfer. The hacker would have to retrieve authentication credentials for two separate individuals.

By enforcing Least Privilege, no one person can perform all the steps independently. The check signer never gets blank checks. The check writer can't add payments to the ledger. Individual checks are numbered and all are accounted for. No person can act alone to spend company money. At best, they can insert a bill into the payment process, which leaves an obvious trail.

SEPARATION OF DUTY WITH ENCRYPTION

Our file encryption program can implement a simple form of Separation of Duty. For example, Bob only wants Alice and Tina to look at the encrypted file if *both* are present.

In other words, neither Tina nor Alice have permission to look at the file by themselves. They can't decrypt the file unless both provide their passphrases, one after the other.

Alice and Tina each choose their own secret passphrase. We will use these passphrases to construct two different KEKs, one to wrap keys for Alice and the other to wrap keys for Tina.

To implement Separation of Duty, we use key splitting. Again, the file encryption program has to include this procedure. The encryption takes place as follows:

- Generate a CEK as usual.
- Encrypt the file as usual.
- Generate another random key and use it to split the CEK.
- Wrap one of the split keys with Alice's passphrase KEK.
- Wrap the other split key with Tina's passphrase KEK.

To decrypt, the program first collects the passphrases from Alice and Tina. If both are present and provide their passphrases, the program can unwrap the two key splits. Once unwrapped, it xors the two together. This produces the CEK, so the program can decrypt the file.

8.2.4 DVD Key Handling

We first encountered the DVD Content Scrambling System in Section 7.5. DVD-CSS uses a combination of key wrapping and key splitting to store encryption keys on a DVD. The first set of keys resides on the hidden first track of the DVD (Figure 8.9).

The first important key on the DVD is the "disk key." It is a random key generated for the specific DVD. The hidden track contains a set of 409 wrapped disk keys. Each key is encrypted using a secret "player key" assigned to a particular manufacturer of DVD players. When a player loads a DVD, it searches the hidden track for the disk key wrapped with its player key. The player unwraps the disk key and then calculates the

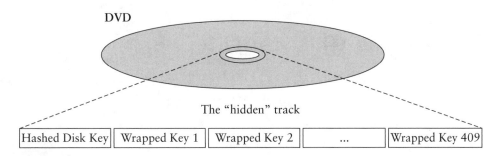

Figure 8.9

Keys on the DVD hidden track.

key's hash. If the answer matches the "hashed disk key" on the hidden track, then the player has decrypted the disk key.

The DVD's actual contents are encrypted separately using a "title key" and a set of "sector keys." Each sector on the DVD is encrypted with its own sector key. This key is saved in the sector's header, split with the title key. Figure 8.10 illustrates the process of decrypting a DVD sector.

The DVD producer begins with a digitized film or other program material in plaintext; then the producer generates a title key. The program material is encrypted, sector by sector, each using a separately generated key. The key is split with the title key and saved with the encrypted sector.

The producer now may share the encrypted program material with potential publishers. The program material doesn't need special protection because it has been encrypted. The producer must simply ensure that the title key remain secret.

To publish a DVD, the DVD publisher receives the program material from the producer. The publisher's staff work with the encrypted program material. They do not need the title key to construct the DVD for publication.

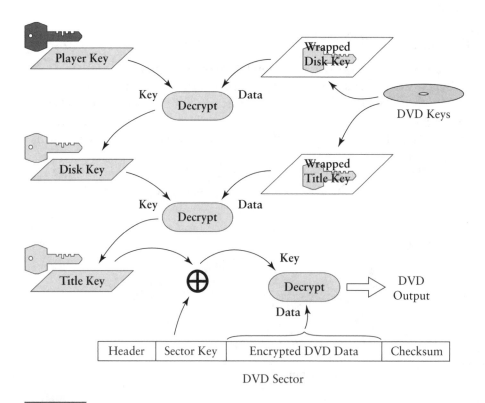

Figure 8.10

Decrypting a DVD sector.

To finalize the disk for publication, the publisher generates a disk key. The key then is encrypted with the 409 player keys and written to the hidden track. This allows any approved DVD player to retrieve the disk key. The disk key is specific to that particular edition of the DVD; the publisher may change it in later editions.

The publisher also saves a wrapped copy of the title key on the disk. The publisher wraps the title key with the disk key and saves the wrapped key on the disk.

8.3 Public-Key Cryptography

When we encrypt with a secret key algorithm, the security resides in the key, and our data remains secret if our key remains secret. We often call this *secret-key cryptography*. With *public-key cryptography*, clever mathematics allow us to share a crypto key publicly and still keep information safe.

Here is an example with Bob and Alice:

Alice, Bob, and their friends share files through a collection of USB drives that hang on hooks on a cork board. Different people use different crypto techniques.

Alice read up on public-key techniques, acquired some software, and has convinced Bob to use it. Alice's software constructed two encryption keys for her. One is a *private key* that she keeps secret from everyone, including Bob. The other is a *public key* that she can share with everyone in the suite. She created a file called "Alice's Key" that she leaves on the USB drive.

However, Alice's keys don't let her *send* secret messages, they only let her *receive* secret messages. To send a secret message to Alice, Bob takes her public key and encrypts the message with it. He puts the message in the shared USB drive. Alice uses her *private key* to decrypt the message (Figure 8.11).

There are two essential points here. First, when the sender uses the ***public key***, the recipient must use the ***private key***. Eve, like everyone else, can retrieve Alice's public key. When she tries to use it to decrypt Bob's message, all she sees is garbage. Because we use two keys and the keys are different, we call this ***asymmetric cryptography***.

The second essential point is that we create the private key first. We derive the public key from the private key (Figure 8.12). In some cases, the private key may be any random number within a particular range. In other cases, we calculate the private key from one or more randomly selected values.

The asymmetry in public-key cryptography allows us to produce ***digital signatures***. For example, Alice can use her private key to encrypt some information; the ciphertext yields the digital signature. Anyone with Alice's public key can decrypt one of Alice's signatures and verify that her personal, private key had encrypted it.

Table 8.1 summarizes important differences between secret-key and public-key cryptography.

All public-key algorithms rely on a mathematical trick. The algorithms use mathematical functions that are relatively easy to calculate but very difficult to invert. Although cryptography always has had one-way functions, researchers like to call these

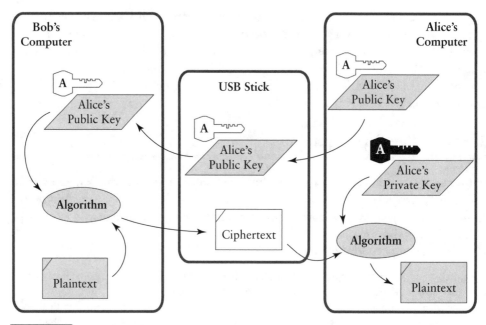

Figure 8.11

Public-key encryption.

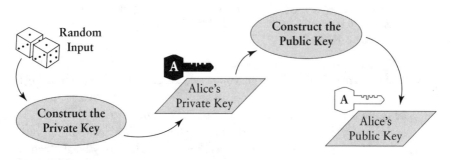

Figure 8.12

Constructing the public/private key pair.

"trapdoor one-way functions." In other words, they have the one-way essence of cryptography, plus a second element that is easy or hard depending on the information you have.

Consider the problem of "prime factors." All integers are either prime numbers or they are composite numbers made up of two or more primes. If we have a list of prime factors in a number (2, 3, 5, and 11, for example), it's straightforward to multiply them

TABLE 8.1 Comparison of secret–key and public–key crypto		
Type	Secret Key	Public Key
Symmetry	Symmetric	Asymmetric
Number of keys	There is one crypto key; the sender and recipient both use it.	There are two crypto keys; the sender uses one and the recipient uses the other.
Key secrecy	The *secret key* is always kept secret.	The *private key* is kept secret. The *public key* is published and shared.
Calculating efficiency	Requires a great deal of calculation using relatively small numbers.	Requires a great deal of calculation using very, very large numbers.
Typical key sizes	128–256 bits	1024–4096 bits
Unique identities	Every member of the cryptonet uses the same key; it is impossible to distinguish one member from another.	Each user may have a unique private key; only the corresponding public key works with a given private key.

together to yield 330. On the other hand, it takes far more computational steps—and a more subtle procedure—to undo the multiplications and retrieve the primes.

This task becomes much, much harder as the numbers grow large—and this becomes the basis of many public-key techniques. We often form the private key from one or two very large prime numbers. We form the public key by calculating a result from those primes.

When we introduced encryption in Chapter 7, we classified symmetric algorithms into categories in Figure 7.2. Asymmetric algorithms fit into categories according to the mathematics they use, but in practice, we use the names of the prevailing algorithms. This is shown in Figure 8.13.

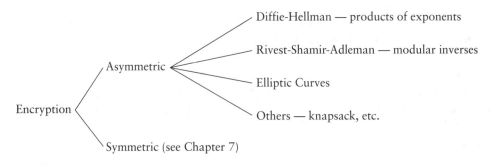

Diffie-Hellman — products of exponents

Rivest-Shamir-Adleman — modular inverses

Asymmetric

Elliptic Curves

Others — knapsack, etc.

Encryption

Symmetric (see Chapter 7)

Figure 8.13

Asymmetric encryption algorithms.

ATTACKING PUBLIC KEYS

Because the techniques rely on mathematical tricks, the encryption is likewise vulnerable to mathematical tricks. Most public-key techniques get their strength from the fact that it's hard to factor primes. Thus, we can attack many of these techniques by trying to factor primes. Compare this to trial-and-error attacks on secret-key algorithms: We must try *every* key in the range of possible keys. If we have a 200-bit secret key, we try, on average, 2^{199} keys to crack it. The effort to crack a secret key increases *exponentially* as we add more possible keys, doubling each time we add a bit.

If we have a 200-bit *public* key, we perform a search akin to prime factoring, which requires far fewer than 2^{199} trials. In fact, the effort increases *logarithmically* as we add more possible keys. Thus, it is much easier to crack a 200-bit public key than a 200-bit secret key. Today, recommended public keys are 10 or even 20 times larger than comparable secret keys.

Public-key cryptography does not replace secret-key cryptography. The public-key techniques do certain things very well, but they do other things very poorly. Modern systems use public keys to wrap secret keys and to construct digital signatures. Even these tasks must take place under very restricted circumstances; otherwise, attackers can use mathematical trickery to overcome the cryptographic protection.

Secret-key encryption exchanges the problem of keeping data secret for the problem of managing the secret encryption key. Public-key encryption often exchanges the problem of managing secret keys with the problem of correctly identifying the public keys. If Eve substitutes her own public key for Alice's key, she can eavesdrop on Bob's conversations.

8.3.1 Sharing a Secret: Diffie-Hellman

The first successful public-key algorithm was not an encryption algorithm in any normal sense. The algorithm, developed by Whitfield Diffie and Martin Hellman at Stanford University, lets two endpoints share a single secret value without sending any secrets back and forth. Although this doesn't actually encrypt information, it provides a shared secret. We generally refer to the algorithm by its inventors' names, **Diffie-Hellman**, and occasionally abbreviate it D-H. The endpoints then use the shared secret as a key in a symmetric cipher like AES. In Figure 8.14, we show the public key in white and the secret key in black.

Unlike the earlier example, both participants must have a public/private key pair. Each one multiplies their own private key by the other's public key to compute the shared secret. Even though each has a different public/private key pair, the trapdoor nature of the computation yields an identical result.

Here is how Bob sends Alice a message:

1. Alice picks a private key value and calculates the matching public-key value. She puts the public-key value on the USB drive in a file named "Alice's Key."

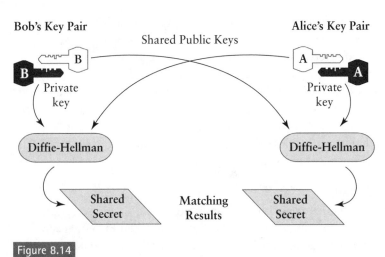

Bob's Key Pair   Shared Public Keys   Alice's Key Pair

Figure 8.14

Procedure for Diffie-Hellman secret sharing.

2. Before he can exchange messages with Alice, Bob also must produce a pair of keys. He saves his private key on his computer and puts the public key in a USB file named "Bob's Key."

3. Bob retrieves Alice's key file from the USB drive. To find their shared secret key, he takes Alice's public key and applies the Diffie-Hellman calculation. That yields a result that's unique between Bob and Alice (Figure 8.14, left side).

4. Bob uses this unique value as a secret key to encrypt his file using AES. He names the file "To Alice."

To recover Bob's file, Alice does the following:

1. She retrieves the file from the USB drive. She also retrieves the file containing Bob's public key.

2. Alice takes Bob's public key and applies the Diffie-Hellman calculation. This yields the same secret value that Bob calculated (Figure 8.14, right side). This serves as the secret encryption key.

3. Alice retrieves the "To Alice" file, plugs the secret encryption key into AES, and decrypts the file.

PERFECT FORWARD SECRECY

In Section 8.1.1, we talked about rekeying: how we need to change encryption keys regularly. If we use the same key continuously, we create more and more ciphertext that could be used to crack that key. If we produce smaller amounts of ciphertext with each key, we make the cryptanalyst's job much harder.

Over the years, cryptographers have designed many ways to rekey. Some techniques work poorly; if attackers recover one or more keys, they can use them to find later keys. The best techniques aren't affected if attackers recover earlier keys.

If an attacker manages to recover one of the system's keys and that key provides no information that helps crack future keys, then the system has **perfect forward secrecy**. If two endpoints generate a new set of Diffie-Hellman key pairs to establish a new, shared secret key, then the system has perfect forward secrecy.

The **Internet Key Exchange** protocol (IKE), discussed in Chapter 14, uses Diffie-Hellman to negotiate keys. Its implementation achieves perfect forward secrecy.

VARIATIONS OF DIFFIE-HELLMAN

Although the classic Diffie-Hellman algorithm can only produce a shared secret, other variations provide encryption and digital signatures. A variant called El Gamal can encrypt data or construct digital signatures. The U.S. **Digital Signature Standard** (DSS) is based on a variant of El Gamal.

8.3.2 Diffie-Hellman: The Basics of the Math

Although the mathematical details of Diffie-Hellman aren't essential to understand its use, we will provide an overview. The magic in Diffie-Hellman arises from properties of **modular exponentiation.** Exponentiation by itself, of course, refers to raising a number to a power. **Modular arithmetic** refers to arithmetic operations that are truncated relative to a particular value. The one-time pads encountered in Section 7.3.3 use modular arithmetic; the "add-without-carry" operation is a modular operation. Here is a calculation of modular exponentiation:

$$P = g^s \bmod N$$

In this equation, we raise the number g to the power s. We then calculate the modulus of this based on a large prime number, N. The modulus is essentially the remainder in an integer divide operation; thus, we discard any part of the result larger than the large prime N.

In high school mathematics, we learned that:

$$(g^x)^y = g^{xy} = (g^y)^x$$

The same relation holds for modular exponentiation. However, it is incredibly more difficult to invert the modular exponentiation. The logarithm is the inverse of exponentiation, and the prime modulus operation makes exponentiation especially hard to invert. This is called the "discrete logarithm problem," and it is as difficult in practice as factoring very large numbers. This provides the "trapdoor" so that the Diffie-Hellman result is easy to compute if you have the private key.

In a Diffie-Hellman calculation, the value s is the *private key* value. It is a randomly chosen value less than N. Each endpoint has its own, unique, private key, and we calculate the public key from it. The public key consists of the following:

g—the generator, a public, shared value; often $g = 2$

N—the modulus, a very large prime number, also shared

P—the unique public value computed from the private key s

The values g and N must be shared within the community of users. If Kevin uses different values than everyone else, he can't compute a shared key with the others. Moreover, s must be less than N.

Let's look at what happens when Bob and Alice try to communicate. Bob has a secret value S_{Bob}, and Alice has a secret value S_{Alice}. The following calculation produces their public keys:

$$P_{Bob} = g^{s_{Bob}} \bmod N$$

$$P_{Alice} = g^{s_{Alice}} \bmod N$$

Now, Alice and Bob can share their public keys and calculate their shared secret. Both keys must use the same values for g and N. Each calculates the shared secret by raising the other's public key by the power of their own private key. The following three steps show how the calculation reduces to identical results:

Alice: Bob:

Step 1: $(P_{Bob})^{s_{Alice}} \bmod N = (P_{Alice})^{s_{Bob}} \bmod N$

Step 2: $(g^{s_{Bob}} \bmod N)^{s_{Alice}} \bmod N = (g^{s_{Alice}} \bmod N)^{s_{Bob}} \bmod N$

Step 3: $(g^{s_{Bob}})^{s_{Alice}} \bmod N = (g^{s_{Alice}})^{s_{Bob}} \bmod N$

The structure of the Diffie-Hellman computation is relatively simple compared to secret-key encryption. The RC4 cipher requires two sets of loops, compared to Diffie-Hellman's two exponentiations and a modulus. Stronger secret-key algorithms like AES are even more complex, as we will see in Chapter 9. Public key calculations become challenging because they use significantly larger numbers than those in secret-key cryptography.

This simplicity opens Diffie-Hellman up to attacks unless we are very careful in the implementation. There are numerous mathematical restrictions on the numbers to use. In practice, people don't tend to use Diffie-Hellman for long-term public keys. More often, Diffie-Hellman is used to create a temporary public/private key pair for a particular transaction.

8.3.3 Elliptic Curve Cryptography

Elliptic curve cryptography has practical similarities to Diffie-Hellman, but calculates over an elliptic curve instead of over a finite field. A discrete elliptic curve, in general, is an equation in x and y of the form:

$$(y^2 = x^2 + ax + b) \pmod p$$

We begin by publicly sharing a particular elliptic curve with predefined values for a, b, and p. There is also a "base point" (x, y) on that curve that serves as another public parameter. These are all very large numbers; they match the key size in length.

Given the public parameters, we can establish a shared secret key using a variation of the Diffie-Hellman procedure. We also can construct a digital signature.

To construct a shared secret, for example, Bob and Alice begin by each selecting a random secret value that is less than p. Alice multiplies her secret value A by (x, y) on the discrete curve to yield her public key (x_A, y_A). Bob does the same with his secret multiplier B to yield his public key (x_B, y_B).

To construct the shared secret key, each multiplies their secret key by the other's published product, all on the elliptic curve:

$$A(x_B, y_B) = B(x_A, y_A)$$

This yields the same pair of points for both Bob and Alice. They use the result to generate their shared secret key.

Finite field techniques like Diffie-Hellman are dramatically weaker, bit for bit, than comparable symmetric-key encryption. That is why Diffie-Hellman keys have at least 10 times as many bits as symmetric keys to provide comparable resistance to trial-and-error attacks.

Elliptic curve cryptography, however, resists trial-and-error attacks with much smaller key sizes. A comparable elliptic curve key may have only two to three times as many bits as a symmetric key of comparable strength. This is because the elliptic curve discrete logarithm problem is harder to solve.

In the United States, NIST and NSA have established standards for using elliptic curve cryptography in government and military applications. This is called "Suite B." The suite includes standards for key negotiation and for digital signatures using an elliptic curve. Suite B uses the following standard curve:

$$(y^2 = x^2 + 3x + b) \pmod p$$

The published standards describe how to use elliptic curve cryptography with 256-bit and 384-bit keys. According to NIST, the 256-bit keys provide comparable security to AES using a 128-bit key, and the larger 384-bit keys are comparable to AES using a 192-bit key. The NIST recommendations actually suggest using slightly larger keys, but these sizes meet their minimum requirements.

8.4 RSA: Rivest-Shamir-Adleman

After studying Diffie and Hellman's 1976 paper describing the public-key cryptography problem and their initial solution, three researchers at MIT, Ron Rivest, Adi Shamir, and Len Adleman, began searching for an improved approach. After several months, they found a very flexible technique that performs asymmetric encryption and decryption. The basic technique, like Diffie-Hellman, uses modular exponentiation.

RSA public and private keys both consist of pairs of numbers. Each pair contains two of the following:

N—the modulus, part of both RSA key pairs

e—the public exponent, part of the RSA public key

d—e's *modular inverse*, the secret part of the private key

There is no g as there was in Diffie-Hellman; we exponentiate the plaintext message itself to produce the ciphertext. Given a message M, we produce ciphertext C as follows:

$$C = M^e \bmod N$$

Decryption uses exactly the same calculation. We simply raise the ciphertext C to the power d:

$$M = C^d \bmod N$$

In fact, we can freely switch between encrypting with the public or private keys as long as we decrypt with the other key:

- We can encrypt with the public key (e, N).

  To decrypt, we use the private key (d, N).
- We can encrypt with the private key (d, N).

  To decrypt, we use the public key (e, N).

In practice, RSA returns us to the example in Figure 8.11: Alice leaves her public key for Bob, and he uses it to encrypt a secret message to her. Bob does not need a public/private key pair himself to use Alice's public key. All he needs is her public key. Moreover, people don't need to share g or N values. In fact, the N value must be unique.

Although the calculations look simple, they are, in fact, difficult to perform. When we exponentiate a message containing more than a few bits, the calculated result exceeds the capacity of the arithmetic operations in typical computers. Thus, these simple-looking calculations require special software.

Digital Signatures

What does it mean for Alice to encrypt data with her *private key* and share that with others? It means that anyone with her public key can decrypt the data. This doesn't keep the encrypted data secret, but it demonstrates that Alice, the owner of the private key, was the one who encrypted the data. We use this in Section 8.5 to construct a "digital signature" to attest to the authenticity of some data.

RSA Applications

RSA's flexibility has led to its widespread use. When we visit a website with an "https:" prefix, we use a cryptographic protocol based on RSA. When a web browser highlights a website name and declares the site's name is verified, it uses RSA. Popular encryption programs, notably PGP, use public-key encryption to simplify the sharing of encrypted files.

Despite RSA's flexibility, especially compared to Diffie-Hellman, we don't really want to encrypt messages directly with it. In other words, the example in Figure 8.11 is actually a bad idea; we don't want to encrypt a simple message like "Pay $100" itself with RSA. In practice, it's not safe to encrypt certain types of messages with RSA. The mathematical design of RSA makes some messages easy to crack; we'll discuss this further in Section 8.4.2.

8.4.1 Encapsulating Keys with RSA

Aside from mathematical risks, there is a simple and obvious reason *not* to encrypt common messages with an RSA public key. Consider the following:

> Bob wants to meet with Alice, and he doesn't want others to know the meeting time. Alice agrees to retrieve the meeting time from a file encrypted with her public key.
>
> Eve knows about the meeting and wants to know when it will happen. She knows the message contains a time of day, so she performs a type of dictionary attack: She creates a whole collection of files, each containing a different time of day. She encrypts each file with Alice's public key. The encrypted file containing "7:32 PM" is identical to the file Bob encrypted. Thus, Eve uncovers the meeting time without knowing Alice's private key.

Here is the lesson: We don't want to encrypt *predictable* data with a public key. We should only encrypt random, unpredictable data. A well-chosen secret key is random and unpredictable. Thus, we often use RSA to encrypt secret keys. This is another form of key wrapping; we use a public key as the KEK. This is often called *key encapsulation*, with the term *key wrapping* used when the KEK is a secret key. However, this textbook uses *key wrapping* as a general term for either case.

In Figure 8.15, Bob tries again to send a secret message. This time, he encrypts the message with a secret AES key and wraps that key with RSA.

To send the message, Bob follows these steps:

1. Bob generates a random number to use as an AES key.
2. He encrypts the message using AES.
3. He retrieves Alice's public key.
4. He encrypts the random AES key with Alice's public key. This wraps the key.
5. He saves the encapsulated key in the file, and names it "To Alice."

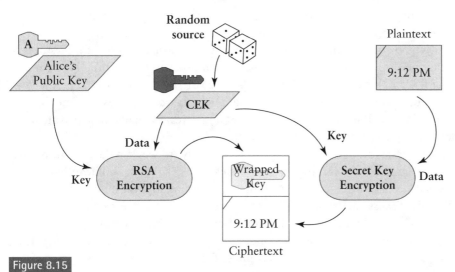

Encapsulating a key with Alice's RSA public key.

Bob doesn't need his own public/private key pair to send Alice a message. To read the message, Alice reverses the process, as shown in Figure 8.16. Unlike secret-key decryption, we use exactly the same RSA calculation for both encryption and decryption.

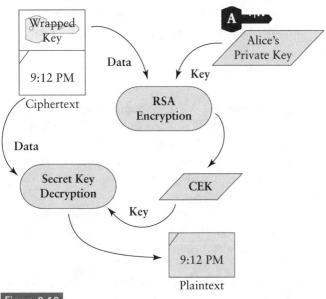

Retrieving the key with Alice's RSA private key.

Sometimes we may refer to an RSA operation as "decryption," but in fact, it uses exactly the same computation. The only difference is in the keys we use.

RSA has two obvious benefits over Diffie-Hellman in sharing a secret key. First, both Bob and Alice need to create and share public keys in order to make Diffie-Hellman work. Using RSA, Bob can encrypt a file to Alice without having to create a public key himself. Second, RSA lets them use a new and different shared secret every time Bob encrypts a file. With Diffie-Hellman, one of them must create a new public/private key pair if they want to use a different shared secret.

Although the basic idea is simple, there are several ways to weaken the key wrapping. For example, we weaken the security if we wrap a secret key that is significantly smaller than the public key. The safer strategy is to include padding to meet minimum-size constraints. We will discuss such vulnerabilities in general in the next section. Several standards organizations, including RSA Laboratories and NIST, have combined the latest risks and recommendations to produce standard techniques for safe key wrapping. It is always best to rely on the latest of such recommendations.

8.4.2 An Overview of RSA Mathematics

Although both Diffie-Hellman and RSA use modular exponentiation, the actual encryption/decryption involves a different mathematical concept: *modular inverses*. In conventional algebra, we say that a and b are inverses if $a = 1/b$. In other words, $a \times b = 1$.

In modular arithmetic, if d and e are modular inverses, given the modulus N, then $d \times e = 1 \bmod N$.

For example, assume M is the message we want to encrypt. We raise it to the power e mod N to encrypt it. This yields ciphertext C. To decrypt it, we raise it to the power of d mod N. The modular inverses cancel each other out, leaving the message M. Here is a simplified view of RSA decryption:

$$C^d = (M^e)^d = M^{(e \times d)} = M^{(1)} = M$$

The missing elements are the modulus operations. A real RSA computation calculates the exponentiation and then takes the result mod N. The exponents e and d are inverses only with respect to the mod N.

Unlike Diffie-Hellman, RSA performs an explicit encrypt or decrypt operation. Both operations use the same calculation. In one case, we use the public exponent e, in the calculation. In the other case, we use d, the private exponent.

Figure 8.17 illustrates the process of constructing a set of RSA keys for Alice. The large primes P and Q produce the modulus N and the modular inverse d. The chosen value for e influences the modular inverse and also becomes part of the public key pair.

The modulus N is the fundamental part of the RSA public key. We start producing a key pair by constructing N. We choose two very large prime numbers; we'll call them P and Q. The size of the public key is determined by the size of those two primes. Once P and Q are multiplied together, they should be so large that it isn't practical to factor N

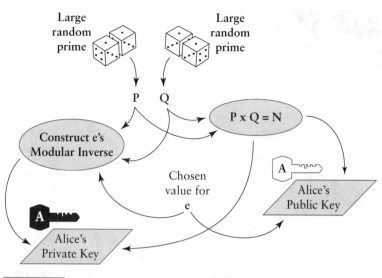

Figure 8.17

Constructing an RSA key pair.

and find them. We increase our resistance to attack by choosing two primes of a similar (large) size.

The *e* value often is chosen to be a prime close to a power of 2, like 3 or 65,537. The *d* value is calculated using the "totient function" $\phi(x) = (P - 1)(Q - 1)$. If we don't have the two *P* and *Q* factors, we can't calculate *d* easily.

BRUTE FORCE ATTACKS ON RSA

The most obvious way to attack an RSA public key is to try to factor the modulus *N*; that is, to find its prime factors *P* and *Q*. This has turned many mathematicians into cryptanalysts, as they attempt to find ever faster ways to factor extremely large numbers.

The Original Challenge

In 1977, Rivest described the RSA algorithm to Martin Gardner (1914–2010), a well-known writer for *Scientific American* magazine. Gardner published a popular column on mathematical games and puzzles and wrote up their technique in his column. He also talked about attacking the public key by factoring the modulus. The designers confidently predicted that a number with as many as 129 decimal digits couldn't be cracked in the foreseeable future. As a puzzle, they provided a message encrypted with a 129-digit public key and offered a $100 reward to anyone who solved it.

Seven years later, an international team of volunteers used the combined power of 1600 machines to crack the code. The effort took 8 months. RSA Laboratories, a research organization started by the algorithm's designers, issued a series of related

TABLE 8.2 Comparable Key Sizes		
Secret Key	RSA & D-H Public Key	Elliptic Curve
80	1024	160
112	2048	224
128	3072	256
192	7680	384
256	15,360	512

challenges starting in 1991, each with a cash prize. The intent was to promote research into number theory, factorization, and related techniques, and it helped gauge the practical strength of the RSA technique. In 2007, the laboratory stopped awarding prizes, though researchers continue to work at factoring the challenge numbers. As of 2010, the largest number factored was "RSA-768," a 768-bit number.

The Factoring Problem

Bit for bit, it is much easier to factor a large number than to brute-force crack a secret key of the same size. This is easy to see if we work out a simple strategy for factoring numbers. In practice, we don't factor a number by dividing it by *every* number less than it is; we speed up things dramatically by dividing by numbers less than or equal to its *square root*. We also skip over all numbers that are obviously not primes. Thus, the number of trials for secret keys may double whenever we add another bit to the key size, but the number of trials in a factoring attack doesn't increase nearly as fast.

Selecting a Key Size

If we use a public key to wrap a secret key, we should choose key sizes that are comparably strong. The public key should be at least as hard to crack as the secret key. In fact, the public key should be harder to crack because it will probably have a longer lifetime. Table 8.2 lists secret key sizes along with the size of a comparable public key modulus N. The values are taken from recommendations by NIST.

As a practical matter, the equivalence of strength between different sized keys means that a successful trial-and-error attack requires the same average number of trials. To crack a public key of n bits, we don't perform 2^{n-1} trials (remember, we include the "–1" because, on average, we only need to try *half* of the keys). We look at the size of the comparable secret key, and *that* key size indicates the number of trials. For example, if the Diffie-Hellman key contains 2048 bits, then the comparable secret key size is 112 bits. The average number of trials is then 2^{112-1}.

Research suggests that it takes as much effort to crack RSA as it takes to search for large prime numbers, and that leads to estimates like those in Table 8.2. As long as these techniques require a great deal of computation time, RSA should provide safe encryption. Some researchers have suggested that *quantum cryptanalysis* techniques could provide a shortcut for attacking RSA encryption. These techniques use notions of simultaneous computations within a "soup" of quantum elements to search a vast number of possibilities for a cryptographic solution. However, there is as yet no practical technique to produce such a computation and extract the desired solution from the myriad of non-solutions.

OTHER ATTACKS ON RSA

RSA is the product of mathematical tricks, so, of course, mathematical tricks can bring it down. In other words, RSA is vulnerable to mathematical attack if we use it in certain unfortunate ways:

- **Small plaintext attack**

  If the public key value is 3 and the message length is less than a third the length of the modulus N, a shortcut attack can recover the message. In particular, if the message is smaller than the cube root of N, then we quickly recover the message after calculating N's cube root.

  We avoid this attack by padding smaller data items with random bits before we encrypt them. For example, to encrypt a small, secret key, we encrypt a larger random value and discard the bits we don't need.

- **Small private key attack**

  If the private key d value is relatively small, there is a mathematical shortcut for recovering it. In practice, the private exponent is around the same size as N, and the public exponent is relatively small.

- **Timing attack**

  The private key's value directly affects the execution time of the RSA algorithm. If Eve is trying to decrypt an RSA-encrypted message and she accurately measures the computation time, it gives her information about the private key value.

- **Chosen ciphertext**

  If Eve can trick Bob into encrypting or decrypting a message of hers with his private key and retrieve the result, she can use that result to crack another message. For example, if Alice encrypted a message to Bob, Eve can construct a separate message that is mathematically related to Alice's message. After Bob applies his own private key to Eve's message, she can use the result to decrypt the message from Alice.

- **Bogus primes**

  RSA uses extremely large prime numbers to construct a key. If we use a composite number instead of a prime, attackers have a far easier time trying to crack the private key. The primes that make up an RSA key are so large that it isn't feasible to prove beyond all doubt that a chosen number is in fact prime. Instead, we rely on mathematical tests to reduce the risk that the chosen number isn't really a prime.

Researchers have reported other vulnerabilities over the years; those with a clear practical application lead to changes in RSA implementations. Starting in 1991, RSA Laboratories published the Public Key Cryptography Standards (PKCS), a set of documents describing best practices for using RSA, Diffie-Hellman, and other public-key techniques. These are routinely updated to reflect the latest recommendations.

8.5 Data Integrity and Digital Signatures

Consider the following:

> Bob borrows $3 from Kevin. Bob writes himself a reminder note that says "I owe Kevin $3." He saves it in a file on his USB drive. Bob encrypts the file with RC4 or some other stream cipher.
>
> A week later he pays back the $3. Before he deletes the note, he looks at it again. Now it says "I owe Kevin $7."

If Kevin, for example, knows exactly what the file says, then he can change its contents bit by bit without knowing the encryption key. This is sometimes called the *bit-flipping attack* (Figure 8.18).

Because stream ciphers encrypt the data bit by bit, we can reverse a bit in the plaintext by reversing the corresponding ciphertext bit. In this particular case, we want to change the $3 to $7, tricking Bob into repaying an extra $4. This requires that we change a single bit in a single ASCII character in the encrypted file.

$$\text{Plaintext "3" } 00110011$$
$$\oplus$$
$$\underbrace{\text{Key Stream } 11010110}$$

$$\text{Ciphertext } 11100101$$
$$\text{Change the encrypted "3" to "7" } \overbrace{11100001}$$
$$\underbrace{\text{Key Stream } 11010110}$$
$$\oplus$$
$$\text{Plaintext "7" } 00110111$$

Figure 8.18

Bit-flipping attack on encryption with xor.

The lower bits of the ASCII character "3" are "0011," which by itself is equal to three in binary. The lower bits of the ASCII character "7" are "0111," which equals seven in binary. If we change that single bit from 0 to 1, we add 4 to the binary value. In the figure, we invert the ciphertext bit corresponding to that plaintext bit. When we decrypt the message, the "3" comes out as a "7."

Bit-flipping only works reliably if two facts are true. First, we must be working with a stream cipher. If we decrypt the data one bit at a time, then we invert a decrypted plaintext bit by inverting the corresponding ciphertext bit.

Second, we must know exactly what the plaintext says, so that we change exactly the bits we want. Even if we don't know what the entire encrypted file says, we might be able to make a few significant changes that don't scramble the file's contents. The recipient might detect our changes if the decrypted plaintext looks garbled.

In Section 5.3.3, we examined checksums, CRCs, and other ways to detect random errors. These techniques detect errors caused by failures of underlying hardware, and some errors caused by software flaws. Computers became useful only after they reached an incredibly high degree of internal reliability. Although modern computers, hard drives, USB sticks, and other devices are very reliable, there are still many cases where they need to check for errors.

However, checksums and CRCs are intended to detect accidental changes caused by unpredictable failures. By themselves they can't detect intentional, malicious changes. If attackers are intent on tricking the system, they can simply recompute the error check to match the changed data.

8.5.1 Detecting Malicious Changes

To detect malicious changes, we must prevent attackers from knowing how to accurately revise the CRC or other error check value. The obvious approach is to add a secret to the process, as in Figure 8.19. Without knowing the secret, attackers won't know how to accurately revise the check value.

The attacker can't modify both the text and the check value without knowing *exactly* what the file says. Any mistake could make the checksum fail. If the attacker *does* know exactly what the file says, then he can replace its contents with a different message and a new checksum, just by flipping appropriate bits as shown in Figure 8.18.

Software distributed on the Internet occasionally takes a different approach; it publishes the check value on a website next to a link for the downloaded file. If Alice, for example, downloads a program, she can calculate the file's check value and compare it with the value published on the website. This strategy poses a problem: What if an attacker replaces the good file with a subverted one whose check value matches the original file's check value? This problem leads us to one-way hash functions.

ONE-WAY HASH FUNCTIONS

We encountered one-way hash functions in Section 6.2.1 when protecting passwords from disclosure. While a checksum or CRC tries to detect random changes to a file, a

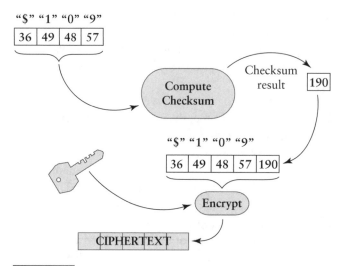

Figure 8.19

Data encrypted with its checksum.

one-way hash tries to detect *any* change to a file. If its contents change a little or a lot, its hash value changes *unpredictably*. Thus, an attacker can't modify a file and preserve its hash value. Sites that publish check values for downloadable files usually publish an SHA or MD5 hash value. Although MD5 is no longer recommended for high-security applications, it still provides a much safer check value than we get from a CRC value.

As shown in Table 6.2, hash values are very large; the smallest is 16 bytes long, and more recent functions yield much longer results. The large results are intended to make it as hard as possible to produce two different but similar documents that yield the same hash value.

For example, imagine that Bob uses a one-way hash that yields an 8-bit check value. He owes Kevin $10, and Kevin provides him with an IOU, based on the template shown in Figure 8.20. Bob computes the hash, saves it, and gives the IOU file to Kevin for safe keeping.

The flowery language allows Kevin to make numerous substitutions in the text, yielding hundreds of different hash values. If Kevin changes the amount from $10 to anything else, he can probably find a different flowery statement that yields the same hash value as the signed message. Kevin then replaces the original IOU message with the new one, and the original hash value doesn't detect the difference.

Kevin's trickery works because the output of the one-way hash is too small. An effective one-way hash yields so many possible values that it's impractical to search for a document with a matching value. A 160-bit hash, like that produced by the Secure Hash Algorithm, SHA, yields too large of a search space. If Bob used SHA, Kevin would have

$$\begin{Bmatrix} \text{Greetings,} \\ \text{To whom it may concern,} \end{Bmatrix}$$

I, Bob, $\begin{Bmatrix} \text{do} \\ \text{do hereby} \end{Bmatrix}$ declare that I $\begin{Bmatrix} \text{borrowed} \\ \text{have borrowed} \end{Bmatrix} \begin{Bmatrix} \text{money} \\ \text{cash money} \end{Bmatrix}$

from my $\begin{Bmatrix} \text{friend} \\ \text{pal} \end{Bmatrix}$ Kevin in the amount of \$10, and that $\begin{Bmatrix} \text{I} \\ \text{I hereby} \end{Bmatrix}$ agree to

$\begin{Bmatrix} \text{pay} \\ \text{reimburse} \end{Bmatrix}$ the $\begin{Bmatrix} \text{lender} \\ \text{esteemed lender} \end{Bmatrix}$ forthwith.

Figure 8.20

An IOU with an adjustable check value.

to construct 2^{160} different versions of the file to try to find a matching hash. That isn't practical.

BIRTHDAY ATTACKS

A more practical approach to this is the ***birthday attack***. The name comes from the "birthday paradox," a classic parlor game. If we have a group of about two dozen people, the odds are good that at least two have their birthday on the same day. This may not seem obvious, because the chances of someone having a particular birthday are 1 in 365. We narrow the odds if we search a group to find *any two people* with the same birthday.

This attack lets Kevin take advantage of the fact that *he* creates the IOU file. He doesn't simply create a single file and then search 256 alternatives for a match. Instead, he randomly creates files of both types until two of them yield the same hash value.

According to the birthday paradox, when we're searching for a match among K elements, we only have to search $\sqrt{K}$ random elements until a match becomes likely. If we have an n-bit number, then a match is likely if we search approximately $2^{n/2}$ elements. Therefore, in Kevin's case, he'll probably construct two matching IOUs after trying around 16 times.

If Bob decides to use a 64-bit hash value, Kevin's work gets a lot harder, but it's not really impossible. He "only" has to search about 4 billion alternatives (2^{32}) before he's likely to hit a matching pair.

When we do this search for document check values, we search at random to try to find *any* two documents with the same check value. If we can find two such documents, one can masquerade as the other, based on its check value. This doesn't necessarily yield a practical attack on documents protected with one-way hash values, but it illustrates a possible risk.

The birthday attack is the reason why one-way hash values are so large. To avoid a birthday attack, the value must contain twice as many bits as the largest number of attempts in a practical birthday attack. If 2^{80} guesses seem implausible, then a 160-bit hash value should be safe.

8.5.2 Detecting a Changed Hash Value

If Bob simply saves the hash value in an IOU file, he won't necessarily detect a malicious change. The forger could simply compute the new hash value that matches the new text. Bob would have to memorize a hash in order to tell if someone changed it.

Hash values aren't easy to memorize; they are long, random-looking binary values. Such values are great for security but terrible to remember. Bob needs to incorporate some secret information into the process, information that only he knows. If he encrypts the hash value with secret information, no one can change it reliably. Figure 8.21 illustrates the construction of an encrypted hash.

Bob can store the actual message in plaintext, assuming the actual information isn't secret. The hash value will be an incomprehensible block of data that he stores with the readable text. He can compute the hash and encrypt it to check the integrity of the text.

If we use a strong one-way hash and effective encryption, the operation in Figure 8.21 should provide some protection. However, we can't use a stream cipher in situations like this, because the attacker knows the message text. The hash value is vulnerable to a known plaintext attack. The attacker can simply recompute the hash on the current message, and xor the hash with the encrypted hash to recover the key stream. Then the attacker can compose a new message, calculate its hash, and use the key stream to reencrypt the corrected hash.

One way to avoid this is to use a strong block cipher instead of a stream cipher. We study block ciphers in Chapter 9.

KEYED HASH

A much easier approach avoids encryption all together. Instead, we include the secret information in the hashed data. We call this a *keyed hash*. We don't need to perform a

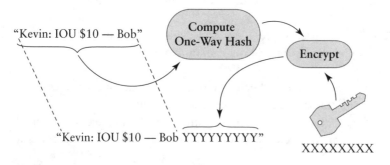

"Kevin: IOU $10 — Bob"

Compute One-Way Hash

Encrypt

"Kevin: IOU $10 — Bob YYYYYYYYY"

XXXXXXXX

Figure 8.21

Encrypting a hash—two steps.

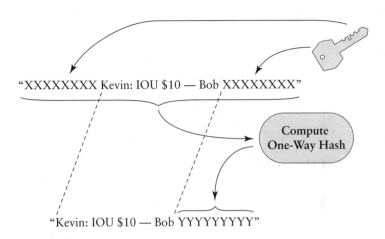

Figure 8.22

Keying a hash—one step.

separate encryption step, hash the passphrase, or incorporate a nonce. Figure 8.22 illustrates an early approach to do this.

The process works as follows. First, we place a copy of the secret at the beginning of a buffer. Next, we place the text we want to protect in the buffer. We follow it with another copy of the secret. Then we compute the hash over the whole buffer, including both copies of the secret. We reduce risks from weaker hash functions if we place the secret at both the beginning and end of the text.

A keyed hash is easy to implement because it relies on only a single cryptographic function: the one-way hash. However, this is also a source of weakness. While hash functions are designed to produce a different hash if someone omits the first and/or last few bytes, some functions are less reliable than others. Thus, the result might not always rely on the presence of the secret keys. Internet security protocols described in Chapter 14 use a more sophisticated technique for keyed hashing.

8.5.3 Digital Signatures

A keyed hash gives us a way to verify that some of our own data has not been modified by an attacker—or at least it hasn't been modified by someone who doesn't share the secret key. This technique is moderately useful, but it doesn't let mutually suspicious people verify information.

For example, Bob can't share a secret key with his bank in order to verify electronic checks or digitized bank statements. Bob could write the check and use his secret to "sign" it, and the bank could verify it with that same secret. Later, though, either Bob or the bank could forge a different version of the same check using the same secret key. The

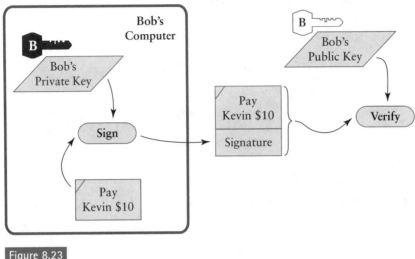

Figure 8.23

Signing a check with a digital signature.

forged version could have a different amount, date, or recipient. It is impossible to tell if the bank produced the forgery or if Bob did.

A digital signature, on the other hand, uses asymmetric keys to sign or verify digital data. If Bob has a bank account that accepts his digital signature, he uses his private key to sign his checks. Anyone can then use his public key to verify his signature (Figure 8.23).

For example, Bob writes a $10 check to Kevin. He provides an electronic copy to Kevin, his bank, or both. When Kevin gets the check, he uses Bob's public key to verify the check's signature. When the bank gets the check, it also uses Bob's public key to verify the signature. In fact, it doesn't matter whether the bank gets a copy of the check from Bob, Kevin, or someone else. No matter how many hands the electronic check passes through, the digital signature confirms that it contains exactly what Bob said it should: the date, the amount, and "Pay Kevin."

We create digital signatures with two cryptographic building blocks. In Figure 8.24, Bob creates a digital signature using his RSA private key. First, he calculates the one-way hash of the data to sign. Second, he encrypts the hash using his private key.

Anyone can verify the digital signature using Bob's public key. For example, Bob's bank can verify an electronically signed check as shown in Figure 8.25. The bank recalculates the one-way hash and decrypts the digital signature. The two answers match if the check has not changed since Bob signed it.

Note that RSA is subject to the same weaknesses when encrypting a one-way hash as it is when encrypting a secret encryption key. In both cases, we must be sure to encrypt a value that contains more bits than the public key's N value. This may involve either padding the hash value with additional, randomly generated data or by using a sufficiently

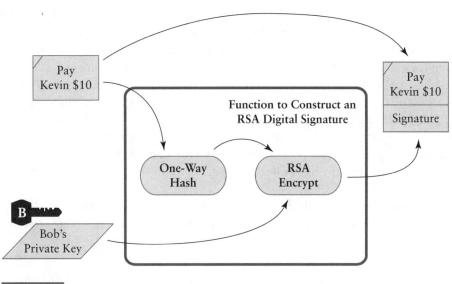

Figure 8.24

Constructing an RSA digital signature.

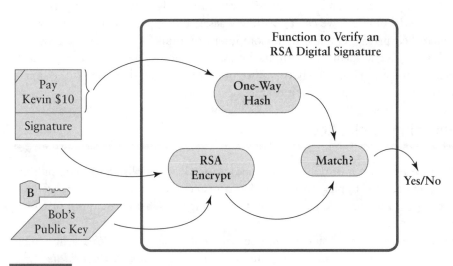

Figure 8.25

Verifying an RSA digital signature.

large hash value. As with key wrapping, there are established standards for constructing
RSA digital signatures. We provide the strongest and safest signatures by following the
latest standards and recommendations.

So far, we have used RSA public-key encryption to produce digital signatures, though this is not the only public-key algorithm for digital signatures. In the United States, NIST created the Digital Signature Standard (DSS), which provides an alternative to RSA. As noted earlier, DSS implements a variant of the El Gamal cipher, which is based on Diffie-Hellman. When signing a document, the DSS requires a random input value in addition to the text being signed. Unlike a nonce, this value must be truly random and unpredictable by the attacker.

A DSS digital signature requires a similar process to an RSA signature. First, we compute a one-way hash of the document, then we find a random number to use. The DSS algorithm has three inputs: the hash value, the random number, and the signer's private key.

The process becomes vulnerable if we ever reuse a random value for two different signatures. This is unlikely in practice as long as we always choose a large, truly random number.

Nonrepudiation

A digital signature provides the strongest practical indication that the key's owner signed the digital data. This is why some use digital signatures to provide nonrepudiation. If we can assume that only one person controls a particular private key, then we can argue that anything signed by that person was knowingly signed by that person.

In practice, unfortunately, we can't absolutely assert that a particular person always controls what their private key will sign. Computer programs may be subverted, which could result in signing a document without the owner's knowledge. We can only assert nonrepudiation if we can completely trust the computing system that applies the signature. Commercial systems rarely merit that level of trust.

8.6 Publishing Public Keys

We get the most benefit out of public-key cryptography if we publish and share public keys. This allows anyone to pick up a public key and encrypt a message to someone else. Attackers can't use the public key to decrypt the message, at least not without breaking the system.

On the other hand, secrecy isn't the only security risk. There is also a trick in which an attacker actively intercepts all traffic. This is often called a ***man-in-the-middle attack***. It is also known as the ***bucket brigade attack***. Figure 8.26 provides a diagram of the action.

Here is how it works:

Bob wants to send another secret message to Alice, and Eve wants to intercept it. Eve took Alice's USB drive and replaced the file titled "Alice's Key." It now contains *Eve's* public key instead of Alice's public key.

Bob retrieves the file titled "Alice's Key." He uses it to wrap the secret key that encrypts his message. He saves the wrapped key and his message in a file titled "To Alice."

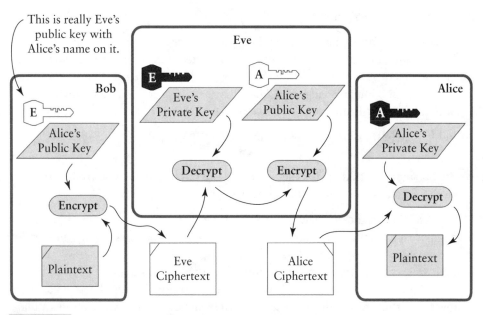

Figure 8.26

Eve performs a bucket brigade attack.

Later, before Alice returns, Eve takes the USB drive again. She retrieves the file titled "To Alice" and unwraps Bob's secret encryption key using *her* private key; then she rewraps the key using *Alice's* public key. She replaces the file on the USB drive.

When Alice returns, she uses her own private key to unwrap Bob's secret key, then she decrypts and reads the message.

Meanwhile, Eve uses her own unwrapped copy of Bob's secret key to decrypt and read the message herself.

Essentially, someone intercepts the public keys traveling in one direction and the secret messages traveling in the other. What Eve has done is distribute a forgery: The file claims to contain Alice's public key but in fact it contains Eve's public key.

Eve's success depends on tricking Bob into using Eve's public key while thinking it is Alice's public key. Once Bob has encrypted the message with Eve's key, Eve must reencrypt it with Alice's key. Otherwise, Alice won't be able to read the message, uncovering Eve's trick.

There are several different strategies for preventing such attacks or for reducing their risks. One approach might be to restrict distribution of public keys so that only authorized people get them. This eliminates many benefits of public-key cryptography. Another approach is to publish individual keys widely so that people can double check their own copies for validity. This also isn't practical, because public keys are enormous blocks of random-looking binary data. They won't contain patterns or structures for people to recognize and remember.

8.6.1 Public-Key Certificates

The favored solution for authenticating public keys was first proposed by an MIT student in 1978. Undergraduate Loren Kohnfelder suggested that we embed public keys in specially constructed credentials called ***public-key certificates***. We use digital signatures to verify a certificate's integrity. Figure 8.27 shows the construction of a certificate.

At a minimum, a certificate contains three pieces of information:

1. A public key (symbolized by the key marked "A")
2. The name of the public key's owner ("Alice")
3. A digital signature that covers the name and the public key (symbolized by the seal with the initial "C" matching the signer's key).

To construct a certificate, we calculate the hash over the owner's name and public key, then we use a private key to construct the signature. Anyone may verify the certificate if they have the appropriate public key.

Although we can use a certificate containing the minimum amount of information, typical modern public-key certificates contain several additional fields. These fields help clarify how the certificate should be used and provide flexibility in creating and validating them. Additional fields generally include:

- The name of the trusted person or entity who issued and signed the certificate, usually a *certificate authority*, or CA, described later.
- A date range during which the certificate is valid
- Specifications of the crypto algorithms used to sign the certificate
- Indication of the certificate's purpose and approved uses

Whether we know it or not, typical web surfers use public-key certificates constantly. Whenever a browser establishes a secure connection with a website, it uses a public-key certificate to verify the site's identity and to retrieve the site's public key. The browser

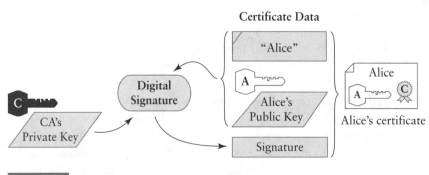

Figure 8.27

Constructing a public-key certificate for Alice.

then uses the key to establish a secure, encrypted connection. We explore this further in Chapter 14.

However, we don't need networks to use certificates. A certificate allows us to authenticate a public key: to confirm that it belongs to a particular individual. We can perform such a test without a network connection.

CERTIFICATE AUTHORITIES

The certificate's signature poses an important question: Who *does* sign a public-key certificate? The signature attests to the fact that the name and public key go together. The signer must be someone trustworthy enough to associate names and keys accurately. Often, the signer is a **trusted third party**, a person or organization whom we trust for certain things. For example, a bank is a trusted third party for handling various financial transactions. If a friend introduces us to someone new, the friend is acting as a trusted third party.

In the world of certificates, the trusted third party is often a **certificate authority** (CA). This is a person or entity that issues certificates on behalf of some organization. Inside a company, the CA could be a trustworthy administrator who issues certificates to employees. There are also commercial authorities that sell certificates for use in Internet commerce.

As is often the case with crypto, public-key certificates replace one really difficult problem with a hopefully easier problem. We no longer have to worry about authenticating the public keys we use; instead, we must ensure that we have the correct CA public keys to authenticate certificates.

Internet e-commerce sites use public-key certificates to authenticate their sites when establishing a secure web connection. The Netscape Navigator was the first browser to use public-key certificates. The Navigator relied on a single CA (RSA Data Security, Inc.) and included its public key in the browser's executable code. Modern browsers contain an entire collection of keys, each belonging to a separate certificate authority (see Chapter 14).

At the very least, public key owners can sign their own certificates. These are called *self-signed certificates*. If Bob receives a self-signed certificate directly from Alice, as opposed to retrieving it from an unattended USB drive, then the certificate is likely to be valid. Bob simply has to ensure that no one hacks his computer and messes with the collection of certificates.

8.6.2 Chains of Certificates

Once we have a public key for a certificate authority, we can authenticate any certificate signed by that authority. However, the authority could get incredibly busy signing certificates, especially in an extremely large organization. We can spread the work by allowing the authority to delegate its work to others. We do this by issuing certificates to these subsidiary certificate authorities.

For example, the company Amalgamated Widget distributes public-key certificates in this fashion. Each department has its own administrator who serves as a CA and issues certificates to people in that department. To establish the system, Amalgamated took the following steps:

1. Each CA generates its own public/private key pair.
2. The initial CA, or *root certificate authority*, signs a public-key certificate for each of the departmental CAs.
3. When someone wants a certificate, they ask their departmental CA to sign it. The departmental CA is usually an IT administrator.

When users send email, they sign it with their private key. In order to authenticate it, each email client in Amalgamated contains a copy of a single public key: the root CA's public key. This key can't authenticate individual user certificates by itself, because the root CA doesn't sign every certificate. Instead, it lets us check the certificate that signed the certificate. We call this series of signed certificates a *certificate chain*.

If Alice receives an email from an official in human resources (HR), her email software authenticates the email by authenticating the certificate chain. This takes place by checking the following signatures:

- The root CA signed the HR admin's certificate.
- The HR admin's certificate signed the HR official's certificate.
- The HR official signed the email to Alice.

Figure 8.28 illustrates the process. Note that each certificate must identify the CA who signed it. We use that field to choose the right certificate for verifying the signature.

The checking process starts at the lower left of the diagram and progresses through each digital signature:

- The email is from the HR official. We retrieve the official's public key from the official's personal certificate.
- We authenticate the email by checking its digital signature, using the official's public key.
- The official's personal certificate was signed by the HR department's admin. We retrieve the admin's pubic key from the admin's CA certificate.
- We authenticate the official's certificate by checking its digital signature, using the public key of the HR department's admin.
- The HR department admin's CA certificate was signed by Amalgamated's root CA. The root CA's public key is built in to Amalgamated's email application software.
- We authenticate the admin's CA certificate by checking its digital signature, using the root CA's public key.

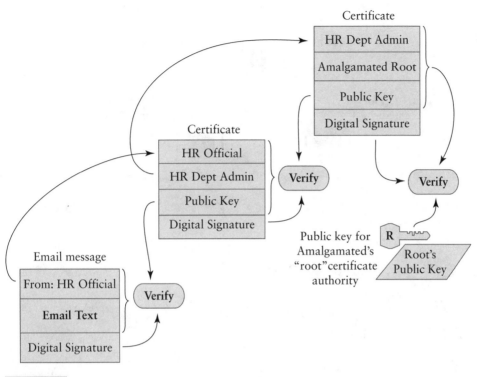

Figure 8.28

Authenticating an email using a certificate chain.

If any check fails, then we can't authenticate the email. A failure may indicate that someone is using an expired certificate or it may indicate a forgery.

CERTIFICATE HIERARCHY

Public-key cryptography provides safe and convenient encryption as long as we can trust the public keys we use. When we have a *public-key infrastructure* (PKI), we have the tools to validate public keys and to use them safely. The exact form of an effective infrastructure has produced a lot of debate over the years.

When public-key certificate systems were first proposed, many experts anticipated a single, global PKI. Individual public-key systems would be part of a giant hierarchy with a single root. All public-key software would carry a single, well-known public key belonging to a universal "root" certificate authority. All national, regional, corporate, and local authorities would have certificates signed by that universal authority. Figure 8.29 illustrates this structure.

In practice, no single authority ever emerged. There were several reasons for this, including the fact that there was no real business, economic, or strategic benefit to adopting a single, universal root authority. Another problem was that different

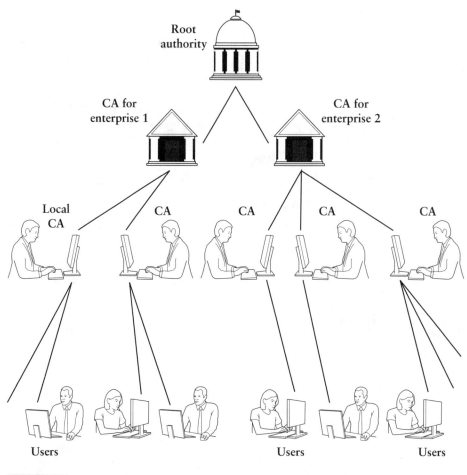

A certificate hierarchy that spans multiple enterprises.

applications demanded different levels of assurance. Multimillion dollar commercial transactions and logins to a personal blog site are both protected with the same public-key technology, but they don't require the same level of caution (and expense) when issuing public-key certificates.

Today, there remains no single, universal root authority. Nonetheless, certificate hierarchies are alive and well. Many large-scale public-key systems use a certificate hierarchy. Internet web browsers contain a database of root public keys, and these often serve as the starting point for hierarchies of authorities.

WEB OF TRUST

When Phil Zimmerman published "Pretty Good Privacy" in 1991, it was partially a political statement. Zimmerman believed that individual freedom would depend in the future on strong cryptography. He wanted cryptography available to the public at large, and usable in a grassroots manner. He didn't want a system that relied on a centralized authority, like a certificate hierarchy with a single root, but he still needed a way to assure the identity of public keys.

To solve the problem, PGP implemented a ***web of trust***. No single person was universally trusted to sign certificates. Instead, individual users made up their own minds about who they trusted to sign certificates. Each certificate could contain as many signatures as the owner desired. Each user would collect certificates from their friends and colleagues. They then could use those certificates to verify signatures on new certificates they receive (Figure 8.30).

The technique relies on Transitive Trust to decide whether a certificate is valid or not. For example, Alice wants to encrypt information for Tina without meeting her in person. She has a copy of every signed certificate in Figure 8.30. Honest Abe signed Alice's own certificate. Abe also signed Carl's certificate, and Carl signed Tina's. If Alice trusts Abe's judgement, then she might accept Tina's certificate, because Abe seems to trust Carl.

The certificate-signing process became a sort of social activity; crypto geeks would arrange "key signing parties" or sign keys when thrown together in a social event. The practice waned after several years, as other assurance techniques replaced it. One

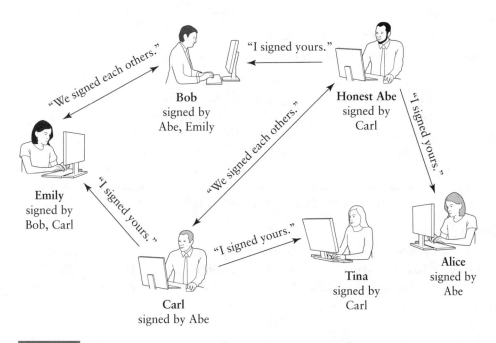

Figure 8.30

A web of trust.

alternative was for people to publish a "key fingerprint" that provided several bytes of the key in hexadecimal. Even these small portions of the key were random enough to make it unlikely that two people would have identical key fingerprints. Moreover, the mathematics of key construction make it impractical to try to create a key with a particular fingerprint. Thus, an attacker couldn't try to masquerade by constructing a public key with a particular fingerprint.

Another alternative was to incorporate email addresses into the certificate process and to use them to increase assurance. The PGP Corporation, which now sells PGP as a commercial product, maintains a PGP key directory on the Internet. When Bob submits his PGP key, the directory validates it by contacting him via the email address in his certificate. Once the email address is validated, the directory adds its own signature to the certificate. Anyone with the directory's certificate can verify any certificate retrieved from the directory.

SELF-SIGNED CERTIFICATES

As described earlier, anyone can produce their own public-key certificate and sign it themselves, yielding a self-signed certificate. Although these are convenient to construct, they also are easy for an attacker to forge. A self-signed certificate only is useful if it is going to be used over time for a series of transactions. As we perform these transactions successfully, we develop increased confidence in the certificate's validity.

There are two cases in which a self-signed certificate provides useful assurance:

1. If the certificate contains other data that we can independently verify
2. If the certificate is used for a series of transactions

For example, there is a website called the PGP Directory. It keeps a public collection of signed PGP certificates. It requires all self-signed certificates to contain an email address. The directory verifies the email address before concluding that the certificate is valid.

If we use a self-signed certificate for a few low-risk transactions, this increases our confidence in its accuracy. If we are sure that the certificate's real owner is the one performing the transactions, then we can at least be confident that those sorts of transactions may take place reliably. On the other hand, we can't assume that a self-signed certificate really belongs to 3M Corporation simply because the signer sells us Post-it notes.

TRICKERY WITH CERTIFICATES

Although public-key certificates provide strong cryptography to protect their information, attackers have found several ways to abuse certificates. Such attacks usually affect authenticated software updates (described in the next section) or secure connections to websites. We discuss these techniques in Section 16.2.3.

8.6.3 Authenticated Software Updates

Software updates pose a serious challenge. If we apply subverted updates to our operating system, we can install malicious software, back doors, and Trojan horses.

Public-key cryptography provides an effective mechanism for authenticating software updates. Figure 8.31 illustrates the basic mechanism for signing and verifying a software update.

If we trust the vendor to create reliable updates, then we can fully automate the update process. We create a set of processes that accept an update file from any user and apply the update. The processes use the vendor's public key to authenticate the update. If the authentication succeeds, a process automatically applies those updates.

The mechanism requires the following components:

- A public/private key pair that the software vendor uses to sign software update files.
- A software update package: trustworthy software that validates the digital signature on a software update file and, if the signature is valid, applies the updates.
- A copy of the vendor's public key that resides inside the update package.
- A digital signature applied by the vendor to every software update file.

The software update process further relies on the appropriate arrangement of processes inside the computer. Figure 8.32 illustrates one approach.

We break the software update process into three steps. First, Bob or some other user retrieves the update file from a disk or the Internet and starts the update. Second, the validation process copies the update software into a protected block of RAM and checks its digital signature. If the signature checks out, the update process runs, and updates the system files.

This is a simple example of an *assured pipeline*, a series of processes that use Least Privilege and Separation of Duty to perform a security-critical task in separate steps.

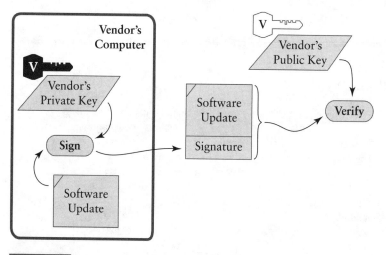

Figure 8.31

Procedure for verifying a software update.

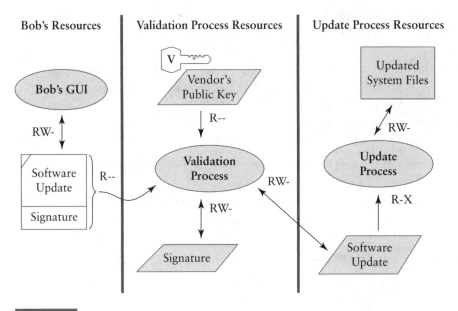

Bob's Resources   Validation Process Resources   Update Process Resources

Figure 8.32

A set of processes for trusted software update.

Bob can start the update process, but his processes lack the rights to patch the system files directly. The validation process validates the authenticity and integrity of the update software before it allows it to execute. Once the process verifies that the update software comes from the vendor, the update process is allowed to run.

8.7 Resources

 IMPORTANT TERMS INTRODUCED

assured pipeline	key encapsulation	public-key certificate
asymmetric cryptography	key rollover	public-key cryptography
birthday attack	key splitting	quantum cryptanalysis
bit-flipping attack	key wrapping	rekeying
bucket brigade attack	keyed hash	reused key stream
certificate chain	man-in-the-middle attack	root certificate authority
cryptonet	modular exponentiation	self-signed certificate
cryptoperiod	modular inverse	Separation of Duty
digital signature	perfect forward secrecy	trusted third party
elliptic curve cryptography	private key	web of trust
internal key	public key	

ACRONYMS INTRODUCED

CA—Certification authority
CEK—Content encrypting key
D-H—Diffie-Hellman
DSS—Digital Signature Standard
HR—Human resources
IKE—Internet Key Exchange
KEK—Key encrypting key
PKCS—Public Key Cryptography Standards
PKI—Public-key infrastructure
PPTP—Point to Point Tunnelling Protocol
RSA—Rivest, Shamir, Adleman

8.7.1 Review Questions

R1. Summarize the challenges of key management.

R2. If we need a 16-byte key, why should we hash a 20-byte passphrase?

R3. Explain the reused key stream problem.

R4. Describe the role of the nonce in preventing reused key streams when using the same passphrase to encrypt different files.

R5. Describe how key wrapping may be applied to file encryption.

R6. What is the difference between key splitting and key wrapping?

R7. Summarize the reasons for rekeying an encrypted file.

R8. Describe the different categories of asymmetric encryption algorithms and how they are used in practice.

R9. What information must be shared to implement Diffie-Hellman key sharing? What is the result?

R10. What information must be shared to exchange a wrapped key using RSA?

R11. What information must be shared to validate a digital signature using RSA?

R12. What information must be available to validate a chain of certificates?

R13. Describe the differences between a hierarchical PKI and one that relies on a web of trust.

R14. Explain how one might establish trust in a self-signed certificate.

8.7.2 Exercises

E1. We want to calculate the amount of "secret entropy" in different implementations of file encryption—that is, the amount of truly secret, unpredictable information used to produce the ciphertext. We need a 16-byte secret key to encrypt the file. Use the estimate of three letters per character (Section 6.4.2) when estimating the entropy in text.

a. Assume we encrypt the file with a 24-letter text passphrase truncated as shown in Figure 8.1.

b. Assume we encrypt the file with a 24-letter text passphrase hashed as shown in Figure 8.2.

c. Assume we encrypt the file with a 24-letter text passphrase hashed with a nonsecret nonce as shown in Figure 8.5.

E2. Redraw Figure 8.6 to show how to *decrypt* a ciphertext file that contains a wrapped key. Be sure to include all necessary components from the original diagram and omit any unnecessary components.

E3. Redraw Figure 8.6 to incorporate passphrases collected from *two* separate users. Combine the passphrases so that the encrypted file can be decrypted if *either* passphrase is provided. This allows someone who knows *either* passphrase to decrypt the file.

E4. Redraw Figure 8.6 to incorporate passphrases collected from *two* separate users. Combine the passphrases to implement Separation of Duty. The encrypted file should be decrypted only if *both* passphrases are provided.

E5. Assume that we can perform 10 million trials/second on our desktop machine. How long will it take us to crack a 1024-bit Diffie-Hellman key? Use the information in Table 8.2.

E6. Bob plans to use Diffie-Hellman to construct a shared secret to encrypt a file shared with Alice. Eve wants to perform a bucket brigade attack and read the shared file.

a. Draw a diagram similar to Figure 8.14 showing how Eve takes part as an invisible participant of the Diffie-Hellman exchange between Bob and Alice.

b. Based on your answer to (a), draw a diagram showing how the contents of Bob's file is shared with Alice.

E7. Bob's little brother loves crypto, especially public-key technology, but he doesn't understand how some of it works. He wrote his own encryption program, shown in Figure 8.33. Draw a diagram showing how Bob could decrypt this message. Omit unnecessary steps.

E8. Bob signed an IOU with a digital signature. The signature uses a 2048-bit RSA key and a 128-bit hash.

a. How many trials should it take, on average, to crack the RSA key?

b. How many trials should it take, on average, for a birthday attack to succeed against a 128-bit hash?

c. Given the previous answers, which is weaker—the hash or the RSA key?

E9. PGP uses public keys to wrap the content key when encrypting a file. Bob wants to share a file with Tina and Alice. He has public keys from each of them. Draw a diagram showing how the file is encrypted and the keys wrapped so that either Tina or Alice may decrypt the file.

E10. Amalgamated Widget has entered a partnering agreement with Foonley Corporation. As a result, email encryption will interoperate between Amalgamated and Foonley. Instead of inserting a second

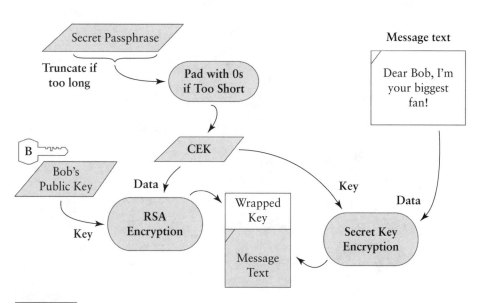

Figure 8.33

Little brother's encryption program.

root key into everyones' email software, Amalgamated has published a certificate containing Foonley's root key, signed by Amalgamated's root. Draw a diagram showing how a certificate signed by Foonley's root is thus validated using Amalgamated's root key.

E11. Identify one or more DRM systems that you use yourself. Describe any problems that occurred using them.

ENCRYPTING VOLUMES

ABOUT THIS CHAPTER

In this chapter, we look at the problem of protecting an entire storage device, as opposed to protecting individual files. We look at the following:

- Risks and policy alternatives for protecting drive contents
- Block ciphers that achieve high security
- Block cipher encryption modes
- Hardware for volume encryption
- Software for volume encryption

9.1 Securing a Volume

When we examined file systems in Section 5.1, Bob and Tina suspected that their survey report was leaked through file scavenging: Someone looked at the "hidden" places on the hard drive. We can avoid such attacks and protect everything on the hard drive, including the boot blocks, directory entries, and free space, if we encrypt the entire drive volume.

Note how we use the word *volume* here: It refers to a block of drive storage that contains its own file system. It may be an entire hard drive, a single drive partition, a removable USB drive, or any other mass storage device. If the system "sees" the volume as a single random-access storage device, then we can protect it all by encrypting it all. We sometimes call this *full-disk encryption* (FDE) because we often apply it to hard drives, but it applies to any mass storage volume (Figure 9.1).

File encryption lets us protect individual files from a strong threat. If we encrypt a particular file, then attackers aren't likely to retrieve its contents, except in two cases. First, there is the file-scavenging problem noted previously. Second, people often forget things, and file encryption is a forgettable task.

In many cases, sensitive data is vulnerable simply because nobody bothered to encrypt it. Even when users encrypt some of their data files, it's not likely that they have

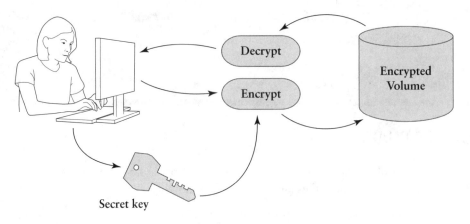

Secret key

Figure 9.1

A hard drive volume with full-disk encryption (FDE).

encrypted *all* of their sensitive files. It is challenging to identify the files at risk and to remember which ones to encrypt.

The principal benefit of encrypting a whole volume is that the encryption takes place automatically. When we plug in a removable encrypted drive or we start up the operating system, the drive encryption system retrieves the volume's encryption keys and mounts the volume. If the keys aren't available, then the volume can't be used. Once the volume is mounted, the data is encrypted and decrypted automatically. The user doesn't need to decide which files to encrypt. In fact, the user doesn't even have the choice of saving a plaintext file; *everything* on the volume is encrypted, including the directories and free space.

Volume encryption is convenient but it does not solve every security problem. For example, it protects Bob if the attacker physically opens up his tower computer and connects directly to his hard drive. Disk encryption does not protect Bob from a Trojan program that copies files to a separate, unencrypted storage device, like a USB stick.

To put volume encryption in context with other security measures, we look at risks and policy trade-offs. First, we will look at risks facing an unencrypted volume. Next, we look at policy trade-offs between volume encryption, file encryption, and file-based access control.

9.1.1 Risks to Volumes

There are three general risks we address with volume encryption:

1. Losing the storage device
2. An eavesdropper that looks at the volume without the operating system in place
3. Discarding a hard drive or other device without wiping it

The first risk is everyones' worst-case scenario: Our computer is stolen. Laptops especially seem likely to "sprout legs and walk away." While our first worry might be the cost of replacing the laptop, many people also worry about identity theft. Some thieves exploit the data stored on the hard drive to masquerade as the laptop's owner. Identity theft is a booming business, and personal computers often contain extensive financial records and lists of online passwords.

The theft risk poses even greater problems for large organizations. A stolen laptop may contain large databases of sensitive information about customers. According to statistics collected for the first half of 2009, there were 19 incidents in the United States where a misplaced or stolen laptop placed databases at risk. The incidents involved private companies, schools, hospitals, and government agencies at all levels. The smallest data loss involved 50 personal records, while one incident involved over a million records.

If a stolen computer contains a customer database, many companies are required legally to contact all affected customers and warn them that their customer information may have been stolen. If the database includes credit card numbers or Social Security numbers, then the company may need to provide some defense against possible identity theft.

EAVESDROPPING

The eavesdropping problem arises if we can't always keep our drive physically safe, or under appropriate software protection. When Bob and Alice started using file encryption, they decided to keep the encrypted file on a shared USB drive. Because the file was encrypted, they assumed it was safe from eavesdropping. For convenience, they left it on the bulletin board in their suite.

We still may risk eavesdropping even if we don't share a drive on a bulletin board. If we back up the data to a separate drive, we need to physically protect the backup drive. If attackers have physical access to our computer, then we can try to protect our data by protecting our Chain of Control; we can disable booting of other drives and enable file protections. However, these defenses don't protect us if the attacker cracks open the computer's case. An attacker can bypass any BIOS or operating system by connecting the hard drive to a different motherboard.

DISCARDED HARD DRIVES

When we upgrade a computer, we often trade up to a larger hard drive. The old drive disappears along with the old computer, but what about our sensitive data?

Research at MIT by Simson Garfinkel found that countless companies and individuals sell or discard computers without properly erasing the hard drives. The researchers found that most people took very simple steps to "clean" their drive of data before passing the computer onto the next owner. Using "undelete" programs and other file-recovery tools, researchers were able to recover numerous personal and business files.

There are four strategies for cleaning a hard drive of personal data:

1. Delete personal files and "empty the trash."

2. Reformat the hard drive.

3. Run a "disk wipe" program.

4. Physically damage the hard drive so that it can't be read.

The first two strategies yield similar results. As noted earlier, files continue to exist in a ghostly form after they have been deleted. The same is true for reformatting. When we reformat a drive, especially a "quick format," we simply rewrite the first few blocks of the hard drive with a new directory that contains no files. Disk recovery software looks at the other blocks on the disk and tries to reconstruct the previous directories. The attempt often succeeds. Once the directories are restored, the software recovers as many files as possible.

Either of the last two strategies may eliminate the risk of recovered files. We examined disk wiping as part of encrypting a file in Section 7.4.3, but there are also utility programs that wipe a drive by overwriting every one of its blocks. Some hard drives have a built-in mechanism to wipe the drive, but these mechanisms are rarely evaluated for effectiveness. Even with the built-in wipe, an attacker might be able to retrieve data.

Note that it may be challenging to physically destroy a modern hard drive. The major components are metal and are assembled to operate at very high rotational speeds. For all but the more extreme threats, we render the data irrecoverable if we open the drive case and remove all of the drive's read/write heads.

9.1.2 Risks and Policy Trade-Offs

Full-disk encryption clearly protects against scavenging data off of an unprotected hard drive. However, just as file encryption was no cure-all, drive encryption doesn't guarantee our safety. Depending on the risks, we may need one or the other or both.

Simply because some risks call for one type of encryption or another does not mean that the encryption solves our problems. Encryption introduces practical problems, especially with respect to key handling.

At this point we have three practical security measures: access controls enforced by the operating system, file encryption, and drive encryption. We can implement all three, or some combination, depending on the risks. Table 9.1 summarizes the individual alternatives.

Table 9.1 answers the following questions about whether the particular security measure protects against the particular risk:

1. **Hostile users.** Does it protect against hostile, logged-in users trying to steal information from other users on the computer?

2. **Trojans.** Does it protect against data leaking through Trojan horse applications?

3. **Trojan crypto.** Does it protect against Trojan software embedded in the crypto software? The general answer is NO.

4. **External files.** Does it protect files that we copy onto removable storage and carry to other computers?

Risk	Access Control	File Encryption	Volume Encryption
Hostile users	YES	YES	NO
Trojans	NO	YES	NO
Trojan crypto	NO	NO	NO
External files	NO	YES	YES
Lost control	NO	YES	YES
Theft	NO	YES	YES
Recycling	NO	YES	YES

TABLE 9.1 Effectiveness of access control and encryption

5. **Lost control.** If attackers take physical control of the computer and physically disassemble it to attack the hard drive, do we have any protection?

6. **Theft.** This is the ultimate case of lost control. Do our files remain protected?

7. **Recycling.** When we want to sell, discard, or recycle the drive, do our files remain protected so that a scavenger or new owner can't recover them?

Access control clearly plays a role on computers where we have to protect data against hostile users. We also could use file encryption as an alternative to access control. This isn't a good idea in practice. We can only protect files with encryption if we always remember to encrypt them. People often forget to do such things and leave information unprotected. Users must also erase completely all plaintext copies of the sensitive data. This is very hard to ensure.

Moreover, we can't use file encryption to protect critical operating system files or even our application programs. If the operating system doesn't provide access controls, then there's no way to prevent someone from installing a Trojan inside our file encryption software.

Volume encryption provides no real protection against hostile users or Trojans. If the hostile users are on the encrypted system, then they are *inside* the boundary protected by the encryption. They see everything as plaintext anyway. If the access control doesn't restrict hostile users, then volume encryption won't improve matters.

Volume encryption becomes important when we risk losing control of our storage device. Clearly, access control gives little protection if the attacker uses a different operating system or special software to retrieve data from a hard drive. File encryption may protect the encrypted files, but risks remain: We might have forgotten to encrypt a critical file, and there are still risks of scavenging information from scratch files.

IDENTIFYING CRITICAL DATA

There are several ways to identify critical data. In some cases we know already which files we need to protect and which aren't important. However, it's best to develop policy statements that help define critical data.

For example, if we handle information that others deem sensitive (like credit card numbers, health information, or proprietary information), we are obliged to safeguard it. In some cases, there are specific security measures we must use. In all cases, however, we need a way to tell which files might contain the sensitive information, so that we may protect those files.

Critical data should always be marked as such. We should clearly distinguish between critical and noncritical data. This makes it easier to ensure that we adequately protect critical data. For example, we may restrict critical data to specific folders or to folders with particular names.

We also may put readable markings in documents to remind us they contain sensitive information. For example, government agencies routinely put classification markings or other warnings about restricted distribution in the document's page header and/or footer. Law firms may do this for documents that are restricted according to judicial orders. Many companies systematically mark all proprietary information.

We also should physically mark any removable storage volumes that might contain sensitive or critical information. Even if the volume is encrypted, it is essential to easily tell whether sensitive information should—or should not—be stored on a particular volume.

POLICY FOR UNENCRYPTED VOLUMES

If an unencrypted volume contains data we can't afford to leak, then we must guarantee its physical protection. It is very hard to guarantee such protection in practice. We often need to leave hardware unattended, even laptops. This opens the risk of a peeping Tom even if we aren't risking theft. If we don't encrypt the drive and we store sensitive information on it, then we need the policy statements shown in Table 9.2.

In practice, the policy statements should be more specific about the information and storage. Somewhere, our policy should identify what we mean by sensitive data. We should also be more specific about which mass storage devices we protect.

Number	Policy Statement	Risks
	TABLE 9.2 Policy statements for an unencrypted volume	
1	The mass storage device shall be physically protected against eavesdropping and theft at all times.	4, 5, 6
2	The mass storage device shall be completely wiped of data before it is recycled or discarded.	7

Number	Policy Statement	Risks
	TABLE 9.3 Policy statements for volume encryption	
1	Every removable storage volume used for sensitive data shall be fully encrypted.	4
2	The computer's system drive shall be fully encrypted.	5, 6
3	There shall be a mechanism that fully erases and purges the encryption key used to encrypt any mass storage volume.	7

These policy statements are easy to write but difficult to implement. If we keep the drives locked in a private office, we may also have to consider the risks of cleaning people. If the drive is in a laptop, we need a locked cabinet for it, and we should avoid carrying it in public.

POLICY FOR ENCRYPTED VOLUMES

In practice, we can justify volume encryption for almost any computer hard drive or USB drive. Although it may not prevent every attack, it prevents many common risks. In most cases, we can*not* keep a hard drive or laptop safe continuously. As of 2010, however, volume encryption remains a relatively rare and sophisticated feature, though this should change as the technologies evolve.

Table 9.3 presents policy statements for volume encryption. As with the previous statements, a practical policy needs to tell people how to identify sensitive data. Policy and procedures also should provide a way to distinguish between volumes containing sensitive data and those that don't.

Now that we know we need volume encryption, we need to figure out how to implement it. Volume encryption places a serious burden on an encryption algorithm. Most algorithms become vulnerable if we encrypt a great deal of information, especially if it includes known plaintext and duplicated information. This is exactly what happens on a large, encrypted hard drive.

9.2 Block Ciphers

The strongest and most respected modern ciphers are ***block ciphers***. While stream ciphers encrypt bit by bit, block ciphers encrypt fixed-sized blocks of bits. The block cipher takes the block of data and encrypts it into an equal-sized block of data. The old Data Encryption Standard worked with 64-bit blocks of data. The new Advanced Encryption Standard works on 128-bit blocks. To apply a block cipher, we must break the data into block-sized chunks and add padding as needed to match the data to the block size (Figure 9.2).

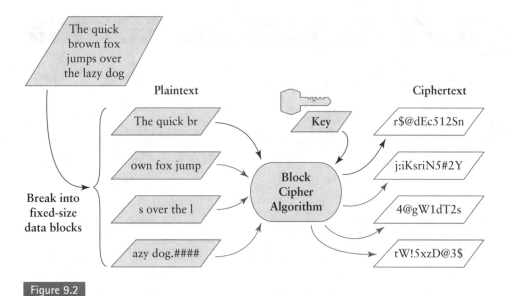

Figure 9.2

Figure 9.2

A block cipher encrypts data in fixed-sized blocks.

In a sense, block ciphers are like the Caesar cipher examined in Section 7.2. We substitute one letter for another, no more and no less, based on the key. We could in theory create a "codebook" for a given key that lists all plaintext values and the corresponding ciphertext values. The book would be impractically huge. For example, if we have a 64-bit block size, the book would have 10^{19} entries. We also would need a different book for each key.

BUILDING A BLOCK CIPHER

Encryption is a systematic scrambling of data. Most block ciphers encrypt by applying a function repeatedly to the plaintext to encrypt. Each repetition is called a *round*.

Before the cipher scrambles the data, it takes the key and produces a *key schedule*. In some cases, the schedule consists of small blocks of the key that the cipher applies to successive rounds. Often, however, the algorithm performs *key expansion* to yield a schedule that is larger than the original key.

Typically, each round uses a successive part of the key schedule. The rounds repeat until the key schedule is exhausted. Here is a general description of the block encryption procedure:

- Generate the key schedule.
- Divide the key schedule into subsections, one per round.
- For each subsection, perform a round:
  - For the first round, take the plaintext as the input text; for the remaining rounds, take the output of the previous round as the input text.

- Take the next unused subsection of the key schedule as the key input.
- Scramble the input text using permutations and substitutions as specified in the encryption algorithm.

The round scrambles the data by applying arithmetic and logical operations, particularly the xor operation. A round often uses both permutations and substitutions to scramble the data. The substitutions may be controlled by special data structures called *S-boxes*. These serve as look-up tables to provide the bits to substitute for particular input bits, given a particular key.

The decryption procedure takes the key and the ciphertext and unscrambles the data. Each round tries to undo the work of a corresponding round in the encryption process. In some algorithms, decryption simply applies the key schedule, the permutations, and the S-boxes in the reverse order.

This procedure highlights three important features of block ciphers:

1. It takes time to change keys, because the procedure must generate a new key schedule for each key.
2. The number of rounds reflect a trade-off between speed and security. More rounds may scramble the data more thoroughly, but each round takes time to execute.
3. Key sizes, block sizes, and the number of rounds performed are built into the procedure. We can't arbitrarily change any of these without redesigning the procedure.

To highlight the third point, compare the flexibility of RC4 to the flexibility of AES. In RC4, the key may contain as few—or as many—bytes as desired. Fewer key bytes provide dramatically inferior encryption. AES supports exactly three key sizes: 128 bits, 192 bits, and 256 bits. The AES procedure performs 10 rounds for a 128-bit key, and additional rounds when using longer keys.

With RC4, we can encrypt a single bit, gigabytes, or more. AES encrypts data in fixed-sized blocks of exactly 128 bits. If we encrypt less than 128 bits, we must pad the data out to 128 bits. AES ciphertext must be a multiple of 128 bits. If we omit part of a ciphertext block, we won't be able to decrypt it correctly.

Despite the inflexibility, AES provides far better encryption than any known stream cipher. Researchers have found numerous shortcomings in RC4. Researchers have studied AES at least as thoroughly, though over a shorter time period, and have found no significant weaknesses.

THE EFFECT OF CIPHERTEXT ERRORS

In Section 7.3.3, we noted how ciphertext errors affect stream ciphers. If we change a single bit of ciphertext, then the corresponding bit will change in the plaintext.

Block ciphers behave differently. There is no one-to-one relationship between individual bits in the plaintext and the ciphertext. The block cipher behaves more like a one-way hash; if we change a single bit in the plaintext, the resulting ciphertext will change dramatically.

Thus, if we encrypt with a block cipher and an error or attack changes a single bit in some ciphertext, it scrambles the entire plaintext data block. In a well-designed block cipher, a change to one input bit will affect bits throughout the output block. This is true when encrypting or decrypting.

Consider, on the other hand, what happens if we rearrange entire blocks of cipher-text. If we rearrange ciphertext bits in a stream cipher, every bit we change will decrypt incorrectly. Stream cipher decryption is sensitive to the order of the data; each bit in the ciphertext must line up with its corresponding bit in the key stream.

In block ciphers, however, we encrypt and decrypt each block independently. Thus, if we change the order of blocks in the ciphertext, we will recover the reordered plaintext as long as we move whole blocks of ciphertext. If we rearrange ciphertext within a block, we lose the entire block when decrypted. As long as whole blocks remain unchanged, the ciphertext decrypts cleanly into plaintext.

9.2.1 Evolution of DES and AES

Section 7.3 introduced the Data Encryption Standard and controversies surrounding its key size. DES was a block cipher that worked on 64-bit blocks using a 56-bit key. The algorithm evolved from "Lucifer," an encryption algorithm developed by IBM. Lucifer implemented rounds, permutations, and S-boxes in a form called a "Feistel structure." It also used a 128-bit key.

DES AND LUCIFER

In the 1970s, the NSA was the only organization in the U.S. government with crypto-graphic expertise, so it was naturally given the job of assessing the algorithm. NSA rec-ommended two changes to Lucifer before making it a national standard. One change was to the S-boxes. A second change was to reduce the key size to 56 bits. The changes were made before the algorithm was approved as a U.S. standard.

As noted earlier, critics immediately decried the 56-bit key as too small. Researchers started cracking DES keys successfully in the 1990s.

The changes to the S-boxes also caused concern. The NSA instructed IBM not to explain why the changes were made. Some observers feared that the changes would give the NSA a secret shortcut to crack DES encryption. If it existed, the shortcut would allow the NSA to crack DES encryption without performing a brute force attack that tried every possible DES key. Any shortcut in a brute force attack would render DES ineffective.

These worries never came true. No shortcut was ever uncovered. Although cryptana-lysts have found attacks that work against DES, none of these attacks are significantly better than a traditional brute force attack.

Looking back, the principal weakness in DES has been its key size. The design con-cepts embodied in DES have stood the test of time. DES has served as a good, working example for future cryptographic designers.

DES was designed to be efficient in hardware. Aside from its key size, this may be its only significant shortcoming. The algorithm required so much low-level bit manipula-tion that some experts believed—or at least hoped—that DES software implementation

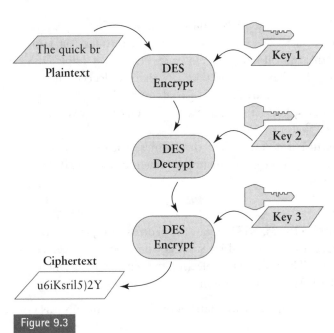

Figure 9.3

Triple DES encryption.

would be too slow to be practical. This proved untrue. Software implementations flourished despite the inefficiencies.

TRIPLE DES

To minimize the risk of the 56-bit encryption key, some organizations tried applying DES several times with different keys. The American National Standards Institute (ANSI) developed a series of standards for using DES. These standards were adopted by the U.S. banking industry. One of these standards included a technique that encrypted data with two or three 56-bit keys instead of a single key (Figure 9.3). This was called Triple DES.

In Triple DES, each DES operation may use a separate 56-bit key. The technique does not simply apply encryption or decryption three times in a row. Instead, the middle step performs the opposite function of the outer steps. The swapped step allows users to operate Triple DES with one, two, or three different 56-bit DES keys.

Here is how we use different numbers of keys with Triple DES:

- One key: Use the same key in all steps. The first two steps invert each other, and the final step performs the encryption.
- Two keys: Use the first key for the first and last steps, and use the second key in the middle step.
- Three keys: Use a different key for each step.

When using three keys, Triple DES requires a 168-bit random key. This may sound significantly stronger than AES with its 128-bit key. In fact, there are attacks on Triple DES that reduce the strength of the 168-bit key to be closer to 112 bits. If Triple DES really worked at the full strength of its key, it would take 2^{168} trials to decrypt the ciphertext. In fact, a more efficient attack only takes 2^{112} trials. When using two keys, Triple DES requires a 112-bit random key. Clever attacks, however, can recover the ciphertext in 2^{80} trials.

Triple DES is less efficient because it performs DES three times. The extra cycles improve security over the original 56-bit key, but the improvement costs a great deal in computing time.

THE DEVELOPMENT OF AES

As DES began to show its age in the 1990s, NIST began the process of replacing it. Unlike the closed, secretive process that produced DES, NIST announced an open competition to produce its replacement. The process for selecting the replacement, called the Advanced Encryption Standard, or AES, had several important features:

- Anyone, anywhere could submit an AES candidate algorithm. Authorship was not limited to U.S. citizens.
- AES candidates must be free of patents or other intellectual property restrictions.
- The design rationale for every AES candidate would be made public, including the rationale for choosing built-in constants, for designing S-boxes, and so on.
- All "unclassified" evaluations of AES candidates would be made public.
- The assessments and relative rankings of AES candidates would be made public.
- The rationale for choosing one candidate over the others to be the new standard would be made public.

Twenty-one candidates were submitted by the June 1998 deadline. Six candidates were eliminated for not meeting requirements. Ten more were eliminated during the first round of evaluation.

AES FINALISTS

The five finalists were announced in 1999:

1. Rijndael, submitted by Joan Daemen of Proton World International and Vincent Rijmen of the Katholieke Universiteit Leuven, in Belgium. NIST ultimately chose Rijndael to become the new AES.
2. MARS, submitted by IBM.
3. RC6, submitted by RSA Laboratories.
4. Serpent, submitted by Ross Anderson of the University of Cambridge, United Kingdom, Eli Biham of Technion, Israel, and Lars Knudsen of the University of California–San Diego.

5. Twofish, submitted by Bruce Schneier, John Kelsey, and Niels Ferguson of Counterpane Internet Security; David Wagner of University of California–Berkeley; Doug Whiting of Hi/Fn; and Chris Hall of Princeton University.

All five finalists were block ciphers designed around the execution of multiple rounds. The final review involved three categories: flexibility, implementation efficiency, and security. There are ways to fairly compare flexibility and efficiency. Each algorithm was assessed as to how easily it could adapt to larger block and key sizes. Although DES was explicitly designed to work efficiently in hardware, the AES candidates were assessed for their efficiency in both hardware and software implementations.

Security assessment posed more of a challenge. It is hard to come up with an objective and appropriate comparison for encryption algorithms. The challenge was to determine which differences in the algorithms might significantly affect their security. One approach was to assess "reduced round" versions of each algorithm. All finalists implemented rounds, and this assessment sought weaknesses in variants that had fewer rounds than were really required.

For example, Rijndael normally performs 10 rounds when encrypting with a 128-bit key. To search for weaknesses, analysts reduced the number of rounds and looked at the result. With Rijndael, the algorithm did not show weaknesses until at least three rounds were omitted. This was not the widest safety margin in terms of rounds, but was judged to provide a good trade-off between security and efficiency.

All five AES finalists have been judged to be excellent block ciphers. Some products and applications use one or another AES finalist and probably provide good security. However, the only algorithm recognized as a national standard by the U.S. government is AES itself, which is a variant of Rijndael.

9.2.2 The RC4 Story

Ron Rivest developed the RC4 algorithm in the late 1980s. As we saw in Chapter 7.3.2, it is a stream cipher and it has been used in numerous products. It is used still occasionally by older web servers and older wireless networks.

Rivest was a cofounder of RSA Data Security, and the company marketed the algorithm. When introduced in 1987, the company offered RC4 as a *trade secret*. A vendor could pay a license fee to RSA and use the algorithm in a product, but they were forbidden to share the RC4 source code with anyone.

When the United States was founded in the late 1700s, the founders favored the notion of *patent protection* for inventions. A patent requires inventors to publish details of their invention. In exchange, the inventor gets a monopoly on its use for roughly 20 years. This promotes science, education, and knowledge, because the invention's principles are made public. It also produces an Open Design so that others can analyze the invention and verify its behavior. The temporary monopoly gives the inventor some time to commercialize the discovery and pay for the costs of development.

A trade secret, on the other hand, is *never* published. In theory, an inventor could keep a permanent monopoly on an invention by keeping it a trade secret. If anyone who shares the secret publishes it, the inventor can sue them for breach of contract. On the other hand, if someone else makes the same discovery independently, the original inventor has no protection.

EXPORT RESTRICTIONS

The trade secret approach proved to be a smart move at the time. Network software vendors realized that their products needed security, and that encryption was the only effective mechanism. However, the U.S. International Traffic in Arms Regulation (ITAR) classified encryption as a weapon of war. Encryption systems, whether in hardware or software, required an export license from the state department. Naturally, the state department turned to the NSA for advice on such licenses. In practice, the state department only allowed exports for use by U.S. companies overseas.

In the early 1990s, software vendors started negotiating with the NSA to establish some type of exportable encryption. NSA eventually adopted an unwritten rule allowing the use of RC4 and an earlier block cipher, RC2 (Rivest's Cipher 2).

The unwritten rule included two additional restrictions. First, if the product used secret encryption keys, the secret part was limited to 40 bits or less. Second, the algorithms had to remain secret or at least unpublished.

RC4 LEAKING, THEN CRACKING

The RC4 algorithm was leaked to the Internet in 1994. The person responsible was never identified. This produced an odd situation. RSA did not officially acknowledge that the leaked algorithm was RC4, so vendors still could tell the NSA that the algorithm was "secret." Today, however, the crypto community accepts the leaked algorithm as being RC4.

The U.S. government still requires licensing of crypto products for export, but the 40-bit key requirement was effectively dropped in 1999. This was fortunate: By 1997, researchers like Ian Goldberg were cracking 40-bit keys in university computing labs. The revised regulations also permitted other crypto algorithms, just as RC4's weaknesses fully emerged.

Before RC4 was leaked, RSA Data Security claimed that its own analyses confirmed its cryptographic strength. However, cracks appeared soon after the algorithm was leaked. Within a year, researchers found sets of "weak keys," all of which generated similar key streams.

In an ideal stream cipher, the entropy in the secret key is spread out among the bits in the stream. For example, we might use a 128-bit key to generate a million-bit key stream. Ideally, we should need to see about 8000 bits of the key stream before we start to detect a bias. In RC4, biases appear in the first bytes of the key stream.

In 2001, several researchers published strategies to attack RC4. When RC4 became the centerpiece of wireless encryption, researchers soon developed practical procedures to crack the encryption. Today, product developers avoid RC4.

LESSONS LEARNED

This story illustrates some important points.

- We can't depend on the algorithm's owner to find its flaws. RSA Security claimed to have performed some analyses that provided favorable results. It was not until third parties analyzed RC4 that problems were found. Notably, RSA Security acted responsibly in the face of these results. Although some vendors intentionally have suppressed information about weaknesses in proprietary crypto algorithms and even threatened legal action against published critiques, there is no evidence that RSA Security ever tried to suppress information about RC4's weaknesses.

- It is harder to find flaws if we limit the number of people investigating the algorithm. Cryptology is a relatively new field in the public sphere. We can't rely on any individual expert—or a handful of experts—to find the flaws in a particular algorithm. The best way to find flaws is to open the search to as many researchers as possible.

- It is hard to keep an algorithm secret. It is not clear how RC4 leaked. Someone may have transcribed a description published by the owner, or someone may have "reverse engineered" a program containing RC4. In 1994, RC4 was being used in Netscape's web browsers. Someone might have picked apart the instructions in the browser that encrypted data and derived the RC4 algorithm from that listing.

It took a few years, but the crypto community found and exploited vulnerabilities in this "secret" algorithm. It is hard to keep a crypto algorithm secret, especially if it resides in software that most people have installed on their computer.

9.2.3 Qualities of Good Encryption Algorithms

Since the development of DES in the 1970s, designers have discussed and reviewed numerous cipher designs. Some have stood the test of time in one form or another. Others, like DES and RC4, have been dropped from newer developments because researchers found problems with them. This is the benefit of Open Design; a larger community of analysts may study algorithms, and hopefully identify the weak ones before attackers take advantage of them.

Large, complex products always pose a challenge to buyers, whether they are automobiles or crypto algorithms. In the case of crypto algorithms, however, we can look for certain qualities that greatly reduce our risks. Here are six qualities of good encryption algorithms:

1. Explicitly designed for encryption.
2. Security does not rely on its secrecy.
3. Available for analysis.
4. Subjected to analysis.
5. No practical weaknesses.

6. Implementation has completed a formal cryptographic evaluation.

Several of these qualities reflect the principle of Open Design.

EXPLICITLY DESIGNED FOR ENCRYPTION

In Section 7.3.2, we constructed a key stream algorithm out of a one-way hash (Figure 7.11). In one sense, this seems like a clever thing to do; the one-way hash output seems random. However, this isn't really what the one-way hash is designed to do. A series of hashes might have unexpected statistical properties. Moreover, the hash feedback is itself vulnerable to a known plaintext attack.

We do *not* build a strong encryption algorithm by reusing a different algorithm for a different purpose. Encryption puts its own requirements on how the algorithm works and what types of patterns are acceptable. Occasionally, we can use an encryption algorithm for a different purpose, like to produce a one-way hash. Even in those cases, we must be careful not to use the algorithm in a way that undercuts its effectiveness.

SECURITY DOES NOT RELY ON ITS SECRECY

This clearly reflects Open Design, Kerckhoff's law, and Shannon's maxim. We build secrecy systems to rely on an independent piece of secret information: the key. If we keep the key secret, then attackers can't efficiently recover the protected information.

If the algorithm's security relies on its secrecy, then everyone who looks at the algorithm will be a member of its cryptonet. This is impractical in countless ways: Not only does it restrict its security analysis, but it makes the algorithm hard to implement and deploy securely.

AVAILABLE FOR ANALYSIS

It is hard to assess the strength of a cryptographic algorithm. Some weak algorithms fall quickly to simple attacks, while others like RC4 survive for a period of time before problems arise. In any case, we can't analyze an algorithm unless we can examine it and see what it does. The first step is to make the algorithm available for analysis. If we prevent or delay that analysis, we risk building products with vulnerable encryption.

We can't rely on the algorithm's owners to analyze the algorithm for us. The owners have to pay for the analysis, and they will only pay as much as necessary for *some* good news. They don't need to be thorough and, in fact, it's not clear what a thorough analysis would entail. If we make the algorithm available for public examination, then a broader community of experts have the opportunity to pass judgement. Potential customers who are interested in the algorithm could arrange their own analyses, which are much more likely to be unbiased than those arranged by the owners.

SUBJECTED TO ANALYSIS

It's not enough to publish an algorithm. Most experts are busy people and aren't going to pick up arbitrary algorithms and analyze them for pleasure. If experts have analyzed the algorithm and published positive results, that gives us a basis for confidence in its behavior.

If recognized experts have been publishing analyses about an algorithm, we have a better reason to trust that algorithm. These analyses should be in peer-reviewed publications where the analyses themselves are studied by experts. If the consensus of these experts supports the algorithm's use, then we can trust it.

No Practical Weaknesses

Cryptographic experts are going to find weaknesses in just about any cryptographic algorithm. This is a natural result: As we use these algorithms in new ways, they become vulnerable to new attacks.

Ideally, the attacks are not relevant to the way we intend to use the algorithm. For example, there are *chosen plaintext* attacks against DES, but they require enormous amounts of data to be effective. The attack doesn't really apply to typical DES implementations. On the other hand, a theoretical weakness in RC4 was cleverly converted by researchers in Darmstadt, Germany, into a real-time attack on commercial wireless network products.

Cryptographic Evaluation

Our checklist for choosing a file encryption program in Section 7.4.4 noted the importance of cryptographic product evaluation. This remains true when using a block cipher. There are "tricks" to using block ciphers that we will discuss further, and the evaluation helps ensure that the developer uses the right tricks to keep the encryption secure.

Unfortunately, no evaluation process is 100 percent foolproof. In fact, different evaluation regimens focus on different issues, and one process may tolerate security flaws that another might reject. For example, the FIPS-140 process focuses primarily on correct implementation of cryptographic mechanisms. It does not always detect and reject even egregious security flaws, such as the authentication weakness found in several encrypted USB products in late 2009.

Choosing an Encryption Algorithm

Here are the general recommendations:

- Use AES if at all possible. AES was subjected to incredible public scrutiny before its selection, which suggests that it will stand the test of time. It is also a U.S. national standard, which provides some legal protection if flaws arise in the algorithm itself.

- Use evaluated cryptographic products if using a certified algorithm. The evaluation process ensures that a trained third party has reviewed the implementation to ensure that the cryptography works correctly.

- Use a well-known, respected algorithm if AES is not available. The best alternatives today are the AES candidates. An older alternative is Triple DES.

- Check recent news and research results in the crypto community regarding the algorithm you want to use. Emerging problems with crypto algorithms have become significant news items in the technical press.

- Do not use "private label" algorithms that have not been published and reviewed by the cryptographic community. There is no way to ensure the effectiveness of such algorithms. Security is riddled with examples of weak proprietary algorithms.

9.3 Block Cipher Modes

Block ciphers suffer from a built-in shortcoming. If we feed a block cipher the same plaintext and the same key, it always yields the same ciphertext. This is what block ciphers do. By itself, this isn't a vulnerability. It becomes a vulnerability when we encrypt data that has block-sized patterns in it.

For example, look at Figure 9.4. On the left, we have a plaintext image, originally rendered in three colors. On the right, we have the ciphertext after it was encrypted with a block cipher. The block cipher transformed the areas of uniform color into distinctive corduroy patterns. Each color in the plaintext yielded its own pattern in the ciphertext. Although this doesn't yield a quality copy of the plaintext image, the ciphertext reveals the essence of the plaintext.

Figure 9.5 shows how this works. We encrypt the text "ABRACARDABRA" with a block cipher that works on 4-byte blocks. Given a particular key, a repeated block of four letters always encrypts to the same ciphertext. In this case, "ABRA" encrypts to the letters "HHIE" every time.

In the early days of encryption, people tried to avoid such patterns by restricting the data being sent. They might use an extra layer of encryption or encourage the radio

Smiley face plaintext image

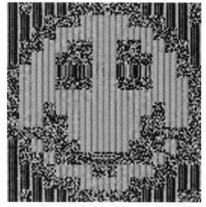

Ciphertext after encrypting the image block-by-block

Figure 9.4

Encryption failure using a block cipher.

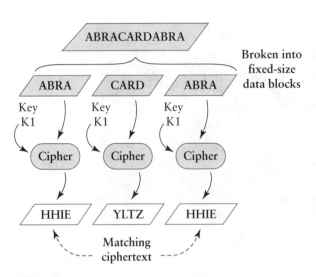

Figure 9.5

Identical blocks encrypt to identical ciphertext.

clerks to rearrange messages to avoid patterns. This is hard to do effectively, because the clerk might change a message's meaning when rearranging its text. In times of stress, when secrecy could be most important, a busy clerk might not rearrange messages at all, and send several in a row with repeated patterns. Cryptanalysts would then focus on messages sent by hurried or careless clerks to crack the encryption.

The most effective way to avoid this problem is to build the solution into the encryption process. The solutions are called block cipher *modes of operation* ("modes" for short). Typically, a mode mixes data together from two separate encryptions. This scrambles the result and eliminates patterns in the ciphertext. This all takes place automatically when applying the mode. Figure 9.6 shows the result of applying a mixing mode while encrypting the smiley face.

Numerous modes have evolved over the years. Here we examine five common modes. Two of these modes are fairly well behaved and are widely used. Two modes generate a key stream that we can use in a stream cipher.

- **Electronic codebook**: encrypts block by block without mixing
- **Output feedback**: generates a key stream
- **Counter**: generates a key stream; **recommended**
- **Cipher feedback**: a mix of stream and block cipher
- **Cipher block chaining**: encrypts in blocks; **recommended**

These modes are specifically intended to keep information confidential. They do not by themselves protect information from modifications. In some cases, ciphertext errors

Encrypted without mixing using
the "electronic codebook"
mode

Encrypted with mixing using
the "cipher block chaining"
mode

Figure 9.6

Using a mixing mode with a block cipher.

or other changes only affect the specific bits modified. In other cases, small changes may damage entire blocks of decrypted plaintext.

When we encrypt data block by block, we call that the *electronic codebook* (ECB) mode. This term arises from the notion that a block cipher acts like a "codebook" in which every block of plaintext has a unique block of ciphertext associated with it. This is much like traditional codebooks published on paper that list plaintext messages and their corresponding code words.

We rarely use ECB mode because block-sized patterns in the plaintext will appear in the ciphertext. We only use ECB when encrypting data that fits within the cipher's block size.

9.3.1 Stream Cipher Modes

Following our discussion in Section 7.3.2, we may use a block cipher to generate a key stream. The simplest approach is the *output feedback* (OFB) mode, shown in Figure 9.7.

Note how it strongly resembles the key stream generator in Figure 7.12. We use the block cipher to generate blocks of ciphertext that serve as the key stream. As shown earlier, we encrypt by applying xor to bits of the plaintext and corresponding bits of the key stream. To decrypt, we generate the matching key stream and apply xor to retrieve the plaintext.

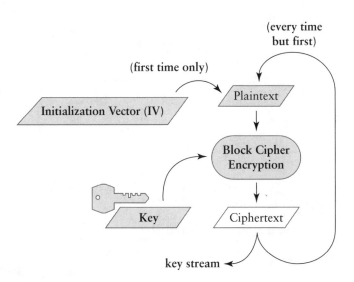

Figure 9.7

Key stream made with OFB (output feedback mode).

Remember from Section 8.2 that we must never encrypt two messages with the same key stream. To avoid this, OFB introduces an extra data item, the *initialization vector* or IV. This is essentially a nonce; we want it to be different from one plaintext message to another and we don't want it to be selected by a potential attacker. If we use the same key and IV for two different messages, we generate the same key stream.

When we use IVs, the ciphertext is always larger than the plaintext. Most applications can accommodate the larger ciphertext, though there are a few cases where the plaintext must match the size of the ciphertext. In those cases, we must use a mode that does not require a separate IV.

Ciphertext Errors

In Section 9.2, we explained how ciphertext errors affect block encryption. Errors behave differently when we use a mode. In OFB, the actual encryption and decryption use xor, so errors behave the same as in other stream ciphers. Mistaken ciphertext bits only affect corresponding plaintext bits. We do not recover the plaintext by running it through the block cipher. We see the same effects if we rearrange ciphertext data; every changed bit will decrypt incorrectly, but the rearrangement affects no other bits.

OFB in Practice

IVs aren't exclusive to OFB; they are used in most modes. When we save the encrypted ciphertext, we must save the IV with it (Figure 9.8). Look at how we generate the key stream; we can't reproduce the same key stream unless we keep the IV. We don't encrypt

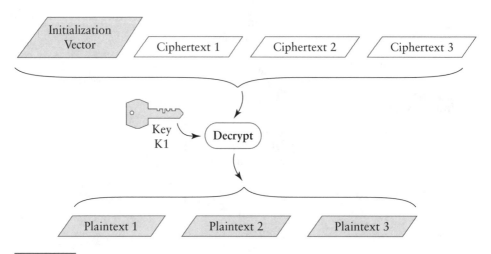

Figure 9.8

Include the IV with the ciphertext when required.

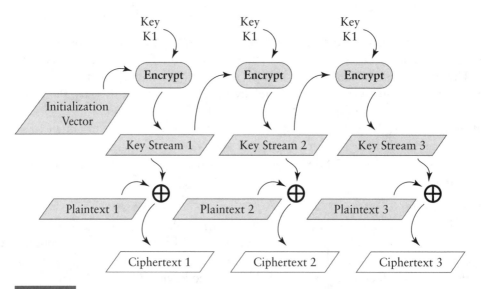

Figure 9.9

Mode encryption diagram: Encrypting with OFB.

the IV; we treat it like a nonce and store it in plaintext form with the corresponding ciphertext.

Figure 9.9 shows OFB encrypting a series of data blocks: Plaintext 1, 2, and 3. We encrypt the initialization vector to produce the first block of key stream bits

(Key Stream 1). We xor those bits with the first block of plaintext, then we use the block cipher on Key Stream 1 to generate the next block of key stream bits. We next apply xor to encrypt the next block of plaintext.

The process repeats until we have encrypted the entire ciphertext. Because we need the initialization vector to decrypt the ciphertext, we must include it with the ciphertext. To decrypt, we apply the same operations, except that we swap the plaintext with the ciphertext.

Note that Figures 9.7 and 9.9 use different ways to illustrate the same cipher mode. The first figure, Figure 9.7, is a *key stream diagram*; it shows how the process generates a key stream. The second figure, Figure 9.9, is a *mode encryption diagram*; it shows how successive blocks of plaintext and ciphertext interact to implement the mode. This second approach most often is used to illustrate modes. Not all modes generate a key stream independent of the message's plaintext and ciphertext, so we can't use the first style to portray every mode.

Weaknesses

OFB is a very simple mode and we encounter security problems if we choose the IV poorly. If, by some chance, an IV appears as the output of the block cipher, then we produce a duplicated key stream.

For example, imagine that we use the value 123456 as our IV. Later, using the same key, we use a different IV in a second message. By coincidence, the second message's key stream generates 123456 as one of its values. Look at what happens when we feed it back to the cipher: From that point on in the message, we use the same key stream as was used in the first message. Fortunately, this is unlikely to happen if the cipher's block size is very large and we often change encryption keys.

COUNTER MODE

Counter (CTR) mode, like OFB, generates a key stream and applies xor to implement a stream cipher (Figure 9.10). Instead of using feedback, the counter mode encrypts successive values of a counter. This eliminates the OFB risk of an accidentally repeated IV and key stream. To avoid this, we *never* encrypt the same counter value with the same key. The initialization vector tells us where to start the counter.

In practice, we can construct the counter in either of two ways. First, we can simply keep a running counter for every block we encrypt with a particular encryption key. We could start at a random value like 12345 and increment the value for each block we encrypt. If we encrypt 100 blocks, the counter will be 12444 when we encrypt the final block. We then use 12445 when we encrypt the 101st block.

For a different approach, we form the counter in two parts. A nonrepeating nonce provides the upper part. We increment the lower part. We may use either approach as long as we can guarantee not to reuse a counter value before we change to a different encryption key.

Because CTR is essentially a key stream generator that encrypts like a conventional stream cipher, it has the same ciphertext error properties as OFB mode.

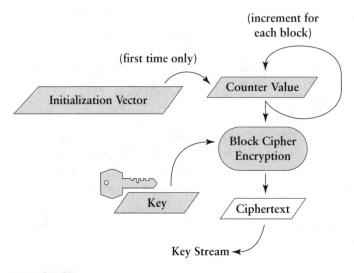

Figure 9.10

Key stream with CTR—the counter mode.

9.3.2 Cipher Feedback Mode

The *cipher feedback* (CFB) mode, shown in Figure 9.11, combines properties of stream ciphers and block ciphers. We generate a key stream one block at a time and combine it

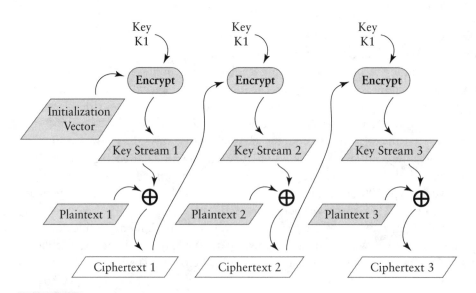

Figure 9.11

Mode encryption diagram for CFB (cipher feedback mode).

with the text using xor. Instead of feeding back the block cipher's output, CFB feeds back the actual ciphertext block. CFB doesn't face the same risk of repeated IVs that we have with OFB. Because each block of encryption depends on both the key stream and the message data, OFB won't repeat the key stream unless we reencrypt exactly the same data with exactly the same IV.

Although we encrypt complete blocks of data to generate the key stream, the plaintext does not have to fit into an integral number of blocks. When we reach the final block, we may encrypt the remaining plaintext and discard any extra key stream bits.

CIPHERTEXT ERRORS

Because CFB feeds the ciphertext through the block cipher to decrypt it, ciphertext errors affect it differently. Remember what happens if we change a *single bit* of a block cipher's input: It affects the entire output block.

Note how CFB ciphertext affects the decrypted plaintext: Each block gets used twice. First, we xor the ciphertext with the key stream. Next, we use the ciphertext as input to the block cipher to produce the next block of key stream.

A single bit error produces two separate changes to the plaintext. First, the corresponding plaintext bit is inverted (as in a stream cipher error). Second, the next block of plaintext is completely scrambled. Thus, we see ***error propagation*** because this single error in the ciphertext damages additional plaintext when we decrypt. The error propagation only affects the following block.

If we rearrange ciphertext blocks encrypted with CFB, we get different results than with a straight block cipher or with a stream cipher. As noted, a misplaced block decrypts incorrectly and causes the block following it to decrypt incorrectly. However, if all subsequent blocks appear in the right order, they will all decrypt correctly. Because of this, CFB is called a "self-synchronizing" cipher; there is a limit to error propagation during decryption, after which the ciphertext decrypts into the correct plaintext. For example, let's switch ciphertext blocks 2 and 3 before decryption and see what happens:

- We retrieve plaintext block 1 correctly from the IV and from ciphertext block 1.
- We generate key stream 2 correctly from ciphertext block 1.
- We incorrectly generate plaintext block 2. We xor key stream 2 with the misplaced ciphertext block 3. This yields nonsense.
- We incorrectly generate key stream 3. We decrypt the misplaced ciphertext block 3, which actually yields key stream 4. We use it in the place of key stream 3.
- We incorrectly generate plaintext block 3. We xor the misplaced key stream 4 with misplaced ciphertext block 2. This yields nonsense.
- We incorrectly generate key stream 4. We decrypt the misplaced ciphertext block 2, which actually yields key stream 3. We use it in the place of key stream 4.
- We incorrectly generate plaintext block 4. We xor the misplaced key stream 3 with the properly placed ciphertext block 4.
- Output returns to normal with plaintext block 5, because the undamaged ciphertext block 4 generates the correct key stream.

Thus, if we swap two adjacent ciphertext blocks, we see errors in three plaintext blocks when we decrypt. The same is true if we change one or more bits in two adjacent ciphertext blocks. The decryption resynchronizes and yields correct plaintext one block past the last ciphertext error.

9.3.3 Cipher Block Chaining

Last, and certainly not least, is the *cipher block chaining* (CBC) mode (Figure 9.12). CBC is one of the oldest and most widely used cipher modes. Unlike the other modes examined, this one is block oriented. To use this mode, the plaintext must be a multiple of the cipher's block size. If it is shorter, we must add padding.

CBC encryption involves two steps. First, we scramble the plaintext by combining each plaintext block with the previous ciphertext block. As shown in the figure, we use xor to combine the plaintext and ciphertext. We combine the first plaintext block, which has no previous ciphertext, with the IV. The second step is block encryption. Its output provides the ciphertext block. We also use this ciphertext block when we encrypt the next plaintext block.

Figure 9.13 illustrates CBC decryption using a *mode decryption diagram*. We start by decrypting the first ciphertext block. Unlike other modes, we actually use the block cipher's decryption procedure to decrypt the ciphertext. We combine the result with the IV to recover the first plaintext block. For subsequent blocks, we first decrypt the ciphertext block, and then we xor the result with the previous ciphertext block.

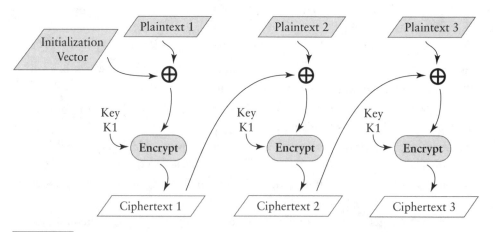

Figure 9.12

Mode encryption diagram for CBC (cipher block chaining).

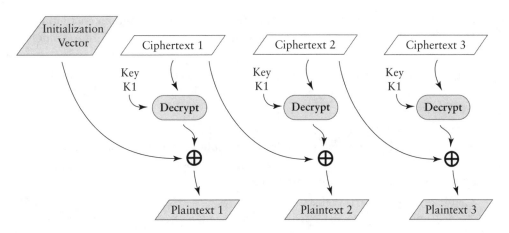

Figure 9.13
Mode decryption diagram for CBC.

Like CFB mode, we use each ciphertext block twice when decrypting. Unlike CFB, both the plaintext and the ciphertext must fit into an integral number of blocks.

Ciphertext Errors
CBC has similar error propagation and self-synchronizing properties to CFB. A single bit error in a ciphertext block will affect both the current block and the next block. Subsequent error-free blocks will decrypt correctly. If we rearrange ciphertext blocks, we lose the corresponding plaintext block contents, plus one block following the ones that moved.

9.4 Encrypting a Volume

The risk and policy discussions in Section 9.1 argue strongly for encrypting storage volumes of all shapes and sizes, but volume encryption also poses some challenges. If a cryptanalyst steals an encrypted drive, there will be gigabytes of ciphertext with which to work. The attacker will be able to guess some of the corresponding plaintext because disk formats are public knowledge. In addition, the attacker can be certain that a great deal of duplicate data resides on the drive, simply because that's what happens on a modern hard drive. If the encrypted drive is a system drive, the attacker might be able to make astute guesses about the drive's contents and make undetectable changes to it.

These risks lead to the following objectives for FDE implementations:

- **Strong encryption**: Use a strong, modern block cipher that can reliably encrypt trillions of bytes of data and more.

- **Large encryption key:** Strong modern ciphers require large, random encryption keys. The ciphers don't provide their strongest security except with fully random keys.
- **High speed:** In practice, this means that we want to encrypt all of the drive's data with the same key. If we switch between keys while encrypting the drive, then we'll have delays awaiting key expansion.
- **Suppress any data patterns:** Use a block cipher mode that mixes data during encryption so that plaintext patterns aren't duplicated in the ciphertext. More-over, it should be impractical for an attacker to choose plaintext data that creates a recognizable pattern in the stored ciphertext.
- **Plaintext size = ciphertext size:** Modern file systems assume they have full access to the disk. We can't steal space from the file system to store IVs, for example.
- **Integrity protection:** This is not the primary concern, but at least it should be hard to make undetectable changes.

In addition, the FDE implementation must handle the crypto keys safely and efficiently. If we have permission to use the encrypted drive, we should be able to supply the keys and mount the drive. When we dismount the drive, the keys should disappear. In hardware implementations, this is tied to the drive hardware status: The drive is "locked" when it is powered off or reset and "unlocked" when its keys are in place and it is mounted for use. We discuss this further as we examine key management and drive hardware issues.

Choosing a Cipher Mode

In order to avoid patterns in the drive's ciphertext, we need to encrypt data differently according to *where* it resides on the hard drive. Conventional cipher modes eliminate patterns by using IVs and chaining. We don't really have a place to store IVs, so we incorporate location information into the encryption instead.

One solution is called a ***tweakable cipher***. A normal cipher takes two inputs: the key and the plaintext, and yields the ciphertext. A tweakable cipher has a third input, the *tweak*, a nonce-like value that modifies the encryption without the cost of changing the encryption key.

In drive encryption, the tweak identifies the disk sector and selects a block within the sector. In practice, we don't really have to design a new block cipher. Instead, we use a block cipher mode to tweak the cipher for us.

Here are two general approaches:

1. Adapt a classic cipher mode. In Section 9.4.2, we adapt CTR and CBC modes to drive encryption.
2. Develop a special, tweakable mode for drive encryption. In Section 9.4.3, we look at the XTS mode, which eliminates shortcomings of CTR and CBC.

HARDWARE VERSUS SOFTWARE

Modern FDE techniques are based in either hardware or software. Hardware-based systems may be built into the hard drive's controller or they may exist as add-on circuits. Software-based systems often operate as a device driver. Both hardware- and software-based techniques share these four properties:

1. Both appear "below" the file system, either at or below the device driver.
2. Both are typically unlocked with a typed passphrase.
3. Both often store their working keys as wrapped keys and use a passphrase to produce the KEK.
4. Both can encrypt the system volume. In both cases, there needs to be special software, or BIOS firmware, that collects the passphrase to unlock the drive.

We discuss hardware-based FDE in Section 9.5. We discuss software-based FDE next.

9.4.1 Volume Encryption in Software

When we look beyond the similarities between hardware and software-based FDE, we find important differences. Because software products reside within the operating system, they have both additional features and additional weaknesses. Here is a listing of some of the better-known FDE software implementations:

- Apple's Macintosh OS-X—can create encrypted drives and "virtual disks" through its Disk Utility.
- Microsoft BitLocker—an optional feature of certain higher-end versions of Microsoft Windows.
- PGPDisk—a commercial package from the company that sells PGP email encryption software. The program uses the same public-key certificates to wrap disk keys that it uses to wrap email encryption keys.
- TrueCrypt—a highly regarded open-source FDE package.

Figure 9.14 illustrates how the software FDE product fits into an input/output operation. This is a variant of Figure 5.18. In this example, we store the actual data on a hard drive partition. The file system treats the FDE package like another type of hardware. When the file system writes data to the FDE, the FDE software encrypts the data, then it passes the ciphertext to the actual hard disk driver. When the file system reads data, it sends the request to the FDE driver. The driver retrieves the corresponding cluster from the hard drive, decrypts it, and passes it back to the file system.

In addition to the driver, the FDE software includes other utility functions. There is typically an application to mount and dismount encrypted drives. This software requests the passphrase and then uses it to unwrap the drive's encryption keys (Figure 9.15). If the FDE software can encrypt the system volume, there is also an installation program and a loader for bootstrapping the encrypted system volume. In better implementations, the installation program encrypts the system volume while

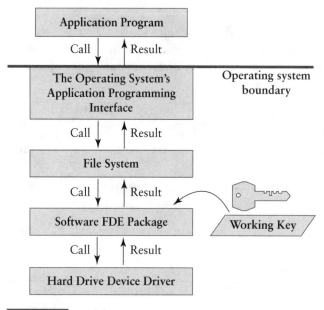

Figure 9.14

Full disk encryption in software.

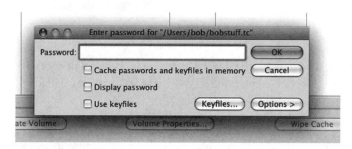

Figure 9.15

Password prompt to mount an encrypted volume.

the system is running, and then updates the bootstrap sectors to boot from the encrypted system volume.

FILES AS ENCRYPTED VOLUMES

A modern file system treats a physical device—or a partition on that device—as a collection of numbered clusters. The inside of a file is also a collection of numbered clusters. If we can make access to the file look like access to a partition, then we can store a file system *inside* a file.

We then can encrypt the file system inside the file using FDE. We call this a *file-hosted volume* as compared to a *device-hosted volume*. If we store the volume on an entire hard drive or a drive partition, it is device hosted. If we store the volume on a file within our file system, then it is file hosted.

Many FDE packages, including TrueCrypt, PGP, and OS-X, support both device-hosted and file-hosted volumes. Such packages have a utility program that opens the file, and the encrypting driver redirects disk accesses to the file. This is called a *loop device*; the system must "loop" through the file system twice to read a file stored on a file-hosted volume.

Bob has created a file-hosted TrueCrypt volume. He started up the "mount" utility, which prompts him for a password, as shown in Figure 9.15. Once Bob types the password, TrueCrypt opens the file, attaches it to its encrypting driver, and directs all accesses to the file. Encrypted drives often are treated as removable drives and formatted with FAT, but most systems allow the owner to apply a different file format.

9.4.2 Adapting an Existing Mode

Existing cipher modes need a third input: an IV or a counter value. To write the data, we need to generate the value and pass it to the encryption mode. To read the data, we need to regenerate the same value and use it again for decryption.

Because we read and write hard drives on a per-sector basis, we process the block modes on the same basis. Thus, we can derive IVs or counters from the sector's address on the hard drive.

DRIVE ENCRYPTION WITH COUNTER MODE

Counter mode produces a key stream by encrypting successive values of a counter. We then encrypt or decrypt by using xor with the key stream. To avoid ciphertext patterns, we must produce a unique counter value for every 128 bits of data on the hard drive. We assume each sector contains 512 bytes, so we have 32 separately encrypted blocks of data in every sector.

This yields a tweakable cipher mode. If we encrypt the same data to store on the same 128-bit block in a particular sector of the drive, we always produce the same ciphertext. This makes writing much more efficient. To achieve this, the mode establishes a separate tweak value for every 128-bit block of encrypted data on the drive. In Counter mode, the tweak value is the counter.

Constructing the Counter

The counter value must be unique for every 128-bit block on the device. To do this, the counter incorporates the sector number and the block's index number within the sector. We construct the counter in three parts:

1. The counter's low-order digits select a single block within the sector. There are 32 blocks of 128 bits each in a standard sector containing 512 bytes. We assign the five lowest bits in the counter to select a block within the sector.
2. The middle digits in the counter select the sector on the hard drive.
3. The remaining high-order digits in the counter will contain a nonce that remains constant for all sectors on the hard drive.

Let's plan ahead: Assume that the arrangement needs to work with hard drives that contain up to an exabyte of storage.

- 1 exabyte = 1 quintillion bytes = 10^{18}
- 1 exabyte's approximate size in binary = 2^{60}
- Number of 512-byte sectors = $2^{60} / 512 = 2^{60} / 2^9 = 2^{51}$

To produce unique counter values for every sector on a 1-exabyte hard drive, we need a 51-bit counter. To uniquely count each AES block on a sector requires another 5 bits. We use a nonce to set the other 72 bits in the 128-bit counter value. The counter value yields the 128-bit block that we encrypt (Figure 9.16).

We never actually increment a counter value when we encrypt a sector on the hard drive. Instead, we calculate the counter value based on the sector's numerical address and the index of the block within the sector.

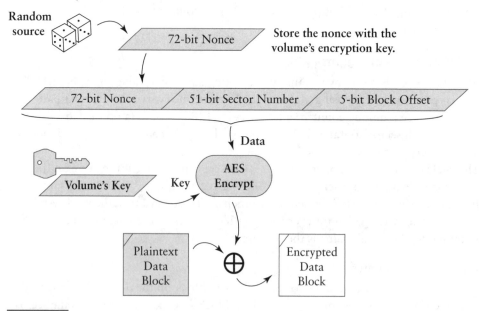

Encrypting disk data with AES and Counter mode.

We insert the nonce in the high-order bits in the counter. We encrypt this assembly of bits to get the 128 bits of key stream. We xor the key stream to encrypt or decrypt the corresponding data.

An Integrity Risk

A major problem with Counter mode is that it relies on a simple xor operation. An attacker can use a bit-flipping attack to replace known data on the drive.

For example, Kevin knows that a certain computer system stores the bootable operating system in a particular place. Because it's easiest to administer systems if they're all alike, Kevin knows the *exact* data contents of the bootable operating system. Thus, he can extract the encrypted data and use a plaintext copy of the system to isolate the key stream. Then he simply reencrypts a modified version of the operating system using that same key stream and returns the system to its owner. When the owner reboots, the computer decrypts and runs the modified operating system.

In practice, hard drive encryption can't protect 100 percent against integrity attacks. However, this sort of attack is so simple to implement that it is worth preventing.

DRIVE ENCRYPTION WITH CBC MODE

CBC does not produce a tweakable mode. We can't encrypt or decrypt individual blocks on a sector with CBC as we can with a tweakable mode. Moreover, the same plaintext will yield different ciphertext even when saved in the same place on the drive, because the ciphertext depends on adjacent ("chained") data during encryption.

However, CBC provides a well-understood cryptographic mechanism. We encrypt a sector at a time and use the sector number as the IV. A prototype hard drive encryptor built for the U.S. government in the early 1990s used this approach with a variant of the CFB mode.

Our first challenge is to ensure unique IVs across the entire volume. One encryption product cut corners and used only 16 bits of the sector number to distinguish the IV. This produced identical IVs for disk sectors that were exactly 65,536 sectors apart.

However, trouble emerges even if we use the entire, unique block number for the IV. The problem is subtle and, in some applications, relatively minor: An attacker can "leak" information through the ciphertext. Specifically, an attacker can construct data that combines with the IV during encryption in a way that stores predictable ciphertext values on different sectors of the drive. Although this might not lead to immediate trouble in many environments, it indicates an unnecessary weakness. We eliminate it by making the IV hard to predict.

Linux-based drive encryption software developed a technique to address this. The solution encrypts the sector number with "salt" to construct the IV, yielding the acronym "ESSIV." In this case, the "salt" is a hashed copy of the volume key (Figure 9.17). In the diagram, CBC encryption has three inputs: the data, the key, and the IV.

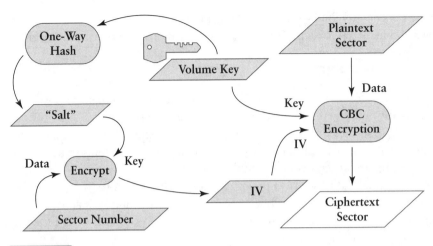

Figure 9.17

Sector encryption with CBC and ESSIV.

Integrity Issues with CBC Encryption

Section 9.3.3 described the error propagation properties of CBC in general terms. The matter becomes more interesting if we apply them to rearranging data on disk sectors.

When CBC encounters an error while decrypting, the error affects the encrypted block containing the error and the following block. After that, decryption continues without error. If we rearrange blocks on a disk sector, there will be garbage in the blocks at the point of rearrangement and the rest will decrypt normally.

This does not pose as large a risk as the bit-flipping attack on CTR mode. An attacker can modify CTR-encrypted data cleanly without leaving telltale blocks of garbage. Moreover, hard drive behavior makes it impractical to prevent all possible integrity attacks.

9.4.3 A "Tweakable" Encryption Mode

The XTS cipher mode evolved from work on tweakable cipher modes over several years. The acronym actually is derived from three other acronyms. This mode was based on an earlier mode called "Xor-Encrypt-Xor" implemented as a "Tweaked Codebook Mode" with "Ciphertext Stealing."

Although XTS may work in a broad range of applications, we focus here on disk encryption using the AES algorithm. XTS handles its tweak input in two parts: One part selects a large chunk of data, like a sector, and the other part selects a single block for encryption by the block cipher. In our case, blocks within a sector are 128 bits each to work with AES. Figure 9.18 shows an encryption operation for a selected 128-bit block within a numbered disk sector.

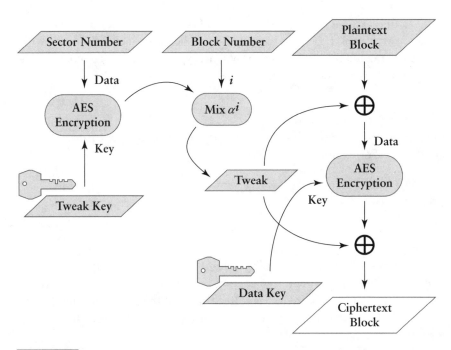

XTS mode to encrypt data on a disk sector.

There are essentially two parts to the XTS mode: generating the tweak and doing the encryption or decryption. We use two keys, one for each part. We generate the tweak the same way for encryption and decryption, as shown in the upper left of the diagram. We encrypt the sector number and then we combine it with the block number to construct the tweak. To perform the encryption, we xor the tweak with the plaintext, encrypt it, and xor the tweak with the ciphertext. We reverse that process to decrypt.

The "mix" operation shown in the figure is a modular multiplication of the encrypted sector number by α^i, where i is the block within the sector. The value α was chosen for its mathematical properties, so that the resulting mix is effective but only requires a small number of adds, shifts, and loops.

The phrase "Ciphertext Stealing" refers to the strategy for handling partial AES data blocks. If individual sectors do not end on a 128-bit boundary, then the mode takes special steps to encrypt or decrypt the partial block at the end of the sector. Those steps combine ciphertext from the previous block with the partial block. Here we only look at the case where we encrypt or decrypt full AES blocks. Partial blocks are rarely a problem because sectors are 512 bytes or a multiple of that size.

IEEE Standard 1619-2007 specifies the details of the XTS mode, and NIST published a recommendation for its use (NIST SP 800-37E). There is no requirement to use the XTS mode as opposed to the others, but it poses a stronger challenge to attackers.

Although it is hard to rearrange blocks successfully in CTR mode, attackers can easily mount a bit-flipping attack on it. Even though it isn't practical to attack CBC mode with bit-flipping, some rearranged blocks on a sector will decrypt correctly. XTS mode resists both bit-flipping and block rearrangement.

9.4.4 Residual Risks

Volume encryption can provide strong protection but, like all security measures, includes residual risks. For example:

- Untrustworthy encryption
- Encryption integrity
- Leaking the plaintext
- Data integrity

We address the first one by picking a quality volume encryption product. We can address the second by using hardware-based encryption (Section 9.5); otherwise, we depend on the security of our operating system. Regardless of the encryption implementation, the third risk relies on the security of our operating system. The fourth requires additional security measures.

Additional risks arise as we examine key management issues. Those are addressed in Section 9.6.

UNTRUSTWORTHY ENCRYPTION

This problem arises if the encryption implementation is faulty. The encryption might use a weak algorithm or apply the algorithm in a way that weakens its protection.

Early commercial volume encryption often used DES encryption. These drives appeared around the turn of the millennium. Ironically, this was shortly after researchers demonstrated the DES Cracker. Although a few volume encryptors used Triple DES, those that relied on 56-bit keys provided relatively weak encryption.

The evolution of AES produced a whole suite of strong block ciphers: the AES finalists and AES itself. These ciphers appear in many modern products. Even though these ciphers are strong, they require an appropriate encryption mode to suppress patterns in the ciphertext.

We reduce the risk of untrustworthy encryption by using certified products. In the United States, the recognized certification is under the latest FIPS 140 standard (FIPS 140-2 is the version as of 2011). Government agencies and most financial institutions are required to use FIPS 140 certified products. Many other countries recognize FIPS 140 certification, and some have implemented their own version of the certification. Note, however, that FIPS 140 only applies to U.S. government standard algorithms, including AES, and not to the AES finalists.

ENCRYPTION INTEGRITY

Even if the product implements a quality algorithm with an appropriate mode, an attacker might be able to weaken, disable, or bypass the encryption. Thus, the stored data is either weakly encrypted or not encrypted at all.

This is a particular risk for software-based encryption. We must install the software correctly and then rely on the operating system to protect its integrity.

Hardware-based products, described in Section 9.5, are far less vulnerable to these types of attacks. To disable or bypass the encryption, attackers would need to attack the driver controller circuitry. This poses a serious challenge for most attackers.

LOOKING FOR PLAINTEXT

Robert H. Morris (1932–2011), an NSA chief scientist, liked to repeat a popular saying among his colleagues: "Rule 1 for cryptanalysis: Check for plaintext." In other words, the smart attacker doesn't start by trying to crack the encryption. The attacker first looks for an opportunity to retrieve the data *before* encryption or *after* decryption. File encryption yields a number of opportunities to look for plaintext if the attacker shares a computer with the target. This is true especially when using full-disk encryption.

When we use full-disk encryption, everyone on the computer sees the drive's contents as plaintext. This is a case of Transitive Trust: When we rely exclusively on full-disk encryption, we implicitly trust everyone who shares the computer.

DATA INTEGRITY

We examined three different modes for encrypting data at the volume level. By including tweaks in volume encryption, we make it impractical to rearrange sectors on the volume. Even though we use the same key to encrypt and decrypt all sectors, the tweaks make the encryption specific to individual sectors.

Within an encrypted sector, the different modes face different integrity problems. CTR mode suffers the worst because we can apply the bit-flipping attack to it. If we know the plaintext contents of a sector, we can change those contents to anything else by flipping the appropriate ciphertext bits. In CBC mode, we can rearrange blocks in a sector, and most blocks will decrypt correctly.

Even though XTS mode doesn't allow us to arrange data within a block, it shares an integrity problem with the other two modes. An attacker always can rewrite the data on a sector with an *older* copy of that sector.

For example, we might make a complete copy of an encrypted volume. Later, we examine the volume to see which sectors have changed. We can rewrite any of those changed sectors with their earlier contents. The earlier contents will decrypt correctly, because they were encrypted with the same key and tweak.

This attack in which we rewrite a sector with older data will work successfully against all three disk encryption modes. It poses a real security challenge. Fortunately, this is not a major risk and not the risk for which we encrypt our drives.

9.5 Encryption in Hardware

If we want to protect our files with encryption and we want the encryption built in, it makes sense to incorporate it into the drive hardware. We call such a device a *self-encrypting drive* (Figure 9.19).

We want the encrypted drive to work with our computer exactly as if it were a normal, nonencrypted drive, with one exception: We want our data protected if the drive is unattended or stolen. In practice, we do this by erasing the encryption key when the drive is unplugged or reset. This "locks" the data on the drive. When we plug in the drive or power it on, we must provide the encryption key to "unlock" the drive.

The locking mechanism is tied to the fundamental problem of all crypto security: How do we manage the keys? If we have a relatively bulky drive, we could store the key on a removable flash memory, either on a card or plugged into a separate USB port. If we encrypt a smaller device, like a USB flash drive, then we need a different strategy for handling the keys. We examine different key management approaches in Section 9.6.

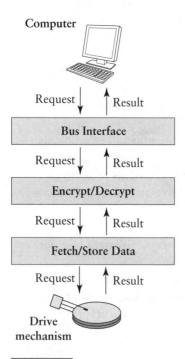

Figure 9.19

Internal functions of a self-encrypting drive.

RECYCLING THE DRIVE

Drive encryption makes it very easy to recycle the drive. The owner directs the controller to purge itself of every copy of the current encryption key and of the associated nonces and IVs. Once finished, there is no practical way to decrypt any data on the hard drive. The drive may still be used, but the owner must produce a new encryption key and reformat the drive's file system.

9.5.1 The Drive Controller

To add encryption to the hard drive, we make no changes to the physical hard drive mechanism. All changes are made to the hard drive controller. Section 5.3.1 described the operation of a typical hard drive controller circuit. A self-encrypting drive shares many of the same features and introduces three changes:

1. Algorithms to encrypt and decrypt the stored data, described earlier.
2. Mechanisms to manage "locking" and "unlocking" the drive, described in Section 9.5.2.
3. Mechanisms to handle the encryption key, described in Section 9.6.

Figure 9.20 shows the hardware block diagram of a self-encrypting drive controller. This is a revision of Figure 5.4, which shows the controller for a nonencrypting drive. The connections between the different components pass commands (marked "C"), data (marked "D"), or keys (marked "K").

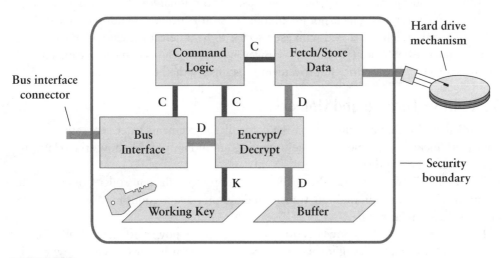

Figure 9.20

Block diagram of a self-encrypting drive controller.

SECURITY BOUNDARY

The security boundary indicates the area within which the drive performs its security activities. As long as attackers don't disturb anything inside that boundary, the controller protects the data on the drive.

Actions outside the boundary should not affect the security of the drive. The drive should reject invalid commands or requests to decrypt data when the drive is locked. If the attacker tries to bypass the controller and read data directly from the drive mechanism, the attacker will only retrieve unreadable, encrypted data. The attacker should not be able to trick the drive into decrypting data by modifying data stored on the drive mechanism.

DRIVE FORMATTING

Drive encryption usually does not affect a hard drive's low-level formatting. The sector headers can remain in plaintext. The sector checksum is calculated on the ciphertext as it is stored on the drive.

High-level formatting places the file system on the drive. Whenever the drive discards a previous encryption key and starts using a new one, all previous data becomes unreadable. The owner then must reformat the file system and start over with an empty drive.

When we change keys and reformat the file system, we don't need to rewrite the drive's sectors with new ciphertext encrypted with the new key. When we reformat the file system, it marks unused sectors as being "free." The operating system then assumes that all such sectors contain garbage. The indecipherable ciphertext in the free sectors is rewritten as the sectors are allocated to new files.

Although most commercial products will use conventional low-level formatting, a drive manufacturer could incorporate a modified sector format to improve security. Additional data might be stored with each sector to help detect the case where an attacker rewrites older sector contents. However, such measures come at the expense of storage capacity. The security improvement must justify the loss of capacity.

9.5.2 Drive Locking and Unlocking

To implement locking and unlocking, the controller implements three separate states: power off, locked, and unlocked. The state diagram in Figure 9.21 shows the relationship between these states.

The arrows between states indicate the events that move the controller from one state to another. The arrows in the state transition diagram must account for every event that may take place in any state.

Initially, the controller's power is off, so it starts in the power-off state. While the power is off, the controller ignores everything until it receives power. When power arrives, the controller starts running and enters the locked state. The controller enters the unlocked state only when the key is made available to the controller. While unlocked, either a reset signal or a loss of power will lock the drive effectively. We keep the drive's data secure by only supplying the key when conditions are right. Section 9.6 discusses strategies for controlling the encryption key.

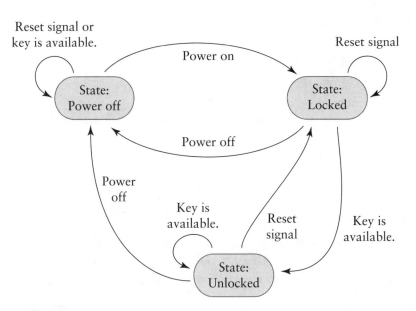

Encrypting Volumes

Figure 9.21

Self-encrypting drive controller's state diagram.

Once the controller has unlocked the drive, the computer can read data from the drive. Here is an overview of the process of reading encrypted data from the hard drive. We start with the computer telling the hard drive controller to read data from a sector.

- The interface logic receives the command over the bus. It extracts the details of the command and passes them to the command logic. The command logic sees that it is a "read" operation and that it requests a particular sector.
- The command logic directs the read/write logic to move the heads to a particular track.
- The command logic tells the crypto logic to prepare to read data from a particular sector.
- The crypto logic sets up the encryption to read that sector. As the data arrives from the disk head, the logic decrypts the data and stores it in the buffer.
- As data becomes available in the buffer, the crypto logic feeds it back to the interface logic, which packages the data and delivers it back to the computer.

9.6 Managing Encryption Keys

Encryption keys pose a challenge in any crypto product. This section reviews the following topics:

- Key generation

- Rekeying
- Key storage, in Section 9.6.1.
- Booting an encrypted drive, in Section 9.6.2
- Residual key management risks, in Section 9.6.3.

Now we examine the issues of key generation and rekeying in drive encryption. The challenges and solutions are similar in software and hardware implementations, so we examine both together.

KEY GENERATION

We have many options for storing and handling keys, but it is best to generate the crypto keys automatically, using a true random number generator. Even though it is challenging to generate truly random numbers inside a typical CPU, software designers have found ways to do this by measuring unpredictable activities inside the operating system. Some software products, like TrueCrypt, prompt the user to perform some "random" actions. The software monitors those actions and generates the keying material from them.

Self-encrypting drives may use custom electronic circuits to generate keys. The designers can construct circuits that generate high-quality, truly random numbers. Such circuits often measure noise from a circuit with unpredictable noise patterns. The same circuits also can generate nonces or IVs to use with block cipher modes.

REKEYING

In Section 8.1.1, we talk about the need to change encryption keys occasionally. By their very nature, encrypted hard drives provide a vast amount of ciphertext encrypted with a single key. NIST recommendations suggest to rekey hard drives at least every 2 years. In some environments, this may correspond with the drive's useful life span. Thus, we might simply coordinate rekeying with drive replacement.

True rekeying poses a challenge on a hard drive because it would take an extremely long time. The controller would have to read each sector on the drive, decrypt it, reencrypt it with the new key, and write it back. Although it might be possible to use the drive during rekeying, it would require very careful implementation by the software designer or drive manufacturer.

Drive vendors rarely provide a rekeying feature. Instead, the owner can change keys by copying the drive to a different self-encrypting drive. The new drive will generate a new key when we start it up. Once we have copied the data onto the new drive, we can rekey the old drive and reuse it, which eliminates the old key. Some systems use "RAID" techniques to provide redundancy (see Section 13.5) and, in many cases, the administrator may simply swap a new, blank drive for the old one and let the RAID system reconstruct the removed drive.

9.6.1 Key Storage

Drive encryption systems manage two types of key storage: ***working key storage*** and ***persistent key storage***. The working key storage provides the key for the encryption algorithm. In a software implementation, we try to keep this block of RAM in storage at all times. We *never* want the operating system to "swap" this RAM to temporary storage, especially on an unencrypted hard drive. The TrueCrypt software package includes detailed instructions on how to protect working key storage.

Working Key Storage in Hardware

Matters are somewhat simpler for hardware-based drive encryption. Figure 9.20 shows the storage area for the working key inside the drive's security boundary. The working key resides in *volatile* storage. It is automatically erased whenever the drive is reset or shut down.

The persistent key storage provides *nonvolatile* memory to preserve a protected copy of the drive key even when power is turned off. When we mount a drive or unlock it, the key is retrieved from persistent key storage and moved to working key storage. When we are finished with the drive, the working key is erased.

The working key storage is inside the drive's security boundary. The storage area should be protected from access while the drive is unlocked. This may involve ***anti-tamper*** features. For example, the controller may be encapsulated in plastic to prevent an attacker from probing its electronics while it operates. The controller may even include circuits to detect if coverings are removed that otherwise protect the working key storage from tampering. DVD players have used similar encapsulation techniques to protect their internal keys.

PERSISTENT KEY STORAGE

A truly secure encryption key can't possibly be memorized. At best, we might encode a key from a long, memorized phrase, but that's not practical as a general rule. Practical drive encryption requires a strategy for storing the drive keys safely and conveniently. Here are three common strategies:

1. Storing the key in "protected storage"
2. Wrapping the key using a passphrase
3. Storing the key in a file or removable storage device

All three are used in some form in some products. The first approach seems riskiest, because it is hard to protect a block of storage. The second approach is similar to authentication using "something you know." The third approach is similar to authentication using "something you have."

Protected Storage

This approach usually is restricted to hardware products, because it is difficult to enforce storage protection in a pure software product. The product stores the keys in persistent storage inside the drive's security boundary. Upon receipt of an established "unlock code," the drive retrieves the keys from protected storage and provides them to the encryption subsystem. When properly implemented, this approach should provide adequate security. Unfortunately, it is not always implemented reliably.

In late 2009, researchers at SySS, a German security firm, found that several self-encrypting USB drives relied on a predefined, unvarying unlock code. The unlocking process relied on AES encryption to transform the user's password into the unlock code. However, the transformation process always yielded the same unlock code, *regardless of the original password*. Thus, an attacker simply had to know the standard unlock code in order to access *any* USB drive of that design. The details are discussed further in Section 9.6.3.

Key Wrapping

Key wrapping provides a simple, general-purpose approach for storing and protecting persistent key storage. We introduced key wrapping in Section 8.2.2. We can use a passphrase to generate a KEK. When the encryption system retrieves the wrapped key, it uses the KEK to decrypt (unwrap) the drive's encryption key. The encryption system stores the unwrapped key in the working key storage.

If we allow two or more different people to use the drive, we can generate separately wrapped drive keys for each user. The drive protects each set of wrapped keys with its own passphrase. This allows us to grant or revoke access to additional users without having to change the passphrases of other users. Not all products allow this, but it provides us with a safe way of extending access to the drive.

Wrapped keys provide an important security benefit: The encryption key is never unwrapped except when the drive actually is using it. This serves a useful purpose even in hardware-based encryption. If the unwrapped key resides in persistent memory, an attacker with strong electronics experience might be able to read the key. A sophisticated attacker won't need the controller to read the drive data. Instead, the attacker can extract the encrypted data and decrypt it elsewhere.

Wrapped keys provide an interesting balance of risks and benefits. Because we use passphrases, we can select a memorable phrase that we never need to write down. We still face the risk of losing our credentials: If we lose or otherwise forget the passphrase, we can't unwrap the keys and unlock the drive. However, we also may have the option of creating extra passphrases, including one we write down and store in a strongly protected location, like a safe or lock box.

Managing Removable Keys

If the drive uses removable storage for persistent key storage, then the drive can monitor the presence of the removable key. When the key appears, the drive becomes available; when the removable key disappears, the drive locks itself. Otherwise, the drive behaves exactly like a normal, nonencrypting volume.

Removable keys are less common in software-based volume encryption products. TrueCrypt supports "keyfiles," which contain additional entropy used to construct the working encryption key. The keyfile must be present to mount its associated volume.

It seems rare to see removable keys in the current generation of self-encrypting drives. It was common in older designs. Today, a drive would probably store external keys on a commercial flash memory. The drive may have a socket for a flash memory card or a USB socket for a USB drive.

The owner controls and protects the drive by carefully handling the key. If Alice has such a drive in her laptop, she would have to insert the flash memory containing the key before she could boot the hard drive. Whenever Alice leaves her laptop unattended, she needs to remove the flash memory. She then must either take the flash memory with her or store it in a safe place. An attacker who finds the flash memory can boot her laptop.

Alice faces two problems with this flash memory. First, there is the risk of losing it. If she loses the flash memory and she has no copies of her hard drive's key, she loses the contents of her hard drive. There is no practical way to read the encrypted hard drive once its key is lost.

Alice can make backup copies of her encryption key to avoid the risk of loss. However, this introduces a second problem. Every copy Alice makes of her drive's key will increase the risk of someone else finding it and making a copy.

9.6.2 Booting an Encrypted Drive

Laptops really need encrypted hard drives; they are the devices most prone to theft. Most owners treat them as very personal objects and store sensitive personal information on them, as well as sensitive company information the owner needs. Laptops have always been targets of theft, both for their intrinsic resale value and for their contents. In the 1990s, laptops stolen at the Reagan National Airport reportedly commanded a premium of two to three times their purchase price in certain criminal circles.

If the encrypted drive uses external keys, booting is simple, as noted earlier. The owner installs the key and the laptop boots normally. Without the key, the drive remains locked.

If the drive uses internal keys, matters are more complicated. When we plug in a removable encrypted drive or file-hosted volume, we run a program to collect a passphrase and mount the drive. We don't have this option when we boot from the encrypted drive; there is no operating system. We need a program that runs during the bootstrap process. This is called *preboot authentication*.

PREBOOT AUTHENTICATION

When the BIOS bootstraps an encrypted drive, it must run a preboot authentication program. There are two strategies for providing preboot authentication:

1. Integrate the program into the BIOS
2. Include the program on a separate, bootable, plaintext partition

The operator might not notice a difference in the boot process between these alternatives. Both run essentially the same preboot authentication program. The principal difference is where the program resides. The BIOS-based program is stored in the BIOS-ROM on the motherboard. The plaintext partition takes up space on the hard drive and boots from there.

BIOS Integration

Vendors who integrate self-encrypting drives into large-volume commercial products probably will integrate the preboot authentication into the BIOS. Modern systems are designed so that vendors can easily customize the BIOS.

Disk-Based Authentication

If the encrypted drive is an "aftermarket" upgrade, either hardware or software, then the BIOS-based software might not be available. For example, TrueCrypt provides a preboot authentication program that resides on the hard drive.

The drive-resident program requires a small plaintext partition on the hard drive, separate from the larger, encrypted partition, shown in Figure 9.22. This plaintext partition contains a bootstrap program. When we boot this hard drive, the BIOS loads the boot program from the plaintext partition. This program collects the volume's passphrase and uses it to decrypt and boot the operating system.

If the encryption is hardware based, then the boot program collects the passphrase and delivers it to the hard drive. The hard drive then unlocks itself and the boot process proceeds from the unlocked hard drive.

The preboot authentication program does not need to restrict itself to passphrases or passwords. If the drive supports more sophisticated authentication (like tokens or biometrics), then the preboot program can provide those credentials instead. The drive controller would need to maintain a database of appropriate base secrets and must have the appropriate software to match the secrets to the credentials.

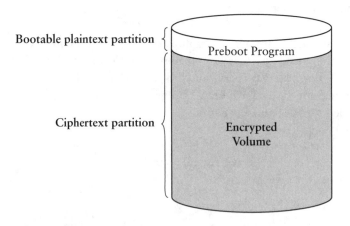

Figure 9.22

Preboot authentication with software encryption.

Automatic Reboot

Computers that serve a lot of people or that perform a vital task really need to be running at all times. If such a computer crashes and restarts, we want it back and running as quickly as possible.

For example, a network server or firewall might suffer a power failure. When power returns, the machine may try to reboot automatically. This is simple if the key resides on a removable flash memory. We simply leave the memory plugged in to the hard drive.

If the drive uses wrapped keys or some other mechanism that requires authentication, we don't want to delay the reboot waiting for preboot authentication. To reboot automatically, the drive must keep a plaintext, unwrapped copy of the drive's encryption key during the crash and restart. The controller then retrieves the key and automatically unlocks the drive.

This option might not protect the hard drive if someone steals it. However, it still provides important protection because we can effectively erase the drive simply by erasing all copies of the encryption keys. It may otherwise be impractical to recycle a modern, large-capacity hard drive.

9.6.3 Residual Risks to Keys

After the volume encryption product implements its protections and we take into account the risks identified earlier, the following four risks remain:

1. Recycled password attack
2. Intercepted passphrase
3. Intercepted keys
4. Built-in master key

Recycled Password Attack

On a self-encrypting hard drive, the wrapped key resides in an inaccessible storage area built into the drive controller. Attackers are unlikely to be able to retrieve those wrapped keys. On software-encrypted volumes, the wrapped key often is stored in the volume's partition or file. An attacker may collect such wrapped keys and try to attack them off-line.

The owner of the encrypted volume can't protect against such an attack by changing the volume's password. A password change simply rewraps the same encryption key with a different password. Instead, the owner must reencrypt the volume with a new key.

Intercepted Passphrase

Passphrase interception risks exist in both software and hardware implementations. Figure 9.23 illustrates the points of risk.

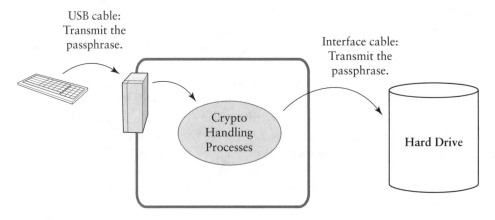

Figure 9.23

Passphrase interception risks.

1. Install a keystroke logger on the USB cable that connects the keyboard to the computer. The attacker could use a logger like those discussed in Section 6.2.2.
2. Sniff the passphrase inside the computer during the volume-mounting process. This may attack preboot authentication software or OS-based drive-mounting software.
3. Eavesdrop on the drive interface cable and intercept a passphrase being sent to a self-encrypting drive.

The first two risks apply to both hardware and software FDE. The third risk only applies to hardware FDE.

INTERCEPTED KEYS

This risk affects hardware and software FDE differently. Most hardware products don't face this risk because the key never leaves the drive. There may be technical attacks that can extract keys from the electronics, but they require a highly motivated threat. The risk is much greater, of course, if the hardware uses removable keys; then we face the risk of an attacker stealing the key or making a copy of it.

The major software FDE risks involve scavenging keys from RAM. These risks manifest themselves in three ways:

1. Eavesdrop on a software encryption process.
2. Scavenge keys from swap files.
3. Scavenge keys from a powered-off RAM: a *cold-boot attack*.

Eavesdrop on the Encryption Process

While the driver encrypts and decrypts data from the volume, it uses the key schedule derived from the secret key. If another process can eavesdrop on the driver, the process can sniff the key schedule and derive the secret key from it.

Sniffing Keys from Swap Files

Most modern operating systems use the hard drive to store blocks of RAM in certain cases. Many systems use "paging files" or "swap files," which store blocks of a process' working RAM if the process is blocked for a period of time. Other systems will write RAM to the hard drive when the system goes into a *hibernate* state, in which the system pauses its operation and allows it to resume later.

If the encryption driver's RAM is written to the hard drive, then the key schedule—and possibly the key itself—also may be written to the hard drive.

Some products provide recommendations on how to avoid such problems. Truecrypt, for example, provides options to disable paging and hibernation.

Cold-Boot Attack

Modern RAMs are not designed to retain their contents after power is turned off. In fact, however, typical RAMs may retain their contents for several minutes, and we can extend retention time by cooling down the RAM chips.

In 2008, researchers at Princeton University demonstrated techniques to retrieve RAM contents after the computer had been powered off. They then extracted drive encryption keys from RAM and used them to decrypt an encrypted drive. This is called a *cold-boot attack*. The attack does not necessarily work against hardware-based systems unless the RAM still contains the drive's passphrase.

It may be difficult to avoid such attacks in all cases. The basic defense is to dismount encrypted drives whenever there is a risk of theft or loss. If the computer is in "sleep" mode with encrypted drives mounted, then the keys also reside in the sleeping RAM. The attacker then can extract the keys from RAM or from saved data on the hard drive.

THE "MASTER KEY" RISK

In late 2009, security researchers discovered that several encrypted USB drive products used an egregiously bad authentication protocol. When the drive enrolled a particular password to authenticate a user or administrator, the drive constructed a special "challenge" value that it subsequently used to authenticate that user.

To authenticate, the drive issued the challenge, and the drive mounting software constructed the response by encrypting the challenge using the user's enrolled passphrase. If the drive received the right response, it unlocked the drive.

The problem was that the right response was *always* the same. The challenge was tailored to the password to yield the required response. Therefore, the drive always sent a specific challenge to verify a specific passphrase and expected a specific response regardless of the chosen passphrase.

An attacker could build a simplified version of the drive-mounting software that omitted the password entirely. When it sent the standard response, the drive would unlock without a password.

9.7 Resources

 IMPORTANT TERMS INTRODUCED

antitamper	key stream diagram	preboot authentication
block cipher	loop device	round
device-hosted volume	mode decryption diagram	S-box
error propagation	mode encryption diagram	self-encrypting drive
file-hosted volume	modes of operation	trade secret
key expansion	patent protection	tweakable cipher
key schedule	persistent key storage	working key storage

ACRONYMS INTRODUCED

ANSI—American National Standards Institute
CBC—Cipher block chaining mode
CFB—Cipher feedback mode
CTR—Counter mode
ECB—Electronic codebook mode
ESSIV—Encrypted sector salt initialization vector
FDE—Full-disk encryption
ITAR—International Traffic in Arms Regulations
IV—Initialization vector
OFB—Output feedback mode
RC2—Rivest's Cipher 2
XTS—Xor-Encrypt-Xor Tweaked Codebook Mode with Ciphertext Stealing

9.7.1 Review Questions

R1. Explain the difference between file encryption and volume encryption.

R2. Explain the fundamental difference between block and stream ciphers.

R3. Describe the steps performed in a typical block cipher.

R4. We encrypt some data with a block cipher. The ciphertext suffers a 1-bit error. How does this affect the plaintext after we decrypt the ciphertext?

R5. Briefly summarize the development of DES and AES.

R6. Does Triple DES yield the same result as single DES if we use a single 56-bit key? Why?

R7. Briefly summarize the history of RC4 and what it tells us about the development of secure encryption algorithms.

R8. Summarize the six qualities of good encryption algorithms.

R9. What is the purpose of block cipher mixing modes?

R10. Describe a simple way to produce a key stream using a block cipher.

R11. Briefly describe the common cipher modes.

R12. Summarize the objectives of a typical FDE implementation.

R13. Explain how software FDE fits into the operating system, relative to other components like the file system and device drivers.

R14. Compare the behavior of CTR, CBC with ESSIV, and XTS modes when encrypting a volume.

R15. Summarize residual risks to information protected by volume encryption. Include key-handling risks.

R16. Summarize the differences between a standard drive controller and a self-encrypting drive controller.

R17. Explain how the boot process takes place when booting a system mounted on an encrypted volume.

9.7.2 Exercises

E1. Search the Internet for the description of a cryptographic algorithm, not including AES, DES, or RC4.

  a. Is it a block or a stream cipher? Provide its "vital statistics," including the supported block sizes and key sizes.

  b. Assess the algorithm in terms of the six recommended properties of an encryption algorithm. For each property, describe how and why the algorithm fulfills—or doesn't fulfill—each property.

E2. Look up the "Feistel structure" and describe how it is related to the structure of block ciphers given in Section 9.2.

E3. For each of the general types of attacks listed in Figure 1.6, describe how volume encryption helps resist that attack. Is there any attack that volume encryption might make more likely to occur?

E4. Tables 3.3 and 3.4 describe the security policy for Bob's tower computer in the suite's common room. Consider the risks

that led to this policy. Does Bob's situation justify volume encryption? Why or why not?

E5. Draw a mode encryption diagram illustrating encryption with CTR mode. Where needed, include a function that increments the counter.

E6. Draw a mode decryption diagram for CFB mode.

E7. We have encrypted a three-block message with CFB mode. A 1-bit error occurred in the second ciphertext block. Draw a mode decryption diagram that shows which plaintext bits are affected by error propagation.

E8. We have encrypted a five-block message with CFB mode. An attacker rearranged blocks 2 and 3. Draw a mode decryption diagram that shows which plaintext bits are affected by error propagation.

E9. We have encrypted a three-block message with CBC mode. A 1-bit error occurred in the second ciphertext block. Draw a mode decryption diagram that shows which plaintext bits are affected by error propagation.

E10. We have encrypted a five-block message with CBC mode. An attacker rearranged blocks 2 and 3. Draw a mode decryption diagram that shows which plaintext bits are affected by error propagation.

E11. Find the detailed technical specifications for a commercial hard drive. The specifications will indicate the drive's size in bytes or sectors and its maximum data transfer speed.

   a. Identify the hard drive by brand and model number. Identify the drive's size in bytes and its maximum data transfer speed.

   b. A simple drive-wiping program will simply write random data over every sector on a hard drive. Given the specifications, calculate how long it would take to wipe all of the data on the drive.

   c. A stronger program that tries to "purge" the data may write a series of three different data patterns to each sector. Calculate how long it would take to purge all of the data on the drive.

   d. Assume that the hard drive is encrypted. How long would it take to "rekey" the data on the drive?

E12. Supertech has produced a 10 exabyte hard drive. To support the larger capacity, they had to change the sector size to 4096 bytes. Design a counter layout like that shown in Figure 9.16 to support Counter mode encryption on this drive.

E13. We want to implement a drive controller that includes persistent key storage to store wrapped keys. The design is based on the controller diagram shown in Figure 9.20.

   a. Redraw Figure 9.20 to include the persistent key storage and any other components required for wrapped keys. Include all data paths necessary to support wrapped keys. Be sure to mark paths to indicate if they carry commands, data, or keys. Clearly indicate the security boundary to show which components reside inside and outside the boundary.

   b. Using the components in your diagram, give a step-by-step description of drive unlocking.

   c. Is the persistent key storage inside or outside the security boundary? Why?

E14. Locate the description of a self-encrypting drive product. Identify the encryption algorithm and cipher mode used. Describe how the drive manages encryption keys. Identify any product certifications held by that product (FIPS 140, for example).

E15. Search the Internet and find a "suspicious" volume encryption product. Identify the elements of the product description that suggest the product may not be reliable.

CONNECTING COMPUTERS

ABOUT THIS CHAPTER

This chapter introduces computer networking and some basic issues in network security. We look at the following:

- Digital networking and reliable transmission
- Building and operating a small-scale LAN
- Reliability and error detection
- Network protocols and the protocol stack
- Network applications and resource sharing

10.1 The Network Security Problem

In this chapter, we graduate from isolated computers to the problems of networked computers. This brings us closer to the entire range of modern information security risks and thus increases the complexity of the problem. For now, we narrow our focus to *local area networks* (LANs).

The modern local network emerged at the same time and place as the modern personal computer: in the 1970s at Xerox Corporation's Palo Alto Research Center, commonly called PARC. Researchers at PARC produced the Alto, the prototype of today's personal computer (Figure 10.1). PARC installed a prototype *Ethernet* to connect the Altos together. Alto users shared printers, files, and other resources across this early LAN.

Local networks became an essential desktop feature in the 1980s. Office desktops rarely had Internet connections until the late 1990s, but all had LANs to share files and printers. In most cases, these LANs used improved Ethernet products.

When we talk about computer networks, even the simplest network has two parts: the hosts and the links. A *host* is a computer connected to the network. A *link* is a component that connects the host to other hosts or to the networks. The simplest network consists of two hosts with a single wire linking them. More complex networks may include separate devices that connect multiple hosts together or that connect networks together.

Figure 10.1

The Xerox Alto.

Even today, wired network connections remain popular. As wireless connections improve in speed and reliability, so do wired connections. It seems likely that a wired LAN always will run faster and more reliably than wireless. It is easier to control and protect a signal on a wire. Wireless LAN signals, on the other hand, must compete with other sources of electronic signals and noise, including motors, microwave ovens, audio/video equipment, and so on. Not only do physical wires isolate a LAN from random noise and interference, they also protect it from outsiders. When we wire up a LAN, it is usually inside a building. We can lock the LAN away from outsiders. We can keep track of which computers we attach to the LAN and which we omit.

As networks grow larger, however, it becomes harder to keep track of its computers. Most wired networks use standard plugs and jacks. If someone has an unused jack that's connected to the network, it's easy to connect another computer. Some organizations try to keep a strict accounting of every authorized computer, but many don't. A malicious visitor can easily plug in to an unused jack; now the network is no longer isolated from attacks.

The rest of this section reviews the following:

- Possible attacks on the network
- Defending the network via physical protection
- Defending hosts against attack

The rest of the chapter gives a tutorial on networking fundamentals. These technical details will give us a better understanding of the risks and how our defenses work.

10.1.1 Basic Network Attacks and Defenses

Figure 1.6 in Chapter 1 lists six general attack types, all of which apply to networks. However, we place a different emphasis on these threats, so we examine them in a different order:

- **Physical theft.** Someone steals network hardware, like wires, hubs, or other equipment that keeps the network running.
- **Subversion.** Someone modifies or otherwise takes over part of the network so that it enables an attack. For example, an attacker might reroute traffic to allow its interception. Note that in networking, this threat involves *physical* or *logical* changes to network components. It does not involve changes to network traffic.

- **Disclosure.** An attacker's computer intercepts copies of network data intended for others. Even if most network traffic is benign, this type of eavesdropping may yield passwords or other data that enables a more serious attack.
- **Forgery.** Someone constructs a bogus message or modifies a legitimate message as part of an attack. For example, a bogus order could send merchandise without collecting payment.
- **Masquerade.** A person tricks the network into sending messages claiming to be originated by someone else. In the networking environment, this behaves like a particular type of forgery.
- **Denial of service.** An attack that makes some or all of the network unusable. Typical attacks either flood parts of the network with traffic or render network components unusable.

EXAMPLE: SHARING EVE'S PRINTER

Let us consider the attacks and their risks in terms of a specific problem:

> Eve has brought in a networked printer. It's an old printer that must be wired into a network. Kevin has some extra networking gear, so the suitemates have strung wires among their desks.
>
> To get things going, the suitemates must buy some paper and toner. Kevin manages to scrounge up a ream or two of paper. Tina collects $10 from each suitemate to buy a new toner cartridge.
>
> They want to restrict access to people in the suite and block access by people who haven't paid part of the toner cost.

Let's apply the security process to the suite's new printer. The assets are the toner and the paper. The risk is that outsiders—those who didn't chip in to pay for toner—will use up the toner.

Policy Statements

There are three statements in the policy:

1. All suitemates shall contribute to the printer supplies.
2. All suitemates shall have access to the printer.
3. Printer access shall only be granted to suitemates.

Potential Controls

In Chapter 2, Figure 2.13 lists six general categories of security controls. These same categories provide basic network defenses.

- **Physical**—physically isolating parts—or all—of the computers and network from potential threats.
- **Mechanical**—providing physical access via locked doors.
- **Logical**—restricting network behavior according to the origin or contents of a request: a user, a computer, or a network-oriented program. Network services use access rules to validate permissions before taking action.

- **Functional**—restricting network activity by not implementing risky actions.
- **Procedural**—protecting the network with operating procedures. For example, only trustworthy people get a key to the room with computers and the network.
- **Cryptographic**—using cryptography to protect network activities. We introduce this in Chapter 14.

What types of controls do the policy statements require? The first statement relies on procedural control. Tina collects money from everyone, and then she goes to the store and buys the cartridge. Leftover money might buy paper or be saved until next time.

10.1.2 Physical Network Protection

The remaining policy statements to protect the suite's printer rely on physical controls. Figure 10.2 shows that the network resides entirely inside the suite. Only suitemates may enter the suite; the school's procedures only issue keys to suitemates and a few trustworthy employees. Suite guests are escorted by a suitemate, and suitemates aren't likely to give away printer access to others. Computers can only print on the printer if they connect to the network. Computers can only connect to the network via a physical wire to one of the network ports.

Frank lives in a nearby suite and he hates having to walk down flights of stairs to pick up a few pages of printout. He would like to hook his computer up to Eve's printer. He won't get a key to the suite; he's willing to bang on the door when he needs a print-out.

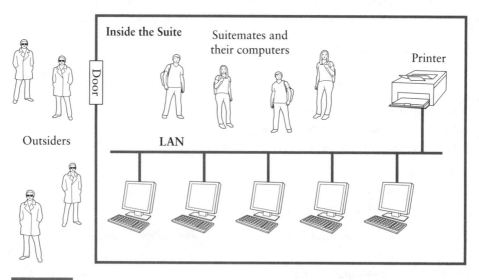

Figure 10.2

Physical protection of a LAN.

Frank's hookup clearly violates the existing policy, but the suitemates could agree to it. After all, it's cheaper to buy toner if more people contribute. They could rewrite the policy to say "suitemates and Frank."

However, that poses another problem. Without Frank wired in, all wiring is inside the suite and under the direct, physical control of the suitemates. If they extend a wire outside the suite, they have to worry about attacks on that wire.

PROTECTING EXTERNAL WIRES

Many companies implement a LAN for their employees' computers. If the company resides inside a single building, the LAN benefits from the building's physical protection. If the company has two adjacent buildings, they can run a network cable between the buildings. Now, however, they have to worry about attacks on the outside cable. Cables often run inside physically strong enclosures, like metal conduits.

An attacker must be highly motivated to break into a metal conduit. Although most attackers are not, sites may face this risk if their networks carry classified defense information. A network requires special physical protections if it carries information through areas open to people not allowed access to that information. We discuss this in greater detail in Section 17.5.

Not only do wires need protection, but the networking equipment needs protection, too. The suite's printer network relies on a few low-cost switches to hook up the computers. If Frank has physical access to a switch and passes a wire through his wall, then he can hook into the network regardless of the suite's approval. However, he would still have some explaining to do when he tried to pick up a printout.

The suitemates verify the integrity of their network by looking at its physical condition. They must account for every device wired in to it. An extra wire suggests an unauthorized user.

The suite's printing network focuses entirely on printing. There are no risks or policy statements related to privacy, eavesdropping, or disclosure. However, some network users may use it for private matters, like printing a tax return or a love letter. This shouldn't pose a problem as long as the suitemates may be trusted.

10.1.3 Host and Network Integrity

This is another important part of modern network security. We must ensure that all host computers on the network are virus-free and can resist obvious attacks. Although this isn't as much of a problem on a small, isolated network like that in the suite, it remains a risk.

> The U.S. military protects its classified networks against attack by isolating them from other networks. If a worm infects millions of computers on the Internet, it won't infect the classified networks. There is no effective connection from the Internet to the classified networks, so there is no way for the infection to enter the classified networks.
>
> In December 2008, the classified networks were in fact infected, reportedly by the "agent.btz" worm. The infection was eventually traced to a USB flash drive that was plugged into a U.S. military laptop at a base in the Mideast. When plugged in, the laptop automatically

ran a program on the drive that infected the computer and its connected network at the U.S. Central Command. The worm soon spread through both classified and unclassified networks.

Shortly after the attack, military commands issued orders forbidding the use of portable USB drives on military computers.

In Section 3.2.4, we reviewed different types of malware, some of which propagate using a USB drive. The same strategy penetrated sensitive U.S. military networks.

NETWORK WORMS

The suitemates aren't going to worry about worm infestation because it didn't appear in their risk assessment and it doesn't figure in to their security policy. As we work with larger and larger networks, we are exposed to a much larger—and riskier—user community. At some point, worms become a serious risk; then we must ensure that we keep computer software patched and up to date. Worms thrive on errors in older, unpatched network software.

Like viruses, worms copy themselves to other places and spread from those other places. While viruses may infect USB drives, diskettes, and application programs, worms infect host computers. When a worm starts running, it takes these four steps:

1. Decide how to locate computers on the network.
2. Send messages to each computer to determine if it has particular security weaknesses. This may consist of simply trying various attacks; this is how the Morris worm operated.
3. If a computer is vulnerable to one of its attacks, the worm penetrates the computer.
4. After penetrating the computer, the worm installs a back door to give control to an attacker.

Note that worms search *automatically* for vulnerable computers. If a computer has not been patched to fix its vulnerabilities, a worm will probably find the computer while scanning the network. This could happen in a matter of minutes.

Early network worms often served no particular purpose. Many were intended to illustrate nothing more than a particular programmer's prowess at designing malware. In fact, early virus and worm authors often were caught because they bragged to others in black-hat hacker discussion groups. Today, however, worms serve a practical if illegal purpose: They help people construct botnets.

BOTNETS

Many of the malware packages discussed in Section 3.2.4 create and operate botnets for monetary gain. To create a botnet, the attackers must infiltrate host computers via a worm, virus, or Trojan. The malware then installs a *rootkit*, software that remains hidden and that provides backdoor control of the computer. The infected host computer becomes a *bot*, a working member of the botnet. Although the most dangerous rootkits have administrative control of a bot, some operate simply as a user. In either case, the rootkit gives the botnet controller the software to control the bot.

A host often becomes a bot because its owner is careless about computer security. For example, the owner might not keep the software up to date and leave it open to worm attacks—or the owner might install an infected USB drive or click on an email-based attack.

A bot's owner usually doesn't realize that the computer is part of a botnet. Successful backdoor software is stealthy and has no obvious effect on the computer's behavior. If the software degrades the computer's behavior, the bot's owner may try to get the computer fixed. The diagnosis and repair process often uncovers the rootkit, allowing the backdoor software to be removed.

Botnets in Operation

A botnet controller may ask its bots to do any of several things. Most bots can download additional malware. This allows the botnet controller to modify the bot to resist attacks on it and to add capabilities. Typical botnets may perform one or more of these operations:

- Steal authentication credentials from the bot's owner. The ZeuS botnet focuses primarily on this theft.
- Harass the bot's owner with pop-up windows. Sometimes the pop-up is simply advertising. In some cases, the pop-up claims to be a virus warning. The bot's owner then is offered antivirus software that's actually additional malware. Some botnets actually charge the bot's owner for this malware download.
- Send spam (see Section 15.3.1).
- Perform *distributed denial of service* (DDOS) attacks. Such attacks transmit a modest amount of data from each bot to the target system. If the botnet has thousands or tens of thousands of bots, the target system may be overwhelmed by the traffic load.

Botnets are often in competition with one another. No botnet wants to share a victim host with another botnet. If a host computer contains two or more bot packages, then their combined effect may slow the computer down and make the owner aware that there's trouble. If a botnet penetrates a host belonging to another botnet, the new one will try to remove the other network's bot software.

Fighting Botnets

Botnets routinely lose bots as individuals replace infected computers or install security software that detects and removes the bot software. However, this doesn't normally affect a large, healthy botnet. The operators continue to locate and incorporate new machines that replace the ones lost.

The most effective way of fighting botnets so far has been to go after a botnet's control mechanism. Botnet operators use a special set of hosts to send commands to the botnet. These command hosts are usually a botnet's weak point.

Between 2008 and 2010, several organizations made a special effort to cripple bot-nets involved in spam production. The effort shut down servers used by Pushdo/Cutwail botnet, a ZeuS organization, and the "Bredolab" botnet. This decreased global spam levels at least 40 percent between August and October 2010.

THE INSIDER THREAT

Do any of the suitemates pose a network-based threat to other suitemates? Eve, for example, is curious about everyone and everything. She owns the printer. What if she sets up the printer to give her copies of everything it prints? This would be an insider threat. Eve is part of a community that more or less trusts its members. The security environment assumes that people will follow the rules, both written and unwritten.

Many networks don't know they have an insider threat until something unfortunate happens. For example, Eve might be able to program the printer server to send copies of everything to her own computer. If Bob prints his tax forms, the printer sends a copy to Eve, too. If Bob or anyone else finds out, the suite needs to reassess its risk environment.

Eve might not be the only insider threat. If the suite as a whole said "No" to Frank's proposal, but his friend Kevin is willing to help him, Frank might still join the network. Kevin could let Frank's network wire pass through his bedroom wall and connect it to a network switch inside his room. Outside, it still looks as if a single network wire goes to Kevin. No one knows Frank is hooked up as long as Kevin intercepts Frank's printouts before anyone else sees them. This violates the suite's printer policy, which still relies on the suite's residents for enforcement.

10.2 Transmitting Information

The 20th century saw the genesis of truly global information networks. There was a telephone in almost every home in the industrialized world. Most phones could connect to almost any other phone on the planet. However, the first information networks arose even earlier to support telegraph messages.

The first true telegraph sent messages a letter at a time via sets of flags; the electrical telegraph coded letters as a series of clicks. Telephones easily replaced telegraphs in many places because the telegraph required skilled operators. To send or receive a mes-sage, the operator had to convert it between written text and telegraph code. Speed and reliability depended on operator skill, and good operators were hard to find.

This posed a particular challenge to stock brokers and other investors. Money was made or lost by responding quickly to price fluctuations. For many years, brokers relied on runners to bring price information to their offices, and it wasn't practical for brokers to keep a staff of telegraph operators.

In 1867, Edward Callahan produced a device to convert telegraph signals directly into printed text. This became the first "stock ticker," which printed stock transactions onto a stream of "ticker tape." In 1874, Frenchman Émile Baudot patented his "print-ing telegraph" that used a keyboard to transmit telegraph messages. A series of

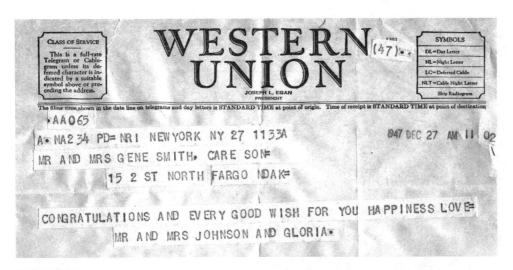

Figure 10.3

A mid-20th century telegram from New York to Fargo.

improvements led to electromechanical teletypes that fully automated telegraph transmission. By World War I, teletypes had replaced telegraph keys in major telegraph offices. The receiving office printed out the message and pasted it to a telegram form to deliver to the recipient (Figure 10.3).

While the ticker tape system broadcast the same messages to numerous recipients, most telegraph messages traveled between one sender and recipient. For example, Bob's great uncle in New York might have needed to send a telegram to his cousin in Boston. Because the cities are a few hundred miles apart and do a lot of business with each other, there was a telegraph line (a network link) directly connecting the two cities.

To send the telegram, Bob's great uncle wrote out the message and handed it to a telegraph clerk. The clerk collected payment, found a teletype, and connected it to the Boston link (Figure 10.4). The clerk typed the message in the New York office, which simultaneously typed out on a teletype in the Boston office. A clerk at that office dispatched a courier to take the telegram to the cousin's address.

If Bob's great uncle needed to telegraph wedding congratulations to his niece in Fargo, North Dakota, the process was more difficult. The great uncle still wrote out the message, handed it to the clerk, and paid for it.

However, the price was much higher because the message traveled farther and needed additional handling to reach its destination. At the time, Fargo was too far away and too obscure to have a direct line from New York. Instead, the telegram had to travel through a network of links that connected telegraph offices in major cities. Each office collected the message and retransmitted it down a link to take it closer to Fargo. As we

Figure 10.4

A clerk connects a teletype to a network link.

can see on the telegram in Figure 10.3, it took almost a half hour to send a telegram halfway across the continent, crossing one time zone.

This example highlights a major difference between telegraph and telephone networks. A telephone conversation required a complete, end-to-end connection between both phones. The network had to establish the connection and keep it working for the duration of the call. Telegrams, on the other hand, were more like letters. The sender and recipient didn't have to be present at the instant of transmission. The message didn't have to traverse the network all at once; it could travel in stages.

When we combine this perspective of older networks with the capabilities of modern computer networks, we find three different strategies for sending data across a network.

1. *Message switching*—used by postal and telegraph networks.
2. *Circuit switching*—used by traditional telephone networks.
3. *Packet switching*—used by modern computer and cell phone networks.

We examine each of these here.

10.2.1 Message Switching

Postal systems and classical teletype networks use message switching. In the postal system, each letter or parcel moves as a single, indivisible unit. Each time a batch of mail is sorted, each letter is redirected to another office that brings it closer to its destination.

Moreover, the sender and recipient don't have to arrange a specific time to send and receive individual messages. The messages may arrive and wait for delivery. In the previous section, Bob's great uncle sent a telegram to his niece in distant Fargo. The niece did not abandon the wedding party to attend the telegram's arrival. The message reached the office at an unpredictable time and was delivered to the new bride by messenger.

Like letters and parcels, each telegram is a single, indivisible unit. The great uncle's telegram travels through the network as a single message. The message might traverse several offices on its trip across the country. Instead of retyping the message, the offices punched each incoming message on a stream of paper tape (Figure 10.5).

Then an operator placed the punched tape in a machine connected to the message's next destination, and the machine automatically retyped the message.

To send the great uncle's message, the clerk in the New York office first connects a teletype to a westbound link leading to Pittsburgh or some other city closer to Fargo. The clerk types in the message and it prints out in the Pittsburgh office. From there, another clerk relays the message to another office, perhaps in Chicago, moving the message even closer to Fargo.

Electronic mail systems use the same approach. When we send an email, the system handles and delivers the message as a single unit. We never receive part of an email; the system only handles and delivers complete messages.

Figure 10.5

Teletype clerks check a message on paper tape.

Message switching has the following advantages:

- Independent receipt. Sender and recipient don't have to arrange a specific time to exchange a message.
- Completeness. The network delivers the entire message to the recipient or nothing at all. The network isn't designed to handle partial messages.

Message switching has these disadvantages:

- Size limits. Message size may be limited by equipment capacities. Longer messages are much harder to handle and are more likely to encounter errors.
- Longer delays. Each node must collect the entire message before it can forward it to another node in the network. This prevents the network from delivering different parts of a long message in parallel, which would reduce its delivery time.

10.2.2 Circuit Switching

Telephone systems traditionally use circuit switching. This dates back to the earliest telephones. When connecting a phone call, the network establishes a specific circuit to carry that individual call from the originating phone to the destination. This is because the network must carry the analog sound signals produced by the two speakers. The sound must travel as fast as possible between the phones. Even a short delay may make it hard for the speakers to carry on a conversation.

To create a circuit for a phone call, the network assigns pieces of the network to that specific call (Figure 10.6). It assigns wires in each network link that connects the two phones. It also assigns circuitry inside each exchange.

Whenever either person speaks, the electric signal passes along the link from the phone to the local exchange. From there, it travels across a circuit to take it to the network link leading to the next exchange that carries the call. This continues until it reaches the local exchange at the other end of the call. The signal then passes along the link that connects to the call's recipient. When either party hangs up the phone, the network reclaims the circuits and data links for use in another phone call.

The 20th century telephone system was so successful that their network engineers had trouble seeing the possible benefits of other networking strategies. Many such experts argued strongly against the use of packet-switching technology when it was new. Their connection-oriented network reliably supported a broad range of services, so their argument seemed plausible at the time.

Circuit switching provided these advantages:

- Rapid connections. The network could quickly establish a connection between any two endpoints.
- Low delays. The network could transmit and receive voice messages with very low delays. The network was designed to keep delays low so that subscribers could have natural conversations that were not plagued by delays.

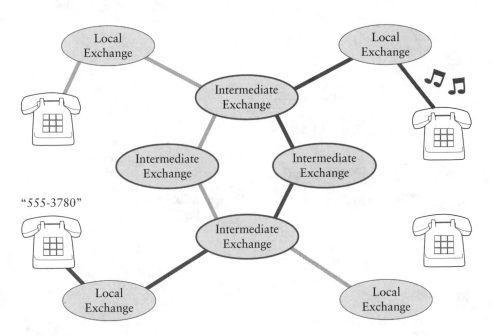

Figure 10.6

A phone call makes a circuit between two phones.

- Multiple messages. Once the endpoints were connected, they could exchange numerous messages.

Circuit switching also had these disadvantages:

- Concurrent receipt. The sender can't send a message until the recipient is present to receive it.
- High overhead. The network had to set aside the resources to carry a person's voice even while the person wasn't actually speaking.

10.2.3 Packet Switching

Packets are blocks of digital data that are neither too large nor too small to handle efficiently. Each packet travels across the network independently. Small messages travel as a single packet. Larger messages are broken into pieces, and each travels in its own packet (Figure 10.7).

This is a completely different approach from either message switching or circuit switching. This strategy emerged in the 1960s as researchers imagined new ways to build self-managing computer networks.

Packet switching is similar to sending messages on postcards. We can easily send a short message, but a very long message poses a challenge. We still can send the message,

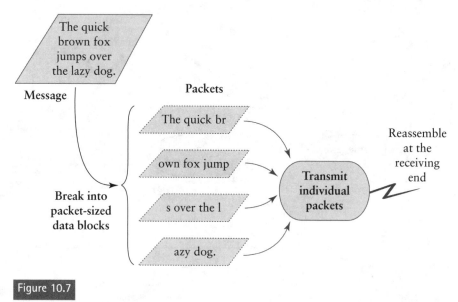

Figure 10.7

A packet network sends messages a packet at a time.

but we must write part of it on each card, and then send the cards individually. Each postcard travels through the postal service (the network) separately. The recipient can start reading the message as soon as the first postcard arrives, but won't be able to finish reading until *all* postcards arrive.

From the network's point of view, a packet needs the same basic information as a postcard:

- The destination—required, or the network can't deliver it.
- Damage detection—implicit in postcards, because we see any tears, smudges, or other injuries.
- The data to carry—optional, but a card seems pointless without it.
- The sender—optional information; the sender writes down a claimed identity but the claim is not always trustworthy.

Every packet contains a special data area, the *packet header*, which contains this information. The network itself may use the header information, or it may be used by the recipient host.

Packet switching provides these advantages:

- Resource efficiency. The network only sets aside enough resources to handle individual packets.
- Flexible routing. Each packet may be routed individually even if all packets are going to the same destination. If network conditions change while packets are in transit, each may take the best path the network finds for that packet.

- Parallel transmission. When we send a series of packets to the network, each packet starts on its way as soon as it is received.
- Service flexibility. We can build an efficient circuit or message switched service with a packet service.

Packet switching also has these disadvantages:

- Reliability. Either the endpoint hosts or the network itself must have an additional protocol to guarantee reliable and orderly transmission.
- Variable delay. Different packets traverse the network at different rates. There is no way to control or even predict the delay encountered.
- Concurrent receipt. The network only delivers packets to recipients who are actively accepting them. The sender may send packets without knowing if the recipient is available; if the recipient can't or won't accept the packets, then they are discarded.

Like postcards, it's possible to lose packets in a computer network. Technology is never 100 percent effective, and packets can disappear into a network without a trace. Likewise, the post office won't know which postcards, if any, disappeared.

The simplest and lowest cost packet networks, like Ethernet, take no special steps to detect lost packets and ensure their delivery. When the network does not take steps to ensure reliable delivery, we call the packets *datagrams*.

Other early networks, including those promoted by telephone companies, tried to ensure that all packets were delivered in the order they were sent. This required additional information in packet headers, and a set of rules to identify packets that were—or were not—received. This provides a *protocol*, a set of rules to establish effective communication.

To provide reliable packet delivery, the reliability protocol had to be incorporated either into the network or into the endpoint hosts. Several early networks incorporated reliability protocols. However, experience showed that the system achieved higher reliability by placing that task in the endpoint hosts. Thus, the network itself focused on packet delivery, and the endpoints kept track of packet order and verified packet delivery.

Mix-and-Match Network Switching

Different types of communication require different types of handling. Regardless of the underlying network, we often have to transmit messages, send a stream of data, or send a number of short messages to many destinations. Although message, circuit, or packet switching may seem ideal for specific types of traffic, we can in fact carry any type of traffic atop any type of switching.

The first packet-switching networks were built atop the circuit-switched telephone network using leased lines. Today, many telephone networks rely on packet-switched backbone networks to provide circuit-oriented connections. We also use the packet-switched Internet to provide reliable circuit-oriented connections between hosts and to deliver message-switched email. Researchers even have encapsulated packets in messages to provide packet switching atop message-switched systems.

10.3 Putting Bits on a Wire

Digital systems store and transmit bits. Analog systems store and transmit a value within some range. Digital systems store values more reliably because they self-correct.

When a circuit handles an *analog signal*, it can be hard to tell if the signal's value is correct or if it has picked up some noise. The analog signal could carry any value within its range; if a "glitch" of some sort changes the signal a little, there is no way to detect and correct that change.

When handling a *digital signal*, the electronic circuits can self-correct minor errors. We use analog electrical signals to represent digital data. For example, the circuit in Figure 10.8 treats a 0 volt signal as digital 0 and a 3 volt signal as a digital 1.

A typical glitch might modify the 0 volt signal by a few percent while it travels from one part of a circuit to another. The resulting signal might reach 0.1 volts. However, even if the glitch changes the signal by 30 percent, the value still represents a 0 bit. The

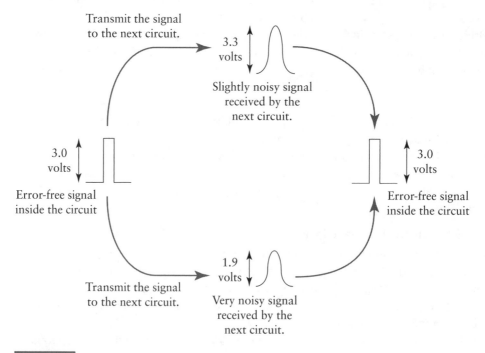

Digital circuits self-correct minor signal glitches.

next stage of the circuit will correct the value back to 0 volts. This is how digital circuits self-correct.

This also illustrates how circuits convert between analog and digital signals. To transmit a digital value within an analog signal (for example, to transmit on a phone line), we *modulate* the analog signal to reflect the digital signal value. To convert the analog signal back to its digital value, a receiving circuit *demodulates* the signal. Again, minor glitches may modify the analog signal, but the circuit can self-correct. The acronym *modem* describes a device to send digital data on an analog link: a "<u>mo</u>dulator-<u>dem</u>odulator."

Synchronous Versus Asynchronous Links

We build network links out of wires, optical fibers, and broadcast radio signals. When we transmit digital data, we code the bits into signals that travel reliably across the link. If we use a simple coding like the one in Figure 10.8 (3.0 volts = a 1 bit; otherwise it's a 0 bit), how do we tell when the link carries data? If nothing is being sent, we might expect the wire to carry 0 volts. On the other hand, maybe the sender is sending a really large number of 0 bits for some reason. And if the signal swings up suddenly, how many 1 bits does that represent?

Some network links, especially in older systems, sent data continuously. These were called *synchronous* links. Any time a receiver looked at the data link, it would be carrying data from the sender. If there was in fact no usable data to send, then the link transmitted a special "Idle" message that told the recipient to ignore the data.

Older teletypes and newer, faster networks use *asynchronous* links. A teletype line carried no current except when sending a typed character. When the clerk typed on the teletype keyboard, it sent the typed character as a sequence of signals. The first signal was a "1" value that indicated the start of a character. After the start signal, the character code of 0s and 1s followed, each bit a few milliseconds long. At the end, the current returned to a zero level until the next character was typed. Modern network devices, like the Ethernet, are also asynchronous, but they use more sophisticated signalling techniques.

10.3.1 Wireless Transmission

Wireless or radio transmissions format binary data in the same way as wired transmissions. We define a particular pair of signals as representing 0 and 1, respectively. The transmitter produces the exact signal, and the receiver looks for a signal near a 1 or 0.

Wireless systems fall into four general categories:

1. Low power, local connections
2. Directional connections, like microwave
3. Terrestrial wide-area broadcast radios
4. Satellite-based networks

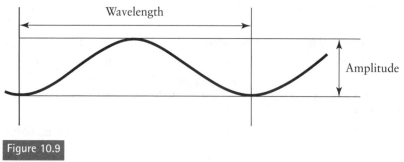

Figure 10.9

Amplitude and wavelength.

FREQUENCY, WAVELENGTH, AND BANDWIDTH

Sounds and radio signals travel in waves (Figure 10.9). When we speak of *frequency*, we refer to the rate at which the wave cycles from beginning to end. Higher frequencies, thus, have shorter wavelengths. We describe frequency in terms of cycles per second; the unit of measure is **Hertz** (Hz).

We call the wave's measured height its *amplitude*. The simplest way to transmit sound with a radio is to vary the amplitude to match the change in sound.

The earliest radios transmitted Morse code, so they essentially broadcast a series of binary "on" and "off" signals. The data transmission rate was expressed in *baud*, which counts the number of symbols transmitted per second. The term was named for Emile Baudot (1845–1903), the French teletype inventor.

Early equipment sent data one bit at a time, and not very quickly by modern standards; the maximum data rate, or **bandwidth**, was around 100 bits/sec. By the 1970s, traditional telephone circuits transmitted digital data at 300 baud. However, clever designs embedded multiple values in each signal, yielding a bandwidth of 1200 bits/sec, and then 19,200 bits/sec.

As designers tried to transmit more and more data over a narrow signal channel, they hit a limit; we can transmit bits at best at *half* the rate of the underlying signal. For example, if a radio circuit is limited to transmitting at 80,000 Hz or less, then its maximum bandwidth is 40,000 bits/sec. This restriction allows the receiver to reliably distinguish between the presence and absence of a signal.

AM AND FM RADIO

Traditionally, radio transmissions are assigned to specific frequency bands for specific purposes. In the United States, the Federal Communications Commission (FCC) assigns radio frequencies. Traditionally, each radio and television (TV) station is assigned a particular frequency for their broadcasts.

Each station has exclusive use of that frequency band within its approved broadcast range. Stations in nearby cities used different frequencies, but a station in a distant city

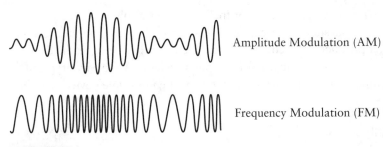

Amplitude Modulation (AM)

Frequency Modulation (FM)

Figure 10.10

AM and FM wave forms.

may reuse a particular frequency. In theory, the transmitters in the respective cities should not be strong enough to interfere with each others' signals.

Older transmission systems used amplitude modulation (AM) to transmit signals. To receive an AM signal, the radio tuned to a specific frequency. Variations in the signal strength (the amplitude) at that frequency carried the variations in the sound being transmitted (Figure 10.10).

These variations in turn vibrated the magnetic coil in the radio's speaker to produce sound. Unfortunately, any other transmissions on the same frequency will distort the signal. Such transmissions occur naturally through lightning and artificially through electric motors and other modern appliances. This makes AM radios more vulnerable to static and other distortion.

In the 1930s, radio designer Edwin Armstrong developed an improved radio that used frequency modulation (FM). This technique transmitted sound by subtly varying the transmission frequency around the transmitter's basic frequency (Figure 10.10). This approach was far less vulnerable to static and yielded a much clearer and more reliable signal. Subsequent broadcast systems, like television, used FM transmission.

FREQUENCY SHARING

Not all radio systems use dedicated frequencies. Public two-way radio systems often share frequency bands with one another. Each type of radio has its assigned channels within its authorized frequency range. If too many radio users are on one channel, users can switch to another. Examples include the "citizen's band" (CB), marine band, and some commercial two-way radio bands. System users had to be licensed by the FCC; the licensing process is supposed to ensure that radio users know how to share the channels effectively and not interfere with one another unnecessarily.

Digital networks can share frequencies very efficiently. The transmitters can take steps to avoid transmitting at the same time as other stations. High bandwidth techniques can keep transmissions short, giving other stations an opportunity to share the channel. Fortunately these techniques work well, because many digital devices share a relatively small number of channels.

The FCC assigned digital devices a section of the low-power appliance frequency band. Local wireless networks share their channels with portable digital phones, garage door openers, and other products. The channels operate efficiently as long as the devices are designed for efficient channel sharing. For example, wireless LAN devices typically use a multiplexing technique that minimizes interference when multiple devices use the same frequency.

RADIO PROPAGATION AND SECURITY

Wires have a natural advantage when it comes to security; attackers can't eavesdrop or worse, unless they physically reach the wires. If we physically protect the wires, we protect our network traffic.

Wireless networking is therefore vulnerable to external attacks. Anyone within radio range who uses compatible wireless networking equipment can use our LAN, eavesdrop on our traffic, and even interfere with our messages. Fortunately, modern wireless systems incorporate cryptographic security, as described in Chapter 14. Since being introduced in the late 1990s, wireless security has improved dramatically. This is fortunate because early implementations contained serious vulnerabilities. There is off-the-shelf software available for cracking the earliest wireless LAN encryption.

10.3.2 Transmitting Packets

Figure 10.11 shows the format of a typical packet, which is similar to the disk sector format introduced in Figure 5.5. Like a disk sector, the packet contains three sections: the header, the data, and the checksum. Like a disk sector, we handle a packet as a single, independent data item. The checksum allows us to detect data errors using the same techniques we applied to disk sectors in Section 5.3.3.

Packet headers contain more data than sector headers. A typical packet header contains the following:

- Address of the packet's sender
- Address of the packet's recipient
- Control information to keep the recipient up to date on the status of transmissions

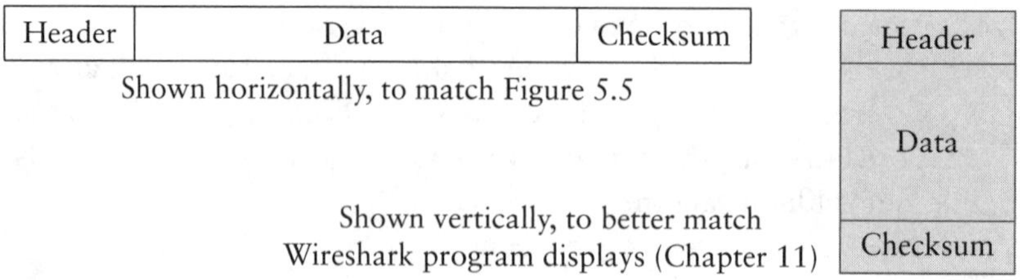

Header	Data	Checksum

Shown horizontally, to match Figure 5.5

Shown vertically, to better match
Wireshark program displays (Chapter 11)

Header
Data
Checksum

Figure 10.11

Basic packet format.

Many networks use special hardware and software that processes packets without ever looking at the data they carry. However, we mustn't make decisions about handling packets based on faulty data in the header, especially if the data is caused by an error. To avoid this, some networks include a separate checksum in the packet's header. When the network processes a header, it verifies the checksum. If the checksum fails to match its expected value, the network discards the packet.

ACKNOWLEDGMENT PROTOCOL

If the network system is to provide reliable transmission, there must first be a way to detect the success or failure of delivery. We generally send a message called an *acknowledgment*, or ACK, back to the sender to indicate successful receipt.

When a packet arrives at its destination, the recipient verifies the packet's checksum. If the checksum fails, it discards the packet. If the packet arrives intact, the recipient transmits the ACK. For this very simple example, the recipient sends a separate ACK packet for each data packet received. Figure 10.12 illustrates this protocol using a *sequence diagram.*

In the sequence diagram, the messages flow between the two network endpoints over a period of time. We begin at the top of the diagram, with the host on the left sending a data packet containing the message "Pay $109." Time progresses as we

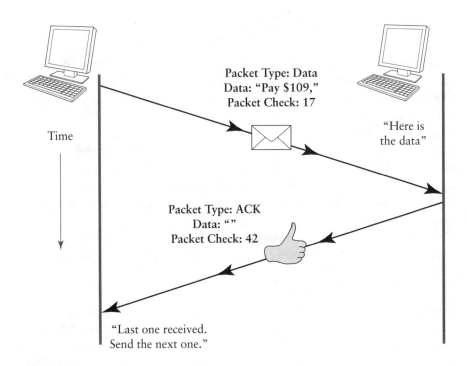

Figure 10.12

A sequence diagram showing a simple ACK protocol.

move downward. The arrow from left to right moving downward shows the data packet traveling to its destination. Midway, the packet arrives at the destination host, who responds with an "ACK" packet. The exchange ends at the lower left, when the ACK arrives at the sender, telling it to send the next packet.

This simple protocol ensures that the sender and recipient both understand the status of the transmission. This is a basic example of *distributed processing*; two computers, remote from one another, exchange information to achieve a shared goal. In this case, the goal is simple: Ensure that data moves from one computer to the other.

We make the protocol more efficient if we revise it to transmit several packets at once, without awaiting individual ACKs. We can number the individual packets, and the sender indicates the packet number when sending ACKs. The Internet's *Transmission Control Protocol*, or TCP, uses a similar strategy. TCP numbers each byte consecutively. When sending an ACK, it transmits the number of the *next* byte it expects to receive. If it receives a packet out of order, it does not report its bytes as received until the earlier packets arrive. We study TCP further in Chapter 12.

NETWORK EFFICIENCY AND OVERHEAD

When we assess the efficiency of different networks, we look at the ratio of the total number of bits the system can carry and the amount of end-user data actually carried. In packet networks, we calculate packet efficiency with the following ratio:

$$\frac{\text{Size of the data field in bits}}{\text{Total packet size in bits}}$$

Packet efficiency provides a simple estimate of network efficiency. Packet headers and checksums represent networking overhead. The users choose the data to send in the data field, and the rest of the packet is required to make the network operate. Thus, we try to make the packet header as small as possible, but no smaller.

Packet efficiency isn't the only element in network efficiency. We introduce other inefficiencies if we omit essential information. For example, we could omit the sender's address from packets. In theory, the network only needs the recipient's address to deliver a packet. In practice, however, it makes sense to include both addresses. Some networking hardware uses the sender's address to ensure that responses go to the correct host. Moreover, the recipient host needs the address of the claimed sender in order to respond with an acknowledgment or with other data. If omitted from the packet header, the sending host would still need to provide the information in the data field.

10.3.3 Recovering a Lost Packet

Whenever a host sends a packet, it sets a deadline for receiving the corresponding ACK. If the recipient doesn't return an ACK by then, the sender assumes the packet was lost or damaged somehow. The sender then resends the packet. This is called a *timeout* mechanism.

Some protocols also use a "negative ACK," or NAK, packet. If the recipient knows that the packet should have arrived or the packet arrives with an intact header but damaged data, then the recipient may send a NAK. Most protocols rely on a timeout instead because the recipient host can't detect all lost packets. For example, the host might not expect another packet or might not know when the next packet *should* arrive. If the host receives a packet with a damaged header, it won't know what host sent the damaged packet.

Network traffic moves most efficiently if we avoid sending unnecessary packets. Even so, a recipient shouldn't delay in sending ACKs. The recipient should process all packets it has received and try to send ACKs in a single batch. However, the recipient should never wait for "just one more" packet before sending an ACK.

As noted earlier when discussing TCP, the hosts must uniquely mark each packet to indicate the data items they contain. Ideally, the marking indicates the order in which the packets were sent. This allows the recipient to put packets in the correct order. It also allows the recipient to detect duplicate packets. An inevitable side effect of retransmission is that we will occasionally create duplicate packets.

If the ACK is delayed too long, the sender will retransmit the packet. This yields the right result if the packet was actually lost. If the ACK was lost or simply delayed, the retransmission creates a duplicate packet. The sequence diagram in Figure 10.13 shows how this happens.

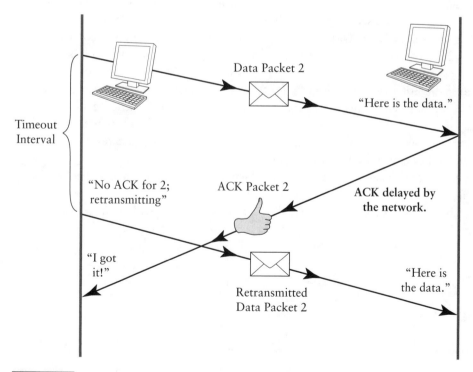

Figure 10.13

A delayed ACK yields a duplicated packet.

The sending host transmits a series of packets. The sender sends packet 2, and the recipient sends the ACK in a timely manner. Unfortunately, the network delays the ACK packet for some reason. Because the sender doesn't receive the ACK within the timeout interval, it retransmits packet 2. The recipient then receives a second copy of packet 2.

Although this may look troubling, it is exactly how the protocol should work. Each host only sees the packets it actually receives, and it can't track the status of packets it has sent. The only way a host knows *anything* about its packets is if another host, or node, sends it a packet to indicate what happened. It may seem inconvenient or complicated to deal with duplicates, but it is the price we pay for reliable data transmission.

Modern networks rely on the endpoints to retransmit lost packets, but this is effective only if packets are very rarely lost. Most modern LANs provide adequate reliability and rarely need to retransmit a packet.

10.4 Ethernet: A Modern LAN

Most modern LANs use a form of the Ethernet network. When originally developed at Xerox PARC, Ethernet provided a bus network using a ***coaxial cable*** ("coax"). This is the same type of cable used with cable TV connections: an insulated metallic jacket surrounding an insulated core with a single, thick wire. Each host computer connected to the shared coax. Modern Ethernet rarely uses coax, but it often still uses a bus connection (Figure 10.14).

Because the Ethernet uses a bus, the hosts must take turns using it. To send a message, a host first listens to the bus to ensure that no other hosts are sending a message. If the bus is silent, the host sends its message. While sending, the host listens to the bus. Ideally, the host will hear only the packet that it sends itself. This indicates that the other hosts should hear the packet clearly, including the destination host.

Because Ethernet uses a bus, all hosts can hear all packets. Each packet header contains the source address of the sending host and the destination address of the receiving host. Each host listens for its own, distinctive destination address. If a packet contains a

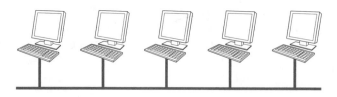

Figure 10.14

The Ethernet LAN connects hosts on a bus.

host's destination address, then its network interface will copy the entire packet into the host's RAM. If the packet contains some other destination address, the network interface ignores the packet.

TODAY'S ETHERNET

Although the Ethernet was originally a proprietary protocol created and promoted by particular companies, it is now an industry standard that covers a broad range of networking technologies. Local and metropolitan networks fall under the IEEE 802 standard, and the 802.3 standard covers coax-based Ethernet as well as modern versions using copper wires or optical fibers. Wireless networking falls under IEEE 802.11. In general, 802 networks use similar packet structures. This allows the hardware to change dramatically while not requiring major software changes.

Wired

Wired Ethernet networks use cables containing twisted pairs of wires and telephone-style "registered jack" RJ-45 plugs and jacks. Ethernet devices usually are marked to indicate their operating speed and the type of connectors it requires. Here are networks commonly seen in household and small business computing equipment:

- 1000baseT—1000 Mb/second (1 Gb/sec), using RJ-45
- 100baseT—100 Mb/sec, using RJ-45
- 10baseT—10 Mb/sec, using RJ-45

A few older networks might use 10base2, based on the original Ethernet coaxial cable.

Optical

Faster networks may use *optical fiber* instead of copper wires. These networks transmit messages using lasers along fibers that carry the light waves even around cable bends. Optical technology achieves the highest performance of today's networks.

Wireless

The 802.11 wireless network technology evolved during the 1990s. Today, it appears in several common variants:

- 802.11b—2.4 GHz frequency; maximum 11 Mb/s data rate
- 802.11.g—2.4 GHz frequency; maximum 54 Mb/s data rate
- 802.11n—2.4 and 5 GHz; maximum 150 Mb/s data rate

The *Wi-Fi* trademark appears on many, but not all, 802.11-compatible products. The Wi-Fi Alliance is an industry group that promotes 802.11 technology and establishes product interoperability standards. A device becomes "Wi-Fi Certified" if it passes the alliance's interoperability tests. Although the term Wi-Fi is not synonymous with 802.11 wireless networking, many circles treat it as such.

10.4.1 Wiring a Small Network

Most modern computers include a built-in Ethernet interface that provides a 100baseT or 1000baseT connection. To build a small network, we connect to one of these types of nodes:

- *Network switch*—high-speed node that connects pairs of hosts together using the Ethernet LAN protocol.
- *Network hub*—lower-speed node that shares Ethernet packets among the connected hosts. These usually are restricted to 100baseT or 10baseT speeds.

We can build a small network of four, five, eight, or a few more hosts, with a single node. The node provides a single RJ-45 socket for each connection. Figure 10.15 shows the sockets on the back of a typical device. To connect more computers, we connect the switch or hub to either another switch or another hub. It is easy to build a small network this way.

There is, however, a limit to how, and how many, switches and hubs we can connect to create a network. Larger networks require careful design. In particular, the network must form a hierarchy of nodes. This provides exactly one route between every pair of endpoints. If we cross-connect branches of the hierarchy, the nodes won't be able to route the packets reliably and will lose packets.

NETWORK CABLES

Wiring for telephone and computer networks fall into standard grades and categories. The lowest are for traditional home telephone wiring. A modern high-speed 100baseT network requires *Category 5* wiring, nicknamed "Cat 5." Faster networks, like 1000baseT, require *Category 5 Enhanced* ("Cat 5 E"), or Category 6 wiring. These

Figure 10.15

RJ-45 connectors on an Ethernet hub.

categories indicate the number of strands of wire, the wire sizes, the insulation, and how they are twisted together.

Traditionally, Ethernet-style RJ-45 cables are directional; the connection to the computer drives the electricity in a particular direction on each wire. When we plug the cable into another device, it must be wired to accept the signals in the opposite direction. For example, we can't always plug the ends of one cable into two computers; both will send a signal "outward" on the same wire.

This is true of the hub shown in Figure 10.15. The numbered ports can connect to a computer; they are called *downlinks*. The leftmost port, marked "Out to Hub," is an *uplink*, which may plug into a downlink on another hub or switch.

Cable directions are less of a problem with recent equipment. Newer, faster 1000baseT switches and network interfaces often can detect the signal direction. This allows us to use any available port to connect switches together.

10.4.2 Ethernet Frame Format

A *frame* is a single data packet on an Ethernet. At the electronic level, an Ethernet interface transmits each frame asynchronously. There are framing signals that mark the beginning and end of each frame. A frame begins with a "preamble" containing 7 bytes' worth of alternating 1s and 0s, followed by a special data byte to mark the start of the frame. The network marks the frame's end with the "idle" signal.

Once a LAN interface receives an Ethernet packet, it interprets the contents as shown in Figure 10.16. This is the "Ethernet II" format, which is the common format in modern LANs.

Because the Ethernet idle signal indicates the packet's start and end, the frame itself doesn't need a built-in length field. Some implementations use the "Type" field to contain the length, but Ethernet II packets don't interpret it that way. Instead, it relies on

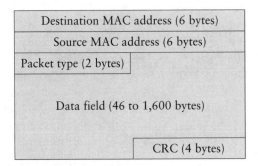

Figure 10.16

Ethernet packet ("frame") contents.

the hardware to find the packet length, and uses those results to find the end of the data field and the 4-byte CRC value.

LAN Addressing

Addresses are very important in Ethernet, because they let each host sort its own traffic out from other host traffic. If we think of the network hardware as our "communications medium," then the address provides us with *media access control* (MAC). Because of this, we typically call an Ethernet address a *MAC address*.

Most network interfaces contain a built-in MAC address. These addresses must be unique. If two hosts had the same MAC address, they could not distinguish between each other's traffic on the LAN. To ensure uniqueness, each manufacturer is assigned a range of addresses. Each manufacturer assigns a unique address within their assigned range to every interface they manufacture.

Address Format

The standard MAC address contains 48 bits arranged as shown in Figure 10.17. The first 24 bits identify the manufacturer. The remaining 24 bits are assigned by the manufacturer to the individual LAN interfaces they manufacture.

Because MAC addresses are assigned in blocks of bits and bytes, it is most convenient to refer to them in hexadecimal notation. The entire address consists of 12 hex characters grouped in 8-bit pairs. A typical address in hex notation might be:

00:17:F2:00:C3:F9.

The following are a few of the 24-bit (3 byte) identifiers assigned to major manufacturers:

- 00:01:02 3Com Corporation
- 00:01:42 Cisco Systems
- 00:02:B3 Intel Corporation
- 00:06:5B Dell Computer
- 00:17:F2 Apple Computer

This is by no means a complete list; the latest list is over 1500 pages long. Many larger vendors, including those just listed, actually have two or more blocks of addresses assigned to them. The additional blocks ensure that no vendor, no matter how large, has

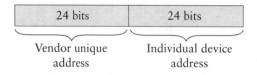

Figure 10.17

MAC address format.

to reassign an older MAC address to a newer product. Thus, every MAC address is unique, no matter when it was assigned.

In addition to the individual interface addresses, the Ethernet also uses a preassigned address of FF:FF:FF:FF:FF:FF to indicate packets that should be broadcast to all hosts on the LAN. If a packet uses this as the destination address, then all Ethernet interfaces will accept the packet as if it were addressed to them individually.

MAC ADDRESSES AND SECURITY

Because MAC addresses are unique and assigned by the hardware manufacturer, they would seem to provide an ideal unique identifier for every network device. In fact, some firewall and gateway products will block or pass network traffic based on MAC addresses (see Section 12.4.2).

For example, the suite might be able to configure Eve's printer so that it only accepts packets from computers belonging to suitemates. We enter the accepted MAC addresses into a network traffic filtering device or perhaps into the printer itself.

Unfortunately, this isn't very reliable in practice. Most Ethernet interfaces actually allow the computer software to change the built-in Ethernet address to a different value. For example, Henry is Frank's roommate, and he knows Bob's MAC address. He also knows that he's not in the suite. Because he's Frank's roommate and Frank has connected to the printer's network, Henry also has access to the printer. He can print things on the printer by connecting to the suite network and masquerading as Bob's computer.

10.4.3 Finding Host Addresses

Except for switches and hubs, every device on an Ethernet LAN has a unique MAC address. We often can find the addresses by inspecting the device. Because MAC addresses are assigned by the manufacturer, we may find the MAC address printed on a label attached to the LAN plug. When a network printer prints a network status page, the page often includes the MAC address.

Most computer systems have one or more utility programs that can retrieve its MAC address. Systems have keyboard commands to display network addresses as well as window- and menu-based commands.

ADDRESSES FROM KEYBOARD COMMANDS

All Unix-derived operating systems, including Linux and Mac OS-X, provides the MAC addresses by typing "ifconfig" into a command shell. The output is dense and arcane, but we will find the contraction "ether" followed by a six-byte hexadecimal MAC address.

On Microsoft Windows, we must start an MS-DOS command window to perform keyboard commands. The MS-DOS command "ipconfig" prints out address information. Figure 10.18 shows the printout of this command; the command itself is underlined. The MAC address is listed under the "Ethernet Adapter" as "Physical Address."

```
Microsoft Windows [Version 6.1.7600]
Copyright (c) 2009 Microsoft Corporation.  All rights reserved.

C:\Users\bob>ipconfig /all

Windows IP Configuration

     Host Name . . . . . . . . . . . . : BobWin7
     Primary Dns Suffix  . . . . . . . : comcast.net
     Node Type . . . . . . . . . . . . : Hybrid
     IP Routing Enabled. . . . . . . . : No
     WINS Proxy Enabled. . . . . . . . : No
     DNS Suffix Search List. . . . . . : smat.us

Ethernet adapter Local Area Connection:

     Connection-specific DNS Suffix  . :
     Description . . . . . . . . . . . : Intel(R) PRO/1000 MT Network Connection
     Physical Address. . . . . . . . . : 00-35-3C-29-35-20
     DHCP Enabled. . . . . . . . . . . : Yes
     Autoconfiguration Enabled . . . . : Yes
     Link-local IPv6 Address . . . . . : fe80::3be3:9c73:55d8:6832%11(Preferred)
     IPv4 Address. . . . . . . . . . . : 10.20.30.28(Preferred)
     Subnet Mask . . . . . . . . . . . : 255.255.255.0
     Lease Obtained. . . . . . . . . . : Saturday, May 01, 2010 12:01:09 PM
     Lease Expires . . . . . . . . . . : Sunday, May 02, 2010 12:01:09 PM
     Default Gateway . . . . . . . . . : 10.20.30.10
     DHCP Server . . . . . . . . . . . : 10.20.30.10
     DHCPv6 IAID . . . . . . . . . . . : 234901590
     DHCPv6 Client DUID. . . . . . . . : 00-01-00-01-BB-23-4F-26-00-35-3C-29-35-20

     DNS Servers . . . . . . . . . . . : 10.20.30.10
     NetBIOS over Tcpip. . . . . . . . : Enabled
```

Figure 10.18

Windows command to retrieve host addresses.

ADDRESSES FROM MAC OS

We also may find the addresses with Mac OS "System Preferences" by following these steps:

- Open "System Preferences."
- Select "Network."
- On the left-hand side of the screen are the network interfaces. Choose the one of interest: It should be active ("green"). This will display basic information about that interface.
- Click the "Advanced" button in the lower right. That displays a set of tabs giving information about different network services and protocols.
- Click the "Ethernet" tab on the far right. This will display the MAC address.

ADDRESSES FROM MICROSOFT WINDOWS

Microsoft also provides a graphical interface. We find the addresses by examining the network interface, which we may reach through the "Network and Sharing Center." Open the "Network and Sharing Center" and follow the steps depending on what you see.

- Look on the right-hand side. If there is a section in the upper middle saying "Access Type: Internet" and "Connections: Local-Area Connection," then:
  - Click on the "Local Area Connection" to display the Network Status for that device.
- Otherwise, look on the left-hand side. There is a list of links to other functions.
  - Click on "Manage network connections." This opens a display of physical network devices.
  - Right click on the local networking device. This produces a context menu. Select "Status" from the menu to display the Network Status for that device.
- In the middle left of the Network Status window, there is a "Details" button. Click on the button.
- This opens the "Network Connection Details" window. The third or fourth line lists the "Physical Address," which gives the MAC address.

10.4.4 Handling Collisions

Host computers use two mechanisms to share the Ethernet reliably and safely. First, the hosts listen before transmitting as noted earlier. Second, the hosts look for *collisions* and automatically retransmit their packet if they detect one. A collision occurs if two or more hosts try to transmit a packet at once. This can happen even if both hosts listen before transmitting; they might be far enough apart so that one host doesn't detect that the other has started.

Hosts will detect a collision because they listen while they transmit. If they don't hear their own packet on the network as they transmit, they know the signal has been mixed with another host's transmission. When this happens, the host immediately stops transmission, then it picks a random amount of time to wait. Once that wait time expires, the host tries to transmit again. If the network is busy, the host waits for the other host to finish. Otherwise, it transmits its packet again.

If the host detects another collision, it randomly picks another wait time, but doubles the possible range of the wait time. Thus, if it collides again and again, it will wait longer and longer before it tries again. Eventually it will find the network idle, and it will transmit its packet. This is called "exponential backoff."

Wireless Collisions

A wireless LAN faces a more significant collision problem. At first, it may seem like a similar problem with a similar solution: The transmitter simply needs to listen for an idle channel before it transmits. However, the packet travels between two devices, and they may be far away from one another. Even if the transmitter hears an idle channel, the receiver might be in range of a different, and active, transmitter.

The wireless protocol takes two steps to address this problem. First, the transmitter and intended recipient both transmit messages to warn away other traffic. Figure 10.19 illustrates the procedure. Second, the recipient will immediately request a retransmission if a transmission fails.

In Figure 10.19, Host 1 wants to send a message to Host 2. At about the same time, Host 3 wants to send a message to Host 2. Hosts 1 and 3 are out of radio range of one another, and Host 2 is between them.

Before sending the actual data packet, Host 1 transmits a warning message called **Request to Send** (RTS). The message is addressed to Host 2. The RTS message is small so that it wastes a minimum amount of bandwidth. The message warns Host 2, and everyone else in radio range of Host 1, that a packet is coming. Because Host 3 is out of radio range, it doesn't see the RTS.

When Host 2 sees the RTS, it responds with a **Clear to Send** (CTS) message. This tells Host 1 that it's ready to receive the message. It also warns everyone within its radio range that Host 2 is awaiting a message from Host 1. Host 3 sees the CTS message and delays its transmission.

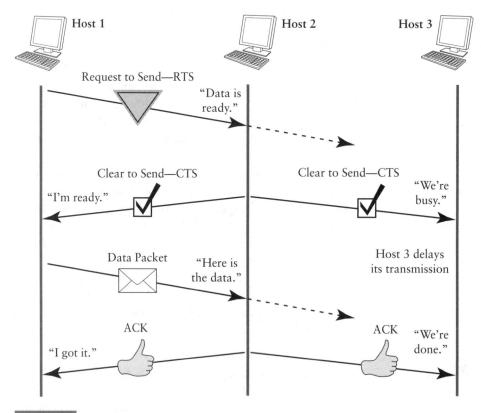

Figure 10.19

Wireless protocol for avoiding collisions.

Upon receiving the CTS, Host 1 transmits its packet. Host 2 waits for the packet to arrive and sends an ACK when it arrives successfully. Because Host 3 hears the ACK, it now knows that Host 1 is through sending its message. Host 3 then may send its own RTS, announcing data it wants to send to Host 2.

Wireless Retransmission

If, after sending the CTS, Host 2 never receives the data packet or it receives a garbled packet, it sends Host 1 a NAK. The wireless protocol is one in which NAKs serve a practical purpose. Host 2 knows that it should receive a packet, and it can reliably tell Host 1 whether the packet arrived. Moreover, wireless transmission is much less reliable than wired transmissions. These retransmissions make the wireless system reliable enough for effective Internet communications.

10.5 The Protocol Stack

In Section 5.6, we saw how operating system designers mastered complexity by organizing the complicated details of OS software into layers. Network designers use the same strategy to produce the network's *protocol stack*. As with the I/O system, the protocol stack forms an hourglass structure (Figure 10.20).

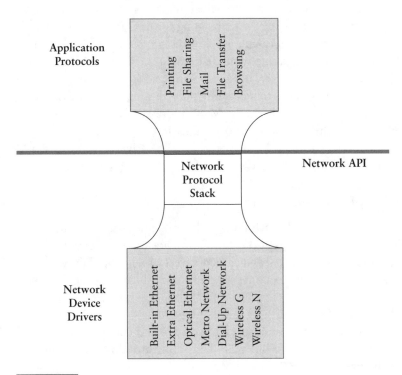

Figure 10.20

"Hourglass" structure of network protocols.

At the bottom of the stack we have device drivers, all for network devices. At the top, we have *application protocols*, which are network protocols designed to do a specific computing task, like file sharing, email, printing, or web access.

The network protocol stack itself focuses on services shared by device drivers on the bottom and applications on the top. In the LAN world, the stack contains two essential protocols:

- *Transport protocol*—associates a packet with an application process and may also detect broken or duplicate packets.
- *Link protocol*—Formats the packets for actual transmission and handles MAC addresses for the hosts.

As a message traverses the protocol stack on the way to the device driver, each layer applies its own formatting (Figure 10.21). This often appears as an additional header prefixed to the outgoing message data.

For example, imagine that we are sending an email message. The application layer inserts fields in the email message's header. It opens a connection to an email server and adds more heading information to identify and route the message.

The transport layer collects enough of the message (including the application header) to fill up a packet. The layer leaves the data undisturbed except perhaps to split it into separate packets. It adds its own transport header, which indicates the application process using this connection, and includes any ACKs pending for data from the recipient. The header also may include a checksum calculated over the packet's data. The layer then passes the packet to the link layer along with the destination address. If the message fills several packets, the transport layer fills up as many packets as needed.

The link layer accepts packets one at a time, each with its destination address. The layer adds a header to the packet that includes the MAC addresses for the source and destination hosts and indicates the type of transport header in the packet.

Then the link layer passes the packet to the device driver. The driver tells the network interface to transmit the packet across the network.

10.5.1 Relationships Between Layers

As data travels down the protocol stack, each layer adds its distinctive "envelope" around the data. When the packet arrives at the destination host, the actual data is inside this series of envelopes, each added by a protocol layer. Moving up the recipient's protocol stack, each layer removes and examines the envelope added by its twin in the sending host.

In practice, most layers simply add a header and don't actually "envelop" the enclosed data. Protocol layers on different hosts communicate and cooperate by sharing data in their respective headers. William Stallings illustrates this with a simple analogy, shown in Figure 10.22.

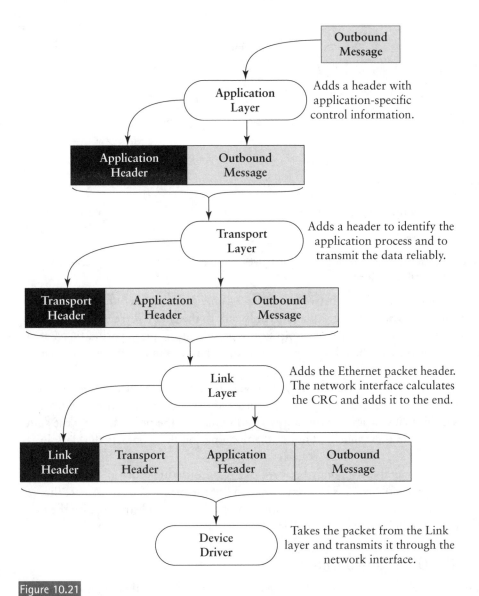

Adds a header with application-specific control information.

Adds a header to identify the application process and to transmit the data reliably.

Adds the Ethernet packet header. The network interface calculates the CRC and adds it to the end.

Takes the packet from the Link layer and transmits it through the network interface.

Figure 10.21

Each protocol layer adds a header to the packet.

Monday evening finds all the suitemates in their rooms preparing for exams that week. No one went down to dinner, and now the dining room is closed. Tina suggests ordering pizza. After some negotiation, Bob writes down the consensus on pizzas to order and collects money.

Bob phones the pizza parlor. The order clerk talks to Bob, collects the order, and negotiates the price. The total is less than the money Bob collected, so Bob agrees to the order.

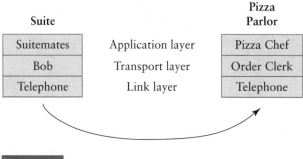

Figure 10.22

Protocol layers in ordering pizza.

> The order clerk turns to the pizza chef and gives him the order for the suite's pizzas. The chef prepares and cooks them.

The essential relationship is between suitemates and the pizza chef: the chef executes the suitemates' desires—but the suitemates only talk to the chef indirectly, through Bob and the order clerk. Even if they were physically present at the pizza parlor, the chef wouldn't talk directly to the table about their order; she stays in the kitchen and makes pizzas.

The order clerk keeps customers from annoying the chef and ensures the orderly collection and payment of pizza orders. Bob has ordered from him several times before and knows his style, so it's easiest for the suite to let Bob handle the order. Because the suitemates are, in fact, in their suite and not in the pizza parlor, Bob contacts the clerk by phone.

Figure 10.22 suggests an analogy between our pizza-ordering protocol layers and the local network protocol layers. The "practical end" of the protocol is, of course, the application layer. The transport layer enforces some reliability and structure on the data transfer, while the link layer simply carries data.

10.5.2 The OSI Protocol Model

When the network community speaks of protocol layers, it relates them to a recognized set of layers called the *Open Systems Interconnect* (OSI) *model*. Here are the layers, numbered from bottom to top:

1. **Physical layer**—the physical wiring and signalling between nodes. For example, Cat 5 cables are wired differently from 4-wire telephone cables.

2. **Data link layer**—manages the structure and content of data carried by the physical layer. Though OSI includes the word "data" in the title, we will continue to call it the *link layer*. Ethernet frames are an example of a data link protocol.

3. **Network layer**—manages intranetwork routing of packets. The ***Internet Protocol*** (IP) resides at this layer, and we sometimes call it the "internet layer."

4. **Transport layer**—associates packets with specific application processes in end-point hosts, and ensures reliability. The TCP protocol resides at this layer.

5. **Session layer**—handles a set of transport connections used for a particular purpose; rarely used today.

6. **Presentation layer**—reformats host data to meet network-wide standards and vice versa; rarely used today.

7. **Application layer**—provides a specific service to the user on a host computer. Examples include email and web protocols.

There are several mnemonics for remembering the seven protocol layers; for example:

Please Do Not Throw Sausage Pizza Away.

When people speak of "Layer 2" or "Layer 7" network activities, they are referring to the corresponding OSI layers. The simple LAN protocols in this chapter only use four protocol layers, as shown in Figure 10.23. We add Layer 3 when we work with internet protocols.

The hubs and switches that make up a wired LAN are "Layer 2" devices. They carry the transport and application data while paying no attention to its contents. The transport layers at the endpoint hosts ensure the reliable transmission of the application data.

We make two simplifying assumptions when using these protocol layers. First, we treat the physical layer as consisting entirely of link wiring or radio transmissions. Second, we consider everything above the fourth layer, the transport layer, to be part of the application.

Because the physical layer consists of physical phenomena, we implement physical or mechanical security controls at the physical layer. All other controls are the realm of higher-level protocols.

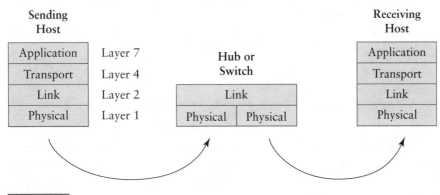

Figure 10.23

Protocol software layers on a simple LAN.

In the world of protocol software, we distinguish between the protocol stack and other components. The protocol stack contains the network software integrated into the operating system. Everything above it is application software. Below it are the device drivers. The link layer may be part of the protocol stack, and it also may be part of the associated device drivers, depending on the network.

THE ORPHANED LAYERS

Modern network applications have evolved dramatically since the OSI model first appeared. In fact, the OSI model predates the Internet itself. The operating system incorporates Layers 2, 3, and 4 into the protocol stack. Application software takes responsibility for the higher layers. However, there are no modern protocols that reside in Layers 5 and 6 and also provide their assigned functions.

If we interpret Layers 5 and 6 in the context of modern networking, they handle these two functions:

* Sessions (Layer 5): persistent dialogs between pairs of hosts; each dialog is made up of multiple interactions at lower protocol layers.
* Consistent presentation (Layer 6): the ability to receive standard information from the network and reformat it to display correctly on the host's desktop.

Web browsers have developed their own mechanisms to handle sessions and to handle platform-specific differences for presenting information. On the Web, we implement sessions to provide individuals with personalized "shopping carts" when visiting an e-commerce site. The web session mechanism associates a particular shopping cart with a particular user desktop. If someone else visits the same site with a different computer or with a different login from the same computer they receive their own shopping cart.

Most web applications implement sessions using "cookies," a special mechanism built into web browsers. We discuss this mechanism further in Section 16.3.2.

Web software provides compatible graphics for different systems by providing custom browser software to run on the different platforms. For example, Apple distributes both a Macintosh and a Windows version of their Safari browser. Mozilla distributes different versions of the Firefox browser for Windows, Macintosh, and for different versions of Unix and Linux.

10.6 Network Applications

Most of us are familiar with web browsers and email clients; we know how to visit websites and send email. Both of these, however, illustrate only half of the networking task: Web pages must reside somewhere and email messages must be delivered somehow. Web and email services operate in a mode called *client/server*. Our desktop or laptop host (the *client*) requests a network service from a distinctive host (the *server*) with the hardware and/or software to provide that service (Figure 10.24).

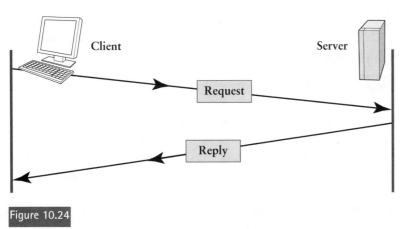

A client requests service and the server replies.

For example, when Bob wants to print on the shared printer, he directs his printing software at that printer. Inside the OS, the software makes a connection to the printer's server software, then the OS sends the file to the printer's server, which feeds it to the printer.

The security issues in client/server protocols generally arise from the challenges of network resource sharing. We discuss those challenges in Section 10.6.1.

Servers

The server software provides services for one or more clients. If a client needs service, it contacts the server and requests the service. If the server can provide the service, it does so and sends the result to the client.

The server has a well-known location, or it has one that is easily found. On the Internet, well-known servers have well-known names (google.com, amazon.com, whitehouse.gov, and so on). Resources on local networks don't tend to have well-known names. For example, we can't just assume that the printer has the name "Printer," because there may, in fact, be two printers on the same LAN. We might even have two printers of exactly the same make and model. Instead, LANs often use broadcast protocols to locate resources like printers and shared file storage; then the clients choose the desired resource from a list of locally available resources.

Peer-to-Peer

Client/server isn't the only strategy for providing network services. Internet file transfer and sharing programs like "Bittorrent" use a different strategy called *peer-to-peer*. In this approach, a server may become a client, and a client may become a server. In essence, the peer-to-peer software package includes both client and server capabilities.

For example, people use Bittorrent to download really large files, like ready-to-run images of Linux hard drives. If dozens of clients all try to download the file from the same server, the server will bog down as it sends the same block of data to dozens of different hosts. With Bittorrent, the hosts work cooperatively to download the file. The server itself may provide different parts of the file to different clients, and these clients in turn distribute those parts to other clients. Thus, each client makes a small demand on the main server, and comparably small demands on the other clients.

NETWORK APPLICATIONS AND INFORMATION STATES

Section 3.5.3 introduced the three fundamental information states: Processing, Storage, and Transmission. Section 7.1.3 described how the states related to encryption. Networking also affects our interpretation of information states.

In that earlier section, we drew a state diagram that did not allow a transition directly from Processing to Transmission. That restriction is not true for network applications. Such programs can send and receive data across the network, thus making the transition between Processing and Transmission.

As noted earlier, information faces risks when it leaves a protected environment. Thus, the network application can put data at risk by changing it to the transmission state: by sending it across a network.

10.6.1 Resource Sharing

In the 1960s and 1970s, the U.S. government spent a great deal of research money on computer networking because it offered a way to share scarce and expensive computer resources among researchers all over the country. In the 1980s and 1990s, the same argument justified installing LANs in offices. Everyone on the network could share a common hard drive; this was important back when hard drives cost $100 per megabyte. Quality printers also were expensive, so printer sharing was another benefit.

Figure 10.25 illustrates the basic notion behind network printer sharing. The box on the top of the figure is Kevin's computer with its own, directly connected printer. When his word processor tries to print the paper he's written, it uses the Printer API to pass the paper to the printer driver. Like any good API, the Printer API provides an abstraction that hides the details of printing from the word processor.

When Bob tries to print his own paper, his word processor also passes the paper through the Printer API. In this case, however, Bob has selected the network printer. Invisible to the word processor, the paper is passed to the "print client," which contacts the "print server" across the LAN. The server accepts the paper and passes it to the printer driver. The printer itself can't tell, and doesn't care, whether the paper came across the network or not.

Network systems use the same general strategy to share all sorts of computer resources:

- **Resource API**—presents a uniform way to use the resource, regardless of whether it is present on the computer or shared over the network.
- **Client**—software contacted by the API to access the resource across the network.
- **Server**—software visible to clients on the network that provides the resource to those clients.

Kevin's computer with a directly connected printer

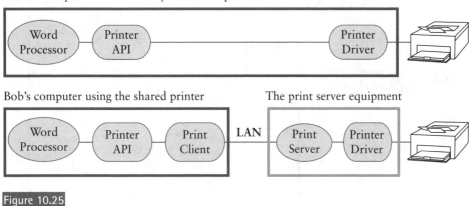

Bob's computer using the shared printer   The print server equipment

Figure 10.25

A directly connected printer versus sharing one across a LAN.

Simple versions of resource sharing would allow anyone on the LAN to use the resource if they had the client software. More sophisticated systems implement access controls. Some systems control access according to the host computer making the request, while others make decisions based on an authenticated user identity. Access controls on resources can be as simple or complex as any established for files, as described in Chapters 3 and 4.

10.6.2 Data and File Sharing

Although many may share printing resources and some may share other I/O or computing resources, data sharing is often a primary requirement. In earlier days, we might share a hard drive to provide additional file storage at a lower cost. Today, cheap hard drives make this unnecessary. Instead, we share hard drives so that we can share data and files.

All modern operating systems provide file-sharing features: One host can connect to another to read and write some of its files. This is a client/server operation. The clients open and close files as if they reside on their own hosts. However, instead of retrieving the file from a local hard drive, they retrieve the file from a "network drive:" a drive on a different computer whose contents are available through the network. In practice, the "drive" is usually a shared folder. Although the shared folder may look like a drive on the client side, the only shared files are those residing in the selected folder on the server side.

When using network drives, the servers exchange data with the clients and update the files. For example, Alice could connect to the suite's LAN, allowing both Bob and Alice to share files on each other's computers. Bob treats Alice's laptop as a server while Alice's laptop uses Bob's desktop as a server.

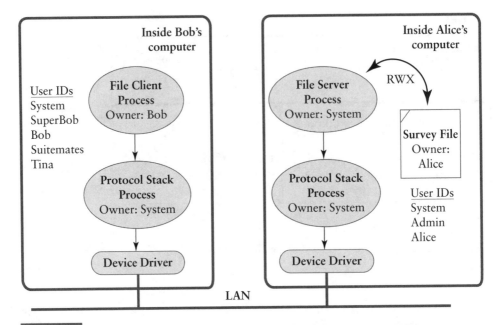

Figure 10.26

Sharing files on a LAN.

File sharing poses a security risk: If a host contains unprotected files, the file service makes them accessible to attackers who connect to the network. Because of this, many modern systems disable file sharing. A computer's owner must activate file sharing before it can be used.

Figure 10.26 illustrates the network software for a simple file-sharing service. Bob and Alice are working on another survey, and Bob wants to retrieve the copy of the survey file residing on Alice's computer.

On Bob's side, he runs a client process that requests the file from Alice's computer. Bob doesn't actually see the client process. Typical systems like Microsoft Windows let Bob select shared folders available to him on other peoples' computers; this is called "mapping" a network drive. Desktop software displays the network drive next to his other local drives. Internally, it activates the client process that accesses the remote files. When Bob tries to retrieve a file from Alice's computer, the file client contacts Alice's server software.

When Alice configured her computer to allow file sharing, it activated the server software. When Bob mapped one of Alice's shared folders, he told Alice's server that he wanted to access its shared files. When Bob retrieves a particular file, the server software retrieves the file and transmits its contents to Bob.

If Bob modifies the file, his client transmits the changes to Alice's file server process. The server process in turn updates the file on Bob's behalf.

DELEGATION: A SECURITY PROBLEM

The arrangement in Figure 10.26 poses a problem. If we look at the File Server Process in Alice's computer, we see it is run by the System process. Thus, the File Server Process has unrestricted access to Alice's shared files. In fact, the process has unrestricted access to *all* of Alice's files.

Matters aren't any better if we change the process owner to be Alice. We don't want the process to use Alice's permissions when working on Bob's behalf. We want it to enforce Bob's rights when running on Bob's behalf. This is the ***delegation problem***.

Ideally, Alice should be able to specify access restrictions on shared files. The File Server Process should enforce these restrictions. However, this gives the process the same access control powers as the file system itself. If a remote user can trick the File Server into granting access, then the file system won't protect the file.

Moreover, how can the File Server enforce different access permissions on different users, when the users aren't actually present on the host computer? The first step is to identify the remote users who make file-sharing requests. The second step is to ensure that the File Server enforces access rights on file sharing.

Figure 10.27 illustrates one strategy to do this. First, Alice configures her system to recognize Bob as a user. The second step is to use Bob's access rights when he accesses the shared files. We can do this by running the File Server under Bob's local user name.

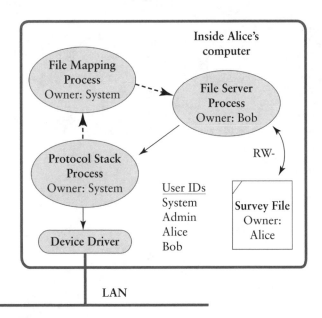

Figure 10.27

One way to delegate access to a file server.

When Bob maps a network drive on Alice's computer, the process requires him to log into Alice's computer. The mapping process collects the user name and password before it maps the drive. The user name must be one that exists on Alice's computer; she must set up a user identity for Bob. In some systems, the mapping process starts a separate File Server Process that uses Bob's user ID. This is shown by the dashed lines in Figure 10.27.

When Bob actually requests the survey file, the client puts his identity information into the request. The client then directs the request at Bob's File Server Process on Alice's computer. The process tries to retrieve the file. If Bob has permission to retrieve the file, then the process also has that permission, and it successfully retrieves the file. Otherwise, the access fails and the server returns an error message to Bob's client.

10.7 Resources

IMPORTANT TERMS INTRODUCED

analog signal	downlink	peer-to-peer
application protocol	Ethernet	protocol
bandwidth	frame	protocol stack
bot	host	rootkit
circuit switching	link	sequence diagram
client	link protocol	server
client/server	MAC address	timeout
collision	message switching	transport protocol
datagram	network hub	uplink
delegation problem	network switch	Wi-Fi
digital signal	optical fiber	
distributed processing	packet switching	

ACRONYMS INTRODUCED

ACK—Acknowledgment

AM—Amplitude modulation

Cat 5—Category 5

Cat 5 E—Category 5, Enhanced

CB—Citizen's band

coax—Coaxial cable

CTS—Clear to Send

DDOS—Distributed denial of service attack

FCC—Federal Communications Commission

FM—Frequency modulation

Hz—Hertz
IP—Internet Protocol
LAN—Local area network
MAC—Media access control
modem—Modulator-demodulator
NAK—Negative acknowledgment
OSI—Open Systems Interconnect
PARC—Palo Alto Research Center
RJ-45—Registered Jack 45
RTS—Request to Send
TCP—Transmission control protocol
TV—Television

10.7.1 Review Questions

R1.   For each of the six types of attacks, give an example of how the attack occurs on a network.

R2.   Summarize and compare the three techniques for transmitting information on communications networks.

R3.   Explain the differences between analog signals and digital signals, between parallel and serial links, and between synchronous and asynchronous communications.

R4.   Explain the difference between baud and bandwidth.

R5.   Explain how a typical acknowledgement protocol works, and why it provides reliable data transmission. How can the protocol produce duplicate packets?

R6.   Briefly describe the different types of Ethernet LAN systems in use.

R7.   Describe the fields in an Ethernet packet.

R8.   Explain how collisions are handled on a wireless LAN. Compare it to how collisions are handled on a wired Ethernet LAN.

R9.   Explain the relationship between layers of software in the network protocol stack and headers appearing in a packet.

R10. List the seven layers in the OSI protocol model in order from lowest to highest.

R11. Give examples of client/server and peer-to-peer network applications.

R12. Describe a typical approach to resource sharing on a network. What is the delegation problem?

10.7.2 Exercises

Note: Some exercises are marked with restrictions. Exercises marked "Small LANs only" should only be performed on a small LAN where the student has permission to perform the assignment, often a household LAN.

E1.   (Small LANs only.) Identify a small, local network that you use. Ideally, it should be a household network with at least one node. Determine the node's make and model. Visit the manufacturer's website and determine whether it provides switch, hub, and/or wireless interconnection between endpoints (switches and hubs are described in Section 10.4). Which is it?

E2. Using a host computer connected to a network, determine the following:

a. Manufacturer of the host's equipment

b. Host's MAC address

c. The vendor who assigned the MAC address. (Determine this from the "vendor unique address" in the MAC address.)

E3. (Small LANs only.) Identify a small, local network that you use. It should contain only a few hosts and no more than two network nodes. Do the following:

a. Identify a physical perimeter that provides some protection to that network.

b. Draw a diagram of the hosts, nodes, and links.

E4. Given the maximum size of an Ethernet packet (Figure 10.16), calculate the packet efficiency.

E5. Many early timesharing computers provided connections across LANs and other networks. Many of these computers accepted data typed at a keyboard one character at a time. Thus, many of the messages sent to these systems contained no more than 1 byte's worth of actual data, after all headers were removed. If we transmit the smallest possible Ethernet packet, and it only contains *1 byte* of data, what is the packet efficiency?

NETWORKS OF NETWORKS

CHAPTER

11

ABOUT THIS CHAPTER

This chapter introduces Internet technology, which connects every computer network to every other one at some level. To understand this, we cover the following topics:

- Network topology
- Basic Internet structure and routing
- Internet host addressing
- Network inspection tools

11.1 Building Information Networks

Some people believe the global telegraph network was the first Internet, but the telephone network was the first to reach into most homes and workplaces. Unlike the telegraph, the telephone became part of the social and cultural fabric of modern life in the mid-20th century, much like the Internet has become today.

Because of this, classic elements of telephone technology became familiar social and cultural concepts, much like the word "multitasking" was inherited from computing. These concepts include switchboards, party lines, area codes, and toy "tin can" telephones. Each of these reflect a particular way of organizing a network. Each arose during the 19th and 20th centuries as telephone engineers faced the problem of connecting phones together into a network.

The telephone exchange was the network's fundamental building block (Figure 11.1). Every phone was wired to an exchange, which connected it to other phones. Although phone calls, especially on wired phones, may seem familiar and even trivial, the underlying network has always demanded the highest performance from available technology.

To make a call, the telephone network establishes a connection between the two telephones. A telephone transmitter converts the speaker's voice into electrical signals that follow the connection across the network. The receiver at the other end converts the signals into sounds. The signals travel across the network with very little delay. If the network delays the signal too much, people have trouble carrying on a conversation.

Figure 11.1

Switchboards were the first exchanges.

NETWORK TOPOLOGY: EVOLUTION OF THE PHONE NETWORK

It's easy to connect things together. It's hard to maintain order while connecting them together. A network's *topology* refers to the structure of its connections. The simplest phone system might contain only phones and wires, but larger networks need intermediate devices to make order out of chaos.

By the end of the 20th century, the phone network had tried every major technique for connecting calls. The challenge was to interconnect the telephone exchanges so that calls could be handled quickly and efficiently.

Traditionally, the phone network uses different terms that we use in computer networking. While we talk about *hosts* on a computer network, we talk about phones in the phone network. What we call *nodes* on a computer network are called exchanges or "central offices" on the phone network. Links on a computer network are called "lines" or "trunks" on the phone network.

Once we get past the differences in terminology, the same network structures appear in both worlds. The most common ones fall into the five categories listed below. Although we will talk about phones and hosts, we will use the more general term *endpoint* for either. We will use the terms *node* and *link* to talk about structures:

- *Point-to-point network* connects exactly two endpoints together. This also is called a *dedicated line*.
- *Star network* connects three or more endpoints through a central node. All messages pass through the central node.
- *Bus network* connects all endpoints to a single, shared communications medium. This is like a telephone "party line" or a two-way radio on a shared radio channel.
- *Tree network* connects endpoints through a hierarchy of nodes. Geographical networks often work this way, with neighborhood, city, metropolitan, and regional nodes.
- *Mesh network* connects endpoints through a network of arbitrarily connected nodes. Although a tree connects only upward or downward in a hierarchy, a mesh has arbitrary connections to other nodes.

Over the years, network designers have implemented other, more specific topologies, including rings, "butterflies," and "hypercubes." These specialized topologies solve specific design problems in particular systems. In general, however, the five structures listed previously are seen in familiar information networks.

Certain features and properties vary from one network topology to another. Here is a summary of properties that work well or poorly depending on the network's topology:

- Growth. It is easier to add endpoints to some topologies than to others.
- Addressing. Some topologies implicitly provide addresses to nodes and endpoints.
- Routing. It is easier to route a connection between endpoints in some topologies than others.
- Privacy. Some networks don't keep network traffic private as well as others.
- Authenticity. Some networks are better than others at reliably identifying the source of a connection.

11.1.1 Point-to-Point Network

With both telegraphy and telephones, the earliest connections were with point-to-point links. The simplest example is the "tin can telephone," a toy that first appeared in the mid-1800s (Figure 11.2). In 1844, Samuel Morse prevailed on the U.S. Congress to pay for a demonstration telegraph line between Washington and Baltimore. This is also a classic point-to-point connection.

The earliest commercial phone systems were entirely point to point. A customer bought the two phones and then arranged to string wires between the desired endpoints. To speak to two or more destinations, the customer bought additional sets of phones, one for each destination.

Point-to-point networks have certain advantages:

- No nodes—we don't need separate network hardware, just the endpoints.
- No addressing problems—since the network only has "us" and "them," we always know who we're talking to.
- Authenticity—given that the link only talks to one other endpoint, we always know who is on the other end.
- Privacy—the link carries the connection between the endpoints, and does not disclose it to other endpoints.

Figure 11.2

Point-to-point network: A tin can telephone.

These networks also have major shortcomings:

- Difficult to expand—assuming we want all endpoints to be able to connect to each other. To add another endpoint, you add point-to-point links between the current endpoints and the new one. The number of links grows exponentially as you add more subscribers.
- Broadcasting is impossible—if we want to broadcast to every connected endpoint, we need to replicate the message over each link. Each link only knows of its own endpoint.

Traditional point-to-point networks also were called *dedicated line* networks because links were not shared among endpoints. This appeals to some customers for security reasons. A dedicated network link seems more secure because the traffic does not route information onto a public network where it might be misrouted or otherwise intercepted by others. In practice, modern dedicated lines have an unshared connection to the vendor's network, and the line's connection is specially routed within the network to keep the traffic separate from other customers' traffic. In fact, however, the dedicated line may share the same links in the public network as other customers' traffic.

Today, point-to-point computer links are relatively rare. They also are rare in phone systems. Point-to-point phones are mostly limited to a few office intercoms. The earliest computer network systems used point-to-point links to connect individual mainframe computers or to connect a mainframe with a smaller utility computer. As noted previously, modern dedicated lines aren't as dedicated as in earlier days, so customers tend to choose alternatives.

11.1.2 Star Network

Telephone vendors did not really prosper until they started offering a phone "service" by which they connected any customer's phone to any other phone. These services arose in cities connecting businesses and wealthier households. All phones connected into a single central exchange. There, a switchboard operator answered all calls and manually connected a caller to the desired destination phone. This arrangement forms a "star" with the exchange serving as a central node (Figure 11.3).

As phone systems connected more customers, they became more useful and valuable to those customers. This is what we now call the *network effect*: A product or service becomes more and more valuable to its customers as more and more use it. Robert Metcalfe, a pioneer in computer networking, coined *Metcalfe's law*, which suggests that a network's value increases with the square of the number of devices it handles.

The star topology requires an addressing scheme to distinguish between the different connections. Early phone systems easily determined the source address of each call; they knew which wire carried the call in to the switchboard. The problem was to identify the destination address. On manual switchboards, the operator literally asked the caller for the destination address by saying, "Number, please."

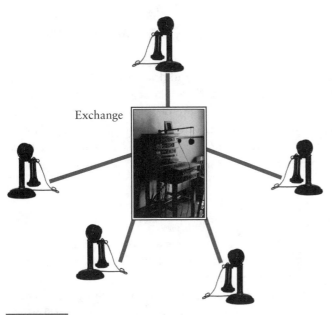

Exchange

Figure 11.3

Star network.

Starting in the 1890s, human operators were replaced by dial-operated "step-by-step" switches. The caller provided the destination address by dialing a phone number. The step-by-step switches counted pulses in the dialed number and used them to automatically connect local phone calls.

The star has important benefits:

- Allows growth. We can connect several phones or hosts together using a single networking system.
- One link per device. We only need one link to connect a phone or host to the network.
- Privacy. Traffic flows only on the wires that connect the source and destination, and through the node.
- Authenticity. The network can reliably identify an endpoint, based on its physical connection.

The star also has shortcomings:

- Limited growth. The central node needs to switch connections based on addresses. The node's complexity increases dramatically as we connect more and more endpoints.

- Broadcasting. If the central node connects pairs of endpoints, it is hard to give it the option of broadcasting as well. This is especially tricky for analog networks like the phone system.

Although the network itself might know the source and destination of every call, the network did not necessarily share that information. Early phone systems had no practical way to identify a caller to the called phone. Police and other investigators had to follow a complicated "call-tracing" procedure to figure out the endpoints of a call. The procedure became more complicated as call routing became more automated. The tracing procedure did not become simple until computing systems played a major role in call management and routing.

11.1.3 Bus Network

We used the term "bus" earlier to describe I/O connections that connect many devices to a computer. We use this same notion in computer networking. The underlying technique also was used in early, low-cost phone systems.

City-based phone networks often had many wealthier subscribers whose fees could pay for expensive telephone exchanges. Rural phone systems were not so lucky. To reduce wiring costs, the network relied on a "party-line" connection among telephones (Figure 11.4).

On a party line, all phones share the same link. Each phone has its own address, indicated by a distinctive ringing pattern. In the simplest systems, each phone had a hand-cranked ringer.

For example, Old Bob (Bob's great-grandfather) had a farm with a party line. His phone number was "two longs and a short." To call Old Bob, another farmer would crank the ringer to make two long ringing sounds and then a short ringing sound. If Old Bob was near the phone, he would hear that pattern and answer it.

Other people on that phone link also would hear the phone ring. Social etiquette decreed that others should not pick up the phone when someone else's phone rang. In practice, however, party lines were a common source of entertainment and gossip in small communities.

Figure 11.4

Bus or "party-line" network.

All shared resources face a common problem: ***contention***. Only one pair of endpoints can use the party line at a time. To make a call, a subscriber picks up the phone. If the line is silent, it is available to use. If the subscriber hears voices, the line is in use. The polite response is to hang up and try again later. In an emergency, the caller can ask others to hang up.

The bus, and other party-line techniques, have these benefits:

- Easy to add endpoints. A bus probably requires the least overhead of any network when adding another endpoint.
- Possibly node-free. The simplest bus arrangements don't require additional hardware though, in practice, many do use node hardware.
- No routing. All endpoints see all traffic, and they use addressing information to decide whether the traffic is directed at them or at a different endpoint.
- Broadcasting is easy. We can designate a certain address as a "broadcast" address that tells all endpoints to listen in.

Here is a summary of bus shortcomings:

- Contention. All endpoints share a single link and they must take turns. This requires planning and coordination by the endpoints.
- Limited growth. As we add more endpoints, contention grows. At some point, the shared link can't handle all traffic produced by the endpoints.
- Denial of service. One endpoint can monopolize the link and shut out all other endpoints.
- Eavesdropping. All nodes can eavesdrop on each other. They do not even need additional equipment, unless the standard hardware explicitly tries to prevent eavesdropping.
- Masquerade. Addresses often are arbitrary on busses and party lines, because the endpoints themselves may connect arbitrarily. Thus, a subverted endpoint can supply a bogus address.

Ethernet, the most popular local networking system, is based on a bus topology. Ethernet has succeeded despite the shortcomings of busses because it provides reliable, low-cost service for small, private networks.

11.1.4 Tree Network

As the telephone system grew, customers of different exchanges wanted to connect to one another. Over time, the interconnections formed a hierarchy; local exchanges all connected to an "intermediate exchange," which allowed people in the same city to speak to one another (Figure 11.5). If someone in the downtown exchange wanted to speak to the Hillside exchange across town, the downtown exchange routed the call to the city's intermediate exchange. From there, the call was routed to Hillside, and the exchange connected to the called phone.

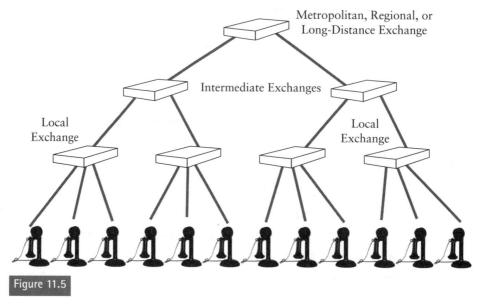

Figure 11.5

Tree network or hierarchy.

As more people wanted to connect, the network added more layers. A citywide exchange could connect calls between intermediate exchanges. Higher-level exchanges interconnected cities with one another. In the early days, subscribers were charged extra money when a call was routed to higher exchanges. Moreover, calls became less automated as they traversed farther on the tree. Long-distance calls relied heavily on human operators until the mid-20th century.

The tree structure allows the network to grow arbitrarily large. Each exchange serves as a "star" for customers or exchanges at the next lower level. Moving upward, each exchange connects to another at the next higher level.

Addressing and routing can be simple in a tree network. For example, we can assign addresses according to a subscriber's location in the hierarchy. Telephone numbers used to work this way. In the "North American Numbering Plan," for example, the lowest four or five digits selected a particular phone line in a local exchange. The next digit or two selected a particular local exchange. The next digits, in turn, could select an intermediate exchange. The highest three digits formed the "area code," which selected a region for long-distance routing.

Hierarchies also suffer from shortcomings. For example, imagine that the middle two phones in Figure 11.5 try to call one another. Even though the phones may be physically nearby, the call must be routed through five separate exchanges. A seemingly local call then must incur the expense of being routed through several layers.

For example, two people may live next door, but still live in different towns with a state boundary between them. If each town has its own phone exchange, then the neighbors' phones will connect to different exchanges in different states. This may make phone calls between the neighbors into long-distance calls.

Another hierarchy problem arose in the United States during the 1990s as cell phones became common. The North American Numbering Plan had assigned area codes nationwide in the mid-20th century while automating long-distance dialing. As vendors sold more and more cell phones, the available phone numbers were quickly used up in major metropolitan areas. To provide for more phones, these areas received additional area codes. This often required assigning new area codes to existing subscribers. Some locales were renumbered two or three times as cell phone usage grew.

Here is a summary of benefits to tree networks:

- Expandable. The network can incorporate an arbitrarily large number of new nodes in an organized way.
- Reliable addresses. Each endpoint can have an explicit address defined by its location in the hierarchy. The network itself can reliably identify the endpoints of every call.
- Simple and reliable routing. Since the addresses reflect an endpoint's location in the hierarchy, it is easy to route calls between any two endpoints.
- Privacy. Connections aren't sent on links accessible to other endpoints.

Here is a summary of shortcomings in tree-shaped networks:

- Inefficiency at the fringes. When two "fringe" endpoints try to communicate, they may need to traverse several levels of the hierarchy even if they are geographically near each other.
- Inflexible addresses. A subscriber can't keep the same address (phone number) when moving. This is especially true when moving between places served by different exchanges.
- Address-based size limits. The size of the network served by a particular part of the hierarchy is limited by the number of exchanges and subexchanges that can fit in the available address space.
- Broadcasting is very hard. Analog broadcasts are impractical; digital broadcasts require a careful network node design. Nodes would have to replicate the broadcast message without accidentally sending duplicates.

Today's telephone system no longer relies so heavily on a hierarchical architecture. Modern networking technology has made it possible to separate telephone locations from telephone numbers, so that a roaming cell phone can receive calls even when in the "wrong" area code.

11.1.5 Mesh

Few phone companies used rigid, unvarying tree structures. Instead, they interconnected exchanges when practical to do so, and they rigged the network to route calls accordingly. Figure 11.6 shows a city network with interconnected local exchanges.

Thus, a downtown subscriber can dial anyone in Hillside, Miltown, or Pier without routing through an intermediate exchange. The Herndon exchange can reach two nearby exchanges, but can't directly reach downtown or the Pier.

The term "mesh" refers to the fact that each node in the network may be connected to one or several other nodes. The interconnections can follow whatever pattern best connects the nodes. In a sense, the tree network is a form of mesh network, but with restrictions on node connections. A mesh network faces different benefits and shortcomings by weakening those restrictions.

A fundamental problem is that the mesh network has no inherent shape or structure. This prevents us from assigning meaningful addresses, like we did on the tree-structured network.

Here is a summary of the benefits:

- Arbitrary size. Like tree networks, there is nothing inherent in the network hardware or structure that limits its size.

- Reliable, authentic addresses. We can assign a unique address to each node and to each endpoint connected to a node; thus, the network can know the source and destination of every call.

- Privacy. Connections aren't sent on links accessible to other endpoints.

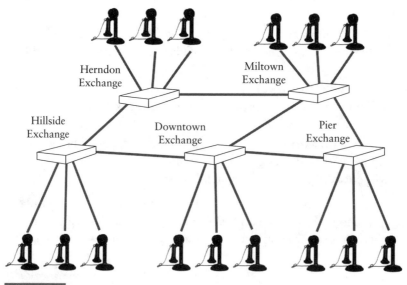

Figure 11.6

A mesh network example.

- Efficient routing. Instead of traversing a hierarchy of nodes, a connection traverses a smaller, even optimal, number of nodes.

Here are limitations to mesh networks:

- Routing gets tricky. Routes can be efficient *in theory*, but that depends on knowing how to route calls efficiently. It is very difficult to implement automatic routing that is fast, efficient, and reliable. Early mesh networks relied on handcrafted routing between a small number of nodes.
- Congestion. Routing has to take into account the amount of traffic on the routes being used. If a few busy endpoints use the same routes, all traffic on that route will slow down. In extreme cases, the network may become too busy to carry any traffic effectively.
- Broadcasting is very hard. Analog broadcasts are impractical; digital broadcasts require a careful network node design. Nodes would have to replicate the broadcast message without accidentally sending duplicates.

11.2 Combining Computer Networks

The telephone system evolved over many decades. It could take years of planning and coordination each time they attempted to interconnect two or more existing networks. Matters could be even worse when connecting networks that developed in different countries or on different continents. The separate networks often used different wiring techniques or voltages or signals to make and route calls. They had to develop a coordinated way to handle the differences before a call from one system could be completed in another.

Early computer systems suffered from the same problem. Different computers had different byte and character sizes; some used sets of 64 characters (6 bits), 128 characters (7 bits), and even 256 characters (8 bits). These evolved from different character sets. One mainframe computer used two different character sets on the same system at the same time: one for batch processing and another for online timesharing terminals.

Many computer vendors developed networking products and technologies in the 1960s and 1970s, including IBM, Honeywell, and DEC. However, these networks rarely worked with equipment from competing vendors. Thus, each network was relatively small or limited in scope. It was difficult to achieve the benefits of a generally available network like today's Internet.

In the late 1960s, the U.S. military, through its Advanced Research Projects Agency (ARPA), developed the ARPANET, an experimental packet-switched computer network. (In later years, the word "Defense" was added to the agency's name, yielding today's acronym DARPA.) The ARPANET connected numerous defense research organizations at universities, military bases, and private companies. The ARPANET was carefully designed so that the network protocols worked seamlessly across a broad range of computing equipment.

Traversing Computer Networks

Users occasionally needed to use one network to reach another. In the 1970s, this often required a personal user account at a computer system that resided on each network. For example, Bob's Uncle Frank worked on a local network at Honeywell Corporation in Minnesota and needed to connect to a remote computer in England. First, he connected his computer to the corporate Multics system and logged in. Given the right permissions, Frank could then use the ARPANET to connect to University College, London (UCL). If he could log in there, he then could open another connection to reach his destination at another site on the U.K. research network.

Such connections were extremely fragile. Interruptions at any gateway host (Multics or UCL) would close the entire connection, as could disruptions on the associated networks. These problems led to the development of modern internet technology. In fact, an early internet demonstration transmitted packets from a vehicle crossing the Golden Gate Bridge in California to a terminal in the Royal Radar Establishment on the U.K. network.

The Internet Emerges

Modern internet technology evolved from research on the ARPANET and the research networks attached to it. As it was, most computers that connected to two or more networks served as gateways for users who needed to reach a destination on another network. The goal of internet research was to route the packets automatically between the networks without intermediate logins.

In a sense, this was like a public highway system. Every town and city had built roads for its citizens. A challenge in the early 20th century was to connect towns and cities together to support reliable automobile travel. In the mid-1920s, state highway officials in the United States coordinated the development of the "U.S. highway system," consisting of numbered roads with well-marked routes. This provided drivers with reliable roads to follow between states and across the country. To become "part of the system," one's driveway or street simply had to reach any other street that reached a U.S. highway.

The same is true for the modern Internet. If a local network uses internet protocols and it connects to *any* network attached to the Internet, then it may send traffic to other Internet hosts.

> **Note on capitalization:** We use lowercase to speak of internet protocols in general. We capitalize the proper name of the global network "the Internet." To carry packets between networks, we use an additional protocol whose proper name is the Internet Protocol (IP).

The Internet was "commercialized" in the early 1990s. Because it started as a research project under U.S. government sponsorship, private companies weren't allowed to use it to explicitly advertise or sell products or to offer services that relied on an Internet connection. Meanwhile, Internet email had become very popular in many circles, and many computer vendors distributed technical data through the Internet. This was enough to justify Internet connections for many organizations. In the United States, the telephone system was a regulated monopoly, which occasionally prevented established telephone companies from offering Internet services. The growing interest in the Internet spawned the first

Internet service providers or ISPs. In the early 1990s, the government privatized the remains of its research network and let the Internet go commercial.

11.2.1 Hopping Between Networks

We often build a LAN around Layer 2 nodes, called switches and hubs. To connect LANs or other integrated networks together, we use Layer 3 routers to move packets between the networks. A router is traditionally called a *gateway*, and many vendors still sell "gateway" products.

Not all networks are LANs. Early networks like the ARPANET covered nations and continents. We call these *wide area networks* or WANs. Each WAN may have a distinct link layer protocol. When we use internet technology to connect two networks with separate link layers together, we call each individual network a *subnet*. The "network" is the combined set of subnets.

Internet routing relies on a simple technical trick and on deploying routers to carry packets between networks. The simple technical trick is to split Layer 2, the link layer, into two parts. The lower part is the regular link layer, with its local MAC addresses. The upper part becomes Layer 3, the *internet layer* (Figure 11.7). Because most modern networks use internet protocols at Layer 3, we may call Layer 3 either the network layer or the internet layer.

When we add a protocol layer, we also add a packet header. Following the link header, the packet now carries an internet header or IP header. The link header still carries a packet from place to place on the subnet. The IP header contains a separate set of source and destination addresses: the *IP addresses*.

Packet addressing and routing on the Internet relies entirely on IP addresses. Although knowing a MAC address allows us to transmit packets across a LAN, we can't use that MAC address to locate a host on a distant LAN. The Internet uses the IP address to direct the packet to the correct LAN.

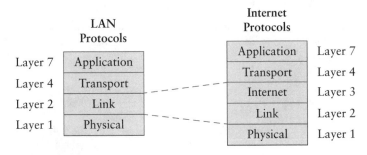

Figure 11.7

Adding a layer to handle internet routing.

When a packet must travel across another network to reach its destination, the link header gets replaced each time it traverses another subnet. The IP header remains largely intact and the remaining packet contents are unchanged.

Figure 11.8 illustrates an example. The figure shows separate LANs, presumably in separate suites, connected by a common router. Bob is on LAN 1, which contains hosts with IP addresses 1.1 through 1.4. Henry is on LAN 2 in his own suite, which hosts IP addresses 2.1 through 2.4.

Bob, on host 1.2, sends packets to Henry on host 2.4. Bob's computer sees that the IP address is not on Lan 1, so it can't send the packet directly to the computer. Instead, the computer addresses it to the router by using the router's MAC address as the packet's destination.

The packet arrives at the router, which strips off the link header. It looks at the IP header and sees that the destination is on LAN 2. The router is attached to LAN 2, so it can deliver the packet directly to its destination. The router looks up the MAC address for host 2.4; then the router constructs a new link header that delivers the packet to host 2.4, its destination.

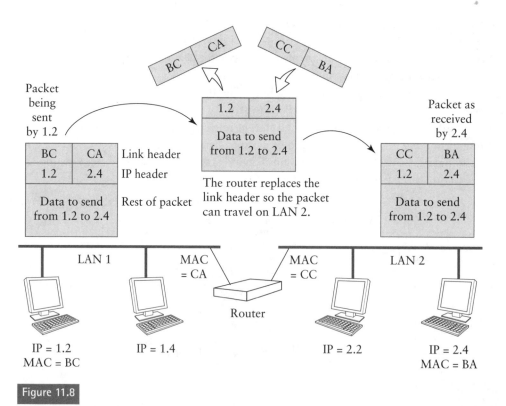

Figure 11.8

Sending a packet from one LAN to another.

Routing Internet Packets

Even though we often focus on routers as the nodes that direct packets around the Internet, every computer that handles internet protocols must do some routing. The internet layer of every such protocol stack contains a *routing table* that chooses a network and/or MAC address for the outgoing packet. Most hosts rely on the Address Resolution Protocol (see Section 11.3.3) to fill in the routing table with addresses on its subnet. Packets destined for other IP addresses go to a default router. This illustrates the basic rule of Internet routing:

> If you don't know how to deliver the packet to its destination, send it to a router that might know how to reach its destination.

No single router knows how to reach every host on the Internet. Most routers know how to route packets to nearby hosts and where to send the remaining packets. A gateway router for a major site may connect to two or more different WANs. Its routing table directs packets to the best WAN to deliver the packet to its destination.

When a packet travels across other networks to reach the network of its destination, it uses those networks as communications links. It doesn't care what else might be happening on those networks. It only cares that the link brings it closer to its destination.

Counting Hops

A router leaves everything past the IP header unchanged. It makes exactly one change to the IP header: It subtracts one from the *time to live* (TTL) field. When first created, the packet's TTL field is set to a large number, as high as 255. Each time the packet passes through a router, the router decrements the TTL field. If the field reaches zero, the router discards the packet.

The TTL field effectively counts the number of "hops" the packet takes through routers. This helps detect packets caught in a "routing loop." If a packet gets caught in such a loop, a router with bad information sends the packet *back* to a router it visited earlier. The packet then is routed again to the router with bad information, which sends it back again.

If a packet is caught in such a loop, its TTL will eventually reach zero, and a router will discard the packet. Often, the router with bad information will correct its routes before the packet's TTL expires.

11.2.2   Evolution of Internet Security

Internet protocols were intended to make it as easy as possible for people to connect to a single, global research network. They succeeded. The Internet was an international network from the moment of its creation. Even though the U.S. military—through DARPA—had funded the Internet's development, they quickly lost control of it as it took on an international scope. Anyone on an Internet-connected host computer could send network traffic to any other Internet host in any country.

Researchers all over the world wanted to use the Internet. In practice, anyone with the money for equipment and a network link could connect to the Internet. Anyone with a moderately plausible "network research" activity could apply to the Internet Assigned Numbers Authority (a network researcher named Jon Postel, 1943–1998) and ask for a block of IP addresses and a domain name.

Although this was incredibly convenient for researchers, it also meant that anyone, researcher or not, could use the Internet. In particular, there has never been a reliable technique to eliminate potential threats from the Internet. In this sense, the Internet literally serves as an "information highway."

Improved U.S. highways in the 1920s and 1930s improved business and personal transportation dramatically, but it also produced a new breed of criminal. Interstate bank robbing was a well-known problem, but the automobile made it much easier to do. Several such robbers were infamous, including Bonnie and Clyde, John Dillinger, and the Karpis gang.

PROTECTING THE ARPANET

The ARPANET pioneered the earliest strategies of Internet security, such as they were. The initial defense was to restrict access to people who had a bona fide reason to use it. This seemed simple at the time, because computers usually resided in locked and guarded computer rooms. Access by computer users was through remote, text-oriented terminals.

To connect to the ARPANET, a site needed an "Interface Message Processor" or IMP (Figure 11.9). This was a $50,000 minicomputer that ran special routing software to carry messages between host computers and the network of IMPs. The IMPs were built by ARPANET contractor Bolt, Beranek, and Newman (BBN).

Each IMP also needed expensive, high-speed, leased lines to connect it to other IMPs in the network. Moreover, a site had to be part of a DOD research program to get

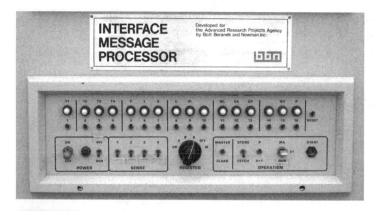

Figure 11.9

Control panel of an ARPANET IMP.

permission to connect to the other IMPs. The DOD made the rules for the ARPANET and required every site to exert some control over who could use the network.

Some sites, especially colleges and universities, did very little to restrict ARPANET access. Although the ARPANET seemed obscure and irrelevant to some, others saw its potential for a broad range of communications tasks. Email evolved on the ARPANET, as did the file sharing that underlies today's World Wide Web.

Email spawned online discussion groups, some that lasted for decades. By allowing broad access, the schools and other sites helped construct a better understanding of what large-scale computer networking could achieve. There was, however, no easy way to use the ARPANET except by having permission to use an ARPANET-connected computer or dial-in port.

EARLY INTERNET ATTACKS

In the Internet's early days, the U.S. government forbade commercial activities on their portion of the Internet. For many years, this essentially prevented formal commercial activities, because the ARPANET carried a great deal of Internet traffic. The only attacks of any significance were thefts of trade secrets and military secrets.

In fact, such attacks occurred in the late 1980s. In Section 4.6, we heard the story of Clifford Stoll, who detected a hacker at Berkeley and tracked him across the Internet back to Germany. The hacker was collecting information from U.S. military and government sites and selling it to Soviet agents.

Also hit was DEC, the company that produced the Vax computer and its VMS operating system. DEC's software development computers were on the Internet, but employees had to use a two-factor authentication system to reach those systems. An attacker hijacked an authenticated connection and used it to steal the VMS source code.

And, of course, there was the Morris worm (Section 2.3). The worm was not intended to bring down the Internet, but it managed to do so. To prevent a recurrence of the worm and to reduce risks of information theft, sites developed tools and techniques to protect themselves.

EARLY INTERNET DEFENSES

On January 1, 1983, the ARPANET protocols all were replaced with internet protocols. At that point, any host connected anywhere on the Internet could open a connection directly to any other host on the Internet. Colleges and universities without military contracts quickly hooked up, and so did many companies in the computing and networking industries.

Access to the Internet is governed by Transitive Trust: If someone provides you with a connection that carries Internet packets, you can use it to communicate with everyone else on the Internet. In fact, once you have that connection you can actually offer Internet connections to others. Internet routers kept long routing lists that directed packets between any two hosts.

As the Internet grew, sites could no longer assume that the network was filled with benign researchers. The Internet population was growing so large and varied that *someone* was going to prove untrustworthy in some sense.

Before the Morris worm incident, sites concerned about security relied on host-based login authentication. Many people thought of the network links themselves as analogous to public streets and trails: We use them but we are cautious; we don't leave valuables unattended, and we keep our doors locked.

Following the well-publicized Internet security incidents in the late 1980s, many sites sought more sophisticated protection. One approach was to scan the packets themselves for indications of bad intent. Early Ethernet users on the Alto network experimented with packet filtering as a way to manage network traffic. Accetta and Rashid at Carnegie-Mellon University developed the "enet" package for Unix, which filtered inbound packets by looking at individual fields. This was the genesis of modern firewalling technology. We examine modern firewall filtering in Section 15.4.

11.2.3 Internet Structure

Following the Internet's commercialization, almost anyone could—and did—become an *Internet service provider* (ISP). In the United States, antitrust laws prevented some telephone companies from becoming ISPs, but other network service companies entered the business, and so did many small-scale operators. In fact, high school students could start an ISP in their basement with a small bank of low-cost dial-in modems. Internet routing helped ensure that any packet could reach any host if any route existed.

The engineering elements of the Internet are the province of the Internet Engineering Task Force (IETF), a largely volunteer organization. The IETF coordinates its engineering standards through an open development process. Initially, the developments focused on decentralized solutions that worked well in the original, research-oriented Internet. As Internet growth exploded in the mid-1990s, decentralized routing bred enormous routing tables in the major ISPs.

Autonomous Systems

Large routing tables pose a serious problem. On the one hand, the large tables allow maximum flexibility when connecting new networks. On the other hand, it takes time to search a large routing table, and this slows down packet delivery. To solve this problem, the Internet moved to a more hierarchical organization built around *autonomous systems* (ASes).

Each AS is essentially an ISP that handles routing between its networking customers. Often these are large telecommunications (telecom) vendors, though ASes may be private or government organizations with large enterprise networks. Originally, the Internet consisted of hosts and networks. Now it consists of hosts, networks, and ASes. Figure 11.10 illustrates this change.

Each AS provides connections between networks and is responsible for routing between those networks. In other words, each AS handles two types of routing:

1. Interior routing—route packets between networks within the AS

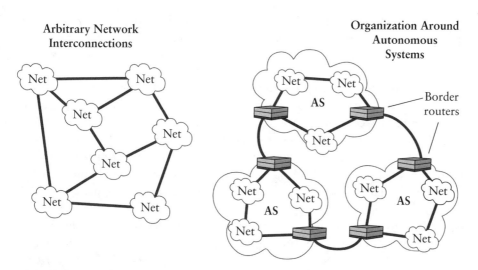

Arbitrary Network
Interconnections

Organization Around
Autonomous
Systems

Figure 11.10

Old and new Internet routing structures.

2. Exterior routing—route packets from a network within the AS to a network on
   another AS

Private networks within an AS are responsible for their own interior routing. The AS
likewise performs its own interior routing between its own routers. The AS generally
provides dedicated network links between its own routers in order to pass traffic
between its customers.

Exterior routing relies on ***border routers***. These routers connect one AS to another.
To route a packet from one AS to another, a router inside the AS forwards the packet to
the appropriate border router, which forwards it to the appropriate AS. If the ASes
aren't directly connected, the border router sends it to an AS that can deliver the packet.

Internet routing mechanisms are designed to detect and recover from routing errors.
However, a really large error can seriously disrupt Internet traffic. The AS structure tries
to reduce such risks by sharing routes among a limited number of other routers.
Although routers within a private network may trust one another, the AS routers do not
generally accept routing information from the private networks. Border routers only
trust traffic from other, connected border routers.

An incident in 1997 illustrates the risks of sharing routes too broadly. An AS border
router in Florida received an extremely large routing update from one of its internal customers. The update was incorrect; it appeared to provide a direct connection to all networks on the Internet via this Florida network.

The border router processed the update and forwarded it to a border router operated
by Sprint, another AS. The Sprint border router distributed the information to other

ASes, which then routed large amounts of traffic to Florida. Because the routing update was large, it propagated slowly and continued to affect Internet traffic for several hours.

ROUTING SECURITY

Although the 1997 routing incident was accidental, it illustrates the lack of sophistication in Internet routing security. The principal security measures restrict the propagation of routing information except among routers that operate as peers.

For example, routers within a private network may exchange routes with one another, but the AS router does not accept routes from the private network. This was one of the mistakes that led to the Florida incident: The Florida AS should not have accepted the routing update from the private network. The problem was made severe by the size and content of the routing update.

A separate peer-to-peer relationship exists between routers within an AS. This allows the AS to establish routes between its customers and its border routers using its own links. Border routers between ASes also share a trust relationship: Each AS must trust the other's border router.

The relationships between AS routers and border routers reflects Transitive Trust between the highest-level routers on the Internet. This is not generally a security problem because all ASes are assumed to share the common objective of routing packets efficiently. Incorrect routes constantly arise by accident. Other routers soon detect the error and establish corrections.

International Rerouting

These trust relationships, combined with the Internet's international nature, mean that packets aren't aware of international boundaries. If a nation contains several well-connected ASes, then that nation's traffic may be routed through other nations.

In April of 2010, China Telecom's border routers briefly distributed routes that redirected 15 percent of the world's Internet destinations through China's routers. Like the Florida incident, the rerouting occurred when the AS published routing information it received from an internal network.

China Telecom and the Chinese government asserted that the incident was accidental. However, the incident was noted in a U.S. government report on the security risks of U.S.–China economic and trade relations. The report discussed several ways in which China might exploit redirected Internet traffic. The report also noted that the rerouting caused a relatively small change in Internet traffic patterns compared to other incidents known to be accidental.

Another incident similar to these occurred in late 2004. An AS in Turkey accidentally rerouted all Internet traffic to itself. This made parts of the Internet unreachable for several hours while the errors were corrected.

Internet experts do not see a simple and effective way of preventing future incidents, whether accidental or not. Such cases usually occur when incorrect routing information from a private network is propagated by an AS. In general, ASes avoid this through careful configuration of border routers. However, there are thousands of border routers, making occasional errors inevitable.

STARTING AN ISP

In the Internet's early days, it was easy to join. Typical networks were educational or research institutions with technical talent but limited resources. A site could simply connect its router to another site's router, and packets would flow. This was why the Internet grew so quickly in its early days.

Almost anyone could become an ISP. This was aided by the fact that U.S. legal restrictions made it difficult for regulated telephone companies to provide Internet service. It opened up the field to entrepreneurs and businesses of all sizes.

This also opened the Internet to abuse by early ISPs. In one case, a bookseller started an ISP that he marketed to other booksellers. Because he was responsible for routing all of their packets and email, he had access to many of their transactions. He used his position to spy on his customers and outbid them for books he wanted.

This behavior was possible because the threat agent actually operated the routers and network links that carried the network traffic. The threat also operated the email server, giving him access to customer email messages. It is possible, though harder, to eavesdrop on email and other traffic without operating the network.

Today it is much harder to start an ISP. One major problem is the shortage of Internet addresses. Following Postel's death in 1998, blocks of Internet addresses were assigned to registrars who doled out addresses to regional ISPs. Because the registrars have assigned all address blocks to ISPs, no free blocks remain. Given that ISPs must assign addresses to customers, a new ISP must acquire a block of addresses from an existing ISP in order to offer services. A new ISP also must fit into the modern routing discipline, either as an autonomous system itself or as a set of networks within another.

11.3 Talking Between Hosts

Computers that support internet protocols tend to use those protocols for all networking, even if they don't connect to the global Internet. The network applications use many Internet conventions when connecting hosts. This section examines several of those conventions:

- Socket interface
- IP address formats
- IP packet format
- Address resolution protocol

SOCKET INTERFACE

All operating systems provide a networking API that allows applications to establish network services and to open connections to services on other hosts.

Many systems use a networking API called the *socket interface*. This interface provides a well-known way of addressing hosts and processes on a computer and of writing client or server software.

Port Numbers

Whenever one process on a host connects to another, each process is assigned a *port number*. If we think of the processes as separate rooms in a hotel, the port number is the room number. The transport layer packet header contains port numbers for both the packet's sending and recipient host. When arriving at the recipient host, the protocol stack uses the port number to direct the incoming packet to the correct process.

Recognized network services are assigned well-known port numbers. To connect to a particular service on a host, the client specifies the port number for that service. The client's stack puts that port number in the outgoing packet along with the client's own port number. Here are port numbers for a few well-known services:

- 21—File transfer protocol, for setting up a file transfer
- 22—Secure shell protocol, to send keyboard commands to a host
- 25—Email protocol, to submit a message for delivery
- 80—World Wide Web

When a client opens a connection to a server, the client sets the recipient's port number in the outbound connection to select the desired service. The client's own port number is selected and assigned by the operating system's protocol stack. The number is usually a five-digit number between 49152 and 65535.

For example, Bob opens a connection to Google's web page. The destination port number is 80, because Bob asks for a web page. The source port number is 51246, chosen randomly by Bob's protocol stack. If Bob opens another connection to Google, it will use the same source port number (80), but the stack randomly chooses *another* port number for the separate connection. The different port numbers keep the different connections separate.

Socket Addresses

We refer to a specific connection or other relationship between two hosts as being a *socket*. We identify a particular socket with its unique *socket address*, which contains the following:

- Transport protocol being used (see Chapter 12)
- Local socket address, which contains:
  - Local IP address or the local network interface to use
  - Local port number
- Remote socket address, which contains:
  - Remote IP address
  - Remote port number

SOCKET API CAPABILITIES

The socket API uses IP addresses and port numbers to establish connections with other hosts. Some functions provide capabilities for clients while others provide capabilities for servers. Here are the major functions:

- connect()—establish a connection to a particular host and port number; used by client software
- listen()—awaits a connection on a particular socket; used by server software
- accept()—when the listen() function detects an incoming connection, this function establishes the connection; used by server software
- read() or recvfrom() or recv()—reads data from an open connection
- write() or sendto() or send()—writes data to an open connection

11.3.1 IP Addresses

When we use internet protocols, our packets contain three different addresses: the MAC address, the IP address, and the port number (Figure 11.11).

In practice, however, our application programs rarely use the MAC addresses. Most applications use some type of socket interface, which uses IP addresses. Although MAC addresses may be sufficient in some cases, the IP address will work as long as there are routers in place and internet protocol software is present. If the hosts are on the same LAN, the internet protocols use an additional protocol to convert the IP address to the MAC address (see Section 11.3.3).

Today, the most common IP addresses are called *IP Version 4* (IPv4) addresses. These addresses are 32 bits long. We represent them with a *dotted decimal notation*. This displays the address as a series of four decimal integers, separated by dots. Each integer represents an 8-bit portion of the IP address. Figure 11.12 illustrates the notation.

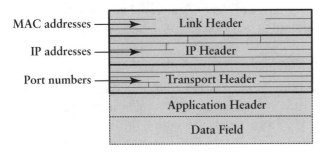

Figure 11.11

Address locations in packet headers.

Dotted decimal notation:
(a 32-bit number)

192.168.1.1

In binary: 1100 0000 - 1010 1000 - 0000 0001 - 0000 0001

Figure 11.12

Dotted decimal notation for Internet addresses.

Here are examples of addresses in dotted decimal notation:

- 74.125.95.99—an address used by Google
- 96.16.114.135—an address used by the White House
- 192.168.1.12—an address used by a home router

IP Version 6

Modern network software actually provides two different IP addresses. Although most of today's Internet traffic uses IPv4 addresses, modern protocol stacks support newer, and longer, addresses in *IP Version 6* (IPv6) format. Although the latest computers and network devices may support Version 6, many hosts and devices only work with IPv4. There are a few institutional and international networks that use Version 6, but the vast majority of Internet services still use IPv4. Thus, when we refer to an "IP address," we mean IPv4.

Version 6 addresses are 128 bits long, four times the size of an IPv4 address. The IPv4 address format was designed in the early 1980s, when the Internet was a relatively small research network. The format started running out of addresses after the Internet "went public" in the mid-1990s. The Internet team that designed Version 6 hope the new address space will last significantly longer.

Version 6 addresses are printed as a group of eight hexadecimal numbers. Each hex number is separated by a colon with leading zeroes suppressed.

11.3.2 IP Packet Format

Figure 11.13 shows major fields in an IP packet. The link header appears before the IP header. The link header's "Packet type" field (see Figure 10.16) indicates that an IP header follows the link header. The IP packet's first field indicates the IP version. In most cases, the packet is for IP Version 4.

Here is a summary of the major field contents:

- Length—the packet's length. The IP header also contains a field that indicates the length of the header by itself.

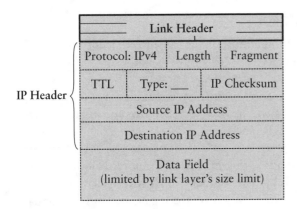

IP Header

Link Header		
Protocol: IPv4	Length	Fragment
TTL	Type: ___	IP Checksum
Source IP Address		
Destination IP Address		
Data Field (limited by link layer's size limit)		

Figure 11.13

Major IP packet fields.

- Fragment—a set of fields to manage the fragmentation and reassembly of IP packets.
- TTL—the time-to-live field described earlier.
- Type—the type of TCP/IP transport protocol carried by this IP packet.
- IP checksum—the checksum of the IP header fields.
- Source IP address—the IP address of the sending host.
- Destination IP address—the IP address of the recipient host.
- Data field—contains the header indicated by the Type field above, and the data contents.

The IP packet may contain an optional set of additional fields called "options" that follow the destination IP address. These rarely appear in packets. If options appear, then the options will be padded with 0 bits to ensure that the header ends on a 32-bit boundary.

PACKET FRAGMENTATION

In a perfect world, all networks will carry the entire IP packet. Occasionally, however, packets must traverse a network with a smaller maximum packet size. If a packet is larger than the network's maximum size, the packet must be broken into smaller packets. The router reformats the packet into fragments small enough to traverse the network. The router puts a copy of the IP header on each fragment. It also fills details to describe each fragment so that the destination host can reassemble them upon receipt.

11.3.3 Address Resolution Protocol

When a host needs to send a packet to another host on the same LAN, its protocol stack must convert the destination's IP address into the correct MAC address. This is the role of the *Address Resolution Protocol* (ARP).

The host uses ARP to construct a table of host MAC addresses on the LAN and their corresponding IP addresses. This table, called the *ARP cache*, allows the network software to insert the correct MAC address when needed.

There are essentially two ARP messages: a request and a response. The ARP request asks for the MAC address that corresponds with a particular IP address. Both use the same simple format, shown in Figure 11.14. The "source" in an ARP packet is *always* the host that sends the packet, and the "target" is always the recipient. Thus, the actual, numeric addresses in an ARP request packet appear in reverse order in the ARP response packet.

The requesting host sends the ARP request as a broadcast packet. This ensures that every host on the LAN will see it. When a host receives the packet, it looks at the queried IP address to see if it matches its own address. If not, the host discards the packet. If the host's own IP address matches the queried address, the host constructs an ARP response packet. The host sends the ARP response packet directly to the requesting host, because it knows the destination MAC address.

The ARP Cache

Every computer using internet protocols contains an ARP cache. This cache lists all of the MAC addresses and corresponding IP addresses collected and used on network traffic by that host. The ARP cache essentially keeps track of every host visited on the LAN. We can examine the ARP cache with the "arp" keyboard command, as shown underlined in Figure 11.15.

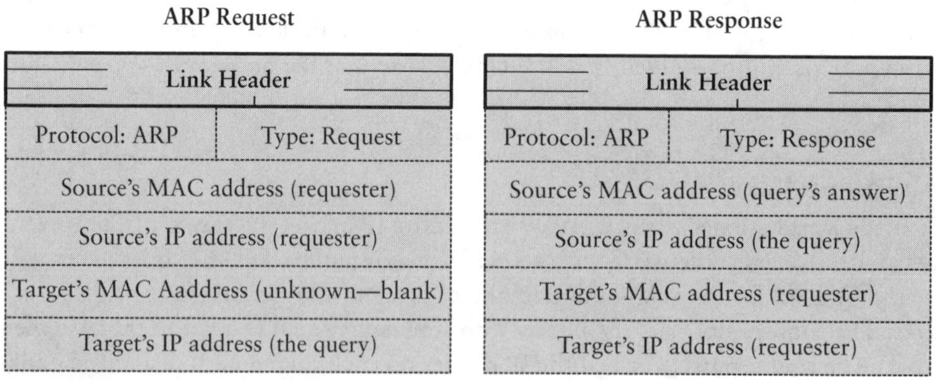

Figure 11.14

ARP packet contents.

```
C:\Users\bob>arp -a

Interface: 10.20.30.28 --- 0xb
  Internet Address        Physical Address      Type
  10.20.30.10             00-1e-ca-3c-1e-47     dynamic
  10.20.30.20             00-11-29-0b-ff-50     dynamic
  10.20.30.22             00-18-41-58-8c-b7     dynamic
  10.20.30.23             00-11-a9-06-af-53     dynamic
  10.20.30.25             00-17-d2-09-bc-fe     dynamic
  239.255.255.250         01-00-3c-7f-ff-fa     static
  239.255.255.253         01-00-3c-7f-ff-fd     static
  255.255.255.255         ff-ff-ff-ff-ff-ff     static

C:\Users\bob>
```

Figure 11.15

Command to display the ARP cache.

If the host's ARP cache has few entries, it is easy to add more. We simply find the IP addresses of other LAN hosts and *ping* them using the "ping" keyboard command. When we ping a host, we send a simple network message that requests a brief response. The ping command requires an IP address. To actually perform the ping, the protocol stack must send an ARP request to resolve the IP request.

Some hosts are configured to ignore ping requests. This is considered a security feature because it makes the host harder to find through simple searching. However, the host will respond to the ARP request even if it ignores the ping.

11.4 Internet Addresses in Practice

Like telephone numbers, there are physical constraints on how we assign numerical IP addresses. Every address contains two parts: the "network bits" and the "host bits" in the address. The upper bits in the address form the network address. The lower bits form the host address.

The distinction between network and host bits is essential for routing packets on the Internet. Routing tables describe how to locate *networks*, not hosts. Once the packet arrives on its destination LAN, we can use ARP to find the right host. The challenge is to reach the network from elsewhere on the Internet.

When a router receives a packet, it extracts the packet's destination IP address, then it sets the host bits to zero, leaving only the network bits. The router searches its routing table using only the network bits of the IP address. To do this, the router must know the dividing line between the network address and the host address.

Network Masks

As the Internet address space was depleted in the 1990s, the address format was revised to introduce a *network mask*: a binary value containing a row of 1 bits to identify the network address bits. Figure 11.16 illustrates a network mask.

In Figure 11.16, the first 20 bits of the mask are set to 1. This indicates that the network address consists of the first 20 bits. The remaining 12 bits select a specific host on that network.

When an organization wants to put a lot of hosts on the Internet, it signs up for a series of IP addresses to assign its hosts. If it needs 500 addresses, then it needs $\log_2(500)$ bits to identify those different hosts. That requires 9 bits. In an IPv4 address, that leaves 21 bits for the network address.

IPv4 Address Classes

Originally, the dividing line between host and network address was always on a byte boundary. This produced three "classes" of IP addresses:

1. Class A. There were 128 of these; each supporting over 16 million hosts on the network.
2. Class B. There were over 16,000 of these; each supporting over 65,000 hosts on the network.
3. Class C. There were over 2 million of these; each supporting 254 hosts on the network.

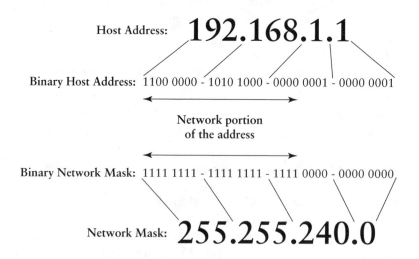

Figure 11.16

Interpreting a network mask.

Class A network addresses were assigned to large or significant organizations involved in Internet development. Even today, many of those addresses still belong to those original organizations.

In practice, the address class arrangement breaks the address space into inconvenient fragments. Network sites would be assigned Class B addresses to support less than 1000 computers, reducing the number of network addresses available to other sites. The network mask allows ISPs to assign smaller blocks of addresses to individual organizations.

11.4.1 Addresses, Scope, and Reachability

In computer science, we use the term "scope" to talk about the range over which something has meaning; a variable's scope inside a program, for example, depends on where and how we define it. When we apply scope to addresses, we indicate the part of the network over which we can use the address to deliver a packet. *Address scope* is based on the protocol layer at which the address is defined. Table 11.1 summarizes the different types of addresses and their corresponding network scopes.

Figure 11.17 illustrates a simple network of Layer 2 and Layer 3 nodes. As in the Ethernet, Layer 2 nodes are hubs and switches. In internet protocols, Layer 3 nodes are routers.

If we have a Layer 2 address, we can reach any device connected to our host via a Layer 2 path. If we have a Layer 3 address, we can reach any host at Layer 2 by using an ARP request to retrieve the MAC address. We also can reach hosts on the other side of a Layer 3 router if the router has a route to that host. This is likely on small networks, like the one shown in Figure 11.17.

When we look at Figure 11.17 in terms of address scope, we find that some hosts can't reach other hosts, depending on the type of address being used. If the hosts only have transport addresses (port numbers, for example), then they don't have enough information to reach another host, even if that host is the only one offering a service on that port. If all hosts have shared Layer 3 addresses (IP addresses) with each other, then all hosts can reach one another.

If we limit the hosts to Layer 2 addresses, however, we run into limitations. A MAC address can't reach another host on the other side of a Layer 3 router, like the one in the

Layer	Address Type	Scope
TABLE 11.1 Scope of addressing information in internet packets		
2	MAC address	Can reach across all interconnected Layer 2 devices
3	IP address	Can traverse Layer 2 devices and Layer 3 routers that contain routes for the destination address
4	Port number	Limited to the transport layers on the endpoints

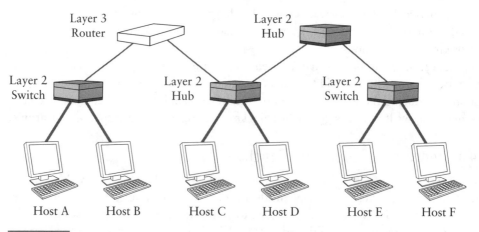

Figure 11.17

Reachability depends on address scope.

Source Host	Destination Host					
	A	**B**	**C**	**D**	**E**	**F**
A	√	√				
B	√	√				
C			√	√	√	√
D			√	√	√	√
E			√	√	√	√
F			√	√	√	√

TABLE 11.2 Layer 2 reachability matrix for Figure 11.17

upper-left corner of the figure. We can illustrate which hosts can reach which with the "reachability matrix" as shown in Table 11.2. There is a check mark if the source host in the left column can reach the given destination host.

11.4.2 Private IP Addresses

Because IPv4 addresses are only 32 bits long, there are approximately 4 billion of them. The global Internet assumes that all such addresses are unique, otherwise, the routers could not decide which host should receive packets with a duplicated address. Unfortunately, the Internet is running out of these *global IP addresses*. These global addresses carry packets directly between Internet hosts.

When a household or small business signs up for Internet service, the ISP usually assigns the customer a single, global IP address. A larger company might request a range of addresses, but in general, there aren't always enough addresses to assign one to each computer. Instead, many networks use *private IP addresses*. These addresses are valid only within the private LAN. When a host on the LAN needs to communicate with a host on the global Internet, the address must be translated to a global IP address.

Most home and small business networks connect to their ISP through a low-cost commercial gateway like the one shown in Figure 11.18. The gateway performs three important functions:

1. Automatically assigns IP addresses to the LAN's hosts using the **Dynamic Host Configuration Protocol** (DHCP).
2. Provides a router to exchange packets between the LAN and the remainder of the Internet.
3. Performs **network address translation** (NAT), which allows the hosts on the LAN to share the global IP address assigned by the ISP.

We examine such gateways and the NAT function further in Section 12.4.

The gateway in Figure 11.18 provides three types of physical network connections. The leftmost RJ-45 port provides an uplink that connects to the Internet. The remaining four RJ-45 ports are downlinks from a built-in switch. These allow four computers, or

Figure 11.18

Typical low-cost commercial gateway.

other switches, to connect to the gateway. Finally, the antenna on the right provides a wireless hub.

Assigning Private IP Addresses

When a host on the LAN boots up or otherwise arrives on the LAN, it uses DHCP to announce its presence on the network. The gateway responds and assigns it an IP address. Instead of assigning a global IP address, the gateway assigns each host a private IP address.

Private IP addresses are assigned out of a special range of addresses dedicated for that purpose. These addresses don't conflict with any other addresses assigned on the Internet, except in other private networks. Private IP addresses fall in the following ranges:

- 10.0.0.0–10.255.255.255: 24 bits of host address
- 172.16.0.0–172.31.255.255: 20 bits of host address
- 192.168.0.0–192.168.255.255: 16 bits of host address

Private IP addresses may *only* be used on a private network. When using private addresses, there must be a gateway between the private network and the rest of the Internet. The gateway must perform NAT to convert the private addresses into recognized, public Internet addresses. If a packet appears on the public Internet with a private IP address, many Internet routers will discard it. Typical gateways like the one in Figure 11.18 handle the translation automatically. We examine NAT in Section 12.4.1.

Dynamic Host Configuration Protocol

When a host boots up or it activates a dormant network interface, it starts by broadcasting a DHCP Query message. The broadcast packet is seen by every host on the LAN, including the gateway. The gateway's DHCP server sees the request and chooses an IP address for the host, then it sends the host a DHCP ACK message, which gives the host its IP address and the addresses of other important services on the LAN.

When assigning private addresses, the DHCP function uses a particular range of addresses and assigns private addresses from that range. When a host opens a connection to a host on the global Internet, the gateway's NAT function converts the host's private IP address to the gateway's public IP address.

11.5 Network Inspection Tools

This section examines two tools for inspecting a computer network. The first tool, *Wireshark*, collects network traffic and displays it as a sequence of packets. The second tool is *nmap*, the "network mapper" utility. Nmap scans a network for host computers and tries to identify the services those computers provide.

Wireshark

Network traffic becomes easier to understand, both for beginners and experts, if we look at the messages firsthand. We use Wireshark to watch hosts exchange packets and to examine individual packets in detail. Wireshark provides a graphical interface organized around a single window, as shown in Figure 11.19.

The Wireshark window contains four major sections. The topmost section provides Wireshark's functions and controls. The remaining three sections display packets or parts thereof:

1. Packet list pane lists the captured packets in sorted order, one packet per line. We can change the sort order by clicking on the column headings.
   - Each line summarizes the packet type and content.
   - The highlighted packet from this list appears in the next three sections.
2. Packet details pane lists the headers in the highlighted packet, one per header.
   - Each line summarizes the header's contents.
   - Each header has an "expand" symbol on the left; clicking the symbol expands the header to display its detailed contents.
3. Packet bytes pane displays the entire packet in hexadecimal and ASCII. When we select part of the packet in the details pane, that part is highlighted in the packet bytes.

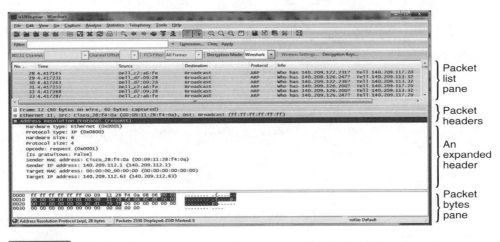

Figure 11.19

Layout of the Wireshark window.

Wireshark contains built-in descriptions of most protocols used on the Internet and by typical commercial equipment. When we expand a header, Wireshark uses its library of descriptions to interpret the packet's contents.

Wireshark provides the following features:

- Opens a *packet capture file* (abbreviated "pcap"), a file containing a collection of network packets.
- Collects packets from a network interface in real time. If Wireshark collects the packets itself, it may save them in a packet capture file for further inspection.
- Displays a list of the captured packets in order of receipt or in other sorted orders.
- Displays the detailed contents of individual packet headers in a readable format.
- Displays the packet contents in raw hexadecimal.

Wireshark is an open-source program available for Windows and Unix-based systems, including Apple's OS-X. The Wireshark website distributes it either as an easy-to-install binary or in source code form. To capture packets, the user must have administrator rights. The user needs no special permission to examine a previously collected packet capture file.

11.5.1 Wireshark Examples

When Wireshark collects a packet or it detects one in a packet capture file, it attaches a time stamp and sequence number to each one. This information appears in the packet list pane and in the first line of the packet details pane. Wireshark lists these as "frame numbers." Figure 11.20 shows the packet details pane for an Ethernet packet.

The second line in the pane provides the basic information about the Ethernet packet: its source and destination MAC addresses. In Figure 11.20, we also see Wireshark's expanded Ethernet header display. These contents appear indented on the lines following the packet's header.

```
▷ Frame 68 (42 bytes on wire, 42 bytes captured)
▽ Ethernet II, Src: Dell_21:24:58 (00:23:ae:21:24:58), Dst: Broadcast (ff:ff:ff:ff:ff:ff)
  ▽ Destination: Broadcast (ff:ff:ff:ff:ff:ff)
      Address: Broadcast (ff:ff:ff:ff:ff:ff)
      .... ...1 .... .... .... .... = IG bit: Group address (multicast/broadcast)
      .... ..1. .... .... .... .... = LG bit: Locally administered address (this is NOT the factory default)
  ▽ Source: Dell_21:24:58 (00:23:ae:21:24:58)
      Address: Dell_21:24:58 (00:23:ae:21:24:58)
      .... ...0 .... .... .... .... = IG bit: Individual address (unicast)
      .... ..0. .... .... .... .... = LG bit: Globally unique address (factory default)
    Type: ARP (0x0806)
▸ Address Resolution Protocol (request)
```

Figure 11.20

Ethernet header displayed in Wireshark.

The expanded Ethernet header doesn't provide much additional information. It indicates some details about the MAC address assignments, and it specifically indicates the type of packet header residing inside the Ethernet packet. In practice, we don't need to see this level of detail. The collapsed header provides us with the source and destination addresses already. The enclosed packet type also is indicated by the type of the packet following the Ethernet header.

ADDRESS RESOLUTION PROTOCOL

ARP is the most common protocol that travels by itself in Ethernet packets. Figure 11.21 shows the Wireshark display of an ARP Request packet.

The packet list effectively summarizes the ARP packet's contents: It identifies the host asking the question and the IP address being queried. The expanded packet shows the details, including the sender's MAC address.

Figure 11.22 displays the ARP Response packet. Again, the packet list summarizes the essential contents. In practice, we rarely need to expand an ARP packet. Note how the contents displayed by Wireshark parallel those shown in Figure 11.21.

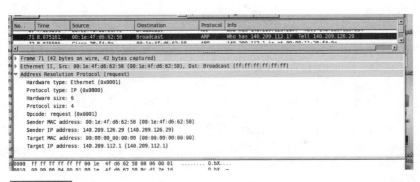

Figure 11.21

ARP Request displayed in Wireshark.

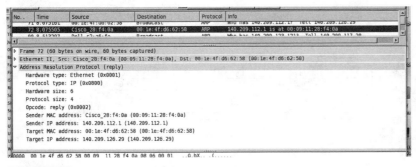

Figure 11.22

ARP Response displayed in Wireshark.

```
Frame 43 (456 bytes on wire, 456 bytes captured)
Ethernet II, Src: Cisco_28:f4:0a (00:09:11:28:f4:0a), Dst: 00:1e:4f:d6:62:58 (00:1e:4f:d6:62:58)
Internet Protocol, Src: 140.209.112.1 (140.209.112.1), Dst: 140.209.126.29 (140.209.126.29)
    Version: 4
    Header length: 20 bytes
  ▷ Differentiated Services Field: 0x00 (DSCP 0x00: Default; ECN: 0x00)
    Total Length: 442
    Identification: 0xaacf (43727)
  ▽ Flags: 0x00
      0... = Reserved bit: Not set
      .0.. = Don't fragment: Not set
      ..0. = More fragments: Not set
    Fragment offset: 0
    Time to live: 255
    Protocol: UDP (0x11)
  ▷ Header checksum: 0x07a2 [correct]
    Source: 140.209.112.1 (140.209.112.1)
    Destination: 140.209.126.29 (140.209.126.29)
▷ User Datagram Protocol, Src Port: bootps (67), Dst Port: bootpc (68)
▷ Bootstrap Protocol
```

Figure 11.23

IP header displayed in Wireshark.

IP HEADER

Figure 11.23 shows an expanded IP header displayed in Wireshark. The essential information is, of course, the host addresses. The expanded header shows the time to live (255), the checksum, and information about fragmentation.

11.5.2 Mapping a LAN with Nmap

It is hard to account for all devices on a large LAN. It remains difficult even if the LAN is in a home or small business. To "map" the LAN, we need to find all IP and MAC addresses on the LAN and identify which machines own which addresses.

If we are working with a LAN that uses a commercial gateway, the gateway may keep a list of LAN devices. Figure 11.24 shows such a list. This list may be a combination of DHCP assignments and ARP discoveries, but it should be reasonably complete.

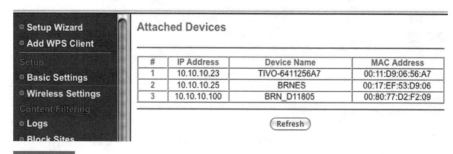

Figure 11.24

Network gateway display of hosts on the LAN.

However, it will not show hosts that have been off-line for a long time. It might not show hosts that never visit the gateway.

The ARP cache is also a good source of information about LAN hosts. It lists every LAN device contacted by the host with the ARP table—but not all hosts visit each other on the LAN. Although most desktops and laptops might visit the printer, the Tivo digital video recorder probably never has. It would be tedious to visit each device and dump its ARP cache. Such a quest would be impractical on a moderately sized LAN.

THE NMAP NETWORK MAPPER UTILITY

Nmap is a well-respected open source utility for mapping computer networks. It also helps with security scanning because it often can identify the versions of network protocol software each host is running. Although we can run nmap from a graphical interface, the features we need are most easily performed with the keyboard command. We type the nmap command as follows:

```
nmap <options> <addresses>
```

<options> may contain a list of options, each prefixed with a hyphen

<addresses> contains a host name, an IP address, or a range of IP addresses in dotted decimal format

Figure 11.25 shows the output of a simple nmap command that identifies a single host to scan.

When we scan a single host, we receive a list of the open ports on that host, the services provided by those ports, and the time required to perform the search.

```
~bob$ nmap 10.20.30.10

Starting Nmap 5.21 ( http://nmap.org ) at 20:05
Nmap scan report for 10.20.30.10
Host is up (0.010s latency).
Not shown: 997 closed ports
PORT    STATE SERVICE
23/tcp open   telnet
53/tcp open   domain
80/tcp open   http

Nmap done: 1 IP address (1 host up) scanned in 0.29 seconds
~bob$
```

Figure 11.25

Output of a simple nmap command.

```
PORT       STATE SERVICE VERSION
427/tcp    open  svrloc?
3703/tcp   open  http     Apache Tomcat/Coyote JSP engine 1.1
6646/tcp   open  unknown
49152/tcp open  msrpc    Microsoft Windows RPC
49153/tcp open  msrpc    Microsoft Windows RPC
49154/tcp open  msrpc    Microsoft Windows RPC
49155/tcp open  msrpc    Microsoft Windows RPC
```

Figure 11.26

Nmap port listing using the -sV option.

```
C:\>nmap 140.209.66.88

Starting Nmap 5.21 ( http://nmap.org ) at 13:01

Note: Host seems down. If it is really up, but blocking our ping
probes, try -PN

Nmap done: 1 IP address (0 hosts up) scanned in 3.19 seconds
```

Figure 11.27

Nmap of a Windows 7 host.

We can select the "service version" option "-sV" to add detail to the list of ports. Nmap will try to guess the specific type and version of protocol software being used on that port (Figure 11.26).

If we give nmap a range of addresses to search, it searches for live hosts and for open ports. If a host ignores its initial ping, it assumes the host is down and goes to the next one. If nmap's ping yields a response, it scans the service ports, testing for open ones. It reports each open port. This continues until it has scanned all ports of all hosts it finds. Figure 11.27 shows what happened when it scanned a running laptop with Windows 7 installed.

Similar things happen when scanning other modern systems. Thus, ping is no longer very reliable for locating live hosts. If we know a host is up, we can direct nmap to scan it anyway by using the "-PN" option. In Figure 11.28, we combine it with the "-O" option, which tells nmap to try to identify the computer's operating system.

```
Nmap scan report for 140.209.66.88
Host is up (0.00s latency).
Not shown: 993 filtered ports
PORT       STATE SERVICE
427/tcp    open  svrloc
3703/tcp   open  unknown
6646/tcp   open  unknown
49152/tcp  open  unknown
49153/tcp  open  unknown
49154/tcp  open  unknown
49155/tcp  open  unknown
Warning: OSScan results may be unreliable because we could not find at
least 1 open and 1 closed port
Device type: general purpose
Running: Microsoft Windows 2008|Vista|7
OS details: Microsoft Windows Server 2008 Beta 3, Microsoft Windows
Vista SP0 or SP1, Server 2008 SP1, or Windows 7
```

Figure 11.28

Nmap of a Windows 7 host with -PN and -O options.

USE NMAP WITH CAUTION

Nmap is designed to search networks for active hosts and to search those hosts for visible services. Although this is useful when managing a network, it is disruptive and troublesome if done unnecessarily. At best, it generates a lot of unnecessary traffic—and we mean *a lot* of traffic, especially when scanning a larger network.

Even worse, it could uncover security weaknesses, which could open the network or its hosts to additional attacks.

Using nmap to scan other hosts on your ISP almost certainly will violate your ISP's Terms of Service. Your ISP then may terminate your Internet service connection.

Using nmap at your school or place of business without permission also may get you into serious trouble. Do not scan hosts on someone else's network without explicit, *written* permission. Thus, if anything goes wrong, you have evidence that your actions were legitimate.

Remember, if you are using nmap on someone else's network, then you are doing security research on their behalf. Your scan results are sensitive data and must not be shared with or leaked to unauthorized people. Keep the information secret and under your personal control.

11.6 Resources

IMPORTANT TERMS INTRODUCED

address scope	internet layer protocol	routing table
ARP cache	IP address	socket address
border router	mesh network	socket interface
bus network	Metcalfe's law	star network
contention	network mask	subnet
dedicated line	ping	topology
dotted decimal notation	point-to-point network	tree network
gateway	port number	Wireshark
global IP address	private IP address	

ACRONYMS INTRODUCED

ARP—Address Resolution Protocol

ARPA—Advanced Research Projects Agency

ARPANET—ARPA Network

AS—Autonomous System

BBN—Bolt, Beranek, and Newman

DARPA—Defense Advanced Research Projects Agency

DHCP—Dynamic Host Configuration Protocol

IETF—Internet Engineering Task Force

IMP—Interface Message Processor

IPv4—IP Version 4

IPv6—IP Version 6

ISP—Internet Service Provider

NAT—Network address translation

nmap—Network mapper

pcap—Packet capture file

telecom—Telecommunications

TTL—Time to live

UCL—University College, London

WAN—Wide area network

11.6.1 Review Questions

R1. Briefly describe and compare the five basic network topologies.

R2. Explain the role of protocol Layer 3 in internet protocols.

R3.   Describe the two parts of an IP address.

R4.   Provide a step-by-step description of how a packet is routed, assuming that it must traverse at least one router.

R5.   Explain the role of autonomous systems and ISPs in the structure of the global Internet.

R6.   What is a socket? How does it relate to a typical networking API?

R7.   Explain the role of port numbers in establishing a connection between two processes.

R8.   Describe the difference between IPv4 and IPv6 addresses. Which is most widely used?

R9.   Explain the role of ARP and how it works.

R10. What is the difference between a global IP address and a private IP address?

R11. Explain the role of the network mask in Internet routing.

R12. Describe the three functions provided by a low-cost commercial Internet gateway product.

11.6.2 Exercises

NOTE: Some exercises are marked with restrictions.

- For some problems, your instructor will provide a Wireshark packet capture file that shows a computer starting up and opening a connection to a web page. You will use that packet capture file in exercises marked "Wireshark."

- Exercises marked "Administrators only" may require administrative access to the computer and/or network where the student performs the assignment.

- Exercises marked "Small LANs only" should only be performed on a small LAN where the student has permission to perform the assignment, often a household LAN.

E1.   Locate and describe a real-world example of each of the five basic network topologies. Do *not* use examples that are in the textbook. Each example should identify a specific system that works today. Identify where the system physically resides and who uses it.

E2.   Follow the route of a packet from your desktop or laptop to a nearby server you often use, probably at school or work. To do this, you use the "tracert" keyboard command on Windows and the "traceroute" keyboard command on Unix-like systems. The command has one argument: the host's name or IP address. Answer the following questions:

a.   Copy and paste the text printed out by the traceroute command.

b.   How many "hops" did the packet take?

c.   Did all hops provide an IP address? Some servers don't respond to traceroute requests.

d.   Examine any readable host names provided for intermediate hops. Do any indicate that the packet took a surprising and possibly long route to reach the destination? If so, identify the distant hops it took.

E3. Use the instructions in Section 10.4.3 to find the MAC address of a desktop or laptop computer you use.

a. Write down the MAC address.

b. Find and write down the IPv4 address; it should be marked as such or with the acronym "inet."

c. Find the network mask. Write it down.

E4. (Administrators only.) Dump the ARP table on the computer you use on your LAN. Now, visit your gateway and dump its list of connected devices (if you don't know how, consult the instruction manual or "help" facility for your gateway). Provide both results as the answer to this question.

E5. (Administrators only.) Start Wireshark running, and activate the packet capture on the LAN interface. Do the following:

a. Locate an ARP Response packet originated by your computer. Provide the following information from the packet:
   • The packet's frame number
   • The requester's IP and MAC addresses
   • The responder's IP and MAC addresses

b. Find the ARP Request packet that produced that response. Provide the following information from that packet:
   • The packet's frame number
   • The requester's IP and MAC addresses
   • The MAC address on the packet

c. Dump the ARP cache on your computer. Provide a copy of that information. You may cut and paste the text if you want, screen capture it, or transcribe it by hand.

E6. (Wireshark.) Locate an ARP Response packet in the capture file.

a. Provide the following information from the packet:
   • The packet's frame number
   • The requester's IP and MAC addresses
   • The responder's IP and MAC addresses

b. Find the ARP Request packet that produced that response. Provide the following information from that packet:
   • The packet's frame number
   • The requester's IP and MAC addresses
   • The MAC address on the packet

E7. (Wireshark.) Locate a pair of packets used by a computer when it first starts using the network. The packets will carry the DHCP protocol, often called "bootp."

a. Identify the packet number that provides the computer's startup information. This would be the packet containing the host's assigned IP address and other information.

b. Provide the source and destination port numbers contained in the packet's UDP header.

c. What is the IP address of the DHCP server that responded?

d. What is the IP address assigned to the computer?

e. Identify the number of the packet that *requests* that information. It should be a broadcast packet sent from the host's MAC address and it should contain a matching transaction number. Wireshark also should provide a link between the two packets.

E8. Find the domain name or IP address of a nearby computer, preferably one in the same room. Send a "ping" to that computer. Use the "ping" keyboard command, which takes a domain name or IP address as its argument. Describe the response displayed by the command. Was the command blocked by a firewall?

E9. Send a "ping" to a distant computer, like an e-commerce or international news site. Use the "ping" command as explained in the previous question. Describe the response displayed by the command. Was the command blocked by a firewall?

E10. Figure 11.29 displays a network of hubs, switches, and gateways. Assume that we are limited to Layer 2 addresses. Fill in a reachability matrix that follows the format of Table 11.2: Put a check mark if the host can reach the destination, given a Layer 2 address.

E11. (Small LANs only.) Run nmap on your LAN. Did it find any hosts? Which hosts did it find? Did it fail to find any hosts that were running at the time?

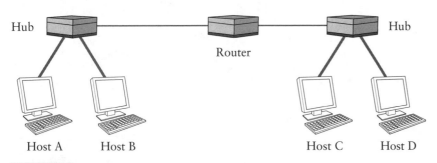

Figure 11.29

Reachability problem.

END-TO-END NETWORKING

ABOUT THIS CHAPTER

This chapter examines transport layer networking, which passes data between processes on different network hosts. We cover the following topics:

- The end-to-end principle in Internet architecture
- Internet packet and transport protocols
- Host naming with the Domain Name System
- Firewalls and network address translation
- Long-distance networking

12.1 "Smart" Versus "Dumb" Networks

When engineers try to design and build more sophisticated systems, they divide the system into components and place different functions in different components. These decisions have far-reaching effects. The telephone system took one approach, and the designers of today's Internet protocols took a different approach.

An individual analog telephone was a fairly simple device that did very little on its own. The telephone network, on the other hand, accepted a dialed phone number, routed and established a connection to the called phone, and managed the conversation. The telephone system was a classic example of a "smart" network with "dumb" endpoints.

The Ethernet, on the other hand, is a "dumb" network. It doesn't tell hosts how to take turns on the network. It doesn't check CRCs on packets. Network switches distinguish packets destined for different hosts on the network, but that is all they do. Hubs do even less work.

The original Ethernet had no circuitry of its own; it was simply a coaxial cable that carried signals between interfaces. Today's hubs and switches are only slightly more sophisticated than that. The lion's share of work is performed by "smart" endpoints: the hosts on the Ethernet.

When first introduced in the 1970s, the Ethernet was greeted with a great deal of skepticism. Some doubted that the collision detection strategy would work well as networks grew larger. Others doubted that the "dumb network" concept made sense.

In fact, the "dumb network" concept arose in part from the attempt in the late 1960s to make the ARPANET a "smart" network. The ARPANET was a mesh network of nodes, and the hosts connected to the nodes. The nodes were small computers that tried to provide a reliable packet delivery service. If the network accepted a message, the network would either deliver it reliably or send an error message indicating the failure. It should never lose a message without indication or deliver a duplicated message.

In practice, the ARPANET was never 100 percent reliable. Because of inevitable timing uncertainties with computer hardware, the host couldn't be 100 percent sure that the network accepted a message. An error message likewise did not 100 percent guarantee that a message had not been delivered.

These shortcomings, though rare, occurred often enough to require special handling in the host's protocol stack. The network could not provide high reliability by itself. Reliability depended on retransmission procedures performed by the endpoint hosts themselves.

THE END-TO-END PRINCIPLE

The failure of network-based reliable transport influenced a central design principle of Internet-oriented networks: the **end-to-end principle**. The concept embodies the notion of dumb networks by placing most network protocols in the connection's endpoint hosts. The network itself simply transmits packets and possibly loses a few on occasion.

The basic concept was proposed in a 1981 paper by Saltzer, Reed, and Clark titled "End-to-End Arguments in System Design." They argued that few mechanisms belonged in the networks themselves, unless justified as performance enhancements. Most mechanisms were more efficiently provided in the endpoint hosts. This approach already was being applied to network applications; all of them consist of services located on endpoint hosts, as discussed in Section 10.6.

Although this philosophy can be taken to extremes, Internet designers apply it pragmatically. The Internet remained a network of more-or-less autonomous routers until traffic grew sharply in the mid-1990s. Then backbone operators reorganized the structure to be "smarter" in order to make routing efficient and reliable.

Although end-to-end retransmissions may work in theory, timeout periods for lost Internet packets are irritatingly long in practice. Thus, lost packets often become visible to users. They become a significant problem if losses occur too often. This is one reason why wireless LANs include a retransmission feature even though TCP also performs retransmissions.

12.2 Internet Transport Protocols

The "hourglass" diagram in Chapter 10 (Figure 10.20) illustrates how internet protocols support a broad range of networking technologies at the bottom and a broad range of applications at the top. Almost all of these rely on the standard network and transport protocols. IP provides global addressing for Internet hosts. TCP and the *User*

Datagram Protocol (UDP) provide data transport between processes on any two of those hosts.

Both TCP and UDP headers carry port numbers that indicate the process sending or receiving the packet at a host. Often the port numbers connect client processes to server processes. When a client opens a connection to a particular server, the client's protocol stack randomly selects the source port. The destination port is chosen according to the application protocol being used; port 80 is traditionally used for web traffic, while port 25 is used to send an email.

USER DATAGRAM PROTOCOL

Not all network traffic requires reliable connections. If a particular application simply needs to exchange unreliable datagrams, we don't use TCP, because it involves unnecessary overhead and possible delays. Some application protocols inherently detect lost or damaged packets and retransmit them as needed. These application protocols use UDP instead of TCP. Figure 12.1 displays the contents of the UDP header.

Figure 12.2 shows a UDP header expanded in Wireshark. As with other simple headers, we learn very little of interest by expanding the header. The principal information is in the port numbers.

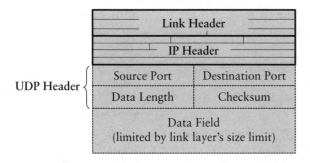

Figure 12.1

UDP packet fields.

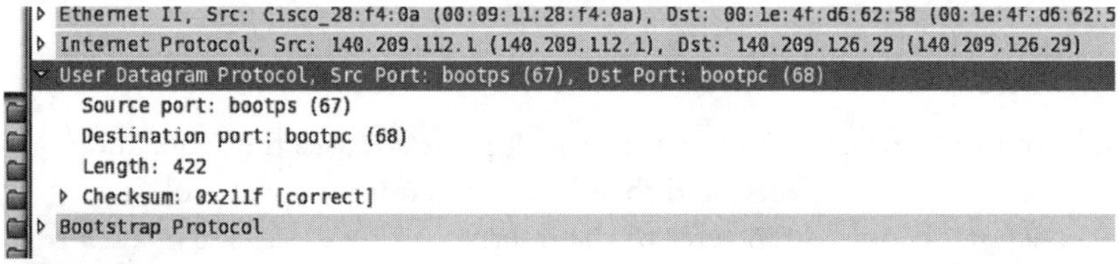

```
▷ Ethernet II, Src: Cisco_28:f4:0a (00:09:11:28:f4:0a), Dst: 00:1e:4f:d6:62:58 (00:1e:4f:d6:62:5
▷ Internet Protocol, Src: 140.209.112.1 (140.209.112.1), Dst: 140.209.126.29 (140.209.126.29)
▽ User Datagram Protocol, Src Port: bootps (67), Dst Port: bootpc (68)
    Source port: bootps (67)
    Destination port: bootpc (68)
    Length: 422
  ▷ Checksum: 0x211f [correct]
▷ Bootstrap Protocol
```

Figure 12.2

UDP header displayed in Wireshark.

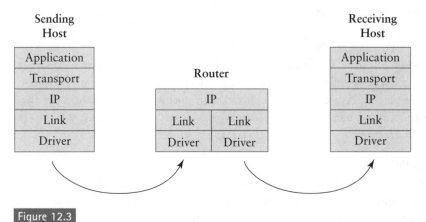

Figure 12.3

Routing and internet protocol layering.

Some might wonder why we should bother having a UDP format at all; it would seem that an application could simply use the IP header itself. The UDP header primarily provides source and destination port numbers. The protocol stack uses port numbers to associate TCP connections with processes; UDP allows it to use the same strategy to deliver UDP packets to processes.

END-TO-END TRANSPORT PROTOCOLS
TCP and UDP are purely end-to-end protocols. No conventional internet router or other intermediate node needs to pay attention to transport headers or those beyond it inside the packet. Figure 12.3 illustrates this clearly; routers do not require a protocol layer above IP in order to carry traffic between networks.

In practice, certain types of network devices do pay attention to higher layer packet headers. Firewalls and NAT devices, for example, use TCP and UDP port numbers. Large-scale sites also may use special "load balancing" routers that distribute traffic among multiple servers; these often use higher level headers to route the traffic. Network intrusion detection systems also look at multiple packet headers to try to detect an attack (see Section 15.5).

12.2.1 Transmission Control Protocol

In Section 10.3.2, we briefly described how a transport protocol uses timeouts and ACKs to ensure reliable packet delivery, and that TCP is the internet protocol that ensures reliable transport. People often refer to the internet protocol stack as "TCP/IP" to acknowledge the presence of both reliable transport (TCP) and internet routing (IP). Figure 12.4 shows the major contents of a TCP packet.

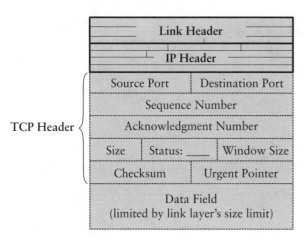

Link Header	
IP Header	

TCP Header

Source Port	Destination Port
Sequence Number	
Acknowledgment Number	
Size	Status: ____	Window Size
Checksum	Urgent Pointer
Data Field (limited by link layer's size limit)	

Figure 12.4

Major TCP packet fields.

Here is a summary of the fields shown:

- Source port—the port number assigned to the sending process.
- Destination port—the port number at the receiving process.
- Sequence number (SEQ)—number assigned to the first byte in the packet; each subsequent byte in the packet is assigned the corresponding sequential number.
- Acknowledgment number—the sequence number of the last byte reliably received by the sender.
- Size—the size of the TCP header.
- Status—a set of flags indicating the roles performed by this packet.
- Window size—indicates the amount of data the sender can accept on this connection.
- Checksum—the checksum for the TCP header and data field.
- Urgent pointer—points to "urgent" data; rarely used.

These same fields appear in the TCP header when expanded by Wireshark. Figure 12.5 shows an expanded TCP header.

SEQUENCE AND ACKNOWLEDGMENT NUMBERS

The sequence and acknowledgment numbers help ensure reliable transmission of all data. The sender sequentially numbers each byte sent in a TCP connection. A packet's SEQ field carries the sequence number of the first byte in each packet. The recipient keeps track of the sequence number of each byte received. The acknowledgment number reports the highest sequence number of all bytes received. When a TCP packet

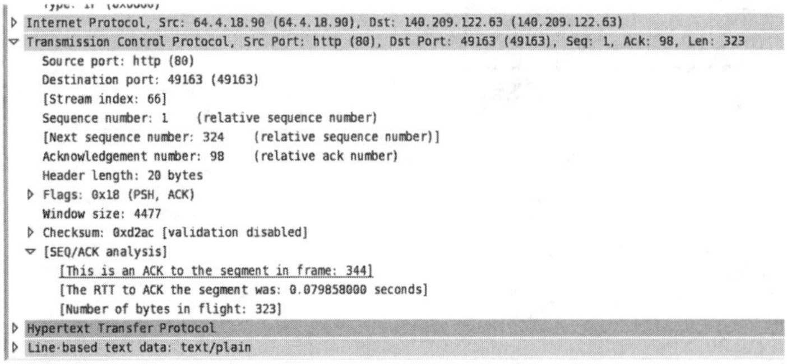

```
   Type: IP (0x0800)
▷ Internet Protocol, Src: 64.4.18.90 (64.4.18.90), Dst: 140.209.122.63 (140.209.122.63)
▽ Transmission Control Protocol, Src Port: http (80), Dst Port: 49163 (49163), Seq: 1, Ack: 98, Len: 323
    Source port: http (80)
    Destination port: 49163 (49163)
    [Stream index: 66]
    Sequence number: 1    (relative sequence number)
    [Next sequence number: 324    (relative sequence number)]
    Acknowledgement number: 98    (relative ack number)
    Header length: 20 bytes
  ▷ Flags: 0x18 (PSH, ACK)
    Window size: 4477
  ▷ Checksum: 0xd2ac [validation disabled]
  ▽ [SEQ/ACK analysis]
      [This is an ACK to the segment in frame: 344]
      [The RTT to ACK the segment was: 0.079858000 seconds]
      [Number of bytes in flight: 323]
▷ Hypertext Transfer Protocol
▷ Line-based text data: text/plain
```

Figure 12.5

TCP header displayed in Wireshark.

acknowledges data from an earlier packet, Wireshark provides a link to that earlier packet in its "SEQ/ACK Analysis."

There is an interesting difference between the packet's actual contents and Wireshark's expanded header. Sequence numbers and acknowledgment numbers are shown *relative* to the start of the connection. Thus, byte 1 in the connection yields sequence number 1 in the expanded Wireshark header.

In fact, when TCP opens a connection, it tries to select a random and hard-to-predict starting sequence number. In the 1990s, attacks developed against firewalls that sent privileged keyboard commands. The receiving hosts accepted the commands, because the source IP address appeared to belong to a trustworthy host. In fact, the source address was forged; the recipient accepted the packet because the attacker accurately guessed the right TCP sequence number. This tricked the recipient's protocol stack into believing that the trusted host had sent the packet as part of an opened connection. This was called the *IP spoofing* attack.

WINDOW SIZE

A fundamental problem in networking is that hosts never operate at exactly the same speed. One host may be a little faster at sending data than the other is at receiving data. If a host sends data too fast, the recipient may lose data as it uses up its available RAM. This is the *flow control* problem.

The window size tells the recipient host how many bytes the sending host may accept in return traffic. Each TCP packet a host receives will acknowledge all bytes received and report the window size: the number of additional bytes it can handle.

TCP CONNECTIONS

Any connection goes through three stages: setup, operation, and termination. The Status flags in a TCP packet indicate its role in the connection. Figure 12.6 shows the complete history of a TCP connection as displayed by a Wireshark packet summary pane.

Source	Destination	Protocol	Info
140.209.122.63	64.4.18.90	TCP	49163 > http [SYN] Seq=0 Win=8192 Len=0 MSS=1460 WS=8
64.4.18.90	140.209.122.63	TCP	http > 49163 [SYN, ACK] Seq=0 Ack=1 Win=1460 Len=0 MSS=1460
140.209.122.63	64.4.18.90	TCP	49163 > http [ACK] Seq=1 Ack=1 Win=65536 Len=0
140.209.122.63	64.4.18.90	HTTP	GET /ncsi.txt HTTP/1.1
64.4.18.90	140.209.122.63	HTTP	HTTP/1.1 200 OK (text/plain)
64.4.18.90	140.209.122.63	TCP	http > 49163 [FIN, ACK] Seq=324 Ack=98 Win=4477 Len=0
140.209.122.63	64.4.18.90	TCP	49163 > http [ACK] Seq=98 Ack=325 Win=65280 Len=0
140.209.122.63	64.4.18.90	TCP	49163 > http [FIN, ACK] Seq=98 Ack=325 Win=65280 Len=0
64.4.18.90	140.209.122.63	TCP	http > 49163 [ACK] Seq=325 Ack=99 Win=4477 Len=0

Figure 12.6

A TCP connection summarized by Wireshark.

Now let us examine this simple connection. Because connections typically take place in a client/server environment, we will call the initiator the client and the recipient the server. The client opens the TCP connection to the server by exchanging a *three-way handshake*: three packets with particular Status flag settings:

- Client sends first packet: SYN ("Synchronize") flag set
- Server sends second packet: both SYN and ACK flags set
- Client sends third packet: ACK flag set

The fourth packet contains data sent by the client to the server ("GET /ncsa.txt"). The fifth packet contains data sent to the client by the server ("HTTP/1.1"). The final packets exchange the FIN ("Finish") flag to close the connection.

Figure 12.7 expands the contents of the TCP flags field. This particular packet has the ACK and the "Push" flags set. The "ACK" flag means that the packet acknowledges an earlier one. The Push flag indicates that the sending application is finished sending data for now.

```
    Header length: 20 bytes
  ▾ Flags: 0x18 (PSH, ACK)
        0... .... = Congestion Window Reduced (CWR): Not set
        .0.. .... = ECN-Echo: Not set
        ..0. .... = Urgent: Not set
        ...1 .... = Acknowledgment: Set
        .... 1... = Push: Set
        .... .0.. = Reset: Not set
        .... ..0. = Syn: Not set
        .... ...0 = Fin: Not set
    Window size: 17376
```

Figure 12.7

TCP flags displayed by Wireshark.

Connection Timeout

Packet delivery is unreliable and host computers also are unreliable. This poses a challenge for network protocols. A host might begin a protocol exchange with another and a packet might get lost. The hosts must be able to recover, instead of waiting forever for a response.

For example, a client begins a three-way handshake, sending a SYN packet to a server. The server responds with the SYN/ACK packet. Then the client shuts down and never responds. This yields a *half-open connection*. The server doesn't quite open the connection, because the final ACK never arrived. The server eventually times out the connection and discards it. Properly designed network protocols provide timeouts for all message exchanges.

12.2.2 Attacks on Protocols

When hosts perform a network protocol, they are like children playing a game while blindfolded. The players can communicate, but those wearing blindfolds can't really tell what is happening. They are limited to spoken messages and can't really see what the others do.

In network protocols, we try to exchange enough messages to tell the hosts what has happened. We don't want to send messages that aren't absolutely necessary. We optimize performance by sending fewer and smaller messages, but we also increase the risk of confusion and chaos.

Internet protocols originally assumed that neither participant was malicious or was trying to trick the other host. Protocols were implemented in the simplest and most obvious ways. This assumption changed dramatically in the late 1980s and the 1990s.

Classic internet protocols, those developed in the early 1980s, often contained vulnerabilities that attackers may exploit. The IETF has overseen improvements to some protocols to eliminate problems and weaknesses. In other cases, we simply can't trust the protocol unless we restrict it to a trustworthy network, or protect it with cryptography (Chapter 14). Attackers have exploited protocols to perform three general types of attacks:

1. Exploit one host's assets to attack a different victim host.
2. Use up the victim host's resources directly.
3. Masquerade as another host or user.

These attacks are completely different from buffer overflow attacks. In those cases, we subvert the Chain of Control and make the CPU perform different instructions. In these attacks, we rely on the network protocols to work the way they were designed to work. We will look at these attacks on a per-protocol basis.

INTERNET CONTROL MESSAGE PROTOCOL

The Internet Control Message Protocol (ICMP) provides status messages that report errors detected while routing internet packets. It also implements the typical "ping"

```
▷ Ethernet II, Src: Cisco_28:f4:0a (00:09:11:28:f4:0a), Dst: Dell_87:38:56 (00:23:ae:87:38:56)
▷ Internet Protocol, Src: 140.209.69.10 (140.209.69.10), Dst: 140.209.122.177 (140.209.122.177)
▽ Internet Control Message Protocol
    Type: 0 (Echo (ping) reply)
    Code: 0 ()
    Checksum: 0x1351 [correct]
    Identifier: 0x0200
    Sequence number: 16909 (0x420d)
  ▽ Data (32 bytes)
      Data: 4142434445464748494A4B4C4D4E4F505152535455565741...
      [Length: 32]
```

Figure 12.8

A "ping" packet shown in Wireshark.

operation and gives routers a way to redirect packets sent by hosts. ICMP packets reside inside IP packets, replacing transport packets like TCP or UDP.

Ping Attacks

To perform a "ping," a host typically sends an ICMP Echo Request packet. The packet contains a block of data that the recipient copies into an Echo Reply and sends back to the original sender. Figure 12.8 illustrates such a packet displayed in Wireshark.

The receipt of the Echo Reply quickly shows that the hosts can reach each other and provides a simple measurement of the transmission delay. Ping has, in fact, been involved in a variety of attacks over the years, mostly causing denial of service.

- **Ping Floods**

  In a "ping flood," one or more hosts conspire to flood a victim with ping requests. The flood of requests keeps the victim's protocol stack and network very busy. Any ping responses the host produces will simply add to the network's congestion. Some networks block pings, or all ICMP messages, to avoid such attacks.

- **Smurf Attack**

  This is a variant of the ping flood in which a single attacker tricks other hosts into attacking the victim. The result is a ping flood, engulfing the victim in a DDOS attack. The attacker sends a *forged* ping request packet; the source host address points at the victim, not the attacker. The destination is a *broadcast* address. This sends the ping request to every computer that receives the broadcast. Thus, every one of these computers sends a ping reply at the victim. The attacker can overwhelm the victim by sending a steady stream of such packets, prompting a continuing flood directed at the victim.

  Internet routing standards expect gateways to discard broadcast packets. This should limit smurf attacks to internal sources. Moreover, hosts often are configured to ignore ping requests sent to broadcast addresses.

- **Ping of Death**

  The "ping of death" is not actually a protocol weakness. It was caused by mishandling of too-large messages, so it was a form of buffer overflow error. The weakness persisted in many protocol stacks until the late 1990s, because it relied on a series of circumstances that never occurred in normal operation. The problem disappeared as protocol stacks were patched to correct the flaw.

Redirection Attacks

ICMP provides error messages so that a router can direct traffic away from itself and toward a different host. Routers may transmit such messages if there are two or more routers visible to the host, but the host sends some of its traffic to the wrong one.

Once an attacker redirects traffic away from the correct router and toward a subverted host, the attacker can intercept, examine, and modify the victim's network traffic. This allows the attacker to take over a victim's TCP connections and masquerade as the victim host or its user.

TCP/IP Attacks

Even though it is simple to forge the source IP address of a UDP packet, it is much harder to believably forge the source of a TCP packet. In general, attackers shouldn't be able to hijack a connection unless they subvert a router that carries the connection's traffic.

- **SYN Flood Attack**

  The attacker sends a series of SYN packets to the victim, each specifying a different socket. The source addresses probably will be forged, because there is no need to process the responses. Each SYN packet produces a half-open connection. The connection persisted until the protocol stack timed it out.

  The attack was very effective when it first emerged in 1996, because victim hosts only had a small number of data structures to handle incoming connections, and those were very quickly used up. Attackers sent SYNs much faster than the victim host would time out the half-open connections.

  The general solution was to improve management of half-open connections. For example, some hosts would discard and reuse the oldest half-open connection if another request came in.

- **Source Routing Attack**

  This is a clever variant of the redirection attacks just noted: The IP header contains an option for "source routing," which allows the sender to direct the traffic through a series of hosts. The attacker forges a packet from a trustworthy host and puts the attacker's host on the packet's route. The attacker directs the packet at the victim. The victim typically will respond using the source route provided in the original packet. This takes the packet back to the attacker's host, enroute to the trustworthy host. The attacker's host simply processes the packet and doesn't forward it further.

There are various approaches to address this risk. For example, hosts might want to discard source routing information when talking to a trusted host. More often, however, we want to rely on cryptographic authentication of the trusted host, which we see in Chapter 14.

- **IP Spoofing Attacks**

  In general, "IP spoofing" refers to any attack that forges the sender's IP address. In an earlier section, we examined a particular spoofing attack that relied on predicting TCP sequence numbers. The attack attempted to send the minimum number of packets necessary to open a connection and provide data; in this case, a series of keyboard commands that enabled the attacker to penetrate the victim host. Because the source address belonged to a trusted host and the sequence numbers looked correct, the victim accepted the data as a legitimate keyboard command from the trusted host.

  In a practical attack, the attacker may open other connections with the victim host to detect the pattern by which the host assigns sequence numbers. Then the attacker floods the victim with packets, each containing a guess at the correct sequence number. Traditionally, the erroneous packets were simply discarded, while the correctly guessed packet was accepted.

12.3 Names on the Internet

When we type an email address or the name of a website, part of the text includes a name with dots, usually suffixed by ".com" or ".edu" or a two-letter abbreviated country name. These are called *domain names*. They are part of an organized collection of names that are unique on the Internet. The names form a hierarchy, as shown in Figure 12.9.

We use domain names most often to identify host computers that provide specific services, particularly web servers and email services. In practice, each name stands for the numerical IP address of the named host.

The *Domain Name System* (DNS) looks up a domain name and retrieves information about it. Application software uses it like a telephone book; we supply a domain name and the DNS retrieves the host's numerical IP address. DNS is an essential part of the Internet; nobody remembers the numerical IP address of Google or Amazon or Microsoft, but everyone knows their domain names. TCP/IP protocols require numerical addresses to open connections, and DNS retrieves the forgettable IP addresses associated with the memorable domain names.

THE NAME SPACE

All domain names include a *top-level domain* (TLD). These are acronyms that more or less reflect the location or purpose of the organization that owns the name. Table 12.1 lists the acronyms for several common TLDs.

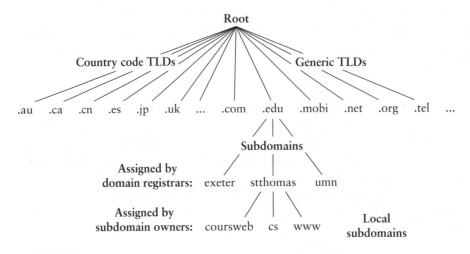

Domain name hierarchy.

TABLE 12.1 Common top-level domain acronyms			
Acronym	Meaning	Type	Usage
ca	Canada	country code	Government or private organizations in that country.
cn	China	country code	Government or private organizations in that country.
uk	United Kingdom	country code	Government or private organizations in that country.
us	United States	country code	Government or private organizations in that country.
com	commercial	generic	Any organization may use this TLD.
edu	educational	generic	Restricted to educational organizations.
net	network	generic	Intended for organizations that provide network services.
org	organization	generic	Intended for noncommercial organizations.
gov	government	generic	Restricted to U.S. federal and state government entities.
mil	military	generic	Restricted to U.S. military organizations.

Figure 12.10

Example format of a three-part domain name.

There are two types of TLDs: generic names and country codes. The generic names are not supposed to be associated with specific countries, although the military and government TLDs are both controlled by the U.S. government alone. Country codes are based on two-letter acronyms defined in the latest version of ISO Standard 3166. Individual countries decide how to manage their own country codes; some allow anyone to register a domain, regardless of location or nationality.

We always construct domain names from right to left, starting with the TLD. Referring to Figure 12.9, we move down the tree as we build the name from right to left. After selecting a TLD, we select a unique subdomain name, like the word "stthomas" in stthomas.edu (Figure 12.10).

Even though there are several schools with "St. Thomas" in their name, there may only be one stthomas.edu. Other organizations may choose the subdomain "stthomas" from other TLDs. For example, as of 2010, the domain name "stthomas.com" was being used to promote tourism in the U.S. Virgin Islands, whose capital is on the island of St. Thomas.

Email addresses contain domain names but those names typically contain only two parts: the subdomain followed by the TLD. Three-part domain names often are used when a site offers several different services. The third, "local" subdomain identifies the service offered. For example, the "www" in Figure 12.10 stands for World Wide Web, and the domain name identifies the stthomas.edu web server.

Local subdomains are controlled by the subdomain owner. Some subdomain owners use them, while others don't. In many cases, the "www" is optional when using a browser: the DNS for the two-part domain name yields the same address as a three-part name beginning with www. For example, stthomas.edu yields the same website as www.stthomas.edu.

Some organizations produce subdomains for subdomains. For example, the University of Minnesota has a website at www.umn.edu, and the computer science and engineering department has its own website at www.cs.umn.edu.

12.3.1 Domain Names in Practice

People and organizations may acquire a domain name by registering it under one of the TLDs. The first step is to find an unregistered name under an existing TLD. For example, Kevin has decided to start a small business on the Internet. He chooses a name and tries to register it under the ".com" domain. His first six name choices were already taken by others, but he settles on "eifsc.com," which hadn't already been registered.

To take possession of his chosen domain name, Kevin contacts a *domain registrar* to register the domain. He pays a registration fee and the registrar creates that name on his behalf. He also provides the registrar with the IP addresses to appear in his DNS entries. The registrar sets up the appropriate DNS entries for Kevin's new domain. As noted in Table 12.1, there are restrictions on the use of some TLDs. For example, Kevin can't register eifsc.edu because he's not an educational organization nor could he register eifsc.mil. These TLDs are managed by special registrars that validate an organization's right to register such names.

The *Internet Corporation for Assigned Names and Numbers*, or ICANN, manages the distribution of domain names and IP addresses. ICANN accredits domain registrars to issue domain names and manage the associated records. Through its subsidiary, the Internet Assigned Numbers Authority, it manages the DNS root and assigns numeric values for protocols and addresses.

USING A DOMAIN NAME

Technically, the domain name provides a memorable substitute for a numerical IP address. In practice, most people think of domain names as standing for websites or as a "home address" for someone's email. It is hard to use DNS itself to link a domain name to a personal web page or email account. In practice, the domain name needs to point to the numerical IP address of the host providing web service or email service.

Many domain registrars provide a service to link a registered domain name to an existing email account or to a web page hosted on a larger site. The registrars implement special hosts to provide this service. The domain name's owner supplies information about their existing email address or web page, and the registrar's server redirects email and web transactions to the appropriate destination. This provides an "alias" for an email address or website.

When handling a website alias, the registrar translates the domain name into a link to a particular web page. For example, Kevin might not have his own host and global IP address. Instead, Kevin has a personal website on "comcast.net" and he wants "eifsc.com" to point to those pages. Using a web-based interface provided by the registrar, Kevin supplies a link to his Comcast home page. After that, the registrar automatically redirects any visit to "eifsc.com" to Kevin's home page at comcast.net.

This allows Kevin to use a personalized domain name with web space he already owns. Many domain registrars also offer web services and will automatically link a personal domain name to the customer's rented web space.

Registrars often also provide email aliases. For example, Kevin has an email account at school, but he wants to also use the email address "kev@eifsc.com." To do this, the registrar provides another web-based interface to establish email forwarding. Kevin selects his domain name "eifsc.com" and gives it the user name "kev." Then he enters his school email address as the email destination.

Whenever the registrar receives email for "eifsc.com," it looks at Kevin's email forwarding requests. If the user name on the email is "kev," then the registrar retrieves Kevin's school email address and forwards the email there.

12.3.2 Looking Up Names

If the DNS serves the same purpose as a telephone book, then we need to examine the lookup process. Every time we type in a link to a web page, we enter a domain name and that name must be converted to an IP address. DNS translations must be fast and accurate.

The lookup process is handled by **domain name resolver** software. The software is part of the standard internet API. Resolver software follows these four steps:

1. The software retrieves the domain name of interest.
2. The software looks up the domain name in the host's cache. Each host keeps a cache of previous domain name queries.
3. If the name isn't in the cache, the host sends a query across the network to its assigned DNS server.
4. The software saves the answer in the cache in case the same query recurs, and it returns the answer to the caller.

The host's DNS server is assigned when the host receives its other internet configuration information, like its IP address and gateway address. The DNS server is identified by its IP address.

If the host must send a DNS query to a server, it sends the query to port 53 at the server's IP address. Typical DNS queries and replies fit in a single packet and are transmitted using UDP. The resolver software sets a timer to detect lost queries, since UDP won't detect lost packets.

There are several kinds of DNS servers. Some are actually resolvers that simply contact other servers for information; these are called *recursive resolvers*. Some contain authoritative answers to some DNS queries but must contact other servers for other queries. In most cases, the resolvers maintain a cache of answers to save time when handling repeated queries.

DNS LOOKUP

Most computer systems have a keyboard command **nslookup** that uses the resolver to look up domain names. The command works in Unix command shells available in OS-X and Linux and in the MSDOS command shell on Windows. Unlike the nmap command examined earlier, nslookup doesn't take a list of options and parameters. Instead, it starts its own command shell that collects domain names to look up.

The following is an example using nslookup on MS-DOS. We underline the commands typed by the user. First, the user Kevin types the nslookup command itself. The program responds by typing the name and IP address of the default name server. In private networks behind a firewall, this will be the local address of the network's gateway.

Because this server address has no domain name, the "Server" name is "Unknown." Then nslookup types a ">" to prompt the user for a domain name:

```
Microsoft Windows [Version 6.1.7600]
Copyright (c) 2009 Microsoft Corporation.  All rights reserved.

C:\Users\kevin>nslookup
Default Server:  UnKnown
Address:  10.20.30.40

>
```

Kevin types in his own domain name to retrieve its IP address:

```
> eifsc.com
Server:  UnKnown
Address:  10.10.10.10

Nonauthoritative answer:
Name:   eifsc.com
Address:  64.202.189.170

>
```

Nslookup responds with a short report of the domain's IP address. If the domain has several IP addresses, the report lists them. For example, a large site like google.com will produce a list of IP addresses. Kevin also may set certain options in the program.

For example, he can tell the program to return "any" domain records it finds instead of only returning the basic IP address record. Figure 12.11 shows what happens when he does this and repeats his query.

12.3.3 DNS Protocol

The ARPANET relied on a file named "HOSTS.TXT" to provide a mapping between host names and their numerical addresses. The early Internet used the same approach, but within a year it was reaching the limits of manageability. Any approach based on a single database would not keep pace with even modest Internet growth.

The proposed solution was a ***distributed database*** to convert host names into numerical addresses. Individual hosts could contact any server in the domain name system. If that server couldn't answer their query, it could redirect the query to a server capable of answering it.

Figure 12.12 shows a Wireshark display of a DNS query response. Like most DNS operations, it travels in a UDP packet. Wireshark provides a link to the corresponding request, which carries a matching transaction ID. The actual query contains the same "queries" section, but lacks the "answers" section. Here, the "answers" section provides the requested IP address.

```
> set type=any
> eifsc.com
Server:  UnKnown
Address:  10.20.30.40

Non-authoritative answer:
eifsc.com         nameserver = ns21.domaincontrol.com
eifsc.com         nameserver = ns22.domaincontrol.com
eifsc.com
        primary name server = ns21.domaincontrol.com
        responsible mail addr = dns.jomax.net
        serial   = 2009032200
        refresh  = 28800 (8 hours)
        retry    = 7200 (2 hours)
        expire   = 604800 (7 days)
        default TTL = 86400 (1 day)
eifsc.com         internet address = 64.202.189.170
eifsc.com         MX preference = 0, mail exchanger = smtp.secureserver.net
eifsc.com         MX preference = 10, mail exchanger =
mailstore1.secureserver.net


ns22.domaincontrol.com  internet address = 208.109.255.11
ns21.domaincontrol.com  internet address = 216.69.185.11
mailstore1.secureserver.net    internet address = 216.69.186.201
smtp.secureserver.net   internet address = 72.167.238.201
>
```

Figure 12.11

Nslookup list of "any" DNS records found for eifsc.com.

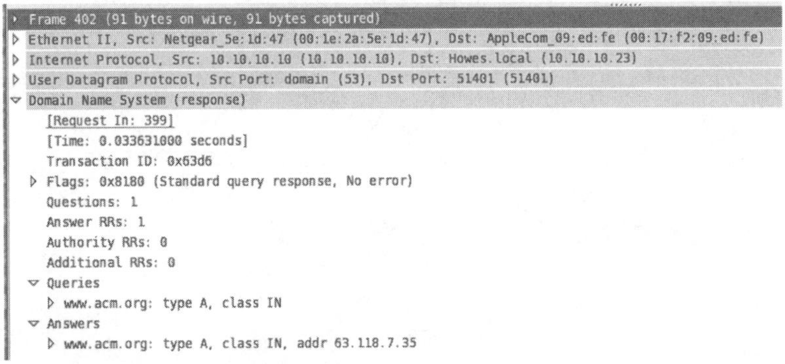

```
▶ Frame 402 (91 bytes on wire, 91 bytes captured)
▷ Ethernet II, Src: Netgear_5e:1d:47 (00:1e:2a:5e:1d:47), Dst: AppleCom_09:ed:fe (00:17:f2:09:ed:fe)
▷ Internet Protocol, Src: 10.10.10.10 (10.10.10.10), Dst: Howes.local (10.10.10.23)
▷ User Datagram Protocol, Src Port: domain (53), Dst Port: 51401 (51401)
▽ Domain Name System (response)
    [Request In: 399]
    [Time: 0.033631000 seconds]
    Transaction ID: 0x63d6
  ▷ Flags: 0x8180 (Standard query response, No error)
    Questions: 1
    Answer RRs: 1
    Authority RRs: 0
    Additional RRs: 0
  ▽ Queries
    ▷ www.acm.org: type A, class IN
  ▽ Answers
    ▷ www.acm.org: type A, class IN, addr 63.118.7.35
```

Figure 12.12

Wireshark display of a DNS response.

Resolving a Domain Name Via Redirection

Names in the DNS form a hierarchy, and different servers are assigned to different sections of the hierarchy. These sections are called "zones." A server assigned to a zone is considered the authority for answering questions about domain names in that zone.

The starting point is, of course, the "root zone" at the top of the hierarchy in Figure 12.9. If we need to resolve a domain name like "www.stthomas.edu" and we don't know where to start, we go to a root server. The root server then refers us to a more specialized server to answer our question. The process repeats until we find the server with the answer.

Figure 12.13 illustrates this iterative lookup process. Our first query goes to the root server. The server looks at the top-level domain in the name: ".edu" in this case. The server doesn't know the whole answer itself, so it refers us to a server with better information.

We send our query a second time, this time to the ".edu" server. This server looks up the subdomain name "stthomas" and finds a server that can answer queries about it.

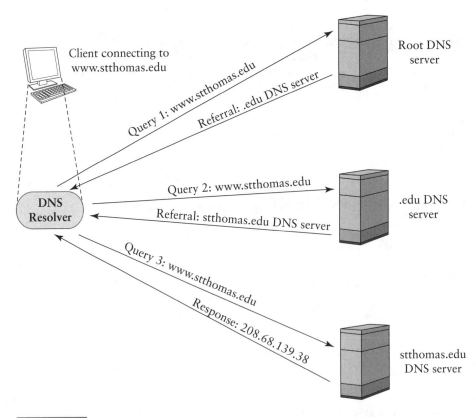

Figure 12.13

Looking up a domain name.

Our second query, like our first, yields a referral to another name server. Our third query goes to the "stthomas.edu" server, which finally returns a response.

Because "stthomas" belongs to a university with a large IT department, it runs its own domain name server. Personal domain names often are directed to a server belonging to a domain registrar. If the subdomain has subdomains, those usually are interpreted by the same server.

Figure 12.13 shows that a domain name query might go through three or more servers in its quest for resolution. Each is responsible for part of the domain name space, and they work together to answer queries. The server responsible for a particular name's meaning can update the information itself without having to update other systems. This is what makes the DNS a distributed database.

By distributing authority to different servers, DNS decentralizes management of different parts of domain names. Authority for "stthomas" or "umn" domain names are delegated to the organizations that own the names. In mid-2011, there were over 130 *million* subdomains registered under the major TLDs. The distributed approach provides a practical way to manage the enormous address space.

DNS REDUNDANCY

Every zone usually has several authoritative servers. If we perform a query and are redirected to another server, the redirection often lists several server IP addresses and we can send our query to any of them. Thus, if one server fails to respond due to excessive load or any other reason, we can contact one of the other servers.

When the zone belongs to an organization, like umn.edu or stthomas.edu, the organization itself is responsible for providing redundant servers. If they don't provide multiple servers and their main server goes down, then no one will be able to resolve their domain names until it recovers.

Shared parts of the name space, like the TLDs, also rely on redundancy. Root zone service is provided by several dozen root servers distributed worldwide. Most TLDs, especially the generic TLDs, also are served by multiple servers.

12.3.4 Investigating Domain Names

Domain names provide the starting point for connecting to entities on the Internet. The names themselves, however, only connect to servers. In order to keep track of domain name ownership, ICANN requires the registration of all owners of domain names. ICANN also requires that the information be posted in a standard Internet database, called the *whois* database.

This database contains ownership, administrative, and technical contact information for domain names, Internet IP address ranges, and Autonomous System identifiers. Figure 12.14 shows the output from a whois query on the domain "stthomas.edu" (some text was suppressed for privacy reasons, but the latest version is available online).

ICANN requires legitimate contact information be associated with the whois record of every domain name. Registrars provide the owner's contact information, but in some

```
Domain Name: STTHOMAS.EDU

Registrant:
    University of St. Thomas
    2115 Summit Avenue
    Mail# xxxx
    St. Paul, MN 55105
    UNITED STATES

Administrative Contact:
    Mxxxx Rxxxxxxxx
    Manager of Operations and Technical Support
    University of St. Thomas
    2115 Summit Ave
    Mail# xxxx
    St. Paul, MN 55105
    UNITED STATES
    mhxxxxxxx@stthomas.edu

Technical Contact:
    Exxx Txxxxx
    Manager of Operations and Technical Support
    University of St. Thomas
    2115 Summit Ave
    Mail # xxxx
    St. Paul, MN 55105
    UNITED STATES
    ejxxxx@stthomas.edu

Name Servers:
    STTHOMAS.EDU            140.209.1.5
    DNS1.STTHOMAS.EDU       140.209.1.17
    NS2.ONVOY.NET

Domain record activated:    12-Sep-1990
Domain record last updated: 03-Jun-2009
Domain expires:             31-Jul-2011
```

Figure 12.14

Whois response for stthomas.edu.

cases, the registrar simply provides its own contact information. This happens if the customer wants to shield their personal information. The registrars provide this service at an extra cost.

The IP address and contact information for the domain name only tells part of a website's story. It does not always identify the website's physical location. This is especially true when organizations rent web service from other organizations. To track down a site's location, we must find the owner of the IP address itself.

The whois service will identify the company owning a particular IP address in terms of the address range. We must use other services to narrow down an address location more precisely. There are also online *geolocation* services that convert IP addresses to more specific physical locations. Typically, these services use a custom database that has collected detailed IP address ranges and associated them with physical street addresses, map coordinates, zip codes, and so on.

12.3.5 Attacking DNS

DNS is a relatively old and widely used Internet component. This makes it a very valuable target. Though vulnerabilities exist, most DNS transactions take place without trouble or interference. Here is a summary of major DNS vulnerabilities:

- Cache poisoning: A resolver receives a bogus response to a DNS query. All subsequent queries will receive the wrong information and redirect connections to the wrong IP address.
- Denial-of-service attack on major DNS servers: Attackers try to disable part or all DNS service in parts of the Internet by attacking major DNS servers.
- DOS attack using a shared resolver: An attacker transmits numerous bogus DNS queries to the shared resolver.

Attacks either trick DNS into returning incorrect information, or they attack DNS services in a way that disrupts other Internet services. We examine each attack and also review proposed DNS security improvements.

DNS information usually is correct because it is hard to trick a resolver into accepting incorrect information. The resolver uses established IP addresses to contact other DNS servers. Those addresses arrive during boot configuration, provided by a trustworthy server, or they are provided through a trustworthy configuration process.

Servers, or malicious hosts posing as servers, can't simply announce DNS information to resolvers. Unlike ARP, the resolvers only look for answers to specific queries. Each query contains a randomly selected client port number and a randomly selected transaction identifier. An attacker must have that information in order to give a bogus answer to a resolver.

CACHE POISONING

This attack provides bogus responses to DNS queries. It takes advantage of the fact that most resolvers contain a cache. If the cache contains bogus data about a host, the resolver will provide the bogus data to all queries about that host.

A simple but inefficient approach to cache poisoning is a form of bucket brigade attack. The attacker sits on a node between the resolver and some DNS servers. When a server sends a response, the attacker modifies the response so that the domain name points to the wrong IP address. In some cases, the attacker can trick the resolver into using the wrong servers to resolve top-level domain names like .com. This allows the attacker to provide bogus answers on a large portion of the names the resolver queries.

A more efficient attack transmits numerous bogus answers to a resolver in hopes of matching a query's port number and transaction number. If the port and transaction numbers are predictable, this attack may work. Some DNS software resists this attack by using truly random values for those numbers and by carefully checking DNS responses against outstanding queries. However, such checks reduce DNS performance, so they are not used everywhere.

Attackers have targeted ISPs and specific sites with cache poisoning attacks. In 2008, the domain name for a security researcher's site was hijacked by poisoning the cache on the ISP's DNS servers. The attack occurred after the site had published details of how to exploit cache poisoning. Similar attacks hit a large ISP in China a few months later. In 2009, a cache poisoning attack redirected traffic to a bogus site masquerading as Brazil's largest bank.

DOS ATTACKS ON DNS SERVERS

In 2002, hundreds of computers worldwide sent thousands of packets to all of the DNS root servers for about an hour. This was a distributed denial of service (DDOS) attack because it relied on numerous separate computers to work together to overwhelm the targets with traffic. The attack briefly interrupted service from all but four of the root servers. Most Internet users saw no service trouble because most DNS queries are answered with cached responses. A similar attack occurred in early 2007. Although the second attack lasted several hours, it affected even fewer root servers.

However, the basic risk remains: Attackers can try to shut down portions of DNS by attacking authoritative servers for different parts of the name space. On Christmas Eve 2009, the DNS provider for amazon.com suffered a DDOS attack. It interfered with access to the Amazon website for about an hour, but only affected visitors in parts of California.

Botnets

DDOS attacks require a large collection of computers to transmit a steady stream of packets. Attackers often rely on botnets to perform such attacks. The attacker may upload special attack software to the individual computers (the "bots") and then direct the attack at a particular DNS or IP address. Such attacks can pose a particular challenge, because the traffic isn't from a single source and may be widely distributed across the network.

DOS ATTACKS AND DNS RESOLVERS

Because DNS resolvers often reside in DNS servers that serve a particular zone of the name space, these machines are targets for attack. However, resolvers also may be tricked into taking part in an *amplification attack*.

In general, an amplification attack is one where the attacker sends a small amount of traffic to a server which responds with a lot of traffic. The attacker forges the packets' return addresses to point to the victim's computer. The server unwittingly sends vast quantities of traffic at the victim on behalf of the attacker.

In a DNS-based amplification attack, the attacker sends thousands of DNS queries to a resolver, with the victim's IP address given as the source of the query. Each query is perhaps 50 bytes long, but the responses may be thousands of bytes long. Thus, the attacker sends a relatively small amount of attack data, and the DNS resolver sends a flood of data to the victim. The attacker can make the attack even more effective by sending a flood of queries to several different resolvers, so that they send the victim an even larger flood of responses.

DNS Security Improvements

DNS is one of the oldest and most heavily used elements of the Internet. As such it is difficult to modify, because so many systems rely on its present structure and operation. However, there are certain steps that many sites and systems take to improve DNS security.

- Randomized requests. The port number and transaction identifier in a DNS request are supposed to be randomly chosen so as to be hard to predict. Not all systems choose them randomly, though software updates have corrected this weakness.

- Limited access to resolvers. An "open resolver" is one that accepts a DNS query from anywhere on the Internet. It is easy to use an open resolver for an amplification attack. Many sites block access to their resolvers so that they are available only to their customers.

- Distributed DNS servers. These provide multiple DNS servers to provide authoritative answers for important domain queries. The major root and TLD domains are covered by multiple servers distributed worldwide. DNS is less vulnerable to DDOS attacks if the attack must target numerous servers in separate locations.

Security improvements also arise from the *DNS Security Extensions* (DNSSEC), which consist primarily of cryptographic techniques for validating DNS transactions. DNSSEC prevents cache poisoning and man-in-the-middle attacks by affixing digital signatures to DNS responses and by providing a certification hierarchy for verifying the signature keys. DNSSEC was first deployed to root servers in 2010.

12.4 Internet Gateways and Firewalls

The original plans for the modern Internet envisioned gateways to connect sites together. They did not envision *firewalls*: gatekeepers at a site's entrance. Figure 12.15 shows a typical configuration for a small network. The network is centered on the gateway, which often includes WiFi wireless LAN support. Most gateways also include a built-in hub or switch that provides downlinks to a few wired computers or other devices. The gateway's uplink connects to the ISP.

In the early days of the Internet, developers found it challenging simply to pass packets between different networks. Protocol and gateway designers did away with every

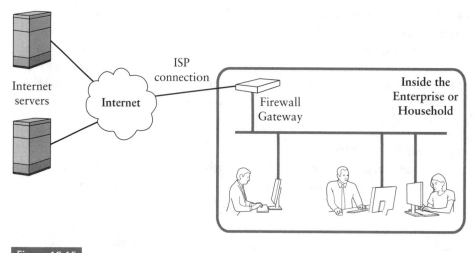

Figure 12.15

A small LAN connects to its ISP through a single gateway.

impediment they could. Today, an Internet packet seems almost alive in its relentless quest to find its destination.

With the evolution of malicious software, all sensible sites try to block potentially hostile traffic. All enterprises, and most households, have installed some type of gateway that contains a firewall. Some install the gateway for protection, though most probably install it for convenience.

A business ISP connection could use any type of service provided by a local telecom company. Typical telecom services are described in Section 12.5. In most households, the connection is either through the local phone company or through the cable TV provider. Traditionally, household computers were connected to the Internet via individual dial-up connections.

Today, many households use *digital subscriber line* (DSL) service, which provides high-speed Internet access simultaneously with telephone service. Many households also use their cable TV provider as ISP via a *cable modem*, which converts Ethernet packets for transmission over cable TV lines. Smaller business networks, and most households, connect to a single ISP.

A gateway provides a simple and convenient way to construct a small LAN. A typical low-cost gateway automatically configures Internet addresses and routes traffic between the LAN and the Internet. Such gateways include network address translation and the DHCP protocol that configures a host's network connections at boot time. Because a typical ISP provides only one globally routeable IP address to a subscriber, all hosts on the subscriber's internal LAN must share that IP address. NAT provides the mechanism to share the address.

Many gateways also contain an event log. This keeps a record of major events, like DHCP address assignments by the ISP and by the gateway itself. This lets the owner track connections by computers on the LAN. Some products also detect certain types of Internet attacks. Typical gateways will email the log to the owner on a periodic basis.

For many people, the gateway lets them take an "install-and-forget" approach to small LANs. The firewall feature of typical gateways may provide the LAN with an extra measure of protection. For these features to work, all hosts must reside on the "LAN" side of the gateway. It is possible technically to add a Layer 2 device (a hub or switch) between the ISP and the site gateway. If, however, we connect a host to that switch, the host probably won't have a working IP address.

Typical low-cost gateway products follow a Default Permit policy for outbound traffic and a Default Deny policy for inbound traffic. Thus, local hosts may initiate communications with external hosts on the Internet, but not vice versa. This does not, by default, allow a small site to host an Internet server. However, typical products may be configured to direct inbound server traffic to local hosts.

12.4.1 Network Address Translation

We introduced NAT briefly in Section 11.4.2. NAT translates the private addresses inside a site to a global Internet address used in packets that travel outside the site. The translation takes place at the site's gateway.

In internet technology, we call a device a *proxy* when it serves as a stand-in for a different internet host. By offering its own IP address for use by hosts inside the site, the gateway serves as a proxy for those hosts.

Sites typically use NAT to provide a number of hosts with global Internet access without assigning a unique global IP address to each one. Hosts inside the site can easily open connections to sites on the global Internet. NAT also provides useful site security because it naturally implements a Default Deny policy on inbound traffic. NAT only accepts inbound traffic if a local host initiated communications with the outside host.

NAT relies on the fact that typical host interactions are started by a client. When a client behind a NAT gateway starts talking to a host on the global Internet, the NAT gateway keeps track of the socket that connects the two hosts. A socket, as described in Section 11.3, associates a particular host and port number with another host and port number. Each socket typically represents a relationship between two processes on the network that are actively communicating with one another.

When we establish a TCP connection, we create a socket that identifies both ends of the connection. When we send UDP traffic, we don't actually create a connection, but there is a socket associated with the traffic. As with TCP, we identify the UDP socket with the two IP addresses and port numbers. Thus, a *socket* is a more general relationship between hosts than a connection.

Figure 12.16 shows how NAT works. A host behind a NAT gateway, on the left, connects to another host on the global Internet, on the right. The example uses 2-byte IP addresses (10.2, 17.8, 27.4) instead of 4-byte addresses for simplicity.

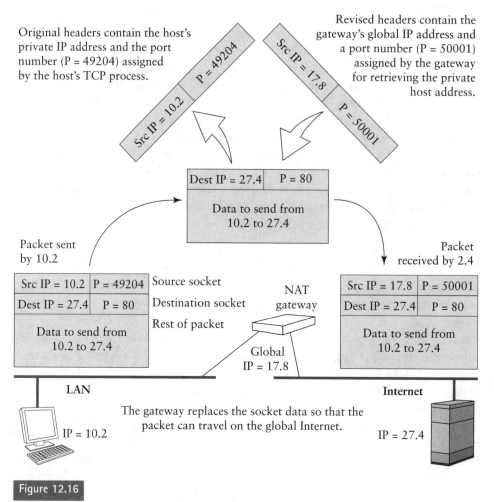

Original headers contain the host's private IP address and the port number (P = 49204) assigned by the host's TCP process.

Revised headers contain the gateway's global IP address and a port number (P = 50001) assigned by the gateway for retrieving the private host address.

Src IP = 10.2 | P = 49204

Src IP = 17.8 | P = 50001

Dest IP = 27.4 | P = 80

Data to send from 10.2 to 27.4

Packet sent by 10.2

| Src IP = 10.2 | P = 49204 |
| Dest IP = 27.4 | P = 80 |

Data to send from 10.2 to 27.4

Source socket

Destination socket

Rest of packet

NAT gateway

Global IP = 17.8

Packet received by 2.4

| Src IP = 17.8 | P = 50001 |
| Dest IP = 27.4 | P = 80 |

Data to send from 10.2 to 27.4

LAN

Internet

The gateway replaces the socket data so that the packet can travel on the global Internet.

IP = 10.2

IP = 27.4

Figure 12.16

Network address translation: Processing the first packet.

Typically, hosts behind a NAT gateway are assigned local IP addresses, like 10.x.x.x, as described in the earlier chapter. Thus, an IP address that starts with 10 must be a local address. The translation process takes place as follows:

- The client process tells the protocol stack to send a packet to the host with global IP address 27.4 on its port 80. This may be a web page request, because port 80 typically is used by web servers.

- The host's protocol stack assigns an arbitrary port number to this side of the socket: port 49204. The stack also fills in the host's IP address of 10.2.

- The host transmits the packet over the LAN. Because the packet's destination is outside the LAN, the packet is directed at the site gateway.

- The gateway begins the NAT process. It assigns a port number to this socket (50001 in this case) and remembers the local host's IP address and chosen port number (IP 10.2, port 49204).

- The gateway rewrites the packet's header to refer to the gateway's global IP address (17.8) and the gateway's chosen port number (50001).

- The gateway forwards the modified packet to the next router on its trip to its destination.

- Upon arrival at the destination host (IP 27.4), the recipient believes that the sending host's IP address is 17.8, because that is what the packet contains. This is, of course, the gateway's address.

When the recipient sends a packet back to the sender, the packet contains the gateway's IP address and port number. When the gateway receives the packet, it looks up the port number in its NAT data. This provides the gateway with the correct local host address and port number. The gateway rewrites the packet header. Then the gateway delivers the packet as if it had always been addressed to IP 10.4, port 49204.

Note that while Figure 12.16 suggests that we are changing the private IP address and port number by substituting a single packet header, that is not what happens. The private IP address resides in the IP header, and the port number is in the TCP/UDP header. NAT must change the appropriate IP address and port in each header.

Configuring DHCP and NAT

Most modern computers rely on DHCP to configure their Internet connection. Because many sites use NAT, they must configure DHCP to assign private IP addresses. Figure 12.17 displays the configuration display for a Linksys commercial wireless gateway, circa 2009. The owner configures the gateway by visiting a web page hosted by the gateway. The figure shows detail from the main setup page. The owner enters the configuration data in fields shown in the large rectangle with the white background.

Here is a summary of the settings shown in the figure:

- **Obtain an IP automatically**—This configures the gateway to use DHCP itself to retrieve its global IP address from the ISP.

- **Host/Domain/MTL**—Optional settings, left blank.

- **Local IP address**—The local IP address assigned to the gateway. Local hosts use this IP address to reach the gateway itself. The network part of this address indicates the network address range to use when assigning local IP addresses. In this example, all addresses are in the range 10.10.10.x.

- **Subnet mask**—As usual, it indicates which address bits select the network; the remaining address bits select hosts. In this case, host addresses are limited to the last byte of the address. This is the best setting for most low-cost gateways.

- **Local DHCP server**—Enabled, so that the gateway provides DHCP service and assigns local addresses.

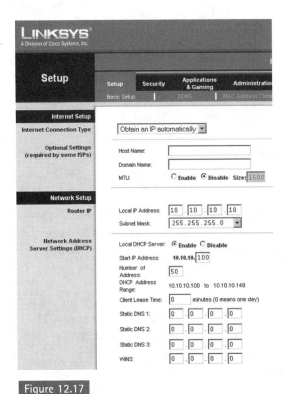

Figure 12.17

Configuring a simple gateway product.

- **Start IP address**—Indicates the lowest IP address assigned by the gateway. This is often the next IP address following the gateway's own address, entered previously.
- **Number of address**—Number of host IP addresses the gateway will assign. The gateway starts at its starting address and assigns this number of addresses, consecutively. All such addresses should be legal addresses. The range must not include the gateway's own local address, entered previously.
- **Client lease time**—The duration during which a host may keep a particular IP address before it expires. The value 0 selects a duration of 1 day.
- **Static DNS, WINS**—Optional IP addresses to identify DNS servers or Windows Internet Name Service (WINS) servers.

Most gateways work as both DHCP clients and as DHCP servers. They contact a DHCP server at the ISP to retrieve their own global IP address, to locate the router they should use for outbound packets, and to locate their DNS servers. The gateways also host DHCP service to assign local IP addresses to hosts on their own local network. Most gateways include a recursive DNS resolver and direct all local DNS queries to the gateway itself. The queries are then resolved by contacting the ISP's servers.

12.4.2 Filtering and Connectivity

NAT by itself provides enough traffic control for most small Internet sites. However, some sites have additional filtering and connectivity requirements, and the gateway provides support for them:

- Packet filtering—block packets that address particular source or destination hosts or that use particular protocols.
- Inbound traffic handling—accept inbound packets that don't belong to a NAT relationship and forward them to a local server host on the LAN.

In both cases, the gateway provides a way to establish rules for handling the desired traffic.

PACKET FILTERING

In general, *packet filtering* is the simplest form of firewall protection. It examines the fields of packet headers individually. If the headers contain particular values, the firewall discards the packet. The filtering may look at any packet headers and filter on these values:

- MAC address—source or destination
- Broadcast transmissions
- Internet Control Message Protocol (ICMP)—an IP protocol that seems to pose more risks than benefits on the modern Internet
- IP address—source or destination
- IP application protocol—inferred from the port numbers

The more sophisticated filters can check any or all of these fields on each packet. They also can apply the filtering selectively, for example, restricting some protocols or hosts to specific time periods. Less-sophisticated products might filter only on port numbers or local IP addresses.

A simple filter allows the owner to identify specific protocols by port number and/or transport type (TCP, UDP, or both) and then to block those particular protocols. The filter also might provide input for ranges of IP addresses or MAC addresses to block.

INBOUND CONNECTIONS

The gateway's NAT function typically ignores unsolicited inbound traffic, which is arguably the most dangerous. If all traffic is solicited by local clients, the traffic is unlikely to be risky, because clients aren't likely to do so from risky locations. However, if we wish to host Internet services within our site, we need a way to retrieve the inbound traffic and direct it to a local server. There are some common ways to do this:

- Default server. The owner configures the gateway to send unexpected traffic to a specific host on the local network. That host is behind the firewall and protected by some of its filtering, but it also responds to connection requests from clients on the Internet.

- Port forwarding. The owner configures the gateway to examine inbound port numbers on traffic. Specific port numbers, or port number ranges, are forwarded to specific local hosts as configured by the owner.
- Universal plug and play (UPnP). This is a set of protocols to allow equipment to share data across the Internet, even in LANs with firewalls and NAT.

As with other types of configuration, a low-cost gateway provides a web-based interface to configure inbound connections.

12.4.3 Software-Based Firewalls

Many vendors also provide software-based firewalls. These are specially privileged applications that monitor the operation of the network protocol stack. It blocks inbound traffic that it recognizes as unsafe or malicious. It may block suspicious actions by network servers or unexpected network activity by any process on the computer. Figure 12.18 illustrates the built-in firewall software on a Macintosh.

Software firewalls originally were third-party products that essentially served the same purpose as external firewalls. In fact, Unix hosts sometimes used the same packet-filtering packages to protect the host itself that were used to implement a network

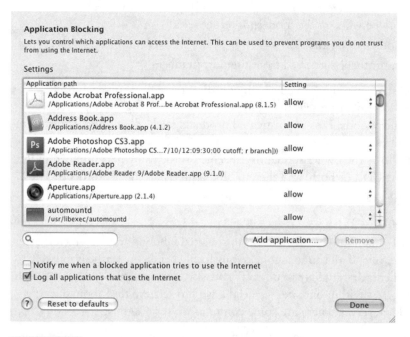

Figure 12.18

Application filtering on a software firewall.

firewall. A typical product would filter inbound network traffic and discard packets directed at risky or unnecessary services. This yields two different types of protection:

1. Controlling inbound connections. This involves filtering services by port number, but it also may filter by host.
2. Controlling applications' network access. This either grants or blocks access to the network by individual applications or processes (Figure 12.18).

As products increased in sophistication, they provided interfaces to permit or deny network access to individual processes. This provided a way to block malicious programs that tried to establish "backdoor" access to a computer. In the 1990s, a program called "Back Orifice" found its way into many Windows systems. Although a few system administrators used it as a way to remotely administer PCs, many attackers used it to construct some of the earliest botnets. A host could block access to Back Orifice by disabling its ability to use the network.

Recent versions of Microsoft Windows include a built-in firewall facility. The facility is preloaded with information about processes that are authorized to use the network. It may ask permission before granting network access to other processes.

Windows Firewall, and most others, will provide a way to manage the list of processes authorized to use the network. Windows calls such processes "exceptions," and the user manages them by manipulating the list of exceptions.

12.5 Long-Distance Networking

Before the days of computing, the earliest networks weren't local networks. To share information in a small area, people simply carried books or papers from one desk to another. Communications networks arose to conquer distance. A modern cell phone tower can connect hand-held phones within 25 miles (40 km). By connecting the tower with the rest of the phone system, the hand-held phone reaches any other phone on the planet (Figure 12.19).

People have used communication networks for thousands of years. For most of history, people wrote messages on paper and sent them as letters. Governments established networks to carry important messages quickly and reliably. In the 5th century BC, the traveler and historian Heroditus described the Persians' network of couriers with the famous phrase:

> ...these are stayed neither by snow nor rain nor heat nor darkness from accomplishing their appointed course with all speed. (*Histories*, Book 8, Ch. 98, Godley translation)

The couriers carried messages in relays, from one post to the next. Although early networks were restricted to government or military traffic, they evolved into today's postal services.

Messages traveled on paper until telegraph systems arose in the late 18th century. The first telegraphs actually used a crude form of optical transmission; telegraphers used large flags to signal between towers constructed across the European countryside. A clerk in one tower watched a distant tower and copied down its signals, while another clerk relayed those signals to the next tower in the network. The process was slow and labor intensive by modern standards, but it transmitted messages much faster than a courier on horseback.

In the 19th century, the telegraph moved from optical to electrical technology. Networks arose on the continents, and then were interconnected by undersea cables. By the end of the 19th century, it was possible to send a telegram between any two major cities on the planet.

This growing web of wires formed the first information network. Unlike the postal system, the telegraph carried the information itself without the paper. To send a telegraph, the sender wrote out the message and paid a telegraph clerk to send it. The clerk then transmitted the message toward its destination. The sender's written message never left the originating office. The receiving office printed out a copy of the telegram and hand-delivered it to the recipient.

By the end of the 19th century, Tesla, Marconi, and other inventors had moved the telegraph to wireless transmission. Thus, we have the three fundamental mechanisms for communicating information without carrying a written message:

1. Optical—transmit data using photons, either visually or by shining a light and measuring the signal.
2. Wire—transmit data using electromagnetic signals across metal wire.
3. Radio—transmit data through the air using nonvisual electromagnetic signals.

Figure 12.19

Cell phone tower.

Although modern communications still relies on these mechanisms, specific technologies were abandoned over the years. Just as the internal combustion engine replaced horse-drawn transportation, modern systems replaced the optical and electrical telegraph systems. Optical systems disappeared in the mid-1800s with the rise of electrical telegraph networks.

Telephone calls, faxes, and email slowly replaced telegrams during the 20th century. By the end of the century, telegrams were used only for formal announcements and congratulations, including weddings, birthdays, and anniversaries. Western Union sent its final telegram in early 2006.

Today's communications technologies are a combination of old and new. Very few old technologies are completely abandoned. Even though telegraph service no longer exists, Morse code still crops up in places. To review modern communications, we will look at these categories of technologies:

- Older—still used, but losing subscribers to newer, lower-cost alternatives
- Mature—today's workhorse technologies
- Evolving—growing, supplanting mature technologies

Although these categories are approximate, they help put the different technologies in a historical perspective.

12.5.1 Older Technologies

Many older technologies still play an important role in modern communications, but they compete poorly with newer techniques. The newer products and systems often offer lower costs or a better mix of features. Older technologies often persist because they are already in place. In some cases, it is cheaper to leave the old system in place than it is to replace it and retrain everyone.

Analog Broadcast Networks

Radio broadcast networks evolved in the early 20th century and were joined mid-century by television broadcasts. The networks actually consisted of individual stations, each assigned a specific frequency channel in the electromagnetic spectrum.

To transmit voice and music, the system used microphones to convert sound into varying amounts of electrical current. These varying currents in turn drove the radio signal. TV used the same technique, but it broke the signal into horizontal lines that scanned across the television tube's surface.

Analog networks took advantage of satellites as soon as the technology was practical. A broadcast satellite accepted a signal from a ground station and repeated it. A receiver anywhere within sight of the satellite could receive the repeated signal, given the right antenna.

Analog networks make inefficient use of the available broadcast spectrum. Moreover, digital techniques provide higher quality service thanks to error detection and correction. Digital television broadcasts have replaced analog broadcasts in parts of the world.

Circuit-Switched Telephone Systems

Even though the telegraph system may have been the first major digital network, it never really reached the technological sophistication of the analog telephone system. As we saw in Section 10.2.2, the telephone network established a call by constructing a circuit between two telephones. The network carried electrical signals produced by a phone's transmitter to the other phone's earpiece and vice versa.

Although certain features of the classic phone network persist in modern systems, much of the underlying technology has been replaced by digital systems. It was difficult to move a given phone number within the network or to provide voice mail services within the network. These features became commonplace as the infrastructure was digitized.

Analog-Based Digital Networks

During the 20th century, companies and other organizations with special communication requirements often leased special communications lines from the telephone company. In some cases, these might connect company phone systems in separate sites, so that an "inside" phone call could connect to a faraway building. Broadcast networks might also lease communications lines to distribute programs to affiliated stations. These same communications lines originally were used for digital networking.

To connect two remote computers, the owner leased a *dedicated line* between them. The telephone company usually provided the modem; the computer manufacturer usually provided the network interface, which exchanged digital signals with the modem. The wiring between a modem and a computer traditionally used "Recommended Standard" RS-232, or the similar V.24 standard from the International Telecommunications Union (ITU).

As computer networking evolved, third-party vendors developed faster, lower-cost modems that worked over conventional telephone lines. Anyone with a computer and a telephone could attach a modem and phone another computer: a dial-up connection. Table 12.2 summarizes differences between dedicated and dial-up lines.

Dial-up connections played an important role in early personal computers: It provided the cheapest network technology available. Many enterprises provided dial-up services of different types. Some provided services without authentication, assuming that no one would know their computer's unlisted phone number. Soon, hobbyists and other curious people found ways to locate and probe these connections.

To reduce the risk of such attacks, system developers looked at different line authentication techniques. An early approach was *dial-back*, in which authorized users could tell the system to call them back at their approved phone. When the caller hung up, the dial-back system would call the user's approved number and connect to their computer. Eventually, some custom modems could take advantage of the "caller ID" feature that reported the caller's phone number.

Microwave Networks

In the 1950s, communications companies developed and installed microwave networks as a substitute for links using copper wire. Microwave networks consist of tall antenna towers within the line of sight of one another, though many miles apart (Figure 12.20).

TABLE 12.2 Dedicated versus dial-up lines	
Dedicated Line	**Dial-Up Line**
Also called "unswitched line"	Also called "switched line"
Typically used a synchronous modem	Typically used an asynchronous modem
Rarely compatible with residential phones	Compatible with residential phones

The signal-handling antenna points at a matching microwave antenna on a distant tower.

Although some such networks belonged to traditional telephone companies, others belonged to competing private companies. Some customers of dedicated telephone lines found it cheaper to build their own microwave networks or to rent microwave links from other vendors. Microwave links were used heavily by radio and television networks and by private organizations needing low-cost long-distance connections. Some organizations installed their own links between offices within a metropolitan area.

The introduction of modern, high-speed optical networks reduced the demand for long-haul microwave networks. The optical systems had much higher bandwidth and provided comparable communications at a much lower cost.

Analog Two-Way Radios

Analog two-way radios, like traditional analog broadcast, were assigned specific frequency bands for specific purposes. For example, municipal police and fire departments were assigned specific bands, as were commercial companies and mobile phones. Different organizations were assigned specific frequencies ("channels") so that they would not interfere with others. A limited number of channels led to scarcity and high costs.

In the United States, frequency assignments were handled by the FCC. Certain channels were set aside for public use, notably the CB and the "family radio service" (FRS) bands. In both cases, the products were intended for personal communications over relatively short distances. A combination of low-cost equipment and popularity leads to crowded channels and difficult communications. Although modern cell phones lack the communal broadcast features of these services, they are more popular for routine two-way communications.

12.5.2 Mature Technologies

Mature communications technologies are used heavily, but replacement technologies loom. These systems may evolve into new and different services or they might fade away like the telegram.

Figure 11.20

Tower with a microwave antenna.

Dedicated Digital Network Links

In the late 1980s, telephone companies began to offer true digital service. In the United States, this included "T1" connections that provided a data speed of 1.544 Mb/sec and eventually "T3" connections at 44.7 Mb/sec. Other countries provided similar capabilities, like the E1/E3 services in Europe. Traditionally, these links provided *exactly* the bandwidth advertised, no more and no less, regardless of whether the customer used it or not.

T1/T3 services were "dedicated line" services. Each rented line connected exactly two endpoints. When customers had to connect to two or more destinations, they had to rent two or more separate lines. Early Internet sites often used a T1/T3 line to connect to their Internet service provider. As Internet services improved, many customers with two or more T1/T3 connections found it cheaper to eliminate extra lines and connect across the Internet.

Although unswitched T1/T3 services are available still in many areas, they often are replaced by "frame relay" or asynchronous transfer mode (ATM) services. The newer services provide similar features to dedicated connections, but may offer lower rates by not guaranteeing the full data transfer rate at all times. Unlike T1/T3 services, both frame relay and ATM support a "switched" service that allows the customer to communicate with multiple destinations.

Cell Phones

The cell phone system uses a network of "cells," each containing antennas to support portable phones. Figure 12.19 shows a typical antenna. Each vertical element supports phone communications on a particular channel. Antennas in busy communities tend to contain many such elements.

Many phone customers own cell phones but do not own a "wired" telephone. In parts of the developing world, cell phones are more common than wired phones, because it is easier to construct and maintain the towers than to install community wiring.

Since its introduction in the early 1980s, cell phones have evolved from an analog to a digital system. Today, the system has evolved to incorporate packet-based network services and Internet access.

Cable TV

Like cell phones, cable systems have evolved from analog to digital systems. Cable networks originally emerged to provide better TV service in remote locations. Connections relied on coaxial cable to carry the signals. Like traditional telephone, this relies on a wired connection. The coaxial cable, however, carries a higher quality signal than conventional phone wiring.

As cable TV offered more programs than broadcast TV, customers paid the premium for a cable connection. Today, cable vendors operate more like communications vendors, offering Internet and telephone service as well as TV.

12.5.3 Evolving Technologies

Newer communications technologies fuel major changes to long-distance communications. It's tricky to predict the future, however. These new technologies could supplant one or more mature technologies or a new innovation may provide a mature technology with new capabilities or economies.

Optical Fiber Networks

Modern optical fiber transmits signals using light waves. The fiber serves as a "light pipe" to carry the signal. Because the fiber must transmit the light signal, it does not bend the same way as traditional wire. On the other hand, optical fiber avoids certain radio interference and induction problems that arise in wired connections. High-quality optical fiber yields a much higher transmission capacity than a comparable wired connection.

An early form of fiber network used the *fiber distributed data interface* (FDDI). These networks used a "ring" topology in which bidirectional connections attached all hosts in a ring. A special LAN protocol coordinated transmissions to allow effective sharing of the network.

Bidirectional Satellite Communications

Digital satellite broadcasts have become commonplace; the equipment is practically free to satellite TV subscribers. Bidirectional communication is a bit more challenging; a compact device must send a signal to a satellite hundreds or thousands of miles overhead. The "Iridium" system deployed a satellite-based cell phone system in the 1990s; subscriber phones worked almost anywhere on the planet. The system was ahead of its time, went bankrupt, and was acquired by the U.S. military. However, the technology and economics may improve in another decade or two, eventually making such a system practical for large-scale commercial deployment.

12.6 Resources

 IMPORTANT TERMS INTRODUCED

cable modem	domain registrar	proxy
distributed database	end-to-end principle	three-way handshake
domain name	flow control	whois
domain name resolver	nslookup	

ACRONYMS INTRODUCED

*See Table 12.1 for acronyms for common top-level domains.

ATM—Asynchronous transfer mode

DNS—Domain Name System

DNSSEC—DNS Security Extensions

DSL—Digital subscriber line
FDDI—Fiber distributed data interface
FIN—Finish TCP flag
FRS—Family radio service
ICANN—Internet Corporation for Assigned Names and Numbers
ICMP—Internet Control Message Protocol
ITU—International Telecommunications Union
RS-232—"Recommended Standard" 232
SEQ—Sequence number
SYN—Synchronize TCP flag
TLD—Top-level domain
UDP—User Datagram Protocol
UPnP—Universal plug and play
WINS—Windows Internet Name Service
www—World Wide Web

12.6.1 Review Questions

R1.   Briefly explain the end-to-end principle.

R2.   Why are there two separate, standard internet transport protocols: TCP and UDP? How are they similar? How are they different?

R3.   Briefly explain how TCP establishes a connection.

R4.   What mechanisms does TCP use to provide acknowledgments and flow control?

R5.   Why do some websites block "ping" requests? Explain whether websites still need to do this.

R6.   Identify and briefly explain two or more denial-of-service attacks that exploit TCP/IP protocols.

R7.   Identify and briefly explain two or more attacks on TCP/IP that may route packets to the wrong hosts.

R8.   Briefly explain the structure and components of a three-part domain name, like www.amawig.com.

R9.   Explain how DNS looks up a domain name using redirection.

R10. Summarize basic attacks on DNS.

R11. Describe how a gateway converts a private IP address into a global IP address using NAT.

R12. What features do a simple, low-cost network gateway provide to protect a small local network from attack?

R13. Why does a typical low-cost network gateway need to provide special mechanisms to handle inbound connections? Why doesn't it simply forward the packets to the chosen host address?

R14. Briefly describe older network technologies. Have you encountered any of these technologies? Briefly describe the encounter.

R15. Briefly describe mature network technologies. Which ones do you use or have you used? Briefly describe your experience.

R16. Briefly describe evolving technologies. Which ones do you use or have you used? Briefly describe your experience.

12.6.2 Exercises

NOTE: For some problems, your instructor will provide a Wireshark packet capture file that shows a computer starting up and opening a connection to a web page. You will use that packet capture file in exercises marked "Wireshark."

E1.   Write two paragraphs describing the circumstances surrounding a documented attack that took advantage of a TCP/IP protocol weakness. The first paragraph should identify who was attacked, where it took place, and when. The second paragraph briefly describes the protocol weakness used in the attack.

E2.   (Wireshark.) Locate a series of packets that establish a TCP connection.

   a. Which packets perform the three-way handshake? Identify them by packet number.

   b. Identify the connection's source and destination port numbers. Identify the application associated with this connection.

   c. Identify a packet, by number, that "acks" data transmitted on this connection. What is the ACK number provided in that packet?

   d. Identify the packet, by number, that sent some of the data "acked" by the packet in the previous question. What is the SEQ number provided in that packet? How many bytes of data were carried in that packet?

E3.   Use "nslookup" or "dnslookup" to look up domain information.

   a. Select a domain name associated with your school or work.

   b. Use the appropriate keyboard command to look up the domain's IP address. Include the command's output as an answer to this question.

   c. What is the numerical IP address associated with this domain name?

E4.   This question explores domain registration.

   a. Construct a legally formatted domain name that has not been registered. What domain name did you choose?

   b. Visit a registrar and confirm that the name has not been registered and is available for sale. Print out the information and offer for sale from the domain registrar.

   c. How much does it cost to register the domain name you chose?

E5.   Select an existing domain name. Look up the owner's "whois" record. Print out the "whois" record. Highlight or otherwise indicate the name and address to contact about this domain.

E6.   We wish to configure our gateway's NAT to assign addresses in the block 10.23.44.x. We want all host addresses on the LAN, including the gateway, to be in the range of 100–150. Identify the fields in Figure 12.17 that must be filled in to achieve this and what values should be filled in to those fields.

E7. (Wireshark.) Find a DNS Response packet. Be sure that it provides an IP address answer to an earlier DNS Query before answering this question.

   a. What is the packet number of this DNS response packet?

   b. What UDP source and destination port numbers appear in this response packet?

   c. What domain name does this packet provide an answer about?

   d. What IP address is provided as an answer?

   e. What is the packet number of the corresponding DNS query?

   f. What UDP source and destination port numbers appear in the query packet?

E8. Figure 12.21 displays a network of hubs, switches, and gateways. When answering the questions, keep in mind the protocol layers provided by these devices. Also,

keep in mind how a NAT gateway handles private and global addresses.

   a. Assuming that we only have MAC addresses for hosts A through D, which can reach which? Fill the answers into a reachability matrix formatted as shown in Table 11.2; put a check mark if the host can reach the destination.

   b. Assuming that we have IP addresses for hosts A through D, which can send an unsolicited packet to which? Fill the answers into a reachability matrix.

E9. Kevin is at a computer behind a NAT gateway. The computer's IP address is 192.168.1.100. He opens a TCP connection to a web server at eifsc.com. Use the standard port number and socket address definition described in Section 11.3.

   a. Using the IP address for eifsc.com looked up in Section 12.3.3 and the source port number of 44366, give the full socket address for the connection to the web server.

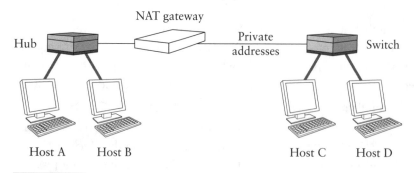

Figure 12.21

Reachability problem.

b. How does a NAT gateway choose a port number for an outgoing packet? Use that technique to choose a port number for this packet.

c. Assume that the NAT gateway has a global IP address of 11.22.33.44. Using the NAT port number chosen in (b), give the full socket address as seen by the server.

E10. Alice is at a computer behind a NAT gateway that has the private IP address 10.23.44.55. The gateway has the first IP address in the range; she has the fifty-fifth. She opens a connection to a file transfer server at 74.125.224.80.

a. Choose a five-digit source port number to be used by Alice's protocol stack.

b. Given the port number chosen for Alice's protocol stack above, give the full socket address as seen on the private side of the gateway. The destination port is the customary port for

setting up a file transfer, as given in Section 11.3.

c. Choose another five-digit port number to be assigned by the NAT to this connection.

d. Assume that the NAT gateway has a global IP address of 11.22.33.44. Using the NAT port number chosen above, give the full socket address as seen on the Internet side of the gateway.

E11. The Internet Assigned Numbers Authority has a web server at whois.iana.org that hosts a "whois" service to retrieve information about generic top-level domains, like .com or .mil, or country-specific domains like .us or .ca.

a. Look up a generic top-level domain. Provide the text output.

b. Look up a country-specific domain for a foreign country. Provide the text output.

ENTERPRISE COMPUTING

ABOUT THIS CHAPTER

Enterprises, whether public or private, commercial or nonprofit, bring important issues to information security. Each consists of a company of people working toward common objectives and sharing a common set of resources. This chapter examines the following aspects of enterprise computing:

- Risks and threats that arise in large groups
- Basic elements of enterprise management
- Physical elements of enterprise security
- Network authentication in an enterprise
- Disaster and contingency planning

13.1 The Challenge of Community

An enterprise is more than a family or a small team sharing a common goal. An enterprise is a larger community of people with different backgrounds, motivations, and desires.

There is an old saying that we don't get to pick our family so it's fortunate that we can pick our friends. Some people, but not all, extend that to coworkers. Happy people work with others they like and respect, but not everyone gets the perfect job. An enterprise has a mix of people; some who are enthusiastic about their team and others who are less enthusiastic.

When we talk about personal computer security, we recognize that responsibility falls entirely on the computer's owner. When we talk about enterprise computer security, responsibility is harder to pin down. Company-appointed administrators may have the authority to modify computers assigned to specific workers, but the administrators can't guarantee a computer's safety. They must depend on the actual computer users to use the computers responsibly.

This poses a huge challenge.

In a company, the principal goal is to strive for the company's goals. No company sets a housekeeping goal, like "keep our computers safe," as a major company goal. The major goals are, of course, based on the reason the enterprise was established.

Commercial enterprises try to make money, nonprofit organizations try to serve a charitable or service objective, and government organizations pursue legislated goals. Although computer security may serve those goals, the security is never an end in itself, not even in organizations that obsess about security.

Because computer security isn't a primary goal, it must compete with primary goals for attention. If an employee must choose between computer security and meeting a deadline for the company president, computer security isn't going to win. Effective security must fit into the fabric of the enterprise's activities, or it will interfere with enterprise goals.

In an enterprise, successful information security strikes a balance between three separate elements:

1. Objectives of the enterprise
2. Risks
3. Costs of security measures

We risk failure if we ignore any of these elements. If we ignore risks in our pursuit of enterprise objectives, we risk our assets. If we ignore the cost of security measures, then we may sacrifice the enterprise objectives even as we reduce risks. If we implement recognized, cost-effective security measures but ignore risks, we either waste money or we open ourselves up to attack—or both.

Within an enterprise, we delegate authority and responsibility for different tasks. The enterprise itself may "own" the information assets and equipment, but it delegates their management to an "information technology" (IT) organization. The IT group takes responsibility for management and administration of computer and network equipment.

This relieves most computer users of many administrative and security responsibilities for their computers. The IT group can't take sole responsibility for computer security, because end users can almost always do things to compromise their computers. We try to address such risks through user training and by ensuring that typical user–computer interactions do not pose risks to users or their systems.

13.1.1 Companies and Information Control

All families and communities have secrets. Often they have to do with reputation: how outsiders view the group. A company also has a reputation and often tries to control it by keeping secrets. Companies have other secrets, too. Those often revolve around economic concerns and legal obligations.

REPUTATION: SPEAKING WITH ONE VOICE

Many people have a love/hate relationship with their job. The company may treat them well for the most part, but there are a few situations that make them unhappy. Not everyone agrees with every decision a company makes, but employees are obligated to honor the company's decision when doing company business.

When entertainment companies publish a production on DVD or other random-access disk, the production often includes interviews and discussions with actors, writers, directors, producers, and other participants. The tradition in these interviews, as in much of show business, is to highlight good work performed by others and to avoid hurt feelings.

Although there are cultural reasons for this, the publisher doesn't want to be held liable in a financial or business sense for these positive statements. For example, a producer might make flattering statements about an actor on the commentary at the same time that the actor is in a legal dispute over appropriate financial compensation. The company doesn't want those positive statements to influence the legal outcome. Thus, a typical DVD includes a statement that commentary represents personal opinion and are not official statements by the publisher.

Most companies find themselves in a similar situation these days. Internet email, discussion forums, and blogs give employees and customers many ways to gripe or express opinions. Sometimes the participants may be highly placed in the company hierarchy. It's always important to distinguish between personal statements and official company statements. Some companies rely primarily on employee common sense, and most employees understand when they can and should speak for the company and when they should highlight their statements as personal opinions.

To summarize, company identity relies on two different processes:

1. Companies need a way to formally identify official company statements. There has to be a way to distinguish official statements from informal, less-binding statements by lower-level employees.

2. Companies need a way to repudiate statements that the public attribute to the company, but that do not reflect the company's current attitude. The company may have reversed a previous attitude, a company statement was misinterpreted, or an unapproved statement from someone related to the company was taken as a company announcement.

COMPANIES AND SECRECY

Companies keep secrets. Some keep more secrets than others. Some, arguably, don't keep as many secrets as they should. Company secrecy falls roughly into four categories:

1. **Obligations**. Companies may have legal or contractual obligations to keep certain types of information secret. Legal obligations address employee privacy, health records privacy, and information that could affect a public company's stock price. Contractual obligations may include trade secrets shared with others, licensed software management, and rules for handling credit card transactions.

2. **Trade secrets**. Companies keep information secret that would give competitors a commercial advantage. These include inventions and processes that may be subject to patent or unpatentable techniques that would benefit competitors. Other trade secrets include business details that might help competitors anticipate price decisions or identify customers that a competitor might try to lure away.

3. **Managing publicity**. As noted previously, companies may keep things secret that might not yield positive publicity.

4. **Secrecy culture**. Some companies have a tradition of keeping their internal activities secret, even without compelling business or legal reasons to do so.

The weight placed on these different types of secrecy will vary from one company to another. It also may be affected by their peers in industry and by the company's history with the media and with secrecy.

Some companies believe that openness is more efficient. It makes life easier for employees and customers; some believe that openness carries a sort of ethical high ground. Other companies believe that secrecy provides an edge over the competition and that it simplifies the task of presenting a consistent public image.

It can be challenging to make secrecy work within a large company, because it may restrict the flow of information management needs to accurately assess the company's health. Even so, many companies thrive with a culture of secrecy, notably 3M and Apple.

Companies emphasize secrecy because management makes it a priority. Employees can't justify the cost and inconvenience of secrecy on their own. One reason for legislation and industry standards for protecting certain types of information: Most companies can't justify secrecy measures without a strong financial and legal inducement.

Accountability

When individuals or organizations lack the motivation to protect information that should be kept secret, evolving laws and regulations try to motivate them by holding them publicly responsible for their failures. A simple and stark example arises from laws that require companies to notify customers whose sensitive information has been lost, leaked, or stolen.

Other regulations, like HIPAA for health care workers, specify procedural and technical measures to protect information and to track the people who use the information. In this case, accountability is tracked to individuals who handle sensitive records. Individuals who mishandle records or intentionally disclose sensitive information may be liable for civil or criminal sanctions.

Need to Know

In general, we don't want to share a secret with others unless we can trust them to keep it secret. In the world of government security (Chapter 17), we are legally obligated *not* to share information with anyone who does not hold the appropriate security clearance. Many companies have rules that restrict certain types of information to specific groups within a company. For example, a company might restrict information about a new product to the product's development team and a handful of senior management. Public companies restrict access to their quarterly financial numbers before their announcement to avoid problems with insider trading.

Every time we share a secret with another person we increase the risk of damage from disclosure. This is the Transitive Trust problem: Everyone who knows a secret may independently decide to share it with someone else. If we tell the wrong person, the secret will leak.

To reduce this risk, critical secrets also are restricted on a ***Need-to-Know*** basis. We may share such secrets only if the recipients clearly need to know the information to fulfill their roles within the enterprise.

In some cases, certain managers make the Need-to-Know decision. The only people who share the secret are those who are specifically granted access to the information. They are not allowed to share it with others; the managers must decide who shares the information.

In many cases, however, the decision to share still falls on the individuals who already know the secret. If Bob and Alice both are working on a project and Alice knows the secret, she may decide herself whether Bob has the Need to Know the secret. This circumstance is more vulnerable to social pressure or social engineering.

13.1.2 Enterprise Risks

In earlier chapters, we discussed the risks in Bob's suite: a small community that behaves like a household. There are different risks in a household than an enterprise, as we saw when developing authentication policies in Section 6.7. In particular, we are more likely to encounter strong threats in an enterprise than in a household. This may simply be because an enterprise often holds more valuable assets, and it may be that people usually avoid households where other members pose a strong threat.

Getting back to risks, let's look at the five general types of attacks and generalize them to cover major types of computer-based attacks on enterprises.

1. **Disclosure**
   - Theft of trade secrets—giving secret company information to competitors. This may include lists of customers or clients as well as secret technical data like product designs or manufacturing processes.
   - Privacy breach—losing information collected by the company about individuals (employees, clients, suppliers, or customers) or giving it to unauthorized recipients.
   - Insider trading—using secret company information to anticipate changes in its publicly traded stock price and buying and selling stock accordingly.
2. **Masquerade**
   - Fraud—using a bogus identity to trick the company into delivering goods or making unnecessary payments.
   - Social engineering—tricking people into providing sensitive information or physical access to company resources.
3. **Service loss**
   - Extortion—interrupting company services and threatening interruption unless the attacker receives a ransom payment.

- Vandalism—attacks on company equipment or services that cause disruptions but aren't tied to ransom payments.
- *Logic bombs*—attacks implemented by employees that take effect unless the employee deactivates them on a regular basis. The bomb triggers if the employee is fired and is not present to deactivate it.

4. **Subversion**
   - Fraud again—an employee might rig the system to provide improper periodic payments and hide them from auditors.
   - Rootkits—employee computers become infested with backdoor software that opens them to other attacks, including theft of authentication credentials or of other sensitive information.
   - Network subversion—someone infiltrates the company's network infrastructure (routers, firewalls, etc.) and uses this access to manipulate network traffic.

5. **Physical theft**
   - Equipment theft—someone steals computing or networking equipment.
   - Laptop theft—someone steals a company laptop, which may contain sensitive company information.

We shall focus on these types of attacks. We can certainly add others to the list, like "embarrassment," possibly caused by disclosure of uncomplimentary information about the company, its management, or employees.

Some experts like to include "ignorance" and "carelessness" as risks to computing systems. Although such behavior occasionally may damage parts of an information system, they usually are enabled by a lack of more specific controls. We discussed Least Privilege in Chapter 4 as a way to reduce desktop virus risks. We also can reduce risks to enterprise assets by enforcing Least Privilege with access restrictions.

Weak controls may allow damage through ignorance or carelessness, but they aren't always the principal cause. Often, such risks simply open the network to more specific attacks. We can't deploy an "anti-ignorance filter" or "anticarelessness scanner" on our network to protect against foolish behavior, so we won't treat ignorance or carelessness as explicit risks.

INSIDERS AND OUTSIDERS

Companies must rely on employees and other hired help to get the work done. To do this, the company grants employees access to company assets. This is a reasonable thing to do; most employees want to do the right thing for the company and keep it healthy. Most employees realize that bad behavior may threaten their jobs. If they are caught stealing or damaging the company, they may be fired. Even if they aren't caught, the company may do poorly and need to eliminate their jobs. Thus, in most cases, employees don't pose a significant threat to a company.

Despite this, employees do occasionally pose an insider threat. We noted such risks in households or dormitories (Chapters 1 and 10), but they are most common and most significant in the work place.

Insider attacks often arise when an employee has special access to a valuable asset. Employees may find themselves in a situation where they believe they can steal from the company and not get caught. Unexpected financial difficulties or risks of layoffs can put otherwise trustworthy employees under a great deal of pressure. Insider threats often arise when these situations collide.

Many of the attacks noted earlier may be mounted by either insiders or outsiders, though insiders have better access to the necessary resources. Financial fraud statistics vary from year to year; sometimes most fraud is external, while at other times most fraud involves insiders. Some attacks, like logic bombs, seem tailor-made for insiders, but also could be launched by outsiders. Viruses and Trojan-based attacks might seem to be more likely to arise externally, but insider access could greatly increase the success of such attacks.

There are three strategies for reducing the risks of insider threats:

1. Monitoring. People are more likely to behave if they think they are being watched. Monitoring may double-check periodic results, like the cash held by cashiers, or may scan for unauthorized activity, like access to nonbusiness websites during business hours.

2. Two-person or multiperson control. Most employee misbehavior is by individuals, not conspiracies. Companies can greatly reduce the risk by involving two or more people in important transactions. This may be procedural, as with checks for accounts payable, in which one person makes the list of checks, another prints the checks, and a third signs them. This also may be implemented with automated systems, as with nuclear missile launching or automated workflow systems.

3. Job rotation. Ongoing cases of employee fraud often rely on "cooking the books" on a regular basis. If a critical activity is performed by different employees in rotation, it is more difficult for one of them to exploit it. There is a notable example of bank fraud that was uncovered when a loyal employee was forced to take some long-neglected vacation. The replacement discovered a serious discrepancy that the regular employee had systematically hid in order to mask an ongoing theft of funds.

Not all internal systems require heavy-duty monitoring or two-person control, but the organization must establish a policy to identify which assets and activities may need this level of protection. As with all policy decisions, it is a tradeoff between the three elements: company objectives, risks, and security costs.

13.1.3 Social Engineering

An Incident: On his way to high school in 1968, Jerry Schneider noticed that the local telephone company piled the most fascinating things into their trash bins: slightly damaged equipment, circuitry, company manuals, and other documents. At first he refurbished discarded equipment and made a modest income reselling it. Then he realized that he could make even more money by reselling brand-new telephone equipment. All he had to do was trick the telephone company into giving him the equipment.

First, Schneider posed as a journalist writing a story about the company's equipment-ordering system to collect additional details of the operation. Later, posing as a company employee, he called the supply organization and asked for telephone numbers and ordering codes so that he could submit orders himself. He then used the automated system to order equipment for his customers, which he promptly resold.

Schneider was caught because a disgruntled employee turned him in. Ultimately, he was held liable for stealing several thousand dollars' worth of equipment and spent 40 days in jail. The telephone company suspected he may have taken over $800,000 worth of equipment, but the automated records were too vague to prove it.

Although Schneider's fraud was jump-started with the discarded company manuals he found, its success relied on his ability to trick the telephone company into disclosing additional information. Schneider was a clean, well-spoken young man, and he spoke convincingly when asking for their help. This is the true sign of social engineering.

A social engineering attack relies on the tension between business objectives and security. When a coworker asks for help, we are inclined to try to help. If we don't, the company may suffer. On the other hand, if we disclose too much, we may put company assets at risk. People often assume that their systems are too complicated for outsiders to exploit.

Following his conviction, Schneider established himself as one of the first white-hat hackers: He started a firm that offered computer security consulting. During a magazine interview with *Fortune* in 1974, Schneider demonstrated how to "hack in" to a remote computer. He tried logging in unsuccessfully a couple of times and then phoned the computer's help line. After several minutes of begging for help, the operator provided him with a password to log in. The reporter protested that he hadn't really broken in. Schneider replied, "Why should I go to all the work of trying to technically penetrate a computer system when it is so easy to con my way in through the time-sharing service personnel?"

This observation is the foundation of social engineering.

Experts at social engineering combine a charming demeanor with technical skills. They must know exactly what information to collect, and what places to visit, to compromise a system. Schneider combined both physical visits to the system under attack and inquiries over the telephone. Here is another example of social engineering; the perpetrator remains unidentified:

An Incident: In 1980, a timesharing company near San Francisco was suddenly plagued with software problems. A repairman, claiming to be from DEC, the computer vendor, appeared. The staff let him in and he worked on the computer. The next day, problems resurfaced, and the staff called DEC headquarters to ask about the repair. The company had no record of the service visit, nor did they have that repairman as an employee.

A sophisticated attack on a computing system often takes place in phases, as we will see in Section 13.5.2. In his book, *The Art of Deception*, famous hacker and social engineer Kevin Mitnick describes several attacks in which the attacker performs an unauthorized credit check through a series of phone calls. For example, he asks one person for information about company office locations, another for a side identity code, and another about credit checking procedures. Combined, the information provides the foundation for the attack. Next, the attacker masquerades as an employee with a crashed terminal and coerces another person to perform a credit check on the targeted individual.

THWARTING SOCIAL ENGINEERING

In Section 13.1.2, we classified social engineering as a form of masquerade. In every social engineering attack, the attacker pretends to be another person or plays an inappropriate role. Typically, the victims don't know the attacker or can't verify the attacker's identity. Classic social engineering attacks take place by telephone. The telephone conveys a great deal of the speaker's personality and that helps reassure the victim that they should comply with the attacker's requests.

The first line of defense, then, can be to require authentication. This applies for people on the phone as well as visitors in person. Then we need to verify that the person has a bona fide need for the service being requested.

Protection against social engineering relies on several different elements. It begins, of course, with policy, but it also reflects implementation decisions. Because social engineering often attacks information related to security, our policy must protect security-related information. Once we have policies and procedures in place to defend against social engineering, we should test them periodically to see if there are weaknesses in the processes. Most people *want* to be helpful, especially to coworkers, and social engineers exploit that.

13.2 Management Processes

In earlier chapters, we applied the security processes to a single person managing a single computer. In practice, of course, people rarely construct a formal, written security analysis for personal assets. These serve simply as exercises to illustrate what happens in large-scale organizations. We can implement our own defenses or share our choices with a small group without putting it all on paper.

We must take more formal steps when we coordinate larger groups of people. We address such problems by applying conventional management techniques. These include:

- Written policies and procedures
- Delegation through a management hierarchy
- Auditing and review

The phrase *policies and procedures* refers to the customary process by which organizations publish guidelines, recommendations, rules, and requirements for performing enterprise activities. In Chapter 1, aircraft hijackings were the subject of policies and procedures published by the airlines. Small organizations simply may publish and distribute such information through memos. Often, a company collects together such information into an employee handbook or even a "Company Standards" document. Some organizations may have several volumes of standards or of policy and procedure documents.

Note that the word "policy" has a different meaning here than in other regions of the information security field. The term refers to two different types of documents in practice:

1. *Policy specifications*—lists of the protections we require. This is how we've been using the term in this textbook. These are technical documents we use to ensure that we implement the right protections.
2. *Policy directives*—collections of rules and other guidance distributed to others to direct their actions. Business and management circles refer to such documents as policies and/or procedures.

Most published "security policies" are policy directives. Many are acceptable use policies (AUPs), like those mentioned in Section 1.6.1. An AUP explains how users may—or may not—use particular enterprise resources. Typical organizations may publish policy directives on the following:

- AUP for enterprise computing equipment, like desktop or laptop computers assigned to individuals
- AUP for Internet web surfing and email
- Procedures for controlling licensed software and other copyrighted material
- Standards and procedures for updating antivirus and other security-critical software
- Standards for password management
- Standards and procedures for employee separation or termination
- Standards and procedures for the physical protection of assets

This is not an exhaustive list of policy directives. Not all companies have published such policies; some might combine a few of these into a single policy or write directives on other security issues.

13.2.1 Security Management Standards

The security community has published international standards for information security management. The standards were developed and published by the ISO and the International Electrotechnical Commission (IEC). The set of standards are called the "27000 series" because they are numbered starting with 27000.

ISO/IEC 27001 establishes the overall standard for an "information security management system" (ISMS). Like policy specifications, 27001 uses the word "shall" to outline requirements an enterprise should fulfill. It also describes how organizations may assess their compliance through formal reviews called *audits*.

This standard establishes processes that continuously assess the enterprise's information security. This follows the example of quality assurance processes discussed in Chapter 1. These same concepts also underlie general-purpose quality-assurance standards like ISO 9001. After an organization implements ISO 27001, they may apply to be formally certified as ISO 27001 compliant. Some potential customers and business partners find it easier to trust an organization that holds such certifications.

ISO/IEC 27002 contains a "Code of Practice" for information security management. Unlike 27001, the Code of Practice provides guidelines and recommendations for information security. The standard is more technical in that it identifies security objectives and, for each objective, one or more controls that may achieve that objective. Thus, 27002 provides more practical guidance on how to fulfill specific objectives with particular technologies or techniques.

A fundamental question posed by any certification standard is whether the benefit is worth the cost. Certification requires extra planning, organization, and documentation. It raises the cost of customary activities. To be worthwhile, it must address a very specific objective. Some organizations pursue it for political or public-relations purposes.

Most, however, only pursue it if the certification is required for specific business purposes. For example, firewall vendors pursued Common Criteria evaluation after various governments made it a requirement of all firewalls they purchased. Some promoters of the 27000 series standards suggest that compliance will make it easier to prove compliance with external mandates, like SOX, HIPAA, or others listed in Section 4.6.2.

EVOLUTION OF MANAGEMENT STANDARDS

The first computer security standards focused on product security. Examples include the Common Criteria and the Orange Book, the latter of which was developed in the 1980s. At the same time, Japanese manufacturers flourished while many U.S. and European manufacturers were failing. As discussed in Section 1.1.2, the Japanese success arose from innovative techniques in product quality improvement.

Meanwhile, the Software Engineering Institute at CMU developed a "Capability Maturity Model" (CMM) for software development. This was a five-level model of how organizations create software. This technique applied the Deming cycle to software development. As organizations achieved higher levels, they enhanced their ability to measure software quality and to improve it.

The CMM did not require specific development activities. Instead, it specified that an organization should assess quality and measure its performance. As an organization achieved higher levels of the CMM, they incorporated more sophisticated techniques to establish and assess quality goals and to improve the quality of their work.

This same philosophy was incorporated into the ISO 9000 standards. Unlike the CMM or later standards like the 27000 series, the ISO 9000 standards were designed to apply continuous quality improvement to *any* industry. The standards identified generic processes that could help an organization improve quality.

The U.S. DOD promoted an extension of the CMM to cover security systems called the "Security Engineering CMM." This became the "System Security Engineering

CMM" and was the subject of ISO/IEC standard 21827. However, the CMM focuses on system and product development; it does not cover the general problem of IT security, like the ISO 27000 standards.

The U.K. government published a "Code of practice for information security management" in 1995. This became the British Standard BS7799 and was the model for today's ISO/IEC 27002. In 1998, a second standard numbered BS7799-2 was published, which provides a management framework like today's ISO/IEC 27001. In 2000, the code of practice was issued internationally as ISO 17799. The management framework was issued internationally in 2005 using the new numbering system as ISO/IEC 27001; then ISO 17799 was revised and reissued as ISO/IEC 27002.

13.2.2 Deployment Policy Directives

The previous section contained a list of over a half-dozen common topics of policy directives. Those particular directives are, however, limited. They all focus on *static* properties of an information system.

We often face a new set of risks when we change or extend the existing system. Companies that handle valuable assets or companies that grow really large, often publish special directives on how to buy, build, and validate a new system before deploying it.

In the most general case, this may be a ***change control process***. Whenever someone needs to modify an important enterprise system, the change goes through the process. A typical process includes analysis, testing, and review, much like the system engineering processes described in Section 1.1.2.

When working with security-critical assets, the process also includes several phases of the security process. This ensures that the new system assesses potential risks and implements practical defenses. When we combine these concerns, we end up with a three-phase process: planning, implementation, and deployment. The process involves these steps:

1. **Planning**
   - Establish system objectives. This is a management-level discussion that determines what the system must do for the enterprise and what resources it may use.
   - Define system requirements. This is a combination of management and technical analysis that outlines more precisely what the system must do and how it must fit into existing systems.
   - Assess risks. This applies the first three phases of the security process to the system being designed. The policy statements may prompt changes to the system requirements.
2. **Implementation**
   - Design the system. This is a technical activity that identifies specific technical solutions to implement the system's features. Once finished, compare the design to the system requirements and the risk assessment to ensure that the design fits our needs.

- Implement the system. This is the technical activity that creates a version of the system.
- Test the system. This is a technical activity that compares the implemented system with its published requirements.

3. **Deployment**
   - Approve the system. This is a management activity that reviews test and analysis results to decide if the system can be deployed.
   - Deploy the system. This is the technical activity that puts the system online.

In practice, the next phase doesn't start until the previous phase reaches a stopping point. For example, the implementation phase doesn't start until initial planning is finished. Like the security process, we may revisit earlier steps when a later step hits a snag.

Individual steps, like design/implement/test, often take place in parallel. For example, one part of the system might still be under design while another is being implemented, and a third is under test. Engineers might be repeating the risk analysis while others are implementing design changes. Some developers may be modifying their component parts while others test the full-scale system using older components.

RISK ACCEPTANCE

Deployment is a crucial step for any security-critical system. Management must decide whether the system's benefits justify the risk of deployment. When a bank deploys or updates its website, management must believe that attackers won't be able to trick the site into doing unauthorized withdrawals. The bank's management must decide if the new system's benefits justify the potential risk of attack.

The decision to accept the risks may be an informal process in some organizations. Other organizations may require additional security testing and analysis before approving a new or modified system. In any case, **document the decision** to accept the risks. This distinguishes between a business decision and a failure of leadership, especially if losses arise from the accepted risk.

13.2.3 Management Hierarchies and Delegation

When an organization grows beyond a handful of people, it often establishes a management hierarchy, with a chief executive at the top. Figure 13.1 illustrates a typical hierarchy.

In Western culture, this tradition dates back to the Roman military legions, if not earlier. Each legion of 6000 men was organized into a hierarchy of cohorts, centuries, and tent groups, each with its own leader. Modern management hierarchies use the same concept with different job titles: chief executive officer (CEO), vice presidents (VPs), heads of divisions or departments, directors, and so on.

Senior management consists of the CEO, the VPs, and possibly others who participate in overall management of the enterprise. "Functional managers" are in charge of a particular component of the enterprise, like a department.

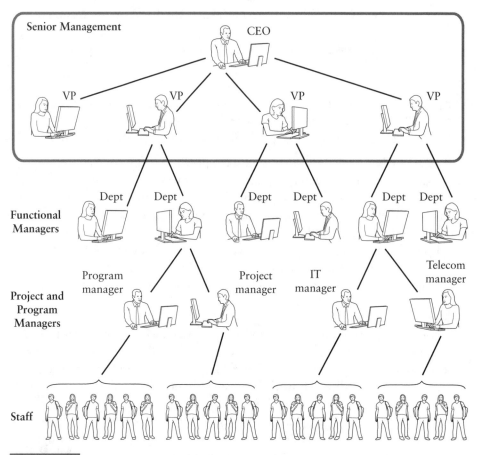

Figure 13.1

Management hierarchy in a larger organization.

An important distinction between lower-level management positions is that some may, or may not, carry responsibilities for budget and staffing. In his part-time job, for example, Bob leads a small development team. Though Bob is nominally responsible for directing the work of team members, Bob has no budget authority nor can he hire or fire people. Bob reports to a project manager, who is responsible for the actual project and its budget. The project manager, in turn, reports to a department manager, who is responsible for staffing, which includes hiring, firing, raises, and performance reviews.

PROFIT CENTERS AND COST CENTERS

Commercial businesses often distinguish between different parts of an organization as being a *profit center* or a *cost center*. A profit center is a division, department, or other component that makes money for the company. In a manufacturing company, for example, each factory or major product line might be organized as a profit center.

The manager of a profit center may have more budget flexibility as long as the center makes the expected level of profit. The manager may decide independently to invest in new equipment and services if they pay for themselves in cost savings.

Cost centers, on the other hand, are business units that do not directly produce revenue or profits. Typical examples include marketing, IT operations, customer service, human resources, and so on. Some enterprises treat all divisions as cost centers.

Implications for Information Security

The difference between a profit center and cost center sheds some light on the problem of investing in information security. If enterprise management does not see significant information security threats, they won't be inclined to invest in security measures. Many enterprises only invest to the degree required by external forces, like HIPAA or PCI-DSS (Section 4.6.2). Compliance is seen as an unavoidable cost of doing business.

In the mid-1990s, however, numerous businesses invested heavily in information security for the World Wide Web. Specifically, the companies purchased Netscape's web encryption technology to protect web-based retail transactions (we introduce Netscape's SSL protocol in Chapter 14). These investments were justified through "profit center" reasoning; the security technology made it safe and practical to offer web-based sales. Because the investment made these new sales possible, a company could bring in more money by investing in this new security technology.

13.2.4 Managing Information Resources

Larger organizations assign particular managers to oversee particular information resources. The lines of authority may follow other organization boundaries. For example, IT resources in the Boston office may be under the Boston division manager or those in factories may be under the individual factory managers. In a different approach, lines of authority may follow technologies, yielding separate managers for servers, for desktops, for telecom, and so on.

These lines of authority determine how the enterprise budgets money for IT equipment and services. This often affects how the enterprise invests in information security. It may be easier to promote enterprise-wide IT security if it is driven by a centralized IT management team. On the other hand, an underfunded centralized IT management structure may hinder security deployment when specific sites or projects have special needs.

When there is an independent IT or technology group within the enterprise, there is usually a senior corporate officer responsible for the group. This may be a chief technical officer (CTO) or a chief information officer (CIO). These individuals are often the focal point for information security leadership as well as IT leadership in general. Ultimately, they are the ones held accountable for proper use of corporate information resources.

All organizations, regardless of size, should strive to distinguish between employees who administer IT and communications systems and those whose work focuses on more direct enterprise goals. This is a form of Least Privilege: An employee should not have administrative access to computers and also use those computers to meet other types of company objectives. Here is an example of the problem:

> At a former summer job, Kevin worked part time as a system administrator and also helped with some new product development. Monday morning, investors were coming in to see an updated presentation on the company's progress. Raj, the technical lead, had given the last presentation, but he was out of town, and his boss told Kevin to do the presentation instead.
>
> Kevin knew that his job depended on giving a good presentation on Monday.
>
> Sunday night, Kevin was prepared to update Raj's old presentation, but he couldn't find it. He had forgotten to ask Raj for a copy before he left town.
>
> Kevin knew Raj kept the file on the computer in his locked office. With administrative access, Kevin should be able to retrieve the file from the computer using file sharing. He went ahead and did so.
>
> The updated presentation was a big success with the investors. Kevin would have kept his job, except that Raj figured out how Kevin had retrieved a copy of the presentation. Kevin was fired because he accessed Raj's computer without permission.

Kevin's acknowledged access to Raj's computer was relatively innocuous. However, it's hard to be sure that Kevin did nothing more than retrieve the required file. Raj's computer contained a number of emails that outlined future business plans, including staffing. Some comments applied to Kevin and were not meant for him to read.

Managing Information Security

Different enterprises take different approaches to managing security. Some have a single security organization headed by a chief information security officer (CISO). This is a member of senior management who is responsible for information security efforts across the enterprise. Others distribute security responsibilities, following the examples of distributed IT responsibilities just described.

Some enterprises, divisions, or locations, maintain a specific security office to centralize security-related activities. Some organizations appoint a security officer who is responsible for all administrative aspects of security. There may be an "infosec officer" who is likewise responsible for information security. This may include physical security, telecom security, and IT security. Others may handle physical security separately and make it part of the physical plant organization. The remaining security areas fall comfortably into information security: network security, computer security, and telephone security.

The auditing staff may or may not be part of the information security staff. Traditionally, auditors are trained as accountants and their job is to analyze a company's financial records. Auditing plays an essential role in information security, because auditing can uncover attacks that resulted in theft through fraud. If an enterprise keeps an auditing staff, the staff usually reports to a special organization that is independent of functional managers. This helps prevent management influence on the results of audit investigations.

13.2.5 Security Audits

Although audits are traditionally associated with accounting and financial records, the word "audit" also applies to certain information security analyses and investigations. In general, the term *security audit* refers to an examination of a system to verify that it complies with its security policy. However, a security-related audit may, in fact, take several different forms:

- An audit against a system-specific security policy (noted previously).
- An audit of software source code to verify compliance with software design standards.
- A review of internal audit logs to search for unusual or unexpected patterns, behaviors, or activities.
- An audit to verify compliance with a specific security standard, like PCI DSS or ISO/IEC 27001.
- A *vulnerability scan* that checks for indications of a list of known vulnerabilities.
- A *penetration test* ("pen test") that tries to penetrate established defenses.

Although many of these measure compliance with internally established protections, some fall into two other categories. First, there are **compliance audits**, in which an outside party verifies that the enterprise follows particular procedures. Second, there are security scans in which an external entity scans the site for vulnerabilities or deploys a "red team" to attempt a technical site penetration.

When we audit our internally established protections, we are auditing against our own security policy. This is part of Phase 5 of the six-phase security process. Such a security audit reviews the security policy against the implementation and verifies that all policy statements are achieved. This essentially measures the enterprise's security against its own rules and objectives.

Many vulnerabilities in computer systems are traced back to flaws in the underlying software. We saw this first in Section 2.3, when the Morris worm exploited carelessness in the "finger" server software. Today, many organizations have established software design standards that try to enforce careful programming techniques. One form of audit is to review software source code to verify its compliance with design standards.

Organizations may perform similar audits against any published standards, policies, or procedures. In fact, one might argue that a policy or procedure can't be implemented effectively unless there is a way to measure and audit compliance.

Audits of audit logs may take many forms. Some organizations simply assign security employees to periodically review the logs for any glaring surprises. Other organizations apply tools to search for patterns or unusual events.

COMPLIANCE AUDITS

Section 4.6.2 discussed external standards, like PCI-DSS or ISO 27001, which involve an audit by an external third party. In the payment card industry, the process is called "assessment." Third-party assessments are performed by a PCI-approved qualified security assessor (QSA). The QSA reviews the system against the PCI-DSS requirements and reports on its compliance or deficiencies. In many cases, however, systems may perform self-assessments.

ISO 27001 provides a certification process through which a third party audits the organization against the standard. The organization begins the process by implementing the published elements of ISO 27001. When all elements are in place and operating, the organization arranges an external audit

SECURITY SCANS

A typical security scan is an automated vulnerability scan in which an analyst scans the network for indicators of known vulnerabilities. The basic concept is similar to the "nmap" tool (Section 11.5.2), except that the scan results are compared against a database of known vulnerabilities. If the scan indicates the presence of a particular version of network software, then the scan reports any vulnerabilities associated with that software.

PCI-DSS has formalized this process. They have established standards for vulnerability scanning and certified security vendors as complying with their standards. Sites that implement PCI-DSS standards may use certified vendors to scan their site for vulnerabilities.

The more classic, and intrusive, security scan is the "pen test," short for penetration test. These are the classic, Hollywood-style attempts to penetrate a secure site through a combination of physical, technical, and social engineering techniques. Some organizations still use these tests to some extent, but they require specialized red teams and can be costly to perform.

13.2.6 Information Security Professionals

Information security is a relatively new field. Until recently, very little training was available. Most people became security professionals by taking on job responsibilities involving security or security technology. Although this still happens occasionally, most employers look for training and/or certification in information security.

Education and certification have an important benefit for a professional; they provide credentials that reflect one's training and expertise. Prospective managers and employers take such credentials into account when filling important positions. Although managers may focus on a prospective hire's most recent experience, credentials provide evidence of a broader range of abilities, which helps an employee move to a different and more challenging position.

Information security professionals play a variety of roles in enterprise security. These roles reflect different types of training and expertise.

- **Implementers**—install, configure, and/or test security hardware and software. This usually requires specialized experience or training with the specific systems being used.

- **Auditors**—examine the condition and contents of an information system, often as part of a financial audit. Financial auditing often requires an education in accounting, though technical computing auditors don't require this background.
- **Forensic investigators**—collect digital evidence and analyze evidence in a manner that preserves its admissability in court. This requires special training courses.
- **Analysts**—develop security plans and analyze existing security architectures. This usually requires a degree from an accredited 2- or 4-year college or university.

Higher-level roles, like those that coordinate large-scale projects or manage security organizations, including senior roles like CISO, are usually open to individuals who prove proficiency at lower-level roles within an enterprise. Organizations usually hire people into such positions who have either proven their capabilities to management directly or have demonstrated prior experience in that role elsewhere.

INFORMATION SECURITY TRAINING

Although experience remains the best teacher, there are a variety of training opportunities in information security:

- **Product-specific training**. These courses often are arranged by product vendors to teach current or potential customers how to use their products. Such courses may last part of a day or for several days. Usually only available to customers who can pay for the training, the training is offered to employees whose job requires it.
- **Hands-on training**. Some organizations, notably SANS Institute, offer a broad range of 1- to 6-day training courses on information security technologies. These courses typically provide hands-on experience using various security tools and techniques. People sign up for these courses individually, though some employers will pay the training costs.
- **College courses**. These generally last several months. Some may involve hands-on training with specific tools, but these courses often pursue higher-level knowledge and understanding. Some employers will pay for college courses.

Product-specific and hands-on training courses are often forms of continuing education and often provide "continuing education credit." Such credits often are required to maintain an ongoing professional certification. Such credits are rarely applicable toward a college degree.

Courses taken at accredited colleges and universities often may apply toward a degree at a comparable institution. Such "transfer credit" is at the discretion of the receiving institution.

Different types of training provide stronger credentials for different types of jobs. Recent hands-on and product-specific courses provide good credentials for immediate job openings involving the tools and skills in the course. By the same token, specific college classes taken recently may qualify the student for a special job opening. Such courses carry less weight over time.

College Degrees

A college degree is a credential that never loses its value. Although specific courses may lose their relevance over time, an earned degree from an accredited institution always carries a prominent place on one's resumé. Many organizations have specific rules regarding the minimum education required for particular jobs. Even though one can certainly found a company like Microsoft or Apple without a college degree and even serve as CEO, such examples are rare.

Colleges that offer information security education in the United States have their curriculum evaluated by the Information Assurance (IA) Courseware Evaluation (IACE) Program. Schools with an active program in information security research may also be identified as a National Center of Academic Excellence in IA Education. Both programs are administered by the NSA. Both programs require that the curriculum meet at least one of the training standards published by the Committee for National Security Systems (CNSS). These standards are discussed briefly in Section 17.3.2.

As described in the Preface, this textbook fulfills the training standards for information systems security professionals.

INFORMATION SECURITY CERTIFICATION

Not all college programs offer a degree with a specific major in information security. In most cases, information security coursework is part of a more general area, like computer science or IT. Such degrees still represent a major achievement by the student, but they do not clearly reflect a student's focus on information security.

Anyone in the information security field may earn a certification. These certifications tend to fall into three categories:

1. **Product-specific certifications.** Microsoft, Cisco, and the other major manufacturers offer certifications to reflect expertise in particular products or product lines.

2. **Hands-on certifications.** Here are a couple of examples:
   - Global information assurance certification (GIAC) program. SANS developed the GIAC as a parallel to their training programs; the certifications show proficiency in topic areas of SANS training programs. GIAC certificates do not require SANS training. Skilled individuals may qualify for certification simply by passing the necessary examination.
   - CompTIA certifications through the Computer Technology Industry Association.

3. **Professional certifications.** These generally require experience in the field as well as passing an examination. Here are a couple of examples:
   - The Certified Information Systems Security Professional (CISSP), administered by the International Information Systems Security Certification Consortium (ISC^2).
   - The Certified Information Security Auditor (CISA), administered by the Information Systems Audit and Control Association (ISACA).

All certifications are temporary. Product-specific certifications may lose their value as new products replace obsolete ones. Other certifications may be retained if the holder complies with continuing education requirements. These help ensure that the individual remains proficient in the field.

GIAC certifications expire after 4 years. To retain the certification without retaking the exam, the holder must complete 36 hours of additional training or other educational activities. The holder may substitute other activities, including work experience, teaching, or writing in the information security field. Most recertifications seem to require additional SANS coursework.

The CISSP maintains a 3-year renewal cycle. To retain the certification, the holder must complete 90 hours of additional training. This training may come from almost any source of information security training, although there are limits to less-formal venues, like vendor presentations. Most CISSPs probably fulfill their training requirements by attending professional conferences in information security.

13.3 Enterprise Issues

Even though individuals and small groups see many of the same problems as larger groups, certain issues become particularly significant. Here, we focus on three particular issues:

1. Personnel security
2. Physical security
3. Software security

These issues become significant as the enterprise community grows large. The role of personnel security obviously grows as the number of personnel grows. The other issues become significant because we must coordinate a number of people.

In our discussions we use the word *employee* to refer to a recognized member of the enterprise. This refers to someone who is an *insider* with respect to the enterprise, someone to whom the enterprise affords some degree of trust. Note that not all participants are employees. Some may be contractors, business partners, or even volunteers in a nonprofit or service organization.

EDUCATION, TRAINING, AND AWARENESS

We ensure that members of the enterprise understand their roles, duties, and benefits through several mechanisms:

- **Culture**. People living in particular cultures have particular expectations of an employer or other enterprise. Most enterprises try to fulfill cultural expectations. When the enterprise takes exception to expectations, it must clearly explain the exceptions to its employees, clients, and other participants.

- **Written instructions.** When an enterprise communicates with outside participants like customers and clients, it provides written explanations. Retail sellers provide "terms and conditions" to potential buyers. Clubs and organizations provide bylaws. Employees often receive, or have access to, an "employee guide" that outlines company rules, benefits, and restrictions. There also may be a large and elaborate set of enterprise policies and procedures.

- **Personal instructions.** Employees usually receive direct instruction from their supervisor regarding their duties and responsibilities. Personnel responsible for other aspects of work, like IT administrators, may provide additional instruction when providing employees with computer and network access. Informal training can demand a great deal of time from existing employees.

- **Formal training.** Some organizations provide formal training courses to teach employees and other participants about special expectations that might be new or peculiar to the organization. This helps ensure consistent behavior. For example, scouting organizations provide training courses for adult leaders. Some organizations provide training to all employees on the use of computer and network resources, instead of relying on terse briefings by IT administrators.

- **Public announcements.** Enterprises often teach employees and participants about new or important activities or responsibilities through periodic announcements. Some announcements simply serve to remind participants of particular rules and obligations.

Every enterprise uses some or all of these techniques to make employees and other participants aware of security issues and obligations.

13.3.1 Personnel Security

Personnel security covers several issues:

- Employee clearances. A *clearance* is a decision to trust someone in a particularly delicate or sensitive capacity. Although this is most common in government and military enterprises, it also takes place in private organizations.

- Employee life cycle. These are actions performed when an employee becomes a member of the enterprise or leaves the enterprise.

- Employee roles. These are actions performed when an employee receives new responsibilities and requires access to different resources.

EMPLOYEE CLEARANCES

All employers collect some information with which to judge the fitness of a potential employee. Some simply ask about illegal drug use, work history, and criminal history on an application form. Some don't even bother to double check the information the applicant provides.

Other employers perform some type of *background investigation* in which they consult third parties to verify the applicant's history. This may involve a drug check, verification of employment history, and a criminal background check. Companies tend to perform the same checks on all employees for particular types of jobs; it doesn't make sense to do background checks on some cash-handling employee applicants and not on others.

Certain jobs may require more extensive background checks. In government and military enterprises, this involves "security clearances" (see Section 17.2). Nongovernment jobs may do additional checks on people employed in security-related or IT-related roles, because such people have exceptional access to sensitive company resources.

Typically, an organization conducts an investigation to ask specific questions. In particular, most organizations want to confirm that the employee has been completely accurate and honest on the employment application. They then may make an employment decision or a decision to appoint someone to a sensitive position, based on information the employee has provided.

If the investigation uncovers information *not* disclosed on the application, such as drug use or criminal convictions, then the combination of a criminal background and dishonesty often will disqualify the applicant. If research finds that the work history is inaccurate, the employer must decide if the dishonesty disqualifies the potential employee. If the employee is hired, the employee's file may contain a note indicating the inaccuracy uncovered in the investigation. This may affect the employee's future options for job positions.

Enterprises also may perform additional investigations before appointing a person to a particularly sensitive or important job, including senior management positions. A vice president at a smaller *Fortune* 500 company once told the author that he was investigated more thoroughly for that promotion than he had been when granted his Top Secret military clearance.

Employee Life Cycle

Life cycle activities mark the beginning and ending of an employee's work at an enterprise. In fact, security-related activities take place even before hiring. The hiring decision itself relies on information about the employee's skills and trustworthiness.

The hiring process almost always involves a personal interview with potential supervisors and managers. Although most supervisors value an interview because the interaction is a good way to assess a potential employee, it also provides an opportunity to authenticate the applicant. Subsequent investigations should use authenticated information about the applicant, like name, address, and date of birth taken from a driver's license or other authentic identity card. Statistically, a person's name, place of residence, and date of birth taken together almost always identify unique individuals.

When employees first start work, their initial contact may often be with people in the company's human resources department. These people may not have encountered the new employees during the hiring process, so they need to repeat the authentication process.

Many companies perform a set of operations known as *provisioning* when a new employee arrives. This may include providing one or more of the following items, tailored to the employee's job responsibilities:

- Company ID card
- Keys to buildings, offices, or storage areas
- User identities on computing systems

In all cases, the provisioning requirements for new employees must be clearly communicated and documented. Those who supply employees with credentials and access rights must know what to provide and must document what actually was provided.

Most companies issue identity cards to employees, and it is essential that the cards accurately reflect individual identities. The card should be issued only after the new employee's identity is independently verified.

Supervisors and managers then grant the new employee access to various physical areas in the enterprise and to information system resources. Different enterprises take different approaches to enrolling new users in information systems. Colleges, large schools, and other large enterprises may automate the enrollment process; the human resources or admissions department provides a list of new users, including personal information about each. The new users self-enroll by providing personal identifying information. Although there is a risk that a third party might masquerade as a new employee or other user, this type of trick often is detected and reported when the legitimate user fails to enroll successfully.

Once the employee has established a user identity in computer systems and on the network, administrators and managers can assign the appropriate access rights to that identity. Certain classes of users may acquire certain rights automatically when they receive access. For example, a school provisions different access rights for instructors than for students.

When an employee or other user leaves the enterprise, we must invert the provisioning process by *decommissioning* the ex-employee's resources. The process isn't always as simple as simply deleting a user identity. Individuals often receive several different types of access, provided through several different mechanisms. Thus, the process often involves the following:

- Changing any shared, memorized secrets that protect resources. This includes safe combinations, shared administrative passwords, alarm codes, and other similar information.
- Retrieving any physical keys, especially master keys, issued to the employee. It's possible, though costly, to change locks if an employee leaves without returning keys. It's often impractical, however, to change locks when a master key goes missing.
- Revoking access to computer and network resources. Sites often simply disable the user's login. Sites rarely delete user identities wholesale, except perhaps for students leaving a school, because the user may have produced valuable files that oth-

ers in the enterprise need. The site might change ownership of the orphaned files and directories.

Employee Roles

Within the enterprise, different employees take on different roles, which in turn give them control over different enterprise assets. Traditionally, the custodial personnel may receive far lower pay than functional managers, but the custodians still have physical access to far more assets than a functional manager. It is not a matter of pay; it is a matter of Least Privilege. The custodian needs keys to offices to vacuum the rugs and empty the trash and to janitor closets to store and clean equipment. The functional manager's job doesn't require all those keys.

The same access concerns apply to computer systems. System managers and administrators usually have unrestricted access to the systems they manage. This is an essential part of the job, because they need power over almost every part of the system to fix broken components.

As noted earlier, however, people with administrative access to computers should not be held responsible for nonadministrative tasks as well. Such obligations could tempt them to bypass access controls to get the job done more efficiently and that undermines system integrity.

Administrators and Separation of Duty

The traditional way to implement a security critical activity is through Separation of Duty. To do this in an automated system, we provide different access rights to the people who perform different steps in the task. Thus, Bob can perform Step 1, but no other steps; Alice can perform Step 2, and Tina can perform Step 3.

However, imagine a situation for which all three steps take place on a single system and rely exclusively on access rights. Kevin, the system administrator, could give himself access to all three steps and complete them by himself—or he could create bogus identities on the system and give them access to the steps.

We resolve this problem by putting parts of the effort outside the scope of Kevin's privileges. Here are some possible strategies:

- Put at least one step on a system that Kevin does not control.
- Restrict Kevin's administrative abilities so that he's more likely to be detected. For example, make the steps require a network-wide identity and prevent Kevin from creating such identities.
- Incorporate crypto into the process. When users complete a step, they must provide a password or construct a digital signature. This blocks Kevin's participation as long as there's no way for him to intercept base secrets.

Partial Insiders

Many organizations have participants who help achieve important goals and make use of enterprise resources, but aren't entirely members of the enterprise. Although large volunteer organizations have a professional staff to oversee valuable assets, some place a great deal of trust in volunteers.

Other organizations hire part-time consultants. Although some consultants receive almost identical treatment as employees (working similar hours, eating in the same lunchroom, attending the same staff meetings), others are brought in periodically and aren't really made part of the enterprise.

In these marginal cases, the enterprise may want to decide which assets may be trusted with these partial insiders. For example, outside consultants might have access to data files for the projects assigned to them. They are also denied access to storage areas containing other projects or future business plans.

13.3.2 Physical Security

Although physical security is important to individuals and to households, it takes on a special importance in enterprises. Because most enterprises are larger than households, they have more resources to physically protect. Another challenge is that physical security is spread across far more people; a mistake by any employee who opens an outside door could risk company assets. Moreover, anyone who has used a company vehicle or copy machine can appreciate how much tougher people treat company equipment than they might treat their own possessions. Here we look at three particular types of enterprise physical protection:

1. Power management
2. Physical protection of information system assets
3. Environmental management

Any of these may, of course, have significant impact on the safety and integrity of information system resources.

POWER MANAGEMENT

Electric power is the lifeblood of information systems. Most systems require consistent and regulated power. Power interruptions may cause denial of service. This leads to the following protections:

- **Protected power controls.** Once power enters the enterprise's secure boundary, it goes into control panels protected with fuses and circuit breakers. These panels may be secured by lock and key simply because the operating currents pose a hazard. The panels also present a possible point of a denial-of-service attack, so service personnel must be trustworthy.

- **Power filtering.** The power supplies in modern computing equipment can adapt to a broad range of voltages, but the equipment works most effectively with reliable, consistent power. Moreover, spikes due to lightning strikes may exceed the power supply's operating range. Thus, power filtering provides important protection.

- **Uninterruptable power systems** (UPS). These were once the exclusive province of larger, enterprise-level computing systems. Today, even households can afford an effective UPS. A high-end UPS may include its own motor-driven generator to handle lengthy power outages. The capacity and duration of a site's UPS depends on their disaster planning (Section 13.5.3).

- **Protected power cabling.** If an enterprise is a particularly attractive target of vandalism or denial-of-service attacks, then they need to protect their power cabling. In some high-security environments, attackers can try to infer sensitive information from a system's power variations. This would call for protected power cabling.

- **Power alarms**. The power system should provide an alarm when it switches from line power to the UPS, and when there are significant changes in the power being provided or being used. Any of these may indicate an impending attack or a risk of losing services. Enterprises may benefit from alarms that provide email, text, or voice mail alerts.

INFORMATION SYSTEM PROTECTION

Physical protection of an enterprise information system begins with Defense in Depth (Section 1.3.3). Most systems reside on desktops, protected by the enterprise's basic physical security boundary. Servers and other critical systems reside inside locked areas, protected from access by most employees.

Following a tradition started in the era of large computer mainframes, many companies maintain an "information system center" or other centralized computer room. The room holds computers that host important network services or that perform other critical activities. Some companies post armed guards, while others rely on intrusion alarms and elaborate access control systems. Some may even implement movie-style biometrics.

There is not always a security benefit to centralizing all critical computing. This is a tradeoff that depends on how computing takes place within the enterprise. If critical activities rely on large, centralized servers, then a central computer center may make sense. In a different approach, critical activities are distributed among separate departments, and each department takes responsibility to provide reliable service. This eliminates the single computer center as a target or as a single point of failure. However, it also means that reliability succeeds or fails piecemeal on the effectiveness of individual departments.

An important problem for both centralized and distributed computing systems is the handling and protection of storage systems, especially backups. This involves several layers of protection:

- **Physical protection of storage systems**. Potential attackers must not have physical access to critical storage systems like file servers.

- **Protection of external storage traffic.** As storage distribution systems become more sophisticated, it becomes easier to physically distribute data at very low levels. If a site transmits low-level storage traffic between protected server rooms, the cabling itself should be shielded from eavesdropping. In many cases, it may be sufficient to use fiber optic connections instead of traditional wiring.

- **Ensure recovery from hardware failures**. This may be provided through technical means like RAID systems (see Section 13.5.1).
- **Ensure recovery from physical disasters**. This includes fires, floods, or storm damage. This requires off-site backups, which themselves must be protected from unauthorized access.

Just as computing may be centralized or distributed, so may be the management of communications. Some sites have central communications centers that have grown from earlier switchboard, teletype, or even telegraph offices. While some communications centers have evolved into call centers, others have evolved into network management centers. Network management, like server systems, provides a critical enterprise service and must be protected from interference. Thus, network management centers often are protected with access controls similar to a computer center.

ENVIRONMENTAL MANAGEMENT

To an environmental manager, computers are simply machines that convert electrical power into heat. To keep the computers working, the air conditioning system must efficiently remove the heat. In colder climates, the computers also must be protected from excessive cold. Thus, these heating, ventilation, and air conditioning (HVAC) systems are essential to computer availability.

Another important part of environmental management is fire safety controls. These consist both of fire alarms to evacuate occupants and fire suppression systems. Fire suppression poses an interesting tradeoff between safety and availability. Classic fire suppression uses water sprinklers, which often render computer systems unusable. More sophisticated chemical-based fire suppression systems don't harm computer data or equipment, but may be toxic to people. Thus, the chemical systems often can't be deployed until people have evacuated an area. It takes careful planning and a firm understanding of fire safety codes to design an effective fire safety system in an information systems environment.

13.3.3 Software Security

Software security involves two important elements: ensuring the security and integrity of software during its development process and ensuring that the coding avoids well-known security problems. Software development security relies on particular types of controls on changes to software. This reduces the risk of unauthorized changes to the software, which could introduce intentional vulnerabilities or other malicious changes. Security problems associated with incorrect coding often arise from coding errors or from carelessness. We try to reduce the risk of such errors through a more formalized coding environment.

SOFTWARE DEVELOPMENT SECURITY

Software development security addresses two particular issues in controlling changes to software:

1. *Revision control*—tracking the changes made to software source code.
2. *Configuration management*—tracking changes to the components selected to be in a software product.

Revision control often is managed by special software that keeps track of all changes made to the source files that produce the software. When a file is first created, the author stores the initial version in the revision control system. Each revision is subsequently stored, keeping track of which changes were applied in which revision.

When it is time to construct a copy of the software, the software builder retrieves the appropriate version of each file from the revision control system. Note that the builder may retrieve either the latest version, or any specifically identified version, of each file.

Configuration Management

The configuration management process specifies the actual components that will go into the final product or into specific versions of the product. At the software level, this may consist of extracting particular files—and particular versions of files—from the revision control system in order to compile and build the system.

This style of configuration management is similar to techniques used in larger-scale system engineering projects. In practice, though, the techniques used in software configuration management are rooted in tools and techniques for software modularity. Individual modules are compiled or built by programs associated with specific source languages. The built modules then are linked together with a "software linker" that hooks procedure calls together. This integrates the modules together into a single, functioning software component.

When a development team decides to produce a new version of a system, they start with an existing version of the system, then they review bug fixes and other improvements made to the system. If a particular change is needed in the new system and the implemented code is acceptable, the team may change the configuration to include the newer version. In making the decision, the team may review the changes made to the code by querying the revision control system.

Once the decisions are made as to the contents of the new version, the build process often is automatic. The build software takes a script that identifies the files and versions and retrieves them from the revision control system, then it runs compilers, linkers, and other software to construct the new version of the product.

Note that the configuration scripts as well as the software source code all are stored in the revision control system. This ensures that all changes are tracked and accounted for systematically.

Most organizations also maintain documentation in a revision control system. Many handle document construction with the same type of integration process that they use for computer software. Because documents often reflect formal decisions about requirements and designs, it is important to track changes. This provides accountability for surprising changes in specifications and designs.

Repeatability and Traceability

This process has significant security implications. It provides a way to trace changes made to software and associate them with the individual who entered them into the system. This provides accountability for significant errors or for changes that appear malicious in nature. It also provides a systematic way to reconstruct any version of the system, if needed for error analysis or forensic purposes.

Even though most file systems and revision control systems support access control lists or similar access restrictions, some organizations rely primarily on their staff to restrict modifications to authorized software components. It is often more practical to leave the software open for modification but to track all modifications carefully. This is an example of a common, though not universally accepted, security dictum: *Trust, but verify.*

In the case of revision control, the system keeps detailed records of who makes what changes. If a change is located that absolutely should not have been made, the system will identify exactly which user submitted that change to the system. Thus, an audit may identify the individual responsible for an improper act, even if the act isn't blocked ahead of time.

FORMALIZED CODING ACTIVITIES

Years ago, computer programming was a refuge for specialized misfits. A manager could provide a description of a programming problem and the programmers—guiding themselves—would complete the project in a matter of days, weeks, or even months. Programming and bug fixing were such arcane activities that managers of the time didn't know how to ride herd over programmers and still keep them productive.

Although some organizations still perform software development in a fairly unstructured environment, many place special constraints on software development. Revision control and configuration management are an obvious example of these constraints. Here are additional constraints intended to improve the code's security and reliability:

- **Coding standards.** Programmers are given a set of rules on how to organize, write, and format their software. The rules also identify functions that they should and should not use in their programs. Older C functions, for example, are responsible for many famous buffer overflow attacks.
- **Code reviews.** Programmers read and comment on each others' code. This has been found to be the most effective approach to finding software flaws.
- **Code analysis procedures.** Tools automatically analyze source code to check compliance with coding standards and to search for known problem areas.
- **Auditing and monitoring.** In addition to code reviews, third parties may perform auditing and monitoring of coding standards to verify that standards are followed and enforced.

Avoiding Risky Practices

When writing code, programmers also take pains to avoid risky coding practices. These include in particular:

- **Do not use unsafe functions**. Old C functions did not check for buffer overflow when moving strings. These functions can't be used safely, so they shouldn't be used at all. This also applies to weak cryptography: Do not use crypto functions that are unreliable or unproven.

- **Validate all input text**. When retrieving text from the user, make certain that it complies with all assumptions regarding its format and content. Text often is passed between programs and interpreted by other software. Many attacks succeed by using unexpected characters that mean nothing to one program but provide an "escape" to take control of another.

- **Use familiar and consistent data formats**. Avoid using special data values to control the program. Allow all data values to have their accepted meaning. Keep in mind that modern character sets may have several similar-looking values to represent a letter, and each may have a different meaning in other languages.

- **Check all error results**. Too many programmers either fail to check function results for errors or ignore significant error codes. This is a difficult but essential part of good programming.

- **Include instrumentation in the code**. While developing the code, write log entries to report the program's status as it executes. This makes it much easier to identify correct (predicted) behavior and to diagnose surprising behavior. The instrumentation also may make it easier for others to check and validate the code.

Although many of these might be detected by code-analysis procedures, not all will be detected. Likewise, one might hope that code reviews catch such things, but the problems aren't always that easy to detect.

Software-Based Access Controls

Security software often implements functions to enforce access controls. These may use a variety of techniques, including the following:

- **Internal security labels**. A *security label* is an identifier that distinguishes data items that require different types of protection. In military circles, the labels may correspond to classification markings like Secret or Top Secret. In other settings, they may correspond to materials such as health information or private information that require special handling.

- **Need-to-Know controls**. These are protections that prevent users from seeing information that they do not specifically need to know. If the system does not need to release sensitive information to a user, it should not display that information. In some cases, this is a matter of identifying the role belonging to the user; in other cases, it involves designing the system according to the roles its users are known to play.

- **Encryption.** Some security software encrypts or decrypts data during processing. The software should take steps to avoid disclosing the decrypted data except to the necessary and authorized recipients. For example, the decrypted data should not be saved on the hard drive unless the user is expected to save an unprotected copy.
- **Integrity checking.** Some security software provides and implements integrity checking. When this is available, the software should perform the check and inform the user of the result. In some environments, the software might need to decide on its own whether to accept data if the integrity is damaged.

13.4 Enterprise Network Authentication

In Chapter 6, we examined different techniques to authenticate people. In general, the user logs in using a personal secret. The secret might be used directly, like a typed password, or it might be encoded in a token or encoded in a fingerprint's pattern. We also examined the implications in choosing one or another technique for household or business purposes. Network authentication poses a new set of problems:

- **Eavesdropping.** Attackers can sniff credentials that pass unprotected across a network.
- **Multiple servers.** We need to use multiple servers: Can we use the same authentication credentials for all of them?
- **Credential updates.** We should be able to change base secrets like passwords or public keys and to revoke credentials of former employees.

A glib answer to the problem might be "Encrypt everything." Unfortunately, this answer simply brings up additional questions. We need to decide how to manage keys. If we share keys among multiple users, we still have a risk of those users eavesdropping on one another. If we give each user a unique key, then we end up with separate keys each time a user connects with a particular server. This yields a nightmarish number of keys to manage and update.

Even though encryption isn't the sole answer, it naturally plays an important role. In practice, network authentication uses encryption to protect passwords in some cases and to generate one-time credentials in other cases.

We address network authentication problems, and others, by choosing from among four basic authentication strategies. These are sometimes called *design patterns*, following the work of architect Christopher Alexander and of the object-oriented software community. Each pattern is constructed from familiar crypto building blocks. Here are the four patterns:

1. **Local:** All components of the system reside within its security boundary, from the input device (keyboard, biometric) to the authentication database. Each local device contains an authentication database that is completely independent from the others.

2. **Direct:** The system contains its own, independent authentication database, but users authenticate to it from remote locations.

3. **Indirect:** The system accepts remote logins, but relies on a separate system, the *authentication server*, to perform the authentication process. The system itself doesn't keep an authentication database for regular users.

4. **Off-line:** This is a variant of direct authentication in which the database uses public-key certificates to authenticate its users.

These four approaches each have their own benefits and shortcomings. Choose one approach or another according to security features and practical benefits of the alternatives. Some alternatives have particular security and usability properties:

- **Security boundary.** Indicate which components of the system require protection to assure the integrity of the authentication decision and to protect the authentication database's secrecy.

- **Crypto requirements.** Different systems may use secret keys or public keys or no crypto at all.

- **Fault tolerance.** If some system components are off-line, some systems still can make authentication decisions.

Another area of tradeoff is in user administration: the challenge of adding and revoking individual users. We shouldn't assess this on a device-by-device basis or we'd always be satisfied with local authentication. Instead, look at the problem of adding or revoking users within the organization responsible for managing the equipment. If we only have to handle a single mainframe, server, or other central device, then matters are simple. They become complicated when we must manage authentication across multiple servers. They become even more difficult if we must administer them across multiple enterprises.

The rest of this section reviews the four design patterns in the light of these properties. First, we briefly review local authentication, and then we review the three patterns used in networks.

LOCAL AUTHENTICATION

Local authentication addresses the simplest situation: when people manipulate the system directly and not remotely. For example, it clearly applies to laptops, phones, and other handheld devices. If we treat an entire desktop computer, including USB cables, as a physical boundary, then we can think of the desktop as providing local authentication (Figure 13.2). This is also the concept implied in most building security systems, because the security system wires often are protected from tampering by the same boundary.

The obvious examples in the computing realm include portable or handheld devices and extend to laptop computers and stand-alone workstations. Less-obvious examples include many physical access control systems, like card-key entry systems, if the system's components rely on physical protection against tampering.

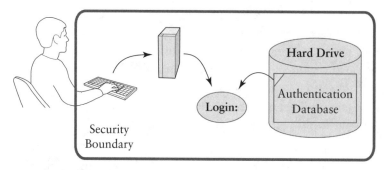

Figure 13.2

Local authentication.

If the system designer really trusts the system's physical security boundary, then local authentication is simple and reliable. Users can choose easier-to-remember passwords because attackers are limited to trial-and-error password guessing. If the attackers can't breach the security boundary, they can't extract passwords stored on the system, encrypted or not. In fact, a reliable boundary eliminates the need for encryption.

A local authentication system can improve its usability by implementing biometric authentication. A major threat against biometrics is to sniff a biometric reading and replay it; the security boundary should eliminate such attacks. However, it does not block other biometric threats. Moreover, physical boundaries are hard to ensure.

For many enterprises, the fundamental shortcoming of local authentication is its administration; each device must be administered individually. If two people need access to a single, secured laptop, then both need authentication credentials. There is no way to revoke a user's access to a particular device except by taking possession of that particular device, changing the necessary authentication credentials, and sharing revised credentials with the remaining users if necessary. The process gets more complex as the user population and the number of devices increase.

13.4.1 Direct Authentication

Direct authentication is the simplest case of remote login over a network (Figure 13.3). We wish to log in to a specific server. The server maintains its own authentication database with its own base secrets. This is a very common authentication pattern; most off-the-shelf web software implements a built-in authentication database, and most companies maintain their own authentication database for customers using their website.

This strategy is appropriate if the server must operate independently of all other enterprise systems or when the following are true:

- The server's proprietor knows who should be allowed to use it ahead of time or can easily make the decision while enrolling a new user.

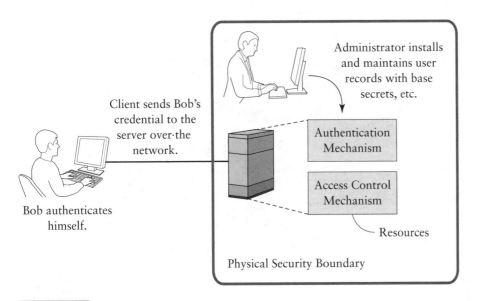

Administrator installs
and maintains user
records with base
secrets, etc.

Client sends Bob's
credential to the
server over·the
network.

Authentication
Mechanism

Access Control
Mechanism

Bob authenticates
himself.

Resources

Physical Security Boundary

Figure 13.3

Direct authentication.

- Each of the proprietor's systems, if the proprietor has more than one, has a unique group of users.

The strategy is common because it is relatively easy to implement. It is self-contained; it doesn't need to interact with other authentication systems. It does not need to comply with many standards or requirements.

In practice, direct authentication simply deploys local authentication across a network. The solution could use any of the implementations described in Chapter 6, though, of course, some are more vulnerable to attack than others. Like all network-based patterns, both the client and the data link are outside the security boundary. In this pattern, as with most authentication, an attacker can almost always subvert the process by subverting the client. Attacks on the data link, however, may be addressed by choosing the appropriate authentication mechanism.

Sniffing attacks on the data link could lead to masquerade if the attacker can replay an authentication credential to log in. This makes both passwords and simple biometrics vulnerable. The challenge-response techniques described in Section 6.5 often are used because they aren't vulnerable to replay attacks. They use cryptography to construct a single-use credential from the base secret. Several vendors, including Microsoft, use challenge-response for network authentication in some products.

Although simple biometrics are vulnerable to replay, some biometrics resist this attack. Such systems compare biometric readings against others recently submitted by the same user and reject exact duplicates. This does not prevent attacks through biometric spoofing (Section 6.6.2) or if the attacker makes subtle changes to the reading.

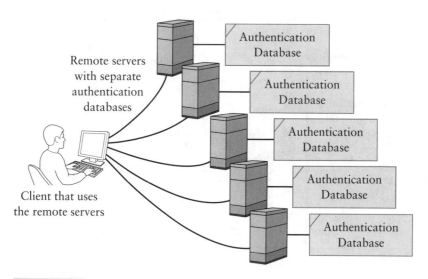

Figure 13.4

Direct authentication scales poorly.

As with local authentication, direct authentication poses a serious administrative burden when the enterprise operates several systems (Figure 13.4). Each system that requires local administration must be updated manually, both to enroll or validate users and to remove former employees. Unix systems, including Linux, traditionally implement local authentication, which becomes direct authentication when performed across a network. Unix vendor Sun Microsystems implemented a system called "Network Information System" (NIS) to reduce the administrative burden of standard Unix authentication. NIS automatically copies and distributes authentication databases between cooperating Unix systems.

13.4.2 Indirect Authentication

The *indirect authentication* pattern tries to solve the scalability problems posed by Figure 13.4. In indirect authentication, the server still demands authentication, but the actual process takes place elsewhere on an authentication server (Figure 13.5).

Although an NIS-type mechanism provides a strategy for administering direct authentication, it scales poorly as the user population expands. At some point, it simply isn't practical to copy the entire database to every system that requires authentication.

The authentication server off-loads the problems of storage, administration, and authentication decision making onto a dedicated server. This solves the problem of managing a user population that uses a variety of authenticated services. Even a site with only two servers will want to avoid the headache of trying to maintain consistency between two separate authentication databases.

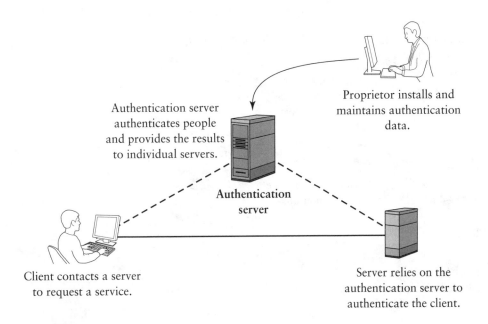

Proprietor installs and
maintains authentication
data.

Authentication server
authenticates people
and provides the results
to individual servers.

**Authentication
server**

Client contacts a server
to request a service.

Server relies on the
authentication server to
authenticate the client.

Figure 13.5

Indirect authentication.

In both local and direct authentication, both the authentication and access control
decisions take place on the same device. This pattern extracts the authentication process
and places it on a separate server. When making an access control decision, other servers rely on the user identity verified by the authentication server. There are three common approaches to indirect authentication:

1. ticket-based
2. service-based
3. redirected

All three of these appear in common systems and products. We generally use one or
another depending on the products we use. A product like Windows or SecurID already
supports a particular technique by virtue of implementing a particular protocol, like
Kerberos or RADIUS.

TICKET-BASED AUTHENTICATION

Modern ticket-based systems implement the *Kerberos* protocol. This was developed in
the 1980s at MIT for authenticating Unix-based desktop systems. When a client wishes
to use a particular service, it contacts the authentication server and requests access to
that service. Figure 13.6 illustrates the process, assuming that the user wants to contact
the mail service to read mail.

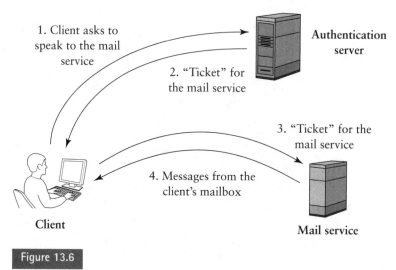

1. Client asks to speak to the mail service

2. "Ticket" for the mail service

Authentication server

3. "Ticket" for the mail service

4. Messages from the client's mailbox

Client

Mail service

Figure 13.6

Ticket-based authentication by Kerberos.

First, the user contacts the authentication server and asks to speak to the mail server. Next, the authentication server issues the client a *ticket*, which is a block of encrypted data intended for the mail service. Tickets are encrypted with secret keys assigned to individual users, clients, and services. The client then contacts the mail service itself and provides a copy of the ticket. The mail service uses its secret key to validate the ticket and ensure that the correct client and user presented it. If the ticket is valid and the client has permission, the service grants the request and delivers the mailbox contents to the client.

Microsoft uses the Kerberos protocol with its "Active Directory," which authenticates users, clients, and services who belong to a Microsoft "domain." When a user logs in to a workstation in a domain, the workstation contacts the Active Directory to authenticate the user and retrieve any needed tickets.

We will revisit Kerberos and ticket-based protocols in Section 14.2.3.

Service-Based Authentication

If Bob deploys a household 802.11 wireless network and enables its encryption features, he will choose a shared secret that the network uses to recognize approved laptops and other wireless devices. It's not practical for large enterprises to share a single secret like that. Instead, enterprises can use a centralized authentication server to validate wireless devices.

Although such systems could use tickets, like Kerberos, they use a different mechanism based on the **RADIUS** ("Remote Authentication Dial-In User") protocol or a newer protocol called "Diameter" (Figure 13.7).

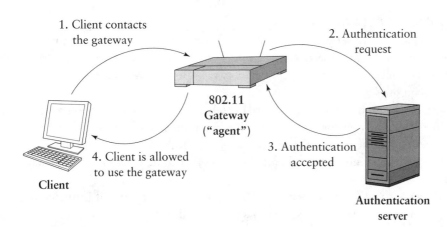

Figure 13.7

Service-based authentication for 802.11 access.

In RADIUS and in similar protocols, the user contacts a service residing on a host. The service operates a software package called an "agent" that mediates the authentication exchange between the client and the authentication server. The agent administers the login process, collects the credentials, and delivers them to the authentication server. If the credentials are correct, the authentication server sends back an "Accept" message.

Service-based authentication appears most often in network-oriented and authentication-oriented products. Many organizations find it much easier to administer 802.11 access centrally via a RADIUS server. Most of the one-time password products encountered in Section 6.5.2, like SecurID and Safeword, use a centralized authentication server.

One-time password tokens typically rely on centralized servers because their accuracy relies on synchronization. For example, each SecurID token uses an internal clock to produce its one-time password, and the clock value may "drift" over time. The central server keeps track of this drift and can resynchronize its drift information if necessary. This would be less reliable if separate servers had to track the drift individually.

REDIRECTED AUTHENTICATION

Many websites use this technique. Although most websites perform direct authentication, others redirect the client's browser to a different website that performs the authentication. Some banks that offer Visa-marked credit cards provide such a service, called "Verified by Visa."

Other websites offer *OpenID* authentication, which redirects authentication to a separate website. Like the other forms of indirect authentication, the authentication server cryptographically protects messages containing the authentication result.

PROPERTIES OF INDIRECT AUTHENTICATION

Aside from the separation of services from authentication, the direct and indirect patterns share many properties. Biometrics are equally risky with both patterns, because the credential passes across a potentially hostile network. Both patterns benefit from cryptographic techniques.

Indirect authentication, however, relies more heavily on cryptography. Because the service host doesn't actually perform the authentication, it must avoid trickery in which an attacker forges an "authentication accepted" message. Both the service and the authentication server must mutually authenticate each other to detect and prevent such forgeries.

Because indirect authentication depends on three hosts instead of two, it is intrinsically less reliable than other techniques. Vendors address this by providing ways to replicate the authentication service on two or more servers.

For many sites, the most important benefit of indirect authentication is that it scales well as an enterprise's computing environment grows. It can scale geographically as well as in terms of the number of hosts it supports and still provide rapid turnaround for new user creation or user revocation.

Scalability falters when the user population spans multiple enterprises. This is because today's indirect authentication products rely on shared secret keys. Because it is impossible to tell how well (or poorly) a third party protects a secret, enterprises rarely want to share such secrets with others who may be competitors in some spheres.

13.4.3 Off-Line Authentication

Off-line authentication provides a practical approach to truly distributed authentication. An enterprise might need to share authentication credentials with other, possibly competing, enterprises. Other approaches rely on shared secrets, which are risky in such a situation. Moreover, indirect techniques rely on authentication servers and some applications may be too broadly distributed or disconnected to rely on central servers. The off-line approach lets servers perform authentication without contacting a third party and still provides a large degree of central control over authentication.

Off-line authentication relies on public-key certificates, using methods introduced in Section 8.6. The enterprise issues public-key certificates to approved users. The enterprise's own certificate authority signs those certificates. Every enterprise application has a copy of the public key for the enterprise's "root" CA. This ensures that every application can authenticate an enterprise certificate. Figure 13.8 illustrates this procedure.

When Bob, as an employee of the enterprise, tries to log in to a service, he provides his public-key certificate. The service uses the root CA's public key to authenticate the certificate, then the service sends Bob's client a challenge. Bob's client "signs" the challenge with his private key to produce the response. The server uses the public key in Bob's certificate to verify the challenge and log him in.

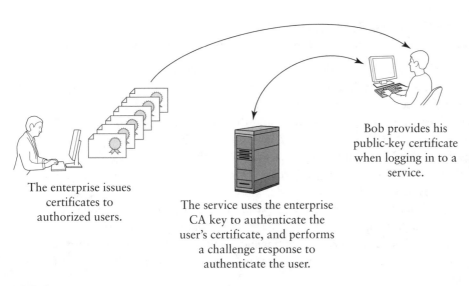

The enterprise issues certificates to authorized users.

The service uses the enterprise CA key to authenticate the user's certificate, and performs a challenge response to authenticate the user.

Bob provides his public-key certificate when logging in to a service.

Figure 13.8

Off-line authentication with public-key certificates.

Web servers and clients use a variant of this to passively authenticate secure web servers. When a client contacts a secure server, the server provides its certificate. The client confirms that the domain name used by the web software to reach the server is the same name that appears in its certificate. In many cases this can detect attempts by an attacker to masquerade as a familiar server. We examine this process further in Section 16.2.2.

The principal benefit of this approach is that it provides centralized authentication authority without a centralized authentication database. The enterprise can enroll a new user by producing a public-key certificate for that user. Neither clients nor servers need to contact a third party to authenticate a certificate. This speeds up service and reduces network traffic. A server can make an authentication decision even in the face of network disruptions. Moreover, the enterprise doesn't need to maintain a highly sensitive online database that is highly attractive to potential attackers.

A problem with this technique is that it is difficult to revoke a public-key certificate. Typical certificate implementations include expiration dates, so this limits the amount of time an invalid certificate might remain in use. If the enterprise needs to revoke a certificate, its only recourse is to announce to the servers that certain certificates have been revoked, using a *revocation list*. Every certificate that the authority has revoked but has not expired must be listed on the revocation list. To identify revoked certificates, applications must download the most recent list and check it when authenticating a certificate. Not all applications pay attention to such lists, unfortunately.

13.5 Contingency Planning

Fires, floods, hurricanes, tornadoes, and other large-scale disasters can devastate a household. They also can devastate an enterprise. Even less-dramatic incidents can close a business: If a fire alarm trips the internal sprinkler system, the water damage alone may destroy essential computing systems and the information they contain.

If a company suffers bad enough data loss to prevent it from transacting business, it may never recover. Half of the companies that suffer such a data loss go out of business within a few years. If a company can't reopen for business within a few weeks, it probably won't recover.

Contingency planning refers to the preparations we make to handle potential disasters, large or small. A small disaster may be when we damage an essential file and must retrieve a backed-up copy. Effective contingency planning addresses small disasters as well as large ones. Contingency planning for individuals or enterprises may include the following:

- Data backup and recovery—ensuring that we can recover essential data if damaged by any sort of disaster
- Incident handling—establishing a procedure to follow if a computer security incident occurs
- Disaster preparation and recovery—ensuring that we can resume essential operations promptly following a disaster

13.5.1 Data Backup and Restoration

Data backup is the starting point for computer system disaster recovery. Once we have a safe and secure copy of essential data, we can recover from most disasters, large and small. Typically, our only losses involve activities since the last backup occurred. Here we examine four backup strategies:

1. File-oriented synchronized backups
2. File-oriented incremental backups
3. Full-image backups
4. RAID as backup

Each of these strategies carries its own benefits and risks. Synchronized backups are quick but tend to be incomplete. Incremental backups may consume time and resources, but provide maximum flexibility. Image backups and RAID provide the easiest recovery from hardware failures. An enterprise may need to apply different strategies to back up different storage resources.

Full Versus Partial Backups

Alice relies on a small number of standard application programs. When she gets a new computer, she installs those two or three applications, copies over her personal files, and she is ready to use the new computer. As long as Alice backs up copies of her working files, it wouldn't take her long to move onto a different computer if she loses her regular computer.

Tina, on the other hand, uses a variety of software development tools, graphics tools, and presentation tools. When she gets a new computer, it can take her 2 or 3 days to install all of her applications. Thus, it is a serious disruption if she loses her computer.

Given these differences, Alice can easily get along with synchronized backups or with the simple user-oriented incremental backups provided by Microsoft Windows. Tina, on the other hand, needs a whole-system backup that lets her restore her entire system. She may achieve this through a full incremental backup or through image backups.

FILE-ORIENTED SYNCHRONIZED BACKUPS

In Section 2.6.3, we examined the process by which Alice backs up files stored on her laptop. Her process tries to preserve recent copies of all of her work even if one of the following occurs:

- Her laptop hard drive fails.
- Her laptop is stolen.
- Her USB drive fails or she loses it.

Alice's strategy produces *synchronized backups*. She backs up a selected collection of files, often gathered into a specific folder or directory. The process preserves two copies of the latest files: one copy on a USB drive and another on a computer's hard drive. The entire process relies heavily on Alice's work habits. If she fails to synchronize her files for a few days and then loses her laptop, she loses the work for those days.

Note that Alice's strategy does not protect against a disaster in her dorm; if a fire or flood inundates her room, she may lose her laptop and both USB drives. We will assume that she is aware of this shortcoming, and that she has accepted the risk.

A realistic backup strategy considers the following issues:

- Deciding what to back up. Do you need to back up everything all the time? Are there things that should be backed up occasionally, while other things are backed up continuously?
- Deciding when and how to back up. A backup process is worthless if it doesn't keep timely backups. Be sure the process works smoothly and consistently.
- Verifying that the system works. We can't assume that the backup system works unless we test it. Some products work correctly in some environments but not in others. A broken backup system doesn't provide the safety we require.
- Arranging both on-site and off-site backups. A building fire or tornado may destroy the building and nearby locations. Keep a periodic backup off-site. Some experts recommend keeping at least one copy at least 100 miles from your site.

An enterprise also should arrange for secure, off-site storage of company archives as well as recent backups. The storage site must be physically secure. The enterprise should have a process for moving data between the archive and company offices.

Off-site backups should "rotate" with on-site storage. Currently, the most practical and cost-effective high-capacity storage devices are often physical hard drives. To reduce the risk of losing data due to failures while in storage, the off-site storage should be periodically recycled and replaced by newer devices.

FILE-ORIENTED INCREMENTAL BACKUPS

Another popular backup strategy is to deploy *incremental backups*, which periodically save all changes made on the system since the previous backup. Typically, the backup software writes the backup files to a separate hard drive. If our main hard drive fails, we should be able to restore the backed-up files onto a replacement hard drive.

Several commercial vendors, including the major security vendors, provide incremental backup products. Microsoft Windows includes a partial incremental backup that saves selected user files. Apple integrated an incremental backup service, called "Time Machine" into OS-X. A number of vendors also offer online incremental backup services, which save the data on remote servers accessible across the Internet.

IMAGE BACKUPS

The simplest information backup strategy is to make an *image backup* of every critical hard drive or other storage device. These are bit-by-bit copies of one mass storage device to another. We then save the copy. If disaster occurs, we retrieve the copy and transcribe it back to the original drive or to a hardware replacement. Image backup has certain benefits:

- Almost every system can perform image backups.
- It is relatively straightforward to create an image backup if the appropriate hardware is available.
- Recovery does not rely on special software; many systems have image-only, bootable systems that can perform image copies.

Unix-based systems, including Apple's OS-X, have a standard text command, "dd," which copies any device to any other. Microsoft also provides an image backup facility in some versions of Windows.

Image backup often poses a challenge for organizations, for these reasons:

- The backup process must copy the *entire* drive. This takes hours for really large, modern hard drives.
- Each time we take a backup, we must copy the entire drive again.
- Not all image backups will allow us to retrieve a specific file from an older backup.

Modern commercial products may address one or more of these shortcomings. Some products use specialized techniques to make the process faster and more efficient.

RAID AS BACKUP

A *redundant array of independent disks* (RAID) storage system contains two or more separate hard drives used together to increase reliability, performance, or both. Different RAID arrangements are numbered; here are some common arrangements:

- RAID 0: "Striping" provides higher performance but lower reliability; requires two or more drives.
- RAID 1: "Mirroring" provides higher reliability and better reading performance; requires two or more drives.
- RAID 4: "Parity disk" provides high reliability and more disk efficiency than RAID 1; requires three or more drives.
- RAID 5: "Distributed parity" also provides high reliability and better efficiency; also requires three or more drives.

A "mirrored RAID" or "RAID 1" system writes all data to two separate hard drives. During reading, the drives can provide data twice as quickly as a single drive. If one drive fails, the other contains a complete copy of the data. This provides the following benefits if a hard drive fails:

- No data is lost.
- The system remains running until the failed drive is replaced.

The major benefit of RAID 1 is reliability. Most hard drives fail after a few years of operation, though a few fail within their first year or two. We can't predict when a particular drive might fail. RAID 1 provides fault tolerance; a drive can fail without us losing our data. To recover, we simply replace the faulty drive. Then the RAID system rewrites the contents of the working drive onto the new drive.

Although this may be an inefficient use of hard drive hardware, it is a cost-effective way to implement reliable storage. For many users, a hard drive failure poses far greater costs than the $100 purchase price of an extra hard drive. Although modern laptops rarely have space for an extra hard drive, most desktop systems can accommodate extra drives. Many systems have built-in circuitry, software, or both, to support RAID.

RAID 1 only provides higher reliability if we promptly replace a failed hard drive. If we run the system without both mirrors, then we lose everything if the second drive fails. There have been many cases of "redundant systems" failing because operators did not replace defective hardware.

Even though RAID protects against hardware failures, there are many important things it does *not* protect against:

- No protection against data damaged by software errors
- No protection against data damaged by user errors
- No off-site data protection

RAID *only* protects against hardware failures. It does not protect against software or operator errors that damage information or files. Thus, RAID doesn't provide full backup protection. Moreover, RAID systems don't directly support off-site backups. It takes special planning and procedures to implement off-site backup with a RAID 1 system.

13.5.2 Handling Serious Incidents

Incidents in general may span the range from minor matters (like rude computing behavior) to major attacks that cause damage. Within a household, we may handle incidents without a formal process. Within an enterprise, a serious incident may impact a number of people. In the past, some companies have suffered because employees tried to cover up significant incidents, hiding them from senior managers.

Enterprises need to establish an incident handling policy. This makes it clear to everyone how to handle incidents and which should be reported to senior management. Problems that don't seriously affect enterprise objectives may be handled within the IT organization. Thus, the policy should include the following:

- How to grade incidents by seriousness
- Who to contact in the IT or security organization when incidents occur
- Roles and responsibilities within IT and within other enterprise departments
- What technical steps to take to mitigate further damage
- What procedural steps to take to report the incident to other enterprise departments or to senior management
- Which incidents should be reported to law enforcement

In general, information on an incident is handled on a Need to Know basis. Public announcements are the province of other departments or of senior management.

EXAMINING A SERIOUS ATTACK

Large-scale attacks consist of four phases:

1. Surveillance. The attacker studies the attack target, collecting information about it.
2. Infiltration. The attacker takes steps to enter the system so that the attack may take place. This by itself "compromises" the system by placing a malicious process within its environment.
3. Execution. The attacker takes the steps needed to achieve the attack's objective.
4. Disengagement. The attacker withdraws, having achieved the attack's objective. Often, this step tries to erase evidence of the attack or eliminate any trail that points to the attacker.

In some cases, the individual steps may seem like attacks by themselves, even if they don't individually cause the loss of an asset. However, the individual steps often compromise the integrity of the system or at least the integrity of its defenses. For example, an intercepted password isn't a lost asset, but it may allow an attack on an asset.

Probes seeking system information, like "nmap scans" (Section 11.5.2), may not seem like significant attacks by themselves. After all, a typical site has enough network capacity to tolerate some level of scanning. However, such behavior may indicate preparation for an attack. Likewise, the appearance of unexpected user identities may not indicate a problem by itself, but it suggests preparation for worse activities in the future.

When analyzing a major attack after it occurs, we may find evidence of earlier attack phases if we study earlier logs. Although an extremely sophisticated attacker might manage to hide all evidence of an attack, not everyone is that clever. Many attackers will leave traces of earlier surveillance or intrusion attempts. Even if the actual, damage-causing attack doesn't leave enough evidence to track the attacker, earlier occurrences may point toward the attacker.

13.5.3 Disaster Preparation and Recovery

A real disaster takes the enterprise systems off-line and prevents business from taking place. Whether caused by an all-out attack on our information systems or a fire, flood, or other natural disaster, a commercial enterprise must recover rapidly to survive. Government and service enterprises likewise must recover quickly, if only to provide the services needed by others affected by disaster.

BUSINESS IMPACT ANALYSIS

A **business impact analysis** (BIA) is a report that assesses the enterprise's ability to recover from a major disaster. This is often the first step in the disaster-planning process. If the enterprise already has plans in place, the BIA provides an assessment of how effectively those plans work. The BIA does the following:

- Estimates the impact of a worst-case scenario on business operations. These include tangible financial impacts and intangible impacts, like those on reputation.
- Identifies work processes affected by such a scenario.
- Estimates how long it will take for the work processes to recover.

A typical BIA is performed by a team that interviews key enterprise personnel and uses the results to construct the report. The BIA proceeds as follows:

- Make a list of major enterprise organizations or business units.
- Within each business unit, identify the business processes it performs.
- For each business process, assess the following:
  - Dependence on IT for operation and support.
  - IT elements required: user population, inputs, outputs, transaction frequencies, etc.
  - Impact on the business if the process doesn't take place for various lengths of time, from 1 hour to 1 month, graded as "significant," "major," or "minor."
  - Identify critical times of the year for that process.
  - Identify interdependencies between this process and other enterprise activities, both in terms of inputs and outputs.

- Identify tangible, financial impacts and intangible impacts.
- Using the process information, identify manpower requirements for recovery, the processes and records required to support critical processes, and the impact the department's processing will have on the enterprise.

The result should provide estimates of the maximum allowable downtime for different enterprise processes. It also will indicate which elements currently have effective recovery plans and which do not.

RECOVERY STRATEGIES

Successful recovery depends on planning and preparation. Enterprises without plans often fail after a disaster. The most effective plans have been tested in practice.

Enterprise plans apply one of the following recovery strategies:

Delayed recovery

A *delayed recovery* requires the least up-front expense, but the enterprise can't resume its computer-based operations immediately. The strategy is to salvage, rent, or buy the equipment needed to resume operations, reinstall systems, software, and databases from backups, and then resume operations. If the existing premises are usable, then the enterprise resumes operations in place. If not, the enterprise rents space for equipment and employees to use.

This approach is what most individuals, households, and extremely small businesses would use. Businesses can prosper after a delayed recovery as long as the delay doesn't last for an extended time.

Cold standby

A *cold standby* is a computing environment, geographically distant from the main site, that we leave idle in case of a disaster. If a disaster occurs, the enterprise activates the cold standby environment, installs its backups, populates the site with employees, and resumes operation.

This approach yields a great deal of equipment that may stand unused for long periods of time. Companies that specialize in disaster services may maintain cold standby environments for their clients, and share them among multiple clients to minimize the expense.

Hot standby

If an enterprise needs to keep operations going at all times despite potential disasters, it implements a *hot standby*. This is essentially a dedicated cold standby site with all equipment already in place and preloaded with the necessary software and data.

Some enterprises might leave the hot standby site idle, but others use such sites to distribute the work. Thus, all sites are operated at all times. If one site goes down due to a disaster, the other site takes over its work and keeps the enterprise in operation.

CONTINGENCY PLANNING PROCESS

Contingency planning covers the entire range of serious incidents from reportable attacks on computer systems to large-scale natural disasters. A contingency plan starts with a BIA as input. The resulting plan also may be called a *business continuity plan* (BCP).

Many of the same elements of incident response also apply to contingency planning. However, contingency planning addresses larger scale problems. In both cases, we look at enterprise objectives for guidance. The objectives help us prioritize the elements of preparation and implementation for disasters and other contingency planning.

The contingency planning process involves the following:

- Identify, characterize, and prioritize critical and essential tasks that must be resumed following a disaster. This should be provided by the BIA.
- Identify roles and responsibilities for developing, approving, and implementing the plan within the enterprise.
- Establish backup requirements for working data and determine how the backups will be retrieved and used to recover from a disaster.
- Develop procedures for off-site processing to resume essential activities.
- Develop a strategy for how to transition from off-site, temporary processes to back-to-routine processes.

Disaster recovery plans, like backup plans, are only effective if they work as intended. The only way to assure that such plans work is to actually try them out. A company can test a delayed recovery plan by renting equipment and trying to set things up in a separate environment. Companies that use standby sites can test their plans by switching over to the standby site as a test. If a company uses distributed sites to provide hot standby, it can test its plan by taking each site off-line and verifying that the other site picks up all the work.

An effective contingency plan is one that is understood and fully supported by senior management. The enterprise must commit resources to the plan for it to succeed. Its implementation following a disaster relies on directions that only senior management can make.

13.6 Resources

 IMPORTANT TERMS INTRODUCED

authentication server	direct authentication	policy directive
background investigation	hot standby	policy specification
change control process	image backup	profit center
clearance	incremental backup	provisioning
cold standby	indirect authentication	revision control
compliance audit	Kerberos	security label
configuration management	local authentication	synchronized backup
contingency planning	logic bomb	ticket
cost center	Need to Know	vulnerability scan
decommissioning	off-line authentication	
delayed recovery	OpenID	

ACRONYMS INTRODUCED

BCP—Business continuity plan

BIA—Business impact analysis

BS—British standard

CEO—Chief executive officer

CIO—Chief information officer

CISA—Certified information security auditor

CISO—Chief information security officer

CMM—Capability Maturity Model

CNSS—Committee for National Security Systems

CompTIA—Computer Technology Industry Association

CTO—Chief technology officer

GIAC—Global information assurance certification

HVAC—Heating, ventilation, and air conditioning

IA—Information assurance

IACE—Information assurance courseware evaluation

IEC—International Electrotechnical Commission

infosec—Information security

ISACA—Information Systems Audit and Control Association

ISC²—International Information Systems Security Certification Consortium

ISMS—Information security management system

NIS—Network Information System

pen test—Penetration test

QSA—Qualified security assessor

RADIUS—Remote Authentication Dial-In User
RAID—Redundant array of independent disks
UPS—Uninterruptable power supply
VP—Vice president

13.6.1 Review Questions

R1. Identify two specific ways in which security for enterprise computing is different from personal computing.

R2. Describe four types of secrecy practiced by enterprises.

R3. Summarize risks that are more significant to enterprises than to individuals.

R4. Describe two techniques to help reduce the insider threat.

R5. Give two examples of social engineering attacks.

R6. List five types of security policy directives often published by organizations.

R7. Briefly summarize the evolution of information security management standards.

R8. Summarize the steps in a typical change control process.

R9. Explain the difference between a profit center and a cost center. How is this distinction relevant to budgeting for information security?

R10. Identify four roles and/or job titles associated with information security management.

R11. Briefly describe five different types of security audits.

R12. Summarize five mechanisms for security education, training, and awareness.

R13. What is the purpose of a background investigation? Do enterprises perform such investigations on all new employees?

R14. What is the relationship between the employee life cycle and security management?

R15. Why is it a challenge to achieve Separation of Duty if all steps take place on a single computer system?

R16. Summarize five methods used to manage electric power.

R17. Identify the four types of protection applied to storage systems.

R18. Explain the role of revision control and configuration management in software development.

R19. Describe methods and techniques used to improve software security.

R20. Identify and describe the four different approaches ("design patterns") for authentication.

R21. Explain the difference between ticket-based and service-based authentication.

R22. Describe different techniques to produce and manage backups.

R23. List the elements of an incident handling policy.

R24. Identify and describe the four phases of a large-scale attack.

R25. Describe the role of a business impact analysis in disaster planning.

R26. List and explain the three basic recovery strategies.

R27. Summarize the five steps in the contingency planning process.

13.6.2 Exercises

Some problems ask about "your organization." For those questions, your organization may be a business you work for or the school you attend.

E1. What types of information does your organization handle that requires confidentiality? Do not guess: Identify types of information that the organization *must* handle. Explain why the organization must handle the information and why it must be kept confidential.

E2. Give an example of a public statement made by a member of your organization. Do you believe that the public statement required prior approval by upper levels of the organization?

E3. Does your organization comply with any national or international quality assurance or information security standards?
  • If so, identify the certifications and when they were last issued.
  • If not, identify at least one standard that the organization could or should comply with. Explain why the standard might apply to the organization.

E4. Draw an organization chart for the top three levels of your organization. The top level should be a chief executive officer or someone with a similar role. Identify the person by name and formal job title. The next two levels need not be complete, but each level should identify the types of roles and job titles at that level. Each level also should identify at least two individuals by name and formal job title.

E5. List four different roles fulfilled by people (employees, students, or other members) in your organization. Be sure to choose roles that require access to different types of information. List the types of information accessed by the people in the different roles.

E6. List four examples of physical security measures used by your organization.

E7. Give three examples of software security issues that could be taught in an introductory programming class.

E8. What authentication pattern is used in your organization when using its computers?

E9. Find out the backup procedures used in your organization. What files and other systems are regularly backed up? Can they retrieve lost files? Are there restrictions on what lost files may be retrieved?

ABOUT THIS CHAPTER

This chapter applies cryptographic techniques to networking. Crypto provides the most effective general-purpose techniques to protect network traffic.

- Role of crypto in communications security
- Impact of using crypto at different protocol layers
- Network key distribution techniques
- Application, network, and link layer crypto
- Policy guidance for crypto application

14.1 Communications Security

In the previous four chapters, we focused on protecting information by keeping threats away from our network. If we connect our network with the Internet, we firewall the connection to try to exclude Internet-based threats—but this doesn't help us when we need to transfer information *between* Internet sites. The data leaves our control, so we need cryptography to protect it.

This is the traditional purpose of encryption: to protect data in motion. Although we introduced encryption in Chapter 7 as a way to protect diaries or copyrighted materials, most of cryptography's history applies to communications security. Julius Caesar created his cipher to protect military dispatches from being read by enemies. The first large-scale application of DES was to protect financial transactions on early computer networks.

In earlier chapters, Alice and Bob shared files on a single computer or by copying files onto a shared USB drive. With a network, Alice and Bob can sit on their own computers and send data directly back and forth. After an unexpected stop at a coffee stand, Bob owes Alice $5. To remind him, Alice emails Bob the following message:

```
Dear Bob,
      Pay me $5.
Alice
```

Figure 14.1 shows the message being sent to Bob's computer from Alice. Their friend Eve continues her inappropriate curiosity about other peoples' business. She also knows

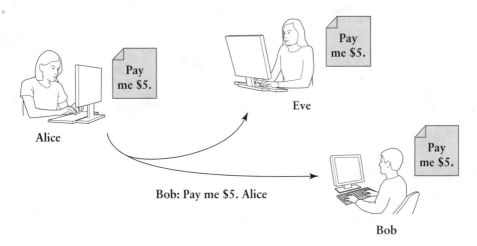

Figure 14.1

A passive attack on an unprotected network message.

enough about networking to intercept a copy of Alice's message. In the best case, such behavior is rude and annoying. In the worst case, the network opens Alice or Bob up to trouble.

Back in Section 10.1.1, we reviewed the six general types of attacks in terms of networks. This attack is a disclosure: Eve has intercepted private information. The attacker simply reads the data without interference. Since Eve simply eavesdropped without interfering with communications, we call this a *passive attack*.

In some cases, disclosure poses no risk. In this case, the message tells nothing salacious or secret about Bob or Alice. The eavesdropping represents a security *incident*, if not an attack.

However, Eve is curious about how Bob reacts to messages like this. Eve constructs a message to Bob telling him to pay *her* $5 (Figure 14.2). Although we would call eavesdropping a passive attack, this is clearly an *active attack*: a network attack in which she forges network traffic. Active attacks may be forgeries or masquerades. If Eve simply pretends to be Alice and takes Alice's $5, then it is a masquerade.

Bob is probably not foolish enough to respond to Eve's message. Alice's message was simply a reminder of something Bob already knew. Eve's message suggests that Bob borrowed money and forgot entirely. Bob ignores the message because he knows it's bogus.

On the other hand, many network messages pass between computer hardware and programs, not between people. Programs are relatively easy to trick, because they know nothing beyond what people tell them.

Imagine what happens if Bob installs a simple cash dispenser on his computer. This allows him to pay people back without actually being present. Alice sends her message and the computer counts out $5 as requested—then Eve sends her message. How do we keep the dispenser from paying her, too? This is the real forgery problem.

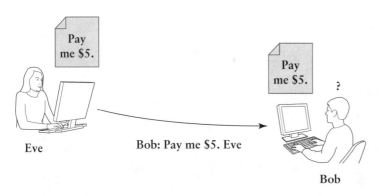

Figure 14.2

An active attack on Bob.

CRYPTOGRAPHIC PROTECTIONS

We use cryptography to apply the following protections to network traffic:

- Confidentiality
- Integrity
- Authenticity
- Nonrepudiation

Crypto techniques originally focused on confidentiality: We kept data secret by encrypting it. Secrecy also may provide a weak type of integrity protection; attackers can't change a message's text reliably without knowing the message's contents already. As we saw in Chapter 7, an attacker who knows the message's contents can modify its contents if we used a stream cipher to protect it.

The remaining three protections don't actually prevent attackers from damaging a packet. Instead, they give us a way to detect such damage. Secret-key techniques allow us to verify data integrity. This in turn gives us some evidence that the data is authentic. We use public-key techniques to unambiguously authenticate a message and associate it with a particular person or entity. The same techniques provide a degree of nonrepudiation: If the message is signed by the entity's public key, then it is hard for the entity to repudiate the message; that is, to deny having produced the signed data.

Some researchers have proposed techniques to block certain denial of service attacks using puzzles or other crypto-like techniques. These may show promise in the future, though none are used widely today.

14.1.1 Crypto by Layers

In Section 13.5, we saw how firewalls handle traffic in terms of protocol layers. Although this is easy to do at lower layers, the firewall must reconstruct parts of the

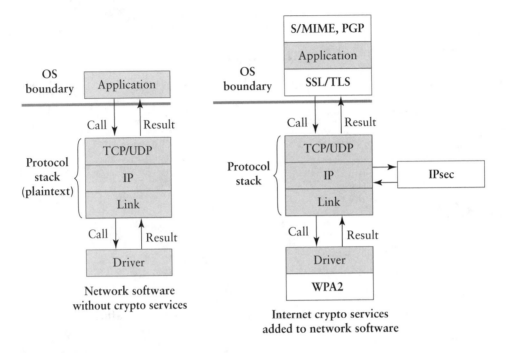

Figure 14.3

Adding cryptography to Internet software.

protocol when interpreting a TCP connection or examining application-level data items. It's hard to scan an email message for viruses without reconstructing the entire message.

Network cryptography also works in relation to protocol layers. We get very different kinds of protection depending on where we apply encryption or verify authenticity within the protocol stack. Today's Internet products provide cryptography at several different layers of the stack, as shown in Figure 14.3.

When we place crypto in different protocol layers, we often balance two important properties: *application transparency* and *network transparency*. If the crypto is "transparent to the application," we can add—or omit—the crypto without making any changes to the application software. Thus, we easily can add encryption without changing the application. When crypto is "transparent to the network," the encrypted traffic may be sent across the Internet. Thus, we can apply our protections and still transmit the data. Some protocols achieve one but not the other, while some achieve both.

Link Layer Encryption and 802.11 Wireless

Traditionally, when someone tried to protect a communications line, they used *link encryption*, which protects point-to-point data links or broadcasts to an exclusive cryptonet. Because it applies protection at the link layer, it is application transparent, and it encrypts *everything* on the link. This was popular in the pre-Internet era, when networked sites often used leased lines. The two endpoints either belonged to the same organization or they had a close relationship, so they trusted each other with encryption keys.

Even though few sites use classic link encryption today, many sites use encryption at the link layer: They encrypt their wireless LAN. As the data link gets more sophisticated, there needs to be control information to manage the encryption. Some of this is essentially plaintext, because it tells the recipient how to decrypt the data. This is true especially for traffic on an 802.11 wireless network. Figure 14.4 illustrates the packet format for encrypted 802.11 data.

Since the introduction of 802.11 products in the late 1990s, there have been a series of security protocols developed. Earlier protocols were not effective against clever attacks on their cryptography. The latest protocol, **Wireless Protected Access, version 2** (WPA2), has resisted attacks, partly by using AES encryption. WPA2 protects the traffic as it travels over the air between the laptop or other wireless host and the network base station.

Link layer encryption techniques, including both link encryptors and WPA2, do not provide network transparency. When a packet destined for the Internet arrives at a wireless gateway or link endpoint, the device strips off the encryption and forwards the packet to its destination. If the encryption were left in place, the routers could not interpret the IP header and route the packet. We look at wireless encryption further in Section 14.5.

Network Layer Encryption and IPsec

When a company needs to connect LANs at two separate sites, the traditional solution was to lease a point-to-point network link between them. Sites couldn't connect across the Internet because the link-level encryption would encrypt the whole packet, including the IP addresses. The only way we can route a packet through protocol stacks is if the appropriate packet headers remain in plaintext.

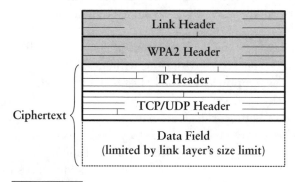

Figure 14.4

A packet with 802.11 link encryption.

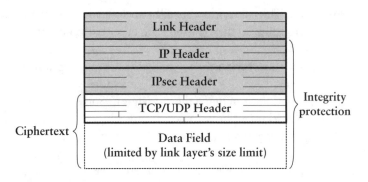

A packet with IPsec protection.

The *IP Security Protocol* was introduced in the mid-1990s to solve this problem. The Internet community generally abbreviates the name as "IPsec" (pronounced eye-pee-seck). Figure 14.5 shows how IPsec cryptography is applied to a packet.

IPsec encryption leaves the link and IP headers in plaintext. The IPsec header provides the information needed to decrypt the packet at the other end. Everything normally following an IP header is encrypted, including the TCP/UDP header and the application data. The IPsec header also contains an integrity check on the IP header contents.

IPsec allows two sites to establish an encrypted connection across the Internet through which they may exchange packets securely. This is called a *virtual private network* (VPN). Some sites also use IPsec to provide a secure connection to workers at home or traveling with laptops. When a computer connects through the VPN, it can see the same network as those physically inside the organization. Sites often implement VPNs by installing encrypting gateways. This off-loads the encryption from most hosts on-site. Traveling laptops still must perform their own IPsec crypto to connect through a site gateway.

IPsec achieves *both* application transparency and network transparency. Any or all Internet application software traffic may be encrypted with IPsec without making any changes to the applications. Because the encryption leaves the IP header in plaintext, the encrypted packets are handled normally by Internet routers.

Although this may seem like the best of both worlds, there remains a problem: Neither the applications nor the users can necessarily tell if messages will be protected or not. This is especially true in sites that use encrypting gateways. Sites often configure specific types of traffic to be encrypted and leave the rest in plaintext. This allows users to exchange IPsec traffic with particular destinations, usually other sites within the organization. The remaining Internet traffic, which is probably directed at public Internet servers, does not use IPsec, because that would not allow connections to public servers.

We look at IPsec further in Section 14.4.

Socket Layer Encryption with SSL/TLS

Socket layer encryption appears outside the OS boundary. It is not part of the operating system, the hardware, or the standard protocol stack shown in Figure 14.3. It is most often part of a networking application, usually a browser. This makes the crypto software much easier to implement and deploy, though it requires modifying the application. We give up application transparency, but we achieve network transparency. The software may also clearly indicate to the user when encryption is being used or not.

Socket layer encryption traditionally is called *Secure Sockets Layer* (SSL), though the modern version of the protocol is called *Transport Layer Security* (TLS). The official SSL protocol is no longer supported, and modern products implement TLS. Despite this, people still refer to the protocol by its traditional acronym, SSL.

We first encountered the socket interface in Section 11.3. The interface resides between the TCP/UDP layer and the applications. Because SSL encrypts the data before it reaches TCP/UDP, the network protocol stack treats it like any other application data: It breaks the data into packets, addresses it with IP and port numbers, and sends it on its way. The receiving host relays the encrypted data to the application indicated by the port number. The receiving host's protocol stack doesn't even pay attention to the fact that the data is encrypted. Figure 14.6 illustrates the packet layout used with SSL encryption.

This is the protocol that usually protects secure web applications. It was developed in 1994 and originally distributed by Netscape Communications, the first company to make serious money out of a commercial crypto product. Netscape produced two products: The Navigator was a browser and the Commerce Server was a web server. These two products introduced SSL.

If Alice visits a website to buy a book, most of her browsing takes place without encryption. When it is time to actually pay for the book, the site redirects her to a web page protected with SSL. Such pages have "https:" as the URL prefix.

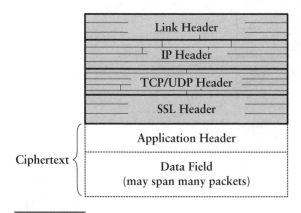

Figure 14.6

A packet with SSL encryption.

SSL was originally a commercial product of Netscape; when the IETF started work on an Internet standard for transport encryption, they adopted the new name and acronym, TLS. Although many people use the terms SSL and TLS interchangeably, the up-to-date protocol is TLS.

Application Layer Encryption with S/MIME or PGP

Arguably, application layer encryption is even older than link encryption: When people first sent encrypted telegrams, they encrypted the message before bringing it to the telegraph office. Telegraph codes date back to the 1800s; Gilbert Vernam produced link encryption for teletypes in the 1920s. Internet email protocols emerged in the late 1980s, before network encryption flourished.

There are many ways to apply encryption at the application level. SSL provides a form of application encryption because the developers usually bundle the SSL software with the application. However, SSL generally appears at the very *bottom* of the application protocol, right at the socket interface. True application layer encryption interacts with the end user.

We call this ***end-to-end crypto***. The application performs the crypto operations at the top of the application layer or even *above* from the protocol stack. This clearly shows the end user whether an individual message or transaction carries crypto protection.

In end-to-end crypto, the actual sender applies the protection and the actual recipient decrypts the message and verifies the digital signature. Applications rely on personal cryptographic keys, while lower-layer crypto uses host-related or network node-related keys.

End-to-end crypto for email, like SSL, sacrifices application transparency for network transparency. Unlike SSL, there may be plaintext application headers that coordinate the handling of the encrypted data (Figure 14.7).

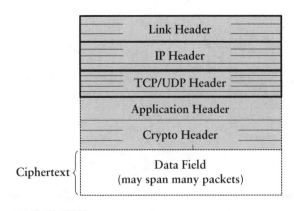

Figure 14.7

A packet with end-to-end crypto.

LAYER-ORIENTED VARIATIONS

Because the different layers encrypt different parts of the packet, they achieve different results. Here is a summary of essential differences. We will examine them further in later sections.

- What protocols actually use this technique?
- Where in the network and/or protocol stack is the plaintext visible?
- Is the encryption transparent to the application?
- Is the encryption transparent to the network, and to what extent? In other words, how much addressing information remains in plaintext?
- Where do the working keys reside?
- How are working keys updated?
- To what degree can we identify or authenticate the source of the packets retrieved from an encrypted connection?

The technical elements noted here may vary from layer to layer and from one crypto algorithm to another. Modern crypto protocols often allow the hosts to choose which crypto algorithms to use for key exchange, authentication, integrity protection, or encryption. The protocols often provide a list of choices called *cipher suites*. Each cipher suite provides a set of algorithms, protocols, and modes that together implement a set of security services. Here are examples:

- Cipher suites in SSL allow the choice of RSA or Diffie-Hellman for key exchange; some still support RC4 encryption, more recent suites support AES.
- Cipher suites for wireless LAN encryption allow the choice of RC4 in three weak alternatives or AES with a strong encryption and integrity protecting mode.

We need to choose our crypto solutions depending on what we need for communication and security. The next section reviews some fundamental administrative and policy issues.

14.1.2 Administrative and Policy Issues

The end of the previous section summarized various technical features of different cryptographic protocols. In practice, however, our security decisions depend on what we're trying to achieve, not on technical features by themselves.

There are six basic issues we need to address when deploying cryptography on the Internet. Some have to do with protection and control, while others have to do with the difficulties of deployment. Here they are:

- **Scope of sniffing protection**. If we use this type of encryption, how thoroughly does it protect the traffic from sniffing?
- **Traffic filtering**. Some environments analyze incoming and outgoing traffic for potential security risks. Encryption interferes with filtering.

- **Automatic encryption.** If we use this type of encryption, must the users activate it, or can it take place automatically?

- **Access to Internet sites.** Can we use the encryption to block user access to Internet sites?

- **End-to-end crypto.** Is the encryption associated with the end users, instead of the host computers or networks?

- **Keying.** Do end users have to manage keys?

Now we talk about each one.

Sniffing Protection

We clearly need to use encryption if we wish to protect against sniffing. Different protocols protect our traffic in different environments. 802.11 wireless encryption protects the wireless transmissions on our LAN, but the gateway removes the encryption before forwarding the data to the Internet. We need to apply encryption at higher protocol levels to protect traffic as it crosses the Internet.

There is, however, a benefit to encrypting as many packet headers as possible: It defeats *traffic analysis*. Attackers rely on traffic analysis when the defenders use encryption that is too difficult to attack. Instead of focusing on message contents, the attackers focus on whatever other traffic properties are visible. Often the attackers can identify the traffic senders and recipients. This by itself may provide significant information. In practice, however, few defenders specifically try to defeat traffic analysis, except some in military and intelligence circles (see Section 17.4.3).

Traffic Filtering

Encryption works against traffic filtering. If the packet is encrypted, the filtering process can't possibly identify sensitive or malicious contents. Some sites that implement both encryption and traffic filtering have configured the filters to decrypt the data, apply the filters, and then forward the data if it passes inspection. This is difficult and poses serious key-management headaches.

Automatic Encryption

People can be very careless about using encryption. Although most employees strive to fulfill their responsibilities in both letter and spirit, encryption is a security measure that many don't understand. Forgetting encryption isn't a security lapse akin to an open door or window; we rarely see the problem. It is an invisible weakness, like a defective burglar alarm.

This makes it easy for people to forget encryption; it's a step that seems to simply slow things down. Communications seem faster, easier, and more reliable without encryption, so there is a strong inducement to omit it.

This is why many applications try to apply encryption automatically. Websites activate encryption automatically when needed to protect an e-commerce transaction. Some enterprise sites automatically encrypt data flowing to other enterprise sites. However, it's not always practical to enable automatic encryption, because it may interfere with other essential, though unencrypted, communications.

Internet Site Access

When the system applies encryption automatically, we don't have to worry about forgetting to encrypt important information. On the other hand, if the system always applies encryption and decryption, we can't communicate with hosts or users who aren't part of the same cryptonet or who don't share the same encryption mechanism. If we automatically encrypt all Internet traffic, we can't communicate with public Internet sites, which don't necessarily use encryption.

End-to-End Crypto

As explained earlier, end-to-end crypto places the security measures in the hands of the sender and recipient. We achieve greater certainty when the end users apply the security measures or validate them through their own direct actions.

Policies should call for end-to-end crypto when we send messages that require clear and reliable accountability. In an end-to-end system, the sender can apply a digital signature and also can apply encryption that only specific recipients can decrypt. This ensures that we clearly and reliably identify the message's author. It also ensures that only the authorized recipients may retrieve the message's contents.

End-to-end message authentication may provide nonrepudiation; that is, to provide strong evidence that a particular user did indeed write a particular message. It is hard for Eve to deny sending a message if it contains her digital signature. Nonrepudiation is one of the generic security services introduced in Section 1.4.2.

End-to-end crypto also is preferred when sending secret information to a small number of specific individuals. The message is less likely to leak if the intended recipients must specifically decrypt the message themselves. A message is more likely to leak if it is decrypted automatically by protocol software.

Keying

The fundamental challenge of any cryptosystem is to create and distribute the keys safely and reliably. In practice, end users hate to handle and manage keys. Passwords are keys, for most practical purposes, and people are notoriously bad at managing passwords. Successful systems put as little keying burden as possible on end users. Before we review different crypto implementations, we will review basic techniques for sharing crypto keys on a network.

14.2 Crypto Keys on a Network

Key management has always posed a challenge for communications networks. Military and intelligence organizations spent much of the 20th century trying out different strategies and discovering their strengths and weaknesses.

Key management comes down to two problems:

1. Ensure that the right people have the right crypto keys
2. Prevent the wrong people from uncovering any crypto keys

It is hard to keep these in balance. An example of this made headlines in late 2009. The Predator drones used by the U.S. military to remotely observe battlefield targets were being monitored by opposing militias. Anyone who could afford the inexpensive software could intercept and watch a drone's video feed. This allowed militias to monitor or evade U.S. military operations.

As the story unfolded, this turned out to be a practical tradeoff between security and usability. The drones had a wireless control channel through which an officer controlled the craft from another continent; that channel was heavily encrypted. The video channel, however, was used by numerous people in the U.S. military, including people in the area covered by the drone. If the video was encrypted, U.S. soldiers on the ground would have less access to it, making their difficult job even harder. There was no practical technique to make *encrypted* video easily available to soldiers on the ground. It was more practical to leave the video feed unprotected.

The Default Keying Risk

Another situation that occasionally crops up with crypto devices (or any devices with built-in secrets) is *default keying*. Some manufacturers install "default" settings for secret keys and passwords. This was especially common among Internet routers until the late 1990s, when attackers penetrated numerous Internet service providers by using the vendors' default passwords.

The problem with default keying should be obvious: *Anyone* who buys the same device has a copy of the same key, unless we change it. Thus, everyone who uses the default key is automatically sharing a cryptonet, whether intentional or not.

Careful vendors make it impossible to use a default key. For example, the device setup process on modern operating systems demand that the user choose an initial administrative password. Earlier systems had default passwords that rarely changed. For example, many minicomputers in the 1970s and 1980s had a built-in administrative account for vendor maintenance personnel: The user name was "FIELD" and the password was always "SERVICE." Site administrators had to explicitly change or remove the account. Otherwise, a knowledgable attacker would have easy entry to their system.

This problem resurfaced in 2010 with SCADA systems ("supervisory control and data acquisition"). These are computer-based devices that control factory equipment and power grids. Certain SCADA products were customarily distributed with default passwords. When security experts raised warnings about SCADA-based viruses and other malware, SCADA system developers had to admit that they were relying on default passwords to control certain large-scale systems.

Key Distribution Objectives

In practice, the two key management problems noted earlier lead to the following two objectives in every key management system:

1. Ensure that keys are changed periodically. This reduces the risk that a cryptanalyst will collect enough ciphertext to crack that particular key. It also reduces the damage caused if the key was leaked without discovering it.

2. Change keys when a key holder should no longer have that key. When we manage physical keys for door locks, we can verify that a key holder returns a physical key. On the other hand, it's easy to make a copy of an encryption key and still return the "original copy." Therefore, we can't tell if a crypto key user has surrendered all copies of that key. The only way to truly revoke their access to the cryptonet is to change the key.

The standard solution is to provide safe and effective techniques to rekey the crypto connections as needed without losing access to the encrypted data. This always has been a tricky problem.

Key Distribution Strategies

In a sense, key distribution is like network wiring; those who share a particular key can exchange data, those without the key are left out. Sharing a particular key is like being on a network bus connection; you can see everything and speak to everyone. However, instead of calling it a bus, we call it a net: a cryptonet. We organize cryptonets in different ways to achieve different results. Here are the basic strategies for managing keys:

- Single cryptonet. Use a single encryption key and distribute it to everyone in the community. This is also known as the *one big cryptonet* strategy. It is easy to establish but very, very hard to maintain.

- Groups of cryptonets. Identify subcommunities and distribute different keys to different subcommunities. Some designers arrange the groups into hierarchies or other structures.

- Pairwise key sharing. Every pair of endpoints gets a unique set of keys. If Bob is going to have an encrypted conversation with his suitemates, he needs a separate key to talk to each one.

- Key distribution center. Every endpoint gets a single secret key, and they use it to talk to a *key distribution center* (KDC). When Bob wants to talk to Alice, his computer contacts the KDC, which creates a unique key to use in his conversation with Alice. The KDC uses Alice's own key to ensure that she can retrieve a readable copy of the key it sent to Bob.

- Public key distribution. Anyone who needs to create authentic traffic or receive encrypted traffic produces a personal public/private key pair and publishes the public key in a certificate. The public key then is used to provide authenticity and secrecy.

Each of these techniques has its own benefits and shortcomings as they try to achieve the overall objectives of key management. Some are open to other security problems.

Key Distribution Techniques

In practice, there are four specific techniques used to implement these different strategies. They are:

1. Manual keying

2. Simple rekeying
3. Secret-key techniques: wrapping, distribution, hashing
4. Public-key techniques: Diffie-Hellman and RSA

All of these techniques have been tried in the past. Many are still widely used today. In practice, however, systems relying on the first two tend to be brittle and subject to failure. Safe and secure systems tend to use more sophisticated techniques.

As we look at these techniques, we will consider this example:

> Alice and Bob live in the same dorm, though on different floors. They are near enough so they can use a wireless LAN connection to talk between their computers. To keep others from listening in, they have been experimenting with key exchange techniques.

14.2.1 Manual Keying: A Building Block

In *manual keying*, we produce one encryption key for each cryptonet or communicating pair and distribute that key to the appropriate endpoints. For example, Alice constructs a hexadecimal crypto key to use with their wireless LAN conversations. She configures her wireless card to use that key. She also writes the key on a sticky note and gives it to Bob.

This is the simplest and most obvious way of distributing keys to encrypt communications. We can use this to implement one or many cryptonets or to deploy pairwise keys to pairs of endpoints. It is often a starting point for crypto keying.

However, this is very hard to do regularly and do safely. To meet our objective of changing keys regularly, we have to distribute keys almost continuously. The more we handle and distribute keys, the more likely the risk of losing or disclosing one.

If we are using cryptonets, we have to worry about getting the keys properly distributed *before* we shift to a new key. Occasionally, one or more endpoints won't get new keys in time.

The most instructive example of manual keying comes from the banking industry.

An Incident: In the late 1970s, a large bank deployed a digital network that used the new Data Encryption Standard to protect its traffic. Initial keys were distributed when the devices were first installed. After a few years, the bank decided to try replacing the original keys with new ones. To do this, they would have to generate and distribute 2000 copies of the new key.

They spent a year planning the rekeying process. The appropriate recipient was identified at each bank. Following older banking procedures, the new key would be sent by registered mail; the safest method available at the time. Each parcel would be acknowledged by the recipient and a signed receipt would be sent back by mail. This would all take place with plenty of time to allow an orderly transition of all sites at once, so that no one would fall off the network.

The result was a disaster. By the time the keys were sent, a number of the intended recipients had retired or changed jobs; their mail was ignored or discarded. Other branches received the keys but failed to send back the receipt. Internationally, the registered mail marking suggested valuable contents, so many parcels were stolen and never arrived at their branches. It took the bank over 2 years to finish the rekeying process.

Although the banker's story involved one big cryptonet, the same problems apply in other cases. If we use pairwise keying or relatively small cryptonets, we replace those keys one pair at a time or one cryptonet at a time. If we have one big cryptonet, we have no choice: We *must* replace all of the keys at once. If anyone has the old key when we shift to the new one, they won't be able to read the new traffic.

To some extent, every cryptosystem will require some type of manual keying. The moral of the story is to do it rarely and to make the most out of manually distributed keys.

14.2.2   Simple Rekeying

There is only one way to avoid rekeying manually: We rekey somehow using the key we already have. In a sense, we use the existing key to "bootstrap" a new key into operation. The simplest approach, called *self-rekeying*, transforms an existing key into a new one. Another approach uses the existing key to distribute a new one. Although both of these strategies yield a nominally different crypto key, both are vulnerable if attackers recover an older key.

These are *not* recommended as crypto building blocks!

SELF-REKEYING

In this technique, everyone on the cryptonet shares the same crypto key and a standard pseudorandom number generator. The PRNG may be based on a one-way hash or other one-way cipher. When it is time to change keys, someone sends an announcement to every endpoint on the cryptonet, then the endpoints all feed the crypto key into the PRNG. The output is used as the new crypto key. Figure 14.8 illustrates the process.

Because each replacement key eventually becomes an expiring key, we have a cycle: We take the output of a PRNG and feed it in as input. This cycle is similar to the weak key stream algorithm examined in Chapter 7 (Figure 7.11). It suffers from the same type of problem: If we recover an earlier part of this sequence, we can reproduce the rest of it.

This technique sacrifices forward secrecy, as discussed in Section 8.3.1. If attackers recover an older key, they can recover every message encrypted with that key *and* everything encrypted with any future key. All they need to do is feed the old key into the PRNG to get the subsequent key and repeat the cycle. Self-rekeying does not ensure forward secrecy.

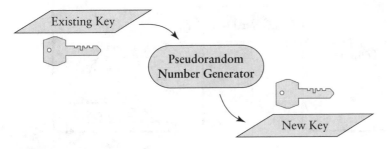

Figure 14.8

Bad idea: Self-rekeying.

The only way self-rekeying provides additional protection is if we also hide the PRNG from attackers. This violates Shannon's maxim, which says the enemy knows our system. However, older military systems occasionally have relied on such assumptions. Self-rekeying sometimes is called *key update* in military circles.

For example, Alice and Bob could agree that every other day they will feed the old crypto key into an MD5 hash and use the starting bytes of the output as their new crypto key. They can do all of this by hand if they share an MD5 program. Of course, if Henry (or someone else) figures out that they're using MD5 and he uncovers an earlier key, then he can read all their messages. Moreover, Henry then could use the key to masquerade as Bob to Alice or as Alice to Bob.

This technique fails when we look at it in the light of our two objectives. Although it does limit the amount of information encrypted with any single key, it provides no protection if attackers recover *any* of our older keys. Moreover, it's almost pointless to self-rekey when people leave the cryptonet. If the people kept copies of old keys, they can use the PRNG to generate all of the future keys.

New Keys Encrypted with Old

This technique is slightly more effective. Its security, however, relies on the ineptitude of one's attackers. It also shares the forward secrecy problem with self-rekeying. This is not a strong basis for security. Instead of using a PRNG, we produce a new, truly random key; then we encrypt the new key using the existing key and distribute it to the cryptonet (Figure 14.9).

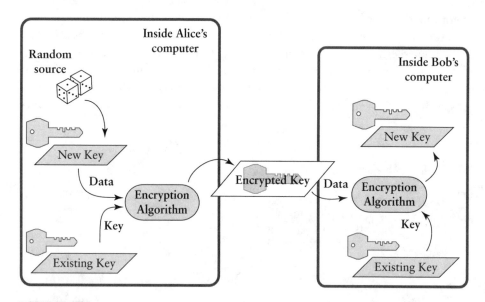

Figure 14.9

Another bad idea: A new key encrypted with an old one.

In this case, Alice generates a new key on her computer. She sends it to Bob over the encrypted wireless LAN, which uses their old crypto key. Bob receives the message. They both agree on a time to enter the new key into their wireless interfaces.

This approach poses more of a challenge to an attacker, especially one with limited resources. However, it's practical to attack this arrangement. If attackers intercept *all* traffic between Bob and Alice and keep the most recent traffic before the keys change, they can unravel each key change. Thus, if they've uncovered an earlier key, they can uncover the subsequent keys.

This is a lot more difficult to attack than self-rekeying. Still, there's no reason to choose a weak key distribution strategy. We might as well choose something without an obvious weakness.

14.2.3 Secret-Key Building Blocks

Banks encountered a great deal of trouble updating and distributing DES encryption keys in the late 1970s and early 1980s. The American Bankers Association promoted a standard for key distribution, which became ANSI X9.17. This standard described several techniques for distributing and validating DES keys. Although the techniques became obsolete, they provide a starting point for secret key management. We will examine the following techniques:

- Key wrapping
- Key distribution centers
- Shared secret hashing

Each of these provides a way to use an existing, shared key to establish a temporary key. Because we use the shared key sparingly and only to produce new working keys, attackers have a much harder time trying to crack it.

These techniques all serve as effective crypto building blocks. Although they do not resist all possible attacks individually, standard crypto protocols combine the building blocks in order to resist the principal attacks. We should strive to use standard crypto protocols whenever possible instead of designing our own.

KEY WRAPPING

Key wrapping uses a KEK to encrypt the key we distribute. We first encountered key wrapping in Section 8.2.2. When encrypting the contents of a file, we encrypt it with a content encrypting key (CEK). We then wrap the CEK with a key encrypting key (KEK) when sharing it. When encrypting network traffic, we use slightly different terms; we encrypt network traffic with a *traffic encrypting key* (TEK). We then wrap the TEK with a KEK when sharing it. Figure 14.10 illustrates the process.

Superficially, Figure 14.10 may look the same as Figure 14.9. The vital difference is that the earlier figure doesn't use a separate KEK. Instead, it uses the previous TEK to encrypt a new TEK. In practice, we must never use a TEK to encrypt another encryption

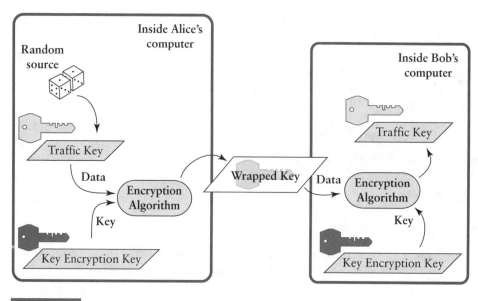

ANSI X9.17: Wrapping a new key for distribution.

key. We only use the KEK to encrypt another key. Although this does not yield "perfect" forward secrecy, it greatly improves security over the pervious techniques.

In a sense, X9.17 doesn't make key distribution significantly easier. If we decide to use the same KEK for many sites, then we face the problems of having one big cryptonet. If we assign a separate KEK to each pair of sites, then the number of distributed keys increases *exponentially* with each new recipient.

KEY DISTRIBUTION CENTER

The KDC eliminates the need to distribute pairwise KEKs to every pair of hosts that wants to communicate. Instead, each host receives a unique "KDC key." If the host needs to communicate with another host, the KDC provides it with two wrapped copies of the same traffic key: One wrapped with the sender's KDC key and the other wrapped with the recipient's KDC key (Figure 14.11).

We first encountered the KDC when discussing ticket-based authentication in Section 13.4.2. The "tickets" issued by a Kerberos authentication server contain the two wrapped keys described previously. Although we can use the shared keys to authenticate the two participants, we also can use them to protect data traffic.

For example, Bob wants to retrieve his email from the mail server, as in the earlier Figure 13.6. He contacts the KDC, which constructs a ticket, as shown in Figure 14.11. Bob forwards the ticket to the mail server, when he connects to it.

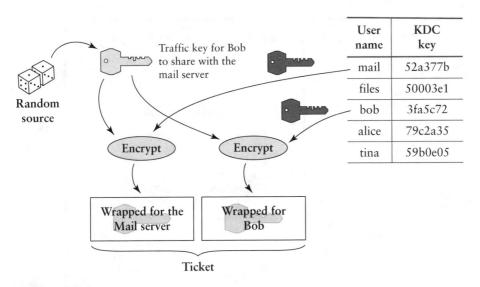

User name	KDC key
mail	52a377b
files	50003e1
bob	3fa5c72
alice	79c2a35
tina	59b0e05

Figure 14.11

Keys wrapped by a key distribution center.

To share the key with the mail server, Bob extracts his wrapped temporary key from
the ticket. He uses his personal KDC key to unwrap the temporary key. The mail server
extracts its own wrapped key from the ticket and uses its own KDC key to unwrap the
temporary key. Now that both have a copy of the temporary key, they can use it to
authenticate each other and to securely transfer email.

This technique is too simple to use by itself. For example, there is no way to detect a
replay attack. If attackers intercept Bob's earlier requests and manage to extract the
wrapped key, then they can intercept his new ticket request and replay the old one. Bob
then uses the previous (leaked) key when he talks to the mail server.

ANSI addressed some of these risks when it standardized a simple KDC for banking
applications in 1985. By then, researchers had moved forward to address other KDC
weaknesses. The Kerberos system was being developed in the mid-1980s, and it incorporated improvements to address the latest vulnerabilities found by researchers. Today,
the X9.17 KDCs are obsolete, but the Kerberos protocol still is being used in numerous
systems, including Microsoft Windows.

SHARED SECRET HASHING

If two sites share a secret, they can combine the shared secret with additional shared
entropy to establish traffic encryption keys. Modern 802.11 wireless systems use this
technique to convert a shared secret into the traffic keys that actually encrypt messages
between wireless hosts.

Figure 14.12 illustrates the process. First, each host generates a random nonce and
sends it to the other. Next, each host uses a one-way hash to combine the shared secret,

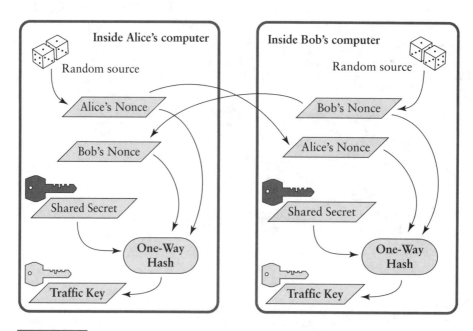

Hashing a shared secret to build a traffic key.

the nonces, and other connection-specific information. We use the hash result to construct our traffic key.

An interesting feature of this technique is that it never transmits a key over the network, whether encrypted or not. An eavesdropper may pick up some of the inputs to the key generation process, including the nonces and well-known connection data like MAC addresses. Without the shared secret, however, there is no way to construct the traffic keys.

Because both Bob and Alice use a new nonce value, there is no way to replay earlier key exchange messages. If an attacker masquerades as Bob, it does no good to replay Bob's earlier nonce. The resulting shared secret still will rely partly on Alice's new nonce value and yield a completely different shared secret.

In practice, two hosts may need two or more keys to carry on a secure conversation. When we need more bits than the one-way hash provides, we repeat the hash process to produce more bits. We retain the bits produced previously and also use them as input to the hash process to produce more output bits.

14.2.4 Public-Key Building Blocks

Section 8.3 introduced the classic public-key cryptographic techniques, Diffie-Hellman and RSA. Both provide ways to establish a shared secret between two endpoints. We can use those techniques to roll over a shared secret key.

Each public-key technique provides slightly different capabilities, benefits, and short-comings. Both are used in fundamental Internet security protocols. When used by them-selves, both of these techniques are vulnerable to "bucket brigade" attacks. In practice, we use these techniques as part of more sophisticated protocols that block or detect such attacks.

SECRET SHARING WITH DIFFIE–HELLMAN

As described in Section 8.3.1, two users can construct a shared secret by sharing Diffie-Hellman public keys. Each combines their own private key with the other's public key to yield the shared secret. Figure 14.13 illustrates the process.

When communicating across a network, we use Diffie-Hellman to construct an *anonymous* temporary shared secret. We do this by constructing a new Diffie-Hellman key pair each time we establish a network session. We don't use a public key out of a certificate, so we can't verify the public key's source.

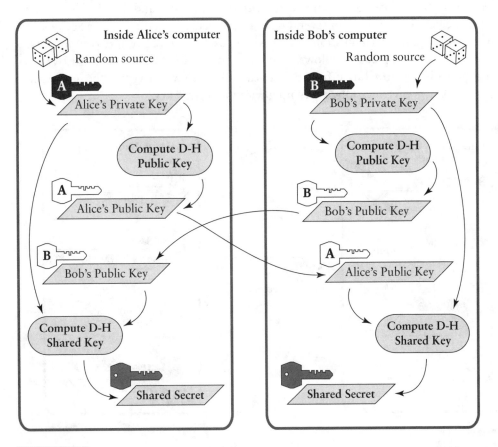

Network Encryption

Figure 14.13

Creating an anonymous Diffie-Hellman shared secret.

Alice generates a random number from which she creates a D-H private key. She then computes the corresponding public key and transmits it to Bob. Inside his own computer, Bob performs the same steps and sends Alice his own public key. They then both perform the D-H shared secret computation.

This produces an identical shared secret inside each computer. Eavesdroppers may intercept the public keys, but they can't construct the shared secret. The only efficient way to construct the secret is by using a public key and a private key.

Because this creates a new shared secret for each session, it provides perfect forward secrecy, as discussed in Section 8.3.1. If an attacker manages to recover the shared secret from a different session, it provides no information about the shared secrets used in other sessions. The Internet Key Exchange (IKE) protocol uses this technique (Section 14.4.3).

WRAPPING A SECRET WITH RSA

As described in Section 8.4.1, if Alice has Bob's RSA public key, Alice can use it to share a secret with Bob. Alice encrypts the secret with the public key and Bob decrypts it with the private key. This appears in several security protocols, including Secure Sockets Layer (SSL). Figure 14.14 illustrates the messages exchanged between two computers.

The process takes place as follows. Alice receives Bob's public key via a trustworthy route, possibly by extracting it from a certificate. Because we encrypted the data with the public key, we retrieve it by decrypting with the private key.

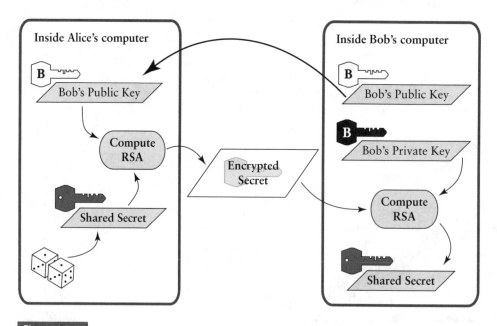

Figure 14.14

Wrapping a shared secret key with RSA.

Thus, *anyone* with Bob's public key can send him information that only he can decrypt. Early public key email mechanisms relied on this asymmetry. SSL also takes advantage of it; individual browsers don't need their own public keys, but they can all send secret information to secured servers.

If we need to authenticate Alice, then we need to take additional steps. On the other hand, we must authenticate Bob's public key before we use it. Otherwise, there is a risk of a bucket brigade attack.

14.2.5 Public-Key Versus Secret-Key Exchanges

Given these two different approaches to key distribution, how do we choose one over the other? In the 1990s, some experts assumed that public keys would replace secret keys everywhere, yet secret key techniques remain popular for many applications. Here we review the advantages of each approach over the other.

CHOOSING SECRET-KEY TECHNIQUES

Secret-key techniques have a longer history than public-key technology. Precomputer techniques were overwhelmingly based on shared secret keys. Public-key cryptography requires a lot of computational power, which brings up the first benefit of secret-key cryptography.

- **Computational resources are limited.**
  Secret-key algorithms require far fewer computing resources than public-key algorithms offering similar security. Secret keys are far smaller. Calculations are much simpler, both for encryption and for key generation. As we strive to fit more and more computing into smaller and smaller spaces, secret-key techniques will arrive in a new, tiny application first.

- **User community is clearly identified ahead of time.**
  Secret-key techniques rely exclusively on shared secrets to keep other things secret. It's not practical to distribute secrets to everyone in a constantly changing community. Therefore, we need to identify our user community and distribute keys to them *before* we can protect our communications.

- **Revocation must be timely and reliable.**
  Because we know who our users are and we know who has which keys, we can revoke a person's access reliably. For cryptonets, we distribute fresh keys to everyone, except to those being revoked. If we are using a key server, like a KDC, we revoke access by deleting those users' KDC keys.

- **Small-user community.**
  If we don't have trustworthy central servers to manage and distribute keys, then key distribution becomes a serious headache as the community grows. We achieve the highest level of security when we minimize the size of our cryptonets and

ideally only have two users in each one. With minimum-sized cryptonets, however, the number of keys grows exponentially as we add new users.

- **Trustworthy central servers are available.**
  If we trust our central servers, we can rely on them to distribute our keys. This makes it easier to manage a large community using secret keys. For example, Microsoft uses the KDC-based Kerberos technology to handle authentication and key distribution within its enterprise LAN products.

CHOOSING PUBLIC-KEY TECHNIQUES

Here are benefits of public-key techniques for key management.

- **User community membership is unpredictable.**
  If we can't identify our user community beforehand, public-key cryptography provides us with ways to "bootstrap" keying material to the new users.

- **Large community *and* untrustworthy server computers.**
  Secret-key techniques become difficult as the user community grows in size, unless we can trust our server systems. Strictly speaking, *any* server can be penetrated by an adequately motivated attacker. If the crypto protects truly critical information, then it might be safer to use public-key cryptography.

- **Inefficient revocation is an acceptable risk.**
  Public-key cryptography is most effective when we can distribute public keys broadly to all potential users. If, however, we need to revoke a public key, we can't guarantee that everyone will hear that the key has been revoked. There are techniques, like revocation lists and online certificate validation services, that reduce the risk of accepting a revoked key. However, such services rob us of a major public-key benefit: the ability to validate and use a key off-line.

14.3 Crypto Atop the Protocol Stack

We achieve very important benefits if we apply cryptography at the very top of the application layer or even above the network protocol stack. It is much easier to develop software as an application instead of making changes to OS or networking software (Figure 14.15). This also provides the benefits of end-to-end crypto.

An important feature of encrypting above the stack is *network transparency*: The encryption doesn't interfere with the network's ability to carry the application's traffic. Figure 14.7 shows this clearly: The packet headers are almost entirely in plaintext, though the data is in ciphertext. This allows the encrypted packets to be treated like any other Internet packets. The routing headers remain comprehensible to the routers, and the TCP headers still allow reliable, orderly delivery.

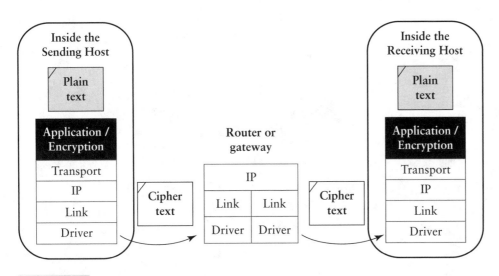

Figure 14.15

Application layer encryption in transit.

PRIVACY-ENHANCED MAIL

Proposals for email encryption arose in the 1980s, often taking advantage of innovations in public-key cryptography. The prototype for end-to-end email encryption was the *Privacy Enhanced Mail* (PEM) protocol. Although PEM supported mail encryption with shared secret keys, its important contribution was to use RSA public keys to wrap the secret key that encrypts a message (Figure 14.16).

Although PEM served as the model for Internet email encryption, it was never widely used itself. The design posed challenges that discouraged its deployment. One problem was that PEM was designed around a single, centralized certification hierarchy. Every PEM email user had to have a public-key certificate issued by a PEM-approved certificate authority. Moreover, there were expenses both in issuing certificates and in licensing of RSA patent rights. RSA Data Security, the company holding the patent rights, offered to issue a certificate and license the patent to any PEM user in exchange for a $25 fee. This went counter to the prevailing customs of the Internet community at that time where most Internet software was free.

PRETTY GOOD PRIVACY

"Pretty Good Privacy" became a de facto standard for email encryption and, in fact, for desktop encryption in general. The original software was distributed free, including its source code. Instead of relying on a hierarchical certification authority, it used the "web of trust" to provide confidence in certificate authenticity. Both the web of trust and certification hierarchies were introduced in Section 8.6.2.

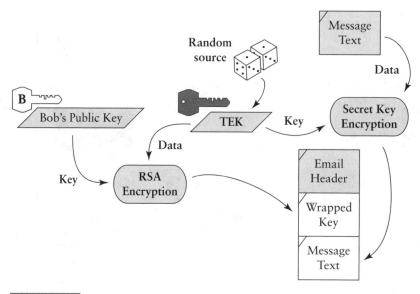

Figure 14.16

Encryption and key wrapping for email to Bob.

Aside from PGP, there are several commercial email products that also provide encryption. Lotus Notes, the desktop email and information management product, provides email encryption and integrity protection based on RSA. Notes was, in fact, the first product to license the RSA algorithm in the 1980s. Microsoft's Outlook Exchange email also can encrypt and sign messages.

S/MIME (*Secure Mulitpart Internet Message Extension*) is an extension to existing Internet email protocols that adds cryptographic protection. Both PGP and S/MIME provide open standards for email security. In addition to free and licensed products from the PGP Corporation, there are other products that implement PGP-style email, notably the Gnu Privacy Guard (GPG). S/MIME is supported by many mailers, including Mozilla's Thunderbird.

ADOPTION OF SECURE EMAIL AND APPLICATION SECURITY

Despite its widespread availability both for free and from vendors, the overwhelming majority of email users can't read encrypted email or verify signatures on messages they receive. Most people simply are resigned to the fact that they can't transmit critical messages via email. Aside from technical experts, few people take the trouble to install secure email software and assign themselves a public-key pair.

Organizations that transmit a number of sensitive messages (like health institutions subject to HIPAA regulations), use email with built-in cryptographic services. The enterprise's IT department handles software distribution and key management and many employees aren't aware of the security measures.

The most successful example of Internet encryption also appears at the application layer: SSL. Unlike email, SSL handles encryption keys automatically and rarely relies on users. Moreover, websites may themselves decide which connections require encryption. Because cryptography requires additional computing power, this lets the site managers optimize performance while providing security where needed.

14.3.1 Transport Layer Security—SSL and TLS

When we limit ourselves to secret-key cryptography, our secure network communications must rely on preshared secrets. We clearly need secure communications if we are to transact business over the Internet. The notorious Internet security incidents of the late 1980s highlighted the risks to Internet traffic. Because CERT started to track security incidents at that time, subsequent incidents simply underscored Internet risks. In 1994, a CERT advisory on password sniffing led the national television news programs to warn "everyone" to change their Internet passwords. Attackers had installed password sniffing software in major Internet service providers.

THE WORLD WIDE WEB

As the World Wide Web evolved in the early 1990s, many observers realized that it could implement an online form of shopping by catalog. At that time, countless companies flourished by printing and distributing product catalogs on paper and by accepting orders over the phone. This early form of "online shopping" firmly established the role of credit cards in ordering products electronically.

The challenge was, of course, to keep the credit cards from leaking to thieves. Although the general public might have let a news report on Internet security pass either unheard or misunderstood, those familiar with the Internet knew better than to risk sensitive data to potential sniffing. Safe and secure Internet shopping required confidentiality for the credit card numbers.

Originally, the World Wide Web was text oriented. The developer, Tim Berners-Lee, was a physicist who developed the technology as a way to publish technical papers and to provide built-in cross-references between related papers. Developers at the National Center for Supercomputer Applications at the University of Illinois realized that they could easily incorporate images into the text-only documents. Most of the changes were in the browser software that displayed the document on the client computer. Their browser, called Mosaic, appealed to nontechnical computer users.

NETSCAPE SOFTWARE

In 1994, Mosaic's developers joined a private company named Netscape Communications to develop a secure browser and web server. The Netscape Commerce Server provided companies with a way to sell products on the Internet and safely collect credit card numbers. The browser, called Netscape Navigator (Figure 14.17), used SSL to establish a secure connection across the Internet.

Figure 14.17

Netscape Navigator software.

Netscape provided the RSA patent holders with 1 percent of the company in exchange for the rights to use RSA in the browser. In 1995, Netscape first offered its stock for sale, and the small company's value quickly rose to over $200 million. Netscape set the stage for overnight stock market success by many Internet companies over the next several years.

SECURE SOCKETS LAYER/TRANSPORT LAYER SECURITY

Website security measures based on SSL and TLS are arguably the world's most widely used cryptographic mechanisms. SSL showed developers how to apply cryptography effectively without troubling end users with key management. As noted earlier, the creators of the SSL protocol no longer support it; today's version is maintained by the IETF under the name Transport Layer Security. However, we will keep with tradition and industry convention and refer to today's protocol as SSL.

Modern SSL supports several different cipher suites that allow selection of different public-key, one-way hash, and secret-key algorithms. Here, however, we focus on the protocols most often used in web applications.

The SSL protocol typically uses RSA to establish a secret shared between the client and server. Once SSL has established the shared secret, it uses a secret-key algorithm to protect the connection's data. Initially, SSL simply wrapped a shared key, much as is shown in Figure 14.14, however, this proved to be vulnerable to several attacks. The modern protocol consists of three parts:

1. Handshake protocol—establishes the shared secret and the keys to be used to protect SSL traffic.

2. Record protocol—transfers information using a symmetric cipher and integrity check.

3. Alert protocol—indicates errors and the end of a secure session.

SSL is designed to work atop a TCP connection; it applies security to an orderly stream of bytes moving between the client and server. However, once the handshake is complete, the client and server use the same shared secret to protect a whole series of TCP connections. This relationship is called an *SSL session*.

In the following sections, we will examine the SSL handshake protocol and the record protocol.

14.3.2 SSL Handshake Protocol

The modern SSL handshake protocol is a combination of shared secret hashing and an RSA-protected key exchange. The client and the server exchange randomly generated nonces, then the client uses the server's public key to transmit a randomly generated secret value. Each one then uses the exchanged data to generate a set of shared secret keys to use.

In Figure 14.18, Alice contacts "the Bank" to transfer some funds. To establish their SSL session, both Alice's client and the Bank's server generate and exchange nonces. Alice's computer then generates a random secret, which it encrypts with the bank's public key.

Once both hosts have received both nonces and the random secret, they each hash the data to construct secret keys to use. The actual process uses a string of predefined data that is combined with the exchanged variables (Figure 14.19). The hash is repeated several times to produce a large "key block" of random data. SSL subdivides the block into separate pieces of random data for every purpose the crypto functions require.

These include keys and data for the following six purposes:

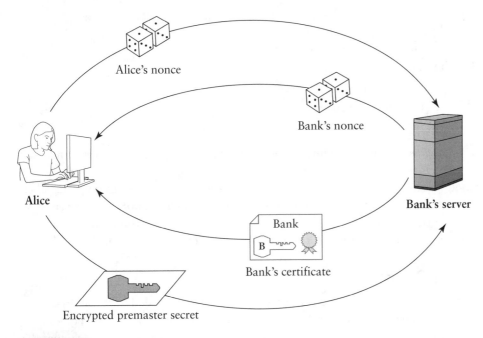

Figure 14.18

The SSL handshake protocol.

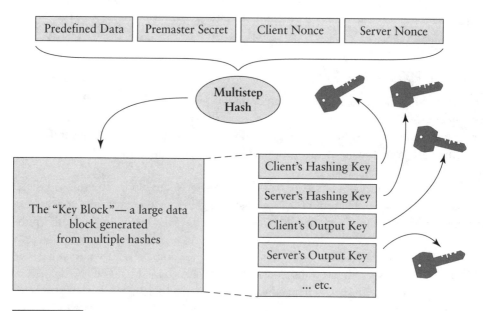

Constructing SSL keys through hashing.

1. Encrypt output from the client
2. Encrypt output from the server
3. Keyed hash of output from the client
4. Keyed hash of output from the server
5. IV for output from the client
6. IV for output from the server

When SSL was developed originally, the designers didn't appreciate the risk of reusing a stream cipher's key stream. They used the shared secret itself directly as the encryption key for traffic in both directions. When the developers realized the mistake, they decided it wasn't significantly more difficult to construct separate keys for encryption and integrity protection in each direction. Although it's not essential to use separate keys for protecting the integrity of a keyed hash, it is often the safest course to take.

14.3.3 SSL Record Transmission

All SSL packets follow a standard format, shown in Figure 14.20. The layout in the figure shows the arrangement for sending encrypted data protected by a block cipher. The first three fields appear in all SSL packets; the "content type" field indicates whether the packet carries data, an alert message, or is negotiating the encryption key.

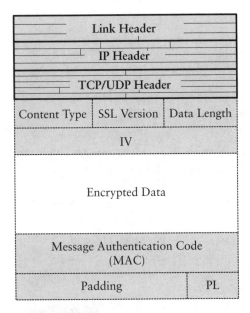

Link Header		
IP Header		
TCP/UDP Header		
Content Type	SSL Version	Data Length
IV		
Encrypted Data		
Message Authentication Code (MAC)		
Padding		PL

Figure 14.20

SSL data packet contents.

The crypto-specific fields provide the information needed to decrypt and verify the packet's data. The first crypto parameter, the IV, is of course used with a block cipher mode. The last parameters, "padding" and "PL," provide padding so that the encrypted data matches the block length. The "PL" field indicates the padding length.

Message Authentication Code

The "message authentication code" field contains the data we use to verify the message's authenticity and integrity. We calculate the code using the types of techniques introduced in Section 8.5.2. The calculation always relies on a shared secret; in this case, we use one of the secrets constructed from the key block.

The acronym "MAC" commonly is used to refer to message authentication codes, even though it clashes with the acronym for Ethernet addresses. To keep the two distinct, the acronym "MAC" by itself will refer to an authentication code, while we will refer to Ethernet addresses as "MAC addresses."

Modern security protocols, including SSL, often use an advanced form of MAC called the *hashed MAC* or HMAC. This code applies the hash twice. The first time the hash combines half of the bits in the key value with the data being protected. The second hash takes the result of the first one and hashes it with the other bits in the key value. Cryptographers have analyzed the function and found that it covers weaknesses that appear in some hash functions when used by themselves, making the MAC more effective.

Data Compression

In addition to encryption and MAC calculation, SSL also applies *compression* to the data. This is a systematic process that reduces the volume of data by taking advantage of redundancy in the plaintext. This reduces the amount of data encrypted and transmitted to make the overall operation more efficient.

APPLICATION TRANSPARENCY AND END-TO-END CRYPTO

SSL rarely achieves true application transparency because it usually is bundled with the client or server software. However, because the protocol fits almost exactly at the network API, it isn't hard to keep the protocol separated from the application. Some vendors even provide external hardware to perform much of the SSL processing before it arrives at the server.

However, SSL illustrates a problem with application transparency: The end user doesn't always know whether the traffic is really protected or not. With email, we can't read encrypted mail unless we take steps to decrypt it; some software won't display a signed email message unless the signature is verified.

There is a sharper separation between SSL cryptography and the applications that use it. Web browsers provide indicators, like a visible padlock or key, to show when cryptography protects a page. However, this proved tricky. The browser may need to open several connections to fill a single page, and some of the connections might not be encrypted. If that happens, should it display the padlock or not?

Modern browsers often display a warning when that happens (Figure 14.21). The figure shows a warning from the Firefox 3 browser. The warning indicates that while some of the page contents are cryptographically protected, other contents are *not* protected.

Figure 14.21

Browser warning about incomplete page encryption.

Also note the lower right-hand corner of the browser window: There is a very tiny padlock superimposed with an exclamation mark (!). The padlock indicates that SSL is being used, and the exclamation mark indicates that not all of the page's contents are cryptographically protected.

Even though email encryption applications may provide end-to-end crypto to users, SSL does not. In SSL, the cryptographic relationship is between a client and server *application*, not between end users. In email, the sender applies cryptography and the recipient removes and validates it.

14.4 Network Layer Cryptography

Network layer cryptography leaves enough of a packet in plaintext to allow routing through the Internet while still protecting the actual data as it travels between hosts. In the Internet community, the standard network layer protocol is IPsec, the IP Security Protocol.

Evolution of Network Layer Encryption IPsec is not the only network layer encryption protocol nor is it the first. The U.S. DOD commissioned a network-layer encryption system for the ARPANET, called the "private line interface." With the deployment of internet protocols, the NSA promoted a series of protocol standards, called the Secure Data Network System (SDNS), that included a protocol similar to IPsec called "Security Protocol 3" (SP3). However, that protocol was never widely used because it encountered deployment and interoperability problems. Moreover, the NSA initially discouraged distribution of the protocol specifications, making it hard to implement.

In the late 1980s, Internet developers produced the Point-to-Point Protocol, or PPP, for carrying IP traffic across serial lines, including dial-up modem connections. Microsoft and a group of other vendors adapted the protocol to use Internet connections as well as dial-up and to provide cryptographic protection of its contents. The new protocol, the Point-to-Point Tunneling Protocol, or PPTP, could connect Windows systems across the Internet and cryptographically protect the connection.

Unfortunately, PPTP contained several design errors, similar to those in early versions of SSL (for an example, return to Section 8.2). However, SSL was promptly revised to eliminate the weaknesses, while flawed versions of PPTP remained in place and supported for years. Products that supported PPTP eventually supported IPsec as a safer alternative.

IPsec was developed and standardized in the mid-1990s. Its development took advantage of lessons learned from the SDNS effort. The developers were familiar with the problems that arose in SSL and PPTP and did not repeat them in the IPsec design.

The principal application of IPsec is the virtual private network. A typical enterprise has a set of central services they provide exclusively to users on the company network. For security reasons they block access to these servers from the Internet. If the enterprise has two or more separate locations, the workers at those locations need to reach those central servers.

In pre-Internet days, larger enterprises might lease a point-to-point connection between headquarters and its other major offices. This gave the offices access to computing resources at headquarters. Leased lines were expensive, however. VPNs provided

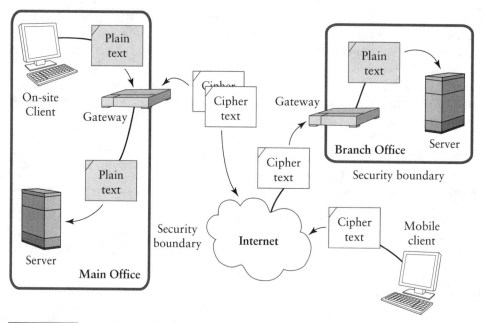

Figure 14.22 |

A small virtual private network.

a lower cost, Internet-based alternative to leased lines. The VPN provided a way to exchange encrypted packets between sites.

Figure 14.22 illustrates a small VPN arrangement. The example shows an enterprise with one main office and one branch office. When people inside one of the offices send messages to the other office, the packets pass through a gateway connected to the Internet. Outbound packets are encrypted and forwarded to the other office. Inbound encrypted packets from the Internet are decrypted and delivered on the office LAN.

The lower right-hand corner shows a mobile client, a device that may operate from one of many unpredictable locations. Many organizations also deploy VPN software on laptops and other mobile clients. This allows the client computer to connect to the enterprise LAN remotely and use its resources. The laptop encrypts the enterprise traffic itself. The enterprise gateway decrypts the laptop's encrypted packets the same as packets from the other gateway.

The encrypting gateways provide *proxy encryption* for the hosts on the enterprise networks. The encryption protects the host traffic, but the hosts themselves don't have to perform the encryption. This is shown in Figure 14.23.

Figure 14.23 shows packet handing in a network that uses an encrypting IPsec gateway. Traffic inside the network is in plaintext. When packets leave the site, they travel through the gateway. Packets destined for other VPN gateways are encrypted on the

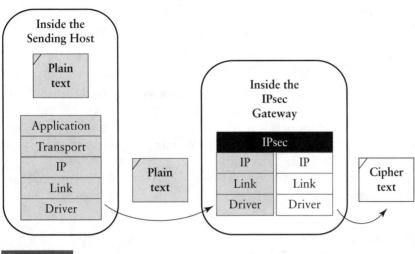

Figure 14.23

IPsec gateway encrypts a packet.

way out. Although the IP header remains in plaintext, the cryptography applies a keyed hash to protect the header from modification.

Because the endpoint hosts aren't doing their own encryption, the gateways don't provide end-to-end crypto. Moreover, the endpoints can't tell for certain if their traffic is being protected or not.

Figure 14.23 illustrates a benefit of moving the cryptography away from the application: We can easily off-load it onto other hardware. Some vendors offer SSL accelerator hardware for websites; no such products are offered for desktops. An IPsec gateway off-loads the cryptography from client and server alike. Not only are desktops relieved of the crypto processing overhead, but they are saved from key management headaches as well.

COMPONENTS OF IPSEC

IPsec itself focuses on data protection. Within IPsec, there are two generic types of protection:

1. Authentication using the Authentication Header (AH)
2. Encapsulation using the *Encapsulating Security Payload* (ESP)

The ESP provides encryption, authentication, or both. The AH provides authentication only; it was included in the standard at a time when encryption technology was more heavily restricted by national governments. Because most products use the ESP, we will discuss it in detail.

IPsec protection relies on shared secret keys. The IKE protocol negotiates the keys and updates them periodically. We will discuss this protocol later in this section.

14.4.1 The Encapsulating Security Payload

Although earlier figures, including Figure 14.5, illustrated a single, straightforward format for an IPsec packet, there are, in fact, several different formats. Even if we omit the AH, the ESP itself has different formats depending on what we need to achieve. There are different formats to handle different encryption and integrity protection techniques and to accommodate different cipher block sizes.

In addition to other ESP format variations, ESP provides two different "modes" for protecting the IP packet it carries:

1. Tunnel mode
2. Transport mode

We discuss each of these after we examine the ESP packet format.

ESP PACKET FORMAT

Figure 14.24 illustrates an ESP header tailored to use a block cipher mode and to provide integrity checking.

Like most packet formats, the ESP puts the control information at the beginning and the integrity check at the end (i.e., the checksum, CRC, or hash value). To allow for block ciphers that require a fixed number of data blocks, there is padding added to the end, too. The end of the packet also includes the "next header" field, which identifies the type of TCP/IP packet encrypted inside the payload data field.

IPsec packets always travel between a pair of hosts that have established a *security association* (SA) between themselves. This association is similar to an SSL session, except that it is between hosts and not between processes. The security association determines which keys, encryption algorithms, and integrity checking techniques the hosts will use. Each security association is established using IKE.

Here is a brief description of the individual packet fields:

- Security Parameter Index (SPI)—a numerical value that associates this packet with a particular SA established between the two hosts.
- Sequence Number—each encrypted packet carries a different sequence number; these are used to detect duplicate packets.
- Initialization Vector (IV)—used with many block cipher modes.
- Payload Data—the headers and data being encrypted.
- TFC Padding—random data appended to the message to improve *traffic flow confidentiality*. This makes traffic analysis more difficult.
- Padding Data—additional padding to ensure the encrypted data fills an integral number of encryption blocks.

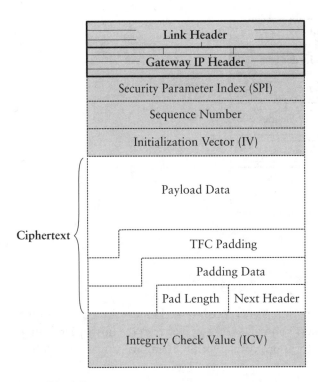

Link Header

Gateway IP Header

Security Parameter Index (SPI)

Sequence Number

Initialization Vector (IV)

Payload Data

Ciphertext {

TFC Padding

Padding Data

Pad Length | Next Header

Integrity Check Value (ICV)

Figure 14.24

IPsec ESP packet contents.

- Pad Length—the number of bytes of padding added to fill out a complete encryption block.
- Next Header—the numeric code for the protocol appearing in the first header in the encrypted payload.
- Integrity Check Value (ICV)—the result of the keyed hash or MAC calculation used to ensure integrity. The ICV covers all the fields shown here, plus most fields of the preceding IP packet header.

Tunnel Mode

In *tunnel mode*, we encrypt the entire IP packet, including the IP header; then we add an IP header to the encrypted packet and direct that packet to the encrypting gateway that will decrypt it. Figure 14.25 shows the resulting packet layout.

When an encrypted, tunnel mode packet arrives, the gateway processes it as follows:

- Discard the plaintext IP header.
- Decrypt the packet inside.
- Route the packet to the destination host based on its decrypted IP header.

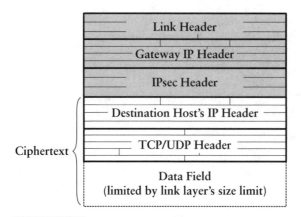

Figure 14.25

Packet layout in IPsec tunnel mode.

Because the packet's actual destination is encrypted, tunnel modes gives some protection against traffic analysis. Attackers still will see traffic between the hosts performing IPsec encryption. If those hosts perform proxy encryption, then this provides less information.

Transport Mode

Transport mode is what we might expect IPsec to do after looking at other encryption protocols: It adds its own header just past the IP header and encrypts everything following its header. Unlike tunnel mode, the process doesn't duplicate any headers, so it is relatively efficient at transporting data. Most implementations provide integrity protection for the IP header even though it isn't encrypted itself.

However, transport mode poses a challenge if the site uses network address translation. If we encrypt a packet before it reaches the NAT gateway, the translation will fail. The gateway may be able to correct the IP header, but it won't be able to correctly modify the encrypted TCP/UDP header. Moreover, the changes to the plaintext IP header will break the packet's integrity check. To use transport mode with NAT, we must apply the encryption after address translation takes place.

14.4.2 Implementing a VPN

Let us consider an example using a small manufacturing company called Amalgamated Widget. Amalgamated has a company headquarters office, a separate research center, and two factories. Each has its own network. Company headquarters has several corporate information servers. The servers are inaccessible except by Amalgamated employees on the company network. Amalgamated connects the individual networks together using an IPsec VPN.

Private IP Addressing

Because global IP addresses are scarce, many enterprises assign private IP addresses to hosts inside the enterprise network. If the enterprise has several separate sites, these sites need to coordinate their IP address management.

Internally, all Amalgamated IP host addresses are assigned from the "Net 10" private address space. The IT department also has arranged its subnets to make IP routing efficient. Each site has its own set of network addresses. Local hosts receive a "Net 10" address on the local network. Thus, every "Net 10" address is unique across Amalgamated.

IPsec Gateways

The gateway device to every Amalgamated network performs IPsec proxy encryption. When a packet with a local IP address is directed to a different Amalgamated site, the gateway uses tunnel mode encryption to encapsulate the packet; then the gateway addresses the IP packet to the other site's gateway. Upon arrival, the receiving gateway discards the packet header, decrypts the packet, and delivers it within the local site.

BUNDLING SECURITY ASSOCIATIONS

In a perfect world, we achieve all of our VPN security objectives with a single IPsec security association. In practice, we may face more complicated situations. For example, we may be operating within an enterprise that provides proxy encryption between sites. Thus, our intrasite enterprise traffic always carries IPsec encryption.

What happens if we use a special third-party product that incorporates IPsec as part of its own, essential security measures? Our traffic will be doubly encrypted as it traverses the Internet. This yields a "bundle" of security associations tied to the Internet packets.

When IPsec was first introduced, U.S. export controls drove product developers to provide completely separate support for integrity protection and for confidentiality. Typical IPsec packets carried two headers: an AH to protect integrity and an ESP to protect confidentiality. Too, there were bundled security associations to coordinate the cipher suites and keys for each set of headers.

14.4.3 Internet Key Exchange Protocol

The IKE protocol establishes the security associations (SAs) between a pair of hosts. The protocol identifies the cryptographic algorithms to use and negotiates keys to use. When keys expire on an active SA, the protocol automatically replaces the old keys with new ones. The IKE process begins with a Diffie-Hellman exchange. This establishes a set of shared secrets that then protect subsequent data exchanges (Figure 14.26).

In this example, Bob is working part-time for a bank and has been given permission to use its VPN connection to work remotely from his laptop. To use the VPN, the laptop first performs an IKE negotiation to establish the security association.

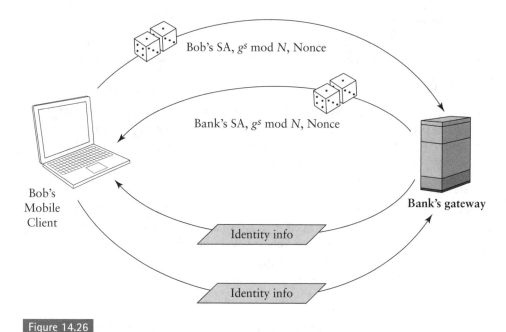

Bob's SA, g^s mod N, Nonce

Bank's SA, g^s mod N, Nonce

Bob's
Mobile
Client

Bank's gateway

Identity info

Identity info

Figure 14.26

Starting an IKE negotiation.

In the first step (shown at the top of Figure 14.26), the laptop assigns a number to its security association, generates a random Diffie-Hellman private key, calculates its public key, and chooses a random nonce. The laptop sends the security association ID number, the D-H public key, and the nonce to the bank's gateway. The bank's gateway responds with the same information, calculated on its side. Each host then derives the D-H shared secret and uses it with the nonce to create a key block, similar to the one in Figure 14.19. From this block, both hosts derive secret keys for protecting the remaining data exchanges. The next exchange is protected by one of the shared keys and provides authentication information for the other host to verify. These may be public-key credentials, a shared secret, or credentials calculated from one of these.

Once the hosts have authenticated each other, they have an IKE security association in place. To use IPsec, however, they must negotiate *another* SA; this one is a "child" SA for use with the IPsec traffic. The negotiation for the child SA establishes the keys to use, the crypto techniques to use, and the other properties of the IPsec association.

The IPsec hosts use IKE to rekey the SA. The hosts keep key expiration timers. When keys expire, a host may negotiate a new child SA to replace the expiring one. At worst, the hosts may repeat the entire IKE transaction, but this isn't really necessary.

14.5 Link Encryption on 802.11 Wireless

Link layer cryptography is perfectly transparent to our applications, but it does not protect our traffic once it leaves our network. The original wireless security measures were both cumbersome and unreliable. Many households and a surprising number of enterprises simply ignored wireless security at first.

> **An Incident:** In 2001, an information security expert was in a waiting room at a local hospital. He opened his laptop to pass the time and noticed that his wireless card had picked up a signal; it connected his laptop to the hospital's internal network. This seems less likely to occur today, given the demands of HIPAA compliance.

WIRELESS DEFENSES

The general objective of wireless defense was to implement a virtual boundary that includes authorized client computers and excludes other clients. Figure 14.27 illustrates this. The boundary includes authorized LAN users. It does not protect packets after they leave the LAN.

Initially, many wireless networks, like that hospital's, relied on Security Through Obscurity. Wireless was a new technology and not present on everyone's laptop. However, anyone with an early wireless card in their laptop could essentially "map" the local wireless LANs. Many programs, including NetStumbler, Cain, and variations of Kismet for Unix-based systems would scan and identify nearby wireless LANs.

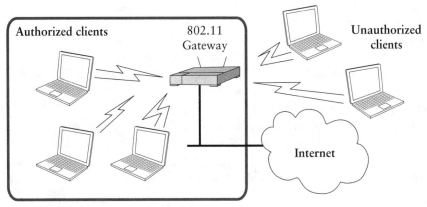

"Virtual" security boundary

Figure 14.27

Wireless LAN security boundary.

We identify wireless LANs by name and the name represents the **_station set identifier_** or SSID. By default, most wireless base stations broadcast a "beacon" message that identifies the LAN's SSID and describes the security measures it uses. This makes it very easy to find unprotected LANs. This type of scanning is called **_wardriving_**.

Base station vendors soon recognized the vulnerability and added a configuration setting to disable beacon broadcasts. LAN users who knew the SSID still could connect to the network. If the user knew the SSID, their laptop could send a "probe request" message to the network with that SSID. If the base station was active and in range, it responded with a "probe response," providing the same information as a "beacon" message.

Disabling the beacon message made wardriving more difficult, but it still allowed attackers to search for easy-to-guess SSIDs. Most vendors choose a well-known default SSID name. For example, Linksys products usually use "linksys" and Netgear products often use "netgear"; thus, disabling the beacon message isn't very effective unless the network has a hard-to-guess SSID.

Initially, many restricted wireless networks avoided using encryption. Instead, they relied on alternatives for access control. For example, some systems kept an inventory of acceptable MAC addresses and ignored packets from hosts with unregistered addresses. The traffic on such networks was completely unprotected otherwise; anyone could eavesdrop on anyone else's traffic. Moreover, an eavesdropper could listen to the traffic and make an inventory of MAC addresses. For example, Eve could make such a list and later reprogram her laptop to use an inactive MAC address. The base station would identify her as an authorized user.

WEP

The first commercial implementation of 802.11 wireless security was called "Wired Equivalent Privacy" (WEP). The name reflected the designer's intent: The security measures were supposed to provide comparable privacy to a wired connection. In fact, the implementation suffered from dramatic weaknesses, and many people found it much harder to configure WEP security than to connect wires.

Networks that used WEP often relied on shared secret keys. Commercial WEP devices could accept up to four separate keys containing either 10 hexadecimal characters (40 bits) or 26 hexadecimal characters (104 bits). WEP used the RC4 cipher and a custom-designed integrity check calculation. Section 9.2.2 reviewed the weaknesses of RC4; the most dramatic demonstrations of cracking RC4 involved rapid penetration of WEP encryption.

WEP also failed to provide a mechanism for temporary keys and rekeying. The shared secret key was combined in a simple way with other information to produce the traffic encryption key. If an attacker deduced the traffic key, he could deduce the shared secret. All keys on the LAN would then need to be changed.

WI-FI PROTECTED ACCESS: WPA AND WPA2

The Wi-Fi Alliance coordinated the replacement of WEP, leading to *Wi-Fi Protected Access*, or WPA. This new protocol included a mechanism to construct traffic keys from a shared secret. There was also an improved MAC to ensure integrity of wireless packets.

Originally, WPA used RC4 and a simple key update protocol. This choice was to provide a partial improvement over WEP that could use existing resources in the current generation of wireless products. It was soon followed by WPA2, which used AES for encryption.

14.5.1 Wireless Packet Protection

Figure 14.4 earlier provided an overview of wireless packet protection. The link header remains in plaintext, plus a cryptographic header. The IP header and all remaining packet contents are encrypted. Figure 14.28 shows the encryption packet format.

WPA2 uses AES encryption with the "counter and CBC MAC" (CCM) mode. This is a block cipher mode providing both encryption and integrity protection. The WPA2 header fields provide the information to implement the mode:

- Packet number—a 48-bit number constructed from the 2-byte and 4-byte fields. We increment it for each packet.

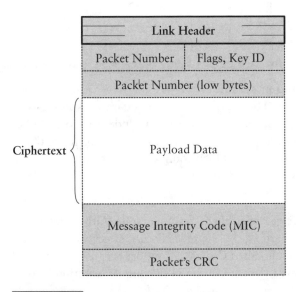

Figure 14.28

WPA2-encrypted packet contents.

- Flags—one flag is used to indicate the packet size
- Key ID—selects one of four preshared key values to use when generating a traffic key.
- Payload Data—the text carried by the packet.
- Message integrity code (MIC)—an integrity check value computed using CCM.
- Packet's CRC—the packet's CRC value computed over the actual data sent. This detects accidental damage to the packet's contents.

CCM uses the same encryption key to both encrypt and perform an integrity check on the message data. Many protocols avoid doing this because it has yielded vulnerabilities in the past. In this case, however, researchers developed arguments that some such modes operate securely. A mathematical proof shows that CCM is as secure as other modes that use one key to protect both confidentiality and integrity.

Encryption Processing

CCM encryption uses Counter mode (Section 9.3.1). The mode constructs a keystream by encrypting a block of counter data using the traffic key; then we encrypt the next block of data by using xor to combine it with the block of keystream. We increment the counter and repeat for the next block, until we have encrypted the packet's plaintext contents. We construct the counter from the following information:

- The 6-byte packet number included in the encryption header. We increment this number for each new packet we send.
- The priority field from the link header fields.
- The packet's source MAC address.
- A block count that we increment for each block of data we encrypt in this packet.

To ensure the security of our encryption, we must *never* use the same counter more than once with any particular traffic key. The counter's structure guarantees this. No two hosts will use the same counter values, because the counter includes the host's MAC address and those are unique. Each host keeps track of packet numbers to ensure that none are repeated for a given key. As long as the block count changes for each block of data encrypted, every encryption uses a different counter value.

Integrity Processing

The CCM integrity computation uses the cipher block chaining mode. Although CBC is vulnerable to certain attacks on its ciphertext, those attacks do not affect its use as an integrity checking procedure. This often is called CBC-MAC mode, because it produces a message authentication code. However, the convention in this implementation is to use the less-confusing acronym MIC for *message integrity check*.

The CCM integrity check is designed to cover all of the encrypted data plus an optional collection of other data that requires authenticity. In WPA2, the MIC verifies the packet's encrypted data plus its MAC addresses, frame control field, and a few other control fields, if present.

To calculate the CBC, we follow the process described in Section 9.3.3, except that we discard all ciphertext blocks except the final one. For each block, we xor the plaintext with the ciphertext of the previous block, and then encrypt the result. That ciphertext is then xor'ed with the next plaintext block. We retain the very last ciphertext result as the MIC value.

When calculating the MIC, we prefix the actual data stream with the packet's MAC addresses and frame control fields. When performing an integrity calculation, the CBC's IV does not have to vary from one packet to the next. In CCM, we use the constant value of 0 for the IV.

Decryption and Validation

The recipient uses the shared traffic encryption key to decrypt an incoming packet. First, the host constructs the counter from the source host's MAC address, the packet priority value, and the packet number in the WPA2 header. Then the host decrypts the packet data.

Once the data is in plaintext, the recipient verifies the MIC. The recipient reconstructs the plaintext data being checked, which includes addresses and other link header data along with the decrypted plaintext. The recipient performs the CBC calculation and checks the result with the MIC transmitted with the packet. The integrity check succeeds if the values match.

14.5.2 Security Associations

Like IPsec, 802.11 calls an ongoing session between two hosts a security association. The hosts are not necessarily user clients or server systems. Either of the hosts might be a wireless base station that connects to a wired network.

In WPA2, the hosts establish the association based on a traffic encrypting key, called the "pairwise transient key." The hosts establish this key in one of two ways. In most cases, both the client endpoints and wireless base stations already share a secret key, and they derive the transient key from the shared secret.

In some enterprises, the shared secret resides in an authentication server. When a user authenticates to a base station, the station contacts the server to produce a temporary shared secret. The client uses the same process as the authentication server to construct a matching temporary secret; then the client and base station produce the pairwise transient key. The authentication server also may tell the base station which SSIDs the client is allowed to use.

ESTABLISHING THE ASSOCIATION

For two hosts to communicate on a secured 802.11 network, they must perform four steps:

1. Locate each other. This involves the beacon or probe messages, which ensure that the two hosts can transmit to one another.

2. Authenticate. In many systems, the two hosts perform an "open" authentication that allows any two hosts to authenticate. This doesn't by itself establish the association, because the hosts haven't established encryption keys. Enterprise systems may perform indirect authentication at this point.

3. Associate. This establishes a relation between a mobile client and a base station. The association indicates that the two are able to exchange wireless traffic.

4. Establish keys. This step constructs a temporary shared secret key from which the hosts generate traffic keys.

In a modern, secured wireless LAN, the hosts must successfully complete all four steps to establish the security association. If the LAN hasn't enabled encryption, then the hosts only perform the first three steps.

ESTABLISHING THE KEYS

Modern wireless LANs often use a protocol called the "four-way handshake" to establish shared secret keys. The process assumes that the two hosts have established a pre-shared key. The technique uses hashed nonces, as described in Section 14.2.3. In Figure 14.29, Alice's mobile client establishes keys with a base station.

The base station begins the four-way handshake after Alice's client and base station perform the "association" step. The first message transmits a nonce and a replay count ("RC" in the figure). We use the replay count to keep things straight if one of the hosts gets lost and starts over.

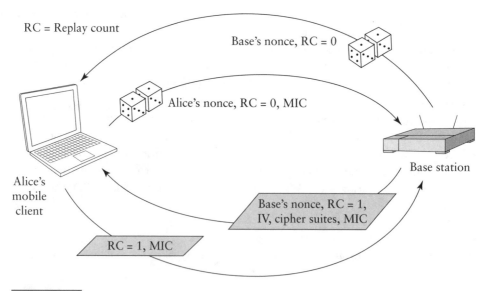

Figure 14.29

Wireless LAN performing a four-way handshake.

In the second step, Alice's client generates its own nonce. Given her nonce and the base station's nonce, her client now has enough data to generate the pairwise transient key. This key is similar to the key block used in SSL; we divide it into specific keys to use in the crypto protocols. The first key we generate and use is a "key confirmation key," which Alice uses to compute the MIC included in the message.

In the third step, the base station computes its own copy of the pairwise transient key. It then responds with a message containing an IV to use in block cipher modes and a list of cipher suites; it retransmits its nonce. The base calculates a MIC using the same key confirmation key, extracted from the transient key.

In the final step, Alice's client increments the replay count and sends the count back in its response, protected by the MIC. At this point, Alice's client has established the security association. Once the base station processes the fourth message correctly, it also establishes the security association.

In most cases, these transient keys remain in place until one host or the other shuts down. The protocol will renegotiate the temporary key only if the underlying master key expires. Preshared keys don't expire until they are replaced.

14.6 Encryption Policy Summary

We began the chapter with a review of network security risks, ending with an overview of policy issues. That list identified six issues, listed here. The remainder of this section reviews how our network cryptography techniques address these issues.

1. Protect selected network traffic from sniffing or eavesdropping.
2. Allow filtering and review of network contents. This is the exact opposite of preventing sniffing. If we allow sniffing, we also allow filtering content review.
3. Automate the encryption decision for users.
4. Permit or deny Internet access to users.
5. Provide end-to-end crypto.
6. Simplify key management.

The specific network crypto solutions examined include the following:

* Link layer encryption on a wireless LAN with WPA2. The security boundaries appear as shown in Figure 14.27.
* Network layer encryption with an IPsec gateway. The security boundaries appear as shown in Figure 14.22.
* Network layer encryption with IPsec on a laptop. The security boundary consists of the laptop's case, plus the site LANs inside any connected VPN.

- "Lower" application layer encryption with SSL. The security boundary includes the user's computer, the server's computer, and the application processes that handle plaintext, encryption, or decryption.
- "Upper" application layer encryption with PGP or S/MIME. It implements roughly the same security boundary as SSL.

The following sections summarize the recommendations in the tables. Each section explains the table's contents.

PREVENT SNIFFING

The different crypto solutions prevent sniffing and eavesdropping in accordance with their security boundaries. The general boundaries fall into three categories:

1. Outsiders—eavesdropping on our wireless LAN traffic from outside our security boundary
2. Other LAN users—eavesdropping by other people sharing our LAN
3. Other Internet users—eavesdroppers who manage to eavesdrop on general Internet traffic, possibly including packets of ours

Table 14.1 shows which techniques prevent sniffing in these different environments. While WPA2 protects all traffic on the wireless LAN, the other solutions only protect traffic that is specifically selected for encryption. PGP, for example, only protects emails that the user has encrypted. IPsec solutions tend to protect traffic according to a policy that applies crypto to specific destination addresses. Plaintext traffic remains unprotected.

TABLE 14.1 Crypto techniques to prevent sniffing

Prevent Sniffing by	WPA2	IPsec Gateway	IPsec Laptop	SSL	PGP S/MIME
Outsiders	YES	No	YES	YES	YES
Other LAN users	No	No	YES	YES	YES
Other Internet users	No	YES	YES	YES	YES

APPLY ENCRYPTION AUTOMATICALLY

Encryption does a terrible job of protecting information if we forget to use it. Some techniques apply crypto automatically and protect our traffic for part or all of its journey. Table 14.2 shows which techniques automatically can protect packets traveling in particular domains.

Encryption interferes with our ability to communicate. If we automatically encrypt everything in a domain, then we can't speak to anyone in that domain who does not

TABLE 14.2 Crypto techniques to automate encryption decisions					
Automatically Encrypt	WPA2	IPsec Gateway	IPsec Laptop	SSL	PGP S/MIME
All LAN traffic	YES	No	No	No	No
All Internet traffic	No	YES	YES	No	No
Selected Internet traffic	No	YES	YES	YES	No
Selected Internet applications	No	No	No	YES	YES
Only by user's request	No	No	No	YES	YES

share keys with us. Moreover, encryption adds to the computational overhead. Although we aren't always as desperate to optimize performance on a desktop or laptop, we want to optimize our servers' performance.

There are two reasons to selectively encrypt:

1. To communicate with hosts that don't encrypt.
2. To omit encryption when the security isn't necessary and the overhead impacts performance. Fortunately, this becomes less and less of an issue as computing performance improves.

ADDITIONAL ISSUES

Table 14.3 summarizes the remaining issues. The first two alternatives look at how different encryption techniques might affect access to public Internet sites. Some organizations, notably the U.S. military, actually rely on encryption to prevent computers on sensitive networks from accessing the Internet.

Many classified military networks connect across the Internet using IPsec and military-grade cryptographic systems. The only packets allowed to enter the classified network from the Internet are those that decrypt properly. All outbound traffic is

TABLE 14.3 Internet access, end-to-end, key handling					
Alternatives	WPA2	Ipsec Gateway	IPsec Laptop	SSL	PGP S/MIME
Allow use of Internet sites	YES	YES	YES	YES	YES
Block use of Internet sites	No	YES	No	No	No
Provide end-to-end crypto	No	No	No	No	YES
Minimize user key distribution	No	YES	No	YES	No

likewise encrypted, which prevents the packets from being processed anywhere except a gateway carrying the matching security association.

End-to-end crypto is, of course, the province of application layer crypto, particularly when the crypto interacts directly with the end user. SSL often is kept at arm's length from the actual user, which makes it less likely to provide end-to-end crypto.

We achieve minimal key distribution with IPsec gateways and with SSL. Most other crypto techniques involve the end user and/or the client machine in the key distribution process. IPsec gateways typically are managed by IT administrators; they provide their protections to user traffic with no user involvement at all. SSL also provides crypto without making the end users manage keying material.

14.7 Resources

 IMPORTANT TERMS INTRODUCED

active attack	link encryption	self-rekeying
application transparency	manual keying	SSL session
cipher suite	network transparency	traffic analysis
compression	one big cryptonet	transport mode
default keying	passive attack	tunnel mode
end-to-end crypto	proxy encryption	wardriving

ACRONYMS INTRODUCED

AH—Authentication Header

CCM—Counter with CBC-MAC

ESP—Encapsulating Security Payload

GPG—Gnu Privacy Guard

HMAC—Hashed message authentication code

ICV—Integrity check value

IPsec—IP Security Protocol

KDC—Key distribution center

MAC—Message authentication code

MIC—Message integrity check

PEM—Privacy-Enhanced Mail

PL—Padding length

PPP—Point-to-Point Protocol

RC—Replay count

S/MIME—Secure Multipart Internet Message Extension

SA—Security association

SDNS—Secure Data Network System
SP3—Security Protocol 3
SPI—Security parameter index
SSID—Station set identifier
SSL—Secure Sockets Layer
TEK—Traffic encrypting key
TFC—Traffic flow confidentiality
TLS—Transport Layer Security
VPN—Virtual private network
WEP—Wired Equivalent Privacy
WPA2—Wireless Protected Access, version 2

14.7.1 Review Questions

R1. Explain the difference between *passive* and *active* attacks on a network. Give an example of each.

R2. Which headers are left in plaintext when we use link encryption? Network encryption? Application encryption?

R3. How is end-to-end encryption different from other types of encryption? At what layer does it take place?

R4. Explain two techniques used for simple rekeying. Why do we avoid simple rekeying?

R5. Explain how key wrapping works on a network. Compare network-based key wrapping with file-based key wrapping.

R6. Describe how to create a shared key using shared secret hashing.

R7. Describe how Diffie-Hellman and RSA are used to share a secret on a network.

R8. Give three circumstances in which secret-key cryptography is a better choice for network encryption.

R9. Describe the SSL key negotiation in terms of the keying techniques introduced in Section 14.2.

R10. Explain how the different IPsec modes apply encryption either *above* or *below* the IP layer.

R11. Describe the IKE protocol in terms of the keying techniques introduced in Section 14.2.

R12. Describe WEP2 key negotiation in terms of the keying techniques introduced in Section 14.2.

R13. Why is key management hard to do when we provide end-to-end crypto?

14.7.2 Exercises

E1. Amalgamated Widget wants to protect the data link when employees visit the company website to work from home. Alice argues for using SSL and Tina argues for using IPsec.

a. List arguments Alice might use in favor of SSL.

b. List arguments Tina might use in favor of IPsec.

E2.   Describe a type of network encryption that you use personally. Explain how the key distribution takes place. Describe the types of information protected.

The next few problems ask about the networking topology portrayed in Figure 14.30. We have two eavesdroppers: Eve and Kevin.

The gateways provide cryptographic protection.

- Gateway A provides WPA2 crypto protection.
- Gateways B and C provide IPsec crypto protection for traffic between Site 1 and Site 2. They provide *no* crypto protection between other Internet destinations.

E3.   Host A sends a plaintext email to the server on Host C. Eve tries to eavesdrop on the following links. On which can she retrieve the plaintext message?

a. Between Host A and Gateway A
b. Between Gateway A and Gateway B
c. Somewhere on the Internet
d. Between Gateway C and Host C

E4.   Kevin has captured crypto keys and he will use them to decrypt an email sent between Host A and Host C and intercepted on the Internet. Which crypto keys will help him?

a. Keys for Gateway A
b. Keys for Gateway B
c. Keys for Gateway C

E5.   Host C provides SSL protection for "secure web" traffic. Kevin intercepts encrypted packets on the Internet from

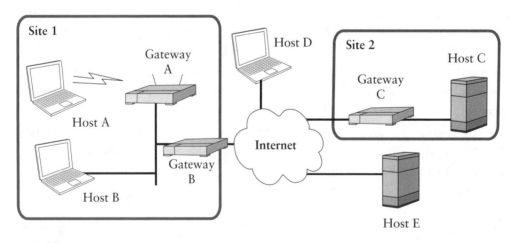

Figure 14.30

Network to use in exercises.

various hosts. Identify which protocol layers are encrypted in each case.

a. From Host A

b. From Host B

c. From Host D

E6. Host E also provides SSL protection for "secure web" traffic, and again, Kevin is intercepting encrypted packets on the Internet. Identify which protocol layers are encrypted in each case:

a. From Host A

b. From Host B

c. From Host D

E7. Redraw Figure 14.16 to show how Bob decrypts the email he receives.

E8. In Figure 14.16, Alice emails encrypted data to Bob. Alice wants to digitally sign the message, too. Draw a revised figure that includes the data and crypto building blocks to show how Alice digitally signs the message.

E9. Figure 14.16 illustrates a way of encrypting email destined to a single recipient. Determine how to encrypt the email so that it may be decrypted by either of *two* recipients. Use the same CEK but wrap it with each recipient's public key.

a. Redraw Figure 14.16 to encrypt the email for two recipients.

b. Draw a diagram showing how one recipient decrypts the email.

E10. Identify a wireless LAN that you use.

a. Describe its effectiveness in coverage and availability.

b. Describe security measures, if any.

c. Is it encrypted? If so, how are keys handled?

E11. Does your organization have a published wireless LAN policy? Review the policy and write a summary of its major points.

E12. Compare the problem of network encryption with hard drive encryption.

a. List aspects of hard drive encryption that make it harder to do than network encryption.

b. List aspects of network encryption that make it harder to do than hard drive encryption.

E13. Hands-on exercise: Pick a particular spot and note its location (street address, cross streets, or other distinctive identification of the location). Use a laptop or other device to identify wireless LANs in that area. Note whether the LANs use any security features like encryption and, if possible, which encryption they use.

E14. (Laptop admins only.) Use Wireshark to "sniff" packets on your wireless LAN. Are the packets encrypted? Which ones are and which ones aren't?

INTERNET SERVICES AND EMAIL

ABOUT THIS CHAPTER

In this chapter, we look at the deployment of Internet services by an enterprise. Email serves as an example of an enterprise capability. The chapter examines the following:

- Fundamentals of Internet service, notably email
- Email formatting and transmission
- Email security issues
- Enterprise firewalling and point of presence

15.1 Internet Services

When typical users think of Internet services, they think of commercial services provided through web pages. A few also may think of email. To provide Internet services, an enterprise connects itself to the Internet and provides hosts for the appropriate services. We discuss Internet connections in Section 15.5.

Network services rely on communications and communications rely on protocols. Our web browsers and email clients are clearly *application programs* and they use *application protocols* to provide their services. In Section 10.5.2, we saw that network applications reside at Layer 7 of the OSI protocol stack.

Not all Layer 7 protocols provide visible services. Both DNS and DHCP, which we encountered in Chapter 12, are Layer 7 protocols. Both usually work invisibly for less-sophisticated Internet users; most people only notice them if they fail.

TRADITIONAL INTERNET APPLICATIONS

Many traditional application protocols, including email and web access, do most of their work by exchanging files between hosts. Each web page is handled as a file when retrieved by a browser. Individual email messages are treated as files when being exchanged between hosts. The protocols exchange the files reliably by using TCP connections. If data is lost while traveling across the network, the hosts negotiate to retransmit the data. Although this occasionally introduces delays in a response, it generally provides acceptable service for traditional Internet applications.

Traditional applications generally follow the client/server model. We use email client software to retrieve or send email, and we use a web browser (client) to retrieve data from web servers. The clients initiate connections to servers and not vice versa.

As Internet services have expanded to provide streaming audio and video media, protocol designers have developed new techniques to provide effective network service. Streaming media do not work well with traditional Internet protocols. We examine this problem briefly in Section 15.5.3.

15.2 Internet Email

Internet email is perhaps the oldest of today's widely used internet applications. Network email sporting an "@" sign originated from Ray Tomlinson of BBN in 1971. Even though raw file transfers accounted for most ARPANET traffic during its history, email was the most familiar and useful ARPANET service to most users.

Although both the ARPANET and today's Internet are packet oriented, email is message oriented. The email system accepts and delivers each message as a single unit. If a message must traverse several email servers, the receiving server collects the entire message before sending it on to the next one.

Internet email standards fall into two categories:

1. *Formatting standards*. These describe the layout of an email message: what headers we use and how we format attachments.

2. *Protocol standards*. These describe how email clients and servers interact to either deliver mail or pick up mail. There is a single standard for email delivery but multiple standards for retrieving email.

The rest of this section will discuss formatting standards. The following section discusses protocol standards.

MESSAGE FORMATTING STANDARDS

Although there are dozens of standards that describe details of Internet email, most build upon other standards. Underlying all email formatting standards is one called "RFC 822," being the 822nd *Request for Comments* published by the ARPANET/ Internet community. Internet protocol standards begin as "Internet Drafts" and become "RFCs" when they are ready for serious consideration by the Internet technical community at large. The RFC becomes a standard after it is accepted by the Internet community.

RFC 822 was published in 1982, which illustrates how old Internet email systems are. Subsequent changes to email format have been extensions to RFC 822. A major extension is the *Multipart Internet Message Extensions* (MIME), which describe how to include email attachments in different formats.

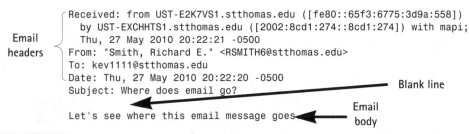

Email
headers

Blank line

Email
body

Figure 15.1

Elements of email format.

Figure 15.1 contains an email message sent from "rsmith6" to "kev1111." An email message consists of two parts: the headers and the body. The headers start at the beginning, of course, and continue until the first blank line appears. The message body follows: a single line of text in this case.

MESSAGE HEADERS

As with individual packets, the "real" data is at the end with increasingly technical headers attached to the beginning. When we first compose a message, we identify the recipient and subject, and we type in the body. Our email client constructs four standard headers:

1. From:
2. To: (also Cc: and Bcc:)
3. Date:
4. Subject:

Modern email clients often insert additional headers for technical reasons. Many include headers describing the format and character set used, so the recipient's email client can distinguish between "richly formatted" email and plain text in different languages. Many also include a "Message ID" so that every email message contains a unique identifier.

When we write an email, the client software constructs those initial headers. Our client software inserts the date and formats the email addresses of the recipients. It also adds the other formatting and identification headers.

The From: Header

The client software is responsible for constructing the "From" field to identify the email's author. Many people own several email addresses. For example, Kevin has five addresses. One address is for his school account. Another address is for his employer. A third belongs to a free email service he uses from a website.

The other two belong to the "eifsc.com" domain name he purchased: Both addresses go to a single mailbox provided by the ISP who handles his domain for him. When Kevin sends an email, his email client lets him choose which address should appear in the "From" field.

Many email clients have no way to validate the "From" field; thus, Kevin could choose any address he wants to appear in that field. For example, he could choose the address of the school's president or of the President of the United States (see Section 15.2.3). However, if anyone sent a reply to his forged From address, it would *not* go to Kevin's email.

The To: Header

We must provide a list of one or more email addresses to receive the message. These addresses may appear in any of three headers: the "To" field, the "Cc" field, or the "Bcc" field. The difference between the To and Cc field in an email is probably a matter of etiquette: Everyone in both lists receives the email. The Bcc field identifies other recipients but doesn't disclose those recipients to others who receive the same email. The client reformats the message to omit the Bcc names before submitting it to an email server for delivery.

Additional Headers

Originally, email clients displayed the entire email, headers and all, because the headers provided essential email details. As email has evolved, new headers have appeared. Many have to do with email formatting and others have to do with email delivery (see Section 15.2.2). The email client produces the formatting headers and email servers add the delivery headers.

Modern email clients don't usually display all email headers. Most clients extract the major headers listed above and display their information at the top of a message. The client hides the remaining headers, though most clients provide a way to examine them.

MIME FORMATTING

MIME formatting allows us to include non-ASCII text and files in email messages. Email messages originally were limited to 7-bit ASCII characters. MIME formatting transforms 8-bit data files into a 7-bit format that travels safely through email software. MIME supports graphically rich emails that include boldface text, italics, bulleted lists, international character sets, and graphics. Figure 15.2 shows a MIME email from Bob's boss.

We can't embed such text directly into an ASCII email. Moreover, we can't transmit 8-bit data files through plain ASCII email. If an email software component only supports 7-bit ASCII characters, it might change the 8th bit. Most application files, like spreadsheets or word processing documents, contain 8-bit data. MIME encoding allows us to send 8-bit application files and graphics by converting the data to a 7-bit ASCII format.

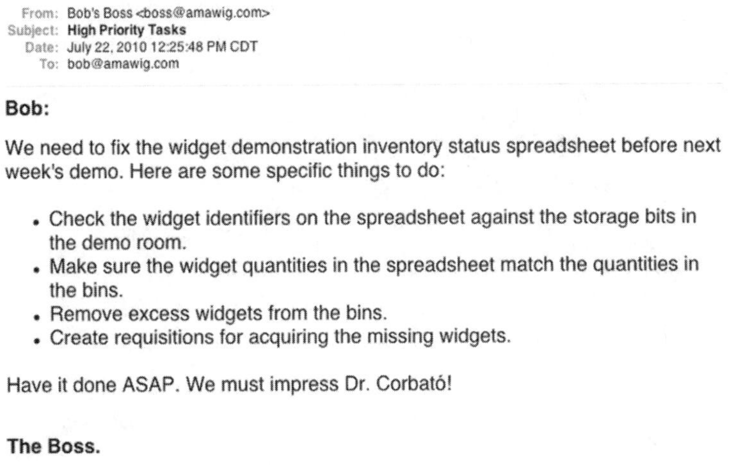

From: Bob's Boss <boss@amawig.com>
Subject: **High Priority Tasks**
Date: July 22, 2010 12:25:48 PM CDT
To: bob@amawig.com

Bob:

We need to fix the widget demonstration inventory status spreadsheet before next
week's demo. Here are some specific things to do:

- Check the widget identifiers on the spreadsheet against the storage bits in
  the demo room.
- Make sure the widget quantities in the spreadsheet match the quantities in
  the bins.
- Remove excess widgets from the bins.
- Create requisitions for acquiring the missing widgets.

Have it done ASAP. We must impress Dr. Corbató!

The Boss.

Figure 15.2

Email in a rich text format.

The email text shown in 15.2 uses a large typeface, a non-ASCII accent character,
bold face, and a bulleted list. Figure 15.3 shows the raw 7-bit ASCII text for this message. We have omitted Received headers and others that aren't relevant here.

The Content-Type header signals the presence of MIME parts. The header first
describes the type of MIME formatting being used. In this case, the message is a *multipart* message, indicating that it has two or more separate sections, each with its own
MIME formatting.

The header also defines a special string, the *boundary marker*, to mark the boundary
between different sections of the message. In this case, the text string starting with
"Apple-Mail" serves as the boundary marker. It divides the message body into two separate sections: the plain text section and the formatted text section.

The message's plain text section begins immediately after the first boundary marker.
The section begins with headers that describe the encoding and character set used in
that section. Following the headers, the section contains a "plain text" version of the
message. The email client constructs this as a convenience in case the recipient's email
client can't display the formatted message in the second section. However, even this
"plain text" is more than ASCII; it uses the ISO 8859-1 character set, which is essentially ASCII extended with common accented characters.

The second boundary marker indicates the start of the second section. Figure 15.3
only shows the beginning lines of that section. The format is "text/html," and "html"
refers to the formatting used on web pages. We describe this further in Section 16.1.

In some systems, the email client uses a web browser—or parts of it—to display html-
style email. This allows such emails to incorporate any formatting that a web page

MIME content type

MIME boundary marker

```
From: Bob's Boss <boss@amawig.com>
Content-Type: multipart/alternative; boundary=Apple-Mail-1-864637676
Subject: High Priority Tasks
Date: Thu, 22 Jul 2010 12:25:48 -0500
Message-Id: <89FB5625-9682-4FA8-9CE3-EC4E9E00255E@amawig.com>
To: bob@amawig.com
Mime-Version: 1.0 (Apple Message framework v1081)


--Apple-Mail-1-864637676
Content-Transfer-Encoding: quoted-printable
Content-Type: text/plain;
        charset=iso-8859-1

Bob:

We need to fix the widget demonstration inventory status spreadsheet =
before next week's demo. Here are some specific things to do:

Check the widget identifiers on the spreadsheet against the storage bits
in the demo room.
Make sure the widget quantities in the spreadsheet match the quantities =
in the bins.
Remove excess widgets from the bins.
Create requisitions for acquiring the missing widgets.

Have it done ASAP. We must impress Dr. Corbat=F3!

The Boss=


--Apple-Mail-1-864637676
Content-Transfer-Encoding: quoted-printable
Content-Type: text/html;
        charset=iso-8859-1

<html><head></head><body style=3D"word-wrap: break-word; =
-webkit-nbsp-mode: space; -webkit-line-break: after-white-space; =
"><b><font class=3D"Apple-style-span" size=3D"5"><span =
class=3D"Apple-style-span" style=3D"font-size: 18px; =
">Bob:</span></font></b><div><br></div><div><font =
class=3D"Apple-style-span" size=3D"5"><span class=3D"Apple-style-span" =
style=3D"font-size: 18px; ">We need to fix the widget demonstration =
inventory status spreadsheet before next week's demo. Here are some =
specific things to do:</span></font></div><div><font =
```

Plain text section

Formatted text section

Figure 15.3

Email text with MIME formatting.

might use. These include variations in type size, weight, and style, as well as special formats like bulleted lists, as we see in the previous figure. However, it also may retrieve and display images from websites and, in some cases, execute scripts or other programs. We discuss those issues further in Section 15.3.

15.2.1 Email Protocol Standards

There are two types of email protocols:

1. *Mailbox protocols*. These describe how email client software on a user's computer retrieves email from a personal mailbox stored on a server.
2. *Delivery protocols*. These describe how email client software takes a message and gives it to an email server for delivery and how servers exchange messages among themselves.

All of these protocols use TCP as the transport protocol. Each has specific port numbers assigned to servers. Most of these protocols initially evolved in the 1980s or early 1990s, and they trust the Internet backbone. Modern sites often provide these protocols with SSL protection. Users may protect the protocol with SSL crypto by connecting to the appropriate port number.

MAILBOX PROTOCOLS

Many email users retrieve their email by visiting their email service using a web browser. Others rely on email client software residing on their computer. Client software uses a *mailbox protocol* to retrieve the email. The protocol logs in to the server containing the user's mailbox. It then examines the mailbox and tells the user what messages are available. Some protocols automatically copy all messages to the user's client. Others leave the messages on the server until the user deletes them.

There are several well-known mailbox protocols, including the Post Office Protocol (POP3), and the Internet Message Access Protocol (IMAP). Other users rely on Microsoft's proprietary email protocol, the "Message API" or MAPI, to access its Exchange Server product. POP3 and IMAP are supported by most email client software, including Mozilla's Thunderbird, Qualcomm's Eudora, Apple Mail on OS-X, and Microsoft's email products.

POP3: An Example

Like all Internet protocols, we find the official description for POP3 in an RFC; this one is RFC 1939, "Post Office Protocol—Version 3." The POP3 protocol includes a strategy to incorporate new features and these are documented in a few later RFCs. However, RFC 1939 describes the fundamentals of POP3 operation.

POP3 is a text-oriented protocol that uses a single connection. The client opens the connection and the server replies with "+OK." The client sends commands and the server responds to each one. Some commands yield a single line response, like those for authenticating. Others yield multiple lines, like those that list available messages or retrieve messages. The server uses a special text marker to indicate the end of the message.

Here is a transcript of a simple POP3 exchange in which Bob's email client finds and retrieves a single email message. We have omitted the email text.

```
01: Server: +OK <8264.4824921587@p3plpop03-
                 07.prod.phx2.secureserver.net>
02: Client: USER bob@amawig.com
03: Server: +OK
04: Client: PASS alice
05: Server: +OK
06: Client: STAT
07: Server: +OK 1 1227
08: Client: UIDL
09: Server: +OK
10: Server: transmits the unique ID of the one and
                 only message
11: Client: LIST
12: Server: +OK
13: Server: transmits the details of the one message
14: Client: RETR 1
15: Server: +OK 1227 octets
16: Server: transmits the text of the first and
                 only message
17: Client: QUIT
18: Server: +OK
```

The client's first real action is to provide the user ID and password in Steps 2 and 4. This immediately indicates a vulnerability: If attackers sniff this connection, they can retrieve Bob's user ID and password. This is why most ISPs today allow users to protect POP3 connections with SSL.

The "STAT" command in Step 6 asks for the amount of mail in the mailbox. The "+OK" response in Step 7 includes the number of messages (1) and the size of the mailbox in bytes (1227). The next two commands, "UIDL" and "LIST," retrieve information about the message to construct the list of available messages.

The "RETR" message in Step 14 includes a message number as an argument and retrieves the single message (Steps 15 and 16). Once Bob's client has retrieved messages, it sends a QUIT command; then the client and server close the connection.

EMAIL DELIVERY

When we create an email message for delivery, we don't place it directly in the recipient's mailbox. Instead, we contact an email server, transmit the message to the server, and let the server deliver it. The email delivery protocol is called the *Simple Mail Transfer Protocol* (SMTP), and it has been the workhorse of Internet email since 1982. These SMTP servers, also called *message transfer agents* (MTAs), form the backbone of Internet email delivery.

The SMTP protocol is extremely simple. We open a connection to the SMTP server and send a series of simple text commands to identify the recipients of the email, then we transmit the email message and close the connection. The server takes responsibility for delivering the message to its recipients.

In simple cases, we connect directly to an MTA and that MTA places the email in the recipient's mailbox. This often happens when sending email between users in the same site. When email must travel across the Internet to a different site, it often passes through a series of MTAs. Section 15.2.2 provides a detailed example of this.

When two MTAs exchange email, they operate in a peer-to-peer relationship. Either MTA can initiate the connection and either can respond. SMTP is a client/server protocol; the MTAs use it as peers because either host can play the role of client or server.

PORT NUMBER SUMMARY

Table 15.1 lists TCP port numbers used by Internet email protocols. The numbers in boldface are listed in the Internet Assigned Numbers. The remaining numbers are part of proposed standards or reflect current customs.

When using POP3 or IMAP, the email client chooses crypto protection, or not, by choosing the appropriate port number. When using SMTP, some sites associate port 465 with SSL protection, though this port has already been assigned to a different protocol.

SMTP does not in fact require a separate port number to support SSL. Recent SMTP servers incorporate a "STARTTLS" command that transforms a plaintext SMTP connection into an SSL-protected one.

15.2.2 Tracking an Email

Although SMTP may be simple by itself, modern email delivery is an elaborate process. Messages rarely flow directly from a client to a server and then directly into the recipient's mailbox. Most emails traverse several MTAs on its trip to its destination. We can track this process by looking at an email's header. For example, let's trace the route of the email in Figure 15.1. We reproduce the email below in Figure 15.4 and underline all headers. The figure also numbers the Received headers in their order of creation.

TABLE 15.1 Port numbers for email protocols

Mail Protocol	Port Number for Traditional Plaintext	Port Number for SSL Protection
SMTP	25, 587	25, 465, 587
POP3	110	995
IMAP	143	993

```
#4  Received: from unknown (HELO MMS01.secureserver.net) ([10.6.12.15])
        (envelope-sender <RSMITH6@stthomas.edu>) by MMS02.secureserver.net
        (qmail-1.03) with SMTP for <kev@eifsc.com>; 28 May 2010 01:22:28 -0000
    X-IronPort-Anti-Spam-Result: Ap4CAKa2/uMOQPqmWdsb2JhbIxUgcRHAa3HYhfh
#3  Received: from USM02.stthomas.edu ([140.209.3.234])
        by MMS01.secureserver.net with ESMTP; 27 May 2010 18:22:28 -0700
#2  Received: from USM01.stthomas.edu (Not Verified[140.209.3.48])
        by USM02.stthomas.edu with MailMarshal (v6,8,2,9371)
        id <B4bff1ad30001>; Thu, 27 May 2010 20:22:27 -0500
#1  Received: from UC123.stthomas.edu ([fe80::65f3:6775:3d9a:558])
        by USM01.stthomas.edu ([2002:8cd1:274::8cd1:274]) with mapi;
        Thu, 27 May 2010 20:22:21 -0500
    From: "Smith, Richard E." <RSMITH6@stthomas.edu>
    To: kev@eifsc.com
    Date: Thu, 27 May 2010 20:22:20 -0500
    Subject: Where does email go?

    Let's see where this email message goes.
```

Figure 15.4

Tracking an email's journey.

As the email travels through the network, each MTA adds a "Received" header to the front of the message. When the MTA creates the header, it includes one or more of the following sections:

- "by" provides the MTA's identity—a domain name and/or IP address, and optionally, the MTA software package being used
- "with" identifies the mail protocol being used, and also may identify the MTA software
- "from" provides the sender's identity—a domain name and/or IP address and possibly a user name if authentication was used when submitting the email for delivery
- "id" provides a local identifier used by the MTA while processing this email message
- Ends with a timestamp

The series of Received headers tells the story of an email's travels in reverse. Figure 15.5 illustrates the trail of our example email as it traversed the four different MTAs.

#1: From UC123 to USM01

The trip begins with the last Received header, which appears right before the From field. The Received header is four lines long; additional lines begin with at least one blank. Here is what it says:

- Received from client UC123, using Microsoft's MAPI
- Arrived at server USM01, running Microsoft Exchange

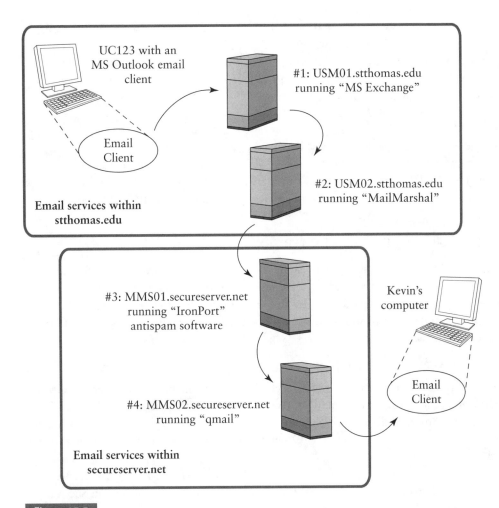

Figure 15.5

Following the email in Figure 15.4.

#2: From USM01 to USM02

Moving upward, the next Received header shows that the Exchange server USM01 uses SMTP to forward the email to USM02, an external email server:

- Received from USM01
- Received by USM02, running MailMarshal

The USM02 server runs a commercial package called MailMarshal that scans both incoming and outgoing email for spam, viruses, or other problems. Now the email leaves stthomas.edu in search of the email service for "eifsc.com," Kevin's personal domain.

We use DNS to look up the email host that serves a particular domain. Although most DNS records we examined in Section 12.3 indicate a general-purpose server at that address, DNS provides additional records to look up email servers. These are called *mail exchange* (MX) records. When USM02 looks up Kevin's domain, the answer directs it to server MMS01 at secureserver.net.

#3: From USM02 to MMS01

Now we move up to the next-to-first Received line. Here the MMS01 server at secure-server.net accepts the incoming email using "ESMTP." This is a generic identifier for "extended" SMTP service. Servers that support ESMTP recognize additional commands to improve email handling security and efficiency. To summarize, the field says:

- Received from USM02
- Received by MMS01 using ESMTP

MMS01 doesn't immediately deliver the message to its next destination. Before forwarding the email, the server applies a commercial antispam package, called "Iron-Port." The package adds its own header to the email; headers that start with an "X" are ignored by standard email software but may be used by specialized, experimental, or proprietary software.

#4: From MMS01 to MMS02

Server MMS02 produces the topmost Received line. It is the final SMTP server to process the email. MMS02 runs "qmail" software. Qmail is an open-source SMTP server that can both forward email and deliver it to local mailboxes. Qmail delivers the email to Kevin's "kev@eifsc.com" mailbox. When Kevin's client retrieves the email, it adds no headers of its own.

Each email may follow its own path and encounter different MTA software. We can track any email using DNS lookups to translate domain names, as shown in Section 12.3.2. We use whois lookups to track down domain owners or IP addresses, as shown in Section 12.3.4. We use web searches to identify MTA software packages.

15.2.3 Forging an Email Message

Figure 15.6 shows an email message received by a Microsoft Outlook email client. Examine the From header. Is it real?

We can't tell by simply looking at the From header. Although this may be an actual email written by the president of the United States, it may also be a forgery. If so, we might find evidence in the Received headers. If the first Received header isn't from the White House, the Executive Office of the President, or a related government entity, the message is a forgery.

The email in Figure 15.6 was displayed by Microsoft Outlook. Like many email clients packages, Outlook filters out the messy and complicated email headers and only displays information from the most familiar ones. Because it hides the Received headers,

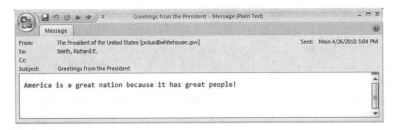

Figure 15.6

Is this really an email from the president of the United States?

we can't immediately judge the message's authenticity. Fortunately, the Outlook desktop client provides an option to retrieve the detailed headers.

Figure 15.7 contains the headers from the "presidential" email as retrieved from the Outlook client. Note that there are two additional headings in the original message: a Message ID and a Return Path, both specifying the White House as the email's source.

However, the forgery becomes obvious when we look at the earliest Received header. When we look up the IP address (circa 2010) we find that it belongs to an ISP in Minneapolis, Minnesota. That is a half a continent away from the White House in Washington, DC. Moreover, the header says that the email originated from the email account of "kev@eifsc.com." That is a surprising identity for the president to use.

We conclude that Kevin forged this email. To produce it, Kevin simply configured his email client to provide the president's email information as one of his "From" addresses.

```
Received: from USM01.stthomas.edu (140.209.3.233) by
 USM02.stthomas.edu (140.209.2.116) with Microsoft SMTP Server
 id 8.1.393.1; Sun, 25 Apr 2010 22:16:20 -0500
Received: from g2host.com (mailfront1.g2host.com[208.42.176.212]) by
 USM02.stthomas.edu with MailMarshal (v6,7,2,8378)id <B4bd505840001>;
 Sun, 25 Apr 2010 22:16:20 -0500
Received: from [98.240.143.111] (account kev@eifsc.com HELO [127.0.0.1])
 by mailfront1.g2host.com (CommuniGate Pro SMTP 5.1.16) with ESMTPSA
 id 150634282 for rsmith6@stthomas.edu; Sun, 25 Apr 2010 22:16:20 -0500
Message-ID: <80EEE093-4468-4020-93AC-ABD63ED4DEC0@whitehouse.gov>
From: The President of the United States <potus@whitehouse.gov>
To: Richard E. Smith <rsmith6@stthomas.edu>
Subject: Greetings from the President
Date: Sun, 25 Apr 2010 22:16:19 -0500
Return-Path: potus@whitehouse.gov
```

Figure 15.7

Headers from the "presidential" email.

He then could write an email and attribute it to the president simply by selecting that From address.

Even though we may identify many forgeries by examining the oldest Received header, we won't detect all forgeries. A more sophisticated attacker could create an even more plausible forgery. The attacker could construct the entire email, including one or more bogus Received headers. The forger could add a Received header that includes a White House source address.

We still might detect such a forgery by carefully analyzing each Received header. If one doesn't clearly refer to the previous one, then we've detected a forgery. However, different MTAs provide different amounts of detail in their Received headers. The forger might produce a believable fake by sending it via an MTA that doesn't clearly identify the source of incoming messages.

AUTHENTICATED EMAIL

The only reliable way to authenticate email is to apply a cryptographic technique to the message itself. The most common approach is for the author to digitally sign the email. Figure 15.8 shows an excerpt from an email that was digitally signed using PGP software. We introduced PGP and other email security protocols in Section 14.3.

The signed portion of the email is carefully marked with the "BEGIN PGP SIGNED MESSAGE" and ends with the signature itself in a special ASCII encoding. The process for signing email is the same one described earlier in Section 8.5. Note that any

From: ZZZZ Management" <management@ZZZZ.org>
Date: September 26, 2008 2:03:39 PM CDT
To: res@cryptosmith.com
Subject: Official: New Credential Announcement

-----BEGIN PGP SIGNED MESSAGE-----
Hash: SHA256

Dear Valued Member,

I am pleased to inform you that ZZZZ launched a brand-new certification program ....

Sincerely,

Executive Director ZZZZ

-----BEGIN PGP SIGNATURE-----
Version: PGP Universal 2.9.0 (Build 397)
Charset: us-ascii

wsBVAwUBSN0x2J/JsGz86uwqAQg4kQgAhoYc5clF7UODXR8MOpAy81x2JVgNDBxo
RXVKA+rjCcjWXdqYZAvRGBt0L4Z2Un65Ts2razE0FnF7pBFusUw4JXOkXLYgpICM
DS0tgnQLpFA+p4QtJnWUgn1xMwQAqM9EeKbsYyyqPZCUS3sycBmLUCuy8mx+nc87
dYgK06SC+lpjRad/k5XysZEd4GesXp+VTx8bey/wAIM8dWfpcC7IlwbWT660fhr0
wpYoa2GGHjVwrPQ+wpzmpJiJ5Spy0+CUgl2Vjgsqexmdrb1SnldtMyY2EZY3k3Ac
cOtSfzkotdT5vhGUuYg35dvdM6TDgHZ923U53mtR6VSdOz0JASLYMQ==
=ttSE
-----END PGP SIGNATURE-----

Figure 15.8

Excerpt from a signed email message.

reformatting of the email text will invalidate the signature. Email servers must be sure to preserve the exact contents of email they transfer or signature checks will fail even on legitimate messages.

PGP is a relatively old program; the simple format shown in Figure 15.8 is peculiar to PGP. There is also an Internet standard for secure email based on a MIME extension, called Secure MIME, or S/MIME, and there is also a MIME extension called "PGP MIME." Most modern email clients support these extensions either directly or though plug-in software. It can, however, be challenging to ensure that all—or most—email recipients have the right software to verify a digital signature.

Secure email poses another challenge because all recipients must have copies of the author's public-key certificate. Many authors simply include the certificate in the email along with the signature or they provide a web link to a site that contains the certificate. Then the recipients can validate the certificate and the signature.

Unfortunately, not all secure email users understand this shortcoming. The email in Figure 15.8 did not include a certificate nor did it provide any way of locating the certificate. Thus, most recipients had no way to validate the email.

15.3 Email Security Problems

The ease of email forgery is not, by itself, a security problem. Remember that typewriters allow anyone to type another person's name on a piece of paper. The problems arise when attackers exploit forgeries to defraud people or take advantage of open systems. In the world of email, there are four major security problems:

1. Connection-based attacks—incidents in which someone sniffs or intercepts another's email session. We can prevent this type of technical attack.
2. Spam—unsolicited email, often—but not always—of a commercial nature. Spam often is used to distribute classic financial frauds.
3. Phishing—email that tries to trick the reader into disclosing confidential identification data.
4. Email viruses—email that contains malicious software that spreads via email.

An unfortunate side effect of easy email forgery is that attackers can distribute emails that claim anyone as the author. Thus, it isn't unknown to receive spam or email viruses that claim to be from well-known and respected computer security experts.

CONNECTION-BASED ATTACKS

Because email protocols use TCP connections, they are vulnerable to attacks on those connections. Given a typical TCP connection, the attacker may sniff its contents, insert or modify data, or even hijack the connection completely.

Even if the account owner handles no sensitive data, the connection carries the login name and password. This gives the attacker the materials needed to hijack the account. No additional attack techniques are really necessary beyond that.

There are RFCs that describe challenge–response authentication techniques to use with email. For example, RFC 2195 suggests a technique to use with IMAP or POP3. Although challenge–response authentication would prevent password sniffing, it does not prevent an attacker from hijacking a connection after it has been authenticated. This is a more challenging attack, because it waits for the moment when the user logs in.

We defend against connection-based attacks by using SSL encryption. SSL prevents sniffing and connection hijacking. It also may prevent attacks in which a site masquerades as the email service in an attempt to capture login credentials, because SSL can authenticate the server. However, masquerade risks may remain if the client does not authenticate the server certificate correctly.

15.3.1 Spam

Unsolicited email, usually called *spam*, relies heavily on the absence of email authentication. Although many jurisdictions have laws in place against distributing spam, a certain community of vendors still rely on spam to generate business. There are organizations that sell prescription drugs without prescriptions or drug alternatives of questionable value or those that promote dubious investments that legitimate brokers won't touch. These vendors operate on questionable legal ground already. They want to attract customers while drawing as little legal attention as possible.

Spam is perfect for advertising such things. The "From" address on the spam email can be completely bogus. Contact information given to potential customers can change with every round of spam sent, making it hard for police or fraud investigators to follow.

CLASSIC FINANCIAL FRAUD

Spam also has become a popular medium for distributing classic financial frauds. Spam often carries investment offers that border on fraudulent; the technique is as old as investing, only the delivery medium makes it seem new.

The same is true for the *advance fee fraud*, typified today by the so-called "Nigerian scam." This scam begins with an email from a wealthy person in a third-world country who needs to transfer tens of millions of dollars to the victim's country. If the victim is willing to transfer the money into their personal bank account, they may keep a "service fee" of 10 percent or even 15 percent of the money. Unfortunately, the funds transfer process requires the payment of various fees and bribes, which the victim is asked to pay up front.

These payments represent the "advance fee." The scam simply seeks to collect a lot of fees allegedly needed to complete the transaction. The actual windfall doesn't really exist. The fraudster demands more and more up-front fee payments until the victim is wiped out or otherwise gives up on the transaction.

Another variant is an email announcing that the victim has won an overseas lottery contest. Again, an advance fee is required to release the lottery funds. In 1997, the U.S.

Secret Service reported that over $100 million had been lost to advance fee scams over the previous 15 months.

A similar fraud took place by mail in the early 1900s; people received letters from an alleged "Spanish prisoner," a wealthy man unjustly imprisoned in Spain. If the victim could forward the fees to support his release from prison, the alleged prisoner would pay a handsome reward. Again, the wealth never existed; the whole point was to collect fees as long as the victim was gullible enough to keep paying.

A clever version of the Spanish Prisoner has arisen recently; it exploits vulnerable email and social networking sites that keep a list of friends' emails. Here is an example:

> Bob received an email from his Uncle Joe. The email says that Joe is in London, and someone has stolen his wallet, luggage, and all of his money. He begs Bob to wire him some money in London so he can buy food and lodging while waiting for the embassy to sort things out.
>
> In fact, Bob's Uncle Joe is at home in Peoria. A fraudster managed to hack into Uncle Joe's email account. The fraudster then sent the email to every address in Uncle Joe's account, masquerading as Uncle Joe—and, unfortunately, Great Aunt Hilda wired money to London for him.

Just about every type of fraud appears in email. There are fraudulent investment offers, fraudulent vendors, fraudulent charities, and so on. No matter how well written the email, keep in mind that there is no way to confirm the email's authorship or accuracy by examining the email alone. A careful examination may detect a forgery, but the examination can't prove the email's authenticity.

EVOLUTION OF SPAM PREVENTION

From a networking perspective, spam is a flood of email directed at unsuspecting recipients. Email administrators at large sites say that the majority of email they process is spam. The better a site can filter out spam before it hits their users' mailboxes, the better the site performs overall. Network administrators often work diligently at eliminating spam.

In the early, precommercial days of the Internet, MTAs accepted connections from anyone. People could easily construct and submit bogus email via such connections. However, the problem was more of a nuisance than a risk. The Internet community valued openness over safety and assurance.

As the Internet became commercial, MTA operators noticed that their servers were spending more and more time processing spam. Moreover, users complained that an increasing proportion of email was spam. Initially, sites tried to control spam through the following strategies:

- Enforce MTA access restrictions. Distinguish between reputable hosts that don't generate spam and hosts that do generate spam. Only allow access by reputable hosts or by those belonging to the ISP's customers. If spam comes from one of the ISP's customers, block access and consider canceling the customer's service.

- Identify consistent patterns in the spam email so that it may be filtered out of legitimate email. Most filtering software marks every email matching a spam pattern, often with a special email header. Email client software uses the mark to sort spam into a separate "junk mail" folder or to delete it.

MTA Access Restriction

The original Internet email design assumed that MTAs were public utility devices available to any Internet user; to send email, the user simply connects to a favored or nearby MTA. Spam distributors took advantage of this in the early days of the Internet.

As the spam problem grew, ISPs established *acceptable use policies* that forbade spam delivery through their systems. Customers who violated the policy were denied email service. To enforce this, the ISPs modified their MTAs to only accept email from approved sources. Individual users had to log in to submit email. ISPs also blocked email connections from spam-friendly MTAs while accepting email from respectable MTAs.

In the mid-1990s, interested ISPs constructed lists of trustworthy and untrustworthy MTAs. These lists were stored in the domain name system. An MTA could retrieve a list by using DNS commands. Different teams manage different MTA lists. Each list reflects a different policy to identify either good ("white") or bad ("black") MTAs. This yields two sets of lists:

1. *Whitelists* identify reputable MTAs or those deemed reputable by the list's maintainer. MTAs would accept email only from hosts who were on the list.
2. *Blacklists* identified MTAs that carried spam. In some cases, the MTAs actually were part of an enterprise that generated or supported spam production. In other cases, the MTAs were unmanaged and easily exploited to transfer spam. Legitimate MTAs avoided accepting email from hosts who were on the list.

Today, spam relies heavily on botnets (see Section 3.2.4). Instead of sending a flood of email through a single MTA, the botnet sends several spam emails from each of its bots. The trickle from individual bots doesn't arouse suspicion, but the overall email flow from the botnet produces the desired quantity of email.

Filtering on Spam Patterns

This is another example of the pattern matching introduced in Section 2.4. When email spam volumes increased dramatically in the 1990s, the spam campaigns often sent the same email message repeatedly to people on a variety of lists. Clever administrators realized that they could eliminate such messages by looking for the repeated email subject lines or contents.

As spam became a more lucrative business, the spam authors adapted their campaigns to defeat simple filters. The email's subject and body would incorporate random data so that messages were superficially different. Antispam software developers fought back by developing more sophisticated filtering and detection techniques. As with other pattern matching systems, the matching falls into two general categories:

1. **Binary matches.** The filter either returns "Match" if the email contains specific text in a particular arrangement and "No Match" otherwise. The matching may

be very sophisticated and include "wild card" values or other context-sensitive tests. Ultimately, however, the filter returns either of the two answers.

2. **Statistical matches**. The filter calculates a likelihood that the email is spam. This often uses "Bayesian filtering," based on Bayes' theorem from the study of statistics. The filter examines individual words in the email and calculates the likelihood that the presence or absence of particular words indicates a spam email. Thus, the filter returns a numerical value.

Antispam developers soon learned that no single rule or technique worked in all cases. Recently, statistics suggest that four out of five emails are in fact spam. The problem is to identify spam emails yet not mistake a legitimate email as spam. This problem of *false positives* makes the detection process especially challenging. There is an ongoing struggle between spam authors and spam filter designers: As the filters get more sophisticated, the spam authors find new ways to trick them.

Modern systems, notably the open-source package SpamAssassin, improve detection by applying numerous filters to each email message. The result yields a *spam score* for that email: A higher positive number indicates spam, while a lower or negative number indicates a legitimate email.

Spam often is handled both at MTAs and at the recipient's email client. In some cases, MTAs have specific information about the format and contents of a particular spam campaign and may be able to safely identify and delete the spam emails. However, such specific information usually isn't available until after the emails have been received and processed.

It is dangerous to have an MTA automatically delete emails suspected of being spam, because the filtering and scoring process isn't 100 percent reliable. The filtering procedure occasionally produces a *false positive* in which it identifies a legitimate email as spam. Because of this, server-based spam detectors often limit themselves to marking likely spam. In some cases, the filter simply may insert the text "[SPAM]" at the beginning of the email's subject line. In other cases, the filter may add a special spam detection heading. For example, Figure 15.4 shows a spam calculation by the proprietary package IronPort.

Email clients may filter spam based on the user's personal experiences and also may take into account the results of MTA-based spam detection. In the first case, a user marks spam emails as spam and the client software applies its own Bayesian filter or other detection technique. This "trains" the client's filter to detect spam. In the second case, the client looks for indicators left by MTA-based spam filters. These may include "[SPAM]" markers or other headers provided by the filters. SpamAssassin, for example, inserts its own header that includes the spam score it calculated.

15.3.2 Phishing

For many people, warning messages from banks cause a lot of anxiety. A troubled bank account can start a cascade of financial troubles touching many other business relationships. The natural reaction is to fix matters as quickly as possible.

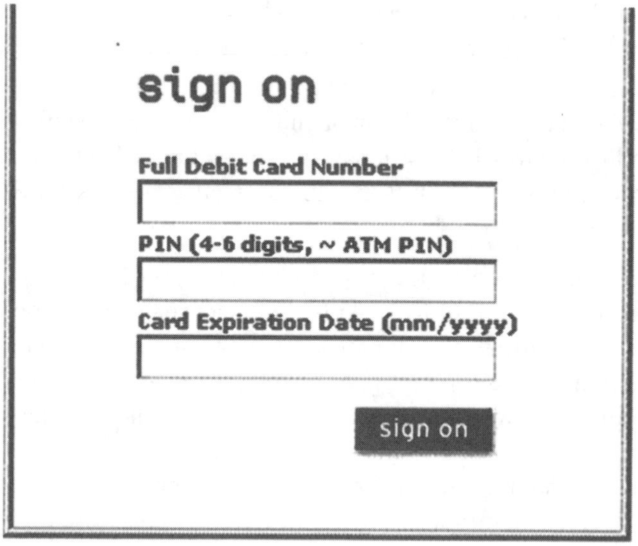

Figure 15.9

A window from an early phishing attack.

However, most people now know that an *email* warning from a bank may simply be a trick: a *phishing* attack. Figure 15.9 illustrates an example. The email link displayed this "sign-on" window atop a bank's actual website.

In fact, the sign-on window was hosted a half a world away from the bank's New York headquarters. The account, PIN, and expiration date were collected for later use in ATM fraud.

Phishing relies to some extent on spam; thousands or even millions of people receive the email. If only a hundred respond, the attack may net thousands of dollars from their bank accounts. In 2009, researchers identified over 150,000 separate phishing attacks. The majority that year were attributed to a single criminal group.

A variant of the phishing attack is the *drive-by download*, described earlier in Section 3.2.4. In this case, the victim simply clicks on a link that visits a website and the web page itself tries to attack the victim's computer. Such attacks succeed if the victim's computer contains a vulnerability that the web page can exploit. Web-based attacks often rely on "scripts" embedded in web pages; we discuss scripts in Section 16.3.1.

Tracking a Phishing Attack

Although attacks directly affect Internet users and their financial institutions, Internet vendors are closely involved in efforts to prevent phishing attacks. To understand these efforts, let us look at the resources used in phishing:

- **Spam email.** This is the medium for distributing the phishing attacks.

- **Website**. This is where the phisher hosts the web page that masquerades as the bank or other institution.
- **Domain name**. The email refers to the site through a domain name.

One way of tracking down those responsible for phishing attacks is to track the resources they use. Even though it's rarely worthwhile to trace spam that involves low-valued crimes, phishing can involve serious money. If the spammer leaves a trail when sending a phish, that trail may be worth following. To counter this risk, phishers must rely on spammers that are exceptionally hard to trace, like those that rely on botnets or other illegal techniques to transmit their spam.

Clearly, a phishing website must be under the control of some ISP somewhere in the world. If we track down the ISP, we should be able to track down the site's owner. In practice, however, many ISPs handle site rental purely online and will rent to anyone whose credit card transaction clears the bank. If the transaction uses a stolen but unreported credit card, the trail leads nowhere.

Like the website, the domain name must lead back to a domain registrar and a genuine individual or organization who registered the domain. Although this ought to provide a link to the phishers, it hasn't always worked that way in practice. There are gaps in the domain registration process, and phishers have found ways to deploy domain names while the actual registration process is incomplete. Thus, attempts to retrieve domain registration information for the phishing site doesn't yield usable whois information.

A typical phishing attack takes place over a matter of hours. The emails are sent, the victims fall for the ruse, account data is collected, and then everything is shut down. The websites disappear. The domains disappear. The data has been collected and moved for safekeeping. This leaves few clues for investigators to follow.

15.3.3 Email Viruses and Hoaxes

An *email virus* is a virus that spreads by email, usually through an attachment. The simplest approach was to attach an executable and to somehow trick the recipient into running it. Another approach was to embed the virus in a document; the virus would be activated when the document was opened. Many email viruses are implemented as macro viruses (Section 3.2.3).

Several early email viruses took advantage of the extensive capabilities of Microsoft's MAPI. Any program or Visual Basic macro could use the API to examine the user's email address book and send email. A virus could create a copy of the virus email and send it to recipients in the user's address book. The first significant virus of this type was named "Melissa" and appeared in early 1999.

In 2000, Bob's Aunt Carol was managing the IT department of a medium-sized company. She had heard about email viruses making the rounds. She was very careful not to click on anything suspicious. The Melissa and ILOVEYOU viruses were obvious and silly. She felt confident that she'd dodged that bullet.

In the cubicle next to her, the mail administrator was monitoring email traffic flow. The mail system was very busy and just keeping up with traffic. A hard drive failure left the server short on storage. If anything happened to slow down the system, mail might back up, fill the disks, and grind the server completely to a halt.

Carol turned to her email. She needed to hire another administrator and an email popped up with the subject "Resume." She opened the message and clicked on the attached Microsoft Word file without another thought.

She waited. Nothing was happening. Microsoft Word was running, but no resume appeared.

Then she heard a cry of anguish from the next cubicle as the email server crashed.

As email viruses evolved, they became more sophisticated on how they appealed to recipients. The "ILOVEYOU" virus masqueraded as a love letter. Many opened it out of curiosity, assuming it was sent to them by mistake. The "Resume" virus appealed to understaffed IT managers, like Aunt Carol. When opened, the virus sent emails to everyone in her lengthy contact list. Although email viruses did not always crash mail systems, they often put them under a great deal of strain.

Virus Execution

When the virus resides inside an email attachment, we infect ourselves if we double-click on the attachment and open it. Some email viruses are simply executable files with misleading names. For example, "Invoice.txt.exe" will appear on some systems as simply "Invoice.txt" if the system is configured to hide file suffixes. It's almost impossible to infect ourselves by opening a text file. If the system hides the real suffix, we might be tricked into running the virus code.

There are a few cases in which it's possible to infect our computer simply by reading an email. For example, early versions of Microsoft's MAPI allowed email messages to embed scripts that could perform virus infections. Emails using html format could include executable scripts. Many email clients block this risk by not implementing script languages or by implementing weakened versions of them.

EMAIL CHAIN LETTERS

A chain letter is a message whose sender asks each recipient to forward to others. Classic chain letters were scams that tried to collect money through a pyramid scheme. Chain emails often simply seek publicity or to produce trouble for a selected victim by producing excessive email traffic.

A common type of chain email claims to promote some charitable activity by generating lots of email traffic. These are almost always bogus; no well-known charity has ever intentionally promoted such an activity. In particular, numerous chain emails have claimed that each email sent will yield a donation for cancer research, or specifically, to the American Cancer Society. Here is a 1997 chain email that illustrates the hoax:

> LITTLE JESSICA MYDEK IS SEVEN YEARS OLD AND IS SUFFERING FROM AN ACUTE AND VERY RARE CASE OF CEREBRAL CARCINOMA. THIS CONDITION CAUSES SEVERE MALIGNANT BRAIN TUMORS AND IS A TERMINAL ILLNESS. THE DOCTORS HAVE GIVEN HER SIX MONTHS TO LIVE.
>
> AS PART OF HER DYING WISH, SHE WANTED TO START A CHAIN LETTER TO INFORM PEOPLE OF THIS CONDITION AND TO SEND PEOPLE THE MESSAGE TO LIVE LIFE TO THE FULLEST AND

ENJOY EVERY MOMENT, A CHANCE THAT SHE WILL NEVER HAVE. FURTHERMORE, THE AMERI-
CAN CANCER SOCIETY AND SEVERAL CORPORATE SPONSORS HAVE AGREED TO DONATE THREE
CENTS TOWARD CONTINUING CANCER RESEARCH FOR EVERY NEW PERSON THAT GETS FOR-
WARDED THIS MESSAGE. PLEASE GIVE JESSICA AND ALL CANCER VICTIMS A CHANCE.
    IF THERE ARE ANY QUESTIONS, SEND THEM TO THE AMERICAN CANCER SOCIETY AT
ACS@AOL.COM

The alleged fund-raising effort never existed. The American Cancer Society received
so many inquiries about this that they posted a web page disavowing it and similar
hoaxes that followed. These hoaxes can generate incredible amounts of email traffic and
yield no charitable results. Fortunately, the listed email address does not actually reach
the American Cancer Society.

Virus Hoax Chain Letters

A peculiar combination of chain letters and email viruses are the *virus hoaxes*. These are
chain letters that encourage recipients to forward a "virus warning" or other security-
related warning to everyone they know. An early form was called "Good Times," and
contained a message like this:

> Happy Chanukah everyone, and be careful out there. There is a virus on America Online being
> sent by E-Mail. If you get anything called "Good Times", DON'T read it or download it. It is a
> virus that will erase your hard drive. Forward this to all your friends. It may help them a lot.

The earliest reported outbreak of "Good Times" was in late 1994, but variants crop
up quite regularly, including one called "Olympic Torch" in 2006 and another called
"Free Money" in 2007. In 2010, a similar virus hoax involving a nonexistent "Christmas tree app" was distributed through social networking sites, notably Facebook.

If an email security warning recommends that it be forwarded to "everyone you
know," then it is a hoax. Legitimate warnings never are distributed through email
acquaintances. They arrive through news announcements or through direct emails from
legitimate system administrators. To forward such an email does no good and often
causes harm, if only by wasting time and resources. If everyone forwards the email, then
everyone receives numerous duplicates in their inbox. Meanwhile, the email service is
kept busy carrying unnecessary messages.

15.4 Enterprise Firewalls

The ARPANET began as a research network in 1969. Within a decade, it was so reliable
that many organizations used it for routine data traffic. The same happened to the Internet in the 1980s.

    Because it was originally a research network, many Internet sites focused on support-
ing and promoting research efforts. Many sites provided public access to some basic
resources and data files. Most sites provided services like "finger" (Section 2.3), email,
and access to shared files. Some sites even allowed outsiders to store files on their file
servers to simplify sharing with the site's own users.

At the same time, computers had become cheap and powerful enough to earn a place on the desktop of most technical professionals. These computers themselves were linked into an enterprise network. Desktops shared printers, central hard drive storage, and an email service. Most networks were local in that they did not connect to other networks or to the Internet.

If a site did connect to the Internet, it usually did so at a single point. The connection usually required an expensive leased line. Within the site, it connected to a host that routed packets and served as a gateway to the site. Originally, this gateway did nothing more than route traffic between the internal LAN and the external Internet.

Only a few sites made any attempt to filter Internet traffic arriving at their site. Most sites allowed packets to move freely between their hosts and the Internet. Moreover, the Internet was so small that no one worried about using up the 4 billion available IP addresses.

EVOLUTION OF INTERNET ACCESS POLICIES

By the late 1980s, the Internet was a very busy international network. There were thousands of private and commercial users as well as government and educational ones. This yielded a major shift in the assets visible on the Internet. Numerous incidents illustrated its vulnerability as well as its promise. For careful sites, this led to major shifts in Internet policy. The policy issues revolved around the following two questions:

1. How do our employees use the Internet to get their jobs done?
2. What services do we offer to Internet users that aid us in achieving our enterprise objectives?

Some organizations essentially unplugged themselves from the Internet, concluding that it served no business purpose. More often, a site might retain email service and block most other services, except perhaps to selected research and development groups. Other organizations took a more selective approach, allowing email and perhaps web surfing, and blocking less-essential activities like ping and the troublesome "finger" service.

As Internet services evolved, especially the World Wide Web, so did the problems and concerns of Internet-connected sites. The web provided access to vast quantities of important and useful information, but also provided a trove of entertainments and distractions. Some organizations tried to restrict or control the sites that users visited through various filtering and monitoring techniques (see Section 16.2.2). The evolution of spam and email viruses also encouraged enterprises to take extra steps in filtering Internet traffic.

A SIMPLE INTERNET ACCESS POLICY

Let us develop a simple policy for the Amalgamated Widget enterprise network. The enterprise has a website and it exchanges email with a few other Internet sites. In order to avoid spam, it only accepts email from its ISP and from the local university. Here is a list of risks Amalgamated in particular wants to avoid through its Internet connection:

1. Attacks on its internal file servers from hackers on the Internet
2. Commercial embarrassment by not having a company website

TABLE 15.2 A simple policy for managing an Internet connection

Policy Number	Policy Statement	Risks
1	Approved MTAs shall be able to deliver mail to enterprise MTAs.	3, 4
2	The marketing, purchasing, and R&D staffs shall have Internet browser access.	5
3	Internet hosts shall be able to visit the corporate external web server.	2
4	Internet hosts shall not be able to open connections to hosts inside the enterprise network.	1

3. Poor customer communication through lack of email

4. Poor email service due to spam

5. Ineffective marketing, purchasing, and R&D staff due to a lack of Internet browser access

These risks yield the Internet access policy shown in Table 15.2.

We implement this policy by controling Internet traffic as it enters and leaves the site. Because all traffic goes through the site gateway, the gateway must implement the controls.

15.4.1 Controlling Internet Traffic

Site policies often apply four different strategies for controlling Internet traffic to and from an enterprise network. A gateway may restrict or allow Internet traffic based on one or more of these strategies:

1. *Host control*—the sending or receiving host address

2. *Service control*—the TCP or UDP service as indicated by the port number

3. *Direction control*—whether the session was initiated inside the private network or from the Internet

4. *Content control*—whether the application data violates specific restrictions

The gateway applies these different controls at different layers of the protocol stack (Figure 15.10).

Host control restricts traffic according to the hosts involved. In theory, this could apply to host addresses in either the link or IP layers. Gateways usually rely on IP addresses and ignore link layer MAC addresses, because MAC addresses aren't retained in a routed packet.

Service control restricts traffic according to the service protocol being used, as indicated by the TCP or UDP port number. Direction control restricts traffic depending on

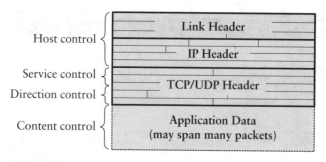

Figure 15.10

Traffic controls involve different packet headers.

whether it originated within the enterprise network or originated from the Internet. Content control restricts traffic based on an analysis of application layer data.

Some site policies use host control as a way to enforce user-based controls. Because most users access the Internet from a personal computer, user-based controls tie the user identity temporarily to a specific IP address. This requires a separate protocol to authenticate the host's user to the gateway.

Direction control is important because most site policies treat inbound connections very differently from outbound connections. We know that outbound connections are opened by hosts inside the enterprise network, so we can trust them to some degree. Inbound connections, on the other hand, may originate from an outsider with malicious intent. Although we might not trust insiders completely, we assume that insiders are less likely to have malicious intent.

Content controls are often used when enterprises need to stem perceived or actual abuses of Internet resources. The most common application is in antispam and email antivirus applications. The antispam software examines incoming email and applies various rules and profiles to detect spam. After detecting it, the software either deletes it or marks it so that recipients can easily filter it out. Antivirus software uses a similar technique by analyzing attachments that may contain viruses. If the attachment matches a possible virus, the software replaces the attachment with a benign substitute, assuming that the recipient did not request the virus email.

Some site policies restrict Internet browsing by users and rely on content control to monitor or enforce that policy. We discuss this further in Section 16.2.

15.4.2 Traffic-Filtering Mechanisms

Firewalls use three mechanisms to filter traffic. The following list presents them in order of increasing complexity.

1. Packet filtering
2. Session filtering
3. Application filtering

Packet filtering was used on the earliest Ethernet LANs in the 1970s, partly to distinguish a host's incoming traffic from the rest of the LAN activity. We filter packets one at a time. We look at the fields of each packet individually, and either accept or reject the packet based on its contents (Figure 15.11).

The firewall may enforce host control, service control, and some degree of content control using a packet filter. The IP header identifies source and destination hosts, and the port number identifies the service being performed. Many sites filter traffic to allow DNS, SMTP, and the *Hypertext Transfer Protocol* (HTTP) used for web traffic, and to reject most other services. Content control is limited to data that is visible in a single packet; packet filtering won't detect unauthorized content that spans multiple packets. Many firewalls ignore the link header because the header would have been replaced if the packet passed through a router.

SESSION FILTERING

In *session filtering*, we keep track of packets exchanged between pairs of sockets; that is, between a pair of hosts using a particular pair of port numbers (Figure 15.12). Some implementations perform "circuit filtering" in which the firewall creates a proxy TCP connection to carry the packets through the firewall. Circuit filters make the filtering decision when establishing the connection; if the filter accepts the connection, then all of its data will pass through the firewall. It is easy to filter on the connection's direction, because the firewall receives and processes the three-way handshake that opens the connection.

Other firewalls implement session filtering with a *stateful packet filter* that maintains connection and session state information instead of actually establishing a connection through the firewall. Stateful filtering bases its decisions on state information developed from previously received packets. The firewall uses this information to make filtering decisions on subsequent packets. In practice, a stateful filter behaves the same as a circuit filter when handling connections: It will allow traffic to flow if it allows the connection to open.

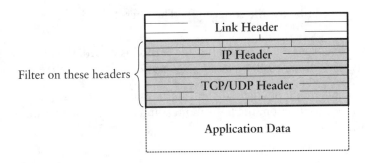

Filter on these headers {

Link Header

IP Header

TCP/UDP Header

Application Data

Figure 15.11

Packet filtering examines individual packet fields.

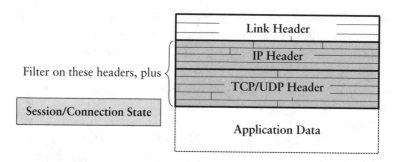

Figure 15.12

Session filtering keeps state across packets.

For example, we have a firewall that blocks incoming connections and only allows its clients to open outbound connections to Internet hosts. Here is how the stateful filter might handle a TCP connection:

- A packet from an internal host arrives at the firewall with its SYN flag set. The filter allows this connection, so it will forward all of its packets after examining them. The filter records the socket information (IP addresses and port numbers) and notes that the socket's session is opening.
- A packet arrives from the Internet for that socket with its SYN and ACK flags set. The filter notes that the session is almost open.
- A packet arrives from the internal host on that socket with its ACK flag set. The filter notes that the socket's session is fully open.
- When subsequent packets arrive in either direction for that session, the filter lets them pass.
- A packet arrives on that socket's session with the FIN flag set. The filter notes that the session is closing.
- More packets are exchanged to close the connection. The filter discards the session.
- If additional packets arrive from the Internet after the session is closed, the filter discards those packets. They do not belong to an open session.

A benefit of stateful filtering is that it handles UDP traffic as well as TCP traffic. Because UDP has no notion of a connection, the firewall must infer the session relationship based on the UDP traffic.

APPLICATION FILTERING

In *application filtering*, the gateway examines the data in application-layer elements when deciding to let data pass (Figure 15.13).

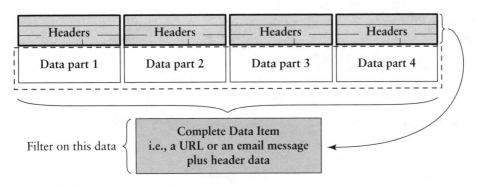

Application filtering applies to multiple packets.

The simplest form is the *application proxy*, a small firewall software component that applies relatively simple tests to smaller application data items. For example, a proxy can apply a blacklist to web URLs or to servers accessed via the file transfer protocol (FTP).

Proxies also provide an effective way to pass complicated protocols through the firewall; FTP, for example, negotiates the port numbers to use for its data connection. An FTP proxy allows the firewall to pass FTP service through while keeping unnecessary FTP ports disabled.

Firewall proxies can easily filter application data that fits into one or two packets. This approach does not allow filtering of arbitrarily large email messages that may contain arbitrarily large attachments. We perform such operations by redirecting the data to a special process that collects the entire message and analyzes it.

Firewalls often redirect all email to a special MTA that handles inbound email. The MTA applies spam and virus filtering software like SpamAssassin (Section 15.3.1) and Ironport (Figure 15.5). All incoming email arrives at the filtering MTA, which filters the email and then forwards it to another MTA for delivery inside the site.

15.4.3 Implementing Firewall Rules

We manage Internet traffic by establishing a list of rules the firewall should enforce. The rules block or allow particular hosts, users, or traffic from certain networks or to restrict connections in particular directions.

Different firewall devices and products use different rule sets, but all have more or less the same semantics. The rule sets are often limited to the firewall-filtering mechanisms just described. Although an antivirus or spam package may apply more complex or sophisticated matching, the firewall rules determine which traffic is directed to those packages for analysis.

Control Number	Type	Direction	Transport protocol	Source Socket		Destination Socket		Policy Number
				Host	Service	Host	Service	
1	Allow	In	All	*	*	dns.amawig.com	DNS	1, 2, 3

TABLE 15.3 Format of simple firewall rules

Table 15.3 shows a simple example of a firewall rule.
Each rule contains seven fields:

1. Control number: numbers the rules so that we may cross-reference them when analyzing our security.
2. Type of rule: either "Allow" or "Deny" to indicate whether the rule explicitly permits or blocks the traffic it describes.
3. Direction: either "In" for traffic inbound to the site from the Internet or "Out" for outboud traffic from the site to the Internet.
4. Transport protocol: either "TCP," "UDP," or "Any."
5. Source socket: identifies the host and service that produced the packet, each in its own column. Either field may match a range of numeric values separated by a hyphen ("-"), or all possible values if a "*" is given.
   - The host identifier may contain an IP address or a domain name.
   - The service appears either as a port number or as a protocol acronym.
6. Destination socket: identifies the host and service intended to receive the packet. Either field may match a range of numeric values separated by a hyphen ("-"), or all possible values if a "*" is given.
   - The host identifier may contain an IP address or a domain name.
   - The service appears either as a port number or as a protocol acronym.
7. Policy number: the number of the corresponding statement in our security policy.

These rules enforce host, service, and direction control. Although the rules aren't designed for a specific firewall brand or model, they assume that the firewall provides session control. The rules also assume that the firewall enforces Deny by Default.

EXAMPLE OF FIREWALL SECURITY CONTROLS

Our example is based on the Amalgamated Widget security policy shown in Table 15.2. The example makes certain assumptions about Amalgamated Widget's enterprise network. We assume that the network has been assigned a block of global Internet addresses in the range 30.40.*.*. In other words, the site may assign any Internet address whose upper half contains 30.40 and may use in the lower 16 bits for individual

TABLE 15.4 Firewall controls to enforce Amalgamated's Internet policy

Control Number	Type	Direction	Transport Protocol	Source Socket		Destination Socket		Policy Number
				Host	Service	Host	Service	
1	Allow	In	All	*	*	dns.amawig.com	DNS	1, 2, 3
2	Allow	Out	All	*	*	*	DNS	1, 2, 3
3	Allow	In	TCP	mail.myisp.net	*	mail.amawig.com	SMTP	1
4	Allow	In	TCP	mail.widget.edu	*	mail.amawig.com	SMTP	1
5	Allow	Out	TCP	mail.amawig.com	*	*	SMTP	1
6	Allow	Out	TCP	30.40.50.*	*	*	HTTP	2
7	Allow	Out	TCP	30.40.60.*	*	*	HTTP	2
8	Allow	Out	TCP	30.40.70.*	*	*	HTTP	2
9	Allow	In	TCP	*	*	www.amawig.com	HTTP	3

host addresses. This allows Amalgamated to assign a global Internet address to every one of its hosts. It does not have to use NAT and private addresses. The firewall security controls in Table 15.4 enforce the Amalgamated policy.

When a packet arrives, the firewall applies the rules in order. If the packet, or its connection, matches one of the rules, the firewall applies the rule. If the rule allows the traffic, the firewall delivers the packet. If the rule denies the traffic, the firewall discards the packet.

This particular firewall implements Deny by Default and then applies the rules in the table. If the firewall does not implement Deny by Default and our policy requires Deny by Default, then the final firewall rule should deny any remaining connections.

Rules 1 and 2 allow DNS packets to enter and leave the site. Standard Internet protocols won't work without DNS. The first rule allows Internet sites to visit the amawig DNS server. The second rule allows any host on the enterprise network to visit any DNS server on the Internet.

Rules 3, 4, and 5 allow email connections between the amawig MTA and other MTAs. Rules 3 and 4 allow the two approved MTAs to connect to the amawig server. Rule 5 allows the amawig MTA to connect to any other MTA. Clients on the enterprise LAN must connect to their own MTA to send email; the firewall doesn't allow access to other MTAs except by the enterprise MTA. In practice, the MTA itself may be configured to only talk to those other two MTAs. We could tighten security by restricting its connections to the other two MTAs.

The next three rules allow outbound HTTP for the three favored groups. The IP addresses with subnets 50, 60, and 70 (the third byte of each address) correspond to host addresses for the three groups allowed to surf the Internet.

The final rule grants Internet visitors access to the enterprise website. Note that neither inbound nor outbound rules permit SSL connections. These require additional rules.

Additional Firewall Mechanisms

A modern enterprise firewall's rule set also will integrate some routing information and a NAT facility. The routing mechanisms allow us to route particular types of traffic to particular hosts or networks. In Table 15.4, all we can do is allow traffic to flow to a particular destination. If we specify the routing, then the traffic flows to the desired destination despite the actual destination address.

Firewall NAT configuration provides similar services to those we discussed in Section 12.4.1. The enterprise firewall provides greater flexibility in assigning addresses and performing translation.

FIREWALL RULE PROLIFERATION

The previous discussion notes a few specific cases for which we could improve the rule set by adding rules. Notably, no one can surf the Web with SSL. In fact, the sample rule set here falls far short of providing typical Internet access even to the privileged groups. There is no FTP support nor access to remote mailboxes via POP3 or IMAP. The firewall also blocks all routing and network management protocols, which may make it difficult for the enterprise to interact with the rest of the Internet.

On the positive side, the rule set implements Deny by Default. The firewall should not allow traffic that we haven't specifically allowed. This also means that we must add rules piecemeal that grant access for every internet application protocol we need to allow. Thus, we add rules as we add capabilities for our users.

It is challenging to manage a firewall rule set. Smaller sites may require only a few—or a few dozen—firewall rules. Larger and more complex sites require a larger and more complex rule set. To some extent, the number of rules depends on the size of the site and the arrangement of its point of presence (see Section 15.5). It also depends on the firewall design itself; some firewall models may describe a complex policy requirement in a single rule, while other models may require several rules to express the same restriction.

In practice, firewall rule sets may range in size from a handful to tens of thousands. Many enterprise firewalls carry 200 or fewer rules, while many others carry a thousand or more. Firewalls that support hundreds of users typically have a couple thousand rules; the largest sites may have tens of thousands of rules.

Firewall rule sets pose an administrative challenge. The system administrators must be able to reliably change rules in response to changes in network organization or changes in security policies. Effective changes must not open vulnerabilities or block needed services.

15.5 Enterprise Point of Presence

The *point of presence* (POP, not to be confused with the POP3 email protocol) is the point at which the enterprise connects to its Internet service. Some enterprises have several points of presence. In some cases, enterprises centralize all Internet traffic so they may treat it all consistently. If the enterprise has multiple sites, all Internet traffic flows to the POP via the enterprise VPN.

Internet Service Providers

Modern ISPs use a variety of technologies to connect to customers. Smaller sites may use the same technology as households: a broadband cable modem connection or a DSL connection. Larger sites may use special, dedicated lines via either copper or optical connections. Many cell phone companies also offer wireless broadband connections to the Internet.

When choosing an ISP, the enterprise needs to consider the amount of Internet traffic they need to support. If the enterprise deploys and manages its own Internet servers on-site, then the POP must handle incoming web traffic as well as outbound browser traffic and email.

When there is a single POP, the ISP treats the enterprise as an autonomous system for routing purposes; all inbound and outbound traffic is routed through the central gateway. Enterprise routing also becomes more complex when there are multiple Internet connections.

The enterprise must arrange its Internet POP to provide both safe and efficient access. There are countless ways to arrange enterprise resources around the POP. The goal is to provide effective outbound access to the Internet and effective inbound access to Internet-visible enterprise services.

The DMZ

Many sites place Internet-visible servers on a special LAN segment called the *demilitarized zone* or DMZ. The name refers to the "no man's land" between two opposing armies that hold an uneasy truce. Although the analogy isn't perfect, the term captures the risky nature of network traffic on the DMZ.

Because outsiders may visit servers on the DMZ, those servers face significantly higher risks than elsewhere on the enterprise network. The POP's arrangement seeks to restrict all risky traffic to the DMZ. Some experts also refer to the DMZ network as a *screened subnet*, because the network is behind an enterprise firewall, but not directly connected to the internal enterprise network.

INTRUSION DETECTION

A site's gateway firewall provides an excellent place to watch for attacks. Even though firewalls try to block attacks by explicitly allowing or blocking specific types of traffic, an *intrusion detection system*, or IDS, searches for more subtle indications of an attack.

Several companies offer commercial IDS products and there is also the open-source product "Snort."

Many products, including Snort, use a similar technique to antivirus programs; they look for patterns in the data that distinctively show up in particular attacks. The network administrator may configure the IDS to try to block the traffic associated with the attack or at least to sound an alarm. Like antivirus software, a pattern-matching IDS won't detect attacks for which there is no preinstalled pattern.

Some products use a statistical approach; they develop profiles of normal network traffic and report unusual changes. This technique can detect new attack techniques without installing new patterns. On the other hand, it won't detect an attack that doesn't affect the network traffic features that it monitors.

There also are distributed IDS systems that collect reports from intrusion sensors spread around the network. The reports go to a central host that may apply either pattern matching or statistical techniques to try to detect intrusions.

A fundamental problem with any pattern-oriented detection technique is that they must be fine-tuned to avoid false alarms. This problem applies to the statistical IDS techniques as well. If the system is too sensitive, it will detect numerous attacks, many of which will be false alarms. If we make the system less sensitive, we receive fewer false alarms, but face a greater risk of not detecting an actual attack.

Intrusion Prevention Systems

A generic IDS simply *reports* a problem, it doesn't respond to it. An *intrusion prevention system* detects an intrusion and automatically implements security measures to block its operation. The simplest case would be to activate filters that block communications with an attacking host. More sophisticated systems may redirect vulnerable traffic or isolate infected host computers.

Data Loss Prevention Systems

Vendors also offer *data loss prevention* systems; instead of looking for inbound intrusions, they watch for unexpected and undesirable outbound data flows. Although some techniques analyze network traffic to detect leaking data, other techniques examine hosts to try to identify and inventory sensitive data, making it easier to track and protect.

15.5.1 POP Topology

A site's point of presence may take many forms. Here are four relatively simple topologies that illustrate common alternatives:

1. Single firewall
2. Bastion host
3. Three-legged firewall
4. Dual firewalls

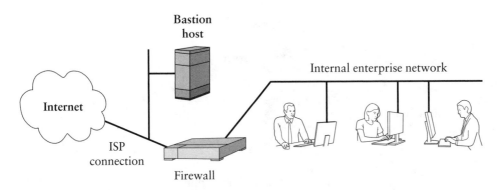

Figure 15.14

Single-firewall topology with an external bastion host.

Single-Firewall Topology

We used this topology when implementing the firewall controls shown in Table 15.4. There is no DMZ; all enterprise servers are inside the firewall. We provide specific firewall rules to focus all inbound Internet traffic to authorized servers. The simple firewall introduced in Section 12.4 (Figure 12.14) implements this topology.

Bastion-Host Topology

Figure 15.14 illustrates an older technique that is less common today. The *bastion host* is a strongly secured host that provides services to the Internet. It relies on careful host configuration and up-to-date patches to resist attacks from the Internet.

When a modern site deploys a bastion host, the bastion provides Internet services. A separate firewall protects the internal enterprise network from Internet-based attacks. This requires a relatively simple firewall configuration, but requires very careful administration of the bastion host.

In older sites, the bastion served as the site's firewall as well as hosting Internet services. The internal network connected to the bastion and it applied firewall filtering to all inbound and outbound traffic.

Sites rarely use bastion hosts today. Typical sites deploy servers on a DMZ. However, most sites "harden" their Internet servers, despite firewall protection, because firewalls can't prevent the entire range of Internet attacks.

Three-Legged Firewall

The three-legged firewall uses a single device to provide separate connections to the ISP, to the internal enterprise network, and to a separate DMZ. Figure 15.15 shows a typical configuration. The arrows show the general policy for allowing connections. All Internet traffic is allowed to reach the DMZ hosts, but is blocked from making

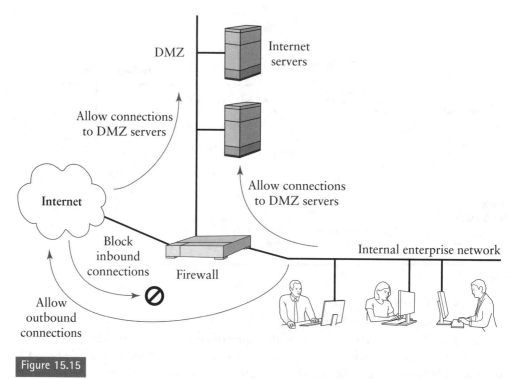

Figure 15.15

Three-legged firewall with a DMZ.

inbound connections to the internal network. Outbound connections can go to the DMZ or to the Internet.

Because the firewall controls access between all three networks, it can also restrict administrative access to the DMZ. The firewall can restrict or block network management protocols from moving between the Internet and the DMZ and only exchange management protocols with the internal network. Unfortunately, however, a great deal of administration now takes place via HTTP and we must allow HTTP traffic onto the DMZ from the Internet.

Dual Firewalls

The dual-firewall topology uses one firewall to protect the entire enterprise from the Internet and a second firewall to protect the internal network from the DMZ. This arrangement is also called a *screened subnet*. Figure 15.16 illustrates the topology. Dual firewalls can enforce the same policies as a three-legged firewall.

Sites may choose this design because a three-legged firewall lacks the performance required. Others choose it because they prefer the Defense in Depth inherent in having two separate devices. Some experts argue that the best approach uses two separate

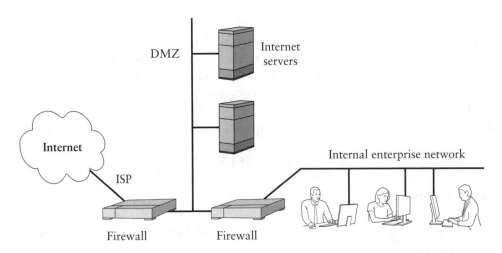

Figure 15.16

Dual-firewall topology with a DMZ.

brands of firewalls, because flaws present in one product might not be present in the other.

Although dual firewalls may have security and performance benefits, they also may be harder to manage. Each has its own set of firewall rules, but the rules must be coordinated to correctly enforce the site's Internet connection policy.

15.5.2 Attacking an Enterprise Site

Many retail stores have antitheft alarms. Expensive merchandise contains special tags that the sales clerk removes when someone buys an item. If someone tries to carry an item out the door without removing the tag, the alarm sounds.

Internet firewalls provide a similar level of protection. They do not protect against every Internet threat. They protect against a set of well-known attacks. They reduce risks by closing certain vulnerabilities.

Over the years, many attacks on firewalls have succeeded. In some cases, firewall improvements have blocked subsequent attacks of that type. In other cases, the attack masquerades as a service that the firewall can't block or it hides under a layer of encryption. Firewalls can't defend against an attack unless they can distinguish the attack from legitimate traffic.

Firewalls do not perform magic. They don't protect the site from all Internet risks or even from highly common ones. Internet worms use the techniques described here to bypass firewalls. We must be sure to protect endpoint hosts and servers as well.

Protocol Attacks

Over the Christmas vacation in 1994, an intruder broke into computers in the San Diego Supercomputer Center. A particular target seemed to be a computer belonging to Tsutomu Shimomura, a security expert who had demonstrated how to reprogram an analog cell phone to eavesdrop on all nearby conversations. The firewall did not detect the attack because the packets appeared to come from *inside* the site: The source IP addresses were for *internal* computers. The attack used IP spoofing, described earlier in Section 12.2.2.

The stream of packets aimed a long series of SYN and ACK packets at one of Shimomura's machines, trying to guess TCP sequence numbers. Finally, the packets struck home and the computer accepted a shell command carried by the attack. The command opened a back door that allowed the attacker into the machine. The attack eventually was attributed to Kevin Mitnick, who was captured and arrested after a lengthy investigation and search.

In a different case, attackers discovered that they could bypass packet filters if the IP packets were broken into two oddly structured fragments. In particular, the packets were too small for the firewall to locate the TCP and UDP port numbers. The firewall checked the first packet in the fragment and let the second packet go through, assuming that it already had checked the port numbers.

In both cases, the firewall allowed attacks through because they took unexpected steps. In the first case, the attacker sent TCP packets with *internal* IP addresses. In the second case, the attacker sent packets that didn't appear to carry port numbers.

Network protocol designers try to make protocols as simple as possible. Simpler protocols are easier to analyze, which makes it easier to find potential problems like these. As we find protocol problems, we modify firewall configurations and rules and patch our protocol stacks to block attacks that they might support.

Tunneling

Tunneling poses a particular challenge for many sites. Site policies generally permit or deny traffic flow based on the *application* being used; many sites allow DNS, email, file transfer, and web traffic. Firewalls generally enforce this by looking at port numbers in the traffic. If a firewall sees port 80, for example, it assumes the connection carries a web transaction.

In practice, however, the endpoint hosts may use port 80 to carry whatever traffic they want. This is the essence of tunneling: Two endpoints use an existing protocol standard to carry different traffic. Some firewalls use proxies to examine traffic more closely and ensure that it contains web-like transactions. Some tunneling software circumvents even this level of filtering by embedding their traffic *inside* web traffic.

Some more-or-less legitimate vendors of gaming or instant message applications use tunneling to circumvent firewalls that would otherwise filter out their traffic. Although network managers may see this as a policy violation, vendors often see this as an improvement in reliability. In some cases, the policy might not have been intended to block their application's traffic and the tunneling ensures reliable connectivity.

It can be very difficult to detect and block undesired tunneling. If the vendor combines tunneling with SSL encryption, there is no practical way to distinguish a legitimate SSL connection from unauthorized tunneling.

National Firewalls

Several nations place a value on protecting their citizens from what they deem offensive material. Some have gone as far as to try to block offensive material from entering the country through the Internet. Although the definition of "offensive" often refers to moral or cultural artifacts, it often applies to political dissent as well.

China's Golden Shield project is perhaps the most ambitious project, if only because of its vast geographical reach and immense population. Also nicknamed "the Great Firewall of China," the project seeks to monitor attempts to retrieve offensive material as well as to block such attempts. Although technical details of China's Shield are not publicized, it apparently blocks access on the basis of web URLs. Hosts who attempt to visit offensive sites may be blocked automatically from network access for as long as 30 minutes following the attempt.

Several other national governments also have deployed national firewalls. In the Mideast, these include Bahrain, Iran, Saudi Arabia, Syria, the United Arab Emirates, and Yemen. Although many countries monitor Internet use and levy fines for prohibited uses, only a few other countries actively filter Internet traffic.

As noted earlier, there are several ways to bypass firewall defenses. The most common approach involves proxies: The client connects to an overseas proxy server. If the client uses SSL encryption, the national firewall can't see the URLs being submitted or the pages in response. National firewalls try to keep ahead of such techniques by blocking connections to known proxy servers.

15.5.3 The Challenge of Real-Time Media

Companies that own the rights to music or video programs face several challenges on the Internet. We examined the digital rights management (DRM) challenge in Section 7.5. Another challenge is to provide a real-time feed of either audio or video media. This challenge also applies to voice over IP (VoIP), through which we use the Internet to provide telephone service.

Unlike traditional Internet services, audio and video are incredibly sensitive to timing. This arises if we listen to different types of mistakes made by novice musicians. One musician plays a piece, keeps with the tempo, and plays a few notes wrong. The other musician plays the same piece, but stops and corrects each wrong note. Most people find it easier to listen to the first musician, because unexpected pauses are much more disruptive to the music. Likewise, people find it very hard to watch a video that arbitrarily pauses and then resumes.

Real-time media has different quality requirements from traditional Internet media. Traditional media rely heavily on 100 percent perfect data transmission with "not unreasonable" delays. Real-time media may tolerate data errors more effectively than it tolerates timing errors. The data errors may cause "dropouts" in which audio or video are garbled. If the dropout is brief enough, then it won't affect the participants' experience.

TCP is not the best transport protocol for real-time media. The IETF has developed the Real-time Transport Protocol (RTP) as an alternative to support streaming media, VoIP, and video teleconferences. Some vendors have implemented their own protocol atop UDP. For example, the Skype telephone application uses UDP packets to transmit custom-formatted audio and video packets between users on a phone call.

Security techniques still are evolving for real-time media. Some systems, like Skype, encrypt all media data. Some streaming systems use encryption to enforce DRM.

15.6 Resources

 IMPORTANT TERMS INTRODUCED

advance fee fraud	formatting standards	session filtering
application filtering	mailbox protocols	spam
application proxy	packet filtering	spam score
blacklist	phishing	stateful packet filter
delivery protocols	protocol standards	tunneling
email virus	screened subnet	whitelist

ACRONYMS INTRODUCED

DMZ—Demilitarized zone

ESMTP—Extended SMTP

FTP—File transfer protocol

HTTP—Hypertext Transfer Protocol

IDS—Intrusion detection system

IMAP—Internet Message Access Protocol

MAPI—Message API

MIME—Multipart Internet Message Extensions

MTA—Message transfer agent

MX—Mail exchange

POP—Point of presence

POP3—Post Office Protocol—version 3

RFC—Request for Comments

RTP—Real-time Transport Protocol

SMTP—Simple Mail Transfer Protocol

VoIP—Voice over IP

15.6.1 Review Questions

R1. Describe the structure of an email message. Identify typical header fields. How does the format mark the end of a message's regular headers?

R2. Explain the purpose and use of MIME in an email message.

R3. Describe a typical strategy for formatting an email message with text features not found in a plaintext file.

R4. Explain the role of mailbox protocols.

R5. Describe how all three types of network switching (message, circuit, and packet) are used in the email system.

R6. Explain how to trace the MTAs through which an email message traveled.

R7. Why is it easy to forge the "From:" header in an email message? Describe how we might spot a forged "From:" header.

R8. Explain the relationship between spam and various types of financial fraud.

R9. Describe how a phishing attack works. Explain the role of the spam email, domain name, and website in the phishing attack.

R10. Explain how email viruses propagate. Explain how email virus hoaxes propagate.

R11. Describe common techniques for identifying and blocking spam.

R12. Identify and describe the three filtering mechanisms used by enterprise firewalls.

R13. Describe the format and contents of rules used by a typical enterprise firewall.

R14. Identify and describe the four basic techniques for arranging an enterprise's Internet point of presence.

R15. Describe two basic techniques that might allow an attacker to bypass a firewall.

15.6.2 Exercises

NOTE: For some problems, your instructor will provide a Wireshark packet capture file that shows a computer starting up and opening a connection to a web page. You will use that packet capture file in exercises marked "Wireshark."

E1. (Wireshark.) Locate a series of packets that retrieve an email message from a mailbox.

  a. What frame numbers perform the three-way handshake to open the connection?

  b. What mailbox protocol does the mail program use?

  c. What is the host name and/or IP address of the email server?

  d. Is there a password or other authentication measure used? If so, identify the frame number—or numbers—and describe what happens.

  e. Identify the frame number of the first packet that retrieves an email message.

E2. (Wireshark.) Locate a series of packets that transmit an email message to a server for delivery.

  a. What frame numbers perform the three-way handshake to open the connection?

b. What is the host name and/or IP address of the email server?

c. Is there a password or other authentication measure used? If so, identify the frame number—or numbers—and describe what happens.

d. What information does the client transmit to the server about the email message aside from the message contents itself?

E3. Retrieve the header from an email message. Highlight the host identifiers (domain names and/or IP addresses) of the MTAs that carried the message.

E4. Find a partner in the class. Construct an email whose "From:" line claims that the email comes from someone else. Email it to your partner; your partner also should construct an email with an inaccurate "From:" line and email it to you. Retrieve the header from that email message. Use the headers to determine the actual source of the email. Indicate the differences between the "From:" line and the header information about the email's delivery.

E5. The Amalgamated Widget site began with a single firewall configuration, using firewall rules as shown in Table 15.4. Then Amalgamated updated the arrangement to use a dual-firewall arrangement like the one shown in Figure 15.16. All servers now reside on the DMZ, with IP addresses in the 30.40.80.x range. Rewrite the firewall rule set to work with the dual-firewall arrangement. Create two sets of rules: one for each firewall. Be sure to block all Internet-to-inside-LAN connections, while still allowing access to appropriate Amalgamated servers. Users on the Internet and on the internal LAN should see no difference in the updated configuration.

E6. Does your organization have an Internet acceptable use policy? Locate and review the policy. Summarize its main points.

E7. Does your organization have an email acceptable use policy? Locate and review the policy. Summarize its main points.

E8. Firewall A is an enterprise firewall with session filtering as described in Section 15.4.2. Firewall B has no features except network address translation and packet filtering.

a. Can both firewalls block inbound connections? Why or why not?

b. Can both firewalls block outbound connections? Why or why not?

c. Can both firewalls allow inbound connections? Why or why not?

d. Can both firewalls allow outbound connections? Why or why not?

THE WORLD WIDE WEB

ABOUT THIS CHAPTER

The World Wide Web provides the technical foundation for most peoples' Internet experience. Modern e-commerce and social media rely primarily on web technologies. This chapter examines the following:

- Fundamentals of hypertext documents
- Web protocols and basic websites
- Modern content management systems
- Assuring the security of web-based activities

16.1 Hypertext Fundamentals

The World Wide Web was the first Internet technology to engage people who were not otherwise computer users. Its popularity arises from ease of use. Most people can read and understand web pages on a computer screen, and they quickly learn how to navigate the Web by clicking on "hypertext links."

The term *hypertext* was coined in the 1970s by computer visionary Ted Nelson, who wanted to improve the computing experience. Nelson proposed computer-aided reading that linked one piece of text to another, making it easy for a reader to pursue a specific interest by jumping between related texts. Nelson credits the idea to the "memex" proposed in a 1945 article by former presidential science adviser Vannevar Bush (1890–1974).

In this section, we study the fundamentals of hypertext and the World Wide Web by examining the following three topics:

1. Web standards
2. Addressing web pages
3. Retrieving a web page

We examine the first topic here and the other two topics in subsequent subsections.

WEB STANDARDS

The hypertext technology beneath the World Wide Web was developed by physicist Tim Berners-Lee, noted in Section 14.3.1. Like email delivery, the Web relies on file transfers. When a browser requests a page, the server transmits a file containing that page. It may take minutes or days for an email to produce a reply, but we receive a rapid response to a web browser's request.

Although file exchange remains the bedrock of web operations, far more technology underlies today's web services. Like email, the Web has two sets of networking standards:

1. **Formatting standards**—how to construct files to be displayed by web browsers. These standards establish different types of *markup languages* that incorporate sophisticated document formatting into simple text-based documents.

2. **Protocol standards**—how hosts communicate in order to display hypertext and locate parts of a hypertext document.

The initial standards were authored by Berners-Lee and were adopted rapidly by the Internet community. Although the IETF is responsible for most internet technical standards, many of the basic web standards are managed by the World Wide Web Consortium (W3C). Founded in 1994, the W3C is supported by an international group of academic and government research institutions.

FORMATTING: HYPERTEXT MARKUP LANGUAGE

The fundamental format on the Web is **Hypertext Markup Language**, with its well-known acronym HTML. Standard, off-the-shelf HTML yields documents that contain formatted text, images, and links to other documents on the Web. Figure 16.1 shows an example of an extremely simple HTML page.

Figure 16.2 shows the HTML source text that produced the simple page. The "markup" aspect of HTML allows us to mark parts of the document to appear in italics, underlined, and so on. We use text elements called *tags* to indicate the format we want. Tags also indicate paragraphs, titles, headings, tables, lists, list elements, and so

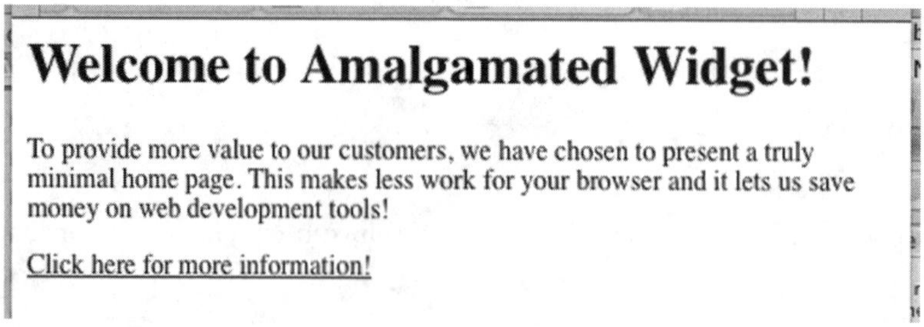

Welcome to Amalgamated Widget!

To provide more value to our customers, we have chosen to present a truly minimal home page. This makes less work for your browser and it lets us save money on web development tools!

Click here for more information!

Figure 16.1

A very, very simple web page.

```
<html>
<head>
<title>Welcome to Amalgamated Widget!</title>
</head>

<body>
<h1>Welcome to Amalgamated Widget!</h1>
<p>To provide more value to our customers, we have chosen to present
a truly minimal home page. This makes less work for your browser and
it lets us save money on web development tools!</p>
<p><a href="about.html">Click here for more information!</a></p>
</body>
</html>
```

Figure 16.2

HTML source text that produced Figure 16.1.

on. Formatted emails, like the one in Figure 15.3 from Chapter 15, use HTML tags to indicate the formatting.

The simplest tag contains its name enclosed in angle brackets. The page text in Figure 16.2 begins with the tags <html>, <head>, and <title>.

We use pairs of tags to delimit the text included in the markup. In Figure 16.2, for example, the third line of text defines the document's title. We start the title with a <title> tag and end it with </title>, which we call the "end tag." The end tag contains the tag's title prefixed with a slash ("/") character.

Traditional web pages begin with the <html> tag to mark the file as containing HTML. The <head> and <title> tags mark introductory data. Some applications only read a page's head tags. The <title> tag places the page's name on the browser's window, but the title does not otherwise appear on the page's display.

The page's <body> contains the displayed text. There are numbered heading tags specifying different heading levels: h1, h2, h3, and so on. The paragraph tag <p> indicates simple text to be formatted into a readable paragraph. This text may be further embellished with boldface, underscores, and so on.

Hypertext Links

An HTML page is hypertext because it contains *hypertext links*, which we will simply call *links*. When we click on a link, we retrieve information from a different page, either on the same web server or on a different server. We use the <a> tag in HTML to construct a link. Figure 16.3 illustrates a simple link. Every link has two parts:

1. **Highlighted text**—when we click our mouse on the highlighted text, the web browser follows the link.
2. **Target**—when the browser follows a link, it retrieves the web page indicated by the link's target.

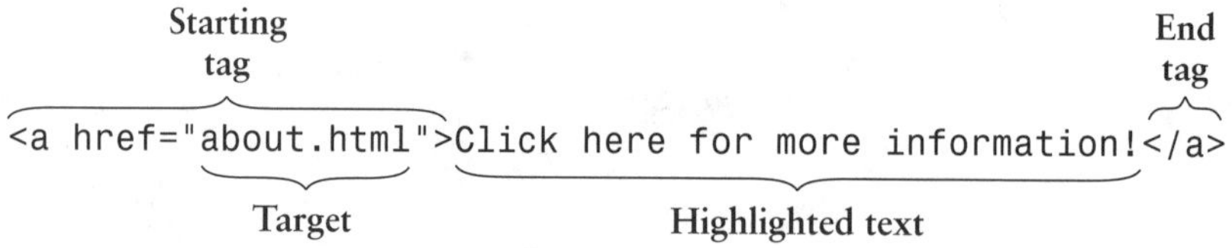

Figure 16.3

A hypertext link from an HTML document.

The starting tag in Figure 16.3 contains the link's target: It is the value of the "href" argument. A tag may carry one or more arguments, each one containing the argument's name, an "=" sign, and the argument's value.

In this case, the link's target is another HTML file named "about.html" stored on the same web server. If a file's link refers to a different web server, then we use a web address as described in Section 16.1.1.

The starting tag and end tag enclose the highlighted text. The end tag never contains arguments, even if they appear in the starting tag.

Most browsers rely on a mouse-based GUI to handle links. If we move our mouse over a link and click on it, the browser follows the link. If we simply place the mouse over the link without clicking, we remain on the current page. Most browsers also provide a discreet status display at the bottom of the browser's window.

When we place the mouse over a link without clicking, most browsers display the target's file name or web address in the status display. This allows us to identify the link's destination before we decide to click on it.

Cascading Style Sheets

Originally, web page authors relied on HTML tags to control both the style and the structure of web pages. Today, most sites use *Cascading Style Sheets*, or CSS files, to control the page's appearance. These files use a distinctive ".css" suffix. Web pages still use the HTML tags to describe the structure and flow of information on the page. The CSS files specify header formatting, typeface selection, bullet formats, and so on.

CSS files provide an easier way to manage web page formats across multiple pages on larger sites. They also provide more effective control over page formatting; for example, CSS allows more precise specification of typefaces and sizes. Even though most browsers still recognize the older HTML formatting tags, most websites avoid using them, because CSS-based formatting is more powerful and easier to manage.

HYPERTEXT TRANSFER PROTOCOL

The Hypertext Transfer Protocol (HTTP) is the fundamental protocol for moving data on the Web. On the client side, we have web browsers like Microsoft's Internet Explorer, Mozilla's Firefox, and Apple's Safari. Because browsers are application programs that run on desktops, anyone may write their own and many other browsers exist. All use

HTTP to exchange data and HTML plus CSS to format the data for display. Different browsers also provide various levels of support for XML, the "Extensible Markup Language."

Web server software may be extremely simple. Virus expert Fred Cohen, for example, implemented a simple HTTP server in only 80 lines of source code. Modern servers that implement SSL and scripting languages are far larger and more complex. Today, there are two widely used web server packages:

1. **Apache**—a full-featured web server maintained and distributed as open source. By most measures, it is the most widely used web server on the Internet.

2. **Internet Information Services** (IIS)—the full-featured commercial web server distributed by Microsoft. IIS supports most of the same web protocols and features as Apache, plus it supports many proprietary extensions. There are IIS websites that only work correctly when visited by Microsoft's Internet Explorer browser.

The major differences between these servers rarely arise in purely static websites. Most of the proprietary extensions in IIS appear when the website uses scripts. We discuss scripts in Section 16.3.

Retrieving Data from Other Files or Sites

When a tag in a web page provides a link or an image, it often refers to a different file. For images, the browser uses HTTP to retrieve the image and then displays it on the page. An HTML file also may retrieve some of its HTML text from another HTML file.

Most important, an HTML file may retrieve its content either from its own server or from any other web server on the Internet. Any HTML tag that accepts a file name also will accept a reference to another page or file elsewhere on the Web.

For example, some websites display advertising that is provided by a separate advertising service. The service tailors the advertising to the specific user who visits the site as well as to the site itself. The website contents come from the server being visited, but the tailored ads come from the servers for the advertising service.

16.1.1 Addressing Web Pages

We locate a web page by typing in that oddly formatted identifier called the *Uniform Resource Locator*, or URL. Figure 16.4 illustrates its basic format.

Although the web community at large calls these identifiers URLs, modern browsers actually use a more general form called the *Uniform Resource Identifier*, or URI. Strictly speaking, a URL specifies a *location* while a URI actually *identifies* a resource. This textbook follows the common usage and calls web page identifiers URLs.

The leftmost part of the URL indicates the *scheme* for interpreting the text following the colon. Typical web-oriented schemes identify the protocol being used to retrieve a page: http, https, ftp, file, and so on. The format to the right of the colon may vary from one scheme to another. Most schemes we use with web pages and resources refer to files stored on servers or hard drives.

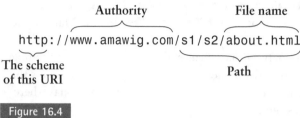

Figure 16.4

Format of a URL, which is a web page URI.

Email URLs

Although web links usually lead to documents or images, some links activate particular applications. An email URL, for example, contains an email address. When we follow an email URL, the browser automatically starts an email client and passes it the email address in the URL. Web pages often provide a "Contact Us" link that contains an email URL.

Figure 16.5 describes the format of an email URL, which follows the format of a URI. To the left of the colon is "mailto," the scheme's name. To the right is an email address. The @ sign separates the user ID from the email server's domain name.

Hosts and Authorities

Returning to the more common URL format in Figure 16.4, the *authority* part of the URL identifies the server containing the resource we want. In most cases, the authority simply contains the domain name of the server. The authority field may contain additional fields as shown in Figure 16.6. Email URLs are the only ones that routinely use the @ sign or anything to the left of it. The port number (shown on the right following a colon) appears occasionally.

As noted in Section 11.3, websites typically provide their service on TCP port number 80. A web server may accept connections on other port numbers and even may serve different pages through different port numbers. If the server does *not* use port 80, the

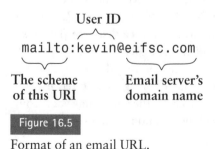

Figure 16.5

Format of an email URL.

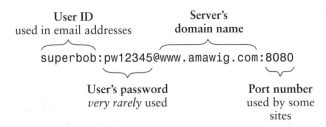

User ID
used in email addresses

Server's
domain name

```
superbob:pw12345@www.amawig.com:8080
```

User's password
very rarely used

Port number
used by some
sites

Figure 16.6

Detailed format of the URL authority field.

URL must include the port number following the domain name, as shown in Figure 16.6.

The user ID and password information are very, very rarely used when retrieving web documents. It is obviously a security risk to embed a reusable password in a URL, because we'll disclose the password whenever we share that URL. Moreover, the password often will travel in plaintext across the Internet. Some browsers, like Firefox, display a warning if a user includes that information in a URL.

Many browsers also allow us to enter a numeric IP address instead of a domain name. For example, many commercial gateways provide web-based administration if we direct the browser to the gateway's IP address. To reach such a web server, we type its IP address in brackets, for example: [192.168.1.1].

Path Name

The authority field ends with a slash and is followed by the file's path name. In Table 3.1 (Chapter 3), we saw how different file systems use different path name delimiters. Most web servers, however, expect to see the slash "/" character as the path name delimiter, even if the server runs atop Windows or Apple's OS-X. The server software interprets the path name and translates it as necessary before passing it to the file system.

Most file systems treat path and file names as being case sensitive. However, not all websites have case-sensitive paths. Many Internet identifiers, notably domain names, ignore case when interpreting the text. Some web servers apply this to URLs. To do so, the server adjusts the path name before passing it to the file system.

Default Web Pages

When we type in a web page location, we want to type as little as possible. We often omit the "http://" suffix to the URL, and most browsers fill it in for us. People often type nothing more than the website's domain name into the browser, and the browser locates its home page.

When we ask a web server for a page, and we don't actually provide a page name, the server tries to guess the page's name. Typical guesses include:

- index.htm, index.html

- home.htm, home.html
- Default.htm

For example, if we type "http://www.amawig.com" into a web browser, the server will eventually retrieve the home page "index.html" because that file is stored in the site's home directory.

Most server software may be configured to look for additional default file names. In dynamic servers, the default names may select scripts to execute (see Section 16.3).

16.1.2 Retrieving a Static Web Page

The simplest websites consist of text files formatted in HTML, possibly combined with image files. When a client requests a page, the server retrieves the file containing that page and performs no additional processing. Many modern sites avoid storing static HTML; instead, they construct the page dynamically, as described in Section 16.3.

When Alice visits a web page, she provides a URL. In a static website, the server converts the URL into a file name reference and retrieves the associated file. If the file contains HTML, the browser interprets it and displays it. Figure 16.7 summarizes the process.

The process involves the following four steps:

1. Alice enters a URL into a browser or selects a link to visit. We will visit the page "http://www.amawig.com/about.html."
2. The browser calls the domain name resolver to retrieve the IP address for www.amawig.com (see Section 12.3.2).
3. The browser opens a connection to the server, using the IP address retrieved by the resolver. The browser connects to the server's port 80, unless a different port

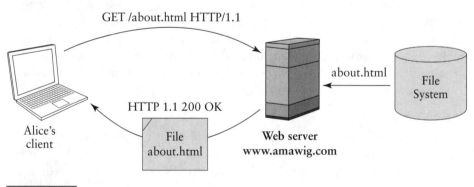

GET /about.html HTTP/1.1

about.html

HTTP 1.1 200 OK

Alice's client

File about.html

Web server www.amawig.com

File System

Figure 16.7

Retrieving a web page using HTTP.

number appeared in the URL. The browser sends an HTTP *GET* command that contains the path name listed in the URL: about.html.

4. The server retrieves the file about.html and transmits its contents across the same connection, then it closes the connection. The browser displays the page.

Earlier in the text, Figure 12.6 used Wireshark to list the packets exchanged during a TCP connection. That particular example shows another HTTP connection. Instead of retrieving a file named "about.html," the Wireshark example retrieves the file "ncsi.txt." Both the GET command and the web page file happen to be small enough to fit in individual packets.

The server's response to a GET command begins with a status message: One line of text that announces whether the GET succeeded or not. If the GET succeeded, then the file's contents follow the line of text.

Building a Page from Multiple Files

When the HTML file refers to other files, the browser must retrieve their contents in order to display the entire page. To retrieve the other files, the browser opens HTTP connections to the appropriate servers and requests the required files.

Originally, each file transfer required a separate connection. As web server traffic grew, however, sites wanted higher efficiency. When a typical web page refers to another file, the file often resides on the same server. The client wastes time and trouble to close one connection when it is immediately going to reopen it to transfer another file. The latest HTTP systems may transfer multiple files through a single connection.

WEB SERVERS AND STATELESSNESS

Basic HTTP is a *stateless protocol*: The basic server software does not keep track of the client's behavior from one connection to the next. There is no notion of a "session" in HTTP. This makes it relatively easy to implement an HTTP server. This also makes it difficult to implement web applications that keep track of a user's behavior across several connections, like "shopping carts." The applications use special techniques we examine in Section 16.3.2.

A static website consists of text files in HTML format plus images stored in standard formats recognized by popular browsers. Common image formats include the Graphics Interchange Format (GIF), Joint Photographic Engineering Group (JPEG) format, and Portable Network Graphics (PNG) format. Most browsers also will retrieve files in raw text format, with the ".txt" file name suffix, and display them in a simple fixed-width text format.

WEB DIRECTORIES AND SEARCH ENGINES

When the World Wide Web was new, the biggest challenge was to find things. In 1993, for example, Bob's Uncle Joe knew that someone had produced an episode guide for *The Twilight Zone* TV series and had posted the file on a website, but there was no way to locate the file without a URL or a helpful link through some other site. In fact, this was how many people initially used personal web pages; they linked to interesting pages in other sites. There was no systematic way to locate information.

In the mid-1990s, two strategies emerged for locating information: directories and search engines. Directories provided a structured listing of websites based on their perceived subject matter. An informal directory developed by two graduate students in 1995 turned into the Yahoo! directory, the most prominent early directory. A *search engine* literally searches every page it can find on the Web and constructs an index of pages that appear relevant to the search. Researchers at DEC's Western Research Center developed Altavista, also in 1995, which was the first effective search engine.

Directories tend to rely on referrals. If Bob wants his web page to appear in a directory, he contacts the directory's owner and provides the URL and description of his site. Some directories automatically add sites. Others assess sites individually to decide if they are appropriate to list.

Directories also may develop structural problems. A well-organized directory provides a list of the "best" sites in every category. Each category's list should be short enough for a typical user to study. In practice, this requires an editor to periodically reorganize different topics as they fill up with individual entries. A large, general-purpose directory may have millions of entries and requires an extremely large team of editors.

Web Crawlers

Search engines, on the other hand, collect information about web content automatically. They use special software that literally "crawls" the Web, following the links it finds in web pages. This software typically is called a **web crawler**, or a *spider*, or even a *robot*. Individual sites may control how search engines handle their site by installing a special file called "ROBOTS.TXT." If the file is present, a well-behaved crawler examines its contents for instructions before crawling the site.

Crime via Search Engine

Search engines pose interesting security problems. If a site posts sensitive information by accident and a page links to it, then anyone can find the information using the search engine. Moreover, a clever search can locate sensitive or malicious information *anywhere* on the Internet. For example, sensitive personal information occasionally appears, including such details as credit card numbers. Card numbers follow a simple format, and they fall into particular numeric ranges depending on the issuing organization. In the past, search engines have allowed searches on those ranges. Such searches might locate pages that were made visible accidentally by an e-commerce site. In other cases, such pages contained information collected by a fraudster.

16.2 Basic Web Security

The Internet is a risky place, and the Web is often the scene of network-based attacks and other security problems. Here we examine four basic aspects of web security:

1. Client policy issues—risks arising from web clients
2. Static website security—risks and defenses for static web pages
3. Server authentication—using SSL to authenticate a server
4. Server masquerades—techniques to masquerade as a particular server using SSL

First, we examine client policy issues. The other aspects appear in subsequent subsections.

CLIENT POLICY ISSUES

In Section 15.4, we looked at the evolution of Internet use policies and the role of firewalls in enforcing them. Here we look more closely at problems arising from clients using web resources. The dilemma remains the same: Many employees use the Web routinely for job-related activities, but the Web also poses risks to productivity. We examine the following issues related to web client use:

- Policy motivations and objectives
- Strategies to manage web use
- The tunneling dilemma

POLICY MOTIVATIONS AND OBJECTIVES

Restrictions on web clients often arise from one or more of the following risks or worries:

- Distractions that divert attention from business tasks
- Network traffic that does not support enterprise objectives
- Inappropriate content that poses legal risks
- Malware that may infect computers via drive-by downloads

There is no doubt that some employees abuse their Internet access by entertaining themselves while they should be at work. However, few reported studies have taken a truly unbiased look at the phenomenon. The available reports and anecdotes suggest that the problem varies widely among organizations and employees and even with the time of year.

Internet Policy Directives

In all cases, employees and other network users must have a clear understanding of the enterprise's expectations. If the organization wishes to enforce standards on Internet behavior, then the organization must define and publish those standards in policy directives. It is difficult to enforce an unwritten policy. It also may be difficult to fire an employee for violating an unwritten policy.

STRATEGIES TO MANAGE WEB USE

When organizations try to manage employees' Internet use, they take three general approaches:

1. Traffic blocking
2. Monitoring
3. Training

Some organizations combine one or more of these techniques. We examine each technique here. Many organizations effectively control web use through a combination of monitoring and training.

Traffic Blocking

Many enterprise networks try to limit web misuse by blocking access to web content. Here are three approaches:

1. **Website whitelist.** This lists *all* websites that employees may visit. It is often impractical to maintain an effective whitelist. It must grant access to every site that the employees might need to get their work done. It is hard to anticipate all sites people might need to visit. If the needed site isn't on the list, a task is delayed while the list is updated.

2. **Content control software** or **website blacklist.** This lists all websites that employees should not visit. Such lists often are built into commercial products and the vendor maintains the list. In some cases, the list classifies sites according to the type of content. The network administrators then may allow access to some types of sites and block access to other types.

3. **Web traffic scanning.** Whitelists and blacklists do not eliminate the risk of malware infections via drive-by downloads. Such attacks even infect legitimate sites on occasion. Web traffic scanners search for malware in the HTML and other files returned to browsers by web servers. However, this introduces a delay in web browsing if the scanning times are excessive.

   In practice, many enterprises and users rely on client-based antivirus software to resist drive-by downloading of malware.

Traffic blocking is rarely 100 percent effective. Users may employ several techniques to disguise their web traffic. These are often the same techniques that people use to ensure personal privacy on the Internet (see Section 16.5). Most employers would be very unhappy with employees who used such techniques to violate the company's acceptable use policy.

Monitoring

In Section 13.3.3, we introduced the maxim *Trust, but Verify.* Instead of restricting user actions ahead of time with web blocking, we monitor their behavior. We use the results of monitoring to ensure that users comply with the web usage policy.

Some sites simply keep a log of URLs visited by users and examine the log for suspicious or inappropriate site names. This is not practical in larger organizations. Some sites use content control software: Instead of using it to block access, the software simply keeps a record of visits. The administrators then can create a report indicating the visits to different types of sites and, if necessary, narrow down visits to specific client computers and desktops.

Training

After we produce a policy directive on web use, we must ensure that the user community understands it. That naturally leads to training. A newly enacted policy requires an initial announcement and explanation to the existing user community. New users learn of the policy during an introductory orientation.

We reinforce the policy training by providing reminders to the user community. An effective reminder indicates that the policy exists and that management pays attention to it. If the enterprises monitors user behavior, then it is worthwhile to remind users of such monitoring. It is particularly effective to provide evidence of such monitoring by reporting general statistics on web use. We improve compliance if people know their work is monitored.

THE TUNNELING DILEMMA

Most Internet-connected networks allow their users to browse the Web. The site's gateways and firewalls are configured to allow such traffic to pass. Some protocols take advantage of this: Instead of using TCP to establish their own, separate connections, the protocols travel *inside* HTTP traffic. We call this *HTTP tunneling*.

Tunneling requires a special-purpose client and a matching server. The client opens an HTTP connection to the server and they exchange packets by embedding them inside the HTTP data (see Figure 16.8).

Some applications have a plausible reason for tunneling. For example, some web applications that exchange XML data may embed the XML within an HTTP tunnel.

To make the tunnel work, client-side software embeds the tunneled data in an HTTP message and sends it to a tunneling server. The server extracts the tunneled data and processes it. To simple firewalls, the exchange looks like a conventional HTTP connection. In fact, the XML tunnel carries more sophisticated XML-formatted data.

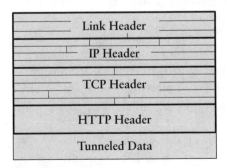

| Link Header |
| IP Header |
| TCP Header |
| HTTP Header |
| Tunneled Data |

Figure 16.8

Packet format for HTTP tunneling.

Although XML tunnels may have a legitimate purpose, other applications use tunneling to circumvent firewall port filtering. For example, there are general-purpose tunneling applications that embed an *entire IP packet* inside the HTTP message. This allows the client to use any application protocol desired. If the local network's firewall blocks applications on most ports except web traffic on port 80, then the general-purpose tunnel bypasses that restriction.

Several open source and commercial packages provide general-purpose HTTP tunneling. The packages allow the user to exchange packets with any Internet host using essentially any protocol. For example, the tunnel could allow a user to communicate via a special-purpose gaming protocol port, even if the local network's firewall blocks that port.

All tunnels, including the general-purpose tunnel, require client software to embed and extract the tunneled data. The client must connect to a server that processes the tunneled data. General-purpose tunnels generally rely on a corresponding server on the public Internet, outside the local network's firewall. Some commercial packages charge a fee to use their tunneling servers.

Firewalling HTTP Tunnels

Sophisticated firewalls and monitoring systems can detect and block some types of tunneling. If the administrators use a website whitelist or can identify tunnel servers, then they can block access to those servers. Some monitoring systems may be able to examine the HTTP traffic itself and recognize tunneling protocols.

Tunneling is a variation of techniques used to achieve higher degrees of privacy while browsing on the Internet. Section 16.5.2 discusses these techniques further.

Some tunneling software uses SSL to encrypt the HTTP traffic. There is no way to detect tunneling encrypted inside such a connection.

16.2.1 Static Website Security

In general, a static website presents the lowest set of risks. Visitors are unlikely to encounter injury from the site, because basic HTML does little more than display data. An HTML file could contain a script and a script could do damage; these are risks of "dynamic" websites (see Section 16.3).

As noted previously, a poorly designed static site might leave sensitive information visible. A website generally consists of a set of files contained within a specific directory hierarchy. We must *never* place files in the site's hierarchy unless we want them visible. Anyone on the Internet can retrieve any file in the hierarchy by adding the path name to the site's URL.

Assuming we've eliminated sensitive information from the site's hierarchy, site defacement remains the major risk faced by static websites. Such attacks modify the site's files so that visitors see different web pages than intended. Figure 16.9 shows the result of an attack on the U.S. Senate's home page in 1999.

You CAN stop ONE,
but you can
NOT stop ALL !

FREE KEVIN   FREE ZYKLON

Select a
Go-Go Girls :)

Figure 16.9

Defaced U.S. Senate website, 1999.

The threat agents are often vandals who simply take advantage of an opportunity to deface the website. In some cases, there may be an economic or political motivation. For example, an unscrupulous competitor might deface another company's web page. The attack on the Senate page does not carry a clear political message, suggesting that the attackers were motivated by vandalism and not political objectives.

An attacker achieves very little by attacking a static website, except perhaps publicity. A successful attack only changes the site's visible contents. The attacker must penetrate the server's security and actually modify the data files stored on the server.

An attacker also may change a website's appearance by redirecting visitors to a *bogus site*; that is, one that masquerades as another site. Instead of actually damaging the U.S. Senate site, the attackers could have redirected visitors to a different website containing their announcements or political messages. Attackers may do this by distributing bogus DNS data that contains the bogus site's IP address or by distributing subverted routing data.

Visitors to a static site face a small number of risks. One risk arises if the site hosts any static files whose contents cause damage simply by reading them. Such "maliciously formatted files" are rare and rely on flaws in the client's display software. In 2004, for example, Microsoft's browsers suffered a buffer overflow when displaying a JPEG file formatted in a particularly extreme manner (the so-called "JPEG of death"). Some attackers constructed malicious JPEGs to try to take advantage of the flaw.

16.2.2 Server Authentication

We select a website to visit by selecting a URL, either by clicking a link or typing it by hand. The URL's authority field contains the web server's domain name—but how do we verify that we are visiting the correct site? If we are visiting an e-commerce site like eBay or Amazon, we don't want to risk our billing information to a bogus site. How can we tell a legitimate site from a bogus one?

Informally, we often can detect a bogus site by looking for errors or inconsistencies. If we know a site well, we probably will be able to spot a fake. However, we won't always detect a fake before we have provided a password or other secret information. Occasionally, a bogus site will practice a little social engineering by alerting us to a "website redesign" as the reason a site looks unfamiliar.

Fortunately, we rarely provide sensitive information except through SSL-protected connections. We examined SSL in Section 14.3. Browsers can authenticate SSL-enabled servers by checking their certificates. Figure 16.10 illustrates the process. When the browser opens an SSL connection, the server sends its certificate. The certificate contains the site's domain name. If the certificate's domain name matches the name in the URL, then the browser accepts the connection.

Although this process usually works successfully, there are cases where the authentication fails. The browser then displays a message to the user indicating that one of the following has happened:

1. Domain names don't match (may be legitimate)
2. Untrusted certificate authority (possibly safe, possibly not)
3. Expired certificate (often still safe to use)
4. Revoked certificate (unsafe to use)
5. Invalid digital signature (unsafe to use)

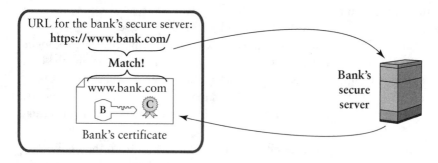

Figure 16.10

Authenticating the web server with SSL.

Mismatched Domain Name: May Be Legitimate

In the first case, the name check shown in Figure 16.10 detects a mismatch and the browser displays a warning. Figure 16.11 shows the warning displayed by the Firefox browser.

In the figure, the URL contained the domain name "www.ccr.gov." Under "Technical Details," the warning notes that the certificate contained the name "www.bpn.gov" instead.

This warning does not always indicate a fraudulent site or even a fraudulent certificate. If the organization has reorganized their site or changed site domain names, then the mismatch may be accidental. Figure 16.11 is an example of such an error; the certificate was issued by the appropriate agency, but contained the wrong domain name.

When the URL and certificate names don't match, we can examine the certificate ourselves and decide its legitimacy. Browsers always provide a mechanism for examining the SSL certificate being used. If we click on "I Understand the Risks" on the Firefox notice, it takes us to another screen that allows display of the certificate. Figure 16.12 shows the certificate associated with this error.

We can decide to trust the certificate in Figure 16.12 based on its contents. The owner and domain name legitimately could apply to this site (the "ccr" site is for U.S. government contractors and the Defense Logistics Agency legitimately might manage that site). The certificate display also indicates that it was signed by a recognized certificate authority: Verisign. When judging a certificate's legitimacy, we consider the following three questions:

1. Is the owning organization a legitimate entity that could reasonably be operating that website? For that matter, is it unlikely that the organization would host a bogus site?

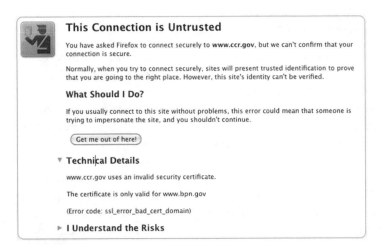

Figure 16.11

Firefox alert for a mismatched certificate name.

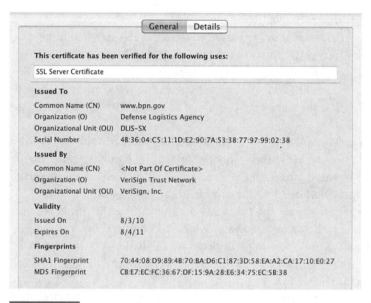

General   Details

This certificate has been verified for the following uses:

SSL Server Certificate

Issued To

Common Name (CN)   www.bpn.gov
Organization (O)   Defense Logistics Agency
Organizational Unit (OU) DLIS–SX
Serial Number   4B:36:04:C5:11:1D:E2:90:7A:53:38:77:97:99:02:38

Issued By

Common Name (CN)   <Not Part Of Certificate>
Organization (O)   VeriSign Trust Network
Organizational Unit (OU) VeriSign, Inc.

Validity

Issued On   8/3/10
Expires On   8/4/11

Fingerprints

SHA1 Fingerprint   70:44:08:D9:89:4B:70:BA:D6:C1:87:3D:58:EA:A2:CA:17:10:E0:27
MD5 Fingerprint   CB:E7:EC:FC:36:67:DF:15:9A:28:E6:34:75:EC:5B:38

Figure 16.12

Certificate information displayed by Firefox.

2. Could the domain name in the certificate legitimately apply to the site selected by the URL? For example, there could be a partial match between the certificate's domain name and the URL's domain name and the browser comparison still could fail. Some certificates allow different local subdomains, while others will only accept a specific subdomain like "www"—or the certificate could include a legitimate variant of the organization's name.

3. Was the certificate issued by a legitimate certificate authority?

If the answer to all three questions is "yes," then the certificate should be trustworthy. The first question may be the hardest to answer without further research. Government agencies or well-known, reputable companies usually are trustworthy in such cases. However, there are so many small companies on the Web that it's hard to identify all of them reliably, much less assess their trustworthiness. Some well-known businesses use a third-party service company to provide sales and "shopping cart" features for their website. Thus, we might end up using an unrecognized company to complete a sale involving a familiar brand name.

The second question is a variant of the first: It is easier to trust the site if the domain names are part of one another. However, a total mismatch doesn't indicate a bogus site if the site's owner is legitimate. The third question is addressed in the next section: the assessment of "untrusted" certificate authorities.

In some cases, there is simply not enough information available to identify a legitimate site with 100 percent confidence. There always will be risks in business transactions, whether on the Web, on the phone, or in person.

Untrusted Certificate Authority: Difficult to Verify

Every valid public-key certificate contains a digital signature. We validate the certificate by checking the signature, using the certificate authority's public key. When SSL was a new technology, it was easy to check certificates. There was only a single authority who issued certificates for SSL and the authority's public key was built into the browser software.

Today, there are hundreds of recognized, reputable certificate authorities. Modern browsers maintain a built-in list of recognized certificate authorities. The left-hand side of Figure 16.13 shows an example of such a list. The list includes a few representative authorities; a typical browser might contain 200 such entries.

The built-in list contains a public-key certificate for each recognized certificate authority. Each certificate contains the name and public key for an authority. The certificate format provides a safe and convenient way to distribute the information.

Figure 16.13 shows how Firefox used its built-in list of authorities to verify the bpn.gov certificate shown in Figure 16.12. Firefox produced an alert (Figure 16.11) indicating that the certificate's name (bpn.gov) did not match the URL name (ccr.gov). Firefox did, however, verify the authenticity of bpn.gov's certificate.

If a certificate authority is *not* in the browser's built-in list, then the browser cannot verify the certificate's digital signature and thus cannot tell if the certificate is legitimate. When this happens, the browser produces a security alert like the one in Figure 16.11. This time, however, the technical details explain that the browser does not trust the authority who issued the certificate.

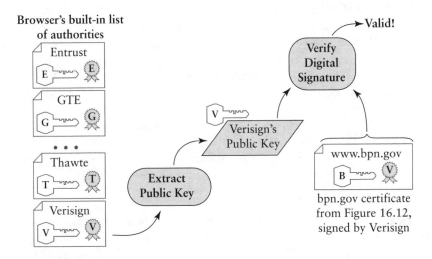

Figure 16.13

Browser authenticates the bpn.gov certificate.

This poses a difficult security problem with no simple answer. The certificate in fact may be legitimate or it may be a *bogus certificate* produced by an attacker. There are two ways an attacker might exploit a bogus certificate in this case:

1. The bogus certificate might be part of a phishing attack: The bogus site may try to trick us into disclosing login information. SSL may protect the connection, but the information we type travels directly to the attacker's system (see Section 15.3.2).

2. The bogus certificate might be part of a bucket brigade attack (see Section 8.6). Again, the attacker might intercept SSL-protected login information for the legitimate site.

On the other hand, both the site and certificate might be genuine. Not all legitimate sites use certificate authorities that appear in the browsers' built-in lists. The U.S. military, for example, may use its own certificate authorities to sign certificates. Public-key certificates for those authorities aren't generally distributed with commercial browsers. Users who regularly visit those sites eliminate the alert by installing the appropriate U.S. military certificate in their browser. This allows the browser to automatically verify the military-issued certificates.

There are two strategies for dealing with an untrusted certificate:

1. **Risky but simple:** Decide to trust the certificate, but treat the site with some suspicion. If the site proves legitimate over several interactions, perhaps it is trustworthy.

2. **Safe but complicated:** Locate an SSL-protected site that can download the missing certificate for the authority. Install the certificate into the browser. Unfortunately, it isn't always simple to locate such sites and certificates.

Expired Certificate: Possibly Bogus, Probably Not

Public-key certificates generally carry a range of effective dates; the certificate in Figure 16.12 was issued on 8/3/10 to expire on 8/4/11. Servers occasionally may use a certificate for a few weeks past its expiration date, and this is usually an administrative oversight. Even though the mistake suggests carelessness on the site's part, it usually does not indicate a bogus site. Avoid certificates that are months or years out of date.

Revoked Certificate: Always Bogus

This error occurs if the certificate authority actually has revoked a certificate. The authority only revokes a certificate following a request from the certificate's owner. This occurs rarely and almost certainly indicates that the certificate is bogus.

Invalid Digital Signature: Always Bogus

This may arise if an attacker simply modifies the public-key certificate directly. For example, the attacker might leave the certificate alone except to substitute one name for another or one public key for another. Any change to the certificate's contents should invalidate the digital signature. This clearly indicates a bogus certificate.

16.2.3 Server Masquerades

A bogus certificate is one whose public key is not exclusively controlled by the individual or enterprise named in the certificate. For example, Kevin wants to create a bogus Amalgamated Widget site. The easiest way for Kevin to create such a site is to omit SSL entirely. Many users won't even notice its absence.

However, Kevin wants to produce a really convincing bogus site and he wants to provide SSL. He uses a software package to construct a public-key certificate containing the name Amalgamated Widget. Because Kevin controls the private key associated with the certificate, it is a bogus certificate.

Many server masquerades rely on bogus certificates. Here are four techniques for tricking users or their browsers into accepting bogus certificates:

1. Bogus certificate authority
2. Misleading domain name
3. Stolen private key
4. Tricked certificate authority

These four techniques are listed in roughly the order of difficulty for the attacker, starting with the easiest.

Section 8.6.3 described a process to verify downloaded software using digital signatures. The technique can authenticate client-side scripts and software updates. Careful software vendors use this technique—or one like it—to protect software while being transmitted across the Internet.

Attackers also may use these four masquerade strategies to produce digitally signed software. When such masquerades succeed, the attacker can distribute malware that appears to be legitimate software.

BOGUS CERTIFICATE AUTHORITY

There are numerous software packages, both open source and commercial, that can construct public-key certificates. Anyone can appoint themselves to be a certificate authority and issue certificates. Kevin did so at the beginning of the section. Once he creates the certificate and inserts the name "www.amawig.com," he can sign it with his personal private key or he can self-sign the certificate with its own private key (see Section 8.6.2).

In either case, typical browsers won't include Kevin's public key in their built-in list of authorities. Thus, the certificate check shown in Figure 16.10 fails and the browser alerts the user.

However, the masquerade still may succeed. The user might not understand the alert and might proceed with the connection regardless. Given the millions of people who use the Internet, it is likely that someone, somewhere will ignore the browser warning and proceed.

MISLEADING DOMAIN NAME

The attacker has a better chance of success if the user doesn't receive a warning from the browser. The attacker avoids the warning by using a public-key certificate that is signed by a legitimate, recognized certificate authority. Kevin can create such a certificate for his masquerade if he uses an intentionally misleading domain name. For example, Kevin might host his bogus amawig.com site at the domain "amavig.com" or "anawig.com." The difference may appear only in the browser's URL window and many users won't notice it.

The only way to detect the misleading name is to look at the URL displayed by the browser and realize that it is wrong. Even experienced computer users might not notice a subtle one-letter change. There are several ways to construct misleading names, and they generally take these forms:

- **Similar but different.** This is the strategy behind Kevin's "anawig.com" domain name.

  The antiphishing tutorial at eBay.com notes how phishers have used the name "signin-ebay.com" to trick users into thinking they had arrived at "sig-nin.ebay.com," which clearly belongs to eBay. Early phishing attempts against Paypal users led to a site named "paypai.com," which was easily misread as "pay-pal.com."

- **Misleading syntax.** Figure 16.6 showed how the domain name in a URL may contain text preceding an @ sign. Phishers have used such names to try to trick users. For example:

  http://www.bank.com@www.phishinghost.com/login.html

  Although this may appear to be a URL leading to www.bank.com, all material to the right of the @ sign really is treated as a user name. In fact, most servers will ignore it. Firefox and other modern web clients produce a warning message when users try to follow URLs containing an @ sign, because it is rarely used except in phishing attempts.

- **Obfuscating syntax.** Programming traditions in the C programming language treat the "null" character (a character whose code is all 0s) as the marker for the end of a text string. Many programs follow this tradition even when underlying standards or protocols do not follow that tradition. For example, the formatting procedures for public-key certificates often allowed null characters in domain names. A security researcher discovered that this trick could hide part of a URL from the browser's user.

We can address some of these problems by tightening the requirements on public-key certificates, like forbidding nulls and other misleading characters. Unfortunately, it's not practical to forbid the registration of like-sounding domain names.

Many of the larger ISPs provide domain registration, SSL certificate issuance, and website hosting services. The operations are fully integrated and automated. If Kevin registers a particular domain name, the ISP also will host a website for the domain and provide it with an SSL certificate. Kevin simply has to pay for everything with a credit card.

If Kevin manages to register a misleading domain name, he easily can set up the bogus site protected with the legitimate-looking SSL certificate. In a technical sense, Kevin isn't using a bogus certificate, though the name suggests that Amalgamated Widget owns it and not Kevin.

This type of attack is hard to prevent ahead of time. Some organizations protect themselves by registering numerous domain names similar to their own and by redirecting those names to their website. Many vendors simply ignore the problem except when a site tries to perform a serious masquerade.

Kevin may be liable for civil and criminal penalties if he sets up the bogus site and tricks Amalgamated's customers. He may be guilty of trademark infringement simply by displaying Amalgamated's logo and other imagery. If he pretends to sell products and collects the money, he may be guilty of fraud.

Even if Kevin manages to hide his ownership of this site and avoid lawsuits or prosecution, Amalgamated may take steps to shut the site down. The company can track down the ISP, contact them, and identify the site as infringing on their trademarks and copyrights. The company also can apply to ICANN to strip Kevin of the misleading domain name. To do so, they must successfully argue that his domain name is too similar to their trademarked name.

STOLEN PRIVATE KEY

This approach requires that Kevin penetrate the amawig.com server somehow and steal a copy of its private key. This makes it trivial to masquerade as the amawig.com server. He distributes Amalgamated Widget's existing public-key certificate and uses the stolen private key to handle the SSL connections.

Technically, the amawig.com certificate becomes bogus as soon as Kevin receives a copy of its private key, because the key is no longer under the control of the legitimate owner. However, the owner probably won't realize this has happened until Kevin's masquerade is detected.

It is not clear how often such thefts occur. There was a notable incident in 2010 involving the Stuxnet worm described in Section 3.2.4. The worm distributed software signed with keys belonging to two Korean hardware vendors. Researchers suspect that the corresponding private keys were stolen by people working for the Stuxnet development team. The keys were used to sign Stuxnet software so that it could masquerade as legitimate device driver software.

TRICKED CERTIFICATE AUTHORITY

Another potential source of trouble is if a reputable certificate authority issues a bogus certificate. If the authority is careless about verifying a buyer's identity or doesn't verify the buyer's authority to use a particular name, then the authority might issue a bogus certificate. Such an attack occurred in 2001 when a soon-to-leave Microsoft employee tricked their certificate authority into issuing a Microsoft-named certificate for a key that he still controlled.

In 2011, an attacker issued bogus certificates by masquerading as a CA affiliate who was authorized to issue certificates. The attacker had intercepted login credentials for a legitimate affiliate. Then he logged in and issued himself nine bogus certificates for well-known sites like Gmail and Yahoo. The attack was made possible because the CA accepted logins via a simple user ID and password. The CA promptly detected the masquerade and issued a security alert, but could not prevent the issuance of the bogus certificates.

16.3 Dynamic Websites

Although static websites fascinated the first web users in the 1990s, they soon were eclipsed by sites offering more dynamic content. Dynamic sites made it easy to update the site's contents continuously and to provide a multimedia experience.

Modern servers construct web pages on demand, based on the visitor's input. If the visitor clicks a particular link or fills out a form, the site constructs the page tailored to the user's selections. Sophisticated sites even take a visitor's earlier activities into account when it builds a page.

Web forms provided the original mechanism for dynamic web output. HTML contains "form" tags that display buttons, text fields, menus, selection boxes, and so on. We construct a web form by including these tags in the page markup. When the page displays, the user may fill in the fields and make selections. The user then may submit the form to the web server by clicking a "Submit" link or button. Otherwise, the user simply may navigate away from the page, often losing the filled-in contents.

WEB FORMS AND POST

When the user clicks "Submit," the browser transmits a special HTTP command called *POST*. This command "posts" the form's fields to the web page. Figure 16.14 shows what happens when Alice fills out a form.

The process takes the following four steps:

1. Alice selects a link that retrieves the form from the server.
2. The server transmits the form to the browser, which displays it to Alice.
3. She fills out the form. When she clicks "Submit," the browser sends the form's fields to the server in the POST command.
4. The server processes the form and sends a reply.

The "Submit" button constructs a URL. Although a typical GET operation simply identifies a path to a file, a typical POST URL contains additional fields. The "?" character marks the beginning of a list of arguments that match up the form's fields. Each field's name serves as an argument name. The POST command passes the argument values contained in the corresponding fields.

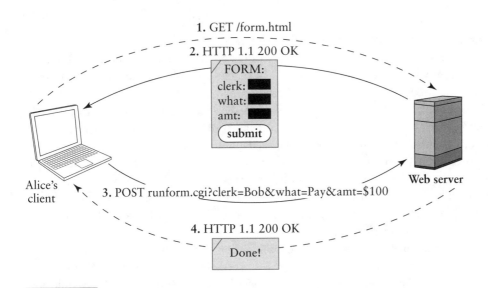

1. GET /form.html

2. HTTP 1.1 200 OK

FORM:
clerk:
what:
amt:
(submit)

Alice's client

Web server

3. POST runform.cgi?clerk=Bob&what=Pay&amt=$100

4. HTTP 1.1 200 OK

Done!

Figure 16.14

Alice chooses, fills out, and submits a form.

The form in this example has three fields: **clerk, what,** and **amt**. Each serves as a variable that receives its field's value. Alice filled in the **clerk** as Bob, the **what** as "Pay," and the amount ("**amt**") as $100. The POST command carries that list of argument values back to the server.

The POST command doesn't literally send the results back to the form's web page on the server; it doesn't copy them back into "form.html." A web page might contain a form, but the page itself is static. It can't process input itself.

Instead, the POST command tells the server to run a command script or other program. Originally, most scripts were in the Perl programming language. Perl is a sophisticated interpreted language that evolved from Unix shell scripts. It still is used heavily for system administration tasks.

When starting the script, the POST command provides the arguments sent by the browser along with their assigned values. The script then performs its actions based on how Alice filled in the form. At minimum, a script might produce a customized page of HTML. The server sends the script's HTML output back to the browser, which displays it to Alice.

16.3.1 Scripts on the Web

As websites became more complex, site builders relied more and more on scripts to simplify site design and operation. Modern sites often use scripts on the server side (called *server-side scripts*) to construct pages with consistent layout and format and including the latest and most accurate contents for that page. Sites also embed scripts in the pages themselves; the client's browser executes those scripts on the user's own computer. Scripts run by the browser are *client-side scripts.*

Server-side scripts have become essential to site construction and operation. Today, few sites actually store their contents as HTML pages. Instead, most links lead to scripts that construct the HTML page contents based on parameters passed with the URL.

Although the examples in the previous section showed arguments passed with POST commands, *any* link or other URL may include a list of arguments. The browser includes those arguments when it sends the GET command.

The server executes a server side script because the URL itself refers to a script or to a page containing a script. Figure 16.15 illustrates the process. When the server encounters a script, it passes the script to the interpreter for that particular scripting language. The script interpreter executes the script. The script's output yields text in HTML format, which the server transmits back to the client.

Some script languages are web specific while others are general-purpose languages adapted to use with websites. Perl is a general-purpose language, as is Java. Scripts written in web-specific languages often look superficially like HTML files. The dynamic elements of the web-specific scripts appear in special tags that aren't part of conventional HTML. The script interpreter intercepts those tags, processes them, and inserts HTML-appropriate text in their place.

Scripting Languages

Initially, web-based scripts used the POST command and a mechanism called the Common Gateway Interface (CGI). The web server executed such commands by calling up scripts with the .cgi suffix. Today, a script may carry one of many suffixes, including:

- PL—Perl
- ASP—Active Server Pages: a web-specific scripting language that supports instructions in Visual Basic, Javascript, and ActiveX, as supported by Microsoft's IIS server

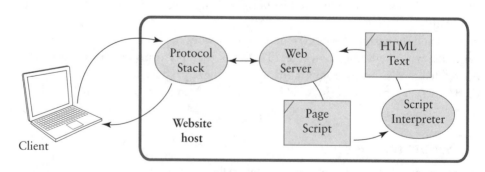

Figure 16.15

Executing a server-side script.

- ASPX—ASP Extended: ASP scripting extended to support Microsoft's ".NET" network programming framework
- PHP—Hypertext Preprocessor, originally called "Personal Home Page" format: a highly popular open-source scripting language used with countless websites
- CFM—Cold Fusion Markup Language: a commercial web-specific scripting language
- JS—Javascript: a web-oriented version of Java
- JSP—Java Server Pages: server-side scripts written in Java
- SSJS—Server Side Javascript: a version of Java tailored for web scripting
- PY—Python: a general-purpose language used for server scripting
- RB—Ruby: another general-purpose language used for server scripting

When a URL refers to a script, it may include one or more arguments. The browser sends these to the server along with the path name in the GET command. The server extracts the path name from the GET command and retrieves the script file. It then extracts the argument list and passes it to the script interpreter along with the path name.

The interpreter executes the script and provides it with the argument list and path name. The script constructs the page based on the arguments it receives.

In some more sophisticated systems, there is a single master script that intercepts *all* incoming HTTP commands. The master script extracts the URL path name and uses it as an argument to determine the page's contents.

CLIENT-SIDE SCRIPTS

Client-side scripts appear as short procedures embedded in an HTML page. The server itself interprets server-side scripts. The server ignores client-side scripts and transmits them to the browser within the web page text. Figure 16.16 shows a simple client-side script written in Javascript.

Most of the web page in the figure consists of conventional HTML. The script begins with the <script> tag. The tag's **type** argument indicates the script language being used (Javascript in this case). The browser interprets everything until the closing </script> tag as part of the script.

The script in the figure uses the "prompt" function to ask the browser's user to type in a name (Figure 16.17); then the script writes out the rest of the web page text, including a personalized message. This takes place entirely within the browser.

This example uses the Javascript language, which most browsers support. Microsoft's browsers also support Visual Basic scripting. Although some browsers support other languages, most client scripts use Javascript.

Client Scripting Risks

Client-side scripting poses special risks because the browser's chain of control passes to the instructions in the web page's script. If the browser visits a malicious website or an

```html
<html>
<head>
<title>simple javascript example</title>
</head>
<h1>Simple Javascript Example</h1>
This page text will be customized just for you!
<p>

<script type="text/javascript">
  var yourname = prompt('What is your name?');
  document.write('JavaScript here, '+yourname+'! What do you want?');
</script>

</html>
```

Figure 16.16

Client-side HTML script in Javascript.

Figure 16.17

Executing the client-side script in Figure 16.16.

attacker saves a malicious script on a legitimate site, then the browser may execute a malicious script. Most scripting languages provide enough programming functions to implement a virus or Trojan capability.

These risks pose an interesting dilemma for web developers. On the one hand, client-side scripts improve efficiency by using the client processor to do the work; they may interact with the user and the client file system without the delays of server interaction. On the other hand, client-side programs could modify and damage files and other resources on the client's host computer. We can increase security by restricting the power of client-side scripting languages, but that reduces their effectiveness.

For example, many sites provide client-side scripts to streamline the uploading of photos or other content. These scripts must be able to select and retrieve files from the host's file system. However, this also opens the host to malicious scripts that might retrieve files without permission.

A particularly common form of client-scripting attack is called ***cross-site scripting*** (abbreviated XSS). In these attacks, the attacker tricks a benign website into feeding a malicious script to the victim's browser. A classic example is when sites allow visitors to post comments and the comments may contain arbitrary HTML text. The attacker either posts the malicious script in a comment or points the comment to a script stored on the attacker's website. The victim's browser loads and executes the attack script simply by visiting the page containing the attacker's comment.

Many sites try to prevent such attacks by limiting the format of posted comments and other user-supplied text. The sites specifically try to filter out scripts or references to scripts. Other defensive strategies try to prevent scripts from doing harm by limiting their capabilities.

"Same Origin" Policy

One defensive strategy that many browsers use is the ***same origin policy***, which grants a script access to resources as long as the resources share the same host, port number, and protocol. If the script tries to retrieve other files from the host, then the script must use the same protocol and port number.

For example, the script can't retrieve a plaintext "http" file if it was retrieved through an encrypted "https" connection. Likewise, a script loaded from "amawig.com" can retrieve other files from that server, but not from "secret.org," even if the browser can reach that server. This reduces the risk of a client-side script from acting as a Trojan that takes advantage of the client's network access rights. Cross-site scripting attacks try to subvert the same origin policy by apparently retrieving the script from a trustworthy website.

Sandboxing

We may also ***sandbox*** the browser to try to reduce these risks. This technique runs the browser in a restricted environment that limits its access to host files and other resources. Some sandboxes block access to all resources outside the sandbox, except those explicitly brought in by the user. Google has built sandboxing into its Chrome browser.

Newer operating systems provide a limited degree of sandboxing when the browser runs as a normal user as opposed to being an administrator. Malicious scripts still may damage the user's personal resources but should not be able to damage system resources. Additional levels of sandboxing may further protect personal resources.

16.3.2 States and HTTP

If HTTP and HTML are essentially stateless, then the output of a web form will depend *entirely* on the data Alice typed in. The form can't collect information from pages Alice visited earlier or forms she previously filled out. This poses a problem for dynamic websites.

For example, Alice visits a site to find a pair of pants and a jacket to go with it. She clicks on a page and selects the pants she wants. Now she navigates to a different page that contains the desired jacket. Because of statelessness, however, the server already has forgotten which pants she wanted.

In fact, we know that modern websites easily keep track of selected merchandise. Most of us realize that sites often track us from one site to the next and use our browsing data to guess our interests and send us targeted advertisements. These actions clearly require "statefulness."

The modern website *shopping cart* keeps track of selected purchases while we browse through a site. The cart mechanism also provides a "checkout" procedure in which we confirm our selections and pay for them electronically.

Beyond shopping carts, Amazon.com pioneered techniques to tailor each page to reflect the interests of each of its visitors. Amazon keeps track of prior searches, of product pages visited, and of purchases. Amazon lists related products and searches on page columns, while the central part of the page focuses on the visitor's selected items or searches.

Browser Cookies

A *browser cookie*, usually just called a "cookie," is a piece of data stored by a browser on behalf of a web server. If the browser has a cookie from a particular web server, then it includes the cookie whenever it sends that server an HTTP message.

The browser won't have a cookie when it visits a server for the very first time. Figure 16.18 shows the client's HTTP GET and the server's response for such an initial visit.

Client's GET

```
GET / HTTP/1.1
Host: www.amawig.com
Accept: text/html,application/xhtml+xml,application/xml;q=0.9,*/*;q=0.8
Accept-Language: en-us,en;q=0.5
Accept-Encoding: gzip,deflate
Accept-Charset: ISO-8859-1,utf-8;q=0.7,*;q=0.7
```

Server's Response

```
HTTP/1.1 200 OK
Date: Mon, 02 Aug 2010 21:51:21 GMT
Server: Apache
Set-Cookie: UID=b8bf3b4b2f3b168e39cd29;
Set-Cookie: SESSION=7daf03bd34cf54; expires=Tue, 03-Aug-2010 21:51:22 GMT
Content-Type: text/html; charset=UTF-8
```
... followed by the HTML page contents

Figure 16.18

The initial website visit produces a cookie.

The client retrieves the home page from Amalgamated Widget as shown in the upper part of Figure 16.18. Because the GET command did not contain cookies already, the server generates cookies for that browser. The server includes the cookies in its response to the GET command, shown under "Server's Response." The response includes two "Set-Cookie" commands that provide two cookies to the browser.

The next time the browser visits the server, it includes the cookies and their corresponding cookie values in its HTTP request. In Figure 16.19, the browser visits the "About" page. Note the cookies included in the last line of the GET request.

When the Amalgamated server receives the request in Figure 16.19, the cookie tells the server that this visitor has visited at least once before. Thus, the cookie provides a simple way of counting visits.

The web browser uses the client computer's file system to maintain a copy of every cookie. The client typically stores the cookies in a folder along with other user-specific data, like the personal desktop background selection, personal email files, desktop layout, and so on. Each user has a personalized database of cookies. Browsers often store the cookies in individual files, each named for the server that owns the cookie. Whenever the browser visits a particular server, it includes the cookies received from that server.

When the client visited the Amalgamated website, the browser received two cookies: the UID cookie and the SESSION cookie. The server uses the first cookie to uniquely identify each visitor. The second cookie lets the site distinguish between separate visits by the same person. The SESSION cookie expires after about 24 hours; when the user visits the site again, the server detects the missing SESSION cookie and issues another one, indicating a new session.

The web server software itself (e.g., Apache or IIS) essentially ignores the cookies; it simply passes them along to scripts that implement a web application for that site. The application scripts may run when the server receives particular HTTP commands and those scripts must interpret the cookies. The example provided here for managing sessions is a simple example; actual sites use different and more sophisticated strategies.

```
GET /about.html HTTP/1.1
Host: www.amawig.com
Accept: text/html,application/xhtml+xml,application/xml;q=0.9,*/*;q=0.8
Accept-Language: en-us,en;q=0.5
Accept-Encoding: gzip,deflate
Accept-Charset: ISO-8859-1,utf-8;q=0.7,*;q=0.7
Cookie: UID=b8bf3b4b2f3b168e39cd29; SESSION=7daf03bd34cf54
```

Figure 16.19

The cookie is added to the header in subsequent visits.

16.4 Content Management Systems

As sites evolved in size and complexity, so did the problem of keeping pages up-to-date and consistent. Sites based on HTML text files face an overwhelming task when updating the overall site appearance, because an update may require individual changes to every page file.

Instead, most modern sites use a *content management system*, or CMS, to manage the site's contents and construct web pages. A CMS-run site is a truly dynamic site; when a user requests a page, the CMS constructs it based on easy-to-change data and parameters.

Instead of storing the website's content in individual HTML page files, the site stores its content in a database. The CMS runs scripts to build pages based on data retrieved from the database. As shown in Figure 16.20, a CMS-based web host contains five separate parts:

1. Protocol stack software—appears in every operating system that hosts web pages.
2. Web server software—appears in every computer that hosts web pages. This implements static HTML, SSL security, and can pass a script to a separate interpreter for execution.
3. Content management system software—receives GET, POST, and other HTTP requests and returns a web page in response.
4. *Database management system* (DBMS) software—stores and retrieves data in a structured manner. This provides a much easier way to handle a variety of site data than a file system by itself.
5. Database—a set of files on the hard drive that contain the site's data, organized and managed by the DBMS.

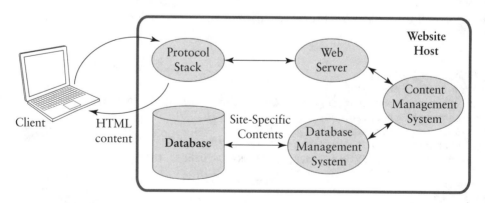

Figure 16.20

Web content management system.

CMS packages often consist of a set of scripts written in an interpreted language. Many are written in PHP, including Drupal, Joomla, and WordPress. When the browser requests a page from a site running one of these packages, the link leads to a PHP script. The PHP interpreter runs the script, which constructs the page's HTML text.

Although there are many commercial CMS systems available, numerous websites rely on open source software. The underlying elements occur so often together that they have earned the acronym "LAMP," which stands for Linux–Apache–MySQL–PHP. A web server based on LAMP uses the components as follows:

- Linux for the server's operating system
- Apache for the web server software
- MySQL for the database management system
- PHP for the web-scripting language

16.4.1 Database Management Systems

A *database* systematically stores data in a structured manner. Most people keep several databases, whether they are aware of it or not; an address book is a database, for example. A database management system is a software package with an effective set of tools for collecting, storing, organizing, and analyzing data. The DBMS manages a set of files that contain the database's data. All operations on the database files take place through the DBMS.

A typical database today organizes its data into tables. Each data table may reside in its own file. Within each table, data is organized into *records* and *fields*. Figure 16.21 shows two tables from a sample database that helps organize a blogging website.

The left table in the figure (marked "Articles") contains five records, each for an article written by one of the users. Each record contains three fields: the article number ("ArticleNo"), the date, and the author. The Users table lists users who may have written articles. Modern *relational* databases provide tools to link records in one table to records in another; this is why arrows link the articles to the authors' entries in the

Articles Table

ArticleNo	Date	Author
101	7/8/9	alice
102	9/9/9	alice
103	8/9/10	bob
104	10/1/10	alice
105	10/10/10	bob

Relations between articles and users (authors)

Users Table

UserID	Password
alice	29ck4cvj2p0
eve	cl40dsk34ow
bob	5ovmerj4i8dk

Figure 16.21

Sample data tables from a sample database.

Users table. The field that identifies one record so that others may link to it is often called a *key field*. The UserID field in the Users table is a key field.

> **History**   Most of the practical problems solved by computers involve databases. Programmers have labored on database problems since the earliest days of electronic computers. In 1951, computer RAMs were so small that they couldn't support modern DBMS functions. Instead, programmers constructed small programs to perform individual DBMS operations. Each program was handcrafted to search for specific fields and sort the data.
>
>   This problem led to the first computer program that itself wrote *another* computer program. The program, called the "Sort Merge Generator," was written in 1951 by Frances "Betty" Holberton (1917–2001). Holberton's program took a description of the key fields in one or more database files and produced a program to merge the files, sorted by their key fields.

Individual database tables are similar to spreadsheets: The rows correspond to records and columns identify fields. Many people routinely use spreadsheets to solve database problems.

STRUCTURED QUERY LANGUAGE

When a program uses a DBMS, it transmits its requests through a specially designed API. Most use a text-oriented interface based on the ***Structured Query Language*** (SQL), a standard in the database community. SQL supports queries to search and extract data from the database plus other operations to add or update data in the database.

The DBMS generally operates as a separate process. Other programs connect to the DBMS through a socket-like interface. The SQL commands arrive via a connection between the program and the DBMS. When the program establishes the connection, it provides a user ID and selects the database to use. The DBMS will check the access permissions for that user ID and establish the connection if allowed.

Figure 16.22 shows a typical SQL query using the SELECT operation. We choose the arguments to SELECT according to what data we want to extract from the database. In the figure, the operation takes place on the database from Figure 16.21. A query's result usually produces a data table.

The SELECT example contains four arguments. The first argument lists the fields returned in the result. There may be one or more fields returned. If the query indicates "*" instead of a list of fields, then the query returns *all* fields.

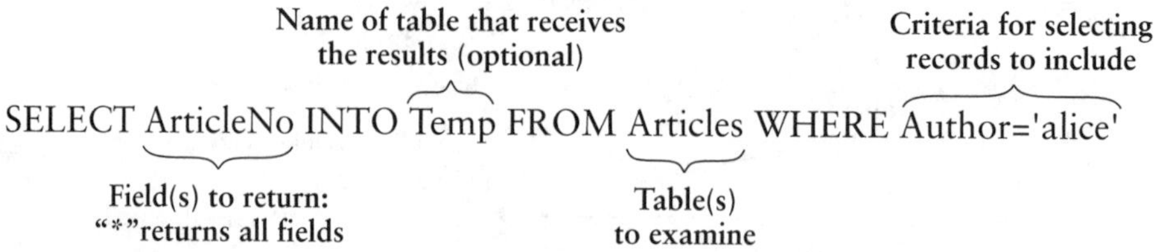

Name of table that receives the results (optional)   Criteria for selecting records to include

SELECT ArticleNo INTO Temp FROM Articles WHERE Author='alice'

Field(s) to return: "*"returns all fields   Table(s) to examine

Figure 16.22

Example of a SELECT command in SQL.

The second argument is optional. The argument, prefixed by INTO, names a table that receives the query's results. The third argument, prefixed by FROM, indicates the table containing the data to be queried. A single database may contain several tables, so this argument always appears.

The final argument, prefixed by WHERE, provides the criteria for selecting records to include in the answer. If we omit WHERE, then the query returns all records and only includes the fields listed in the first argument. The WHERE clause usually compares the contents of a named field in a particular record and accepts that record if the comparison succeeds. A single WHERE clause may perform several comparisons, combined with the logical operators "AND" and "OR."

If we perform the query in Figure 16.22 on the sample tables in Figure 16.21, the result yields a table named Temp. The table contains three records, each with a single ArticleNo field.

Enterprise Databases

Many modern organizations maintain a *data warehouse*, which contains a copy of all of the organization's transaction data for the purpose of analysis and reporting. The analysis process is sometimes called *data mining*, in which analysts seek insight into the organization's operations by studying large quantities of detailed data.

Although not all organizations structure their databases into a data warehouse, all organizations rely heavily on collecting and analyzing enterprise data. To publish an accurate balance sheet for the corporate annual report, the enterprise must systematically collect and analyze the enterprise's financial information.

Database Security

In general, database security relies on the same general concepts and mechanisms as file system security. Most databases require identification and authentication before they accept queries or other operations from remote sources. Sophisticated database systems also maintain "database user" tables that associate individual users with specific access rights. On a database, access rights are similar to those of files and directories described in Section 3.1: the right to create, modify, or delete items and collections thereof.

Databases may, however, enforce more detailed access restrictions. Even though access controls to files might be analogous to those for accessing tables, a database also may restrict a user's right to see or modify particular fields in particular tables. This is similar to allowing a user to modify a spreadsheet, but restricting which *columns* may be modified.

Important challenges in database security are embodied in the terms *aggregation and inference*. If we forbid Eve from looking at certain fields, but still allow her to make queries including those fields, then she may be able to infer the values of hidden fields. For example, we might hide salaries from Eve, but she may still infer salary information by making clever queries. We revisit these problems when we look at the challenge of protecting sensitive information in Section 17.1.1.

16.4.2 Password Checking: A CMS Example

In a CMS, the DBMS stores information about the site's format and page layouts as well as the actual contents to appear on individual pages. One table may contain articles or blog posts while another may contain images or other media.

When the CMS receives a web page request, it uses the path name and any arguments provided as input to a database query. The DBMS returns the text of the selected page article to the CMS, which formats the text into an HTML page.

LOGGING-IN TO A WEBSITE

Most modern websites provide different services and capabilities to different people. The general public may see a site's general contents, but they aren't allowed to add information or make other changes. Most sites require visitors to register and identify themselves before they are allowed to modify the site. (As of 2011, Wikipedia is probably the most famous of the few Internet sites where anonymous visitors may make changes). When revisiting the site, registered users must authenticate themselves; this typically requires a password.

The password database, like other databases on a CMS, resides in a database table. The Users table shown earlier in Figure 16.21 contains the basic data we require: a user ID and a hashed password. Note that the CMS uses hashed passwords in *this* example, but the example in the *next* section does not use hashed passwords.

AN EXAMPLE LOGIN PROCESS

In this example, Alice logs into a CMS-based website. The CMS performs the operation in two parts. The first part displays a web page to collect the user ID and performs a database query to collect the user's database record. The second part displays a separate web page to collect the password and performs a separate database query to verify it.

Figure 16.23 follows the first part of the login process from Alice's browser through the CMS to the database. The process starts in the upper left of the figure. After Alice navigates to the login screen the following steps occur:

1. Alice types her user ID "alice" into the login screen and presses "Enter." The browser has collected Alice's keystrokes. When it receives the "Enter" key, it starts processing the user ID.

2. The browser constructs a POST command to transmit Alice's user ID to the server. The POST command executes the script "checkuserid.php" and passes the value "alice" for the argument **userid**.

   Although not shown here, the POST command also carries a cookie that ties this POST command to the password Alice will enter later.

3. The server receives the POST command and runs the "checkuserid" script. This script takes the argument value assigned to **userid** and inserts it into a database SELECT command. The script sends the SELECT command to the DBMS.

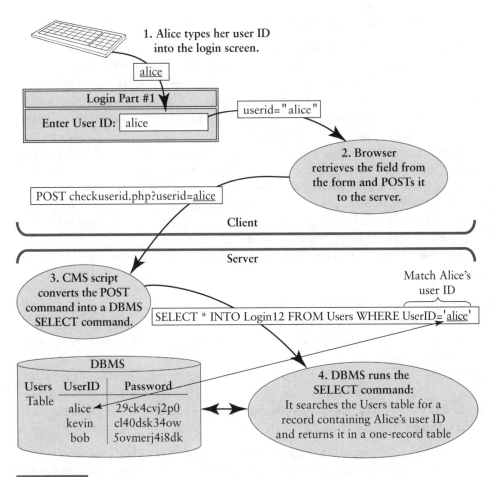

1. Alice types her user ID into the login screen.

alice

Login Part #1

Enter User ID: alice

userid="alice"

2. Browser retrieves the field from the form and POSTs it to the server.

POST checkuserid.php?userid=alice

Client

Server

3. CMS script converts the POST command into a DBMS SELECT command.

Match Alice's user ID

SELECT * INTO Login12 FROM Users WHERE UserID='alice'

DBMS

Users Table	UserID	Password
	alice	29ck4cvj2p0
	kevin	cl40dsk34ow
	bob	5ovmerj4i8dk

4. DBMS runs the SELECT command: It searches the Users table for a record containing Alice's user ID and returns it in a one-record table

Figure 16.23

Alice logs into a CMS-based website.

4. The DBMS executes the SELECT command. The WHERE clause locates Alice's user record. The DBMS saves the result in a temporary table named **Login12**. If **Login12** contains no records, then the login fails. This happens if the SELECT command doesn't find any records with a matching user ID.

If Login12 contains Alice's record, then the CMS continues with the second part of login: It sends Alice's client the password page. The page provides a cookie that associates Alice's browser with the Login12 temporary database table.

The CMS performs the same general steps a second time to check Alice's password. The password travels via a POST command and the CMS embeds it in a SELECT command. The CMS uses the cookie from Alice's POST command to retrieve the Login12 table and complete the login check.

16.4.3 Command Injection Attacks

Although a CMS naturally is vulnerable to the same attacks as any server or other software, it also faces a vulnerability inherent in the basic design. The CMS takes text from a URL and passes it as arguments to scripts. The script interpreter takes that information and interprets it according to the language's rules. A CMS script often produces output in the form of SQL commands that are passed to the DBMS.

Most programs examine and rearrange data as little as possible. This yields smaller and faster programs. For example, a web form collects a user name. The CMS puts the user name into an SQL query to retrieve the user's information. In a perfect world, we pass the user name from the URL to the SQL command with no extra muss or fuss.

In practice, however, this opens a serious vulnerability called a ***command injection*** attack. In such an attack, the attacker provides additional text in a web page field. This extra text is cleverly designed to look either like commands in the CMS's own interpreted language (a PHP or Perl command, for example) or SQL statements to be interpreted by the DBMS.

A PASSWORD-ORIENTED INJECTION ATTACK

Eve now will masquerade as Alice by using a command injection attack. We use the same CMS login process described in the previous section. This time, however, we will omit password hashing.

When Eve performs the first step of the login process, she provides Alice's user ID. The process unfolds exactly as shown in Figure 16.23. The server creates the temporary Login12 table and awaits Alice's password. Figure 16.24 follows the command injection attack as it travels from the client to the DBMS:

1. The website prompts for Alice's password. Instead of typing in a password, Eve types in a specially crafted text string. The first letter "x" represents a guess at Alice's password, but it won't matter what password Eve types there.

2. The browser takes Eve's text string and embeds it in a POST command, assigned to the **pw** argument. The actual text looks like code, because the browser converts it to omit all blanks and URL-like punctuation. The "%27" represents a single quote character and the "+" signs stand in for individual space characters. The POST command also carries a cookie to tell the server which table contains its login record. Most systems do this indirectly; they put a session identifier in the cookie and store the table identifier with other session information.

3. The CMS converts the POST command into a SELECT command to check Alice's password. Eve's text string appears as the underlined text. The CMS sends the command to the DBMS.

4. The DBMS runs the SELECT command. Eve's specially crafted text string recasts the WHERE clause into an expression that is *always true*, regardless of Alice's password.

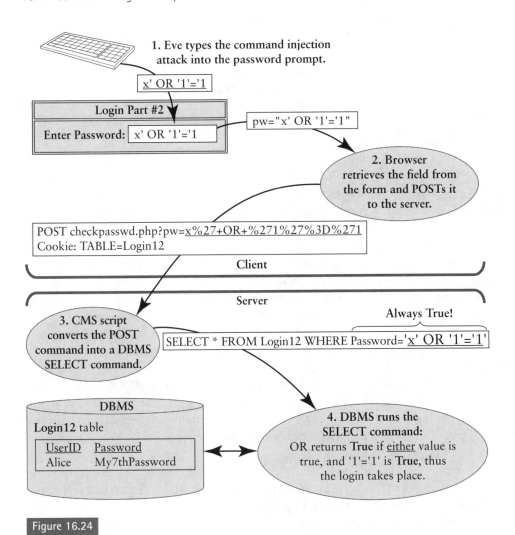

1. Eve types the command injection attack into the password prompt.

x' OR '1'='1

Login Part #2

Enter Password: x' OR '1'='1

pw="x' OR '1'='1"

2. Browser retrieves the field from the form and POSTs it to the server.

POST checkpasswd.php?pw=x%27+OR+%271%27%3D%271
Cookie: TABLE=Login12

Client

Server

Always True!

3. CMS script converts the POST command into a DBMS SELECT command.

SELECT * FROM Login12 WHERE Password='x' OR '1'='1'

DBMS

Login12 table

UserID   Password
Alice   My7thPassword

4. DBMS runs the SELECT command: OR returns **True** if <u>either</u> value is true, and '1'='1' is **True**, thus the login takes place.

Figure 16.24

Login masquerade using a command injection attack.

This type of attack subverts the Chain of Control by tricking the DBMS into interpreting part of the password as an SQL expression. In Section 2.3.1, we saw how a buffer overflow redirects the CPU to execute the wrong instructions; here the command insertion attack redirects the DBMS to perform the wrong password comparison.

INSIDE THE INJECTION ATTACK

Figure 16.25 shows the format of the SELECT command used to verify Alice's password. The FROM clause is filled in from cookie information. The WHERE is completed with the password text.

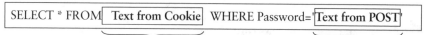

SELECT * FROM Text from Cookie WHERE Password='Text from POST'

The CMS must check these fields carefully before filling
them in or an injection attack may take place.

Figure 16.25

An SQL command injection vulnerability.

If the server hashes passwords, it performs the hash *before* inserting the value into the SELECT command. It is not unusual for a CMS to omit password hashing; some programmers believe it's safest to handle passwords as little as possible. Imprudence leads to disaster here.

Eve's injection attack exploits a feature of the SQL WHERE clause: The clause may perform a simple comparison between a single field and a data value or it may make several comparisons and use the combined results. Eve's attack transforms the WHERE clause from a simple password comparison into a two-part comparison.

On the left of Figure 16.26, we see the simple comparison that happens when Alice types her actual password. On the right, we see the two-part comparison that Eve injects with the typed password.

The two-part comparison uses the "OR" operation to combine the results of two different comparisons. The first part compares the password against an arbitrary value and usually will be logically false—but the second part of the two-part comparison is always logically true. The "OR" operation combines the two comparisons; if *either* is true, then the comparison yields a match.

This example uses a very simple technique to pass the temporary table name from the first part of the login to the second part: It places the table name in a cookie. The second step simply copies the cookie name into the SELECT statement.

This simple approach yields another avenue for command injection. The semicolon character (";") marks the end of a command in SQL. Assume that Eve could intercept

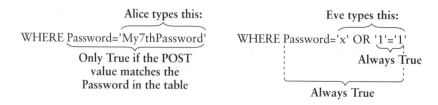

Alice types this:

WHERE Password='My7thPassword'

Only True if the POST
value matches the
Password in the table

Eve types this:

WHERE Password='x' OR '1'='1'

Always True

Always True

Figure 16.26

A password that always matches in SQL.

the HTTP text containing the password, modify it, and send it on its way. She also might attack successfully if she appends a semicolon to the table name and the semicolon is copied into the SELECT command. SQL will treat the semicolon as the end of the statement and simply may signal success. The dangling WHERE clause may or may not produce an error, depending on the DBMS.

RESISTING WEBSITE COMMAND INJECTION

This particular example of command injection relied on plaintext passwords. If the CMS used password hashing, the command injection itself would have been scrambled, defeating the injection.

Large websites, however, may have hundreds or thousands of other text fields. Hashing passwords won't prevent command injections in those other fields. A clever command injection may retrieve *any* information from the site's database, posing serious privacy risks for customers as well as security risks for the site.

Input Validation

Most CMS software tries to eliminate command injections through careful software design. The CMS scripts try to carefully analyze all text typed in by a user to ensure that it carries no hidden threats. These strategies include the following:

- Avoid embedding any typed-in text directly into a command or script statement. Store the text in a variable and refer to the variable instead.
- If text must be used in a script, scan it to identify and remove any "escape" characters that might be interpreted by the script language. For example, the password in Figure 16.24 includes single-quote characters that alter the meaning of the SQL statement.
- If users may post messages to the site (i.e., comments on a blog post), be sure to review the text for risky content. For example, a comment could contain or refer to a malicious script. A user's browser then will execute the script when viewing the comment. This is a type of cross-site scripting attack. Some sites permit users to use a subset of HTML for formatting a comment and filter out all other HTML tags.
- Be cautious about files uploaded by users. A malicious user could upload a file containing a malicious program; it is much easier to trick the CMS to execute a local file than a remote one.

Site security also depends on the integrity of the CMS scripts. An attacker can penetrate the site easily if the operator uploads scripts from an untrustworthy source. Most CMS packages use add-on modules produced by third parties to provide special features. Be sure that the module authors are reputable and trustworthy.

16.5 Ensuring Web Security Properties

Here we examine the challenge of achieving the CIA properties (confidentiality, integrity, availability) on websites. We examine confidentiality and integrity here. A separate section discusses availability and a final section examines web privacy.

WEB CONFIDENTIALITY

Web services face a range of confidentiality problems and related security objectives. Although many web servers offer their contents to any and all potential visitors, some try to restrict access. Any site that collects confidential information from visitors is obliged to protect that information. We examine these cases here.

Serve Confidential Data

Most sites address this problem by identifying trustworthy users. If the user is authorized to retrieve the information, then we trust users to protect it when it arrives on their clients. We can't really prevent a user from making copies of data they retrieve from a website. Sites that implement this type of confidentiality rely on server-based authentication and access control to protect the data on the server and SSL protection on the data while in transit.

A variant of this arises when the site wishes to enforce digital rights management (DRM). SSL only protects data while in transit. It won't prevent sharing through Transitive Trust once a user retrieves the data from the site (see Section 7.5). Most DRM implementations apply the security measures directly to the data. Each authorized user receives a credential that allows decryption under controlled circumstances. In Section 8.2.4, we saw that credentials for DVD buyers were built into DVD player hardware.

Collect Confidential Data

Sites often collect confidential data as part of a retail or financial transaction, though it may occur in other circumstances as well. Although the banking industry has developed a broad range of standards and recommendations for protecting web-based transactions, the best-known standards come from the payment card industry: PCI-DSS (see Section 4.6.2). These standards specify protection within retail establishments that use credit cards as well as websites that use credit cards.

Typical implementations rely on a secure server host and SSL protection on network traffic. The client must support SSL, but otherwise has few restrictions.

WEB INTEGRITY

There are essentially two integrity problems in the web environment: The first is ensuring integrity of data presented by the server; the second is ensuring integrity of data transmitted between the server and client.

We briefly addressed the server integrity problem when discussing static websites: If we can prevent outsiders from modifying the site's files, we can prevent most problems. The problem becomes more complex as sites allow visitors to store data, because this brings up cross-site scripting risks and related attacks. The notion of site integrity should indicate that the site does not pose a risk to visitors.

We maintain the integrity of data in transit by using SSL. Even though TCP by itself ensures integrity in the face of random communications errors, it cannot protect against a malicious attempt to modify traffic. Such assurance requires cryptographic integrity measures.

16.5.1 Web Availability

We classify levels of web service availability into four categories. These categories often suggest both the level of effort and the types of techniques used to improve availability.

1. *Routine availability*: The system may suffer occasional downtime, either expected or unexpected. The system managers take no special steps to ensure availability.

2. *High availability*: The system may experience scheduled downtime, but never experiences unscheduled downtime. Such systems require special designs to mask unexpected failures, possibly through redundancy.

3. *Continuous operation*: The system is designed to operate continuously with no scheduled outages. It might experience unscheduled outages. Such systems often rely on special hardware to allow routine maintenance and component swapping without shutting down the system.

4. *Continuous availability*: The system is designed to experience no outages at all, either scheduled or unscheduled. This requires a combination of the techniques used to achieve both high availability and continuous operation.

Redundancy plays a fundamental role in achieving higher levels of availability. To avoid software-based failures, sites may deploy upgraded software in test environments. The sites then perform functional and stability tests before deploying the revised software. Such testing naturally requires separate systems to host the test environment.

High Availability

For high availability, a system generally incorporates redundant components for processing, storage, and networking. Application processing is distributed among an integrated group of processors called a *cluster*. The system may "load balance" among the processors to increase overall performance while reducing the risk of a crash. If one processor in the cluster crashes, another takes up its work.

Although RAID provides redundancy on a small scale, large-scale sites often rely on *storage area networks* (SANs). These systems use network protocols to distribute disk storage across multiple devices. A modern SAN may distribute hardware geographically to provide higher assurance against a site-specific disaster.

Network redundancy relies on multiple links and routers. In some cases, the site simply deploys multiple devices with standard internetworking protocols. For some types of load-balancing, however, the network may use transport-layer header information to route traffic to particular servers.

Continuous Operation

By itself, high availability does not ensure continuous operation. A RAID-configured hard drive system still may need to be taken off-line in order to replace a failed drive. Other types of routine maintenance may require the whole system be taken off-line, including power system modifications and some network modifications.

We rely on redundancy and special architectures to achieve continuous operation. We build separate systems that rely on separate networking and power connections. We use a SAN to distribute data and to allow ongoing maintenance of the storage system. We use load balancing to distribute the work between separate components, and the load balancing components themselves also must be redundant to allow routine maintenance.

Continuous Availability

We achieve continuous availability by eliminating every reason for the system to shut down, either intentionally or by accident. This combines high-availability design tricks with continuous operation techniques. By itself, continuous operation provides the procedures to perform maintenance without shutting the entire system down. To achieve continuous availability, we must ensure that a second failure can't bring the system down before we fix the first one.

Continuous availability often relies on geographic dispersion; we place redundant servers in geographically separate locations. This reduces the risk of losing service due to a local problem like a power failure or a local disaster like a flood, tornado, or hurricane.

It can be tricky to deploy a dynamic website across geographically distributed locations. Dynamic sites rely on a database that also must be geographically distributed, and database contents may vary in different locations. If the site implements user sessions or shopping carts, then the overall system must ensure that a single session takes place using a particular database.

16.5.2 Web Privacy

One shortcoming of a rigorous, enterprise-focused security engineering process is that it often shifts focus away from risks to customers and other outside individuals. A privacy breach might not damage an enterprise directly, but it may cause significant damage to individuals. This has produced legislation in many regions to protect personal privacy and to hold enterprises accountable for data they store.

In addition, many web users try to preserve privacy through other techniques, notably through anonymity and through "private browsing." We examine these cases here.

CLIENT ANONYMITY

Anonymity is both a blessing and a curse on the Internet. On some occasions, it seems impossible to hold people accountable for Internet misbehavior. On other occasions, it seems impossible to browse without leaving an undesired trail.

People prize anonymity on the Internet for a variety of reasons. A plausible, and often socially acceptable, reason for anonymity is to mask the identity of a political dissenter or anyone who wants to voice an unpopular opinion. Anonymity becomes particularly important in places where political dissenters face injury or arrest. In countries that do not criminalize dissent, anonymity may be used to hide other legal but disreputable activities.

Even though web browsing seems like an anonymous activity to many people, the browser provides servers with many details about its users. Researchers have noted that browsers will report detailed configuration information about the browsing host and the information may be enough to "fingerprint" individual hosts. Although this technique has not seen significant practical use, it might provide circumstantial evidence of a user's visit.

More significantly, the TCP/IP connection must provide the client's numerical IP address. Even if the site applies NAT to the IP address, the address and port number uniquely identify the visit. Law enforcement organizations in the United States suggest that ISPs try to preserve information that ties IP addresses to specific subscribers for at least 6 months so that the data may be available to investigators.

Anonymous Proxies

When people wish to further hide their identities while web browsing, they may use an *anonymous proxy*. To use one, the user configures the browser's proxy setting to direct traffic at the proxy's IP address. The browser essentially "tunnels" the IP packets to the proxy, which forwards the packet after applying NAT to the source address. The receiving server sees the anonymous proxy as the packet's source.

When the server transmits its reply, it directs the packet at the proxy, because that was the address in the inbound packets. The proxy identifies the appropriate browser and sends the packet back to that browser. The user's traffic remains anonymous as long as an eavesdropper can't correlate the server's traffic with that user's traffic. For example, the eavesdropper simply might monitor traffic at the anonymous proxy. The eavesdropper can associate the user and server addresses by comparing the sizes, contents, and timing of the packets.

Client users also must rely on the proxy to protect their identities. If the proxy keeps a record of visitors and their activities, then there is a risk of the anonymous users being unmasked. Moreover, an attacker who subverts a proxy may interfere with user traffic or indulge in extortion of those relying on the proxy's anonymity.

The safest anonymous proxies use a technique called *onion routing*, which routes each connection through a network of proxies. This makes it much more difficult to associate user and server traffic, because connections enter and leave at a variety of points. The Tor network, run by the Electronic Frontier Foundation (EFF), is the best-known anonymous proxy network. According to the EFF, Tor users include casual users desiring additional privacy as well as journalists, law enforcement, intelligence agents, business executives, and political activists.

Sites that resist privacy may restrict access via anonymous proxies. Nations that filter their citizens' web traffic often may try to block access to proxies, because the proxies would circumvent filtering. Wikipedia, the online community encyclopedia, does not allow visitors to edit its articles if visiting via an anonymous proxy, in order to make visitors more accountable for their edits.

PRIVATE BROWSING

Certain companies try to systematically track a user's browsing activity. The primary example is in third-party advertising; the advertiser tries to track each user's visits and then infers a user's interests from the types of sites visited. Advertisers typically use cookies to track user behavior; the advertiser then selects ads to display to each user based on the particular user's behavior.

In a perfectly safe and fully functional environment, the server wants to know as much as possible about each client host. The server wants to know the screen size, the contents of its font library, performance capabilities, data formats supported, and anything else that helps optimize the site's display. Although it isn't always clear what bits of information will significantly improve the client's experience when visiting the site, designers are inclined to share as much information as possible. This makes it hard to ensure privacy.

Moreover, browsers routinely maintain a great deal of information about the sites a user visits. Some information resides in the browser's "history," which may help users locate a site visited earlier. Browsers also maintain an internal cache with copies of pages and images retrieved from the web. This speeds up the process of displaying a site if the user returns to it; only revised files need to be retrieved.

Between its cookies, history, and cache, the browser retains a great deal of information about a user's web visiting behavior. Users that worry about external eavesdroppers monitoring their web browsing also may worry about people searching their client host.

Some browsers provide special features to support private browsing. These may consist of erasing the history, cookies, and cache after the browsing session ends. Other features might restrict which client details the browser reveals.

16.6 Resources

 IMPORTANT TERMS INTRODUCED

anonymous proxy	continuous operation	routine availability
authority	database	same origin policy
bogus certificate	GET	sandbox
bogus site	high availability	scheme
browser cookie	HTTP tunneling	server-side script
client-side script	hypertext	stateless protocol
command injection	hypertext links	web crawler
continuous availability	POST	

ACRONYMS INTRODUCED

ASP—Active Server Pages
ASPX—Active Server Pages, Extended
CFM—Cold Fusion Markup Language
CGI—Common Gateway Interface
CMS—Content management system
CSS—Cascading Style Sheets
DBMS—Database management system
GIF—Graphics Interchange Format
HTML—Hypertext Markup Language
IIS—Internet Information Services
JPEG—Joint Photographic Engineering Group
JS—Javascript
JSP—Java Server Page
LAMP—Linux, Apache, MySQL, PHP
PHP—Personal Home Page/Hypertext Preprocessor
PL—Perl
PNG—Portable Network Graphics
PY—Python
RB—Ruby
SAN—Storage area network
SQL—Structured Query Language
SSJS—Server-side Javascript
URI—Uniform Resource Identifier
URL—Uniform Resource Locator
W3C—World Wide Web Consortium
XML—Extensible Markup Language
XSS—Cross-site scripting

16.6.1 Review Questions

R1.   Describe the respective roles of HTML and HTTP in the World Wide Web.

R2.   Identify and describe five HTML tags.

R3.   Identify and describe the four major components of a URL.

R4.   Describe the four steps the browser takes to retrieve and display a web page.

R5.   Identify and describe three different strategies and techniques to manage web use.

R6.   Explain how the web browser authenticates a server that uses SSL.

R7.   Describe three different techniques for masquerading as a particular host that uses SSL.

R8. Explain the operation of server-side scripts and client-side scripts. How are they the same? How are they different?

R9. How does a website maintain a state for a web visitor's session? For example, how does it ensure that it correctly associates a particular browser with a particular shopping cart?

R10. Describe the basic components of a content management system.

R11. Describe the role of a DBMS and SQL in a content management system.

R12. Explain the steps involved in performing a typical operation in a web CMS, like the one illustrated in Figure 16.23.

R13. Describe how an SQL command injection attack might work.

R14. Summarize the challenges of achieving web confidentiality and integrity.

R15. Describe the four different categories of site availability.

R16. Summarize the basic elements of client anonymity and private browsing.

16.6.2 Exercises

E1. Using an instructor-provided Wireshark packet capture file, locate a series of packets that retrieve a web page.

   a. What frame numbers perform the three-way handshake to open the connection?

   b. What is the host name and/or IP address of the web server?

   c. Identify the frame number containing the GET command.

   d. Does the GET command contain a cookie? How many cookie values does it contain? What name or names are given to the cookie values?

   e. Identify the frame number of the first packet that responds to the GET command.

   f. How many packets are required to transmit the requested page?

E2. Write a simple web page in HTML. Use Figure 16.2 as an example, but customize it to contain different titles, headings, and text. Hand in two items: (1) the page's HTML source text and (2) a copy of the

page produced by the browser after the script has executed.

E3. Visit a website's home page. Note the URL.

   a. Modify the URL to include a user ID (any name will do). Save and hand in any alert that the browser displays. If it displays no alert, simply save and hand in the browser window showing its contents and the modified URL.

   b. Modify the URL to include both a user ID and password. Again, any name will do and use a simple string of letters as the password. Save and hand in any alert that the browser displays. If it displays no alert, simply save and hand in the browser window showing its contents and the modified URL.

E4. Visit an SSL-protected website. Use the browser to display the certificate.

   a. Make a copy of the certificate's contents to hand in.

   b. What is the name of the certificate authority that issued the certificate?

c. Use the browser to display the certificate for that certificate authority. Make a copy of that certificate's contents to hand in, too.

E5. Write a web page that uses Javascript to customize itself. Use Figure 16.16 as an example, but be sure that it produces a different title and different text on the resulting page. Hand in two items: (1) the page's HTML source text, including the script and (2) a copy of the page produced by the browser after the script has executed.

E6. Bob has a web page that contains private information. To protect it from disclosure, he added a client-side script to the beginning of the page. The script checks for a secret password. If the password is wrong, the script won't let the browser display the rest of the page. Explain why or why not this protects Bob's private information.

E7. Redraw Figure 16.20 to show the location and flow of these types of data: HTML, server-side scripts, and SQL.

GOVERNMENTS AND SECRECY

ABOUT THIS CHAPTER

This chapter surveys government information security with a special focus on military-grade secrecy requirements. Although parts of this may apply to other national governments, this chapter focuses on policies and concepts specific to the U.S. government and often to the U.S. defense and intelligence communities. This chapter examines the following aspects of governments and secrecy:

- The secrecy problem as seen by governments and by the defense and intelligence communities
- Security classifications and clearances
- National information security policy issues and typical policy elements
- Communications security in the U.S. defense and intelligence communities
- Special data protection concerns, like media handling and transmission security
- Information security in critical applications

17.1 Secrecy in Government

Governments try to rely on commercial products for most tasks, including information technology. Many countries even rely on a number of commercial technologies for military applications, though nuclear-armed countries tend to spend more money on specialized equipment. In information technology, government secrecy requirements often lead to specialized products, technologies, and equipment.

Government secrecy in the United States evolved during the 20th century. Before World War I, the state department routinely published its communications with embassies and with other governments. Military secrets were few, because military advantage usually resided in physical superiority. When the U.S. Army or Navy went to battle, secrecy and surprise were important, but secrecy played little role in peacetime.

This changed in 1917. On the same day President Woodrow Wilson asked for a declaration of war, an Espionage Act was introduced to Congress. The law made it unlawful to disclose information about national defense. Even though espionage earlier had been handled through laws regarding treason, this established a different offense: a failure to keep a secret.

Following World War II and the development of the atomic bomb, government secrecy took on apocalyptic proportions. If a cold-war adversary could exploit a military secret to make a successful nuclear attack, then the target might be obliterated while the aggressor suffered little damage.

When we talk about risks and threat agents in the national arena, we often speak of *adversaries*. The term refers to threat agents motivated by loyalty to a particular nation or cause who see our nation as a threat. Unlike threat agents associated with private or commercial risks, these agents often are willing to sacrifice their lives to achieve their objectives. Moreover, agents of national governments may have far greater resources behind them than those in private industry.

When we compare the risk of warfare or even nuclear annihilation with risks faced in private and commercial realms, we see why governments put more resources into secrecy. Commercial and private enterprises may be obliged to keep certain secrets, but disclosure doesn't obliterate a nation. Although a disclosed secret could destroy jobs and companies—and possibly lives, there is almost always a way to pay restitution for leaked secrets in the private and commercial sphere. We can't do that with secrets that risk a nation's existence.

This justification arose during the Cold War era and variants of it continue today. This has led to an elaborate bureaucracy for establishing, identifying, and managing secret information as well as an elaborate technical infrastructure to protect secrets. This has had a major impact on government information technology since computers evolved in the 1950s. Military and intelligence agencies also paid for most early computer developments in the United States, United Kingdom, and other countries.

Hostile Intelligence Services

Governments typically face a more sophisticated threat than private enterprises. Companies may, of course, have competitors who systematically try to steal proprietary secrets and confidential company information. However, both the competitors and the companies themselves must limit the effort they put into espionage. Companies thrive on profits and spying is an overhead expense.

A *hostile intelligence service* is a threat agent that collects sensitive information on behalf of a potential adversary. Traditionally, such services worked on behalf of nations. This is not always true; some may work on behalf of nonnational entities, like terrorist organizations or extremist political groups.

Hostile intelligence services may be very well funded when associated with large or wealthy nations. Both the United States and Russia deployed human agents and technical means, including satellites and large-scale code breaking operations to penetrate the others' secrets. Both nations likewise spent large amounts of resources to protect their most critical secrets.

CLASSIFIED INFORMATION

The concept of *classified information* refers to information explicitly protected by particular laws or regulations and marked to indicate its status. Although many governments also have laws to protect private personal information and health care information, neither of these are considered classified. Typically, a government classifies information associated with national security or intelligence activities.

In countries with a culture of openness or free speech, classified information represents an exception in which disclosing information may be a criminal act. Nations often justify this as a significant threat to public safety or order. According to typical laws and regulations, information is classified when its disclosure might cause "serious" or "exceptionally grave" injury to the nation.

In the United States, the free speech guarantee of the Constitution's First Amendment poses a challenge to the secrecy needs of the defense and intelligence communities. Although federal laws and regulations make it possible to prosecute individuals for disclosing classified information, most criminal convictions are limited to those who release more sensitive, "Top Secret" information. There have been few civilian convictions for disclosing less-sensitive—but still classified—information.

17.1.1 The Challenge of Secrecy

Secrecy poses a challenge in two dimensions. First, disclosure is ruled by Transitive Trust; a secret remains secret only if *everyone* who knows it keeps it secret. Second, secrets are easy to leak. There are many ways for a physical fact to leak out, like a scientific formula or the attributes of a machine or weapon. A threat agent may discover the fact independently or accurately infer secret facts through observation and study.

In the 1980s, the novelist Tom Clancy spoke informally with many military experts, observed unclassified military activities, and read extensively about military topics. He had no access to classified information. Nonetheless, military officials claimed that some information appearing in his novels was in fact classified. Clancy says that such information is the product of combining unclassified facts to infer classified ones.

Clancy's experience illustrates the problem of *aggregation and inference*. If we collect a large amount of public information on a classified topic, the *aggregate* of information may contain classified information. We extract the classified information by *inferring* it from the visible facts.

Information rendered to paper or to bits often leaves evidence behind. In Section 7.4.3, we saw how difficult it was to totally erase data from a hard drive. Printed documents may leave telltale information inside the computer that operates the printer and in the printer itself. Photocopy machines may retain thousands of images of previously copied documents.

To keep a secret, we must consider the leakiness of information in general, *plus* we must take account of the carelessness and possible blunders of *everyone* who knows the secret. A typical strategy to protect secrets is to establish a comprehensive set of policies and procedures to manage and protect the secrets. The U.S. Defense Security Service has published a set of such procedures in their 140-page *National Industrial Security Program Operating Manual* or *NISPOM*.

THE DISCIPLINE OF SECRECY

Secrecy processes like those described in the *NISPOM* provide layered defenses to help individuals avoid disclosing secrets. In theory, everyone who handles the secrets uses a similar process, though this is not true in practice. The *NISPOM* describes procedures for private enterprises that handle classified government secrets, but government agencies and military commands make their own rules.

Secrecy procedures often rely on a collection of simple strategies. When we combine the strategies and apply them consistently, the secrets should remain safe. Basic strategies include:

- Secrets are secured by default. Under normal circumstances, keep classified documents locked up so that others can't retrieve them. There are security standards for how long it takes to break into a cabinet approved to store classified information. Always lock up classified documents in approved cabinets except when actually in use. Approved cabinets often resemble safes, complete with combination locks.

- Secrets are never left unattended. If the secret document isn't locked up, then it must remain under the direct physical control of someone authorized to have it. If the authorized person leaves the area, the classified document goes with the authorized person.

- Avoid identifying secrets as secrets. A nonclassified document should avoid referring to a classified document, because it indicates the existence of a secret. When carrying a classified document, hide the cover so that others can't tell it is a classified document.

- Secrets are revealed only in safe places. Discussions of classified information are restricted to rooms declared safe. Exclude cell phone, webcams, and other recording or transmission equipment from the area. Don't work on a classified document except in a closed area that excludes others who might eavesdrop or shoulder surf.

- Verify permissions before sharing. Always check with authorities before sharing classified information with others. Confirm that the intended recipient is both authorized to receive the information and has the appropriate Need to Know.

These five strategies are simple to enumerate. The specific procedures to implement them can become quite detailed. It can be difficult to follow all security procedures, day after day, year after year. People become lax or careless without further help. We address this with two familiar strategies:

1. Defense in Depth. Provide layers of protection; multiple opportunities to detect lapses in security and fix them before classified data actually leaks. For example, people who work with classified materials on a daily basis usually work in a closed area that only allows access to people allowed to share the secrets. If someone for-

gets to lock up a classified document, the document remains in the closed area, inaccessible to unauthorized people.

2. Security awareness. Everyone responsible for protecting secrets must participate in periodic briefings, retraining, or other security awareness activities to help ensure ongoing compliance with procedures.

Practical security procedures recognize the inevitability of human errors and take steps to reduce their risk. Childrens' diaries rarely remain secret because it is hard for anyone to systematically protect a secret, much less a child.

Secrecy and Information Systems

It is extremely difficult to control the spread of secrets—or of any type of information—in an information system. Secrecy seems to pose a simple problem; we use a few trustworthy processes to handle the data and we block access from everything else.

However, such a solution relies on a flawless operating system. We have no such operating system. It relies on flawless applications for constructing and modifying secret documents. Applications mustn't accidentally leave too-secret information in a less-secret document.

This is called the *redaction problem*; how can we remove sensitive information from a document and be confident that we removed *all* of the sensitive information? It is easy to redact a paper document; we simply blank out the information we want to remove (Figure 17.1). Blanking out doesn't always do what we expect in a word-processing program.

A classic example occurred during the Iraq war; the U.S. military released a report about an incident at a checkpoint where civilians were killed. The original report contained a great deal of classified information; it was edited to hide the information and then released to the public. Unfortunately, the editor simply placed black boxes over the sensitive text. In fact, the text was still present in the document's released Adobe Acrobat file, *underneath* the black boxes.

Exposure and Quarantine

Many security experts see secret information as analogous to contagious diseases. Until medical science developed tests to distinguish healthy patients from those carrying such

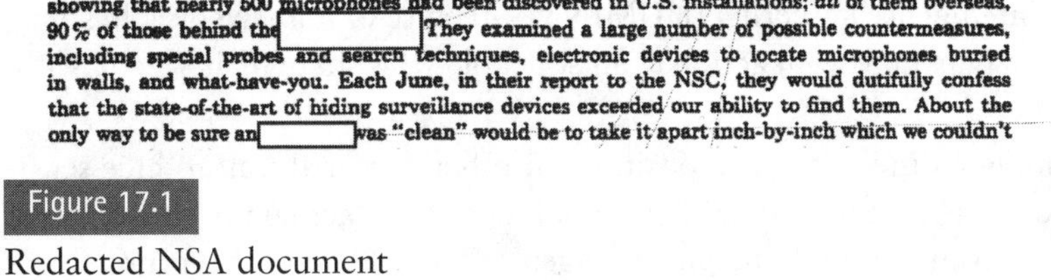

SECRET NOFORN   EO 1.4.(c)

and developing a program to counter them. In the space of a few years, they assembled information showing that nearly 500 microphones had been discovered in U.S. installations; *all* of them overseas, 90% of those behind the [   ] They examined a large number of possible countermeasures, including special probes and search techniques, electronic devices to locate microphones buried in walls, and what-have-you. Each June, in their report to the NSC, they would dutifully confess that the state-of-the-art of hiding surveillance devices exceeded our ability to find them. About the only way to be sure an [   ] was "clean" would be to take it apart inch-by-inch which we couldn't

Figure 17.1

Redacted NSA document

a disease, public health officials would place people in quarantine if they were simply *exposed* to an infected person. Boarding schools routinely shut down for several weeks if a student was diagnosed with an infectious disease. Everyone who came in contact with a sick student was placed in quarantine while sick students were treated. Those not in contact with sick students were sent home to avoid both the sick and the exposed.

Computer systems follow this "exposure and quarantine" model when handling highly sensitive information. If any data in a system is considered highly sensitive, then *all* data on the system is treated as being equally sensitive. If an operator produces a document containing no sensitive data, the operator must take special steps to export the nonsensitive data and nothing else.

Redaction technology is similar to disease testing of a century ago. We can't automatically and reliably ensure that we have removed every bit of sensitive information from a document. The vendor may have some subtle feature or undocumented flaw that retains information in an unexpected place. Thus, if *any* classified information infects a document, we can't be positive that our editing has removed *all* of it.

17.1.2 Information Security and Operations

Governments place a high value on protecting their most important secrets. Hostile governments may place an equally high value on finding that information. Strategies and actions unknown in the world of legitimate commerce are routine in international conflicts, even when countries aren't directly at war. These particularly apply to these situations:

- Intelligence and counterintelligence
- Information operations
- Operations security

The following subsections examine strategies and techniques applied in these challenging environments.

INTELLIGENCE AND COUNTERINTELLIGENCE

The intelligence community uses the whole gamut of "spy tradecraft" to collect information and to try to defeat adversary spies. Although it's customary to collect information about "adversary businesses" in the commercial world, many of these measures are too extreme or are even illegal in the commercial realm. They are routine in the national intelligence communities.

- Human-based intelligence gathering (HUMINT)—the use of human spies. In some cases, companies may take legal action against people who share their secrets with competitors.
- Covers—assuming a different name, position, or other personal trait to hide sensitive information, like a person's actual personal identity or actual job title or position. This is very common with intelligence agents. The CIA does this routinely

with many staff members. Former CIA employees sometimes must provide cover information on a resume when job hunting. In the commercial world, a cover is "misrepresentation" and may be reason to fire the perpetrator.

- Technical surveillance countermeasures—using various techniques to defeat eavesdropping, bugs, wiretapping, or other surveillance techniques. Private and commercial enterprises might do this in extreme situations. Again, technical surveillance often violates the law; if a commercial adversary does it, the victim may pursue legal action against the perpetrator.

- Emergency destruction—the process of destroying information that risks falling into the hands of adversaries. Legitimate private and commercial enterprises rarely have information that is sensitive enough to justify emergency destruction.

Although some or all of these techniques occasionally may arise in private or commercial environments, it is the exception rather than the rule. Military and government agencies rely on them more often because they can't use the same types of financial inducements or legal threats to deter their adversaries.

MILITARY INFORMATION OPERATIONS

Within the U.S. military, *information operations* are intended to influence or actually disrupt the decision making of adversaries. These operations rely on a variety of measures that are rarely used in private or commercial activities. These include:

- Electronic warfare—using the electromagnetic spectrum to jam, mislead, or attack an adversary. This may involve eavesdropping on adversary signals or on jamming them.

- Computer network operations—exploiting and attacking adversary computer networks on one side and defending our own networks from attack on the other.

- Military deception—specific actions taken to mislead an adversary in order to promote the success of a military operation. The deceptions intend to encourage particular actions or inactions on the part of the adversary.

- *Operations security* (OPSEC)—managing publicly visible aspects of military operations to prevent disclosure of sensitive information about the operations. We discuss this further later.

- Psychological operations—conveying selected elements of factual information to foreign audiences to influence their behavior. These operations may appeal to public emotions and motives to try to influence public opinion and the actions of governments and organizations.

Companies and other private organizations may use some of these techniques in a milder, legal form. Advertisements, public relations campaigns, and other activities to manage an enterprise's public image clearly have similar objectives to information operations. In general, however, companies avoid actually violating laws or incurring legal risks, because they may work against promoting the intended public image.

OPERATIONS SECURITY

OPSEC is a process for assessing publicly visible ("friendly") aspects of military operations from the point of view of adversaries to ensure that adversaries can't deduce sensitive information from its publicly visible actions. An OPSEC analysis may restrict public activities or lead to cover-and-deception activities.

A classic example arose during the first Gulf War. In late 1990, as the U.S. military approached the moment of their invasion of Iraqi-held Kuwait, a pizza delivery official reported a sharp spike in nighttime delivery orders around Washington, D.C., and the Pentagon. A related legend claims that pizza orders also spiked prior to troop deployments in Grenada, Panama, and the Middle East and during the Kremlin coup in 1991.

OPSEC experts call these visible side effects of military operations "unclassified indicators." An effective OPSEC program eliminates such indicators. Sometimes we suppress indicators by keeping an operation as secret as possible until implementation. During the 1991 Gulf War, the air strike planning activity was kept secret from the command's Air Force headquarters staff until only a few hours before its execution; this was justified on OPSEC grounds.

Within the U.S. defense community, every major command has an OPSEC program officer who manages the program and coordinates its operation within the command. This includes assessing ongoing activities and operations from an OPSEC standpoint, making assessments of specific programs, and providing awareness and training to the command.

OPSEC planning arises in all operations planning in a military command. A military campaign targets particular strategic and operational objectives and OPSEC planning focuses on ensuring these objectives. The OPSEC planning process is similar to the first four phases in our six-phase security process: (1) identifying critical resources (information, in this case), (2) assessing risks, (3) identifying policy goals, and (4) applying security measures. An "OPSEC assessment" applies the process intensively to a particular operation or activity. The assessment involves a multidisciplined team of experts and the results help assess the organization's OPSEC processes and procedures.

Given the central role that websites, email, and personal cell phones play in modern communications, information security has a significant impact on OPSEC. A careless individual easily may leak information that indicates an upcoming operation or other sensitive activity. In some cases, we prevent this through security training: If people remain aware of data sensitivity, they are less likely to release sensitive information by accident. In other cases, we can monitor websites and other communications to squelch disclosures after the fact.

Another information security aspect is in the choice of media for sharing sensitive information. Users may share OPSEC-sensitive unclassified information safely via restricted and specifically approved chat rooms or other discussion media. Users should never share data on external commercial sites, because the data could leak to adversaries, even if the site resides in a "friendly" country.

17.2 Classifications and Clearances

Security classification and clearance programs are a distinctive feature of military and government information security. The outline of a classification system evolved in Great Britain during the late 19th century. All allied powers adopted similar systems before or during World War I, including the United States.

A modern security classification system has four elements:

1. Classification—identifies a special category of information called "classified information" and identifies *classification levels* that indicate different degrees of risk of disclosure.

2. Protections—specific security measures that prevent physical access to classified information by unauthorized people.

3. Clearances—a process to establish permission to receive classified information in which we investigate individuals to assess their trustworthiness. A person must receive a *security clearance* to be granted access to classified information.

4. Penalties—significant administrative and legal penalties for mishandling or disclosing classified information.

Although commercial organizations occasionally implement similar programs to protect commercial secrets, they are rarely more than a poor imitation. Commercial organizations never need the level of secrecy or assurance demanded in the military and intelligence communities. Moreover, commercial enterprises can't apply the serious penalties a government or military service may establish.

CLASSIFICATION LEVELS

The "classification" part of classification systems assigns different levels to information. In the United States, we classify information into one of three levels. The classification reflects the degree of damage to national security that unauthorized disclosure could reasonably expect to cause:

1. Confidential—"damage"
2. Secret—"serious damage"
3. Top Secret—"exceptionally grave damage"

Although we use the phrase classification level here, other publications often use different phrases to mean the same thing. These include, for example, security level, sensitivity level, security classification, sensitivity label, and classification label.

In principle, the classification decision is supposed to balance the risks of disclosure and the benefits of leaving the information unclassified. Classified information is costly to manage and inconvenient to distribute. Moreover, troubles may arise from failures to share information. The 9/11 Commission noted several cases in which unshared information helped prevent detection of the attacks on New York City and Washington, D.C., ahead of time.

Other Restrictions

Figure 17.1 displayed part of a declassified, formerly secret document. The legend "NOFORN" appears after the classification level. This is an acronym meaning "no foreign distribution." In other words, the material must not be shared with foreign nationals, even if they have a U.S.-approved secret clearance. Documents may contain a variety of such restrictions. Some indicate that recipients first should receive a briefing on how to handle material with such markings. Other legends restrict the document to members of specific projects or programs or to a controlled list of authorized recipients.

For example, some documents are "originator controlled" (abbreviated ORCON). In such cases, the document's originator has the sole authority to grant access to it. This often is applied to intelligence data that could disclose information about the source. The team that manages the intelligence source decides to release the data if the risk of losing their source is justified by the benefit of sharing the intelligence data.

When we establish special restrictions to a program's information, we also may require a special clearance procedure. Although the clearance procedure for Top Secret information is more-or-less standard across the U.S. government, access to special programs and certain types of intelligence may require a more elaborate investigation and clearance process. People often refer to such programs as being classified "above Top Secret."

LEGAL BASIS FOR CLASSIFICATION

Although federal laws passed by Congress make it a criminal act to disclose national security information to adversaries, the classification system is entirely a presidential artifact. The security classification system was established through an executive order issued by the president. Executive orders provide the president with a way to specify how government departments should perform their legally mandated duties. As such, executive orders have the force of law.

As of 2010, the classification system is defined by Executive Order 13526. The order is issued under the president's legal authority as commander-in-chief, because it regulates aspects of national security. The order defines the recognized classification levels, assigns responsibility for classifying information, establishes responsibilities for safeguarding the information, and sets standards for declassifying information.

MINIMIZING THE AMOUNT OF CLASSIFIED INFORMATION

It is easy to misuse security classifications. Once information is classified, the government justifiably may refuse to disclose it in court and, in some cases, to Congress. The U.S. Supreme Court has upheld the government's right to protect classified data even when it may be important evidence in a civil or criminal trial. To minimize abuse, classifiers may not classify information simply to hide embarrassment, waste, fraud, errors, or criminal conduct.

The amount of classified information has grown dramatically over time and it continues to grow. Most U.S. presidents have taken steps to stem the tide when they revise the classification system through a new executive order. These steps fall into three categories:

1. Limit the ability to classify information. In most cases, it is limited to a handful of agency heads, who may delegate it to officials in their agency. However, people who work with classified information may classify a new document that contains information already deemed classified. This is called "derivative classification."

2. Systematically downgrade classified information. Provide a mechanism by which older classified information automatically is downgraded to a lower level over time. Ideally, this eventually leads to the declassification of the oldest classified information, except in special cases.

3. Restrict or forbid reclassification. Occasionally a presidential administration will decide that previously unclassified or declassified data may indeed be sensitive after all; then a collection of formerly unclassified information suddenly sports classification labels. This may be forbidden by executive order, but it may be reversed by a subsequent order.

Significant changes in the U.S. classification system followed the September 11 attacks. These changes tended to increase the amount of classified information. Specific changes slowed down or stopped systematic downgrading, while other changes reclassified previously classified information. Subsequent changes in 2009 reinstituted and clarified earlier rules that automatically downgraded older classified information.

17.2.1 Security Labeling

Anything containing classified information must carry a visible label indicating its classification level. This helps keep the materials safe by making them easy to spot by those responsible for their safety.

Classified devices or equipment likewise carry a label. The outside label indicates the most sensitive information contained therein. If a device contains a single item of Top Secret information, we label it Top Secret.

Classified documents always have standard, colored cover sheets that indicate their classification level. Document cover sheets and paper labels to apply to equipment or other items often use this color code:

- Top Secret—orange or gold
- Secret—red
- Confidential—blue

Document markings are quite elaborate. The DOD publishes a special manual explaining the details (DOD 5200.1-PH). Figure 17.2 shows an unclassified example of classified document markings.

The document's first page briefly explains why the document is classified and how or when it will be declassified. The document's overall classification level also appears at

SECRET

OFFICE OF THE SECRETARY OF DEFENSE
WASHINGTON, DC

MEMORANDUM FOR DASD (I&S)   31 August 1996

SUBJECT: "Classified by" Line (U)

1. **(S)** The third step in properly marking a document is to annotate the original classification authority on the document. This is accomplished by placing the original classification authority on the "Classified by" line. The "Classified by" line should include the name or personal identifier of the actual classifier and their position. If the identification of the originating agency is not apparent on the face of the document, place it *below* the "Classified by" line.

2. **(U)** The original classifier shall identify a concise reason for classification which, at a minimum cites the applicable classification categories in section 1.5 of E.O. 12958 as the basis for classification. Original classifiers must ensure that the exemption category selected is consistent with the reason for classification cited on the document.

Classified by:	Emmett Paige, Jr., ASD(C3I)
Reason:	Military Plans; Foreign Relations
OR	
Reason:	1.5 (a) and (d)
Declassify on:	December 31, XXXX **SECRET**

Figure 17.2

Classified document markings—an unclassified example.

the top and bottom of the first page. If the document contains multiple pages, the overall level also appears at the top and bottom of the back page.

Every page of a classified document carries its classification level on its header and footer. The header and footer simply may repeat the overall classification level of the entire document. However, authors are encouraged to mark pages individually to reflect the highest classification level of information on that particular page. This makes it easier to lower a document's sensitivity by examining the headers to remove more-sensitive pages.

Classified documents also carry "portion markings." These are abbreviated classification levels prefixed to every paragraph. In Figure 17.2, the portion markings indicate that paragraph 1 is classified Secret and paragraph 2 is unclassified. Portion markings are supposed to make redaction easier by distinguishing between more-classified and less-classified information, and by clearly indicating unclassified information.

SENSITIVE BUT UNCLASSIFIED

Governments have several mechanisms to restrict the flow of sensitive information. Laws to protect privacy and to protect health information, for example, establish federal restrictions on data distribution. However, this does *not* make private information classified information. The term "classified information" applies to specific categories of sensitive national security information. Not all sensitive data is classified.

When classification systems first evolved, they included the category "For Official Use Only," abbreviated FOUO. Traditionally, this marking indicates information that should not be released to the public or to the press. The information is intended only for use within the issuing organization and should only be shared with others if there is a Need to Know.

However, FOUO information is *not* classified information. Recipients don't need a security clearance. Recipients only need a bona fide reason to receive the data. Individual organizations may establish their own rules for sharing and handling such information. Rules even may be contradictory between different organizations.

Contradictory rules and other regulatory obstacles cause the executive branch to periodically create a new and different general-purpose term for unclassified information that requires special handling. The term "Sensitive but Unclassified" was popular for many years. More recently, the phrase "Controlled Unclassified Information" has become popular.

Government rules also forbid the export of certain types of information. This usually applies to specialized technical data with obvious and immediate military application. Again, this information is not classified, even though the government restricts its distribution. Such documents usually carry a specific "Export Controlled" or "Export Restricted" marking.

Document authors sometimes format an unclassified document to look like a classified one. They place distribution restrictions in the header and footer, simulating a classification level. They even might include portion markings that abbreviate distribution restrictions, like FOUO, or "U.S. Only" to indicate an export restriction.

These stylistic tricks occasionally confuse people in the government and military community. When the press reports that a hacker retrieved "classified information" from a poorly secured website, the documents almost always are restricted distribution documents formatted to look like classified documents. Sensitivity labels distinguish a classified document from others, but a claim of "leaked classified information" always attracts greater attention.

17.2.2 Security Clearances

A security clearance indicates that an individual is deemed trustworthy and may have access to classified information up to a particular classification level. We call these *hierarchical* levels because access to a higher level grants access to all lower levels. Figure 17.3 shows the arrangement graphically. The arrows indicate that information at a particular level may flow to people with appropriate clearances.

In Figure 17.3, Bob is in the middle with a Secret clearance. He may read Files B and C, because the Secret clearance allows him to read either Secret or Confidential documents. Tina at the bottom with a Confidential clearance can read only File C. Alice on top with a Top Secret clearance may read all three files. Despite clearances, though, any of them might be refused access to a document if they lack the Need to Know.

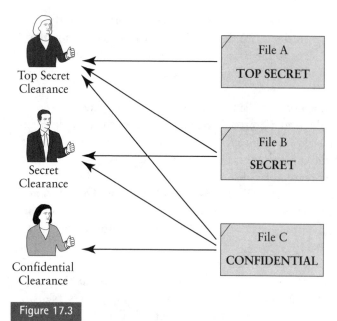

Figure 17.3

Access permissions for security clearances.

A government agency or military command issues someone a security clearance after investigating their background. The investigation begins with a detailed questionnaire that asks about the individual's previous addresses, jobs, education, legal problems, financial condition, family, and acquaintances. The investigation then evaluates the questionnaire and searches for any evidence that might call the individual's loyalty or trustworthiness into question.

Lower-level clearances require shorter and less-detailed investigations. Higher-level clearances require more detailed investigations. In the past, in fact, a private government contractor could perform its own investigation to issue an employee a Confidential clearance. Today, the government performs both Confidential and Secret investigations. Both involve a local and national check of law enforcement databases for criminal history and a credit check to assess financial stability. If a Secret clearance applicant needs access to a special program, then the investigation may be more thorough or include a personal interview.

All Top Secret clearances require a background investigation. A standard Top Secret investigation starts with a detailed questionnaire that reviews the applicant's personal history with a particular focus on the past 10 years. It also collects names of friends, neighbors, and family members who might be interviewed as part of the investigation. An investigator interviews the applicant to discuss information on the application. Other investigators may interview friends, neighbors, and family. Like lower-level clearances, investigators also perform a criminal background and credit check.

For access to information beyond Top Secret, the investigation is even more thorough. The investigation may look more closely at relationships with foreign nationals for spying risks or at lifestyle details for blackmail or extortion risks. The investigation also may include a *polygraph* examination, also known as a lie detector test.

There are two general reasons to refuse a clearance. First, an applicant may have a history or personal traits that place trustworthiness in doubt. For example, applicants may be refused a clearance if they participate in illegal activities (drugs or black-hat hacking, for example) or have a serious criminal record. The second reason for refusal is if the applicant lies to investigators or tries to mislead them. Such dishonesty raises strong questions about an applicant's trustworthiness.

17.2.3 Classification Levels in Practice

We protect classified data according to its sensitivity using Defense in Depth. Lower classification levels require less protection than higher levels. Higher classification calls for additional layers of security or for stronger measures or both.

To protect Confidential documents, we lock them up in a filing cabinet with an approved locking mechanism. We also may store Secret or Top Secret documents in a similar filing cabinet, but we also must provide a periodic guard patrol or an intrusion alarm or both. If we use stronger storage containers, we reduce the need for guards. Access control systems to protect Secret information have less-stringent requirements than those to protect Top Secret information.

Working with Classified Information

When it comes time to work with classified documents, we must use a work area that excludes unauthorized people. If we work in an office, we typically post a sign on the door saying "Restricted Area; Do Not Enter," and we close the door. No one may enter the office unless they have the appropriate clearance.

Ideally, we have a storage container in the office to store our classified documents and other materials. Otherwise, we may need to carry our classified documents past uncleared people. If so, we cover them to hide any classification markings. We want to avoid indicating that we are carrying classified information.

If we have classified material outside of a container, we essentially are shackled to that material. We may not leave it unattended in our restricted area unless there is another authorized person present who will take responsibility for it when we leave. Otherwise, we either bring the classified material with us or we lock it up.

There are very stringent restrictions on working with classified information on computers. Essentially, the *entire computer* is classified at the level of the most sensitive information it contains. We can't connect a computer to any network, unless the network is cleared to handle information at the same level as the computer. We examine these issues further in Section 17.6.

Higher Levels Have Greater Restrictions

At first it may seem that things are easiest if we are cleared for Top Secret and higher and if we arrange everything so that we can handle and store Top Secret and higher information. In theory, this would grant us access to whatever information we need and allow us to produce whatever documents we want. In practice, this arrangement is expensive and highly restricting.

When we accept responsibility for protecting sensitive information, we literally take on a burden. We must take active steps to protect the information and those steps restrict what we may do. Moreover, the burdens—in terms of restrictions on data handling and on our own behavior—become much heavier as the classification level increases.

The office in which we work on Top Secret information may have thick and comfortably soundproof walls, but it doesn't have windows. The door to our office suite is literally a vault door with a combination lock. We can't use a desktop computer to routinely produce unclassified documents if we also use it to create classified documents. Internet access is impossible or severely restricted if the computer handles *any* classified information. Friends and family can't drop in at work unless they have the right security clearances. Otherwise, the guard turns them away at the building's front entrance.

Moreover, there are government agencies ultimately responsible for the classified information and they often take special steps to reduce the risks posed by hostile intelligence services. They monitor our activities as much as is practical, keeping an eye on our offices and our homes. Some agencies may tap our phones to check for unauthorized contacts or other suspicious activities. People cleared for certain programs are even forbidden to travel overseas.

17.2.4 Compartments and Other Special Controls

Besides the hierarchical classification levels, we assign an additional set of classification markings to special types of information. This is how we classify information above Top Secret. The markings may belong to special programs or to intelligence data associated with particular sources or data collection methods. Here are some types of additional classified controls:

- *Sensitive Compartmented Information* (SCI)
- *Special Access Program* (SAP)
- *Special Intelligence* (SI)

First, we will examine these different categories, then we will look at how we interpret combinations of such markings.

SENSITIVE COMPARTMENTED INFORMATION

The word *compartment* refers to a well-known security strategy in the intelligence community. We protect secrets by breaking them up into separate sets and placing each in a separate compartment. We grant different people access to different compartments. If someone in a compartment turns out to be a spy, we only lose the information from the spy's compartment.

If we look at this in terms of earlier concepts and strategies, compartments provide a sort of Least Privilege combined with Separation of Duty. We divide the information into independent elements that people can work on separately (Separation of Duty). We restrict people, even highly trusted and cleared people, to as few compartments as possible (Least Privilege).

SCI Clearances

Access to SCI is the province of the U.S. intelligence community; it establishes the standards and issues the clearances. Top Secret access to SCI often requires an extensive investigation and a polygraph examination. The requirements may be lower for some compartments or for compartments restricted to Secret information.

Clearance procedures become more stringent if the person needs access to multiple compartments. Some intelligence operatives may need access to only a single compartment. Others, like intelligence analysts, may take information from one or more compartments and process it to yield information assigned to a different compartment. Such people face much more stringent investigation and clearance requirements.

For example, people with clearance to a single compartment might not require a polygraph examination. To gain access to one or two compartments, the investigation might call for a "counterintelligence" polygraph examination that focuses on questions about risks of spying. Broader access might require a "full-scope" polygraph examination that probes the person's lifestyle for risks of extortion as well as spy risks.

Example of SCI Processing

Here is a fictional example of how to process intelligence data through a series of compartments. We assume that Bob, Alice, Tina, and Clark all work for an unnamed intelligence agency, spying on the south of Freedonia to develop information about the grape harvest. They all have Top Secret clearances, but they work on different things. Kevin works in the department of agriculture and has a clearance and a Need to Know about the Freedonian grape harvest. Table 17.1 identifies the different workers and their clearances.

The agency assigns separate compartments to collect and process different types of intelligence data. As separate compartments process the data, they make it harder to identify the data's source. This allows the agency to release the data without disclosing exactly *how* they collected the data.

In this example, compartment names may have some relationship to the topic. In practice, the agency may choose the names totally at random, so that the name itself suggests nothing about the associated compartment. However, the compartment names *are* associated with information of particular types, so a spy could infer information by watching compartment names. Therefore, the agency usually classifies the compartment names themselves. Thus, we need the appropriate clearance before we even can look at a document's cover page to see to which compartment it belongs.

Who	Classification Level	Compartments	Duties
Bob	Top Secret	ARGUS, SAUVE	Analyze satellite photos
Alice	Top Secret	BISHOP, KRUG	Analyze HUMINT
Tina	Top Secret	SAUVE, KRUG, MALBEC	Merge satellite and HUMINT data
Clark	Top Secret	MALBEC	Sanitize MALBEC data, add public info
Kevin	Secret	MALBEC	Forecast world grape crop

TABLE 17.1 Fictional example of intelligence agency compartments

Figure 17.4 illustrates the flow of data between the different workers and their compartments. Bob and Alice both analyze raw intelligence data, but they work in different compartments. Bob takes raw satellite images of the south of Freedonia that belong in the ARGUS compartment. He analyzes and sanitizes the images to remove indications of the satellite image's real quality and to omit hints at how to hide information from the satellite, then he moves the result into the SAUVE compartment.

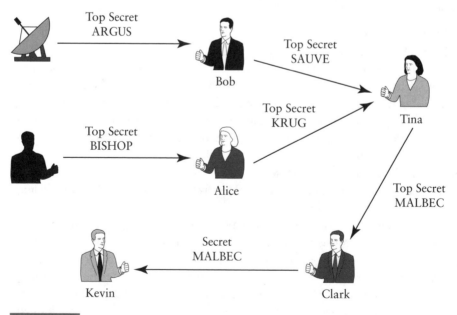

Figure 17.4

Using compartments to process data.

Alice takes intelligence from spies in the grape arbors (compartment BISHOP), analyzes it, and sanitizes it to hide the spies' identities, then she moves the result into the KRUG compartment. Tina takes the somewhat-sanitized data from SAUVE and KRUG, further removes indications of its sources, and produces a combined result for the MALBEC compartment.

Clark is responsible for taking information classified Top Secret MALBEC and sanitizing it so he can hand it over to Kevin. He combines the MALBEC data with published information about the grape harvest. To reduce the information to Secret, he further disguises the actual information sources. Now he can release the data to Kevin, who has a Secret clearance, plus clearance to the MALBEC compartment.

No one on this project belongs to more than three compartments. Tina has the most access to information, but she doesn't have direct access to raw intelligence. Kevin needs to have a special clearance to look at intelligence data, but he only sees it after several layers of sanitization and abstraction. If he sells the information to his friend at the Freedonian embassy, the Freedonian can't quite identify the human agents or infer the quality of the satellite cameras.

Although this arrangement makes the secrets safer, it also makes sharing more difficult between different parts of the government. The intelligence agency wants to keep its assets safe, so it filters high-priority secrets through a sanitization process like this. Lower-priority information may never be analyzed and thus never be shared. Other government agencies, like Homeland Security, have public safety obligations that may be compromised if a potential terrorist threat goes undetected because information failed to be shared.

In any case, when Kevin gets caught for stealing secrets, he's in serious trouble. Moreover, if they used defense satellites to collect the grape harvest information, then the disclosure places defense intelligence assets at risk. Even though it is hard to prosecute a case of disclosing classified information in some cases, the law explicitly forbids disclosing intelligence data that supports national defense. The disclosure could make the defense satellites less effective, even after the layers of sanitization.

Special Access Programs

A special access program is one whose data is released only to individuals specifically cleared by the program's own security office. This includes people working directly on the program, either in the DOD or in the contractors who perform the work. The DOD establishes a SAP when the project relies heavily on secrecy for its success.

Stealth aircraft provide the best recent examples of special access programs. The DOD established a separate SAP to develop particular prototypes and for operational aircraft. Each aircraft has a variety of secret properties associated with how it evades detection. The SAP may grant access when individuals on related projects need access to project details.

Many SAPs, including early stealth aircraft, began as *black programs*. The DOD won't officially acknowledge the existence of a black program. When a black program becomes public, as in the unveiling of stealth aircraft in the late 1980s, the program remains a SAP, but the DOD acknowledges its existence.

When the DOD creates a SAP, especially for a black program, it often creates two different security identifiers for its information: a classified identifier called a *code word* and an unclassified identifier. The classified code word is used within the project. The unclassified identifier usually is constructed from a pair of words, like HAVE BLUE, the name applied to a prototype of the F-117 stealth fighter. The unclassified identifier may be used to identify the project in published budgets or on documents released to people not cleared for code word materials.

SPECIAL INTELLIGENCE

Special Intelligence refers to information about communications security (COMSEC) or communications intelligence (COMINT). These clearances are the province of the NSA. Although they have requirements similar to SCI clearances, the NSA enforces its own, specific requirements.

As with SCI, the agency assigns code words to different types of intelligence or other sensitive information. This tradition dates back at least to World War II. Figure 17.5 shows two decoded messages intercepted from Soviet spy traffic in the 1940s.

Both intercepts originally were classified Top Secret. The left-hand intercept originally was assigned the code word FROTH and later assigned BRIDE. The right-hand intercept also was given two code words, one being VENONA. The other code word was blacked out before the intercept was declassified, suggesting that the other code word was still being used.

There could be several reasons for reassigning a document from one code word to another or for assigning it two separate code words. In the case of FROTH and BRIDE, the intercept apparently started out with the FROTH code word and was changed to

Figure 17.5

Declassified intercepts from the NSA's VENONA project.

BRIDE. In this case, the renaming may have been a response to the Kim Philby incident noted in Section 8.2. Perhaps the NSA replaced the FROTH keyword after Philby fell under suspicion in the 1950s.

ENFORCING ACCESS TO LEVELS AND COMPARTMENTS

A compartment, code word, or SAP identifier indicates that recipients must be cleared for a specific type of information to receive a document so marked. This works the same as other distribution restrictions: to receive the document we must fulfill all of its restrictions.

Figure 17.6 shows how this works. The diagram yields a structure called a *lattice* that shows how the different levels and compartments relate to one another. Computer-based systems that enforce access restrictions on classified information often use a lattice to implement the protections.

For example, Kevin's Secret clearance and his MALBEC clearance allow him to see Secret MALBEC data, but without a Top Secret clearance he can't look at Top Secret MALBEC data. If Kevin also is cleared for the BOONE compartment, then he can read Secret BOONE documents as well. Because he is cleared for both, he also can look at compilations of both that carry a Secret BOONE MALBEC label.

If we have the clearance to read a particular document in the figure, we also can read all documents that point to it and all documents pointing to those documents. For example, Kevin can read the Secret BOONE MALBEC document, so he can read all of

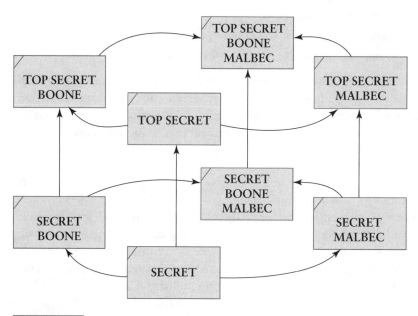

Figure 17.6

A lattice showing compartment clearances.

the Secret documents in the diagram, even those without a compartment name. If we can read Top Secret documents, then we also can read Secret documents. However, if we don't have any compartment clearances, we can't read any compartmented documents, not even the Secret ones.

The same rules apply, regardless of whether we are talking about compartments, SI or SAP code words, or about other distribution restrictions. The hierarchical classification levels apply according to individual security clearances. To read a specific document, we must be authorized for *every* compartment, code word, or other restriction it carries.

17.3 National Policy Issues

In the United States, national policy for telecom and information systems is coordinated by the Committee on National Security Systems (CNSS). The committee traces its roots back to an executive order issued by the president in 1953. Until 2001, the committee was called the National Security Telecommunications and Information Systems Security Committee (NSTISSC). This committee also establishes federal standards for information security training.

To provide an overview of national policy issues, we organize them into the following areas:

- Legal elements
- Personnel roles and responsibilities
- Distinctive threats, vulnerabilities, and countermeasures
- Planning and management

We have covered many of these areas already and will cover others later in this chapter. The next few paragraphs summarize the first three areas listed. The next subsection reviews major facets of national security policy. The final subsections review national planning and management processes for security-critical information systems.

LEGAL ELEMENTS
We encountered legal elements earlier in this chapter with a brief review of the executive order concept and its role in establishing the system for classifying information. We reviewed other legal elements in earlier chapters, including information security legislation and standards in Section 4.6.2 and the overview of legal systems in Section 5.1. Federal agencies face additional requirements intended to reduce the risks of fraud, waste, and abuse by government employees. Although evidence collection and preservation often follow similar standards to private industry if a security incident leads to prosecution, there may be different requirements for applying military or administrative sanctions.

Moreover, the investigative process may vary from one agency to another. Some agencies have an inspector general with broad investigative powers. Others may incorporate investigations and audits into routine operations. In some cases, separate agencies like special prosecutors or the Government Accountability Office (GAO) may have the authority to investigate.

Federal Information Security Management Act

The third part ("Title III") of the 2002 E-Government Act is called the Federal Information Security Management Act (FISMA). The act requires executive branch agencies, including the DOD, to take the following steps to ensure the security of information and systems:

- Plan for security
- Assign security responsibility to appropriate officials in the agency
- Review information system security controls periodically
- Explicitly authorize information systems to operate *before* they go into production and periodically reassess and reauthorize existing systems

FISMA follows a series of legislative acts that promote a risk-based approach to government information security. In other words, government information security must follow a continuous improvement process, like the one studied in this textbook.

NIST Standards and Guidance for FISMA

As of 2010, FISMA implementation is integrated with older security policies and procedures. As implementation progresses, CNSS policies and standards evolve to be consistent with NIST's federal standards (FIPS documents) and recommendations (NIST SP documents) These include:

- FIPS 199: Standards for categorizing the sensitivity of information systems in terms of loss of confidentiality, integrity, and availability.
- FIPS 200: Summary of minimum information system security requirements in terms of 17 general areas. Specifies SP 800-53 as the source of security controls to implement the requirements based on system sensitivity (as defined in FIPS 199).
- NIST SP 800-30: Risk assessment process for information systems, introduced in Section 1.5.2.
- NIST SP 800-37: Establishes a six-step *risk management framework* (RMF) for information systems security.
- NIST SP 800-53: Provides a strategy for selecting security controls within the six-step framework described in SP 800-37.

PERSONNEL ROLES AND RESPONSIBILITIES

U.S. laws and regulations establish executive roles and responsibilities for government agencies and military commands. Agency managers establish specific policies and procedures to implement national requirements and standards. NIST SP 800-37 provides a framework for information security roles, responsibilities, and accountability.

In general, roles and responsibilities in federal agencies are similar to those described for private and commercial organizations in Section 13.2.3. In terms of information security planning and management, federal agencies follow more specific policies and procedures described in later subsections. An agency director or military commander must decide personally whether a system with critical security elements is secure enough to be deployed. This decision is based on a careful analysis of the system design and on extensive testing of its security properties.

Another significant difference between private enterprises and federal agencies is that the federal agencies often have more significant responsibilities for protecting secret information. We examined these in Section 17.1. In terms of personnel, agencies may require individuals to manage OPSEC, information security, and cryptographic resources, depending on the nature of their operations. Agency employees also may be personally accountable for agency information. This typically requires agencies to provide procedures and systems to associate employee actions with access or modification of important or sensitive federal data.

DISTINCTIVE THREATS, VULNERABILITIES, AND COUNTERMEASURES

In general, government agencies face the same information security issues—and apply the same remedies—as other large enterprises and institutions. However, two major differences arise. First, legal elements make the agencies accountable in ways unfamiliar to private organizations. Second, federal agencies often have secrecy obligations far beyond those faced by private organizations or even by local and state governments. We must adjust our security objectives and requirements to include these concerns when we address security in the federal context. Secrecy concerns in particular may lead to particular types of security controls and countermeasures, including the following:

- Communications security, discussed in Section 17.4
- Data protection, discussed in Section 17.5
- Information assurance, discussed in Section 17.6

17.3.1 Facets of National System Security

To support system security in compliance with national standards, it is important to recognize certain essential areas of interest. These include physical security, communications security, information security, and security procedures. The following sections summarize facets that are particularly relevant to national system security. Appropriate security controls for these elements are enumerated in NIST SP 800-53.

Physical Security

Within physical security, the following topics require particular attention in national system security:

- Protection of areas. Physical areas are protected not only to prevent loss of equipment and information within those areas, but also to provide basic TEMPEST protection (Section 17.5.2).

- Protection of equipment. This involves both the physical protection of information against theft, but also to keep proper control of security-critical equipment to ensure its integrity (Section 17.4.2).

- Protection of magnetic media. Physical protection ensures the integrity of magnetic media; Section 17.5 discusses particular media handling issues for sensitive information.

- Backup of data and files. This provides multiple physical copies of critical information, both for copies in physically separate locations and copies for immediate local recovery.

Communications Security

Within communications security, the following topics require particular attention in national system security:

- Protection of data communications. These problems are addressed through physical security and through cryptosystems. We examine cryptosystems further in Section 17.4 and physical security in Section 17.5.

- Protection of voice communications. Although this originally focused on classic analog voice systems, modern voice systems often are hosted atop digital communications backbones. Nonetheless, there remain national standards for analog voice systems deployed within critical federal and defense sites. Moreover, the CNSS has published NSTISSP-101 as a national policy on protecting voice communication. CNSS also has published numerous standards that apply specifically to telephone systems.

- Application of crypto systems. This is addressed further in Section 17.4.

- Protection of keying material. National policies to protect keying material are managed and administered by the NSA. Section 17.4.1 discusses these in detail.

- Transmission security countermeasures. These are measures intended to hide significant patterns in transmission behavior so as to minimize the information disclosed by patterns of crypto-protected communications traffic. This is discussed further in Section 17.4.3.

Information Security

Within information security, the following topics require particular attention in national system security:

- IT security. These traditionally are called *automated information systems* (AIS) in older policy documents.

- Protection of files. In most cases, government applications rely on the conventional measures studied in earlier chapters. In some cases, these are augmented by special measures to protect critical secrets from disclosure (Section 17.6).

- Protection against malicious logic. These are conventional security measures, though in some cases the systems avoid Internet connections, which may affect the nature of the threat. Different agencies and environments may publish specific guidance on antivirus measures and others to resist malicious logic.

- Protection of passwords. Agencies publish their own policies on password management.

Life-Cycle Procedures

National security systems must comply with specific policies for life-cycle procedures. The RMF in NIST SP 800-37 incorporates these into a security process intended for government-wide adoption.

- Policies for acquisition, enterprise architecture, and risk management are discussed in the next section.

- Approval for operation. Critical defense systems must follow national policies outlining a specific approval process. CNSS has published this policy in CNSSP-6; a further discussion appears in Section 17.3.3.

- Reporting security violations. Government agencies establish specific policies and procedures to monitor security activities and to address procedure violations. CNSS has published a recommendation on incident management, CNSS-048-07, a policy on information spills, CNSSP-18, and a list of frequently asked questions on incidents and spills, CNSS-079-07.

17.3.2 Security Planning

Security planning is implemented through life cycle management, plus two additional concerns: budgeting and training. Security system budgeting poses a challenge, particularly in the federal arena. On the one hand, budgeting may follow a conventional cycle when developing or maintaining IT systems in a conventional manner. On the other hand, new threats and vulnerabilities may arise unexpectedly, and new countermeasures may impose unexpected expenses. These must be addressed in agency policies and procedures.

As noted earlier in the section, FISMA legislation is promoting a government-wide transition to standard processes for information security management. These are illustrated in NIST SP 800-37 and 800-53.

System Life-Cycle Management

System life-cycle management involves acquisition, architecture, approval to operate, and risk management. Here are specific CNSS policies that address these areas:

- Acquisition policy. The CNSS has published a policy on system acquisition, NSTISSP-11 (soon to be replaced by CNSS-11), that addresses issues in using commercial technologies for information security in applications that were restricted to government-specific technology under older regulations and standards.

- Enterprise architecture. The CNSS publishes a specific policy on enterprise architecture: CNSSP-21.

- Risk management. The CNSS publishes a specific policy on risk management: CNSSP-22. This is similar to NIST SP 800-30 (see Section 1.5.2).

Government standards organizations also have published guidance for selecting and applying security controls. These documents present a process to identify security measures to apply according to the system's purpose and sensitivity:

- Recommended information system security controls: NIST SP 800-53.

- Federal standard for information security controls: FIPS-200.

- Controls for national security systems: CNSSI-1253.

The process of validating a system's security properties and approving it for operation traditionally are addressed through *certification and accreditation* or C&A. The certification process analyzes the system design and tests the implementation to verify the operation of security controls. The accreditation is a formal acceptance by agency management of the risks inherent in operating the system. This process is covered in the next section.

Security System Training

The CNSS has published security training standards for key roles in information system management, development, and support. These form the basis for federal certification of post-secondary training programs through the NSA's Information Assurance Courseware Evaluation Program. Here are the relevant training standards:

- Information Systems Security Professionals, NSTISSI 4011
- Senior Systems Managers, CNSSI 4012
- System Administrators, CNSSI 4013
- Information Systems Security Officers, CNSSI 4014
- System Certifiers, NSTISSI 4015
- Risk Analysts, CNSSI 4016

Institutions that offer educational programs in information security may submit their curricula for evaluation and certification. The applicant provides an overview of the curriculum and indicates how the different elements cover the requirements for training individuals in one or more of the listed roles.

CNSS also publishes a glossary of standard terms used in information assurance: CNSSI-4009.

The U.S. DOD has published its own standard on the training and certification of information security professionals: DOD Manual 8570.01.

17.3.3 Certification and Accreditation

C&A encompasses the process by which we approve an information system that handles critical or highly sensitive data. Systems to handle classified information typically go through the C&A process. This process may be replaced by NIST's RMF, described in NIST SP 800-37.

The CNSS has published the following policies and instructions on C&A:

- CNSSP-6: National policy on certification and accreditation.
- NSTISSI-1000: National Information Assurance Certification and Accreditation Process (NIACAP).

The C&A process coordinates the efforts of people working to create, validate, and approve the system to serve a particular user population. The process involves the following four roles:

1. System developer—the team responsible for creating the IT system.
2. End user—the people to be served by the IT system.
3. Certifier—the team that analyzes the system's security.
4. *Designated Accrediting Authority* (DAA) or "accreditor"—the person who takes responsibility for the system's correct operation and signs off on approving its operation. This may be an agency head, military site commander, or designee.

There is a representative for each role who participates in planning and implementing the C&A process. These individuals discuss and resolve trade-offs between security, performance, schedule, and budget.

The results of C&A negotiations are captured in the *System Security Authorization Agreement* (SSAA). The document collects all information specific to the system's C&A. It describes the system's security requirements, how the system implements them, and the steps necessary to approve the system for operation. The approval process depends on performing specific design analyses and security tests. The SSAA also captures the test results and notes any residual vulnerabilities or other security issues.

A routine C&A process involves four phases:

1. Definition. The team uses the system's operating objectives and environment to establish its security requirements.
2. Verification. The developers and certifiers analyze and review the system's evolving design and implementation to ensure compliance with security requirements.
3. Validation. The certifier determines that the fully integrated system complies with the security requirements in the SSAA and issues a recommendation. The DAA reviews the analyses, test results, and certifier's recommendation to make the final accreditation decision.

4. Postaccreditation. The process of deploying the system such that it complies with its security requirements consistently during operation and in the face of evolving threats and minor system modifications.

If the validation proceeds successfully, the DAA typically will accredit the system and issue a formal "Approval to Operate" statement. If the validation uncovers problems with the system, the DAA has a more difficult decision, especially if the system fulfills an essential and immediate need. If the system poses too much of a risk in its current state, the DAA simply may refuse to accredit until problems are fixed.

If the user community really needs the system and the DAA agrees that the need justifies the risk, then the DAA may issue an "Interim Approval to Operate" (IATO). To issue interim approval, the DAA requires a plan to remedy the system's shortcomings so that it earns final approval. Some large, complex systems can't be adequately tested before they are placed in operation to some degree. In such cases, the DAA may issue an IATO to permit a complete validation of the system.

NIST RISK MANAGEMENT FRAMEWORK

Military and government agencies are planning to phase out the traditional C&A process and replace it with NIST's RMF. The process consists of the following six steps:

1. Categorize Information Systems: Using guidance from FIPS 199 and NIST SP 800-60 to assign information and systems to security categories.

2. Select Security Controls: Using guidance from FIPS 200 and NIST SP 800-53, choose security controls appropriate to the categories identified in Step 1.

3. Implement Security Controls: NIST SP 800-70 provides a process for standardizing checklists and guidelines for implementing security controls.

4. Assess Security Controls: NIST SP 800-53A recommends assessment procedures for SP 800-53 security controls. This is similar to the certification step of the C&A process.

5. Authorize Information Systems: This is similar to the accreditation step of the C&A process.

6. Monitor Security Controls: This establishes requirements to continuously monitor both the system's security configuration and the system operation to ensure that security measures remain in force and that incidents are detected and addressed.

17.4 Communications Security

The phrase *communications security* (COMSEC) refers to cryptography within the U.S. government and refers particularly to cryptosystems to protect critical government secrets. The CNSS has published the following policies on communications security and cryptography for national security systems:

- Safeguarding COMSEC materials: CNSSP-1

- Granting access to classified crypto information: CNSSP-3
- Use of crypto in high-risk environments: NCSC-5
- Wireless networking: CNSSP-17
- IPsec encryption: CNSSP-19
- Public key infrastructure: CNSSP-25
- Voice communications security: NSTISSP-101

The CNSS also has published the following instructions on communications security and cryptography:

- Public key infrastructure and X.509 certificates: CNSSI-1300
- Security doctrine for FORTEZZA crypto cards: CNSSI-3028
- COMSEC utility program: CNSSI-4007
- Voice-over IP guidelines: CNSSI-5000
- Voice-over IP telephone program: CNSSI-5001
- National COMSEC instruction: NACSI-6002

Although the rules have expanded recently to accept a broader range of civilian systems, the NSA retains authority to assess and approve cryptosystems that protect classified information. The NSA has developed a reputation for setting high standards for cryptographic safety. Some may argue that the standards are too high, but the standards arise from unfortunate experiences in the past.

In the 1950s, researchers determined that poorly designed crypto equipment often transmitted a faint signal that echoed its plaintext. Thus, when the device generated its ciphertext signal, a sensitive receiver could retrieve the plaintext. Cryptanalysis wasn't even necessary. The CIA found out that the Soviet military command in East Germany used such a device. Moreover, the Soviet signal cables ran in an underground tunnel near the Berlin Wall. The CIA promptly dug a secret tunnel under the wall and tapped into the cables.

This attack exploited vulnerabilities in crypto hardware. Today, we often refer to such exploits as *side channel attacks*. To help prevent such problems with U.S. devices, the NSA insists on red/black separation, fault analyses, and other techniques.

A variant of this risk arises from "compromising emanations," a set of problems whose study remained highly classified for several years. Assigned the code word *TEMPEST*, these problems allowed spies to listen to teletypes across the street from a locked communications room or watch the same image displayed on a television tube hundreds of feet away. The problems have proven extremely difficult to eliminate entirely, but many techniques minimize the risks. We examine this problem further in Section 17.5.2.

Although TEMPEST places the plaintext data at risk, we must recognize that the mere flow of traffic may disclose a great deal of information about classified activities. Even without decrypting message traffic, a careful analyst can detect patterns of data flowing between different recipients and associate the amounts and direction of flow with different types of activities. This is the ***transmission security***, or TRANSEC, problem. We discuss this later in this section.

KEY LEAKAGE THROUGH SPYING

Another risk has arisen from leaked keying materials, particularly via spies. In 1976, federal agents arrested a highly cleared employee of a defense contractor for selling secrets to the Soviets. As described in Robert Lindsey's book *The Falcon and The Snowman* and the 1985 film, Christopher Boyce collected expired encryption keys used to protect Top Secret intelligence traffic. He then sold them to Soviet agents through a high school friend.

Both U.S. and Soviet security experts agree that the Walker spy ring, exposed in 1985, was a far more significant leak. Starting in 1967, John A. Walker, then a Navy warrant officer and communications specialist, started selling U.S. crypto materials to the Soviets. When a change of duty removed his access to crypto materials, he recruited others to collect the material for him. Ultimately his spy ring included his brother, his son, and a third naval officer.

Since then, the DOD claims to have spent billions of dollars replacing crypto equipment and revising key management procedures to help prevent a similar leak. Traditional crypto keys were used and then destroyed; a Walker or Boyce could simply pocket the key material and claim it was destroyed. Revised procedures require strict accountability and two-person control for Top Secret keying material.

The following subsections review technical and procedural strategies for ***high-assurance*** cryptography. We use the term *assurance* in information security to refer to the degree of confidence we have in the system's operation. A high-assurance system meets the most stringent standards for protecting information in a critical application. High-assurance cryptography relies on two elements: high-quality equipment and an effective key-management process. We examine each of these in the following subsections.

17.4.1 Cryptographic Technology

The NSA and NIST share responsibility for establishing cryptographic standards to protect U.S. government traffic. The government typically places products and technologies in four categories:

1. Type 1—approved by the NSA for protecting classified and other highly sensitive national security information. The NSA takes responsibility for producing and distributing Type 1 keys. Most Type 1 algorithms are classified. AES is the only unclassified Type 1 algorithm.

2. Type 2—approved by the NSA for protecting unclassified but sensitive government information. The NSA produces and distributes keys for Type 2 applications. The NSA produced a Type 2 algorithm named SKIPJACK in the 1990s.

3. Type 3—commercial products using NIST-approved algorithms and evaluated under an approved process, like FIPS-140 (see Section 7.4.4). DES was a Type 3 algorithm until NIST decertified it.

4. Type 4—commercial products using other, possibly proprietary algorithms. These are not certified by NIST.

Traditionally, the NSA used their own, proprietary cryptographic algorithms and techniques in Type 1 systems. This provided a degree of Security Through Obscurity to protect the data, because the NSA routinely classified the algorithms it developed. This changed recently; newer systems may use AES to protect classified information.

CLASSIC TYPE 1 CRYPTO TECHNOLOGY

In practice, Type 1 cryptography involves more than choosing the correct algorithm. The NSA requires Type 1 products to meet certain design constraints. To receive Type 1 approval, a product also endures a rigorous analysis and review process to ensure correct operation.

Some Type 1 requirements ensure that the device always accurately displays its status to the operator, so the operator can tell if the crypto is disabled or not or has keys installed or not. Other requirements and analyses seek to minimize the risk of plaintext data leaking through poor design choices or through equipment failures.

A common feature of Type 1 products is *red/black separation* (Figure 17.7). The device's design draws a firm boundary between parts of the device that handle plaintext ("red") data and parts that handle ciphertext ("black") data.

The separation helps ensure that plaintext signals aren't transmitted along with the ciphertext. The device isolates the actual encryption and decryption from all other processing.

Type 1 devices also go through a *security fault analysis*. This process searches for simple failures that might disable the encryption or allow plaintext to leak out with the ciphertext.

> **Example:** Two military sites were communicating via teletypes using the Vernam cipher with one-time keys. This particular site had two teletypes: one for typing outbound messages and the other for printing inbound messages. One of the operators noticed that a perfect, plaintext copy of the outbound messages was being typed out on the inbound teletype. At first he assumed that another operator had rewired it to print an extra copy of outbound messages. In fact, a relay at the far station had failed, making it echo back the inbound message *in plaintext* on the return connection.

Fault analysis originated with mechanical and electromechanical crypto devices and evolved to address modern systems. While red/black separation tries to keep red and black data separate, the fault analysis ensures that a simple failure doesn't produce an unintended data path between red and black.

All Type 1 devices provide a simple and reliable way to *zeroize* the device. When we zeroize the device, we erase all of its working encryption keys. The design, analysis, and testing process ensures that the zeroize operation works reliably and that simple hardware failures won't interfere with it.

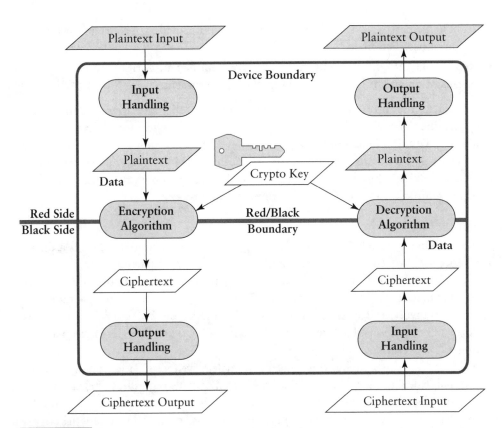

Figure 17.7
Red/black separation in a crypto device.

17.4.2 Crypto Security Procedures

The best crypto technology in the world is easily undermined if threat agents capture the keys used or subvert the crypto equipment. The NSA has established a set of policies and procedures to protect against such risks. These revolve around **COMSEC materials**, a term that applies to both Type 1 crypto hardware and its keys.

If a site or organization needs Type 1 crypto protection, it manages the equipment and keys through a "COMSEC account." This account keeps track of each device and every key assigned to the organization. The organization assigns a specific person the job of **COMSEC custodian**. This custodian has the following duties:

- Identify and keep an inventory of all COMSEC material.
- Provide access to COMSEC material for people who are authorized to access it.
- Ensure that COMSEC material is protected or that it is in the custody of people who may be trusted to protect it.

- Handle the destruction of COMSEC material and provide appropriate documentation of destruction.
- Report all COMSEC incidents to specifically identified authorities, both within the organization and at higher levels in the U.S. government.

In general, an organization handles COMSEC material the same way it handles comparably classified materials. Access is restricted to people specifically authorized to handle and use it. COMSEC materials are protected at all times or they are under the direct physical control of someone authorized to carry them. COMSEC materials never leave a secure site unless they are carefully wrapped and shipped via a highly trusted courier or service. These procedures apply both to equipment and to keys.

TWO-PERSON INTEGRITY

Top Secret keying materials require *two-person integrity* (TPI) controls. This is a form of Separation of Duty that requires two authorized people take part in critical operations. The Boyce and Walker incidents dramatically illustrated the risk of leaking Top Secret keying materials; TPI reduces those risks by having two separate people take part in all activities involving Top Secret crypto keys. In practice, sites assign people to teams to perform TPI operations. Each team member signs a log when they perform an action involving a Top Secret key.

The U.S. military also applies this concept to nuclear weapons. Traditionally called the "two-man rule," military doctrine does not allow anyone, regardless of clearance, to be alone with a nuclear weapon. Sites that contain or control nuclear weapons identify such an area as a *no lone zone*. No one may enter a no lone zone alone; all workers enter such zones in pairs or in larger groups. Figure 17.8 shows a no lone zone warning sign from a Titan missile launch control center.

Figure 17.8

Missile launch control is a no lone zone.

CONTROLLED CRYPTOGRAPHIC ITEMS

A *controlled cryptographic item* (CCI) is a piece of COMSEC equipment tracked through a COMSEC account. We must ensure the safety and integrity of every CCI. This requires continuous physical protection during shipment and deployment. In most cases, we may install a CCI inside a cleared facility.

A CCI is not necessarily a classified device, especially when it contains no working crypto keys. Older devices are classified because they physically implement a classified encryption algorithm in discrete electronic circuits. If a hostile intelligence service steals one, its scientists might be able to reverse-engineer the algorithm.

Modern devices often implement crypto algorithms in software. We can design such devices to store algorithms in an encrypted form. If we don't load the appropriate decryption keys, an attacker can't recover the algorithms. When we prepare such a device for shipment, we remove the algorithm decryption keys.

Modern devices also have antitamper features. These include internal sensors and other checks to detect attempts to tamper with the device's internal circuits. The simplest antitamper mechanisms are physical seals attached to a device's covers. If attackers try to remove a cover, they break the seal, which indicates the tampering. Some devices also have antitamper sensors that may cause the device to zeroize itself.

The COMSEC custodian must inspect the CCI inventory periodically. The custodian must locate each device, check its antitamper indicators, and verify that it resides within an adequately protected location. The custodian must report any tampering with CCIs or any missing equipment.

KEY MANAGEMENT PROCESSES

Type 1 crypto keys may be distributed in either paper or electronic form. Older systems and procedures use paper keys. Newer systems use electronic keys as much as possible. The earliest form of electronic keying was over-the-air rekeying (OTAR). Several Type 1 devices incorporate OTAR, which wraps a new traffic key in a key-encrypting key using a device-specific protocol. More recently, electronic keys may be distributed on electronic storage media or distributed across networks using the Electronic Key Management System (EKMS).

The Walker spy ring flourished when crypto keys were produced and distributed exclusively on paper and entrusted to lone individuals. Digital keys were distributed on punched tape or punched cards. To load a key into a device, the operator connected a paper tape reader to the "key fill" connection and read the tape. A spy easily could copy crypto keys punched on paper by reproducing the pattern of holes in a photograph or photocopy or even by hand.

Since then, the NSA has developed policies and procedures to prevent a repetition of the Walker spy ring. The first major change was to require TPI for all Top Secret keys. The other major change is to minimize and even eliminate paper keys wherever possible. However, existing devices and procedures are hard to eliminate overnight. Paper-based key management will persist as long as end users still rely on older crypto technologies.

Data Transfer Device

As a first step to eliminate keys on paper, the NSA deployed the Data Transfer Device, or DTD. This device uses the same connection as a paper tape reader. Instead of using paper tape, the DTD stores keys internally and transmits them to individual devices by command. Unlike paper tape, the DTD keeps a record every time it transmits a key. This provides better records of a key's distribution and use.

Electronic Key Management System

The NSA established the EKMS to distribute and manage Type 1 crypto keys electronically. EKMS has a central facility at NSA that oversees the system and that establishes certain special-purpose keys used in other parts of the system. Every major site with a COMSEC account has a local management device (LMD) that communicates with the central facility to create and manage keys for local users. The LMD loads keys directly into a transfer device as needed. From there, the COMSEC custodian or authorized clerk may load keys from the transfer device into individual COMSEC devices.

The LMD and the DTD handle these general kinds of keys:

- **Seed key**—a nonsecret key used to generate other keys using unpublished NSA algorithms.
- **Operational key**—a secret key used by a device for crypto operations. Seed keys must be converted into operational keys.
- **Black key**—a "benign" key or one wrapped by a KEK so that it may be handled with less risk of leaking.

Older Type 1 crypto equipment uses operational keys exclusively. In some cases, these devices may support key update or OTAR to periodically replace the working traffic keys. Otherwise, the operators must manually replace the operational key periodically. In some cases, the device stores an internal KEK, which supports the loading of a new operational key in black form. To use seed keys, a device must incorporate the crypto protocols necessary to convert a seed key into an operational key. The seed key and black key procedures reduce key distribution risks because operators don't need to protect those keys from disclosure.

17.4.3 Transmission Security

Transmission security, also called TRANSEC, arose as a communications security issue from two sources:

1. Traffic analysis. Even if we encrypt all traffic, attackers can learn a lot simply by observing communications patterns. They can identify military units and force structure by watching the message flow and infer the tempo of operations from the amount of traffic. This is a confidentiality problem.
2. *Jamming.* Attackers can seriously disrupt operations if they block messages from commanders or from surveillance systems that detect and report targets. This is an availability problem.

Some TRANSEC techniques are clearly extensions of the cryptography we already use. Others are extensions of *electronic warfare* (EW) techniques used in sophisticated weapons platforms. In all cases, the techniques help ensure confidentiality and availability. The most effective general-purpose technique is *spread spectrum*, which also may appear in commercial communications systems and products.

ELECTRONIC WARFARE

To understand the jamming problem, we must take a brief look at the EW environment. Modern defenses rely heavily on radar to detect incoming attacks. A typical modern radar system transmits a microwave radio signal. If the signal bounces off an object (like an airplane or ship), the radar antenna detects the reflected signal and uses it to locate the object in space. The Doppler effect also allows the radar to compute the object's relative motion.

Radars give us important information during military operations, but they also pose a risk. Anyone can easily detect the radar signals, because they are very strong. The signals also clearly point back at the radar's location.

EW begins with detection; we use specially designed receivers to detect transmissions from radar or communications equipment belonging to opposing forces. In either case, a good EW receiver will detect the transmission and the direction to its transmitter. If the transmitter is within missile range, an attacker can easily fire a missile that homes in on the transmitter. The EW receiver also may identify the types of equipment the opposition forces use. Different weapons incorporate particular electronic packages and the electronic signals often are distinctive.

Another part of EW tries to prevent detection of military units by screening them from radar or other sensors. This often involves active jamming or deception of the opponent's radar. In jamming, we transmit a signal that garbles the signal bounced back to the radar. Instead of seeing a clean radar signal that indicates the target's direction, distance, and speed, the opponent sees a noisy bar that indicates the general direction of the jammer itself. A more sophisticated jammer might actually adjust the radar signal so that it indicates a target that's not really there or hide the target entirely.

EW also may attack communications. If we identify frequencies being used by opposing forces, we can transmit noise on those frequencies. If the noise signal is powerful enough, it will drown out the opposition's communications traffic. This poses a serious problem to modern military forces. Most forces use surveillance aircraft to locate and identify targets. If we jam our attackers' communications, they can't direct their aircraft at military targets.

To counter an EW attack, we try to avoid jamming by masking our transmitters from the opposition. There are several techniques to achieve this:

- Low power transmissions. Keep the transmitted signals so low that opponents can't detect them and target them for jamming.

- Burst transmissions. Avoid two-way radio transmissions and rely instead on brief, highly compressed messages. Transmit each message in a very brief burst that is hard to detect and jam before the transmission ends.
- Directional transmissions. Use either directional radio transmissions or optical techniques, like a directed laser, to minimize the likelihood of interception, detection, and jamming. These often are restricted to line-of-sight transmissions.
- Spread spectrum transmissions. Disperse the transmission across a range of frequencies to make it harder to detect. We also may mix noise in with the transmission to make it harder to distinguish the communication traffic from random noise.

Different systems make use of these different techniques, particularly in military applications. Spread spectrum provides the most effective general-purpose protection for both confidentiality and availability.

SPREAD SPECTRUM

Although spread spectrum techniques evolved to resist jamming on the battlefield, they also resist civilian sources of radio interference. As the civilian radio spectrum has grown more crowded, designers have used these techniques to make radio systems more reliable and efficient.

The earliest spread spectrum techniques relied on *frequency hopping*. The transmitter divided the message into separate pieces and transmitted each piece at a different frequency, hopping from one frequency to the next. Eavesdroppers might see a brief, burst-like transmission at a particular frequency, but they wouldn't know which frequency held the next part of the transmission. If we think of this in terms of transmitting data on a "carrier wave," we change the carrier wave's frequency each time we hop.

For example, the transmission might use the range of frequencies between 100 KHz and 200 KHz in 10 Hz increments. This provides 100 possible frequencies to use. The transmitter divides the message into 10 millisecond chunks and sends each one on a different frequency. In a trivial case, the transmitter sends the first chunk at 100 KHz, the second at 110 KHz, the third at 120 KHz, and so on.

In practice, the transmitter uses a pseudorandom sequence to choose the frequencies. The sender and receiver agree on the sequence; they exchange a nonce that selects the sequence to use. In commercial devices, we use the hopping to avoid noisy channels and other forms of interference. These are more-or-less random events, so we can rely on a pseudorandom generator that produces easy-to-compute patterns.

In military applications, the frequency hopping sequence may be controlled by a cryptographic device. The sender and recipient use a shared secret key and a transmitted nonce to produce the sequence. Like all Type 1 keys, management follows COMSEC procedures.

Navigational satellites, older wireless LANs, and some cell phone technologies use a different form of spread spectrum called "direct-sequence spread spectrum," or DSSS. Instead of hopping between frequencies, DSSS applies a function to the carrier wave that spreads the binary data across the signal. The function is a pseudorandom sequence of +1 and −1 signals called "chips" that occur at a higher rate than the underlying binary data rate. Thus, the transmitter uses several chips to encode each bit. The DSSS receiver applies the same pseudorandom sequence of chips to recover the binary data.

17.5 Data Protection

Data can't always be encrypted. Working data must be in plaintext. We need reasonably safe techniques to handle plaintext data and to prevent leakage. Here we review a few examples of special techniques to protect plaintext data:

- Digital storage media
- Protected wiring arrangements
- Unintended data emanations called TEMPEST

MEDIA HANDLING

Storage media include portable or removable hard drives, flash drives, DVDs, and even older media like recordable tapes. If they contain sensitive or classified information, we must treat them like any classified paper or device:

- External marking. We mark all portable media with a visible label indicating the highest classification level of the data it contains. If the level itself contains classified code words or compartment names, then we must keep the media in a cover that protects the names from disclosure.
- Continuous protection. We keep portable media locked up except when we are using it. When not locked up, the media remains under our direct physical control or under the direct physical control of someone else with authorized access to the information.
- Secure transportation. The media never leaves our cleared facility unless we wrap it properly for shipment and transport it via an authorized courier service.

Earlier, we discussed the exposure and quarantine analogy for how classified information affects digital storage: When we "expose" a device to data at a higher classification level, the storage instantly is classified at that level. If the drive contains Confidential information and we store Secret information on it, we must now label it as a Secret drive. If the drive contains Top Secret BOONE data and we store Secret MALBEC data on it, we must now label it Top Secret BOONE MALBEC.

The DOD provides procedures and standards for downgrading or sanitizing media at lower classification levels, like Confidential or Secret. The procedures rely on overwriting, as described in Section 7.4.3.

Media Sanitization and Destruction

However, military and intelligence agencies don't always believe these measures are completely effective. Media containing Top Secret information can't always be sanitized. Some organizations may allow a device containing SCI or code word data to be sanitized and reused with different compartments or code words. However, organizations rarely allow sanitized media to be used in Secret or lower environments. They destroy the media instead.

Media destruction, however, can be a challenge. The NSA has established standards for destroying hard drives and other portable media. Use the following procedures with NSA-approved devices for erasure or destruction:

- Hard drives—either destroy the hard drive or disassemble it and apply a *degausser* (a strong electromagnet for erasing magnetic media) to every recording surface. The disassembly process renders the drive unusable in normal circumstances and the degausser removes the data.
- DVDs and CDs—physically destroy the readable surface or destroy the entire disk using an approved shredder, grinder, or incinerator.
- Diskettes and tapes—use an approved degausser to erase the media or disintegrate in an approved disintegrator.

Although earlier research suggested that flash drives could be easily and reliably sanitized, more recent studies indicate problems. Simple rewriting of flash drives may be adequate for the risks faced in most commercial applications. However, the ongoing recommendation for high-security applications requires that drives be destroyed if they contain highly sensitive information.

17.5.1 Protected Wiring

Informally, it may seem easy to transmit information safely. We connect a wire from Point A to Point B and we watch that wire very, very carefully. In practice, this can be very difficult, especially if we are sending highly classified data through less-protected areas.

For example, a shipboard sensor may need to transmit classified information to an analysis center elsewhere onboard. The natural solution is to run a cable from the sensor to the center. However, we must remember that the cable carries classified information. It probably will travel across parts of the ship where people aren't cleared for the information it carries. What if one of them taps the cable and extracts classified information?

We use a *protected distribution system*, or PDS, to transmit plaintext classified information through an area of lesser classification or control. The PDS provides safeguards to prevent physical access or exploitation of electrical or electronic signals. In practice, a PDS primarily serves to slow down such an attack and to make it visible. National PDS guidance is established in NSTISSI-7003.

The simplest possible PDS consists of a single piece of pipe, conduit, or other uncut enclosure. The pipe carries the cables through the less-cleared area between the closed areas. We run the cables inside the pipe. The cables must reach the full length unbroken between the two closed areas. Any joints, breakout boxes, or other access points to the cables must appear only inside an area cleared for the information carried by the cables.

A simple PDS is appropriate to carry lower-level classified data through uncontrolled areas. They also may carry highly classified data through a controlled area intended for less-classified information. For example, two Top Secret areas may run a simple PDS through a closed area used by people cleared for Secret data.

A typical installation places the PDS in plain sight. This makes it easy to keep the PDS under observation and to inspect it for penetration attempts or possible tapping. Some environments install cameras to continuously monitor the PDS.

Higher-risk environments require a "hardened" PDS. Such installations typically use metal conduit or pipe to protect the cables. Some installations use airtight pipes with controlled air pressure to detect penetration attempts. A pressure sensor monitors the pipe continuously and sounds the alarm if the pressure changes.

In a hardened PDS, all connections or bends between components are completely sealed using welding, epoxy, or other permanent closure. Access covers and breakout boxes must be secured with government-approved combination padlocks. If this level of construction isn't practical, then the PDS must carry an alarm to detect tampering or it must be under continuous 24-hour surveillance.

The PDS provides *physical* protection of the cables and may provide some degree of electromagnetic protection as well. The PDS helps protect the inside cables against exterior eavesdropping. Problems may arise, however, if a PDS carries several cables, and the cables carry data at different classification levels. There are risks of "crosstalk" in which data on one cable may generate signals in a nearby cable. This may leak data from a higher-classified communications line to a lower-classified one. This is a type of TEMPEST problem.

17.5.2 TEMPEST

During World War II, teletype transmissions produced enormous amounts of electronic noise. In fact, researchers easily recovered plaintext messages across the street from a military crypto center in downtown New York City. A properly tuned radio receiver could detect the signals at fairly long distances.

This posed numerous practical problems for military and intelligence organizations. Secure rooms already were overloaded with equipment. It wasn't always affordable or even practical to move communication centers or to take other measures to reduce this "radiation leakage." The security measures often were judged too difficult to implement and skipped due to operational necessities.

Because the problems couldn't be solved quickly or easily, all issues associated with them were classified in the early years of the Cold War. The NSA assigned the problem the code word TEMPEST. Techniques to detect and exploit such signals progressed much faster than techniques to suppress them.

Victor Sheymov, a KGB security expert who defected from Russia in the 1980s, described an unusual set of empty tunnels, too narrow to fit a person, found in the Soviet

Embassy in Beijing. Research eventually determined that the tunnels served as acoustical channels to allow different types of eavesdropping on embassy activities. However, the tunnels may have been for more than simply eavesdropping on conversations. When U.S. researchers found microphones in U.S. embassies, they feared the intent was to eavesdrop on *acoustic* signals from cipher machines or even from typewriters.

TEMPEST does not limit itself to studying electromagnetic signals. It studies all forms of compromising emanations because the signals may arise in many unexpected forms. Although many problems arise from unintended electromagnetic noise, we also face risks from acoustical signals and even from power line variations. These early problems yielded five countermeasures:

1. Shielding. Put shields around the equipment to block acoustical or electromagnetic signals. This was often a problem, because secured spaces tended to be overfilled with equipment already. Adding shields after the fact wasn't always practical.

2. Filtering. Put filters on the power lines and other outbound connections to ensure that sensitive data wasn't radiated through power fluctuations or other signals. In some cases, the filters intentionally limit radiated signals to specific frequency bands ("banding").

3. Masking. Structure the devices to emanate signals that don't distinguish between different data values. Early masking attempts operated several devices at once, in hopes that their combined output would mask individual signals. This rarely was effective. Typically, a device had to be redesigned to radiate a uniform signal.

4. Attenuation. Adjust the device so that it uses less power and radiates a weaker signal. In some cases, we must redesign the equipment to attenuate its emanations without reducing its effectiveness.

5. Zoning. Establish a controlled area between the vulnerable, emanating equipment and potential attackers. In theory, the zone should place threat agents outside the range for detecting exploitable emanations.

The specific requirements for TEMPEST protection vary significantly from one application to another. The rules vary between agencies and projects and according to the sensitivity and perceived risks faced by the site. In some cases, sites could not implement all TEMPEST protections because of impacts on day-to-day operations.

TEMPEST ZONES

The earliest TEMPEST security strategy was to establish a ***zone of control*** around sensitive equipment and restrict access to that area. Following the trouble detected with teletypes in New York, the U.S. Army recommended a 100-foot (30 m) zone of control around communications centers. The zone radiated in all directions, horizontally and vertically. By the mid-1950s, the recommended control zone had doubled in size, though researchers continued to improve their interception capabilities.

A typical standard for TEMPEST zones, based on the document NSTISSAM TEMPEST/2-95, identifies three critical distances:

- Zone A: controlled area of 66 feet (20 m) or less
- Zone B: larger than Zone A and less than 328 feet (100 m)
- Zone C: larger than Zone B

Individual devices then may be evaluated for TEMPEST emanations and categorized into different levels. Zone requirements are derived according to equipment TEMPEST levels.

TEMPEST RED/BLACK

As TEMPEST concepts evolved, a key strategy reflects the red/black technique described in Section 17.4.1. In fact, the Soviet leakage problem that led to the Berlin Tunnel was a TEMPEST red/black problem. Red and black have subtly different meanings in terms of TEMPEST.

- **Red** refers to areas or elements that carry sensitive national security data.
- **Black** refers to areas or elements that do not carry sensitive national security data and that may safely connect or emanate signals to the outside world.

When we look at a secure area in the TEMPEST context, we almost treat it like an enormous crypto device. We keep red and black elements separate so that we can control red device emanations. Unlike crypto devices, however, we try to block all paths so that red data remains in the secure area.

When we run red and black cables in a TEMPEST environment, we need to avoid accidental connections or spillage between different classification levels. We avoid the obvious mistakes by labeling cable connections: We don't want to plug the Top Secret cable into the Secret jack.

TEMPEST SEPARATION

A less-obvious risk arises from "coupling," an electromagnetic phenomenon in which the energy produced by a signal on one wire produces a detectable signal in an adjacent wire. This leads to "crosstalk" in which the signal from one wire is apparent in the other. In typical cases, the problem is an annoyance—crosstalk introduces noise into an otherwise clean signal—but in TEMPEST, it may allow data leakage. We avoid coupling by providing sufficient TEMPEST separation between cables.

One published guideline for protecting highly sensitive data gave the following recommendations for TEMPEST separation between red and black components:

- 2 inches between shielded components, including shielded cables and TEMPEST-approved equipment
- 6 inches between unshielded cables and shielded components, except crypto equipment
- 3 feet between crypto equipment and unshielded cables
- 3 feet between equipment without TEMPEST approval and unshielded cables

Power wiring and supplies also pose a challenge. Power arrives from the public power grid, which powers black circuits. Power circuits feeding the red equipment must be filtered. Moreover, black power lines should not run near red cables or equipment. Following the recommendations just listed, black power lines should be at least 2 inches from shielded components, and at least 6 inches from other components.

Grounding problems also may cause TEMPEST emanations. Electrically, we typically measure voltage as a difference between a given point in the circuit and the proverbial "ground." People working with high-quality audio equipment sometimes may hear noise or distortion if separate components don't really share a common ground. We typically eliminate such problems by wiring the components to a common ground.

Grounding problems in a secure installation can produce undesirable currents, which in turn, may emanate sensitive data. However, we can't solve the problem by simply wiring all the grounds together. We must keep red and black grounds separate, just like we kept the power lines separate. Moreover, TEMPEST rules may call for special filters or other hardware when connecting the red ground to the common (black) ground.

17.6 Trustworthy Systems

Computers are not trustworthy, just as cities are not safe. We might trust parts of them, but riskiness in one part can yield riskiness in others. We build trustworthy environments from the ground up. We start with a safe interior and a reliable boundary. We validate trustworthy members individually before bringing them in.

The U.S. government tried to incorporate such ideas in computer systems when they developed the *Orange Book* standards in the early 1980s. The *Orange Book*'s title began with the phrase "Trusted Computer Systems." The goal was to promote the development of trustworthy systems.

The *Orange Book* defined three general levels of trusted systems, going from least trusted to most trusted:

- C—Provides "discretionary protection" in that file and resource owners may decide individually what to protect and how to share the things they own.
- B—Provides "mandatory protection" in that the system enforces access rights based on security classifications and clearances, regardless of personal access control settings.
- A—Provides "verified protection" in that the mechanisms have been formally verified to correctly enforce the mandatory protection policy.

The *Orange Book* provided a widely accepted notion of what it meant to have a "secure computer." In practice, the notion wasn't useful in most environments. The *Orange Book* focused on mechanisms to protect classified information, a policy problem shared by very few commercial organizations.

REFERENCE MONITOR

Although the *Orange Book* focused on solving a specific problem—protecting classified information—it also promoted a sound foundation for trustworthy computing. This foundation is the ***reference monitor***, a mechanism that *always* enforces its security policy. A reference monitor has the following features:

- Nonbypassable. The reference monitor makes all access control decisions. There is no way to reach a resource, except through the reference monitor.
- Tamperproof. There is no way for attackers or other system users to damage or disable the reference monitor.
- Verified. The reference monitor must be small enough so that we may analyze and test it thoroughly in order to assure that it operates correctly.

When we incorporate the reference monitor into a computing system, we can build a system that reliably enforces its security policy. We call such a system a ***trusted computing base*** or TCB. The TCB provides an effective building block for enforcing confidentiality and integrity policies. These mechanisms do not, however, provide a simple and obvious way of ensuring availability.

HIGH ASSURANCE

A high-assurance system is one whose behavior is verified to comply with its policy. To truly verify the TCB's behavior, we must construct a *formal security policy*; that is, a policy expressed in an unambiguous symbolic form. We also construct a *formal design specification* in the same form. Then, we construct a mathematical proof to show that the design specification enforces the policy.

In practice, the formal design specification describes the system's API. The description reflects the behavior of its inputs, outputs, and internal states when it processes different requests. The policy provides a formal definition of "secure" versus "insecure" system states. We verify the system successfully if the proofs show that the system always remains in a secure state or never enters an insecure state.

This process helps locate flaws at different steps in the software development process. The very act of formalizing the policy and design often uncover misunderstandings on how the system should operate and ambiguities in behavior. Formal methods detect additional flaws while developing the formal proofs. More flaws emerge as developers confirm that the formal specification matches the implemented code. As developers detect and patch flaws, they incorporate the changes into both the code and the formal specifications. This process may detect flaws in the patches themselves.

TRUSTED SYSTEMS TODAY

In this context, a "trustworthy" system is one that always remains in one secure state or another or a system that never enters an insecure state. In practice, very few real-world systems use TCBs. For many years, this was because the standards for TCBs were skewed in favor of systems to share classified information in a controlled manner. More recently, vendors have produced systems that focus on high-integrity operation, though the market still remains small. High-assurance processes also are expensive. In one case, the formal assurance efforts *doubled* a TCB's development cost.

Assurance must always focus on behaviors described in the formal policy. If the policy doesn't ensure reliability, then the formal methods won't verify system reliability. In the TCB just noted, formal assurance accounted for only 19 percent of the flaws detected in the deployed system. Most of those flaws involved security-critical mechanisms to protect classified information and such assurance may be justified in some environments.

Because of the expense and complexity, few modern systems achieve such high levels of assurance. Today, the term "trusted systems" is applied to systems that meet certain analysis and testing requirements defined in terms of the Common Criteria. Many organizations consider systems trustworthy out of necessity; too often critical systems rely on Microsoft Windows and other large commercial operating systems simply because it's affordable. It is relatively expensive and time-consuming to develop a software product using a high-assurance platform.

Modern high-assurance computing systems comply with special Common Criteria Protection Profiles and with other trusted computing standards. For example, some vendors offer products that comply with DO-178B, the accepted standard for high-assurance software in the aircraft industry. Modern high-assurance systems often produce a *separation kernel*—a system that divides processing resources among several isolated subsystems that may only communicate with one another through explicitly established communications links.

NATIONAL STANDARDS

The CNSS has published several standards to establish information assurance requirements for national defense systems:

- Policy for space systems: CNSSP-12, which is mapped to DOD Directive 8581.1
- Policy to provide products to nongovernment users: CNSSP-14
- Policy on assured information sharing: CNSSP-24
- Policy on controlled access protection: NSTISSP-200
- Instruction on reserve equipment: CNSSI-4008

17.6.1 Integrity of Operations

Most computing operations must achieve a certain level of integrity to provide a measure of reliability. As operations become more critical, so do the requirements for high integrity. In a few cases, we seek to achieve the highest possible assurance that operations take place as planned with no accidents or surprises. Nuclear weapons provide the most compelling example; we tolerate as few errors as possible when managing, operating, or moving them. Although a great deal of secrecy surrounds nuclear operations, the motivation is to ensure the correct operation of U.S. nuclear forces.

According to U.S. defense policy, nuclear weapons are supposed to deter attacks by enemy forces by threatening nuclear retaliation. However, the mere existence of nuclear weapons poses an enormous threat: If only one weapon explodes by accident, it could devastate several square miles of land and spread toxic radioactivity over a vast area. To properly control nuclear weapons, we must prevent mistakes or abuse while ensuring that a valid launch order is always carried out.

The risks posed by nuclear weapons are so acute that all activities surrounding them must follow special procedures that include redundant checking. Every operation is checked and verified. Any errors or shortfalls in the procedures may have serious consequences, even if no nuclear-related losses or injuries occur.

Example: In 2007, the U.S. Air Force disciplined 70 airmen for accidentally carrying nuclear-tipped cruise missiles on a B-52 bomber. From one standpoint, the incident was minor: No weapons were launched or detonated and the weapons were always in the custody of appropriate U.S. military forces. On the other hand, the incident took place because several nuclear management procedures were either ignored or botched. One observer speculated that the weapons were essentially missing without being missed for at least 10 hours. If the weapons had left U.S. custody, 10 hours would have allowed thieves to thoroughly cover their trail.

There are two parts to the U.S. military policy for controlling nuclear weapons:

1. Positive control. The weapons shall always be deployed when a legitimate order is given.
2. Force surety (or "negative control"). The weapons shall never be deployed without a legitimate order.

Both parts of the policy pose significant challenges, because both make global statements ("always" and "never"). U.S. nuclear command and control implements these policies through a large collection of interacting procedures. The steps in different procedures require separate personnel to cooperate to implement the policies. This is a sophisticated example of Defense in Depth. The multiple procedures also help verify the work of other personnel. The procedures construct a "cocoon" of protection around the weapons, so that if one procedure fails, others detect and help cover any protective gaps.

Although the 2007 incident reflected failures in several procedures, no one was hurt and no weapons detonated. Moreover, a vigorous response to incidents like the one in 2007 may serve as a warning to commanders who cut corners on nuclear operations.

Nuclear Operations

During the 1960s, the United States and Soviet Union developed nuclear forces to counter the perceived threat posed by each against the other. Both argued that the forces were meant to deter the other from attacking. For both, the worst-case attack was for the opponent to launch a surprise attack that destroyed the other's nuclear missile force. This set the stage for a second attack that devastated what was left of the victim's country.

To prevent such an attack, both forces developed early warning mechanisms to detect incoming bombers or missiles. They also developed mechanisms to ensure a counterattack despite imminent devastation. Part of the counterattack relied on missiles kept on hair-trigger alert. As soon as the incoming attack was detected, the targeted country would launch its nuclear missiles at the attacker. The entire process, from detecting the incoming attack to the launch of counterattacking missiles, was designed to take place in a matter of minutes.

POSITIVE CONTROL

National military commanders in the United States issue an Emergency Action Message, or EAM, when they need to give time-critical orders or other guidance to commanders and combat units. Commanders issue an EAM to order the launch of nuclear weapons or to initiate a drill to exercise the readiness of U.S. nuclear forces.

Formal authority to launch nuclear weapons rests with the president. However, military forces must retain the ability to launch a counterattack if a surprise attack kills the president or places the president out of touch with military forces. Thus, there are several underground and airborne command posts that also are authorized to issue an EAM.

A valid EAM uses a special set of authentication codes. These codes are changed regularly to reduce the risk of forged orders. When an EAM reaches a weapons platform like a missile launch control center or a nuclear submarine, two people must independently authenticate it. Then those two work together, and possibly with others, to implement the attack order. Teamwork serves both to ensure that launches are based on authenticated orders and that the order is carried out as stated.

FORCE SURETY

To prevent the improper use of nuclear weapons, U.S. forces must deal with several risks:

- A nuclear war occurs because of an accidental or unauthorized missile launch.
- An adversary manages to steal a nuclear weapon.
- A nuclear weapon detonates unexpectedly.

Force surety relies heavily on two-person integrity controls. All locations that house nuclear weapons or elements of the nuclear command and control system are no lone zones (Figure 17.8). Military units that handle or use nuclear weapons deploy additional guards and other protective measures. The actual launch of a nuclear weapon requires coordinated action by at least two separate people.

For example, it requires a two-person crew to launch Minuteman nuclear missiles. The equipment literally will not allow the launch if either is absent. Each crew member authenticates the EAM independently, then the crew members strap themselves into their respective chairs in front of their control panels: The panels won't start the launch procedure until then. The panels are placed far enough apart and the steps in the launch procedure are so time-critical that one crew member can't perform the procedure on both panels.

Nuclear weapons also contain special design features to prevent accidental or unauthorized detonation. Weapons follow a two-step process when detonating:

1. Arm the weapon.
2. Detonate the weapon.

An unarmed weapon can't possibly detonate. At most, high explosives inside the weapon might detonate, but this causes orders of magnitude less damage. Missile-based weapons include sensors to track its trajectory. The weapon won't arm itself unless it reaches a planned altitude on its flight path and starts to descend toward its target. This prevents a disaster if the rocket motor fails shortly after launch. If the missile fails to reach the right altitude, it won't arm itself before it crashes. If it crashes on friendly soil, it won't detonate.

The arming procedure on nuclear weapons relies on a secret code. Some weapons use the code to encrypt its timing logic; without the code, the weapon won't perform the precise timing steps needed to produce a nuclear explosion. Without the code, the device can't detonate. This makes accidents with unarmed weapons somewhat less catastrophic and prevents stolen weapons from being detonated by adversaries.

Achieving Nuclear High Assurance

Nuclear weapons pose a particularly difficult assurance problem. We can experiment with parts of the system, but we can't test everything. The U.S. military relies heavily on component testing, crew training, and periodic drills to validate the nuclear command system. Component testing and simulations help ensure the quality of the weapons themselves.

Physical protection follows examples shown earlier for handling critical documents: Keep under continuous control, keep strict accounts, perform regular inventories, and so on. We achieve higher assurance by implementing these procedures redundantly, so that there are multiple accounts, multiple guards, and multiple inventories.

Nuclear assurance is extremely expensive. The day-to-day operating procedures for the nuclear forces primarily pay for keeping the forces alert and ready to respond to an attack. Extra guards protect the weapons and control centers. Extra personnel perform nuclear-related paperwork. Nuclear assurance dramatically increases staff and administrative costs.

Moreover, critical nuclear information is properly classified Top Secret. This includes lower-level details of EAM transmission and validation of weapon system operation and of the nuclear bombs themselves. It is costly to create and distribute up-to-date codes (classified Top Secret) for authenticating an EAM and for arming weapons. Like all nuclear costs, lower assurance is not an acceptable option.

17.6.2 Multilevel Security

Computer-sharing techniques like multitasking and timesharing arose in the 1950s and 1960s in response to extremely high computing costs. Most military and government agencies couldn't afford to dedicate individual computers to specific classified programs. They needed a way to share computers without leaking information between programs or between classification levels.

It is difficult to share classified information on a computer because it is hard to prevent leakage. Transitive Trust produces the most significant leakage threat; people with a higher clearance must not leak information to those who have a lower clearance. The basic problem is the Trojan horse, which we examined in Section 4.5.

The term *multilevel security* (MLS) refers both to the sharing problem and to a particular mechanism to implement that type of sharing. The sharing problem involves two parts:

1. Grant access to a file if its classification level is equal to or less than the clearance assigned to the user.

2. Never allow access to information whose classification level is greater than a user's clearance.

Systems typically implement multilevel security by using the "Bell-LaPadula model." To implement this, we establish security labels that we assign to all processes, users, files, and other resources. The security label reflects the classification level of information. When applied to a user or process, the label reflects a security clearance the user holds. If a user holds a Top Secret clearance, then the user also holds all clearances below that. To implement multilevel security, the Bell-LaPadula model enforces two properties:

1. The Simple Security Property. A process may read from resources whose security label is at or below the process' own security label.

2. The * Property. A process may write to resources whose security label matches or exceeds its own. When speaking, we call this "the star property."

These rules are *always* enforced. For this reason, the multilevel security mechanism often is called *mandatory access control* (MAC). There are other mandatory access control mechanisms, but multilevel security is the most common. Here are examples of mandatory access control with multilevel security:

- If a system administrator has access to administrative mechanisms on a system, but only has a Secret clearance, the Simple Security Property will block all attempts to retrieve Top Secret files. (In practice, it's rarely practical to administer a system without having access and Need to Know for all data stored on the system.)

- If Bob is working with Top Secret information, for example, the * property prevents his processes from writing Top Secret information to Secret files. The * property is intended to block Trojan horse attacks. A Trojan horse might write the data to a different Top Secret file, but that prevents the information from leaking to someone without the proper clearance.

In a sense, multilevel security behaves like volume encryption; we protect everything whether we need to or not. Everything on the system carries a security label and has its accesses checked, even globally shared "unclassified" resources like application program files.

RULE- AND IDENTITY-BASED ACCESS CONTROL

Multilevel security and similar mechanisms sometimes are called "rule-based access control," because they are based on a fixed set of rules that the system enforces continuously. Although mandatory access control is the traditional term and remains widely used, some sources use the other term. To some extent, multilevel security mechanisms are intended to enforce access restrictions on behalf of third parties; the authorities who classified the information.

The two Bell-LaPadula rules are not sufficient by themselves to protect classified information. Access to classified information also is restricted by Need to Know. Most systems rely on conventional file-based access controls, like those in Chapters 3 and 4, to enforce Need to Know. Such rules are often called identity-based access control because they are based on user identities and controlled by the identified owners of files. The *Orange Book* called such rules "discretionary access control" because restrictions are applied at the discretion of those who had access to the files. Today, standards for such controls often refer to them as *controlled access protection*.

COVERT CHANNELS

Multilevel security works effectively only if all data paths between processes are controlled by the system security mechanisms. In fact, most systems provide many unplanned and unexpected ways to communicate between two processes. For example, if the system lets processes take exclusive control of a file, then one process can send a series of signals to the other by holding and releasing particular files. Processes may also communicate by producing delays in other shared resources, like the hard drive or available RAM.

These mechanisms create **covert channels** between processes. The channels aren't restricted by the Bell-LaPadula rules. Successful multilevel security enforcement relies on being able to restrict how processes communicate with each other. Researcher Butler Lampson called this "the confinement problem."

As secure system design evolved in the 1970s and 1980s, researchers developed techniques to locate, assess, and block covert channels. The basic strategy was to eliminate as many shared resources as possible. Designers assessed the remaining shared resources and tried to block or at least restrict any covert channels that arose.

Covert channels provided an additional reason to apply formal methods to system design. A well-designed formal specification helped locate and identify shared resources. Certain types of formal analysis would locate covert channels because they violated the security policy. Unfortunately, no technique could identify all possible covert channels. Experts dispute whether a practical system could eliminate all covert channels.

OTHER MULTILEVEL SECURITY PROBLEMS

Covert channels were not the only persistent problem with multilevel systems. When the government began promoting multilevel systems using the *Orange Book*, it was easy for many people to argue that the highest-rated "A1" systems were secure by definition because they had to meet stringent requirements, including formal security proofs. In fact, *all* multilevel secure systems suffered from two security problems:

1. The virus problem. The Bell-LaPadula rules do not—and cannot—prevent a virus present at a lower classification level from propagating to higher classification levels.

2. The redaction problem. Users routinely rely on large and unreliable application programs to edit classified documents and to create less-classified versions of such documents by removing the more-sensitive data. Unfortunately, the programs were rarely—if ever—analyzed to verify correct behavior. This may lead to unfortunate surprises like the one described in Section 17.1.1.

The redaction problem is very challenging, especially when faced with general purpose, free-format information. There are a handful of automated techniques that can reliably sanitize information of specific types and formats.

17.6.3 Computer Modes of Operation

When we deploy a computer system to process classified information, it is accredited to operate in a particular "mode." The different modes reflect the different types of classified information that might be present on the system and the clearances of potential users. There are four recognized modes. Each represents either tighter security requirements on the data and user community, or tighter requirements on the host computing system.

1. Dedicated
2. System High
3. Compartmented or Partitioned
4. Multilevel

We describe each mode here.

Dedicated Mode

This mode places the fewest requirements on the computer itself, but places the most restrictions on the data being processed and on the user community. A dedicated computer operates on data at or below one classification level. Everyone with access to that computer must be cleared for the data it handles, and must have a Need to Know for all data it handles.

Almost any computer may be used in dedicated mode. All security relies on physical protection. The operating system and hardware do not need to provide authentication, access control, or other security measures.

A computer in dedicated mode may process data at different classification levels for different groups of users, as long as it happens at different times. This is called "periods processing." For example, Secret Project X can use the dedicated mode computer in the mornings, and Top Secret Project Y uses it in the afternoons. The computer must support a procedure that completely erases its storage between periods if it is used for periods processing.

System-High Mode

In this mode, the system may process data at multiple classification levels. The entire user community must be cleared for the highest level present on the system, but they do not all require a Need-to-Know. The system must enforce Need-to-Know controls between users.

Computers used in system-high mode must be evaluated to ensure that they can in fact enforce Need-to-Know restrictions between users. The system must be able to enforce controlled access protection (also called "discretionary" or "identity-based" access control). Most of the better-known commercial operating systems are approved for system-high mode. In general, such systems must undergo a Common Criteria evaluation that assesses the system against the "Controlled Access Protection Profile."

System-high mode is the most common mode used with both computers and computer networks that process classified information. A system-high network must be entirely protected in accordance with the requirements for its classification level. However, because we isolate the network from less-cleared users and networks, we can build the network from commercial products.

The proliferation of system-high networks has led to a new problem: the challenge of *cross-domain sharing*. People working on a network at a higher classification level often produce material for people working at a lower classification level. Separate classification levels represent different domains. This arrangement also is called *multiple single levels* or MSL (in contrast to MLS). Although it may be a challenge to share properly sanitized information without accidentally spilling more-sensitive information, there are reliable and effective ways to sanitize and share certain types of information.

Compartmented or Partitioned Mode

In this mode, everyone who uses the system is cleared for Top Secret and for access to special program or intelligence data. However, the system contains data belonging to different SCI compartments or possessing different intelligence or special program code words. Not all users have formal access permission to all compartments or code words.

This is similar to the multilevel security problem in that users are literally not cleared to see information marked with particular compartments or code words. Because all users have been cleared for data above Top Secret, the risk of spillage is somewhat less than that we face if a Secret user receives Top Secret information.

The system requires multilevel security protections, but does not require the same degree of assurance. To address this, the intelligence community developed the Compartmented Mode Workstation (CMW). A CMW's underlying operating system enforces multilevel data flow between partitions, but does not necessarily concern itself with blocking covert channels. Because a covert channel won't spill data unless someone intentionally implements a program to exploit one, the risk should be minimal in the CMW environment.

Multilevel Mode

In this mode, the system may serve users with different security clearances and may store data which some users aren't cleared to receive. The system must implement a reliable and effective multilevel security mechanism. Today, multilevel servers often appear in two particular applications:

1. Multilevel servers—server systems that provide information to clients operating at different classification levels.
2. Guards—high-assurance firewalls that pass information between different security domains and MSL environments.

These applications easily provide data sharing in the low-to-high direction; users with lesser clearances can easily provide information to users with higher clearances. However, modern military operations require an effective flow of information in the opposite direction: high-to-low.

For example, a combat team is directed to attack a target; their orders may be classified Confidential or Secret. However, the Secret orders are created by an officer at a command post who uses online information from a Top Secret intelligence summary. The Top Secret summary was created from SCI and code-word intelligence that was sanitized by intelligence officers before being sent to the command post.

At each step, someone must sanitize a document and release it to a less-sensitive domain. Although there are some tools to help streamline and automate the release of sanitized documents, the process is hard to automate reliably.

17.7 Resources

 IMPORTANT TERMS INTRODUCED

adversary	COMSEC custodian	hostile intelligence service
aggregation and inference	COMSEC material	information operations
classification level	covert channel	jamming
classified information	cross-domain sharing	no lone zone
code word	degausser	polygraph
compartment	high assurance	red/black separation

redaction problem	separation kernel	zeroize
reference monitor	side channel attack	zone of control
security clearance	spread spectrum	
security fault analysis	TEMPEST	

ACRONYMS INTRODUCED

AIS—Automated information system

C&A—Certification and accreditation

CCI—Controlled cryptographic item

CMW—Compartmented Mode Workstation

COMINT—Communications intelligence

COMSEC—Communications security

DAA—Designated Accrediting Authority

DSSS—Direct sequence spread spectrum

DTD—Data Transfer Device

EAM—Emergency Action Message

EKMS—Electronic Key Management System

EW—Electronic warfare

FOUO—For Official Use Only

GAO—Government Accountability Office

HUMINT—Human-based intelligence gathering

IATO—Interim Approval to Operate

LMD—Local management device

MAC—Mandatory access control

MLS—Multilevel security

MSL—Multiple single levels

NIACAP—National Information Assurance Certification and Accreditation Process

NISPOM—*National Industrial Security Program Operating Manual*

NOFORN—No foreign distribution

NSTISSC—National Security Telecommunications and Information Systems Security Committee

NSTISSI—National Security Telecommunications and Information Systems Instruction

OPSEC—Operations security

ORCON—Originator controlled

OTAR—Over-the-air rekeying

PDS—Protected distribution system

RMF—Risk management framework

SAP—Special Access Program

SCI—Sensitive Compartmented Information

SI—Special Intelligence

SSAA—System Security Authorization Agreement

TCB—Trusted computing base
TPI—Two-person integrity
TRANSEC—Transmission security

17.7.1 Review Questions

R1. Identify information security risks and threat agents that apply particularly to information systems in government organizations.

R2. How is classified information different from other sensitive information?

R3. Summarize the security measures applied to classified information.

R4. Explain the redaction problem and how the exposure and quarantine model applies to sensitive information.

R5. Summarize elements of government and military information operations, of intelligence operations, and of operations security.

R6. Explain the difference between a security classification and a security clearance. How do they interact?

R7. Describe the different types of security markings that may appear on a classified document. Distinguish between genuine classification levels and other markings. What is meant by "above Top Secret?"

R8. Explain how compartments or code words might be used to protect particularly sensitive information.

R9. Summarize the major facets of national information security policy.

R10. Why does the U.S. government put special efforts into COMSEC instead of simply relying on commercial cryptographic products and mechanisms?

R11. Identify features of U.S. COMSEC measures that make them different from commercial practices described in earlier chapters.

R12. Describe the security problems associated with TRANSEC and common techniques used to address them.

R13. Explain the problems related to TEMPEST and five basic techniques used to address those problems.

R14. Identify the basic features of a reference monitor and explain its purpose.

R15. Explain the two parts of the policy used by the U.S. military to ensure the proper management of nuclear weapons.

R16. Explain the multilevel security problem and the Bell-LaPadula model.

R17. Describe the four modes of operation. Identify the most common mode used today.

17.7.2 Exercises

E1. Visit the CNSS website (cnss.gov). Locate the most recently updated policy, instruction, or standard. Identify the document, its date of issue, and briefly describe its topic.

E2. Visit the U.S. Government Accountability Office website (gao.gov). Locate a recent report on information security in the U.S. government. Review the report and briefly describe the information security issue addressed in the report.

E3. Revisit Alice's security policy development in Section 2.6. Assume that Alice's laptop is used for highly sensitive intelligence work instead of class work and personal activities.

    a. Create an appropriate list of risks for that situation.

    b. Create a new policy that addresses those risks, instead of the one shown in Table 2.3.

E4. Assuming that people have the security clearances shown in Table 17.1, and the Need-to-Know, list which people are cleared to read documents with the following classifications:

    a. Secret

    b. Top Secret

    c. Secret KRUG

    d. Secret KRUG MALBEC

    e. Top Secret MALBEC

    f. Secret MALBEC

    g. Secret SAUVE MALBEC

    h. Top Secret ARGUS BISHOP

    i. Top Secret BISHOP KRUG

    j. Top Secret SAUVE MALBEC

Each of the following problems requires the student to watch a particular dramatic film. **Each film typically runs about 2 hours.** Each problem notes the standard running time for the film; this may vary if watched on commercial television. The films are listed chronologically and not by topic or significance.

E5. Watch *Fail Safe* (1964), 112 minutes. Unrated.

    a. How does the "fail safe point" procedure help ensure positive control when launching an attack with bombers?

    b. How does the "fail safe point" procedure help ensure nuclear surety?

    c. What error occurred to cause the bombers to attack Moscow?

    d. Why couldn't the bombers be recalled?

E6. Watch *Dr. Strangelove* (1964), 95 minutes. Unrated.

    a. The film portrays an unintended nuclear attack. Was the attack a failure of positive control or of nuclear surety? Why?

    b. Why did the general try to block the Soviet ambassador from visiting the Pentagon's War Room?

    c. The Soviet ambassador describes their automated doomsday device as intended to be a deterrent for nuclear war. List two reasons why it might serve as a deterrent. List two reasons why it might be a bad choice for a deterrent.

    d. Why did the recall order fail? Was this a failure of nuclear surety or of positive control? Why?

E7. Watch *WarGames* (1983), 114 minutes. Rated PG (USA).

    a. The film opens with an incident in a Minuteman launch control center. Does the incident reflect a failure of positive control or of nuclear surety? Why?

    b. The two teenagers were playing "global thermonuclear war" and they launched simulated missiles at Las Vegas and Seattle. Assume that the computer operator hadn't detected that it was a simulation. What would happen next? What subsequent steps might prevent a missile launch?

c. How did the teenagers find the dial-in port to the WOPR?

d. Should the WOPR have had the dial-in port used in the film? Why or why not? What policies might apply to this situation?

E8. Watch *The Falcon and the Snowman* (1985), 131 minutes. Rated R (USA).

a. Identify two different types of security measures that would have helped prevent theft of the crypto keys.

b. Did the NSA inspector perform a reasonable inspection? Why or why not?

E9. Watch *Crimson Tide* (1995), 116–123 minutes, depending on the release. Rated R (USA).

a. Consider the missile launch procedures portrayed in the film. Is it possible for a single person to launch a nuclear missile? Why or why not?

b. A dispute develops between the captain and executive officer about the interpretation of an EAM. Does this dispute reflect a failure of positive control or of nuclear surety? Why?

c. Under what circumstances should a recipient accept an unauthenticated message? Give an example of a circumstance in which accepting an unauthenticated message would yield the wrong result.

d. Following the final scene but before the credits, the film displays a message explaining a change to the process of authorizing nuclear missile launches. Would this change have prevented the problem portrayed in the film? Why or why not?

Acronyms

This appendix contains all acronyms defined in this textbook. Tables A.1 and A.2 repeat earlier tables that define abbreviations for large numbers (Table 5.1) and top-level domain name acronyms (Table 12.1), respectively.

If we append a lowercase "i" to a large number abbreviation, it represents the corresponding power of two. For example:

2^{20} bytes = 1 MiB
2^{30} bytes = 1 GiB

The right-hand column indicates the chapter in which each acronym was introduced.

3DES—Triple Data Encryption Standard	Chapter 7
ACK—Acknowledgment	Chapter 10
ACL—Access control list	Chapter 4
ACM—Association for Computing Machinery	Chapter 1
AES—Advanced Encryption Standard	Chapter 7
AH—Authentication Header	Chapter 14
AIS—Automated information system	Chapter 17
AM—Amplitude modulation	Chapter 10

TABLE A.1 Abbreviations for large numbers

Abbreviation	Prefix Name	Decimal Size	Size in Thousands	Binary Approximation	Address Variable Size
K	kilo-	10^3	1000	$1024 = 2^{10}$	10
M	mega-	10^6	1000^2	$1024^2 = 2^{20}$	20
G	giga-	10^9	1000^3	$1024^3 = 2^{30}$	30
T	tera-	10^{12}	1000^4	$1024^4 = 2^{40}$	40
P	peta-	10^{15}	1000^5	$1024^5 = 2^{50}$	50
E	exa-	10^{18}	1000^6	$1024^6 = 2^{60}$	60

TABLE A.2 Common top-level domain acronyms

Acronym	Meaning	Type	Usage
ca	Canada	country code	Government or private organizations in that country
cn	China	country code	Government or private organizations in that country
uk	United Kingdom	country code	Government or private organizations in that country
us	United States	country code	Government or private organizations in that country
com	commercial	generic	Any organization may use this TLD
edu	educational	generic	Restricted to educational organizations
net	network	generic	Intended for organizations that provide network services
org	organization	generic	Intended for noncommercial organizations.
gov	government	generic	Restricted to U.S. federal and state government entities
mil	military	generic	Restricted to U.S. military organizations

ANSI—American National Standards Institute   Chapter 9
API—Application programming interface   Chapter 5
ARP—Address Resolution Protocol   Chapter 11
ARPA—Advanced Research Projects Agency   Chapter 11
ARPANET—ARPA Network   Chapter 11
AS—Autonomous system   Chapter 11
ASIS—American Society for Industrial Security   Chapter 1
ASP—Active Server Pages   Chapter 16
ASPX—Active Server Pages, Extended   Chapter 16
ATA—Advanced technology attachment   Chapter 2
ATM—Automated teller machine   Chapter 1
ATM—Asynchronous transfer mode (networking)   Chapter 12
AUP—Acceptable use policy   Chapter 1
b (lowercase)—Suffix indicating storage in bits   Chapter 5
B (uppercase)—Suffix indicating storage in bytes   Chapter 5
BBN—Bolt, Beranek, and Newman   Chapter 11
BCP—Business continuity plan   Chapter 13
BIA—Business impact analysis   Chapter 13
BIOS—Basic Input/Output System   Chapter 2

BPB—BIOS parameter block	Chapter 5
BS—British standard	Chapter 13
B-trees—Balanced trees	Chapter 5
C&A—Certification and accreditation	Chapter 17
CA—Certification authority	Chapter 8
CAST—Carlisle Adams and Stafford Tavares, creators of the CAST encryption algorithm	Chapter 7
Cat 5—Category 5	Chapter 10
Cat 5 E—Category 5, Enhanced	Chapter 10
CB—Citizen's band	Chapter 10
CBC—Cipher block chaining mode	Chapter 9
CCI—Controlled cryptographic item	Chapter 17
CCM—Counter with CBC-MAC	Chapter 14
CD—Compact disk	Chapter 2
CD-R—Recordable CD	Chapter 7
CD-RW—Rewritable CD	Chapter 7
CEK—Content encrypting key	Chapter 8
CEO—Chief executive officer	Chapter 13
CERT—Computer Emergency Response Team	Chapter 2
CERT-CC—CERT Coordinating Center	Chapter 2
CFB—Cipher feedback mode	Chapter 9
CFM—Cold Fusion Markup Language	Chapter 16
CGI—Common Gateway Interface	Chapter 16
CIA—Confidentiality, integrity, availability	Chapter 1
CIA—Central Intelligence Agency	Chapter 7
CIO—Chief information officer	Chapter 13
CISA—Certified information security auditor	Chapter 13
CISO—Chief information security officer	Chapter 13
CISSP—Certified information systems security professional	Chapter 1
CMM—Capability Maturity Model	Chapter 13
CMS—Content management system	Chapter 16
CMU—Carnegie-Mellon University	Chapter 1
CMW—Compartmented Mode Workstation	Chapter 17
CNSS—Committee for National Security Systems	Chapter 13
coax—Coaxial cable	Chapter 10
COMINT—Communications intelligence	Chapter 17
CompTIA—Computer Technology Industry Association	Chapter 13
COMSEC—Communications security	Chapter 17
CPU—Central processing unit	Chapter 2
CRC—Cyclic redundancy check	Chapter 5

CRUD—Create, read, update, delete access rights	Chapter 3
CSS—Cascading Style Sheets	Chapter 16
CTO—Chief technology officer	Chapter 13
CTR—Counter mode	Chapter 9
CTS—Clear to Send	Chapter 10
CTSS—Compatible Time-Sharing System	Chapter 2
CVE—Common Vulnerability Enumeration	Chapter 2
DAA—Designated Accrediting Authority	Chapter 17
DARPA—Defense Advanced Research Projects Agency	Chapter 11
DBMS—Database management system	Chapter 16
DDOS—Distributed denial of service attack	Chapter 10
DEC—Digital Equipment Corporation	Chapter 4
DEP—Data execution prevention	Chapter 2
DES—Data Encryption Standard	Chapter 7
D-H—Diffie-Hellman	Chapter 8
DHCP—Dynamic Host Configuration Protocol	Chapter 11
DMCA—Digital Millennium Copyright Act	Chapter 1
DMZ—Demilitarized zone	Chapter 15
DNS—Domain Name System	Chapter 12
DNSSEC—DNS Security Extensions	Chapter 12
DOD—Department of Defense	Chapter 4
DOS—Denial of Service	Chapter 1
DRM—Digital rights management	Chapter 1
DSL—Digital subscriber line	Chapter 12
DSS—Digital Signature Standard	Chapter 8
DSSS—Direct sequence spread spectrum	Chapter 17
DTD—Data transfer device	Chapter 17
DVD—Digital video disk	Chapter 5
DVD-CSS—DVD content scrambling system	Chapter 7
DVD-R—Recordable DVD	Chapter 7
DVD-RW—Rewritable DVD	Chapter 7
DVI—Digital video interface	Chapter 2
EAM—Emergency Action Message	Chapter 17
ECB—Electronic codebook mode	Chapter 9
ECC—Error correcting code	Chapter 5
EDC—Error detecting code	Chapter 5
EFF—Electronic Frontier Foundation	Chapter 7
EKMS—Electronic Key Management System	Chapter 17
ESC—Escape character	Chapter 2
ESMTP—Extended SMTP	Chapter 15

ESP—Encapsulating Security Payload   Chapter 14

ESSIV—Encrypted sector salt initialization vector   Chapter 9

EW—Electronic warfare   Chapter 17

FAA—Federal Aviation Administration   Chapter 1

FAR—False acceptance rate   Chapter 6

FAT—File allocation table   Chapter 5

FCC—Federal Communications Commission   Chapter 10

FDDI—Fiber Distributed Data Interface   Chapter 12

FDE—Full-disk encryption   Chapter 9

FIN—Finish TCP flag   Chapter 12

FIPS—Federal Information Processing Standard   Chapter 6

FISMA—Federal Information Security Management Act   Chapter 4

FM—Frequency modulation   Chapter 10

FOUO—For Official Use Only   Chapter 17

FRR—False rejection rate   Chapter 6

FRS—Family Radio Service   Chapter 12

FTP—File transfer protocol   Chapter 15

GAO—Government Accountability Office   Chapter 17

GIAC—Global Information Assurance Certification   Chapter 13

GIF—Graphics interchange format   Chapter 16

GLBA—Gramm-Leach-Bliley Act   Chapter 4

GPG—Gnu Privacy Guard   Chapter 14

GUI—Graphical user interface   Chapter 2

HFS+ or HFS Plus—Hierarchal File System Plus   Chapter 5

HIPAA—Health Insurance Portability and Accountability Act   Chapter 4

HMAC—Hashed Message Authentication Code   Chapter 14

HR—Human resources   Chapter 8

HTML—Hypertext Markup Language   Chapter 16

HTTP—Hypertext Transfer Protocol   Chapter 15

HUMINT—Human-based intelligence gathering   Chapter 17

HVAC—Heating, ventilation, and air conditioning   Chapter 13

Hz—Hertz   Chapter 10

I/O—Input/output   Chapter 2

IA—Information assurance   Chapter 13

IATO—Interim Approval to Operate   Chapter 17

IBM—International Business Machines   Chapter 2

ICANN—Internet Corporation for Assigned Names and Numbers   Chapter 12

ICMP—Internet Control Message Protocol   Chapter 12

ICV—Integrity Check Value   Chapter 14

ID—Identity   Chapter 1

IDE—Integrated Drive Electronics	Chapter 2
IDEA—International Data Encryption Algorithm	Chapter 7
IDS—Intrusion detection system	Chapter 15
IEC—International Electrotechnical Commission	Chapter 13
IEEE—Institute of Electrical and Electronics Engineers	Chapter 4
IETF—Internet Engineering Task Force	Chapter 11
IIS—Internet Information Services	Chapter 16
IKE—Internet Key Exchange	Chapter 8
IMAP—Internet Message Access Protocol	Chapter 15
IMP—Interface Message Processor	Chapter 11
infosec—Information security	Chapter 13
IP—Internet Protocol	Chapter 10
IPsec—IP Security Protocol	Chapter 14
IPv4—IP Version 4	Chapter 11
IPv6—IP Version 6	Chapter 11
ISACA—Information Systems Audit and Control Association	Chapter 13
ISC2—International Information Systems Security Certification Consortium	Chapter 13
ISMS—Information security management system	Chapter 13
ISO—International Standards Organization	Chapter 1
ISP—Internet service provider	Chapter 11
IT—Information technology	Chapter 1
ITAR—International Traffic in Arms Regulations	Chapter 9
ITU—International Telecommunications Union	Chapter 12
IV—Initialization vector	Chapter 9
JPEG—Joint Photographic Engineering Group	Chapter 16
JS—Javascript	Chapter 16
JSP—Java server page	Chapter 16
KDC—Key distribution center	Chapter 14
KEK—Key encrypting key	Chapter 8
LAMP—Linux, Apache, MySQL, PHP	Chapter 16
LAN—Local area network	Chapter 10
LMD—Local management device	Chapter 17
MAC—Media access control	Chapter 10
MAC—Message authentication code	Chapter 14
MAC—Mandatory access control	Chapter 17
MAPI—Message API	Chapter 15
MBR—Master boot record	Chapter 3
MD5—Message Digest 5	Chapter 6
MFT—Master file table	Chapter 5

MIC—Message integrity check   Chapter 14

MIME—Multipart Internet Message Extensions   Chapter 15

MIT—Massachusetts Institute of Technology   Chapter 1

MLS—Multilevel security   Chapter 17

MMC—Multimedia card   Chapter 5

modem—Modulator-demodulator   Chapter 10

MSL—Multiple single levels   Chapter 17

MTA—Message transfer agent   Chapter 15

Multics—Multiplexed Information and Computing Service   Chapter 4

MX—Mail exchange   Chapter 15

NAK—Negative acknowledgment   Chapter 10

NAT—Network address translation   Chapter 11

NFSV4—Network File Service, Version 4   Chapter 4

NIACAP—National Information Assurance Certification and
   Accreditation Process   Chapter 17

NIS—Network Information Service   Chapter 13

NISPOM—National Industrial Security Program Operating Manual   Chapter 17

NIST—National Institute of Standards and Technology   Chapter 1

NIST SP—NIST Special Publication   Chapter 4

nmap—Network mapper   Chapter 11

NOFORN—No foreign distribution   Chapter 17

NSA—National Security Agency   Chapter 1

NSTISSC—National Security Telecommunications and
   Information Systems Security Committee   Chapter 17

NSTISSI—National Security Telecommunications and
   Information Systems Security Instruction   Chapter 17

NTFS—NT File System   Chapter 5

OCTAVE—Operationally Critical Threat, Asset, and Vulnerability
   Evaluation   Chapter 1

OFB—Output feedback mode   Chapter 9

OODA—Observe, Orient, Detect, Act   Chapter 1

OpenVMS—Open Virtual Memory System   Chapter 4

OPSEC—Operations security   Chapter 17

ORCON—Originator controlled   Chapter 17

OSI—Open Systems Interconnect   Chapter 10

OTAR—Over-the-air rekeying   Chapter 17

PARC—Palo Alto Research Center   Chapter 10

PC—Program counter   Chapter 2

pcap—Packet capture file   Chapter 11

PCI—Peripheral component interconnect   Chapter 2

PCI DSS—Payment Card Industry Data Security Standard — Chapter 4
PDA—Personal digital assistant — Chapter 1
PDCA—Plan, Do, Check, Act — Chapter 1
PDF—Adobe Portable Document Format — Chapter 3
PDS—Protected distribution system — Chapter 17
PEM—Privacy Enhanced Mail — Chapter 14
pen test—Penetration test — Chapter 13
PGP—Pretty Good Privacy — Chapter 7
PHP—Personal Home Page/Hypertext Preprocessor — Chapter 16
PID—Processor identifier — Chapter 2
PIN—Personal identification number — Chapter 6
PKCS—Public Key Cryptography Standards — Chapter 8
PKI—Public-key infrastructure — Chapter 8
PKZIP—Phil Katz' "Zip" compression program — Chapter 7
PL—Padding length — Chapter 14
PL—Perl — Chapter 16
PLC—Programmable Logic Controller — Chapter 1
PNG—Portable Network Graphics — Chapter 16
POP—Point of presence — Chapter 15
POP3—Post Office Protocol, Version 3 — Chapter 15
POSIX—Portable Operating System Interface (Unix) — Chapter 4
PPP—Point-to-Point Protocol — Chapter 14
PPTP—Point-to-Point Tunneling Protocol — Chapter 8
PRNG—Pseudorandom number generator — Chapter 6
PY—Python — Chapter 16
QSA—Qualified Security Assessor — Chapter 13
RADIUS—Remote Authentication Dial-In User — Chapter 13
RAID—Redundant array of independent disks — Chapter 13
RAM—Random access memory — Chapter 2
RB—Ruby — Chapter 16
RC—Replay count — Chapter 14
RC2—Rivest's Cipher 2 — Chapter 9
RC4—Rivest's Cipher 4 — Chapter 7
RC6—Rivest's Cipher 6 — Chapter 7
RFC—Request for comments — Chapter 15
RFID—Radio frequency identification — Chapter 6
RJ45—Registered Jack 45 — Chapter 10
RMF—Risk management framework — Chapter 17
RO—Read-only access — Chapter 2
ROM—Read-only memory — Chapter 2

RPM—Revolutions per minute	Chapter 5
RS-232—"Recommended Standard" 232	Chapter 12
RSA—Rivest, Shamir, Adleman	Chapter 8
RTP—Real-Time Transport Protocol	Chapter 15
RTS—Request to Send	Chapter 10
RW—Read/write access	Chapter 2
RWX—Read, write, execute access rights	Chapter 3
S/MIME—Secure Multipart Internet Message Extension	Chapter 14
SA—Security association	Chapter 14
SAN—Storage area network	Chapter 16
SANS—SysAdmin and Network Security	Chapter 2
SAP—Special Access Program	Chapter 17
SATA—Serial ATA	Chapter 2
SCADA—Supervisory Control and Data Acquisition	Chapter 1
SCI—Sensitive Compartmented Information	Chapter 17
SD—Secure digital	Chapter 5
SDHC—Secure digital high capacity	Chapter 5
SDNS—Secure Data Network System	Chapter 14
SDS—Scientific Data Systems	Chapter 2
SDXC—Secure Digital Extended Capacity	Chapter 5
SEI—Software Engineering Institute	Chapter 1
SEQ—Sequence number	Chapter 12
SHA-x—Secure Hash Algorithm, x is version or bit size	Chapter 6
SI—Special Intelligence	Chapter 17
SMTP—Simple Mail Transfer Protocol	Chapter 15
SOX—Sarbanes-Oxley Act	Chapter 4
SP3—Security Protocol 3	Chapter 14
SPI—Security parameter index	Chapter 14
SQL—Structured Query Language	Chapter 16
SSAA—System Security Authorization Agreement	Chapter 17
SSID—Station set identifier	Chapter 14
SSJS—Server Side Javascript	Chapter 16
SSL—Secure Sockets Layer	Chapter 14
STO—Security Through Obscurity	Chapter 2
SYN—Synchronize TCP flag	Chapter 12
TCB—Trusted computing base	Chapter 17
TCP—Transmission Control Protocol	Chapter 10
TCSEC—Trusted Computer System Evaluation Criteria	Chapter 4
TEK—Traffic encrypting key	Chapter 14
telecom—Telecommunications	Chapter 11

TFC—Traffic flow confidentiality   Chapter 14
TLD—Top-level domain   Chapter 12
TLS—Transport Layer Security   Chapter 14
TPI—Two-person integrity   Chapter 17
TRANSEC—Transmission security   Chapter 17
TTL—Time to live   Chapter 11
TV—Television   Chapter 10
UAC—User Account Control   Chapter 4
UCL—University College, London   Chapter 11
UDP—User Datagram Protocol   Chapter 12
UFS—Unix file system   Chapter 5
UK—United Kingdom   Chapter 6
UPnP—Universal Plug and Play   Chapter 12
UPS—Uninterruptable power supply   Chapter 13
URI—Uniform Resource Identifier   Chapter 16
URL—Uniform Resource Locator   Chapter 16
USB—Universal Serial Bus   Chapter 1
VGA—Video Graphics Array   Chapter 2
VoIP—Voice Over IP   Chapter 15
VP—Vice president   Chapter 13
VPN—Virtual private network   Chapter 14
W3C—World Wide Web Consortium   Chapter 16
WAN—Wide area network   Chapter 11
WEP—Wired Equivalent Privacy   Chapter 14
WINS—Windows Internet Name Service   Chapter 12
WPA2—Wireless Protected Access, Version 2   Chapter 14
WTC—World Trade Center   Chapter 1
www—World Wide Web   Chapter 12
XML—Extensible Markup Language   Chapter 16
xor—Exclusive or   Chapter 7
XSS—Cross-site scripting   Chapter 16
XTS—Xor-Encrypt-Xor Tweaked Codebook Mode with Ciphertext
    Stealing   Chapter 9

ALTERNATIVE SECURITY TERMS AND CONCEPTS

This appendix provides brief articles on certain concepts relevant to CNSS training standards for information security professionals. It contains the following topics:

- Application-dependent guidance
- Attribution of information
- Comprehensive model of information systems security
- Configuration management of programming standards and control
- Critical and essential workloads
- Threats to systems
- Information identification
- Network security privileges (class, node)
- Object reuse
- Power emergency shutdown
- Procedural controls on documentation, logs, and journals
- Public switched network
- Public versus private networks
- Remanence
- Segregation of duties
- Threats and threat agents
- Transmission security countermeasures

B.1 Application–Dependent Guidance

It is not practical to apply "one size fits all" security to all applications. Off-the-shelf security mechanisms rarely provide sufficient security by themselves. Instead, security-critical activities must incorporate security measures in the applications themselves. We identify those measures as we follow the six-phase security process.

For example, Section 13.1.2 describes the use of two-person or multiperson control. Corporate accounts payable serves as the example application. To increase the security of the application, we use Least Privilege and Separation of Duty.

B.2 Attribution of Information

When we attribute information to a particular entity, whether it is a person or an organization, we make assumptions about that entity's beliefs and intentions. Security errors often arise from incorrect attribution. For example, if a shipping clerk receives a request to deliver a valuable shipment to a particular location, the clerk will set up the delivery if the attribution is correct. An attacker can commit a fraud by tricking the clerk to deliver a shipment to the wrong address.

If we can reliably attribute a collection of information to reliable sources, then our systems can operate reliably when users act on the information to perform tasks, like printing address labels for delivering valuable cargo. Such attribution often rests on authentication techniques. If we require authentication to update the information in a database, then we attribute the information to people with legitimate login privileges. If information carries a digital signature, we attribute it to the individual who signed it: the owner of the private key.

B.3 Comprehensive Model of Information Systems Security

While trying to establish some structure in information security education and training, officials at the DOD developed a "comprehensive model" to incorporate the major aspects of the topic. The result was published in 1991 by Captain John R. McCumber, then of the DOD Joint Staff.

The model organizes familiar elements of information systems and security into three broad categories: critical information characteristics, information states, and security measures. Readers encounter these categories and their elements in different sections of the textbook.

- Critical information characteristics: the CIA properties of information introduced in Section 1.4.2.
  - Confidentiality
  - Integrity
  - Availability

- Information states: the three basic states introduced in Section 3.5.3.
  - Transmission
  - Storage
  - Processing

- Security measures: three categories of security controls introduced in Chapters 1, 2, and 13.
  - Technology (Chapter 1)
  - Policy and Practices (Section 2.6 and Section 13.2)
  - Education, Training, and Awareness (Section 13.2.6 and 17.3.2)

The model views the categories as representing three separate dimensions, each three layers deep. This yields a cube made of smaller cubes, each representing a specific element from each of the three categories. For example, one cube combines Confidentiality, Transmission, and Technology to lead us to Chapter 14, studying Network Encryption. If we examine Integrity, Storage, and Policy and Practices, we find ourselves arranging data backups at the end of Section 2.6.3, or arranging enterprise backup and recovery procedures in Section 13.5.1.

The second security measure is sometimes phrased as "policies, procedures, and practices." Security *practices* are documented through policies and procedures. Although the term *practices* is not specifically used in Section 13.2, the section discusses the ways by which an enterprise establishes uniform practices to ensure security.

B.3.1 The MSR Model

In 2001, Maconachy, Schou, Ragsdale, and Welch augmented the comprehensive model to create the MSR model. The new model renamed the security characteristics to be *security services*, also listed in Section 1.4.2. Nonrepudiation and Authentication were added to the list of services. Information states remained unchanged. Security measures were replaced with *countermeasures*, and that list's third element was replaced with a more general term: People.

The MSR model is part of the ACM's Information Technology 2008 curriculum guidelines.

B.3.2 Applying the Models

In either case, the model provides a way of categorizing other aspects of information security. For example, we could categorize a threat, vulnerability, or attack in terms of a choice from each category. A sniffing vulnerability, for example, might be categorized as involving Confidentiality, Transmission, and Technology again. We locate a likely countermeasure by matching an alternative with the same three categories.

B.4 Configuration Management of Programming Standards and Control

Section 13.3 specifically discusses configuration management and its role in managing the contents of computer software and of its design documentation. Effective organizations also apply configuration management processes to the processes themselves. The documents containing policies, procedures, and programming standards are all kept under configuration control. Changes to the policies and standards must go through an established review process.

B.5 Critical and Essential Workloads

Section 13.5.3 discusses the process of analysis and planning to address the risks of catastrophic interruptions in system operation. The Business Impact Analysis (BIA) identifies critical and essential workloads by looking at business processes. The BIA estimates the impact on the business if a particular process doesn't take place for varying times from one week to 1 month in duration. The impact is graded in terms of "significant," "major," or "minor" to help identify the critical and essential workloads.

B.6 Threats to Systems

The textbook identifies threat agents primarily in terms of motivation: property theft, vandalism, identity theft, and so on (see Section 1.4.1). "Natural" threats may include either environmental or technological hazards that occur due to random-occurring events, including both environmental events and operator or maintenance-related errors in technical systems. Employee-oriented risks include malicious acts by disgruntled employees and accidents caused by or vulnerabilities opened due to careless employees (see Section 13.1.2).

B.7 Information Identification

Many certification and accreditation processes speak of *information identification* as an important part of the process. In this textbook, we *identify assets*, and the assets are typically information or information-related processes.

B.8 Network Security Privileges

A privilege is an access right. In some environments, these rights may be organized into sets called *privilege classes*. Instead of assigning individual rights to processes, the system assigns rights based on the privilege class to which the process belongs.

In a networking environment, it may be difficult to enforce access rights on the basis of process identity. Such identities are generally provided by software on the nodes themselves, and a subverted node may provide bogus identity information. Instead, network security decisions may be enforced on a *node* basis, relying on node addressing information. Thus, particular nodes may be assigned to privilege classes. Access rights are granted to that node's processes based on the node's privilege class.

B.9 Object Reuse

The *object reuse* problem arises when an attacker scavenges sensitive information left in storage areas after an authorized process has finished using the storage areas. The textbook addresses two specific cases of this:

- Undeleting a file, as described in Section 5.4.3. Chapter 5 opens with an example in which Bob and Tina's sensitive file is retrieved by someone who used an undelete utility to retrieve the deleted file.
- File scavenging, introduced in Chapter 5. Undeleting is a form of file scavenging. Some attackers may also extract information by studying the data directly on the disk, in case the file directories no longer point to interesting deleted files.

We can also look at object reuse as a more general problem that applies to any storage area. It's possible to scavenge data from RAM if the operating system provides some RAM that was unchanged after being used by a different process. If the operating system allocates blocks of drive storage to a new file before data is written, it might be possible to read previously written data from those blocks.

Modern operating systems try to prevent object reuse in both RAM and on drive storage:

- RAM—When a process requests a new block of RAM, the OS erases the RAM before giving it to the process.
- Drive storage—when a process opens a new file, the file is empty. If the process tries to read from the empty file, the OS returns no data and reports "end of file." If the process writes data to only the beginning of a data block, the rest of the block is erased before the block is added to the file. This prevents the process from scavenging data left on partially written blocks.

B.10 Power Emergency Shutdown

Section 13.3.2 discusses physical security for enterprise information technology, and it covers the topic of power management.

An important safety element of power systems for information systems is the emergency shutdown mechanism. A typical mechanism removes power from all electrical and electronic equipment in a data center or other room dedicated to information technology equipment. There may be one or more emergency shutdown switches, each placed near a room exit. An emergency shutdown switch may be required in the following installations:

- A larger, wired-in uninterruptable power system.
- A computer room with a raised floor.

The final decision as to the requirement for emergency shutdown often rests with building inspectors who assess safety and compliance with mandatory construction codes. In some cases, an emergency shutdown should *not* be installed. These include systems with these properties:

- Provide safety-critical operations, like fire alarms or 911 emergency calls from building occupants.
- Requires a particular shutdown sequence by individual devices to prevent serious damage.

An emergency shutdown switch may often be optional. In such cases the enterprise should consider whether a shutdown switch really addresses serious risks or whether it poses additional risks to interrupted equipment.

B.11 Procedural Controls on Documentation, Logs, and Journals

Section 4.6.1 focuses on automated methods of logging significant events in an information system. Traditional techniques rely on a paper trail. Documentation, logs, and journals generally provide that paper trail. For example, many organizations require visitors to physically sign a paper log when arriving at a site. The enterprise develops specific procedures for using and preserving that log as an independent record of individuals who visit the site. Written journals may play a similar role. A paper journal may record petty cash handling. Some researchers keep a written and dated record of research activities that may be used in patent filings and disputes.

The enterprise must establish and oversee the procedural controls for these paper records. There must be instructions as to when the records are created and kept, and oversight to ensure that the procedures are followed. When a paper record is full, the procedures indicate how it must be archived or, if obsolete, destroyed.

B.12 Public Switched Network

The term *public switched network* traditionally refers to the circuit-switched telephone network described in Section 10.2.2 and used as examples in Section 11.1. Dial-up connections used the public switched network. Some enterprises could lease a communications line from the public network; this provided a dedicated, high performance connection between two sites. Although such dedicated lines often shared infrastructure with the public network, switched connections could not achieve comparable performance until the introduction of frame relay or asynchronous transfer mode (ATM) service.

B.13 Public Versus Private Networks

A public network is one that connects a variety of different individuals and organizations together. The global Internet and the commercial telephone network are examples of public networks: almost anyone can join the network who can pay for access, and most members can communicate with most other members. Private networks only connect a specific set of endpoints, which may be individuals, hosts, or sites. Different private networks provide different degrees of privacy, as shown in virtual private networks that implement IPsec encryption in Sections 14.4 and 14.6.

B.14 Remanence

Remanence is the measurable signal that remains on a storage device. For example, magnetic remanence on a hard drive refers to the magnetic patterns that indicate the data stored on the drive. This includes both the information intentionally stored as well as data that the operator attempted to erase. When we wish to retain data reliably, remanence indicates the degree to which we succeed. When we wish to erase undesirable data, remanence refers to the device's tendency to retain data despite attempts to erase it. *Optical* remanence refers to the tendency of optical devices, like CDs and DVDs, to retain information.

Section 7.4.3 discusses the challenges of erasing stored information. The section on erasing low-level data and on optical media specifically addresses the problems of remanence on magnetic and optical media.

B.15 Segregation of Duties

This textbook introduces the basic principle of Separation of Duty in Section 8.2.3. This phrasing is somewhat more common in the information security community than "segregation of duties," and it refers to the same fundamental concept. In both cases, we break up a task into separate steps performed by separate individuals or agents. When performed correctly, Separation of Duty reduces the risk of fraud or abuse by requiring multiple people to cooperate for the abuse to occur.

B.16 Threats and Threat Agents

The term *threat* has held two separate definitions in the security community: it may either represent a specific type of attack or damage that threatens an asset, or it may represent an *agent* that is motivated to threaten an asset. The text uses the following terms instead:

- An *attack* is a particular strategy or technique for exploiting or damaging an asset.
- A *risk* is a particular type of attack that threatens an asset.
- A *threat agent* is an active entity that is motivated to attack an asset.

The text introduces these terms in Figure 1.3 on Page 12.

B.17 Transmission Security Countermeasures

This textbook discusses a broad range of technical measures related to transmission security in Section 17.4.3. The basic concept is to provide *pattern forewarning protection*: the communications between units should not reflect patterns of content, amount, or frequency that forewarn adversaries of upcoming actions. If adversaries identify particular patterns of communication that always precede particular unit activities, they are forewarned of those activities.

In the days of voice and telegraph communication, there were two specific transmission security strategies:

- Callsign variations—Units were never called directly by name in radio messages. Instead, each unit had a callsign that could be changed occasionally. If adversaries learned to associate messages to a particular callsign with actions of a particular unit, the changed callsign would reduce their ability to predict our actions.

- Frequency variations—Units periodically change the radio frequencies used to transmit their traffic. This forces adversaries to monitor numerous frequencies, and makes it harder to associate messages on particular frequencies with particular unit activities.

Beyond those techniques, radio operators might "pad" a message with extra text, or send messages with no significant content at all, simply to obscure any patterns in the actual messages being exchanged.

Index

Note: Italicized page locators indicate figures/photos; tables are noted with *t*.

A

Abbreviations, for large numbers, 199*t*
Abnagle, Frank, 13
Above Top Secret classification, 774
Abstraction, I/O system and, 219–220
Acceptable use policy, 32, 576
Access control, 229, 230
  deploying cryptography on Internet and, 628, 629
  effectiveness of encryption and, 387*t*
  strategies for, 60–65
    islands, 60
    puzzles and patterns, 60, 61–63
    vaults, 60, 61
Access control lists, 149–163
  Macintosh OS-X, 152–155
  Microsoft Windows, 156–163
  modern implementation of, 151
  Multics, 150–151
  POSIX, 151–152
Access matrix, 68–69, 115
  for processes, 69*t*
  for shared data section, 71*t*
Access rights, 69–70
  determining, for Microsoft Windows ACLs, 158–159

directory, 95–97
to executable files, 117
file ownership and, 94–95
managing, 114–115
to personal files, *118*
Access rules, ambiguous, 146*t*
Accountability, companies, secrecy, and, 570
Accreditation. *See* Certification and accreditation
Acknowledgment numbers, TCP and, 529–530
Acknowledgment protocol (ACK), *455*, 455–456, *457*, 457, 458, 528
ACLs. *See* Access control lists
Acoustical signals, TEMPEST problem and, 806
Acronyms, memory size names and, 199, 199*t*
Active attacks, 620, *621*
Active Directory, Kerberos protocol and, 604
Active Server Pages, 740
Active Server Pages Extended, 741
Active tokens, search space and, 265–266
ActiveX, 740
Adams, Carlisle, 317
Addressing
  in tree network, 488
  web pages, 719–722
    default web pages, 721–722
    email URLs, 720
    hosts and authorities, 720–721

    path name, 721
Address Resolution Protocol, 495, 506–507
  ARP cache, 506–507
  command to display ARP cache for, *507*
  packet contents and, *506*
Address scope, 509
  reachability dependent on, *510*
Address variables
  memory sizes and, 197–200
  size of, 198
Adleman, Len, 353
Administrative groups, basic file sharing on Windows and, 140
Administrative users, Least Privilege and, 140–143
Administrators, 21, 108
  separation of duty and, 591
Admissible evidence, 181
Adobe Acrobat, 103
Advanced Encryption Standard, 298–299, 316, 329–330, 389
  choosing encryption algorithm and, 399
  development of, 394
  encrypting disk data with, *414*
  finalists, 394–395
  flexibility of RC4 *vs.* flexibility of, 393
  key encapsulation with RSA and, 354, *355*
  key sizes and average cracking times, 299*t*

untrustworthy encryption and, 418

Advanced Research Projects Agency, 491

Advanced Technology Attachment, 45

Advance fee fraud, 688

Adversaries, 766

AES. *See* Advanced Encryption Standard

agent.btz worm, 439–440

Aggregation
    challenge of secrecy and, 767
    database security and, 749

Aircraft hijackings, 35–39
    high-level analysis of
        assets, 36
        implementation, 36
        monitoring, 37
        policy, 36
        recovery, 37
    September 11, 2001, 37–39, *38*

AIS. *See* Automated information systems

Alexander, Christopher, 598

Algorithms, 287
    encryption, qualities of, 397–400
    "private label," cautionary note, 400
    RC4, leaking and cracking, 396, 397

Aliases, website, 538

Altavista, 724

AM. *See* Amplitude modulation

Amazon.com, 744

Ambiguous access rules, 16t

American Bankers Association, 635

American Cancer Society, email hoaxes and, 694–695

American National Standards Institute, 393

Amplification attacks, 546–547

Amplitude, *452*

Amplitude modulation, 453

AM radio, 452–453

AM wave form, *453*

Analog-based digital networks, 558

Analog broadcast networks, 557

Analog signals, 450, 451

Analog two-way radios, 559

Analysts, training and expertise for, 585

Anderson, Ross, 394

Anonymity, client, 758–760

Anonymous Diffie-Helman shared secret, creating, 639, *639*

Anonymous proxies, 759–760

ANSI. *See* American National Standards Institute

ANSI X9.17, 637
    wrapping new keys for distribution and, 635, *636*

Antihacking laws, 31

Anti-tamper, working key storage and, 425

Antivirus software, 6

Apache, 719

API. *See* Application programming interface

Apple II, 100

Apple Macintosh OS-X, 50
    choosing users for group in, *155*

Apple Mail, on OS-X, 679

Apple's HFS Plus, 211–212
    volume format, *212*

Apple's Safari, 718

Application filtering, 698, 700–701, *701*

Application layer, OSI protocol model, 471

Application layer encryption with S/MIME or PGP, 626
    in transit, *643*

Application programming interface, 217

Application programs, 99, 673

Application protocols, 468, 673

Application proxy, 701

Application transparency, 622
    end-to-end crypto and, 650–651
    IPsec and, 624

apps, 2

Arm, hard drive, *188*

Armstrong, Edwin, 453

ARP. *See* Address Resolution Protocol

ARPA. *See* Advanced Research Projects Agency

ARPANET, 491, 492, 493, 526, 540, 651, 674, 695
    IMP, *496*
    protecting, 496–497

ARP cache
    description of, 506
    displaying, command for, *507*

ARP request, displayed in Wireshark, *515*

ARP response, displayed in Wireshark, *515*

Art of Deception, The (Mitnick), 574

AS. *See* Autonomous systems

AS-400, 115

ASCII character set, 248

ASCII email, 676

ASIS International, 11

ASPs. *See* Active Server Pages

ASPX. *See* Active Server Pages Extended

Assessment, 583

Assets
    identifying, 14–15
    student computer example and, 8
    Trojan horse analysis and, 128

Assured pipeline, 377

Asymmetric cryptography, 345

Asymmetric encryption, *288*

Asymmetric encryption algorithm, 347

Asynchronous links, synchronous links *vs.*, 451

Asynchronous transfer mode services, 560

ATA. *See* Advanced Technology Attachment

Atlas computer, 66

Atlas system, 115

ATM cards, 259

ATM services. *See* Asynchronous transfer mode services

Atomic bomb, development of, 766
Attack damage, 20
Attacker, 12
Attacks
  calculating impact of, 27–28, 28t
  defined, 12
  detecting, by reviewing logs, 169–170
Attack strategy, low hanging fruit, 236–237
Attenuation, TEMPEST problem and, 806
Attribute entries, NT file system and, 214
Auditing, 582. See also Security audits
  enterprises and, 596
Audit logs, audits of, 583
Auditors, training and expertise for, 585
Audits, 576
Audit trail, 166
AUP. See Acceptable use policy
Authenticated email, 686–687
Authenticated software updates, 376–378
Authentication, 2, 229–281
  base secret and, 231
  basic external attacks on, 235
  biometric, 268–272
  digest, 262–263
  direct, 600–602
  disk-based, 428
  enterprise network, 598–607
  of hard drive, 185
  indirect, 602–603
    properties of, 606
  local, 599–600
  objective of, 231
  off-line, 606–607
  performing, steps in, 230, 231
  preboot, 427–428
  to protect computer resources, 230
  redirected, 605
  risks and, 234–236
  security services and, 22
  server, 730–734

service-based, 604–605
techniques, examples of, 232t
threats and, 233–234
ticket-based, 603–604
Authentication factors, 231–233
  three-factor authentication, 233
  two-factor authentication, 232–233
  types of, 231–232
Authentication Header, within IPsec, 653
Authentication policy, 272–280
  location and, 274
  password selection and handling, 279–280
    simple passwords, 280
    strong but memorable passwords, 280
    strongest passwords, 280
  strong and extreme threat environments
    constructing policy, 278
    passwords alone for strong threats, 276
    passwords plus biometrics, 277, 277t
    passwords plus tokens, 278, 278t
    strong threats, risks from, 273–274
  weak threat environments
    household policy, 274–275, 274t
    workplace policy: passwords and tokens, 275, 276t
    workplace policy: passwords only, 275, 275t
  weak threats, risks from, 273
Authentication server, 599
Authentication tokens, 258–268
  challenge-response, 259, 262–263
  denial of service, 267, 267t
  one-time password tokens, 259, 264–266

passive, 259–260
vulnerabilities of, 266–268, 267t
  clone credential, 266–267, 267t
  clone or borrow the credential, 266–267, 267t
  denial of service, 267, 267t
  retrieve from backup, 267, 267t
  sniff credential, 267, 267t
  trial and error guessing, 267, 267t
Authenticity, 621
Authorities, email URLs and, 720–721, 721
Automated information systems, 789
Automobiles, computer-controlled, security vulnerabilities with, 3
Autonomous systems, 498–500
Availability
  security services and, 22
  Web, 757–758
Average attack space, 254, 266
Average cracking time, 299

B
Back door, opening for attacker, 54
Backdoor attack, laptop risk assessment and, 26
Back doors, 376
Background investigations, 588, 778
"Back Orifice" program, 555
Backups
  full vs. partial, 608–610
  image, 610
  incremental, 610
  procedure, 78
  RAID as, 611–612
  synchronized, 609–610
Bacon, Francis, 7
Balanced trees (B-trees), 212
Bandwidth, 452
Base secret, 231
Basic language, 100

Basic principle of information security, 6
  Chain of Control, 63–64
  Continuous Improvement, 6
  Defense in Depth, 18
  Deny by Default, 112
  Least Privilege, 15
  Open Design, 62
  Separation of Duty, 341–342
  Transitive Trust, 165
Bastion-host topology, 706, 707
Baudot, Émile, 442, 452
Bayesian filtering, 691
BBN. *See* Bolt, Beranek, and Newman
Bcc field, in emails, 676
BCP. *See* Business continuity plan
Beale, T. J., 286
Beale Papers, 285–286
Bell-LaPadula model, properties enforced by, 814
Bell-LaPadula rules
  covert channels and, 815
  virus problem and, 816
Bell Telephone Laboratories, 143
Berners-Lee, Tim, 645, 716
Beyond Fear (Schneier), 4
BIA. *See* Business impact analysis
Biased password selection, 254–257
  four-digit luggage lock, *256,* 256–257
  independent guesses and, 255
  measuring likelihood, not certainty, 255
Bidirectional satellite communications, 561
Biham, Eli, 394
Bill of Rights, Fourth Amendment of, 181
Binary encryption, 300
Binary exponents, relationship between decimals and, 199
Binary keys, textual keys *vs.,* 329
Binary matches, 690–691
Biological viruses, 101
Biometric authentication, 268–272
  accuracy of, 269–270

fingerprint reader on laptop keyboard, *268*
vulnerabilities of, 271–272
Biometrics, 63
Biometric sensor, 270
Biometric spoofing, 601
Biometric systems, 233
  elements of, *269*
BIOS (Basic Input/Output System), 46, 64
BIOS-integration, preboot authentication and, 427, 428
BIOS parameter block (BPB), 202
Birthday attacks, 363–364
Birthday paradox game, 363
Bit-flipping attacks, 360–361, 418
  on encryption with xor, *360*
BitLocker (Microsoft), 411
Bits, estimating number of, 199–200
Bittorrent, 473–474
Black-hat hackers, defined, 13
Black hats
  exploit and, 125
  windows of vulnerability and, 125
Black Hat USA 2005 Briefings, 34
Blacklists, 690, 726
Black programs, 783–784
Block cipher modes, 400–409
Block ciphers, 389–400
  applying, 389
  building, 390–391
  data encrypted in fixed-sized blocks, *390*
  encryption failure with, *400*
  features of, *391*
  mixing mode used with, *402*
Block encryption procedure, description of, 390–391
Blogs, 569
b (lower case), storage in bytes, 200
Blue Screen of Death, 71
Blu-ray disks, 318
Bogus certificates, 734, 735

Bogus primes attack, on RSA, 359–360
Bogus purchase, laptop risk assessment and, 26
Bogus sites, 546, 729
Bolt, Beranek, and Newman, 496
Boot, 64
Boot blocks, 201–203
  contents of FAT 32 boot block, *202t*
Booting, 46
Bootstrap, defined, 64
Bootstrapping, 46
Border routers, 499
Botnet operators, 21
  identifying specific attacks by, *26t*
Botnets, 13, 440–442
  DDOS attacks on DNS servers and, 546
  fighting, 441–442
  in operation, 441
bots, 440, 441, 546
Boundaries, 9, 15–17
  analyzing, 16–17
  in dorms, 15–16
  insider threats and, 17
  Least Privilege principle and, 15, 16
Boyce, Christopher, 795, 798
Boyd, John, 7
bpn.gov certificate, browser authentication for, *733*
Bredolab botnet, 442
British Standard BS7799, 578
Broadcast networks, 558
Browser cookies, 744–745
  adding to header in subsequent visits, *745*
  defined, *744*
  producing, *744*
Browsers, 718, 721
  sandboxing, 743
Browser software, 472
Browsing, private, 760
B-trees (balanced trees), 212
Bucket brigade attacks, 368, *369*
  bogus certificates and, 734
Buffer overflows, Morris worm and, 54–60

Buffers, 49, 190
Bugs, 123
Built-in file encryption, 309–311
Burst transmissions, countering
  EW attacks and, 802
Bus, 45, 189
Bush, Vannevar, 715
Business continuity plan, 615
Business impact analysis, 613,
  615
Business records, legal issues and,
  182
Bus interface, 190
Bus interface connector, 190
Bus network, 482, *486*, 486–487
  benefits and shortcomings
    with, 487

C

CA. *See* Certificate authority
C&A. *See* Certification and
    authentication
Cable modem, 548
Cables, 45, *46*
  network, 460–461
Cable TV, 560
Cache poisoning, DNS and, 545–
  546
Caesar cipher, 293, 294, 390,
  619
Cain, *659*
Callahan, Edward, 442
Called procedure, 49
Caller ID feature, *558*
Calling procedure, 49
Capability-based security, 114–
  115
Capability(ies), 115–117
  defined, 115
  in practice, 115
  resource-oriented permissions
    and, 116–117
Capability Maturity Model, 577
Capitalization, for Internet
    protocols and, 492
Cascading Style Sheets, 718
CAST, 317
Catch Me if You Can (film), 13
Category 5 Enhanced wiring (Cat
  5 E), 460

Category 5 wiring (Cat 5), 460
CB. *See* Citizen's band
CBC
  calculating, 663
  sector encryption with, *416*
CBC encryption, integrity issues
    with, 416
CBC mode, drive encryption
    with, 414–416
Cc field, in emails, 676
CCI. *See* Controlled
    cryptographic item
CCM. *See* Counter with CBC
    MAC
CD-R (recordable CD), 315
CD-RW (rewritable CD), 315
CDs. *See* Compact disks
CEK. *See* Content encryption key
Cell phones, 54, 560
Cell phone towers, *555*, *556*
Censorware, 113
Central Intelligence Agency, 309,
  770–771, 794
Central processing unit, 44
CEO. *See* Chief executive officer
CERT. *See* Computer Emergency
    Response Team
CERT Advisories, 59
CERT Coordination Center
    (CERT/CC), 59
Certificate authority, 370, 371
  bogus, 735
  subsidiary, 371–373
  tricked, 737–737
  untrusted: difficult to verify,
    733–734
Certificate chain, 372
  digital signatures and, 372–
    373
  email authenticated with, *373*
Certificate hierarchy, for
    spanning multiple
    enterprises, *374*
Certificate names, mismatched,
    Firefox alert for, *731*
Certificates
  bogus, defined, 735
  expired: possibly bogus,
    probably not, 734
  revoked: always bogus, 734

Certification, information
    security and, 586–587
Certification and accreditation
  government communications
    security and, 791,
    792–793
  CNSS policies/instructions
    on, 792
  phases of, 792–793
Certified Information Systems
    Security Professional,
    586, 587
CFB mode. *See* Cipher feedback
    mode
CFM. *See* Cold Fusion Markup
    Language
CGI. *See* Common Gateway
    Interface
Chain letters
  email, 694–695
  virus hoax, 695
Chain of Control, 63–64, 109
  computer viruses and, 101
  executable files and, 100
  subverting, 65
Challenge-response
    authentication, 259,
    260–263, *261*
  challenge-response calculation,
    263
  hand-operated token, *261*
  implementing, 262
  for network, 601
  nonce and, 261
  using challenge-response
    token, *262*
Change control process, 578
Character set, 248
Checks, signing, with digital
    signature, 366
Checksums, 193–194, 242, 361,
    454, 654
  data encrypted with, *362*
  simple, calculating, 194, *194*
Check value, 185, 190
Chief executive officer, 579, *580*
Chief information officer, 581
Chief information security
    officer, 582, 585
Chief technical officer, 581

China Telecom, 500
Chosen ciphertext attack, on
    RSA, 359
Christian canon law, 180
Chrome browser (Google),
    sandboxing and, 743
CIA. *See* Central Intelligence
    Agency
CIA properties, 22
CIO. *See* Chief information
    officer
Cipher block chaining, 401, 408–
    409
    mode decryption diagram for,
    409
    mode encryption diagram for,
    408
Cipher feedback, 401
Cipher feedback code, mode
    encryption diagram for,
    406
Cipher feedback mode, 406–408
    ciphertext errors, 407–408
Cipher machine, Friedman with,
    296
Cipher mode, choosing, 410
Ciphers, *288, 289*
    Caesar, 293, 294
    stream, 302–305
    substitution, *288, 289,* 293
    Vignère, 294–296
Cipher suites, 627
Ciphertext, 287
    identical blocks encrypting to
        identical ciphertext, *401*
    IV included with, when
        required, *404*
    key wrapping and, 338
    symmetric encryption and,
        290
Ciphertext errors
    for CBC, 409
    for CFB, 407–408
    effects of, 306, 391–392
    for OFB, 403
Ciphertext Stealing, 416, 417
Circuit board, hard drive
    controller, 189
Circuit filtering, 699

Circuit-switched telephone
    systems, *557*
Circuit switching, 444, 446–447
    advantages with, 446–447
    disadvantages with, 447
Cisco, 34
    certifications through, 586
CISO. *See* Chief information
    security officer
CISSP. *See* Certified Information
    Systems Security
    Professional
Citizen's band, 453, 559
Civil complaint, 181
Civil law, 180
Civil War, Confederate cipher
    used during, *294,*
    294–296
Clancy, Tom, 767
C language, 58, 103
Classification levels, 773–774
    enforcing access to, 785–786
Classifications and clearances,
    773–786
    classification levels, 773–774
    classification levels in
        practices, 779–780
    compartments and other
        special controls, 780–786
    security clearances, 777–779
    security labeling, 775–777
Classification system, legal basis
    for, 774
Classified information
    computer modes of operation
        and, 816–818
    compartmented or
        partitioned mode and,
        816, 817–818
    dedicated mode, 816–817
    multilevel mode, 816, 818
    system-high mode, 816,
        817
    government secrecy and, 767
    minimizing amount of,
        774–775
    security labeling and,
        775–776
    working with, 779

Clearances
    defined, 588
    employee, 588–589
    modern security classification
        system and, 773
    security, 777–779
Clear to Send, 466
Client
    network services and, 472
    resource sharing and, 474
    service request and reply, 473
Client anonymity, 758–760
Client policy issues, Web security
    and, 725
Client/server mode, 472
Client-side scripts, 740, 741–743
    executing, 742
    HTML, in Javascript, 742
    risks with, 741–743
    "same origin" policy and, 743
    sandboxing and, 743
Clone credential
    authentication tokens and,
        266–267, 267t
    biometric authentication and,
        271
Cluster chain, 203
Clusters, 757
    building FAT files from,
        203–206
    in file, FAT pointing to, *205*
    on hard drive, *191*
    NT file system and, 213
    parts of files in, *204*
    storage of, 204
    Unix file system, 209
CMM. *See* Capability Maturity
    Model
CMS. *See* Content management
    systems
CMW. *See* Compartmented
    Mode Workstation
CNSS. *See* Committee on
    National Security
    Systems
Coaxial cable, 458
Cobol, 103
Code analysis procedures, 596
Code reviews, 596

Codes, *288, 289, 293*
Codes of conduct, 32
Code word, classified, 784
Coding activities, formalized
  enterprises and, 596–598
    auditing and monitoring,
      596
    avoiding risky practices, 597
    code analysis procedures,
      596
    code reviews, 596
    coding standards, 596
    software-based access
      controls, 597–598
Coding standards, 596
Cohen, Fred, 100, 719
Cold-boot attacks, 430, 431
Cold Fusion Markup Language,
  741
Cold standby, 614
Cold War
  government secrecy and,
    766
  nuclear operations during,
    811–812
  TEMPEST problem and, 805
College degrees, information
  security field, 586
Collisions
  avoiding, wireless protocol
    for, 466
  handling, 465–467
    wireless collisions, 465–467
    wireless retransmission, 467
Command injection attacks,
  752–755
  defined, 752
  inside of, 753–755
  login masquerade and, 753
  password-oriented, 752–753
  resisting website command
    injection, input
    validation, 755
Command logic, 190
  reading encrypted data from
    hard drive and, 423
Commercial enterprises,
  information security and,
  568
Committee on National Security
  Systems, 586, 786

C&A policies and instructions,
  792
communications security and
  cryptography instructions
  by, 794–795
communications security
  policies published by,
  793–794
information assurance
  requirements for national
  defense systems, 810
Common Criteria, 151
Common Criteria certification,
  172
Common Criteria evaluation,
  577
Common Criteria Protection
  Profiles, modern high-
  assurance computing
  systems and, 810
Common Gateway Interface,
  740
Common law, 180
Common Vulnerability
  Enumeration (CVE)
  database, 59–60
Communication networks,
  history behind, 555–557
Communications intelligence
  (COMINT), 784
Communications security
  (COMSEC), 619–629,
  784, 793–803
  crypto by layers, 621–627
    application layer encryption
      with S/MIME or PGP,
      626
    link layer encryption and
      802.11 wireless, 622–623
    network layer encryption
      and IPsec, 623–624
    socket layer encryption with
      SSL/TLS, 625–626
    cryptographic technology,
      795–796
    crypto security procedures for,
      797–800
    key leakage through spying,
      795
    layer-oriented variations in,
      627

national system security and,
  789
transmission security and,
  800–803
Compact access rules, 119,
  119
  for isolation policy, 121*t*
Compact disks, 45
  companies and secrecy, 569–
    571
  erasure or destruction of, 804
Companies and information
  control, 568–571
  accountability, 570
  managing publicity, 570
  Need to Know, 570–571
  obligations, 569
  reputation: speaking with one
    voice, 568–569
  secrecy culture, 570
  trade secrets, 569
Company ID cards, 590
Company identity, processes tied
  to, 569
Company statements (official),
  personal statements *vs.*,
  569
Compartmented mode, computer
  modes of operation and,
  816, 817–818
Compartmented Mode
  Workstation, 818
Compartments, 780
  clearances, lattice of, 785
  data processing with, 782
  enforcing access to, 785–786
Compatible Time-Sharing
  System, 65, 232, 236,
  237
Competitors, 21
Compiler, 103
Compliance, 581
Compliance audits, 583–584
Compression, 650
Compromised systems, 12, 13,
  178
Compromising emanations,
  TEMPEST and, 794
CompTIA certification, 586
Computer-based encryption,
  298–308

Advanced Encryption
    Standard, 298–299
Data Encryption Standard,
    298
exclusive or, 300–302
key stream security, 305–306
one-time pad, 306–308
predicting cracking speeds,
    299–300
stream ciphers, 302–305
Computer customization, 14
Computer dissection, 44–45
Computer Emergency Response
    Team, 59, 645
Computer modes of operation
    classified information and,
        816–818
    compartmented or
        partitioned mode, 816,
        817–818
    dedicated mode, 816–817
    multilevel mode, 816, 818
    system-high mode, 816, 817
Computer networking, 435–478
    Ethernet: modern LAN, 458–
        467
    network applications, 472–
        478
    network security problem,
        435–442
    protocol stack, 467–472
    putting bits on a wire, 450–
        458
    transmitting information,
        442–450
Computer network operations,
    military information
    operations and, 771
Computer networks
    combining, 491–501
    emergence of Internet, 492–
        493
    evolution of Internet security,
        495–498
    early Internet attacks, 497
    early Internet defenses,
        497–498
    protecting the ARPANET,
        496–497
    hopping between, 493–495

counting hops, 495
routing Internet packets,
    495
traversing, 492
Computers
    classified information and,
        779
    executing machine instruction
        in, 47
    programs and, 43–49
    working insides of, 44
Computer Technology Industry
    Association, 586
Computer viruses, 63, 100–103
    malicious viruses, 102–103
    removable storage devices and,
        6
    virus infection, 100–102
COMSEC. See Communications
    security
COMSEC materials, 797
Con artists, 21
Concurrency problem, 216
Confederate Army, Vignère
    cipher used by, 294–296
Confederate cipher disk,
    reproduction of, 294
Conficker or Downadup, 6, 104,
    105
Confidential classification, 773
Confidential clearances, 778
Confidential documents,
    protecting, 779
Confidential information, color
    code for, 775
Confidentiality, 621
    security services and, 22
    on the Web, 756
Configuration management
    process
    enterprises and, 595–596
    repeatability and traceability
        in, 596
    software development security,
        595
Connection-based email attacks,
    687–688
Consent to search, 182
Consultants, enterprises and,
    592

Containers, 96
Content control, Internet traffic
    control and, 697
Content control software, 113,
    726
Content encryption key, 339
    KEK encryption of, key
        wrapping and, 338
    Separation of Duty and, 343
Contention, bus network and,
    487
Content management systems,
    746, 746–755
    database management systems,
        747–749
    description of, 746–747
    password checking: example,
        750–751
    logging-in to website, 750
    login process, 750–751,
        751
Content-Type header, MIME
    formatting in Internet
    email and, 677
Contingency planning, 608–616
    components of, 608
    data backup and restoration,
        608–612
    full-oriented incremental
        backups, 610
    full vs. partial backups,
        608–610
    image backups, 610
    RAID as backup, 611–612
    disaster preparation and
        recovery, 613–615
    business impact analysis,
        613–614
    process for, 615
    recovery strategies, 614
    handling serious incidents,
        612–613
Continuous availability, 757,
    758
Continuous Improvement, roots
    of, 6–7
Continuous operation, 757, 758
Contractual obligations,
    companies, secrecy, and,
        569

Contributor rights, basic file sharing on Windows and, 138

Controlled access protection, 815

Controlled Access Protection Profile, system-high mode of operation and, 817

Controlled cryptographic item, 799

Controlled sharing, 106–107, 135–143
  basic, on Windows, 137–138
    administrative groups, 140
    user groups, 139–140
  Least Privilege and administrative users, 140–143
  sharing dilemma, 136–137
  tailored file security policies, 136

Control section, 48
  shared by two processes, 69

Cookies, 472, 760
  browser, 744, 744–745, 745

Co-owner rights, basic file sharing on Windows and, 138

Corbató, Fernando, 65, 232

Corporate espionage, 766

COSMEC custodian, duties of, 797–798

Cost centers, 580–581

Counterintelligence, 770–771

Counterintelligence polygraph examination, SCI clearances and, 781

Counter mode, 401, 405
  CCM encryption and, 662
  drive encryption with, 413–415
  constructing counter, 413–415
  integrity risk, 415
  encrypting disk data with, 414
  key stream with, 406

Counter with CBC MAC, 661–662

Country codes, 537

Coupling, 807

Covers, 770–771

Covert channels, multilevel security and, 815–816

CPU. See Central processing unit

Crackers, defined, 13

Cracking feasibility, different degrees of, 251t

Cracking speeds, 251–252
  predicting, 299–300

CRCs. See Cyclic redundancy checks

Credentials, 229, 234, 235
  guessing, 266
  sniffing, 235, 236, 243–244

Credential updates, enterprise network authentication and, 598

Credit cards, 259
  online shopping and, 645

Crime, via search engines, 724

Criminal background checks, 589

Criminal complaints, 181

Critical data, identifying noncritical data vs., 388

Cross-domain sharing, system-high mode of operation and, 817

Cross-site scripting, 743

Crosstalk, TEMPEST separation and, 807

CRUD (Create, read, update, delete access rights), 95

Cryptanalysis, 305
  encryption and, 293–297

Crypto atop protocol, 642–651
  adoption of secure email and application security, 644–645
  Pretty Good Privacy, 643–644
  privacy-enhanced mail, 643
  SSL handshake protocol, 647–648
  SSL record transmission, 648–651
  transport layer security—SSL and TLS, 645–647

Cryptograms, 293

Cryptographic building blocks, 242–243

challenge-response, 260–264

Diffie-Hellman secret sharing, 348–351, 639–640

digital signature, 365–368

exclusive-or, 300–302

key distribution center, 636–637

key wrapping, 338–341, 635–636

manual keying, 632–633

one-way hash function, 240–243

RSA, 353–354

RSA secret wrapping, 354–356, 640–641

shared secret hashing, 637–638

stream cipher, 302–305

Cryptographic function, 241

Cryptographic product evaluation, 317
  of encryption algorithms, 399–400

Cryptographic protections, 621

Cryptographic randomness, 250

Cryptographic technology governments, secrecy and, 795–796
  classic Type I crypto technology, 796

Cryptography, 61, 285, 325. See also Encryption; Public-key cryptography
  asymmetric, 345
  deploying on Internet, issues related to, 627–628
    access to Internet sites, 628
    automatic encryption, 628
    end-to-end crypto, 628
    keying, 628
    scope of sniffing protection, 627
    traffic filtering, 627
  elliptic curve, 353
  high-assurance, 795
  indirect authentication and, 606
  Open Design and, 62–63
  secret-key, 345

symmetric, *288, 288,* 347
Cryptography by layers,
    621–626
    adding cryptography to
        Internet software, *622*
    application layer encryption
        with S/MIME or PGP,
        626
    link layer encryption and
        802.11 wireless,
        622–623
    network layer encryption and
        IPsec, 623–624
    socket layer encryption with
        SSL/TLS, 625–626
Crypto keys
    on a network, 629–642
        manual keying, 632–633
        public-key building blocks,
            638–641
        public-key *vs.* secret-key
            exchanges, 641–642
        secret-key building blocks,
            635–638
        simple rekeying, 633–635
    Walker spy ring and, 799
Crypto logic, reading encrypted
        data from hard drive and,
        423
Cryptology, 296, 397
Cryptonets, 326
    rekeying and, 327
Cryptoperiods, 327, 328
    key wrapping and, 340
Crypto security procedures,
        797–800
    controlled cryptographic
        items, 799
    key management processes,
        799–800
        data transfer device, 800
        electronic key management
            system, 800
    two-person integrity, 798
CSS. *See* Cascading Style Sheets
CTO. *See* Chief technical officer
CTR mode. *See* Counter mode
CTS. *See* Clear to Send
CTSS. *See* Compatible Time-
        Sharing System

Culture, enterprise community
        and, 587
Custodians, physical access and,
        591
Cutler, Dave, 146
Cutwail. *See* Pushdo/Cutwail
Cyclic redundancy checks, 195,
        242, 361, 654
Cylinder, 188

D
DAA. *See* Designated
        Accrediting/Authority
Daemen, Joan, 394
DARPA, 491, 495
Data
    file sharing and, 475–476
    hiding with partitions, 197
    sharing, 70–71
Data backup and restoration
    file-oriented incremental
        backups, 610
    full *vs.* partial backups,
        608–610
    image backups, 610
    RAID as backup, 611–612
Database management systems,
        747–749
    database security and, 749
    enterprise databases and, 749
    Structured Query Language
        and, 748–749
Database management system
        software, 746
Databases, 747
    enterprise, 749
    relational, 747–748
Database security, 749
Data compression, SSL record
        transmission and, 650
Data Encryption Standard, 298,
        299, 305, 389
    evolution of, 392–394
    Lucifer and, 392–393
    triple, 393–394
Data execution prevention, 58
Data files, executable files *vs.*, 97
Datagrams, 449
Data integrity, encrypting a
        volume and, 419

Data link layer, OSI protocol
        model, 470
Data loss prevention systems, 706
Data mining, 749
Data processing, compartments
        used for, 782
Data protection, 803–804
    media handling, 803
    media sanitization and
        destruction, 803–804
Data recovery, low-level,
        preventing, 314
Data section, 48
Data storage, on hard drive,
        185–200
Data tables, 747
    sample, from sample database,
        747
Data Transfer Device, keys
        handled by, 800
Data warehouses, 749
Daughterboards, 44, *44*
DDOS. *See* Distributed denial of
        service attacks
DEC. *See* Digital Equipment
        Corporation
Decimals, relationship between
        binary exponents and,
        199
Decommissioning, 590
Decryption, 285, 356. *See also*
        Encryption
    for cipher block chaining
        mode, 408, *409*
    of DVD sector, *344*
    of files, security boundaries
        for, *312*
    RSA, 356
    of stream ciphers, 392
    symmetric encryption and,
        290
Decryption algorithm, 287
Dedicated digital network links,
        560
Dedicated lines, 482, 484,
        558
    dial-up lines *vs.,* 558*t*
Dedicated mode, computer
        modes of operation and,
        816–817

Default Deny policy, low-cost gateway products and, 549
Default file protection
Microsoft Windows ACLs and, 159–163
dynamic ACLs, 160–162
inherited rights, 159
moving and copying files, 162–163
Default keying, 630
Default permit, 114
Default Permit policy, low-cost gateway products and, 549
Defense, 12
Defense in Depth, 18–19
control of nuclear weapons and, 811
discipline of secrecy and, 768–769
physical protection of enterprise information system and, 593
protecting classified data and, 779
two-factor authentication and, 233
Defense secrecy restrictions, 32
Defragment utility, 192
Degaussers, 804
Delayed recovery, 614
Delegation, of access to file server, 477
Delegation problem, 477
Deleting files, FAT directories and, 206–207
Delivery protocols, 679, 680–681
Demilitarized zone, 705
dual-firewall topology with, 708, 709
three-legged firewall with, 708, 708
Deming, W. Edwards, 7
Deming cycle, 7, 577
Denial of service, 23, 235, 437
authentication tokens and, 267, 267t
biometric authentication and, 271
bus network and, 487

distributed, 441
DNS resolvers and, 546–547
on DNS servers, 545, 546
file protection policies and, 108
power interruptions and, 592
Dennis, Jack, 115
Deny access, for Microsoft Windows ACLs, 157–159, 158
Deny by Default, 112–114
Microsoft Windows ACLs and, 159
opposite of, 113–114
DEP. See Data execution prevention
Department of Defense, 151, 170, 497, 651
FISMA and, 787
media sanitization procedures/ standards of, 803
Password Management Guideline, 245
security labeling and, 775–776
special access programs and, 783
Department of Homeland Security, US-CERT and, 59
Deployment, security-critical systems and, 579
Deployment policy directives, 578–579
risk acceptance and, 579
steps related to, 578–579
deployment, 579
implementation, 578–579
planning, 578
Derivative classification, 775
DES. See Data Encryption Standard
DESCHALL, 298, 299
DES Cracker, 252, 298, 299, 418
Designated Accrediting/ Authority, 792, 793
Design features, of dispatcher, 83
Design patterns, types of, 598–599
Detective controls, 166
Device drivers, 53, 99

Device-hosted volume, 413
Device independence, I/O devices and, 215
D-H. See Diffie-Hellman
DHCP. See Dynamic Host Configuration Protocol
Dial-back, 558
Dial-up connections, 558
Dial-up lines, dedicated lines vs., 558t
Diameter protocol, 604
Diaries, encrypted, 286–287
Dictionary attacks, 252
analysis of, 253
by Morris worm, 253, 257
Diffie, Whitfield, 348, 353
Diffie-Hellman, 347, 348–351, 368, 632, 638
background and description of, 348–349
cipher suites in SSL and, 627
IKE process and, 657, 658
math basics and, 350–351
perfect forward secrecy and, 349–350
procedure for secret sharing, 349
RSA vs., secret key sharing and, 356
secret sharing with, 639, 639–640
variations of, 350
Digest authentication, 262–263
Digital circuits, minor signal glitches self-corrected with, 450
Digital devices, turning off, 184
Digital Equipment Corporation, 146, 491, 497
Digital evidence, 181–185
collecting legal evidence, 182–184
documenting the scene, 183–184
securing the scene, 183
Fourth Amendment and, 181–182
procedures, 184–185
authenticating a hard drive, 185
Digital forensics, 178, 179

Digital Millennium Copyright Act, 31, 35
Digital networks, 453, 558
Digital rights management, 31, 317–320, 711, 756
DVD Content Scrambling System, 319–320
policy dilemmas, 318–319
Digital satellite broadcasts, 561
Digital signals, 450, 451
Digital signatures, 345, 350, 365–368, 370
chains of certificates and, 372–373
invalid: always bogus, 734
nonrepudiation and, 368
RSA, verifying, 367
RSA and, 353–354
signing a check with, 366
in valid public-key certificates, 733
Digital Signature Standard, 350, 368
Digital steganography, 61
Digital subscriber line, 548
Digital systems, 450
Digital video disks, 195
erasure or destruction of, 804
Digital Video Interface, 45
Direct authentication, 601
description of, 600–601
poor scaling with, 602
sniffing attacks and, 601
Direct connect tokens, 263, 263–264
Direct design pattern, 599
Directional transmissions, countering EW attacks and, 802
Direction control, Internet traffic control and, 697
Directories, 724
access rights for, 95–97
Unix, 210–211
Unix permission flags and, 144
Directory name formats, 93t
Directory ownership, 96
Directory path, 92–93
Direct-sequence spread spectrum, 802, 803

Disaster preparation and recovery, 613–614
business impact analysis, 613–614
data backup and restoration, 608–612
recovery strategies, 614
Disclosure, 23, 108, 437
Disclosure attacks, 571, 620
Discrete logarithm problem, 350
Discretionary access control, 815
Disengagement, serious attacks and, 612
Disk-based authentication, 428
Diskettes
erasure or destruction of, 804
virus-infected, 102
Disk keys, on DVDs, 343
Disk platers, 187, 187
Dismount, 216
Dispatcher, 66
design features of, 83
Dispatching procedure, 83–84
Distributed database, 540
Distributed denial of service attacks, 441
on DNS servers, 546
Distributed DNS servers, 547
Distributed processing, 456
DMCA. See Digital Millennium Copyright Act
DMZ. See Demilitarized zone
DNS. See Domain Name System
Document markings, security labeling and, 775–776, 776
DOD. See Department of Defense
Domain names, 535
common top-level domain acronyms, 536t
constructing, 537
hierarchy of, 536
investigating, 543–545
looking up, 539–540, 542
misleading, 736
mismatched: may be legitimate, 731–733

Firefox alert for mismatched certificate name, 731
phishing and, 693
resolver software, 539
resolving via redirection, 542–543
taking possession of, 538
three-part, example format, 537
using, 538–539
Domain Name System, 535, 673
attacking
cache poisoning, 545–546
DOS attacks on DNS resolvers, 545–547
DOS attacks on DNS servers, 545
DNS protocol, 540–543
DNS redundancy, 543
Wireshark display of DNS response, 541
DNS Security Extensions (DNS-SEC), 547
security improvements for, 547
Domain registrar, 538
Doorknob rattling, 236
Dorms, boundaries in, 15–16, 16
DOS. See Denial of service
Dotted decimal notation, 503
examples of addresses in, 504
for Internet addresses, 504
Downadup or Conficker, 104, 105
Downlinks, 461
"Downloads" subdirectory, 93
Draper, John, 13
Drive-by downloads, 104, 692
Drive controller, 189
adding encryption to hard drive and, 421
Drive encryption
with CBC mode, 414–416
with counter mode, 413–415
constructing counter, 413–415
integrity risk, 415
Drive formatting, encryption in hardware and, 422

Drive locking/unlocking, encryption in hardware and, 422–423
DRM. *See* Digital rights management
Drupal, 747
DSL. *See* Digital subscriber line
DSS. *See* Digital Signature Standard
DSSS. *See* Direct-sequence spread spectrum
DTD. *See* Data Transfer Device
Dual firewalls, 706, 708–709, *709*
Due diligence, fault and, 179
"Dumb" networks, "smart" networks *vs.*, 525–526
Duplicated packet, delayed ACK and, *457*
DVD content protection, *319*
DVD Content Scrambling System (DVD-CSS), 318, 319–320, 343
DVD key handling, 343–345
  decrypting DVD sector, *344*
  finalizing disk for publication, 344–345
  keys on DVD hidden track, *343*
DVD publisher, 344
DVD-R (recordable DVD), 315
DVD-RW (rewritable DVD), 315
DVDs. *See* Digital video disks
DVI. *See* Digital Video Interface
Dynamic ACLs, Microsoft Windows, 160–162
Dynamic Host Configuration Protocol, 511, 512, 673
  configuring, NAT and, 551–552
Dynamic inheritance, moving and copying files and, 162–163
Dynamic link libraries (.dll), 70, 99
Dynamic websites, 738–745
  scripts on the Web, 739–743
  states and HTTP, 743–745
  web forms and POST, 738–739

E
EAM. *See* Emergency Action Message
Eavesdropping
  bus network and, 487
  on encryption process, 430
  enterprise network authentication and, 598
  risks to volumes and, 384, 385
ECB. *See* Electronic codebook mode
ECCs. *See* Error correcting codes
e-commerce, public-key certificates and, 371
EDCs. *See* Error detecting codes
Education, for information security professionals, 585–586
EFF. *See* Electronic Frontier Foundation
E-Government Act (2002), 787
802.11 access, service-based authentication for, *605*
802.11 link encryption, packet with, *623*
802.11 wireless
  link encryption on, 658–665
  link layer encryption and, 622–623
802.11 wireless network technology, 459
EKMS. *See* Electronic Key Management System
Electrical telegraph, 442
Electric power management, in enterprises, 592–593
Electromechanical encryption, 296–297
Electronic codebook mode, 401, 402
Electronic Frontier Foundation, 298, 759
Electronic keying, early forms of, 799
Electronic Key Management System, 799, 800
Electronic warfare, 771, 801–802
El Gamal cipher, 350, 368
Elliptic curve cryptography, 353

Elliptic curves, *347*
email, 445, 569. *See also* Internet email
  aliases, 538
  authenticated, 686–687
    with certificate chain, *373*
  signed, excerpt from, *686*
  spam and, 13
  tracking, 681–684, *682*, *683*
    from MMS01 to MMS02, 684
    from UC123 to USM01, 682
    from USM01 to USM02, 683–684
    from USM02 to MMS01, 684
Email chain letters, 694–695
email format, elements of, *675*
email infection, Trojan malware and, 104
email messages, forging, 684–687, *685*
email protocol, port numbers for, 502
email security problems, 687–695
  connection-based attacks, 687–688
  phishing, 691–693
  spam, 688–691
  viruses and hoaxes, 693–695
email text, with MIME formatting, *678*
email URLs, 720, *720*, *721*
Email viruses
  defined, 693
  execution of, 694
Embezzlement, 14
Embezzlers, 21, 108
Emergency Action Message, 812, 813
Emergency destruction, 771
Employee clearances, 588–589
Employee life cycle, 588, 589–591
Employee roles, 588, 591
Employees, insider attacks and, 573
Employment history, verification of, 589
Encapsulating Security Payload, 653, 654–656

packet format, 654–656
   transport mode, 656
   tunnel mode, 655–656
Encapsulation of keys
   with RSA
      public key, 355
      retrieving key with RSA
         private key, 355
Encrypted diary: process
      example, 286–287
Encrypted drive
   automatic reboot, 429
   booting, 427–429
   preboot authentication, 427
      BIOS integration, 427, 428
      disk-based authentication,
         427, 428
Encrypted sector salt
      initialization vector. See
      ESSIV
Encrypting gateways, 624
Encrypting a hash, two steps for,
      364
Encrypting volumes, 409–419
   adapting an existing mode,
      413–416
      drive encryption with CBC
         mode, 415–416
      drive encryption with
         counter mode, 413–415
   block cipher modes, 400–409
   block ciphers, 389–400
   choosing a cipher mode,
      410
   encryption in hardware,
      420–423
      drive controller, 421–422
      drive locking and
         unlocking, 422–423
   FDE implementations,
      objectives for, 409–410
   hardware vs. software, 411
   managing encryption keys,
      423–431
      booting an encrypted drive,
         427–429
      key generation, 424
      key storage, 425–427
      rekeying, 424
      residual risks to keys, 429–
         431

password volume for
      mounting, 412
   policy for, 389
   policy statements for, 389t
   residual risks, 418–419
      data integrity, 419
      encryption integrity, 419
      looking for plaintext, 419
      untrustworthy encryption,
         418
   securing a volume, 383–389
   in software, 411–413
      files as encrypted volumes,
         412–413
      "tweakable" mode, 416–418
Encryption, 2, 62, 285–320. See
      also Cryptography; See
      also Decryption;
      Network encryption
   asymmetric, 288, 289, 345,
      347
   automatic, deploying
      cryptography on Internet
      and, 628
   automatic application of, 666–
      667, 667t
   binary, 300
   categories of, 288–289
   for cipher block chaining
      mode, 408, 408
   computer-based, 298–308
   cryptanalysis and, 293–297
   digital rights management and,
      317–320
   effective, 290–291
   effectiveness of access control
      and, 387t
   for email, 644
   encrypted diary: process
      example, 286–287
   enterprise network
      authentication and, 598
   file encryption software, 309–
      317
   information states and, 291–
      292, 292
   procedure diagram of, 288
   process view of, 289
   public-key, 346, 348
   secret-key, 348
   security software and, 598

selective, reasons for, 667
Separation of Duty with,
      342–343
symmetric, 347
   process diagram of, 290
traditional purpose of, 619
untrustworthy, 418
with xor, bit-flipping attack
      on, 360
Encryption algorithms, 265, 347
   categories of, 288
   good, qualities of, 397–400
      available for analysis, 397,
         398
      cryptographic evaluation,
         398, 399
      explicitly designed for
         encryption, 397, 398
      no practical weaknesses,
         397, 399
      security does not rely on its
         secrecy, 397, 398
      subjected to analysis, 397,
         398–399
Encryption application
      programs, 311–313
   ensuring secure file encryption,
      312–313
   protecting the secret key, 313
Encryption key management,
      423–431
   automatic reboot, 429
   booting an encrypted drive,
      427–429
   key generation, 424
   key storage, 425
   persistent key storage, 425–
      427
      key wrapping, 426
      managing removable keys,
         426–427
      protected storage, 425–426
   preboot authentication, 427–
      428
      BIOS integration, 428
      disk-based authentication,
         428
   rekeying, 424
   residual risks to keys, 429–431
      intercepted keys, 429,
         430–431

intercepted passphrase, 429–430

"master key" risk, 431

recycled password attack, 429

Encryption keys, 287

distributing, 328

nonces used for constructing, *336*

text used for, 329–331

software checklist for key handling, 331

taking advantage of longer passphrases, 330–331

End tags, HTML, 717

End-to-end crypto, 642, 668

application transparency and, 650–651

deploying cryptography on Internet and, 628, 629

description of, 626

packet with, 626

End-to-end networking, 525–561

Internet gateways and firewalls, 547–555

Internet transport protocols, 526–535

long-distance networking, 555–561

names on the Internet, 525–547

"smart" *vs.* "dumb" networks, 525–526

End-to-end principle, 526

End-to-end transport protocols, 528

English Common Law, 180, 182

Enigma cipher machine (German), 297

Enigma (film), 297

Enterprise computing, 567–616

challenge of community, 567–575

contingency planning, 608–615

enterprise issues, 587–598

enterprise network authentication, 598–607

management processes, 575–587

Enterprise databases, 749

Enterprise firewalls, 695–704

Enterprise issues, 587–588

education, training, and awareness, 587–588

culture, 587

formal training, 588

personal instructions, 588

public announcements, 588

written instructions, 588

personnel security, 587, 588–592

physical security, 587, 592–594

software security, 587, 594–598

Enterprise network authentication, 598–607

credential updates and, 598

crypto requirements and, 599

direct authentication and, 600–602

eavesdropping and, 598

fault tolerance and, 599

indirect authentication and, 602–603

local authentication and, 599–600

multiple servers and, 598

off-line authentication and, 606–607

redirected authentication and, 605

security boundary and, 599

service-based authentication and, 604–605

ticket-based, 603–604

Enterprise point of presence, 705–712

attacking an enterprise site, 709–711

demilitarized zone, 705

Internet service providers, 705

intrusion detection, 705–706

POP topology, 706–709

real-time media challenge and, 711–712

Enterprise risks, 571–573

disclosure attacks and, 571

insiders and outsiders, 572–573

masquerade attacks and, 571

physical theft, 572

service loss attacks and, 571–572

subversion attacks, 572

Enterprises

defined, 567

information security and, 567

Enterprise security, influences on, 2

Enterprise sites

attacking, 709–711

protocol attacks, 710

tunneling, 710–711

Entropy, bias and, 253–254

Environmental management, enterprises and, 594

Environmental risks, 21

E1/E3 services (Europe), 560

Equipment theft, at workplace, 572

Error correcting codes, 195

Error detecting codes, 195

Error detection and correction, 192–195

checksums, 193–194

cyclic redundancy checks, 195

error correcting codes, 195

parity checking, 192–193

by using odd parity on nine-track tape, *193*

Error propagation, 407

Escape character (ESC), 64

ESP. *See* Encapsulating Security Payload

Espionage, one-time pads and, 307

Espionage Act, 765

ESP packet contents, *655*

Essay file, information states of, *123*

ESSIV, 415

sector encryption with, *416*

Ethernet, 435, 449, 458–459

bus topology and, 487

as "dumb" network, 525

frame format, 461–463

address format, 462–463

LAN addressing, 462

MAC addresses and security, 463

LAN connecting hosts on a bus, *458*

optical fiber, 459
packet (frame) contents, *461*
wired networks, 459
wireless network technology, 459
Ethernet connection, 45
Ethernet header, in Wireshark, *514, 515*
Ethernet hub, RJ-45 connectors on, *460*
Ethical issues in security analysis, 31–35
  laws, regulations, and codes of conduct, 31–32
  searching for vulnerabilities, 32–33
  sharing or publishing vulnerabilities, 33–35
Eudora (Qualcomm), 679
Event, 168
Event logging, in operating system, *169*
Event logging mechanism, major elements of, 168–169
Event logs
  for gateways, 548–549
  Microsoft Windows, *166*
Evidence, admissible, 181
EW. *See* Electronic warfare
Exceptions, *555*
Exclusive or (xor) cipher, 300–302, *301, 333*
  eliminating key streams with, *334*
  encrypting image with, *301*
  encryption with, bit-flipping attack on, *360*
  key splitting with, *341*
Executable files, 97–106
  access rights to, 117
  data files *vs.*, 97
  types of, 99–100
  virus infection in, *101*
Execute right, 99
Execution, serious attacks and, 612
Execution access rights, 98–100
Executive Order 13526, classification system defined by, 774

Expired certificates, possibly bogus, probably not, 734
Explicit denial, 147
Exploit, 125
Exponentiation, 350
Export Controlled marking, 777
Export Restricted marking, 777
Exposure and quarantine model, secrecy, information systems and, 769–770, 803
Extended SMTP (ESMTP), 684
Extensible Markup Language, 719
Extents
  Apple's HFS+ and, 211–212
  NT file system and, 213
Exterior routing, autonomous systems and, 499
External files
  effectiveness of access control and encryption, 387*t*
  securing a volume and, 386
External security requirements, 170–172
  laws, regulations, and industry rules, 171
  security process and, 171–172
External storage traffic, protection of, 593–594
External wires, protecting, 439
ext3 file system (Linux), 209
Extortion, 571
Extreme threats, 234
  key management and, 326
  key strength and, 333
Extremist political groups, 766

F
FAA. *See* Federal Aviation Administration
Facebook, 105, 695
Factories, security risks and, 3
Fair use, 318
Falcon and The Snowman, The (Lindsey), 795
False acceptance rate, 270
False positives problem, spam and, 691
False rejection rate, 270

Family radio service bands, 559
FAR. *See* False acceptance rate
FAT. *See* File allocation table
FAT 12, 195, 200, 203, 207
  Microsoft's FAT file system formats, 203*t*
  volume layout and, 201
FAT 16, 200, 207
  flash storage and, 205
  Microsoft's FAT file system formats, 203*t*
  volume layout and, 201
FAT 32, 200, 203
  boot block, contents of, 202
  flash storage and, 205
  Microsoft's FAT file system formats, 203*t*
FAT directories, 206–207
  deleting files, 206–207
  long file names, 206
  undeleting files, 207
FAT file system, 195
FAT-formatted volume, layout of, *201*
Fault, due diligence and, 179
FBI. *See* Federal Bureau of Investigation
FCC. *See* Federal Communications Commission
FDDI. *See* Fiber distributed data interface
FDE. *See* Full-disk encryption
Feature extraction, biometric authentication and, 269
Federal Aviation Administration, 36, 37
Federal Bureau of Investigation, 287
Federal Communications Commission, 452, 454, 559
Federal Information Processing Standard 180, 241
Federal Information Security Management Act, 171, 787
  NIST standards and guidance for, 787

summary of, 787

Feistel structure, 392

Ferguson, Niels, 395

Fetch/store data, 190

Fiber distributed data interface, 561

Fields, in data tables, 747

File allocation table, 195

File allocation table: example file system, 200–207

   boot blocks, 201–203

      FAT and array of address variables, 202–203

      FAT format alternatives, 203

   building files from clusters, 203–206

      cluster storage, 204

      example, 204–205

      FAT and flash storage, 205–206

   contents of FAT 32 boot block, 202t

   FAT directories, 206–207

      deleting files, 206–207

      long file names, 206

      undeleting files, 207

   volume layout, 201

File encryption

   enabling on Windows, 310

   secure, ensuring, 312–313

File encryption keys

   hashing passphrases for, 330

   passphrase used for, 329

File encryption programs

   choosing, 315–317

      cryptographic product evaluation, 317

      file encryption security checklist, 316–317

      software security checklist, 316

File encryption security checklist, 316–317

File encryption software, 309–317

   built-in file encryption, 309–311

choosing file encryption program, 315–317

   cryptographic product evaluation, 317

   file encryption security checklist, 316–317

   software security checklist, 316

encryption application programs, 311–313

   ensuring secure file encryption, 312–313

   protecting the secret key, 313

erasing a plaintext file, 313

erasing optical media, 315

preventing low-level data recovery, 314

requirements for key handling in, 331

risks that demand overwriting, 314

uses for, 309

File folders, 91

File-hosted volume, 413

File management, I/O system and, 54

File names, 92–93

   formats for, 93t

File-oriented incremental backups, 610

File-oriented synchronized backups, 609–610

File ownership, 96

   access rights and, 94–95

File permission flags, 143–148

   for compact access rules, 119

   set of, 118

File protection

   initial, 95

   from various threats, 108

Files. *See also* Sharing files; Storing files

   access rights for, 95

   as encrypted volumes, 412–413

   encrypting with wrapped keys, 339

   executable, 97–106

loss of, laptop risk assessment and, 26

moving/copying, dynamic inheritance and, 162–163

security controls for, 111–117

sharing and protecting, 106–111

   policies for, 108–111

File scavenging, 178

File security controls, 117–123

   file permission flags, 117–120

   policy enforcement and, 120–121, 120t

   states and state diagrams, 121–123

File server, delegating access to, 477

File sharing

   data and, 475–476

   on LAN, 476

   on Microsoft Windows Vista, 138

   security risk with, 476

File-sharing policy, security controls for, 148, 149t

File synchronization software, 78, 80

File system objectives, conflicting, 209

File systems, 91–97

   categories of, 93

   design goals for, 208–209

File system software, I/O system and, 216

File transfer protocol

   application proxy and, 701

   port numbers for, 502

Filtering

   connectivity and

      inbound connections, 553–554

      packet filtering, 553

      TEMPEST problem and, 806

Financial data, 14

Finger, exploiting, 56–57

Finger attack, 252

Finger overflow, 55–56

Fingerprint, 232t

Finger process, attacking computer via, *56*
Finger program, *55*
Finger service
buffer overflow in, *57*
data section for, *55*
Finish TCP flag (FIN), 531
FIPS documents, 787
FIPS-180. *See* Federal Information Processing Standard 180
FIPS 140 certified products, 418
FIPS 140-2, 317
Firefox, 472, 718, 721
alert for mismatched certificate names, *731, 733*
certificate information displayed by, *732*
Fires, 608
Firewall filtering, 498
Firewall proxies, 701
Firewall rules
implementing, 701–704
format of simple firewall rules, 702, *702t*
proliferation of, 704
Firewalls, 547, 709
dual, 706, 707–708, *708*
enterprise, 695–704
HTTP tunnels and, 728
national, 711
single, 706, 707, *707*
software-based, 554–555
three-legged, 706, 707–708, *708*
Firewall security controls, example of, 702–704, *703t*
Firewall vendors, Common Criteria evaluation and, 577
Firmware, 46
First Amendment, government secrecy and, 767
FISMA. *See* Federal Information Security Management Act
Flags, wireless packet protection and, 662
Flash drives, 192
Flash storage, FAT and, 205–206

Floods, 608
Flow control problem, 530
FM. *See* Frequency modulation
FM radio, 452–453
FM wave form, *453*
Force surety, nuclear weapons and, 811, 812–813
Forensic investigators, training and expertise for, 585
Forgeries, *23,* 437, 620, 687
distributing, 369
of email messages, 684–687, *685*
file protection policies and, 108
Formal design specification, 809
Formal security policies, 809
Formatting standards
for Internet email, 674
for the Web, 716
For Official Use Only, 777
Fortran, 103
FOUO. *See* For Official Use Only
Fourth Amendment, surveillance and seizure restrictions and, 181–182
Four-way handshake, wireless LANs and, 664, *664*
Fragmentation, 192
partitioning and, 197
Frame, defined, 461
Frame relay services, 560
Fraud, 571, 572
financial, 688–689
workplace, 573, 574
Free Money virus hoax, 695
Free-space management, 208
Frequency, 452
Frequency analysis, 294
Frequency hopping, 802
Frequency modulation, 453
Frequency sharing, 453
Friedman, William, 297
with cipher machine, *296*
From: header, for Internet email, 675–676
FRR. *See* False rejection rate
FRS bands. *See* Family radio service bands

Full-disk encryption, 383, 386
hard drive volume with, *384*
techniques for, hardware *vs.* software, 411
Full-scope polygraphy examination, SCI clearances and, 781
Functional managers, 579, *580*

G
GAO. *See* Government Accountability Office
Gardner, Martin, 357
Garfinkel, Simson, 385
Gates, Bill, 100
Gateways, 493, 547
construction of small LANs and, 548
filtering, connectivity and, 553–554
functions of, 511–512
Internet traffic control and, 697
low-cost commercial, *511*
simple, configuring, *552*
Generic names, 537
Geolocation services, 545
GET command, 723
scripts and, 741
GIAC. *See* Global information assurance certification
GIIF. *See* Graphics Interchange Format
GLBA. *See* Gramm-Leach-Bliley Act
Global information assurance certification, 586, 587
Global information networks, genesis of, in 20th century, 442
Global IP addresses, 511
Global policies, 108
Gnu, 143
Gnu Privacy Guard, 644
Goldberg, Ian, 396
Gold Bug, The (Poe), 285, 293, 294
Golden Shield project (China), 711

Good Times virus hoax, 695
Government
  information security, security
      classification and
      clearances and, 773
  secrecy in
      classified information,
        767
      evolution of, in 20th
        century U.S., 765
      hostile intelligence services,
        766
      intelligence and
        counterintelligence,
        770–771
      military information
        operations, 771
      operations security, 772
Government Accountability
    Office, 787
GPG. See Gnu Privacy Guard
Gramm-Leach-Bliley Act,
    171
Graphical user interface, 50
Graphics Interchange Format,
    723
Great Britain, evolution of
    classification system in,
    773
Grounding problems, TEMPEST
    emanations and, 808
Group rights, 139
  Unix file permissions, 144,
    144
  VMS file permission flags,
    145
Guards, multilevel servers and,
    818
Guessing
  authentication tokens and,
    267, 267t
  biometric authentication and,
    271
GUI. See Graphical user interface
Gulf War (1991), operations
    security during, 772
Guy, Mike, 239

H
Hackers

black-hat, 13
  defined, 13
  white-hat, 574
Half-open connection, 532
Hall, Chris, 395
Hands-on certifications, 586
Hard drive, 45
  authenticating, 185
  cleaning of personal data,
    385–386
  discarded, risks to volumes
    and, 384, 385–386
  dissecting, 188–189
  erasure or destruction of,
    804
  formatting, 190–192
    flash drives, 192
    high-level format, 191
    low-level format, 190,
      190
  history behind and description
    of, 186–189
  magnetic recording, tapes and,
    185–186
  mechanism, 188
  partitions, 195–197
    hiding data with, 197
    partitioning and
      fragmentation, 197
    partitioning in modern
      systems, 196–197
    partitioning to support
      older drive formats, 195–
      196
  rekeying, 424
  sectors and clusters on, 191,
    191
  speeds for, 190
  storing data on, 185–200
  typical, 187
Hard drive controller, 189–190
  hardware block diagram of,
    189
Hard drive volume, with full-disk
    encryption, 384
Hardened protected distribution
    systems, 805
Hardware, 14
  block diagram, 189, 189
  encryption in, 420–423

drive controller, 421
    drive formatting, 422
    recycling the drive, 421
    security boundary, 422
    working key storage in, 425
Hardware failures, ensuring
    recovery from, 594
Hardware theft, laptop risk
    assessment and, 26
Hash
    encrypting, two steps, 364
    keying, one step, 365
Hashed MAC, 649
Hash functions, modern,
    241–242, 242t
Hashing, 632
    constructing SSL keys through,
      648
    secret keys, 637–638
      to build a traffic key, 638
Hashing passphrase, for file
    encryption key, 330
Hash values, 241, 242t, 654
    changed, detecting, 364
    keyed hash, 364–365, 365
Header, 190
Head tags, HTML, 717
Health Insurance Portability and
    Accountability Act, 171,
    570, 577, 581
Heating, ventilation, and air
    conditioning, 594
Hebern, Edward, 296
Hellman, Martin, 348, 353
Heroditus, 555
Hertz (Hz), 452
HFS+. See Hiearchical file system
    plus
Hibernation state, 431
Hiearchical directory, 91
Hiearchical file system plus, 208,
    211–212
Hierarchical file systems, 208
Hierarchical levels, security
    clearances and, 777
High-assurance cryptography,
    795
High-assurance systems, 809
High availability, 757
High-level analysis, 8

High-level format, 191
    fragmentation, 192
    quick format, 192
Highlighted tag, hypertext links, 717
HIPAA. *See* Health Insurance Portability and Accountability Act
Hiring process, 589
HMAC. *See* Hashed MAC
Hoaxes, email, 695
Holberton, Frances Betty, 748
Honeywell Corporation, 491, 492
Hops, counting, 495
Host, 435
    network integrity and, 439–440
Host addresses
    finding, 463–465
        addresses from keyboard commands, 463
        addresses from Mac OS, 464
        addresses from Microsoft Windows, 465
        retrieving, Windows command for, *464*
Host control, Internet traffic control and, 697
Hostile intelligence services, 766
Hostile users
    effectiveness of access control, encryption and, *387t*
    securing a volume and, 386
Hosts
    address resolution protocol, 506–507
    behind NAT gateways, 550–551
    email URLs and, 720–721
    IP addresses and, 503–504
    IP packet format, 504–505
        packet fragmentation, 505
    talking between, 501–507
        socket addresses, 502
        socket API capabilities, 503
        socket interface, 501–502
HOSTS.TXT, 540
Hotel room card keys, 259

Hot standby, 614
Hourglass
    I/O and file systems, *215*, 215–216
    network protocols, 467
Household security policy, for weak threat environments, 274–275, *274t*
Housemates, 108
HR. *See* Human resources
HTML. *See* Hypertext Markup Language
HTTP. *See* Hypertext Transfer Protocol
HTTP tunneling
    description of, 727–728
    firewalling and, 728
    packet format for, 727
Hubs, for wired LANs, 471
Human-based intelligence gathering, 770
Human resources, 372
HUMINT. See Human-based intelligence gathering
Hunter's dilemma, 4
Hurricanes, 608
HVAC. *See* Heating, ventilation, and air conditioning
Hypercubes (topology), 482
Hypertext, coining of term for, 715
Hypertext fundamentals, 715–724
    addressing Web pages, 719–722
    formatting: Hypertext Markup Language, 716–718
    Hypertext Transfer Protocol, 718
    retrieving static web pages, 722–723
    Web directories and search engines, 723–724
    Web servers and statelessness, 723
    Web standards, 716
Hypertext links, 717–718, *718*
Hypertext Markup Language, 716, 743

Cascading Style Sheets, 718
    formatting with, 716–717
    hypertext links, 717–718, *718*
    source text, 717
Hypertext Transfer Protocol, 699, 718–719
    retrieving data from other files or sites, 719
    retrieving web page with, 722
    states and, 743–745
        browser cookies, 744–745

I
IATO. *See* Interim Approval to Operate
IBM, 65, 491
IBM System/38, 115
ICANN. *See* Internet Corporation for Assigned Names and Numbers
ICV. *See* Integrity Check Value
IDE. *See* Integrated Drive Electronics
IDEA. *See* International Data Encryption Algorithm
Identity-based access control, multilevel security and, 815
Identity theft, 14
    laptop risk assessment and, 26
    stolen laptops and, 385
Identity thieves, 21
    identifying specific attacks by, *26t*
IDS. *See* Intrusion detection system
IEC. *See* International Electrotechnical Commission
IEEE. *See* Institute for Electrical and Electronics Engineers
IETF. *See* Internet Engineering Task Force
IIS. *See* Internet Information Services
IKE Protocol. *See* Internet Key Exchange Protocol
ILOVEYOU virus, 693, 694

Image backups, 610
Image formats, common, 723
IMAP. *See* Internet Message
    Access Protocol
IMP. *See* Interface Message
    Processor
Implementation
    student's computer example
        and, 9
    Trojan horse analysis and,
        128–129
Implementers, training and
    expertise for, 584
Inbound connections, *553–554*
Incidents, aftermath of, 178–179
Incomplete page encryption,
    browser warning about,
    650
Incremental backups, 610
Independent guesses, making, 255
Index variable, 198
Indirect authentication, 602–606,
    603
    description of, 602–603
    properties of, 606
    redirected authentication, 605
    service-based authentication,
        604–605
    ticket-based authentication,
        603–604
Indirect design pattern, 599
Industrial systems, security risks
    and, 3
Inference
    challenge of secrecy and, 767
    database security and, 749
Infiltration, serious attacks and,
    612
Information, general types of
    attacks on, *23*
Information Assurance (IA)
    Courseware Evaluation
    Program, 586
Information networks
    building, 481–491
        bus network, 486–487
        mesh network, 490–491
        network topology, 482
        point-to-point network,
            483–484

star network, 484–486
tree network, 487–489
Information resources
    management, 581–582
    lines of authority and, 581
    managing information security
        and, 582
Information security
    Continuous Improvement
        principle and, 6
    national system security and,
        789–790
Information security architecture,
    17–18
Information security
    management system,
    576
Information security
    professionals, 584–587
    college degrees for, 586
    information security
        certification for, 586–587
    information security training
        for, 585
    training and expertise of, 584–
        585
Information security training
    college courses, 585
    hands-on training, 585
    product-specific training,
        585
Information states, 122–123
    encryption and, 291–292, *292*
        illustrating policy with state
            diagram, 291
        proof of security, 292
    of essay file, *123*
    network applications and, 474
Information system center, 593
Information system protection,
    593–594
Information systems
    audits of, 168
    secrecy and, 769–770
Information Systems Audit and
    Control Association, 586
Information transmission, 442–
    450
    circuit switching, 446–447
    message switching, 444–446

packet switching, 447–450
Infosec officer, 582
Inheritance, static, 159
Inherited rights
    ACLs and, 159
    adding to, in Windows ACL,
        162
Initialization vector, 403
    ESP packet format and, 654
Inodes, 209–210
Input/output
    device independence and,
        215
    file system software and,
        214–222
    hourglass design and, *215,*
        215–216
    security and, 221–222
        file access restrictions, 222
        restricting devices
            themselves, 221–222
        restricting parameters in I/O
            operations, 222
    software layering and,
        217–220
        abstraction, 219–220
        example of, 217
        layering logic, 218–219
    typical operation, 220–221
        call operating system, 220
        driver starts actual I/O
            device, 221
        I/O operation ends, 221
        OS constructs the I/O
            operation, 220–221
Input/output (I/O) circuits, *44, 45*
Input/output (I/O) connections,
    44
Insider attacks, 573
Insider threats, 17, 442
    reducing risks of, 573
Insider trading, 571
Institute for Electrical and
    Electronics Engineers,
    144
Integrated Drive Electronics, 45
Integrity
    of computer hardware, 9
    security services and, 22,
        621

Web, 756–757

Integrity checking, security software and, 598

Integrity check value, 185
    ESP packet format and, 655

Integrity of operations, 810–813
    achieving nuclear high assurance, 813
    force surety and, 812–813
    for nuclear operations, 811–812
    positive control and, 812

Intelligence gathering, 770–771

Interactive guessing, 245

Interface logic, reading encrypted data from hard drive and, 423

Interface Message Processor, 496, 496, 497

Interim Approval to Operate, 793

Interior routing, autonomous systems and, 498

Internal keys, 330
    changing, 335–336
    with nonces, software checklist for, 337–338

Internal security labels, 597

International Data Encryption Algorithm, 317

International Electrotechnical Commission, 576

International Information Systems Security Certification Consortium (ISC²), 586

International rerouting, 500–501

International Standards Organization, 7

International Telecommunications Union, 558

International Traffic in Arms Regulation, 396

Internet. See also Names on the Internet; Web security; World Wide Web
    emergence of, 491, 492–493
    old and new routing structures, 499

Internet access policies
    evolution of, 696
    simple, 696–697, 697t

Internet addresses
    in practice, 507–509
        IPv4 address classes, 508–509
        network masks, 508, 508

Internet applications, traditional, 673–674

Internet Assigned Numbers Authority, 496

Internet-based networking, 2

Internet Control Message Protocol
    attacks on
        ping attacks, 533–534
        ping floods, 533
        ping of death, 534
        redirection attacks, 534
        smurf attack, 533

Internet Corporation for Assigned Names and Numbers, 538, 543, 737

Internet email, 674–687
    authenticated email, 686–687
    categories of standards for, 674
    elements of format for, 675
    forging email messages, 684–686
    message formatting standards, 674–675
    message headers, 675–676
        additional headers, 676
        From: header, 675–676
        To: header, 676
    MIME formatting, 676–679
    protocol standards, 679–681
        email delivery, 680–681
        mailbox protocols, 679–680
        port number summary, 681
    tracking an email, 681–684

Internet Engineering Task Force, 498, 626, 646, 712, 716

Internet Explorer, 718

Internet gateways and firewalls, 547–565

filtering and connectivity, 553–554
    inbound connections, 553–554
    packet filtering, 553
network address translation, 549–552
    configuring DHCP and, 551–552
    overview of, 547–549
    small LAN connects its ISP through a single gateway, 548
software-based, 554–555

Internet Information Services, 719

Internet Key Exchange Protocol, 350, 640, 657–658
    starting negotiation, 658

Internet layer, 493, 493

Internet Message Access Protocol, 679, 681

Internet packets
    routing, 495
    scope of addressing information in, 509t

Internet policy directives, Web security and, 725

Internet Protocol, 470, 492, 493, 493
    displayed in Wireshark, 516
    layering, routing and, 528

Internet routing, 528

Internet security
    early attacks on Internet, 497
    early defense of Internet, 497–498
    evolution of, 495–498
    protecting the ARPANET, 496–497

Internet service providers, 493, 498
    enterprise point of presence and, 705
    starting, 501

Internet services, 673–674

Internet software, cryptography added to, 622

Internet Storm Center, 60

Internet structure, 498–501

autonomous systems, 498–500
routing security, 500–501
starting an ISP, 501
Internet traffic control, 696–697
gateways and, 697
packet headers and, *698*
Internet transport protocols, 526–535
attacks on protocols, 532–535
Transmission Control Protocol, 528–532
User Datagram Protocol, 526–528
Interpreter, 103
Interpreter program, 99
Intruders, catching, 167
Intrusion detection systems, 705–706
Intrusion prevention systems, 706
Invisible partitions, 197
I/O management, operating system and, 53
I/O system, 53–54
IOU, with adjustable check value, *363*
IP. *See* Internet Protocol
IP addresses, 493, 503–504
address locations in packet headers, *503*
dotted decimal notation for, *504*
global, 511
IP version 6, 504
private, 510–512
assigning, 512
dynamic host configuration protocol, 512
virtual private networks and, 657
IP packet format, 504–505
major field contents, 504–505
major IP packet fields, *505*
packet fragmentation, 505
IPsec gateways, 665
encryption of packet and, *653*
virtual private networks and, 657
IP Security Protocol (IPsec), 651

classified military networks and, 667
components of, 653–654
network layer encryption and, 623–624
packet protected with, *624*
IP spoofing attacks, 530, 535
IP version 4 (IPv4), 503, 508
IP version 6 (IPv6), 504
Iraq war, redaction problem and, 769
Ironport, 684, 701
ISACA. *See* Information Systems Audit and Control Association
Islamic law, 180
Islands, 60, 66, 113, 114
ISMS. *See* Information security management system
ISO. *See* International Standards Organization
ISO 9001, 577
ISO 27000, 171
ISO 27001, 7, 583, 584
ISO 27002, 7
ISO 8859-1 character set, 677
ISO/IEC 21827, 578
ISO/IEC 27001, 576, 577, 578
ISO/IEC 27002, 578
Isolation and mediation, islands and, 60
Isolation policy
compact access rules for, 121*t*
enforcing, security controls and, 120–121, 120*t*
ISPs. *See* Internet service providers
ITAR. *See* International Traffic in Arms Regulation
Iteration, security process and, 6
ITU. *See* International Telecommunications Union
IV. *See* Initialization vector

J
Jamming, 800
electronic warfare and, 801–802

spread spectrum techniques and, 802
Japanese manufacturers, Deming cycle and, 7
Java, 103
buffer overflows checked with, 58
Javascript, 103, 740, 741
client-side HTML script in, 742
Jerusalem virus, 102
Jewish law, 180
Job rotation, reducing risk of insider threats and, 573
Joint Photographic Engineering Group, 723
Joomla, 747
JPEG. *See* Joint Photographic Engineering Group
"JPEG of death," 730
JS. *See* Javascript

K
Kaplan, Ray, 13
Katz, Phil, 315
KDC. *See* Key distribution center
KEKs. *See* Key encrypting keys
Kelsey, John, 395
Kerberos, 115, 603, 637
ticket-based authentication by, *604*
Kerckhoff's principle, 62, 288, 290, 398
Kernel mode, 66
Keyboard commands, host addresses from, 463
Keyboards, 45
Key distribution
objectives, 630–631
problem, 325
strategies, 631
techniques, 631–632
Key distribution centers, 631, 635, 636–637
keys wrapped in, 637
Keyed hash, 364–365
Key encrypting keys, 339
encryption of CEK, key wrapping and, *338*
key encapsulation with RSA and, 354

key wrapping and, 635, 636
Separation of Duty and, 343
wrapped keys and, 426
Key expansion, 390
Key field, in User tables, 748
Keyfiles, 426
Key fingerprint, 376
Key handling, software checklist
    for, 331
Key ID, wireless packet
    protection and, 662
Keying
    deploying cryptography on
       Internet and, 628, 629
    hash, one step, *365*
Key leakage, through spying,
    795
Key management, 325–333
    cryptonets and, 326
    cryptoperiods and, 328
    distributing new keys, 328
    key-sharing procedures for,
       327
    key strength and, 332–333
    levels of risk in, 326
    problems related to, 629–630
    public-key cryptography and,
       328–329
    rekeying and, 327–328
    text used for encryption keys,
       329–331
Key rollover, 327
Keys. *See also* Wrapped keys
    combining with nonces,
       336–337
    on DVD hidden track, *343*
    employees and, 590
    encapsulation with RSA,
       354–356, *355*
    intercepted, 430–431
    internal, 330
    new
       distributing, 328
       encrypted with old, *634,*
       634–635
    private, 345
    public, 345
    sniffing from swap files, 431
Key schedule, 390
Key-sharing procedures, 327

Key sizes
    comparable, *358t*
    selecting, 358–359
Key splitting, 340
    with xor, *341*
Key storage
    persistent, 425–427
       key wrapping, 426
       managing removable keys,
       426–427
       protected storage, 425–426
Key stream, 302
    diagram of, *405*
    eliminating with "xor," *334*
    generating, *303*
    improved, from one-way hash,
       304
Key stream security, 305–306
    RC4 biases
       effects of ciphertext errors,
       306
       pseudo-random number
       generators, 305–306
Key strength, operating
    recommendations,
    332–333
Keystroke loggers, 243, *244*
Key update, 634
Key wrapping, 328, 338–341,
    354, 426, 632, 635–636
    cryptoperiods and, 340
    for email, *644*
    KEK encrypting CEK, *338*
    in key distribution centers, *637*
    key splitting and, 340
    multiple recipients and,
       339–340
    software checklist for,
       340–341
Kismet, 659
Klein, Daniel, password study by,
    257–258, 332
Knapsack, *347*
Knudsen, Lars, 394
Kohnfelder, Loren, 370
Kuwait, 772

L
LAMP, 747
Lampson, Butler, 68, 115

Lampson's matrix, 68
LAN addressing, 462
Language-based password bias,
    estimating, 257–258
LANs. *See* Local area networks
Laptops, encrypted hard drives
    and, 427
Laptop theft, at workplace,
    572
Large numbers, abbreviations
    for, *199t*
Large-scale attacks, phases of,
    612
Lattice, of compartment
    clearances, 785, *785*
Layer 2 devices, 471
Layer 2 nodes, 493
Layer 3 routers, 493
Layer 7 protocols, network
    applications and, 673
Layered defense, 18
Layoffs, insider threats and,
    573
Layout information, executable
    files and, 98
Least Privilege, 342, 572
    access rights and, 96–97
    administrative users and,
       140–143
       administration of regular
       users, 141–142
       user account control on
       Windows, 142–143
    boundaries and, 15, 16
    compartments and, 781
    execute right and, 99
    information resources
       management and, 582
    sharing dilemma and, 137
Legal disputes
    resolving, 180–181
    security incidents and,
       180–181
Legal evidence
    collecting at scene, 183
       documenting the scene,
       183–184
       securing the scene, 183
Legal obligations, companies,
    secrecy, and, 569

Legal systems, categories of, 180
Lie detector tests, security
    clearances and, 779
Life-cycle procedures, national
    system security and, 790
Lindsey, Robert, 795
Lines, on phone network, 482
Link, 435
LinkedIn, ZeuS and, 105
Link encryption
    on 802.11 wireless, 658–665
        Wired Equivalent Privacy,
            660
        wireless defenses, 659–660
        wireless LAN security
            boundary, 659
        wireless packet protection,
            661–663
        Wi-Fi protected access: WPA
            and WPA₂, 661
Link layer encryption, 802.11
    wireless and, 622–623
Link protocol, 468
Linksys, 660
Linksys commercial wireless
    gateway, settings for,
    551, 552
Linux, 50, 143, 472
    ext3 file system, 209
    local authentication and, 602
    truly random sources and,
        250
Linux, Apache, MySQL, PHP.
    See LAMP
Linux systems, synchronization
    programs for, 80
Lisp, 99, 103
LMDS. See Local management
    device
Load-balancing, high Web
    availability and, 757
Load balancing routers, 528
Local area networks, 435, 436
    file sharing on, 476
    mapping with nmap, 516,
        516–519
    physical protection of, 438
    protecting external wires, 439
    protocols, 493, 493

sending a packet from one to
    another, 494, 494
simple, protocol software
    layers on, 471
small, firewalls and, 548–549
wireless security boundary,
    659
Local authentication, 599–600,
    600
    benefits and shortcomings
        with, 600
    description of, 599
Local design pattern, 598
Local management device, keys
    handled by, 800
Log entry, 168
Logging events, 167–170
Logic bombs, 572
login feature, 11
Login process, 230
Long-distance networking, 555–
    561
    evolving technologies
        bidirectional satellite
            communications, 561
        optical fiber networks, 561
    mature technologies
        cable TV, 560
        cell phones, 560
        dedicated digital network
            links, 560
    older technologies
        analog-based digital
            networks, 558
        analog broadcast networks,
            557
        analog two-way radios, 559
        circuit-switched telephone
            systems, 557
        microwave networks, 558–
            559
    overview of, 555–557
Long file names, FAT directories
    and, 206
Loop device, 413
Lost control
    effectiveness of access control
        and encryption, 387t
    securing a volume and, 387

Lost files, laptop risk assessment
    and, 26
Lost packets, recovering, 456–
    458
Lottery fraud, 688–689
Lotus Notes, 644
Lower bound, 254
Low hanging fruit, 236
Low-level format
    on hard drive, 190
    of hard drive sector, 190
Low power transmissions,
    countering EW attacks
    and, 801
Lucifer, DES and, 392–393
Luggage lock, four-digit, 256,
    256–257
Lynn, Michael, 34

M
MAC. See Mandatory access
    control; Media access
    control; Message
    authentication code
MAC address
    format for, 462
    network interfaces and, 462
    security and, 463
    uniqueness of, 463
Machine instructions, 43
Macintosh
    file and directory name
        formats for, 93t
    synchronization programs for,
        80
    System Monitor application
        on, 53
Macintosh OS-X, 143, 411,
    413
Macintosh OS-X ACLs,
    152–155, 153
    modifying rights on entry, 154
Mac OS, host addresses from, 464
Macros, 103
Macro viruses, 103–104
    email viruses implemented as,
        695
Macro Virus Protection
    (Microsoft), 104

Macrovision copy protection, 318, 320

Magic number, executable files and, 97

Magnetic recording and tapes, hard drives and, 185–186

Magnetic stripe cards, 232t, 259

Magnetic tape drive, *186*

Mailbox protocols, 679
  POP3: an example, 679–680

Mail exchange, 684

Mainframe computers, 67

Maintenance crews, 21

Major attacks, handling, 612–613

Malicious acquaintances, 21, 108
  identifying specific attacks by, 26t

Malicious changes
  detecting, 361–364
    birthday attacks, 363–364
    one-way hash functions, 361–363

Malicious software. *See* Malware

Malicious viruses, 102–103

Malware, 65, 104–106, 376, 548. *See also* Botnets
  Conficker or Downadup, 104, 105
  exploit, 125
  pattern detection, 63
  Pushdo/Cutwail, 104, 105
  Stuxnet, 104, 106
  Waledac, 104, 105
  Web traffic scanning and, 726
  ZeuS, 105–106

Management hierarchies and delegation, 579–581
  in larger organization, *580*
  profit centers and cost centers, 580–581
    implications for information security, 581

Management processes, 575–576
  auditing and review, *575*
  delegation through management hierarchy, *575*
  written policies and procedures, *575*

Mandatory access control, multilevel security and, 814

Man-in-the-middle attack, 368

Manual keying, 631, 632–633

Manufacturing systems, security risks and, 3

Mapping, of network drive, 476

Marine band, 453

Markup languages, 716

MARS, 317, 394

Mask, 151

Masking, TEMPEST problem and, 806

Masquerade attacks, 571
  direct authentication and, 601

Masquerades, *23*, 437, 620
  bus network and, 487
  file protection policies and, 108
  server, 735–738
  social engineering and, 571, 575

Massachusetts Institute of Technology, 13, 59

Master Boot Record, 102

Master file table, 212, *213*

"Master key" risk, 431

Master keys, employees and, 590

MBR. *See* Master Boot Record

McAfee, 316

MD5 hash value, 362

Meddlers, risk assessment and, 12

Media access control, 462

Media sanitation and destruction, 803–804

Mediation, 180

Melissa virus, 693

Memory mapped I/O, 221

Memory size names, acronyms and, 199, 199t

Memory sizes, address variables and, 197–200

Mesh network, 482, *490*, 490–491
  benefits with, 490–491
  limitations with, 491

Message API (MAPI), 679

Message authentication code, SSL record transmission and, 649–650

Message Digest 5 (MD5), 241, 242t

Message headers
  for Internet email, 675–676
    From: header, 675–676
    To: header, 676

Message integrity check, 662
  calculating, 663

Message switching, 444–446
  advantages and disadvantages of, 446

Message transfer agents, 680, 681

Metcalfe, Robert, 484

Metcalfe's law, 484

MFT. *See* Master file table

MIC. *See* Message integrity check

Mice, 45

Michelangelo virus, 102

Microcomputers, 67

Microphones, 557

Microsoft Corporation, 50, 100
  certifications through, 586
  FAT file system formats, 203
  Point to Point Tunnelling Protocol, 335

Microsoft email products, 679

Microsoft Windows, 810
  basic file sharing, 137–138
  dynamic link libraries (.dll), 70
  enabling file encryption, *310*
  file and directory name formats, *93t*
  host addresses, 465
  resource oriented permissions, *116*
  security event log, *166*
  SYSTEM user identity, 120
  Task Manager, 53
    process display, *141*
  user account control, 142–143

Microsoft Windows ACLs, *156*, 156–163
  advanced security settings for, *160*
  default file protection, 159–163

dynamic ACLs, 160–162
inherited rights, 159
moving and copying files,
    162–163
denying access, 157–159
determining access rights,
    158–159
effective, building, 159
evolution of, 156–157
for survey folder, 161, *161*
Microwave, 451
Microwave antenna, tower with,
    559
Microwave networks, 558–559
Military deception, 771
Military information operations,
    771
Military-issued certificates, 734
Military security, security
    classification and
    clearances and, 773
MIME. *See* Multipart Internet
    Message Extensions
MIME formatting
    Internet email and, 676–679
        description of, 676
        email in rich text format,
            677
        email text with, *678*
Minicomputers, 67
Minuteman nuclear missiles,
    force surety and, 812–
    813
Mirrored RAID, 611
Missile launch control, no lone
    zone and, 798, *798*
MIT. *See* Massachusetts Institute
    of Technology
Mitnick, Kevin, 13, 574
Mix-and-match network
    switching, 449–450
Mixing mode, using with block
    cipher, *402*
MLS. *See* Multilevel security;
    Multiple single levels
MMC. *See* Multimedia card
Mode decryption diagram, for
    cipher block chaining,
    409
Mode encryption diagram, 405

Modem, 451, *558*
Modes of operation, block
    cipher, 401
Modular arithmetic, 350
    on a number circle, *308*
    one-time pads and, 307–308
Modular exponentiation,
    calculation of, 350
Modular inverse, 353, 356
Modularity, 218
Money mules, 106
Monitoring
    enterprises and, 596
    reducing risk of insider threats
        and, 573
    student's computer example
        and, 9–10
    Trojan horse analysis and, 129
Monitoring system, 165–172
    catching an intruder, 167
    event logging, 166
    external security requirements,
        170–172
    logging events, 167–270
Moore, Gordon, 187
Moore's law, 187, 195, 251,
    298, 299, 300, 305
Morris, Robert H., 419
Morris, Robert T., 55, 56
Morris worm, 64, 120, 170, 252,
    257, 497, 498, 583
    buffer overflows and, 55–60
    dictionary attack by, *253, 257*
    programming of, 55
    release of, 58
    security alerts about, 59–60
    shellcode for, 57–58
Morse, Samuel, 483
Morse code, 452, 557
Mosaic, 645
Moss, Jeff, 13
Motherboard, *44, 44–45*
Motorola Corporation, 7
Mount, 216
Mozilla, 472
MS-DOS, 50
    drive partitioning, example of,
        196
    file and directory name
        formats, *93t*

MTA access restrictions, 690
MTAs. *See* Message transfer
    agents
Multics ACLs, *150*, 150–151
Multics timesharing system,
    241
Multilevel mode, computer
    modes of operation and,
    816, 818
Multilevel security, 814–816
    covert channels, 815–816
    mandatory access control
        with, examples of,
        814–815
    other problems related to, 816
    rule- and identity-based access
        control, 815
Multilevel servers, 818
Multimedia card, 206
Multipart Internet Message
    Extensions, 674
Multiperson control, reducing
    risk of insider threats
    and, 573
Multiple servers, enterprise
    network authentication
    and, 598
Multiple single levels, system-
    high mode of operation
    and, 817
Multitasking, 50, 65, 814
MX. *See* Mail exchange
MySpace, ZeuS and, 105

N
NAK. *See* Negative
    acknowledgment
Names on the Internet, *See also,*
    Domain names; Domain
    Name; 535–547
    attacking DNS, 545–547
    cache poisoning, 545–546
    DNS security
        improvements, 547
    DOS attacks and DNS
        resolvers, 546–547
    DOS attacks on DNS
        servers, 546
    common top-level domain
        acronyms, *536t*

DNS protocol, 540–543
    DNS redundancy, 543
    resolving domain name via
        redirection, 542–543
    domain names
        hierarchy of, *536*
        investigating, 543–545
        in practice, 537–539
        three-part, *537*
        using, 538–539
    looking up, 539–540
    name space, *535, 537*
Napoleonic law, 180
NAT. *See* Network address
        translation
National Center of Academic
        Excellence, in IA
        education, 586
National defense systems, CNSS
        standards for information
        assurance requirements,
        810
National firewalls, 711
*National Industrial Security
        Program Operating
        Manual,* 768
National Information Assurance
        Certification and
        Accreditation Process,
        792
National policy issues, 786–788
    certification and accreditation,
        792–793
    distinctive threats,
        vulnerabilities, and
        countermeasures, 788
    facets of national system
        security, 788–790
    legal elements, 786–787
    personnel roles and
        responsibilities, 788
    security planning, 790–791
National security, legal basis for
        classification system and,
        774
National Security Agency, 241,
        299, 334, 651
    cryptographic standards and,
        794, 795, 796

declassified intercepts from
        VENONA project, *784*
    elliptic curve cryptography
        standards, 352
    Information Assurance
        Courseware Evaluation
        Program, 791
    Lucifer and, 392
    media erasure/destruction
        procedures approved by,
        804
    redacted document, 769
    Type 1 cryptographic products
        and, 796
National security information,
        32
National Security
        Telecommunications and
        Information Systems
        Instruction
    7003, national PDS guidance
        and, 804
National Security
        Telecommunications and
        Information Systems
        Security Committee, 786
National system security
    facets of, 788–790
        communications security,
        789
        information security, 789–
        790
        life-cycle procedures, 790
        physical security, 789
National Treasure (film), 285
Natural threats, 21
Needham, Roger, 239
Need to Know
    classified information and,
        777
    access to, 815
    companies, secrecy, and,
        570–571
    controls, 597
    dedicated mode of operation
        and, 816
Negative acknowledgment
    lost packet recovery and, 456,
        457

wireless retransmission and,
        467
Nelson, Ted, 715
Netgear products, 660
Netscape Commerce Server,
        645
Netscape Communications, 625,
        626, 645
Netscape Navigator, 645, *646*
    public-key certificates and,
        371
Netscape software, 645–646
NetStumbler, 659
Network address translation,
        511, 512, 549–552
    processing first packet with,
        550
Network applications, 472–478,
        673
    data and file sharing,
        475–476
    delegation and, 477–478
    information states and, 474
    peer-to-peer strategy and,
        473–474
    resource sharing and,
        474–475
    servers and, 473
Network-based guessing, 246
Network cables, 460–461
Network defenses
    cryptographic, 438
    functional, 438
    logical, 437
    mechanical, 437
    physical, 437
    procedural, 438
Network effect, 484
Network efficiency, overhead
        and, 456
Network encryption, 619–668
    administrative and policy
        issues, 627–628
    communications security,
        619–629
    crypto atop protocol stack,
        642–651
    crypto keys on a network,
        629–642

encryption policy summary, 665–668

link encryption on 802.11 wireless, 659–665

network layer cryptography, 651–658

Network hub, 460

Network Information System, 602

Network inspection tools, 512–519

nmap, 512, 517–519

Wireshark, 512, 513–517

Network integrity, host and, 439–440

Network layer, OSI protocol model, 470

Network layer cryptography, 651–658

encapsulating security payload, 654–656

implementing a VPN, 656–657

Internet Key Exchange protocol, 657–658

Network layer encryption, IPsec and, 623–624

Network layer protocols, evolution of, 651

Network mapper utility, 517

Network masks
defined, 508
interpreting, 508

Network message, unprotected, passive attack on, 620

Network protocol process, I/O system and, 54

Network protocols
attacks on, 532–535
hourglass structure of, 467

Network security problem, 435–442

basic network attacks and defenses, 436–438

host and network integrity, 439–442

botnets, 440–442

insider threat, 442

network worms, 440

physical network protection, 438–439

protecting external wires, 439

Networks of networks, 481–520

building information networks, 481–491

combining computer networks, 491–501

Internet addresses in practice, 507–512

network inspection tools, 512–519

talking between hosts, 501–507

Network subversion, at workplace, 572

Network switch, 460

Network topology
evolution of phone network, 482–483

summary of properties for, 483

Network transparency, 622

crypto atop protocol stack and, 642

IPsec and, 624

Network worms, 440

Next Header, ESP packet format and, 655

NFSV4 (Network File Service, version 4), 151

NIACAP. See National Information Assurance Certification and Accreditation Process

"Nigerian scam," 688

9/11 Commission, 773

NIS. See Network Information System

NISPOM. See National Industrial Security Program Operating Manual

NIST, 317, 356

cryptographic standards, 795

elliptic curve cryptography standards, 352

risk assessment steps and, 29–30

risk management framework, steps in, 793

NIST's federal standards, guidance for FISMA and, 787

NIST Special Publication, 171

nmap, 512

mapping LAN with, 516, 516–519

network mapper utility, 517

output of simple command, 517

port listing using -sV option, 518

using with caution, 519

of Windows 7 host, 518

with -PN and -O options, 519

nmap scans, 613

Nodes, 482

No foreign distribution (NOFORN), 774

No lone zone, 798, 798

Nonces, 261

constructing encryption keys and, 336

four-way handshakes and, 664, 664, 665

internal keys with, software checklist for, 337–338

keys combined with, 336–337

Nondisclosure agreements, 32

Nonrepudiation, 621

digital signatures and, 368

security services and, 22

North American Numbering Plan, 488, 489

Norton, 316

NSA. See National Security Agency

nslookup, 539–540

nslookup list, of "any" DNS records found for eifsc.com, 541

NSTISSC. *See* National Security Telecommunications and Information Systems Security Committee

NSTISSI. *See* National Security Telecommunications and Information Systems Instruction

NT file system (NTFS), 208, 212–214, *213*

Nuclear threat, government secrecy and, 766

Nuclear weapons
  detonating, two-step process for, 813
  integrity of operations and, 810–813
    achieving nuclear high assurance, 813
    force surety and, 812–813
    nuclear operations, 811–812
    positive control and, 812
  no lone zone and, 798, *798*
  risks posed by, 811
  U.S. military policy for control of, 811

Numbers
  large, abbreviations for, 199*t*
  truly random, *251*

O

Objects, 111, 112

OCTAVE Allegro, 30

OCTAVE framework, phases of, 30

OCTAVE process, development of, 30

Odd parity, detecting error in, 193, *193*

OFB mode. *See* Output feedback mode

Off-line attack, 246

Off-line authentication, 606–607
  description of, 606
  with public-key certificates, 606, *607*

Off-line design pattern, 599

Off-line password cracking, 246–247

Olympic Torch virus hoax, 695

One big cryptonet strategy, 631

One-time pads, 306–308
  modular arithmetic and, 307–308, *308*
  practical, 308
  Soviet espionage and, 307, 333

One-time password tokens, 259, 264–268
  attacking, 266
  generating one-time password, *265*
  SecurID, *264*

One-way hashes, 239, 285, 336
  improved key stream from, *304*

One-way hash functions, 240–243
  cryptographic, 330
  detecting malicious changes and, 361–363
  performance of, 243
  procedure diagram of, *241*

Onion routing, 759

Online shopping, 645

OODA loop, 7

Open Design, 398
  cryptography and, 62–63
  description of, 62

OpenID authentication, 605

Open source software, 143

Open Systems Interconnect model, layers of, 470–471

OpenVMS
  development of, 146
  file permission flags, *145*

Operating system layers, procedure calls between, *218*

Operating systems, 50, 53–54
  access rights for files provided by, *95*
  event logging in, *169*

I/O system, 53–54
  security features with, 68

Operating systems kernel, 99

Operations security, 771, 772

Operator errors, 65

Opportunistic attacks, 237

OPSEC. *See* Operations security

Optical fiber, 459

Optical fiber networks, 561

Optical mechanisms, for communicating information, 556

Optical media, erasing, 315

Optical networks, 559

Orange Book, 151, 170, 577, 808, 815, 816

Originator controlled (ORCON), 774

Orphaned layers, 472

OSI model. *See* Open Systems Interconnect model

OS-X, resource oriented permissions, *116*

OS-X padlock, unlocking with administrator's password, 142, *142*

OTAR. *See* Over-the-air rekeying

Other rights, in Unix, 144

Outlook Exchange (Microsoft), 644

Output feedback, 401

Output feedback mode, 402
  encrypting with, *404*
  key stream made with, *403*
  in practice, 403–405
  weaknesses with, 405

Over-the-air rekeying, 799, 800

Overwriting, risks related to, 314

Owner rights
  basic file sharing on Windows, 137
  permission flags and, 118, *118*
  in practice, 119–120
  Unix file permissions, 144, *144*
  VMS file permission flags, *145*

P

Packet addressing, IP addresses and, 493
Packet capture file (pcap), 514
Packet efficiency, 456
Packet filtering, 553, 698, 699, 699
Packet headers, 448
    address locations in, 503
    data in, 454
    traffic controls and, 698
Packet number, wireless packet protection and, 661
Packets
    acknowledgment protocol, 456–457
    basic format of, 454
    defined, 447
    with 802.11 link encryption, 623
    with end-to-end crypto, 626
    fragmentation of, 505
    IPsec gateway and encryption of, 653
    with IPsec protection, 624
    network efficiency and overhead, 456
    sending from one LAN to another, 494, 494
    with SSL encryption, 625
    transmitting, 454–456
    wireless protection of, 661–663
Packet's CRC value, wireless packet protection and, 662
Packet switching, 444, 447–450
    advantages with, 448–449
    disadvantages with, 449
    mix-and-match network switching, 449–450
Padding Data, ESP packet format and, 654
Padding length, ESP packet format and, 655
Page table, 66
Paging files, 431
Pairwise transient key, 663

Parallel wiring, serial wiring vs., 46
PARC (Palo Alto Research Center), 435, 458
Parity checking, 192–193
Partial insiders, enterprises and, 591–592
Partitioned mode, computer modes of operation and, 816, 817–818
Partitioning
    fragmentation and, 197
    in modern systems, 196–197
Partitions
    hard drive, 195–197
    hiding data with, 197
Passive attacks, 23
    defined, 620
    on unprotected network message, 620
Passive authentication tokens, 259–260, 260
Passive tokens, search space and, 265
Passphrase interception
    risks to keys and, 429–430, 430
    cold-boot attacks, 431
    eavesdropping on encryption process, 430
    sniffing keys from swap files, 431
Passphrases, 249, 249
    hashing for file encryption key, 330
    key strength and, 332
    longer, taking advantage of, 330–331
    reusing, 335
    using for file encryption key, 329
    wrapped keys and, 426
Password bias
    entropy and, 253–254
    language-based, estimating, 257–258
Password bias attacks, 252–258

Password checking
    CMS example
        logging-in to website, 750
        login process, 750–751, 751
Password cracking, 246
Password cracking utilities, 253
Password guessing, 244–252
    cracking speeds, 251–252
    DOD password guideline, 245
    interactive guessing, 245
    network-based guessing, 246
    off-line password cracking, 246–247
    password search space, 247–249
    stories about, 244–245
    truly random password selection, 249–251
Password hashes, off-line trial-and-error attack on, 246
Password hashing, 239–240
    in practice, 240
    procedure diagrams, 239, 240
Password Management Guideline (DOD), 245
Password-oriented injection attacks, 752–753
    password that always matches in SQL, 754
Passwords, 232
    cracking, 332
    memorized, 232t
    selection and handling of, 279–280
    typing, masking space for, 238
Password search space, 247–249
Password systems
    conventional, 2
    evolution of, 237–244
    one-way hash functions, 240–243
    password hashing, 239–240
    sniffing credentials, 243–244
Password theft, laptop risk assessment and, 26
Patch, defined, 124
Patching process, 124

Patching security flaws, 123–126
Patent protection, 395
Path name, email URLs and, 721
Pattern-based access control, 63
Patterns, 60
Payload data
    ESP packet format and, 654
    wireless packet protection and, 662
Payment Card Industry Data Security Standard, 171, 581, 583, 584
PC. *See* Program counter
PCI. *See* Peripheral Component Interconnect
PCI DSS. *See* Payment Card Industry Data Security Standard
PDAs. *See* Personal digital assistants
PDCA cycle, 7
PDF. *See* Portable Document Format
PDS. *See* Protected distribution system
Peer-to-peer strategy, network services and, 473–474
PEM. *See* Privacy Enhanced Mail
Penalties, modern security classification system and, 773
Penetration test (pen test), 583, 584
Pepys, Samuel, encrypted diaries of, 287, 290
Perfect forward secrecy, Diffie-Hellman and, 349–350
Periods processing, dedicated mode of operation and, 817
Peripheral Component Interconnect, 45
Perl, 99, 740
Permission flags, 117–119, *118*, *119*
    ambiguities and, 146–147
    examples of, 147–148
Permutations, rounds and, 391

Persistent key storage, 425–427
    key wrapping, 426
    managing removable keys, 426–427
    protected storage, 425–426
Personal computers
    evolution of, 67
    identity theft and, 385
    security on, 67
Personal data, cleaning hard drive of, 385–386
Personal digital assistants, security problems and, 2
Personal files, access rights to, *118*
Personal Home Page/Hypertext Preprocessor, 99, 103, 741, 747
Personal identification numbers, 231, 232*t*
Personal statements, official company statements *vs.*, 569
Personnel security, 587, 588–592
    administrators and separation of duty, 591
    employee clearances, 588–589
    employee life cycle, 589–591
    employee roles, 591
    partial insiders, 591–592
PGP. *See* Pretty Good Privacy
PGP Directory, 376
PGPDisk, 411
PGP MIME, 687
Philby, Kim, 334, 785
Phishing, 687, 691–693
    bogus certificates and, 734
    misleading syntax and, 736
    tracking attacks of, 692–693
    window from early phishing attack, *692*
Phone phreaks, defined, 13
Photo ID cards, pattern-based access control and, 63
PHP. *See* Personal Home Page/ Hypertext Preprocessor

Physical disasters, ensuring recovery from, 594
Physical layer, OSI protocol model, 470
Physical network protection, 438–439
    external wires, 439
    for LAN, *438*
Physical security
    in enterprises, 592–594
    environmental management, 594
    information system protection, 593–594
    power management, 592–593
    national system security and, 789
Physical theft, *23*, 436, 572
Ping, 507
Ping attacks, ICMP and, 533–534
Ping floods, ICMP and, 533
Ping of death, 534
Ping packet, displayed in Wireshark, *533*
PINs. *See* Personal identification numbers
Pins, input/output and, 45
PKI. *See* Public-key infrastructure
PKZIP, 315
PL. *See* Padding length; Perl
Plaintext, 287
    encrypting a volume and looking for, 419
    symmetric encryption and, *290*
Plaintext files, erasing, 313–315
Planning, security process and, 5
Platters, hard drive, 187, *187*, 188, *188*
PLCs. *See* Programmable logic controllers
PNG. *See* Portable Network Graphics
Poe, Edgar Allen, 285, 293
Pointer variables, 198

Point of presence, enterprise, 705–712

Point-to-point network, 482, 483, 483–484

advantages with, 483

disadvantages with, 484

Point-to-Point Tunneling Protocol, 335, 651

Policy

student's computer example and, 9

Trojan horse analysis and, 128

Policy coverage, verifying, 76

Policy directives, 576

Policy specifications, 576

Polygraph examinations, security clearances and, 779

POP. *See* Point of presence

POP3, 679–680, 681

POP topology, 706–709

bastion host, 706, 707

dual firewalls, 706, 708–709, 709

single firewall, 706, 707, 707

three-legged firewall, 706, 707–708, 708

Portable Document Format, 103

Portable Network Graphics, 723

Portable Operating System Interface, 144

Portion markings, for classified documents, 776

Port numbers, 502

for email protocols, 681, 681*t*

User Datagram Protocol and, 527, 528

Positive control, nuclear weapons and, 811, 812

POSIX. *See* Portable Operating System Interface

POSIX ACLs, 151–152

access control entries in, 152*t*

Postal systems, 556

message switching and, 444

POST command

example login process and, 750, 751

password-oriented injection attacks and, 752

web forms and, 738–739, 739

Postel, Jon, 496, 501

Post Office Protocol, version 3. *See* POP3

Potter, Beatrix, encrypted diary of, 286–287, 289, 290, 291, 293, 294

Power alarms, 593

Power cabling, protected, 593

Power filtering, types of, 592–593

Power grids, security risks and, 3

PPP. *See* Point-to-Point Protocol

PPTP. *See* Point-to-Point Tunneling Protocol

Preboot authentication

encrypted drives and, 427–428

BIOS integration, 427, 428

disk-based authentication, 427, 428

with software encryption, 428

Predator drones, 630

Presentation layer, OSI protocol model, 471

Pretty Good Privacy, 316, 374–376, 687

application layer encryption with, 626

crypto atop protocol stack and, 643–644

Prime factors problem, public-key cryptography and, 346–347

Printers, 45

directly connected vs. sharing across LAN, 475

sharing, risks related to, 437

policy statements, 437

potential controls, 437–438

Privacy

reasonable expectation of, 182

tailored policies and, 109

Web, 758–760

Privacy breach, 571

laptop risk assessment and, 25

Privacy Enhanced Mail, crypto atop protocol stack and, 643

Private action, 180

Private browsing, 760

Private IP addresses

assigning, 512

networks and use of, 511

virtual private networks and, 657

Private keys, 345

stolen, 737

Private key value, in Diffie-Hellman calculation, 351

"Private label" algorithms, cautionary note, 400

Private/public key pair, constructing, *346*

Private searches, 182

PRNGs. *See* Pseudorandom number generators

Procedure diagrams, 240

of encryption, *288*

of one-way hash function, *241*

Process diagrams, 240

Processes

access matrix for, 69*t*

active, observing, 52–53

control section shared by, 69

data section shared by, 70

partial list of, displayed by Unix ps command, 52

programs and, 49–50

running two at once, 51

switching between, 51–53

Process examples

student's computer, 7–11

assets, 8

implementation, 9

monitoring, 9–10

policy, 9

recovery, 10

risks, 8

Processing state, 122

Process management, operating system and, 53

Process protection

dispatcher's design description, 83–84

design features, 83

dispatching procedure, 83–84

functional security controls, 83

policy for, 82, 82*t*

risk assessment and, 81–82

security controls for, 84–85, 84*t*

security plan for, 80–85

Process state, 51

Product-specific certifications, 586, 587

Professional certifications, 586

Profit centers, 580–581

information security and, 581

Program counter, 47

Programmable logic controllers, 3

Programmed I/O, 222

Programming languages, 103

Programs

computers and, 43–49

executing, 47–48

procedures and, 48–49

processes and, 49–50

separate control and data sections, 48, *48*

sharing, 68–70

access matrix and, 68–69

access rights and, 69–70

Program size, executable files and, 97

Project and program managers, *580*

Property thieves, 26*t*

Protected distribution systems, 804–805

Protected power controls, 592

Protecting files, policies for, 108–111

Protections, modern security classification system and, 773

Protocol attacks, 710

Protocol layers

headers added to packets with, *469*

in ordering pizza, 469–470, *470*

Protocols, defined, 449

Protocol stack, 467–472

adoption of secure email and application security, 644–645

crypto on top of, 642–651

hourglass structure of, 467, *467*

OSI protocol model, 470–472

Pretty Good Privacy, 643–644

privacy-enhanced mail, 643

relationships between layers, 468–471

SSL handshake protocol, 647–648

SSL record transmission, 648–651

transport layer security—SSL and TLS, 645–647

Protocol standards

for Internet email, 674

for the Web, 716

Provisioning requirements, 590

Proxies, 549

anonymous, 759–760

encryption of, 652

firewall, 701

ps command (Unix), 53

partial list of processes displayed by, *52*

Pseudorandom number generators, 250, 306

key stream security and, 305–306

self-rekeying and, 633, 634

Pseudorandom numbers, 250

Psychological operations, 771

Public announcements, enterprise community and, 588

Publicity, companies, secrecy, and, 570

Public-key building blocks, 638–641

secret sharing with Diffie-Hellman, 639–640

wrapping a secret key with RSA, *640,* 640–641

Public-key certificates, 115, 370

certificate authorities, 371

constructing, 370, *370*

expired: possibly bogus, probably not, 734

information in, 370

off-line authentication with, 606, 607

secure email and, 687

self-signed, 376

trickery with, 376

valid, digital signatures in, 733

Public-key cryptography, 328–329, 345–352

asymmetric encryption algorithms, 347

attacking public keys, 348

constructing public/private key pair, *346*

Diffie-Hellman, 348–351

elliptic curve cryptography, 352

secret-key cryptography *vs.*, 347*t*

secret-key *vs.* public-key crypto, 347*t*

Public-key encryption, 348

Public-key infrastructure, 373

Public keys, 311, 345

attacking, 348

distribution of, 631

encryption of, *346*

publishing, 368–378

authenticated software updates, 376–378

certificate authorities, 371

certificate hierarchy, 373–374

chains of certificates, 371–373

public-key certificates, 370–371

self-signed certificates, 376

trickery with certificates, 376

web of trust, 374–376

techniques, 632

Public-key techniques, choosing, 642

Public opinion, psychological operations and, 771
Public/private key pair, constructing, *346*
Pushdo/Cutwail, 104, 105, 442
Puzzles, 60
Python (PY), 99, 103, 741

Q
Qualified security assessor (QSA), 583–584
Quantum computing techniques, key cracking and, 252
Quantum cryptanalysis, 359

R
Radar signals, risks related to, 801
Radio, 556, 557
  AM and FM, 452–453
  analog two-way, 559
  frequency sharing and, 453
  propagation and security, 454
Radio frequency identification, 259–260
Radio interference, spread spectrum techniques and, 802
Radio signals, 452, *452*
Radio transmissions, 451
RADIUS, 604–605
RAID, as backup, 611–612
RAID system, 424
RAID 1 system, reliability of, 611
RAM. *See* Random access memory
RAM management, operating system and, 53
RAM protection, 66
Random access, hard drives and, 186–187
Random access memory, 44, *44*, 45, 230
  separating data and control, 48
  sniffing keys from swap files, 431
Random password selection, 249–251

Rational Doors, 76
Rational security decisions, 3, 5
Rax system (Boston University), 237
RC. *See* Replay count
RC2, 396
RC4, 304–305, 329, 333, 335, 338, 351
  cracking
    rapid penetration of WEP encryption and, 660
    flexibility of AES *vs.* flexibility of, 393
RC4 biases, 305
  effects of ciphertext errors, 306
  pseudorandom number generators and, 305–306
RC4 story, 395–397
  export restrictions, 396
  leaking, then cracking of algorithm, 396
  lessons learned, 397
RC6, 317, 394
Reachability
  address scope dependent on, *510*
  Layer 2 reachability matrix, *510t*
Reader rights, basic file sharing on Windows and, 138
Reading, shared, tailored policies and, 109
Read-only memory, 46
Read-only (RO) access restriction, 68
Read-only sharing, 111
Read right, 96
Read/write head, hard drive, 186, 187, *187*, *188*
Read/write (RW) access, 69
Real-time media, challenge of, 711–712
Real-time Transport Protocol, 712
Reasoned paranoia, 5
Recommendations, 29
Recommended Standard 232 (RS-232), 558

Records, in data tables, 747
Recovery
  disaster preparation and, 613–614
    business impact analysis, 613–614
    strategies for, 614
  from hardware failures, 594
  from physical disasters, 594
  student's computer example and, 10
  Trojan horse analysis and, 129
Recovery phase, 177–181
  aftermath of an incident, 178–179
    digital forensics, 179
    fault and due diligence, 179
  compromised systems, 178
  incidents and damage, 178
  legal disputes, 180–181
Recursive resolvers, 539
Recycled password attacks, wrapped keys and, 429
Recycle folder, 177
Recycling
  effectiveness of access control and encryption, 387t
  securing a volume and, 387
Recycling drive, 421
Redacted NSA document, 769
Redaction problem, 769
  multilevel security and, 816
Redaction technology, disease testing and, 770
Red/black separation, in crypto device, 796, 797
Redirected authentication, 605–606
Redirection attacks, ICMP and, 534
Red team, 170
Redundant array of independent disks. *See* RAID
Reference monitor, features of, 809
Registration, websites and, 750
Rekeying, 327–328
  true, encryption key management and, 424
Relational databases, 747–748

Relativistic security decisions, 3, 4
Religious law, 180
Remediation, 178
Removable keys, managing, 426–427
Removable storage devices, computer viruses and, 6
Replay count, 664
Reputation, companies and, 568–569
Request for Comments, 674
Request to Send, 466
Resource API, 474
Resource-oriented permissions, 116–117
Resource sharing, 474–475
Retrieve from backup, 239
    authentication tokens and, 267, 267t
    biometric authentication and, 271
Retrieve from backup attack, 235, 236
Return address, 49
Reused keys
    avoiding, 335–338
        changing the internal key, 335–336
        combining the key with a nonce, 336–337
        software checklist for internal keys using nonces, 337–338
Reused key stream, 333, 334
Reused key stream problem, 333–345
Revision control, software development security and, 595, 596
Revocation list, 607
Revolutions per minute, 190
RFCs. See Request for Comments
RFID. See Radio frequency identification
Ribbon cables, 46
Rich text format, email in, 677
Rights, 112
Rijimen, Vincent, 394
Rijndael, 317, 394, 395

Riley, Francis, 35
Ring topology, 482
Risk assessment, 11–20
    authentication threats and, 234
    identifying assets, 14–15
    identifying goals, 14
    NIST recommendation, 29–30
    OCTAVE process, 30–31
    overview, 19–20
    process, 19
    security architecture, 17–19
    security boundaries, 15–17
Risk identification, 20–23
    security properties, services, and attacks, 22–23
    threat agents, 20–22
Risk management framework, 787
Risks
    authentication and, 234–236
    identifying, 11–12, 12
    to laptop: example, 24–29
        calculating relative significance of attacks, 27–29
        estimating impact of attacks, 27
        estimating likelihood of individual attacks, 27
        identifying computing assets, 25
        identifying threat agents and potential attacks, 25–27
    prioritizing, 23–31
        sneak thief example, 23–24
        steps in, 24
    specific security policy statements related to, 110, 110t
    student computer example and, 8
    Trojan horse analysis and, 128
Ritchie, Dennis, 143, 237, 238
Rivest, Ron, 241, 304, 353, 357, 395
Rivest's Cipher 2. See RC2
Rivest's Cipher 4. See RC4
Rivest's Cipher 6. See RC6

Rivest-Shamir-Adleman, 347, 353–360, 632, 638
    applications with, 354
    bogus primes attacks on, 359–360
    brute force attacks on, 357–359
        factoring problem, 358
        original challenge, 357–358
        selecting key size, 358–359
    chosen ciphertext attacks on, 359
    cipher suites in SSL and, 627
    constructing key pair, 357
    Diffie-Hellman vs., secret key sharing and, 356
    digital signatures and, 353–354
    encapsulating keys with, 354–356
    overview of mathematics, 356–357
    small plaintext attack on, 359
    small private key attack on, 359
    timing attack on, 359
    wrapping secret key with, 640, 640–641
RJ-45 connectors, on Ethernet hub, 460
RMF. See Risk management framework
ROM. See Read-only memory
Roman law, 180
Roommates, attacks by, 26t
Root certificate authority, 372
Root directory, 91
Rootkits, 440, 572
Root zone, 542
Rotor machines, 296, 297, 297
Round, 390, 391
Routers, 34
    border, 499
    load balancing, 528
Routine availability, 757
Routing
    autonomous systems and, 498–499
    Internet, 493
    Internet packets, 495

Internet protocol layering and, *528*

mesh network and, 491

in tree network, 488

Routing security, 500

   international rerouting, 500–501

Routing table, 495

RPM. *See* Revolutions per minute

RSA. *See* Rivest-Shamir-Adleman

RSA Data Security, 395, 396, 397

RSA digital signature

   constructing, *367*

   verifying, *367*

RSA Laboratories, 356, 357, 394

RSA private key, digital signature created with, 366

RS 232. *See* Recommended Standard 232

RTP. *See* Real-time Transport Protocol

RTS. *See* Request to Send

Ruby, 741

Rule-based access control, multilevel security and, 815

Rule-based security decisions, 3, *4*

S

SA. *See* Security association

Safari browser, 472, 718

Safeguards, 12

Safeword, 605

Same origin policy, scripts on the Web and, 743

Sandboxing, scripts on the Web and, 743

SANs. *See* Storage area networks

SANS Institute, 60

SAP. *See* Special Access Program

Sarbanes-Oxley Act, 171, 577

Satellite-based networks, 451

Satellite communications, bidirectional, 561

S-boxes, 391, 392

SCADA devices. *See* Supervisory control and data acquisition devices

SCADA systems, 630

Schemes, web-oriented, 718

Schneider, Jerry, 573, 574

Schneier, Bruce, 4, 395

Schwartz, Randall, 33

SCI. *See* Sensitive Compartmented Information

Scientific Data Systems, 69

Scope, 509, *509t*

Screened subnet, 708

Scripting languages, 99–100, 103, 740–741

Script kiddy, 13, 108

Scripts on the Web, 739–743

   client-side scripts, 741–743

   cross-site scripting, 743

   scripting languages, 740–741

   server-side scripts, 739–740

SDHC. *See* Secure digital high capacity

SDNS. *See* Secure Data Network System

SDS. *See* Scientific Data Systems

SDXC. *See* Secure digital extra capacity

Search engines

   crime via, 724

   Web directories and, 723–724

Search space

   active tokens and, 265–266

   passive tokens and, 265

   password, 247–249

   for random passwords or passphrases, *249t*

Secrecy

   challenge of, 767–768

   companies and, 569–571

     accountability, 570

     culture of, 570

     managing publicity, 570

     Need to Know, 570–571

     obligations, 569

     trade secrets, 569

   discipline of, 768–769

information systems and, 769–770

   exposure and quarantine, 769–770

Secrecy in government, 765–772

   classifications and clearances, 773–786

     classification levels, 773–774

     classification levels in practice, 779–780

     compartments and other special controls, 780–786

     security clearances, 777–779

     security labeling, 775–777

   classified information, 767

   communications security, 793–803

   data protection, 803–808

   hostile intelligence services, 766

   information security and operations, 770–772

   intelligence and counterintelligence, 770–771

   military information operations, 771

   operations security, 772

   national policy issues, 786–793

   trustworthy systems, 808–818

Secret classification, 773

Secret documents, storing, 779

Secret information, color codes for, 775

Secret investigations, 778

Secret-key building blocks, 635–638

   key distribution centers, 636–637

   key wrapping, 635–636

   shared secret hashing, 635, 637–638

Secret-key cryptography, 345

   public-key cryptography *vs.*, *347t*

Secret-key encryption, 348
Secret keys
    protecting, 313
    shared, symmetric
        cryptography and, 290
    symmetric encryption and,
        290
    techniques, 632
Secret-key techniques
    choosing, 641–642
    data integrity verified with,
        621
Secret sharing, Diffie-Hellman
    and, 348–350
Sector encryption, with CBC and
    ESSIV, 416
Sector keys, on DVD, 344
Sectors, on hard drive, 188, 191,
    191
Secure Data Network System,
    651
Secure digital extra capacity,
    206
Secure digital high capacity, 206
Secure digital (SD) card, 206
Secure email and application
    security, adoption of,
    644–645
Secure Hash Algorithms, 241,
    362
Secure MIME (S/MIME), 626,
    687
Secure Multipart Internet
    Message Extension, 644
Secure shell protocol, port
    numbers for, 502
Secure Sockets Layer, 646–647
    authenticating web server
        with, 730
    cipher suites in, 627
    socket layer encryption with,
        625, 625–626
    transport layer and, 645–647
SecurID, 603, 605
    one-time password token, 264,
        264
Security
    capability-based, 115

I/O devices and, 221–222
    file access restrictions,
        222
    restricting devices
        themselves, 221–222
    restricting parameters in I/O
        operations, 222
    for operating system, 54
    on personal computers, 67
Security analysis, ethical issues
    in, 31–35
Security architecture, 17–19
Security architecture study, 18
Security associations, 654,
    663–665
    bundling, 657
    establishing, 663–664
    establishing keys for,
        664–665
    IKE protocol and, 657
Security audits, 583–584
    compliance audits, 583–584
    security scans, 584
Security awareness, discipline of
    secrecy and, 769
Security boundary, encryption in
    hardware and, 422
Security choices, types of, 3
Security clearances, 773, 777–
    779
    access permissions for, 778
    refusing, 779
Security controls
    to enforce isolation policy,
        120–121, 120t
    for file-sharing policy, 148,
        149t
    for process protection, 84–85,
        84t
    for shared project files, 148t
Security controls for files
    capabilities, 115–117
        in practice, 115
        resource-oriented
            permissions, 116–117
    deny by default, 112–114
    managing access rights,
        114–115

Security decisions, making, 3–5
Security Engineering CMM,
    577
Security event log, Microsoft
    Windows, 166
Security examples, aircraft
    hijacking, 35–39
Security fault analysis, 796
Security flaws
    exploits and, 124–125
    patching, 123–126
Security goals, 9, 14
Security label, defined, 597
Security labeling, 775–777
    sensitive but unclassified,
        776–777
Security logs, 167
Security management standards,
    576–578
    evolution of, 577–578
Security Parameter Index, ESP
    packet format and, 654
Security plan, 72
    defined, 18
    for process protection,
        80–85
Security planning, 790–791
    security system training, 791
    system life-cycle management,
        790–791
Security policies
    authentication and, 233
    role of, 9
Security policy and
        implementation, 71–80
    constructing security policy,
        75
    overview, 71–72
    policy construction, 76–77, 76t
    risk analysis, 73–75
        course work/shared server:
            files lost, 75
        course work/shared server:
            stolen work, 74–75
        laptop computer: back
            door, 74
        laptop computer: hardware
            theft, 73–74

proprietary software:
hardware theft, 74
USB drive: hardware theft,
74
security controls, 77–80, 79*t*
backup procedure, 78
categories of, 77
security plan, construction of,
72–73
writing security policy, 73
Security process, *See also,*
Six-phase security
process; 5–6
phases of, *5*
Security requirement, 9
Security scans, 584
Security system training,
standards and
educational programs
for, 791
"Security theater," 4
Security Through Obscurity, 61,
62, 290, 659
Seek right, 96
Seizure, collecting evidence and,
181
SELECT command
example login process and,
750, 751
password-oriented injection
attacks and, 752, 753,
754
in Structured Query Language,
748, *748*
Self-encrypting drive, 420
internal functions of, *420*
Self-encrypting drive controller
block diagram of, *421*
state diagram of, *423*
Self-rekeying, *633,* 633–634
Self-signed certificates, 371, 376
Self-synchronizing ciphers, 407
Senate website, defaced, 1999,
729
Senior management, 579, *580*
Sensitive but unclassified
information, 776–777
Sensitive Compartmented
Information, 780–783
clearances related to, 781

example of intelligence agency
compartments, 782*t*
processing example for, 781–
783
Separation kernel, 810
Separation mechanisms, 65–66
program modes, 66
RAM protection, 66
Separation of Duty, 341–343
administrators and, 591
compartments and, 781
for early nuclear missile, 341,
342
with encryption, 342–343
two-person integrity controls
and, 798
September 11, 2001 airline
hijackings, 37–39, *38,*
38*t*
September 11, 2001 terrorist
attacks, U.S.
classification system in
wake of, 775
Sequence diagram,
acknowledgment
protocol and, 456
Sequence numbers (SEQs), 529
ESP packet format and, 654
TCP and, 529–530
Sequential access, 186
Serial ATA cables, 46, *46*
Serial ATA (SATA), 45
Serial wiring, parallel wiring *vs.,*
46
Serious attacks, handling within
enterprises, 612–613
Serpent, 317, 394
Server authentication, 730–734
expired certificate: possibly
bogus, probably not, 734
invalid digital signatures:
always bogus, 734
mismatched domain name,
731–733
revoked certificate: always
bogus, 734
with SSL, 730, *730*
untrusted certificate authority:
difficult to verify, 733–
734

Server masquerades, 735–738
bogus certificate authority,
735
misleading domain name,
736–737
stolen private key, 737
tricked certificate authority,
737–738
Servers
multilevel, 818
network services and, 472, 473
resource sharing and, 474
Server Side Javascript, 741
Server-side scripts, 739–740
executing, *740*
Service-based authentication,
604–605
for 802.11 access, *605*
Service control, Internet traffic
control and, 697
Service loss attacks, 571
Service request and reply, client
and, *473*
Session filtering, 698, 699–700,
700
Session layer, OSI protocol
model, 471
setuid operation, 142
SHA. *See* Secure Hash Algorithm
SHA-0, 242, 242*t*
SHA-1, 242, 242*t*
SHA-224, 242, 242*t*
SHA-256, 242, 242*t*
SHA-384, 242, 242*t*
SHA-512, 242, 242*t*
"Shall," security policy and use
of, 73
Shamir, Adi, 353
Shannon, Claude, 62, 306
Shannon entropy, 253
Shannon's maxim, 63, 398, 634
Shared computer, user isolation
policy for, 109–111, 110*t*
Shared files, Macintosh ACL for,
153
Shared libraries, 99
Shared reading, tailored policies
and, 109
Shared secret hashing, 635, 637–
638

Shared secret keys, symmetric
cryptography and, 290
Shared updating, tailored policies
and, 109
access control lists, 149–155
Sharing files, 135–173
controlled sharing, 135–143
controls on, 106–107, 107
file permission flags, 143–148
Microsoft Windows ACLs,
156–163
monitoring system and,
165–172
objectives for policies related
to, 107
policies for, 108–111
risks and, 108
Trojan horses, 163–165
SHA-x. See Secure Hash
Algorithms
Shell, 50
Shell script, 103
Shewhart, Walter A., 7
Sheymov, Victor, 805
Shielding, TEMPEST problem
and, 806
Shopping, online, 645
Shopping carts, 472, 744
Shoulder surfing, 234
SI. See Special Intelligence
Side channel attacks, 794
SIM card, 232t
Simple Mail Transfer Protocol,
680, 681
Simple rekeying, 632
Simple Security Property,
multilevel security and,
814
Single-firewall topology, 706,
707, 707
Six phase security process, 5,
5–11
analyze risks, 8, 19, 19–29
establish security policy, 9,
71–77
identify assets, 8, 14–15
implement defenses, 9, 77–80
monitor defenses, 9–10, 165–
170

recover from attacks, 10, 177–
179
Six Sigma process, 7
SKIPJACK, 796
Skype, 712
Small networks, wiring,
460–461
Small plaintext attack, on RSA,
359
Small private key attack, on RSA,
359
Smart card, 232t
"Smart" networks, "dumb"
networks vs., 525–526
Smart phones, security problems
and, 2
S/MIME. See Secure MIME
SMTP. See Simple Mail Transfer
Protocol
Smurf attack, ICMP and, 533
Snake oil products, 308
Sniff, 234, 236
Sniff credential
authentication tokens and,
267, 267t
biometric authentication and,
271
Sniffing, 687
credentials, 243–244
direct authentication and,
601
email messages, 680
preventing, 666, 666t
Sniffing protection, deploying
cryptography on Internet
and scope of, 627, 628
Social engineering, 240, 571,
573–575
examples of, 573–574
thwarting, 575
Social forgery, laptop risk
assessment and, 26
Socket addresses, 502
Socket API capabilities, functions
of, 503
Socket interface, 501–502
Socket layer encryption, with
SSL/TLS, 625, 625–626
Software, 14

Capability Maturity Model
and, 577
content control, 726
database management system,
746
domain name resolver, 539
Netscape, 645–646
Web server, 719
Software-based access controls
encryption, 598
integrity checking, 598
internal security labels, 597
Need-to-Know controls, 597
Software-based firewalls, 554–
555
application filtering on, 554
Software bugs, 65
Software layers, 217
abstraction and, 219–220
example of, 217
layering logic, 218–219
Software patch, 124
Software security
enterprises and, 594–598
elements of, 594
formalized coding activities,
596–598
software development
security, 595–596
Software security checklist, 316
Software updates
authenticated, 376–378
trusted, set of processes for,
378
verifying, 377
Solaris operating system, 143
Sort Merge Generator, 748
Source routing attack, 534–535
Soviet agents, key leakage
through spying and, 795
Soviet espionage, one-time pads
and, 307, 333
Soviet Union, nuclear operations
during Cold War and,
811–812
SOX. See Sarbanes-Oxley Act
Spam, 13, 687, 688–691
evolution in prevention of,
689–691

filtering on spam patterns, 690–691

MTA access restriction, 690

financial fraud, 688–689

phishing and, 692

SpamAssassin, 691, 701

Spam score, 691

Spanish Prisoner fraud, 689

Special Access Program, 780, 783–784

Special Intelligence, 780, 784–785

SPI. *See* Security Parameter Index

Spreadsheets

complex risk assessments and, 28

first programs, 100

Spread spectrum, 801, 802–803

SP3. *See* Security Protocol 3

Spying

corporate *vs.* government, 766

key leakage through, 795

Spy tradecraft, 770

SQL. *See* Structured Query Language

SSAA. *See* System Security Authorization Agreement

SSID. *See* Station set identifier

SSJS. *See* Server Side Javascript

SSL. *See* Secure Sockets Layer

SSL alert protocol, 646

SSL data packet contents, *649*

SSL handshake protocol, 646, *647*, 647–648

SSL keys, constructing through hashing, *648*

SSL record transmission, 646, 648–651

application transparency and end-to-end crypto, 650–651

data compression, 650

message authentication code, 649–650

SSL session, 646

Stack, 49

Staff, in larger organizations, *580*

Stallings, William, 468

Standards, 29

Stanford University, 59

Star network, 482, 484–486, *485*

benefits with, 485

shortcomings with, 485–486

State diagrams, 121, 291

door's operation shown with, *122*

policy illustrated with, 291–292

of software vulnerability, *126*

Stateful packet filter, 699, 700

Statelessness, 744

Stateless protocol, 723

States, 121, 291

information, 122–123

Static inheritance, 159

Static website security, 728–730

Station set identifier, 660

Statistical matches, 691

Stealing, 572

Stealth aircraft, special access programs and, 783–784

Steganography, 61, *61*, 62

STO. *See* Security through Obscurity

Stock tickers, first, 442

Stolen authentication database attacks, 240

Stolen computers, risks to volumes and, 384, 385

Stolen private keys, 737

Stolen work, laptop risk assessment and, 25

Stoll, Clifford, 167, 169, 497

Storage area networks, 757, 758

Storage device, lost, risks to volumes and, 384, 385

Storage state, 122

Storage systems, physical protection of, 593

Storing files, 177–223

data stored on hard drive, 185–200

digital evidence, 181–185

FAT: example file system, 200–207

input/output and file system software, 214–222

modern file systems, 207–214

recovery: phase six, 177–181

aftermath of an incident, 178–179

legal disputes, 179–181

Stream cipher modes, 402–405

ciphertext errors, 403

OFB in practice, 403–405

weaknesses with, 405

Stream ciphers, *302*, 302–305, 391, 392

Strict layering, 218

Strong threats, 234

key management and, 326

key strength and, 332–333

policies for

passwords alone, 276, 277*t*

passwords plus biometrics, 277, 277*t*

passwords plus tokens, 278, 278*t*

Structured Query Language, 748–749

SELECT command in, 748, *748*

Stuxnet, 3, 6, 104, 106, 737

Subdomains, 537

Subjects, 112

Subnets, 493

Substitution ciphers, *288*, 289, 293

Substitutions, rounds and, 391

Subversion, *23*, 436

file protection policies and, 108

Subversion attacks, 572

Suite B, 352

Suitmates, 108

identifying specific attacks by, 26*t*

Sun's Solaris operating system, 50

Superblock, 209

Supervisory control and data acquisition devices, 3

Supreme Court, classified data and, 774

Surveillance

collecting evidence and, 181

serious attacks and, 612

Survey files, policy additions for tailored sharing of, 148*t*

Swap files, sniffing keys from, 431

Switchboards, *482*

Switches, for wired LANs, 471

Symmetric encryption, *288,* 288–289, *347*
  process diagram of, *290*

SYN/ACK packet, 532

Synchronized backups, 609–610

Synchronous links, asynchronous links *vs.,* 451

SyncToy (Microsoft), 80

SYN flood attack, 534

SYN packet, 532

Syntax, misleading or obfuscating, 736

SySS, 426

System-high mode, computer modes of operation and, 816, 817

System life-cycle management, 790–791
  acquisition policy, 790–791
  enterprise architecture, 791
  risk management, 791

System logs, 167

System rights
  permission flags and, 118, *118*
  in practice, 119–120
  VMS file permission flags, *145*

System Security Authorization Agreement, 792

System Security Engineering CMM, 577–578

Systems engineering process, 5

SYSTEM user identity, 120

T

Tags, HTML, 716–717

Tailored file security policies, 136

Tailored policies, 108, 109

Tailored sharing of survey files, policy additions for, 148*t*

Tapes, erasure or destruction of, 804

Target, hypertext links, 717

Tavares, Stafford, 317

TCB. *See* Trusted computing base

TCP. *See* Transmission Control Protocol

TCP connections, stateful filters and, 700

TCP flags, Wireshark display, *531*

TCP/IP, 528

TCP/IP attacks, 534–535
  IP spoofing attacks, 535
  source routing attacks, 534–535
  SYN flood attacks, 534

TCSEC. *See Trusted Computer System Evaluation Criteria*

Technical surveillance countermeasures, 771

TEK. *See* Traffic encrypting key

Telecom, 498

Telegrams, 445
  from New York to Fargo, *443,* 443–444
  sending, *443,* 443–444

Telegraph, 442–444, 556

Telegraph codes, 626

Telephone networks, 557
  network topology: evolution of, 482–483
  telegrams *vs.,* 444

Telephones, 442

Telephone system
  circuit switching and, 446, *447*
  evolution of, 491
  as "smart" network with "dumb" end-points, 525

Teletype machines, Unix developers working on, 237, *238*

Teletype networks, message switching and, 444

Teletypes, 300, 443, *444, 445*
  link encryption for, 626

Television, 452, 557
  cable, 560
  satellite, 561

TEMPEST attacks, 244

TEMPEST problem, 794, 803

countermeasures relative to, 806

crosstalk, PDS and, 805

history behind, 805–806

TEMPEST protection, 789

TEMPEST red/black problem, 807

TEMPEST separation, between red and black components, 807–808

TEMPEST zones, 806–807

Temporary permissions, for administrative powers, 141

Terrorism, September 11, 2001 airline hijackings, 37–39, *38, 38t*

Terrorist organizations, 766

Text, using for encryption keys, 329–331

Textual keys, binary keys *vs.,* 329

TFC. *See* Traffic flow confidentiality

TFC Padding, ESP packet format and, 654

Theft, 436
  effectiveness of access control and encryption, 387*t*
  of laptops, 427
  risks to volumes and, 384, 385
  securing a volume and, 387
  stolen private keys, 737
  workplace, 572

Thieves, 20, 21
  risk assessment and, 12

Third-party assessments, 583–584

Thompson, Ken, 143, 237, *238*

Threat agents, 8, 12, 17, 20–22
  hostile intelligence service, 766
  identifying specific attacks by, 26*t*

Threats, authentication and, 233–234

3DES. *See* Triple Data Encryption Standard

Three-factor authentication, 233

Three-legged firewall, 706, 707–708, *708*

Three-way handshake, 531
Thunderbird, 644, 679
Ticket, 604
Ticket-based authentication, 604–604
  by Kerberos, *604*
Timeouts, 456, 528
Timesharing, 814
Time to live, *495*
Timing attack, on RSA, 359
Titan missile launch control center, no lone zone and, *798*
Titan timesharing system (University of Cambridge), 237–238
Titan II nuclear missile, Separation of Duty for, 341, *342*
Title keys, on DVD, 344
Title tags, HTML, 717
TLDs. *See* Top-level domains
TLS. *See* Transport Layer Security
To: header, for Internet email, 676
Tomlinson, Ray, 674
T1 connections, *560*
Top-level domains, *535*
  DNS redundancy and, 543
  types of, 537
Topology, 482
Top Secret classification, 773, 774
Top Secret clearances, 778
Top Secret documents, storing, 779
Top Secret information
  color codes for, 775
  compartmented or partitioned mode of operation and, 817
  greater restrictions and, 780
Top Secret keying materials, two-person integrity controls and, 798
Tornadoes, 608
TPI controls. *See* Two-person integrity controls
Track, 188, *188*

Trade-off analysis, security process and, 5
Trade secrets, 395–396
  companies, secrecy, and, 569
  theft of, 571
Traffic analysis, 628
Traffic blocking, 726
Traffic encrypting key, 635
Traffic filtering, deploying cryptography on Internet and, 627, 628
Traffic-filtering mechanisms, 698–701
  application filtering, 698, 700–701, *701*
  packet filtering, 698, 699
  session filtering, 698, 699–700, *700*
Traffic flow confidentiality, TFC Padding and, 654
Training, information security, 585
TRANSEC. *See* Transmission security
Transitive Trust, 165
  cryptonets and, 326
  disclosure and, 767
  Internet access and, 497
  leakage threat and, 814
  routing security and, 500
  secrecy and, 570–571
  web of trust and, 375
Transmission Control Protocol, 456, 457, 527, 528–532
  connections, 530–531
  connection timeout, 532
  as end-to-end protocol, 528
  header displayed in Wireshark, *530*
  packet fields, 529, *529*
  sequence and acknowledgment numbers and, 529–530
  TCP flags displayed in Wireshark, *531*
  window size, 530
Transmission security, 795, 800–803
  electronic warfare and, 801–802
  jamming and, 800

  spread spectrum, 802–803
  traffic analysis, 800
Transmission state, 122
Transmitting information. *See* Information transmission
Transport layer, OSI protocol model, 471
Transport Layer Security, 646–647
  socket layer encryption with, 625–626
  transport layer and, 645–647
Transport mode, Encapsulating Security Payload and, 654, 656
Transport protocol, 468
Transposition cipher, *288, 289*
Trash folder, 177
Treason, Espionage Act and, 765–766
Tree network, 487–489, *488*
  benefits and shortcomings with, 489
Triple Data Encryption Standard, 317, 399, 418
  encryption, *393,* 393–394
Trojan crypto
  effectiveness of access control and encryption, 387t
  securing a volume and, 386
Trojan horses, *127,* 163–165, 376, 440
  access rights applied to files, 164t
  effectiveness of access control and encryption, 387t
  preventing access by, file encryption and, 309
  securing a volume and, 386
  security process applied to, 128–129
  Trojan game copies secret files, *164*
Trojan infection, 104
Troy, fall of, analyzing security failure in, 129
TrueCrypt, 315, 411, 413, 424, 425, 426, 428, 431
Truly random numbers, *251*

Trunks, on phone network, 482
Trust, but Verify maxim, 726
Trusted Computer System Evaluation Criteria (Orange Book), 151
Trusted computing base, 809
Trusted systems, contemporary, 809–810
Trusted third party, 371
Trustworthy systems
  government, national defense and, 808–818
    computer modes of operation, 816–818
    integrity of operations, 810–813
    multilevel security, 814–816
T3 connections, 560
TTL. *See* Time to live
Tunneling, 710–711
  HTTP, dilemma of, 727–728
Tunnel mode
  Encapsulating Security Payload and, 654, 655–656
  IPsec, packet layout in, *656*
TV. *See* Television
Tweakable cipher, 410
Tweakable encryption mode, 416–418
Two-factor authentication, 232–233
Twofish, 317, 395
Two-person integrity controls, Top Secret keying materials and, 798
Two-way radio bands, 453

U
UAC. *See* User account control
UCL. *See* University College (London)
UDP. *See* User Datagram Protocol
UFS. *See* Unix file system
Unclassified indicators, 772
Undelete program, 178
Undeleting files, FAT directories and, 207

Underlying system policy, for shared computers, 109, 109*t*
Unencrypted volumes, policy for, 388–389, 388*t*
Uniform Resource Identifiers, 719, *720*, 721
Uniform Resource Locators, 719
  email, 720
  format of, *720*
Uninterruptible power systems, 593
United States, nuclear operations during Cold War and, 811–812
Universal plug and play (UPnP), 554
Universal Serial Bus, 45
University College (London), 492
University of California (Berkeley), 59
Unix, 143, 472
  commands for adjusting file's rights, 145
  denying access on, 157
Unix-based systems, 50
  root directories for, 91
Unix directory listing command "ls," 145
Unix file permissions, for typical file, *144*
Unix file systems, 208, 209–211
  directories, 210–211
  inodes, 209–210
  local authentication and, 602
Unix-like systems, file and directory name formats, 93*t*
Unix ps command, partial list of processes displayed by, *52*
Unix "root" account, 142
Unix-style permission flags, POSIX ACL system tied to, 151
Unix timesharing system, developers of, 237, *238*
Unix volume format, classic, *210*
Unpatched flaws, time line for attacking, *125*

Untrustworthy encryption, 418
Updating, shared, tailored policies and, 109
Uplinks, 461
Upper bound, 247
UPS. *See* Uninterruptible power systems
URIs. *See* Uniform Resource Identifiers
URLs. *See* Uniform Resource Locators
U.S. Air Force, 241
U.S. Army, 765
  TEMPEST zones and, 806
U.S. Army Security Agency, 333, 334
U.S. Defense Security Service, 767
U.S. Navy, 765
U.S. State Department, 765
USB. *See* Universal Serial Bus
USB direct connect challenge-response tokens, *263*, 263–264
USB drives, 6
USB password token, 232*t*
US-CERT, 59
Usenet News system, macro viruses and, 104
User account control
  pop-up window, *143*
  on Windows, 142–143
User Datagram Protocol, 526–528
  as end-to-end protocol, 528
  header displayed in Wireshark, *527*
  packet fields, *527*
User file-sharing policy, 111
User groups, basic file sharing on Windows and, 139–140
User identities (user IDs), 66–67, 229, 590
UserID field, in User tables, 748
User interface, I/O system and, 54
User isolation policy, for shared computers, 109–111, 110*t*
User mode, 66

User rights, 144
Utilities, security risks and, 3

V
Vandalism, workplace, 572
Vandals, 20, 21
Van Horn, Earl, 115
Vaults, 60, 61, 114
VENONA project (NSA),
    declassified intercepts
    from, *784*
Verification, security process
    and, 6
"Verified by Visa" service, 605
Verisign, 731
Vernam, Gilbert, 300, 301, 302,
    333, 626
Vernam cipher, 796
VGA. *See* Video Graphics Array
Vice president, 579, *580*
Video displays, 45
Video Graphics Array, 45
Vignère cipher, 294–296
Virtual private networks, 624,
    651–652
    bundling security associations,
        657
    implementing, 656–657
    IPsec gateways and, 657
    private IP addressing and, 657
    small, *652*
Viruses, 2, 63, 440
    biological, 101
    computer, 100–103
    diskette infected with, *102*
    email, 687, 693–695
    infection by, 100–102
    macro, 103–104
    malicious, 102–103
Virus hoaxes, 695
Virus infection, in executable
    program file, *101*
Visicalc, 100
Visual Basic, 100, 103, 740
Voice over IP (VoIP), 711
Volume layout, FAT formatted,
    201
Volumes. *See also* Encrypting
    volumes

risks and policy trade-offs,
    386–389
    identifying critical data, 388
    policy for encrypted
        volumes, 389
    policy for unencrypted
        volumes, 388–389
    risks to, 384–386
    discarded hard drives,
        385–386
    eavesdropping, 385
    securing, 383–389
VP. *See* Vice president
VPNs. *See* Virtual private
    networks
Vulnerabilities, 236
    of authentication tokens,
        26–267, *267t*
    of biometric authentication,
        271–272
    for DVD CSS arrangement,
        320
    searching for, 32–33
    sharing or publishing,
        33–35
Vulnerability, 12
Vulnerability scan, 583

W
Wagner, David, 395
Waledac, 104, 105
Walker, John A., 795, 798
Walker spy ring, preventing
    repetition of, 799
WANs. *See* Wide area networks
Ward, James B., 285
Wardriving, 660
WarGames (film), 54
Wavelength, 452, *452*
Weak threats, 234
    key management and, 326
    key strength and, 332
Web availability categories
    continuous availability, 757,
        758
    continuous operation, 757,
        758
    high availability, 757
    routine availability, 757

Web browsers, 673, 718
Web content management
    system, 746
Web crawlers, 724
Web directories, search engines
    and, 723–724
Web forms, POST command
    and, 738–739, *739*
Web integrity, 756–757
Web of trust, 374–376, *375*
Web pages, 472
    addressing, 719–722
    default, 721–722
    simple, *716*
    static, retrieving, 722–724
        building a page from
            multiple files, 723
        crime via search engines,
            724
        with HTTP, 722
        web crawlers, 724
        Web directories and search
            engines, 723–724
        Web servers and
            statelessness, 723
Web privacy, 758–760
    client anonymity, 758–760
        anonymous proxies, 759–
            760
        private browsing, 760
Web security issues, 724–738
    client policy issues, 725
    server authentication,
        730–734
    server masquerades, 735–738
    static website security,
        728–730
    tunneling dilemma, 727–728
    Web use strategies, 725–727
Web security properties
    ensuring, 756–760
        Web confidentiality, 756
        Web integrity, 756–757
        Web availability, 757–758
        Web privacy, 758–760
Web servers, statelessness and,
    723
Web server software, 719
Website aliases, 538

Website command injection, resisting, input validation and, 755

Websites. *See also* Content management systems
  dynamic, 738–745
  phishing and, 693
  registration and, 750

Website whitelist, 726

Web software, 472

Web standards, 716

Web traffic scanning, 726

Web use strategies, 725–727
  monitoring, 726–727
  traffic blocking, 726
  training, 727

WEP. *See* Wired Equivalent Privacy

Wesley, Charles, encrypted diary of, 287, 290, 291

Western Union, 556

Western Union telegram, *443*

White-hat hackers, 13, 574

White hats, windows of vulnerability and, 125

Whitelists, 690, 726

Whiting, Doug, 395

whois database, 543–545

whois response for stthomas.edu, *544*

Whole-system backups, 609

Wide area networks, 493, 495

Wi-Fi, 459

Wi-Fi Alliance, 459, 661

Wi-Fi Protected Access, 661

Wikipedia, 759

Wilson, Woodrow, 765

Wily Hacker, 167, 169, 170

Window of vulnerability, 125
  defined, 126
  state diagram of, *126*

Windows. *See* Microsoft Windows

Windows-based systems, 50

Windows Internet Name Service, 552

Window size, TCP and, 530

Windows NT operating system, 212

Windows system drive, root directory folder for, *92*

Windows Vista
  file sharing on, *138*
  user account control on, 142

Windows XP Pro, editing "Survey" user group on, *139*

Winer, David, 298

WINS. *See* Windows Internet Name Service

Wired Equivalent Privacy, 660

Wired Ethernet networks, 459

Wired mechanisms, for communicating information, 556

Wired network connections, popularity of, 436

Wireless collisions, handling, 465–467

Wireless connections, 436

Wireless LAN encryption, cipher suites for, 627

Wireless defenses, 659–660

Wireless network technology, 459

Wireless packet protection, 661–663
  decryption and validation, 663
  encryption processing, 662
  integrity processing, 662–663

Wireless Protected Access, version 2, 623, 661, 665
  encrypted packet contents, *661*

Wireless retransmission, 467

Wireless systems, categories of, 451

Wireless transmission, 451–454, 556
  AM and FM radio, 452–453
  frequency, wavelength, and bandwidth, 452
  frequency sharing, 453–454
  radio propagation and security, 454

Wireshark, 512, 513–516, 723
  ARP request displayed in, *515*

ARP response displayed in, *515*

DNS response display on, *541*

Ethernet header displayed in, *514*

examples, 514–515

features of, 514

IP header displayed in, *516*

ping packet shown in, *533*

TCP connection summarized by, *531*

TCP flags displayed by, *531*

TCP header displayed in, *530*

UDP header displayed in, *527*

window for
  layout of, *513*
  sections of, 513

WordPress, 747

Word-processor program, execution access rights and, 98–100

Work data, 14

Work factor, 248

Working key storage, 425

Workplace security policy
  passwords and tokens, 275, 276t
  passwords only, 275, 275t

World rights
  permission flags and, 118, *118*
  Unix file permissions, 144, *144*
  VMS file permission flags, *145*

World Trade Center, September 11, 2001 terrorist attack on, 37, *37*

World War I, 765
  security classification systems during, 773

World War II, 766
  British spying network in Germany during, 332
  German Enigma cipher machine used during, 297, *297*
  special intelligence and, 784
  TEMPEST problem and, 805

World Wide Web, 497, 537, 645, 696, 715–761. *See also* Internet
  basic Web security, 724–738
  content management systems, 746–755
  dynamic websites, 738–745
  ensuring Web security properties, 756–760
  hypertext fundamentals, 715–724
  information security investments for, 581
  port numbers for, 502
World Wide Web Consortium, 716
Worm propagation, 104
Worms, 55, 65
  Morris worm, 55–60, 497, 498, 583
  network, 440
  Stuxnet, 3, 6, 737
WPA. *See* Wi-Fi Protected Access

WPA2. *See* Wireless Protected Access, version 2
Wrapped keys
  cryptoperiods and, 340
  key splitting and, 340
  multiple recipients and, 339–340
  recycled password attacks and, 429
  risks and benefits with, 426
  with RSA, *640*, 640–641
  software checklist for, 340–341
Write right, 96
W3C. *See* World Wide Web Consortium
WWW. *See* World Wide Web

X
Xerox Corporation, 435, 458
XML. *See* Extensible Markup Language
XML tunnels, 727, 728

xor. *See* Exclusive or (xor) cipher
Xor-Encrypt-Xor, 416
XTS
  cipher mode and, evolution of, 416
  encrypting data on a disk sector and, *417*
  two parts to, 417

Y
Yahoo!, 724

Z
Zbot malware, 105
Zero-day exploit, 125, 126
Zeroize, 796
ZeuS, 105–106, 243, 441
Zimmerman, Phil, 316, 374
Zone of control, 806
Zones, 542
Zoning, TEMPEST problem and, 806

CREDITS

CHAPTER 1
1.1 © Michal Kowalski/ShutterStock, Inc.; **1.7** © Ken Tannenbaum/ShutterStock, Inc.

CHAPTER 2
2.1 (left) © iStockphoto/Thinkstock; **2.1 (middle)** © Péter Gudella/Dreamstime.com; **2.3 (right)** © iStockphoto/Thinkstock; **2.5** Used with permission from Microsoft; **2.10 (right)** Courtesy of Department of Defense; **2.11 (left)** Used with permission from Microsoft; **2.11 (right)** Used with permission from Microsoft.

CHAPTER 3
3.1 Used with permission from Microsoft; **3.2** Used with permission from Microsoft. **3.11 (left)** Screenshot reprinted with permission from Apple Inc.; **3.11 (right)** Used with permission from Microsoft; **3.20** Courtesy of Project Gutenberg

CHAPTER 4
4.1 Used with permission from Microsoft; **4.2** Used with permission from Microsoft; **4.3** Used with permission from Microsoft; **4.4** Screenshot reprinted with permission from Apple Inc.; **4.5** Used with permission from Microsoft; **4.10** Screenshot reprinted with permission from Apple Inc.; **4.11** Screenshot reprinted with permission from Apple Inc.; **4.12** Screenshot reprinted with permission from Apple Inc.; **4.13** Used with permission from Microsoft; **4.14** Used with permission from Microsoft; **4.15** Used with permission from Microsoft; **4.16** Used with permission from Microsoft; **4.17** Used with permission from Microsoft; **4.19** Used with permission from Microsoft.

CHAPTER 5
5.1 Photographed by Dr. Richard Smith at the Computer History Museum, California.

CHAPTER 6
6.4 Courtesy of Boston University; **6.5** Reprinted with permission of Alcatel-Lucent USA Inc.; **6.8** Photo courtesy of KeyGhost.com

CHAPTER 7

7.6 Courtesy of Library of Congress, Prints & Photographs Division [LC-USZ62-93385]; **7.7** Photographed by Dr. Richard Smith at the Computer History Museum, California; **7.14** Used with permission from Microsoft.

CHAPTER 8

8.8 Courtesy of the Titan Missile Museum.

CHAPTER 9

9.15 Screenshot reprinted with permission from Apple Inc.

CHAPTER 10

10.1 Photographed by Dr. Richard Smith at the Computer History Museum, California; **10.3** © Western Union Holdings Inc.; **10.4** Library of Congress, Prints & Photographs Division, FSA/OWI Collection, LC-USW3- 032342-E; **10.5** Library of Congress, Prints & Photographs Division, FSA/OWI Collection, LC-USW3- 032343-E

CHAPTER 11

11.1 Courtesy of Library of Congress, Prints & Photographs Division, [LC-DIG-ggbain-01423]; **11.2** Reproduced from Boy's Book of Science, John Pepper; **11.3 (ins)** © Holly Kuchera/ShutterStock, Inc.; **11.3 (main)** © 2009fotofriends/ShutterStock, Inc.; **11.9** Photographed by Dr. Richard Smith at the Computer History Museum, California; **11.19** © Wireshark Foundation; **11.20** © Wireshark Foundation; **11.21** © Wireshark Foundation; **11.22** © Wireshark Foundation; **11.23** © Wireshark Foundation; **11.24** © Netgear.

CHAPTER 12

12.2 © Wireshark Foundation; **12.5** © Wireshark Foundation; **12.6** © Wireshark Foundation; **12.7** © Wireshark Foundation; **12.8** © Wireshark Foundation; **12.12** © Wireshark Foundation; **12.17** © Linksys; **12.18** Screenshot reprinted with permission from Apple Inc.

CHAPTER 14

14.17 © AOL Inc.; **14.21** Screenshot reprinted with permission from Apple Inc.

CHAPTER 15

15.6 Used with permission from Microsoft.

CHAPTER 17

17.1 Courtesy of the U.S. National Security Agency. Accessed on August 19, 2011 at [http://www.nsa.gov/public_info/_files/cryptologic_histories/history_comsec.pdf]; **17.2** Courtesy of the U.S. Department of Defense. Accessed on August 19, 2011 at [www.dtic.mil/dtic/pdf/customer/STINFOdata/DoD5200_1ph.pdf]; **17.5** Courtesy of the U.S. National Security Agency; **17.8** Courtesy of the Titan Missile Museum.